Lecture Notes in Artificial Intelligence 3651

Edited by J. G. Carbonell and J. Siekmann

Subseries of Lecture Notes in Computer Science

Robert Dale Kam-Fai Wong Jian Su
Oi Yee Kwong (Eds.)

Natural Language Processing – IJCNLP 2005

Second International Joint Conference
Jeju Island, Korea, October 11-13, 2005
Proceedings

Series Editors

Jaime G. Carbonell, Carnegie Mellon University, Pittsburgh, PA, USA
Jörg Siekmann, University of Saarland, Saarbrücken, Germany

Volume Editors

Robert Dale
Macquarie University
Centre for Language Technology
Division of Information and Communication Sciences
Sydney NSW 2109, Australia
E-mail: rdale@ics.mq.edu.au

Kam-Fai Wong
Chinese University of Hong Kong
Department of Systems Engineering and Engineering Management
Shatin, N.T., Hong Kong
E-mail: kfwong@se.cuhk.edu.hk

Jian Su
Natural Language Synergy Lab
Institute for Infocomm Research
21 Heng Mui Keng Terrace, Singapore, 119613
E-mail: sujian@i2r.a-star.edu.sg

Oi Yee Kwong
City University of Hong Kong
Language Information Sciences Research Centre
Tat Chee Avenue, Kowloon, Hong Kong
E-mail: rlolivia@cityu.edu.hk

Library of Congress Control Number: 2005932752

CR Subject Classification (1998): I.2.7, I.2, F.4.3, I.7, J.5, H.3, F.2

ISSN 0302-9743
ISBN-10 3-540-29172-5 Springer Berlin Heidelberg New York
ISBN-13 978-3-540-29172-5 Springer Berlin Heidelberg New York

Springer is a part of Springer Science+Business Media

springeronline.com

Printed in Germany

Typesetting: Camera-ready by author, data conversion by Scientific Publishing Services, Chennai, India
Printed on acid-free paper SPIN: 11562214 06/3142 5 4 3 2 1 0

From the Conference Chair

The Second International Joint Conference on Natural Language Processing (IJCNLP 2005) was prepared to serve as a linking device for advanced research cooperation as well as a sharing device under the AFNLP (Asian Federation of NLP) flag and among worldwide NLP communities.

The twenty-first century, introducing a new international economic world, is experiencing a leap forward in the world of knowledge. The technology of NLP has been achieving rapid growth through the accumulated industrialization experiences and vivid deeper research. We believe this progress is not only contributing to the knowledge society, but also playing an important role in economic growth through awakening the infrastructure of knowledge of the human brain and language functions.

Following the success of IJCNLP 2004, IJCNLP 2005 has made further progress. Not only do we have a big submission increase, but also more invited talks and more tutorials are organized. All these could not have happened without a lot of effort from the conference committees. I'd like to take this opportunity to express my sincere gratitude to the organizing chair Jong-Hyeok Lee, the program co-chairs Robert Dale and Kam-Fai Wong, the publication co-chairs Jian Su and Oi Yee Kwong, and all the other committee chairs for supporting IJCNLP 2005 enthusiastically. It is also my pleasure to thank the AFNLP President Benjamin T'sou, the Vice-President Jun'ichi Tsujii, and the Conference Coordination Committee chair Keh-Yih Su for their continuous advice.

Furthermore, I greatly appreciate the support from the sponsors of this conference: Jeju Province Local Government, KAIST, KISTI, ETRI, Microsoft Korea, Microsoft Japan, and Mobico & Sysmeta.

Last, we look forward to the active participation from you, the honorable guests, to make this conference a successful event.

October 2005

Key-Sun Choi
Conference Chair
IJCNLP 2005

Preface

The Theme of IJCNLP 2005:
"NLP with Kimchee", a Conference with a Unique Flavor

Welcome to IJCNLP 2005, the second annual conference of the Asian Federation of Natural Language Processing (AFNLP). Following the success of the first conference held in the beautiful city of Sanya, Hainan Island, China, in March 2004, IJCNLP 2005 is held in yet another attractive Asian resort, namely Jeju Island in Korea, on October 11–13, 2005 — the ideal place and season for appreciating *mugunghwa*, the rose of Sharon, and the national flower of Korea.

On behalf of the Program Committee, we are excited to present these proceedings, which collect together the papers accepted for oral presentation at the conference. We received 289 submissions in total, from 32 economies all over the world: 77% from Asia, 11% from Europe, 0.3% from Africa, 1.7% from Australasia and 10% from North America. We are delighted to report that the popularity of IJCNLP has significantly increased this year, with an increase of 37% from the 211 submissions from 16 economies and 3 continents received for IJCNLP 2004.

With such a large number of submissions, the paper selection process was not easy. With the very considerable assistance of our 12 area chairs — Claire Gardent, Jamie Henderson, Chu-Ren Huang, Kentaro Inui, Gary Lee, Kim-Teng Lua, Helen Meng, Diego Mollá, Jian-Yun Nie, Dragomir Radev, Manfred Stede, and Ming Zhou — and the 133 international reviewers, 90 papers (31%) were accepted for oral presentation and 62 papers (21%) were recommended as posters. The accepted papers were then assigned to 27 parallel sessions leading to a very solid three-day technical program. Four invited speeches were added to further strengthen the program; we are honored this year to have invited Bill Dolan (USA), Seyoung Park (Korea), Karen Spärck Jones (UK) and Hozumi Tanaka (Japan), all world-renowned researchers in their areas, to present their views on the state of the art in natural language processing and information retrieval.

IJCNLP 2005 is obviously a sizable international conference. The work of the Program Committee would not have been so smooth without the unfailing support of the other team members. In particular, we would like to thank Key-Sun Choi (General Chair) and Jong-Hyeok Lee (Organizing Committee Chair) for their continuous backing and their prompt responses to our numerous requests for information and assistance. Thanks are due to the Publication Committee Co-chairs, Jian Su and Oi Yee Kwong, for serving as the bridge between Springer, the authors, and the Program Committee. We are also very grateful to Benjamin T'sou, the President of AFNLP, for his invaluable advice at various stages in the development of the conference.

We hope you will take advantage of every aspect of IJCNLP 2005: the program and the presentations; the proceedings and the papers; the meetings and the people; the resort and the mugunghwa, as well as the food — especially the kimchee. Enjoy it ☺.

October 2005

Robert Dale and Kam-Fai Wong
Program Committee Co-chairs
IJCNLP 2005

Conference Organization

Conference Chair	Key-Sun Choi (KAIST, Korea)
Organizing Chair	Jong-Hyeok Lee (POSTECH, Korea)
Program Co-chairs	Robert Dale (Macquarie University, Australia)
	Kam-Fai Wong (Chinese University of Hong Kong, Hong Kong)
Publication Co-chairs	Jian Su (Institute for Infocomm Research, Singapore)
	Oi Yee Kwong (City University of Hong Kong, Hong Kong)
Publicity Co-chairs	Hiroshi Nakagawa (University of Tokyo, Japan)
	Jong C. Park (KAIST, Korea)
Financial Co-chairs	Hyeok-Cheol Kwon (Busan National University, Korea)
	Takenobu Tokunaga (Tokyo Institute of Technology, Japan)
Poster and Demo Co-chairs	Rajeev Sangal (IIIT, India)
	Dekang Lin (Google, USA)
	Maosong Sun (Tsinghua University, China)
Tutorial Chair	Dekai Wu (HKUST, Hong Kong)
Workshop Co-chairs	Yuji Matsumoto (NAIST, Japan)
	Laurent Romary (LORIA, France)
Exhibition Co-chairs	Seung-Shik Kang (Kookmin University, Korea)
	Tetsuya Ishikawa (University of Tsukuba, Japan)

Program Committee

Program Co-chairs

Robert Dale, Macquarie University, Australia
Kam-Fai Wong, Chinese University of Hong Kong, Hong Kong

Area Chairs

Claire Gardent, CNRS/LORIA, Nancy, France
(Dialogue and Discourse)
James Henderson, University of Geneva, Switzerland
(Parsing and Grammatical Formalisms)
Chu-Ren Huang, Academia Sinica, Taiwan
(Semantics and Ontology)
Kentaro Inui, Nara Institute of Science and Technology, Japan
(Text and Sentence Generation)
Gary Geunbae Lee, POSTECH, Korea
(Text Mining and Information Extraction)
Kim-Teng Lua, COLIPS, Singapore
(POS Tagging, WSD and Word Segmentation)
Helen Meng, Chinese University of Hong Kong, Hong Kong
(Spoken Language Processing)
Diego Mollá, Macquarie University, Australia
(Question Answering)
Jian-Yun Nie, University of Montreal, Canada
(Information Retrieval)
Dragomir Radev, University of Michigan, USA
(Text Summarization and Opinion Extraction)
Manfred Stede, University of Potsdam, Germany
(Machine Translation)
Ming Zhou, Microsoft Research Asia, China
(NLP Applications)

Reviewers

Jan Alexandersson
John Bateman
Farah Benamara
Emily Bender
Kalina Bontcheva
Johan Bos
Paul Buitelaar
Harry Bunt
John Carroll
Yee Seng Chan
Berlin Chen
Hsin-Hsi Chen
John Chen
Ruey-Cheng Chen
Pu-Jen Cheng
Lee-Feng Chien
Key-Sun Choi
Charles Clarke

Eric de la Clergerie
Mike Collins
Robert Dale
Angelo Dalli
Thierry Declerck
Minghui Dong
Mark Dras
Terumasa Ehara
Christiane Fellbaum
Guo Hong Fu
Jianfeng Gao
Claire Gardent
Ulrich Germann
Sanda Harabagiu
Donna Harman
James Henderson
Graeme Hirst
Julia Hockenmaier
Chu-Ren Huang
Kentaro Inui
Shuichi Itahashi
Dong Hong Ji
Hongyan Jing
Noriko Kando
Hideki Kashioka
Tatsuya Kawahara
Frank Keller
Jin-dong Kim
Alistair Knott
Wessel Kraaij
Sadao Kurohashi
Oi Yee Kwong
Wai Lam
Helen Langone
Mirella Lapata
Gary Geunbae Lee
Alessandro Lenci
Gina Levow
Haizhou Li
Mu Li
Wei Li
Wenjie Li
Elizabeth Liddy
Chin-Yew Lin
Dekang Lin
Charles Ling
Qun Liu
Ting Liu
Yang Liu
Wai-Kit Lo
Vincenzo Lombardo
Jin Kiat Low
Kim-Teng Lua
Robert Luk
Yajuan Lv
Qing Ma
Bernardo Magnini
Yuval Marom
Yuji Matsumoto
Kathleen McCoy
Helen Meng
Paola Merlo
Diego Mollá
Josiane Mothe
Dragos Munteanu
Mark-Jan Nederhof
Ani Nenkova
Hwee Tou Ng
Jian-Yun Nie
Takashi Ninomiya
Douglas Oard
Kiyonori Ohtake
Alessandro Oltramari
Miles Osborne
Patrick Paroubek
Adam Pease
Gerald Penn
Massimo Poesio
Dragomir Radev
Deepak Ravichandran
Fuji Ren
Fabio Rinaldi
Rajeev Sangal
Rolf Schwitter
James Shaw
Claude Shen
Melanie Siegel
Khalil Sima'an
Virach Sornlertlamvanich
Manfred Stede
Kristina Striegnitz
Maosong Sun
Richard Sutcliffe
Bing Swen
Simone Teufel
Thanaruk Theeramunkong
Takenobu Tokunaga
Jun'ichi Tsujii
Yoshimasa Tsuruoka
Gertjan van Noord
Jose Luis Vicedo
Chao Wang
Hsin-Min Wang
Hui Wang
Jenq-Haur Wang
Bonnie Webber
David Weir
Fuliang Weng
Janyce Wiebe
Florian Wolf
Kam-Fai Wong
Yunqing Xia
Jie Xu
Kazuhide Yamamoto
Chris Yang
Hongyuan Zha
ChengXiang Zhai
Weidong Zhan
Jie Zhang
Min Zhang
Yujie Zhang
Zhu Zhang
Tiejun Zhao
GuoDong Zhou
Liang Zhou
Ming Zhou
Ingrid Zukerman

Sponsors

Jeju Province Local Government
Korea Advanced Institute of Science and Technology (KAIST)
Korea Institute of Science and Technology Information (KISTI)
Electronics and Telecommunications Research Institute (ETRI)
Microsoft Korea
Microsoft Japan
Mobico & Sysmeta

Table of Contents

Information Retrieval

Corpus-Based Parsing

Web Mining

Rule-Based Parsing

Disambiguation

Text Mining

Document Analysis

Ontology and Thesaurus

Relation Extraction

Text Classification

Transliteration

Machine Translation – I

Question Answering

Morphological Analysis

Machine Translation – II

Text Summarization

Named Entity Recognition

Linguistic Resources and Tools

Discourse Analysis

Semantic Analysis – I

NLP Applications

Tagging

Semantic Analysis – II

Language Models

Spoken Language

Terminology Mining

A New Method for Sentiment Classification in Text Retrieval

Yi Hu[1], Jianyong Duan[1], Xiaoming Chen[1,2], Bingzhen Pei[1,2], and Ruzhan Lu[1]

[1] Department of Computer Science and Engineering,
Shanghai Jiao Tong University, Shanghai, China, 200030
[2] School of Computer Science and Engineering,
Guizhou University, Guiyang, China, 550025
{huyi, duan_jy, chen-xm, peibz, rz-lu}@cs.sjtu.edu.cn

Abstract. Traditional text categorization is usually a topic-based task, but a subtle demand on information retrieval is to distinguish between positive and negative view on text topic. In this paper, a new method is explored to solve this problem. Firstly, a batch of Concerned Concepts in the researched domain is predefined. Secondly, the special knowledge representing the positive or negative context of these concepts within sentences is built up. At last, an evaluating function based on the knowledge is defined for sentiment classification of free text. We introduce some linguistic knowledge in these procedures to make our method effective. As a result, the new method proves better compared with SVM when experimenting on Chinese texts about a certain topic.

1 Introduction

Classical technology in text categorization pays much attention to determining whether a text is related to a given topic [1], such as sports and finance. However, as research goes on, a subtle problem focuses on how to classify the semantic orientation of the text. For instance, texts can be for or against "racism", and not all the texts are bad. There exist two possible semantic orientations: positive and negative (the neutral view is not considered in this paper). Labeling texts by their semantic orientation would provide readers succinct summaries and be great useful in intelligent retrieval of information system.

Traditional text categorization algorithms, including Naïve Bayes, ANN, SVM, etc, depend on a feature vector representing a text. They usually utilize words or n-grams as features and construct the weightiness according to their presence/absence or frequencies. It is a convenient way to formalize the text for calculation. On the other hand, employing one vector may be unsuitable for sentiment classification. See the following simple sentence in English:

— Seen from the history, the great segregation is a pioneering work.

Here, "segregation" is very helpful to determine that the text is about the topic of racism, but the terms "great" and "pioneering work" may just be the important hints for semantic orientation (support the racism). These two terms probably contribute

R. Dale et al. (Eds.): IJCNLP 2005, LNAI 3651, pp. 1 – 9, 2005.

less to sentiment classification if they are dispersed into the text vector because the relations between them and "segregation" are lost. Intuitively, these terms can provide more contribution if they are considered as a whole within the sentence. We explore a new idea for sentiment classification by focusing on sentences rather than entire text.

"Segregation" is called as Concerned Concept in our work. These Concerned Concepts are always the sensitive nouns or noun phrases in the researched domain such as "race riot", "color line" and "government". If the sentiment classifying knowledge about how to comment on these concepts can be acquired, it will be helpful for sentiment classification when meeting these concepts in free texts again. In other words, the task of sentiment classification of entire text has changed into recognizing the semantic orientation of the context of all Concerned Concepts.

We attempt to build up this kind of knowledge to describe different sentiment context by integrating extended part of speech (EPOS), modified triggered bi-grams and position information within sentences. At last, we experiment on Chinese texts about "racism" and draw some conclusions.

2 Previous Work

A lot of past work has been done about text categorization besides topic-based classification. Biber [2] concentrated on sorting texts in terms of their source or source style with stylistic variation such as author, publisher, and native-language background.

Some other related work focused on classifying the semantic orientation of individual words or phrases by employing linguistic heuristics [3][4]. Hatzivassiloglou et al worked on predicting the semantic orientation of adjectives rather than phrases containing adjectives and they noted that there are linguistic constraints on these orientations of adjectives in conjunctions.

Past work on sentiment-based categorization of entire texts often involved using cognitive linguistics [5][11] or manually constructing discriminated lexicons [7][12]. All these work enlightened us on the research on Concerned Concepts in given domain.

Turney's work [9] applied an unsupervised learning algorithm based on the mutual information between phrases and the both words "excellent" and "poor". The mutual information was computed using statistics gathered by a search engine and simple to be dealt with, which encourage further work with sentiment classification.

Pang et al [10] utilized several prior-knowledge-free supervised machine learning methods in the sentiment classification task in the domain of movie review, and they also analyzed the problem to understand better how difficult it is. They experimented with three standard algorithms: Naïve Bayes, Maximum Entropy and Support Vector Machines, then compared the results. Their work showed that, generally, these algorithms were not able to achieve accuracies on the sentiment classification problem comparable to those reported for standard topic-based categorization.

3 Our Work

3.1 Basic Idea

As mentioned above, terms in a text vector are usually separated from the Concerned Concepts (***CC*** for short), which means no relations between these terms and CCs. To avoid the coarse granularity of text vector to sentiment classification, the context of each CC is researched on. We attempt to determine the semantic orientation of a free text by evaluating context of CCs contained in sentences. Our work is based on the two following hypothesizes:

- H_1. A sentence holds its own sentiment context and it is the processing unit for sentiment classification.
- H_2. A sentence with obvious semantic orientation contains at least one Concerned Concept.

H_1 allows us to research the classification task within sentences and H_2 means that a sentence with the value of being learnt or evaluated should contain at least one described CC. A sentence can be formed as:

$$word_{-m} word_{-(m-1)} ... word_{-1} CC_i word_1 ... word_{(n-1)} word_n \ . \tag{1}$$

CC_i (given as an example in this paper) is a noun or noun phrase occupying the position 0 in sentence that is automatically tagged with extended part of speech (***EPOS*** for short)(see section 3.2). A word and its tagged EPOS combine to make a 2-tuple, and all these 2-tuples on both sides of CC_i can form a sequence as follows:

$$\begin{bmatrix} word_{-m} \\ epos_{-m} \end{bmatrix} \begin{bmatrix} word_{-(m-1)} \\ epos_{-(m-1)} \end{bmatrix} \cdots \begin{bmatrix} word_{-1} \\ epos_{-1} \end{bmatrix} CC_i \begin{bmatrix} word_1 \\ epos_1 \end{bmatrix} \cdots \begin{bmatrix} word_{(n-1)} \\ epos_{(n-1)} \end{bmatrix} \begin{bmatrix} word_n \\ epos_n \end{bmatrix} . \tag{2}$$

All the words and corresponding EPOSes are divided into two parts: m 2-tuples on the left side of CC_i (from –m to -1) and n 2-tuples on the right (from 1 to n). These 2-tuples construct the context of the Concerned Concept CC_i.

The sentiment classifying knowledge (see sections 3.3 and 3.4) is the contribution of all the 2-tuples to sentiment classification. That is to say, if a 2-tuple often co-occurs with CC_i in training corpus with positive view, it contributes more to positive orientation than negative one. On the other hand, if the 2-tuple often co-occurs with CC_i in training corpus with negative view, it contributes more to negative orientation. This kind of knowledge can be acquired by statistic technology from corpus.

When judging a free text, the context of CC_i met in a sentence is respectively compared with the positive and negative sentiment classifying knowledge of the same CC_i trained from corpus. Thus, an evaluating function $\boldsymbol{E}$ (see section 3.5) is defined to evaluate the semantic orientation of the free text.

3.2 Extended Part of Speech

Usual part of speech (POS) carries less sentiment information, so it cannot distinguish the semantic orientation between positive and negative. For example, "hearty" and "felonious" are both tagged as "adjective", but for the sentiment classification, only the tag “adjective” cannot classify their sentiment. This means different adjective has different effect on sentiment classification. So we try to extend words’ POS (EPOS) according to its semantic orientation.

Generally speaking, empty words only have structural function without sentiment meaning. Therefore, we just consider substantives in context, which mainly include nouns/noun phrases, verbs, adjectives and adverbs. We give a subtler manner to define EPOS of substantives. Their EPOSes are classified to be positive orientation (PosO) or negative orientation (NegO). Thus, “hearty” is labeled with “pos-adj”, which means PosO of adjective; “felonious” is labeled with “neg-adje”, which means NegO of adjective. Similarly, nouns, verbs and adverbs tagged with their EPOS construct a new word list. In our work, 12,743 Chinese entries in machine readable dictionary are extended by the following principles:

- To nouns, their PosO or NegO is labeled according to their semantic orientation to the entities or events they denote (pos-n or neg-n).
- To adjectives, their common syntax structure is {Adj.+Noun*}. If adjectives are favor of or oppose to their headwords (Noun*), they will be defined as PosO or NegO (pos-adj or neg-adj).
- To adverbs, their common syntax structure is {Adv.+Verb*/Adj*.}, and Verb*/Adj*. is headword. Their PosO or NegO are analyzed in the same way of adjective (pos-adv or neg-adv).
- To transitive verb, their common syntax structure is {TVerb+Object*}, and Object* is headword. Their PosO or NegO are analyzed in the same way of adjective (pos-tv or neg-tv).
- To intransitive verb, their common syntax structure is {Subject*+InTVerb}, and Subject* is headword. Their PosO or NegO are analyzed in the same way of adjective (pos-iv or neg-iv).

3.3 Sentiment Classifying Knowledge Framework

Sentiment classifying knowledge is defined as the importance of all 2-tuples <*word, epos*> that compose the context of CC_i (given as an example) to sentiment classification and **every** Concerned Concept like CC_i has its own positive and negative sentiment classifying knowledge that can be formalized as a 3-tuple K:

$$K := (CC, S^{pos}, S^{neg}) \ . \tag{3}$$

To CC_i, its S_i^{pos} has concrete form that is described as a set of 5-tuples:

$$S_i^{pos} := \left\{ (< word_\xi, epos_\xi >, wordval_\xi, eposval_\xi, \alpha_\xi^{left}, \alpha_\xi^{right}) \right\} \ . \tag{4}$$

Where S_i^{pos} represents the positive sentiment classifying knowledge of CC_i, and it is a data set about all 2-tuples <*word, epos*> appearing in the sentences containing CC_i in training texts with positive view. In contrast, S_i^{neg} is acquired from the training texts with negative view. In other words, S_i^{pos} and S_i^{neg} respectively reserve the features for positive and negative classification to CC_i in corpus.

In terms of S_i^{pos}, the importance of $< word_\xi, epos_\xi >$ is divided into $wordval_\xi$ and $eposval_\xi$ (see section 4.1) which is estimated by modified triggered bi-grams to fit the long distance dependence. If $<word_\xi, epos_\xi>$ appears on the left side of CC_i, the "side" adjusting factor is α_i^{left}; if it appears on the right, the "side" adjusting factor is α_i^{right}. We also define another factor β (see section 4.3) that denotes dynamic "positional" adjusting information during processing a sentence in free text.

3.4 Contribution of <*word, epos*>

If a <*word, epos*> often co-occurs with CC_i in sentences in training corpus with positive view, which may means it contribute more to positive orientation than negative one, and if it often co-occurs with CC_i in negative corpus, it may contribute more to negative orientation.

We modify the classical bi-grams language model to introduce long distance triggered mechanism of $CC_i \rightarrow <word, epos>$. Generally to describe, the contribution ***c*** of each 2-tuple in a positive or negative context (denoted by ***Pos_Neg***) is calculated by (5). This is an analyzing measure of using multi-feature resources.

$$c(<word, epos> | CC_i, Pos\_Neg) := \alpha\beta \exp\left(\Pr(<word, epos> | CC_i, Pos\_Neg)\right) \quad \alpha, \beta > 0 \,. \tag{5}$$

The value represents the contribution of <*word, epos*> to sentiment classification in the sentence containing CC_i. Obviously, when α and β are fixed, the bigger Pr(<*word, epos*>|CC_i, *Pos_Neg*>) is, the bigger contribution *c* of the 2-tuple <*word, epos*> to the semantic orientation Pos_Neg (one of {positive, negative} view) is.

It has been mentioned that α and β are adjusting factor to the sentiment contribution of pair <*word, epos*>. α rectifies the effect of the 2-tuple according to its appearance on which side of CC_i, and β rectifies the effect of the 2-tuple according to its distance from CC_i. They embody the effect of "side" and "position". Thus, it can be inferred that even the same <*word, epos*> will contribute differently because of its side and position.

3.5 Evaluation Function *E*

We propose a function *E* (equation (6)) to evaluate a free text by comparing the context of every appearing *CC* with the two sorts of sentiment context of the same *CC* trained from corpus respectively.

$$E = (1/N) \sum_{i=1}^{N} \left(Sim(S_i', S_i^{pos}) - Sim(S_i', S_i^{neg}) \right) \,. \tag{6}$$

N is the number of total Concerned Concepts in the free text, and *i* denotes certain CC_i. *E* is the semantic orientation of the whole text. Obviously, if $E \geq 0$, the text is to be regarded as positive, otherwise, negative.

To clearly explain the function *E*, we just give the similarity between the context of CC_i (S_i') in free text and the **positive** sentiment context of the same CC_i trained from corpus. The function *Sim* is defined as follows:

$$Sim(S_i^{'},S_i^{pos}) = \left(\prod_{\xi=-1}^{-m}\alpha_\xi^{left}\beta_\xi^{left}\right)\exp\left(\sum_{\xi=-1}^{-m}\Pr(<word_\xi,epos_\xi>|CC_i,positive)\right) + \left(\prod_{\gamma=1}^{n}\alpha_\gamma^{right}\beta_\gamma^{right}\right)\exp\left(\sum_{\gamma=1}^{n}\Pr(<word_\gamma,epos_\gamma>|CC_i,positive)\right). \quad (7)$$

$\left(\prod_{\xi=-1}^{-m}\alpha_\xi^{left}\beta_\xi^{left}\right)\exp\left(\sum_{\xi=-1}^{-m}\Pr(<word_\xi,epos_\xi>|CC_i,positive)\right)$ is the positive orientation of the left context of CC_i, and $\left(\prod_{\gamma=1}^{n}\alpha_\gamma^{right}\beta_\gamma^{right}\right)\exp\left(\sum_{\gamma=1}^{n}\Pr(<word_\gamma,epos_\gamma>|CC_i,positive)\right)$ is the right one. Equation (7) means that the sentiment contribution **c** of **each** <*word, epos*> calculated by (5) in the context of CC_i within a sentence in free text, which is $S_i^{'}$, construct the overall semantic orientation of the sentence together. On the other hand, $Sim(S_i^{'},S_i^{neg})$ can be thought about in the same way.

4 Parameter Estimation

4.1 Estimating Wordval and Eposval

In terms of CC_i, its sentiment classifying knowledge is depicted by (3) and (4), and the parameters *wordval* and *eposval* need to be leant from corpus. Every calculation of Pr(<*word, epos*>|CC_i, *Pos_Neg*) is divided into two parts like (8) according to statistic theory:

$$\Pr(<word_\xi,epos_\xi>|CC_i,Pos\_Neg)=\Pr(epos_\xi\,|\,CC_i,Pos\_Neg)\times\Pr(word_\xi\,|\,CC_i,Pos\_Neg,epos_\xi)\cdot(8)$$

$eposval := \Pr(epos_\xi\,|\,CC_i,Pos\_Neg)$ and $wordval := \Pr(word_\xi\,|\,CC_i,Pos\_Neg,epos_\xi)$.

The "*eposval*" is the probability of $epos_\xi$ appearing on both sides of the CC_i and is estimated by Maximum Likelihood Estimation (MLE). Thus,

$$\Pr(epos_\xi\,|\,CC_i,Pos\_Neg)=\frac{\#(epos_\xi,CC_i)+1}{\sum_{epos}\#(epos,CC_i)+|EPOS|}. \quad (9)$$

The numerator in (9) is the co-occurring frequency between $epos_\xi$ and CC_i within sentence in training texts with Pos_Neg (certain one of {positive, negative}) view and the denominator is the frequency of co-occurrence between all EPOSes appearing in CC_i 's context with Pos_Neg view.

The "*wordval*"is the conditional probability of $word_\xi$ given CC_i and $epos_\xi$ which can also be estimated by MLE:

$$\Pr(word_\xi\,|\,CC_i,Pos\_Neg,epos_\xi)=\frac{\#(word_\xi,epos_\xi,CC_i)+1}{\sum_{word}\#(word,epos_\xi,CC_i)+\sum_{word}1}. \quad (10)$$

The numerator in (10) is the frequency of co-occurrence between $< word_{\xi}, epos_{\xi} >$ and CC_i, and the denominator is the frequency of co-occurrence between all possible words corresponding to $epos_{\xi}$ appearing in CC_i 's context with Pos_Neg view.

For smoothing, we adopt add–one method in (9) and (10).

4.2 Estimating α

The α_{ξ} is the adjusting factor representing the different effect of the $< word_{\xi}, epos_{\xi} >$ to CC_i in texts with Pos_Neg view according to the side it appears, which means different side has different contribution. So, it includes α_{ξ}^{left} and α_{ξ}^{right} :

$$\alpha_{\xi}^{left} = \frac{\#\text{ of } < word_{\xi}, epos_{\xi} > \text{ appearing on the left side of } CC_i}{\#\text{ of } < word_{\xi}, epos_{\xi} > \text{ appearing on both sides of } CC_i}, \tag{11}$$

$$\alpha_{\xi}^{right} = \frac{\#\text{ of } < word_{\xi}, epos_{\xi} > \text{ appearing on the right side of } CC_i}{\#\text{ of } < word_{\xi}, epos_{\xi} > \text{ appearing on both sides of } CC_i}. \tag{12}$$

4.3 Calculating β

β is positional adjusting factor, which means different position to some *CC* will be assigned different weight. This is based on the linguistic hypothesis that the further a word get away from a researched word, the looser their relation is. That is to say, β ought to satisfy an **inverse proportion** relationship with position.

Unlike *wordval, eposval* and α which are all private knowledge to some CC, β is a dynamic positional factor which is independent of semantic orientation of training texts and it is only depend on the position from CC. To the example CC_i, β of $< word_{\mu}, epos_{\mu} >$ occupying the μth position on its left side is β_{μ}^{left}, which can be defined as:

$$\beta_{\mu}^{left} = (1/2)^{|\mu|-1}(2-(1/2)^{m-1})^{-1} \quad \mu = -1 \sim -m\,. \tag{13}$$

β of $< word_{\upsilon}, epos_{\upsilon} >$ occupying the υth position on the right side of CC_i is β_{υ}^{right}, which can be defined as:

$$\beta_{\upsilon}^{right} = (1/2)^{\upsilon-1}(2-(1/2)^{n-1})^{-1} \quad \upsilon = 1 \sim n\,. \tag{14}$$

5 Test and Conclusions

Our research topic is about "Racism" in Chinese texts. The training corpus is built up from Chinese web pages and emails. As mentioned above, all these extracted texts in corpus have obvious semantic orientations to racism: be favor of or oppose to. There are 1137 texts with positive view and 1085 texts with negative view. All the Chinese texts are segmented and tagged with defined EPOS in advance. They are also marked positive/negative for supervised learning. The two sorts of texts with different view are respectively divided into 10 folds. 9 of them are trained and the left one is used for test.

For the special domain, there is no relative result that can be consulted. So, we compare the new method with a traditional classification algorithm, i.e. the popular SVM that uses bi-grams as features. Our experiment includes two parts: a part experiments on the relatively "long" texts that contain more than 15 sentences and the other part experiments on the "short" texts that contain less than 15 sentences. We choose "15" as the threshold to distinguish long or short texts because it is the mathematic expectation of "length" variable of text in our testing corpus. The recall, precision and F1-score are listed in the following Experiment Result Table.

Table. Experiment Result

	Texts with Positive View (more than 15 sentences)		Texts with Negative View (more than 15 sentences)	
	SVM	Our Method	SVM	Our Method
Recall(%)	80.6	73.2	68.4	76.1
Precision(%)	74.1	75.3	75.6	73.8
F1-score(%)	77.2	74.2	71.82	74.9
	Texts with Positive View (less than 15 sentences)		Texts with Negative View (less than 15 sentences)	
	SVM	Our Method	SVM	Our Method
Recall(%)	62.1	63.0	62.1	69.5
Precision(%)	65.1	70.1	59.0	62.3
F1-score(%)	63.6	66.4	60.5	65.7

The experiment shows that our method is useful for sentiment classification, especially for short texts. Seen from the table, when evaluating texts that have more than 15 sentences, for enough features, SVM has better result, while ours is averagely close to it. However, when evaluating the texts containing less than 15 sentences, our method is obviously superior to SVM in either positive or negative view. That means our method has more potential value to sentiment classification of short texts, such as emails, short news, etc.

The better result owes to the fine description within sentences and introducing linguistic knowledge to sentiment classification (such as EPOS, α and β), which proved the two hypothesizes may be reasonable. We use modified triggered bi-grams to describe the importance among features ({<word, epos>}) and Concerned Concepts, then construct sentiment classifying knowledge rather than depend on statistic algorithm only.

To sum up, we draw the following conclusions from our work:

- Introducing more linguistic knowledge is helpful for improving statistic sentiment classification.

- Sentiment classification is a hard task, and it needs subtly describing capability of language model. Maybe the intensional logic of words will be helpful in this field in future.
- Chinese is a language of concept combination and the usage of words is more flexible than Indo-European language, which makes it more difficult to acquire statistic information than English [10].
- We assume an independent condition among sentences yet. We should introduce a suitable mathematic model to group the close sentences.

Our experiment also shows that the algorithm will become weak when no *CC* appears in sentences, but this method is still deserved to explore further. In future, we will integrate more linguistic knowledge and expand our method to a suitable sentence group to improve its performance. Constructing a larger sentiment area may balance the capability of our method between long and short text sentiment classification.

Acknowledgement. This work is supported by NSFC Major Research Program 60496326: Basic Theory and Core Techniques of Non Canonical Knowledge and also supported by National 863 Project (No. 2001AA114210-11).

References

1. Hearst, M.A.: Direction-based text interpretation as an information access refinement. In P. Jacobs (Ed.), *Text-Based Intelligent Systems: Current Research and Practice in Information Extraction and Retrieval.* Mahwah, NJ: Lawrence Erlbaum Associates (1992)
2. Douglas Biber: Variation across Speech and Writing. Cambridge University Press (1988)
3. Vasileios Hatzivassiloglou and Kathleen McKeown: Predicting the semantic orientation of adjectives. In Proc. of the 35th ACL/8th EACL (1997) 174-181
4. Peter D. Turney and Michael L. Littman: Unsupervised learning of semantic orientation from a hundred-billion-word corpus. Technical Report EGB-1094, National Research Council Canada (2002)
5. Marti Hearst: Direction-based text interpretation as an information access refinement. In Paul Jacobs, editor, Text-Based Intelligent Systems. Lawrence Erlbaum Associates (1992)
6. Bo Pang and Lillian Lee: A Sentimental Education: Sentiment Analysis Using Subjectivity Summarization Based on Minimum Cuts. Proceedings of the 42nd ACL (2004) 271--278
7. Sanjiv Das and Mike Chen: Yahoo! for Amazon: Extracting market sentiment from stock message boards. In Proc. of the 8th Asia Pacific Finance Association Annual Conference (2001)
8. Vasileios Hatzivassiloglou, Janyce Wiebe: Effects of Adjective Orientation and Gradability on Sentence Subjectivity. COLING (2000) 299-305
9. Peter Turney: Thumbs up or thumbs down? Semantic orientation applied to unsupervised classication of reviews. In Proc. of the ACL (2002)
10. Bo Pang, Lillian Lee and Shivakumar Vaithyanathan: Thumbs up? Sentiment Classification using Machine Learning Techniques. In Proc. Conf. on EMNLP (2002)
11. Warren Sack: On the computation of point of view. In Proc. of the Twelfth AAAI, page 1488. Student abstract (1994)
12. Richard M. Tong: An operational system for detecting and tracking opinions in on-line discussion. Workshop note, SIGIR Workshop on Operational Text Classification (2001)

Topic Tracking Based on Linguistic Features

Fumiyo Fukumoto and Yusuke Yamaji

Interdisciplinary Graduate School of Medicine and Engineering,
Univ. of Yamanashi, 4-3-11, Takeda, Kofu, 400-8511, Japan
fukumoto@yamanashi.ac.jp, g03mk031@ccn.yamanashi.ac.jp

Abstract. This paper explores two linguistically motivated restrictions on the set of words used for topic tracking on newspaper articles: named entities and headline words. We assume that named entities is one of the linguistic features for topic tracking, since both topic and event are related to a specific *place* and *time* in a story. The basic idea to use headline words for the tracking task is that headline is a compact representation of the original story, which helps people to quickly understand the most important information contained in a story. Headline words are automatically generated using headline generation technique. The method was tested on the Mainichi Shimbun Newspaper in Japanese, and the results of topic tracking show that the system works well even for a small number of positive training data.

1 Introduction

With the exponential growth of information on the Internet, it is becoming increasingly difficult to find and organize *relevant* materials. Tracking task, i.e. starts from a few sample stories and finds all subsequent stories that discuss the target topic, is a new line of research to attack the problem. One of the major problems in the tracking task is how to make a clear distinction between a *topic* and an *event* in the story. Here, an event refers to the subject of a story itself, i.e. a writer wants to express, in other words, notions of who, what, where, when, why and how in the story. On the other hand, a topic is some unique thing that occurs at a specific place and time associated with some specific actions [1]. It becomes *background* among stories. Therefore, an event drifts, but a topic does not. For example, in the stories of 'Kobe Japan quake' from the TDT1 corpus, the event includes early reports of damage, location and nature of quake, rescue efforts, consequences of the quake, and on-site reports, while the topic is Kobe Japan quake.

A wide range of statistical and machine learning techniques have been applied to topic tracking, including k-Nearest Neighbor classification, Decision Tree induction [3], relevance feedback method of IR [12,13], hierarchical and non-hierarchical clustering algorithms [20], and a variety of Language Modeling [15,5,10,17]. The main task of these techniques is to tune the parameters or the threshold for binary decisions to produce optimal results. In the TDT context, however, parameter tuning is a tricky issue for tracking. Because only the small number of labeled positive stories is available for training. Moreover, the well-known past experience from IR that notions of who, what, where, when, why, and how may not make a great contribution to the topic tracking task [1] causes this fact, i.e. a topic and an event are different from each other.

R. Dale et al. (Eds.): IJCNLP 2005, LNAI 3651, pp. 10–21, 2005.

This paper explores two linguistically motivated restrictions on the set of words used for topic tracking on newspaper articles: named entities and headline words. A topic is related to a specific *place* and *time*, and an event refers to notions of who(*person*), where(*place*), when(*time*) including what, why and how in a story. Therefore, we can assume that named entities is one of the linguistic features for topic tracking. Another linguistic feature is a set of headline words. The basic idea to use headline words for topic tracking is that headline is a compact representation of the original story, which helps people to quickly understand the most important information contained in a story, and therefore, it may include words to understand what the story is about, what is characteristic of this story with respect to other stories, and hopefully include words related to both topic and event in the story. A set of headline words is automatically generated. To do this, we use a technique proposed by Banko [2]. It produces coherent summaries by building statistical models for content selection and surface realization. Another purpose of this work is to create Japanese corpus for topic tracking task. We used Mainichi Shimbun Japanese Newspaper corpus from Oct. to Dec. of 1998 which corresponds to the TDT3 corpus. We annotated these articles against the 60 topics which are defined by the TDT3.

The rest of the paper is organized as follows. The next section provides an overview of existing topic tracking techniques. We then describe a brief explanation of a headline generation technique proposed by Banko et al. [2]. Next, we present our method for topic tracking, and finally, we report some experiments using the Japanese newspaper articles with a discussion of evaluation.

2 Related Work

The approach that relies mainly on corpus statistics is widely studied in the topic tracking task, and an increasing number of machine learning techniques have been applied to the task. CMU proposed two methods: a k-Nearest Neighbor (kNN) classifier and a Decision-Tree Induction (dtree) classifier [1,20,3]. Dragon Systems proposed two tracking systems; one is based on standard language modeling technique, i.e. unigram statistics to measure story similarity [18] and another is based on a Beta-Binomial model [10]. UMass viewed the tracking problem as an instance of on-line document classification, i.e. it classifies documents into categories or classes [4,8,19,9,14]. They proposed a method including query expansion with multi-word features and weight-learning steps for building linear text classifiers for the tracking task [13]. These approaches, described above, seem to be robust and have shown satisfactory performance in stories from different corpora, i.e. TDT1 and TDT2. However, Carbonell claims that something more is needed if the system is intended for recognizing topic drift [3]. Yang et al. addressed the issue of difference between early and later stories related to the target event in the TDT tracking task. They adapted several machine learning techniques, including k-Nearest Neighbor(kNN) algorithm and Rocchio approach [21]. Their method combines the output of a diverse set of classifiers and tuning parameters for the combined system on a retrospective corpus. The idea comes from the well-known practice in information retrieval and speech recognition of combining the output of a large number of systems to yield a better result than the individual system's output. They reported that the new variants of kNN reduced up to 71% in weighted error rates on the TDT3-dryrun corpus.

GE R&D proposed a method for topic tracking by using summarization technique, i.e. using *content compression* rather than on corpus statistics to detect relevance and assess topicality of the source material [16]. Their system operates by first creating a topic tracking query out of the available training stories. Subsequently, it accepts incoming stories, summarizes them topically, scores the summaries(passages) for content, then assesses content relevance to the tracking query. They reported stories whose compressed content summaries clear the empirically established threshold are classified as being 'on topic'. Unlike most previous work on summarization which focused on extractive summarization: selecting text spans - either complete sentences or paragraphs - from the original story, this approach solves a problem for extractive summarization, i.e. in many cases, the most important information in the story is scattered across multiple sentences. However, their approach uses frequency-based term weighting. Therefore, it is not clear if the method can identify the most important information contained in a story.

These methods, described above, show that it is crucial to develop a method for extracting words related to both topic and event in a story. Like other approaches, our method is based on corpus statistics. However, our method uses two linguistically motivated restrictions on the set of words: named entities and headline words. We assume that named entities is one of the linguistic features for topic tracking, since both topic and event are related to a specific $place$ and $time$ in a story. Another linguistic feature is a set of headline words. The basic idea to use headline words is that headline is a compact representation of the original story, and therefore, it may include words to understand what the story is about, and hopefully include words related to both topic and event in the story.

3 Generating Headline

Banko et al. proposed an approach to summarization capable of generating summaries shorter than a sentence. It produces by building statistical models for *content selection* and *surface realization*. We used their method to extract headline words. Content selection requires that the system learns a model of the relationship between the appearance of words in a story and the appearance of corresponding words in the headline. The probability of a candidate headline, H, consisting of words $(w_1,w_2,\cdots,w_n)$, can be computed:

$$P(w_1,\cdots,w_n) = \prod_{i=1}^{n} P(w_i \in H \mid w_i \in D) \cdot P(len(H) = n) \cdot \prod_{i=2}^{n} P(w_i \mid w_1,\cdots,w_{i-1}) \quad (1)$$

In formula (1), the first term denotes the words selected for the headline, and can be computed:

$$P(w_i \in H \mid w_i \in D) = \frac{P(w_i \in D \mid w_i \in H) \cdot P(w_i \in H)}{P(w_i \in D)} \quad (2)$$

where H and D represent the bags of words that the headline and the story contain. Formula (2) shows the conditional probability of a word occurring in the headline given that the word appeared in the story. It has been estimated from a suitable story/headline corpus. The second term in formula (1) shows the length of the resulting headline, and can also be learned from the source story. The third term shows the most likely sequencing of the words in the content set. Banko et al. assumed that the likelihood of a word in the story is independent of other words in the headline. Surface realization is to estimate the probability of any particular surface ordering as a headline candidate. It can be computed by modeling the probability of word sequences. Banko et al. used a bigram language model. When they estimate probabilities for sequences that have not been seen in the training data, they used back-off weights [6].

Headline generation can be obtained as a weighted combination of the content and structure model log probabilities which is shown in formula (3).

$$arg\ max_H(\alpha \cdot \sum_{i=1}^{n} \log(P(w_i \in H \mid w_i \in D)) + \beta \cdot \log(P(len(H) = n)) + \gamma \cdot \sum_{i=2}^{n} \log(P(w_i \mid w_{i-1}))) \quad (3)$$

To generate a headline, it is necessary to find a sequence of words that maximizes the probability, under the content selection and surface realization models, that it was generated from the story to be summarized. In formula (3), cross-validation is used to learn weights, α, β and γ for a particular story genre.

4 Extracting Linguistic Features and Tracking

We explore two linguistically motivated restrictions on the set of words used for tracking: named entities and headline words.

4.1 Extracting Named Entities and Generating Headline Words

For identifying named entities, we use CaboCha [7] for Japanese Mainichi Shimbun corpus, and extracted Person Name, Organization, Place, and Proper Name.

Headline generation can be obtained as a weighted combination of the content and structure model log probabilities shown in formula (3). The system was trained on the 3 months Mainichi Shimbun articles((27,133 articles from Jan. to Mar. 1999) for Japanese corpus. We estimate α, β and γ in formula (3) using 5 cross-validation[1]. Fig. 1 illustrates sample output using Mainichi Shimbun corpus. Numbers to the right are log probabilities of the word sequence.

4.2 Tracking by Hierarchical Classification

In the TDT tracking task, the number of labeled positive training stories is small (at most 16 stories) compared to the negative training stories. Therefore, the choice of *good* negative stories from a large number of training data is an important issue to detect subject shifts for a binary classifier such as a machine learning technique, Support Vector Machines(SVMs) [22]. We apply hierarchical classification technique to the training data.

[1] In the experiment, we set α, β, γ to 1.0, 1.0, 0.8, respectively.

<Headline> パキスタン (Pakistan) カシミール問題解決へ (Kashimir issue)
第 3 パーティ仲裁国 (third party mediation) と会合 (meeting) </Headline>
イスラマバード, パキスタンは 2 週間以内に, 燐国インドについて話合いを持つ, すなわちパキスタンは第 3 国の仲裁国に対してインドとパキスタンで起きた過去の戦争に関するカシミール問題に対して調査するよう強く迫った...
(ISLAMABAD, Pakistan, Less than two weeks ahead of fresh talks with its uneasy neighbor India, Pakistan pressed on Saturday for international mediation in the thorny Kashmir issue, the flashpoint of two previous wars between the two countries...)
[Generated title words]
2: カシミール (Kashimir) 問題 (issue) -6.83
3: 第 3 (third) パーティ (party) 仲裁 (mediation) -11.97
4: カシミール (Kashimir) インド (India) Islamabad 再開 (resume) -23.84
5: カシミール (Kashimir) インド (India) 再開 (resume) イスラマバード (Islamabad) カシミール (Kashimir) -33.36
6: カシミール (Kashimir) インド (India) 再開 (resume) イスラマバード (Islamabad) カシミール (Kashimir) イスラム教 (Muslim) -38.32

Fig. 1. Simple story with original headline and generated output

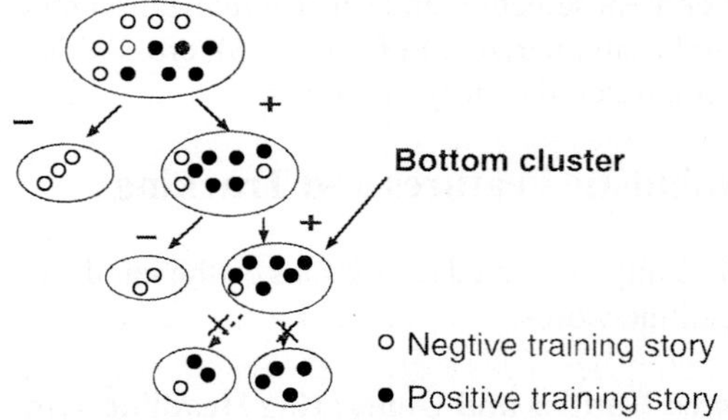

Fig. 2. Graphical representation of hierarchical classification

A hierarchical decomposition of a classification problem can be used to set the negative set for discriminative training. We use partitioning clustering algorithm, k-means ($k = 2$) which partitions a training data into clusters where similar stories are found in the same cluster and separated from dissimilar stories. Fig. 2 illustrates hierarchical classification of training data with k-means. Each level in Fig. 2 denotes the result obtained by a simple k-means (k=2) algorithm, and consists of two clusters: one is a cluster which includes positive and negative stories. Another is a cluster with only negative stories, each of these are dissimilar with the positive stories. The algorithm involves iterating through the data that the system is permitted to classify during each iteration. More specifically:

1. In the training data which includes all the initial positive training stories, select two initial seeds $\mathbf{g}$ and $\bar{\mathbf{s}}_i$, where $\mathbf{g}$ is a vector of the center of gravity on positive training stories, and $\bar{\mathbf{s}}_i$ is a vector of the negative training story which has the smallest value(as measured by cosine similarity) between $\bar{\mathbf{s}}_i$ and $\mathbf{g}$. The center of gravity $\mathbf{g}$ is defined as:

$$\mathbf{g} = (g_1, \cdots, g_n) = (\frac{1}{p}\sum_{i=1}^{p} s_{i1}, \cdots, \frac{1}{p}\sum_{i=1}^{p} s_{in}) \tag{4}$$

where s_{ij} $(1 \leq j \leq n)$ is the TF$*$IDF value of word j in the positive story $\mathbf{s}_i$.

2. Apply k-means (k=2) to the training data.
3. For the cluster which includes positive stories, iterate step 1 and 2 until positive training stories are divided into two clusters[2].

Tracking involves a training phase and a testing phase. During the training phase, we employ the hierarchy which is shown in Fig. 2 by learning separate classifiers trained by SVMs. '± 1' in Fig. 2 denotes binary classification for stories at each level of the hierarchy. Each test story is judged to be negative or positive by using these classifiers to greedily select sub-branches until a leaf is reached. Once, the test story is judged to be negative, tracking is terminated. When the test story is judged to be positive by using a classifier of the bottom cluster, a cluster is divided into two: positive and negative stories. For each training data in the bottom cluster and test stories, we extract named entities and headline words. The result of training data is used to train SVMs and a classifier is induced. Each test story which also consists of a set of words produced by named entities and generating headline word procedures is judged to be negative or positive by using the classifier. This procedure, tracking, is repeated until the last test story is judged.

5 Experiments

5.1 Experiments Set Up

We chose the TDT3 corpus covering October 1, 1998 to December 31, 1998 as our gold standard corpus for creating Japanese corpus. The TDT3 corpus, developed at LDC, is a larger and richer collection, consisting of 34,600 stories with 60 manually identified topics. The stories were collected from 2 newswire, 3 radio programs and 4 television programs. We then create a Japanese corpus, i.e. we annotate Mainichi Shimbun Japanese Newspaper stories from October 1, 1998 to December 31, 1998 against the 60 topics. Not all the topics could have seen over the 3 months Japanese Newspaper stories. Table 1 shows 20 topics which are included in the Japanese Newspaper corpus.

'Topic ID' in Table 1 denotes ID number defined by the TDT3. The evaluation for annotation is made by three humans. The classification is determined to be correct if the majority of three human judges agrees. The Japanese corpus consists of 27,133 stories. We used it in the experiment. We obtained a vocabulary of 52,065 unique words after tagging by a morphological analysis, Chasen [11].

5.2 Basic Results

Table 2 summarizes the results using all words for each sequence that maximizes the probability, i.e. 14 sequences in all. The results were obtained using the standard TDT

[2] When the number of positive training stories(N_t) is 1, iterate step 1 and 2 until the depth of the tree in the hierarchy is identical to that of N_t=2.

Table 1. Topic Name

Topic ID	Topic name	Topic ID	Topic name
30001	Cambodian government coalition	30003	Pinochet trial
30006	NBA labor disputes	30014	Nigerian gas line fire
30017	North Korean food shortages	30018	Tony Blair visits China in Oct.
30022	Chinese dissidents sentenced	30030	Taipei Mayoral elections
30031	Shuttle Endeavour mission for space station	30033	Euro Introduced
30034	Indonesia-East Timor conflict	30038	Olympic bribery scandal
30042	PanAm lockerbie bombing trial	30047	Space station module Zarya launched
30048	IMF bailout of Brazil	30049	North Korean nuclear facility?
30050	U.S. Mid-term elections	30053	Clinton's Gaza trip
30055	D'Alema's new Italian government	30057	India train derailment

Table 2. The results

N_t	Prec.	Rec.	F	Miss	F/A	N_t	Prec.	Rec.	F	Miss	F/A
1	.000	.000	.000	1.000	.0000	8	.858	.432	.575	.568	.0001
2	.846	.040	.077	.960	.0000	16	.788	.520	.626	.480	.0004
4	.905	.142	.245	.858	.0000	Avg.	.679	.227	.305	.663	.0001

evaluation measure. 'N_t' denotes the number of positive training stories where N_t takes on values 1, 2, 4, 8 and 16. The test set is always the collection minus the N_t = 16 stories. 'Miss' denotes Miss rate, which is the ratio of the stories that were judged as YES but were not evaluated as YES for the run in question. 'F/A' shows false alarm rate, which is the ratio of the stories judged as NO but were evaluated as YES. 'Prec.' is the ratio of correct assignments by the system divided by the total number of system's assignments. 'F'(pooled avg) is a measure that balances recall(Rec.) and precision, where recall denotes the ratio of correct assignments by the system divided by the total number of correct assignments. We recall that a generated headline is a sequence of words that maximizes the probability. We set the maximum number of word sequence by calculating the average number of the original titles, and obtained the number of 15 words. The minimum number of words in a sequence is two. Fig. 3 illustrates the extracted headline for each sequence. Box in Fig. 3 shows a word, and 'arg max P(x)' denotes the maximum probability of a candidate headline. For example, the extracted sequence

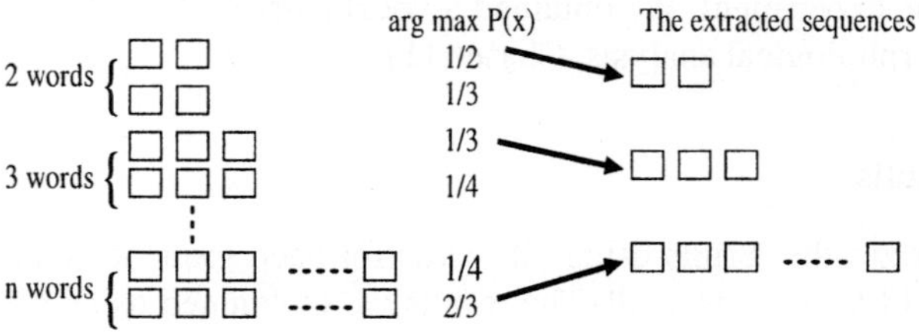

Fig. 3. The extracted headline for each sequence

of two words is the sequence whose maximum probability is $\frac{1}{2}$. Table 2 shows that our method is more likely to be effective for higher values of N_t, while F-score was 0 when $N_t = 1$.

5.3 Title Words

Our approach using the headline generation is to find a sequence of words that maximizes the probability. It can be produced for an arbitrary number of words. We recall that Table 2 shows the result using each sequence that maximizes the probability. However, when $N_t = 1$, the result was not good, as the F-score was zero. We thus conducted the following two experiments to examine the effect of the number of words in a sequence: (1) the tracking task using all words, each of which is the element of only one sequence that maximizes the probability(Fig. 4) and (2) the tracking using various number of word sequences(Fig. 5). In (2), we tested different number of words in a sequence, and we chose six words that optimized the global F-score. The results are shown in Tables 3 and 4.

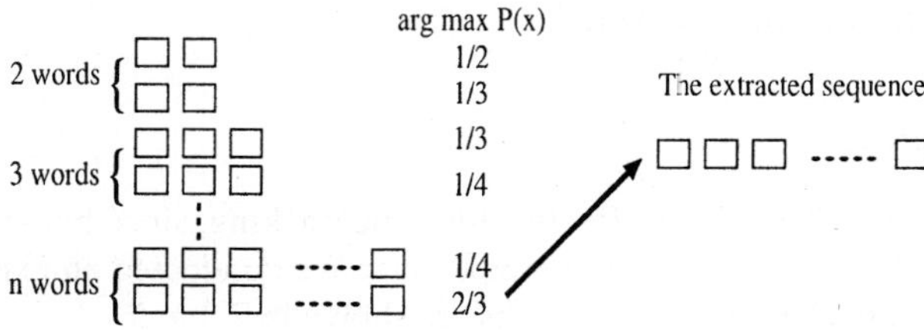

Fig. 4. The extracted headline for maximizing the probability

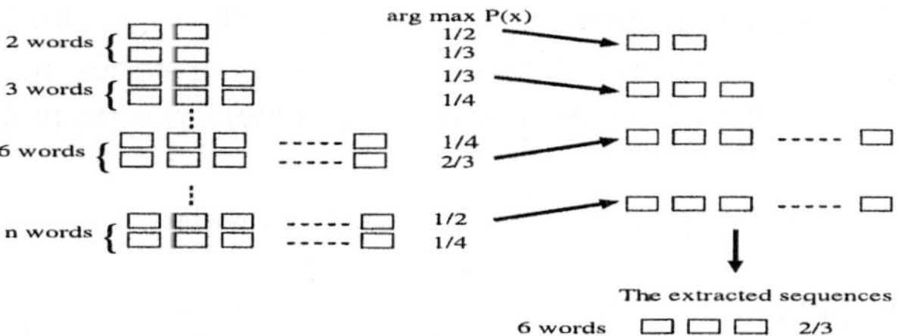

Fig. 5. The extracted headline for various sequences

Table 3 shows the tracking result using only one sequence of words that maximizes the probability, and Table 4 shows the result of six words. In Table 3, the average number of words which maximizes the probability for all the training data is 4.4, and the result is similar to that of Table 4. We can see from both Tables 3 and 4 that when the number of words in a sequence is small, the result has no effect with the number of positive training data, since the range of F-score in Table 3 is $0.415 \sim 0.478$, and that in Table 4

Table 3. The result using title words with high probabilities

N_t	Prec.	Rec.	F	Miss	F/A	N_t	Prec.	Rec.	F	Miss	F/A
1	.466	.375	.415	.626	.0005	8	.702	.372	.487	.628	.0003
2	.591	.402	.478	.599	.0003	16	.604	.393	.476	.607	.0007
4	.674	.340	.452	.660	.0003	Avg.	.607	.376	.462	.624	.0004

Table 4. The result using 3 title words

N_t	Prec.	Rec.	F	Miss	F/A	N_t	Prec.	Rec.	F	Miss	F/A
1	.608	.378	.465	.622	.0003	8	.687	.334	.453	.662	.0003
2	.652	.365	.466	.635	.0002	16	.734	.397	.516	.603	.0004
4	.709	.336	.456	.664	.0002	Avg.	.678	.362	.471	.637	.0003

is 0.453 $\sim$ 0.516. On the other hand, as we can see from Table 2, when the number of title words is large, the smaller the number of positive training data is, the worse the result is. To summarize the evaluation, the best result is when we use a sequence which consists of a small number of words, six words.

5.4 Named Entities

We assume that named entities is effective for topic tracking, since both topic and event are related to a specific *place* and *time* in a story. We conducted an experiment using various types of named entities. The results are shown in Table 5.

Table 5 shows the tracking result using six words which is the output of the headline generation with some named entities. In Table 5, 'Org', 'Per', 'Loc', 'Proper' denotes organization, person, location, and proper name, respectively. 'None' denotes the baseline, i.e. we use only the output of the headline generation, six words. Table 5 shows that the best result was when we use 'Org', 'Person', and 'Proper' with $N_t = 16$, and the F-score is 0.717. When N_t is larger than 8 positive training stories, the method which uses six title words with named entities consistently outperforms the baseline. When N_t

Table 5. Combination of Named Entities

Named entities	N_t [F-measure]					Avg.	Named entities	N_t [F-measure]					Avg.
	1	2	4	8	16			1	2	4	8	16	
Org Per Loc Proper	.138	.302	.377	.589	.673	.416	Per Loc	.237	.379	.453	.565	.647	.456
Org Per Loc	.138	.307	.391	.586	.668	.418	Per Proper	.437	**.474**	.542	.580	.671	.541
Org Per Loc	.118	.187	.296	.590	**.717**	.382	Loc Proper	.440	.461	.496	.647	.633	.535
Org Loc Proper	.159	.342	.350	.607	.667	.471	Org	.143	.205	.270	.561	.606	.357
Per Loc Proper	.239	.397	.458	.574	.652	.464	Per	**.498**	**.497**	.517	.543	.629	.537
Org Per	.112	.178	.288	.579	.704	.372	Loc	.439	.459	.485	.561	.612	.511
Org Loc	.165	.350	.342	.594	.657	.422	Proper	**.486**	**.473**	.470	.453	.557	.488
Org Proper	.143	.229	.235	.548	.638	.359	None	.465	.466	.456	.453	.516	.471

Table 6. The result with v.s. without hierarchical classification

With hierarchy						Without hierarchy					
N_t	Prec.	Rec.	F	Miss	F/A	N_t	Prec.	Rec.	F	Miss	F/A
1	.695	.422	.525	.578	.0002	1	.669	.396	.498	.604	.0002
2	.707	.475	.568	.526	.0002	2	.671	.394	.497	.606	.0002
4	.835	.414	.554	.586	.0001	4	.747	.396	.517	.605	.0002
8	.823	.523	.639	.477	.0002	8	.709	.440	.543	.560	.0003
16	.819	.573	.674	.428	.0003	16	.818	.511	.629	.489	.0003
Avg.	.776	.481	.592	.519	.0001	Avg.	.723	.427	.537	.573	.0002

Table 7. The result with a hierarchy was worse than that of without a hierarchy

		With hierarchy			Without hierarchy		
Topic	N_t	**F/A**	Prec.	F	**F/A**	Prec.	F
Pinochet trial	16	.0003	.828	.870	.0002	.837	.875
Taipei Mayoral elections	4	.0004	.333	.400	.0002	1.000	.667
Taipei Mayoral elections	8	.0003	.333	.500	.0002	1.000	.667
North Korean food shortages	16	.0002	.700	.298	.0001	.700	.304

is smaller than 4 positive training stories, the result was improved when we add 'Per' and 'Proper' to the baseline. This indicates that these two named entities are especially effective for topic tracking.

5.5 Hierarchical Classification

We recall that we used partitioning clustering algorithm, k-means ($k = 2$) to balance the amount of positive and negative training stories used per estimate. To examine the effect of hierarchical classification using k-means, we compare the result with and without a hierarchy. Table 6 shows the results using the same data, i.e. we use the output of headline generation, six words, and named entities, Person name, and Proper name.

Overall, the result of 'with hierarchy' was better than that of 'without hierarchy' in all N_t values. On the other hand, there are four topics/N_t patterns whose results with hierarchical classification were worse than those of without a hierarchy. Table 7 shows the result. The F/A for all results with a hierarchy were lower than those without a hierarchy. One reason behind this lies iteration of a hierarchical classification, i.e. our algorithm involves iterating through the data that the system is permitted to classify during each iteration. As a result, there are a few negative training data in the bottom cluster, and the test stories were judged as NO but were evaluated as YES. We need to explore a method for determining the depth of the tree in the hierarchical classification, and this is a rich space for further investigation.

5.6 Comparative Experiments

The contribution of two linguistically motivated restrictions on the set of words is best explained by looking at other features. We thus compared our method with two baselines:

Table 8. Comparative experiment

Method	Prec.	Rec.	F	Miss	F/A	Method	Prec.	Rec.	F	Miss	F/A
Stories	.875	.026	.057	.974	.0000	Headlines and NE	.835	.414	.554	.586	.0001
Original headlines	.911	.190	.315	.810	.0000						

Table 9. N_t and F-measure

Method	N_t					Method	N_t				
	1	2	4	8	16		1	2	4	8	16
Stories	-5%	-5%	-	+45%	+61%	Headlines and NE	-2%	-2%	-	+2%	+11%
Original headlines	-26%	-16%	-	+22%	+34%						

(1) all words in the stories as features, and (2) the original headlines in the stories as features[3]. Table 8 shows each result, when N_t = 4. 'Stories' shows the result using all words in the stories and 'Original headlines' shows the result using the original headlines in the stories. 'Headlines and NE' denotes the best result obtained by our method, i.e. the output of headline generation, six words, and named entities, Person and Proper name. Table 8 shows that our method outperformed the other two methods, especially attained a better balance between recall and precision. Table 9 illustrates changes in pooled F1 measure as N_t varies, with N_t = 4 as the baseline. Table 9 shows that our method is the most stable all N_t training instances before N_t = 16, especially our method is effective even for a small number of positive training instances for per-source training: it learns a good topic representation and gains almost nothing in effectiveness beyond N_t = 16.

6 Conclusion

We have reported an approach for topic tracking on newspaper articles based on the two linguistic features, named entities and headlines. The result was 0.776 average precision and 0.481 recall, especially our method is effective even for a small number of positive training instances for per-source training in the tracking task. Future work includes (i) optimal decision of seed points for k-means clustering algorithm, (ii) exploring a method to determine the depth of the tree in the hierarchical classification, and (iii) applying the method to the TDT3 corpus.

References

1. J.Allan and J.Carbonell and G.Doddington and J.Yamron and Y.Yang: Topic Detection and Tracking Pilot Study Final Report. Proc. of the DARPA Workshop. (1997)
2. M.Banko and V.Mittal and M.Witbrock: Headline Generation Based on Statistical Translation. Proc. of ACL-2000. (2000) 318–325

[3] In both cases, we used hierarchical classification to make our results comparable with these two results.

3. J.Carbonell and Y.Yang and J.Lafferty and R.D.Brown and T.Pierce and X.Liu: CMU Report on TDT-2: Segmentation, Detection and Tracking, Proc. of the DARPA Workshop, (1999)
4. D.R.Cutting, D.R.Karger and L.O.Pedersen and J.W.Tukey: Scatter/Gather: a Cluster-based Approach to Browsing Large Document Collections . Proc. of ACM SIGIR-1992. (1992) 318–329
5. H.Jin and R.Schwartz and S.Sista and F.Walls: Topic Tracking for Radio, TV Broadcast, and Newswire. Proc. of the DARPA Broadcast News Transcription and Understanding Workshop. (1999)
6. S.Katz: Estimation of Probabilities from Sparse Data for the Language Model Component of a Speech Recognizer. IEEE Transactions on Acoustics, Speech and Signal Processing. **24** (1987)
7. T.Kudo and Y.Matsumoto: Fast Methods for Kernel-Based Text Analysis. Proc. of the ACL-2003. (2003) 24–31
8. D.D.Lewis: An Evaluation of Phrasal and Clustered Representations on a Text Categorization Task. Proc. of the ACM SIGIR-1994. (1994) 37–50
9. D.D.Lewis and R.E.Schapire and J.P.Callan and R.Papka: Training Algorithms for Linear Text Classifiers. Proc. of the ACM SIGIR-1996. (1996) 298–306
10. S.A.Lowe: The Beta-binomial Mixture Model and its Application to TDT Tracking and Detection. Proc. of the DARPA Workshop. (1999)
11. Y.Matsumoto and A.Kitauchi and T.Yamashita and Y.Haruno and O.Imaichi and T.Imamura: Japanese Morphological Analysis System Chasen Mannual. NAIST Technical Report NAIST-IS-TR97007. (1997)
12. D.W.Oard: Topic Tracking with the PRISE Information Retrieval System. Proc. of the DARPA Workshop. (1999)
13. R.Papka and J.Allan: UMASS Approaches to Detection and Tracking at TDT2. Proc. of the DARPA Workshop. (1999)
14. R.E.Schapire: BoosTexter: A Boosting-based System for Text Categorization. Journal of Machine Learning. (1999)
15. R.Schwartz and T.Imai and L.Nguyen and J.Makhoul: A Maximum Likelihood Model for Topic Classification of Broadcast News. Proc. of Eurospeech. (1996) 270–278
16. T.Strzalkowski and G.C.Stein and G.B.Wise: GE.Tracker: A Robust, Lightweight Topic Tracking System. Proc. of the DARPA Workshop. (1999)
17. Yamron and Carp: Topic Tracking in a News Stream. Proc. of the DARPA Broadcast News Transcription and Understanding Workshop. (1999)
18. J.P.Yamron and I.Carp and L.Gillick and S.Lowe and P.V.Mulbregt: Topic Tracking in a News Stream. Proc. of the DARPA Workshop. (1999)
19. Y. Yang: Expert Network: Effective and Efficient Learning from Human Decisions in Text Categorization and Retrieval. Proc. of the ACM SIGIR-1994. (1994) 13–22
20. Y.Yang and T.Pierce and J.Carbonell: A Study on Retrospective and On-Line Event Detection. Proc. of the ACM SIGIR-1998. (1998) 28–36
21. Y.Yang and T.Ault and T.Pierce and C.W.Lattimer: Improving Text Categorization Methods for Event Tracking. Proc. of the ACM SIGIR-2000. (2000) 65–72
22. V.Vapnik: The Nature of Statistical Learning Theory. Springer. (1995)

The Use of Monolingual Context Vectors for Missing Translations in Cross-Language Information Retrieval

Yan Qu[1], Gregory Grefenstette[2], and David A. Evans[1]

[1] Clairvoyance Corporation, 5001 Baum Boulevard, Suite 700, Pittsburgh, PA, 15213, USA
{yqu, dae}@clairvoyancecorp.com
[2] LIC2M/SCRI/LIST/DTSI/CEA, B.P.6, 92265 Fontenay-aux-Roses Cedex, France
{Gregory.Grefenstette}@cea.fr

Abstract. For cross-language text retrieval systems that rely on bilingual dictionaries for bridging the language gap between the source query language and the target document language, good bilingual dictionary coverage is imperative. For terms with missing translations, most systems employ some approaches for expanding the existing translation dictionaries. In this paper, instead of lexicon expansion, we explore whether using the context of the unknown terms can help mitigate the loss of meaning due to missing translation. Our approaches consist of two steps: (1) to identify terms that are closely associated with the unknown source language terms as *context* vectors and (2) to use the translations of the associated terms in the context vectors as the surrogate translations of the unknown terms. We describe a query-independent version and a query-dependent version using such monolingual context vectors. These methods are evaluated in Japanese-to-English retrieval using the NTCIR-3 topics and data sets. Empirical results show that both methods improved CLIR performance for short and medium-length queries and that the query-dependent context vectors performed better than the query-independent versions.

1 Introduction

For cross-language text retrieval systems that rely on bilingual dictionaries for bridging the language gap between the source query language and the target document language, good bilingual dictionary coverage is imperative [8,9]. Yet, translations for proper names and special terminology are often missing in available dictionaries. Various methods have been proposed for finding translations of names and terminology through transliteration [5,11,13,14,16,18,20] and corpus mining [6,7,12,15,22]. In this paper, instead of attempting to find the candidate translations of terms without translations to expand existing translation dictionaries, we explore to what extent simply using text context can help mitigate the missing translation problem and for what kinds of queries. The context-oriented approaches include (1) identifying words that are closely associated with the unknown source language terms as *context* vectors and (2) using the translations of the associated words in the context vectors as the surrogate translations of the unknown words. We describe a query-independent

R. Dale et al. (Eds.): IJCNLP 2005, LNAI 3651, pp. 22 – 33, 2005.

version and a query-dependent version using such context vectors. We evaluate these methods in Japanese-to-English retrieval using the NTCIR-3 topics and data sets. In particular, we explore the following questions:

- Can translations obtained from context vectors help CLIR performance?
- Are query-dependent context vectors more effective than query-independent context vectors for CLIR?

In the balance of this paper, we first describe related work in Section 2. The methods of obtaining translations through context vectors are presented in Section 3. The CLIR evaluation system and evaluation results are presented in Section 4 and Section 5, respectively. We summarize the paper in Section 6.

2 Related Work

In dictionary-based CLIR applications, approaches for dealing with terms with missing translations can be classified into three major categories. The first is a do-nothing approach by simply ignoring the terms with missing translations. The second category includes attempts to generate candidate translations for a subset of unknown terms, such as names and technical terminology, through phonetic translation between different languages (i.e., transliteration) [5,11,13,14,16,18,20]. Such methods generally yield translation pairs with reasonably good accuracy reaching about 70% [18]. Empirical results have shown that the expanded lexicons can significantly improve CLIR system performance [5,16,20]. The third category includes approaches for expanding existing bilingual dictionaries by exploring multilingual or bilingual corpora. For example, the "mix-lingual" feature of the Web has been exploited for locating translation pairs by searching for the presence of both Chinese and English text in a text window [22]. In work focused on constructing bilingual dictionaries for machine translation, automatic translation lexicons are compiled using either clean aligned parallel corpora [12,15] or non-parallel comparable corpora [6,7]. In work with non-parallel corpora, contexts of source language terms and target language terms and a seed translation lexicon are combined to measure the association between the source language terms and potential translation candidates in the target language. The techniques with non-parallel corpora save the expense of constructing large-scale parallel corpora with the tradeoff of lower accuracy, e.g., about 30% accuracy for the top-one candidate [6,7]. To our knowledge, the usefulness of such lexicons in CLIR systems has not been evaluated.

While missing translations have been addressed in dictionary-based CLIR systems, most of the approaches mentioned above attempt to resolve the problem through dictionary expansion. In this paper, we explore non-lexical approaches and their effectiveness on mitigating the problem of missing translations. Without additional lexicon expansion, and keeping the unknown terms in the source language query, we extract context vectors for these unknown terms and obtain their translations as the surrogate translations for the original query terms. This is motivated by the pre-translation feedback techniques proposed by several previous studies [1,2]. Pre-translation feedback has been shown to be effective for resolving translation ambiguity, but its effect on recovering the lost meaning due to missing translations has not been empirically evaluated. Our work provides the first empirical results for such an evaluation.

3 Translation via Context Vectors

3.1 Query-Independent Context Vectors

For a source language term *t*, we define the context vector of term *t* as:

$$C_t = \langle t_1, t_2, t_3, t_4, ..., t_i \rangle$$

where terms t_1 to t_i are source language terms that are associated with term *t* within a certain text window in some source language corpus. In this report, the associated terms are terms that co-occur with term *t* above a pre-determined cutoff threshold.

Target language translations of term *t* are derived from the translation of the known source language terms in the above context vectors:

$$trans(t) = <trans(t_1), trans(t_2), ..., trans(t_n)>$$

Selection of the source language context terms for the unknown term above is only based on the association statistics in an independent source language corpus. It does not consider other terms in the query as context; thus, it is query *independent*. Using the Japanese-to-English pair as an example, the steps are as follows:

1. For a Japanese term *t* that is unknown to the bilingual dictionary, extract concordances of term *t* within a window of *P* bytes (we used *P=200* bytes or 100 Japanese characters) in a Japanese reference corpus.
2. Segment the extracted Japanese concordances into terms, removing stop-words.
3. Select the top *N* (e.g., N=5) most frequent terms from the concordances to form the context vector for the unknown term *t*.
4. Translate these selected concordance terms in the context vector into English to form the pseudo-translations of the unknown term *t*.

Note that, in the translation step (Step 4) of the above procedure, the source language association statistics for selecting the top context terms and frequencies of their translations are not used for ranking or filtering any translations. Rather, we rely on the Cross Language Information Retrieval system's disambiguation function to select the best translations in context of the target language documents [19].

3.2 Query-Dependent Context Vectors

When query context is considered for constructing context vectors and pseudo-translations, the concordances containing the unknown terms are re-ranked based on the similarity scores between the window concordances and the vector of the known terms in the query. Each window around the unknown term is treated as a document, and the known query terms are used. This is based on the assumption that the top ranked concordances are likely to be more similar to the query; subsequently, the context terms in the context vectors provide better context for the unknown term. Again, using the Japanese-English pair as an example, the steps are as follows:

1. For a Japanese term t unknown to the bilingual dictionary, extract a window of text of P bytes (we used $P=200$ bytes or 100 Japanese characters) around every occurrence of term t in a Japanese reference corpus.
2. Segment the Japanese text in each window into terms and remove stopwords.
3. Re-rank the window based on similarity scores between the terms found in the window and the vector of the known query terms.
4. Obtain the top N (e.g., N=5) most frequently occurring terms from the top M (e.g., M=100) ranking windows to form the Japanese context vector for the unknown term t.
5. Translate each term in the Japanese context vector into English to form the pseudo-translations of the unknown term t.

The similarity scores are based on Dot Product.

The main difference between the two versions of context vectors is whether the other known terms in the query are used for ranking the window concordances. Presumably, the other query terms provide a context-sensitive interpretation of the unknown terms. When M is extremely large, however, the query-dependent version should approach the performance of the query-independent version.

We illustrate both versions of the context vectors with topic 23 (金大中大統領の対アジア政策 "President Kim Dae-Jung's policy toward Asia") from NTCIR-3:

First, the topic is segmented into terms, with the stop words removed:

金大中；大統領；アジア；政策

Then, the terms are categorized as "known" vs. "unknown" based on the bilingual dictionary:

```
Unknown:
Query23: 金大中
Known:
Query23:大統領
Query23:アジア
Query23:政策
```

Next, concordance windows containing the unknown term 金大中 are extracted:

経済危機克服へ３項目ーー韓国の金大中・次期大統領、雇用促進など提示
【ソウル３１日大澤文護】韓国の金大中（キムデジュン）次期大統領はく
【ソウル３１日大澤文護】韓国の金大中（キムデジュン）次期大統領は
経世済民」の書を記者団に見せる金大中・次期大統領＝ＡＰ
……

Next, the text in each window is segmented by a morphological processor into terms with stopwords removed [21].

In the query-independent version, we simply select the top 5 most frequently occurring terms in the concordance windows. The top 5 source language context terms for 金大中 are:

3527:金
3399:大中
3035:大統領
2658:韓国
901:キムデジュン[1]

Then, the translations of the above context terms are obtained from the bilingual dictionary to provide pseudo-translations for the unknown term 金大中, with the relevant translations in italics:

金大中 ≅ 金 ⇒ gold
金大中 ≅ 金 ⇒ metal
金大中 ≅ 金 ⇒ money
金大中 ≅大中 ⇒ ∅
金大中 ≅ 大統領 ⇒ chief executive
金大中 ≅ 大統領 ⇒ president
金大中 ≅ 大統領 ⇒ presidential
金大中 ≅ 韓国 ⇒ korea
金大中 ≅キムデジュン ⇒ ∅

With the query-dependent version, the segmented concordances are ranked by comparing the similarity between the concordance vector and the known term vector. Then we take the 100 top ranking concordances and, from this smaller set, select the top 5 most frequently occurring terms. This time, the top 5 context terms are:

1391:大統領
1382:金
1335:大中
1045:韓国
379:キムデジュン

In this example, the context vectors from both versions are the same, even though the terms are ranked in different orders. The pseudo-translations from the context vectors are:

金大中 ≅ 大統領 ⇒ chief executive
金大中 ≅ 大統領 ⇒ president
金大中 ≅ 大統領 ⇒ presidential
金大中 ≅ 金 ⇒ gold
金大中 ≅ 金 ⇒ metal
金大中 ≅ 金 ⇒ money
金大中 ≅大中 ⇒ ∅
金大中 ≅ 韓国 ⇒ korea
金大中 ≅キムデジュン ⇒ ∅

[1] Romanization of the katakana name キムデジュン could produce a correct transliteration of the name in English, which is not addressed in this paper. Our methods for name transliteration can be found in [18,20].

4 CLIR System

We evaluate the usefulness of the above two methods for obtaining missing translations in our Japanese-to-English retrieval system. Each query term missing from our bilingual dictionary is provided with pseudo-translations using one of the methods. The CLIR system involves the following steps:

First, a Japanese query is parsed into terms[2] with a statistical part of speech tagger and NLP module [21]. Stopwords are removed from query terms. Then query terms are split into a list of known terms, i.e., those that have translations from bilingual dictionaries, and a list of unknown terms, i.e., those that do not have translations from bilingual dictionaries. Without using context vectors for unknown terms, translations of the known terms are looked up in the bilingual dictionaries and our disambiguation module selects the best translation for each term based on coherence measures between translations [19].

The dictionaries we used for Japanese to English translation are based on edict[3], which we expanded by adding translations of missing English terms from a core English lexicon by looking them up using BabelFish[4]. Our final dictionary has a total of 210,433 entries. The English corpus used for disambiguating translations is about 703 MB of English text from NTCIR-4 CLIR track[5]. For our source language corpus, we used the Japanese text from NTCIR-3.

When context vectors are used to provide translations for terms missing from our dictionary, first, the context vectors for the unknown terms are constructed as described above. Then the same bilingual lexicon is used for translating the context vectors to create a set of pseudo-translations for the unknown term t. We keep all the pseudo-translations as surrogate translations of the unknown terms, just as if they really were the translations we found for the unknown terms in our bilingual dictionary.

We use a corpus-based translation disambiguation method for selecting the best English translations for a Japanese query word. We compute coherence scores of translated sequences created by obtaining all possible combinations of the translations in a source sequence of n query words (e.g., overlapping 3-term windows in our experiments). The coherence score is based on the mutual information score for each pair of translations in the sequence. Then we take the sum of the mutual information scores of all translation pairs as the score of the sequence. Translations with the highest coherence scores are selected as best translations. More details on translation disambiguation can be found in [19].

Once the best translations are selected, indexing and retrieval of documents in the target language is based on CLARIT [4]. For this work, we use the dot product function for computing similarities between a query and a document:

---

[2] In these experiments, we do not include multiple-word expression such as 戦争犯罪 (*war crime*) as terms, because translation of most compositional multiple-word expressions can be generally constructed from translations of component words (戦争 and 犯罪) and our empirical evaluation has not shown significant advantages of a separate model of phrase translation.

[3] http://www.csse.monash.edu.au/~jwb/j_edict.html

[4] http://world.altavista.com/

[5] http://research.nii.ac.jp/ntcir/ntcir-ws4/clir/index.html

$$sim(P, D) = \sum_{t \in P \cap D} W_P(t) \bullet W_D(t) \cdot \quad (1)$$

where $W_P(t)$ is the weight associated with the query term t and $W_D(t)$ is the weight associated with the term t in the document D. The two weights are computed as follows:

$$W_D(t) = TF_D(t) \bullet IDF(t) . \quad (2)$$

$$W_P(t) = C(t) \bullet TF_P(t) \bullet IDF(t) . \quad (3)$$

where IDF and TF are standard inverse document frequency and term frequency statistics, respectively. *IDF(t)* is computed with the target corpus for retrieval. The coefficient *C(t)* is an "importance coefficient", which can be modified either manually by the user or automatically by the system (e.g., updated during feedback).

For query expansion through (pseudo-) relevance feedback, we use pseudo-relevance feedback based on high-scoring sub-documents to augment the queries. That is, after retrieving some sub-documents for a given topic from the target corpus, we take a set of top ranked sub-documents, regarding them as relevant sub-documents to the query, and extract terms from these sub-documents. We use a modified Rocchio formula for extracting and ranking terms for expansion:

$$Rocchio(t) = IDF(t) \times \frac{\sum_{D \in DocSet} TF_D(t)}{NumDoc} \quad (4)$$

where *IDF(t)* is the Inverse Document Frequency of term t in reference database, *NumDoc* the number of sub-documents in the given set of sub-documents, and $TF_D(t)$ the term frequency score for term t in sub-document D.

Once terms for expansion are extracted and ranked, they are combined with the original terms in the query to form an expanded query.

$$Q_{new} = k \times Q + Q_{exp} \quad (5)$$

in which Q_{new}, Q_{orig}, Q_{exp} stand for the new expanded query, the original query, and terms extracted for expansion, respectively. In the experiments reported in Section 5, we assign a constant weight to all expansion terms (e.g., 0.5)

5 Experiments

5.1 Experiment Setup

For evaluation, we used NTCIR-3 Japanese topics[6]. Of the 32 topics that have relevance judgments, our system identifies unknown terms as terms not present in our expanded Japanese-to-English dictionary described above. The evaluation of the

[6] http://research.nii.ac.jp/ntcir/workshop/OnlineProceedings3/index.html

effect of using context vectors is based only on the limited number of topics that contain these unknown terms. The target corpus is the NTCIR-3 English corpus, which contains 22,927 documents. The statistics about the unknown terms for short (i.e., the title field only), medium (i.e., the description field only), and long (i.e., the description and the narrative fields) queries are summarized below. The total number of unknown terms that we treated with context vectors was 83 (i.e., 6+15+62).

	Short	Medium	Long
No. of topics containing unknown terms	5[7]	14[8]	24[9]
Avg No. of terms in topics (total)	3.2 (16)	5.4 (75)	36.2 (86.9)
Avg. No. of unknown terms (total)	1 (6)	1.1 (15)	2.6[10] (62)

For evaluation, we used the mean average precision and recall for the top 1000 documents and also precision@30, as defined in TREC retrieval evaluations.

We compare three types of runs, both with and without post-translation pseudo-relevance feedback.

- Runs without context vectors (baselines)
- Runs with query-dependent context vectors
- Runs with query-independent context vectors

5.2 Empirical Observations

Tables 1-4 present the performance statistics for the above runs. For the runs with translation disambiguation (Tables 1-2), using context vectors improved overall recall, average precision, and precision at 30 documents for **short** queries. Context vectors moderately improved recall, average precision (except for the query independent version), and precision at 30 documents for **medium** length queries.

For the long queries, we do not observe any advantages of using either query-dependent or query-independent versions of the context vectors. This is probably because the other known terms in long queries provide adequate context for recovering the loss of missing translation of the unknown terms. Adding candidate translations from context vectors only makes the query more ambiguous and inexact.

When all translations were kept (Tables 3-4), i.e., when no translation disambiguation was performed, we only see overall improvement in recall for short and medium-length queries. We do not see any advantage of using context vectors for improving average precision or precision at 30 documents. For longer queries, the performance statistics were overall worse than the baseline. As pointed out in [10], when all translations are kept without proper weighting of the translations, some terms get more favorable treatment than other terms simply because they contain more translations. So, in models where all translations are kept, proper weighting schemes should be developed, e.g., as suggested in related research [17].

---

[7] Topics 4, 23, 26, 27, 33.

[8] Topics 4, 5, 7, 13, 14, 20, 23, 26, 27, 28, 29, 31, 33, 38.

[9] Topics 2, 4, 5, 7, 9, 13, 14, 18, 19, 20, 21, 23, 24, 26, 27, 28, 29, 31, 33, 37, 38, 42, 43, 50.

[10] The average number of unique unknown terms is 1.4.

Table 1. Performance statistics for short, medium, and long queries. Translations were disambiguated; no feedback was used. Percentages show change over the baseline runs.

No Feedback	**Recall**	**Avg. Precision**	**Prec@30**
Short			
Baseline	28/112	0.1181	0.05
With context vectors (query independent)	43/112 (+53.6%)	0.1295 (+9.7%)	0.0667 (+33.4%)
With context vectors (query dependent)	43/112 (+53.6%)	0.1573 (+33.2%)	0.0667 (+33.4)
Medium			
Baseline	113/248	0.1753	0.1231
With context vectors (query independent)	114/248 (+0.9%)	0.1588 (-9.5%)	0.1256 (+2.0%)
With context vectors (query dependent)	115/248 (+1.8%)	0.1838 (+4.8%)	0.1282 (+4.1%)
Long			
Baseline	305/598	0.1901	0.1264
With context vectors (query independent)	308/598 (+1.0%)	0.1964 (+3.3%)	0.1125 (-11.0%)
With context vectors (query dependent)	298/598 (-2.3%)	0.1883 (-0.9%)	0.1139 (-9.9%)

Table 2. Performance statistics for short, medium, and long queries. Translations were disambiguated; for pseudo-relevance feedback, the top 30 terms from top 20 subdocuments were selected based on the Rocchio formula. Percentages show change over the baseline runs.

With Feedback	**Recall**	**Avg. Precision**	**Prec@30**
Short			
Baseline	15/112	0.1863	0.0417
With context vectors (query independent)	40/112 (+166.7%)	0.1812 (-2.7%)	0.0417 (+0.0%)
With context vectors (query dependent)	40/112 (+166.7%)	0.1942 (+4.2%)	0.0417 (+0.0%)
Medium			
Baseline	139/248	0.286	0.1513
With context vectors (query independent)	137 (-1.4%)	0.2942 (+2.9%)	0.1538 (+1.7%)
With context vectors (query dependent)	141 (+1.4%)	0.3173 (+10.9%)	0.159 (+5.1%)
Long			
Baseline	341/598	0.2575	0.1681
With context vectors (query independent)	347/598 (+1.8%)	0.2598 (+0.9%)	0.1681 (+0.0%)
With context vectors (query dependent)	340/598 (-0.3%)	0.2567 (-0.3%)	0.1639 (-2.5%)

Table 3. Performance statistics for short, medium, and long queries. All translations were kept for retrieval; pseudo-relevance feedback was not used. Percentages show change over the baseline runs.

No Feedback	Recall	Avg. Precision	Prec@30
Short			
Baseline	33/112	0.1032	0.0417
With context vectors (query independent)	57/112 (+72.7%)	0.0465 (-54.9%)	0.05 (+19.9%)
With context vectors (query dependent)	41/112 (+24.2%)	0.1045 (-0.2%)	0.0417 (+0%)
Medium			
Baseline	113/248	0.1838	0.0846
With context vectors (query independent)	136/248 (+20.4%)	0.1616 (-12.1%)	0.0769 (-9.1%)
With context vectors (query dependent)	122/248 (+8.0%)	0.2013 (+9.5%)	0.0769 (-9.1%)
Long			
Baseline	283	0.1779	0.0944
With context vectors (query independent)	295/598 (+4.2%)	0.163 (-8.4%)	0.0917 (-2.9%)
With context vectors (query dependent)	278/598 (-1.8%)	0.1566 (-12.0%)	0.0931 (-1.4%)

Table 4. Performance statistics for short, medium, and long queries. All translations were kept for retrieval; for pseudo-relevance feedback, the top 30 terms from top 20 subdocuments were selected base on the Rocchio formula. Percentages show change over the baseline runs.

With Feedback	Recall	Avg. Precision	Prec@30
Short			
Baseline	40/112	0.1733	0.0417
With context vectors (query independent)	69/112 (+72.5%)	0.1662 (-4.1%)	0.1583 (+279.6%)
With context vectors (query dependent)	44/112 (+10.0%)	0.1726 (-0.4%)	0.0417 (+0.0%)
Medium			
Baseline	135/248	0.2344	0.1256
With context vectors (query independent)	161/248 (+19.3%)	0.2332 (-0.5%)	0.1333 (+6.1%)
With context vectors (query dependent)	139/248 (+3.0%)	0.2637 (+12.5%)	0.1154 (-8.1%)
Long			
Baseline	344/598	0.2469	0.1444
With context vectors (query independent)	348/598 (+1.2%)	0.2336 (-5.4%)	0.1333 (-7.7%)
With context vectors (query dependent)	319/598 (-7.3%)	0.2033 (-17.7%)	0.1167 (-19.2%)

6 Summary and Future Work

We have used context vectors to obtain surrogate translations for terms that appear in queries but that are absent from bilingual dictionaries. We have described two types of context vectors: a query-independent version and a query-dependent version. In the empirical evaluation, we have examined the interaction between the use of context vectors with other factors such as translation disambiguation, pseudo-relevance feedback, and query lengths. The empirical findings suggest that using query-dependent context vectors together with post-translation pseudo-relevance feedback and translation disambiguation can help to overcome the meaning loss due to missing translations for short queries. For longer queries, the longer context in the query seems to make the use of context vectors unnecessary.

The paper presents only our first set on experiments of using context to recover meaning loss due to missing translations. In our future work, we will verify the observations with other topic sets and database sources; verify the observations with other language pairs, e.g., Chinese-to-English retrieval; and experiment with different parameter settings such as context window size, methods for context term selection, different ways of ranking context terms, and the use of the context term ranking in combination with disambiguation for translation selection.

References

1. Ballesteros, L., and Croft, B.: Dictionary Methods for Cross-Language Information Retrieval. In Proceedings of Database and Expert Systems Applications (1996) 791–801.
2. Ballesteros, L., Croft, W. B.: Resolving Ambiguity for Cross-Language Retrieval. In Proceedings of SIGIR (1998) 64–71.
3. Billhardt, H., Borrajo, D., Maojo, V.: A Context Vector Model for Information Retrieval. Journal of the American Society for Information Science and Technology, 53(3) (2002) 236–249.
4. Evans, D. A., Lefferts, R. G.: CLARIT–TREC Experiments. Information Processing and Management, 31(3) (1995) 385–395.
5. Fujii, A., Ishikawa, T.: Japanese/English Cross-Language Information Retrieval: Exploration of Query Translation and Transliteration. Computer and the Humanities, 35(4) (2001) 389–420.
6. Fung, P.: A Statistical View on Bilingual Lexicon Extraction: From Parallel Corpora to Non-parallel Corpora. In Proceedings of AMTA (1998) 1–17.
7. Fung, P., Yee, L. Y.: An IR Approach for Translating New Words from Nonparallel, Comparable Texts. In Proceedings of COLING-ACL (1998) 414–420.
8. Hull, D. A., Grefenstette, G.: Experiments in Multilingual Information Retrieval. In Proceedings of the 19th Annual International ACM SIGIR Conference on Research and Development in Information Retrieval (1996) 49–57.
9. Grefenstette, G.: Evaluating the Adequacy of a Multilingual Transfer Dictionary for Cross Language Information Retrieval. In Proceedings of LREC (1998) 755–758.
10. Grefenstette, G.: The Problem of Cross Language Information Retrieval. In G. Grefenstette, ed., Cross Language Information Retrieval, Kluwer Academic Publishers (1998) 1–9.

11. Grefenstette, G., Qu, Y., Evans, D. A.: Mining the Web to Create a Language Model for Mapping between English Names and Phrases and Japanese. In Proceedings of the 2004 IEEE/WIC/ACM International Conference on Web Intelligence (2004) 110–116.
12. Ido, D., Church, K., Gale, W. A.: Robust Bilingual Word Alignment for Machine Aided Translation. In Proceedings of the Workshop on Very Large Corpora: Academic and Industrial Perspectives (1993) 1–8.
13. Jeong, K. S., Myaeng, S, Lee, J. S., Choi, K. S.: Automatic Identification and Back-transliteration of Foreign Words for Information Retrieval. Information Processing and Management, 35(4) (1999) 523–540.
14. Knight, K, Graehl, J.: Machine Transliteration. Computational Linguistics: 24(4) (1998) 599–612.
15. Kumano, A., Hirakawa, H.: Building an MT dictionary from Parallel Texts Based on Linguistic and Statistical Information. In Proceedings of the 15th International Conference on Computational Linguistics (COLING) (1994) 76–81.
16. Meng, H., Lo, W., Chen, B., Tang, K.: Generating Phonetic Cognates to Handel Named Entities in English-Chinese Cross-Language Spoken Document Retrieval. In Proc of the Automatic Speech Recognition and Understanding Workshop (ASRU 2001) (2001).
17. Pirkola, A., Puolamaki, D., Jarvelin, K.: Applying Query Structuring in Cross-Language Retrieval. Information Management and Processing: An International Journal. Vol 39 (3) (2003) 391–402.
18. Qu, Y., Grefenstette, G.: Finding Ideographic Representations of Japanese Names in Latin Scripts via Language Identification and Corpus Validation. In Proceedings of the 42nd Annual Meeting of the Association for Computational Linguistics (2004) 183–190.
19. Qu, Y., Grefenstette, G., Evans, D. A.: Resolving Translation Ambiguity Using Monolingual Corpora. In Peters, C., Braschler, M., Gonzalo, J. (eds): Advances in Cross-Language Information Retrieval: Third Workshop of the Cross-Language Evaluation Forum, CLEF 2002, Rome, Italy, September 19–20, 2002. Lecture Notes in Computer Science, Vol 2785. Springer (2003) 223–241.
20. Qu, Y., Grefenstette, G., Evans, D. A: Automatic Transliteration for Japanese-to-English Text Retrieval. In Proceedings of the 26th Annual International ACM SIGIR Conference on Research and Development in Information Retrieval (2003) 353–360.
21. Qu, Y., Hull, D. A., Grefenstette, G., Evans, D. A., Ishikawa, M., Nara, S., Ueda, T., Noda, D., Arita, K., Funakoshi, Y., Matsuda, H.: Towards Effective Strategies for Monolingual and Bilingual Information Retrieval: Lessons Learned from NTCIR-4. ACM Transactions on Asian Language Information Processing. (to appear)
22. Zhang, Y., Vines, P: Using the web for automated translation extraction in cross-language information retrieval. In Proceedings of the 27th Annual International ACM SIGIR Conference on Research and Development in Information Retrieval (2004) 162–169.

Automatic Image Annotation Using Maximum Entropy Model

Wei Li and Maosong Sun

State Key Lab of Intelligent Technology and Systems,
Department of Computer Science and Technology, Tsinghua University,
Beijing 100084, China
wei.lee04@gmail.com, sms@mail.tsinghua.edu.cn

Abstract. Automatic image annotation is a newly developed and promising technique to provide semantic image retrieval via text descriptions. It concerns a process of automatically labeling the image contents with a pre-defined set of keywords which are exploited to represent the image semantics. A Maximum Entropy Model-based approach to the task of automatic image annotation is proposed in this paper. In the phase of training, a basic visual vocabulary consisting of blob-tokens to describe the image content is generated at first; then the statistical relationship is modeled between the blob-tokens and keywords by a Maximum Entropy Model constructed from the training set of labeled images. In the phase of annotation, for an unlabeled image, the most likely associated keywords are predicted in terms of the blob-token set extracted from the given image. We carried out experiments on a medium-sized image collection with about 5000 images from Corel Photo CDs. The experimental results demonstrated that the annotation performance of this method outperforms some traditional annotation methods by about 8% in mean precision, showing a potential of the Maximum Entropy Model in the task of automatic image annotation.

1 Introduction

Last decade has witnessed an explosive growth of multimedia information such as images and videos. However, we can't access to or make use of the relevant information more leisurely unless it is organized so as to provide efficient browsing and querying. As a result, an important functionality of next generation multimedia information management system will undoubtedly be the search and retrieval of images and videos on the basis of visual content.

In order to fulfill this "intelligent" multimedia search engines on the world-wide-web, content-based image retrieval techniques have been studied intensively during the past few years. Through the sustained efforts, a variety of state-of-the-art methods employing the query-by-example (QBE) paradigm have been well established. By this we mean that queries are images and the targets are also images. In this manner, visual similarity is computed between user-provided image and database images based on the low-level visual features such as color, texture, shape and spatial relationships. However, two important problems still remain. First, due to the limitation of object recognition and image understanding, semantics-based image segmentation algorithm

R. Dale et al. (Eds.): IJCNLP 2005, LNAI 3651, pp. 34–45, 2005.

is unavailable, so segmented region may not correspond to users' query object. Second, visual similarity is not semantic similarity which means that low-level features are easily extracted and measured, but from the users' point of view, they are non-intuitive. It is not easy to use them to formulate the user's needs. We encounter a so-called semantic gap here. Typically the starting point of the retrieval process is the high-level query from users. So extracting image semantics based on the low-level visual features is an essential step. As we know, semantic information can be represented more accurately by using keywords than by using low-level visual features. Therefore, building relationship between associated text and low-level image features is considered to an effective solution to capture the image semantics. By means of this hidden relationship, images can be retrieved by using textual descriptions, which is also called query-by-keyword (QBK) paradigm. Furthermore, textual queries are a desirable choice for semantic image retrieval which can resort to the powerful text-based retrieval techniques. The key to image retrieval using textual queries is image annotation. But most images are not annotated and manually annotating images is a time-consuming, error-prone and subjective process. So, automatic image annotation is the subject of much ongoing research. Its main goal is to assign descriptive words to whole images based on the low-level perceptual features, which has been recognized as a promising technique for bridging the semantic gap between low-level image features and high-level semantic concepts.

Given a training set of images labeled with text (e.g. keywords, captions) that describe the image content, many statistical models have been proposed by researchers to construct the relation between keywords and image features. For example, co-occurrence model, translation model and relevance-language model. By exploiting text and image feature co-occurrence statistics, these methods can extract hidden semantics from images, and have been proven successful in constructing a nice framework for the domain of automatic image annotation and retrieval.

In this paper, we propose a novel approach for the task of automatic image annotation using Maximum Entropy Model. Though Maximum Entropy method has been successfully applied to a wide range of application such as machine translation, it is not much used in computer vision domain, especially in image auto annotation.

This paper is organized as follows: Section 2 presents related work. Section 3 describes the representation of labeled and unlabeled images, gives a brief introduction to Maximum Entropy Model and then details how to use it for automatically annotating unlabeled images. Section 4 demonstrates our experimental results. Section 5 presents conclusions and a comment for future work.

2 Related Work

Recently, many statistical models have been proposed for automatic image annotation and retrieval. The work of associating keywords with low-level visual features can be addressed from two different perspectives.

2.1 Annotation by Keyword Propagation

This kind of approach usually formulates the process of automatic image annotation as one of supervised classification problems. With respect to this method, accurate annotation information is demanded. That is to say, given a set of training images labeled with semantic keywords, detailed labeling information should be provided. For example, from training samples, we can know which keyword corresponds to which image region or what kind of concept class describes a whole-image. So each or a set of annotated keyword can be considered as an independent concept class, followed by training each class model with manually labeled images, then the model is applied to classify each unlabeled image into a relevant concept class, and finally producing annotation by propagating the corresponding class words to unlabeled images.

Wang and Li [8] introduced a 2-D multi- resolution HMM model to automate linguistic indexing of images. Clusters of fixed-size blocks at multiple resolution and the relationships between these clusters is summarized both across and within the resolutions. To annotate the unlabeled image, words of the highest likelihood is selected based on the comparison between feature vectors of new image and the trained concept models. Chang et al [5] proposed content-based soft annotation (CBSA) for providing images with semantic labels using (BPM) Bayesian Point Machine. Starting with labeling a small set of training images, an ensemble of binary classifier for each keyword is then trained for predicting label membership for images. Each image is assigned one keyword vector, with each keyword in the vector assigned a confidence factor. In the process of annotation, words with high confidence are considered to be the most likely descriptive words for the new images. The main practical problem with this kind of approaches is that a large labeled training corpus is needed. Moreover, during the training and application stages, the training set is fixed and not incremented. Thus if a new domain is introduced, new labeled examples must be provided to ensure the effectiveness of such classifiers.

2.2 Annotation by Statistical Inference

More recently, there have been some efforts to solve this problem in a more general way. The second approach takes a different strategy which focuses on discovering the statistical links between visual features and words using unsupervised learning methods. During training, a roughly labeled image datasets is provided where a set of semantic labels is assigned to a whole image, but the word-to-region information is hidden in the space of image features and keywords. So an unsupervised learning algorithm is usually adopted to estimate the joint probability distribution of words and image features.

Mori et al [4] were the earliest to model the statistics using a co-occurrence probabilistic model, which predicate the correct probability of associating keywords by counting the co-occurrence of words with image regions generated using a fixed-size blocks. Blocks are vector quantized to form clusters which inherit the whole set of keywords assigned to each image. Then clusters are in turn used to predict the keywords for unlabeled images. The disadvantage is that the model is a little simple and the rough fixed-size blocks are unable to model objects effectively, leading to poor annotation accuracy. Instead of using fixed-size blocks, Barnard et al [1] performed Blobworld segmentation and Normalized cuts to produce semantic meaningful regions. They constructed a hierarchical model via EM algorithm. This model combines both asymmetric clustering model which maps words and image regions into clusters and symmetric clustering model which models the joint distribution of words and regions. Duygulu et al [2] proposed a translation model to map keywords to individual image regions. First, image regions are created by using a segmentation algorithm. For each region, visual features are extracted and then blob-tokens are generated by clustering the features for each region across whole image datasets. Each image can be represented by a certain number of these blob-tokens. Their Translation Model uses machine translation model lof IBM to annotate a test set of images based on a large number of annotated training images. Another approach using cross-media relevance models (CMRM) was introduced by Jeon et al [3]. They assumed that this could be viewed as analogous to the cross-lingual retrieval problem and a set of keywords $\{w_1, w_2, ..., w_n\}$ is related to the set of blob-tokens $\{b_1, b_2, ..., b_n\}$, rather than one-to-one correspondence between the blob-tokens and keywords. Here the joint distribution of blob-tokens and words was learned from a training set of annotated images to perform both automatic image annotation and ranked retrieval. Jeon et al [9] introduced using Maximum Entropy to model the fixed-size block and keywords, which gives us a good hint to implement it differently. Lavrenko et al [11] extended the cross-media relevance model using actual continuous-valued features extracted from image regions. This method avoids the clustering and constructing the discrete visual vocabulary stage.

3 The Implementation of Automatic Annotation Model

3.1 The Hierarchical Framework of Automatic Annotation and Retrieval

The following Fig. 1 shows the framework for automatic image annotation and keyword-based image retrieval. Given a training dataset of images labeled with keywords. First, we segment a whole image into a collection of sub-images, followed by extracting a set of low-level visual features to form a feature vector to describe the visual content of each region. Second, a visual vocabulary of blob-tokens is generated by clustering all the regions across the whole dataset so that each image can be represented by a number of blob-tokens from a finite set of visual symbols. Third, both textual information and visual information is provided to train the Maximum Entropy model, and the learned model is then applied to automatically generate keywords to describe the semantic content of an unlabeled image based on the low-level features. Consequently, both the users' information needs and the semantic content of images can be represented by textual information, which can resort to the powerful text IR techniques to implement this cross-media retrieval, suggesting the importance of textual information in semantics-based image retrieval.

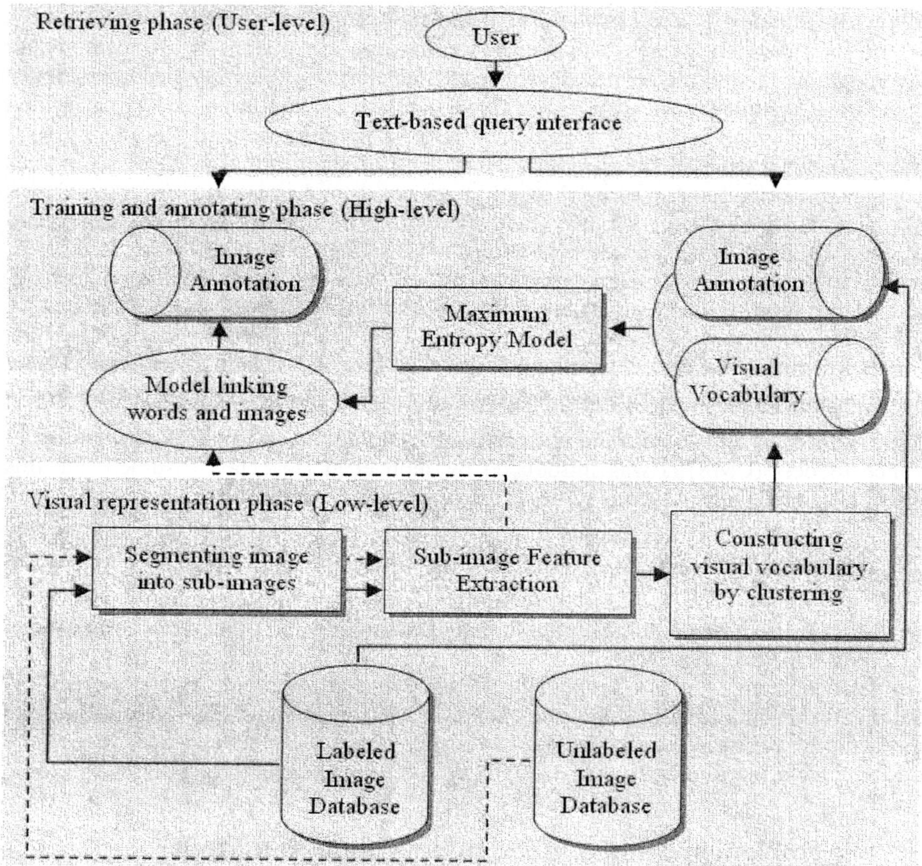

Fig. 1. Hierarchical Framework of Automatic Annotation and Retrieval

→ learning correlations between blob-tokens and textual annotations
- - -→ applying correlations to generate annotations for unlabeled images

3.2 Image Representation and Pre-processing

A central issue in content-based image annotation and retrieval is how to describe the visual information in a way compatible with human visual perception. But until now, no general framework is proposed. For different tasks and goals, different low-level features are used to describe and analyze the visual content of images. On the whole, there are two kinds of interesting open questions remain unresolved. First, what feature sets should be selected to be the most expressive for any image region. Second, how blob-tokens can be generated, that is to say, how can one create such a visual vocabulary of blob-tokens to represent each image in the collection using a number of symbols from this finite set? In our method, we carried out these following two steps: First, segment images into sub-images, Second, extract appropriate features for any sub-images, cluster similar regions by k-means and then use the centroid in each cluster as a blob-token. The first step can be employed by either using a segmentation algorithm to produce semantically meaningful units or partitioning the image into fixed-size rectangular grids. Both methods have pros and cons, a general purpose segmentation algorithm may produce semantic regions, but due to the limitation in computer vision and image processing, there are also the problems of erroneous and unreliable region segmentation. The advantage of regular grids is that is does not need to perform complex image segmentation and is easy to be conducted. However, due to rough fixed-size rectangular grids, the extracted blocks are unable to model objects effectively, leading to poor annotation accuracy in our experiment.

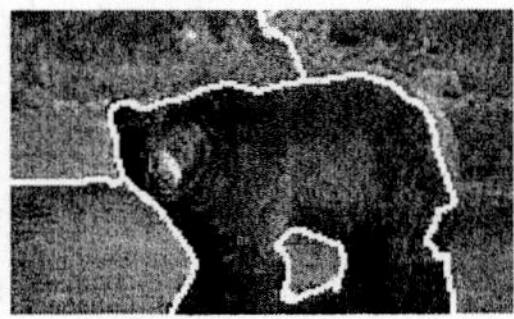
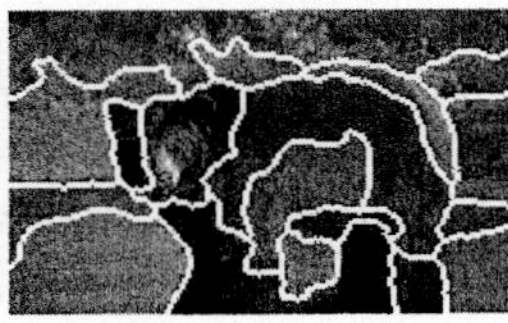

Fig. 2. Segmentation Results using Normalized cuts and JSEG

In this paper, we segment images into a number of meaningful regions using Normalized cuts [6] against using JSEG. Because the JSEG is only focusing on local features and their consistencies, but Ncuts aims at extracting the global impression of an image data. So Ncuts may get a better segmentation result than JSEG. Fig. 2 shows segmentation result using Normalized cuts and JSEG respectively, the left is the original image, the mid and the right are the segmentation result using Ncuts and JSEG respectively. After segmentation, each image region is described by a feature vector formed by HSV histograms and Gabor filters. Similar regions will be grouped together based on k-means clustering to form the visual vocabulary of blob-tokens. Too much clusters may cause data sparseness and too few can not converge. Then each of the labeled and unlabeled images can be described by a number of blob-tokens, instead of the continuous-valued feature vectors. So we can avoid the image data modeling in a high-dimensional and complex feature space.

3.3 The Annotation Strategy Based on Maximum Entropy

Maximum Entropy Model is a general purpose machine learning and classification framework whose main goal is to account for the behavior of a discrete-valued random process. Given a random process whose output value y may be influenced by some specific contextual information x, such a model is a method of estimating the conditional probability.

$$p(y \mid x) = \frac{1}{Z(x)} \prod_{j=1}^{k} \alpha_j^{f_j(x,y)} \tag{1}$$

In the process of annotation, images are segmented using normalized cuts, every image region is represented by a feature vector consisting of HSV color histogram and the Gabor filters, and then a basic visual vocabulary containing 500 blob-tokens is generated by k-means clustering. Finally, each segmented region is assigned to the label of its closest blob-token. Thus the complex visual contents of images can be represented by a number of blob-tokens. Due to the imbalanced distribution of keywords frequency and the data sparseness problem, the size of the pre-defined keyword vocabulary is reduced from 1728 to 121 keywords, by keeping only the keywords appearing more than 30 times in the training dataset.

We use a series of feature function $f_{\mathrm{FC,\ Label}}(b_i, w_j)$ to model the co-occurrence statistics of blob-tokens b_i and keywords w_j, where FC denote the context of feature constraints for each blob-token. The following example represents the co-occurrence of the blob-token b_* and the keyword "water" in an image *I*.

$$f_{\mathrm{FC_w,\ water}}(b_i, w_j) = \begin{cases} 1 & if\ w_j == 'water'\ and\ FC_w(b_i) == true \\ 0 & otherwise \end{cases} \quad (2)$$

If blob-token b_i satisfies the context of feature constraints and keyword "water" also occurs in image *I*. In other words, if the color and texture feature components are coordinated with the semantic label 'water', and then the value of the feature function is 1, otherwise 0.

The following Fig. 3 shows the annotation procedure that using MaxEnt captures the hidden relationship between blob-tokens and keywords from a roughly labeled training image sets.

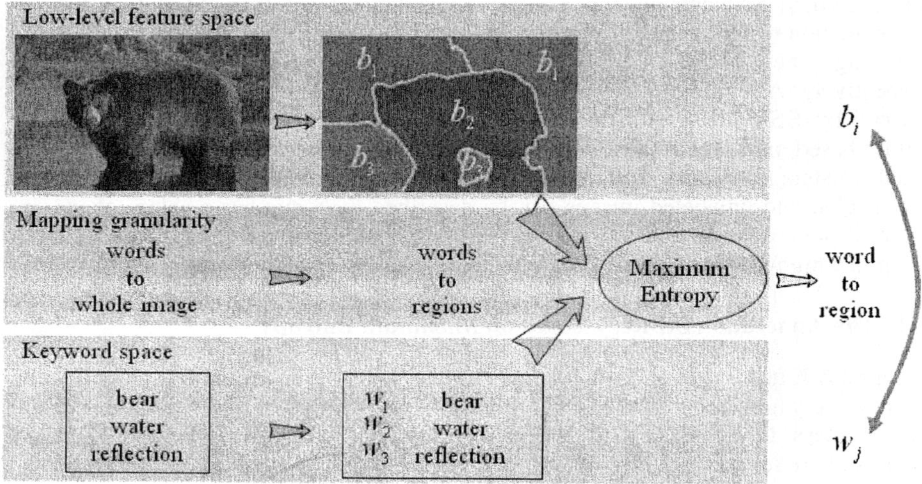

Fig. 3. Learning the statistics of blob-tokens and words

In the recent past, many models for automatic image annotation are limited by the scope of the representation. In particular, they fail to exploit the context in the images and words. It is the context in which an image region is placed that gives it meaningful interpretation.

In our annotation procedure, each annotated word is predicted independently by the Maximum Entropy Model, word correlations are not taken into consideration. However, correlations between annotated words are essentially important in predicting relevant text descriptions. For example, the words "trees" and "grass" are more likely to co-occur than the words "trees" and "computers". In order to generate appropriate annotations, a simple language model is developed that takes the word-correlation information into account, and then the textual description is determined not only by the model linking keywords and blob-tokens but also by the word-to-word correlation. We simply count the co-occurrence information between words in the pre-defined textual set to produce a simple word correlation model to improve the annotation accuracy.

4 Experiments and Analysis

We carried out experiments using a mid-sized image collection, comprising about 5,000 images from Corel Stock Photo CDs, 4500 images for training and 500 for testing. The following table 1 shows the results of automatic image annotation using Maximum Entropy.

Table 1. Automatic image annotation results

Images	Original Annotation	Automatic Annotation
	sun city sky mountain	Sun sky mountain clouds
	flowers tulips mountain sky	Flowers sky trees grass
	tufa snow sky grass	snow sky grass stone
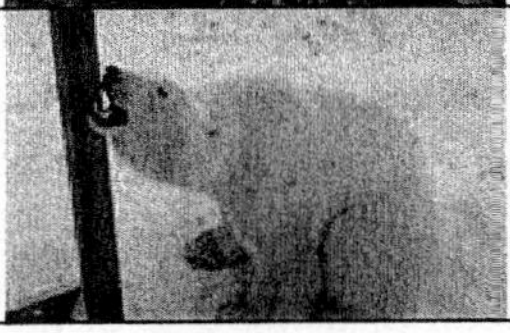	polar bear snow post	bear snow sky rocks

For our training datasets, the visual vocabulary and the pre-defined textual set contain 500 blob-tokens and 121 keywords respectively, so the number of the training pairs (b_i, w_j) is 60500. After the procedure of feature selection, only 9550 pairs left. For model parameters estimation, there are a few algorithms including Generalized Iterative Scaling and Improved Iterative Scaling which are widely used. Here we use Limited Memory Variable Metric method which has been proved effective for Maximum Entropy Model [10]. Finally, we can get the model linking blob-tokens and keywords, and then the trained model $p(y|x)$ is applied to predict textual annotations $\{w_1, w_2, \ldots, w_n\}$ given an unseen image formed by $\{b_1, b_2, \ldots, b_m\}$.

To further verify the feasibility and effectiveness of Maximum Entropy model, we have implemented the co-occurrence model as one of the baselines whose conditional probability $p(w_j|b_i)$ can be estimated as follows:

$$p(w_j|b_i) = \frac{p(b_i|w_j)p(w_i)}{\sum_{k=1}^{N} p(b_i|w_k)p(w_i)} \approx \frac{(m_{ij}/n_j)(n_j/N)}{\sum_{k=1}^{N}(m_{ik}/n_k)(n_k/N)} = \frac{m_{ij}}{\sum_{k=1}^{N} m_{ik}} = \frac{m_{ij}}{M_i} \tag{3}$$

Where m_{ij} denote the co-occurrence of b_i and w_j, n_j denote the occurring number of w_j in the total N words.

The following Fig. 4 shows the some of the retrieval results using the keyword '*water*' as a textual query.

Fig. 4. Some of retrieved images using '*water*' as a query

The following Fig. 5 and Fig. 6 show the precision and recall of using a se of high-frequency keywords as user queries. We implemented two statistical models to link blob-tokens and keywords.

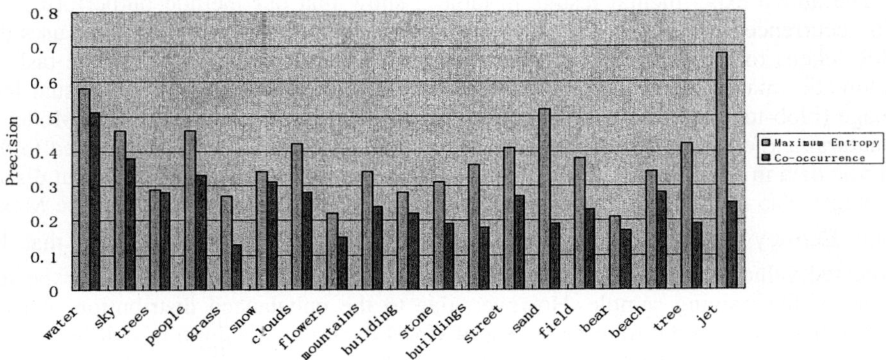

Fig. 5. Precision of retrieval using some high-frequency keywords

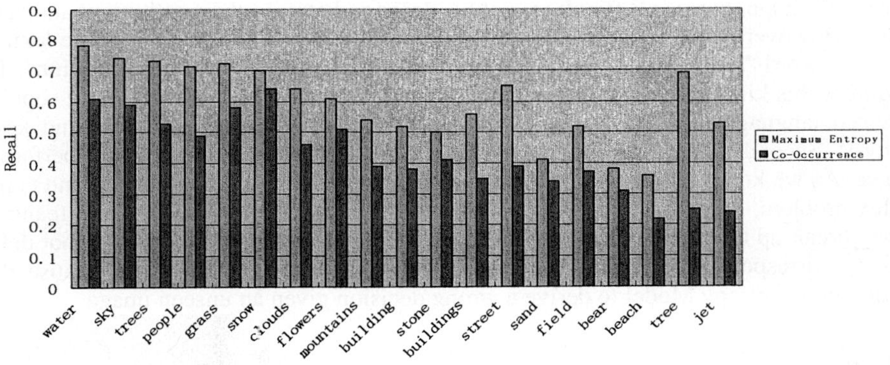

Fig. 6. Recall of retrieval using some high-frequency keywords

The annotation accuracy is evaluated by using precision and recall indirectly. After posing a keyword query for images, the measure of precision and recall can be defined as follows:

$$precision = \frac{A}{A+B} \qquad recall = \frac{A}{A+C} \tag{4}$$

Where A denote the number of relevant images retrieved, B denote the number of irrelevant images retrieved, C denote the number of relevant images not retrieved in the image datasets, and images whose labels containing the query keyword is considered relevant, otherwise irrelevant.

Table 2. Experimental results with average precision and mean

Method	Mean precision	Mean recall
Co-occurrence	0.11	0.18
Maximum Entropy	0.17	0.25

The above experimental results in table 2 show that our method outperforms the Co-occurrence model [4] in the average precision and recall. Since our model uses the blob-tokens to represent the contents of the image regions and converts the task of automatic image annotation to a process of translating information from visual language (blob-tokens) to textual language (keywords). So Maximum Entropy Model is a natural and effective choice for our task, which has been successfully applied to the dyadic data in which observations are made from two finite sets of objects. But disadvantages also exist. There are two fold problems to be considered. First, since Maximum Entropy is constrained by the equation $p(f) = \tilde{p}(f)$, which assumes that the expected value of output of the stochastic model should be the same as the expected value of the training sample. However, due to the unbalanced distribution of keywords frequency in the training subset of Corel data, this assumption will lead to an undesirable problem that common words with high frequency are usually associated with too many irrelevant blob-tokens, whereas uncommon words with low frequency have little change to be selected as annotations for any image regions, consider word "sun" and "apple" , since both words may be related to regions with "red" color and "round" shape, but it is difficult to make a decision between the word "sun" and "apple". However, since "sun" is a common word as compared to "apple" in the lexical set, the word "sun" will definitely used as the annotation for these kind of regions. To address this kind of problems, our future work will mainly focus on the more sophisticated language model to improve the statistics between image features and keywords. Second, the effects of segmentation may also affect the annotation performance. As we know, semantic image segmentation algorithm is a challenging and complex problem, current segmentation algorithm based on the low-level visual features may break up the objects in the images, that is to say, segmented regions do not definitely correspond to semantic objects or semantic concepts, which may cause the Maximum Entropy Model to derive a wrong decision given an unseen image.

5 Conclusion and Future Work

In this paper, we propose a novel approach for automatic image annotation and retrieval using Maximum Entropy Model. Compared to other traditional classical methods, the proposed model gets better annotation and retrieval results. But three main challenges are still remain:

1) Semantically meaningful segmentation algorithm is still not available, so the segmented region may not correspond to a semantic object and region features are insufficient to describe the image semantics.
2) The basic visual vocabulary construction using k-means is only based on the visual features, which may lead to the fact that two different semantic objects with similar visual features fall into the same blob-token. This may degrade the annotation quality.
3) Our annotation task mainly depend on the trained model linking image features and keywords, the spatial context information of image regions and the word correlations are not fully taken into consideration.

In the future, more work should be done on image segmentation techniques, clustering algorithms, appropriate feature extraction and contextual information between regions and words to improve the annotation accuracy and retrieval performance.

Acknowledgements

We would like to express our deepest gratitude to Kobus Barnard and J.Wang for making their image datasets available. This research is supported by the National Natural Science Foundation of China under grant number 60321002 and the National 863 Project of China under grant number 2001AA114210-03, and the ALVIS Project co-sponsored by EU PF6 and NSFC.

References

1. K. Barnard, P. Dyugulu, N. de Freitas, D. Forsyth, D. Blei, and M. I. Jordan. Matching words and pictures. Journal of Machine Learning Research, 3: 1107-1135, 2003.
2. P. Duygulu, K. Barnard, N. de Freitas, and D. Forsyth. Ojbect recognition as machine translation: Learning a lexicon fro a fixed image vocabulary. In Seventh European Conf. on Computer Vision, 97-112, 2002.
3. J. Jeon, V. Lavrenko and R. Manmatha. Automatic image annotation and retrieval using cross-media relevance models. In Proceedings of the 26th intl. SIGIR Conf, 119-126, 2003.
4. Y. Mori, H. Takahashi, and R. Oka, Image-to-word transformation based on dividing and vector quantizing images with words. First International Workshop on Multimedia Intelligent Storage and Retrieval Management, 1999.
5. Edward Chang, Kingshy Goh, Gerard Sychay and Gang Wu. CBSA: Content-based soft annotation for multimodal image retrieval using bayes point machines. IEEE Transactions on Circuts and Systems for Video Technology Special Issue on Conceptual and Dynamical Aspects of Multimedia Content Descriptions, 13(1): 26-38, 2003.
6. J. shi and J. Malik. Normalized cuts and image segmentation. IEEE Transactions On Pattern Analysis and Machine Intelligence, 22(8): 888-905, 2000.
7. A. Berger, S. Pietra and V. Pietra. A maximum entropy approach to natural language processing. In Computational Linguistics, 39-71, 1996.
8. J. Li and J. A. Wang. Automatic linguistic indexing of pictures by a statistical modeling approach. IEEE Transactions on PAMI, 25(10): 175-1088, 2003.
9. Jiwoon Jeon, R. Manmatha. Using maximum entropy for automatic image annotation. In proceedings of third international conference on image and video retrieval, 24-31, 2004.
10. Robert Malouf. A comparison of algorithms for maximum entropy parameter estimation. In Proceedings of the 6th Workshop on Computational Language Learning, 2003.
11. V. Lavrenko, R. Manmatha and J. Jeon. A model for learning the semantics of pictures. In Proceedings of the 16th Annual Conference on Neural Information Processing Systems, 2004.

Corpus-Based Analysis of Japanese Relative Clause Constructions

Takeshi Abekawa[1] and Manabu Okumura[2]

[1] Interdisciplinary Graduate School of Science and Engineering,
Tokyo Institute of Technology, Japan
abekawa@lr.pi.titech.ac.jp
[2] Precision and Intelligence Laboratory,
Tokyo Institute of Technology, Japan
oku@pi.titech.ac.jp

Abstract. Japanese relative clause constructions (RCC's) are defined as being the NP's of structure 'S NP', noting the lack of a relative pronoun or any other explicit form of noun-clause demarcation. Japanese relative clause modification should be classified into at least two major semantic types: case-slot gapping and head restrictive. However, these types for relative clause modification cannot apparently be distinguished. In this paper we propose a method of identifying a RCC's type with a machine learning technique. The features used in our approach are not only representing RCC's characteristics, but also automatically obtained from large corpora. The results we obtained from evaluation revealed that our method outperformed the traditional case frame-based method, and the features that we presented were effective in identifying RCC's types.

1 Introduction

Japanese relative clause constructions (RCC's) are defined as being the NP's of structure 'S NP', noting the lack of a relative pronoun or any other explicit form of noun-clause demarcation[1]. Japanese relative clause constructions should be classified into at least two major semantic types: case-slot gapping and head restrictive. However, these types for relative clause constructions cannot apparently be distinguished.

Given the types of Japanese relative clause constructions and a corpus of Japanese relative clause construction instances, we present a machine learning based approach to classifying RCC's. We present a set of lexical and semantic features that characterize RCC's, and integrate them as a classifier to determine RCC types. We use decision tree learning as the machine learning algorithm.

Distinguishing case-slot gapping and head restrictive relative clauses, or resolving the semantic relationship between the relative clause and its head noun has several application domains, such as machine translation from Japanese[5]. It also has a place in text understanding tasks, such as splitting a long sentence into multiple shorter sentences, and removing less important clauses to shorten a sentence[6].

R. Dale et al. (Eds.): IJCNLP 2005, LNAI 3651, pp. 46–57, 2005.

Previously, relative clauses had been analyzed with rule-based methods that utilized case frames[5,2]. Using hand-crafted rules and knowledge creates several problems: the high cost of constructing them, and lower scalability and coverage.

Recently, due to the availability of very large corpora, corpus-based and machine learning-based approaches have been actively investigated[7]. Cooccurrence information between nouns and verbs can be calculated from the syntactically parsed corpus, and this information can be used preferentially instead of hand-crafted case frames to determine whether a noun can be the filler of a case-slot of a verb[7,11].

However, merely using the cooccurrence information between nouns and verbs instead of case frames cannot provide a good solution to the analysis of Japanese relative clauses. Clauses with high occurrence probability of the main verb and the head noun can sometimes be head restrictive. Moreover, just because the head noun can be the filler of a case-slot of the verb does not always mean that the clause as case-slot gapping. We have to rely on several different clues in order to realize accurate classification. Therefore, in this paper we present eight features are effective in classifying case-slot gapping and head restrictive relative clauses. Most of the features can be automatically acquired by statistically analyzing a corpus as explained in section 4.

In section 2 we first describe the nature of Japanese RCC's, and in section 3 we outline previous work on the analysis of Japanese relative clauses. In section 4 we explain the features that we present in this paper, and in section 5 we explain the machine learning-based classifier, which uses the features in section 4. In section 6 we describe the evaluation of the system and discuss the experimental results.

2 Japanese Relative Clause Constructions

Japanese relative clause constructions have the structure '*S NP*', and constitute a noun phrase as a whole. We will term the modifying *S* the "relative clause", the modified *NP* the "head NP", and the overall NP a "relative clause construction" or RCC[2]. Example RCCs are:

(a) さんまを　焼く　男
saury　grill　man
"the man$_i$ who φ_i grills a saury"

(b) 誰もが　知っている　情報
everyone　know　information
"the information$_i$ which everyone knows ϕ_i"

(c) さんまを　焼く　匂い
saury　grill　smell
"the smell of saury grilled"

RCC should be classified into at least two major semantic types: case-slot gapping and head restrictive. With case-slot gapping RCC's (also called '**inner**' relative clauses[14]), the head NP can be considered to have been gapped from a case slot subcategorized by the main verb of the relative clause. Head restrictive RCC's (also called '**outer**' relative clause[14]) occur when the relative clause modifies the head NP. In (a), the head NP "" (man) can be the subject of the main verb of the relative clause, and in (b), the head NP "" (information) can be object of the main verb. These RCC type are 'inner' relative clauses. In (c) the head NP "" (smell) cannot fill the gap in the relative clause, and RCC type is 'outer'.

The inherent difficulty in determining the type of RCC derives from the fact that these two types of RCC are syntactically identical. Even if the relative clause has case-slot gapping, the type of that clause is not always 'inner', because in Japanese the main verb of the relative clause has often zero pronoun. We thus have to disambiguate the individual RCC instances.

3 Related Work

Previous work on analyzing Japanese relative clauses has used case frames as useful information. They have first tried to find the case frame for the main verb of the relative clause and embedded the nouns in the clause into its case-slots. The head noun is then tried to be embedded into the remaining case-slot in the case frame. To determine whether a relative clause instance is 'outer' clause, they have beforehand constructed a dictionary of the nouns that can be modified by 'outer' clause, such as ""(purpose), or ""(opinion). In one approach[5], the instance is determined to be 'outer' clause, if the head noun is included in the dictionary, regardless of the main verb of the relative clause. In another approach[12], the instance is determined to be 'outer', if the head noun cannot be embedded into a case-slot and the head noun is included in the dictionary.

Recently, cooccurrence information between verbs and nouns has been used in analysis. Kawahara and Kurohashi[7] automatically extracted case frames from very large corpora, and used the case frames to analyze Japanese relative clauses. However, they judged the instances as 'outer' clauses, only if case-slot filling did not succeed.

Murata[11] presented a statistical method of classifying whether the relative clause is an 'inner' or an 'outer' clause. However this method cannot correctly classify 'outer' relative clause which had high cooccurrence probability of the main verbs and the head nouns.

4 Feature Set to Classify RCC Type

In this section, we present eight features that can be considered to be effective in classifying 'inner' and 'outer' relative clauses.

1. **Degree of possibility where the head noun can be modified by the 'outer' relative clause (degree of 'outerness').**

In Japanese, there are two ways of modification between verbs and nouns: nouns modify verbs by filling a case-slot (noun → verb), and verbs modify nouns in

Table 1. Comparison of the number of cooccurring verbs

	relative clauses		case-slots	
noun	freq.	verb No.	freq.	verb No.
(intent)	8,732	941	14,216	677
(fact)	5,454	1,448	7,301	754
(preparation)	2,268	428	2,720	74
(people)	6,681	1,367	10,026	1,998
(city)	1,172	449	3,688	857
(television)	2,740	707	30,627	2,228

relative clauses (verb → noun). Some pairs of a verb and a noun can cooccur only in RCC, and cannot cooccur by filling a case-slot of the verb. For example, noun "準備" (preparation) and verb "走る" (run) can cooccur with each other as the main verb of a relative clause and its head noun, as in "走る準備" (preparation for running), though the noun cannot fill any case-slots of the verb, as in *"準備が走る" (*preparation runs). For nouns, some verbs only cooccur in relative clauses, and a number of such verbs tend to be modified by 'outer' clauses.

Table 1 shows the occurrence frequency of sample nouns and the number of their cooccurring verbs in the relative clauses or in the case-slot relations. For nouns that do not tend to be modified by 'outer' clauses, such as "人々"(people), "都市" (city), and "テレビ"(television), the ratio between the frequency and the number of verbs is almost the same between the relative clause and case-slot cases. On the contrary, for nouns that tend to be modified by 'outer' clauses, such as "意向"(intent), "事実" (fact), and "用意"(preparation), the number of verbs is much bigger in relation to clause cases, although the frequency is smaller. The reason may be, as previously explained, that some verbs cooccur with the nouns that tend to be modified by the 'outer' clause only in relative clause constructions.

Therefore, we can measure the likelihood that the noun will be modified by 'outer' relative clauses, by calculating the difference in the frequency distribution of verbs cooccurring in relative clauses against the frequency distribution of verbs cooccurring in the case-slot relation (If the difference is larger, the probability that the noun can be modified by the 'outer' relative clause becomes larger).

We calculate the likelihood as $J(P_k(v|n), P_m(v|n))$, the Jensen-Shannon distance between the cooccurrence probability where nouns fill the case-slots of verbs($P_k(v|n)$) and the cooccurrence probability where verbs cooccur with nouns in relative clauses($P_m(v|n)$). Given two probability distributions p,q, the Jensen-Shannon distance is defined by the following formula[9]:

$$J(p,q) = \frac{1}{2}\left[D(p||\frac{p+q}{2}) + D(q||\frac{p+q}{2})\right]. \quad (1)$$

$D(p||q)$ is the Kullback-Leibler distance and defined by the following formula[3]:

$$D(p||q) = \sum_i p_i \log \frac{p_i}{q_i}. \quad (2)$$

Table 2. 'outerness' of example nouns

noun	意向 (intent)	事実 (fact)	用意 (preparation)	人々 (people)	都市 (city)	テレビ (television)
$J(P_k, P_m)$	0.546	0.360	0.616	0.160	0.155	0.159

We use the Jensen-Shannon distance rather than the Kullback-Leibler distance, because the former is symmetric and has stability in various sizes of probability distribution experimentally. $P_k(v|n)$ and $P_m(v|n)$ are calculated as follows:

$$P_k(v|n) = \frac{f_k(n, v)}{f_k(n)}, \tag{3}$$

$$P_m(v|n) = \frac{f_m(n, v)}{f_m(n)}, \tag{4}$$

where $f_k(n, v)$ is the cooccurrence frequency where noun n fills a case-slots of verb v, and $f_k(n)$ is the frequency of the noun that occurs in the case-slot of verbs. Similarly, $f_m(n, v)$ and $f_m(n)$ are the frequencies for relative clause constructions. Table 2 shows the 'outerness' of sample nouns. The values of the nouns that are often modified by 'outer' clauses are higher than those of the nouns which tend to be modified by 'inner' clauses.

2. **Cooccurrence information between head noun and main verb of relative clause.**

For a relative clause instance to be an 'inner' clause, the head noun has to fill a case-slot of the main verb of the relative clause. Consider the following two examples:

(a) 共鳴する 音
resonate sound
"the sound$_i$ that ϕ_i resonates"

(b) 破壊する 音
destruct sound
"the destruction sound"

In (a), "音" (sound) can be the subject ("が" case) of the main verb "共鳴する" (resonate). On the contrary, in (b) "音" cannot fill any case-slots of the main verb "破壊する" (destruct) and can be considered to be modified by the 'outer' relative clause. Therefore, if the head noun can fill a case-slot of the main verb, the relation can be more plausibly assessed as 'inner'.

Whether a noun can fill a case-slot of a verb has been traditionally determined using case frames. However, we use the cooccurrence information between the head noun and the main verb. In this paper, the cooccurrence between nouns and verbs is measured by mutual information. Taking into account the information on case particles, mutual information is calculated with the following formula:

$$I(n, k; v) = \log \frac{p(n, k, v)}{p(n, k)p(v)}, \tag{5}$$

where $p(n,k)$ is the probability that noun n will cooccur with case particle k and $p(n,k,v)$ is the cooccurrence probability for noun n, case particle k and verb v, and $p(v)$ is the occurrence probability for verb v. The following seven case particles were taken into account: ("が","を","に","で","へ","と", and "から"). This is because only these case-slots can, in fact, be gapped to the head noun to construct the relative clause.

3. **Which case-slots are already filled for main verb by nouns in relative clause.**

As previously explained, if the head noun can fill the case-slot of the main verb of the relative clause, the RCC instance can be judged as an 'inner' clause. However, if the case-slot that the head noun can fill is already filled by the noun in the relative clause, and hence unavailable for case-slot gapping, the rule cannot be applied. Consider, for example, the following two cases:

(a) 聞いてきた 話
hear story
"the story$_i$ that (someone) heard ϕ_i"

(b) 落語を 聞いてきた 話
Japanese comic story hear story
"the story that (someone) heard a Japanese comic story"

In (a), since "話" (story) can fill the object ("を" case) case-slot of the main verb "聞く" (hear), the relation can be judged as 'inner'. However, in (b), since the object ("を" case) case-slot of the main verb "聞く" is already filled by the noun "落語" (Japanese comic story), and "話" cannot fill any case-slot, the instance is judged as 'outer'.

Taking the situation into account, if a noun in the relative clause fills a case-slot of the main verb, the mutual information for the case-slot is set to a very small value M_{min}.

4. **Whether the head noun is modified by modifiers other than the relative clause (other modifier).**

Previous work on analyzing Japanese relative clauses has taking into account only the head noun, and has not taking into account modifiers other than the relative clause. Consider the following two examples:

(a) 彼に 話す 目的
him talk purpose
"the purpose that (someone) talk (something) to him"
"the purpose$_i$ that (someone) talk ϕ_i to him"

(b) 彼に 話す 旅行の 目的
him talk trip purpose
"the purpose of the trip $_i$ that (I) talk ϕ_i to him"

(a) has two interpretations. The first interpretation is that "目的" (purpose) do not fill the remaining case-slots of the main verb "話す" (talk) and can be considered to be modified by the 'outer' relative clause. The second interpretation is that "目的" can be the direct object("を" case) of the main verb "話す" and can be considered to be modified by the 'inner' relative clause. On the contrary, (b) has only the interpretation of 'inner'.

If the head noun is modified by modifiers other than the relative clause, such as adjectives, compound nouns, and "AB"(B of A), the relative clause type tends to be 'inner'. The function of 'outer' relative clause describes the content of the head noun. If the head noun is modified by a modifier, the relative clause need not describe it. Therefore, the type of relative clause tends to be 'inner'.

To implement the idea, we define a feature 'other modifier'. If the head noun is modified by any modifiers other than the relative clause, its value is 1, otherwise, 0[3].

5. Whether head noun tends to be modified

As for the nouns which tend to be modified by 'outer' relative clauses, the relative clauses describe the content of the head nouns. It is difficult to understand their meaning without any modification. Therefore we calculate the percentage to what degree nouns are modified by any modifier in large corpora. Table 3 shows the percentage for example nouns.

Table 3. Percentage of modification

意向 (intention)	分野 (field)	テレビ (television)	彼 (he)	Average of all nouns
0.983	0.973	0.287	0.155	0.460

The percentages of nouns "意向"(intention) and "分野"(field), which tend to be modified by 'outer' relative clause, are close to 1, that is to say, such nouns must have any modification. We consider, the higher this percentage, the higher the possibility that the noun is modified by 'outer' relative clause.

6. Percentage where "という" is inserted between relative clause and head nouns

"という" is a function expression that is sometimes inserted between relative clauses and head nouns. Table 4 shows the percentage where "という" cooccurs with example nouns.

Table 4. The percentage of "という" cooccurring with noun

意見 (opinion)	噂 (rumor)	場所 (place)	人々 (people)	Average of all nouns
0.335	0.246	0.007	0.008	0.007

[3] In the experiment, we use syntactic annotated corpus. Therefore, other modifier elements are already identified.

The percentages of nouns "意見"(opinion) and "噂"(rumor), which tend to be modified by 'outer' relative clause, are higher than the average. We consider, the higher this percentage, the higher possibility that the noun is modified by 'outer' relative clause.

7. Whether head noun tends to be modified by past-tensed relative clauses(tense information)

Some nouns tend to be modified by past-tense relative clauses, and others tend to be modified by those in the present tense. Consider, for example, the following two nouns: "計画"(plan) and "記憶" (memory). Both nouns are considered to imply the concept of time (future or past) [4] .

Table 5. Tense of main verb and distribution of inner/outer

	計画 (plan)		記憶 (memory)	
tense	inner	outer	inner	outer
present	6	89	12	**0**
past	5	**0**	5	83

For each of the two nouns "計画"(plan) and "記憶"(memory), we examined 100 relative clause instances that had the noun as the head noun (Table 5).If the head noun implies the concept of time, the tense of the main verb of the relative clause tends to coincide with this concept. Furthermore, note that the tense of the main verb of 'outer' relative clauses is the same as the time concept of the head noun. From this, if the noun tends to be modified by a specific-tense relative clause, the relative clause tends to be 'outer', and if the tense of the main verb contradicts the time concept of the head noun (tense of frequently modified relative clauses), the relative clause should be determined as 'inner'.

To implement this idea, we first calculated deviations in the distribution of tense for the relative clauses. The percentage of past-tense main verbs in all relative clauses, R_{past}, and the average for all the nouns were calculated. Table 6 shows the results for sample nouns.

Table 6. Percentage of past-tense main verbs

計画 (plan)	記憶 (memory)	場所 (place)	人々 (people)	Average of all nouns
0.032	0.958	0.333	0.422	0.322

For a head noun which does not imply the concept of time ("場所" (place) and "人々"(people)), the percentage is near average. On the contrary, "計画"(plan) and "記憶"(memory) which imply the concept of time have an extreme value.

[4] In Japanese, there are just two tense surface markers: present and past. Therefore, future tense is indicated by the present tense on the surface.

Taking into account the actual tense of the relative clause instances, we calculated the following score:

$$V_{past} \begin{cases} R_{past} - AVG_{past} \text{ in case of present tense} \\ AVG_{past} - R_{past} \text{ in case of past tense} \end{cases} \tag{6}$$

For a head noun not implying the concept of time, in either tense of the main verb, the score is rather low, and a decision on inner/outer might not be affected by the score. For a head noun implying the concept of time, the absolute value of the score is rather large, and if the tense of the main verb is the same as the time concept, the score becomes negative; otherwise the score becomes positive.

8. **Whether main verb has a sense of 'exclusion'**

The last feature is for identifying exceptional 'outer' relative clause. Consider the following two examples:

(a) 日本を 除く アジア諸国
Japan except Asian countries
"Asian countries except Japan"

(b) 怪我人を 除いた 乗客
injured people except passenger
"the passenger except injured people"

These examples are 'outer' relative clauses, and this RCC type is identified by the main verb which has sense of exclusion. There are a few verbs which indicate the RCC type by itself. Therefore, we defined a feature 'excluding verb'. If the main verb contains a character '除' (which has sense of exclusion), the feature is set to 1, otherwise, 0.

5 Machine Learning Based Classifier for RCC Type

We integrated the eight features in described the last section and used the machine learning approach to determine the RCC type. We used C5.0[13] as the machine learning algorithm.

C5.0 is a decision-tree based classification system that has been used in natural language processing, such as text classification, chunking, text summarization, and ellipsis resolution[10]. C5.0 takes a set of training instances with a feature vector and correct type as input, and induces a classifier which characterizes the given feature space.

Since we use only eight features, we think even the state of the art machine learning method like SVM would yield almost the same accuracy as decision-tree. Furthermore decision-tree are more easily interpreted by human than SVMs.

6 Evaluation

6.1 Experiment

Cooccurrence and other statistical information used in this work were calculated from the corpus of a collection of twenty-two years of newspaper articles. The corpus was parsed with KNP[8], which is a rule-based Japanese syntactic parser. The cooccurrence information we obtained was as follows: the number of $f_k(n,v)$ was about 60.8 million, and the number of $f_m(n,v)$ was about 12.4 million.

The data used in the evaluation was a set of RCC instances randomly extracted from the EDR corpus[4] which had syntactically analyzed. Then, a label, whether the relative clause is 'inner' or 'outer', was manually annotated. The statistics on the data are shown in Table 7. Evaluation with C5.0 was carried out by way of 5-fold cross validation.

Table 7. Statistics on evaluation data

Total	Inner	Outer
749	580	169

Table 8. Experimental results

		Inner		Outer	
	accuracy	precision	recall	precision	recall
Baseline	0.774	0.774	1.000	-	-
Cooccurrence information only	0.787	0.836	0.906	0.520	0.366
Case frame	0.830	0.868	0.921	0.657	0.521
Our approach	0.902	0.931	0.942	0.794	0.762

```
...excluding verb = 1: outer(exceptinal type) (22/2)
 :.excluding verb = 0:
   :..outerness <= 0.212: inner (444/6)
      outerness >  0.212:
      :..other modifier = 1: inner (84/17)
         other modifier = 0:
         :..cooccurrence("を" case) >  -9.10: inner (28/4)
            cooccurrence("を" case) <= -9.10:
            :..percentage of "という" >  0.027: outer (105/14)
               percentage of "という" <= 0.027:
               :..percentage of modified <= 0.735: inner (25/2)
                  percentage of modified >  0.735:
                  :..cooccurrence("が" case) <= -13.1:outer (31/5)
                     cooccurrence("が" case) >  -13.1:inner (10/2)
```

Fig. 1. Generated decision tree

The baseline we used determines all instances as 'inner' relative clauses. We also compared our approach with the traditional method with case frames, and a method that uses only cooccurrence information (features 2 and 3 in section 4. An evaluation measure is an accuracy, which is defined as the number of correctly identified RCCs divided by the number of all RCCs. And for inner/outer relative clauses, precision and recall are calculated.

$$Precision = \frac{\#\text{number of correctly identified relative clauses}}{\#\text{number of inner/outer attempted by system}}$$

$$Recall = \frac{\#\text{number of correctly identified relative clauses}}{\#\text{number of inner/outer relative clauses}}$$

The results are shown in Table 8. The generated decision tree from all instances is shown in Figure 1. The last values on each line, for example '22/2' and '444/6', indicated 'number of applied examples / number of misclassification'.

6.2 Discussion

Accuracy of our approach is higher than that of the traditional approach. Our approach works well especially for identifying 'outer' relative clause. Furthermore, using only cooccurrence information could not yield better performance for 'outer' relative clause. Therefore, we conclude that the features in our approach can effectively identify the 'outer' relative clause.

Figure 1 shows that the most contributive feature except 'excluding verb' is the degree of 'outerness'. This feature can classify many instances with high accuracy (98.6%=438/444). If the degree of 'outerness' is smaller than certain threshold, RCC type is 'inner' with high probability.

The second contributing feature is the 'other modifier'. If modifiers other than the relative clause exist, RCC type is 'inner'. However, the accuracy of this feature is not so good compared with other features.

We unfortunately could not find the 'tense information' in our decision tree. We consider the reason to be that nouns which imply the concept of time are very few, and there might be no instances which contain them.

7 Conclusions

In this paper, we presented eight lexical and semantic features that characterized RCC, and we integrated them using machine learning approach to determine the RCC type.

Evaluation proved that our approach outperformed the traditional case frame-based method, and the features that we presented were effective in classifying types into 'inner' and 'outer' relative clauses.

After identification of 'inner' clauses, case identification will be necessary for semantic analysis. This will be considered in future work.

References

1. Baldwin, T., Tokunaga, T. and Tanaka, H.: The parameter-based analysis of Japanese relative clause constructions. In IPSJ SIGNote on Natural Language **134**-8 (1999) 55-62
2. Baldwin, T.: Making Sense of Japanese Relative Clause Constructions. In Proceedings of the Second Workshop on Text Meaning and Interpretation (2004) 49-56.
3. Dagan, I., Lee, L. and Pereira, F.: Similarity-based models of word cooccurrence probabilities. Machine Learning **34** (1999) 65-81
4. EDR.: EDR electronic dictionary technical guide. Technical Report TR045, Japanese Electronic Dictionary Research Institute Ltd (1995)
5. Ikehara, S., Shirai, S., Yokoo, A. and Nakaiwa, H.: Toward an MT system without pre-editing effect of new methods in ALT-J/E . In Proceedings of the Third Machine Translation Summit (1991)
6. Ishizako, T., Kataoka, A., Masuyama, S., Yamamoto, K. and Nakagawa, S.: Reduction of overlapping expressions using dependency relations. Natural Language Processing **7**(4) (2000) 119-142. (in Japanese)
7. Kawahara, D. and Kurohashi, S.: Fertilization of case frame dictionary for robust Japanese case analysis. In Proceedings of the 19th International Conference on Computational Linguistics (2002) 425-431
8. Kurohashi, S. and Nagao, M.: Kn parser: Japanese dependency/case structure analyzer. In Proceeding of the International Workshop on Sharable Natural Language Resources (1994) 48-55
9. Lin, J.: Divergence measures based on the shannon entropy. IEEE TRANSACTIONS ON INFORMATION THEORY. **37**(1) (1991) 145-151
10. Manning, C. and Schutze, H.: Foundations of Statistical Natural Language Processing. MIT Press (1999)
11. Murata, M.: Extraction of negative examples based on positive examples automatic detection of mis-spelled Japanese expressions and relative clauses that do not have case relations with their heads . In IPSJ SIGNote on Natural Language **144**-15 (2001) 105-112. (in Japanese)
12. Narita, H.: Parsing Japanese clauses modifying nominals. In IPSJ SIGNote on Natural Language **99**-11 (1994) 79-86. (in Japanese)
13. Quinlan, J.: C4.5: Programs for Machine Learning. Morgan Kaufmann (1993)
14. Teramura, H.: Rentai-shuushoku no shintakusu to imi. No.**1-4**. Nihongo Nihonbunka **4-7** (1975-1978) (in Japanese)

Parsing Biomedical Literature*

Matthew Lease and Eugene Charniak

Brown Laboratory for Linguistic Information Processing (BLLIP),
Brown University, Providence, RI USA
{mlease, ec}@cs.brown.edu

Abstract. We present a preliminary study of several parser adaptation techniques evaluated on the GENIA corpus of MEDLINE abstracts [1,2]. We begin by observing that the Penn Treebank (PTB) is lexically impoverished when measured on various genres of scientific and technical writing, and that this significantly impacts parse accuracy. To resolve this without requiring in-domain treebank data, we show how existing domain-specific lexical resources may be leveraged to augment PTB-training: part-of-speech tags, dictionary collocations, and named-entities. Using a state-of-the-art statistical parser [3] as our baseline, our lexically-adapted parser achieves a 14.2% reduction in error. With oracle-knowledge of named-entities, this error reduction improves to 21.2%.

1 Introduction

Since the advent of the Penn Treebank (PTB) [4], statistical approaches to natural language parsing have quickly matured [3,5]. By providing a very large corpus of manually labeled parsing examples, PTB has played an invaluable role in enabling the broad analysis, automatic training, and quantitative evaluation of parsing techniques. However, while PTB's Wall Street Journal (WSJ) corpus has historically served as the canonical benchmark for evaluating statistical parsing, the need for broader evaluation has been increasingly recognized in recent years. Furthermore, since it is impractical to create a large treebank like PTB for every genre of interest, significant attention has been directed towards maximally reusing existing training data in order to mitigate the need for domain-specific training examples. These issues have been most notably explored in parser adaptation studies conducted between PTB's WSJ and Brown corpora [6,7,8,9].

As part of our own exploration of these issues, we have been investigating statistical parser adaptation to a novel domain: biomedical literature. This literature presents a stark contrast to WSJ and Brown: it is suffused with domain-specific vocabulary, has markedly different stylistic constraints, and is often written by non-native speakers. Moreover, broader consideration of technical literature shows this challenge and opportunity is not confined to biomedical literature

* We would like to thank the National Science Foundation for their support of this work (IIS-0112432, LIS-9721276, and DMS-0074276), as well as thank Sharon Goldwater and our anonymous reviewers for their valuable feeback.

R. Dale et al. (Eds.): IJCNLP 2005, LNAI 3651, pp. 58–69, 2005.

alone, but is also demonstrated by patent literature, engineering manuals, and field-specific scientific discourse. Through our work with biomedical literature, we hope to gain insights into effective techniques for adapting statistical parsing to technical literature in general.

Our interest in biomedical literature is also motivated by a real need to improve information extraction in this domain. With over 15 million citations in PubMed today, biomedical literature is the largest and fastest growing knowledge domain of any science. As such, simply managing the sheer volume of its accumulated information has become a significant problem. In response to this, a large research community has formed around the challenge of enabling automated mining of the literature [10,11]. While the potential value of parsing has often been discussed by this community, attempts to employ it thus far appear to have been limited by the parsing technologies employed. Reported difficulties include poor coverage, inability to resolve syntactic ambiguity, unacceptable memory and speed, and difficulty in hand-crafting rules of grammar [12,13]. Perhaps the most telling indicator of community perspective came in a recent survey's bleak observation that efficient and accurate parsing of unrestricted text appears to be out of reach of current techniques [14].

In this paper, we show that broad, accurate parsing of biomedical literature is indeed possible. Using an off-the-shelf WSJ-trained statistical parser [3] as our baseline, we provide the first full-coverage parse accuracy results for biomedical literature, as measured on the GENIA corpus of MEDLINE abstracts [1,2]. Furthermore, after showing that PTB is lexically impoverished when measured on various genres of scientific and technical writing, we describe three methods for improving parse accuracy by leveraging lexical resources from the domain: part-of-speech (POS) tags, dictionary collocations, and named-entities. Our general hope is that lexically-based techniques such as these can provide alternative and complementary value to treebank-based adaptation methods such as co-training [9] and sample selection [15]. Our lexically-adapted parser achieves a 14.2% reduction in error over the baseline, and in the case of oracle-knowledge of named-entities, this reduction improves to 21.2%.

Section 2 describes the GENIA corpus in detail. In Section 3, we present unknown word rate experiments which measure the coverage of PTB's grammar on various genres of scientific and technical writing. Section 4 describes our methods for lexical adaptation and their corresponding effects on parse accuracy. Section 5 concludes with a discussion challenges and opportunities for future work.

2 The GENIA Corpus

The GENIA corpus [1,2] consists of MEDLINE abstracts related to transcription factors in human blood cells. Version `3.02p` of the corpus includes 1999[1] abstracts (18,545 sentences, 436,947 words) annotated with part-of-speech (POS)

[1] The reported total of 2000 abstracts includes repetition of article ID 97218353.

tags and named-entities. Named-entities were labelled according to a corpus-defined ontology, and the POS-tagging scheme employed is very similar to that used in PTB (see Section 4.1).

Using these POS annotations and PTB guidelines [16], we hand-parsed 21 of these abstracts (215 sentences) to create a pilot treebank for measuring parse accuracy. We performed the treebanking using the GRAPH[2] tool developed for the Prague Dependency Treebank. Initial bracketing was performed without any form of automation. Following this, our baseline parser [3] was used to propose alternative parses. In cases where hand-generated parses conflicted with those proposed by the parser, hand-parses were manually corrected, or not corrected, according to PTB bracketing guidelines. Our pilot treebank is publicly available[3].

Subsequent to this, the Tsujii lab released its own beta version treebank, which includes 200 abstracts (1761 sentences) from the original corpus. This treebanking was performed largely in accordance with PTB guidelines (perhaps the most significant difference being constituent labels NAC and NX were excluded in favor of NP). Because there is no redundancy in the coverage of the Tsuijii lab's treebank and our own pilot treebank (and by chance, NAC and NX do not occur in our pilot treebank either), we have combined the two treebanks to maximize our evaluation treebank (see Table 3).

An additional note is required regarding our use of named-entities (Section 4.3). Entity annotations (not available in the treebank) were obtained from the earlier 3.02p version of the corpus. Any sentences that did not match between the two versions of the corpus (due to differences in tokenization or other variations) were discarded. The practical impact of this was negligible, as only 25 sentences had to be discarded[4].

3 Unknown Words

Casual reading of technical literature quickly reveals a rich, field-specific vocabulary. For example, consider the following sentence taken from GENIA:

> The study of NF-kappaB showed that oxLDLs led to a decrease of activation-induced p65/p50 NF-kappaB heterodimer binding to DNA, whereas the presence of the constitutive nuclear form of p50 dimer was unchanged.

To quantitatively measure the size and field-specificity of domain vocabulary, we extracted the lexicon contained in WSJ sections 2-21 and evaluated the unknown word rate (by token) for various genres of technical literature. Results are given in Table 1.

---

[2] http://quest.ms.mff.cuni.cz/pdt/Tools/Tree_Editors/Graph

[3] http://www.cog.brown.edu/Research/nlp

[4] Because our preliminary use of named-entities assumes oracle-knowledge, this experiment was carried out on the development section only, thus only the development section was reduced in this way.

Table 1. Unknown word rate on various technical corpora given WSJ 2-21 lexion

Corpus	Unknown Word Rate
WSJ sect. 24	2.7
Brown-DEV	5.8
Brown sect. J	7.3
CRAN	10.0
CACM	10.7
DOE	16.7
GENIA	25.5

Brown-DEV corresponds to a balanced sampling of the Brown corpus (see Table 4). Section J of Brown contains "Learned" writing samples and demonstrated the highest rate of any single Brown section. CRAN contains 1400 abstracts in the field of aerodynamics, and CACM includes 3200 abstracts from Communications of the ACM [17]. DOE contains abstracts from the Department of Energy, released as part of PTB. GENIA here refers to 333 abstracts (IDs 97449161-99101008) not overlapping our treebank. As this table shows, unknown word rate clearly increases as we move to increasingly technical domains. Annecdotal evaluation on patent literature suggests its unknown rate lies somewhere between that of DOE and GENIA.

While these results appear to indicate WSJ is lexically impoverished with respect to increasingly technical domains, it was also necessary to consider the possibility that the results were simply symptomatic of technical domains having very large lexicons. If such were the case, we would expect to see these domains demonstrate high unknown word rates even in the presence of a domain-specific lexicon. To test this hypothesis, we contrasted unknown word rates on GENIA using lexicons extracted from WSJ sections 2-21, Brown (training section from Table 4), and from GENIA itself (1,333 abstracts: IDs 90110496-97445684)[5]. Results are presented in Table 2.

Table 2. Unknown word rate on GENIA using lexicons extracted from WSJ, Brown, and GENIA

Lexicon	Size	Unknown Word Rate
Brown	25K	28.2
WSJ	40K	25.5
Brown+WSJ	50K	22.4
GENIA	15K	5.3
Brown+WSJ+GENIA	60K	4.6

[5] While this set of abstracts does overlap the Tsujii treebank, this experiment was run prior to the treebank's release.

Although the unknown word rate in the presence of in-domain training for GENIA (5.3%, Table 2) is nearly twice that of out-of-domain training (2.7%, Table 1), suggesting a larger lexicon does indeed exist, it is also strikingly clear that WSJ and Brown provide almost no lexical value to the domain: expanding GENIAs lexicon by 45,000 new terms found in WSJ and Brown produced only a meager 0.7% reduction in unknown word rate. Contrast this with the enormous reduction achieved through using GENIA's lexicon instead of the WSJ or Brown lexicons (Table 2).

4 Parser Adaptation

In this section, we present three methods for parser adaptation motivated by the results of our unknown word rate experiments (Section 3). The goal of these adaptations is to help an off-the-shelf PTB-trained parser compensate for the large amount of domain-specific vocabulary found in technical literature, specifically biomedical text. To accomplish this without depending on in-domain treebank data, we consider three alternative (and less expensive) domain-specific knowledge sources: part-of-speech tags, dictionary collocations, and named-entities. We report on the results of each technique both in isolation and in combination.

We adopt as our baseline for these experiments the publicly available Charniak parser [3] trained on WSJ sections 2-21 of the Penn Treebank. Our division of the GENIA corpus into development and test sets is shown in Table 3. Analysis was carried out on the development section, and the test section was reserved for final evaluation. Parse accuracy was measured using the standard PARSEVAL metric of bracket-bracket scoring, assuming the usual conventions regarding punctuation [18]. Statistical significance for each experiment was assessed using a two-tailed paired t-test on sentence-averaged f-measure scores. Since our evaluation treebank excludes `NX` and `NAC` constituent labels in favor of `NP` (Section 2), for all experiments

Table 3. Division of the GENIA combined treebank into development and test sections

Source	Section	Abstract IDs	Sentences
Pilot	Development	99101510-99120900	215
Tsujii	Development	91079577-92060325	732
Tsujii	Test	92062170-94051535	1004

Table 4. Brown corpus division. Training and evaluation sections were obtained from Gildea [7]. The development (and final training) section was created by extracting every tenth sentence from Gildea's training corpus.

	POS-Train	Development	Test
Sentences	19637	2181	2425

Table 5. PARSEVAL f-measure scores on the GENIA development section using the adaptation methods described in Section 4. Statistical significance of individual adaptations are compared against no adaptation, and combined adaptations are compared against the best prior adaptation. As the p values indicate, all of the adaptions listed here produced a significant improvement in parse accuracy.

Adaptation	F-measure	Error reduction	Significance
none	78.3	–	–
lexicon	78.6	1.4	$p = 0.002$
no NNP	79.1	3.7	$p = 0.002$
train POS	80.8	11.5	$p < 0.001$
entities	80.9	12.0	$p < 0.001$
no NNP, train POS	81.5	14.7	$p = 0.043$
no NNP, train POS, entities	82.9	21.2	$p < 0.001$

Table 6. Final PARSEVAL f-measure results on GENIA compared with scores on Brown and WSJ sect. 23. In all cases, the parser was trained on WSJ sect. 2-21 with the over-parsing parameter set to 21x over-parsing. Adapted GENIA results includes POS adaptations only (oracle-type entity adaptation was not used). Adapted Brown results use POS re-training on Brown train section.

Corpus	F-measure	Error reduction	Significance
GENIA-unadapted	76.3	–	–
GENIA-adapted	79.6	14.2	$p < 0.001$
Brown-unadapted	83.4	–	–
Brown-adapted	84.1	4.1	$p = 0.002$
WSJ	89.5	–	–

(including baseline) we post-processed parser output to collapse these label distinctions[6]. Results from our various experiments are summarized in Table 5.

Final results of our adapted parser are given in Table 6. For comparison with standard benchmarks, parser performance was also evaluated on WSJ section 23 and on Brown. Table 4 shows our division of the Brown corpus.

4.1 Using POS Tags

Part-of-speech tags provide an important data feature to statistical parsers [3,5]. Since technical and scientific texts introduce a significant amount of domain-specific vocabulary (Section 3), a POS-tagger trained only on everyday

[6] While PTB examples could be similarly pre-processed prior to training, thereby reducing the search space while parsing, the reduction would be minor and would mean giving up a potentially useful distinction in syntactic contexts.

English is immediately at a disadvantage for tagging such text. Indeed, our off-the-shelf PTB-trained parser achieves only 84.6% tagging accuracy on GENIA. Consequently, our simple first adaptation step was to retrain the parser's POS-tagger on the 1,778 GENIA abstracts not present in the combined treebank (in addition to WSJ sections 2-21). This simple fix raised tagging accuracy to 95.9%. Correspondingly, parsing accuracy improved from 78.3% to 80.8% (Table 5).

While such POS-retraining is a direct remedy to learning appropriate tags for new vocabulary, it is only a partial fix to a larger problem. In particular, the trees found in PTB codify a relationship between PTB POS tags and constituent structure, and any mismatch between the tagging schemata used in PTB and that used by our new corpus could result in misapplication or underutilization of the bracketing rules acquired by the parser during training. To overcome this, it is necessary to introduce an additional mapping step which converts between the two POS tagging schemata. For closely related schemata, this mapping may be trivial, but this cannot be assumed without a carefully analysis of tag distribution and usage across the two corpora.

In the case of GENIA, the tagging guidelines used were based on PTB and only subsequently revised (to improve inter-annotator agreement), so while differences do exist, the problem is much less significant than the general case of arbitrarily different schemata. Reported differences include treatment of hyphenated, partial, and foreign terms, and most notably, the distinction between proper (NNP) and common (NN) nouns [2]. In order to quantitatively assess the degree to which these and other revisions were made to the tagging scheme, we extracted the POS distribution for 333 GENIA abstracts (as used in our unknown word rate experiments from Section 3). From this distribution, we learned that NNP almost never occurs in GENIA. This meant that our PTB-trained parser would be unable to leverage PTB's constituent structure examples examples that involved proper nouns.

As a preliminary remedy, we simply relabeled all proper nouns as common in PTB and re-trained the parser. This improved tagging accuracy to 96.4% and parsing accuracy to 81.5% (Table 5). We should note, however, that this solution is not ideal. While it does allow use of PTB's NNP-examples, it does so at the cost of confusing legitimate differences in the syntactic distribution of common and proper nouns in English (as reflected by a 0.7% loss in accuracy on WSJ evaluation when using this NN-NNP conflated training data). Clearly it would be better if GENIA's nouns could be re-tagged to preserve this distinction while preserving inter-annotator agreement. A first step in this direction would be to perform this re-tagging automatically based on determiner usage and GENIA's entity annotations, with success measured by the corresponding impact on parse accuracy. This, along with a more careful analysis of tagging differences, remains for future work.

We have also evaluated parser performance under the oracle condition of perfect tags. This was implemented as a soft constraint so that the parser's joint probability model could overrule the oracle tag for cases in which no parse could be found using it (cases of annotator error or data sparsity). Using the oracle tag 99.8% of the time (in addition to other POS adaptations) had almost no impact on parse accuracy, suggesting that further POS-related improvements in parse accuracy will only come from the sort of careful analysis of the tagging schemata discussed above.

4.2 Using a Domain-Specific Lexicon

Another strategy we employed for lexical adaptation was the use of a domain-specific dictionary. For biomedicine, such a dictionary is available from the National Library of Medicine: the Unified Medical Language System (UMLS) SPECIALIST lexicon [19]. Covering both general English as well as biomedical vocabulary, the SPECIALIST lexicon contains over 415,000 entries (including orthographic and morphological variants). Entries are also assigned one of eleven POS categories specified as part of the lexicon.

Given our finding from Section 4.1 that even oracle POS tags would do little to improve upon our re-trained POS tagger, we did not make use of lexicon POS tags. Instead, we restricted our use of the lexicon to extracting collocations. We then added a hard-constraint to the parser that these collocations could not be cross-bracketed and that each collocation must represent a flat phrase with no internal sub-constituents. This approach was motivated by a couple of observations. On one hand, we observed cases where the parser would be confused by long compound nouns; in desperation to find the start of a verb phrase, it would sometimes use part of the compound to head a new verb phrase. Unfortunately, WSJ sections 2-21 contain approximately 500 verb phrases headed by present-participle verbs mistagged as nouns, thus making this bizarre bracketing rule statistically viable. A second observation was the frequency with which we saw the terms "in vivo" and "in vitro" (treebanked as foreign adjverbial or adjectival collocations) mis-analyzed. Even in biomedical texts, "in" appears far more often as a preposition than as part of such collocations, and as such, is almost always mis-parsed in these collocational contexts to head a prepositional phrase. Our hope was that by preventing such collocations from being cross-bracketted, we could prevent this class of parsing mistakes.

We found use of lexical collocations did yield a small (0.3%) but statistically significant improvement in performance over the unmodified parser (Table 5). However, when combined with either POS or entity adaptations, the lexicon's impact on parsing accuracy was statistically insignificant. Our interpretation of this latter result is that the primary limitation of the lexicon is coverage, despite its size. That is, when either of the other adaptations were used, the lexicon did not offer much beyond them. It is not surprising that oracle-knowledge of entities (Section 4.3) provided greater coverage than the generic dictionary, and the improvement in tagging from POS adaptation (sharper tag probabilities) helped somewhat in preventing the verb-ification of some of the long compound nouns. While the lexicon was the only adaptation to correctly fix "in vivo" type mistakes, these phrases alone were not sufficiently frequent to provide a statistically significant improvement in parse accuracy on top of other adaptations. As such, the primary value of this method would be in cases where such a lexicon is available but POS tags and labelled entities are not.

4.3 Using Named-Entities

The primary focus of the GENIA corpus is to support training and evaluation of automatic named-entity recognition. As such, a variety of biologically meaningful terms have been annotated in the corpus according to a corpus-defined ontology. Given the availability of these annotations, we were interested in considering the extent to which they could be used as a source of lexical information for parser adaptation.

Given the problems described earlier with regard to lexical collocations being cross-bracketted by our off-the-shelf PTB-trained parser (Section 4.2), our hope was that named-entities could be used similarly to lexical collocations in helping to prevent this class of mistakes. To put it another way, we hoped to exploit the correlation between named-entities and noun phrase (NP) boundaries. A common preprocessing step in detecting named-entities is to use a chunker to find NPs. Our approach was to do the reverse: to use named-entities as a feature for finding NP boundaries.

Our initial plan was to use the same strategy we had used with dictionary collocations: to add a hard-constraint to the parser that a named-entity could not be cross-bracketed and had to represent a flat phrase with no internal sub-constituents. However, we found upon closer inspection that the entities often did contain substructure (primarily parenthetical acronyms), and so we relaxed the flat-constituent constraint and enforced only the cross-bracketing constraint.

As a preliminary step, we evaluated the utility of this method using oracle-knowledge of named-entities. By itself, this method was roughly equivalent to POS re-training in improving parsing accuracy from 78.3% to 80.9% (Table 5). But when combined with POS adaptations, use of named-entities provided another significant improvement in performance, from 81.5% to 82.9%. Clearly this is a promising avenue for further work, and it will be interesting to see how much of this benefit from the oracle case can be realized when using automatically detected entities.

5 Discussion

We have found only limited use of parsing reported to date for biomedical literature, thus it is difficult to compare our parsing results against previous work in parsing this domain. To the best of our knowledge, only one other wide-coverage parser has been applied to biomedical literature: Grover et al. report 99% coverage using a hand-written grammar with a statistical ranking component [20]. We do not know of any quantitative accuracy figures reported for this domain other than those described here.

For those interested in mining the biomedical literature, the next important step will be assessing the utility of PTB-style parsing compared to other parsing models that have been employed for information extraction. There has been promising work in using PTB-style parses for information extraction by inducing predicate-argument structures from the output parses [21]. It will be interesting to see for the biomedical domain how these predicate-argument structures compare to those induced by other grammar formalisms currently in use, such as HPSG [22].

The next immediate extension of our work is to evaluate use of detected named-entities in place of the oracle case described in Section 4.3, replacing the current hard-constraint with a soft-constraint confidence term to be incorporated into the parser's generative model. Performance of named-entity recognition on GENIA was recently studied as part of a shared task at BioNLP/NLPBA 2004. The best system achieved 72.6% f-measure [23], though note that this task required both detection and classification of named-entities. As our usage of entities does not require classification, this number should be considered a lower-bound in the context of our usage model. We expect this level of accuracy should be sufficient to improve parse scores, though how much of the oracle benefit we can realize remains to be seen.

There are also interesting POS issues meriting further investigation. As discussed in Section 4.1, we would like to find a better solution to the lack of proper noun annotations in GENIA, perhaps by detecting proper nouns using determiners and labelled entities. More careful analysis of the differences between the PTB and GENIA tagging schemata is also needed. Additionally, there are interesting issues regarding how POS tags are used by the parsing model. Whereas the Collins' model [5] treats POS tagging as an external preprocessing step (a single best tag is input to the parsing model), the Charniak model [3] generates tag hypotheses as part of its combined generative model, and thus considers multiple hypotheses in searching for the best parse. The significance of this is that other components of the generative model can influence tag selection, and Charniak has reported adding this feature to his simulated version of the Collins model improved its accuracy by 0.6% [24]. However, this result was for in-domain evaluation; the picture becomes more complicated when we begin parsing out-of-domain. If we have an in-domain trained POS-tagger, we might not want a combined model trained on out-of-domain data overruling our tagger's predictions. One option may be introducing a weighting factor into the generative model to indicate the degree of confidence assigned to our tagger relative to the other components of the combined model.

Another issue for further work is the parsing of paper titles. In the GENIA development section, only 28% of the titles are sentences whereas 71% are noun phrases. This distribution is radically different than the rest of the corpus, which is heavily dominated by sentence-type utterances. As headlines are even more rare in our WSJ training data than titles are in GENIA (since WSJ contains full article text), our parser performs miserably at utterance-type detection (i.e. correctly labelling the top-most node in the parse tree): 58.6%. Correspondingly, parse accuracy on titles is only 69.1%, which represents a statistically significant decrease in accuracy in comparison to the entire development section ($p = 0.038$). In investigating this, we noticed an oddity in GENIA in that most titles were encoded in the corpus with an ending period that did not exist in the original papers the corpus was derived from. By removing these periods, we improved utterance-type detection to 77.9%. While parse accuracy rose to 72.0%, this was statistically insignificant ($p = 0.082$). The solution we would like to move towards is to respect the legitimate distributional differences between title and non-title utterances and parameterize the parser differently for the two cases. Generally speaking, such "contextual parsing" might allow us to improve parsing accuracy more widely by parameterizing our parser differently based on where the current utterance fits in the larger discourse. This example of period usage in titles also highlights a broader issue that seemingly innocuous issues in corpus preparation can have significant impact when parsing. As a further example of this, the choice to (at times) separately tokenize term-embedded parentheses in GENIA creates unnecessary attachment ambiguity in the resulting parenthetical phrases. For example, in the phrase "C3a and C3a(desArg)", "C3a(desArg)" is tokenized as "C3a (desArg)", which produces ambiguity as to whether the parenthetical should attach low (to the latter "C3a") or high (to the compound "C3a and C3a"). Issues such as these remind us to be mindful of the relationship between corpus preparation and parsing, as well as downstream processing, and that some issues which appear difficult to resolve while parsing might be handled more easily at another stage in the processing pipeline.

We view biomedical and other technical texts as providing an interesting set of challenges and questions for future parsing research. An interesting introduction to some of these challenges, supported by examples drawn from the domain, can be found in [25]. A significant question for consideration is the degree to which these challenges are related to domain knowledge vs. stylistic norms of the genre. For example, [2] reports that whereas POS determination required domain expertise, prepositional phrase (PP)-attachment could be largely determined even by non-biologists. Our own treebanking experience left us with the opposite impression. For example, in the phrase "gene expression and protein secretion of IL-6", should the PP attach high (IL-6 *gene expression and protein secretion*) or low (gene expression and IL-6 *protein secretion*)? Domain knowledge appears to be necessary here for correct resolution. In contrast to this, POS tags appear to be a distributional rather than a semantic concern. Issues like this highlight how little we really understand currently about the parameters of corpus variation. How do the frequencies of different syntactic constructions vary by genre, and are there key structural variations at work? How do we effectively adapt parsers in response? These issues remain important topics for future investigation.

References

1. Kim, J.d., Ohta, T., Tateisi, Y., Tsujii, J.: Genia corpus - a semantically annotated corpus for bio-textmining. Bioinformatics (Supplement: Eleventh International Conference on Intelligent Systems for Molecular Biology) **19** (2003) i180–i182
2. Tateisi, Y., Ohta, T., dong Kim, J., Hong, H., Jian, S., Tsujii, J.: The genia corpus: Medline abstracts annotated with linguistic information. In: Third meeting of SIG on Text Mining, Intelligent Systems for Molecular Biology (ISMB). (2003)
3. Charniak, E.: A maximum-entropy-inspired parser. In: Proc. NAACL. (2000) 132–139
4. Marcus, M., Santorini, B., Marcinkiewicz, M.A.: Building a large annotated corpus of English: The Penn Treebank. Computational Linguistics **19** (1993) 313–330

5. Collins, M.: Discriminative reranking for natural language parsing. In: Proc. ICML. (2000) 175–182
6. Ratnaparkhi, A.: Learning to parse natural language with maximum entropy models. Machine Learning **34** (1999) 151–175
7. Gildea, D.: Corpus variation and parser performance. In: Proceedings of the 2001 Conference on Empirical Methods in Natural Language Processing. (2001) 167–202
8. Roark, B., Bacchiani, M.: Supervised and unsupervised pcfg adaptation to novel domains. In: Proceedings of HLT-NAACL. (2003) 205–212
9. Steedman, M., Hwa, R., Clark, S., Osborne, M., Sarkar, A., Hockenmaier, J., Ruhlen, P., Baker, S., Crim, J.: Example selection for bootstrapping statistical parsers. In: Proceedings of HLT-NAACL. (2003) 331–338
10. de Bruijn, B., Martin, J.: Literature mining in molecular biology. In: Proceedings of the European Federation for Medical Informatics (EFMI) Workshop on Natural Language Processing in Biomedical Applications. (2002)
11. Hirschman, L., Park, J., Tsujii, J., Wong, L., Wu, C.: Accomplishments and challenges in literature data mining for biology. Bioinformatics **18** (2002) 1553–1561
12. Yakushiji, A., Tateisi, Y., Miyao, Y., Tsujii, J.: Event extraction from biomedical papers using a full parser. In: Pacific Symposium on Biocomputing. (2001) 408–419
13. Daraselia, N., Yuryev, A., Egorov, S., Novichkova, S., Nikitin, A., Mazo, I.: Extracting human protein interactions from medline using a full-sentence parser. Bioinformatics **20** (2004) 604–611
14. Shatkay, H., Feldman, R.: Mining the biomedical literature in the genomic era: An overview. Journal of Computational Biology **10** (2003) 821–855
15. Hwa, R.: Learning Probabilistic Lexicalized Grammars for Natural Language Processing. PhD thesis, Harvard University (2001)
16. Bies, A., Ferguson, M., Katz, K., MacIntyre, R.: Bracketting Guideliness for Treebank II style Penn Treebank Project. Linguistic Data Consortium. (1995)
17. Buckley, C.: Implementation of the smart information retrieval system. Technical Report 85-686, Cornell University (1985)
18. Goodman, J.: Parsing inside-out. PhD thesis, Harvard University (1998)
19. McCray, A.T., Srinivasan, S., Browne, A.C.: Lexical methods for managing variation in biomedical terminologies. In: Proceedings of the 18th Annual Symposium on Computer Applications in Medical Care (SCAMC). (1994) 235–239
20. Grover, C., Lapata, M., Lascarides, A.: A comparison of parsing technologies for the biomedical domain. Journal of Natural Language Engineering (2002)
21. Surdeanu, M., Harabagiu, S., Williams, J., Aarseth, P.: Using predicate-argument structures for information extraction. In: Proceedings of the 41st Annual Meeting of the Association for Computational Linguistics (ACL-03). (2003) 8–15
22. Miyao, Y., Ninomiya, T., Tsujii, J.: Corpus-oriented grammar development for acquiring a head-driven phrase structure grammar from the penn treebank. In: Proc. of IJCNLP-04. (2004) 684–693
23. Zhou, G., Su, J.: Exploring deep knowledge resources in biomedical name recognition. In: Proceedings of the Joint Workshop on Natural Language Processing in Biomedicine and its Applications (JNLPBA-04). (2004)
24. Charniak, E.: Statistical parsing with a context-free grammar and word statistics. In: Proceedings of the Fourteenth National Conference on Artificial Intelligence, Menlo Park, AAAI Press/MIT Press (1997)
25. Park, J.C.: Using combinatory categorical grammar to extract biomedical information. IEEE Intelligent Systems **16** (2001) 62–67

Parsing the Penn Chinese Treebank with Semantic Knowledge

Deyi Xiong[1,2], Shuanglong Li[1,3],
Qun Liu[1], Shouxun Lin[1], and Yueliang Qian[1]

[1] Institute of Computing Technology, Chinese Academy of Sciences,
P.O. Box 2704, Beijing 100080, China
{dyxiong, liuqun, sxlin}@ict.ac.cn
[2] Graduate School of Chinese Academy of Sciences
[3] University of Science and Technology Beijing

Abstract. We build a class-based selection preference sub-model to incorporate external semantic knowledge from two Chinese electronic semantic dictionaries. This sub-model is combined with modifier-head generation sub-model. After being optimized on the held out data by the EM algorithm, our improved parser achieves 79.4% (F1 measure), as well as a 4.4% relative decrease in error rate on the Penn Chinese Treebank (CTB). Further analysis of performance improvement indicates that semantic knowledge is helpful for nominal compounds, coordination, and N◇V tagging disambiguation, as well as alleviating the sparseness of information available in treebank.

1 Introduction

In the recent development of full parsing technology, semantic knowledge is seldom used, though it is known to be useful for resolving syntactic ambiguities. The reasons for this may be twofold. The first one is that it can be very difficult to add additional features which are not available in treebanks to generative models like Collins (see [1]), which are very popular for full parsing. For smaller tasks, like prepositional phrase attachment disambiguation, semantic knowledge can be incorporated flexibly using different learning algorithms (see [2,3,4,5]). For full parsing with generative models, however, incorporating semantic knowledge may involve great changes of model structures. The second reason is that semantic knowledge from external dictionaries seems to be noisy, ambiguous and not available in explicit forms, compared with the information from treebanks. Given these two reasons, it seems to be difficult to combine the two different information sources–*treebank* and *semantic knowledge*–into one integrated statistical parsing model.

One feasible way to solve this problem is to keep the original parsing model unchanged and build an additional sub-model to incorporate semantic knowledge from external dictionaries. The modularity afforded by this approach makes it easier to expand or update semantic knowledge sources with the treebank

R. Dale et al. (Eds.): IJCNLP 2005, LNAI 3651, pp. 70–81, 2005.

unchanged or vice versa. Further, the combination of the semantic sub-model and the original parsing model can be optimized automatically.

In this paper, we build a class-based selection preference sub-model, which is embedded in our lexicalized parsing model, to incorporate external semantic knowledge. We use two Chinese electronic dictionaries and their combination as our semantic information sources. Several experiments are carried out on the Penn Chinese Treebank to test our hypotheses. The results indicate that a significant improvement in performance is achieved when semantic knowledge is incorporated into parsing model. Further improvement analysis is made. We confirm that semantic knowledge is indeed useful for nominal compounds and coordination ambiguity resolution. And surprisingly, semantic knowledge is also helpful to correct Chinese N◇V mistagging errors mentioned by Levy and Manning (see [12]). Yet another great benefit to incorporating semantic knowledge is to alleviate the sparseness of information available in treebank.

2 The Baseline Parser

Our baseline parsing model is similar to the history-based, generative and lexicalized Model 1 of Collins (see [1]). In this model, the right hand side of lexicalized rules is decomposed into smaller linguistic objects as follows:

$$P(h) \rightarrow \#L_n(l_n)...L_1(l_1)H(h)R_1(r_1)...R_m(r_m)\# \ .$$

The uppercase letters are delexicalized nonterminals, while the lowercase letters are lexical items, e.g. head word and head tag (part-of-speech tag of the head word), corresponding to delexicalized nonterminals. $H(h)$ is the head constituent of the rule from which the head lexical item h is derived according to some head percolation rules.[1] The special termination symbol # indicates that there is no more symbols to the left/right. Accordingly, the rule probability is factored into three distributions. The first distribution is the probability of generating the syntactic label of the head constituent of a parent node with label P, head word Hhw and head tag Hht:

$$Pr_H(H|P, Hht, Hhw) \ .$$

Then each left/right modifier of head constituent is generated in two steps: first its syntactic label M_i and corresponding head tag M_iht are chosen given context features from the parent (P), head constituent (H, Hht, Hhw), previously generated modifier ($M_{i-1}, M_{i-1}ht$) and other context information like the direction (dir) and distance[2] (dis) to the head constituent:

[1] Here we use the modified head percolation table for Chinese from Xia (see [6]).

[2] Our distance definitions are different for termination symbol and non-termination symbol, which are similar to Klein and Manning (see [7]).

$$Pr_M(M_i, M_iht|HC_M) \ .$$

where the history context HC_M is defined as the joint event of

$$P, H, Hht, Hhw, M_{i-1}, M_{i-1}ht, dir, dis \ .$$

Then the new modifier's head word M_ihw is also generated with the probability:

$$Pr_{M_w}(M_ihw|HC_{M_w}) \ .$$

where the history context HC_{M_w} is defined as the joint event of

$$P, H, Hht, Hhw, M_{i-1}, M_{i-1}ht, dir, dis, M_i, M_iht \ .$$

All the three distributions are smoothed through Witten-Bell interpolation just like Collins (see [1]). For the distribution Pr_M, we build back-off structures with six levels, which are different from Collins' since we find our back-off structures work better than the three-level back-off structures of Collins. For the distribution Pr_{M_w}, the parsing model backs off to the history context with head word Hhw removed, then to the modifier head tag M_iht, just like Collins. Gildea (see [9]) and Bikel (see [10]) both observed that the effect of bilexical dependencies is greatly impaired due to the sparseness of bilexical statistics. Bikel even found that the parser only received an estimate that made use of bilexical statistics a mere 1.49% of the time. However, according to the wisdom of the parsing community, lexical bigrams, the word pairs (M_ihw, Hhw) are very informative with semantic constraints. Along this line, in this paper, we build an additional class-based selectional preference sub-model, which is described in section 3, to make good use of this semantic information through selectional restrictions between head and modifier words.

Our parser takes segmented but untagged sentences as input. The probability of unknown words, $Pr(uword|tag)$, is estimated based on the first character of the word and if the first characters are unseen, the probability is estimated by absolute discounting.

We do some linguistically motivated re-annotations for the baseline parser. The first one is marking non-recursive noun phrases from other common noun phrases without introducing any extra unary levels (see [1,8]). We find this basic NP re-annotation very helpful for the performance. We think it is because of the annotation style of the Upenn Chinese Treebank (CTB). According to Xue et al. (see [11]), noun-noun compounds formed by an uninterrupted sequence of words POS-tagged as NNs are always left flat because of difficulties in determining which modifies which. The second re-annotation is marking basic VPs, which we think is beneficial for reducing multilevel VP adjunction ambiguities (see [12]).

To speed up parsing, we use the beam thresholding techniques in Xiong et al. (see [13]). In all cases, the thresholding for completed edges is set at $ct = 9$ and incomplete edges at $it = 7$. The performance of the baseline parser is 78.5% in terms of F1 measure of labeled parse constituents on the same CTB training and test sets with Bikel et al. (see [14])

3 Incorporating Semantic Knowledge

In this section, we describe how to incorporate semantic knowledge from external semantic dictionaries into parsing model to improve the performance. Firstly, we extract semantic categories through two Chinese electronic semantic dictionaries and some heuristic rules. Then we build a selection preference sub-model based on extracted semantic categories. In section 3.3, we present our experiments and results in detail. And finally, we compare parses from baseline parser with those from the new parser incorporated with semantic knowledge. We empirically confirm that semantic knowledge is helpful for nominal compound, coordination and POS tagging ambiguity resolution. Additionally, we also find that semantic knowledge can greatly alleviate problems caused by data sparseness.

3.1 Extracting Semantic Categories

Semantic knowledge is not presented in treebanks and therefore has to be extracted from external knowledge sources. We have two Chinese electronic semantic dictionaries, both are good knowledge sources for us to extract semantic categories. One is the HowNet dictionary[3], which covers 67,440 words defined by 2112 different sememes. The other is the "TongYiCi CiLin" expanded version (henceforth CiLin)[4], which represents 77,343 words in a dendrogram.

HowNet (HN): Each sememe defined by the HowNet is regarded as a semantic category. And through the hypernym-hyponym relation between different categories, we can extract semantic categories at various granularity levels. Since words may have different senses, and therefore different definitions in HowNet, we just use the first definition of words in HowNet. At the first level HN1, we extract the first definitions and use them as semantic categories of words. Through the hypernym ladders, we can get HN2, HN3, by replacing categories at lower level with their hypernyms at higher level. Table 1 shows information about words and extracted categories at different levels.

CiLin (CL): CL is a branching diagram, where each node represents a semantic category. There are three levels in total, and from the top down, 12 categories in the first level (CL1), 97 categories in the second level (CL2), 1400 categories in the third level (CL3). We extract semantic categories at level CL1, CL2 and CL3.

HowNet+CiLin: Since the two dictionaries have different ontologies and representations of semantic categories, we establish a strategy to combine them: HowNet is used as a primary dictionary, and CiLin as a secondary dictionary. If a word is not found in HowNet but found in Cilin, we will look up other words from its synset defined by CiLin in HowNet. If HowNet query succeeds, the corresponding semantic category in HowNet will be assigned to this word.

[3] http://www.keenage.com/.

[4] The dictionary is recorded and expanded by Information Retrieval Laboratory, Harbin Institute of Technology.

Table 1. Sizes and coverage of words and semantic categories from different semantic knowledge sources

	Data	HN1	HN2	HN3	CL1	CL2	CL3
words in train	9522		6040			6469	
words in test	1824		1538			1581	
words in both	1412		1293			1310	
classes in train	-	1054	381	118	12	92	1033
classes in test	-	520	251	93	12	79	569
classes in both	-	504	248	93	12	79	552

According to our experimental results, we choose HN2 as the primary semantic category set and combine it with CL1, CL2 and CL3.

Heuristic Rules (HR): Numbers and time expressions are recognized using simple heuristic rules. For a better recognition, one can define accurate regular expressions. However, we just collect suffixes and feature characters to match strings. For example, Chinese numbers are strings whose characters all come from a predefined set. These two classes are merged into HowNet and labelled by semantic categories from HowNet.

In our experiments, we combine HN2, CL1/2/3, and HR as our external sources. In these combinations {HN2+CL1/2/3+HR}, all semantic classes come from the primary semantic category set HN2, therefore we get the same class coverage that we obtain from the single source HN2 but a bigger word coverage. The number of covered words of these combinations in {*train, test, both*} is {7911, 1672, 1372} respectively.

3.2 Building Class-Based Selection Preference Sub-model

There are several ways to incorporate semantic knowledge into parsing model. Bikel (see [15]) suggested a way to capture semantic preferences by employing bilexical-class statistics, in other words, dependencies among head-modifier word classes. Bikel did not carry it out and therefore greater details are not available. However, the key point, we think, is to use classes extracted from semantic dictionary, instead of words, to model semantic dependencies between head and modifier. Accordingly, we build a similar bilexical-class sub-model as follows:

$$Pr_{class}(C_{M_ihw}|C_{Hhw}, Hht, M_iht, dir) \ .$$

where C_{M_ihw} and C_{Hhw} represent semantic categories of words M_ihw and Hhw, respectively. This model is combined with sub-model Pr_{M_w} to form a mixture model P_{mix}:

$$Pr_{mix} = \lambda Pr_{M_w} + (1-\lambda)Pr_{class} \ . \quad (1)$$

λ is hand-optimized, and an improvement of about 0.5% in terms of F1 measure is gained. However, even a very slight change in the value of λ, e.g. 0.001, will have a great effect on the performance. Besides, it seems that the connection between entropy, i.e. the total negative logarithm of the inside probability of trees, and F1 measure, is lost, while this relation is observed in many experiments. Therefore, automatic optimization algorithms, like EM, can not work in this mixture model. The reason, we guess, is that biclass dependencies among head-modifier word classes seem too coarse-grained to capture semantic preferences between head and modifier. In most cases, a head word has a strong semantic constraints on the concept κ of mw, one of its modifier words, but that doesn't mean other words in the same class with the head word has the same semantic preferences on the concept κ. For example, the verb *eat* impose a selection restriction on its object modifier[5]: it has to be solid food. On the other hand, the verb *drink* specifies its object modifier to be liquid beverage. At the level HN2, verb *eat* and *drink* have the same semantic category *metabolize*. However, they impose different selection preferences on their PATIENT roles.

To sum up, bilexical dependencies are too fine-grained when being used to capture semantic preferences and therefore lead to serious data sparseness. Biclass dependencies, which result in an unstable performance improvement, on the other hand, seem to be too coarse-grained for semantic preferences. We build a class-based selection preference model:

$$Pr_{sel}(C_{M_i hw}|Hhw, P) \ .$$

This model is similar to Resnik (see [2]). We use the parent node label P to represent the grammatical relation between head and modifier. Besides, in this model, only modifier word is replaced with its semantic category. The dependencies between head word and modifier word class seem to be just right for capturing these semantic preferences.

The final mixture model is the combination of the class-based selection preference sub-model Pr_{sel} and modifier-head generation sub-model Pr_{M_w}:

$$Pr_{mix} = \lambda Pr_{M_w} + (1-\lambda) Pr_{sel} \ . \qquad (2)$$

Since the connection between entropy and F1 measure is observed again, EM algorithm is used to optimize λ. Just like Levy (see [12]), we set aside articles 1-25 in CTB as held out data for EM algorithm and use articles 26-270 as training data during λ optimization.

3.3 Experimental Results

We have designed several experiments to check the power of our class-based selection preference model with different semantic data sources. In all experiments, we first use the EM algorithm to optimize the parameter λ. As mentioned above, during parameter optimization, articles 1-25 are used as held out data and articles 26-270 are used as training data. Then we test our mixture model with optimized parameter λ using the training data of articles 1-270 and test data of articles 271-300 of length at most 40 words.

[5] According to Thematic Role theory, this modifier has a PATIENT role.

Table 2. Results for incorporating different semantic knowledge sources. The baseline parser is described in Sect. 2. in detail.

	Baseline	HN1	HN2	HN3	CL1	CL2	CL3
F1(%)	78.5	78.6	79.1	78.9	77.5	78.7	78.8

Table 3. Results for combinations of different semantic knowledge sources

	Baseline	HN2+CL1+HR	HN2+CL2+HR	HN2+CL3+HR
F1(%)	78.5	79.2	79.4	79.3

Firstly, we carry out experiments on HowNet and CiLin, separately. Experimental results are presented in Table 2. As can be seen, CiLin has a greater coverage of words than that of HowNet, however, it works worse than HowNet. And at the level CL1, coarse-grained classes even yield degraded results. It's difficult to explain this, but the main reason may be that HowNet has a fine-grained and substantial ontology while CiLin is designed only as a synset container.

Since HowNet has a better semantic representation and CiLin better coverage, we want to combine them. The combination is described in Sect. 3.1, where HN2 is used as the primary semantic category set. Words found by CiLin and heuristic rules are labelled by semantic categories from HN2. Results are shown in Table 3. Although external sources HN2+CL1/2/3+HR have the identical word coverage and yield exactly the same number of classes, the different word-class distributions in them lead to the different results.

Due to the combination of HN2, CL2 and HR, we see that our new parser with external semantic knowledge outperforms the baseline parser by 0.9% in F1 measure. Given we are already at the 78% level of accuracy, an improvement of 0.9% is well worth obtaining and confirms the importance of semantic dependencies on parsing. Further, we do the significance test using Bikel's significance tester[6] which is modified to output p-value for F1. The significance level for F-score is at most $(43376+1)/(1048576+1) = 0.041$. A second 1048576 iteration produces the similar result. Therefore the improvement is statistically significant.

3.4 Performance Improvement Analysis

We manually analyze parsing errors of the baseline parser (BP) as well as performance improvement of the new parser (IP) with semantic knowledge from the combination of HN2, CL2 and HR. Improvement analysis can provide an additional valuable perspective: how semantic knowledge helps to resolve some ambiguities. We compare BP and IP on the test data parse by parse. There are 299 sentences of length at most 40 words among the total 348 test sentences. The two parsers BP and IP found different parses for 102 sentences, among which

[6] See http://www.cis.upenn.edu/ dbikel/software.html

Table 4. Frequency of parsing improvement types. *AR* represents *ambiguity resolution.*

Type	Count	Percent(%)
Nominal Compound *AR*	19	38
Coordination *AR*	9	18
N◇V *AR* in *N◇V+noun*	6	12
Other *AR*	16	32

IP yields better parse trees for 47 sentences according to the gold standard trees. We have concentrated on these 47 sentences and compared parse trees found by *IP* with those found by *BP*. Frequencies of major types of parsing improvement is presented in Table 4. Levy and Manning (see [12])(henceforth L&M) observed the top three parsing error types: NP-NP modification, Coordination and N◇V mistagging, which are also common in our baseline parser. As can be seen, our improved parser can address these types of ambiguities to some extent through semantic knowledge.

Nominal Compounds (NCs) Disambiguation: Nominal compounds are notorious "every way ambiguous" constructions.[7] The different semantic interpretations have different dependency structures. According to L&M, this ambiguity will be addressed by the dependency model when word frequencies are large enough to be reliable. However, even for the treebank central to a certain topic, many very plausible dependencies occur only once.[8] A good technique for resolving this conflict is to generalize the dependencies from word pairs to word-class pairs. Such generalized dependencies, as noted in section 3.2, can capture semantic preferences, as well as alleviate the data sparseness associated with standard bilexical statistics. In our class-based selection preference model, if the frequency of pair $[C_{Mhw}, Hhw]$[9] is large enough, the parser can interpret nominal compounds correctly, that is, it can tell which modify which.

NCs are always parsed as flatter structures by our baseline parser, just like the tree a. in Figure 1. This is partly because of the annotation style of CTB, where there is no NP-internal structure. For these NCs without internal analysis, we re-annotated them as basic NPs with label NPB, as mentioned in section 2. This re-annotation really helps. Another reason is that the baseline parser, or the modifier word generating sub-model P_{M_w}, can not capture hierarchical semantic dependencies of internal structures of NCs due to the sparseness of bilexical dependencies. In our new parser, however, the selection preference model is able to build semantically preferable structures through word-class dependency statistics. For NCs like (n_1, n_2, n_3), where n_i is a noun, dependency structures

[7] "Every way ambiguous" constructions are those for which the number of analyses is the number of binary trees over the terminal elements. Prepositional phrase attachment, coordination, and nominal compounds are all "every way ambiguous" constructions.

[8] Just as Klein et al. (see [8]) said, one million words of training data just isn't enough.

[9] Henceforth, $[s_1, s_2]$ denotes a dependency structure, where s_1 is a modifier word or its semantic class (C), and s_2 is the head word.

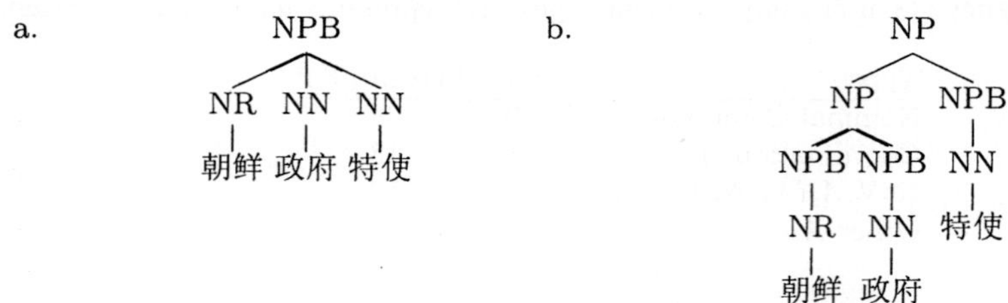

Fig. 1. Nominal Compounds: The North Korean government's special envoy. a. is the incorrect flat parse, b. is the right one in corpus

$\{[C_{n_1}, n_2], [C_{n_1}, n_3], [C_{n_2}, n_3]\}$ will be checked in terms of semantic acceptability and semantically preferable structures will be built finally. For more complicated NCs, similar analysis follows.

In our example (see Fig. 1.), the counts of word dependencies *[朝鲜/North Korea, 政府/government]* and *[朝鲜/North Korea,特使/special envoy]* in the training data both are 0. Therefore, it is impossible for the baseline parser to have a preference between these two dependency structures. On the other hand, the counts of word-class dependencies *[来源值,政府/government]*, where 来源值 is the semantic category of 朝鲜 in HN2, is much larger than the counts of *[来源值,特使/special envoy]* and *[组织,特使/special envoy]*, where 组织 is the semantic category of 政府 in the training data. Therefore, the dependency structure of *[朝鲜/North Korea, 政府/government]* will be built.

Coordination Disambiguation: Coordination is another kind of "every way ambiguous" construction. For coordination structures, the head word is meaningless. But that doesn't matter, since semantic dependency between the spurious head and modifier will be used to measure the meaning similarity of coordinated structures. Therefore, our selection preference model still works in coordination constructions. We have also found VP coordination ambiguity, which is similar to that observed by L&M. The latter VP in coordinated VPs is often parsed as an IP due to *pro*-drop by the baseline parser. That is, the coordinated structure *VP* is parsed as: $VP^0 \rightarrow VP^1 IP^2$. This parse will be penalized by the selection preference model because the hypothesis that the head word of IP^2 has a similar meaning to the head word of VP^1 under the grammatical relation VP^0 is infrequent.

N◇V-ambiguous Tagging Disambiguation: The lack of overt morphological marking for transforming verbal words to nominal words in Chinese results in ambiguity between these two categories. L&M argued that the way to resolve this ambiguity is to look at more external context, like some function words, e.g. adverbial or prenominal modifiers, co-occurring with N◇V-ambiguous words. However, in some cases, N◇V-ambiguous words can be tagged correctly without external context. Chen et al. (see [16]) studied the pattern of *N◇V+noun*, which will be analyzed as a *predicate-object* structure if *N◇V* is a verb and a *modifier-noun* structure if *N◇V* is a noun. They found that in most cases, this pattern can

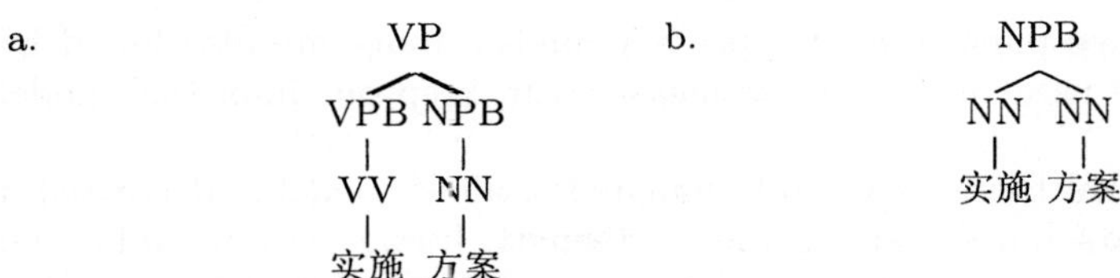

Fig. 2. N◇V-ambiguity: a. implement plans (incorrect parse) versus b. implementation plans (corpus)

Table 5. Previous Results on CTB parsing for sentences of length at most 40 words

	LP	LR	F1
Bikel and Chiang 2000	77.2	76.2	76.7
Levy and Manning 2003	78.4	79.2	78.8
Present work	80.1	78.7	79.4
Bikel Thesis 2004	81.2	78.0	79.6
Chiang and Bikel 2002	81.1	78.8	79.9

be parsed correctly without any external context. Furthermore, they argued that semantic preferences are helpful for the resolution of ambiguity between these two different structures. In our selection preference model, semantic preferences interweave with grammatical relations. These semantic dependencies impose constraints on the structure of the pattern *N◇V+noun* and therefore on the POS tag of *N◇V*. Figure 2 shows our new parser can correct N◇V mistagging errors occurring in the pattern of *N◇V+noun*.

Smoothing: Besides the three ambiguity resolution noted above, semantic knowledge indeed helps alleviate the fundamental sparseness of the lexical dependency information available in the CTB. For many word pairs *[mod,head]*, whose count information is not available in the training data, the dependency statistics of head and modifier can still work through the semantic category of *mod*. During our manual analysis of performance improvement, many other structural ambiguities are addressed due to the smoothing function of semantic knowledge.

4 Related Work on CTB Parsing

Previous work on CTB parsing and their results are shown in table 5. Bikel and Chiang (see [14]) used two different models on CTB, one based on the modified BBN model which is very similar to our baseline model, the other on Tree Insertion Grammar (TIG). While our baseline model used the same unknown word threshold with Bikel and Chiang but smaller beam width, our result outperforms theirs due to other features like distance, basic NP re-annotation used by our baseline model. Levy and Manning (see [12]) used a factored model with rich re-annotations guided by error analysis. In the baseline model, we also used several re-annotations but find most re-annotations they suggested do not fit our model. The three parsing error types expounded above are also found by L&M. However, we used more efficient measures to keep our improved model from these errors.

The work of Bikel thesis (see [10]) emulated Collins' model and created a language package to Chinese parsing. He used subcat frames and an additional POS tagger for unseen words. Chiang and Bikel (see [17]) used the EM algorithm on the same TIG-parser to improve the head percolation table for Chinese parsing. Both these two parsers used fine-tuned features recovered from the treebank that our model does not use. This leads to better results and indicates that there is still room of improvement for our model.

5 Conclusions

We have shown that how semantic knowledge may be incorporated into a generative model for full parsing, which reaches 79.4% in CTB. Experimental results are quite consistent with our intuition. After the manual analysis of performance improvement, the working mechanism of semantic knowledge in the selection preference model is quite clear:

1. Using semantic categories extracted from external dictionaries, the class-based selection preference model first generalizes standard bilexical dependencies, some of which are not available in training data, to word-class dependencies. These dependencies are neither too fine-grained nor too coarse-grained compared with bilexical and biclass dependencies, and really help to alleviate fundamental information sparseness in treebank.
2. Based on the generalized word-class pairs, semantic dependencies are captured and used to address different kinds of ambiguities, like nominal compounds, coordination construction, even N$\diamond$V-ambiguous words tagging.

Our experiments show that generative models have room for improvement by employing semantic knowledge. And that may be also true for discriminative models, since these models can easily incorporate richer features in a well-founded fashion. This is the subject of our future work.

Acknowledgements

This work was supported in part by National High Technology Research and Development Program under grant #2001AA114010 and #2003AA111010. We would like to acknowledge anonymous reviewers who provided helpful suggestions.

References

1. Michael Collins. 1999. Head-Driven Statistical Models for Natural Language Parsing. PhD thesis, University of Pennsylvania.
2. Philip Stuart Resnik. 1993. Selection and Information: A Class-Based Approach to Lexical Relationships. PhD thesis, University of Pennsylvania, Philadelphia, PA, USA.

3. Sanda Harabagiu. 1996. An Application of WordNet to Prepositional Attachement. In *Proceedings of ACL-96*, June 1996, Santa Cruz CA, pages 360-363.
4. Yuval Krymolowski and Dan Roth. 1998. Incorporating Knowledge in Natural Language Learning: A Case Study. In *COLING-ACL'98 Workshop on Usage of WordNet in Natural Language Processing Systems*,Montreal, Canada.
5. Mark McLauchlan. 2004. Thesauruses for Prepositional Phrase Attachment. In *Proceedings of CoNLL-2004*,Boston, MA, USA, 2004, pp. 73-80.
6. Fei Xia. 1999. Automatic Grammar Generation from Two Different Perspectives. PhD thesis, University of Pennsylvania.
7. Dan Klein and Christopher D. Manning. 2002. Fast Exact Natural Language Parsing with a Factored Model. In *Advances in Neural Information Processing Systems 15 (NIPS-2002)*.
8. Dan Klein and Christopher D. Manning. 2003. Accurate Unlexicalized Parsing. In *Proceedings of ACL-03*.
9. Daniel Gildea. 2001. Corpus variation and parser performance. In *Proceedings of EMNLP-01*, Pittsburgh, Pennsylvania.
10. Daniel M. Bikel. 2004a. On the Parameter Space of Generative Lexicalized Statistical Parsing Models. PhD thesis, University of Pennsylvania.
11. Nianwen Xue and Fei Xia. 2000. The Bracketing Guidelines for Chinese Treebank Project. Technical Report IRCS 00-08, University of Pennsylvania.
12. Roger Levy and Christopher Manning. 2003. Is it harder to parse Chinese, or the Chinese Treebank? In *Proceedings of ACL-03*.
13. Deyi Xiong, Qun Liu and Shouxun Lin. 2005. Lexicalized Beam Thresholding Parsing with Prior and Boundary Estimates. In *Proceedings of the 6th Conference on Intelligent Text Processing and Computational Linguistics (CICLing)*, Mexico City, Mexico, 2005.
14. Daniel M. Bikel and David Chiang. 2000. Two statistical parsing models applied to the chinese treebank. In *Proceedings of the Second Chinese Language Processing Workshop*, pages 1-6.
15. Daniel M. Bikel. 2004b. Intricacies of Collins' Parsing Model. to appear in *Computational Linguistics*.
16. Kejian Chen and Weimei Hong. 1996. Resolving Ambiguities of Predicate-object and Modifier-noun Structures for Chinese V-N Patterns. in Chinese. In *Communication of COLIPS*, Vol.6, #2, pages 73-79.
17. David Chiang and Daniel M. Bikel. 2002. Recovering Latent Information in Treebanks. In *proceedings of COLING*,2002.

Using a Partially Annotated Corpus to Build a Dependency Parser for Japanese

Manabu Sassano

Fujitsu Laboratories, Ltd., 4-1-1, Kamikodanaka, Nakahara-ku,
Kawasaki 211-8588, Japan
sassano@jp.fujitsu.com

Abstract. We explore the use of a partially annotated corpus to build a dependency parser for Japanese. We examine two types of partially annotated corpora. It is found that a parser trained with a corpus that does not have any grammatical tags for words can demonstrate an accuracy of 87.38%, which is comparable to the current state-of-the-art accuracy on the Kyoto University Corpus. In contrast, a parser trained with a corpus that has only dependency annotations for each two adjacent *bunsetsus* (chunks) shows moderate performance. Nonetheless, it is notable that features based on character n-grams are found very useful for a dependency parser for Japanese.

1 Introduction

Corpus-based supervised learning is now a standard approach to build a system which shows high performance for a given task in NLP. However, the weakness of such approach is to need an annotated corpus. Corpus annotation is labor intensive and very expensive. To reduce or avoid the cost of annotation, various approaches are proposed, which include unsupervised learning, minimally supervised learning (e.g., [1]), and active learning (e.g., [2,3]).

To discuss clearly the cost of corpus annotation, we here consider a simple model of the cost:

$$\text{annotation cost} \propto \sum_t c(t)n(t)$$

where t is a type of annotation such as POS tagging, chunk tagging, etc., $c(t)$ is a cost per type t annotation, and $n(t)$ is the number of type t annotation.

Previous work to tackle the problem of annotation cost has mainly focused on reducing $n(t)$. For example, in active learning, useful examples to be annotated are selected based on some criteria, and then the number of examples to be annotated is considerably reduced. In contrast, we here focus on reducing $c(t)$ instead of $n(t)$. Obviously, if some portion of annotations are not given, the performance of a NLP system will deteriorate. The question here is how much the performance deteriorates. Is there a good trade-off between saving the cost and losing the performance?

Minimizing portions of annotations is also very important from the point of view of engineering. Suppose that we want to build an annotated corpus to make a parser for some real-world application. The design and strategy of corpus annotation is crucial in order to get a good parser while saving the cost. Furthermore, we have to keep in mind

R. Dale et al. (Eds.): IJCNLP 2005, LNAI 3651, pp. 82–92, 2005.

the maintenance cost of both the corpus and the parser. For example, we may find some errors in the annotations and the design of linguistic categories. In this situation fewer annotations lead to saving the cost because the corpus is more stable and less prone to errors.

The main purpose of this study is to explore the use of a partially annotated corpus to build a dependency parser for Japanese. In this paper, we describe experiments to investigate the feasibility of a partially annotated corpus. In addition, we propose features for parsing which are based on character n-grams. Even if grammatical tags are not given, a parser with these features demonstrates better performance than does the maximum entropy parser [4] with full grammatical features. Similarly, we have conducted experiments on *bunsetsu* (described in Sect. 2.1) chunking trained with a corpus which does not have grammatical tags. After that, we have tested a parser trained with a corpus which is partially annotated for dependency structures.

2 Parsing Japanese

2.1 Syntactic Properties of Japanese

The Japanese language is basically an SOV language. Word order is relatively free. In English the syntactic function of each word is represented with word order, while in Japanese postpositions represent the syntactic function of each word. For example, one or more postpositions following a noun play a similar role to declension of nouns in German, which indicates a grammatical case.

Based on such properties, the concept of *bunsetsus*[1] was devised and has been used to describe the structure of a sentence in Japanese. A *bunsetsu* consists of one or more content words followed by zero or more function words. By defining a bunsetsu like that, we can analyze a sentence in a similar way that is used when analyzing the grammatical role of words in inflecting languages like German.

Thus, strictly speaking, bunsetsu order rather than word order is free except the bunsetsu that contains the main verb of a sentence. Such bunsetsu must be placed at the end of the sentence. For example, the following two sentences have an identical meaning: (1) Ken-ga kanojo-ni hon-wo age-ta. (2) Ken-ga hon-wo kanojo-ni age-ta. (-ga: subject marker, -ni: dative case particle, -wo: accusative case particle. English translation: Ken gave a book to her.) Note that the rightmost bunsetsu 'age-ta,' which is composed of a verb stem and a past tense marker, has to be placed at the end of the sentence.

We here list the constraints of Japanese dependency including ones mentioned above.

C1. Each bunsetsu has only one head except the rightmost one.
C2. Each head bunsetsu is always placed at the right hand side of its modifier.
C3. Dependencies do not cross one another.

These properties are basically shared also with Korean and Mongolian.

[1] The word 'bunsetsu' in Japanese is composed of two Chinese characters, i.e., 'bun' and 'setsu.' 'Bun' means a sentence and 'setsu' means a segment. A 'bunsetsu' is considered to be a small syntactic segment in a sentence. A *eojeol* in Korean [5] is almost the same concept as a bunsetsu. Chunks defined in [6] for English are also very similar to bunsetsus.

2.2 Typical Steps of Parsing Japanese

Because Japanese has the properties above, the following steps are very common in parsing Japanese:

S1. Break a sentence into morphemes (i.e. morphological analysis).
S2. Chunk them into bunsetsus.
S3. Analyze dependencies between these bunsetsus.
S4. Label each dependency with a semantic role such as agent, object, location, etc.

Note that since Japanese does not have explicit word delimiters like white spaces, we first have to tokenize a sentence into morphemes and at the same time give a POS tag to each morpheme (S1). Therefore, when building an annotated corpus of Japanese, we have to decide boundaries of each word (morpheme) and POS tags of all the words.

3 Experimental Setup

3.1 Parsing Algorithm

We employ the Stack Dependency Analysis (SDA) algorithm [7] to analyze the dependency structure of a sentence in Japanese. This algorithm, which takes advantage of C1, C2, and C3 in Sect. 2.1, is very simple and easy to implement. Sassano [7] has proved its efficiency in terms of time complexity and reported the best accuracy on the Kyoto University Corpus [8]. The SDA algorithm as well as Cascaded Chunking Model [9] is a shift-reduce type algorithm.

The pseudo code of SDA is shown in Fig. 1. This algorithm is used with any estimator that decides whether a bunsetsu modifies another bunsetsu. A trainable classifier, such as an SVM, a decision tree, etc., is a typical choice for the estimator.

3.2 Corpus

To facilitate comparison with previous results, we used the Kyoto University Corpus Version 2 [8]. Parsers used in experiments were trained on the articles on January 1st through 8th (7,958 sentences) and tested on the articles on January 9th (1,246 sentences). The articles on January 10th were used for development. The usage of these articles is the same as in [4,10,9,7].

3.3 Choice for Classifiers

We use SVMs [11] for estimating dependencies between two bunsetsus because they have excellent properties. One of them is that combinations of features in an example are automatically considered with polynomial kernels. Excellent performance has been reported for many NLP tasks including Japanese dependency parsing, e.g., [9]. Please see [11] for formal descriptions of SVMs.

3.4 SVM Setting

Polynomial kernels with the degree of 3 are used and the misclassification cost is set to 1.

```
//
// Input: N: the number of bunsetsus in a sentence.
//     w[]: an array that keeps a sequence of bunsetsus in the sentence.
//
// Output: outdep[]: an integer array that stores an analysis result,
//     i.e., dependencies between the bunsetsus. For example, the
//     head of w[j] is outdep[j].
//
// stack: a stack that holds IDs of modifier bunsetsus
//     in the sentence. If it is empty, the pop method
//     returns EMPTY (−1).
//
// function estimate_dependency(j, i, w[]):
//     a function that returns non-zero when the j-th
//     bunsetsu should modify the i-th bunsetsu.
//     Otherwise returns zero.
//
procedure analyze(w[], N, outdep[])
// Push 0 on the stack.
stack.push(0);
// Variable i for a head and j for a modifier.
for (int i = 1; i < N; i++) {
  // Pop a value off the stack.
  int j = stack.pop();
  while (j != EMPTY && (i == N − 1 || estimate_dependency(j, i, w))) {
    // The j-th bunsetsu modifies the i-th bunsetsu.
    outdep[j] = i;
    // Pop a value off the stack to update j.
    j = stack.pop();
  }
  if (j != EMPTY)
    stack.push(j);
  stack.push(i);
}
```

Fig. 1. Pseudo code of the Stack Dependency Analysis algorithm. Note that "i == N − 1" means the i-th bunsetsu is the rightmost one in the sentence. Any classifiers can be used in estimate_dependency().

4 Dropping POS Tags

First we conducted experiments on dropping POS tags. In corpus building for a parser, disambiguating POS tags is one of time consuming tasks. In addition, it takes much time to prepare guidelines for POS tagging. Furthermore, in the case of a Japanese corpus, we will need more time because we have to deal with word boundaries as well as POS tags. Therefore, it would be desirable to avoid or reduce POS annotations while minimizing the loss of performance of the parser.

4.1 Features

To examine the effect of dropping POS tags, we built the following four sets of features and measured parsing performance with these feature sets.

Standard Features. By the "standard features" here we mean the feature set commonly used in [4,10,12,9,7]. We employ the features below for each bunsetsu:

1. Rightmost Content Word - major POS, minor POS, conjugation type, conjugation form, surface form (lexicalized form)
2. Rightmost Function Word - major POS, minor POS, conjugation type, conjugation form, surface form (lexicalized form)
3. Punctuation (periods, and commas)
4. Open parentheses and close parentheses
5. Location - at the beginning of the sentence or at the end of the sentence.

In addition, features as to the gap between two bunsetsus are also used. They include: distance, particles, parentheses, and punctuation.

Words-Only Features. If POS tags are not available, we have to use only tokens (words) as features. In addition, we cannot identify easily content words and function words in a bunsetsu. Therefore, we here chose the simplest form of feature sets. We constructed a bag of words in each bunsetsu and then used them as features. For example, we assume that there are three words in a bunsetsu: *keisan* (computational), *gengogaku* (linguistics), *no* (of). In this case we get $\{keisan, gengogaku, no\}$ as features.

Character N-Gram Features. Next we constructed a feature set without word boundaries or POS tags. In this feature set, we can use only the character string of a bunsetsu. At first glance, such a feature set is silly and it seems that a corpus without POS tags cannot yield a good parser. It is because no explicit syntactic information is given.

Can we extract good features from a string? We found useful ideas in Sato and Kawase's papers [13,14]. They define a similarity score between two sentences in Japanese and use it for ranking translation examples. Their similarity score is based on character subsequence matching. Just raw character strings are used and neither morphological analysis, POS tagging, nor parsing is applied. Although no advanced analysis was applied, they had good results enough for translation-aid. In [13], DP matching based scores are investigated, and in [14], the number of common 2-grams and 3-grams of characters between two sentences is incorporated into a similarity score.

In our experiments we use blended n-grams which are both 1-grams and 2-grams. All the 1-grams and 2-grams from the character string of a bunsetsu are extracted as features. For example, suppose we have a bunsetsu the string of which is a sequence of three characters: *kano-jo-no* where '-' represents a boundary between Japanese characters and this string is actually written with three characters in Japanese. The following features are extracted from the string: *kano*, *jo*, *no*, $-*kano*, *kano-jo*, *jo-no*, *no*-$, where '$' represents a bunsetsu boundary.

Combination of "Standard Features" and Character N-grams. The fourth feature set that we have investigated is a combination of "standard features" and character n-grams, which are described in the previous subsection.

4.2 Results and Discussion

Performance of parsers trained with these feature sets on the development set and the test set is shown in Table 1. For comparison to previous work we use the standard measures for the Kyoto University Corpus: dependency accuracy and sentence accuracy. The dependency accuracy is the percentage of correct dependencies and the sentence accuracy is the percentage of sentences, all the dependencies in which are correctly analyzed.

Table 1. Performance on Development Set and Test Set

	Dev. Set		Test Set	
Feature Set	Dep. Acc.	Sent. Acc.	Dep. Acc.	Sent. Acc.
"Standard"	88.97	46.18	88.72	45.28
Bag of Words (Words Only)	85.22	35.02	84.43	34.95
Character N-Grams	87.79	42.66	87.38	40.84
"Standard" + Character N-Grams	89.72	47.04	89.07	46.89

To our surprise, the parser with the feature set based on character n-grams achieved an accuracy of 87.38%, which is very good. Although this is worse than that of "standard feature set," the performance is still surprising. We considered POS tags were essential for parsing. Why so successful?

The reason would be explained by the writing system of Japanese and its usage. In modern Japanese text mainly five different scripts are used: kanji, hiragana, katakana, Arabic numerals, and Latin letters. Usage of these scripts indicates implicitly the grammatical role of a word. For example, kanji is mainly used to represent nouns or stems of verbs and adjectives. It is never used for particles, which are always written in hiragana. Essential morphological and syntactic categories are also often indicated in hiragana. Conjugation forms of verbs and adjectives are represented with one or two hiragana characters. Syntactic roles of a bunsetsu are often indicated by the rightmost morpheme in it. Most of such morphemes are endings of verbs or adjectives, or particles. In other words, the rightmost characters in a bunsetsu are expected to indicate the syntactic role of a bunsetsu.

Bunsetsu Chunking. After we observed the results of the experiments on parsing, a new question arose to us. Can we chunk tokens to bunsetsus without POS tags, too? We carried out additional experiments on bunsetsu chunking. Following [15], we encode bunsetsu chunking as a tagging problem. In bunsetsu chunking, we use the chunk tag set {`B`, `I`} where `B` marks the first word of some bunsetsu and words marked `I` are inside a bunsetsu. In these experiments on bunsetsu chunking, we estimated the chunk tag of each word using a SVM from five words and their derived attributes. These five words are a word to be estimated and its two preceding/following words. Features are extracted from the followings for each word: word (token) itself, major POS, minor POS, conjugation type, conjugation form, the leftmost character, the character type of the leftmost character, the rightmost character, and the character type of the rightmost character. A character type has a value which indicates a script. It can be either kanji, hiragana, katakana, Arabic numerals, or Latin letters.

We conducted experiments with four sets of features. Performance on the development set and the test set is shown in Table 2. We used the same performance measures as in [16]. Precision (p) is defined as the percentage of words correctly marked B among all the words that the system marked B. Recall (r) is defined as the percentage of words correctly marked B among all the words that are marked B in the training set. F-measure is defined as: F-measure $= 2pq/(p+q)$.

Table 2. Bunsetsu Chunking Performance on Development Set and Test Set. Grammatical tags include POS tags and conjugation types/forms.

Feature Set	Dev. Set (F)	Test Set (F)
Surface Form + Grammatical Tags	99.58	99.57
Surface Form Only	97.65	97.02
Surface Form + Char. Features (No Grammatical Tags)	99.09	99.07
Mixed	99.64	99.64

The bunsetsu chunker with surface forms only yielded worse performance than did that with the grammatical tags including major/minor POS and conjugation type/form. However, the chunker with character features achieved good performance even if grammatical tags are not available. In addition, the feature set in which all the available features are used gives the best among the feature sets we tested. Again we found that features based on characters compensate performance deterioration caused by no grammatical tags.

We have found that both a practical parser and a practical bunsetsu chunker can be constructed from a corpus which does not have POS information. This means we can make a parser for Japanese which is less dependent on a morphological analyzer. It would be useful for improving the modularity of an analysis system for Japanese.

5 Dropping Longer Dependency Annotations

As previous work [4,17] reports, approximately 65% of bunsetsus modify the one on their immediate right hand side. From this observation, we simplify dependency annotations. For each bunsetsu we give either the D tag or O where bunsetsus marked D modify the one on their immediate right hand side and bunsetsus marked O do not.

	Ken-ga	*kanojo-ni*	*ano*	*hon-wo*	*age-ta.*
	Ken-subj	to her	that	book-acc	gave.
ID	0	1	2	3	4
Head	4	4	3	4	-
{D, O}	O	O	D	D	-

Fig. 2. Sample sentence with dependency annotations. Bunsetsus marked D modify the one on their immediate right hand side and bunsetsus marked O do not. An English translation is "Ken gave that book to her."

Figure 2 shows a sample sentence with dependency annotations. This encoding scheme represents some portion of the dependency structure of a sentence. Annotating under this scheme is easier than selecting the head of each bunsetsu. We examined usefulness of this type of partially annotated corpus following the encoding scheme above.

5.1 Using Partial Dependency Annotations

The SDA algorithm, which we employ for experiments, can work with a partially annotated corpus to parse a sentence in Japanese[2]. In training, first we construct a training set only from dependency annotations between two adjacent bunsetsus. We ignore relations between two bunsetsus which have a longer dependency. After that, we train a classifier for parsing from the training set. In testing, we use the classifier for both two adjacent bunsetsus and other pairs of bunsetsus.

5.2 Results and Discussion

Performance on the development set and the test set are shown in Table 3.

The parser trained with the partially annotated corpus yielded good performance. However, its accuracy is considerably worse than that of the parser with the fully annotated corpus. This tendency is clearer in terms of sentence accuracy. To examine differences in terms of quantity, we plot the learning curves with the two corpora. The curves are shown in Fig. 3.

Table 3. Performance of parsers trained with the fully annotated corpus and the partially annotated corpus

	# of Training	Dev. Set		Test Set	
Training Set	Examples	Dep. Acc.	Sent. Acc.	Dep. Acc.	Sent. Acc.
Full	98,689	88.97	46.18	88.72	45.28
Adjacent Annotations Only	61,899	85.65	38.00	85.50	38.58

How many sentences which are partially annotated do we need in order to achieve a given accuracy with some number of fully annotated sentences? It is found that we need 8 – 17 times the number of sentences when using the partially annotated corpus instead of the fully annotated one. If hiring linguistic experts for annotation is much more expensive than hiring non experts, or it is difficult to find a large enough number of experts, this type of partially annotated corpus could be useful.

The naive approach we examined was not so effective in the light of the number of sentences to be required. However, we should note that a partially annotated corpus is easier to maintain the consistency of annotations.

6 Related Work

In this section we briefly review related work from three points of view, i.e., parsing performance, the use of partially annotated corpora, and the use of character n-grams.

[2] Cascaded Chunking Model [9] also can be applicable to use a partially annotated corpus.

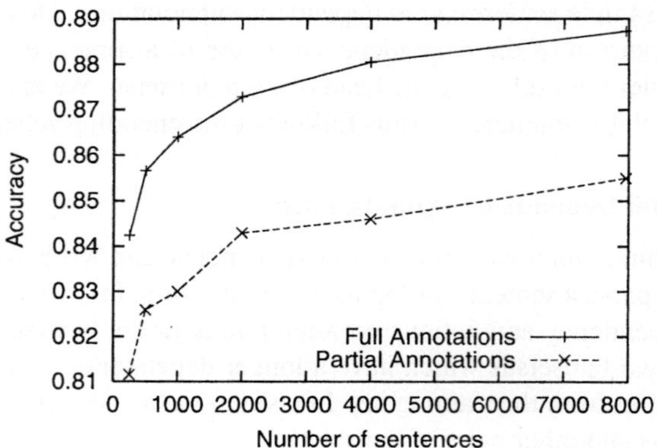

Fig. 3. Learning curves of parsers trained with the partially annotated corpus and the fully annotated corpus

Parsing Performance. Although improvement of the performance of a parser is not a primary concern in this paper, comparison with other results will indicate to us how practical the parser is. Table 4 summarizes comparison to related work on parsing accuracy. Our parsers demonstrated good performance although they did not outperform the best. It is notable that the parser which does not use any explicit grammatical tags outperforms one by [4], which employs a maximum entropy model with full grammatical features given by a morphological analyzer.

Table 4. Comparison to related work on parsing accuracy. KM02 = Kudo and Matsumoto 2002 [9], KM00 = Kudo and Matsumoto 2000 [12], USI99 = Uchimoto et al. 1999 [4], Seki00 = Sekine 2000 [18], and Sass04 = Sassano 2004 [7].

	Algorithm/Model/Features	Acc.(%)
This paper	Stack Dependency Analysis (cubic SVM) w/ char. n-grams	89.07
	Stack Dependency Analysis (cubic SVM) w/ char. n-grams, no POS	87.38
Sass04	Stack Dependency Analysis (cubic SVM) w/ various enriched features	89.56
KM02	Cascaded Chunking (cubic SVM) w/ dynamic features	89.29
KM00	Backward Beam Search (cubic SVM)	89.09
USI99	Backward Beam Search (MaxEnt)	87.14
Seki00	Deterministic Finite State Transducer	77.97

Use of Partially Annotated Corpora. Several papers address the use of partially annotated corpora. Pereira and Schabes [19] proposed an algorithm of inferring a stochastic context-free grammar from a partially bracketed corpus. Riezler et al. [20] presented a method of discriminative estimation of an exponential model on LFG parses from partially labeled data.

Our study differs in that we focus more on avoiding expensive types of annotations while minimizing the loss of performance of a parser.

Use of Character N-grams. Character n-grams are often used for POS tagging of unknown words, unsupervised POS tagging, and measures of string similarity. The number of common n-grams between two sentences is used for a similarity measure in [14]. This usage is essentially the same as in the spectrum kernel [21], which is one of string kernels [22].

7 Conclusion

We have explored the use of a partially annotated corpus for building a dependency parser for Japanese. We have examined two types of partially annotated corpora. It is found that a parser trained with a corpus that does not have any grammatical tags for words can demonstrate an accuracy of 87.38%, which is comparable to the current state-of-the-art accuracy. In contrast, a parser trained with a corpus that has only dependency annotations for each two adjacent bunsetsus shows moderate performance. Nonetheless, it is notable that features based on character n-grams are found very useful for a dependency parser for Japanese.

References

1. Yarowsky, D.: Unsupervised word sense disambiguation rivaling supervised methods. In: Proc. of ACL-1995. (1995) 189–196
2. Thompson, C.A., Califf, M.L., Mooney, R.J.: Active learning for natural language parsing and information extraction. In: Proc. of the Sixteenth International Conference on Machine Learning. (1999) 406–414
3. Tang, M., Luo, X., Roukos, S.: Active learning for statistical natural language parsing. In: Proc. of ACL-2002. (2002) 120–127
4. Uchimoto, K., Sekine, S., Isahara, H.: Japanese dependency structure analysis based on maximum entropy models. In: Proc. of EACL-99. (1999) 196–203
5. Yoon, J., Choi, K., Song, M.: Three types of chunking in Korean and dependency analysis based on lexical association. In: Proc. of the 18th Int. Conf. on Computer Processing of Oriental Languages. (1999) 59–65
6. Abney, S.P.: Parsing by chunks. In Berwick, R.C., Abney, S.P., Tenny, C., eds.: Principle-Based Parsing: Computation and Psycholinguistics. Kluwer Academic Publishers (1991) 257–278
7. Sassano, M.: Linear-time dependency analysis for Japanese. In: Proc. of COLING 2004. (2004) 8–14
8. Kurohashi, S., Nagao, M.: Building a Japanese parsed corpus while improving the parsing system. In: Proc. of the 1st LREC. (1998) 719–724
9. Kudo, T., Matsumoto, Y: Japanese dependency analysis using cascaded chunking. In: Proc. of CoNLL-2002. (2002) 63–69
10. Sekine, S., Uchimoto, K., Isahara, H.: Backward beam search algorithm for dependency analysis of Japanese. In Proc. of COLING-00. (2000) 754–760
11. Vapnik, V.N.: The Nature of Statistical Learning Theory. Springer-Verlag (1995)
12. Kudo, T., Matsumoto, Y.: Japanese dependency structure analysis based on support vector machines. In: Proc. of EMNLP/VLC 2000. (2000) 18–25
13. Sato, S.: CTM: An example-based translation aid system. In: Proc. of COLING-92. (1992) 1259–1263

14. Sato, S., Kawase, T.: A high-speed best match retrieval method for Japanese text. Technical Report IS-RR-94-9I, Japan Advanced Institute of Science and Technology, Hokuriku (1994)
15. Ramshaw, L.A., Marcus, M.P.: Text chunking using transformation-based learning. In: Proc. of VLC 1995. (1995) 82–94
16. Murata, M., Uchimoto, K., Ma, Q., Isahara, H.: Bunsetsu identification using category-exclusive rules. In: Proc. of COLING-00. (2000) 565–571
17. Maruyama, H., Ogino, S.: A statistical property of Japanese phrase-to-phrase modifications. Mathematical Linguistics **18** (1992) 348–352
18. Sekine, S.: Japanese dependency analysis using a deterministic finite state transducer. In: Proc. of COLING-00. (2000) 761–767
19. Pereira, F., Schabes, Y.: Inside-outside reestimation from partially bracketed corpora. In: Proc. of ACL-92. (1992) 128–135
20. Riezler, S., King, T.H., Kaplan, R.M., Crouch, R., III, J.T.M., Johnson, M.: Parsing the Wall Street Journal using a lexical-functional grammar and discriminative estimation techniques. In: Proc. of ACL-2002. (2002) 271–278
21. Leslie, C., Eskin, E., Noble, W.S.: The spectrum kernel: A string kernel for SVM protein classification. In: Proc. of the 7th Pacific Symposium on Biocomputing. (2002) 564–575
22. Lodhi, H., Saunders, C., Shawe-Tayor, J., Cristianini, N., Watkins, C.: Text classification using string kernels. Journal of Machine Learning Research **2** (2002) 419–444

Entropy as an Indicator of Context Boundaries —An Experiment Using a Web Search Engine—

Kumiko Tanaka-Ishii

Graduate School of Information Science and Technology,
University of Tokyo
kumiko@i.u-tokyo.ac.jp

Abstract. Previous works have suggested that the uncertainty of tokens coming after a sequence helps determine whether a given position is at a context boundary. This feature of language has been applied to unsupervised text segmentation and term extraction. In this paper, we fundamentally verify this feature. An experiment was performed using a web search engine, in order to clarify the extent to which this assumption holds. The verification was applied to Chinese and Japanese.

1 Introduction

The theme of this paper is the following assumption:

The uncertainty of tokens coming after a sequence helps determine whether a given position is at a context boundary. (A)

Intuitively, the variety of successive tokens at each character inside a word monotonically decreases according to the offset length, because the longer the preceding character n-gram, the longer the preceding context and the more it restricts the appearance of possible next tokens. On the other hand, the uncertainty at the position of a word border becomes greater and the complexity increases, as the position is out of context. This suggests that a word border can be detected by focusing on the differentials of the uncertainty of branching. This assumption is illustrated in Figure 1. In this paper, we measure this uncertainty of successive tokens by utilizing the entropy of branching (which we mathematically define in the next section).

This assumption dates back to the fundamental work done by Harris [6] in 1955, where he says that when the number of different tokens coming after every prefix of a word marks the maximum value, then the location corresponds to the morpheme boundary. Recently, with the increasing availability of corpora, this characteristic of language data has been applied for unsupervised text segmentation into words and morphemes. Kempe [8] reports an experiment to detect word borders in German and English texts by monitoring the entropy of successive characters for 4-grams. Many works in unsupervised segmentation utilise the fact that the branching stays low inside words but increases at a word or morpheme border. Some works apply this fact in terms of frequency [10] [2], while others utilise more sophisticated statistical measures: Sun et al. [12] use mutual information; Creutz [4] use MDL to decompose Finnish texts into morphemes.

R. Dale et al. (Eds.): IJCNLP 2005, LNAI 3651, pp. 93–105, 2005.

This assumption seems to hold not only at the character level but also at the word level. For example, the uncertainty of words coming after the word sequence, "The United States of", is small (because the word America is very likely to occur), whereas the uncertainty is greater for the sequence "computational linguistics", suggesting that there is a context boundary just after this term. This observation at the word level has been applied to term extraction by utilising the number of different words coming after a word sequence as an indicator of collocation boundaries [5] [9].

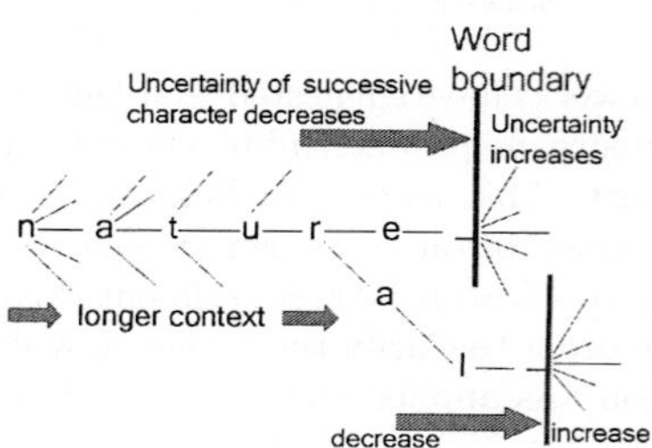

Fig. 1. Intuitive illustration of a variety of successive tokens and a word boundary

As can be seen in these previous works, the above assumption (A) seems to govern language structure both microscopically at the morpheme level and macroscopically at the phrase level. Assumption (A) is interesting not only from an engineering viewpoint but also from a language and cognitive science viewpoint. For example, some recent studies report that the statistical, innate structure of language plays an important role in children's language acquisition [11]. Therefore, it is important to understand the innate structure of language, in order to shed light on how people actually acquire it.

Consequently, this paper verifies assumption (A) in a fundamental manner. We address the questions of why and to what extent (A) holds. Unlike recent, previous works based on limited numbers of corpora, we use a web search engine to obtain statistics, in order to avoid the sparseness problem as much as possible. Our discussion focuses on correlating the entropy of branching and word boundaries, because the definition of a word boundary is clearer than that of a morpheme or phrase unit. In terms of detecting word boundaries, our experiments were performed in character sequence, so we chose two languages in which segmentation is a crucial problem: Chinese which contains only ideograms, and Japanese, which contains both ideograms and phonograms. Before describing the experiments, we discuss assumption (A) in more detail.

2 The Assumption

Given a set of elements χ and a set of n-gram sequences χ_n formed of χ, the conditional entropy of an element occurring after an n-gram sequence X_n is defined as

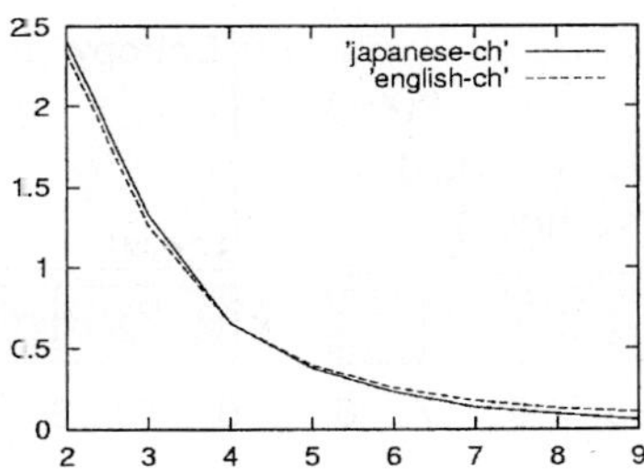

Fig. 2. Decrease in $H(X|X_n)$ for characters when n is increased

$$H(X|X_n) = -\sum_{x_n \in \chi_n} P(X_n = x_n) \sum_{x \in \chi} P(X = x|X_n = x_n) \log P(X = x|X_n = x_n)$$

where $P(X = x)$ indicates the probability of occurrence of x.

A well-known observation on language data states that $H(X|X_n)$ decreases as n increases [3]. For example, Figure 2 shows the entropy values as n increases from 1 to 9 for a character sequence. The two lines correspond to Japanese and English data, from corpora consisting of the Mainichi newspaper (30 MB) and the WSJ (30 MB), respectively. This phenomenon indicates that X will become easier to estimate as the context of X_n gets longer. This can be intuitively understood: it is easy to guess that "e" will follow after "Hello! How ar", but it is difficult to guess what comes after the short string "He".

The last term $-\log P(X = x|X_n = x_n)$ in formula above indicates the information of a token of x coming after x_n, and thus the branching after x_n. The latter half of the formula, the local entropy value for a given x_n

$$H(X|X_n = x_n) = -\sum_{x \in \chi} P(X = x|X_n = x_n) \log P(X = x|X_n = x_n), \quad (1)$$

indicates the average information of branching for a *specific* n-gram sequence x_n. As our interest in this paper is this local entropy, we denote simply $H(X|X_n = x_n)$ as $h(x_n)$ in the rest of this paper.

The decrease in $H(X|X_n)$ globally indicates that given an n-length sequence x_n and another $(n+1)$-length sequence y_{n+1}, the following inequality holds *on average*:

$$h(x_n) > h(y_{n+1}). \quad (2)$$

One reason why inequality (2) holds for language data is that there is *context* in language, and y_{n+1} carries a *longer context* as compared with x_n. Therefore, if we suppose that x_n is the prefix of x_{n+1}, then it is very likely that

$$h(x_n) > h(x_{n+1}) \quad (3)$$

holds, because the longer the preceding n-gram, the longer the *same* context. For example, it is easier to guess what comes after x_6="natura" than what comes after x_5 = "natur". Therefore, the decrease in $H(X|X_n)$ can be expressed as the

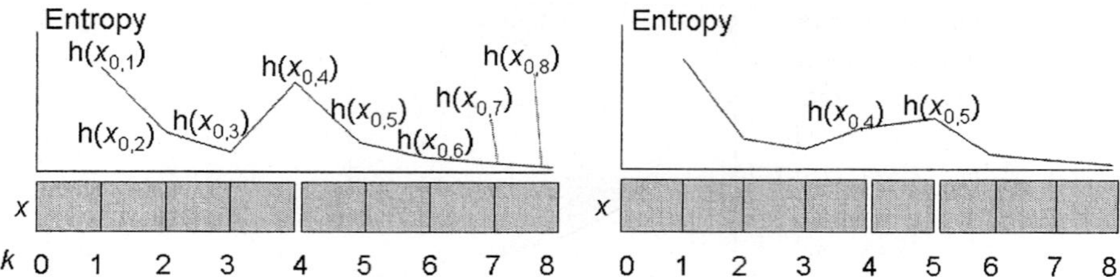

Fig. 3. Our model for boundary detection based on the entropy of branching

concept that if the context is longer, the uncertainty of the branching decreases on average. Then, taking the logical contraposition, if the uncertainty does not decrease, the context is not longer, which can be interpreted as the following:

> If the complexity of successive tokens increases, the location is at the context border. (B)

For example, in the case of x_7 = "natural", the entropy h("natural") should be larger than h("natura"), because it is uncertain what character will allow x_7 to succeed. In the next section, we utilise assumption (B) to detect the context boundary.

3 Boundary Detection Using the Entropy of Branching

Assumption (B) gives a hint on how to utilise the branching entropy as an indicator of the context boundary. When two semantic units, both longer than 1, are put together, the entropy would appear as in the first figure of Figure 3. The first semantic unit is from offsets 0 to 4, and the second is from 4 to 8, with each unit formed by elements of χ. In the figure, one possible transition of branching degree is shown, where the plot at k on the horizontal axis denotes the entropy for $h(x_{0,k})$ and $x_{n,m}$ denotes the substring between offsets n and m.

Ideally, the entropy would take a maximum at 4, because it will decrease as k is increased in the ranges of $k < 4$ and $4 < k < 8$, and at $k = 4$, it will rise. Therefore, the position at $k = 4$ is detected as the "local maximum value" when monitoring $h(x_{0,k})$ over k. The boundary condition after such observation can be redefined as the following:

B$_{max}$ Boundaries are locations where the entropy is locally maximised.

A similar method is proposed by Harris [6], where morpheme borders can be detected by using the local maximum of the number of different tokens coming after a prefix.

This only holds, however, for semantic units longer than 1. Units often have a length of 1: at the character level, in Japanese and Chinese, there are many one-character words, and at the word level, there are many single words that do not form collocations. If a unit has length 1, then the situation will look like the second graph in Figure 3, where three semantic units, $x_{0,4}$, $x_{4,5}$ $x_{5,8}$, are present, with the middle unit having length 1. First, at $k = 4$, the value of h increases.

At $k = 5$, the value may increase or decrease, because the longer context results in an uncertainty decrease, *though an uncertainty decrease does not necessarily mean a longer context.* When h increases at $k = 5$, the situation would look like the second graph. In this case, the condition B_{max}will not suffice, and we need a second boundary condition:
$\mathrm{B}_{increase}$ Boundaries are locations where the entropy is increased.
On the other hand, when h decreases at $k = 5$, then even $\mathrm{B}_{increase}$cannot be applied to detect $k = 5$ as a boundary. We have other chances to detect $k = 5$, however, by considering $h(x_{i,k})$ where $0 < i < k$. According to inequality (2), then, a similar trend should be present for plots of $h(x_{i,k})$, assuming $h(x_{0,n}) > h(x_{0,n+1})$; then, we have

$$h(x_{i,n}) > h(x_{i,n+1}), \quad \text{for} \quad 0 < i < n. \tag{4}$$

The value $h(x_{i,k})$ would hopefully rise for some i if the boundary at $k = 5$ is important, although $h(x_{i,k})$ can increase or decrease at $k = 5$, just as in the case for $h(x_{0,n})$.

Therefore, when the target language consists of many one element units, $\mathrm{B}_{increase}$is crucial for collecting all boundaries. Note that boundaries detected by $\mathrm{B}_{max}$are included in those detected by the condition $\mathrm{B}_{increase}$.

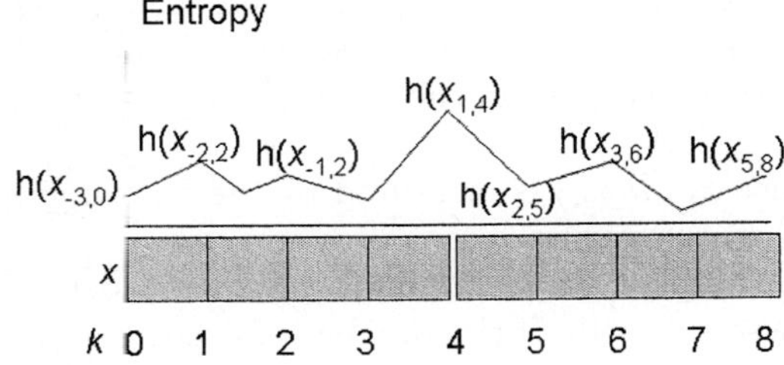

Fig. 4. Kempe's model for boundary detection

Kempe's detection model is based solely on the assumption that the uncertainty of branching takes a local maximum at a context boundary. Without any grounding on this assumption, Kempe [8] simply calculates the entropy of branching for a fixed length of 4-grams. Therefore, the length of n is set to 3, $h(x_{i-3,i})$ is calculated for all i, and the maximum values are claimed to indicate the word boundary. This model is illustrated in Figure 4, where the plot at each k indicates the value of $h(x_{k-3,k})$. Note that at $k = 4$, the h value will be highest. It is not possible, however, to judge whether $h(x_{i-3,i})$ is larger than $h(x_{i-2,i+1})$ in general: Kempe's experiments show that the h value simply oscillates at a low value in such cases.

In contrast, our model is based on the monotonic decrease in $H(X|X_n)$. It explains the increase in h at the context boundary by considering the entropy decrease with a longer context.

Summarising what we have examined, in order to verify assumption (A), which is replaced by assumption (B), the following questions must be answered experimentally:

Q1 Does the condition described by inequality (3) hold?
Q2 Does the condition described by inequality (4) hold?
Q3 To what extent are boundaries extracted by B_{max}or $B_{increase}$?

In the rest of this paper, we demonstrate our experimental verification of these questions.

So far, we have considered only regular order processing: the branching degree is calculated for *successive* elements of x_n. We can also consider the reverse order, which involves calculating h for the *previous* element of x_n. In the case of the previous element, the question is whether the head of x_n forms the *beginning* of a context boundary. We use the subscripts *suc* and *prev* to indicate the regular and reverse orders, respectively. Thus, the regular order is denoted as $h_{suc}(x_n)$, while the reverse order is denoted by $h_{prev}(x_n)$.

In the next section, we explain how we measure the statistics of x_n, before proceeding to analyze our results.

4 Measuring Statistics by Using the Web

In the experiments described in this paper, the frequency counts were obtained using a search engine. This was done because the web represents the largest possible database, enabling us to avoid the data sparseness problem to the greatest extent possible.

Given a sequence x_n, $h(x_n)$ is measured by the following procedure.

1. x_n is sent to a search engine.
2. One thousand snippets, at maximum, are downloaded and x_n is searched for through these snippets. If the number of occurrences is smaller than N, then the system reports that x_n is unmeasurable.
3. The elements occurring before and after x_n are counted, and $h_{suc}(x_n)$ and $h_{prev}(x_n)$ are calculated.

N is a parameter in the experiments described in the following section, and a higher N will give higher precision and lower recall. Another aspect of the experiment is that the data sparseness problem quickly becomes significant for longer strings. To address these issues, we chose N=30.

The value of h is influenced by the indexing strategy used by a given search engine. Defining $f(x)$ as the frequency count for string x as reported by the search engine,

$$f(x_n) > f(x_{n+1}) \tag{5}$$

should usually hold if x_n is a prefix of x_{n+1}, because all occurrences of x_n contain occurrences of x_{n+1}. In practice, this does not hold for many search engines, namely, those in which x_{n+1} is indexed separately from x_n and an occurrence of x_{n+1} is not included in one of x_n. For example, the frequency count of "mode" does not include that of "model", because it is indexed separately. In particular,

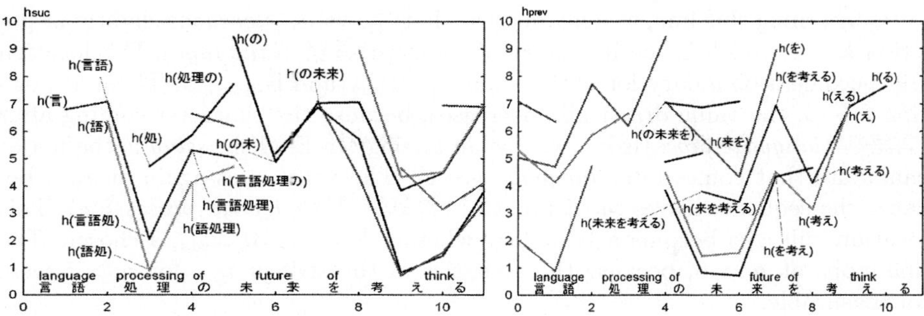

Fig. 5. Entropy changes for a Japanese character sequence (left:regular; right:reverse)

search engines use this indexing strategy at the string level for languages in which words are separated by spaces, and in our case, we need a search engine in which the count of x_n includes that of x_{n+1}. Although we are interested in the distribution of tokens coming after the string x_n and not directly in the frequency, a larger value of $f(x_n)$ can lead to a larger branching entropy.

Among the many available search engines, we decided to use AltaVista, because its indexing strategy seems to follow inequality (5) better than do the strategies of other search engines. AltaVista used to utilise string-based indexing, especially for non-segmented languages. Indexing strategies are currently trade secrets, however, so companies rarely make them available to the public. We could only guess at AltaVistafs strategy by experimenting with some concrete examples based on inequality (5).

5 Analysis for Small Examples

We will first examine the validity of the previous discussion by analysing some small examples. Here, we utilise Japanese examples, because this language contains both phonograms and ideograms, and it can thus demonstrate the features of our method for both cases.

The two graphs in Figure 5 show the actual transition of h for a Japanese sentence formed of 11 characters: $x_{0,11}$ =" 言語処理の未来を考える"(*We think of the future of* (*natural*) *language processing* (*studies*)). The vertical axis represents the entropy value, and the horizontal axis indicates the offset of the string. In the left graph, each line starting at an offset of $m+1$ indicates the entropy values of $h_{suc}(x_{m,m+n})$ for $n > 0$, with plotted points appearing at $k = m + n$. For example, the leftmost solid line starting at offset $k = 1$ plots the h values of $x_{0,n}$ for $n > 0$, with m=0 (refer to the labels on some plots):

$x_{0,1}$ = 言
$x_{0,2}$ = 言語
...
$x_{0,5}$ = 言語処理の,

with each value of h for the above sequence $x_{0,n}$ appearing at the location of n.

Concerning this line, we may observe that the value *increases* slightly at position $k = 2$, which is the boundary of the word"言語"(*language*). This location will become a boundary for both conditions, $B_{max}$and $B_{increase}$. Then, at position $k = 3$, the value drastically decreases, because the character coming after "言語処"(*language proce*) is limited (as an analogy in English, *ssing* is the major candidate that comes after *language proce*). The value rises again at $x_{0,4}$, because the sequence leaves the context of "言語処理" (*language processing*). This location will also become a boundary whether B_{max}or $B_{increase}$is chosen. The line stops at $n = 5$, because the statistics of the strings $x_{0,n}$ for $n > 5$ were unmeasurable.

The second leftmost line starting from $k = 2$ shows the transition of the entropy values of $h_{suc}(x_{1,1+n})$ for $n > 0$; that is, for the strings starting from the second character "語", and so forth. We can observe a trend similar to that of the first line, except that the value also increases at 5, suggesting that $k = 5$ is the boundary, given the condition $B_{increase}$.

The left graph thus contains 10 lines. Most of the lines are locally maximized or become unmeasurable at the offset of $k = 5$, which is the end of a large portion of the sentence. Also, some lines increase at $k = 2$, 4, 7, and 8, indicating the ends of words, which is correct. Some lines increase at low values at 10: this is due to the verb "考える" (*think*), whose conjugation stem is detected as a border.

Similarly, the right-hand graph shows the results for the reverse order, where each line ending at $m - 1$ indicates the plots of the value of $h_{prev}(x_{m-n,m})$ for $n > 0$, with the plotted points appearing at position $k = m - n$. For example, the rightmost line plots h for strings ending with "る" (from $m = 11$ and $n = 10$ down to 5):

$x_{10,11}$ = る
$x_{9,11}$ = える
...
$x_{6,11}$ = 来を考える
$x_{5,11}$ = 未来を考える,

where $x_{4,11}$ became unmeasurable. The lines should be analysed from back to front, where the increase or maximum indicates the *beginning* of a word. Overall, the lines ending at 4 or 5 were unmeasurable, and the values rise or take a maximum at $k = 2$, 4 or 7.

Note that the results obtained from the processing in each direction differ. The forward pass detects 2,4,5,7,8, whereas the backward pass detects 2,4,7. The forward pass tends to detect the *end* of a context, while the backward pass typically detects the *beginning* of a context. Also, it must be noted that this analysis not only shows the segmenting position but also the structure of the sentence. For example, a rupture of the lines and a large increase in h are seen at $k = 5$, indicating the large semantic segmentation position of the sentence. In the right-hand graph, too, we can see two large local maxima at 4 and 7. These segment the sentence into three different semantic parts.

```
1. 开放|的|中国|符合|美国|的|利益
2. 伟大|的|无产阶级|革命家
3. 全国|人民|的|大力|支援
4. 一个|家庭|如果|不|团结

   -----------

5. 医学|教育|国際協力|研究|センター
   Center for international cooperative medical education
6. 人工物|工学|研究|センター
   Center for studies on artifact engineering
7. バチ|こいて|最悪
   He lied, so I feel really bad (colloquial)
8. マキコ|の|今カレ|って|パー件売る|とか
   I heard that Makiko's current boyfriend is going to
   sell party tickets
   (colloquial in Japanese high school female students)
9. 売れ残り|リスク|が|大きい|海外|市場|より
   ...rather than overseas' market, where the leftover
   risk is higher
10. 携帯|先進国|の|はず|が|ドコモ|の|独自|方式|の|せい|で
   We have been a country with advanced cell phone.
   However, NTT has adopted its own method, so...
11. 漢文|電子|大藏經 系列
   one sort of Chinese Buddhist script in electronic form
12. 本師|釋迦牟尼|佛 佛牙|舍利
   teeth bones of a sort a Buddha
```

Fig. 6. Other segmentation examples

On these two graphs, questions Q1 through Q3 from §3 can be addressed as follows. First, as for Q1, the condition indicated by inequality (3) holds in most cases where all lines decrease at $k = 3, 6, 9$, which correspond to inside words. There is one counter-example, however, caused by conjugation. In Japanese conjugation, a verb has a prefix as the stem, and the suffix varies. Therefore, with our method, the endpoint of the stem will be regarded as the boundary. As conjugation is common in languages based on phonograms, we may guess that this phenomenon will decrease the performance of boundary detection.

As for Q2, we can say that the condition indicated by inequality (4) holds, as the upward and downward trends at the same offset k look similar. Here too, there is a counter-example, in the case of a one element word, as indicated in §3. There are two one-word words $x_{4,5}$= "の" and $x_{7,8}$= "を", where the gradients of the lines differ according to the context length. In the case of one of these words, h can rise or fall between two successive boundaries indicating a beginning and end. Still, we can see that this is complemented by examining lines starting from other offsets. For example, at $k = 5$, some lines end with an increase.

As for Q3, if we pick boundary condition B_{max}, by regarding any unmeasurable case as $h = -\infty$, and any maximum of any line as denoting the boundary, then the entry string will be segmented into the following:

言語 (*language*)|処理 (*processing*)|の (*of*)|未来 (*future*)|を (*of*)|考える (*think*).

This segmentation result is equivalent to that obtained by many other Japanese segmentation tools. Taking $B_{increase}$as the boundary condition, another boundary is detected in the middle of the last verb "考え | る (*think*, segmented at the stem of the verb)". If we consider detecting the word boundary, then this segmentation is incorrect; therefore, to increase the precision, it would be better to apply a threshold to filter out cases like this. If we consider the morpheme level, however, then this detection is not irrelevant.

These results show that the entropy of branching works as a measure of context boundaries, not only indicating word boundaries, but also showing the sentence structure of multiple layers, at the morpheme, word, and phrase levels.

Some other successful segmentation examples in Chinese and Japanese are shown in Figure 6. These cases were segmented by using B_{max}. Examples 1 through 4 are from Chinese, and 5 through 12 are from Japanese, where '|' indicates the border. As this method requires only a search engine, it can segment texts that are normally difficult to process by using language tools, such as institution names (5, 6), colloquial expressions (7 to 10), and even some expressions taken from Buddhist scripture (11, 12).

6 Performance on a Larger Scale

6.1 Settings

In this section, we show the results of larger-scale segmentation experiments on Chinese and Japanese. The reason for the choice of languages lies in the fact that the process utilised here is based on the key assumption regarding the semantic aspects of language data. As an ideogram already forms a semantic unit as itself, we intended to observe the performance of the procedure with respect to both ideograms and phonograms. As Chinese contains ideograms only, while Japanese contains both ideograms and phonograms, we chose these two languages.

Because we need correct boundaries with which to compare our results, we utilised manually segmented corpora: the People's Daily corpus from Beijing University [7] for Chinese, and the Kyoto University Corpus [1] for Japanese.

In the previous section, we calculated h for almost all substrings of a given string. This requires $O(n^2)$ searches of strings, with n being the length of the given string. Additionally, the process requires a heavy access load to the web search engine. As our interest is in verifying assumption (B), we conducted our experiment using the following algorithm for a given string x.

1. Set $m = 0$, n=1.
2. Calculate h for $x_{m,n}$
3. If the entropy is unmeasurable, set $m = m + 1$,$n = m + 2$, and go to step 2.
4. Compare the result with that for $x_{m,n-1}$.
5. If the value of h fulfils the boundary conditions, then output n as the boundary. Set $m = m + 1$, $n = m + 2$, and go to 2.
6. Otherwise, set $n = n + 1$ and go to 2.

The point of the algorithm is to ensure that the string length is not increased once the boundary is found, or if the entropy becomes unmeasurable. This algorithm becomes $O(n^2)$ in the worst case where no boundary is found and all substrings are measurable, although this is very unlikely to be the case. Note that this

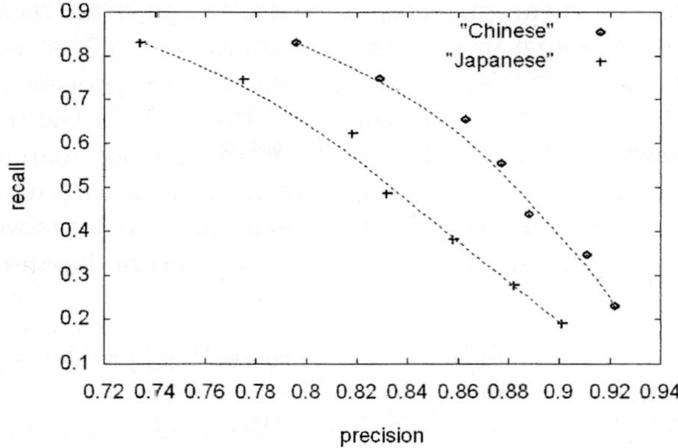

Fig. 7. Precision and recall of word segmentation using the branching entropy in Chinese and Japanese

algorithm defines the regular order case, but we also conducted experiments in reverse order, too.

As for the boundary condition, we utilized $B_{increase}$, as it includes B_{max}. A threshold *val* could be set to the margin of difference:

$$h(x_{n+1}) - h(x_n) > val. \tag{6}$$

The larger *val* is, the higher the precision, and the lower the recall. We varied *val* in the experiment in order to obtain the precision and recall curve.

As the process is slow and heavy, the experiment could not be run through millions of words. Therefore, we took out portions of the corpora used for each language, which consisted of around 2000 words (Chinese 2039, Japanese 2254). These corpora were first segmented into phrases at commas, and each phrase was fed into the procedure described above. The suggested boundaries were then compared with the original, correct boundaries.

6.2 Results

The results are shown in Figure 7. The horizontal axis and vertical axes represent the precision and recall, respectively. The figure contains two lines, corresponding to the results for Japanese or Chinese. Each line is plotted by varying *val* from 0.0 to 3.0 with a margin of 0.5, where the leftmost points of the lines are the results obtained for val=0.0.

The precision was more than 90% for Chinese with $val > 2.5$. In the case of Japanese, the precision deteriorated by about 10%. Even without a threshold ($val = 0.0$), however, the method maintained good precision in both languages.

The locations indicated incorrectly were inside phonogram sequences consisting of long foreign terms, and in inflections in the endings of verbs and adjectives. In fact, among the incorrect points, many could be detected as correct segmentations. For example, in Chinese, surnames were separated from first names by our procedure, whereas in the original corpus, complete names are regarded as single words. As another example in Chinese, the character "家" is used to indicate "-ist" in English, as in "革命家" (revolutionist) and our process suggested that there is a border in between "革命" and "家". However, in the original corpus, these words are not segmented before "家" but are instead treated as one word.

Unlike the precision, the recall ranged significantly according to the threshold. When *val* was high, the recall became small, and the texts were segmented into larger phrasal portions. Some successful examples in Japanese for *val*=3.0 are shown in the following.

- 地方分権など | 大きな | 課題がある (There are | big | problems | such as power decentralizaion.)
- 今は解散の時期ではない | と考えている (We think that | it is not the time for breakup).

The segments show the global structure of the phrases, and thus, this result demonstrates the potential validity of assumption (B). In fact, such sentence segmentation into phrases would be better performed in a word-based manner, rather than a character-based manner, because our character-based experiment mixes the word-level and character-level aspects at the same time. Some previous works on collocation extraction have tried boundary detection using branching [5]. Boundary detection by branching outputs tightly coupled words that can be quite different from traditional grammatical phrases. Verification of such aspects remains as part of our future work.

Overall, in these experiments, we could obtain a glimpse of language structure based on assumption (B) where semantic units of different levels (morpheme, word, phrase) overlaid one another, as if to form a fractal of the context. The entropy of branching is interesting in that it has the potential to detect all boundaries of different layers within the same framework.

7 Conclusion

We conducted a fundamental analysis to verify that the uncertainty of tokens coming after a sequence can serve to determine whether a position is at a context boundary. By inferring this feature of language from the well-known fact that the entropy of successive tokens decreases when a longer context is taken, we examined how boundaries could be detected by monitoring the entropy of successive tokens. Then, we conducted two experiments, a small one in Japanese, and a larger-scale experiment in both Chinese and Japanese, to actually segment words by using only the entropy value. Statistical measures were obtained using a web search engine in order to overcome data sparseness.

Through analysis of Japanese examples, we found that the method worked better for sequences of ideograms, rather than for phonograms. Also, we observed that semantic layers of different levels (morpheme, word, phrase) could potentially be detected by monitoring the entropy of branching. In our larger-scale experiment, points of increasing entropy correlated well with word borders especially in the case of Chinese. These results reveal an interesting aspect of the statistical structure of language.

References

1. Kyoto University Text Corpus Version 3.0, 2003. http://www.kc.t.u-tokyo.ac.jp/nl-resource/corpus.html.
2. R.K. Ando and L. Lee. Mostly-unsupervised statistical segmentation of japanese: Applications to kanji. In *ANLP-NAACL*, 2000.
3. T.C. Bell, J.G. Cleary, and I. H. Witten. *Text Compression.* Prentice Hall, 1990.
4. M. Creutz and Lagus K. Unsupervised discovery of morphemes. In *Workshop of the ACL Special Interest Group in Computational Phonology*, pages 21–30, 2002.
5. T.K. Frantzi and S. Ananiadou. Extracting nested collocations. *16th COLING*, pages 41–46, 1996.
6. S.Z. Harris. From phoneme to morpheme. *Language*, pages 190–222, 1955.
7. ICL. People daily corpus, beijing university, 1999. Institute of Computational Linguistics, Beijing University http://162.105.203.93/Introduction/ corpustagging.htm.
8. A. Kempe. Experiments in unsupervised entropy-based corpus segmentation. In *Workshop of EACL in Computational Natural Language Learning*, pages 7–13, 1999.
9. H. Nakagawa and T. Mori. A simple but powerful automatic termextraction method. In *Computerm2: 2nd International Workshop on Computational Terminology*, pages 29–35, 2002.
10. S. Nobesawa, J. Tsutsumi, D.S. Jang, T. Sano, K. Sato, and M Nakanishi. Segmenting sentences into linky strings using d-bigram statistics. In *COLING*, pages 586–591, 1998.
11. J.R. Saffran. Words in a sea of sounds: The output of statistical learning. *Cognition*, 81:149–169, 2001.
12. M. Sun, Dayang S., and B. K. Tsou. Chinese word segmentation without using lexicon and hand-crafted training data. In *COLING-ACL*, 1998.

Automatic Discovery of Attribute Words from Web Documents

Kosuke Tokunaga, Jun'ichi Kazama, and Kentaro Torisawa

Japan Advanced Institute of Science and Technology (JAIST),
Asahidai 1-1, Nomi, Ishikawa, 923-1292 Japan
{kosuke-t, kazama, torisawa}@jaist.ac.jp

Abstract. We propose a method of acquiring attribute words for a wide range of objects from Japanese Web documents. The method is a simple unsupervised method that utilizes the statistics of words, lexico-syntactic patterns, and HTML tags. To evaluate the attribute words, we also establish criteria and a procedure based on question-answerability about the candidate word.

1 Introduction

Knowledge about how we recognize objects is of great practical importance for many NLP tasks. Knowledge about *attributes*, which tells us from what viewpoints objects are usually understood or described, is one of such type of knowledge. For example, the attributes of *car* objects will be *weight*, *engine*, *steering wheel*, *driving feel*, and *manufacturer*. In other words, attributes are items whose values we want to know when we want to know about the object. More analytically, we tend to regard A as an attribute for objects of class C when A works as if function $v = A(o), o \in C$ where v is necessary to us to identify o (especially to distinguish o from $o'(\neq o) \in C$). Therefore, obvious applications of attributes are ones such as summarization [1,2] and question-answering [3]. Moreover, they can be useful as features in word clustering [4] or machine learning. Although the knowledge base for attributes can be prepared manually (e.g., WordNet [5]), problems are cost and coverage. To overcome these, we propose a method that automatically acquires attribute knowledge from the Web.

To acquire the attributes for a given class, C (e.g., *car*), the proposed method first downloads documents that contain class label C (e.g., "car") from the Web.[1] We extract the candidates of attribute words from these documents and score them according to the statistics of words, lexico-syntactic patterns, and HTML tags. Highly scored words are output as attributes for the class. Lexico-syntactic patterns and other statistics have been used in other lexical knowledge acquisition systems [3,4,6,7,8]. We specifically used lexico-syntactic patterns involving the Japanese postposition "no" as used in [8] such as "C no A" where A is an attribute word, which is almost equivalent to pattern "A of C" used in [7] to

[1] We use C to denote both the class and its class label (the word representing the class). We also use A to denote both the attribute and the word representing it.

R. Dale et al. (Eds.): IJCNLP 2005, LNAI 3651, pp. 106–118, 2005.

find part-whole relations. Novel features of our method are its use of Web search engines to focus on documents highly relevant to the class and its use of statistics concerning attribute words and surrounding HTML tags.

One of the difficulties in studying attribute knowledge is that there are no standard definitions of attributes, or criteria for evaluating obtained attributes. In this paper, we propose a simple but effective definition of attributes that matches our motivation and applications, i.e., whether we can ask a question about the attribute and whether there is an answer to that question (*question answerability*). For example, one can ask as "Who is the manufacturer of this car?", and someone might answer "Honda", because we want to know the *manufacturer* when we concerned about cars. We designed a procedure for evaluating attributes based on this idea. As the literature points out [9,10], attributes can include many types of relations such as property (e.g., *weight*), part-of (e.g., *engine*), telic (e.g., *driving feel*), and agentive (e.g., *manufacturer*). However, we ignored type distinctions in this study. First, because attributes are useful even if the type is not known, and second, because defining attributes as one of these types and evaluating them only complicates the evaluation process, making the results unstable. The use of linguistic tests to define attributes is not that new. Woods [11] devised a test on whether we can say "The A of o is v." Although we followed this procedure, we focused more on attributes that are important for our understanding of an object by using *question-answerability* as our criterion.

2 Acquisition Method

2.1 Basic Observations on Attributes

Our method is based on the following three observations.

1. Attributes tend to occur in documents that contain the class label and not in other documents.
2. Attributes tend to be emphasized by the use of certain HTML tags or occur as items in HTML itemizations or tables in Web documents.
3. Attributes tend to co-occur with the class label in specific lexico-syntactic patterns involving the postposition "no."

2.2 Extraction of Candidate Words

To acquire the attributes of class C, we first download documents that contain class label C using a Web search engine, according to the first observation. We refer to this set of documents as a *local document set* ($LD(C)$). All the nouns appearing in the local document set are regarded as candidates of attribute words. Here, the nouns are words tagged as "proper nouns", "sahen nouns" (nouns that can become a verb with the suffix "suru"), "location", or "unknown" (e.g., words written in katakana) by a Japanese morphological analyzer, JUMAN [12]. Note that we restricted ourselves to single word attributes in this study. The obtained candidate words are scored in the next step.

Table 1. Lexico-syntactic patterns for attribute acquisition. (We added possible English translations for the patterns in parenthesis).

C no A ha (A of C [*verb*])	C no A de (by A of C)	C no A e (to A of C)
C no A ga (A of C [*verb*])	C no A made (even/until A of C)	C no A、(A of C,)
C no A wo ([*verb*] A of C)	C no A kara (from A of C)	
C no A ni (at/in A of C)	C no A yori (from/than A of C)	

2.3 Ranking of Candidate Words

We rank the candidate words according to a score that reflects the observations described in Sect. 2.1. The overall score takes the following form.

$$V(C, A) = n(C, A) \cdot f(C, A) \cdot t(C, A) \cdot dfidf(C, A), \quad (1)$$

where A is the candidate word to be scored and C is the class. $n(C, A)$ and $f(C, A)$ are scores concerning lexico-syntactic patterns. $t(C, A)$ is a score concerning the statistics of HTML tags to reflect the second observation. Finally, $dfidf(C, A)$ is the score related to word statistics. This reflects the first observation. By multiplying these sub-scores, we expect that they will complement each other. We will explain the details on these sub-scores in the following.

As previously mentioned, we use lexico-syntactic patterns including the Japanese postposition "no" as clues. The patterns take the form "C no A $POST$" where $POST$ is a Japanese postposition or a punctuation mark.[2] The actual patterns used are listed in Table 1. Score $n(C, A)$ is the number of times C and A co-occur in these patterns in the local document set $LD(C)$.

Score $f(C, A)$ requires more explanation. Roughly, $f(C, A)$ is the number of times C and A co-occur in the patterns without the last postposition (i.e., pattern "C no A") collected from 33 years of parsed newspaper articles.[3] Note that pattern matching was done against the parsed dependency structures.[4] The reason this score was used in addition to $n(C, A)$ was to obtain more reliable scores by increasing the number of documents to be matched. This may sound contradictory to the fact that the Web is the largest corpus in the world. However, we found that we could not obtain all the documents that contained the class label because existing commercial Web search engines return URLs for a very small fraction of matched documents (usually up to about 1,000 documents). Although we could use hit counts for the patterns, we did not do this to avoid overloading the search engine (each class has about 20,000 candidate words).

Score $t(C, A)$ is the number of times A appears in $LD(C)$ surrounded by HTML tags. More precisely, we count the number of times A appears in the form: "<*tag1*>*A*<*tag2*>" where the number of characters between HTML tags

[2] Note that there are actually no spaces between words in Japanese. The spaces are for easier understanding.

[3] Yomiuri newspaper 1987–2001, Mainichi newspaper 1991–1999, and Nikkei newspaper 1983–1990; 3.01 GB in total. We used a Japanese dependency parser [13].

[4] The differences from $n(C, A)$ were introduced to reuse the existing parsed corpus.

```
<B>タイ風・カレー</B><BR>材料<BR>鶏肉 400g, なす 2 個, バイマックルー 2 枚, ナン
プラー大さじ 1.5<BR>赤唐辛子 1.5 本, 砂糖小さじ 1, ココナッツミルク, バジル<P>スパ
イス<BR>コリアンダー, クミン<P>作り方<BR><OL><LI>材料をペースト状にして, カレー
```

Fig. 1. Example HTML document

(i.e., the length of A) is 20 at maximum. The tags (<*tag1*> and <*tag2*>) can be either a start tag (e.g., <A>) or an end tag (e.g., </A>). This score is intended to give high values for words that are emphasized or occur in itemizations or tables. For example, in the HTML document in Fig. 1, the words "タイ風・カレー (Thai-curry)", "材料 (ingredient)", "スパイス (spice)", "コリアンダー, クミン (coriander, cumin)", and "作り方 (recipe)" are counted.

Finally, $dfidf(C, A)$, which reflects the first observation, is calculated as:

$$dfidf(C, A) = df(A, LD(C)) \cdot idf(A), \quad idf(A) = \log \frac{|G|}{df(A,G)}.$$

$df(A, X)$ denotes the number of documents where A appears in documents X. G is a large set of randomly collected Web documents, which we call the *global document set*. We derived this score from a similar score, which was used in [14] to measure the association between a hypernym and hyponyms.

3 Evaluation Criteria

This section presents the evaluation criteria based on *question-answerability* (QA tests). Based on the criteria, we designed an evaluation procedure where the evaluators were asked to answer either by yes or no to four tests at maximum, i.e., a hyponymy test (Sect. 3.4), a QA test (Sect. 3.1) and a suffix augmented QA test (Sect. 3.2) followed by a generality test (Sect. 3.3).

3.1 Question-Answerability Test

By definitions we used, attributes are what we want to know about the object. Therefore, if A is an attribute of objects of class C, we can arrange questions (consisting of A and C) that require the values for A as the answer. Then someone should be able to answer the questions. For example, we can ask "Who is the director of this movie?" because *director* is an attribute of *movie*. The answer might be someone such as "Stanley Kubrick." We designed the QA test shown in Fig. 2 to assess the correctness of attribute A for class C based on this criterion. Several points should be noted. First, since the value for the attribute is actually defined for the object instance (i.e., $v = A(o), o \in C$), we should qualify class label C using "kono (this)" to refer to an object instance of class C.

Second, since we cannot know what question is possible for A beforehand, we generate all the question types listed in Fig. 2 and ask whether any of them are acceptable.

Are any of the following questions grammatically correct, natural, and answerable?
1. この C の A は何? (kono C no A ha nani?/What is the A of this C?)
2. この C の A は誰? (kono C no A ha dare?/Who is the A of this C?)
3. この C の A はいつ? (kono C no A ha itu?/When is the A of this C?)
4. この C の A はどこ? (kono C no A ha doko?/Where is the A of this C?)
5. この C の A はどれ? (kono C no A ha dore?/Which is the A of this C?)
6. この C の A はいくつ? (kono C no A ha ikutu?/How many is the A of this C?)
7. この C の A はどう? (kono C no A ha dou?/How much is the A of this C?)

Fig. 2. Question-answerability Test

Third, the question should be *natural* as well as grammatically correct. Naturalness was explained to the evaluators as positively determining whether the question can be their first choice in usual conversations. In our point of view, attributes should be important items for people in describing objects. We assumed that attributes that conformed to the naturalness criterion would be such important attributes. For example, *stapler* is not an attribute of *company* in our sense, although almost all companies own *staplers*. Our naturalness criterion can reflect this observation since the question "What is the stapler of this company?" is unnatural as a first question when talking about a company, and therefore we can successfully conclude that *stapler* is not an attribute. Note that Woods' linguistic test [11] (i.e., whether "the attribute of an object is a value" can be stated or not) cannot reject *stapler* since it does not have the naturalness requirement (e.g., we can say "the stapler of [used by] SONY is Stapler-X").[5] In addition, note that such importances can be assessed more easily in the QA test, since questioners basically ask what they think is important at least at the time of utterance. However, we cannot expect such an implication even though the declarative sentence is acceptable.

Finally, the answer to the question does not necessarily need to be written in language. For example, values for attributes such as *map*, *picture*, and *blueprint* cannot be written as language expressions but can be represented by other media. Such attributes are not rare since we obtain attributes from the Web.

3.2 Suffix Augmented QA Test

Some attributes that are obtained can fail the QA test even if they are correct, especially when the surface form is different from the one they actually mean. This often occurs since Japanese is very elliptic and our method is restricted to single word attributes. For example, the word seito (students) can be used to represent the attribute seito suu (number of students) as in the sentence below.

kono	gakko	no	seito	ha	500	nin
this	school	of	students	is	500	NUM

(The number of students of this school is 500.)

[5] *Stapler* might be an important attribute of companies for stationery sellers. However, we focus on attributes that are important for *most people* in *most situations*.

– 数 (number of) 方法 (method for) 名 (name of) 者 (-er)
– 時間 ([amount of] time of) 時刻 (time of) 時期 (period of) 場所 (location of)
– 金額 (amount of money for) 程度 (degree of) 具合 (state of)
– の〜さ (nominalized adjectives e.g., "height of" "prettiness of")

Fig. 3. Allowed augmentation

These attributes whose parts are elided (e.g., seito representing seito suu) are also useful since they are actually used in sentences as in the above example. Therefore, they should be assessed as correct attributes in some way. Although the most appropriate question for seito representing seito suu is (6) in Fig. 2, it is unfortunately ungrammatical since ikutu cannot be used for the number of persons. Therefore, seito representing seito suu will fail the QA test.[6]

In Japanese, most of the elided parts can be restored by adding appropriate suffixes (as "suu" (number of) in the previous example) or by adding "no" + nominalized adjectives. Thus, when the attribute word failed the first QA test, we asked the evaluators to re-do the QA test by choosing an appropriate suffix or a nominalized adjective from the list of allowed augmentations and adding it to the end of the evaluated word. Figure 3 lists the allowed augmentations.[7,8]

3.3 Generality Test

Although our primal aim was to acquire the attributes for a given class, i.e., , to find attributes that are common to all the instances of the class, we found, in preliminary experiments, that some uncommon (but interesting) attributes were assessed as correct according to the QA test depending on the evaluator. An example is *subtitle* for the class *movie*. Strictly speaking, *subtitle* is not an attribute of all movies, since all movies do not necessarily have subtitles. For example, only foreign films have subtitles in Japan. However, we think this attribute is also useful in practice for people who have a keen interest in foreign films. Thus, the evaluators were asked whether the attribute was common for most instances of the class when the attribute was judged to be correct in the QA test. We call attributes that passed this generality test *general attributes*, and those that failed but passed the QA test *relaxed attributes* (note that general attributes is a subset of relaxed attributes). We compare the accuracies for the relaxed and general attributes in the experiments.

[6] Seito (representing *students*) might pass the QA test with question type (2) in Fig. 2. However, this is not always the case since some evaluators will judge the question to be unnatural.

[7] Postposition "no (of)" before the suffix is also allowed to be added if it makes the question more natural.

[8] The problem here might not occur if we used many more question types in the first QA test. However, we did not do this to keep the first QA test simple. With the same motivation, we kept the list of allowed suffixes short (only general and important suffixes). The uncovered cases were treated by adding nominalized adjectives.

3.4 Hyponymy Test

Finally, we should note that we designed the evaluation procedure so that the evaluators could be asked whether candidate A is a hyponym of C before the QA tests. If A is a hyponym of C, we can skip all subsequent tests since A cannot be an attribute of C. We added this test because the output of the system often contains hyponyms and these tend to cause confusion in the QA tests since expression "C no A" is natural even when A is a hyponym of C (e.g., "anime no Dragon Ball (Dragon Ball [of/the] anime)").

4 Experiments

4.1 Experimental Setting

We first selected 32 word classes from 1,589 classes acquired from the Web with an automatic hypernym-hyponym acquisition method [14]. Here, we regarded the hypernym as the class label. Since our purpose was just to evaluate our method for classes from the Web, we selected classes that were obtained successfully. We randomly chose the 22 classes listed in Table 2 for human evaluation from these 32 classes.[9] The hyponyms were used to help the evaluators to disambiguate the meaning of class labels (if ambiguity existed).

To collect $LD(C)$, we used the Web search engine goo (http://www.goo.ne.jp). The size of $LD(C)$ was 857 documents (URLs) on class average. There were about $20,000$ candidate words on class average. As global document set G required for the calculation of $dfidf(C, A)$, we used 1.0×10^6 randomly downloaded Web documents.

Table 2. Classes used in evaluation

都市 (city), 博物館 (museum), 祝日 (national holiday), 警察 (police), 施設 (facility), 大学 (university), 新聞 (newspaper), ごみ (garbage), 神社 (shrine), 鳥 (bird), 病院 (hospital), 植物 (plant), 川 (river), 小学校 (elementary school), 曲 (music tune), 図書館 (library), 支店 (branch office), サイト (web site), 町 (town), センサー (sensor), 研修 (training), 自動車 (car)

We output the top 50 attributes for each class ranked with our proposed method and with alternative methods that were used for comparison. We gathered outputs for all the methods, removing duplication (i.e., taking the set union) to achieve efficient evaluation, and re-sorted them randomly to ensure that the assessment was unbiased. Four human evaluators assessed these gathered attributes class-by-class in four days using a GUI tool implementing the evaluation procedure described in Sect. 3. There were a total of $3,678$ evaluated attributes. Using the evaluation results, we re-constructed the evaluations for the top 50 for each method. The kappa value [15], which indicates inter-evaluator agreement, was 0.533 for the general attribute case and 0.593 for the relaxed attribute case. According to [15], these kappa values indicate "moderate" agreement.

[9] This selection was due to time/cost limitations.

4.2 Accuracy of Proposed Method

Figure 4 has accuracy graphs for the proposed method for relaxed attributes. The graph on the left shows per-evaluator precision when the top n (represented by x axis) attributes were output. The precision is the average over all classes. Although we cannot calculate the actual recall, the x axis corresponds to approximate recall. We can see that ranking with the proposed method has a positive correlation with human evaluation, although the assessments varied greatly depending on the evaluator. The graph on the right shows curves for average (with standard deviation), 3-consensus, and 4-consensus precision. 3-consensus (4-consensus) is precision where the attribute is considered correct by at least three (four) evaluators. Figure 5 has graphs for the general attribute case the same as for the relaxed case. Although there is a positive correlation between ranking with the proposed method and human evaluators, the precision was, not surprisingly, lower than that for the relaxed case. In addition, the lower kappa value (0.533 compared to 0.593 for the relaxed case) indicated that the generality test was harder than the QA tests.

The accuracy of the proposed method was encouraging. Although we cannot easily determine which indicator is appropriate, if we use the majority rule (3-

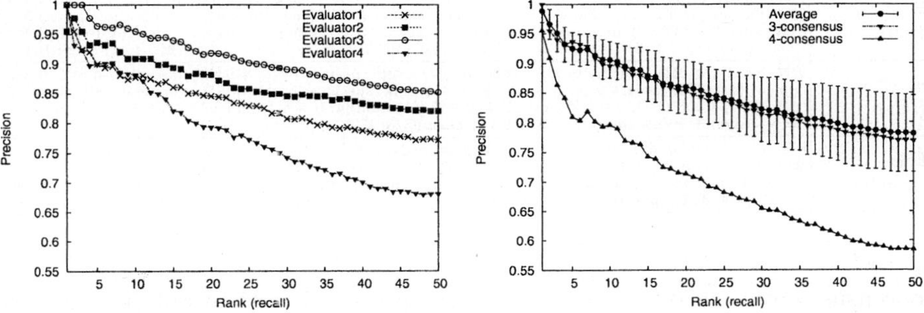

Fig. 4. Accuracy of relaxed attributes

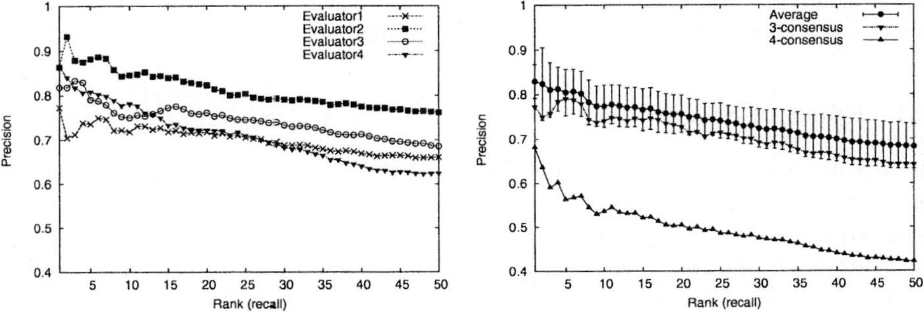

Fig. 5. Accuracy of general attributes

Table 3. Top 20 attributes of several classes obtained by proposed method

Classes	Attributes
鳥 (bird)	写真 (picture)[4/4] 名前 (name)[4/2] 種類 (sort)[4/4] イラスト (illustration)[3/3] 特徴 (characteristics)[4/4] 病気 (disease)[4/2] 生活 (life)[4/4] 話題 (topic)[3/2] 関係 (relation)[0/0] イメージ (image)[4/4] 巣 (nest)[4/4] 鳴き声 (song)[4/4] 姿 (shape)[4/4] 情報 (info.)[4/4] 世界 (world)[0/0] 声 (song)[4/4] 動物 (animal)[0/0] ページ (page)[3/2] 生態 (ecology)[4/4] 羽 (wing)[4/4]
病院 (hospital)	ホームページ (home page)[4/1] 施設 (facility)[3/3] 情報 (info.)[4/4] 紹介 (intro.)[4/4] 窓口 (info. desk)[4/4] 認定 (authorization)[3/3] 名称 (name)[4/2] 医師 (doctor)[4/4] 精神科 (psychiatry)[4/2] 評判 (reputation)[4/4] 対応 (handling)[4/4] 電話 (phone)[2/2] 診療 (medical care)[4/4] 治療 (treatment)[4/4] 医療 (medical service)[3/3] 機能 (function)[3/3] 院長 (director)[4/4] 評価 (valuation)[4/4] 診察 (medical examination)[4/4] ページ (page)[2/2] 管理 (admin.)[4/3] 一部 (part)[1/1]
植物 (plant)	名前 (name)[4/2] 種類 (species)[4/4] 写真 (picture)[4/4] 種子 (seed)[4/4] 栽培 (cultivation)[4/3] 観察 (observation)[4/3] 特徴 (characteristics)[4/4] 説明 (explanation)[4/4] 画像 (image)[4/4] 調査 (surveillance)[4/3] データ (data)[4/4] 進化 (evolution)[3/3] 解説 (description)[4/4] リスト (list)[2/2] 葉 (leaf)[4/3] 保存 (preservation)[2/2] デザイン (design)[1/1] 生育 (growth)[4/4]
川 (river)	水位 (water level)[4/4] 上流 (upstream)[4/4] 名前 (name)[4/2] 環境 (environment)[4/4] 水質 (water quality)[4/4] 歴史 (history)[4/4] 源流 (head stream)[4/4] 写真 (picture)[4/4] 水 (water)[4/4] 水面 (surface)[4/4] 場所 (location)[4/4] 流れ (current)[4/4] 水辺 (waterside)[4/4] 水源 (river head)[4/4] 四季 (four seasons)[3/3] 特徴 (characteristics)[4/4] 中 (inside)[1/1] ほとり (streamside)[4/4] 自然 (nature)[4/4] せせらぎ (babbling)[4/4]
小学校 (elementary school)	活動 (activity)[4/4] 取り組み (efforts)[4/3] 運動会 (athletic meeting)[4/4] 子ども (child)[4/4] ホームページ (home page)[4/0] 校長 (head teacher)[4/4] 教室 (classroom)[4/4] 校歌 (school song)[4/4] 児童 (student)[4/4] 校舎 (school building)[4/4] 行事 (event)[4/4] 学習 (learning)[3/3] 給食 (feeding service)[4/3] ページ (page)[2/2] 体育館 (gym)[4/4] 学級 (class)[3/3] メール (mail)[0/0] 学年 (grade)[1/1] 始業式 (opening ceremony)[4/4] 音楽 (music)[2/2]
曲 (music tune)	歌詞 (lyrics)[4/1] タイトル (title)[4/2] 演奏 (performance)[4/4] リスト (list)[0/0] イメージ (image)[4/4] 作詞 (lyrics writing)[4/1] 楽譜 (musical score)[4/4] 名前 (name)[4/2] 内容 (content)[3/3] ジャンル (genre)[4/4] 情報 (info.)[4/4] ポイント (point)[4/4] 世界 (world)[1/1] メロディー (melody)[4/4] 最後 (end)[3/2] 題名 (title)[4/2] 中 (inside)[0/0] 作曲 (composition)[4/4] テーマ (theme)[4/4] データ (data)[4/2]
図書館 (library)	資料 (source material)[4/4] ホームページ (home page)[4/2] ページ (page)[3/1] 歴史 (history)[4/4] 設置 (establishment)[4/4] システム (system)[4/4] 蔵書 (book stock)[4/4] コピー (copy)[2/2] 本 (book)[4/4] 場所 (location)[4/4] 利用 (use)[4/4] サービス (service)[4/4] データベース (database)[4/3] 図書 (book)[4/4] 新聞 (newspaper)[4/4] 休館 (close)[4/4] 目録 (catalog)[3/3] 展示 (display)[4/2] 施設 (facility)[2/2] 情報 (info.)[4/4]
町 (town)	人口 (population)[4/4] 歴史 (history)[4/4] ホームページ (home page)[4/0] 観光 (sightseeing)[4/4] 情報 (info.)[3/3] 財政 (finance)[4/4] 施設 (facility)[4/4] 文化財 (heritage)[4/2] 環境 (environment)[4/4] 温泉 (hot spring)[3/1] 話題 (topic)[3/2] 四季 (four seasons)[3/3] イベント (event)[4/3] 図書館 (library)[4/3] 文化 (culture)[4/4] 風景 (landscape)[4/4] シンボル (symbol)[4/3] 産業 (industry)[4/3] 農業 (agriculture)[4/2] 議会 (town council)[3/3]
センサー (sensor)	情報 (info.)[4/4] 感度 (sensitivity)[4/3] 種類 (sort)[4/3] 位置 (position)[4/4] 取り付け (install)[4/4] 開発 (development)[4/4] 精度 (accuracy)[4/4] サイズ (size)[4/4] 仕様 (specification)[4/4] 温度 (temperature)[2/1] データ (data)[4/4] セット (set)[4/4] 設置 (install)[4/4] 機能 (function)[4/4] 技術 (technology)[4/4] 特長 (feature)[4/4] ページ (page)[3/3] 高さ (height)[3/2] 採用 (adoption)[3/3] 応用 (application)[4/4]
研修 (training)	内容 (content)[4/4] 目的 (purpose)[4/4] 実施 (practice)[4/4] テーマ (theme)[4/3] プログラム (program)[4/4] 講師 (lecturer)[4/4] 予定 (plan)[4/4] 名称 (name)[4/2] メニュー (menu)[4/4] 報告 (report)[4/4] 対象 (target)[4/4] 成果 (outcome)[4/4] 充実 (satisfaction)[2/2] 場 (place/atmosphere)[3/3] あり方 (state of existence)[2/2] 詳細 (detail)[4/4] 機会 (opportunity)[1/1] 定員 (capacity)[4/4] 受講 (participation)[4/4] ほか (other)[0/0]

consensus in our case) employed in [7], the proposed method obtained relaxed attributes with 0.852 precision and general attributes with 0.727 precision for the top 20 outputs. Table 3 lists the top 20 attributes obtained with the proposed method for several classes. The numeral before (after) "/" is the number of evaluators who judged the attribute as correct as a relaxed (general) attribute. We can see that many interesting attributes were obtained.

4.3 Effect of Scores

In this analysis, we assessed the effect that sub-scores in Eq. (1) had on the acquisition accuracy by observing the decrease in precision when we removed each score from Eq. (1). First, we could observe a positive effect for most scores in terms of the precision averaged over evaluators. Moreover, interestingly, the tendency of the effect was very similar for all evaluators, even though the assessments varied greatly depending on the evaluator as the previous experiment showed. Due to space limitations, we will only present the latter analysis here.

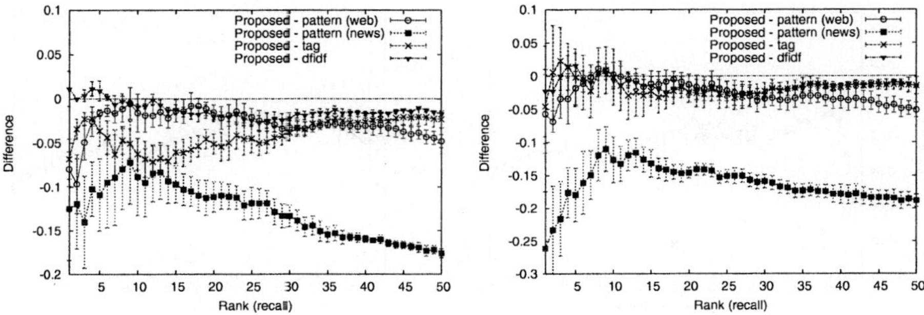

Fig. 6. Effect of scores. Left: relaxed attribute. Right: general attribute.

We calculated the change in precision "per evaluator", and then calculated the averaged change, i.e., the change averaged over evaluators. Figure 6 plots the averaged change and standard deviations. The effect of $n(C, A)$ is represented by "Proposed - pattern (web)", that of $f(C, A)$ by "Proposed - pattern (news)", that of $t(C, A)$ by "Proposed - tag", and that of $dfidf(C, A)$ by "Proposed - dfidf". In the relaxed attribute case, we can see that most of the scores were effective at almost all ranks regardless of the evaluator (negative difference means positive effect). The effect of $f(C, A)$ and $t(C, A)$ was especially remarkable. Although $n(C, A)$ has a similar curve to $f(C, A)$, the effect is weaker. This may be caused by the difference in the number of documents available (As we previously described, we currently cannot obtain a large number of documents from the Web). The effect $dfidf(C, A)$ had was two-fold. This contributed positively at lower ranks but it contributed negatively at higher ranks (around the top 1-5). In the general attribute case, the positive effect became harder to observe although the tendency was similar to the relaxed case. However, we can see that $f(C, A)$ still contributed greatly even in this case. The effect of $t(C, A)$, on the other hand, seems to have weakened greatly.

4.4 Effect of Hypernym

If we have a hypernym-hyponym knowledge base, we can also collect the local document set by using the hyponyms in the class as the keywords for the search engine instead of using the class label (hypernym). In this experiment, we compared the proposed method with this alternative. We collected about the same number of documents for the alternative method as for the proposed method to focus on the quality of collected documents. We used hyponyms with the alternative method instead of class label C in patterns for $n(C, A)$ (thus $n(Hs, A)$ to be precise). $f(C, A)$ was unchanged. Figure 7 plots the results in the same way as for the previous analysis (i.e., difference from the proposed method). We can see that the class label is better than hyponyms for collecting local documents at least in the current setting.

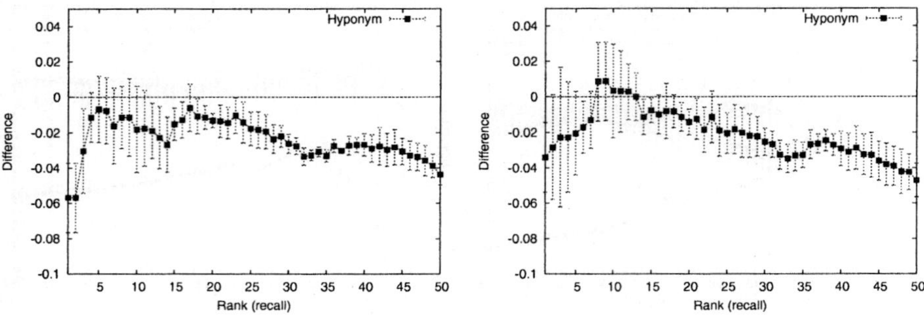

Fig. 7. Effect of hypernyms. Left: relaxed case. Right: general case.

5 Discussion

5.1 Related Work

Several studies have attempted to acquire attributes or attribute-value pairs [1,3,7,8,16]. Yoshida [1] proposed a method of integrating tables on the Web. Although his method consequently acquired attributes, he did not evaluate the accuracy of attributes. Yoshida et al. [16] proposed a method of identifying attribute-value pairs in Web documents. However, since this method only identified the attributes obtained with the method in [1], the coverage might be bounded by the coverage of tables for attributes. Moreover, these methods did not utilize the statistics for words or lexico-syntactic patterns as ours did. Takahashi et al. [8] extracted triples $(object, attribute, value)$ from newspaper articles using lexico-syntactic patterns and statistical scores. However, they focused only on proper nouns and selected the attribute candidates manually. Freishmann et al. [3] extracted attribute-value pairs with a high degree of precision by filtering the candidates extracted with lexico-syntactic patterns by using a model learned with supervised learning. Although this approach is promising, their method was limited to person names and we must prepare training data to apply the method to other types of objects.

5.2 Future Directions

Clues based on QA tests. The current ranking, Eq. (1), does not exploit the observation behind the criteria in Sect. 3. Only the lexico-syntactic patterns "C no A" slightly reflect the criteria. Higher accuracy might be achieved by using patterns that directly reflect the QA tests, e.g., statistics from FAQ lists. The hyponym tests in Sect. 3.4 can also be reflected if we use a hyponymy database. In addition, it is not surprising that the proposed method was not efficient at acquiring general attributes since the score was not meant for that (although the use of class labels might be a contributing factor, ambiguous class labels cause problems at the same time). The hyponym database might be exploited to measure the generality of attributes.

Full use of the Web. The current method cannot use all Web documents due to limitations with search engines. The more Web documents we have, the more useful the score $n(C, A)$. We are currently planning to prepare our own non-restricted Web repository. Using this, we would also like to elaborate on the comparison described in Sect. 4.4 between the use of hypernyms (class labels) and hyponyms (instance words) in collecting the local document set.

Assessment of Coverage. Currently, the actual recall with the proposed method is unknown. It will be important to estimate how many attributes are needed for practical applications, e.g., by manually analyzing the use of pattern "C no A" exhaustively for a certain class, C. In addition, since we selected classes that were successfully obtained with a hyponymy acquisition method, we cannot deny the possibility that the proposed method has been evaluated for the classes for which reliable statistics can easily be obtained. Thus, the evaluation of more difficult (e.g., more infrequent) classes will be an important future work.

Type Acquisition. What types of questions and what types of suffix augmentations are possible for a given attribute (i.e., the type of attribute value) might also be useful, e.g., in value extraction and in determining type of the attribute (in the sense of "property or part-of"). This was left for the evaluators to chose arbitrarily in this study. We would like to extract such knowledge from the Web using similar techniques such as word statistics and lexico-syntactic patterns.

6 Conclusion

We presented a method of acquiring attributes that utilizes statistics on words, lexico-syntactic patterns, and HTML tags. We also proposed criteria and an evaluation procedure based on question-answerability. Using the procedure, we conducted experiments with four human evaluators. The results revealed that our method could obtain attributes with a high degree of precision.

References

1. Yoshida, M.: Extracting attributes and their values from web pages. In: Proc. of the ACL 2002 Student Research Workshop. (2002) 72–77
2. Yoshida, M., Torisawa, K., Tsujii, J.: Integrating tables on the world wide web. Transactions of the Japanese Society for Artificial Intelligence **19** (2004) 548–560
3. Fleischman, M., Hovy, E., Echihabi, A.: Offline strategies for online question answering: Answering questions before they are asked. In: Proc. of ACL 2003. (2003) 1–7
4. Almuhareb, A., Poesio, M.: Attribute-based and value-based clustering: An evaluation. In: Proc. of EMNLP 2004. (2004) 158–165
5. Fellbaum, C., ed.: WordNet: An electronic lexical database. The MIT Press (1998)

6. Hearst, M.A.: Automatic acquisition of hyponyms from large text corpora. In: Proc. of COLING '92. (1992) 539–545
7. Berland, M., Charniak, E.: Finding parts in very large corpora. In: Proc. of ACL '99. (1999)
8. Takahashi, T., Inui, K., Matsumoto, Y.: Automatic extraction of attribute relations from text (in Japanese). IPSJ, SIG-NLP. NL-164 (2004) 19–24
9. Guarino, N.: Concepts, attributes and arbitrary relations: some linguistic and ontological criteria for structuring knowledge base. Data and Knowledge Engineering (1992) 249–261
10. Pustejovsky, J.: The Generative Lexicon. The MIT Press (1995)
11. Woods, W.A.: What's in a Link: Foundations for Semantic Networks. In: Representation and Understanding: Studies in Cognitive Science. Academic Press (1975)
12. Kurohashi, S., Nagao, M.: Japanese morphological analysis system JUMAN version 3.61 manual (1999)
13. Kanayama, H., Torisawa, K., Mitsuishi, Y., Tsujii, J.: A hybrid Japanese parser with hand-crafted grammar and statistics. In: Proc. of COLING 2000. (2000) 411–417
14. Shinzato, K., Torisawa, K.: Acquiring hyponymy relations from web documents. In: Proc. of HLT-NAACL04. (2004) 73–80
15. Landis, J.R., Koch, G.G.: The measurement of observer agreement for categorial data. Biometrics **33** (1977) 159–174
16. Yoshida, M., Torisawa, K., Tsujii, J.: Chapter 10 (Extracting Attributes and Their Values from Web Pages). In: Web Document Analysis. World Scientific (2003)

Aligning Needles in a Haystack: Paraphrase Acquisition Across the Web

Marius Paşca and Péter Dienes

Google Inc.,
1600 Amphitheatre Parkway,
Mountain View, California, 94043, USA
{mars, dienes}@google.com

Abstract. This paper presents a lightweight method for unsupervised extraction of paraphrases from arbitrary textual Web documents. The method differs from previous approaches to paraphrase acquisition in that 1) it removes the assumptions on the quality of the input data, by using inherently noisy, unreliable Web documents rather than clean, trustworthy, properly formatted documents; and 2) it does not require any explicit clue indicating which documents are likely to encode parallel paraphrases, as they report on the same events or describe the same stories. Large sets of paraphrases are collected through exhaustive pairwise alignment of small needles, i.e., sentence fragments, across a haystack of Web document sentences. The paper describes experiments on a set of about one billion Web documents, and evaluates the extracted paraphrases in a natural-language Web search application.

1 Introduction

The information captured in textual documents frequently encodes semantically equivalent ideas through different lexicalizations. Indeed, given the generative power of natural language, different people employ different words or phrases to convey the same meaning, depending on factors such as background knowledge, level of expertise, style, verbosity and personal preferences. Two equivalent fragments of text may differ only slightly, as a word or a phrase in one of them is paraphrased in the other, e.g., through a synonym. Yet even small lexical variations represent challenges to any automatic decision on whether two text fragments have the same meaning, or are relevant to each other, since they are no longer lexically identical. Many natural-language intensive applications make such decisions internally. In document summarization, the generated summaries have a higher quality if redundant information has been discarded by detecting text fragments with the same meaning [1]. In information extraction, extraction templates will not be filled consistently whenever there is a mismatch in the trigger word or the applicable extraction pattern [2]. Similarly, a question answering system could incorrectly discard a relevant document passage based on the absence of a question phrase deemed as very important [3], even if the passage actually contains a legitimate paraphrase.

R. Dale et al. (Eds.): IJCNLP 2005, LNAI 3651, pp. 119–130, 2005.

In information retrieval, deciding whether a text fragment (e.g., a document) is relevant to another text fragment (i.e., the query) is crucial to the overall output, rather than merely useful within some internal system module. Indeed, relevant documents or passages may be missed, due to the apparent mismatch between their terms and the paraphrases occurring in the users' queries. The previously proposed solutions to the mismatch problem vary with respect to the source of the data used for enriching the query with alternative terms. In automatic query expansion, the top documents provide additional query terms [4]. An alternative is to attempt to identify the concepts captured in the queries and find semantically similar concepts in external resources, e.g., lexical databases [5,6]. This paper explores a different direction, namely the unsupervised acquisition of large sets of paraphrases from unstructured text within Web documents, and their exploitation in natural-language Web search.

We present a lightweight method for unsupervised extraction of paraphrases from arbitrary, textual Web documents. The method taps the textual contents provided by millions of anonymous Web document contributors. The remainder of the paper is structured as follows. After a condensed overview of the paraphrase acquisition method and a contrast to previous literature in Section 2, Section 3 presents the method in more detail. Section 4 describes evaluation results when applying the method to textual documents from a Web repository snapshot of the Google search engine.

2 Method at a Glance

The proposed acquisition method collects large sets of word and phrase-level paraphrases via exhaustive pairwise alignment of small needles, i.e., sentence fragments, across a haystack of Web document sentences. The acquisition of paraphrases is a side-effect of the alignment.

In the example in Figure 1, if two sentence fragments have common word sequences at both extremities, then the variable word sequences in the middle are potential paraphrases of each other. A significant advantage of this extraction mechanism is that it can acquire paraphrases from sentences whose information content overlaps only partially, as long as the fragments align. Indeed, the source sentences of the paraphrase (*withdrew from*, *pulled out of*), as well as of (*took effect*, *came into force*), are arguably quite different overall in Figure 1. Moreover, the sentences are part of documents whose content intersection is very small.

In addition to its relative simplicity when compared to more complex, sentence-level paraphrase acquisition [7], the method introduced in this paper is a departure from previous approaches in several respects. First, the paraphrases are not limited to variations of specialized, domain-specific terms as in [8], nor are they restricted to a narrow class such as verb paraphrases [9]. Second, as opposed to virtually all previous approaches, the method does not require high-quality, clean, trustworthy, properly-formatted input data. Instead, it uses inherently noisy, unreliable Web documents. The source data in [10] is also a set of Web documents. However, it is based on top search results collected

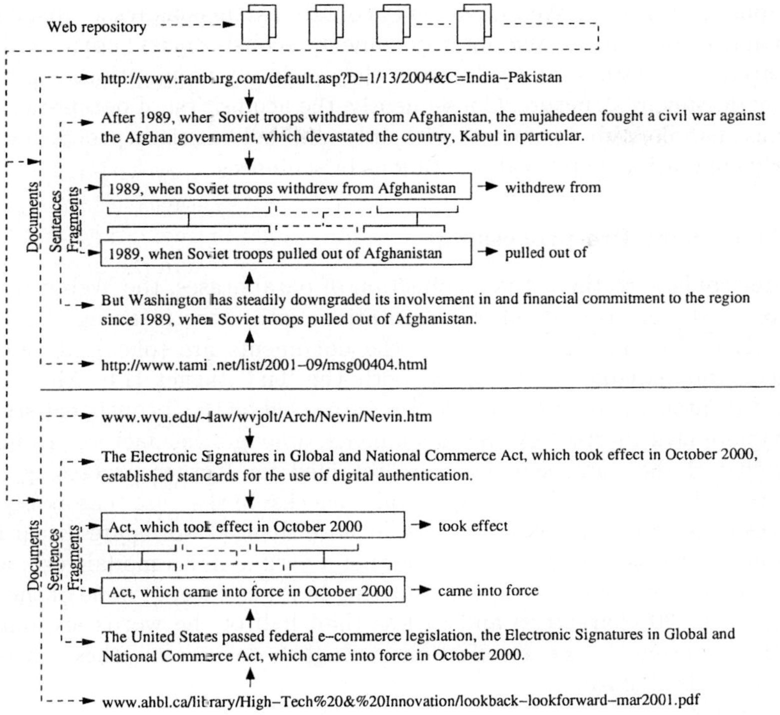

Fig. 1. Paraphrase acquisition from unstructured text across the Web

from external search engines, and its quality benefits implicitly from the ranking functions of the search engines. Third, the input documents here are not restricted to a particular genre, whereas virtually all other recent approaches are designed for collections of parallel news articles, whether the articles are part of a carefully-compiled collection [11] or aggressively collected from Web news sources [12]. Fourth, the acquisition of paraphrases in this paper does not rely on external clues and attributes that two documents are parallel and must report on the same or very similar events. Comparatively, previous work has explicit access to, and relies strongly on clues such as the same or very similar timestamps being associated to two news article documents [11], or knowledge that two documents are translations by different people of the same book into the same language [13].

3 Mining the Web for Paraphrases

The use of the Web as input data source strongly impacts the design of the method, since the average Web document is much noisier and less reliable than documents in standard textual collections. Furthermore, the separation of useful textual information from other items within the document is trivial in standard collections. In contrast, Web documents contain extraneous HTML information, formatting errors, intra- and inter-document inconsistencies, spam and other adversarial information, and in general they lack any assumptions regarding a common document structure. Consequently, the acquisition of paraphrases must be robust, handle Web documents with only minimal linguistic processing, avoid expensive operations, and scale to billions of sentences.

3.1 Document Pre-processing

As a pre-requisite to the actual acquisition of paraphrases, the Web documents are converted from raw string representations into more meaningful linguistic units. After filtering out HTML tags, the documents are tokenized, split into sentences and part-of-speech tagged with the TnT tagger [14]. Many of the candidate sentences are in fact random noise caused by the inconsistent structure (or complete lack thereof) of Web documents, among other factors. To improve the quality of the data, sentences are retained for further processing only if they satisfy the following lightweight sanity checks: 1) they are reasonably sized: sentences containing less than 5 words or more than 30 words are discarded; 2) they contain at least one verb that is neither a gerund nor a modal verb; 3) they contain at least one non-verbal word starting in lower-case; 4) none of the words is longer than 30 characters; and 5) less than half of the words are numbers. Since the experiments use a collection of English documents, these checks are geared towards English.

3.2 Acquisition via Text Fragment Alignment

At Web scale, the number of sentences that pass the fairly aggressive sanity checks during document pre-processing is still extremely large, easily exceeding one billion. Any brute-force alignment of all pairs of document sentences is therefore unfeasible. Instead, the acquisition of paraphrases operates at the level of text fragments (ngrams) as shown in Figure 2.

The extraction algorithm roughly consists of the following three phases:

- Generate candidate ngrams from all sentences (steps 1 through 5 in Figure 2);
- Convert each ngram into a ready-to-align pair of a variable fragment (a candidate paraphrase) and a constant textual anchor (steps 6 through 13);
- Group the pairs with the same anchors; collect the variable fragments within each group of pairs as potential paraphrases of one another (steps 14 to 20).

The algorithm starts with the generation of candidate ngrams, by collecting all possible ngrams such that their length varies within pre-defined boundaries. More precisely, an ngram starts and ends in a fixed number of words (L_C); the count of the additional (ngram) words in-between varies within pre-defined limits (Min_P and Max_P, respectively).

The concatenation of the fixed-length left (Cst_L) and right (Cst_R) extremities of the ngram forms a textual **anchor** for the variable fragment (Var) in the middle. The variable fragment becomes a potential candidate for a paraphrase:

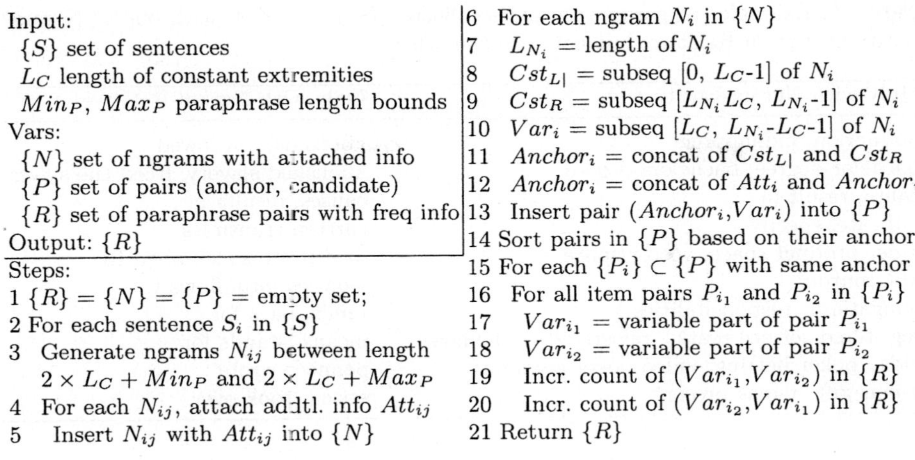

Input:
$\{S\}$ set of sentences
L_C length of constant extremities
Min_P, Max_P paraphrase length bounds
Vars:
$\{N\}$ set of ngrams with attached info
$\{P\}$ set of pairs (anchor, candidate)
$\{R\}$ set of paraphrase pairs with freq info
Output: $\{R\}$
Steps:
1 $\{R\} = \{N\} = \{P\}$ = empty set;
2 For each sentence S_i in $\{S\}$
3 Generate ngrams N_{ij} between length $2 \times L_C + Min_P$ and $2 \times L_C + Max_P$
4 For each N_{ij}, attach addtl. info Att_{ij}
5 Insert N_{ij} with Att_{ij} into $\{N\}$
6 For each ngram N_i in $\{N\}$
7 L_{N_i} = length of N_i
8 $Cst_{L|}$ = subseq $[0, L_C\text{-}1]$ of N_i
9 Cst_R = subseq $[L_{N_i} L_C, L_{N_i}\text{-}1]$ of N_i
10 Var_i = subseq $[L_C, L_{N_i}\text{-}L_C\text{-}1]$ of N_i
11 $Anchor_i$ = concat of $Cst_{L|}$ and Cst_R
12 $Anchor_i$ = concat of Att_i and $Anchor_i$
13 Insert pair ($Anchor_i$,Var_i) into $\{P\}$
14 Sort pairs in $\{P\}$ based on their anchor
15 For each $\{P_i\} \subset \{P\}$ with same anchor
16 For all item pairs P_{i_1} and P_{i_2} in $\{P_i\}$
17 Var_{i_1} = variable part of pair P_{i_1}
18 Var_{i_2} = variable part of pair P_{i_2}
19 Incr. count of (Var_{i_1},Var_{i_2}) in $\{R\}$
20 Incr. count of (Var_{i_2},Var_{i_1}) in $\{R\}$
21 Return $\{R\}$

Fig. 2. Algorithm for paraphrase acquisition from Web document sentences

(S_1) *Together they form the Platte River ,which eventually flows into the Gulf of Mexico.*
$\underbrace{\textit{,which eventually}}_{Cst_L}$ $\underbrace{\textit{flows}}_{Var}$ $\underbrace{\textit{into the Gulf}}_{Cst_R}$

Whenever the anchors of two or more ngrams are the same, their variable fragments are considered to be potential paraphrases of each other, thus implementing a const-var-const type of alignment.

3.3 Alignment Anchors

According to the simplified discussion from above, the algorithm in Figure 2 may align two sentence fragments *"decided to read the government report published last month"* and *"decided to read the edition published last month"* to incorrectly produce *government report* and *edition* as potential paraphrases of each other. To avoid such alignments, Steps 4 and 12 of the algorithm enrich the anchoring text around each paraphrase candidate, namely by extending the anchors to include additional information from the source sentence. By doing so, the anchors become longer and more specific, and thus closer to expressing the same information content. In turn, this reduces the chances of any two ngrams to align, since ngram alignment requires the complete matching of the corresponding anchors. In other words, the amount of information captured in the anchors is a trade-off between coverage (when anchors are less specific) and accuracy of the acquired paraphrases (when the anchors are more specific). At the low end, less specific anchors include only immediate contextual information. This corresponds to the algorithm in Figure 2, when nothing is attached to any of the ngrams in Step 4. At the high end, one could collect all the remaining words of the sentence outside the ngram, and attach them to more specific anchors in Step 4. This is equivalent to pairwise alignment of full-length sentences.

We explore three different ways of collecting additional anchoring information from the sentences:

Table 1. Examples of paraphrase pairs collected from the Web with one of Ngram-Entity or Ngram-Relative, but not with the other

Only with Ngram-Entity	Only with Ngram-Relative
abduction, kidnapping	abolished, outlawed
bachelor degree, bachelors degree	abolished slavery, freed the slaves
cause, result in	causes, results in
indicate, specify	carries, transmits
inner product space, vector space	died from, succumbed to
kill, murder	empties into, flows to
obligations, responsibilities	funds, pays for
registered service marks, registered trademarks	means, stands for
video poker betting, video poker gambling	penned, wrote
x-mas gift, x-mas present	seized, took over

- Ngram-Only: The anchor includes only the contextual information assembled from the fixed-length extremities of the ngram. Nothing else is attached to the anchor.
- Ngram-Entity: In addition to Ngram-Only, the anchor contains the preceding and following named entities that are nearest to the ngram. Sentences without such named entities are discarded. The intuition is that the ngram contains information which relates the two entities to each other.
- Ngram-Relative: On top of Ngram-Only, the anchor includes the remaining words of the adverbial relative clause in which the variable part of the ngram appears, e.g., *"when Soviet Union troops pulled out of Afghanistan"*, or *"which came into force in 2000"* in Figure 1. The clause must modify a named entity or a date, which is also included in the anchor. Sentences not containing such clauses are rejected. [1] The intuitive motivation in that the entity is related to part of the ngram via the adverbial particle.

For illustration, consider the earlier example of the sentence S_1 from Section 3.2. With Ngram-Entity, *Platte River* (preceding entity) and *Mexico* (following entity) are included in the anchor. In comparison, with Ngram-Relative the additional information combines *Platte River* (entity) and *of Mexico* (remainder of relative clause). In this example, the difference between Ngram-Entity and Ngram-Relative happens to be quite small. In general, however, the differences are more significant. Table 1 illustrates paraphrases collected from the Web by only one of the two anchoring mechanisms.

To ensure robustness on Web document sentences, simple heuristics rather than complex tools are used to approximate the additional information attached to ngrams in Ngram-Entity and Ngram-Relative. Named entities are approximated by proper nouns, as indicated by part-of-speech tags. Adverbial relative clauses, together with the entities or dates they modify, are detected according to a small set of lexico-syntactic patterns which can be summarized as:

$\langle [\mathit{Date}|\mathit{Entity}]\ [,|\text{-}|(|\text{nil}]\ [\mathit{Wh}]\ \mathit{RelClause}\ [,|\text{-}|)|.]\rangle$

[1] By discarding many sentences, Ngram-Relative sacrifices recall in favor of precision.

where *Wh* is one of *who*, *when*, *which* or *where*. The patterns are based mainly on *wh*-words and punctuation. The matching adverbial clause *RelClause* must satisfy a few other constraints, which aim at avoiding, rather than solving, complex linguistic phenomena. First, personal and possessive pronouns are often references to other entities. Therefore clauses containing such pronouns are discarded as ambiguous. Second, appositives and other similar pieces of information are confusing when detecting the end of the current clause. Consequently, during pattern matching, if the current clause does not contain a verb, the clause is either extended to the right, or discarded upon reaching the end of the sentence.

4 Evaluation

The input data for paraphrase acquisition is a collection of 972 million Web documents, from a Web repository snapshot of the Google search engine taken in 2003. All documents are in English. The parameters controlling the length of the ngrams and candidate paraphrases, introduced in Figure 2, are L_C=3, Min_P=1 and Max_P=4. [2] The anchors use additional information from the sentences, resulting in separate runs and sets of paraphrases extracted with Ngram-Only, Ngram-Entity and Ngram-Relative respectively. The experiments use a parallel programming model [15]. The extracted paraphrase pairs that co-occur very infrequently (i.e., in less than 5 unique ngram pairs) are discarded.

4.1 Quantitative Results

The sanity checks applied in document pre-processing (see Section 3.1) discard a total of 187 billion candidate sentences from the input documents, with an average of 3 words per sentence. In the case of Ngram-Only, paraphrases are extracted from the remaining 9.5 billion sentences, which have 17 words on average. As explained in Section 3.3, Ngram-Entity and Ngram-Relative apply a set of additional constraints as they search the sentences for more anchoring information. Ngram-Entity discards 72 million additional sentences. In contrast, as many as 9.3 billion sentences are rejected by the constraints encoded in Ngram-Relative.

The number of paraphrase pairs extracted from the Web varies with the particular kind of anchoring mechanism. The simplest one, i.e., Ngram-Only, produces 41,763,994 unique pairs that co-occur in at least 5 different ngrams. With Ngram-Relative, the output consists of 13,930 unique pairs. In comparison, Ngram-Entity generates 101,040 unique pairs. Figure 3 shows that the number of acquired paraphrases varies more or less linearly in the size of the input data.

The large majority of the paraphrase pairs contain either two single-word phrases (40% for Ngram-Entity, and 49% for Ngram-Relative), or one single-word and one multi-word phrase (22% for Ngram-Entity, and 43% for Ngram-Relative). Table 2 illustrates the top paraphrase pairs with two multi-word phrases, after removal of paraphrases containing only stop words, or upper/lower

[2] No experiments were performed with higher values for Max_P (to collect longer paraphrases), or higher/lower values for L_C (to use more/less context for alignment).

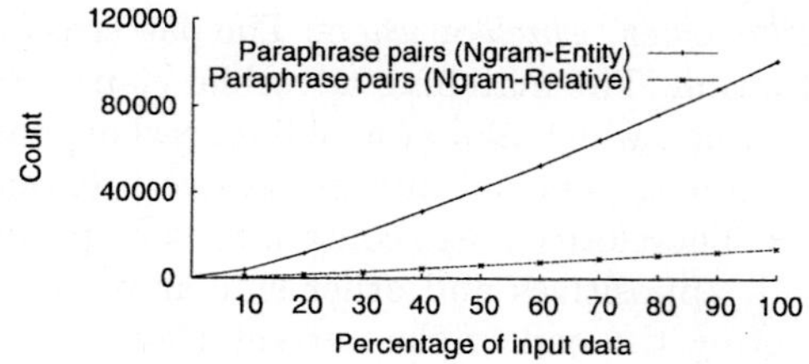

Fig. 3. Variation of the number of acquired paraphrase pairs with the input data size

Table 2. Top ranked multi-word paraphrase pairs in decreasing order of frequency of co-occurrence

#	Ngram-Entity	Ngram-Relative
1	DVD Movie, VHS Movie	became effective, took effect
2	betting is excited, wagering is excited	came into force, took effect
3	betting is, wagering is	became effective, went into effect
4	betting is excited, gambling is excited	became effective, came into force
5	Annual Meeting of, meeting of	became effective, came into effect
6	center of, centre of	entered into force, took effect
7	betting is, gambling is	one hour, two hours

case variation. Top multi-word phrases extracted by Ngram-Relative tend to be self-contained syntactic units. For instance, *entered into force* is a verb phrase in Table 2. In contrast, many of the top paraphrases with Ngram-Entity end in a linking word, such as the pair (*center of, centre of*). Note that every time this pair is extracted, the smaller single-word paraphrase pair that folds the common linking word into the anchor, e.g., (*center, centre*), is also extracted.

4.2 Quality of Paraphrases

Table 2 shows that the extracted paraphrases are not equally useful. The pair (*became effective, took effect*) is arguably more useful than (*one hour, two hours*). Table 3 is a side-by-side comparison of the accuracy of the paraphrases with Ngram-Only, Ngram-Entity and Ngram-Relative respectively. The values are the result of manual classification of the top, middle and bottom 100 paraphrase pairs from each run into 11 categories. The first six categories correspond to pairs classified as correct. For instance (*Univeristy, University*) is classified in class (1); (*Treasury, treasury*) in (2); (*is, are*) in (3); (*e-mail, email*) in (4); and (*can, could*) in (5). The pairs in class (6) are considered to be the most useful; they include (*trip, visit*), (*condition, status*), etc. The next three classes do not contain synonyms but are still useful. The pairs in (7) are siblings rather than direct synonyms; examples are (*twice a year, weekly*) and (*French, welsh*). Furthermore, modal verbs such as (*may, should*), numbers, and prepositions like (*up, back*) also fall under class (7). Many of the 63 pairs classified as siblings

Table 3. Quality of the acquired paraphrases

Classification of Pairs	Ngram-Only			Ngram-Entity			Ngram-Relative		
	Top 100	Mid 100	Low 100	Top 100	Mid 100	Low 100	Top 100	Mid 100	Low 100
(1) Correct; punct., symbols, spelling	1	5	11	12	6	20	18	11	15
(2) Correct; equal if case-insensitive	0	5	0	27	2	11	9	2	14
(3) Correct; both are stop words	4	0	0	3	0	1	1	0	0
(4) Correct; hyphenation	0	1	4	10	35	8	2	19	43
(5) Correct; morphological variation	8	1	10	9	10	20	20	15	6
(6) Correct; synonyms	16	8	21	5	32	14	33	23	6
Total correct	29	20	46	66	85	74	83	70	84
(7) Siblings rather than synonyms	63	29	19	32	8	15	5	7	7
(8) One side adds an elaboration	0	0	3	0	0	0	1	2	1
(9) Entailment	0	3	2	0	0	1	3	1	0
Total siblings	63	32	24	32	8	16	9	10	8
(10) Incorrect; antonyms	6	0	2	0	1	4	4	3	4
(11) Incorrect; other	2	48	28	2	6	6	4	17	4
Total incorrect	8	48	30	2	7	10	8	20	8

with Ngram-Only in Table 3 are precisely such words. Class (8) contains pairs in which a portion of one of the elements is a synonym or phrasal equivalent of the other element, such as (*poliomyelitis globally*, *polio*) and (*UNC*, *UNC-CH*), whereas (9) captures what can be thought of as entailment, e.g., (*governs*, *owns*) and (*holds*, *won*). Finally, the last two classes from Table 3 correspond to incorrect extractions, due to either antonyms like (*lost*, *won*) and (*your greatest strength*, *your greatest weakness*) in class (10), or other factors in (11).

The aggregated evaluation results, shown in bold in Table 3, suggest that Ngram-Only leads to paraphrases of lower quality than those extracted with Ngram-Entity and Ngram-Relative. In particular, the samples from the middle and bottom of the Ngram-Only paraphrases contain a much higher percentage of incorrect pairs. The results also show that, for Ngram-Entity and Ngram-Relative, the quality of paraphrases is similar at different ranks in the paraphrase lists sorted by the number of different ngrams they co-occur in. For instance, the total number of correct pairs has comparable values for the top, middle and bottom pairs. This confirms the usefulness of the heuristics introduced in Section 3.3 to discard irrelevant sentences with Ngram-Entity and Ngram-Relative.

4.3 Paraphrases in Natural-Language Web Search

The usefulness of paraphrases in Web search is assessed via an existing experimental repository of more than 8 million factual nuggets associated with a date. Repositories of factual nuggets are built offline, by matching lightweight, open-domain lexico-semantic patterns on unstructured text. In the repository used in this paper, a factual nugget is a sentence fragment from a Web document, paired with a date extracted from the same document, when the event encoded in the

Table 4. Impact of expansion of the test queries (QH/QL=count of queries with higher/lower scores than without expansion, NE=Ngram-Entity, NR=Ngram-Relative)

Max. nr. disjunctions per expanded phrase	QH		QL		Score	
	NE	NR	NE	NR	NE	NR
1 (no paraphrases)	0	0	0	0	52.70	52.70
2 (1 paraphrase)	17	8	7	6	64.50	57.62
3 (2 paraphrases)	22	13	6	9	70.38	60.46
4 (3 paraphrases)	23	15	6	7	71.42	60.39
5 (4 paraphrases)	26	18	12	5	71.73	63.35

sentence fragment occurred according to the text, e.g., ⟨*1937, Golden Gate was built*⟩, and ⟨*1947, Bell Labs invented the transistor*⟩.

A test set of temporal queries is used to extract direct results (dates) from the repository of factual nuggets, by matching the queries against the sentence fragments, and retrieving the associated dates. The test queries are all queries that start with either *When* or *What year*, namely 207 out of the total count of 1893 main-task queries, from the Question Answering track [16] of past editions (1999 through 2002). The metric for measuring the accuracy of the retrieved results is the de-facto scoring metric for fact-seeking queries, that is, the reciprocal rank of the first returned result that is correct (in the gold standard) [16]. If there is no correct result among the top 10 returned, the query receives no credit. Individual scores are aggregated (i.e., summed) over the entire query set.

In a series of parallel experiments, all phrases from the test queries are expanded into Boolean disjunctions with their top-ranked paraphrases. Query words with no paraphrase are placed into the expanded queries in their original form. The other query words are expanded only if they are single words, for simplicity. Examples of implicitly-Boolean queries expanded disjunctively, before removal of stop words and *wh*-words, are:

– When did Amtrak (begin | start | began | continue | commence) (operations | operation | activities | Business | operational)?
– When was the De Beers (company | Co. | firm | Corporation | group) (founded | established | started | created | co-founded)?

Table 4 illustrates the impact of paraphrases on the accuracy of the dates retrieved from the repository of factual nuggets associated with dates. When compared to non-expanded queries, paraphrases consistently improve the accuracy of the returned dates. Incremental addition of more paraphrases results in more individual queries with a better score than for their non-expanded version, and higher overall scores for the returned dates. The paraphrases extracted with Ngram-Entity produce scores that are higher than those of Ngram-Relative, due mainly to higher coverage. Since the temporal queries represent an external, objective test set, they provide additional evidence regarding the quality of paraphrases in a practical application.

5 Conclusion

The Web has gradually grown into a noisy, unreliable, yet powerful resource of human knowledge. This knowledge ranges from basic word usage statistics to intricate facts, background knowledge and associated inferences made by humans reading Web documents. This paper describes a method for unsupervised acquisition of lexical knowledge across the Web, by exploiting the numerous textual forms that people use to share similar ideas, or refer to common events. Large sets of paraphrases are collected through pairwise alignment of ngrams occurring within the unstructured text of Web documents. Several mechanisms are explored to cope with the inherent lack of quality of Web content. The quality of the extracted paraphrases improves significantly when the textual anchors used for aligning potential paraphrases attempt to approximate, even at a very coarse level, the presence of additional information within the sentences. In addition to the known role of the extracted paraphrases in natural-language intensive applications, the experiments in this paper illustrate their impact in returning direct results to natural-language queries.

The final output of the extraction algorithm lacks any distinction among paraphrases that apply to only one of the several senses or part of speech tags that a word or phrase may have. For instance, *hearts*, *center* and *middle* mix the medical and positioning senses of the word heart. Conversely, the extracted paraphrases may capture only one sense of the word, which may not match the sense of the same word in the queries. As an example, in the expansion of one of the test queries, *"Where is the massive North Korean (nuclear|atomic) (complex|real) (located|situated|found)?"*, a less-than-optimal paraphrase of *complex* not only provides a sibling rather than a near synonym, but may incorrectly shift the focus of the search towards the mathematical sense of the word (*complex* versus *real* numbers). Aggregated contextual information from the source ngrams could provide a means for selecting only some of the paraphrases, based on the query. As another direction for future work, we plan to revise the need for language-dependent resources (namely, the part of speech tagger) in the current approach, and explore possibilities of minimizing or removing their use for seamless transfer of the approach to other languages.

References

1. Hirao, T., Fukusima, T., Okumura, M., Nobata, C., Nanba, H.: Corpus and evaluation measures for multiple document summarization with multiple sources. In: Proceedings of the 20th International Conference on Computational Linguistics (COLING-04), Geneva, Switzerland (2004) 535–541
2. Shinyama, Y., Sekine, S.: Paraphrase acquisition for information extraction. In: Proceedings of the 41st Annual Meeting of the Association of Computational Linguistics (ACL-03), 2nd Workshop on Paraphrasing: Paraphrase Acquisition and Applications, Sapporo, Japan (2003) 65–71
3. Paşca, M.: Open-Domain Question Answering from Large Text Collections. CSLI Studies in Computational Linguistics. CSLI Publications, Distributed by the University of Chicago Press, Stanford, California (2003)

4. Mitra, M., Singhal, A., Buckley, C.: Improving automatic query expansion. In: Proceedings of the 21st ACM Conference on Research and Development in Information Retrieval (SIGIR-98), Melbourne, Australia (1998) 206–214
5. Schutze, H., Pedersen, J.: Information retrieval based on word senses. In: Proceedings of the 4th Annual Symposium on Document Analysis and Information Retrieval. (1995) 161–175
6. Zukerman, I., Raskutti, B.: Lexical query paraphrasing for document retrieval. In: Proceedings of the 19th International Conference on Computational Linguistics (COLING-02), Taipei, Taiwan (2002) 1177–1183
7. Barzilay, R., Lee, L.: Learning to paraphrase: An unsupervised approach using multiple-sequence alignment. In: Proceedings of the 2003 Human Language Technology Conference (HLT-NAACL-03), Edmonton, Canada (2003) 16–23
8. Jacquemin, C., Klavans, J., Tzoukermann, E.: Expansion of multi-word terms for indexing and retrieval using morphology and syntax. In: Proceedings of the 35th Annual Meeting of the Association of Computational Linguistics (ACL-97), Madrid, Spain (1997) 24–31
9. Glickman, O., Dagan, I.: Acquiring Lexical Paraphrases from a Single Corpus. In: Recent Advances in Natural Language Processing III. John Benjamins Publishing, Amsterdam, Netherlands (2004) 81–90
10. Duclaye, F., Yvon, F., Collin, O.: Using the Web as a linguistic resource for learning reformulations automatically. In: Proceedings of the 3rd Conference on Language Resources and Evaluation (LREC-02), Las Palmas, Spain (2002) 390–396
11. Shinyama, Y., Sekine, S., Sudo, K., Grishman, R.: Automatic paraphrase acquisition from news articles. In: Proceedings of the Human Language Technology Conference (HLT-02), San Diego, California (2002) 40–46
12. Dolan, W., Quirk, C., Brockett, C.: Unsupervised construction of large paraphrase corpora: Exploiting massively parallel news sources. In: Proceedings of the 20th International Conference on Computational Linguistics (COLING-04), Geneva, Switzerland (2004) 350–356
13. Barzilay, R., McKeown, K.: Extracting paraphrases from a parallel corpus. In: Proceedings of the 39th Annual Meeting of the Association for Computational Linguistics (ACL-01), Toulouse, France (2001) 50–57
14. Brants, T.: TnT - a statistical part of speech tagger. In: Proceedings of the 6th Conference on Applied Natural Language Processing (ANLP-00), Seattle, Washington (2000) 224–231
15. Dean, J., Ghemawat, S.: MapReduce: Simplified data processing on large clusters. In: Proceedings of the 6th Symposium on Operating Systems Design and Implementation (OSID-04), San Francisco, California (2004) 137–150
16. Voorhees, E., Tice, D.: Building a question-answering test collection. In: Proceedings of the 23rd International Conference on Research and Development in Information Retrieval (SIGIR-00), Athens, Greece (2000) 200–207

Confirmed Knowledge Acquisition Using Mails Posted to a Mailing List

Yasuhiko Watanabe, Ryo Nishimura, and Yoshihiro Okada

Ryukoku University, Seta, Otsu, Shiga, 520-2194, Japan
watanabe@rins.ryukoku.ac.jp

Abstract. In this paper, we first discuss a problem of developing a knowledge base by using natural language documents: wrong information in natural language documents. It is almost inevitable that natural language documents, especially web documents, contain wrong information. As a result, it is important to investigate a method of detecting and correcting wrong information in natural language documents when we develop a knowledge base by using them. In this paper, we report a method of detecting wrong information in mails posted to a mailing list and developing a knowledge base by using these mails. Then, we describe a QA system which can answer how type questions based on the knowledge base and show that question and answer mails posted to a mailing list can be used as a knowledge base for a QA system.

1 Introduction

Because of the improvement of NLP, research activities which utilize natural language documents as a knowledge base become popular, such as QA track on TREC [1] and NTCIR [2]. However, these QA systems assumed the user model where the user asks what type questions. On the contrary, there are a few QA systems which assumed the user model where the user asks how type question, in other words, how to do something and how to cope with some problem [3] [4] [7]. There are several difficulties in developing a QA system which answers how type questions, and we focus attention to two problems.

First problem is the difficulty of extracting evidential sentences by which the QA system answers how type questions. It is not difficult to extract evidential sentences by which the QA system answers what type questions. For example, question (Q1) is a what type question and "Naoko Takahashi, a marathon runner, won the gold medal at the Sydney Olympics" is a good evidential sentence for answering question (Q1).

(Q1) Who won the gold medal in women's marathon
 at the Sydney Olympics?
(DA1–1) Naoko Takahashi.

It is not difficult to extract this evidential sentence from natural language documents by using common content words and phrases because this sentence and question (Q1) have several common content words and phrases. On the contrary, it is difficult to extract evidential sentences for answering how type questions

R. Dale et al. (Eds.): IJCNLP 2005, LNAI 3651, pp. 131–142, 2005.

only by using linguistic clues, such as, common content words and phrases. For example, it is difficult to extract evidential sentences for answering how type question (Q2) because there may be only a few common content words and phrases between the evidential sentences and question (Q2).

(Q2) How can I cure myself of allergy?
(DA2–1) You had better live in a wooden floor.
(O2–1–1) Keep it clean.
(O2–1–2) Your room is always dirty.
(DA2–2) Drink two spoonfuls of vinegar every day.
(QR2–2–1) I tried, but, no effect.

To solve this problem, [3] and [4] proposed methods of collecting knowledge for answering questions from FAQ documents and technical manuals by using the document structure, such as, a dictionary-like structure and if-then format description. However, these kinds of documents requires the considerable cost of developing and maintenance. As a result, it is important to investigate a method of extracting evidential sentences for answering how type questions from natural language documents at low cost. To solve this problem, we proposed a method of developing a knowledge base by using mails posted to a mailing list (ML) [8]. We have the following advantages when we develop knowledge base by using mails posted to a mailing list.

- it is easy to collect question and answer mails in a specific domain, and
- there is some expectation that information is updated by participants

Furthermore, we developed a QA system and show that mails posted to a mailing list can be used as a knowledge base by which a QA system answers how type questions [8].

Next problem is wrong information. It is almost inevitable that natural language documents, especially web documents, contain wrong information. For example, (DA3–1) is opposed by (QR3–1–1).

(Q3) How I set up my wheel mouse for the netscape ?
(DA3–1) You can find a setup guide in the Dec. issue of SD magazine.
(QR3–1–1) I cannot use it although I modified
/usr/lib/netscape/ja/Netscape according to the guide.

Wrong information is a central problem of developing a knowledge base by using natural language documents. As a result, it is important to investigate a method of detecting and correcting wrong information in natural language documents. In this paper, we first report a method of detecting wrong information in question and answer mails posted to a mailing list. In our method, wrong information in the mails are detected by using mails which ML participants submitted for correcting wrong information in the previous mails. Then, the system gives one of the following confirmation labels to each set of question and their answer mails:

positive label shows the information described in a set of a question and its answer mail is confirmed by the following mails,
negative label shows the information is opposed by the following mails, and
other label shows the information is not yet confirmed.

Our knowledge base is composed of these labeled sets of a question and its answer mail. Finally, we describe a QA system: It finds question mails which are similar to user's question and shows the results to the user. The similarity between user's question and a question mail is calculated by matching of user's question and the significant sentence extracted from the question mail. A user can easily choose and access information for solving problems by using the significant sentences and confirmation labels.

2 Mails Posted to a Mailing List

There are mailing lists to which question and answer mails are posted frequently. For example, in Vine Users ML, several kinds of question and answer mails are posted by participants who are interested in Vine Linux [1]. We intended to use these question and answer mails for developing knowledge base for a QA system because

– it is easy to collect question and answer mails in a specific domain,
– it is easy to extract reference relations among mails,
– there is some expectation that information is updated by participants, and
– there is some expectation that wrong information in the previous mails is pointed out and corrected by participants.

However, there is a problem of extracting knowledge from mails posted to a mailing list. As mentioned, it is difficult to extract knowledge for answering how type questions from natural language documents only by using linguistic clues, such as, common content words and phrases. To solve this problem, [3] and [4] proposed methods of collecting knowledge from FAQ documents and technical manuals by using the document structure, such as, a dictionary-like structure and if-then format description. However, mails posted to a mailing list, such as Vine Users ML, do not have a firm structure because questions and their answers are described in various ways. Because of no firm structure, it is difficult to extract precise information from mails posted to a mailing list in the same way as [3] and [4] did. However, a mail posted to ML generally has a significant sentence. A significant sentence of a question mail has the following features:

1. it often includes nouns and unregistered words which are used in the mail subject.
2. it is often quoted in the answer mails.
3. it often includes the typical expressions, such as,

[1] Vine Linux is a linux distribution with a customized Japanese environment.

(a) (*ga* / *shikasi* (but / however)) + ⋯ + *mashita* / *masen* / *shouka* / *imasu* (can / cannot / whether / current situation is) + .
(ex) *Bluefish de nihongo font ga hyouji deki masen.* (I cannot see Japanese fonts on Bluefish.)
(b) *komatte* / *torabutte* / *goshido* / *?* (have trouble / is troubling / tell me / ?)
(ex) *saikin xstart ga dekinakute komatte imasu* (In these days, I have trouble executing xstart.)

4. it often occurs near the beginning.

Before we discuss the significant sentence in answer mails, we classified answer mails into three types: (1) direct answer (DA) mail, (2) questioner's reply (QR) mail, and (3) the others. Direct answer mails are direct answers to the original question. Questioner's reply mails are questioner's answers to the direct answer mails. Suppose that (Q2) in Section 1 and its answers are question and answer mails posted to a mailing list, respectively. In this case, (DA2–1) and (DA2–2) are DA mails to (Q2). (QR2–2–1) is a QR mail to (DA2–2). (O2–1–1) and (O2–1–2) are the others.

In a DA mail, the answerer gives answers to the questioner, such as (DA2–1) and (DA2–2). Also, the answerer often asks the questioner back when the question is imperfect. As a result, significant sentences in DA mails can be classified into two types: answer type and question type sentence. They have the following features:

- it often includes the typical expressions, such as,
  - answer type sentence
    - *dekiru* / *dekinai* (can / cannot)
    - *shita* / *shimashita* / *shiteimasu* / *shiteimasen* (did / have done / doing / did not do)
    - *shitekudasai* / *surebayoi* (please do / had better)
  - question type sentence
    - *masuka* / *masenka* / *desuka* (did you / did not you / do you)
- it is often quoted in the following mails.
- it often occurs after and near to the significant sentence of the question mail if it is quoted.

In a QR mail, the questioner shows the results, conclusions, and gratitude to the answerers, such as (QR2–2–1), and sometimes points out wrong information in a DA mail and correct it, such as, (QR2–2–1) and (QR3–1–1). A significant sentence in a QR has the following features:

- it often includes the typical expressions.
  - *dekita* / *dekimasen* (could / could not)
  - *arigatou* (thank)
- it often occurs after and near to the significant sentence of the DA mail if it is quoted.

Taking account of these features, we proposed a method of extracting significant sentences from question mails and their DA mails by using surface clues [8]. Then, we showed, by using the significant sentences extracted from question and their DA mails, the system can answer user's questions or, at least, give a good hint to the user. In this paper, we show that wrong information in a set of a question mail and its DA mail can be detected by using the QR mail. Then, we examined whether a user can easily choose and access information for solving problems with our QA system. In the next section, we will explain how to extract significant sentences from QR mails by using surface clues and confirm information in a set of a question mail and its DA mail.

3 Confirmation of Question and Answer Mails Posted to ML

Information in a set of a question and its DA mail is confirmed by using the QR mail in the next way:

step 1. extract a question mail, and its DA and QR mails by using reference relations and sender's email address.

step 2. extract sentences from each mail by detecting periods and blank lines.

step 3. check each sentence whether it is quoted in the following mails.

step 4. extract the significant sentence from the question mail by using surface clues, such as, words in the subject, quotation in the DA mails, and clue expressions in the same way as [8] did.

step 5. extract the significant sentence from the DA mail by using surface clues, such as, quotation in the QR mail, and clue expressions in the same way as [8] did.

step 6. calculate the significant score of each sentence in the QR mail by applying the next two rules. The sentence which has the largest score is selected as the significant sentence in the QR mail.

- **rule 6–1:** a rule for typical expressions. Give n points to sentences which include n clue expressions in Figure 1.
- **rule 6–2:** when two or more sentences have the largest score by applying rule 6–1, (1) give 1 point to the sentence which is located after and the nearest to the significant sentence in the DA mail if it is quoted, or (2) give 1 point to the sentence which is the nearest to the lead.

step 7. give one of the following confirmation labels to the set of the question and DA mail.

- **positive label** is given to the set of the question and its DA mail when the significant sentence in the QR mail has type 1 clue expressions in Fig 1.
- **negative label** is given to the set of the question and its DA mail when the significant sentence in the QR mail has type 2 clue expressions in Fig 1.
- **other label** is given to the set of the question and its DA mail when the significant sentence in the QR mail has neither type 1 nor type 2 clue expressions in Fig 1.

type 1 expressions

- ··· + *dekiru / dekita* (can / could).
- ··· + *kaiketsu suru / shita* (solve / solved).
- ··· + *tsukaeru / tsukaeta* (be usable).
- ··· + *umaku iku / itta / ikimashita* (go / went well).

type 2 expressions

- ··· + *dekinai / dekinakatta* (cannot / could not).
- ··· + *kaiketsu shinai / shinakatta* (do/did not solve).
- ··· + *tsukaenai / tsukaenai / tsukaemasen* (not be usable).
- ··· + *umaku ikanai / ikanakatta* (do/did not go well).

Fig. 1. Clue expressions for extracting a significant sentence from a QR mail

For evaluating our method, we selected 100 examples of question mails in Vine Users ML. They have 121 DA mails, each of which has one QR mail.

First, we examined whether the results of determining the confirmation labels were good or not. The results are shown in Table 1. Table 2 shows the type and number of incorrect confirmation. The reasons of the failures were as follows:

- there were many significant sentences which did not include the clue expressions.
- there were many sentences which were not significant sentences but included the clue expressions.
- some question mails were submitted not for asking questions, but for giving some news, notices, and reports to the participants. In these cases, there were no answer in the DA mail and no sentence in the QR mail for confirming the previous mails.
- questioner's answer was described in several sentences and one of them was extracted, and
- misspelling.

Next, we examined whether these significant sentences and the confirmation labels were helpful in choosing and accessing information for solving problems. Our QA system put the significant sentences in reference order, such as,

(Q4) *vedit ha, sonzai shinai file wo hirakou to suru to core wo haki masuka.*
(Does vedit terminate when we open a new file?)
(DA4–1) *hai, core dump shimasu.* (Yes, it terminates.)
(DA4–2) *shourai, GNOME ha install go sugu tsukaeru no desu ka?*
(In near future, can I use GNOME just after the installation?)

Then, we examined whether a user can easily choose and access information for solving problems. In other words, we examined whether

- there was good connection between the significant sentences or not, and
- the confirmation label was proper or not.

For example, (Q4) and (DA4–1) have the same topic, however, (DA4–2) has a different topic. In this case, (DA4–1) is a good answer to question (Q4). A user

Table 1. Results of determining confirmation labels

type	correct	incorrect	total
positive	35	18	53
negative	10	4	14
other	48	6	54

Table 2. Type and number of incorrect confirmation

incorrect	type and number of correct answers			
confirmation	positive	negative	other	total
positive	–	4	14	18
negative	2	–	2	4
other	4	2	–	6

Table 3. Results of determining confirmation labels to the proper sets of a question and its DA mail

labeling result	positive	negative	other	total
correct	29	8	27	64
failure	4	4	15	23

can access the document from which (DA4–1) was extracted and obtain more detailed information. As a result, the set of (Q4) and (DA4–1) was determined as correct. On the contrary, the set of (Q4) and (DA4–2) was a failure. In this experiment, 87 sets of a question and its DA mail were determined as correct and 34 sets were failures. The reasons of the failures were as follows:

- wrong significant sentences extracted from question mails, and
- wrong significant sentences extracted from DA mails.

Failures which were caused by wrong significant sentences extracted from question mails were not serious. This is because there is not much likelihood of matching user's question and wrong significant sentence extracted from question mails. On the other hand, failures which were caused by wrong significant sentences extracted from DA mails were serious. In these cases, significant sentences in the question mails were successfully extracted and there is likelihood of matching user's question and the significant sentence extracted from question mails. Therefore, the precision of the significant sentence extraction was emphasized in this task.

Next, we examined whether proper confirmation labels were given to these 87 good sets of a question and its DA mail or not, and then, we found that proper confirmation labels were given to 64 sets in them. The result was shown in Table 3.

We discuss some example sets of significant sentences in detail. Question (Q5) in Figure 2 has two answers, (DA5–1) and (DA5–2). (DA5–1) is a suggestion to

(Q5) *sound no settei de komatte imasu.*
(I have much trouble in setting sound configuration.)
(DA5–1) *mazuha, sndconfig wo jikkou shitemitekudasai.*
(First, please try 'sndconfig'.)
(QR5–1–1) *kore de umaku ikimashita.* (I did well.)
(DA5–2) *sndconfig de, shiawase ni narimashita.*
(I tried 'sndconfig' and became happy.)

(Q6) *ES1868 no sound card wo tsukatte imasu ga, oto ga ookisugite komatte imasu.* (My trouble is that sound card ES1868 makes a too loud noise.)
(DA6–1) *xmixer wo tsukatte kudasai.* (Please use xmixer.)
(QR6–1–1) *xmixer mo xplaycd mo tsukaemasen.*
(I cannot use xmixer and xplaycd, too.)

Fig. 2. Examples of the significant sentence extraction

the questioner of (Q5) and (DA5–2) explains answerer's experience. The point to be noticed is (QR5–1–1). Because (QR5–1–1) contains type 1 expression in Figure 1, it gives a positive label to the set of (Q5) and (DA5–1). It guarantees the information quality of (DA5–1) and let the user choose and access the answer mail from which (DA5–1) was extracted.

Example (Q6) is an interesting example. (DA6–1) in Figure 2 which was extracted from a DA mail has wrong information. Then, the questioner of (Q6) confirmed whether the given information was helpful or not, and then, posted (QR6–1–1) in order to point out and correct the wrong information in (DA6–1). In this experiment, we found 16 cases where the questioners posted reply mails in order to correct the wrong information, and the system found 10 cases in them and gave negative labels to the sets of the question and its DA mail.

4 QA System Using Mails Posted to a Mailing List

4.1 Outline of the QA System

Figure 3 shows the overview of our system. A user can ask a question to the system in a natural language. Then, the system retrieves similar questions from mails posted to a mailing list, and shows the user the significant sentences which were extracted from the similar question and their answer mails. A user can easily choose and access information for solving problems by using the significant sentences and the confirmation labels. The system consists of the following modules:

Knowledge Base. It consists of

- question and answer mails (50846 mails),
- significant sentences (26334 sentences: 8964, 13094, and 4276 sentences were extracted from question, DA, and QR mails, respectively),
- confirmation labels (4276 labels were given to 3613 sets of a question and its DA mail), and
- synonym dictionary (519 words).

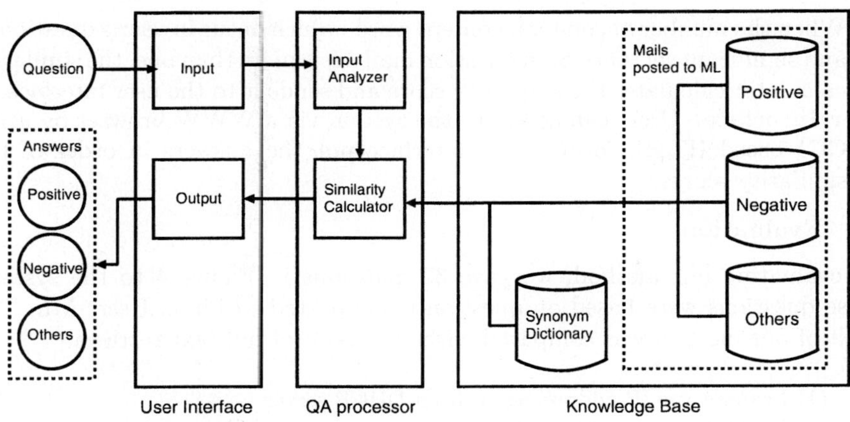

Fig. 3. System overview

QA processor. It consists of input analyzer and similarity calculator.

Input analyzer transforms user's question into a dependency structure by using JUMAN[6] and KNP[5].

Similarity calculator calculates the similarity between user's question and a significant sentence in a question mail posted to a mailing list by using their common content words and dependency trees in the next way:

The weight of a common content word t which occurs in user's question Q and significant sentence S_i in the mails M_i $(i = 1 \cdots N)$ is:

$$w_{WORD}(t, M_i) = tf(t, S_i) \log \frac{N}{df(t)}$$

where $tf(t, S_i)$ denotes the number of times content word t occurs in significant sentence S_i, N denotes the number of significant sentences, and $df(t)$ denotes the number of significant sentences in which content word t occurs.

Next, the weight of a common modifier-head relation in user's question Q and significant sentence S_i in question mail M_i is:

$$w_{LINK}(l, M_i) = w_{WORD}(modifier(l), M_i) + w_{WORD}(head(l), M_i)$$

where $modifier(l)$ and $head(l)$ denote a modifier and a head of modifier-head relation l, respectively.

Therefore, the similarity score between user's question Q and significant sentence S_i of question mail M_i, $SCORE(Q, M_i)$, is set to the total weight of common content words and modifier-head relations which occur user's question Q and significant sentence S_i of question mail M_i, that is,

$$SCORE(Q, M_i) = \sum_{t \in T_i} w_{WORD}(t, M_i) + \sum_{l \in L_i} w_{LINK}(l, M_i)$$

where the elements of set T_i and set L_i are common content words and modifier-head relations in user's question Q and significant sentence S_i in question mail M_i, respectively.

When the number of common content words which occur in user's question Q and significant sentence S_i in question mail M_i is more than one, the similarity calculator calculates the similarity score and sends it to the user interface.

User Interface. Users can access to the system via a WWW browser by using CGI based HTML forms. User interface put the answers in order of the similarity scores.

4.2 Evaluation

For evaluating our method, we gave 32 questions in Figure 4 to the system. These questions were based on question mails posted to Linux Users ML. The result of our method was compared with the result of full text retrieval

(1) I cannot get IP address again from DHCP server.
(2) I cannot make a sound on Linux.
(3) I have a problem when I start up X Window System.
(4) Tell me how to restore HDD partition to its normal condition.
(5) Where is the configuration file for giving SSI permission to Apache ?
(6) I cannot login into proftpd.
(7) I cannot input kanji characters.
(8) Please tell me how to build a Linux router with two NIC cards.
(9) CGI cannot be executed on Apache 1.39.
(10) The timer gets out of order after the restart.
(11) Please tell me how to show error messages in English.
(12) NFS server does not go.
(13) Please tell me how to use MO drive.
(14) Do you know how to monitor traffic load on networks.
(15) Please tell me how to specify kanji code on Emacs.
(16) I cannot input \ on X Window System.
(17) Please tell me how to extract characters from PDF files.
(18) It takes me a lot of time to login.
(19) I cannot use lpr to print files.
(20) Please tell me how to stop making a backup file on Emacs.
(21) Please tell me how to acquire a screen shot on X window.
(22) Can I boot linux without a rescue disk?
(23) Pcmcia drivers are loaded, but, a network card is not recognized.
(24) I cannot execute PPxP.
(25) I am looking for FTP server in which I can use chmod command.
(26) I do not know how to create a Makefile.
(27) Please tell me how to refuse the specific user login.
(28) When I tried to start Webmin on Vine Linux 2.5, the connection to localhost:10000 was denied.
(29) I have installed a video capture card in my DIY machine, but, I cannot watch TV programs by using xawtv.
(30) I want to convert a Latex document to a Microsoft Word document.
(31) Can you recommend me an application for monitoring resources?
(32) I cannot mount a CD-ROM drive.

Fig. 4. 32 questions which were given to the system for the evaluation

Table 4. Results of finding a similar question by matching of user's question and a significant sentence

	Test 1	Test 2	Test 3
our method	9	15	17
full text retrieval	5	5	8

(a) the number of questions which were given the proper answer

	Test 1	Test 2	Test 3
our method	9	25	42
full text retrieval	5	9	15

(b) the number of proper answers

	positive	negative	other	positive & negative
Test 1	2	2	5	0
Test 2	9	4	12	0
Test 3	10	5	25	2

(c) the number and type of labels given to proper answers

Test 1. by examined first answer
Test 2. by examined first three answers
Test 3. by examined first five answers

Table 4 (a) shows the number of questions which were given the proper answer. Table 4 (b) shows the number of proper answers. Table 4 (c) shows the number and type of confirmation labels which were given to proper answers.

In Test 1, our system answered question 2, 6, 7, 8, 13, 14, 15, 19, and 24. In contrast, the full text retrieval system answered question 2, 5, 7, 19, and 32. Both system answered question 2, 7 and 19, however, the answers were different. This is because several solutions of a problem are often sent to a mailing list and the systems found different but proper answers. In all the tests, the results of our method were better than those of full text retrieval. Our system answered more questions and found more proper answers than the full text retrieval system did. Furthermore, it is much easier to choose and access information for solving problems by using the answers of our QA system than by using the answers of the full text retrieval system.

Both systems could not answer question 4, "Tell me how to restore HDD partition to its normal condition". However, the systems found an answer in which the way of saving files on a broken HDD partition was mentioned. Interestingly, this answer may satisfy a questioner because, in such cases, our desire is to save files on the broken HDD partition. In this way, it often happens that there are gaps between what a questioner wants to know and the answer, in several aspects, such as concreteness, expression and assumption. To overcome the gaps, it is important to investigate a dialogue system which can communicate with the questioner.

References

1. TREC (Text REtrieval Conference) : http://trec.nist.gov/
2. NTCIR (NII-NACSIS Test Collection for IR Systems) project: http://research.nii.ac.jp/ntcir/index-en.html
3. Kurohashi and Higasa: Dialogue Helpsystem based on Flexible Matching of User Query with Natural Language Knowledge Base, 1st ACL SIGdial Workshop on Discourse and Dialogue, pp.141-149, (2000).
4. Kiyota, Kurohashi, and Kido: "Dialog Navigator" A Question Answering System based on Large Text Knowledge Base, 19th COLING (COLING02), pp.460-466, (2002.8).
5. Kurohashi and Nagao: A syntactic analysis method of long Japanese sentences based on the detection of conjunctive structures, Computational Linguistics, 20(4),pp.507-534, (1994).
6. Kurohashi and Nagao: JUMAN Manual version 3.6 (in Japanese), Nagao Lab., Kyoto University, (1998).
7. Mihara, fujii, and Ishikawa: Helpdesk-oriented Question Answering Focusing on Actions (in Japanese), 11th Convention of NLP, pp. 1096–1099, (2005).
8. Watanabe, Sono, Yokomizo, and Okada: A Question Answer System Using Mails Posted to a Mailing List, ACM DocEng 2004, pp.67-73, (2004).

Automatic Partial Parsing Rule Acquisition Using Decision Tree Induction*

Myung-Seok Choi, Chul Su Lim, and Key-Sun Choi

Korea Advanced Institute of Science and Technology, 373-1 Guseong-dong, Yuseong-gu, Daejeon 305-701, Republic of Korea
{mschoi, cslim}@kaist.ac.kr kschoi@cs.kaist.ac.kr

Abstract. Partial parsing techniques try to recover syntactic information efficiently and reliably by sacrificing completeness and depth of analysis. One of the difficulties of partial parsing is finding a means to extract the grammar involved automatically. In this paper, we present a method for automatically extracting partial parsing rules from a tree-annotated corpus using decision tree induction. We define the partial parsing rules as those that can decide the structure of a substring in an input sentence deterministically. This decision can be considered as a classification; as such, for a substring in an input sentence, a proper structure is chosen among the structures occurred in the corpus. For the classification, we use decision tree induction, and induce partial parsing rules from the decision tree. The acquired grammar is similar to a phrase structure grammar, with contextual and lexical information, but it allows building structures of depth one or more. Our experiments showed that the proposed partial parser using the automatically extracted rules is not only accurate and efficient, but also achieves reasonable coverage for Korean.

1 Introduction

Conventional parsers try to identify syntactic information completely. These parsers encounter difficulties when processing unrestricted texts, because of ungrammatical sentences, the unavoidable incompleteness of lexicon and grammar, and other reasons like long sentences. Partial parsing is an alternative technique developed in response to these problems. This technique aims to recover syntactic information efficiently and reliably from unrestricted texts by sacrificing completeness and depth of analysis, and relying on local information to resolve ambiguities [1].

Partial parsing techniques can be roughly classified into two groups. The first group of techniques involves partial parsing via finite state machines [2,3,9,10]. These approaches apply the sequential regular expression recognizer to an input sentence. When multiple rules match an input string at a given position,

* This research was supported in part by the Ministry of Science and Technology, the Ministry of Culture and Tourism, and the Korea Science and Engineering Foundation in Korea.

R. Dale et al. (Eds.): IJCNLP 2005, LNAI 3651, pp. 143–154, 2005.

the longest-matching rule is selected. Therefore, these parsers always produce a single best analysis and operate very fast. In general, these approaches use a hand-written regular grammar. As would be expected, manually writing a grammar is both very time consuming and prone to have inconsistencies.

The other group of partial parsing techniques is text chunking, that is, recognition of non-overlapping and non-recursive cores of major phrases (chunks), by using machine learning techniques [4,7,8,13,15,17]. Since Ramshaw and Marcus [15] first proposed formulating the chunking task as a tagging task, most chunking methods have followed this *word-tagging* approach. In base noun phrase chunking, for instance, each word is marked with one of three chunk tags: I (for a word inside an NP), O (for outside of an NP), and B (for between the end of one NP and the start of another) as follows[1]:

In (early trading) in (Hong Kong) (Monday), (gold) was quoted at ($ 366.50) (an ounce).
In$_O$ early$_I$ trading$_I$ in$_O$ Hong$_I$ Kong$_I$ Monday$_B$,$_O$ gold$_I$ was$_O$ quoted$_O$ at$_O$ \$$_I$ 366.50$_I$ an$_B$ ounce$_I$.$_O$

With respect to these approaches, there have been several studies on automatically extracting chunking rules from large-scale corpora using transformation-based learning [15], error-driven pruning [7], the ALLiS top-down inductive system [8]. However, it is not yet clear how these approaches could be extended beyond the chunking task.

In this paper, we present a method of automatically extracting partial parsing rules from a tree-annotated corpus using the decision tree method. Our goal is to extract rules with higher accuracy and broader coverage. We define the partial parsing rules as those that can establish the structure of a substring in an input sentence deterministically. This decision can be considered as a classification; as such, for a substring in an input sentence, a proper structure is chosen among the structures occurred in the corpus, as extended from the *word-tagging* approach of text chunking. For the classification, we use decision tree induction with features of contextual and lexical information. In addition, we use negative evidence, as well as positive evidence, to gain higher accuracy. For general recursive phrases, all possible substrings in a parse tree are taken into account by extracting evidence recursively from a parse tree in a training corpus. We induce partial parsing rules from the decision tree, and, to retain only those rules that are accurate, verify each rule through cross-validation.

In many cases, several different structures are assigned to the same substring in a tree-annotated corpus. Substrings for coordination and compound nouns are typical examples of such ambiguous cases in Korean. These ambiguities can prevent us from extracting partial parsing rules that cover the substrings with more than one substructure and, consequently, can cause the result of partial parsing to be limited to a relatively shallow depth. In this work, we address this problem by merging substructures with ambiguity using an underspecified representation.

---

[1] This example is excerpted from Tjong Kim Sang [17].

This underspecification leads to broader coverage without deteriorating either the determinism or the precision of partial parsing.

The acquired grammar is similar to a phrase structure grammar, with contextual and lexical information, but it allows building structures of depth one or more. It is easy to understand; it can be easily modified; and it can be selectively added to or deleted from the grammar. Partial parsing with this grammar processes an input sentence deterministically using longest-match heuristics. The acquired rules are then recursively applied to construct higher structures.

2 Automatic Rule Acquisition

To start, we define the rule template, the basic format of a partial parsing rule, as follows:

$$left\ context \mid substring \mid right\ context \longrightarrow substructure$$

This template shows how the *substring* of an input sentence, surrounded by the *left context* and the *right context*, constructs the *substructure*. The *left context* and the *right context* are the remainder of an input sentence minus the *substring*. For automatic learning of the partial parsing rules, the lengths of the *left context* and the *right context* are restricted to one respectively. Note that applying a partial parsing rule results in a structure of depth one or more. In other words, the rules extracted by this rule template reduce a substring into a subtree, as opposed to a single non-terminal; hence, the resultant rules can be applied more specifically and strictly.

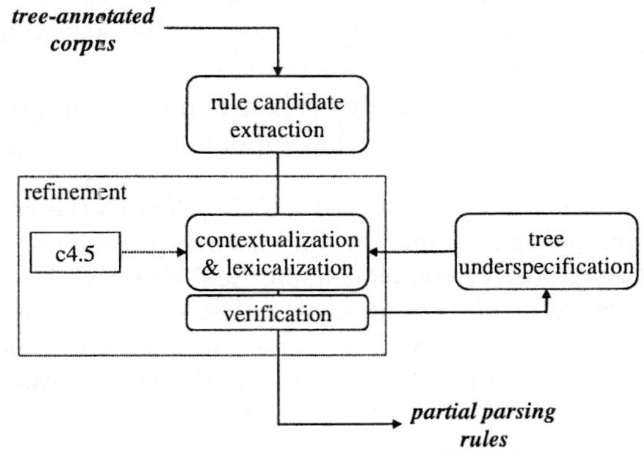

Fig. 1. Procedure for extracting partial parsing rules

Figure 1 illustrates the procedure for the extraction of partial parsing rules. First, we extract all possible rule candidates from a tree-annotated corpus, compliant with the rule template. The extracted candidates are grouped according to their respective substrings. Next, using the decision tree method, these candidates are enriched with contextual and lexical information. The contextualized and lexicalized rules are verified through cross-validation to retain only those rules that are accurate. The successfully verified accurate rules become the final partial parsing rules. Remaining rules that cannot be verified are forwarded to the tree underspecification step, which merges tree structures with hard ambiguities. As seen in Fig. 1, the underspecified candidates return to the refinement step. The following subsections describe each step in detail.

2.1 Extracting Candidates

From the tree-annotated corpus, we extract all the possible candidates for partial parsing rules in accordance with the rule template. Scanning input sentences annotated with its syntactic structure one by one, we can extract the substructure corresponding to every possible substring at each level of the syntactic structure. We define level 0 as part-of-speech tags in an input sentence, and level n as the nodes whose maximum depth is n. If no structure precisely corresponds to a particular substring, then a null substructure is extracted, which represents negative evidence.

Figure 2 shows an example sentence[2] with its syntactic structure[3] and some of the candidates for the partial parsing rules extracted from the left side of the example. In this figure, the first partial parsing rule candidate shows how the substring 'npp' can be constructed into the substructure 'NP'. S_{null} denotes negative evidence.

The extracted rule candidates are gathered and grouped according to their respective substrings. Figure 3[4] shows the candidate groups. In this figure, G_1 and G_2 are the group names, and the number in the last column refers to the frequency that each candidate occurs in the training corpus. Group G_1 and G_2 have 2 and 3 candidates, respectively. When a particular group has only one candidate, the candidate can always be applied to a corresponding substring

[2] 'NOM' refers to the nominative case and 'ACC' refers to the accusative case. The term 'npp' denotes personal pronoun; 'jxt' denotes topicalized auxiliary particle; 'ncn' denotes non-predicative common noun; 'jco' denotes objective case particle; 'pvg' denotes general verb; 'ef' denotes final ending; and 'sf' denotes full stop symbol. For a detailed description of the KAIST corpus and its tagset, refer to Lee [11]. The symbol '+' is not a part-of-speech, but rather a delimiter between words within a word phrase.

[3] In Korean, a word phrase, similar to bunsetsu in Japanese, is defined as a spacing unit with one or more content words followed by zero or more functional words. A content word indicates the meaning of the word phrase in a sentence, while a functional word—a particle or a verbal-ending—indicates the grammatical role of the word phrase. In the KAIST corpus used in this paper, a functional word is not included in the non-terminal that the preceding content word belongs to, following the restricted representation of phrase structure grammar for Korean [12]. For example, a word phrase "*na*/npp + *neun*/jxt" is annotated as "(NP *na*/npp) + *neun*/jxt", as in Fig. 2.

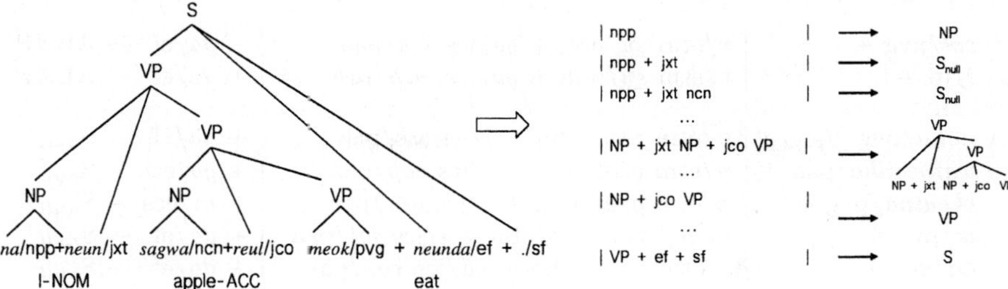

Fig. 2. An example sentence and the extracted candidates for partial parsing rules

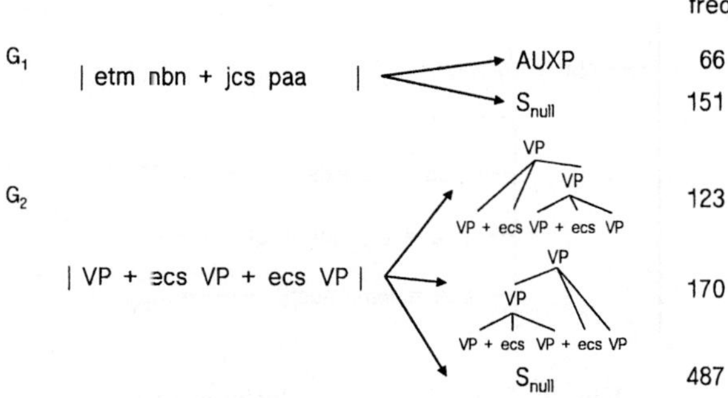

Fig. 3. Groups of partial parsing rules candidates

deterministically. In contrast, if there is more than one candidate in a particular group, those candidates should be enriched with contextual and lexical information to make each candidate distinct for proper application to a corresponding substring.

2.2 Refining Candidates

This step refines ambiguous candidates with contextual and lexical information to make them unambiguous.

First, each candidate needs to be annotated with contextual and lexical information occurring in the training corpus, as shown in Fig. 4. In this figure, we can see that a substring with lexical information such as '*su*/nbn' unambiguously constitutes the substructure 'AUXP'. We use the decision tree method, C4.5 [14], to select the important contextual and lexical information that can facilitate the establishment of unambiguous partial parsing rules. The features used in the decision tree method are the lexical information of each terminal or

[4] The term 'etm' denotes adnominalizing ending; 'nbn' denotes non-unit bound noun; 'jcs' denotes subjective case particle; 'paa' denotes attributive adjective; 'ecs' denotes subordinate conjunctive ending; and 'AUXP' denotes auxiliary phrase.

sal/pvg +	*r*/etm *su*/nbn + *ga*/jcs ***iss***/paa	+ *da*/ef	→ AUXP
i/jp +	*r*/etm *su*/nbn + *ga*/jcs ***eop***/paa	+ *da*/ef	→ AUXP
nolla/pvg +	*n*/etm *jeok*/nbn + *i*/jcs *iss*/paa	+ *da*/ef	→ S_{null}
wanjeonha/paa +	*n*/etm *geot*/nbn + *i*/jcs *eop*/paa	+ *go*/ecc	→ S_{null}
kkeutna/pvg +	*n*/etm *geut*/nbn + *i*/jcs *ani*/paa	+ *ra*/ecs	→ S_{null}
ik/pvg +	*neun*/etm *geut*/nbn + *i*/jcs *jot*/paa	+ *da*/ef	→ S_{null}
ha/xsv +	*r*/etm *nawi*/nbn + *ga*/jcs *eop*/paa	+ *da*/ef	→ S_{null}

Fig. 4. Annotated candidates for the G_1 group rules

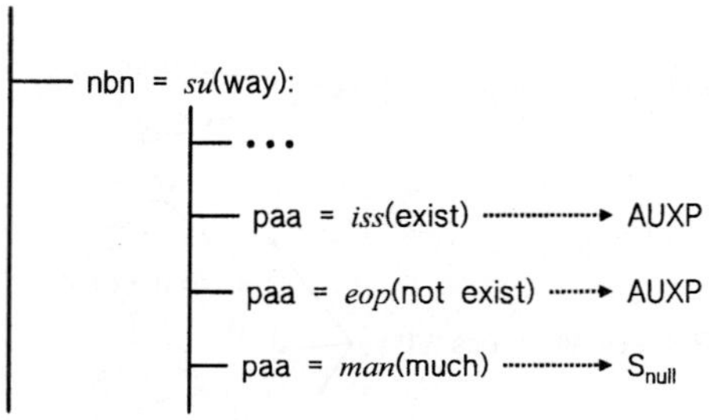

nbn = *su*(way):
- ...
- paa = *iss*(exist) → AUXP
- paa = *eop*(not exist) → AUXP
- paa = *man*(much) → S_{null}

Fig. 5. A section of the decision tree

non-terminal for the *substring*, and the parts-of-speech and lexical information for the *left context* and the *right context*. Lexical information of a non-terminal is defined as the part-of-speech and lexical information of its headword.

Figure 5 shows a section of the decision tree learned from our example substring. The deterministic partial parsing rules in Fig. 6 are extracted from the decision tree. As shown in Fig. 6, only the lexical entries for the second and the fourth morphemes in the substring are selected as additional lexical information, and none of the contexts is selected in this case. We should note that the rules induced from the decision tree are ordered. Since these ordered rules do not interfere with those from other groups, they can be modified without much difficulty.

etm ***su***/nbn + jcs ***iss***/paa	⟶ AUXP
etm ***su***/nbn + jcs ***eop***/paa	⟶ AUXP
etm ***su***/nbn + jcs ***man***/paa	⟶ S_{null}

Fig. 6. Partial parsing rules extracted from a section of the decision tree in Fig. 5

After we enrich the partial parsing rules using the decision tree method, we verify them by estimating the accuracy of each rule to filter out less deterministic rules. We estimate the error rates (%) of the rule candidates via a 10-fold cross validation on the training corpus. The rule candidates of the group with an error rate that is less than the predefined threshold, θ, can be extracted to the final partial parsing rules. The candidates in the group G_2 in Fig. 3 could not be extracted as the final partial parsing rules, because the estimated error rate of the group was higher than the threshold. The candidates in G_2 are set aside for tree underspecification processing. Using the threshold θ, we can control the number of the final partial parsing rules and the ratio of the precision/recall trade-off for the parser that adopts the extracted partial parsing rules.

2.3 Dealing with Hard Ambiguities: The Underspecified Representation

The group G_2 in Fig. 3 has one of the attachment ambiguities, namely, consecutive subordinate clauses. Figure 7 shows sections of two different trees extracted from a tree-annotated corpus. The two trees have identical *substrings*, but are analyzed differently. This figure exemplifies how an ambiguity relates to the lexical association between verb phrases, which is difficult to annotate in rules. There are many other syntactic ambiguities, such as coordination and noun phrase bracketing, that are difficult to resolve with local information. The resolution usually requires lexical co-occurrence, global context, or semantics. Such ambiguities can deteriorate the precision of partial parsing or limit the result of partial parsing to a relatively shallow depth.

Rule candidates with these ambiguities mostly have several different structures assigned to the same substrings under the same non-terminals. In this paper, we refer to them as *internal syntactic ambiguities.* We manually examined the patterns of the internal syntactic ambiguities, which were found in the KAIST corpus as they could not be refined automatically due to low estimated accuracies. During the process, we observed that few internal syntactic ambiguities could be resolved with local information.

In this paper, we handle internal syntactic ambiguities by merging the candidates using tree intersection and making them underspecified. This underspecified representation enables an analysis with broader coverage, without deterio-

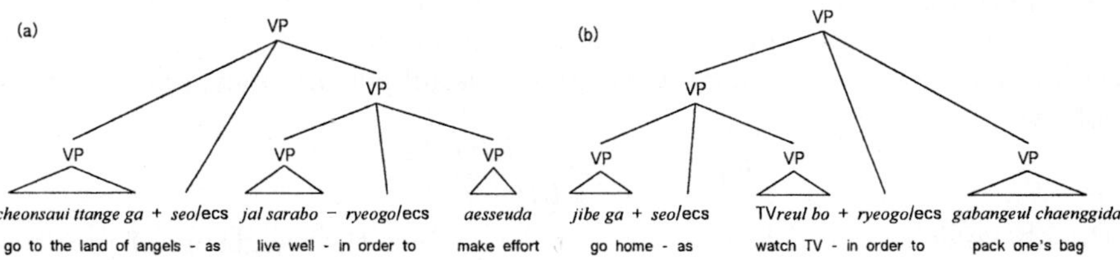

Fig. 7. Examples of internal syntactic ambiguities

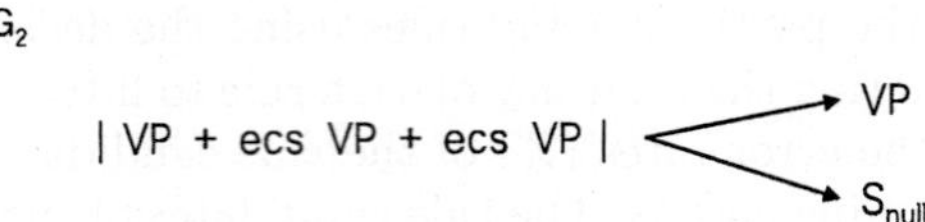

Fig. 8. Underspecified candidates

rating the determinism or the precision of partial parsing. Since only different structures under the same non-terminal are merged, the underspecification does not harm the structure of higher nodes. Figure 8 shows the underspecified candidates of group G_2. In this figure, the first two rules in G_2 are reduced to the merged 'VP'. Underspecified candidates are also enriched with contextual and lexical information using the decision tree method, and they are verified through cross-validation, as described in Sect. 2.2. The resolution of internal syntactic ambiguities is forwarded to a module beyond the partial parser. If necessary, by giving all possible structures of underspecified parts, we can prevent a later processing from re-analyzing the parts. Any remaining candidates that are not selected as the partial parsing rules after all three steps are discarded.

3 Experimental Results

We have performed experiments to show the usefulness of automatically extracted partial parsing rules. For our evaluations, we implemented a naive partial parser, using TRIE indexing to search the partial parsing rules. The input of the partial parser is a part-of-speech tagged sentence and the result is usually the sequence of subtrees. At each position in an input sentence, the parser tries to choose a rule group using longest-match heuristics. Then, if any matches are found, the parser applies the first-matching rule in the group to the corresponding substring, because the rules induced from the decision tree are ordered.

In our experiments, we used the KAIST tree-annotated corpus [11]. The training corpus contains 10,869 sentences (289,362 morphemes), with an average length of 26.6 morphemes. The test corpus contains 1,208 sentences, with an average length of 26.0 morphemes. The validation corpus, used for choosing the threshold, θ, contains 1,112 sentences, with an average length of 20.1 morphemes, and is distinct from both the training corpus and the test corpus.

The performance of the partial parser was evaluated using PARSEVAL measures [5]. The F measure, a complement of the E measure [16], is used to combine precision and recall into a single measure of overall performance, and is defined as follows:

$$F_\beta = \frac{(\beta^2 + 1) * LP * LR}{\beta^2 * LP + LR}$$

In the above equation, β is a factor that determines the weighting of precision and recall. Thus, $\beta < 1$ is used to weight precision heavier than recall, $\beta > 1$ is used to weight recall heavier than precision, and $\beta = 1$ is used to weight precision and recall equally.

Table 1. Precision/Recall with respect to the threshold, θ, for the validation corpus

θ	# of rules	precision	recall	$F_{\beta=0.4}$
6	18,638	95.5	72.9	91.6
11	**20,395**	**95.1**	**75.1**	**91.7**
16	22,650	94.2	78.0	91.6
21	25,640	92.6	83.3	91.2
26	28,180	92.0	84.7	90.9

Table 2. Experimental results of the partial parser for Korean

Grammar	precision	recall	$F_{\beta=0.4}$	$F_{\beta=1}$
baseline	73.0	72.0	72.9	72.5
depth 1 rule only	95.2	68.3	90.3	79.6
not underspecified	95.7	71.6	91.4	81.9
underspecified	**95.7**	**73.6**	**91.9**	**83.2**
underspecified (in case θ=26)	92.2	83.5	90.9	87.6
PCFG	80.0	81.5	80.2	80.7
Lee [11]	87.5	87.5	87.5	87.5

The parsing result can be affected by the predefined threshold, θ (described in Sect. 2.2), which can control both the accuracy of the partial parser and the number of the extracted rules. Table 1 shows the number of the extracted rules and how precision and recall trade off for the validation corpus as the threshold, θ, is varied. As can be seen, a lower threshold, θ, corresponds to a higher precision and a lower recall. A higher threshold corresponds to a lower precision and a higher recall. For a partial parser, the precision is generally favored over the recall. In this paper, we used a value of 11 for θ, where the precision was over 95% and $f_{\beta=0.4}$ was the highest. The value of this threshold should be set according to the requirements of the relevant application.

Table 2 presents the precision and the recall of the partial parser for the test corpus when the threshold, θ, was given a value of 11. In the baseline grammar, we selected the most probable structure for a given substring from each group of candidates. The "depth 1 rule only" grammar is the set of the rules extracted along with the restriction, stating that only a substructure of depth one is permitted in the rule template. The "underspecified" grammar is the final version of our partial parsing rules, and the "not underspecified" grammar is the set of the rules extracted without the underspecification processing. Both PCFG and Lee [11] are statistical full parsers of Korean, and Lee enriched the grammar using contextual and lexical information to improve the accuracy of a parser. Both of them were trained and tested on the same corpus as ours was for comparison. The performance of both the "not underspecified" grammar and the "underspecified" grammar was greatly improved compared to the baseline grammar and PCFG, neither of which adopts contextual and lexical information in their rules. The "not underspecified" grammar performed better than the "depth 1 rule only" grammar. This indicates that increasing the depth of a rule is helpful in partial parsing, as in the case of a statistical full parsing, Data-Oriented Parsing [6]. Comparing the "underspecified" grammar with the "not underspecified" grammar, we can see that underspecification leads to broader coverage, that is, higher recall. The precision of the "underspecified" grammar was above 95%. In other words, when a parser generates 20 structures, 19 out of 20 structures are correct. However, its recall dropped far beyond that of the statistical full parser [11]. When we set θ to a value of 26, the underspecified grammar slightly outperformed that of the full parser in terms of $f_{\beta=1}$, although the proposed partial parser does not always produce one complete parse tree[5]. It follows from what has been said thus far that the proposed parser has the potential to be a high-precision partial parser and approach the performance level of a statistical full parser, depending on the threshold θ.

The current implementation of our parser has a $O(n^2 m_r)$ worst case time complexity for a case involving a skewed binary tree, where n is the length of the input sentence and m_r is the number of rules. Because m_r is the constant, much more than two elements are reduced to subtrees of depth one or more in each level of parsing, and, differing from full parsing, the number of recursions in the partial parsing seems to be limited[6], we can parse in near-linear time. Figure 9 shows the time spent in parsing as a function of the sentence length[7].

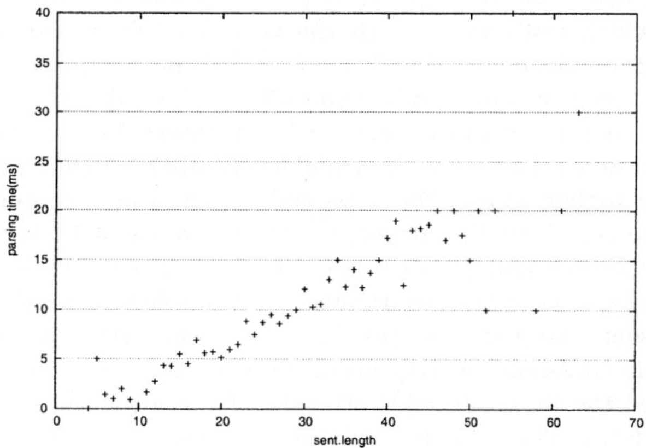

Fig. 9. Time spent in parsing

Lastly, we manually examined the first 100 or so errors occurring in the test corpus. In spite of underspecification, the errors related to conjunctions and

[5] In the test corpus, the percentage that our partial parser (θ=26) produced one complete parse tree was 70.9%. When θ=11, the percentage was 35.9%.

[6] In our parser, the maximum number of recursion was 10 and the average number of recursion was 4.47.

[7] This result was obtained using a Linux machine with Pentium III 700MHz processor.

attachments were the most frequent. The errors of conjunctions were mostly caused by *substrings* not occurring in the training corpus, while the cases of attachments lacked contextual or lexical information for a given *substring*. These errors can be partly resolved by increasing the size of the corpus, but it seems that they cannot be resolved completely with partial parsing. In addition, there were errors related to noun phrase bracketing, date/time/unit expression, and either incorrectly tagged sentences or inherently ambiguous sentences. For date, time, and unit expressions, manually encoded rules may be effective with partial parsing, since they appear to be used in a regular way. We should note that many unrecognized phrases included expressions not occurring in the training corpus. This is obviously because our grammar cannot handle unseen substrings; hence, alleviating the sparseness in the *sequences* will be the goal of our future research.

4 Conclusion

In this paper, we have proposed a method of automatically extracting the partial parsing rules from a tree-annotated corpus using a decision tree method. We consider partial parsing as a classification; as such, for a substring in an input sentence, a proper structure is chosen among the structures occurred in the corpus. Highly accurate partial parsing rules can be extracted by (1) allowing rules to construct a subtree of depth one or more; (2) using decision tree induction, with features of contextual and lexical information for the classification; and (3) verifying induced rules through cross-validation. By merging substructures with ambiguity in non-deterministic rules using an underspecified representation, we can handle syntactic ambiguities that are difficult to resolve with local information, such as coordination and noun phrase bracketing ambiguities. Using a threshold, θ, we can control the number of the partial parsing rules and the ratio of the precision/recall trade-off of the partial parser. The value of this threshold should be set according to the requirements of the relevant application. Our experiments showed that the proposed partial parser using the automatically extracted rules is not only accurate and efficient, but also achieves reasonable coverage for Korean.

References

1. Abney, S.P.: Part-of-speech tagging and partial parsing. Corpus-Based Methods in Language and Speech. Kluwer Academic Publishers (1996)
2. Abney, S.P.: Partial parsing via finite-state cascades. Proceedings of the ESSLLI '96 Robust Parsing Workshop (1996) 8–15
3. Aït-Mokhtar, S., Chanod, J.P.: Incremental finite-state parsing. Proceedings of Applied Natural Language Processing (1997) 72–79
4. Argamon-Engelson, S., Dagan, I., Krymolowski, Y.: A memory-based approach to learning shallow natural language patterns. Journal of Experimental and Theoretical AI **11**(3) (1999) 369–390

5. Black, E., Abney, S., Flickenger, D., Gdaniec, C., Grishman, R., Harrison, P., Hindle, D., Ingria, R., Jelinek, F., Klavans, J., Liberman, M., Marcus, M., Roukos, S., Santorini, B., Strzalkowski, T.: A procedure for quantitatively comparing the syntactic coverage of English grammars. Proceedings of the DARPA Speech and Natural Language Workshop (1991) 306–311
6. Bod, R.: Enriching Linguistics with Statistics: Performance Models of Natural Language. Ph.D Thesis. University of Amsterdam (1995)
7. Cardie, C., Pierce, D.: Error-driven pruning of treebank grammars for base noun phrase identification. Proceedings of 36th Annual Meeting of the Association for Computational Linguistics and 17th International Conference on Computational Linguistics (1998) 218–224
8. Déjean, H.: Learning rules and their exceptions. Journal of Machine Learning Research **2** (2002) 669–693
9. Hindle, D.: A parser for text corpora. Computational Approaches to the Lexicon. Oxford University (1995) 103–151
10. Hobbs, J.R., Appelt, D., Bear, J., Israel, D., Kameyama, M., Stickel, M., Tyson, M.: Fastus: A cascaded finite-state transducer for extracting information from natural-language text. Finite-State Language Processing. The MIT Press (1997) 383–406
11. Lee, K.J.: Probabilistic Parsing of Korean based on Language-Specific Properties. Ph.D. Thesis. KAIST, Korea (1998)
12. Lee, K.J., Kim, G.C., Kim, J.H., Han, Y.S.: Restricted representation of phrase structure grammar for building a tree annotated corpus of Korean. Natural Language Engineering **3**(2) (1997) 215–230
13. Muñoz, M., Punyakanok, V., Roth, D., Zimak, D.: A learning approach to shallow parsing. Proceedings of the 1999 Joint SIGDAT Conference on Empirical Methods in Natural Language Processing and Very Large Copora (1999) 168–178
14. Quinlan, J.R.: C4.5: Programs for Machine Learning. Morgan Kaufmann Publishers (1993)
15. Ramshaw, L.A., Marcus, M.P.: Text chunking using transformation-based learning. Proceedings of Third Wordkshop on Very Large Corpora (1995) 82–94
16. van Rijsbergen, C.: Information Retrieval. Buttersworth (1975)
17. Tjong Kim Sang, E.F.: Memory-based shallow parsing. Journal of Machine Learning Research **2** (2002) 559–594

Chunking Using Conditional Random Fields in Korean Texts

Yong-Hun Lee, Mi-Young Kim, and Jong-Hyeok Lee

Div. of Electrical and Computer Engineering POSTECH and AITrc,
San 31, Hyoja-dong, Nam-gu, Pohang, 790-784, R. of Korea
{yhlee95, colorful, jhlee}@postech.ac.kr

Abstract. We present a method of chunking in Korean texts using conditional random fields (CRFs), a recently introduced probabilistic model for labeling and segmenting sequence of data. In agglutinative languages such as Korean and Japanese, a rule-based chunking method is predominantly used for its simplicity and efficiency. A hybrid of a rule-based and machine learning method was also proposed to handle exceptional cases of the rules. In this paper, we present how CRFs can be applied to the task of chunking in Korean texts. Experiments using the STEP 2000 dataset show that the proposed method significantly improves the performance as well as outperforms previous systems.

1 Introduction

Text chunking is a process to identify non-recursive cores of various phrase types without conducting deep parsing of text [3]. Abney first proposed it as an intermediate step toward full parsing [1]. Since Ramshaw and Marcus approached NP chunking using a machine learning method, many researchers have used various machine learning techniques [2,4,5,6,10,11,13,14]. The chunking task was extended to the CoNLL-2000 shared task with standard datasets and evaluation metrics, which is now a standard evaluation task for text chunking [3].

Most previous works with relatively high performance in English used machine learning methods for chunking [4,13]. Machine learning methods are mainly divided into the generative approach and conditional approach. The generative approach relies on generative probabilistic models that assign a joint probability $p(X,Y)$ of paired input sequence and label sequence, X and Y respectively. It provides straightforward understanding of underlying distribution. However, this approach is intractable in most domains without strong independence assumptions that each input element is independent from the other elements in input sequence, and is also difficult to use multiple interacting features and long-range dependencies between input elements. The conditional approach views the chunking task as a sequence of classification problems, and defines a conditional probability $p(Y|X)$ over label sequence given input sequence. A number of conditional models recently have been developed for use. They showed better performance than generative models as they can handle many arbitrary and overlapping features of input sequence [12].

A number of methods are applied to chunking in Korean texts. Unlike English, a rule-based chunking method [7,8] is predominantly used in Korean because of its well-developed function words, which contain information such as grammatical

R. Dale et al. (Eds.): IJCNLP 2005, LNAI 3651, pp. 155 – 164, 2005.

relation, case, tense, modal, etc. Chunking in Korean texts with only simple heuristic rules obtained through observation on the text shows a good performance similar to other machine learning methods [6]. Park et al. proposed a hybrid of rule-based and machine learning method to handle exceptional cases of the rules, to improve the performance of chunking in Korean texts [5,6].

In this paper, we present how CRFs, a recently introduced probabilistic model for labeling and segmenting sequence of data [12], can be applied to the task of chunking in Korean texts. CRFs are undirected graphical models trained to maximize conditional probabilities of label sequence given input sequence. It takes advantage of generative and conditional models. CRFs can include many correlated, overlapping features, and they are trained discriminatively like conditional model. Since CRFs have single exponential model for the conditional probability of entire label sequence given input sequence, they also guarantee to obtain globally optimal label sequence. CRFs successfully have been applied in many NLP problems such as part-of-speech tagging [12], text chunking [13,15] and table extraction from government reports [19].

The rest of this paper is organized as follows. Section 2 gives a simple introduction to CRFs. Section 3 explains how CRFs is applied to the task of chunking in Korean texts. Finally, we present experimental results and draw conclusions.

2 Conditional Random Fields

Conditional Random Fields (CRFs) are conditional probabilistic sequence models first introduced by Lefferty et al [12]. CRFs are undirected graphical models, which can be used to define the joint probability distribution over label sequence given the entire input sequence to be labeled, rather than being directed graphical models such as Maximum Entropy Markov Models (MEMMs) [11]. It relaxes the strong independence assumption of Hidden Markov Models (HMMs), as well as resolves the label bias problem exhibited by MEMMs and other non-generative directed graphical models such as discriminative Markov models [12].

2.1 Fundamentals of CRFs

CRFs may be viewed as an undirected graphical model globally conditioned on input sequence [14]. Let $X=x_1x_2x_3...x_n$ be an input sequence and $Y=y_1y_2y_3...y_n$ a label sequence. In the chunking task, X is associated with a sequence of words and Y is associated with a sequence of chunk types. If we assume that the structure of a graph forms a simple first-order chain, as illustrated in Figure 1, CRFs define the conditional probability of a label sequence Y given an input sequence X by the Hammersley-Clifford theorem [16] as follows:

$$p(Y \mid X) = \frac{1}{Z(X)} \exp\left(\sum_i \sum_k \lambda_k f_k(y_{i-1}, y_i, X, i) \right) \tag{1}$$

where $Z(X)$ is a normalization factor; $f_k(y_{i-1}, y_i, X, i)$ is a feature function at positions i and i-1 in the label sequence; λ_k is a weight associated with feature f_k.

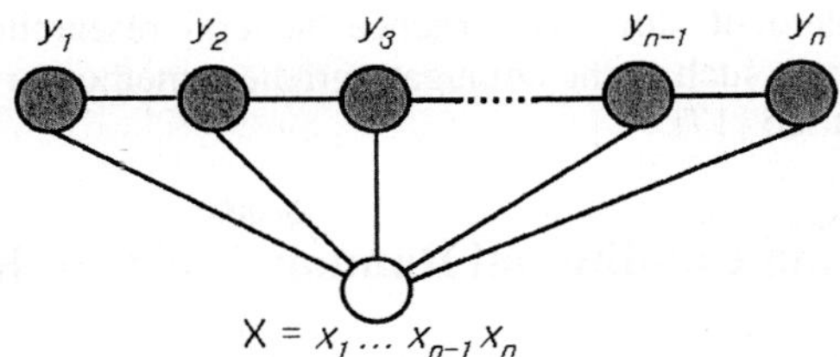

Fig. 1. Graphical structure of chain-structured CRFs

Equitation 1, the general form of a graph structure for modeling sequential data, can be expanded to Equation 2,

$$p(Y \mid X) = \frac{1}{Z(X)} \exp\left(\sum_i \sum_k \lambda_k t_k(y_{i-1}, y_i, X, i) + \sum_i \sum_k \mu_k s_k(y_i, X, i) \right) \quad (2)$$

where $t_k(y_{i-1}, y_i, X, i)$ is a transition feature function of the entire input sequence and the labels at positions i and i-1 in the label sequence; $s_k(y_i, X, i)$ is a state feature function of the label at position i and the observed input sequence; and λ_k and μ_k are parameters to be estimated from training data. The parameters λ_k and μ_k play similar roles to the transition and emission probabilities in HMMs [12]. Therefore, the most probable label sequence for input sequence X is Y^* which maximizes a posterior probability.

$$Y^* = \arg\max_Y P_\lambda(Y \mid X) \quad (3)$$

We can find Y^* with dynamic programming using the Viterbi algorithm.

2.2 Parameter Estimation for CRFs

Assuming the training data $\{(X^{(n)}, Y^{(n)})\}$ are independently and identically distributed, the product of Equation 1 over all training sequences is a likelihood function of the parameter λ. Maximum likelihood training chooses parameter values such that the log-likelihood is maximized [10]. For CRFs, the log-likelihood $L(\lambda)$ is given by

$$\begin{aligned} L(\lambda) &= \sum_n \log P_\lambda(Y^{(n)} \mid X^{(n)}) \\ &= \sum_n \left[\sum_i \sum_k \lambda_k f_k(y_{i-1}^{(n)}, y_i^{(n)}, X^{(n)}, i) - \log Z(X^{(n)}) \right] \end{aligned} \quad (4)$$

It is not possible to analytically determine the parameter values that maximize the log-likelihood. Instead, maximum likelihood parameters must be identified using an iterative technique such as iterative scaling [12] or gradient-based methods [13,14].

Lafferty et al. proposed two iterative scaling algorithms to find parameters for CRFs. However, these methods converge into a global maximum very slowly. To overcome this problem of slow convergence, several researchers adopted modern optimization algorithms such as the conjugate-gradient method or the limited-memory BFGS(L-BFGS) method [17].

3 Chunking Using Conditional Random Fields in Korean Texts

We now describe how CRFs are applied to the task of chunking in Korean texts. Firstly, we explore characteristics and chunk types of Korean. Then we explain the features for the model of chunking in Korean texts using CRFs. The ultimate goal of a chunker is to output appropriate chunk tags of a sequence of words with part-of-speech tags.

3.1 Characteristics of Korean

Korean is an agglutinative language, in which a word unit (called an eojeol) is a composition of a content word and function word(s). Function words – postpositions and endings – give much information such as grammatical relation, case, tense, modal, etc. Well-developed function words in Korean help with chunking, especially NP and VP chunking. For example, when the part-of-speech of current word is one of determiner, pronoun and noun, the following seven rules for NP chunking in Table 1 can find most NP chunks in text, with about 89% accuracy [6].

Table 1. Rules for NP chunking in Korean texts

No	Previous eojeol	Chunk tag of current word
1	determiner	I-NP
2	pronoun	I-NP
3	noun	I-NP
4	noun + possessive postposition	I-NP
5	noun + relative postfix	I-NP
6	adjective + relative ending	I-NP
7	others	B-NP

For this reason, boundaries of chunks are easily found in Korean, compared to other languages such as English or Chinese. This is why a rule-based chunking method is predominantly used. However, with sophisticated rules, the rule-based chunking method has limitations when handling exceptional cases. Park et al. proposed a hybrid of the rule-based and the machine learning method to resolve this problem [5,6]. Many recent machine learning techniques can capture hidden characteristics for classification. Despite its simplicity and efficiency, the rule-based method has recently been outdone by the machine learning method in various classification problems.

3.2 Chunk Types of Korean

Abney was the first to use the term 'chunk' to represent a non-recursive core of an intra-clausal constituent, extending from the beginning of constituent to its head. In

Korean, there are four basic phrases: noun phrase (NP), verb phrase (VP), adverb phrase (ADVP), and independent phrase (IP) [6]. As function words such as postposition or ending are well-developed, the number of chunk types is small compared to other languages such as English or Chinese. Table 2 lists the Korean chunk types, a simple explanation and examples of each chunk type.

Table 2. The Korean chunk types

No	Category	Explanation	Example
1	NP	Noun Phrase	**[NP저 아름다운 여인을]** [보세요]. ([the beautiful woman] [look])
2	VP	Verb Phrase	[지붕이] [몽땅] **[VP내려앉아 있다]**. ([the roof] [completely] [has fallen in])
3	ADVP	Adverb Phrase	[새가] **[ADVP 매우 높이]** [날고 있다]. ([a bird] [very high] [is flying])
4	IP	Independent Phrase	**[IP 와]**, [이거] [정말] [맛있다]. ([wow] [this] [very] [is delicious])

Like the CoNLL-2000 dataset, we use three types of chunk border tags, indicating whether a word is outside a chunk (O), starts a chunk (B), or continues a chunk (I). Each chunk type XP has two border tags: B-XP and I-XP. XP should be one of NP, VP, ADVP and IP. There exist nine chunk tags in Korean.

3.3 Feature Set of CRFs

One advantage of CRFs is that they can use many arbitrary, overlapping features. So we take advantage of all context information of a current word. We use words, part-of-speech tags of context and combinations of part-of-speech tags to determine the chunk tag of the current word,. The window size of context is 5; from left two words to right two words. Table 3 summarizes the feature set for chunking in Korean texts.

Table 3. Feature set for the chunking in Korean texts

Word	POS tag	Bi-gram of tags	Tri-gram of tags
$w_{i-2}= w$ $w_{i-1}= w$ $w_i= w$ $w_{i+1}= w$ $w_{i+2}= w$	$t_{i-2}= t$ $t_{i-1}= t$ $t_i= t$ $t_{i+1}= t$ $t_{i+2}= t$	$t_{i-2}= t', t_{i-1}= t$ $t_{i-1}= t', t_i= t$ $t_i= t', t_{i+1}= t$ $t_{i+1}= t', t_{i+2}= t$	$t_{i-2}= t'', t_{i-1}= t', t_i= t$ $t_{i-1}= t'', t_i= t', t_{i+1}= t$ $t_i= t'', t_{i+1}= t', t_{i+2}= t$

4 Experiments

In this section, we present experimental results of chunking using CRFs in Korean texts and compare the performance with previous systems of Park et al [6]. To make a fare comparison, we use the same dataset as Park et al [6].

4.1 Data Preparation

For evaluation of our proposed method, we use the STEP 2000 Korean chunking dataset (STEP 2000 dataset)[1], which is converted from the parsed KAIST Corpus [9].

Table 4. Simple statistics on the STEP 2000 dataset

Information	Value
POS tags	52
Words	321,328
Sentences	12,092
Chunk tags	9
Chunks	112,658

그	npp	B-NP	his
의	jcm	I-NP	postposition: possessive
책	ncn	I-NP	book
은	jxt	I-NP	postposition: topic
파기	ncpa	B-VP	destructed
되	xsv	I-VP	be
었	ep	I-VP	pre-final ending : past
다	ef	I-VP	ending : declarative
.	sf	O	

Fig. 2. An example of the STEP 2000 dataset

The STEP 2000 dataset consists of 12,092 sentences. We divide this corpus into training data and test data. Training data has 10,883 sentences and test data has 1,209 sentences, 90% and 10% respectively. Table 4 summarizes characteristics of the STEP 2000 dataset. Figure 2 shows an example sentence of the STEP 2000 data-set and its format is equal to that of CoNLL-2000 dataset. Each line is composed of a word, its part-of-speech (POS) tag and a chunk tag.

4.2 Evaluation Metric

The standard evaluation metrics for chunking performance are precision, recall and F-score ($F_{\beta=1}$) [3]. F-score is used for comparisons with other reported results. Each equation is defined as follows.

---

[1] STEP is an abbreviation of *Software Technology Enhancement Program*. We download this dataset from http://bi.snu.ac.kr/~sbpark/Step2000. If you want to know the part-of-speech tags used in the STEP 2000 dataset, you can reference KAIST tagset [9].

$$precision = \frac{\#\ of\ \ correct\ \ chunks}{\#\ of\ \ chunks\ \ in\ output} \quad (5)$$

$$recall = \frac{\#\ of\ \ correct\ \ chunks}{\#\ of\ \ chunks\ \ in\ test\ \ data} \quad (6)$$

$$F_{\beta=1} = \frac{2 \times recall\ \times precision}{recall\ + precision} \quad (7)$$

4.3 Experimental Results

Experiments were performed with C++ implementation of CRFs (FlexCRFs) on Linux with 2.4 GHz Pentium IV dual processors and 2.0Gbyte of main memory [18]. We use L-BFGS to train the parameters and use a Gaussian prior regularization in order to avoid overfitting [20].

Table 5. The performance of proposed method

Chunk tag	Precision	Recall	F-score
NP	94.23	94.30	94.27
VP	96.71	96.28	96.49
ADVP	96.90	97.02	96.96
IP	99.53	99.07	99.30
All	95.42	95.31	95.36

Total number of CRF features is 83,264. As shown in Table 5, the performances of most chunk type are 96~100%, very high performance. However, the performance of NP chunk type is lowest, 94.27% because the border of NP chunk type is very ambiguous in case of consecutive nouns. Using more features such as previous chunk tag should be able to improve the performance of NP chunk type.

Table 6. The experimental results of various chunking methods[2]

	HMMs	DT	MBL	Rule	SVMs	Hybrid	CRFs
Precision	73.75	92.29	91.41	91.28	93.63	94.47	95.42
Recall	76.06	90.45	91.43	92.47	91.48	93.96	95.31
F-score	74.89	91.36	91.38	91.87	92.54	94.21	95.36

Park et al. reported the performance of various chunking methods [6]. We add the experimental results of the chunking methods using HMMs-bigram and CRFs. In Table 6, F-score of chunking using CRFs in Korean texts is 97.19%, the highest

[2] Performances of all methods except HMMs and CRFs are cited from the experiment of Park et al [6]. They also use the STEP 2000 dataset and similar feature set. Therefore, the comparison of performance is reasonable.

performance of all. It significantly outperforms all others, including machine learning methods, rule-based methods and hybrid methods. It is because CRFs have a global optimum solution hence overcoming the label bias problem. They also can use many arbitrary, overlapping features.

Figure 3 shows the performance curve on the same test set in terms of the precision, recall and F-score with respect to the size of training data. In this figure, we can see that the performance slowly increases in proportion to the size of training data.

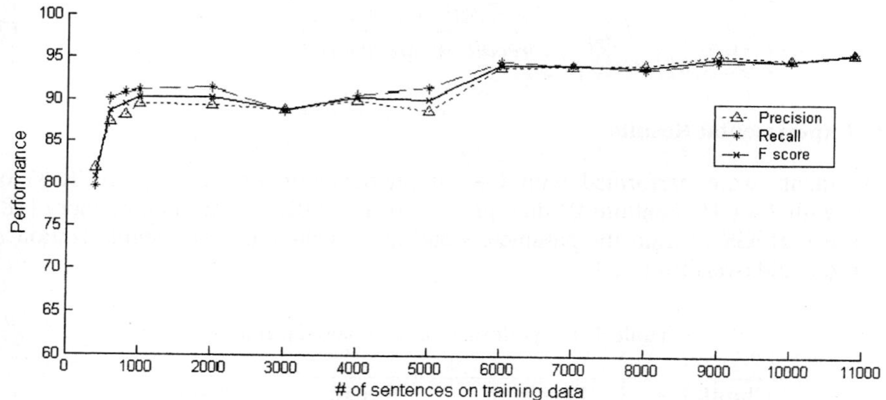

Fig. 3. The performance curve respect to the size of training data

In the experiment, we can see that CRFs can help improve the performance of chunking in Korean texts. CRFs have many promising properties except for the slow convergence speed compared to other models. In the next experiment, we have tried to analyze the importance of each feature and to make an additional experiment with various window sizes and any other useful features.

5 Conclusion

In this paper, we proposed a chunking method for Korean texts using CRFs. We observed that the proposed method outperforms other approaches. Experiments on the STEP 2000 dataset showed that the proposed method yields an F-score of 95.36%. This performance is 2.82% higher than that of SVMs and 1.15% higher than that of the hybrid method. CRFs use a number of correlated features and overcome the label bias problem. We obtained a very high performance using only small features. Thus, if we use more features such as semantic information or collocation, we can obtain a better performance.

From the experiment, we know that the proposed method using CRFs can significantly improve the performance of chunking in Korean texts. CRFs are a good framework for labeling an input sequence. In our future work, we will investigate how CRFs can be applied to other NLP problems: parsing, semantic analysis and spam filtering. Finally, we hope that this work can contribute to the body of research in this field.

Acknowledgements

This work was supported by the KOSEF through the Advanced Information Technology Research Center (AITrc) and by the BK21 Project.

References

1. S. Abney: Parsing by chunks. In R. Berwick, S. Abney, and C. Tenny, editors, Principle-based Parsing. Kluwer Academic Publishers (1991).
2. L. A. Ramashaw and M. P. Marcus: Text chunking using transformation-based learning. Proceedings of the Thired ACL Workshop on Very Large Corpora (1995).
3. E. F. Tjong Kim Sang and S. Buchholz: Introduction to the CoNLL-2000 shared task: Chunking. Proceedings of CoNLL-2000 (2000) 127-132.
4. T. Kudo and Y. Matsumoto: Chunking with support vector machines. Proceedings of NAACL2001, ACL (2001).
5. Park, S.-B. and Zhang, B.-T.: Combining a Rule-based Method and a *k*-NN for Chunking Korean Text. Proceedings of the 19th International Conference on Computer Processing of Oriental Languages (2001) 225-230.
6. Park, S.-B. and Zhang, B.-T.: Text Chunking by Combining Hand-Crafted Rules and Memory-Based Learning. Proceedings of the 41st Annual Meeting of the Association for Computational Linguistics (2003) 497-504.
7. H.-P. Shin: Maximally Efficient Syntactic Parsing with Minimal Resources. Proceedings of the Conference on Hangul and Korean Language Information Processing (1999) 242-244.
8. M.-Y. Kim, S.-J. Kang and J.-H. Lee: Dependency Parsing by Chunks. Proceedings of the 27th KISS Spring Conference (1999) 327-329.
9. J.-T. Yoon and K.-S. Choi: Study on KAIST Corpus, CS-TR-99-139, KAIST CS (1999).
10. A. L. Berger, S. A. Della Pietra and V. J. Della Pietra: A maximum entropy approach to natural language processing. Computational Linguistics, 22(1) (1996) 39-71.
11. Andrew McCallum, D. Freitag and F. Pereira: Maximum entropy Markov models for information extraction and segmentation. Proceedings of International Conference on Machine Learning , Stanford, California (2000) 591-598.
12. John Lafferty, Andrew McCallum and Fernando Pereira: Conditional Random Fields: Probabilistic Models for Segmenting and Labeling Sequence Data. Proceedings of the 18th International Conference on Machine Learning (2001) 282-289.
13. Fei Sha and Fernando Pereira: Shallow Parsing with Conditional Random Fields. Proceedings of Human Language Technology-NAACL, Edmonton, Canada (2003).
14. Hanna Wallach: Efficient Training of Conditional Random Fields. Thesis. Master of Science School of Cognitive Science, Division of Informatics. University of Edinburgh (2002).
15. Yongmei Tan, Tianshun Yao, Qing Chen and Jingbo Zhu: Applying Conditional Random Fields to Chinese Shallow Parsing. The 6th International Conference on Intelligent Text Processing and Computational Linguistics (CICLing-2005) . LNCS, Vol.3406, Springer, Mexico City, Mexico (2005) 167-176.
16. J. Hammersley and P. Clifford. Markov fields on finite graphs and lattices. Unpublished manuscript (1971).

17. D. C. Liu and J. Nocedal: On the limited memory bfgs method for large-scale optimization. Mathematic Programming, 45 (1989) 503-528.
18. Hieu Xuan Phan and Minh Le Nguyen: FlexCRFs: A Flexible Conditional Random Fields Toolkit. http:://www.jaist.ac.jp/~hieuxuan/flexcrfs/flexcrfs.html (2004).
19. D. Pinto, A. McCallum, X. Wei and W. B. Croft: Table extraction using conditional random fields. Proceedings of the ACM SIGIR (2003).
20. S. F. Chen and R. Rosenfeld: A Gaussian prior for smoothing maximum entropy models. Technical Report CMU-CS-99-108, Carnegie Mellon University (1999).

High Efficiency Realization for a Wide-Coverage Unification Grammar*

John Carroll[1] and Stephan Oepen[2]

[1] University of Sussex
[2] University of Oslo and Stanford University

Abstract. We give a detailed account of an algorithm for efficient tactical generation from underspecified logical-form semantics, using a wide-coverage grammar and a corpus of real-world target utterances. Some earlier claims about chart realization are critically reviewed and corrected in the light of a series of practical experiments. As well as a set of algorithmic refinements, we present two novel techniques: the integration of subsumption-based local ambiguity factoring, and a procedure to selectively unpack the generation forest according to a probability distribution given by a conditional, discriminative model.

1 Introduction

A number of wide-coverage precise bi-directional NL grammars have been developed over the past few years. One example is the LinGO English Resource Grammar (ERG) [1], couched in the HPSG framework. Other grammars of similar size and coverage also exist, notable examples using the LFG and the CCG formalisms [2,3]. These grammars are used for generation from logical form input (also termed tactical generation or realization) in circumscribed domains, as part of applications such as spoken dialog systems [4] and machine translation [5].

Grammars like the ERG are lexicalist, in that the majority of information is encoded in lexical entries (or lexical rules) as opposed to being represented in constructions (i.e. rules operating on phrases). The semantic input to the generator for such grammars, often, is a bag of lexical predicates with semantic relationships captured by appropriate instantiation of variables associated with predicates and their semantic roles. For these sorts of grammars and 'flat' semantic inputs, lexically-driven approaches to realization – such as Shake-and-Bake [6], bag generation from logical form [7], chart generation [8], and constraint-based generation [9] – are highly suitable. Alternative approaches based on semantic head-driven generation and more recent variants [10,11] would work less well for lexicalist grammars since these approaches assume a hierarchically structured input logical form.

Similarly to parsing with large scale grammars, realization can be computationally expensive. In his presentation of chart generation, Kay [8] describes one source of potential inefficiency and proposes an approach for tackling it. However, Kay does not report on a verification of his approach with an actual grammar. Carroll et al. [12]

* Dan Flickinger and Ann Copestake contributed a lot to the work described in this paper. We also thank Berthold Crysmann, Jan Tore Lønning and Bob Moore for useful discussions. Funding is from the projects COGENT (UK EPSRC) and LOGON (Norwegian Research Council).

R. Dale et al. (Eds.): IJCNLP 2005, LNAI 3651, pp. 165–176, 2005.

$$\langle h_1, \\ \{ h_1\text{:proposition\_m}(h_2),\ h_3\text{:\_run\_v}(e_4, x_5),\ h_3\text{:past}(e_4), \\ h_6\text{:\_the\_q}(x_5, h_7, h_8),\ h_9\text{:\_athlete\_n}(x_5),\ h_9\text{:\_young\_a}(x_5),\ h_9\text{:\_polish\_a}(x_5) \}, \\ \{ h_2 =_q h_3,\ h_8 =_q h_9 \} \rangle$$

Fig. 1. Simplified MRS for an utterance like *the young Polish athlete ran* (and variants). Elements from the bag of EPs are linked through both scopal and 'standard' logical variables.

present a practical evaluation of chart generation efficiency with a large-scale HPSG grammar, and describe a different approach to the problem which becomes necessary when using a wide-coverage grammar. White [3] identifies further inefficiencies, and describes and evaluates strategies for addressing them, albeit using what appears to be a somewhat task-specific rather than genuine wide-coverage grammar. In this paper, we revisit this previous work and present new, improved algorithms for efficient chart generation; taken together these result in (i) practical performance that improves over a previous implementation by two orders of magnitude, and (ii) throughput that is near linear in the size of the input semantics.

In Section 2, we give an overview of the grammar and the semantic formalism we use, recap the basic chart generation procedure, and discuss the various sources of potential inefficiency in the basic approach. We then describe the algorithmic improvements we have made to tackle these problems (Section 3), and conclude with the results of evaluating these improvements (Section 4).

2 Background

2.1 Minimal Recursion Semantics and the LinGO ERG

Minimal Recursion Semantics (MRS) [13] is a popular member of a family of flat, underspecified, event-based (neo-Davidsonian) frameworks for computational semantics that have been in wide use since the mid-1990s. MRS allows both underspecification of scope relations and generalization over classes of predicates (e.g. two-place temporal relations corresponding to distinct lexical prepositions: English *in May* vs. *on Monday*, say), which renders it an attractive input representation for tactical generation. While an in-depth introduction to MRS is beyond the scope of this paper, Figure 1 shows an example semantics that we will use in the following sections. The truth-conditional core is captured as a flat multi-set (or 'bag') of *elementary predications* (EPs), combined with generalized quantifiers and designated *handle* variables to account for scopal relations. The bag of EPs is complemented by the handle of the top-scoping EP (h_1 in our example) and a set of 'handle constraints' recording restrictions on scope relations in terms of dominance relations.

The LinGO ERG [1] is a general-purpose, open-source HPSG implementation with fairly comprehensive lexical and grammatical coverage over a variety of domains and genres. The grammar has been deployed for diverse NLP tasks, including machine translation of spoken and edited language, email auto response, consumer opinion tracking (from newsgroup data), and some question answering work.[1] The ERG uses MRS

[1] See `http://www.delph-in.net/erg/` for background information on the ERG.

as its meaning representation layer, and the grammar distribution includes treebanked versions of several reference corpora – providing disambiguated and hand-inspected 'gold' standard MRS formulae for each input utterance – of which we chose one of the more complex sets for our empirical investigations of realization performance using the ERG (see Section 4 below).

2.2 The Basic Procedure

Briefly, the basic chart generation procedure works as follows. A preprocessing phase indexes lexical entries, lexical rules and grammar rules by the semantics they contain. In order to find the lexical entries with which to initialize the chart, the input semantics is checked against the indexed lexicon. When a lexical entry is retrieved, the variable positions in its relations are instantiated in one-to-one correspondence with the variables in the input semantics (a process we term Skolemization, in loose analogy to the more general technique in theorem proving; see Section 3.1 below). For instance, for the MRS in Figure 1, the lookup process would retrieve one or more instantiated lexical entries for *run* containing h_3:_run_v(e_4, x_5). Lexical and morphological rules are applied to the instantiated lexical entries. If the lexical rules introduce relations, their application is only allowed if these relations correspond to parts of the input semantics (h_3:past(e_4), say, in our example). We treat a number of special cases (lexical items containing more than one relation, grammar rules which introduce relations, and semantically vacuous lexical items) in the same way as Carroll et al. [12].

After initializing the chart (with inactive edges), active edges are created from inactive ones by instantiating the head daughter of a rule; the resulting edges are then combined with other inactive edges. Chart generation is very similar to chart parsing, but what an edge covers is defined in terms of semantics, rather than orthography. Each edge is associated with the set of relations it covers. Before combining two edges a check is made to ensure that edges do not overlap: i.e. that they do not cover the same relation(s). The goal is to find all possible inactive edges covering the full input MRS.

2.3 Complexity

The worst-case time complexity of chart generation is exponential (even though chart parsing is polynomial). The main reason for this is that in theory a grammar could allow any pair of edges to combine (subject to the restriction described above that the edges cover non-overlapping bags of EPs). For an input semantics containing n EPs, and assuming each EP retrieves a single lexical item, there could in the worst case be $O(2^n)$ edges, each covering a different subset of the input semantics. Although in the general case we cannot improve the complexity, we can make the processing steps involved cheaper, for instance efficiently checking whether two edges are candidates for being combined (see Section 3.1 below). We can also minimize the number of edges covering each subset of EPs by 'packing' locally equivalent edges (Section 3.2).

A particular, identifiable source of complexity is that, as Kay [8] notes, when a word has more than one intersective modifier an indefinite number of its modifiers may be applied. For instance, when generating from the MRS in Figure 1, edges corresponding to the partial realizations *athlete*, *young athlete*, *Polish athlete*, and *young Polish athlete* will all be constructed. Even if a grammar constrains modifiers so there is only one valid ordering, or the generator is able to pack equivalent edges covering the same EPs, the number of edges built will still be 2^n, because all possible complete and incomplete phrases will be built. Using the example MRS, ultimately useless edges such as *the young athlete ran* (omitting *Polish*) will be created.

Kay proposes an approach to this problem in which edges are checked before they are created to see if they would 'seal off' access to a semantic index (x_5 in this case) for which there is still an unincorporated modifier. Although individual sets of modifiers still result in exponential numbers of edges, the exponentiality is prevented from propagating further. However, Carroll et al. [12] argue that this check works only in limited circumstances, since for example in (1) the grammar must allow the index for *ran* to be available all the way up the tree to *How*, and simultaneously also make available the indexes for *newspapers*, *say*, and *athlete* at appropriate points so these words could be modified[2].

(1) *How quickly did the newspapers say the athlete ran?*

Carroll et al. describe an alternative technique which adjoins intersective modifiers into edges in a second phase, after all possible edges that do not involve intersective modification have been constructed by chart generation. This overcomes the multiple index problem described above and reduces the worst-case complexity of intersective modification in the chart generation phase to polynomial, but unfortunately the subsequent phase which attempts to adjoin sets of modifiers into partial realizations is still exponential. We describe below (Section 3.3) a related technique which delays processing of intersective modifiers by inserting them into the generation forest, taking advantage of dynamic programming to reduce the complexity of the second phase. We also present a different approach which filters out edges based on accessibility of *sets* of semantic indices (Section 3.4), which covers a wider variety of cases than just intersective modification, and in practice is even more efficient.

Exponential numbers of edges imply exponential numbers of realizations. For an application task we would usually want only one (the most natural or fluent) realization, or a fixed small number of good realizations that the application could then itself select from. In Section 3.5 we present an efficient algorithm for selectively unpacking the generation forest to produce the n-best realizations according to a statistical model.

3 Efficient Wide-Coverage Realization

3.1 Relating Chart Edges and Semantic Components

Once lexical lookup is complete and up until a final, post-generation comparison of results to the input MRS, the core phases of our generator exclusively operate on typed feature structures (which are associated to chart edges). For efficiency reasons, our algorithm avoids any complex operations on the original logical-form input MRS. In order to best guide the search from the input semantics, however, we employ two techniques that relate components of the logical form to corresponding sub-structures in the feature

[2] White [3] describes an approach to dealing with intersective modifiers which requires the grammarian to write a collection of rules that 'chunk' the input semantics into separate modifier groups which are processed separately; this involves extra manual work, and also appears to suffer from the same multiple index problem.

structure (FS) universe: (i) Skolemization of variables and (ii) indexing by EP coverage. Of these, only the latter we find commonly discussed in the literature, but we expect some equivalent of making variables ground to be present in most implementations.

As part of the process of looking up lexical items and grammar rules introducing semantics in order to initialize the generator chart, all FS correspondences to logical variables from the input MRS are made 'ground' by specializing the relevant sub-structure with Skolem constants uniquely reflecting the underlying variable, for example adding constraints like [SKOLEM *"x5"*] for all occurrences of x_5 from our example MRS. Skolemization, thus, assumes that distinct variables from the input MRS, where supplied, cannot become co-referential during generation. Enforcing variable identity at the FS level makes sure that composition (by means of FS unification) during rule applications is compatible to the input semantics. In addition, it enables efficient pre-unification filtering (see 'quick-check' below), and is a prerequisite for our index accessibility test described in Section 3.4 below.

In chart *parsing*, edges are stored into and retrieved from the chart data structure on the basis of their string *start* and *end* positions. This ensures that the parser will only retrieve pairs of chart edges that cover compatible segments of the input string (i.e. that are adjacent with respect to string position). In chart *generation*, Kay [8] proposed indexing the chart on the basis of logical variables, where each variable denotes an individual entity in the input semantics, and making the edge coverage compatibility check a filter. Edge coverage (with respect to the EPs in the input semantics) would be encoded as a bit vector, and for a pair of edges to be combined their corresponding bit vectors would have to be disjoint.

We implement Kay's edge coverage approach, using it not only when combining active and inactive edges, but also for two further tasks in our approach to realization:

- in the second phase of chart generation to determine which intersective modifier(s) can be adjoined into a partially incomplete subtree; and
- as part of the test for whether one edge subsumes another, for local ambiguity factoring (see Section 3.2 below)[3].

In our testing with the LinGO ERG, many hundreds or thousands of edges may be produced for non-trivial input semantics, but there are only a relatively small number of logical variables. Indexing edges on these variables involves bookkeeping that turns out not to be worthwhile in practice; logical bit vector operations on edge coverage take negligible time, and these serve to filter out the majority of edge combinations with incompatible indices. The remainder are filtered out efficiently before unification is attempted by a check on which rules can dominate which others, and the *quick-check*, as developed for unification-based parsing [14]. For the quick-check, it turns out that the same set of feature paths that most frequently lead to unification failure in parsing also work well in generation.

---

[3] We therefore have four operations on bit vectors representing EP coverage ($\mathcal{C}$) in chart edges:

- concatenation of edges e_1 and $e_2 \rightarrow e_3$: $\mathcal{C}(e_3) = \text{OR}(\mathcal{C}(e_1), \mathcal{C}(e_2))$;
- can edges e_1 and e_2 combine? $\text{AND}(\mathcal{C}(e_1), \mathcal{C}(e_2)) = 0$;
- do edges e_1 and e_2 cover the same EPs? $\mathcal{C}(e_1) = \mathcal{C}(e_2)$;
- do edges $e_1, \ldots, e_n$ cover all input EPs? $\text{NOT}(\text{OR}(\mathcal{C}(e_1), \ldots, \mathcal{C}(e_n)) = 0$.

3.2 Local Ambiguity Factoring

In chart parsing with context free grammars, the parse forest (a compact representation of the full set of parses) can only be computed in polynomial time if sub-analyses dominated by the same non-terminal and covering the same segment of the input string are 'packed', or factored into a single unitary representation [15]. Similar benefits accrue for unification grammars without a context free backbone such as the LinGO ERG, if the category equality test is replaced by feature structure subsumption [16][4]; also, feature structures representing the derivation history need to be *restricted* out when applying a rule [17]. The technique can be applied to chart realization if the input span is expressed as coverage of the input semantics. For example, with the input of Figure 1, the two phrases in (2) below would have equivalent feature structures, and we pack the one found second into the one found first, which then acts as the representative edge for all subsequent processing.

(2) *young Polish athlete* | *Polish young athlete*

We have found that packing is crucial to efficiency: realization time is improved by more than an order of magnitude for inputs with more than 500 realizations (see Section 4). Changing packing to operate with respect just to feature structure equality rather than subsumption degrades throughput significantly, resulting in worse overall performance than with packing disabled completely: in other words, equivalence-only packing fails to recoup the cost of the feature structure comparisons involved.

A further technique we use is to postpone the creation of feature structures for active edges until they are actually required for a unification operation, since many end up as dead ends. Oepen and Carroll [18] do a similar thing in their 'hyper-active' parsing strategy, for the same reason.

3.3 Delayed Modifier Insertion

As discussed in Section 2.3, Carroll et al. [12] adjoin intersective modifiers into each partial tree extracted from the forest; their algorithm searches for partitions of modifier phrases to adjoin, and tries all combinations. This process adds an exponential (in the number of modifiers) factor to the complexity of extracting each partial realization.

This is obviously unsatisfactory, and in practice is slow for larger problems when there are many possible modifiers. We have devised a better approach which delays processing of intersective modifiers by inserting them into the generation forest at appropriate locations before the forest is unpacked. By doing this, we take advantage of the dynamic programming-based procedure for unpacking the forest to reduce the complexity of the second phase. The procedure is even more efficient if realizations are unpacked selectively (section 3.5).

3.4 Index Accessibility Filtering

Kay's original proposal for dealing efficiently with modifiers founders because more than one semantic index may need to be accessible at any one time (leading to the

[4] Using subsumption-based packing means that the parse forest may represent some globally inconsistent analyses, so these must be filtered out when the forest is unpacked.

alternative solutions of modifier adjunction, and of chunking the input semantics – see Sections 2.3 and 3.3).

However, it turns out that Kay's proposal can form the basis of a more generally applicable approach to the problem. We assume that we have available an operation collect-semantic-vars() that traverses a feature structure and returns the set of semantic indices that it makes available[5]. We store in each chart edge two sets: one of semantic variables in the feature structure that are *accessible* (that is, they are present in the feature structure and could potentially be picked by another edge when it is combined with this one), and a second set of *inaccessible* semantic variables (ones that were once accessible but no longer are). Then,

- when an active edge is combined with an inactive edge, the accessible sets and inaccessible sets in the resulting edge are the union of the corresponding sets in the original edges;
- when an inactive edge is created, its accessible set is computed to be the semantic indices available in its feature structure, and the variables that used to be accessible but are no longer in the accessible set are added to its inaccessible set, i.e.

```
tmp ← edge.accessible;
edge.accessible ← collect-semantic-vars(edge.fs)
edge.inaccessible ← (tmp \ edge.accessible) ∪ edge.inaccessible
```

- immediately after creating an inactive edge, each EP in the input semantics that the edge does not (yet) cover is inspected, and if the EP's index is in the edge's inaccessible set then the edge is discarded (since there is no way in the future that the EP could be integrated with any extension of the edge's semantics).

A nice property of this new technique is that it applies more widely than to just intersective modification: for instance, if the input semantics were to indicate that a phrase should be negated, no edges would be created that extended that phrase without the negation being present. Section 4 shows this technique results in dramatic improvements in realization efficiency.

3.5 Selective Unpacking

The selective unpacking procedure outlined in this section allows us to extract a small set of n-best realizations from the generation forest at minimal cost. The global rank order is determined by a conditional Maximum Entropy (ME) model – essentially an adaptation of recent HPSG parse selection work to the realization ranking task [19]. We use a similar set of features to Toutanova and Manning [20], but our procedure differs from theirs in that it applies the stochastic model *before unpacking*, in a guided search through the generation forest. Thus, we avoid enumerating all candidate realizations. Unlike Malouf and van Noord [21], on the other hand, we avoid an approximative beam search during forest creation and guarantee to produce exactly the n-best realizations (according to the ME model). Further looking at related parse selection work, our procedure is probably most similar to those of Geman and Johnson [22] and Miyao and

[5] Implementing collect-semantic-vars() can be efficient: searching for Skolem constants throughout the full structure, it does a similar amount of computation as a single unification.

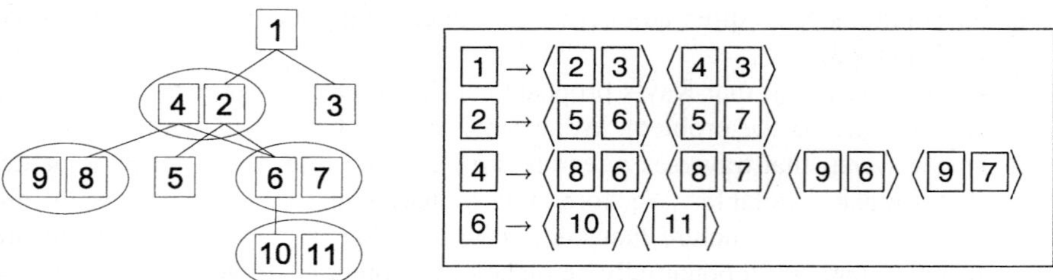

Fig. 2. Sample generator forest and sub-node decompositions: ovals in the forest (on the left) indicate packing of edges under subsumption, i.e. edges $\boxed{4}$, $\boxed{7}$, $\boxed{9}$, and $\boxed{11}$ are *not* in the generator chart proper. During unpacking, there will be multiple ways of instantiating a chart edge, each obtained from cross-multiplying alternate daughter sequences locally. The elements of this cross-product we call *decomposition*, and they are pivotal points both for stochastic scoring and dynamic programming in selective unpacking. The table on the right shows all non-leaf decompositions for our example generator forest: given two ways of decomposing $\boxed{6}$, there will be three candidate ways of instantiating $\boxed{2}$ and six for $\boxed{4}$, respectively, for a total of nine full trees.

Tsujii [23], but neither provide a detailed discussion of the dependencies between locality of ME features and the complexity of the read-out procedure from a packed forest.

Two key notions in our selective unpacking procedure are the concepts of (i) *decomposing* an edge locally into candidate ways of instantiating it and of (ii) nested contexts of 'horizontal' search for ranked *hypotheses* (i.e. uninstantiated edges) about candidate subtrees. See Figure 2 for examples of edge decomposition, but note that the 'depth' of each local cross-product needs to correspond to the maximum required context size of ME features; for ease of exposition, our examples assume a context size of no more than depth one (but the algorithm straightforwardly generalizes to larger contexts). Given one decomposition – i.e. a vector of candidate daughters to a token construction – there can be multiple ways of instantiating each daughter: a parallel index vector $\langle i_0 \ \ldots \ i_n \rangle$ serves to keep track of 'vertical' search among daughter hypotheses, where each index i_j denotes the i-th instantiation (hypothesis) of the daughter at position j. Hypotheses are associated with ME scores and ordered within each nested context by means of a local agenda (stored in the original representative edge, for convenience). Given the additive nature of ME scores on complete derivations, it can be guaranteed that larger derivations including an edge e as a sub-constituent on the *fringe* of their local context of optimization will use the best instantiation of e in their own best instantiation. The second-best larger instantiation, in turn, will be obtained from moving to the second-best hypothesis for *one* of the elements in the (right-hand side of the) decomposition. Therefore, nested local optimizations result in a top-down, exact n-best search through the generation forest, and matching the 'depth' of local decompositions to the maximum required ME feature context effectively prevents exhaustive cross-multiplication of packed nodes.

The main function hypothesize-edge() in Figure 3 controls both the 'horizontal' and 'vertical' search, initializing the set of decompositions and pushing initial hypotheses onto the local agenda when called on an edge for the first time (lines 11 – 17). Furthermore, the procedure retrieves the current next-best hypothesis from the agenda (line 18), generates new hypotheses by advancing daughter indices (while skipping over

```
1  procedure selectively-unpack-edge(edge , n) ≡
2    results ← ⟨ ⟩; i ← 0;
3    do
4      hypothesis ← hypothesize-edge(edge , i); i ← i + 1;
5      if (new ← instantiate-hypothesis(hypothesis)) then
6        n ← n − 1 results ← results ⊕ ⟨new⟩;
7    while (hypothesis and n ≥ 1)
8    return results;

9  procedure hypothesize-edge(edge , i) ≡
10   if (edge.hypotheses[i]) return edge.hypotheses[i];
11   if (i = 0) then
12     for each (decomposition in decompose-edge(edge)) do
13       daughters ← ⟨ ⟩; indices ← ⟨ ⟩
14       for each (edge in decomposition.rhs) do
15         daughters ← daughters ⊕ ⟨hypothesize-edge(edge, 0)⟩;
16         indices ← indices ⊕ ⟨0⟩;
17       new-hypothesis(edge, decomposition, daughters, indices);
18   if (hypothesis ← edge.agenda.pop()) then
19     for each (indices in advance-indices(hypothesis.indices)) do
20       if (indices ∈ edge.indices) then continue
21       daughters ← ⟨ ⟩;
22       for each (edge in hypothesis.decomposition.rhs) each (i in indices) do
23         daughter ← hypothesize-edge(edge, i);
24         if (not daughter) then
25           daughters ← ⟨ ⟩; break
26         daughters ← daughters ⊕ ⟨daughter⟩;
27       if (daughters) then new-hypothesis(edge, decomposition, daughters, indices)
28     edge.hypotheses[i] ← hypothesis;
29     return hypothesis;

30 procedure new-hypothesis(edge , decomposition , daughters , indices) ≡
31   hypothesis ← new hypothesis(decomposition, daughters, indices);
32   edge.agenda.insert(score-hypothesis(hypothesis), hypothesis);
33   edge.indices ← edge.indices ∩ {indices};
```

Fig. 3. Selective unpacking procedure, enumerating the *n* best realizations for a top-level result *edge* from the generation forest. An auxiliary function decompose-edge() performs local cross-multiplication as shown in the examples in Figure 2. Another utility function not shown in pseudo-code is advance-indices(), another 'driver' routine searching for alternate instantiations of daughter edges, e.g. advance-indices(⟨0 2 1⟩) → {⟨1 2 1⟩ ⟨0 3 1⟩ ⟨0 2 2⟩}. Finally, instantiate-hypothesis() is the function that actually builds result trees, replaying the unifications of constructions from the grammar (as identified by chart edges) with the feature structures of daughter constituents.

configurations seen earlier) and calling itself recursively for each new index (lines 19 – 27), and, finally, arranges for the resulting hypothesis to be cached for later invocations on the same *edge* and *i* values (line 28). Note that we only invoke instantiate-hypothesis() on complete, top-level hypotheses, as the ME features of Toutanova and Manning [20] can actually be evaluated *prior* to building each full feature structure. However, the procedure could be adapted to perform instantiation of sub-hypotheses within each local search, should additional features require it. For better efficiency, our instantiate-hypothesis() routine already uses dynamic programming for intermediate results.

4 Evaluation and Summary

Below we present an empirical evaluation of each of the refinements discussed in Sections 3.2 through 3.5. Using the LinGO ERG and its '*hike*' treebank – a 330-sentence

Table 1. Realization efficiency for various instantiations of our algorithm. The table is broken down by average ambiguity rates, the first two columns showing the number of items per aggregate and average string length. Subsequent columns show relative cpu time of one- and two-phase realization with or without packing and filtering, shown as a *relative multiplier* of the baseline performance in the *1p+f+* column. The rightmost column is for selective unpacking of up to 10 trees from the forest produced by the baseline configuration, again as a factor of the baseline. (The quality of the selected trees depends on the statistical model and the degree of overgeneration in the grammar, and is a completely separate issue which we do not address in this paper).

Aggregate	**items** ♯	**length** ϕ	**1p−f−** ×	**2p−f−** ×	**1p−f+** ×	**1p+f−** ×	**2p+f−** ×	**1p+f+** *s*	**n=10** ×
500 < *trees*	9	23.9	31.76	20.95	11.98	9.49	3.69	31.49	0.33
100 < *trees* ≤ 500	22	17.4	53.95	36.80	3.80	8.70	4.66	5.61	0.42
50 < *trees* ≤ 100	21	18.1	51.53	13.12	1.79	8.09	2.81	3.74	0.62
10 < *trees* ≤ 50	80	14.6	35.50	18.55	1.82	6.38	3.67	1.77	0.89
0 ≤ *trees* ≤ 10	185	10.5	9.62	6.83	1.19	6.86	3.62	0.58	0.95
Overall	**317**	**12.9**	**35.03**	**20.22**	**5.97**	**8.21**	**3.74**	**2.32**	**0.58**
Coverage			**95%**	**97%**	**99%**	**99%**	**100%**	**100%**	**100%**

collection of instructional text taken from Norwegian tourism brochures – we benchmarked various generator configurations, starting from the 'gold' standard MRS formula recorded for each utterance in the treebank. At 12.8 words, average sentence length in the original *'hike'* corpus is almost exactly what we see as the average length of all paraphrases obtained from the generator (see Table 1); from the available reference treebanks for the ERG, *'hike'* appears to be among the more complex data sets.

Table 1 summarizes relative generator efficiency for various configurations, where we use the best-performing *exhaustive* procedure *1p+f+* (one-phase generation with packing and index accessibility filtering) as a baseline. The configuration *1p–f–* (one-phase, no packing or filtering) corresponds to the basic procedure suggested by Kay [8], while *2p–f–* (two-phase processing of modifiers without packing and filtering) implements the algorithm presented by Carroll et al. [12]. Combining packing and filtering clearly outperforms both these earlier configurations, i.e. giving an up to 50 times speed-up for inputs with large numbers of realizations. Additional columns contrast the various techniques in isolation, thus allowing an assessment of the individual strengths of our proposals. On low- to medium-ambiguity items, for example, filtering gives rise to a bigger improvement than packing, but packing appears to flatten the curve more. Both with and without packing, filtering improves significantly over the Carroll et al. two-phase approach to intersective modifiers (i.e. comparing columns *2p–f–* and *2p+f–* to *1p–f+* and *1p+f+*, respectively), thus confirming the increased generality of our solution to the modification problem. Finally, the benefits of packing and filtering combine more than merely multiplicatively: compared to *1p–f–*, just filtering gives a speed-up of 5.9, and just packing a speed-up of 4.3. At 25, the product of these factors is well below the overall reduction of 35 that we obtain from the combination of both techniques.

While the rightmost column in Table 1 already indicates that 10-best selective unpacking further improves generator performance by close to a factor of two, Figure 4 breaks down generation time with respect to forest creation vs. unpacking time. When plotted against increasing input complexity (in terms of the 'size' of the input MRS), forest creation appears to be a low-order polynomial (or better), whereas exhaustive

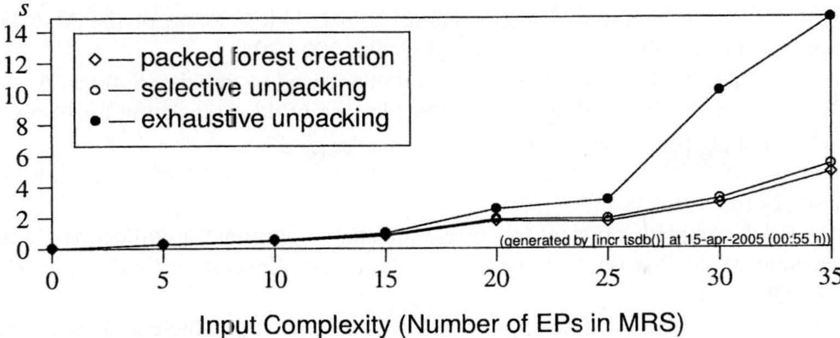

Fig. 4. Break-down of generation times (in seconds) according to realization phases and input complexity (approximated in the number of EPs in the original MRS used for generation). The three curves are, from 'bottom' to 'top', the average time for constructing the packed generation forest, selective unpacking time (using $n = 10$), and exhaustive unpacking time. Note that both unpacking times are shown as increments on top of the forest creation time.

unpacking (necessarily) results in an exponential explosion of generation time: with more than 25 EPs, it clearly dominates total processing time. Selective unpacking, in contrast, appears only mildly sensitive to input complexity and even on complex inputs adds no more than a minor cost to total generation time. Thus, we obtain an overall observed run-time performance of our wide-coverage generator that is bounded (at least) polynomially. Practical generation times using the LinGO ERG average below or around one second for outputs of fifteen words in length, i.e. time comparable to human production.

References

1. Flickinger, D.: On building a more efficient grammar by exploiting types. Natural Language Engineering **6 (1)** (2000) 15 – 28
2. Butt, M., Dyvik, H., King, T.H., Masuichi, H., Rohrer, C.: The Parallel Grammar project. In: Proceedings of the COLING Workshop on Grammar Engineering and Evaluation, Taipei, Taiwan (2002) 1 – 7
3. White, M.: Reining in CCG chart realization. In: Proceedings of the 3rd International Conference on Natural Language Generation, Hampshire, UK (2004)
4. Moore, J., Foster, M.E., Lemon, O., White, M.: Generating tailored, comparative descriptions in spoken dialogue. In: Proceedings of the 17th International FLAIRS Conference, Miami Beach, FL (2004)
5. Oepen, S., Dyvik, H., Lønning, J.T., Velldal, E., Beermann, D., Carroll, J., Flickinger, D., Hellan, L., Johannessen, J.B., Meurer, P., Nordgård, T., Rosén, V.: Som å kapp-ete med trollet? Towards MRS-based Norwegian – English Machine Translation. In: Proceedings of the 10th International Conference on Theoretical and Methodological Issues in Machine Translation, Baltimore, MD (2004)
6. Whitelock, P.: Shake-and-bake translation. In: Proceedings of the 14th International Conference on Computational Linguistics, Nantes, France (1992) 610 – 616
7. Phillips, J.: Generation of text from logical formulae. Machine Translation **8** (1993) 209 – 235

8. Kay, M.: Chart generation. In: Proceedings of the 34th Meeting of the Association for Computational Linguistics, Santa Cruz, CA (1996) 200 – 204
9. Gardent, C., Thater, S.: Generating with a grammar based on tree descriptions. A constraint-based approach. In: Proceedings of the 39th Meeting of the Association for Computational Linguistics, Toulouse, France (2001)
10. Shieber, S., van Noord, G., Pereira, F., Moore, R.: Semantic head-driven generation. Computational Linguistics **16** (1990) 30 – 43
11. Moore, R.: A complete, efficient sentence-realization algorithm for unification grammar. In: Proceedings of the 2nd International Natural Language Generation Conference, Harriman, NY (2002) 41 – 48
12. Carroll, J., Copestake, A., Flickinger, D., Poznanski, V.: An efficient chart generator for (semi-)lexicalist grammars. In: Proceedings of the 7th European Workshop on Natural Language Generation, Toulouse, France (1999) 86 – 95
13. Copestake, A., Flickinger, D., Sag, I., Pollard, C.: Minimal Recursion Semantics. An introduction. (1999)
14. Kiefer, B., Krieger, H.U., Carroll, J., Malouf, R.: A bag of useful techniques for efficient and robust parsing. In: Proceedings of the 37th Meeting of the Association for Computational Linguistics, College Park, MD (1999) 473 – 480
15. Billot, S., Lang, B.: The structure of shared forests in ambiguous parsing. In: Proceedings of the 27th Meeting of the Association for Computational Linguistics, Vancouver, BC (1989) 143 – 151
16. Oepen, S., Carroll, J.: Ambiguity packing in constraint-based parsing. Practical results. In: Proceedings of the 1st Conference of the North American Chapter of the ACL, Seattle, WA (2000) 162 – 169
17. Shieber, S.: Using restriction to extend parsing algorithms for complex feature-based formalisms. In: Proceedings of the 23rd Meeting of the Association for Computational Linguistics, Chicago, IL (1985) 145 – 152
18. Oepen, S., Carroll, J.: Performance profiling for parser engineering. Natural Language Engineering **6 (1)** (2000) 81 – 97
19. Velldall, E., Oepen, S., Flickinger, D.: Paraphrasing treebanks for stochastic realization ranking. In: Proceedings of the 3rd Workshop on Treebanks and Linguistic Theories, Tübingen, Germany (2004)
20. Toutanova, K., Manning, C.: Feature selection for a rich HPSG grammar using decision trees. In: Proceedings of the 6th Conference on Natural Language Learning, Taipei, Taiwan (2002)
21. Malouf, R., van Noord, G.: Wide coverage parsing with stochastic attribute value grammars. In: Proceedings of the IJCNLP workshop Beyond Shallow Analysis, Hainan, China (2004)
22. Geman, S., Johnson, M.: Dynamic programming for parsing and estimation of stochastic unification-based grammars. In: Proceedings of the 40th Meeting of the Association for Computational Linguistics, Philadelphia, PA (2002)
23. Miyao, Y., Tsujii, J.: Maximum entropy estimation for feature forests. In: Proceedings of the Human Language Technology Conference, San Diego, CA (2002)

Linguistically-Motivated Grammar Extraction, Generalization and Adaptation

Yu-Ming Hsieh, Duen-Chi Yang, and Keh-Jiann Chen

Institute of Information Science, Academia Sinica, Taipei
{morris, ydc, kchen}@iis.sinica.edu.tw

Abstract. In order to obtain a high precision and high coverage grammar, we proposed a model to measure grammar coverage and designed a PCFG parser to measure efficiency of the grammar. To generalize grammars, a grammar binarization method was proposed to increase the coverage of a probabilistic context-free grammar. In the mean time linguistically-motivated feature constraints were added into grammar rules to maintain precision of the grammar. The generalized grammar increases grammar coverage from 93% to 99% and bracketing F-score from 87% to 91% in parsing Chinese sentences. To cope with error propagations due to word segmentation and part-of-speech tagging errors, we also proposed a grammar blending method to adapt to such errors. The blended grammar can reduce about 20~30% of parsing errors due to error assignment of pos made by a word segmentation system.

Keywords: Grammar Coverage, Ambiguity, Sentence Parsing, Grammar Extraction.

1 Introduction

Treebanks provide instances of phrasal structures and their statistical distributions. However none of treebanks provide sufficient amount of samples which cover all types of phrasal structures, in particular, for the languages without inflectional markers, such as Chinese. It results that grammars directly extracted from treebanks suffer low coverage rate and low precision [7]. However arbitrarily generalizing applicable rule patterns may cause over-generation and increase ambiguities. It may not improve parsing performance [7]. Therefore a new approach of grammar binarization was proposed in this paper. The binarized grammars were derived from probabilistic context-free grammars (PCFG) by rule binarization. The approach was motivated by the linguistic fact that adjuncts could be arbitrarily occurred or not occurred in a phrase. The binarized grammars have better coverage than the original grammars directly extracted from treebank. However they also suffer problems of over-generation and structure-ambiguity. Contemporary grammar formalisms, such as GPSG, LFG, HPSG, take phrase structure rules as backbone for phrase structure representation and adding feature constraints to eliminate illegal or non-logical structures. In order to achieve higher coverage, the backbone grammar rules (syntactic grammar) are allowed to be over-generation and the feature constraints (semantic grammar for world knowledge) eliminate superfluous structures

R. Dale et al. (Eds.): IJCNLP 2005, LNAI 3651, pp. 177 – 187, 2005.

and increase the precision of grammar representation. Recently, probabilistic preferences for grammar rules were incorporated to resolve structure-ambiguities and had great improvements on parsing performances [2, 6, 10]. Regarding feature constrains, it was shown that contexture information of categories of neighboring nodes, mother nodes, or head words are useful for improving grammar precision and parsing performances [1, 2, 7, 10, 12]. However tradeoffs between grammar coverage and grammar precision are always inevitable. Excessive grammatical constraints will reduce grammar coverage and hence reduce parsing performances. On the other hand, loosely constrained grammars cause structure-ambiguities and also reduce parsing performances. In this paper, we consider grammar optimization in particular for Chinese language. Linguistically-motivated feature constraints were added to the grammar rules and evaluated to maintain both grammar coverage and precision. In section 2, the experimental environments were introduced. Grammar generalization and specialization methods were discussed in section 3. Grammars adapting to pos-tagging errors were discussed in section 4. Conclusions and future researches were stated in the last section.

2 Research Environments

The complete research environment, as shown in the figure 1, comprises of the following five modules and functions.

a) Word segmentation module: identify words including out-of-vocabulary word and provide their syntactic categories.
b) Grammar construction module: extract and derive (perform rule generalization, specialization and adaptation processes) probabilistic grammars from treebanks.
c) PCFG parser: parse input sentences.
d) Evaluation module: evaluate performances of parsers and grammars.
e) Semantic role assignment module: resolve semantic relations for constituents.

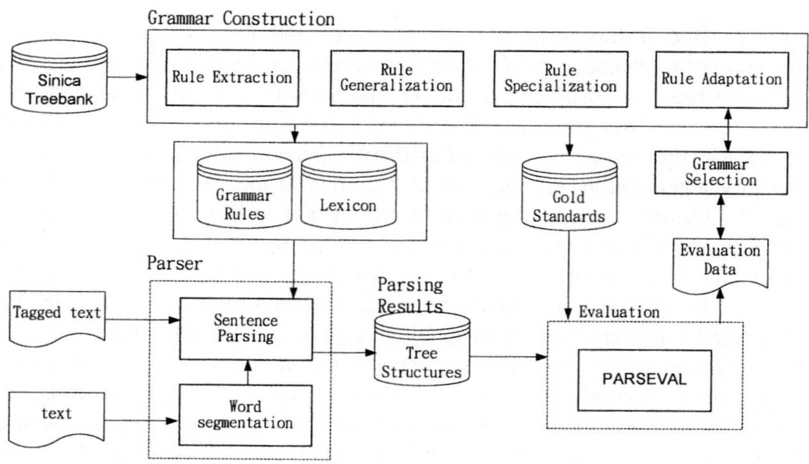

Fig. 1. The system diagram of CKIP parsing environment

2.1 Grammar Extraction Module

Grammars are extracted from Sinica Treebank [4, 5]. Sinica Treebank version 2.0 contains 38,944 tree-structures and 230,979 words. It provides instances of phrasal structures and their statistical distributions. In Sinica Treebank, each sentence is annotated with its syntactic structure and semantic roles for constituents in a dependency framework. Figure 2 is an example.

e.g. 他 叫 李四 撿 球
Ta jiao Li-si jian qiu.
"He asked Lisi to pick up the ball."
Tree-structure:
S(agent:NP(Head:Nh:他)|Head:VF:叫|goal:NP(Head:Nb:李四)|theme:VP(Head:VC:撿 goal:NP(Head:Na:球)))

Fig. 2. A sample tree-structure

Since the Treebank cannot provide sufficient amount of samples which cover all types of phrasal structures, it results that grammars directly extracted from treebanks suffer low coverage rate [5]. Therefore grammar generalization and specialization processes are carried out to obtain grammars with better coverage and precision. The detail processes will be discussed in section 3.

2.2 PCFG Parser and Grammar Performance Evaluation

The probabilistic context-free parsing strategies were used as our parsing model [2, 6, 8]. Calculating probabilities of rules from a treebank is straightforward and we use maximum likelihood estimation to estimate the rule probabilities, as in [2]. The parser adopts an Earley's Algorithm [8]. It is a top-down left-to-right algorithm. The results of binary structures will be normalized into a regular phrase structures by removing intermediate nodes, if used grammars are binarized grammars. Grammar efficiency will be evaluated according to its parsing performance.

2.3 Experiments and Performance Evaluation

Three sets of testing data were used in our performance evaluation. Their basic statistics are shown in Table 1. Each set of testing data represents easy, hard and moderate respectively.

Table 1. Three sets of testing data were used in our experiments

Testing data	Sources	hardness	# of short sentence (1-5 words)	# of normal sentences (6-10 words)	# of long sentences (>11 words)	Total sentences
Sinica	Balanced corpus	moderate	612	385	124	1,121
Sinorama	Magazine	harder	428	424	104	956
Textbook	Elementary school	easy	1,159	566	25	1,750

The following parser and grammar performance evaluation indicators were used in our experiments:

- LP(Labeled Precision)

$$LP = \frac{\text{\# of correct phrases labeled by the parser}}{\text{\# of phrases labeled by the parser}}$$

- LR(Labeled Recall)

$$LR = \frac{\text{\# of correct phrases labeled by the parser}}{\text{\# of phrases in the testing data}}$$

- LF(Labeled F-measure)

$$LF = \frac{LP * LR * 2}{LP + LR}$$

- BP(Bracketed Precision)

$$BP = \frac{\text{\# of pairs of brackets correctly made by the parser}}{\text{\# of pairs of brackets made by the parser}}$$

- BR(Bracketed Recall)

$$BR = \frac{\text{\# of pairs of brackets correctly made by the parser}}{\text{\# of pairs of brackets in the gold standard of the testing data}}$$

- BF(Bracketed F-measure)

$$BF = \frac{BP * BR * 2}{BP + BR}$$

Additional indicators regarding coverage of grammars:

- RC-Type：type coverage of rules

$$\text{RC - Type} = \frac{\text{\# of rules types in both testing data and grammar rules}}{\text{\# of rule types in testing data}}$$

- RC-Token：token coverage of rules

$$\text{RC - Token} = \frac{\text{\# of rules tokens in both testing data and grammar rules}}{\text{\# of rule tokens in testing data}}$$

The token coverage of a set of rules is the ceiling of parsing algorithm to achieve. Tradeoff effects between grammar coverage and parsing F-score can be examined for each set of rules.

3 Grammar Generalization and Specialization

By using above mentioned research environment, we intend to find out most effective grammar generalization method and specialization features for Chinese language. To extend an existing or extracted grammar, there are several different approaches. A naïve approach is to generalize a fine-grained rule to a coarse-grained rule. The approach does not generate new patterns. Only the applicable patterns for each word were increased. However it was shown that arbitrarily increasing the applicable rule patterns does increase the coverage rates of grammars, but degrade parsing performance [5]. A better approach is to generalizing and specializing rules under linguistically-motivated way.

3.1 Binary Grammar Generation, Generalization, and Specialization

The length of a phrase in Treebank is variable and usually long phrases suffer from low probability. Therefore most PCFG approaches adopt the binary equivalence grammar, such as Chomsky normal form (CNF). For instance, a grammar rule of S→ NP Pp Adv V can be replaced by the set of equivalent rules of {S→Np R0, R0→Pp R1, R1→Adv V}. The binarization method proposed in our system is different from CNF. It generalizes the original grammar to broader coverage. For instance, the above rule after performing right-association binarization[1] will produce following three binary rules {S→Np S', S'→Pp S', S'→Adv V}. It results that constituents (adjuncts and arguments) can be occurred or not occurred at almost any place in the phrase. It partially fulfilled the linguistic fact that adjuncts in a phrase are arbitrarily occurred. However it also violated the fact that arguments do not arbitrarily occur. Experimental results of the Sinica testing data showed that the grammar token coverage increased from 92.8% to 99.4%, but the labeling F-score dropped from 82.43% to 82.11% [7]. Therefore feature constraints were added into binary rules to limit over-generation caused by recursively adding constituents into intermediate-phrase types, such as S' at above example.

Feature attached rules will look like following:

$S'_{\text{-left:Adv-head:V}} \rightarrow \text{Adv V};$
$S'_{\text{-left:Pp-head:V}} \rightarrow \text{Pp } S'_{\text{-left:Adv-head:V}};$

The intermediated node $S'_{\text{-left:Pp-head:V}}$ says that it is a partial S structure with leftmost constituent Pp and a phrasal head V. Here the leftmost feature constraints linear order of constituents and the head feature implies that the structure patterns are head word dependent. Both constraints are linguistically plausible. Another advantage of the feature-constraint binary grammar is that in addition to rule probability it is easy to implement association strength of modifier word and head word to evaluate plausibility of derived structures.

3.2 Feature Constraints for Reducing Ambiguities of Generalized Grammars

Adding feature constraints into grammar rules attempts to increase precision of grammar representation. However the side-effect is that it also reduces grammar coverage. Therefore grammar design is balanced between its precision and coverage. We are looking for a grammar with highest coverage and precision. The tradeoff depends on the ambiguity resolution power of adopted parser. If the ambiguity resolution power of adopted parser is strong and robust, the grammar coverage might be more important than grammar precision. On the other hand a weak parser had better to use grammars with more feature constraints. In our experiments, we consider grammars suited for PCFG parsing. The follows are some of the most important linguistically-motivated features which have been tested.

[1] The reason for using right-association binarization instead of left-association or head-first association binarization is that our parsing process is from left to right. It turns out that parsing speed of right associated grammars is much faster than left-associated grammars for left-to-right parsing.

Head (*Head feature*): Pos of phrasal head will propagate to all intermediate nodes within the constituent.
Example:S(NP(Head:Nh:他)|S'$_{-VF}$(Head:VF:叫|S'$_{-VF}$(NP(Head:Nb:李四)| VP(Head:VC:撿| NP(Head:Na:球)))))
Linguistic motivations: Constrain sub-categorization frame.

Left (*Leftmost feature*): The pos of the leftmost constitute will propagate one–level to its intermediate mother-node only.
Example:S(NP(Head:Nh:他)|S'$_{-Head:VF}$(Head:VF:叫|S'$_{-NP}$(NP(Head:Nb:李四)| VP(Head:VC:撿| NP(Head:Na:球)))))
Linguistic motivation: Constraint linear order of constituents.

Mother (*Mother-node*): The pos of mother-node assigns to all daughter nodes.
Example:S(NP$_{-S}$(Head:Nh:他)|S'(Head:VF:叫|S'(NP$_{-S}$(Head:Nb:李四)|VP$_{-S}$(Head:VC: 撿| NP$_{-VP}$(Head:Na: 球)))))
Linguistic motivation: Constraint syntactic structures for daughter nodes.

Head0/1 (*Existence of phrasal head*): If phrasal head exists in intermediate node, the nodes will be marked with feature 1; otherwise 0.
Example:S(NP(Head:Nh: 他)|S'$_{-1}$(Head:VF: 叫 |S'$_{-0}$(NP(Head:Nb: 李 四)|VP(Head:VC: 撿| NP(Head:Na: 球)))))
Linguistic motivation: Enforce unique phrasal head in each phrase.

Table 2. Performance evaluations for different features

	(a)Binary rules without features			(b)Binary+Left		
	Sinica	Snorama	Textbook	Sinica	Sinorama	Textbook
RC-Type	95.632	94.026	94.479	95.074	93.823	94.464
RC-Token	99.422	99.139	99.417	99.012	98.756	99.179
LP	81.51	77.45	84.42	86.27	80.28	86.67
LR	82.73	77.03	85.09	86.18	80.00	87.23
LF	82.11	77.24	84.75	86.22	80.14	86.94
BP	87.73	85.31	89.66	90.43	86.71	90.84
BR	89.16	84.91	90.52	90.46	86.41	91.57
BF	88.44	85.11	90.09	90.45	86.56	91.20
	(c)Binary+Head			(d)Binary+Mother		
	Sinica	Snorama	Textbook	Sinica	Sinorama	Textbook
RC-Type	94.595	93.474	94.480	94.737	94.082	92.985
RC-Token	98.919	98.740	99.215	98.919	98.628	98.857
LP	83.68	77.96	85.52	81.87	78.00	83.77
LR	83.75	77.83	86.10	82.83	76.95	84.58
LF	83.71	77.90	85.81	82.35	77.47	84.17
BP	89.49	85.29	90.17	87.85	85.44	88.47
BR	89.59	85.15	90.91	88.84	84.66	89.57
BF	89.54	85.22	90.54	88.34	85.05	89.01

Each set of feature constraint added grammar is tested and evaluated. Table 2 shows the experimental results. Since all features have their own linguistic motivations, the result feature constrained grammars maintain high coverage and have improving grammar precision. Therefore each feature more or less improves the parsing performance and the feature of leftmost daughter node, which constrains the linear order of constituents, is the most effective feature. The Left-constraint-added grammar reduces grammar token-coverage very little and significantly increases label and bracket f-scores.

It is shown that all linguistically-motivated features are more or less effective. The leftmost constitute feature, which constraints linear order of constituents, is the most effective feature. The mother-node feature is the least effective feature, since syntactic structures do not vary too much for each phrase type while playing different grammatical functions in Chinese.

Table 3. Performances of grammars with different feature combinations

	(a) Binary+Left+Head1/0			(b) Binary+Left+Head		
	Sinica	Sinorama	Textbook	Sinica	Sinorama	Textbook
RC-Type	94.887	93.745	94.381	92.879	91.853	92.324
RC-Token	98.975	98.740	99.167	98.173	98.022	98.608
LF	86.54	79.81	87.68	86.00	79.53	86.86
BF	90.69	86.16	91.39	90.10	86.06	90.91
LF-1	86.71	79.98	87.73	86.76	79.86	87.16
BF-1	90.86	86.34	91.45	90.89	86.42	91.22

Table 4. Performances of the grammar with most feature constraints

	Binary+Left+Head+Mother+Head1/0		
	Sinica	Sinorama	Textbook
RC-Type	90.709	90.460	90.538
RC-Token	96.906	96.698	97.643
LF	86.75	78.38	86.19
BF	90.54	85.20	90.07
LF-1	88.56	79.55	87.84
BF-1	92.44	86.46	91.80

Since all the above features are effective, we like to see the results of multi-feature combinations. Many different feature combinations were tested. The experimental results show that none of the feature combinations outperform the binary grammars with Left and Head1/0 features, even the grammar combining all features, as shown in the Table 3 and 4. Here LF-1 and BF-1 measure the label and bracket f-scores only on the sentences with parsing results (i.e. sentences failed of producing parsing results are ignored). The results show that grammar with all feature constraints has better LF-1 and BF-1 scores, since the grammar has higher precision. However the total performances, i.e. Lf and BF scores, are not better than the simpler grammar with feature constraints of Left and Head1/0, since the higher precision grammar losses slight edge on the grammar coverage. The result clearly shows that tradeoffs do exist between grammar precision and coverage. It also suggests that if a feature constraint can improve grammar precision a lot but also reduce grammar coverage a lot, it is better to treat such feature constraints as a soft constraint instead of hard constraint. Probabilistic preference for such feature parameters will be a possible implementation of soft constraint.

3.3 Discussions

Feature constraints impose additional constraints between constituents for phrase structures. However different feature constraints serve for different functions and have different feature assignment principles. Some features serve for local constraints, such as Left, Head, and Head0/1. Those features are only assigned at local intermediate nodes. Some features are designed for external effect such as Mother Feature, which is assigned to phrase nodes and their daughter intermediate nodes. For instances, NP structures for subject usually are different from NP structures for object in English sentences [10]. NP attached with Mother-feature can make the difference. NP_S rules and NP_{VP} rules will be derived each respectively from subject NP and object NP structures. However such difference seems not very significant in Chinese. Therefore feature selection and assignment should be linguistically-motivated as shown in our experiments.

In conclusion, linguistically-motivated features have better effects on parsing performances than arbitrarily selected features, since they increase grammar precision, but only reduce grammar coverage slightly. The feature of leftmost daughter, which constraints linear order of constituents, is the most effective feature for parsing. Other sub-categorization related features, such as mother node and head features, do not contribute parsing F-scores very much. Such features might be useful for purpose of sentence generation instead of parsing.

4 Adapt to Pos Errors Due to Automatic Pos Tagging

Perfect testing data was used for the above experiments without considering word segmentation and pos tagging errors. However in real life word segmentation and pos tagging errors will degenerate parsing performances. The real parsing performances of accepting input from automatic word segmentation and pos tagging system are shown in the Table 5.

Table 5. Parsing performances of inputs produced by the automatic word segmentation and pos tagging

	Binary+Left+Head1/0		
	Sinica	Sinorama	Textbook
LF	76.18	64.53	73.61
BF	84.01	75.95	84.28

The naïve approach to overcome the pos tagging errors was to delay some of the ambiguous pos resolution for words with lower confidence tagging scores and leave parser to resolve the ambiguous pos until parsing stage. The tagging confidence of each word is measured by the following value.

Confidence value= $\frac{P(c_{1,w})}{P(c_{1,w})+P(c_{2,w})}$, where $P(c_{1,w})$ and $P(c_{2,w})$ are probabilities assigned by the tagging model for the best candidate $c_{1,w}$ and the second best candidate $c_{2,w}$.

The experimental results, Table 6, show that delaying ambiguous pos resolution does not improve parsing performances, since pos ambiguities increase structure ambiguities and the parser is not robust enough to select the best tagging sequence. The higher confidence values mean that more words with lower confidence tagging will leave ambiguous pos tags and the results show the worse performances. Charniak et al [3] experimented with using multiple tags per word as input to a treebank parser, and came to a similar conclusion.

Table 6. Parsing performances for different confidence level of pos ambiguities

	Confidence value=0.5		
	Sinica	Sinorama	Textbook
LF	75.92	64.14	74.66
BF	83.48	75.22	83.65
	Confidence value=0.8		
	Sinica	Sinorama	Textbook
LF	75.37	63.17	73.76
BF	83.32	74.50	83.33
	Confidence value=1.0		
	Sinica	Sinorama	Textbook
LF	74.12	61.25	69.44
BF	82.57	73.17	81.17

4.1 Blending Grammars

A new approach of grammar blending method was proposed to cope with pos tagging errors. The idea is to blend the original grammar with a newly extracted grammar derived from the Treebank in which pos categories are tagged by the automatic pos tagger. The blended grammars contain the original rules and the extended rules due to pos tagging errors. A 5-fold cross-validation was applied on the testing data to tune the blending weight between the original grammar and the error-adapted grammar. The experimental results show that the blended grammar of weights 8:2 between the original grammar and error-adapted grammar achieves the best results. It reduces about 20%~30% parsing errors due to pos tagging errors, shown in the Table 7. The pure error-adapted grammar, i.e. 0:10 blending weight, does not improve the parsing performance very much

Table 7. Performances of the blended grammars

	Error-adapted grammar i.e. blending weight (0:10)			Blending weight 8:2		
	Sinica	Sinirama	Textbook	Sinica	Sinirama	Textbook
LF	75.99	66.16	71.92	78.04	66.49	74.69
BF	85.65	77.89	85.04	86.06	77.82	85.91

5 Conclusion and Future Researches

In order to obtain a high precision and high coverage grammar, we proposed a model to measure grammar coverage and designed a PCFG parser to measure efficiency of the grammar. Grammar binarization method was proposed to generalize rules and to increase the coverage of context-free grammars. Linguistically-motivated feature constraints were added into grammar rules to maintain grammar rule precision. It is shown that the feature of leftmost daughter, which constraints linear order of constituents, is the most effective feature. Other sub-categorization related features, such as mother node and head features, do not contribute parsing F-scores very much. Such features might be very useful for purpose of sentence generation instead of parsing. The best performed feature constraint binarized grammar increases the grammar coverage of the original grammar from 93% to 99% and bracketing F-score from 87% to 91% in parsing moderate hard testing data. To cope with error propagations due to word segmentation and part-of-speech tagging errors, a grammar blending method was proposed to adapt to such errors. The blended grammar can reduce about 20~30% of parsing errors due to error assignment of a pos tagging system.

In the future, we will study more effective way to resolve structure ambiguities. In particular, consider the tradeoff effect between grammar coverage and precision. The balance between soft constraints and hard constraints will be focus of our future researches. In addition to rule probability, word association probability will be another preference measure to resolve structure ambiguity, in particular for conjunctive structures.

Acknowledgement

This research was supported in part by National Science Council under a Center Excellence Grant NSC 93-2752-E-001-001-PAE and National Digital Archives Program Grant NSC93-2422-H-001-0004.

References

1. E. Charniak, and G. Carroll, "Context-sensitive statistics for improved grammatical language models." In Proceedings of the 12th National Conference on Artificial Intelligence, AAAI Press, pp. 742-747, Seattle, WA, 1994,
2. E. Charniak, "Treebank grammars." In Proceedings of the Thirteenth National Conference on Artificial Intelligence, pp. 1031-1036. AAAI Press/MIT Press, 1996.

3. E. Charniak, and G. Carroll, J. Adcock, A. Cassanda, Y. Gotoh, J. Katz, M. Littman, J. Mccann, "Taggers for Parsers", Artificial Intelligence, vol. 85, num. 1-2, 1996.
4. Feng-Yi Chen, Pi-Fang Tsai, Keh-Jiann Chen, and Huang, Chu-Ren, "Sinica Treebank." Computational Linguistics and Chinese Language Processing, 4(2):87-103, 2000.
5. Keh-Jiann Chen and, Yu-Ming Hsieh, "Chinese Treebanks and Grammar Extraction." the First International Joint Conference on Natural Language Processing (IJCNLP-04), March 2004.
6. Michael Collins, "Head-Driven Statistical Models for Natural Language parsing." Ph.D. thesis, Univ. of Pennsylvania, 1999.
7. Yu-Ming Hsieh, Duen-Chi Yang and Keh-Jiann Chen, "Grammar extraction, generalization and specialization. (in Chinese)"Proceedings of ROCLING 2004.
8. Christopher D. Manning and Hinrich Schutze, "Foundations of Statistical Natural Language Processing." the MIT Press, Cambridge, Massachusetts, 1999.
9. Mark Johnson, "PCFG models of linguistic tree representations." Computational Linguistics, Vol.24, pp.613-632, 1998.
10. Dan Klein and Christopher D. Manning, "Accurate Unlexicalized Parsing." Proceeding of the 4lst Annual Meeting of the Association for Computational Linguistics, pp. 423-430, July 2003.
11. Honglin Sun and Daniel Jurafsky, "Shallow Semantic Parsing of Chinese." Proceedings of NAACL 2004.
12. 12.Hao Zhang, Qun Liu, Kevin Zhang, Gang Zou and Shuo Bai, "Statistical Chinese Parser ICTPROP." Technology Report, Institute of Computing Technology, 2003.

PP-Attachment Disambiguation Boosted by a Gigantic Volume of Unambiguous Examples

Daisuke Kawahara and Sadao Kurohashi

Graduate School of Information Science and Technology, University of Tokyo,
7-3-1 Hongo Bunkyo-ku, Tokyo, 113-8656, Japan
{kawahara, kuro}@kc.t.u-tokyo.ac.jp

Abstract. We present a PP-attachment disambiguation method based on a gigantic volume of unambiguous examples extracted from raw corpus. The unambiguous examples are utilized to acquire precise lexical preferences for PP-attachment disambiguation. Attachment decisions are made by a machine learning method that optimizes the use of the lexical preferences. Our experiments indicate that the precise lexical preferences work effectively.

1 Introduction

For natural language processing (NLP), resolving various ambiguities is a fundamental and important issue. Prepositional phrase (PP) attachment ambiguity is one of the structural ambiguities. Consider, for example, the following sentences [1]:

(1) a. Mary ate the salad with a fork.

b. Mary ate the salad with croutons.

The prepositional phrase in (1a) "with a fork" modifies the verb "ate", because "with a fork" describes how the salad is eaten. The prepositional phrase in (1b) "with croutons" modifies the noun "the salad", because "with croutons" describes the salad. To disambiguate such PP-attachment ambiguity, some kind of world knowledge is required. However, it is currently difficult to give such world knowledge to computers, and this situation makes PP-attachment disambiguation difficult. Recent state-of-the-art parsers perform with the practical accuracy, but seem to suffer from the PP-attachment ambiguity [2, 3].

For NLP tasks including PP-attachment disambiguation, corpus-based approaches have been the dominant paradigm in recent years. They can be divided into two classes: supervised and unsupervised. Supervised methods automatically learn rules from tagged data, and achieve good performance for many NLP tasks, especially when lexical information, such as words, is given. Such methods, however, cannot avoid the sparse data problem. This is because tagged data are not sufficient enough to discriminate a large variety of lexical information. To deal with this problem, many smoothing techniques have been proposed.

R. Dale et al. (Eds.): IJCNLP 2005, LNAI 3651, pp. 188–198, 2005.

The other class for corpus-based approaches is unsupervised learning. Unsupervised methods take advantage of a large number of data that are extracted from large raw corpora, and thus can alleviate the sparse data problem. However, the problem is their low performance compared with supervised methods, because of the use of unreliable information.

For PP-attachment disambiguation, both supervised and unsupervised methods have been proposed, and supervised methods have achieved better performance (e.g., 86.5% accuracy by [1]). Previous unsupervised methods tried to extract reliable information from large raw corpora, but the extraction heuristics seem to be inaccurate [4, 5]. For example, Ratnaparkhi extracted unambiguous word triples of (verb, preposition, noun) or (noun, preposition, noun), and reported that their accuracy was 69% [4]. This means that the extracted triples are not truly unambiguous, and this inaccurate treatment may have led to low PP-attachment performance (81.9%).

This paper proposes a PP-attachment disambiguation method based on an enormous amount of truly unambiguous examples. The unambiguous examples are extracted from raw corpus using some heuristics inspired by the following example sentences in [6]

(2) a. She sent him into the nursery to gather up his toys.
    b. The road to London is long and winding.

In these sentences, the underlined PPs are unambiguously attached to the double-underlined verb or noun. The extracted unambiguous examples are utilized to acquire precise lexical preferences for PP-attachment disambiguation. Attachment decisions are made by a machine learning technique that optimizes the use of the lexical preferences. The point of our work is to use a "gigantic" volume of "truly" unambiguous examples. The use of only truly unambiguous examples leads to statistics of high-quality and good performance of disambiguation in spite of the learning from raw corpus. Furthermore, by using a gigantic volume of data, we can alleviate the influence of the sparse data problem.

The remainder of this paper is organized as follows. Section 2 briefly describes the globally used training and test set of PP-attachment. Section 3 summarizes previous work for PP-attachment. Section 4 describes a method of calculating lexical preference statistics from a gigantic volume of unambiguous examples. Section 5 is devoted to our PP-attachment disambiguation algorithm. Section 6 presents the experiments of our disambiguation method. Section 7 gives the conclusions.

2 Tagged Data for PP-Attachment

The PP-attachment data with correct attachment site are available [1]. These data were extracted from Penn Treebank [7] by the IBM research group [8]. Hereafter, we call these data "IBM data". Some examples in the IBM data are shown in Table 1.

[1] Available at ftp://ftp.cis.upenn.edu/pub/adwait/PPattachData/

Table 1. Some Examples of the IBM data

v	n_1	p	n_2	attach
join	board	as	director	V
is	chairman	of	N.V.	N
using	crocidolite	in	filters	V
bring	attention	to	problem	V
is	asbestos	in	product	N
making	paper	for	filters	N
including	three	with	cancer	N

Table 2. Various Baselines and Upper Bounds of PP-Attachment Disambiguation

method	accuracy
always N	59.0%
N if p is "of"; otherwise V	70.4%
most likely for each preposition	72.2%
average human (only quadruple)	88.2%
average human (whole sentence)	93.2%

The data consist of 20,801 training and 3,097 test tuples. In addition, a development set of 4,039 tuples is provided. Various baselines and upper bounds of PP-Attachment disambiguation are shown in Table 2. All the accuracies except the human performances are on the IBM data. The human performances were reported by [8].

3 Related Work

There have been lots of supervised approaches for PP-attachment disambiguation. Most of them used the IBM data for their training and test data.

Ratnaphakhi et al. proposed a maximum entropy model considering words and semantic classes of quadruples, and performed with 81.6% accuracy [8]. Brill and Resnik presented a transformation-based learning method [9]. They reported 81.8% accuracy, but they did not use the IBM data [2]. Collins and Brooks used a probabilistic model with backing-off to smooth the probabilities of unseen events, and its accuracy was 84.5% [10]. Stetina and Nagao used decision trees combined with a semantic dictionary [11]. They achieved 88.1% accuracy, which is approaching the human accuracy of 88.2%. This great performance is presumably indebted to the manually constructed semantic dictionary, which can be regarded as a part of world knowledge. Zavrel et al. employed a nearest-neighbor method, and its accuracy was 84.4% [12]. Abney et al. proposed a boosting approach, and yielded 84.6% accuracy [13]. Vanschoenwinkel and Manderick introduced a kernel method into PP-attachment disam-

[2] The accuracy on the IBM data was 81.9% [10].

biguation, and attained 84.8% accuracy [14]. Zhao and Lin proposed a nearest-neighbor method with contextually similar words learned from large raw corpus [1]. They achieved 86.5% accuracy, which is the best performance among previous methods for PP-attachment disambiguation without manually constructed knowledge bases.

There have been several unsupervised methods for PP-attachment disambiguation. Hindle and Rooth extracted over 200K (v, n_1, p) triples with ambiguous attachment sites from 13M words of AP news stories [15]. Their disambiguation method used lexical association score, and performed at 75.8% accuracy on their own data set. Ratnaparkhi collected 910K unique unambiguous triples (v, p, n_2) or (n_1, p, n_2) from 970K sentences of Wall Street Journal, and proposed a probabilistic model based on cooccurrence values calculated from the collected data [4]. He reported 81.9% accuracy. As previously mentioned, the accuracy was possibly lowered by the inaccurate (69% accuracy) extracted examples. Pantel and Lin extracted ambiguous 8,900K quadruples and unambiguous 4,400K triples from 125M word newspaper corpus [5]. They utilized scores based on cooccurrence values, and resulted in 84.3% accuracy. The accuracy of the extracted unambiguous triples are unknown, but depends on the accuracy of their parser.

There is a combined method of supervised and unsupervised approaches. Volk combined supervised and unsupervised methods for PP-attachment disambiguation for German [16]. He extracted triples that are possibly unambiguous from 5.5M words of a science magazine corpus, but these triples were not truly unambiguous. His unsupervised method is based on cooccurrence probabilities learned from the extracted triples. His supervised method adopted the backed-off model by Collins and Brooks. This model is learned the model from 5,803 quadruples. Its accuracy on a test set of 4,469 quadruples was 73.98%, and was boosted to 80.98% by the unsupervised cooccurrence scores. However, his work was constrained by the availability of only a small tagged corpus, and thus it is unknown whether such an improvement can be achieved if a larger size of a tagged set like the IBM data is available.

4 Acquiring Precise Lexical Preferences from Raw Corpus

We acquire lexical preferences that are useful for PP-attachment disambiguation from a raw corpus. As such lexical preferences, cooccurrence statistics between the verb and the prepositional phrase or the noun and the prepositional phrase are used. These cooccurrence statistics can be obtained from a large raw corpus, but the simple use of such a raw corpus possibly produces unreliable statistics. We extract only truly unambiguous examples from a huge raw corpus to acquire precise preference statistics.

This section first mentions the raw corpus, and then describes how to extract truly unambiguous examples. Finally, we explain our calculation method of the lexical preferences.

4.1 Raw Corpus

In our approach, a large volume of raw corpus is required. We extracted raw corpus from 200M Web pages that had been collected by a Web crawler for a month [17]. To obtain the raw corpus, each Web page is processed by the following tools:

1. sentence extracting
   Sentences are extracted from each Web page by a simple HTML parser.
2. tokenizing
   Sentences are tokenized by a simple tokenizer.
3. part-of-speech tagging
   Tokenized sentences are given part-of-speech tags by Brill tagger [18].
4. chunking
   Tagged sentences are chunked by YamCha chunker [19].

By the above procedure, we acquired 1,300M chunked sentences, which consist of 21G words, from the 200M Web pages.

4.2 Extraction of Unambiguous Examples

Unambiguous examples are extracted from the chunked sentences. Our heuristics to extract truly unambiguous examples were decided in the light of the following two types of unambiguous examples in [6].

(3) a. She sent him into the nursery to gather up his toys.

b. The road to London is long and winding.

The prepositional phrase "into the nursery" in (3a) must attach to the verb "sent", because attachment to a pronoun like "him" is not possible. The prepositional phrase "to London" in (3b) must attach to the noun "road", because there are no preceding possible heads.

We use the following two heuristics to extract unambiguous examples like the above.

- To extract an unambiguous triple (v, p, n_2) like (3a), a verb followed by a pronoun and a prepositional phrase is extracted.
- To extract an unambiguous triple (n_1, p, n_2) like (3b), a noun phrase followed by a prepositional phrase at the beginning of a sentence is extracted.

4.3 Post-processing of Extracted Examples

The extracted examples are processed in the following way:

- For verbs (v):
  - Verbs are reduced to their lemma.
- For nouns (n_1, n_2):
  - 4-digit numbers are replaced with <year>.

  - All other strings of numbers were replaced with <num>.
  - All words at the beginning of a sentence are converted into lower case.
  - All words starting with a capital letter followed by one or more lower case letters were replaced with <name>.
  - All other words are reduced to their singular form.
- For prepositions (p):
  - Prepositions are converted into lower case.

As a result, 21M (v, p, n_2) triples and 147M (n, p, n_2) triples,in total 168M triples, were acquired.

4.4 Calculation of Lexical Preferences for PP-Attachment

From the extracted truly unambiguous examples, lexical preferences for PP-attachment are calculated. As the lexical preferences, pointwise mutual information between v and "p n_2" is calculated from cooccurrence counts of v and "p n_2" as follows[3]:

$$I(v, pn_2) = \log \frac{\frac{f(v,pn_2)}{N}}{\frac{f(v)}{N}\frac{f(pn_2)}{N}} \tag{1}$$

where N denotes the total number of the extracted examples (168M), $f(v)$ and $f(pn_2)$ is the frequency of v and "p n_2", respectively, and $f(v, pn_2)$ is the cooccurrence frequency of v and pn_2.

Similarly, pointwise mutual information between n_1 and "p n_2" is calculated as follows:

$$I(n_1, pn_2) = \log \frac{\frac{f(n_1,pn_2)}{N}}{\frac{f(n_1)}{N}\frac{f(pn_2)}{N}} \tag{2}$$

The preference scores ignoring n_2 are also calculated:

$$I(v, p) = \log \frac{\frac{f(v,p)}{N}}{\frac{f(v)}{N}\frac{f(p)}{N}} \tag{3}$$

$$I(n_1, p) = \log \frac{\frac{f(n_1,p)}{N}}{\frac{f(n_1)}{N}\frac{f(p)}{N}} \tag{4}$$

5 PP-Attachment Disambiguation Method

Our method for resolving PP-attachment ambiguity takes a quadruple (v, n_1, p, n_2) as input, and classifies it as V or N. The class V means that the prepositional

[3] As in previous work, simple probability ratios can be used, but a preliminary experiment on the development set shows their accuracy is worse than the mutual information by approximately 1%.

phrase "p n_2" modifies the verb v. The class N means that the prepositional phrase modifies the noun n_1.

To solve this binary classification task, we employ Support Vector Machines (SVMs), which have been well-known for their good generalization performance [20].

We consider the following features:

- LEX: word of each quadruple
  To reduce sparse data problems, all verbs and nouns are pre-processed using the method stated in Section 4.3.
- POS: part-of-speech information of v, n_1 and n_2
  POSs of v, n_1 and n_2 provide richer information than just verb or noun, such as inflectional information.
  The IBM data, which we use for our experiments, do not contain POS information. To obtain POS tags of a quadruple, we extracted the original sentence of each quadruple from Penn Treebank, and applied the Brill tagger to it. Instead of using the correct POS information in Penn Treebank, we use the POS information automatically generated by the Brill tagger to keep the experimental environment realistic.
- LP: lexical preferences
  Given a quadruple (v, n_1, p, n_2), four statistics calculated in Section4.4, $I(v, pn_2)$, $I(n_1, pn_2)$, $I(v, p)$ and $I(n_1, p)$, are given to SVMs as features.

6 Experiments and Discussions

We conducted experiments on the IBM data. As an SVM implementation, we employed SVM^{light} [21]. To determine parameters of SVM^{light}, we run our method on the development data set of the IBM data. As the result, parameter j, which is used to make much account of training errors on either class [22], is set to 0.65, and 3-degree polynomial kernel is chosen. Table 3 shows the experimental results for PP-attachment disambiguation. For comparison, we conducted several experiments with different feature combinations in addition to our proposed method "LEX+POS+LP", which uses all of the three types of features. The proposed method "LEX+POS+LP" surpassed "LEX", which is the standard supervised model, and furthermore, significantly outperformed all other

Table 3. PP-Attachment Accuracies

LEX	POS	LP	accuracy
√			85.34
√	√		85.05
		√	83.73
	√	√	84.66
√		√	86.44
√	√	√	**87.25**

Table 4. Precision and Recall for Each Attachment Site ("LEX+POS+LP" model)

class	precision	recall
V	1067/1258 (84.82%)	1067/1271 (83.95%)
N	1635/1839 (88.91%)	1635/1826 (89.54%)

Table 5. PP-Attachment Accuracies of Previous Work

	method	accuracy
our method	SVM	87.25%
supervised		
Ratnaphakhi et al., 1994	ME	81.6%
Brill and Resnik, 1994	TBL	81.9%
Collins and Brooks, 1995	back-off	84.5%
Zavrel et al., 1997	NN	84.4%
Stetina and Nagao, 1997	DT	88.1%
Abney et al., 1999	boosting	84.6%
Vanschoenwinkel and Manderick, 2003	SVM	84.8%
Zhao and Lin, 2004	NN	86.5%
unsupervised		
Ratnaparkhi, 1998	-	81.9%
Pantel and Lin, 2000	-	84.3%

ME: Maximum Entropy, TBL: Transformation-Based Learning,
DT: Decision Tree, NN: Nearest Neighbor

configurations (McNemar's test; $p < 0.05$). "LEX+POS" model was a little worse than "LEX", but "LEX+POS+LP" was better than "LEX+LP" (and also "POS+LP" was better than "LP"). From these results, we can see that "LP" worked effectively, and the combination of "LEX+POS+LP" was very effective. Table 4 shows the precision and recall of "LEX+POS+LP" model for each class (N and V).

Table 5 shows the accuracies achieved by previous methods. Our performance is higher than any other previous methods except [11]. The method of Stetina and Nagao employed a manually constructed sense dictionary, and this conduces to good performance.

Figure 1 shows the learning curve of "LEX" and "LEX+POS+LP" models while changing the number of tagged data. When using all the training data, "LEX+POS+LP" was better than "LEX" by approximately 2%. Under the condition of small data set, "LEX+POS+LP" was better than "LEX" by approximately 5%. In this situation, in particular, the lexical preferences worked more effectively.

Figure 2 shows the learning curve of "LEX+POS+LP" model while changing the number of used unambiguous examples. The accuracy rises rapidly by 10M unambiguous examples, and then drops once, but after that rises slightly. The best score 87.28% was achieved when using 77M unambiguous examples.

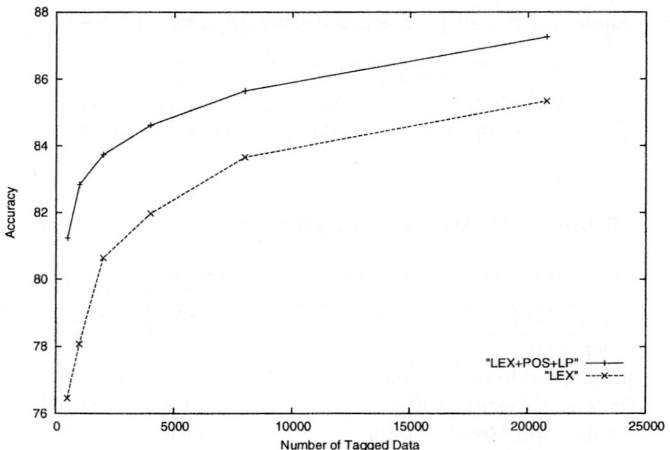

Fig. 1. Learning Curve of PP-Attachment Disambiguation

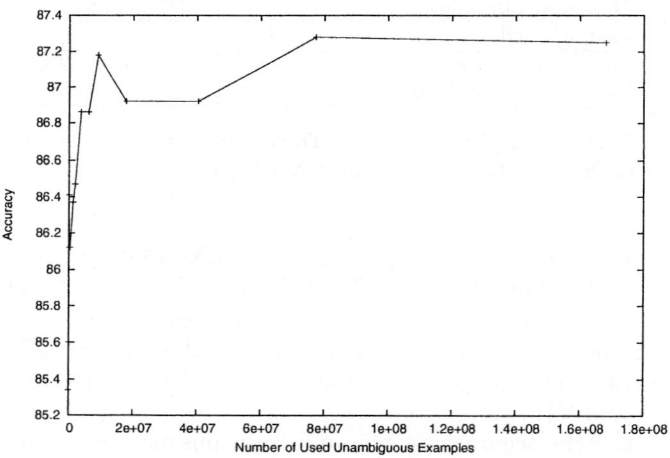

Fig. 2. Learning Curve of PP-Attachment Disambiguation while changing the number of used unambiguous examples

7 Conclusions

This paper has presented a corpus-based method for PP-attachment disambiguation. Our approach utilizes precise lexical preferences learned from a gigantic volume of truly unambiguous examples in raw corpus. Attachment decisions are made using a machine learning method that incorporates these lexical preferences. Our experiments indicated that the precise lexical preferences worked effectively.

In the future, we will investigate useful contextual features for PP-attachment, because human accuracy improves by around 5% when they see more than just a quadruple.

Acknowledgements

We would like to thank Prof. Kenjiro Taura for allowing us to use an enormous volume of Web corpus. We also would like to express our thanks to Tomohide Shibata for his constructive and fruitful discussions.

References

1. Zhao, S., Lin, D.: A nearest-neighbor method for resolving pp-attachment ambiguity. In: Proceedings of the 1st International Joint Conference on Natural Language Processing. (2004) 428–434
2. Collins, M.: Head-Driven Statistical Models for Natural Language Parsing. PhD thesis, University of Pennsylvania (1999)
3. Charniak, E.: A maximum-entropy-inspired parser. In: Proceedings of the 1st Meeting of the North American Chapter of the Association for Computational Linguistics. (2000) 132–139
4. Ratnaparkhi, A.: Statistical models for unsupervised prepositional phrase attachment. In: Proceedings of the 17th International Conference on Computational Linguistics. (1998) 1079–1085
5. Pantel, P., Lin, D.: An unsupervised approach to prepositional phrase attachment using contextually similar words. In: Proceedings of the 38th Annual Meeting of the Association for Computational Linguistics. (2000) 101–108
6. Manning, C., Schütze, H.: Foundations of Statistical Natural Language Processing. MIT Press (1999)
7. Marcus, M., Santorini, B., Marcinkiewicz, M.: Building a large annotated corpus of English: the Penn Treebank. Computational Linguistics **19** (1994) 313–330
8. Ratnaparkhi, A., Reynar, J., Roukos, S.: A maximum entropy model for prepositional phrase attachment. In: Proceedings of the ARPA Human Language Technology Workshop. (1994) 250–255
9. Brill, E., Resnik, P.: A rule-based approach to prepositional phrase attachment disambiguation. In: Proceedings of the 15th International Conference on Computational Linguistics. (1994) 1198–1204
10. Collins, M., Brooks, J.: Prepositional phrase attachment through a backed-off model. In: Proceedings of the 3rd Workhop on Very Large Corpora. (1995) 27–38
11. Stetina, J., Nagao, M.: Corpus based pp attachment ambiguity resolution with a semantic dictionary. In: Proceedings of the 5th Workhop on Very Large Corpora. (1997) 66–80
12. Zavrel, J., Daelemans, W., Veenstra, J.: Resolving pp attachment ambiguities with memory-based learning. In: Proceedings of the Workshop on Computational Natural Language Learning. (1997) 136–144
13. Abney, S., Schapire, R., Singer, Y.: Boosting applied to tagging and pp attachment. In: Proceedings of 1999 Joint SIGDAT Conference on Empirical Methods in Natural Language Processing and Very Large Corpora. (1999) 38–45

14. Vanschoenwinkel, B., Manderick, B.: A weighted polynomial information gain kernel for resolving pp attachment ambiguities with support vector machines. In: Proceedings of the 18th International Joint Conference on Artificial Intelligence. (2003) 133–138
15. Hindle, D., Rooth, M.: Structural ambiguity and lexical relations. Computational Linguistics **19** (1993) 103–120
16. Volk, M.: Combining unsupervised and supervised methods for pp attachment disambiguation. In: Proceedings of the 19th International Conference on Computational Linguistics. (2002) 1065–1071
17. Takahashi, T., Soonsang, H., Taura, K., Yonezawa, A.: World wide web crawler. In: Poster Proceedings of the 11th International World Wide Web Conference. (2002)
18. Brill, E.: Transformation-based error-driven learning and natural language processing: A case study in part-of-speech tagging. Computational Linguistics **21** (1995) 543–565
19. Kudo, T., Matsumoto, Y.: Chunking with support vector machines. In: Proceedings of the 2nd Meeting of the North American Chapter of the Association for Computational Linguistics. (2001) 192–199
20. Vapnik, V.: The Nature of Statistical Learning Theory. Springer (1995)
21. Joachims, T.: 11. In: Making Large-Scale Support Vector Machine Learning Practical, in Advances in Kernel Methods - Support Vector Learning. MIT Press (1999) 169–184
22. Morik, K., Brockhausen, P., Joachims, T.: Combining statistical learning with a knowledge-based approach – a case study in intensive care monitoring. In: Proceedings of the 16th International Conference on Machine Learning. (1999) 268–277

Adapting a Probabilistic Disambiguation Model of an HPSG Parser to a New Domain

Tadayoshi Hara[1], Yusuke Miyao[1], and Jun'ichi Tsujii[1,2,3]

[1] Department of Computer Science, University of Tokyo,
Hongo 7-3-1, Bunkyo-ku, Tokyo 113-0033, Japan
[2] CREST, JST (Japan Science and Technology Agency),
Honcho, 4-1-8, Kawaguchi-shi, Saitama 332-0012, Japan
[3] School of Informatics, University of Manchester,
POBox 88, Sackville St, Manchester, M60 1QD, UK

Abstract. This paper describes a method of adapting a domain-independent HPSG parser to a biomedical domain. Without modifying the grammar and the probabilistic model of the original HPSG parser, we develop a log-linear model with additional features on a treebank of the biomedical domain. Since the treebank of the target domain is limited, we need to exploit an original disambiguation model that was trained on a larger treebank. Our model incorporates the original model as a reference probabilistic distribution. The experimental results for our model trained with a small amount of a treebank demonstrated an improvement in parsing accuracy.

1 Introduction

Natural language processing (NLP) is being demanded in various fields, such as biomedical research, patent application, and WWW, because an unmanageable amount of information is being published in unstructured data, i.e., natural language texts. To exploit latent information in these, the assistance of NLP technologies is highly required. However, an obstacle is the lack of portability of NLP tools. In general, NLP tools specialized to each domain were developed from scratch, or adapted by considerable human effort. This is because linguistic resources for each domain, such as a treebank, have not been sufficiently developed yet. Since dealing with various kinds of domains is an almost intractable job, sufficient resources can not be expected.

The method presented in this paper is the development of disambiguation models of an HPSG parser by combining a disambiguation model of an original parser with a new model adapting to a new domain. Although the training of a disambiguation model of a parser requires a sufficient amount of a treebank, its construction requires a considerable human effort. Hence, we exploit the original disambiguation model that was trained with a larger, but domain-independent treebank. Since the original disambiguation model contains rich information of general grammatical constraints, we try to use its information in developing a disambiguation model for a new domain.

R. Dale et al. (Eds.): IJCNLP 2005, LNAI 3651, pp. 199–210, 2005.

Our disambiguation model is a log-linear model into which the original disambiguation model is incorporated as a reference distribution. However, we cannot simply estimate this model, because of the problem that has been discussed in studies of the probabilistic modeling of unification-based grammars [1,2]. That is, the exponential explosion of parse candidates assigned by the grammar makes the estimation intractable. The previous studies solved the problem by applying a dynamic programming algorithm to a packed representation of parse trees. In this paper, we borrow their idea, and define reference distribution on a packed structure. With this method, the log-linear model with a reference distribution can be estimated by using dynamic programming.

In the experiments, we used an HPSG parser originally trained with the Penn Treebank [3], and evaluated a disambiguation model trained with the GENIA treebank [4], which consisted of abstracts of biomedical papers. First, we measured the accuracy of parsing and the time required for parameter estimation. For comparison, we also examined other possible models other than our disambiguation model. Next, we varied the size of a training corpus in order to evaluate the size sufficient for domain adaptation. Then, we varied feature sets used for training and examined the parsing accuracy. Finally, we compared the errors in the parsing results of our model with those of the original parser.

In Section 2, we introduce the disambiguation model of an HPSG parser. In Section 3, we describe a method of adopting reference distribution for adapting a probabilistic disambiguation model to a new domain. In Section 4, we examine our method through experiments on the GENIA treebank.

2 An HPSG Parser

The HPSG parser used in this study is *Enju* [5]. The grammar of Enju was extracted from the Penn Treebank [3], which consisted of sentences collected from The Wall Street Journal [6]. The disambiguation model of Enju was trained on the same treebank. This means that the parser has been adapted to The Wall Street Journal, and would be difficult to apply to other domains such as biomedical papers that include different distribution of words and their constraints.

In this study, we attempted the adaptation of a probabilistic disambiguation model by fixing the grammar and the disambiguation model of the original parser. The disambiguation model of Enju is based on a feature forest model [2], which is a maximum entropy model [7] on packed forest structure. The probability, $p_E(t|s)$, of producing the parse result t for a given sentence s is defined as

$$p_E(t|s) = \frac{1}{Z_s} \exp\left(\sum_i \lambda_i f_i(t,s)\right)$$

$$Z_s = \sum_{t' \in T(s)} \exp\left(\sum_i \lambda_i f_i(t',s)\right),$$

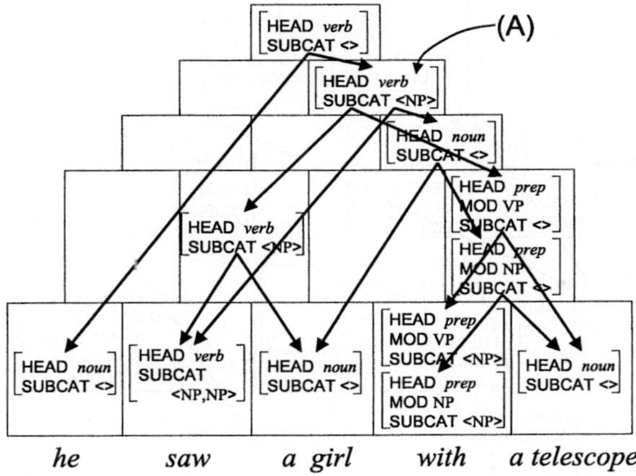

Fig. 1. Chart for parsing *"he saw a girl with a telescope"*

where $T(s)$ is the set of parse candidates assigned to s. The feature function $f_i(t, s)$ represents the characteristics of t and s, while the corresponding model parameter λ_i is its weight. Model parameters were estimated so as to maximize the log-likelihood of the training data.

Estimation of the above model requires a set of training pairs $\langle t_s, T(s)\rangle$, where t_s is the correct parse for the sentence s. While t_s is provided by a treebank, $T(s)$ is computed by parsing each s in the treebank. However, the simple enumeration of $T(s)$ is impractical because the size of $T(s)$ is exponential to the length of s.

To avoid an exponential explosion, Enju represented $T(s)$ in a packed form of HPSG parse trees [5]. In chart parsing, partial parse candidates are stored in a *chart*, in which phrasal signs are identified and packed into an equivalence class if they are determined to be equivalent and dominate the same word sequence. A set of parse trees is then represented as a set of relations among equivalence classes. Figure 1 shows a chart for parsing *"he saw a girl with a telescope"*, where the modifiee (*"saw"* or *"girl"*) of *"with"* is ambiguous. Each feature structure expresses an equivalence class, and the arrows represent immediate-dominance relations. The phrase, *"saw a girl with a telescope"*, has two ambiguous subtrees (A in the figure). Since the signs of the top-most nodes are equivalent, they are packed into the same equivalence class. The ambiguity is represented as two pairs of arrows that come out of the node.

A packed chart can be interpreted as an instance of a feature forest [2]. A feature forest represents a set of exponentially-many trees in an "and/or" graph of a tractable size. A feature forest is formally defined as a tuple $\langle C, D, R, \gamma, \delta\rangle$, where C is a set of conjunctive nodes, D is a set of disjunctive nodes, $R \subseteq C$ is a set of root nodes[1], $\gamma : D \rightarrow 2^C$ is a conjunctive daughter function, and $\delta : C \rightarrow 2^D$ is a disjunctive daughter function.

[1] For the ease of explanation, the definition of root node is slightly different from the original.

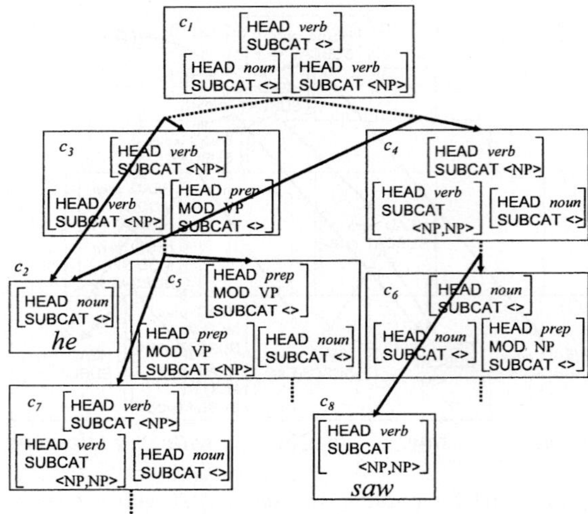

Fig. 2. Packed representation of HPSG parse trees in Figure 1

Figure 2 shows (a part of) the HPSG parse trees in Figure 1 represented as a feature forest. Square boxes are conjunctive nodes, dotted lines express a disjunctive daughter function, and solid arrows represent a conjunctive daughter function.

Based on the definition, parse tree t of sentence s can be represented as the set of conjunctive nodes in the feature forest. The probability $p_E(t|s)$ is then redefined as

$$p_E(t|s) = \frac{1}{Z_s} \exp\left(\sum_{c \in t} \sum_i \lambda_i f_i(c) \right)$$

$$Z_s = \sum_{t' \in T(s)} \exp\left(\sum_{c \in t'} \sum_i \lambda_i f_i(c) \right),$$

where $f_i(c)$ are alternative feature functions assigned to conjunctive nodes $c \in C$. By using this redefined probability, a dynamic programming algorithm can be applied to estimate $p(t|T(s))$ without unpacking the packed chart [2].

Feature functions in feature forest models are designed to capture the characteristics of a conjunctive node. In HPSG parsing, it corresponds to a tuple of a mother and its daughters. Enju uses features that are combinations of the atomic features listed in Table 1. The following combinations are used for representing the characteristics of the binary/unary rule applications.

$$f_{\text{binary}} = \left\langle \begin{array}{l} \text{RULE,DIST,COMMA,} \\ \text{SPAN}_h, \text{SYM}_h, \text{WORD}_h, \text{POS}_h, \text{LE}_h, \\ \text{SPAN}_n, \text{SYM}_n, \text{WORD}_n, \text{POS}_n, \text{LE}_n \end{array} \right\rangle$$

$$f_{\text{unary}} = \langle \text{RULE,SYM,WORD,POS,LE} \rangle$$

where suffix h and n means a head daughter and a non-head daughter, respectively.

Table 1. Templates of atomic features

RULE	the name of the applied schema
DIST	the distance between the head words of the daughters
COMMA	whether a comma exists between daughters and/or inside of daughter phrases
SPAN	the number of words dominated by the phrase
SYM	the symbol of the phrasal category (e.g. NP, VP)
WORD	the surface form of the head word
POS	the part-of-speech of the head word
LE	the lexical entry assigned to the head word

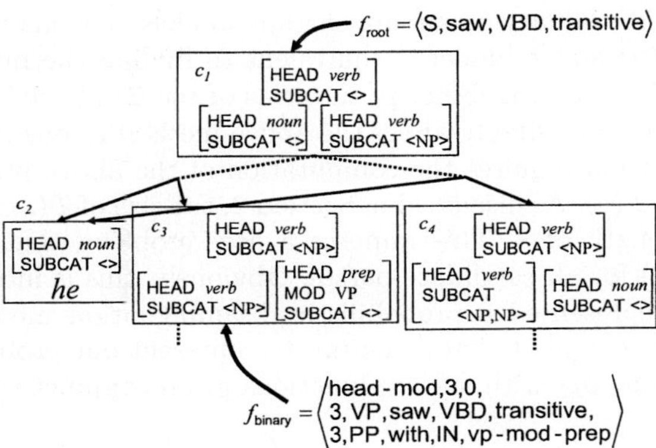

Fig. 3. Example features

In addition, the following feature is used for expressing the condition of the root node of the parse tree.

$$f_{\text{root}} = \langle \text{SYM,WORD,POS,LE} \rangle$$

Figure 3 shows example features: f_{root} is the feature for the root node, in which the phrase symbol is S and the surface form, part-of-speech, and lexical entry of the lexical head are *"saw"*, VBD, and a transitive verb, respectively. The f_{binary} is the feature for the binary rule application to *"saw a girl"* and *"with a telescope"*, in which the applied schema is the Head-Modifier Schema, the head daughter is VP headed by *"saw"*, and the non-head daughter is PP headed by *"with"*, whose part-of-speech is IN and the lexical entry is a VP-modifying preposition.

3 Re-training of Disambiguation Models

The method of domain adaptation is to develop a new maximum entropy model with incorporating an original model as a reference probabilistic distribution. The idea of adaptation using a reference distribution has already been presented in several studies [8,9]. When we have a reference probabilistic model $p_0(t|s)$ and are making a new model $p_M(t|s)$, the probability is defined as

$$p_M(t|s) = \frac{1}{Z'_s} p_0(t|s) \exp\left(\sum_j \rho_j g_j(t', s)\right)$$

$$\text{where} \quad Z'_s = \sum_{t' \in T(s)} p_0(t'|s) \exp\left(\sum_j \rho_j g_j(t', s)\right).$$

Model parameters, ρ_j, are estimated so as to maximize the likelihood of the training data as in ordinary maximum entropy models. The maximization of the likelihood with the above model is equivalent to finding the model p_M that is closest to the reference probability p_0 in terms of the Kullback-Leibler distance.

However, we cannot simply apply the above method to our task because the parameter estimation requires the computation of the above probability for all parse candidates $T(s)$. As discussed in Section 2, the size of $T(s)$ is exponentially related to the length of s. This imposes a new problem, that is, we need to enumerate $p_0(t|s)$ for all candidate parses. Obviously, this is intractable.

Since Enju represented a probabilistic disambiguation model in a packed forest structure, we exploit that structure to represent our probabilistic model. That is, we redefine p_M with feature functions g_j on conjunctive nodes as

$$p_M(t|s) = \frac{1}{Z'_s} p_0(t|s) \exp\left(\sum_{c \in t} \sum_j \rho_j g_j(c)\right)$$

$$\text{where} \quad Z'_s = \sum_{t' \in T(s)} p_0(t|s) \exp\left(\sum_{c \in t'} \sum_j \rho_j g_j(c)\right).$$

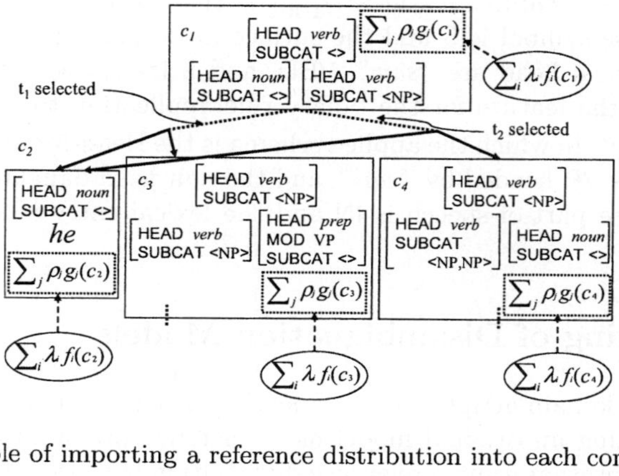

Fig. 4. Example of importing a reference distribution into each conjunctive node

As described in Section 2, the original model, $p_E(t|s)$, is expressed in a packed structure as

$$p_E(t|s) = \frac{1}{Z_s} \exp\left(\sum_{c\in t}\sum_i \lambda_i f_i(c)\right)$$

$$\text{where} \quad Z_s = \sum_{t'\in T(s)} \exp\left(\sum_{c\in t}\sum_i \lambda_i f_i(c)\right).$$

Then, $p_0(t|s)$ is substituted by $p_E(t|s)$, and $p_M(t|s)$ is formulated as

$$\begin{aligned} p_M(t|s) &= \frac{1}{Z'_s}\left\{\frac{1}{Z_s}\exp\left(\sum_{c\in t}\sum_i \lambda_i f_i(c)\right)\right\}\exp\left(\sum_{c\in t}\sum_j \rho_j g_j(c)\right) \\ &= \frac{1}{Z'_s\cdot Z_s}\exp\left(\sum_{c\in t}\sum_i \lambda_i f_i(c) + \sum_{c\in t}\sum_j \rho_j g_j(c)\right) \\ &= \frac{1}{Z''_s}\exp\left\{\sum_{c\in t}\left(\sum_i \lambda_i f_i(c) + \sum_j \rho_j g_j(c)\right)\right\} \end{aligned}$$

$$\text{where} \quad Z''_s = Z_s \cdot Z'_s = \sum_{t\in T(s)} \exp\left\{\sum_{c\in t}\left(\sum_i \lambda_i f_i(c) + \sum_j \rho_j g_j(c)\right)\right\}.$$

With this form of $p_M(t|s)$, a dynamic programing algorithm can be applied. For example, we show how to obtain probabilities of parse trees in the case of Figure 4. For ease, we assume that there are only two disjunctive daughters (dotted lines) that are of the top conjunctive node. The left disjunctive node introduces a parse tree t_1 that consists of conjunctive nodes $\{c_1, c_2, c_3, \dots\}$, and the right one, t_2 that consists of $\{c_1, c_2, c_4, \dots\}$. To each conjunctive node c_k, a weight from the reference distribution $\sum_i \lambda_i f_i(c_k)$ is assigned. Probability $p_M(t_1|s)$ and $p_M(t_2|s)$ are then given as

$$\begin{aligned} p_M(t_1|s) = \frac{1}{Z''_s}\exp\Bigg\{&\left(\sum_i \lambda_i f_i(c_1) + \sum_j \rho_j g_j(c_1)\right) + \left(\sum_i \lambda_i f_i(c_2) + \sum_j \rho_j g_j(c_2)\right) \\ &+ \left(\sum_i \lambda_i f_i(c_3) + \sum_j \rho_j g_j(c_3)\right) + \cdots\Bigg\} \end{aligned}$$

$$\begin{aligned} p_M(t_2|s) = \frac{1}{Z''_s}\exp\Bigg\{&\left(\sum_i \lambda_i f_i(c_1) + \sum_j \rho_j g_j(c_1)\right) + \left(\sum_i \lambda_i f_i(c_2) + \sum_j \rho_j g_j(c_2)\right) \\ &+ \left(\sum_i \lambda_i f_i(c_4) + \sum_j \rho_j g_j(c_4)\right) + \cdots\Bigg\}. \end{aligned}$$

4 Experiments

We implemented the method described in Section 3. The original parser, Enju, was developed on Section 02-21 of the Penn Treebank (39,832 sentences)[5]. For the training of our model, we used the GENIA treebank [4], which consisted of 500 abstracts (4,446 sentences) extracted from MEDLINE. We divided the GENIA treebank into three sets of 400, 50, and 50 abstracts (3,524, 455, and 467 sentences), and these sets were used respectively as training, development, and final evaluation data. The method of Gaussian MAP estimation [10] was used for smoothing.

The meta parameter σ of the Gaussian distribution was determined so as to maximize the accuracy on the development set. In the following experiments, we measured the accuracy of predicate-argument dependencies on the evaluation set. The measure is labeled precision/recall (LP/LR), which is the same measure as previous work [11,5] that evaluated the accuracy of lexicalized grammars on the Penn Treebank.

First, we measured the accuracy of parsing and the time required for parameter estimation. Table 2 compares the results of the following estimation methods.

Table 2. Accuracy and time cost for various estimation methods

	F-score		Training	Parsing time (sec.)	
	GENIA Corpus	Penn Treebank	time (sec.)	GENIA Corpus	Penn Treebank
Our method	86.87	86.81	2,278	611	3,165
Combined	86.32	86.09	29,421	424	2,757
GENIA only	85.72	42.49	1,694	332	8,183
Original model	85.10	87.16	137,038	515	2,554

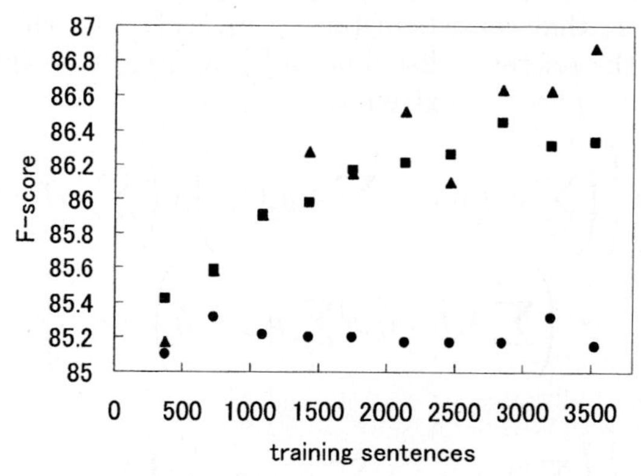

Fig. 5. Corpus size vs. Accuracy

Table 3. Accuracy with atomic feature templates

Features	LP	LR	F-score	diff.
RULE	85.42	84.87	85.15	+0.05
DIST	85.29	84.77	85.03	−0.07
COMMA	85.45	84.86	85.15	+0.05
SPAN_h+SPAN_n	85.58	85.02	85.30	+0.20
SYMBOL_h+SYMBOL_n	85.01	84.56	84.78	−0.32
WORD_h+WORD_n	86.59	86.07	86.33	+1.23
WORD_h	85.48	84.98	85.23	+0.13
WORD_n	85.44	84.64	85.04	−0.06
POS_h+POS_n	85.23	84.77	85.00	−0.10
LE_h+LE_n	85.42	85.06	85.24	+0.14
None	85.39	84.82	85.10	

Table 4. Accuracy with the combination of RULE and other features

Features	LP	LR	F-score	diff.
RULE+DIST	85.41	84.85	85.13	+0.03
RULE+COMMA	85.92	85.15	85.53	+0.43
RULE+SPAN_h+SPAN_n	85.33	84.82	85.07	−0.03
RULE+SYMBOL_h+SYMBOL_n	85.43	85.00	85.21	+0.11
RULE+WORD_h+WORD_n	87.12	86.62	86.87	+1.77
RULE + WORD_h	85.74	84.94	85.34	+0.24
RULE + WORD_n	85.10	84.60	84.85	−0.25
RULE−POS_h+POS_n	85.51	85.08	85.29	+0.19
RULE+LE_h+LE_n	85.48	85.08	85.28	+0.18
None	85.39	84.82	85.10	

Our method: training with our method
Combined: training Enju model with the training corpus replaced by the combination of the GENIA corpus and the Penn Treebank
GENIA only: training Enju model with the training corpus replaced by the GENIA corpus only
Original Model: training an original Enju model

The table shows the accuracy and the parsing time for the GENIA corpus and the Penn Treebank Section 23, and also shows the time required for the training of the model. The additional feature used in our method was RULE+WORD_h+ WORD_n, which will be explained later. In the "Combined" method, we could not train the model with the original training parameters ($n = 20$, $\epsilon = 0.98$ in [5]) because the estimator ran out of memory. Hence, we reduced the parameters to $n = 10$, $\epsilon = 0.95$.

For the GENIA corpus, our model gave the higher accuracy than the original model and the other estimation methods, while for the Penn Treebank, our model gave a little lower accuracy than the original model. This result indicates that our model was more adapted to the specific domain. The "GENIA only"

Table 5. Accuracy with the combination of WORD and another feature

Features	LP	LR	F-score	diff.
WORD_h+WORD_n+RULE	87.12	86.62	86.87	+1.77
WORD_h+WORD_n+DIST	86.41	85.86	86.14	+1.04
WORD_h+WORD_n+COMMA	86.91	86.38	86.64	+1.54
WORD_h+WORD_n+SPAN_h+SPAN_n	85.77	85.22	85.49	+0.39
WORD_h+WORD_n+SYMBOL_h+SYMBOL_n	86.58	85.70	86.14	+1.04
WORD_h+WORD_n+POS_h+POS_n	86.53	85.99	86.26	+1.16
WORD_h+WORD_n+LE_h+LE_n	86.16	85.68	85.92	+0.82
None	85.39	84.82	85.10	

Table 6. Errors in our model and Enju

	Total errors	Common errors	Errors not in the other model
Our model	1179	1050	129
Original model	1338	1050	288

method gave significantly lower accuracy. We expect that the method clearly lacked the amount of the training corpus for obtaining generic grammatical information.

The "Combined" method achieved the accuracy close to our method. However, it is notable that our method took much less time for the training of the model since ours did not need to handle the Penn Treebank. Instead, our method exploited the original model of Enju, which was trained on the Penn Treebank, and this resulted in much less cost of training.

Next, we changed the size of the GENIA treebank for training: 40, 80, 120, 160, 200, 240, 280, 320, 360, and 400 abstracts. Figure 5 shows the accuracy when the size of the training data was changed. We can say that, for those feature sets giving remarkable accuracy in the experiments, the accuracy edged upwards with the size of the training corpus, and the trend does not seem to converge even if more than 400 abstracts exist. If we choose more complex feature sets for higher accuracy, data sparseness will occur and an even larger corpus will be needed. These findings indicate that we can further improve the accuracy by using a larger treebank and a proper feature set.

Table 3 shows the accuracy of models with only atomic feature templates. The bottom of the table gives the accuracy attained by the original parser. When we focus on the WORD features, we can see the combination of WORD_h and WORD_n improved the accuracy significantly, although each of the features by itself did not improve so much. DIST, SYMBOL, and POS feature templates lowered the accuracy. The other feature templates improved the accuracy, though not as well as the WORD templates.

Table 4 shows that the RULE feature combined with one or more other features often gave a little higher accuracy than the RULE feature gave by itself, though not as well as the WORD features.

Table 5 shows that the WORD features combined with one or more other features gave remarkable improvement to the accuracy as a whole. RULE and COMMA features gave even higher accuracy than with only the WORD features. Our results revealed that the WORD features were crucial for the adaptation to the biomedical domain. We expect that this was because the biomedical domain had a different distribution of words, while more generic grammatical constraints were not significantly different from other domains.

Table 6 shows the comparison of the number of errors of our model with those of the original model in parsing the GENIA corpus. Though our model gave less errors than the original model, our model introduced a certain amount of new errors. In future work, we need to investigate manually those errors to find more suitable feature templates without losing the information in the original model.

5 Conclusions

We have presented a method of adapting a domain-independent HPSG parser to a biomedical domain. Since the treebank of the new domain was limited, we exploited an original disambiguation model. The new model was trained on a biomedical treebank, and was combined with the original model by using it as a reference distribution of a log-linear model. The experimental results demonstrated our new model was adapted to the target domain, and was superior to other adaptation methods in accuracy and the cost of training time. With our model, the parsing accuracy for the target domain improved by 1.77 point with the treebank of 3,524 sentences. Since the accuracy did not seem to saturate, we will further improve the accuracy by increasing the size of the domain-dependent treebank. In addition, the experimental results showed that the WORD feature significantly contributed to the accuracy improvement.

We examined only a few feature templates, and we must search for further more feature templates. Not only the new combinations of the atomic features but also new types of features, which may be domain-dependent such as named entities, will be possible.

References

1. Geman, S., Johnson, M.: Dynamic programming for parsing and estimation of stochastic unification-based grammars. In: Proc. 40th ACL. (2002)
2. Miyao, Y., Tsujii, J.: Maximum entropy estimation for feature forests. In: Proc. HLT 2002. (2002)
3. Marcus, M., Kim, G., Marcinkiewicz, M.A., MacIntyre, R., Bies, A., Ferguson, M., Katz, K., Schasberger, B.: The Penn Treebank: Annotating predicate argument structure. In: ARPA Human Language Technology Workshop. (1994)
4. Kim, J.D., Ohta, T., Teteisi, Y., Tsujii, J.: Genia corpus - a semantically annotated corpus for bio-textmining. Bioinformatics **19** (2003) i180–i182
5. Miyao, Y., Tsujii, J.: Probabilistic disambiguation models for wide-coverage HPSG parsing. In: Proc. ACL 2005. (2005)

6. Miyao, Y., Ninomiya, T., Tsujii, J.: Corpus-oriented grammar development for acquiring a Head-driven Phrase Structure Grammar from the Penn Treebank. In: Proc. IJCNLP-04. (2004)
7. Berger, A.L., Pietra, S.A.D., Pietra, V.J.D.: A maximum entropy approach to natural language processing. Computational Linguistics **22** (1996) 39–71
8. Jelinek, F.: Statistical Methods for Speech Recognition. The MIT Press (1998)
9. Johnson, M., Riezler, S.: Exploiting auxiliary distributions in stochastic unification-based grammars. In: Proc. 1st NAACL. (2000)
10. Chen, S., Rosenfeld, R.: A gaussian prior for smoothing maximum entropy models. Technical Report CMUCS-99-108, Carnegie Mellon University (1999)
11. Clark, S., Curran, J.R.: Parsing the WSJ using CCG and log-linear models. In: Proc. 42nd ACL. (2004)

A Hybrid Approach to Single and Multiple PP Attachment Using WordNet

Akshar Bharathi, Rohini U.[1], Vishnu P.[1], S.M. Bendre[2], and Rajeev Sangal[1]

[1] International Institute of Information Technology,
Hyderabad, India
rohini@research.iiit.net, vishnu@students.iiit.net, sangal@iiit.net
[2] University of Hyderabad, Hyderabad, India
bendre@iiit.net

Abstract. The problem of prepositional phrase attachment is crucial to various natural language processing tasks and has received wide attention in the literature. In this paper, we propose an algorithm to disambiguate between PP attachment sites. The algorithm uses a combination of supervised and unsupervised learning along with the WordNet information, which is implemented using a back-off model. Our use of the available sources of lexical knowledge base in combination with large un-annotated corpora generalizes the existing algorithms with improved performance. The algorithm achieved average accuracy of 86.68% over three test data sets with 100% recall. It is further extended to deal with the multiple PP attachment problem using the training based on single PP attachment sites and showed improvement over the earlier works on multiple pp attachment.

1 Introduction

Prepositional phrase (PP) attachment problem addresses structural ambiguity in natural language processing which is a major source of errors in parsing. The goal of PP attachment is to decide the attachment site of a given PP in the sentence. For example, consider the following sentences

a) *Mary ate the salad with a fork.*
b) *Mary ate the salad with croutons.*

In sentence a), the PP '*with a fork*' attaches to the verb *eat* rather than the noun *salad* and is called adverbial attachment. In sentence b), the PP '*with croutons*' attaches to *salad* rather than *eat* and is called adjectival attachment.

1.1 Related Work

The problem of disambiguation between the PP attachment sites has received wide attention in natural language processing. Many rule-based methods, statistical methods which comprise of supervised and unsupervised methods and hybrid methods are proposed for the ambiguity resolution.

R. Dale et al. (Eds.): IJCNLP 2005, LNAI 3651, pp. 211–222, 2005.

The prominent among the supervised methods which use annotated corpora for ambiguity resolution is the transformation-based approach by Brill and Resnik [1] with reported accuracy of 80% and the back-off approach to smoothen the probabilities of unseen attachments by Collins and Brooks [2] with reported accuracy of 84.5%. Ratnaparakhi et al [7] considered lexical information within the verb phrase and used maximum entropy model to achieve the accuracy of 81.6%. Stetina and Nagao [9] used the WordNet thesaurus and sense tagged corpus to achieve the accuracy of 88.1% using a decision tree for classification. Though supervised methods dominate unsupervised methods in performance and the accuracy achieved by Stetino and Nagao [9] is close to the human accuracy of 88.2% reported by Ratnaparakhi et al [7], the non-availability of large amount of annotated corpus is a serious limitation.

On the other hand, the unsupervised methods use un-annotated corpus and infer attachment site based on the lexical association. Hindle and Rooth [4] used the lexical associations of verbs and nouns by computing co-occurrence frequencies, which resulted in 82% correct attachments for a set of around 3000 test cases from the Penn Tree bank. Pantel and Lin [6] proposed an iterative approach using unsupervised training data. The algorithm uses contextually similar words derived from a collocation database and a corpus based thesaurus for classification with 84% accuracy. Zavrel et al [11] proposed a nearest-neighbor algorithm using memory based learning with an accuracy of 84.4%. Zhao and Lin [12] also used nearest-neighbor approach using various similarity measures and the algorithm achieved 86.5% accuracy using the cosine of mutual information as the similarity measure. Srinivas and Bhattacharya [8] extracted unambiguous data from raw corpus based on heuristics, expanded it using WordNet and used it as a training set, which yielded an accuracy of 83.86% on test data prepared by Ratnaparakhi et al [7]. Volk [10] combined the supervised and unsupervised approaches and used the back-off model for disambiguation on German corpus, achieving an accuracy of about 81% with a small annotated corpus of 10,000 sentences.

1.2 Proposed Approach

In this paper, we propose an approach which combines the strength of supervised and unsupervised approaches and also uses WordNet information whenever available to improve the disambiguation of attachment of a given PP. Our approach handles the problem of sparse data and the use of WordNet significantly differs from the earlier approaches (Stetino and Nagao [9]; Srinivas and Bhattacharya [8]).

The training phase consists of supervised and unsupervised learning from annotated and un-annotated corpora and computing supervised and unsupervised scores. The supervised scores for quadruplets, triplets and pairs are analogous to the scores considered by Collins and Brooks [2]. Further, information is iteratively extracted from the un-annotated corpus and is used to compute unsupervised scores for triplets and pairs. In addition, synonyms of verb and nouns present in a quadruplet are extracted from WordNet and their supervised and unsupervised scores are appropriately used to compute supervised and unsupervised WordNet scores respectively. All the calculated scores effectively give probability estimates of verb and noun attachments in the given situation. A convex combination of all these scores is used for disambiguation of the attachment of a given PP using a back-off model similar to Volk [10]. The approach achieves an accuracy of 86.5% on the test data in [7] containing 2998 quadruplets. The algorithm was also tested on two other data sets and achieved an average accuracy of 86.68% with 100% recall over all three data sets.

We further extend the algorithm to handle the problem of multiple PP attachment. A sentence often contains multiple prepositions, increasing the number of possible attachment sites and thus complicating the PP attachment problem further. For instance, out of 1223 sentences extracted from Penn Tree Bank, containing at least one preposition, all had two prepositions and 43% had three prepositions. The problem of multiple PP attachment has not received much attention in the literature. To our knowledge, there is a single reported attempt by Merlo et al [5] to disambiguate attachment sites in case of multiple PPs in a sentence. They used generalized back-off approach, re-using the single PP attachment training information for multiple PP attachment and achieved an accuracy of 84.3% for first PP, 69.6% for the second and 43.6% for the third PP on data extracted from Penn Tree Bank.

Our extended algorithm when run on the data extracted from Penn Tree Bank showed the accuracy of 86.5% for the first PP, 71.9% for the second and 58% for the third PP. The algorithm was also applied to the test data used by Merlo et al [5] and resulted in the accuracy of 88.99% for the first PP and 73.4% for the second PP. The noun belonging to the last PP in the sentence is not available in this test data and hence the accuracy of our algorithm for the third PP could not be calculated. The algorithm showed improvement over the accuracy achieved by Merlo et al for the first two PPs.

The rest of the paper is organized as follows. Section 2 briefly discusses the single and multiple PP attachment problem and Section 3 describes the training data. Section 4 details the supervised and unsupervised learning. Section 5 presents the disambiguation algorithm for single PP attachment and its evaluation. Section 6 discusses the extension of the single PP algorithm to multiple PP attachment problem and its evaluation and the conclusions are presented in Section 7.

2 Characterizing the PP-Attachment Problem

We first consider the single PP attachment problem. Given a sentence with a single PP, the sentence is typically reduced to a quadruplet (V, N, P_1, N_1) where V is the head verb, N is the head noun of the of the object of V, P_1 is a preposition and N_1 is the head noun of the PP (Ratnaparakhi et al [7]; Pantel and Lin [6]; Volk [10], among others). Thus, the PP attachment problem simplifies to the binary classification task of attaching the PP (P_1, N_1) to V (adverbial attachment) or to N (adjectival attachment).

In case a sentence contains multiple prepositions, the attachment sites for all the PPs need to be determined. An average English sentence usually contains multiple verbs as well as multiple PPs. For example, consider the following sentence from Penn Tree Bank,

ACET will shortly be opening a new office in the east end of London to serve clients in North and East London

which has three PPs and two verbs. The general structure of a sentence having multiple PPs can be represented by

$$V_a \;\; N_a \;\; P_1 \;\; N_1 \;\; P_2 \;\; N_2 \;\; \cdots \;\; V_g \;\; N_g \;\; P_k \;\; N_k \;\; \cdots$$

As a result, there is a multi-fold increase in the possible attachment sites for the second and subsequent PPs. In particular, for the sentence above, the representation is

$$V_a \;\; N_a \;\; P_1 \;\; N_1 \;\; P_2 \;\; N_2 \;\; V_b \;\; N_b \;\; P_3 \;\; N_3$$

and the possible attachments for the preposition phrases can be listed as

- $(P_1, N_1) \;\; \rightarrow \;\; V_a,\; N_a$
- $(P_2, N_2) \;\; \rightarrow \;\; V_a,\; N_a,\; N_1$
- $(P_3, N_3) \;\; \rightarrow \;\; V_a,\; V_b,\; N_2,\; N_b$

For instance, the possible attachment sites for the preposition *'of'* (P_2) in the sentence above are *open, office, end.* The increase in the number of possible attachment sites of subsequent PPs complicates the problem. Also, the presence of multiple verbs in the sentence further adds to the existing complexity. Note that the attachment ambiguity of the first PP (P_1, N_1) is the same as that of a single PP discussed earlier.

We assume that the attachment of a PP in a sentence is independent of the attachment of any other PP that occurs before or after it in the sentence. However, we use a few linguistic rules to rule out certain possible attachment sites, which are discussed in detail in Section 6.

3 Data Description

As mentioned earlier, our approach is a combination of supervised and unsupervised methods which uses two annotated and un-annotated corpora each.

The first annotated corpus[1] consists of 20,801 tagged quadruplets (V, N, P_1, N_1) from Wall Street Journal(WSJ), extracted from Penn Tree bank by the group at IBM. This corpus has been extensively used in earlier works on PP attachment (Ratnaparkhi et al [7]; Stetina and Nagao [9]; Zavrel et al [11], among others). The second annotated corpus consists of 1800 sentences extracted from texts G and H of British National Corpus (BNC)[2] and manually tagged by us. The first un-annotated corpus consists of 40,000 untagged sentences from WSJ . Our second un-annotated corpus consists of around 37 million words extracted from the texts A, B, C and D of BNC.

[1] ftp://ftp.cis.upenn.edu/pub/adwait/PPattachData

[2] http://www.natcorp.ox.ac.uk

For testing the single PP attachment algorithm, we considered three data sets. The first data set (data set I) is from the Penn Tree Bank (WSJ), consisting of 2998 tagged quadruplets collected by Ratnaparkhi [7]. The second data set (data set II) consists of manually tagged 1209 sentences which we extracted from Penn Tree Bank using TGrep2 [3]. For the third data set (data set III), we consider 4583 quadruplets corresponding to the first PP attachments from the test data used by Merlo et al [5][4]. The first test data for multiple PP attachment algorithm (data set IV) consists of 1223 manually annotated sentences extracted automatically from the Penn Tree Bank. In addition, we also tested the algorithm on the data (data set III) used by Merlo et al [5].

4 Learning from Training Data

In this section, we introduce the supervised and unsupervised scores based on supervised and unsupervised learning methods.

4.1 Supervised Learning

Initially, a few preprocessing steps such as morphing, converting all words to lower case, replacing numbers and years by a common token 'NUMBER' etc were carried out on the annotated corpora. The frequencies of quadruplets, triplets, pairs and prepositions for noun and verb attachment were calculated. Based on these frequencies, we compute the following supervised and unsupervised scores analogous to [2].

$$DV = f(0, V, P_1, N_1) + f(0, N, P_1, N_1) + f(0, V, N, P_1)$$
$$DN = f(1, V, P_1, N_1) + f(1, N, P_1, N_1) + f(1, V, N, P_1)$$

where f stands for frequency of occurrence of the triplet in data, 0 stands for verb attachment and 1 for noun attachment. The supervised verb and noun scores for triplets are

$$V_{sup_N}(V, P_1, N_1) = \frac{DV}{DV + DN}, \quad N_{sup_V}(N, P_1, N_1) = \frac{DN}{DV + DN} \tag{1}$$

The subscripts N and V in sup_N and sup_V in (1) above stand for the exact N and V present in the quadruplet, indicating the dependence of the scores on N or V respectively.

Similarly, we compute the scores for the pairs (V, P_1), (N, P_1) and preposition P_1 which are denoted by $V_{sup_{N,N_1}}(V, P_1), N_{sup_{V,N_1}}(N, P_1)$ and $V_{sup}(P_1)$, $N_{sup}(P_1)$ respectively.

---

[3] http://tedlab.mit.edu/ dr/TGrep2/

[4] http://www.latl.unige.ch/personal/cathy_f.html

4.2 Unsupervised Learning

In order to learn from un-annotated corpus, we carried out an iterative approach analogous to Pantel and Lin [6] with modified scores. Each sentence of the un-annotated corpus was parsed using Minipar[5] ignoring the PP attachments. The parsed sentences were used to extract the quadruplets of the form (V, N, P_1, N_1) for every existing PP (P_1, N_1). Each of the extracted quadruplet was reduced to two triplets (V, P_1, N_1) and (N, P_1, N_1) and an initial value of 0.5 was assigned to each triplet. The value of 0.5 can be interpreted as the initial probability that the PP (P_1, N_1) gets a verb or a noun attachment. If only one triplet is extracted from a parsed sentence, a value of 1 is assigned to it. Let $V_{value}(V, P_1, N_1)$ be the sum of the initial values assigned to (V, P_1, N_1) over the entire corpus and similarly we compute $N_{value}(N, P_1, N_1)$. For a specific triplet (V, P_1, N_1), we define proportion as

$$Prop(V, P_1, N_1) = \frac{V_{value}(V, P_1, N_1)}{\sum_{v_i} V_{value}(v_i, P_1, N_1)} \tag{2}$$

where v_i ranges over all verbs occurring with the PP (P_1, N_1) in the un-annotated corpus. $Prop(V, P_i, N_1)$ is an empirical estimate of the probability that the PP (P_1, N_1) occurs with this specific verb V. These proportions are analogous to the frequencies defined by Pantel and Lin [6], but unlike them, we retain P_1 and N_1 in the computations. We believe that N_1 provides context information and as pointed out by Collins and Brooks [2], the preposition P_1 plays a major role in deciding the attachment.

Starting with the initial value in (2), we iteratively modify *Prop* for V by modifying V_{value} to $Prop(V, P_1, N_1) + \sum_{n_i} Prop(V, P_1, n_i) + \sum_{v_i} Prop(v_i, P_1, N_1) + \sum_{v_i, n_i} Prop(v_i, P_1, n_i)$. Effectively, this is a back-off smoothing to get better expectations of V_{value} from the unsupervised corpus. Note that the computation of V_{value} is the Expectation-step and estimating probabilities through *Prop* is the Maximization-step of the EM algorithm. By using back-off smoothing of V_{value} in between, we modify the expectations computed in the E-step. The iterations are continued till the value of $Prop(V, P_1, N_1)$ stabilizes. The stabilized value gives a smoothed estimate of the probability mentioned earlier. $Prop(N, P_1, N_1)$ is computed on the same lines using N_{value}.

From the *Prop* values of triplets thus obtained, we calculate the unsupervised scores for triplets as,

$$V_{unsup}(V, P_1, N_1) = \frac{Prop(V, P_1, N_1)}{\sum_{v_i} Prop(v_i, P_1, N_1)} \tag{3}$$

$$N_{unsup}(N, P_1, N_1) = \frac{Prop(N, P_1, N_1)}{\sum_{n_i} Prop(n_i, P_1, N_1)} \tag{4}$$

where the sum in the denominator of (3) is over all the verbs which co-occur with (P_1, N_1) in the training set. The unsupervised scores for pairs are calculated on the same lines and we skip the details here..

---

[5] http://www.cs.ualberta.ca/ lindek/minipar.htm

The resulting database at the end of the learning stage consists of triples and pairs with their corresponding supervised and unsupervised scores.

5 Single PP Attachment

We now propose an algorithm for the disambiguation of attachment sites for a single PP. As mentioned earlier, the algorithm combines the information learnt from supervised and unsupervised learning with that of WordNet.

Methods incorporating WordNet in PP attachment algorithm have been proposed earlier by Stetina and Nagao [9] for sense disambiguation in constructing a decision tree for PP attachment disambiguation, and Srinivas and Bhattacharya [8] to expand the training set size by replacing each word in the training set by its synonyms. As mentioned earlier, our use of WordNet significantly differs from the above two approaches.

For disambiguation, if the given quadruplet (V, N, P_1, N_1) is present in the annotated corpus, it is assigned the attachment given by the annotated corpus. Otherwise the sets of synonyms are extracted from WordNet for each of V, N and N_1, which we denote by $\mathcal{C}_V$, $\mathcal{C}_N$ and $\mathcal{C}_{N_1}$ respectively. Using the quantities defined in (1)-(4) for the two triplets (V, P_1, N_1) and (N, P_1, N_1), we define WordNet scores for V and N as follows

$$WV_i(V,P_1,N_1)=\begin{cases} \sum_{v_i\in\mathcal{C}_V}\sum_{n_i\in\mathcal{C}_N}\sum_{n1_i\in\mathcal{C}_{N_1}} \frac{g(V_{sup_{n_i}}(v_i,P_1,n1_i))}{|\mathcal{C}_V|*|\mathcal{C}_N|*|\mathcal{C}_{N_1}|} & \text{if } i = sup \\ \sum_{v_i\in\mathcal{C}_V}\sum_{n1_i\in\mathcal{C}_{N_1}} \frac{g(V_{unsup}(v_i,P_1,n1_i))}{|\mathcal{C}_V|*|\mathcal{C}_{N_1}|} & \text{if } i = unsup \end{cases} \tag{5}$$

$$WN_i(N,P_1,N_1)=\begin{cases} \sum_{v_i\in\mathcal{C}_V}\sum_{n_i\in\mathcal{C}_N}\sum_{n1_i\in\mathcal{C}_{N_1}} \frac{g(N_{sup_{v_i}}(n_i,P_1,n1_i))}{|\mathcal{C}_V|*|\mathcal{C}_N|*|\mathcal{C}_{N_1}|} & \text{if } i = sup \\ \sum_{v_i\in\mathcal{C}_V}\sum_{n1_i\in\mathcal{C}_{N_1}} \frac{g(N_{unsup}(n_i,P_1,n1_i))}{|\mathcal{C}_V|*|\mathcal{C}_{N_1}|} & \text{if } i = unsup \end{cases} \tag{6}$$

If any of the triplets is not present in the training corpus, the score is taken to be zero. The function g used in the scores in (5) and (6) is an appropriate weight function. In particular, one can consider binary functions of the type $g(V_{sup_{n_i}}) = 1$ if $V_{sup_{n_i}} > N_{sup_{v_i}}$ and 0 otherwise. We consider the convex combinations of the scores introduced in (1) to (6) above to define the final scores which are used for the disambiguation and are given by

$$FinalVScore_i(V.P_1,N_1) = \alpha\ WV_i(V,P_1,N_1) + (1-\alpha)\ V_i(V,P_1,N_1) \tag{7}$$
$$FinalNScore_i(N,P_1,N_1) = \alpha\ WN_i(N,P_1,N_1) + (1-\alpha)\ N_i(N,P_1,N_1) \tag{8}$$

where α is an appropriately chosen value between 0 and 1 and i is *sup* or *unsup* as the case may be. For the pairs (V, P_1), (N, P_1) and (P_1, N_1) extracted from the given quadruple (V, N, P_1, N_1), the WordNet scores and the final scores are calculated on similar lines. The details of the score calculations for the pairs are presented in Appendix.

To summarize, the disambiguation algorithm is as follows. Given a quadruplet, if the preposition is *'of'*, a noun attachment is assigned irrespective of the verb. Next, if the quadruplet exits in the supervised data the tagged attachment is assigned. Else, a back-off model is employed using the final supervised scores first and then unsupervised scores if needed, at each stage of the model. Also, at each stage, if *FinalVScore* is larger than *FinalNScore*, verb attachment is assigned and noun attachment otherwise. If no attachment is assigned up to the pair stage, the algorithm goes to Level B, where the site is assigned based on the attachment given to the preposition in the annotated corpus. If this leads to a tie, the algorithm goes to Level C, where the default attachment of noun is given to the PP, since it has been reported that choosing noun as the attachment site yields an accuracy of 58.96% [6].

The combination of information from corpora and WordNet used in the algorithm also takes care of the sparse data. We believe that this kind of combination of information helps in disambiguating the attachment even when there is a narrow difference in the noun and verb attachment scores. In Table 1 below, we present the number and percentage of quadruplets identified and the accuracy of the algorithm at each stage of the algorithm for the three test data sets I, II and III described in Section 3. To make certain that our test data sets II and III are not overlapping with the training data set, we did not consider the supervised quadruplets identified by the algorithm for calculating the precision for these two data sets. Hence, the precision reported for data set II is for 863 sentences and that for data set III is for 2481 sentences. The precision increases by about 2-3% when supervised quadruplets are considered.

Table 1. Single PP Attachment : Stage-wise Results

Data set Size	I (Ratnaparkhi) 2998		II (WSJ) 1209		III (Merlo et al) 4583	
Stage	Identified (%)	Accuracy (%)	Identified (%)	Accuracy (%)	Identified (%)	Accuracy (%)
'of'(noun)	29.45	95.1	42.34	99.21	31.96	99.86
Sup Quad	2.33	85.7	28.61	87.57	45.86	89.72
Sup Trip	18.21	84.2	14.39	79.31	8.42	83.28
UnSup Trip	2.33	81.41	2.56	61.29	3.09	64.08
Sup Pair	36.45	82.43	5.54	67.16	5.73	82.5
Unsup Pair	3.73	72.32	2.73	60.60	1.57	72.22
Default(B, C)	7.47	65.1	3.80	34.78	2.68	54.47

Table 2. Single PP Attachment : Overall Results

	Data set I		Data set II		Data set III	
Accuracy	Precision	Recall	Precision	Recall	Precision	Recall
Without Default	**86.32%**	92%	**89.35%**	94.66%	**90.79%**	95.04%
With Default	84.6%	**100%**	86.44%	**100%**	88.99%	**100%**

Table 2 below gives overall precision for the three data sets with and without default stage of level B and C. As anticipated, the precision increases with lower recall.

The average precision over all three data sets is 86.68 % for 100% recall and removing the default stages B and C from the algorithm increases the average precision to 88.82% with 93.9% recall. Though the precision for the data set III is surprisingly high, the precision for the data set I did not surpass the human accuracy of 88.2% reported by Ratnaparkhi et al [7].

6 Extension to Multiple PP Attachments

In this section, we discuss the extension of the proposed single PP attachment algorithm to handle the multiple PP attachment ambiguity. We assume that the decision of the attachment site of one PP in a sentence is independent of the attachment sites of the other PPs in the same sentence. This assumption allows us to use the single PP training data for multiple PP attachment problem. It also enhances the performance of the algorithm by reducing the possible attachment sites for the PPs. Before discussing the algorithm, we present the rules used for reducing possible attachment sites of PPs.

We first resolve the ambiguity among multiple verbs by using clause boundary information, since a preposition can attach only to elements within a clause. The clause boundary information is extracted from the phrase structure tree given by Collins parser. The accuracy of clause boundary identification of Collins parser is reported to be 85% ([3]). Given a test sentence, we identify the clause in which a preposition falls and rule out the other verbs as possible attachment sites, reducing the possibility of multiple verbs as attachment sites. For instance, the clause boundaries for the example sentence of Section 2 are

ACET [will shortly be opening a new office in the east end of London [to serve clients in North and East London]]

The second PP '*in North and East London*' falls in the clause headed by the verb '*serve*', which rules out the verb '*open*' as a possible attachment site.

The preposition may still have a verb and multiple nouns as its attachment sites within the same clause. Though we assume independence of PP attachments, we make use of linguistic knowledge to rule out certain attachment sites. We apply a rule which does not allow edges corresponding to the attachments to cross. For instance, in a structure of the type

$$V_a \;\; N_a \;\; P_1 \;\; N_1 \;\; P_2 \;\; N_2$$

if (P_1, N_1) attaches to V_a then (P_2, N_2) cannot attach to N_a. In the above example, if the PP (P_1, N_1) '*in the east end*' attaches to '*open*', then the PP '*of London*' can not attach to '*office*'. Though the above rule further reduces the possible attachment sites, the ambiguity in the attachment sites of the preposition still persists.

As a first step towards using the single PP algorithm, we construct all possible quadruplets using the verb and available nouns with this PP. For instance, if the possible attachment sites of (P_2, N_2) are V_a, N_a and N_1, then the quadruplets constructed are (V_a, N_a, P_2, N_2), (V_a, N_1, P_2, N_2).

Given any multiple PP sentence, the attachment site of the first preposition is decided based on the algorithm described in Section 5. For each of the subsequent PPs, we first run the single PP attachment algorithm for all the constructed quadruplets. If all the quadruplets give verb as its attachment, adverbial attachment is assigned for the PP. If the attachments given by quadruplets are contradictory, we compute $\lambda Score$ for each of the quadruplet, defined as

$$\lambda Score(V, N, P_1, N_1) = \beta\ E_1 + (1 - \beta)\ E_2$$

where β is an appropriately selected normalizing constant between 0 and 1, E_1 is $FinalVScore_i$ for the quadruplet (V, N, P_1, N_1) and E_2 is $FinalNScore_i$ for the quadruplet (V, N, P_1, N_1) defined in (7) and (8), where i is *sup* or *unsup*, as the case may be. We pick the quadruplet with highest $\lambda Score$ and the PP attachment given by this quadruplet is assigned to the PP.

The above approach was tested using data set IV (Section 3) of 1223 sentences from WSJ, extracted from Penn Tree Bank. All sentences have at least two PPs and 43% of them have three PPs. As mentioned in Section 3, we considered data set III [5] of tuples extracted from 4583 sentences consisting of two or three PPs. The noun belonging to the last PP in the sentence is not available in this test data. Hence only those tuples with two or more PPs could be used to test the accuracy of the attachment of first PP. Similarly, to test for accuracy of the attachment of the second PP, we had to use tuples from the sentences with three PPs. Since all the tuples had a maximum of three PPs only, the accuracy of our algorithm for the attachment of the third PP could not be calculated for data set III. Table 3 presents the performance of our algorithm on data sets IV and III.. Note that analogous to the single PP case, the recall including the default

Table 3. Multiple PP Attachment Results

Data set	IV (WSJ)			III (Merlo et al)		
	PP_1	PP_2	PP_3	PP_1	PP_2	PP_3
Total no. of PPs	1223	1223	523	2581	430	–
Correct	1058	880	303	2208	316	-
Precision	**86.5%**	**71.9%**	**58%**	**88.99%**	**73.4%**	–

is 100% here. The accuracy of PP_1 is similar to the accuracy reported for the single PP attachment (Tables 1 and 2). For the first and the second PP of the test data III, the algorithm achieved 88.99% and 73.4% accuracy respectively. The corresponding accuracies using the algorithm by Merlo et al [5] are 84.3% and 69.6% respectively. The reported accuracy for the third PP is 43.6% and we believe that with the availability of the noun in the third PP, our algorithm would have achieved higher accuracy.

7 Conclusions

In this work, we have looked at the problems of both single PP attachment as well as multiple PP attachment. We combine both supervised and unsupervised methods along with the WordNet information in our algorithm. Our use of WordNet information significantly differs from the earlier approaches using WordNet. The training data from annotated corpora contains quadruplets with PP attachment information, whereas in case of unsupervised training, the data consists of co-occurrence information about the PP and its attachment sites. The training data sets have been extracted from WSJ as well as BNC. Two existing test data sets ([7], [5]) and a third data set extracted from WSJ were used for evaluating the accuracy of the algorithm. The precision of 86.32% with a recall of 92% was achieved on Ratnaparkhi's dataset [7] consisting of 2998 quadruplets. We achieved the average precision of 86.68% with 100% recall and the average of precision of 88.82% with 93.9% recall on the three data sets.

Multiple PP attachment problem was reduced to a problem of stepwise attachment of PPs from left to right within a clause. As a result, the single PP attachment algorithm can be extended to disambiguate each PP attachment site. Based on the attachment decisions for the earlier PPs, certain later PP attachments are ruled out because of non-crossing of attachments. On the test data consisting of 1223 sentences extracted from WSJ the algorithm achieved the precision of 86.5% for the first PP and 71.9% and 58% respectively for subsequent PPs with 100% recall. The algorithm was also tested on the data set used in [5] and showed improvement over the accuracy by the earlier algorithm. Annotated corpus plays an important role in reaching these levels of accuracy and a larger annotated corpus would help in improving this accuracy.

In conclusion, the algorithm shows significant improvement over earlier approaches to single and multiple PP attachment problem. Using thesaurus in place of WordNet is likely to improve the performance further since a thesaurus typically gives larger number of synonyms and does not provide subdivision of senses as fine as WordNet. This possibility is currently being investigated.

While considering second and subsequent PPs in a multiple PP sentence, the quadruplets that are formed do not have information that the noun at a possible attachment site may or may not be an object of the verb. For example, consider the sentence *He put the book on flowers on table.* The PP '*on flowers*' attaches to the noun '*book*' where as '*on the table*' attaches to the verb '*put*'. With the verb like '*put*', both prepositions '*on*' are highly likely to be attached to '*put*' because of the mandatory requirement of the verb frame. Thus the availability of verb frame information will make the task of PP attachment easier. Incorporation of such syntactic information would require a change in the algorithm and may be attempted in the future. In the presence of coordinate structure of two nouns or nous or verbs, our algorithm uses only the last element (noun or verb) in the coordinated structure. Handling of coordinate structure will also be pursued in future.

References

1. Brill, E., Resnik, P.: A Rule based Approach to PP Attachment Disambiguation. In Proceedings of COLING (1994)
2. Collins, M., Brooks, J.: PP Attachment Through a Backed-Off Model. In Proceedings of the Third Workshop on Very Large Corpora (1995)
3. Collins, M.: Head-Driven Statistical Models for Natural Language Processing. Ph.D. Thesis, University of Pennsylvania (1999)
4. Hindle, H., Roth, M.: Structural Ambiguity and Lexical Relations. Computational Linguistics **19** (1993) 103–120
5. Merlo, P., Crocker, M., Berthouzoz, C.: Attaching Multiple Prepositional Phrases:Generalized Backed-off Estimation. In Proceedings of the 2nd conference on Empirical Methods in Natural Language Processing(EMNLP-2) (1997) 149–155
6. Pantel, P., Lin, D.: An Unsupervised Approach to Prepositional Phrase attachment using contextually similar words. In Proceedings of ACET(2000) 101–108
7. Ratnaparkhi, A., Reynar, J., Roukos, S.: Maximum Entropy Model for Prepositional Phrase Attachment. In Proceedings of the ARPA Workshop on Human Language Technology (1994)
8. Srinivas, M., Bhattacharya, P.: Unsupervised PP Attachment Disambiguation Using Semantics. In *Recent Advances in Natural Language Processing*, Allied Publications, New Delhi, India (2004)
9. Stetina, J., Nagao, M.: Corpus Based PP Attachment Ambiguity Resolution with a Semantic Dictionary. In Proceedings of the Fifth Workshop on Very Large Corpora (1997) 66–80
10. Volk, M.,: Combining unsupervised and supervised methods for PP attachment disambiguation. In Proceedings of COLING-2002, Taipei (2002)
11. Zavrel, J., Daelemans, W.: Memory-based Learning: Using similarity for smoothing. In Proceedings of 35th annual meeting of the ACL, Madrid (1997)
12. Zhao, S., Lin, D.: A Nearest Neighbour Method for Resolving PP-Attachment Ambiguity. In Proceedings of the First International Joint Conference on Natural Language Processing (2004)

Appendix . WordNet Scores for Pairs

The initial scores for verb and noun based on annotated corpus are $V_{sup_{N,N_1}}(V, P_1)$, $N_{sup_{V,N_1}}(N, P_1)$ and those using un-annotated corpus are $V_{unsup}(V, P_1)$ and $N_{unsup}(N, P_1)$. WordNet scores for pairs are calculated analogous to those in (5) and (6), given by

$$WV_i(V, P_1) = \begin{cases} \sum_{v_i \in \mathcal{C}_V} \sum_{n_i \in \mathcal{C}_N} \sum_{n1_i \in \mathcal{C}_{N_1})} \frac{g(V_{sup_{n_i,n1_i}}(v_i, P_1))}{|\mathcal{C}_V| * |\mathcal{C}_{N_1}| * |\mathcal{C}_N|} & \text{if i = sup} \\ \sum_{v_i \in \mathcal{C}_V} \frac{g(V_{unsup}(v_i, P_1))}{|\mathcal{C}_V|} & \text{if i = unsup} \end{cases}$$

$$WN_i(N, P_1) = \begin{cases} \sum_{v_i \in \mathcal{C}_V} \sum_{n_i \in \mathcal{C}_N} \sum_{n1_i \in \mathcal{C}_{N_1}} \frac{g(N_{sup_{v_i,n1_i}}(n_i, P_1))}{|\mathcal{C}_N| * |\mathcal{C}_{N_1}| * |\mathcal{C}_N|} & \text{if i = sup} \\ \sum_{n_i \in \mathcal{C}_N} \frac{g(N_{unsup}(n_i, P_1))}{|\mathcal{C}_N|} & \text{if i = unsup.} \end{cases}$$

Similar to final triplet scores in (7) and (8), the final pair scores are

$$FinalVScore_i(V, P_1) = \alpha\ WV_i(V, P_1) + (1 - \alpha)\ V_i(V, P_1)$$
$$FinalNScore_i(N, P_1) = \alpha\ WN_i(N, P_1) + (1 - \alpha)\ N_i(N, P_1)$$

Period Disambiguation with Maxent Model

Chunyu Kit and Xiaoyue Liu

Department of Chinese, Translation and Linguistics,
City University of Hong Kong, 83 Tat Chee Ave., Kowloon, Hong Kong
{ctckit, xyliu0}@cityu.edu.hk

Abstract. This paper presents our recent work on period disambiguation, the kernel problem in sentence boundary identification, with the maximum entropy (Maxent) model. A number of experiments are conducted on PTB-II WSJ corpus for the investigation of how context window, feature space and lexical information such as abbreviated and sentence-initial words affect the learning performance. Such lexical information can be automatically acquired from a training corpus by a learner. Our experimental results show that extending the feature space to integrate these two kinds of lexical information can eliminate 93.52% of the remaining errors from the baseline Maxent model, achieving an F-score of 99.8227%.

1 Introduction

Sentence identification is an important issue in practical natural language processing. It looks simple at first glance since there are a very small number of punctuations, namely, period ("."), question mark ("?"), and exclamation ("!"), to mark sentence ends in written texts. However, not all of them are consistently used as sentence ends. In particular, the use of the dot "." is highly ambiguous in English texts. It can be a full stop, a decimal point, or a dot in an abbreviated word, a numbering item, an email address or a ULR. It may be used for other purposes too. Below are a number of examples from PTB-II WSJ Corpus to illustrate its ambiguities.

(1) `Pierre Vinken, 61 years old, will join the board as a nonexecutive director Nov. 29.`
(2) `The spinoff also will compete with International Business Machines Corp. and Japan's Big Three -- Hitachi Ltd., NEC Corp. and Fujitsu Ltd.`
(3) `The government's construction spending figures contrast with a report issued earlier in the week by McGraw-Hill Inc.'s F.W. Dodge Group.`

Frequently, an abbreviation dot coincides with a full stop, as exemplified by "Ltd." in (2) above. A number followed by a dot can be a numbering item, or simply a normal number at sentence end.

In contrast to ".", "!" and "?" are rarely ambiguous. They are seldom used for other purposes than exclamation and question marks. Thus, the focus of

R. Dale et al. (Eds.): IJCNLP 2005, LNAI 3651, pp. 223–232, 2005.

sentence identification is on period disambiguation to resolve the ambiguity of ".": Whenever a dot shows up in a text token, we need to determine whether or not it is a true period. It is a yes-no classification problem that is suitable for various kinds of machine learning technology to tackle.

Several approaches were developed for sentence splitting. These approaches can be categorized into three classes: (1) rule-based models consisting of manually constructed rules (e.g., in the form of regular expression), supplemented with abbreviation lists, proper names and other relevant lexical resources, as illustrated in [1]; (2) machine learning algorithms, e.g., decision tree classifiers [11], maximum entropy (Maxent) modelling [10] and neural networks [8], among many others; and (3) syntactic methods that utilize syntactic information, e.g., [6] is based on a POS tagger. The machine learning approaches are popular, for period disambiguation is a typical classification problem for machine learning, and the training data is easily available.

Our research reported in this paper explores how context length and feature space affects the performance of the Maxent model for period disambiguation. The technical details involved in this research are introduced in Section 2, with a focus on feature selection and training algorithm. Section 3 presents experiments to show the effectiveness of context length and feature selection on learning performance. Section 4 concludes the paper with our findings: putting frequent abbreviated words or sentence-initial words into the feature space significantly enhances the learning performance, and using a three-word window context gives better performance than others in terms of the F-score. The best combination of the two kinds of lexical information achieves an F-score of 99.8227%, eliminating 93.5% remaining errors from the baseline Maxent model.

2 Feature Selection

The problem of period disambiguation can be formulated as a statistical classification problem. Our research is aimed at exploring the effectiveness of Maxent model [2,12] tackling this problem when trained with various context length and feature sets.

Maxent model is intended to achieve the most unbiased probabilistic distribution on the data set for training. It is also a nice framework for integrating heterogeneous information into a model for classification purpose. It has been popular in NLP community for various language processing tasks since Berger et al. [2] and Della Pietra et al. [3] presenting its theoretical basis and basic training techniques. Ratnaparkhi [9] applied it to tackle several NL ambiguity problems, including sentence boundary detection. Wallach [14] and Malouf [4] compared the effectiveness of several training algorithms for Maxent model.

There are a number of full-fledged implementations of Maxent models available from the Web. Using the OpenNLP MAXENT package from `http://maxent.sourceforge.net/`, acknowledged here with gratitude, we are released from the technical details of its implementation and can concentrate on examining the effectiveness of context length and feature space on period disambiguation. Basically, our exploration is carried out along the following working procedure: (1) prepare a set of training data in terms of the feature space we choose; (2) train the Maxent model, and test its performance with a set of testing data; (3) examine the errors in the test outcomes and adjust the feature space for the next round of training and testing towards possible improvement.

2.1 Context and Features

To identify sentence boundaries, a machine learner needs to learn from the training data the knowledge whether or not a dot is a period in a given context . Classification decision is based on the available contextual information. A context is the few tokens next to the target. By "target" we refer to the "." to be determined whether or not it is a period, and by "target word" (or "dotted word") we refer to the token that carries the dot in question. The dot divides the target word into prefix and suffix, both of which can be empty. Each dot has a *true* or *false* answer for whether it is a true period in a particular context, as illustrated by the following general format.

$$[\text{ preceding-words prefix}\texttt{.}\text{suffix following-words }] \rightarrow \text{Answer: } \textit{true/false}\ . \quad (1)$$

Contextual information comes from all context words surrounding the target dot, including its prefix and suffix. However, instead of feeding the above contextual items to a machine learner as a number of strings for training and testing, extracting special and specific features from them for the training is expected to achieve more effective results. To achieve a learning model as unbiased as possible, we try to extract as many features as possible from the context words, and let the training algorithm to determine their significance. The main cost of using a large feature set is the increase of training time. However, this may be paid off by giving the learner a better chance to achieve a better model.

Table 1. Features for a context word

Feature	Description	Example
`IsCap`	Starting with a capital letter	`On`
`IsRpunct`	Ending with a punctuation	`Calgary,`
`IsLpunct`	Starting with a punctuation	`‘‘We`
`IsRdot`	Ending with a dot	`billions.`
`IsRcomma`	Ending with a comma	`Moreover,`
`IsEword`	An English word	`street`
`IsDigit`	An numeric item	`25%, 36`
`IsAllCap`	Consisting of only capital letters (& dots)	`WASHINGTON`

The feature set for a normal context word that we have developed through several rounds of experiments along the above working procedure are presented in Table 1. Basically, we extract from a word all features that we can observe from its

Table 2. Features for a target word

Feature	Description	Example
`IsHiphenated`	Containing a dash	`non-U.S.`
`IsAllCap`	Consisting of only capital letters (& dots)	`D.C.`
`IsMultiDot`	Containing more than one dot	`N.Y.,`
`prefixIsNull`	A null prefix	`.270`
`prefixIsRdigit`	Ending with a digit	`45.6`
`prefixIsRpunct`	Ending with a punctuation	`0.2%.`
`prefixIsEword`	An English word	`slightly.`
`prefixIsCap`	Starting with a capital letter	`Co.`
`suffixIsNull`	A null suffix	`Mr.`
`suffixIsLdigit`	Starting with a digit	`78.99`
`suffixIsLpunct`	Starting with a punctuation	`Co.'s`
`suffixIsRword`	Ending with a word	`Calif.-based`
`suffixIsCap`	Starting with a capital letter	`B.A.T`

text form. For feature extraction, this set is applied equally, in a principled way, to all context words. The feature set for both parts of a target word is highly similar to that for a context word, except for a few specific to prefix and/or suffix, as given in Table 2, of 13 features in total. The data entry for a given dot, for either training or testing, consists of all such features from its target word and each of its context words. Given a context window of three tokens, among which one is target word, there are 2×8+13=29 features, plus an answer, in each data entry for training.

After feature extraction, each data entry originally in the form of (1) is turned into a more general form for machine learning, as shown in (2) below, consisting of a feature value vector and an answer.

$$f:[f_1=v_1, f_2=v_2, f_3=v_3, \cdots, f_n=v_n] \rightarrow a\text{: } \textit{true/false}\ . \tag{2}$$

Accordingly, the Maxent model used in our experiments has the following distribution in the exponential form:

$$p(a|f) = \frac{1}{Z(f)}\exp(\sum_i \lambda_i \delta(f_i, a))\ , \tag{3}$$

where λ_i is a parameter to be estimated for each i through training, the feature function $\delta_i(f_i, a) = v_i$ for the feature f_i in a data entry $f \rightarrow a$, and the normalization factor

$$Z(f) = \sum_a \exp(\sum_i \lambda_i \delta(f_i, a))\ . \tag{4}$$

2.2 Abbreviation List and Sentence-Initial Words

In addition to the above features, other types of contextual information can be helpful too. For example, abbreviated words like "Dr.", "Mr." and "Prof."

may give a strong indication that the dot they carry is very unlikely to be a period. They may play the role of counter-examples. Another kind of useful lexical resource is sentence-initial words, e.g., "The", "That" and "But", which give a strong indication that a preceding dot is very likely to be a true period.

In order to integrate these two kinds of lexical resource into the Maxent model, we introduce two multi-valued features, namely, `isAbbr` and `isSentInit`, for the target word and its following word, respectively. They are both multi-valued feature function. A list of abbreviated words and a list of sentence-initial words can be easily compiled from a training corpus. Theoretically, the larger the lists are, the better the learning performance could be. Our experiments, to be reported in the next section, show, however, that this is not true, although using the most frequent words in the two lists up to a certain number does lead to a significant improvement.

3 Experiments and Results

3.1 Corpus

The corpus used for our experiments is the PTB-II WSJ corpus, a refined version of PTB [5]. It is particularly suitable for our research purpose. In contrast to BNC and Brown corpus, the WSJ corpus indeed contains many more dots used in different ways for various purposes. Sentence ends are clearly marked in its POS tagged version, although a few mistakes need manual correction. Among 53K sentences from the corpus, 49K end with ".". This set of data is divided into two for training and testing by the ratio of 2:1. The baseline performance by brute-force guess of any dot as a period is 65.02% over the entire set of data.

3.2 Baseline Learning Performance

Our first experiment is to train a Maxent model on the training set with a three-word context window in terms of the features in Tables 1 and 2 above. The performance on the open test is presented in Table 3. It is the baseline performance of the Maxent model.

Table 3. Baseline learning performance of Maxent model

Precision (%)	Recall (%)	F-score (%)
97.55	96.97	97.26

3.3 Effectiveness of Context Window

To examine how context words affect the learning performance, we carry out a number of experiments with context windows of various size. The experimental results are presented in Fig. 1, where x stands for the position of target word and

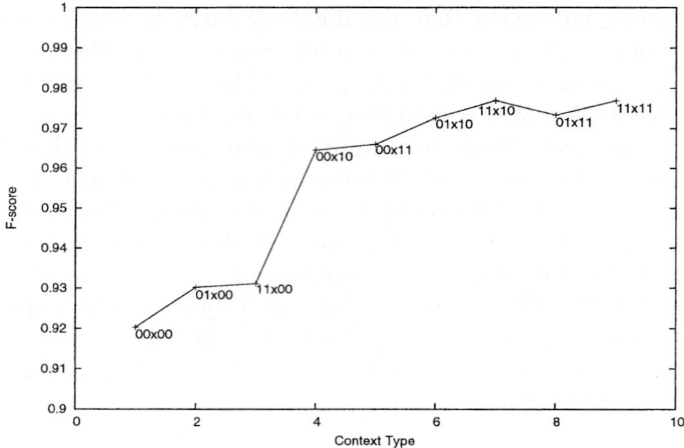

Fig. 1. Effectiveness of context window

1 for a context word in use. For example, `01x10` represents a context window consisting of a target word, its preceding and following words. Each such window is itself a context type.

We can observe from the results that (1) the features extracted from the target word itself already lead the Maxent model to an F-score beyond 92%, (2) the context words preceding the target word are less effective, in general, than those following the target, and (3) combining context words on both sides outperforms those on only one side. The best three context types and the correspondent performance are presented in Table 4. Since they are more effective than others, the experiments to test the effectiveness of abbreviated words and sentence-initial words are based on them.

Table 4. Outperforming context types and their performance

Context Type	`01x10`	`11x10`	`11x11`
F-score (%)	97.2623	97.6949	97.6909

3.4 Effectiveness of Abbreviated Words

Information about whether a target word is an abbreviation plays a critical role in determining whether a dot is truly a period. To examine the significance of such information, an abbreviation list is acquired from the training data by dotted word collection, and sorted in terms of the difference of each item's occurrences in the middle and at the end of a sentence. It is assumed that the greater this difference is, the more significant a dotted word would be as a counter-example. In total, 469 such words are acquired, among which many are not really abbreviated words. A series of experiments are then conducted by adding the next 50 most frequent dotted words to the abbreviation list for model training each time. To utilize such

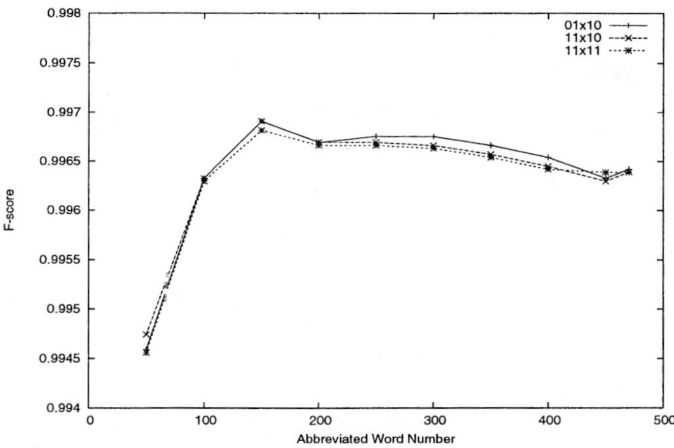

Fig. 2. Effectiveness of abbreviation list

Table 5. Effectiveness of abbreviation list

Context Type	`01x10`	`11x10`	`11x11`
F-score (%)	99.6908	99.6908	99.6815
Increase	+2.4285	+1.9959	+1.9906

lexical resource, a multi-valued feature `isAbbr` is introduced to the feature set to indicate whether a target word is in the abbreviation list and what it is. That is, all words in the list actually play a role equivalent to individual bi-valued features, under the umbrella of this new feature.

The outcomes from the experiments are presented in Fig. 2, showing that performance enhancement reaches rapidly to the top around 150. The performance of the three best context types at this point is given in Table 5, indicating that an abbreviation list of 150 words leads to an enhancement of 1.99–2.43 percentage points, in comparison to Table 4. This enhancement is very significant at this performance level. Beyond this point, the performance goes down slightly.

3.5 Effectiveness of Sentence-Initial Words

In a similar way, we carry out a series of experiments to test the effectiveness of sentence-initial words. In total, 4190 such words (word types) are collected from the beginning of all sentences in the training corpus. Every time the next 200 most frequent words are added to the sentence-initial word list for training, with the aid of another multi-valued feature `isSentInit` for the context word immediately following the target word.

Experimental outcomes are presented in Fig. 3, showing that the performance maintains roughly at the same level when the list grows. Until the very end,

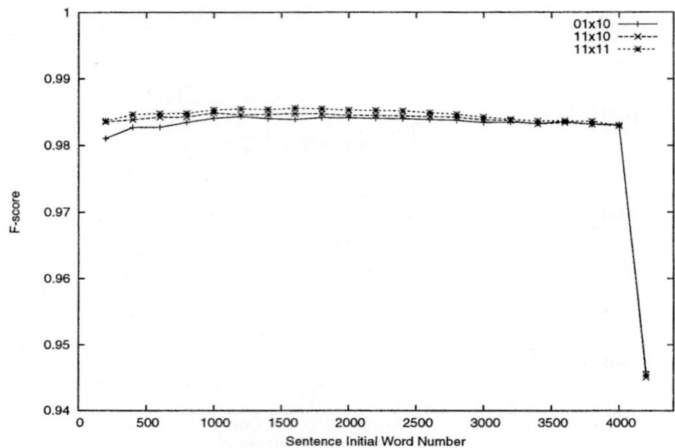

Fig. 3. Effectiveness of sentence-initial words

Table 6. Performance enhancement by sentence-initial words

Context Type	01x10	11x10	11x11
List size	1200	1000	1200
F-score (%)	98.4307	98.4868	98.5463
Increase	+1.1784	+0.7919	+0.8554

when those most infrequent (or untypical) sentence-initial words are added, the performance drops rapidly. The numbers of sentence-initial words leading to the best performance with various context types are presented in Table 6. This list of words lead to a significant performance enhancement of 0.79–1.18 percentage points, in comparison to Table 4.

3.6 Combination of Two Lists

Through the experiments reported above we find the optimal size of abbreviation list and sentence-initial words, both in the order of their frequency ranks, in each context type of our interests. The straightforward combination of these two lists in terms of these optimal sizes leads to almost no difference from using abbreviation list only, as presented in Table 7.

Table 7. Performance from simple combination of the two lists

Context Type	01x10	11x10	11x11
Sentence-initial words	1200	1000	1200
Abbreviation list	150	150	150
F-score (%)	99.7064	99.7156	99.6912

Table 8. Performance from various size combination of the two lists

Sentence-initial words	Abbreviation list	F-score 01x10	11x10	11x11
100	200	99.7646%	99.7738%	99.7707%
100	400	99.7125%	99.7033%	99.7002%
100	600	99.7033%	99.6971%	99.6971%
100	800	99.6788%	99.6941%	99.6911%
100	1000	99.6696%	99.6818%	99.6696%
100	1200	99.6635%	99.6574%	99.6544%
150	200	99.8013%	99.7890%	99.7921%
150	400	99.7431%	99.7339%	99.7369%
150	600	99.7431%	99.7370%	99.7370%
150	800	99.7401%	99.7309%	99.7278%
150	1000	99.7156%	99.7156%	99.7064%
150	1200	99.7064%	99.7034%	99.6912%
200	200	99.8227%	99.7890%	99.7921%
200	400	99.7584%	99.7461%	99.7339%
200	600	99.7523%	99.7431%	99.7339%
200	800	99.7462%	99.7370%	99.7340%
200	1000	99.7309%	99.7125%	99.7064%
200	1200	99.7095%	99.6973%	99.6911%

To explore the optimal combination of the two lists, a series of experiments are carried out near each list's optimal size. The results are presented in Table 8, showing that the best combination is around 200 words from each list and any deviation from this point would lead to observable performance declination. The best performance at this optimal point is 99.8227% F-score, achieved with the `01x10` context type, which is significantly better than the best performance using any single list of the two.

Comparing to the baseline performance of the Maxent model in Table 4, we can see that this improvement increases only 99.8227 - 97.2623 = 2.5604 percentage points. Notice, however, that it is achieved near the ceiling level. Its particular significance lies in the fact that $\frac{99.8227-97.2623}{100-97.2623} = 93.52\%$ remaining errors from the baseline model are further eliminated by this combination of the two lists, both of which are of a relatively small size.

4 Conclusions

We have presented in the above sections our recent investigation into how context window, feature space and simple lexical resources like abbreviation list and sentence-initial words affect the performance of the Maxent model on period disambiguation, the kernel problem in sentence identification. Our experiments on PTB-II WSJ corpus suggest the following findings: (1) the target word itself provides most useful information for identifying whether or not the dot it carries is a true period, achieving an F-score beyond 92%; (2) unsurprisingly, the most useful context words are the two words next to the target word, and the context words to its right is more informative in general than those to its left; and (3) extending the feature space to utilize lexical information from the most frequent 200 abbreviated words and sentence-initial words, all of which can be straightforwardly collected from the training corpus, can eliminate 93.52% remaining errors from the baseline model in the open test, achieving an F-score of 99.8227%.

Acknowledgements

The work described in this paper was supported by the Research Grants Council of HKSAR, China, through the CERG grant 9040861 (CityU 1318/03H). We wish to thank Alex Fang for his help.

References

1. Aberdeen, J., Burger, J., Day, D., Hirschman, L., Robinson, P., and Vilain, M.: Mitre: Description of the alembic system used for muc-6. In *Proceedings of the Sixth Message Understanding Conference (MUC-6)*, Columbia, Maryland. Morgan Kaufmann (1995)
2. Berger, A., Pietra, S.D., and Pietra, V.D.: A maximum entropy approach to natural language processing. *Computational linguistics.* (1996) 22(1):39–71
3. Della Pietra, S., Della Pietra, V., and Lafferty, J.: Inducing features of random fields. *Transactions Pattern Analysis and Machine Intelligence.* (1997) 19(4): 380–393
4. Malouf, R.: A comparison of algorithms for maximum entropy parameter estimation. In *Proceedings of CoNLL-2002*, Taipei, Taiwan (2002) 49–55
5. Marcus, M.P., Santorini, B., and Marcinkiewicz, M.A.: Building a large annotated corpus of english: The penn treebank. *Computational Linguistics.* (1993) 19(2): 313–329
6. Mikheev, A.: Tagging sentence boundaries. In *Proceedings of the First Meeting of the North American Chapter of the Association for Computational Linguistics (NAACL'2000).* (2000)
7. Mitchell, T.: *Machine Learning.* McGraw Hill, New York (1997)
8. Palmer, D.D. and Hearst, M.A.: Adaptive Multilingual Sentence Boundary Disambiguation. *Computational Linguistics.* (1997) 23(2):241–267
9. Ratnaparkhi, A.: *Maximum entropy models for natural language ambiguity resolution.* Ph.D. dissertation, University of Pennsylvania (1998)
10. Reynar, J.C. and Ratnaparkhi, A.: A maximum entropy approach to identifying sentence boundaries. In *Proceedings of the Fifth Conference on Applied Natural Language Processing*, Washington, D.C. (1997)
11. Riley, M.D.: Some applications of tree-based modelling to speech and language indexing. In *Proceedings of the DARPA Speech and Natural Language Workshop.* Morgan Kaufmann (1989) 339–352
12. Rosenfeld, R.: *Adaptive statistical language modeling: A Maximum Entropy Approach.* PhD thesis CMU-CS-94. (1994)
13. Van Rijsbergen, C.J.: *Information Retrieval.* Butterworths, London (1979)
14. Wallach, H.M.: *Efficient training of conditional random fields.* Master's thesis, University of Edinburgh (2002)

Acquiring Synonyms from Monolingual Comparable Texts

Mitsuo Shimohata[1] and Eiichiro Sumita[2]

[1] Oki Electric Industry Co., Ltd.,
2-5-7, Honmachi, Chuo-ku, Osaka City, Japan
shimohata363@oki.com

[2] ATR Spoken Language Translation Research Laboratories,
2-2-2 Hikaridai, Keihanna Science City, Kyoto, Japan
eiichiro.sumita@atr.jp

Abstract. This paper presents a method for acquiring synonyms from monolingual comparable text (MCT). MCT denotes a set of monolingual texts whose contents are similar and can be obtained automatically. Our acquisition method takes advantage of a characteristic of MCT that included words and their relations are confined. Our method uses contextual information of surrounding one word on each side of the target words. To improve acquisition precision, *prevention of outside appearance* is used. This method has advantages in that it requires only part-of-speech information and it can acquire infrequent synonyms. We evaluated our method with two kinds of news article data: sentence-aligned parallel texts and document-aligned comparable texts. When applying the former data, our method acquires synonym pairs with 70.0% precision. Re-evaluation of incorrect word pairs with source texts indicates that the method captures the appropriate parts of source texts with 89.5% precision. When applying the latter data, acquisition precision reaches 76.0% in English and 76.3% in Japanese.

1 Introduction

There is a great number of synonyms, which denote a set of words sharing the same meaning, in any natural language. This variety among synonyms causes difficulty in natural language processing applications, such as information retrieval and automatic summarization, because it reduces the coverage of lexical knowledge. Although many manually constructed synonym resources, such as WordNet [4] and Roget's Thesaurus [12], are available, it is widely recognized that these knowledge resources provide only a small coverage of technical terms and cannot keep up with newly coined words.

We propose a method to acquire synonyms from monolingual comparable text (MCT). MCT denotes sets of different texts[1] that share similar contents. MCT are appropriate for synonym acquisition because they share not only many

[1] In this paper, "text" can denote various text chunks, such as documents, articles, and sentences.

R. Dale et al. (Eds.): IJCNLP 2005, LNAI 3651, pp. 233–244, 2005.

synonymous words but also the relations between the words in a each text. Automatic MCT construction can be performed in practice through state-of-the-art clustering techniques [2]. News articles are especially favorable for text clustering since they have both titles and date of publication.

Synonym acquisition is based on a distributional hypothesis that words with similar meanings tend to appear in similar contexts [5]. In this work, we adopt loose contextual information that considers only the surrounding one word from each side of the target words. This narrow condition enables extraction from source texts[2] that have different structures. In addition, we use another constraint, *prevention of outside appearance*, which reduces improper extraction by looking over outside places of other texts. This constraint eliminates many non-synonyms having the same surrounding words by chance. Since our method does not cut off acquired synonyms by frequency, synonyms that appear only once can be captured.

In this paper, we describe related work in Sect. 2. Then, we present our acquisition method in Sect. 3 and describe its evaluation in Sect. 4. In the experiment, we provide a detailed analysis of our method using monolingual parallel texts. Following that, we explain an experiment on automatically constructed MCT data of news articles, and conclude in Sect. 5

2 Related Work

Word Clustering from Non-comparable Text

There have been many studies on computing similarities between words based on their distributional similarity [6,11,7]. The basic idea of the technique is that words sharing a similar characteristic with other entities form a single cluster [9,7]. A characteristic can be determined from relations with other entities, such as document frequency, co-occurrence with other words, and adjectives depending on target nouns.

However, this approach has shortcomings in obtaining synonyms. First, words clustered by this approach involve not only synonyms but also many near-synonyms, hypernyms, and antonyms. It is difficult to distinguish synonyms from other related words [8]. Second, words to be clustered need to have high frequencies to determine similarity, therefore, words appearing only a few times are outside the scope of this approach. These shortcomings are greatly reduced with synonym acquisition from MCT owing to its characteristics.

Lexical Paraphrase Extraction from MCT

Here, we draw comparisons with works sharing the same conditions for acquiring synonyms (lexical paraphrases) from MCT. Barzilay et al. [1] shared the same conditions in that their extraction relies on local context. The difference is that

[2] We call texts that yield synonyms as "source texts."

their method introduces a refinement of contextual conditions for additional improvement, while our method introduces two non-contextual conditions.

Pang et al. [10] built word lattices from MCT, where different word paths that share the same start nodes and end nodes represent paraphrases. Lattices are formed by top-down merging based on structural information. Their method has a remarkable advantage in that synonyms do not need to be surrounded with the same words. On the other hand, their method is not applicable to structurally different MCTs.

Shimohata et al. [13] extracted lexical paraphrases based on the substitution operation of edit operations. Text pairs having more than three edit distances are excluded from extraction. Therefore, their method considers sentential word ordering. Our findings, however, suggest that local contextual information is reliable enough for extracting synonyms.

3 Synonym Acquisition

Synonym extraction relies on word pairs that satisfy the following three constraints: (1) agreement of context words; (2) prevention of outside appearance; and (3) POS agreement. Details of these constraints are described in the following sections. Then, we describe refinement of the extracted noun synonyms in Sect. 3.4.

3.1 Agreement of Context Words

Synonyms in MCTs are considered to have the same context since they generally share the same role. Therefore, agreement of surrounding context is a key feature for synonym extraction. We define contextual information as surrounding one word on each side of the target words. This minimum contextual constraint permits extraction from MCT having different sentence structures.

Figure 1 shows two texts that have different structures. From this text pair, we can obtain the following two word pairs WP-1 and WP-2 with context words (synonym parts are written in bold). These two word pairs placed in different parts would be missed if we used a broader range for contextual information.

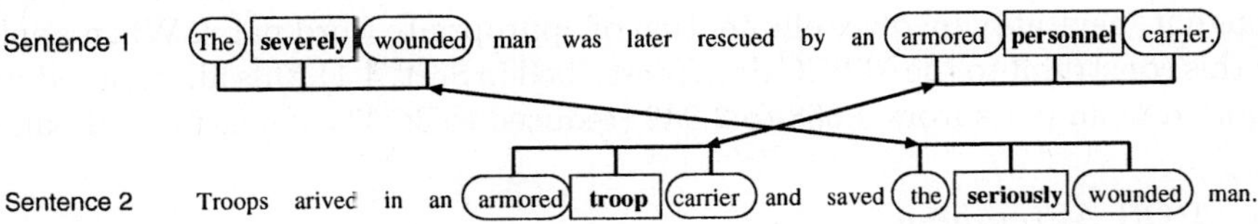

Fig. 1. Extracting Synonyms with Context Words

WP-1 "the **severely** wounded" ⇔ "the **seriously** wounded"
WP-2 "armored **personnel** carrier" ⇔ "armored **troop** carrier"

Words are dealt with based on their appearance, namely, by preserving their capitalization and inflection. Special symbols representing "Start-of-Sentence" and "End-of-Sentence" are attached to sentences. Any contextual words are accepted, but cases in which the surrounding words are both punctuation marks and parentheses/brackets are disregarded.

3.2 Prevention of Outside Appearance

Prevention of outside appearance is a constraint based on characteristics of MCT. It filters incorrect word pairs by looking into outside of synonym words and context words in the other text (we call this outside region the "outside part."). This constraint is based on the assumption that an identical context word — either a noun, verb, adjective, or adverb — appears only once in a text. Actually, our investigation of English texts in the Multiple-Translation Chinese Corpus data (MTCC data described in Sect. 4.1) proves that 95.2% of either nouns, verbs, adjectives, or adverbs follow this assumption.

This constraint eliminates word pairs that have a word satisfying the following two constraints.

C1 The word appears in the outside part of the other text.
C2 The word does not appear in the synonym part of the other text.

The constraint C1 means that the word in the outside part of the other text is considered as a correspondent word, and a captured word is unlikely to be corresponding. In other words, appearance of the word itself is more reliable than local context coincidence. The constraint C2 means that if the word is included in the synonym part of the other text, this word pair is considered to capture a corresponding word independent of the outside part.

Figure 2 illustrates an example of outside appearance. From S1 and S2, the word pair "Monetary Union" and "Finance Minister Engoran" can be extracted. However, the word "Monetary" in S1 does appear in the synonym part of S2 but does appear in another part of S2. This word pair is eliminated due to outside appearance. However, if the word appears in the synonym part of S2, it remains independent of the outside part.

This constraint is a strong filtering tool for reducing incorrect extraction, although it inevitably involves elimination of appropriate word pairs. When applying this constraint to the MTCC data (described in Sect. 4.1), this filtering reduces acquired noun pairs from 9,668 to 2,942 (reduced to 30.4% of non-filtered pairs).

3.3 POS Agreement

Word pairs to be extracted should have the same POS. This is a natural constraint since synonyms described in ordinary dictionaries share the same POS. In addition, we focus our target synonym on content words such as nouns, verbs, adjectives, and adverbs. A definition of each POS is given below.

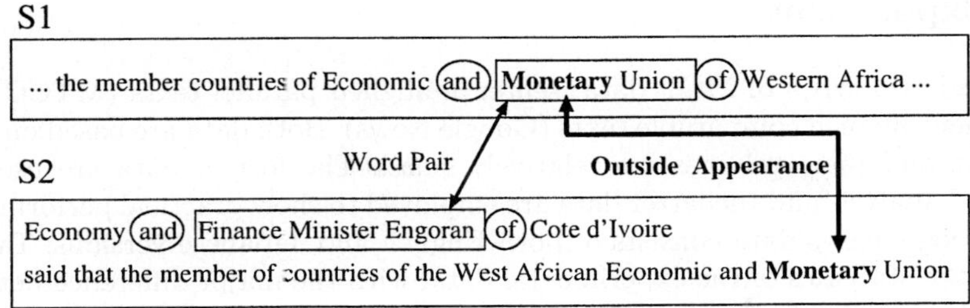

Fig. 2. Text Pair Having Outside Appearance

Nouns	Consist of a noun sequence. Length of sequences is not limited.
Verbs	Consist of one verb.
Adjectives	Consist of one adjective.
Adverbs	Consist of one adverb.

The word pair WP-1 satisfies the constraint for adverbs, and WP-2 satisfies that for nouns. The MCT in Fig. 1 can produce the word pair "the **severely wounded** man" and "the **seriously wounded** man." This word pair is eliminated because the synonym part consists of an adverb and an adjective and does not satisfy the constraint.

3.4 Refinement of Noun Synonym Pairs

Acquired noun pairs require two refinement processes, incorporating context words and eliminating synonyms that are subsets of others, since nouns are allowed to contain more than one word.

After the extraction process, we can obtain noun pairs with their surrounding context words. If these context words are considered to be a part of compound nouns, they are incorporated into the synonym part. A context word attached to the front of the synonym part is incorporated if it is either a noun or an adjective. One attached to the back of the synonym part is incorporated if it is a noun. Thus, when the noun pair "air **strike** operation" = "air **attack** operation" is extracted, both context words remain since they are nouns.

Next, a noun pair included in another noun pair is deleted since the shorter noun pair is considered a part of the longer noun pair. If the following noun pairs Noun-1 and Noun-2 are extracted[3], Noun-1 is deleted by this process.

Noun-1 "British High" ⇔ "British Supreme"
Noun-2 "British High Court" ⇔ "British Supreme Court"

[3] All words in these expressions belong to "proper noun, singular" (represented as NNP in the Penn Treebank manner).

4 Experiment

We used two types of MCT data: sentence-aligned parallel texts (MTCC) and document-aligned comparable texts (Google News). Both data are based on news articles, and their volumes are relatively small. The former data are used for detailed analysis and the latter data are employed to show practical performance. The Google News data consists of both English and Japanese versions. Table 1 shows the statistics of the experimental data, with the major difference between MTCC and Google News data being "Words per Text." The text length of Google News data is much longer than MTCC data since texts in Google News data denote a whole article whereas those in MTCC data denote a sentence.

These two English data and the one Japanese data originally contained plain text data. We applied the Charniak parser [3] to the English data and Chasen[4] to the Japanese data to obtain POS information. It should be noted that we do not use any information except that of POS from parsed results.

Table 1. Statistics of Three Experimental Data

	MTCC	Google News (E)	Google News (J)
Text Clusters	993	61	88
Texts	10,655	394	417
Words	302,474	176,482	127,482
Texts per Cluster (Mean)	10.7	6.5	4.7
Words per Text (Mean)	28.4	447.9	305.7
(Variance)	364.5	64591.3	55495.7

MTCC: Multiple-reference Data from LDC

4.1 Multiple-Translation Chinese Corpus

The Linguistic Data Consortium (LDC) releases several multiple-translation corpora to support the development of automatic means for evaluating translation quality. The Multiple-Translation Chinese Corpus[5] (MTCC) is one of those, and it contains 105 news stories and 993 sentences selected from three sources of journalistic Mandarin Chinese text. Each Chinese sentence was independently translated into 11 English sentences by translation teams. We applied the Charniak parser to these 10,923 translations and obtained 10,655 parsed results. This data comprises high-quality comparable texts, namely parallel texts.

We applied our method to the data and obtained 2,952 noun pairs, 887 verb pairs, 311 adjective pairs, and 92 adverb pairs. Samples of acquired synonyms are shown in Appendix A. Roughly speaking, the number of acquired word pairs for each POS is proportional to the frequency of occurrence for that POS in the MTCC data.

[4] http://chasen.naist.jp/hiki/ChaSen/

[5] Linguistic Data Consortium (LDC) Catalog Number LDC2002T01.

Extracted word pairs were manually evaluated by two methods: evaluation with source texts and without source texts. First, an evaluator judged whether extracted word pairs were synonyms or not without source texts. If two words could be considered synonyms in many cases, they were marked "yes," otherwise "no." The criterion for judgment conformed to that of ordinary dictionaries, i.e., the evaluator judges whether given a word pair would be described as a synonym by an ordinary dictionary. Therefore, word pairs heavily influenced by the source texts are judged as "no," since these word pairs are not synonymous in general situations. Morphological difference (e.g. singular/plural in nouns) is not taken into consideration.

Next, word pairs evaluated as non-synonyms were re-evaluated with their source texts. This evaluation is commonly used in paraphrase evaluation [1,10]. When word pairs could be considered to have the same meaning for the given sentence pair, the evaluator marked "yes," otherwise "no." This evaluation clarifies the ratio of the these two causes of incorrect acquisition.

1. The method captures proper places in sentences from source texts, but the semantic difference between words in this place pair exceeds the range of synonyms.
2. The method captures improper places in sentences from source texts that have the same local context by chance.

An example of evaluation with source texts and without source texts is shown in Fig. 3. Samples of this evaluation are also shown in Appendix A.

The precision, the ratio of "yes" to the total, on MTCC data by each POS is shown in Fig. 4, where the All POS precision with source texts reaches 89.5%. This result suggests that our method could capture proper places of MCT pairs with this level of precision. However, this precision falls to 70.0% without source texts that represents synonym acquisition precision. This is because some of the extracted word pairs have a hypernymous relationship or have great influence on context in source texts.

Acquired word pairs include those occurring only once since our method does not cut off according to word frequency. The amount of those occurring only once accounts for 88.8% of the total. This feature is advantageous for acquiring proper nouns; acquired word pairs including proper nouns account for 63.9% of the total noun pairs.

Word pair judged as non-synonym	
Synonym-1	Muslim robe
Synonym-2	sarong
Source Text Pair	
Sentence-1	A resident named Daxiyate wears a turban and **Muslim robe**.
Sentence-2	A citizen named Daciat wore a Moslem hat and **sarong**.

Fig. 3. Example of Evaluation with Source Texts

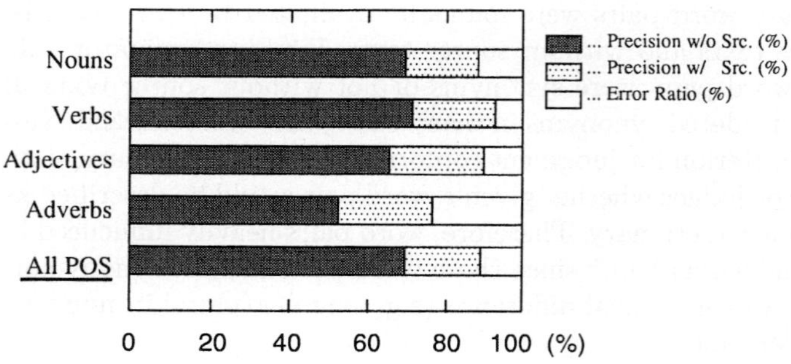

Fig. 4. Precisions for MTCC Data

Here, we discuss our method's coverage of all the synonyms in the training data. Since it is very difficult to list all synonyms appearing in the training data, we substitute identical word pairs for synonym pairs to estimate coverage. We counted identical word pairs from all MCT pairs (Total) and those that have the same context words (Same Context). The ratio of "Same Context" to "Total" denotes coverage of our method and it was found to be 27.7%. If the tendency of local context for identical word pairs is equal to that of synonym word pairs, our method can capture 27.7% of the embedded synonyms in the training data.

We looked up acquired word pairs in WordNet[6], a well-known publicly available thesaurus, to see how much general synonym knowledge is included in the acquired synonyms. We could obtain 1,001 different word pairs of verbs, adjectives, and adverbs after unifying conjugation[7]. WordNet knows, i.e., both words are registered as entries, 951 word pairs (95.0%) among the 1,001 acquired pairs. The thesaurus covers, i.e., both words are registered as synonyms, 205 word pairs (21.6%) among 951 known pairs. This result shows that our method can actually capture general synonym information. The remaining acquired word pairs are still valuable since they include either general knowledge not covered by WordNet or knowledge specific to news articles. For example, extracted synonym pairs, "express"="say," "present"="report," and "decrease"="drop" are found from the data and are not registered as synonyms in WordNet.

4.2 Google News Data

We applied our method to Google News data acquired from "Google News, [8]" provided by Google, Inc. This site provides clustered news articles that describe the same events from among approximately 4,500 news sources worldwide.

[6] http://www.cogsci.princeton.edu/~wn/

[7] Acquired nouns are excluded from the consulting since many proper names are acquired but are not covered in WordNet.

[8] English version: http://news.google.com/
Japanese version: http://news.google.com/nwshp?ned=jp

From the Google News site, we gathered articles with manual layout-level checking. This layout-level checking eliminates unrelated text such as menus and advertisements. Our brief investigation found that clustered articles often have a small overlap in described facts since each news site has its own interest and viewpoint in spite of covering the same topic.

We use entire articles as "texts" and do not employ an automatic sentence segmentation and alignment tool. This is because the results derived from automatic sentence segmentation and alignment on the Google News data would probably be unreliable, since the articles greatly differ in format, style, and content. Since our method considers only one-word-length context in each direction, it can be applied to this rough condition. On the other hand, this condition enables us to acquire synonyms placed at distant places in articles.

The next issue for the experimental conditions is the range for outside-appearance checking. Following the condition of MTCC data, the outside-appearance checking range covers entire texts, i.e., outside appearance should be checked throughout an article. However, this condition is too expensive to follow since text length is much longer than that of MTCC data. We tested various ranges of 0 (no outside-appearance checking), 10, 20, 40, 70, 100, 200, and unlimited words. Figure 5 illustrates the range of outside-appearance checking.

We limit the words to be tested to nouns since the acquired amounts of other POS types are not sufficient. Acquired noun pairs are evaluated without source

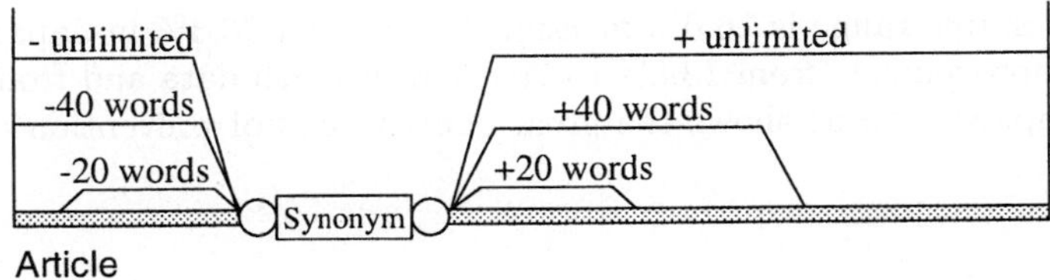

Fig. 5. Range for Outside-Appearance Checking

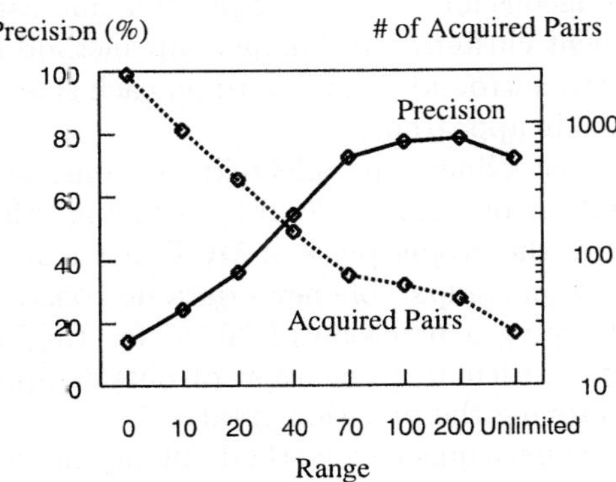

Fig. 6. Precisions of Google (E) by Outside-Appearance Checking Range

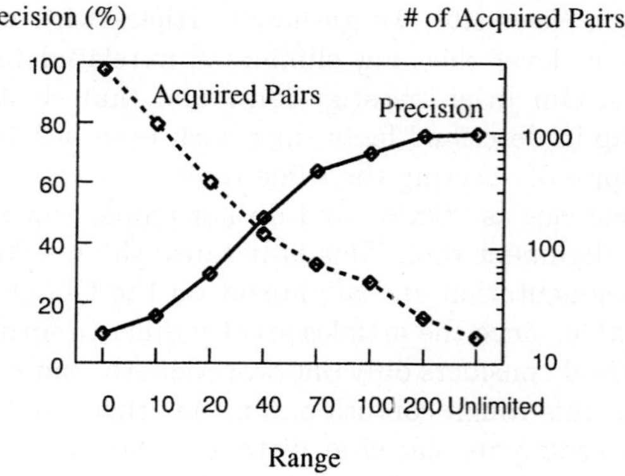

Fig. 7. Precisions of Google (J) by Outside-Appearance Checking Range

texts. Appendix B shows examples. Figures 6 and 7 display the amount and precision for acquired nouns in each range of English data and Japanese data, respectively.

The tendencies of these two data are similar, as the range expands, precision increases and the amount of acquired pairs decreases at an exponential rate. When the range is close to unlimited, precision levels off. The average precision at this stable range is 76.0% in English data and 76.3% in Japanese. The precision improvement (from 13.8% to 76.0% in English data and from 9.5% to 76.3% in Japanese data) shows the great effectiveness of prevention of outside appearance.

5 Conclusions

We proposed a method to acquire synonyms from monolingual comparable texts. MCT data are advantageous for synonym acquisition and can be obtained automatically by a document clustering technique. Our method relies on agreement of local context, i.e., the surrounding one word on each side of the target words, and prevention of outside appearance.

The experiment on monolingual parallel texts demonstrated that the method acquires synonyms with a precision of 70.0%, including infrequent words. Our simple method captures the proper place of MCT text pairs with a precision of 89.5%. The experiment on comparable news data demonstrated the robustness of our method by attaining a precision of 76.0% for English data and 76.3% for Japanese data. In particular, prevention of outside-appearance played an important role by improving the precision greatly.

The combination of our acquisition method, an automatic document clustering technique, and daily updated Web texts enables automatic and continuous synonym acquisition. We believe that the combination will bring great practical benefits to NLP applications.

Acknowledgment

The research reported here was supported in part by a contract with the National Institute of Information and Communications Technology entitled "A study of speech dialogue translation technology based on a large corpus".

References

1. R. Barzilay and K. McKeown. Extracting paraphrases from a parallel corpus. In *Proc. of ACL-01*, pages 50–57, 2001.
2. M.W. Berry, editor. *Survey of Text Mining Clustering, Classification, and Retrieval.* Springer, 2004.
3. E. Charniak. A maximum-entropy-inspired parser. In *Proc. of the 1st Conference of the North American Chapter of the Association for Computational Linguistics*, 2000.
4. C. Fellbaum. *WordNet: An Electronic Lexical Database.* MIT Press, 1998.
5. Z. Harris. *Mathematical Structures of Language.* Interscience Publishers, 1968.
6. D. Hindle. Noun classification from predicate-argument structures. In *Proc. of ACL-90*, pages 268–275, 1990.
7. D. Lin. Automatic retrieval and clustering of similar words. In *Proc. of COLING-ACL 98*, pages 768–774, 1998.
8. D. Lin, S. Zhao, L. Qin, and M. Zhou. Identifying synonyms among distributionally similar words. In *Proc. of the 18th International Joint Conference on Artificial Intelligence (IJCAI)*, pages 1492–1493, 2003.
9. C.D. Manning and H. Schütze, editors. *Foundations of Statistical Natural Language Processing*, pages 265–314. MIT Press, 1999.
10. B. Pang, K. Knight, and D. Marcu. Syntax-based alignment of multiple translations: Extracting paraphrases and generating new sentences. In *Proc. of HLT-NAACL 2003*, pages 181-188, 2003.
11. F. Pereira, N. Tishby, and L. Lee. Distributional clustering of English words. In *Proc. of ACL-93*, pages 183–190, 1993.
12. P.M. Roget. *Roget's International Thesaurus.* Thomas Y. Crowell, 1946.
13. M. Shimohata and E. Sumita. Identifying synonymous expressions from a bilingual corpus for example-based machine translation. In *Proc. of the 19th COLING Workshop on Machine Translation in Asia*, pages 20–25, 2002.

Appendix

A Samples of Acquired Words from MTCC and Their Evaluation

	Synonym-1	Synonym-2	Evaluation
Nouns	press conference	news conference	Yes
	foreign funds	foreign capital	Yes
	complete	finish	Yes
	disclose	reveal	Yes
	military officials	military officers	No
	Sunday radio program	Sunday TV program	No

Verbs	indicate	show	Yes
	believe	think	Yes
	cease	stop	Yes
	consider	study	No
	believe	trust	No
Adjectives	basic	essential	Yes
	notable	significant	Yes
	massive	substantial	Yes
	active	good	No
	direct	strong	No
Adverbs	currently	now	Yes
	certainly	definitely	Yes
	extremely	very	Yes
	now	officially	No
	absolutely	entirely	No

B Samples of Acquired Nouns from Google News (E) and Their Evaluation

	Synonym-1	Synonym-2	Evaluation
Nouns	Karzai	President Karzai	Yes
	Abu Omar	Abu Umar	Yes
	relief effort	relief mission	Yes
	Muslim community	Muslim minority	No
	World Food Program	World Health Organization	No

A Method of Recognizing Entity and Relation

Xinghua Fan[1, 2] and Maosong Sun[1]

[1] State Key Laboratory of Intelligent Technology and Systems,
Tsinghua University, Beijing 100084, China
fanxh@tsinghua.org.cn, sms@mail.tsinghua.edu.cn
[2] State Intellectual Property Office of P.R. China, Beijing, 100088, China

Abstract. The entity and relation recognition, i.e. (1) assigning semantic classes to entities in a sentence, and (2) determining the relations held between entities, is an important task in areas such as information extraction. Subtasks (1) and (2) are typically carried out sequentially, but this approach is problematic: the errors made in subtask (1) are propagated to subtask (2) with an accumulative effect; and, the information available only in subtask (2) cannot be used in subtask (1). To address this problem, we propose a method that allows subtasks (1) and (2) to be associated more closely with each other. The process is performed in three stages: firstly, employing two classifiers to do subtasks (1) and (2) independently; secondly, recognizing an entity by taking all the entities and relations into account, using a model called the Entity Relation Propagation Diagram; thirdly, recognizing a relation based on the results of the preceding stage. The experiments show that the proposed method can improve the entity and relation recognition in some degree.

1 Introduction

The entity and relation recognition, i.e. assigning semantic classes (e.g., person, organization and location) to entities in a sentence and determining the relations (e.g., born-in and employee-of) that hold between entities, is an important task in areas such as information extraction (IE) [1] [2] [3] [4], question answering (QA) [5] and story comprehension [6]. In a QA system, many questions concern the specific entities in some relations. For example, the question that "Where was Poe born?" in TREC-9 asks for the location entity in which Poe was born. In a typical IE task in constructing a job database from unstructured texts, the system are required to extract many meaningful entities like titles and salary from the texts and to determine how these entities are associated with job positions.

The task of recognizing entity and relation is usually treated as two separate subtasks carried out sequentially: (1) to recognize entities using an entity recognizer, and (2) to determine the relations held between them. This approach has two shortcomings. Firstly, the errors made in subtask (1) will be propagated to subtask (2) with an accumulative effect, leading to a loss in performance of relation recognition. For example, if "Boston" is mislabeled as a person, it will never have chance to be classified as the location of Poe's birthplace. Secondly, the information available only in

R. Dale et al. (Eds.): IJCNLP 2005, LNAI 3651, pp. 245 – 256, 2005.

subtask (2) cannot be used for subtask (1). For example, if we feel difficult to determine whether the entity X is a person or not, but we can determine that there exists a relation born-in between X and China easily, it is obvious that we can claim that X must be a person.

To address the problems described above, this paper presents a novel approach which allows subtasks (1) and (2) to be linked more closely together. The process is separated into three stages. Firstly, employing two classifiers to perform subtasks (1) and (2) independently. Secondly, recognizing an entity by taking all the entities and relations into account using a particularly designed model called the Entity Relation Propagation Diagram. And, thirdly, recognizing a relation based on the results of the preceding step.

The rest of the paper is organized as follows. Section 2 defines the problem of entity and relation recognition in a formal way. Section 3 describes the proposed method of recognizing entity and relation. Section 4 gives the experimental results. Section 5 is the related work and comparison. Section 6 is conclusions.

2 The Problem of Entity and Relation Recognition

Conceptually, the entities and relations in a sentence can be viewed, while taking account of the mutual dependencies among them, as a labeled graph in Fig. 1.

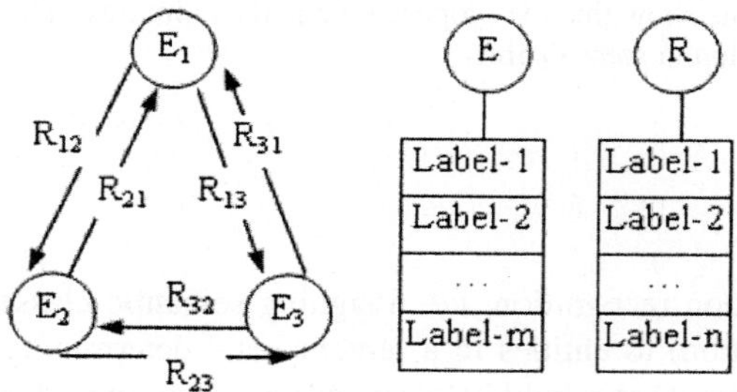

Fig. 1. Concept view of the entities and relations among them

In Fig.1, a node represents an entity and a link denotes the relation held between two entities. The arrowhead of a link represents the direction of the relation. Each entity or relation has several attributes, which are structured as a list of the node or the edge. These attributes can be classified into two classes. Some of them that are easy to acquire, such as words in an entity and parts of speech of words in a context, are called local attributes; the others that are difficult to acquire, such as semantic classes of phrases and relations among them, are called decision attributes. The issue of entity and relation recognition is to determine a unique value for each decision attribute of all entities and relations, by considering the local attributes of them. To describe the problem in a formal way, we first give some basic definitions as follows.

Definition 1 (Entity). An entity can be a single word or a set of consecutive words with a predefined boundary. A sentence is a linked list, which consists of words and entities. Entities in a sentence are denoted as E_1, E_2 ... according to their order, with values ranging over a set of entity class C^E. For example, the sentence in Fig. 2 has three entities: E_1= "Dole", E_2= "Elizabeth" and E_3= "Salisbury, N.C.". Note that it is not easy to determine the entity boundaries [7]. Here we assume that it has been solved and its output serves as the input to our model.

Dole 's wife, Elizabeth , is naive of Salisbury, N.C.

E_1 E_2 E_3

Fig. 2. A sentence that have three entities

Definition 2 (Relation). In this paper, we only consider the relation between two entities. An entity pair (E_i. E_j) represents a relation R_{ij} from entity E_i and E_j, where E_i is the first argument and E_j is the second argument. Relation R_{ij} takes its value that ranges over a set of relation class C^R. Note that (E_i, E_j) is an ordered pair, and there exist two relations R_{ij} =(E_i, E_j) and R_{ji} =(E_j, E_i) between entities E_i and E_j.

Definition 3 (Class). The class of an entity or relation is its decision attribute, which is one of the predefined class set and is unknown before being recognized. We denote the sets of predefined entity class and relation class as C^E and C^R respectively. C^E has one special element other-ent, which represents any unlisted entity class. For algorithmic reasons, we suppose all elements in C^E are mutually exclusive. Similarly, C^R also has one special element other-rel, which represents that the two involved entities are irrelevant or their relation class is undefined. For algorithmic reasons, we suppose all elements in C^R are mutually exclusive. In fact, because the class of an entity or a relation is only a label that we want to predict, if an entity or a relation have more than one labels simultaneously, to satisfy the constraint that all elements in C^E or C^R are mutually exclusive, we can separate it into several cases and construct several predefined entity class sets and relation class sets.

The classes of entities and relations in a sentence must satisfy some constraints. For example, if the class of entity E_1, which is the first argument of relation R_{12}, is a location, then the class of relation R_{12} cannot be born-in because the class of the first argument in relation R_{12} has to be a person.

Definition 4 (Constraint). A constraint is a 5-tuple $(\mathrm{R}, \varepsilon^1, \varepsilon^2, \alpha_\mathrm{R}, \alpha_\varepsilon)$. The symbols are defined as follows. $\mathrm{R} \in C^R$ represents the class of relation R. $\varepsilon^1, \varepsilon^2 \in C^E$ represents the classes of the first argument E_i and the second argument E_j in the relation R respectively. $\alpha_R \in [0,1]$ is a real number that represents a joint conditional probability distribution $\alpha_\mathrm{R} = \Pr\{\varepsilon^1, \varepsilon^2 \mid \mathrm{R}\}$. $\alpha_\varepsilon \in [0,1]$ is a real number that represents a conditional probability distribution $\alpha_\varepsilon = \Pr\{\mathrm{R} \mid \varepsilon^1, \varepsilon^2\}$. Note that α_R and α_ε need not to be specified manually and can be learned from an annotated training dataset easily.

Definition 5 (Observation). We denote the observations of an entity and a relation in a sentence as O^E and O^R respectively. O^E or O^R represent all the "known" local attributes of an entity or a relation, e.g., the spelling of a word, parts of speech, and semantic related attributes acquired from external resources such as WordNet. The observations O^E and O^R can be viewed as a random event, and $\Pr\{O^E\} = \Pr\{O^R\} \equiv 1$ because O^E and O^R in a sentence are known.

Based on the above definitions, the issue of entity and relation recognition can be described in a formal way as follows. Suppose in a sentence, the set of entity is $\{E_1, E_2 \ldots E_n\}$, the set of relation is $\{R_{12}, R_{21}, R_{13}, R_{31}, \ldots, R_{1n}, R_{n1}, \ldots, R_{n-1,n}, R_{n,n-1}\}$, the predefined sets of entity class and relation class are $C^E = \{e_1, e_2, \ldots e_m\}$ and $C^R = \{r_1, r_2, \ldots r_k\}$ respectively, the observation of entity E_i is O_i^E, and the observation of relation R_{ij} is O_{ij}^R. n, m and k represent the number of entity, the number of the predefined entity class and the number of the predefined relation class respectively. The problem is to search the most probable class assignment for each entity and each relation of interest, given the observations of all entities and relations. In other words, the problem is to solve the following two equations, using two kinds of constraint knowledge $\alpha_R, \alpha_\varepsilon$ and the interaction among entities and relations.

$$e = \arg\max_d \Pr\{E_i = e_d \mid O_1^E, O_2^E, \cdots, O_n^E, O_{12}^R, O_{21}^R, \cdots, O_{1n}^R, O_{n1}^R, \cdots, O_{n-1,n}^R, O_{n,n-1}^R\} \quad (1)$$

$$r = \arg\max_d \Pr\{R_{ij} = r_d \mid O_1^E, O_2^E, \cdots, O_n^E, O_{12}^R, O_{21}^R, \cdots, O_{1n}^R, O_{n1}^R, \cdots, O_{n-1,n}^R, O_{n,n-1}^R\} \quad (2)$$

In (1), d =1, 2, …, m, and in (2), d=1, 2, …, k.

3 The Proposed Method

Because the class assignment of a single entity or relation depends not only on local attributes itself, but also on those of all other entities and relations, the equations (1) and equation (2) cannot be solved directly. To simplify the problem, we present the following method consisting of three stages. Firstly, employ two classifiers to perform entity recognition and relation recognition independently. Their outputs are the conditional probability distributions $\Pr\{E \mid O^E\}$ and $\Pr\{R \mid O^R\}$, given the corresponding observations. Secondly, recognize an entity by taking account of all entities and relations, as computed in the previous step. This is achieved by using the model Entity Relation Propagation Diagram (ERPD). And, recognize a relation based on the results of the second step at last.

In this paper, we concentrate on the processes at the second and the third stages, assuming that the process at the first stage is solved and its output are given to us as input. At the second stage, the aim of introducing ERPD is to estimate the conditional probability distribution $\Pr\{E \mid ERPD\}$ given the constraint α_R in Definition 5 and the sets $\{\Pr\{E_i \mid O^{E_i}\}\}$ and $\{\Pr\{R_{ij} \mid O^{R_{ij}}\}\}$ (i, j=1,…,n), as computed at the first stage. For the readability, suppose $\Pr\{E \mid ERPD\}$ is given, the entity recognition equation (1) becomes the equation (3).

$$e = \begin{cases} \arg\max_d \Pr\{E_i = e_d \mid O^{E_i}\} & RV > \theta \\ \arg\max_d \Pr\{E_i = e_d \mid ERPD\} & RV \le \theta \end{cases} \quad (3)$$

where θ is a threshold determined by the experiment. RV∈ [0, 1] is a real number, called the reliable value, representing the belief degree of the output of the entity recognizer at the first stage. Suppose the maximum value of the conditional probability distribution $\Pr\{E \mid O^E\}$ is V_m and the second value is V_s, RV is defined as:

$$RV = \frac{V_m - V_s}{V_m + V_s} \quad (4)$$

The reason of introducing RV is due to a fact that only for ambiguous entities, it is effective by taking the classes of all entities in a sentence into account. "Reliable Value" measures whether an entity is ambiguous.

At the third stage, the basic idea of recognizing a relation is to search the probable relation given its observation, under a condition of satisfying the constraints imposed by the results of entity recognition at the second stage. The relation recognition equation (2) becomes the equation (5).

$$r = \arg\max_k \Pr\{R = r^k \mid O_R\} \times W_R \quad (5)$$

$$W_R = \begin{cases} 1 & \text{if } \Pr\{r \mid \varepsilon^1, \varepsilon^2\} > 0 \\ 0 & \text{if } \Pr\{r \mid \varepsilon^1, \varepsilon^2\} = 0 \end{cases}$$

where $\varepsilon^1, \varepsilon^2$ is the results of entity recognition at the second stage, $\Pr\{r \mid \varepsilon^1, \varepsilon^2\}$ is constraint knowledge α_ε in Definition 4, and W_R is the weight of the constraint knowledge.

In the following sections, we present ERPD and two algorithms to estimate the conditional probability distribution $\Pr\{E \mid ERPD\}$.

3.1 The Entity Relation Propagation Diagram

To represent the mutual dependencies among entities and relations, a model named the Entity Relation Propagation Diagram that can deal with cycles, similar to the Causality Diagram [8][9] for the complex system fault diagnosis, is developed for entity and relation recognition.

The classes of any two entities are dependent on each other through the relations between them, while taking account of the relations in between. For example, the class of entity E_i in Fig. 3 (a) depends on the classes of relations R_{ji} between entities E_i and E_j, and the classes of relations R_{ij} and R_{ji} depend on the classes of entities E_i and E_j. This means that we can predict the class of a target entity according to the class of its neighboring entity, making use of the relations between them. We further introduce the relation reaction intensity to describe the prediction ability of this kind.

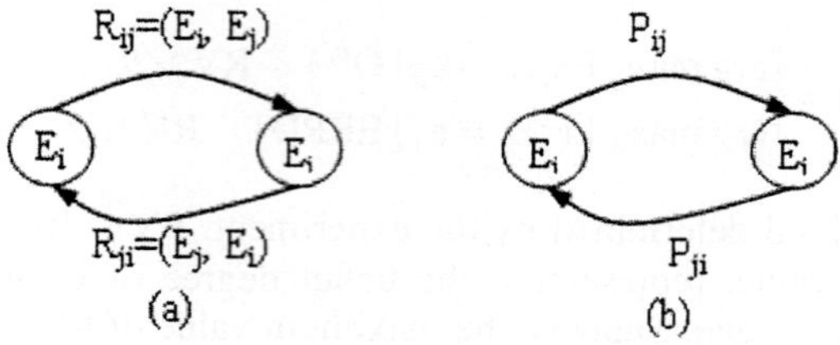

Fig. 3. Illustration of relation reaction

Definition 6 (Relation Reaction Intensity). We denote the relation reaction intensity from entity E_i to entity E_j as P_{ij}, which represents the ability that we guess the class of E_j if we know the class of its neighboring entity E_i and the relation R_{ij} between them. The relation reaction intensity could be modeled using a condition probability distribution $P_{ij}=\Pr\{E_j|E_i\}$.

The element p_{ij}^{kl} of P_{ij} represents the conditional probability $\Pr\{E_j=e_l|E_i=e_k\}$:

$$p_{ij}^{kl}=\Pr\{E_j=e_l|E_i=e_k\}=\sum_{t=1}^{N}\frac{\Pr\{R_{ij}=r_t\}\Pr\{E_i=e_k,E_j=e_l|R_{ij}=r_t\}}{\Pr\{E_i=e_k\}}$$

according to Definition 5:

$$\Pr\{R_{ij}=r_t\}=\Pr\{R_{ij}=r_t|O_{ij}^R\},\ \Pr\{E_i=e_k\}=\Pr\{E_i=e_k|O_i^E\}$$

Then, we have:

$$p_{ij}^{kl}=\sum_{t=1}^{N}\frac{\Pr\{R_{ij}=r_t|O_{ij}^R\}\Pr\{E_i=e_k,E_j=e_l|R_{ij}=r_t\}}{\Pr\{E_i=e_k|O_i^E\}} \tag{6}$$

where $r_t\in C^R$, N is the number of relations in relation class set. In equation (6), $\Pr\{E_i=e_k,E_j=e_l|R_{ij}=r_t\}$ represents the constraint knowledge α_R among entities and relations. $\Pr\{R_{ij}=r_t|O_{ij}^R\}$ and $\Pr\{E_i=e_k|O_i^E\}$ represent the outputs at the first stage.

Definition 7 (Observation Reaction Intensity). We denote the observation reaction intensity as the conditional probability distribution $\Pr\{E|O^E\}$ of an entity class, given the observation, which is the output at the first stage.

The Entity Relation Propagation Diagram (ERPD). is a directed diagram that allows cycles. As illustrated in Fig. 4, the symbols used in the ERPD are defined as follows. A circle node represents an event variable that can be any one from a set of mutually exclusive events, which all together cover the whole sample space. Here, an event variable represents an entity, an event represents a predefined entity class, and the whole sample space represents the set of predefined entity classes. Box node represents a basic event which is one of the independent sources of the associated event variable. Here, a basic event represents the observation of an entity. Directed arc represents a linkage event variable that may or may not enable an input event to cause the corresponding output event. The linkage event variable from an event variable to another event variable represents the relation reaction intensity in Definition 6. And, the linkage event variable from a basic event to the corresponding event variable represents the observation reaction intensity in Definition 7. All arcs pointing to a node are in a logical OR relationship.

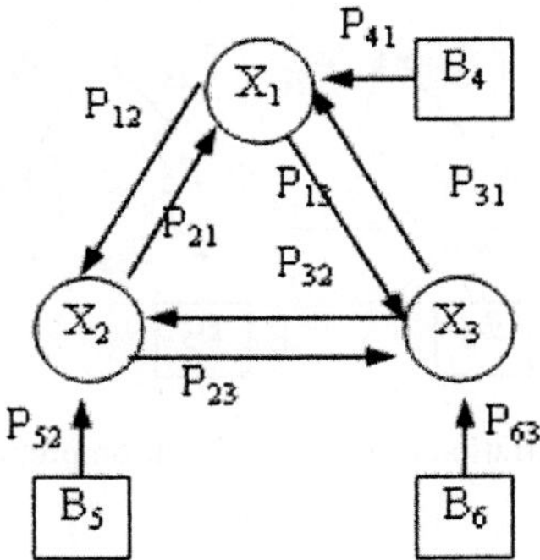

Fig. 4. Illustration of the Entity Relation Propagation Diagram

Now, we present two algorithms to compute the conditional probability distribution $\Pr\{E \mid ERPD\}$, one is based on the entity relation propagation tree, and the other is the directed iteration algorithm on ERPD.

3.2 The Entity Relation Propagation Tree

The Entity Relation Propagation Tree (ERPT). is a tree decomposed from an ERPD, which represents the relation reaction propagation from all basic events to each event variable logically. Each event variable in the ERPD corresponds to an ERPT. For example, the ERPT of X_1 in Fig. 4 is illustrated in Fig. 5. The symbols used in the ERPT are defined as follows. The root of the tree, denoted as Circle, is an event variable corresponding to the event variable in the ERPD. A leaf of the tree, denoted as Box, is a basic event corresponding to the basic event in the ERPD. The middle node of the tree, denoted as Diamond, is a logical OR gate variable, which is made from an event variable that has been expanded in the ERPD, and, the label in Diamond corresponds to the label of the expanded event variable. The directed arc of the tree corresponds to the linkage event variable in the ERPD. All arcs pointing to a node are in a logical OR relationship. The relation between the directed arc and the node linked to it is in logical AND relationship.

To decompose an ERPD into entity relation propagation trees, firstly we decompose the ERPD into mini node trees. Each event variables in the ERPD corresponds to a mini node tree, in which the root of the mini tree is the event variable in concern at present, and the leaves are composed of all neighboring basic events and event variables that are connected to the linkage event variables pointing to the top event variables. Secondly, expand a mini node tree into an entity relation propagation tree, i.e., the neighboring event variables in the mini node tree are replaced with their corresponding mini trees. During expanding a node event variable, when there are loops, Rule BreakLoop is applied to break down the loops.

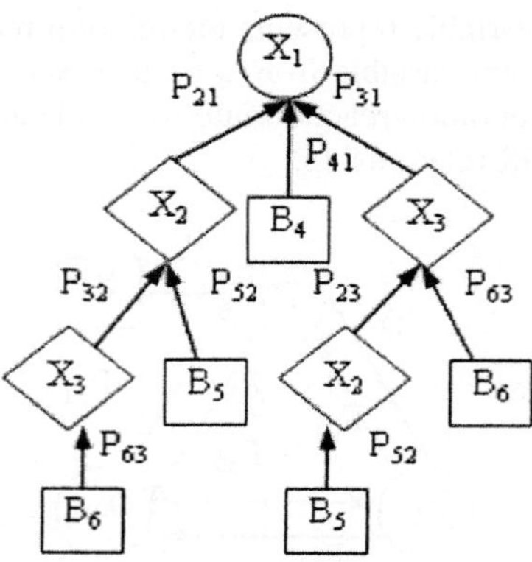

Fig. 5. Illustration of the entity relation propagation tree

Rule BreakLoop. An event variable cannot propagate the relation reaction to itself. Rule 1 is derived from a law commonsense - one can attest that he is sinless. When such a loop is encountered, the descendant event variable, which is same as the head event variable of the loop, is treated as a null event variable, together with its connected linkage event variable to be deleted.

Compute the Conditional Probability Distribution in an ERPT. After an ERPD is decomposed into entity relation propagation trees, the conditional probability distribution $\Pr\{E \mid ERPD\}$ becomes $\Pr\{E \mid ERPT\}$. When an event variable X_i has more than one input, these inputs will be in logic OR relationship, as defined in the ERPD. Since these inputs are independent, there exists such a case that one input causes X_i to be an instance X_i^k while another input causes X_i to be an instance X_i^l, this would be impossible because X_i^k and X_i^l are exclusive. In the real world, the mechanism, in which X_i can response to more than one independent input properly, is very complicated and may vary from one case to another. To avoid this difficulty, a basic assumption is introduced.

Assumption. When there is more than one input to X_i, each input will contribute a possibility to X_i. For each input, its contribution to this possibility equals to the probability that it causes X_i directly, as if the other inputs do not exist. The final possibility that X_i occurs is the sum of the possibilities from all inputs.

Suppose an event variable X has m inputs, and the probability distributions of all linkage event variables, linked basic events or event variables are P_i and Pr $\{X_i\}$ respectively, i=1,2...m. Based on the above assumption, the formula for computing the probability distribution of X can be derived as:

$$\begin{bmatrix} \Pr\{X^1\} \\ \vdots \\ \Pr\{X^n\} \end{bmatrix} = \mathrm{Norm}(\sum_{i=1}^{m} P_i \times \begin{bmatrix} \Pr\{X_i^1\} \\ \vdots \\ \Pr\{X_i^n\} \end{bmatrix}) \tag{7}$$

where, Norm () is a function that normalizes the vector in {}, and n is the state number of X.

So, the probability distribution Pr{E | ERPT} of the variable X in the corresponding ERPT can be computed in the following steps. Firstly, to find the middle node sequence in the corresponding ERPT in the depth-first search; secondly, according to the sequence, for each middle node, equation (7) is applied to compute its probability distribution. In this procedure, the previous results can be used for the latter computation.

3.3 The Directed Iteration Algorithm on ERPD

The idea is to compute the probability distribution of the event variable on the ERPD directly, without decomposing the ERPD to some ERPTs. The aim is to avoid the computational complexity of using ERPT. This is achieved by adopting an iteration strategy, which is the same as that used in the loopy belief network [10].

The Directed Iteration Algorithm. is as follows: Firstly, only take the basic event as input, and initialize each event variable according to formula (7), i.e., assigning an initialized probability distribution to each event variable. Secondly, take the basic event and the probability distributions of all neighboring nodes computed in the previous step as input, and iterate to update the probability distributions of all nodes in ERPD in parallel according to formula (7). Thirdly, if none of the probability distribution of all nodes in ERPD in successive iterations changes larger than a small threshold, the iteration is said to converge and then stops.

4 Experiments

Dataset. The dataset in our experiments is the same as the Roth's dataset "all" [11], which consists of 245 sentences that have the relation kill, 179 sentences that have the relation born-in and 502 sentences that have no relations. The predefined entity classes are other-ent, person and location, and the predefined relation classes are other-rel, kill and born-in. In fact, we use the results at the first stage in our method as the input, which are provided by W. Yih.

Experiment Design. We compare five approaches in the experiments: Basic, Omniscient, ERPD, ERPD* and BN. The Basic approach, which is a baseline, tests the performance of the two classifiers at the first stage, which are learned from their local attributes independently. The Omniscient approach is similar to Basic, the only deference is that the classes of entities are exposed to relation classifier and vice versa. Note that it is certainly impossible to know the true classes of an entity and a relation in advance. The BN is the method based on the belief network, -- we follow the BN method according to the description in [11]. The ERPD is the proposed method based on ERPT, and the ERPD* is the proposed method based on the directed iteration algorithm. The threshold of RV is 0.4.

Results. The experimental results are shown in Table 1. It can be seen from the table that 1) it is very difficult to improve the entity recognition because BN and Omniscient almost do not improve the performance of Basic; 2) the proposed method can improve the precision, which is thought of being more important than the recall for the task of recognizing entity; 3) the relation recognition can be improved if we can improve the entity recognition, as indicated by the comparisons of Basic, ERPD and Omniscient; 4) the proposed method can improve the relation recognition, and it performance is almost equal to that of BN; 5) the performance of ERPD and ERPD* is almost equal, so the directly iteration algorithm is effective.

Table 1. Experimental results

Approach	Person			Location		
	Rec	Prec	F_1	Rec	Prec	F_1
Basic	90.9	89.2	90.0	83.8	83.8	83.6
ERPD	**90.9**	**89.2**	**90.0**	**74.7**	**91.0**	**81.9**
ERPD*	90.7	89.1	89.9	75.3	90.9	82.3
BN	87.7	90.7	89.1	83.4	83.2	83.1
Omniscient	90.9	89.5	90.1	83.8	84.5	84.0
Approach	Kill			Born-in		
	Rec	Prec	F_1	Rec	Prec	F_1
Basic	59.1	68.0	62.8	65.1	72.9	68.4
ERPD	**57.6**	**81.4**	**66.6**	**64.0**	**84.9**	**72.4**
ERPD*	56.9	81.2	66.1	64.0	83.9	72.0
BN	53.9	85.5	65.7	63.0	86.6	72.4
Omniscient	59.1	81.3	67.8	65.1	86.1	73.5

5 Related Work and Comparison

Targeting at the problems mentioned above, a method based on the belief network has been presented in [11], in which two subtasks are carried out simultaneously. Its procedure is as follows: firstly, two classifiers are trained for recognizing entities and relations independently and their outputs are treated as the conditional probability distributions for each entity and relation, given the observed data; secondly, this information together with the constraint knowledge among relations and entities are represented in a belief network [12] and are used to make global inferences for all entities and relations of interest. This method is denoted BN in our experiments.

Although BN can block the error propagation from the entity recognizer to the relation classifier as well as improve the relation recognition, it cannot make use of the information, which is only available in relation recognition, to help entity recognition. Experiments show that BN cannot improve entity recognition.

Comparing to BN, the proposed method in this paper can overcome the two shortcomings of it. Experiments show that it can not only improve the relation recognition, but also improve the precision of entity recognition. Moreover, the model ERPD could be more expressive enough than the belief network for the task of recognizing entity and relation. It can represent the mutually dependences between entities and relations by introducing relation reaction intensity, and can deal with a loop without the limitation of directed acyclic diagram (DAG) in the belief network. At the same time, the proposed method can merge two kinds of constraint knowledge (i.e. α_R and α_ε in Definition 4), but the method based on belief network can only use α_ε. Finally, the proposed method has a high computation efficiency while using the directed iteration algorithm.

6 Conclusions

The subtasks of entity recognition and relation recognition are typically carried out sequentially. This paper proposed an integrated approach that allows the two subtasks to be performed in a much closer way. Experimental results show that this method can improve the entity and relation recognition in some degree.

In addition, the Entity Relation Propagation Diagram (ERPD) is used to figure out the dependencies among entities and relations. It can also merge some constraint knowledge. Regarding to ERPD, two algorithms are further designed, one is based on the entity relation propagation tree, the other is the directed iteration algorithm on ERPD. The latter can be regarded as an approximation of the former with a higher computational efficiency.

Acknowledgements

We would like to express our deepest gratitude to Roth D. and Yih W. for making their dataset available for us. The research is supported in part by the National 863 Project of China under grant number 2001AA114210-03, the National Natural Science Foundation of China under grant number 60321002, and the Tsinghua-ALVIS Project co-sponsored by the National Natural Science Foundation of China under grant number 60520130299 and EU FP6.

References

1. Chinchor, N. MUC-7 Information Extraction Task Definition. In Proceeding of the Seventh Message Understanding Conference (MUC-7), Appendices, 1998.
2. Califf, M. and Mooney, R. Relational Learning of Pattern-match Rules for Information Extraction. In Proceedings of the Sixteenth National Conference on Artificial Intelligence and Eleventh Conference on Innovative Applications of Artificial Intelligence, 328-334, Orlando, Florida, USA, AAAI Press, 1999.
3. Freitag, D. Machine Learning for Information Extraction in Informal Domains. Machine learning, 39(2/3): 169-202, 2000.
4. Roth, D. and Yih, W. Relational Learning via Prepositional Algorithms: An Information Extraction Case Study. In Proceedings of the Seventeenth International Joint Conference on Artificial Intelligence, 1257-1263, Seattle, Washington, USA, Morgan Kaufmann, 2001.
5. Voorhees, E. Overview of the Trec-9 Question Answering Track. In The Ninth Text Retrieval Conference (TREC-9), 71-80, 2000.

6. Hirschman, L., Light, M., Breck, E. and Burger, J. Deep Read: A Reading Comprehension System. In Proceedings of the 37th Annual Meeting of Association for Computational Linguistics, 1999.
7. Abney, S.P. Parsing by Chunks. In S. P. Abney, R. C. Berwick, and C. Tenny, editors, Principle-based parsing: Computation and Psycholinguistics, 257-278. Kluwer, Dordrecht, 1991.
8. Xinghua Fan. Causality Diagram Theory Research and Applying it to Fault Diagnosis of Complexity System, Ph.D. Dissertation of Chongqing University, P.R. China, 2002.
9. Xinghua Fan, Zhang Qin, Sun Maosong, Huang Xiyue. Reasoning Algorithm in Multi-Valued Causality Diagram, Chinese Journal of Computers, 26(3), 310-322, 2003.
10. Murphy, K., Weiss, Y., and Jordan, M. Loopy Belief Propagation for Approximate Inference: An empirical study. In Proceeding of Uncertainty in AI, 467-475, 1999.
11. Roth, D. and Yih, W. Probability Reasoning for Entity & Relation Recognition. In Proceedings of 20th International Conference on Computational Linguistics (COLING-02), 835-841, 2002.
12. Pearl, J. Probability Reasoning in Intelligence Systems. Morgan Kaufmann, 1988.

Inversion Transduction Grammar Constraints for Mining Parallel Sentences from Quasi-Comparable Corpora*

Dekai Wu[1] and Pascale Fung[2]

[1] Human Language Technology Center, HKUST,
Department of Computer Science
[2] Department of Electrical and Electronic Engineering,
University of Science and Technology, Clear Water Bay, Hong Kong
dekai@cs.ust.hk, pascale@ee.ust.hk

Abstract. We present a new implication of Wu's (1997) Inversion Transduction Grammar (ITG) Hypothesis, on the problem of retrieving truly parallel sentence translations from large collections of highly *non*-parallel documents. Our approach leverages a strong language universal constraint posited by the ITG Hypothesis, that can serve as a strong inductive bias for various language learning problems, resulting in both efficiency and accuracy gains. The task we attack is highly practical since non-parallel multilingual data exists in far greater quantities than parallel corpora, but parallel sentences are a much more useful resource. Our aim here is to mine truly parallel sentences, as opposed to comparable sentence pairs or loose translations as in most previous work. The method we introduce exploits Bracketing ITGs to produce the first known results for this problem. Experiments show that it obtains large accuracy gains on this task compared to the expected performance of state-of-the-art models that were developed for the less stringent task of mining comparable sentence pairs.

1 Introduction

Parallel sentences are a relatively scarce but extremely useful resource for many applications including cross-lingual retrieval and statistical machine translation. Parallel sentences, or *bi-sentences* for short, can be exploited for a wealth of applications ranging from mining term translations for cross-lingual applications, to training paraphrase models and inducing structured terms for indexing, query processing, and retrieval.

Unfortunately, far more is available in the way of monolingual data. High-quality parallel corpora are currently largely limited to specialized collections of government (especially UN) and certain newswire collections, and even then relatively few bi-sentences are available in tight sentence-by-sentence translation.

* This work was supported in part by the Hong Kong Research Grants Council through grants RGC6083/99E, RGC6256/00E, DAG03/04.EG09, and RGC6206/03E.

R. Dale et al. (Eds.): IJCNLP 2005, LNAI 3651, pp. 257–268, 2005.

Increasingly sophisticated methods for extracting loose translations from non-parallel monolingual corpora—and in particular, what have been called *comparable sentence pairs*—have also recently become available. But while loose translations by themselves already have numerous applications, truly parallel sentence translations provide invaluable types of information for the aforementioned types of mining and induction, which cannot easily be obtained from merely loose translations or comparable sentence pairs. In particular, truly parallel bi-sentences are especially useful for extracting more precise syntactic and semantic relations within word sequences.

We present a new method that exploits a novel application of *Inversion Transduction Grammar* or *ITG* expressiveness constraints (Wu 1995 [1], Wu 1997 [2]) for mining monolingual data to obtain tight sentence translation pairs, yielding accuracy significantly higher than previous known methods. We focus here on very non-parallel *quasi-comparable* monolingual corpora, which are available in far larger quantities but are significantly more difficult to mine than either noisy parallel corpora or comparable corpora. The majority of previous work has concerned *noisy parallel corpora* (sometimes imprecisely also called "comparable corpora"), which contain non-aligned sentences that are nevertheless mostly bilingual translations of the same document. More recent work has examined *comparable corpora*, which contain non-sentence-aligned, non-translated bilingual documents that are topic-aligned. Still relatively few methods attempt to mine quasi-comparable corpora, which contain far more heterogeneous, very non-parallel bilingual documents that could be either on the same topic (in-topic) or not (off-topic).

Our approach is motivated by a number of desirable characteristics of ITGs, which historically were developed for translation and alignment purposes, rather than mining applications of the kind discussed in this paper. The ITG Hypothesis posits a strong language universal constraint that can act as a strong inductive bias for various language learning problems, resulting in both efficiency and accuracy gains. Specifically, the hypothesis asserts that sentence translation between any two natural languages can be accomplished within ITG expressiveness (subject to certain conditions). So-called *Bracketing ITGs* (BITG) are particularly interesting in certain applications such as the problem we consider here, because they impose ITG constraints in language-independent fashion, and do not require any language-specific linguistic grammar. (As discussed below, Bracketing ITGs are the simplest form of ITGs, where the grammar uses only a single, undifferentiated non-terminal.)

The key modeling property of bracketing ITGs that is most relevant to the task of identifying parallel bi-sentences is that they assign strong preference to candidate sentence pairs in which nested constituent subtrees can be recursively aligned with a minimum of constituent boundary violations. Unlike language-specific linguistic approaches, however, the shape of the trees are driven in unsupervised fashion by the data. One way to view this is that the trees are hidden explanatory variables. This not only provides significantly higher robustness than more highly constrained manually constructed grammars, but also makes the model widely applicable across languages in economical fashion without a large investment in manually constructed resources.

Moreover, for reasons discussed by Wu [2], ITGs possess an interesting intrinsic combinatorial property of permitting roughly up to four arguments of any frame to be transposed freely, but not more. This matches suprisingly closely the preponderance of linguistic verb frame theories from diverse linguistic traditions that all allow up to four arguments per frame. Again, this property falls naturally out of ITGs in language-independent fashion, without any hardcoded language-specific knowledge. This further suggests that ITGs should do well at picking out translation pairs where the order of up to four arguments per frame may vary freely between the two languages. Conversely, ITGs should do well at rejecting candidates where (1) too many words in one sentence find no correspondence in the other, (2) frames do not nest in similar ways in the candidate sentence pair, or (3) too many arguments must be transposed to achieve an alignment—all of which would suggest that the sentences probably express different ideas.

Various forms of empirical confirmation for the ITG Hypothesis have emerged recently, which quantitatively support the qualitative cross-linguistic characteristics just described across a variety of language pairs and tasks. Zens and Ney (2003) [3] show that ITG constraints yield significantly better alignment coverage than the constraints used in IBM statistical machine translation models on both German-English (Verbmobil corpus) and French-English (Canadian Hansards corpus). Zhang and Gildea (2004) [4] found that unsupervised alignment using Bracketing ITGs produces significantly lower Chinese-English alignment error rates than a syntactically supervised tree-to-string model [5]. Zhang and Gildea (2005) [6] show that lexicalized ITGs can further improve alignment accuracy. With regard to translation rather than alignment accuracy, Zens *et al.* (2004) [7] show that decoding under ITG constraints yields significantly lower word error rates and BLEU scores than the IBM constraints. Chiang (2005) [8] obtains significant BLEU score improvements via unsupervised induction of hierarchical phrasal bracketing ITGs. Such results partly motivate the work we discuss here.

We will begin by surveying recent related work and reviewing the formal properties of ITGs. Subsequently we describe the architecture of our new method, which relies on multiple stages so as to balance efficiency and accuracy considerations. Finally we discuss experimental results on a quasi-comparable corpus of Chinese and English from the topic detection task.

2 Recent Approaches to Mining Non-parallel Corpora

Recent work (Fung and Cheung 2004 [9]; Munteanu *et al.* 2004 [10]; Zhao and Vogel 2002 [11]) on extracting bi-sentences from comparable corpora is largely based on finding on-topic documents first through similarity matching and time alignment.

However, Zhao and Vogel used a corpus of Chinese and English versions of news stories from the Xinhua News agency, with “roughly similar sentence order of content". This corpus can be more accurately described as a noisy parallel corpus. Munteanu *et al.* used comparable corpora of news articles published within the same 5-day window. In both cases, the corpora contain documents on the same matching topics; unlike our present objective of mining quasi-comparable corpora, these other methods assume corpora of on-topic documents.

Munteanu *et al.* first identify on-topic document pairs by looking at publication date and word overlap, then classify all sentence pairs as being parallel or not parallel, using a maximum entropy classifier trained on parallel corpora. In contrast, the method we will propose identifies candidate sentence pairs without assuming that publication date information is available, and then uses the ITG constraints to automatically find parallel sentence pairs without requiring any training.

It is also difficult to relate Munteanu *et al.*'s work to our present objective because they do not directly evaluate the quality of the extracted bi-sentences (they instead look at performance of their machine translation application); however, as with Fung and Cheung, they noted that the sentences extracted were not truly parallel on the whole.

In this work, we aim to find parallel sentences from much more heterogenous, very non-parallel quasi-comparable corpora. Since many more multilingual text collections available today contain documents that do not match documents in the other language, we propose finding more parallel sentences from off-topic documents, as well as on-topic documents. An example is the TDT corpus, which is an aggregation of multiple news sources from different time periods.

3 Inversion Transduction Grammars

Formally, within the expressiveness hierarchy of transduction grammars, the ITG level of expressiveness has highly unusual intrinsic properties as seen in Figure 1. Wu [2] showed that the ITG class is an equivalence class of subsets of syntax-directed transduction grammars or SDTGs (Lewis and Stearns 1968 [12]), equivalently defined by meeting any of the following three conditions: (1) all rules are of rank 2, (2) all rules are of rank 3, or (3) all rules are either of *straight* or *inverted* orientation (and may have *any* rank). Ordinary unrestricted SDTGs allow any permutation of the symbols on the right-hand side to be specified when translating from the input language to the output language. In contrast, ITGs only allow two out of the possible permutations. If a rule is straight, the order of its right-hand symbols must be the same for both languages (just as in a *simple SDTG* or *SSDTG*). On the other hand, if a rule is inverted, then the order is left-to-right for the input language and right-to-left for the output language. Since inversion is permitted at any level of rule expansion, a derivation may intermix productions of either orientation within the parse tree. The ability to compose multiple levels of straight and inverted constituents gives ITGs much greater expressiveness than might seem at first blush, as indicated by the growing body of empirical results mentioned earlier.

A simple example may be useful to fix ideas. Consider the following pair of parse trees for sentence translations:

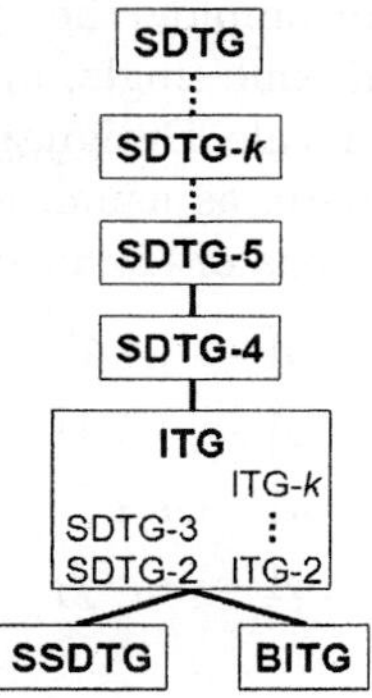

Fig. 1. The ITG level of expressiveness constitutes a surprisingly broad equivalence class within the expressiveness hierarchy of transduction grammars. The simple monolingual notion of "context-free" is too coarse to adequately categorize the bilingual case of transduction grammars. The expressiveness of a transduction grammar depends on the maximum rank k of rules, i.e., the maximum number of nonterminals on the right-hand-side. SDTG-k is always more expressive than SDTG-(k-1), except for the special case of the ITG class which includes both SDTG-2 and SDTG-3. In contrast, for monolingual CFGs, expressiveness is not affected by rank, as shown by the existence of a binary Chomsky normal form for any CFG. A binary normal form exists for ITGs but not SDTGs.

[[[The Authority]$_{NP}$ [will [[be accountable]$_{VV}$ [to [the [[Financial Secretary]$_{NN}$]$_{NNN}$]$_{NP}$]$_{PP}$]$_{VP}$]$_{VP}$]$_{SP}$.]$_{S}$

[[[管理局]$_{NP}$ [将会 [[向 [[[财政 司]$_{NN}$]$_{NNN}$]$_{NP}$]$_{PP}$ [负责]$_{VV}$]$_{VP}$]$_{VP}$]$_{SP}$ 。]$_{S}$

Even though the order of constituents under the inner VP is inverted between the languages, an ITG can capture the common structure of the two sentences. This is compactly shown by writing the parse tree together for both sentences with the aid of an ⟨⟩ angle bracket notation marking parse tree nodes that instantiate rules of inverted orientation:

[[[The/εAuthority/管理局]$_{NP}$ [will/将会 ⟨[be/εaccountable/负责]$_{VV}$ [to/向 [the/ε [[Financial/财政Secretary/司]$_{NN}$]$_{NNN}$]$_{NP}$]$_{PP}$ ⟩$_{VP}$]$_{VP}$]$_{SP}$ ./。]$_{S}$

In a weighted or stochastic ITG (SITG), a weight or a probability is associated with each rewrite rule. Following the standard convention, we use a and b to denote probabilities for syntactic and lexical rules, respectively. For example, the probability of the rule NN $\overset{0.4}{\rightarrow}$ [A N] is $a_{\mathrm{NN}\rightarrow[\mathrm{A\ N}]} = 0.4$. The probability of a lexical rule A $\overset{0.001}{\rightarrow}$ x/y is $b_{\mathrm{A}}(x, y) = 0.001$. Let W_1, W_2 be the vocabulary sizes of the two languages, and $\mathcal{N} = \{A_1, \ldots, A_N\}$ be the set of nonterminals with indices $1, \ldots, N$.

Polynomial-time algorithms are possible for various tasks including translation using ITGs, as well as bilingual parsing or *biparsing*, where the task is to build the highest-scored parse tree given an input bi-sentence.

For present purposes we can employ the special case of Bracketing ITGs, where the grammar employs only one single, undistinguished "dummy" nonterminal category for any non-lexical rule. Designating this category A, a Bracketing ITG has the following form (where, as usual, lexical transductions of the form $A \rightarrow e/f$ may possibly be singletons of the form $A \rightarrow e/\epsilon$ or $A \rightarrow \epsilon/f$).

$$
\begin{aligned}
A &\rightarrow [AA] \\
A &\rightarrow \langle AA \rangle \\
A &\rightarrow \epsilon, \epsilon \\
A &\rightarrow e_1/f_1 \\
&\dots \\
A &\rightarrow e_i/f_j
\end{aligned}
$$

Broadly speaking, Bracketing ITGs are useful when we wish to make use of the structural properties of ITGs discussed above, without requiring any additional linguistic information as constraints. Since they lack differentiated syntactic categories, Bracketing ITGs merely constrain the *shape* of the trees that align various nested portions of a sentence pair. The only linguistic knowledge used in Bracketing ITGs is the purely lexical set of collocation translations. Nevertheless, the ITG Hypothesis implies that biparsing truly parallel sentence pairs with a Bracketing ITG should typically yield high scores. Conversely, some non-parallel sentence pairs could be ITG-alignable, but any significant departure violating constituent boundaries will be downgraded.

As an illustrative example, in the models employed by most previous work on mining bi-sentences from non-parallel corpora, the following pair of sentences (found in actual data arising in our experiments below) would receive an inappropriately high score, because of the high lexical similarity between the two sentences:

Chinese president Jiang Zemin arrived in Japan today for a landmark state visit .
江泽民 将 是 到 日本 做 国事访问 的 首 位 中国 国家 主席 。
(*Jiang Zemin will be the first Chinese national president to pay a state vist to Japan.*)

However, the ITG based model is sensitive enough to the differences in the constituent structure (reflecting underlying differences in the predicate argument structure) so that our experiments show that it assigns a low score. On the other hand, the experiments also show that it successfully assigns a high score to other candidate bi-sentences representing a true Chinese translation of the same English sentence, as well as a true English translation of the same Chinese sentence.

4 Candidate Generation

An extremely large set of pairs of monolingual sentences from the quasi-comparable monolingual corpora will need to be scanned to obtain a useful

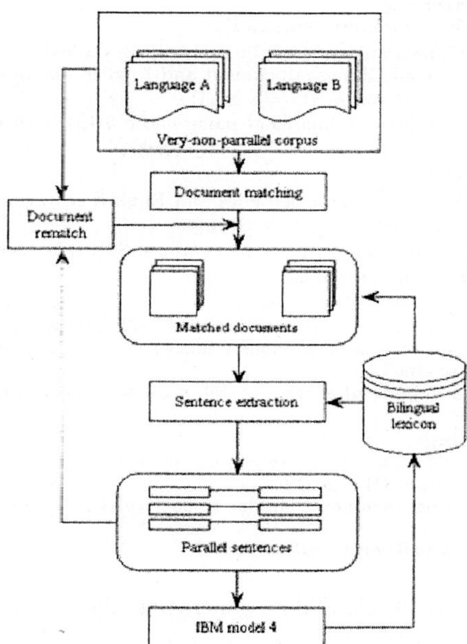

Fig. 2. Candidate generation overview. The iterative bootstrapping algorithm first mines loosely parallel sentence pairs from quasi-comparable corpora that contain both on-topic and off-topic documents. In a preprocessing step, documents that are believed to be on the same topic according to their similarity score are extracted, then "parallel" pairs are mined from these matched documents. The extracted sentences are used to bootstrap the entire process iteratively in two ways: (1) they are used to update a bilingual lexicon, which is then used again to reprocess the documents to be matched again; (2) any document pairs that are found to contain at least one "parallel" sentence pairs are considered to be on-topic, and added to the matched document set. Note that step (2) adds to the on-topic document set certain document pairs that are not considered to be on-topic by document matching scores.

number of parallel sentences, since obviously, the overwhelming majority of the n^2 possible sentence pairs will *not* be parallel. It is infeasible to run the ITG biparsing algorithm on n^2 candidate sentence pairs. Therefore a multi-stage algorithm is needed that first generates likely candidates using faster heuristics, and then biparses the candidates to obtain the final high-precision results.

We base our candidate generation on a method that Fung and Cheung (2004) developed for extracting loose translations (comparable sentence pairs) from quasi-comparable corpora [9], as shown in Figure 2. We selected this model because it produces the highest known accuracy on that task.

Figure 3 outlines the algorithm in greater detail. In the following sections, we describe the document pre-processing step followed by each of the subsequent iterative steps of the algorithm.

1. **Initial document matching**
   For all documents in the comparable corpus D:
   - Gloss Chinese documents using the bilingual lexicon (Bilex)
   - For every pair of glossed Chinese document and English documents:
     - compute *document similarity* => S(i,j)
   - Obtain all matched bilingual document pairs whose S(i,j) > threshold1 => D2
2. **Sentence matching**
   For each document pair in D2:
   - For every pair of glossed Chinese sentence and English sentence:
     - compute *sentence similarity* => S2(i,j)
   - Obtain all matched bilingual sentence pairs whose S2(i,j) > threshold2 => C1
3. **EM learning of new word translations**
   For all bilingual sentences pairs in C1, do:
   - Compute *translation lexicon probabilities* of all bilingual word pairs =>S3(i,j)
   - Obtain all bilingual word pairs previously unseen in Bilex and whose S3(i,j) > threshold3 => L1, and update Bilex
   - Compute *sentence alignment scores* => S4; if S4 does not change then return C1 and L1, otherwise continue
4. **Document re-matching**
   - Find all pairs of glossed Chinese and English documents which contain parallel sentences (anchor sentences) from C1 => D3
   - Expand D2 by finding documents similar to each of the document in D2
   - D2 := D3
5. **Goto 2 if termination criterion not met**

Fig. 3. Candidate generation algorithm

Document preprocessing. The documents are word segmented with the Linguistic Data Consortium (LDC) Chinese-English dictionary 2.0. The Chinese document is then glossed using all the dictionary entries. When a Chinese word has multiple possible translations in English, it is disambiguated using an extension of Fung *et al.*'s (1999) method [13].

Initial document matching. The aim of this step is to roughly match the Chinese-English documents pairs that are on-topic, in order to extract parallel sentences from them. Following previous work, cosine similarity between document vectors is used to judge whether a bilingual document pair is on-topic or off-topic.

Both the glossed Chinese document and English are represented in word vectors, with term weights. Pair-wise similarities are calculated for all possible Chinese-English document pairs, and bilingual documents with similarities above a certain threshold are considered to be comparable. Comparable documents are often on-topic.

Sentence matching. All sentence pair combinations within the on-topic documents are considered next in the selection process. Each sentence is again represented as word vectors. For each extracted document pair, pair-wise cosine similarities are calculated for all possible Chinese-English sentence pairs. Sentence pairs above a set threshold are considered parallel and extracted from the documents. Since cosine similarity is computed on translated word pairs within the sentence pairs, the better our bilingual lexicon is, the more accurate the sentence similarity will be. In the following section, we discuss how to find new word translations.

EM lexical learning from matched sentence pairs. This step updates the bilingual lexicon according to the intermediate results of parallel sentence extraction. New bilingual word pairs are learned from the extracted sentence pairs based on an EM learning method. In our experience any common method can be used for this purpose; for the experiments below we used the GIZA++ [14] implementation of the IBM statistical translation lexicon Model 4 of Brown *et al.* (1993) [15].

This model is based on the conditional probability of a source word being generated by the target word in the other language, based on EM estimation from aligned sentences. Zhao and Vogel (2002) showed that this model lends itself to adaptation and can provide better vocabulary coverage and better sentence alignment probability estimation [11]. In our work, we use this model on the intermediate results of parallel sentence extraction, i.e., on a set of aligned sentence pairs that may or may not truly correspond to each other.

We found that sentence pairs with high alignment scores are not necessarily more similar than others. This might be due to the fact that EM estimation at each intermediate step is not reliable, since we only have a small amount of aligned sentences that are truly parallel. The EM learner is therefore weak when applied to bilingual sentences from very non-parallel quasi-comparable corpora.

Document re-matching. This step implements a "find-one-get-more" principle, by augmenting the earlier matched documents with document pairs that are found to contain at least one parallel sentence pair. We further find other documents that are similar to each of the monolingual documents found. The algorithm then iterates to refine document matching and parallel sentence extraction.

Convergence. The IBM model parameters, including sentence alignment score and word alignment scores, are computed in each iteration. The parameter values eventually stay unchanged and the set of extracted bi-sentence candidates also converges to a fixed size. The iteration then terminates and returns the last set of bilingual sentence pairs as the generated candidate sentences.

5 ITG Scoring

The ITG model computes scores upon the set of candidates generated in the preceding stage. A variant of the approach used by Leusch *et al.* (2003) [16] allows us to forego training to estimate true probabilities; instead, rules are simply given unit weights. This allows the scores computed by ITG biparsing to be interpreted as a generalization of classical Levenshtein string edit distance, where inverted block transpositions are also allowed. Even without probability estimation, Leusch *et al.* found excellent correlation with human judgment of similarity between translated paraphrases.

As mentioned earlier, biparsing for ITGs can be accomplished efficiently in polynomial time, rather than the exponential time required for classical SDTGs. The biparsing algorithm employs a dynamic programming approach described by Wu [2]. The time complexity of the algorithm in the general case is $\Theta\left(T^3V^3\right)$ where T and V are the lengths of the two sentences. This is a factor of V^3 more than monolingual chart parsing, but has turned out to remain quite practical for corpus analysis, where parsing need not be real-time.

6 Experiments

Method. For our experiments we extracted the bi-sentences from a very non-parallel, quasi-comparable corpus of TDT3 data which consists of transcriptions of news stories from radio and TV broadcasts in both English and Chinese channels during the period 1998-2000. This corpus contained approximately 290,000 English sentences and 110,000 Chinese sentences. This yields over 30 billion possible sentence pairs, so a multi-stage approach is clearly necessary.

Experience showed that the lexicon learned in the candidate generation stage, while adequate for candidate generation, is not of sufficient quality for biparsing due to the non-parallel nature of the training data. However, any translation lexicon of reasonable accuracy can be used. For these experiments we employed the LDC Chinese-English dictionary 2.0.

To conduct as blind an evaluation as possible, an independent annotator separately produced gold standard labels for a random sample of approximately 300 of the top 2,500 candidate sentence pairs proposed by the generation stage. The annotator was instructed to accept any semantically equivalent translations, including non-literal ones. Inspection had shown that sentence pair candidates longer than about 15 words were practically never truly parallel translations, so these were a priori excluded by the sampling in order to ensure that precision/recall scores would be more meaningful.

Results. Under our method any desired tradeoff between precision and recall can be obtained. Therefore, rather than arbitrarily setting a threshold, we are interested in evaluation metrics that can show whether the ITG model is highly effective at any desired tradeoff points. Thus, we assess the contribution of ITG ranking by computing standard uninterpolated average precision scores used to evaluate the effectiveness of ranking methods. Specifically, in this case, this is the expected value of precision over the rank positions of the correctly identified truly parallel bi-sentences:

$$\text{uninterpolated average precision} = \frac{1}{\mid T \mid} \sum_{i \in T} \text{precision at rank}\,(i) \qquad (1)$$

where T is the set of correctly identified bi-sentences.

Our method yielded an uninterpolated average precision of 64.7%. No direct comparison of this figure is possible since previous work has focused on the rather different objectives of mining noisy parallel or comparable corpora to extract comparable sentence pairs and loose translations. However, we can understand the improvement by comparing against scores obtained using the cosine-based lexical similarity metric which is typical of the majority of previous methods for mining non-parallel corpora, including that of Fung and Cheung (2004)[9]. Evaluating the ranking produced under this more typical score yielded

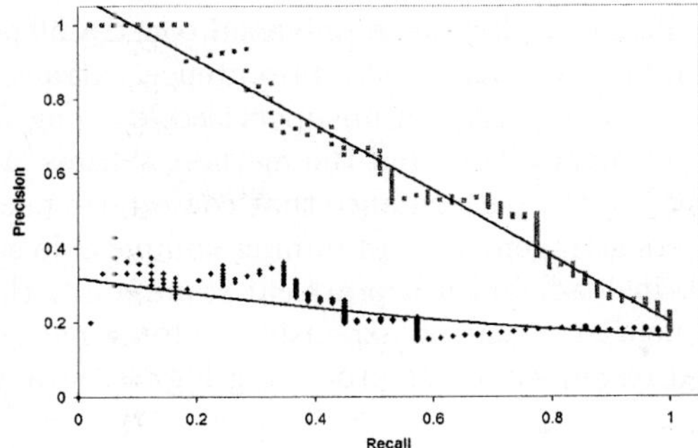

Fig. 4. Precision-recall curves for the ITG model (upper curve) versus traditional cosine model (lower curve); see text

an uninterpolated average precision of 24.6%. This suggests that the ITG based method could produce significant accuracy gains if applied to many of the existing non-parallel corpus mining methods.

Figure 4 compares precision versus recall curves obtained with rankings from the ITG model compared with the more traditional cosine lexical similarity model. The graph reveals that at all levels, much higher precision can be obtained using the ITG model. Up to 20% recall, the ITG ranking produces bi-sentences with perfect precision; in contrast, the cosine model produces 30% precision. Even at 50% recall, the ITG ranked bi-sentences have above 65% precision, as compared with 21% for the cosine model.

As can be seen from the following examples of extracted bi-sentences (shown with rough word glosses), the ITG constraints are able to accommodate nested inversions accounting for the cross-linguistic differences in constituent order:

It is time to break the silence.
现在 呢，是 打破 沉默 的 时候 了 。
(*Now* topical , *is break silence* genitive *time* aspectual .)

I think that's what people were saying tonight.
我 认为 这 是 人们 今晚 所 说 的话 。
(*I think this is people today by say* genitive *words* .)

If the suspects are convicted, they will serve their time in Scotland.
如果 两 名 嫌疑 人 被 判 有罪，就 得 在 苏格兰 服刑 。
(*If two* classifier *suspected person* bei-particle *sentence guilty, then must in Scotland serve time* .)

7 Conclusion

We have introduced a new method that exploits generic bracketing Inversion Transduction Grammars giving the first known results for the new task of mining truly parallel sentences from very non-parallel quasi-comparable corpora.

The method takes the strong language universal constraint posited by the ITG Hypothesis as an inductive bias on the bi-sentence extraction task which we anticipate will become a key stage in unsupervised learning for numerous more specific models. Experiments show that the method obtains large accuracy gains on this task compared to the performance that could be expected if state-of-the-art models for the less stringent task of mining comparable sentence pairs were applied to this task instead. From a practical standpoint, the method has the dual advantages of neither requiring expensive training nor requiring language-specific grammatical resources, while producing high accuracy results.

References

1. Wu, D.: An algorithm for simultaneously bracketing parallel texts by aligning words. In: ACL-95, Cambridge, MA (1995)
2. Wu, D.: Stochastic inversion transduction grammars and bilingual parsing of parallel corpora. Computational Linguistics **23** (1997)
3. Zens, R., Ney, H.: A comparative study on reordering constraints in statistical machine translation. In: ACL-03, Sapporo (2003) 192–202
4. Zhang, H., Gildea, D.: Syntax-based alignment: Supervised or unsupervised? In: COLING-04, Geneva (2004)
5. Yamada, K., Knight, K.: A syntax-based statistical translation model. In: ACL-01, Toulouse, France (2001)
6. Zhang, H., Gildea, D.: Stochastic lexicalized inversion transduction grammar for alignment. In: ACL-05, Ann Arbor (2005) 475–482
7. Zens, R., Ney, H., Watanabe, T., Sumita, E.: Reordering constraints for phrase-based statistical machine translation. In: COLING-04, Geneva (2004)
8. Chiang, D.: A hierarchical phrase-based model for statistical machine translation. In: ACL-05, Ann Arbor (2005) 263–270
9. Fung, P., Cheung, P.: Mining very-non-parallel corpora: Parallel sentence and lexicon extraction via bootstrapping and em. In: EMNLP-2004, Barcelona (2004)
10. Munteanu, D.S., Fraser, A., Marcu, D.: Improved machine translation performance via parallel sentence extraction from comparable corpora. In: NAACL-04. (2004)
11. Zhao, B., Vogel, S.: Adaptive parallel sentences mining from web bilingual news collections. In: IEEE Workshop on Data Mining. (2002)
12. Lewis, P.M., Stearns, R.E.: Syntax-directed transduction. Journal of the Association for Computing Machinery **15** (1968) 465–488
13. Fung, P., Liu, X., Cheung, C.S.: Mixed-language query disambiguation. In: ACL-99, Maryland (1999)
14. Och, F.J., Ney, H.: Improved statistical alignment models. In: ACL-2000, Hong Kong (2000)
15. Brown, P.F., DellaPietra, S.A., DellaPietra, V.J., Mercer, R.L.: The mathematics of statistical machine translation. Computational Linguistics **19** (1993) 263–311
16. Leusch, G., Ueffing, N., Ney, H.: A novel string-to-string distance measure with applications to machine translation evaluation. In: MT Summit IX. (2003)

Automatic Term Extraction Based on Perplexity of Compound Words

Minoru Yoshida[1,2] and Hiroshi Nakagawa[1,2]

[1] Information Technology Center, University of Tokyo,
7-3-1 Hongo, Bunkyo-ku, Tokyo 113-0033
[2] JST CREST, Honcho 4-1-8, Kawaguchi-shi, Saitama 332-0012
mino@r.dl.itc.u-tokyo.ac.jp, nakagawa@dl.itc.u-tokyo.ac.jp

Abstract. Many methods of term extraction have been discussed in terms of their accuracy on huge corpora. However, when we try to apply various methods that derive from frequency to a small corpus, we may not be able to achieve sufficient accuracy because of the shortage of statistical information on frequency. This paper reports a new way of extracting terms that is tuned for a very small corpus. It focuses on the structure of compound terms and calculates perplexity on the term unit's left-side and right-side. The results of our experiments revealed that the accuracy with the proposed method was not that advantageous. However, experimentation with the method combining perplexity and frequency information obtained the highest average-precision in comparison with other methods.

1 Introduction

Term extraction, which is the task of extracting terminology (or technical terms) from a set of documents, is one of major topics in natural language processing. It has a wide variety of applications including book indexing, dictionary generation, and keyword extraction for information retrieval systems.

Most automatic term extraction systems make a sorted list of candidate terms extracted from a given corpus according to the "importance" scores of the terms, so they require scores of "importance" for the terms. Existing scores include TF-IDF, C-Value [1], and FLR [9]. In this paper, we propose a new method that involves revising the definition of the FLR method in a more sophisticated way. One of the advantages of the FLR method is its size-robustness, i.e, it can be applied to small corpus with less significant drop in performance than other standard methods like TF and IDF, because it is defined using more fine-grained features called term units. Our new method, called FPP, inherit this property while exhibiting better performance than FLR.

At the same time, we also propose a new scheme for evaluating term extraction systems. Our idea is to use summaries[1] of articles as a gold standard. This strategy is based on the assumption that *summaries of documents can*

[1] In more detail, an article revised for display on mobile phones.

R. Dale et al. (Eds.): IJCNLP 2005, LNAI 3651, pp. 269–279, 2005.

serve as collections of important terms because, in writing summaries, people may make an original document shorter by dropping unnecessary parts of original documents, while retaining essential fragments. Thus, we *regard* a term in an original document to be important if it also appears in the summary.

2 Term Extraction

Term extraction is the task of extracting important terms from a given corpus. Typically, term extraction systems first extract *term candidates*, which are usually the noun phrases detected by handcrafted POS sequence patterns, from the corpus. After that, term candidates are sorted according to some *importance* score. Important terms, (i.e., terms that appear in the summary, in our problem setting,) are desired to be ranked higher than others. In this paper we focus on the second step, i.e., term candidate sorting by importance scores. We propose a new score of term importance by modifying an existing one in a more sophisticated manner.

In the remainder of this paper, a term candidate is represented by $W = w_1 w_2 \cdots w_n$ where w_i represents a *term unit* contained in W, and n is the number of term units contained in W. Here, *a term unit* is the basic element comprising term candidates that is not further decomporsable without destruction of meaning. Term units are used to calculate of the LR score that is explained in the next section.

3 Related Work

Many methods of term scoring have been proposed in the literature [7] [3] [4]. Methods that use corpus statistics have especially emerged over the past decade due to the increasing number of machine-readable documents such as news articles and WWW documents. These methods can be mainly categorized into the following three types according to what types of features are used to calculate the scores.

- Measurement by frequencies
- Measurement by internal structures of term candidates
- Combination of the above

3.1 Score by Frequency: TF

Frequency is one of the most basic features of term extraction. Usually, a term that appears frequently is assumed to be important. We introduce a score of this type: $tf(W)$.

$tf(W)$ represents the *TF(Term Frequency)* of W. It is defined as *the number of occurrences of W in all documents.* Note that $tf(W)$ is the result of the brute force counting of W occurrences. This method, for example, counts the term *natural* even if it is merely part of another phrase such as *natural language processing*.[2]

3.2 Score by Internal Structures in Term Candidates: LR

An LR method [9] is based on the intuition that some words are used as term units more frequently than others, and a phrase that contains such "good" term units is likely to be important. The left score $l(w_i)$ of each term unit w_i of a target term is defined as the number (or the number of types) of term units connected to the left of w_i (i.e., appearing just in the left of w_i in term candidates), and the right score $r(w_i)$ is defined in the same manner.[3] An LR score $lr(w_i)$ is defined as the geometric mean of left and right scores:

$$lr(w_i) = \sqrt{l(w_i)r(w_i)}$$

The total LR score of W is defined as a geometric mean of the scores of term units as:

$$LR(W) = (lr(w_1)lr(w_2)\cdots lr(w_n))^{\frac{1}{n}}.$$

An example of LR score calculation is given in the next section.

3.3 Mixed Measures

C-Value. C-Value[1] is defined by the following two expressions:

$t(W)$: frequency of terms that contain W,
$c(W)$: number of types of terms that contain W.

Note that $t(W)$ does not count W itself. Intuitively, $t(W)$ is the degree of being part of another term, and $c(W)$ is the degree of being part of various types of terms.

C-Value is defined by using these two expressions in the following way.

$$c\text{-}val(W) = (n-1) \times \left(tf(W) - \frac{t(W)}{c(W)}\right)$$

Note that the value is zero where $n = 1$. MC-Value [9] is a modified version of C-Value adapted for use in term collections that include the term of length 1 (i.e., $n = 1$).

$$MC\text{-}val(W) = n \times \left(tf(W) - \frac{t(W)}{c(W)}\right)$$

We used MC-Value in the experiments because our task was to extract terms regardless of whether each term is one-word term or not.

---

[2] We can also use another frequency score F(Frequency), or $f(W)$, that is defined as the number of *independent* occurrences of W in all documents. (*Independent* means that W is not included in any larger term candidate.) However, we observed that $f(W)$ (or the combination of $f(W)$ and another score) had no advantage over $tf(W)$ (or the combination of $tf(W)$ and another score) in the experiments,so in this paper we omit scores that are the combination of $f(W)$ and other scores.

[3] In addition, we apply the adding-one smoothing to both of them to avoid the score being zero when w_i has no connected terms.

FLR. The LR method reflects the number of appearances of term units, but does not reflect that of a whole term itself. For example, even if "natural language" is more frequent than "language natural" and the former should be given a higher score than the latter, LR cannot be used to do this.

An FLR method [9] was proposed to overcome this shortcoming of LR. It reflects both the frequencies and inner structures of terms. $FLR(W)$ is defined as the product of $LR(W)$ and $tf(W)$ as:

$$FLR(W) = tf(W)LR(W).$$

4 Our Method: Combining Types and Frequencies via Entropy

4.1 Preliminaries: Token-LR and Type-LR

Figure 1 outlines example statistics for term unit connections. For example, the term *disaster information* appeared three times in the corpus.

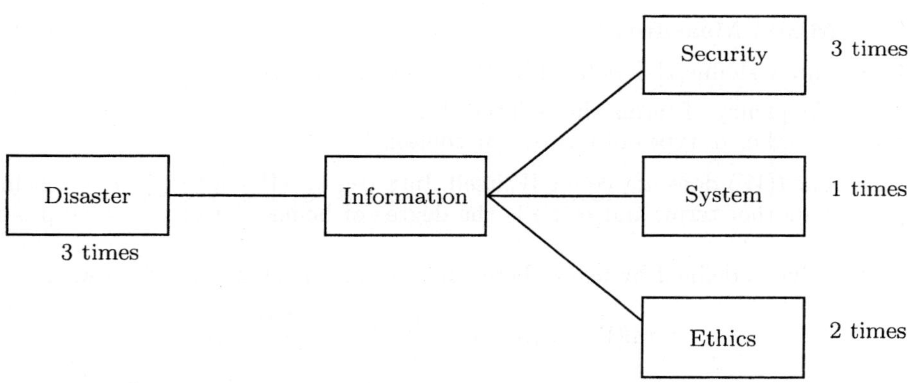

Fig. 1. An example of statistics for term unit connections

LR scores have two versions: Token-LR and Type-LR. Token-LR (and Type-LR) are calculated by simply counting the frequency (and the types) of terms connected to each term unit, respectively. In this case, a Type-LR score for the term unit "information" is

$$l(information) = 1 + 1^4, \quad r(information) = 3 + 1, \quad LR(information) = \sqrt{8},$$

and a Token-LR score is

$$l(information) = 3 + 1, \quad r(information) = 6 + 1, \quad LR(information) = \sqrt{28}.$$

[4] Note that the adding-one smoothing is applied.

Type-LR cannot reflect frequencies which suggest whether there are *specially important* connecting terms or not. However, Token-LR cannot reflect the number of types that suggest the variety of connections. To solve these shortcomings with LR measures, we propose a new kind that combines these two through *perplexity.*

4.2 Term Extraction by Perplexity

Our method is based on the idea of perplexity [8]. The score of a term is defined by the *left perplexity* and *right perplexity* of its term units. In this subsection we first give a standard definition of the perplexity of language, from which our left and right perplexity measures are derived. After that, we describe how to score terms by using these perplexities.

Perplexity of language. Assume that language L is information source that produces word lists of length n and each word list is produced independently with probability $P(w_1^n)$. Then, the entropy of language L is calculated as:

$$H_0(L) = -\sum_{w_1^n} P(w_1^n) \log P(w_1^n).$$

The entropy per word is then calculated as:

$$H(L) = -\frac{1}{n} \sum_{w_1^n} P(w_1^n) \log P(w_1^n).$$

This value indicates the number of bits needed to express each word generated from L. Perplexity of language L is defined using $H(L)$ as:

$$Perplexity = 2^{H(L)}.$$

Perplexity can be seen as the average number of types of words that follow each preceding word. The larger the perplexity of L, the less predictable the word connection in L.

Left and right perplexity. Assume that k types of unit words can connect to the right of w_i (see Figure 2).

Also assume that R^i is a random variable assigned to the i-th term unit which represents its right connections and takes its value from the set $\{r_1, r_2, \cdots, r_k\}$. Then, entropy $H(R^i)$ is calculated as:

$$H(R^i) = -\sum_{j=1}^{k} P(r_j) \log_2 P(r_j)$$

Note that we define $0 \log 0 = 0$, according to the fact that $x \log x \rightarrow 0$ where $x \rightarrow 0$.

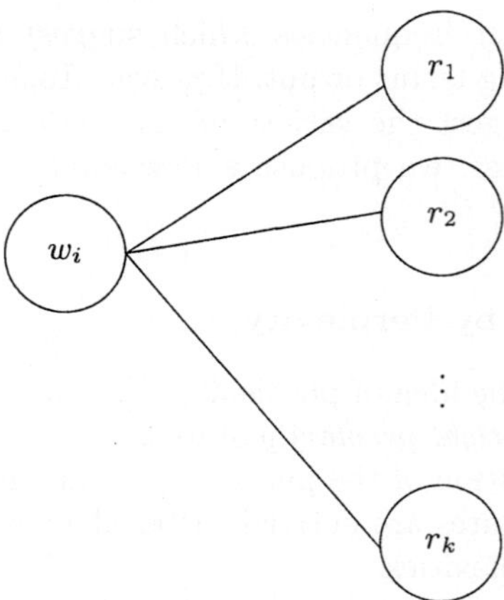

Fig. 2. Example of term unit and term units connected to its right

This entropy value can be thought of as a variety of terms that connect to the right of w_i, or, more precisely, the number of bits needed to describe words that connect to the right of w_i.

Then right perplexity $pp_r(w_i)$ of term unit w_i is defined as

$$pp_r(w_i) = 2^{H(R^i)}.$$

This value can be seen as the number of branches, in the sense of information theory, of right-connection from w_i. It naturally reflects both the frequency and number of types of each connection between term units.

Random variable L^i for the left connections is defined in the same manner. The perplexity for left connections is thus defined as:

$$pp_l(w_i) = 2^{H(L^i)}.$$

Term Score by Perplexity. We define our measure by substituting l and r in the definition of LR with pp_l and pp_r. First, a combination of left and right perplexities is defined as the geometric mean of both:

$$pp(w_i) = (pp_l(w_i) \cdot pp_r(w_i))^{\frac{1}{2}}.$$

After that, perplexity score $PP(W)$ for W is defined as the geometric mean of all $pp(w_i)$s:

$$PP(W) = \left[\prod_{i=1}^{n} pp(w_i)\right]^{\frac{1}{n}}.$$

We used $\log PP(W)$ instead of $PP(W)$ to make implementation easier. Notice that $\log x$ is a monotonic (increasing) function of x.

$$PP(W) = \left[\prod_{i=1}^{n}\{pp_l(w_i) \cdot pp_r(w_i)\}^{\frac{1}{2}}\right]^{\frac{1}{n}}$$

$$\Rightarrow \log_2 PP(W) = \frac{1}{n}\log_2\left(\prod_{i=1}^{n}\{pp_l(w_i) \cdot pp_r(w_i)\}^{\frac{1}{2}}\right)$$

$$\Rightarrow \log_2 PP(W) = \frac{1}{2n}\sum_{i=1}^{n}(\log_2 pp_l(w_i) + \log_2 pp_r(w_i))$$

Using $pp_r(w_i) = 2^{H(R^i)}$ and $pp_l(w_i) = 2^{H(l^i)}$, we obtain

$$\log_2 PP(W) = \frac{1}{2n}\sum_{i=1}^{n}\left(H(R^i) + H(L^i)\right).$$

The right side means the sum of the left and right entropies of all term units.

4.3 Term Extraction by Perplexity and TF

Perplexity itself serves as a good score for terms, but combining it with TF, which is a measure from another point of view, can provide a still better score that reflects both the inner structures of term candidates and their frequencies which are regarded as global information about the whole corpus.

Our new score, $FPP(W)$, which is a combination of PP and TF, is defined as their product:

$$FPP(W) = tf(W)PP(W)$$

$$\Rightarrow \log_2 FPP(W) = \log_2 tf(W) + \log_2 PP(W)$$

$$\Rightarrow \log_2 FPP(W) = \log_2 tf(W) + \frac{1}{2n}\sum_{i=1}^{n}\left(H(R^i) + H(L^i)\right)$$

We avoided the problem of $\log_2 tf(W)$ being undefined with $tf(W) = 0$ [5] by applying the adding-one smoothing to $tf(W)$. Therefore, the above definition of $\log FPP(W)$ changed as follows:

$$\log_2 FPP'(W) = \log_2(tf(W) + 1) + \frac{1}{2n}\sum_{i=1}^{n}\left(H(R^i) + H(L^i)\right).$$

We used this $\log_2 FPP'(W)$ measure for evaluation.

[5] This situation occurs when we want to score a new term candidate from outside of corpus.

5 Experiments

5.1 Test Collection

We collected news articles and their summaries from the Mainichi Web News from April, 2001 to March, 2002. The articles were categorized into four genres: Economy, Society, World, and Politics. A shorter version of each article was provided for browsing on mobile phones. Articles for mobile phones were written manually from the original ones, which were shorter versions of the original articles adapted to small displays. We regard them as summaries of the original articles and used them to evaluate whether the extracted terms were correct or not. If a term in the original article was also in the summary, the term was correct, and incorrect if otherwise. Each article had a size of about 300 letters and each summary had a size of about 50.

Table 1 lists the number of articles in each category.

Table 1. Number of articles in test collection

	Economy	Society	World	Politics
# of articles	4,177	5,952	6,153	4,428

5.2 Experimental Setup

We used test data on the various numbers of articles to investigate how the performance of each measure changed according to corpus size. A corpus of each size was generated by singly adding an article randomly selected from the corpus of each genre. We generated test data consisting of 50 different sizes (from 1 to 50) for each genre. The average number of letters in the size 50 corpus was about 19,000, and the average number of term candidates was about 1,300. We used five different seed numbers to randomly select articles. The performance of each method was evaluated in terms of recall and precision, which were averaged over the five trials.

5.3 Preprocessing: Term Candidate Extraction

Each article was preprocessed with a morphological analyzer, the Chasen 2.3.3.[2] The output of Chasen was further modified according to heuristic rules as follows.

- Nouns and undefined words were extracted for further processes and other words were discarded.
- Suffixes and prefixes were concatenated to their following and preceding words, respectively.

The result was a set of term candidates to be evaluated with the term importance scores described in the previous sections.

We applied the following methods to the term candidates: F, TF, DF (Document Frequency) [8], LR, MC-Value, FLR, TF-IDF [8], PP, and FPP'.

5.4 Evaluation Method

We used average precision [8] for the evaluation. Let D be a set of all the term candidates and $D_q \subseteq D$ be a set of the correct ones among them. The extracted term was correct if it appeared in the summary. Then, the average precision can be calculated in the following manner.

$$\text{Average-Precision} = \frac{1}{|D_q|} \sum_{1 \le k \le |D|} \left\{ r_k \times \left(\frac{1}{k} \sum_{1 \le i \le k} r_i \right) \right\}$$

where $r_i = 1$ if the i-th term is correct, and $r_i = 0$ if otherwise.

Note that the total number of correct answers was $|D_q|$. The next section presents the experimental results obtained by average precision.

Table 2. Average precision on corpus of 1, 10, and 50 articles. Each cell contains results for the Economy/World/Society/Politics genres.

Measure	SIZE=1	SIZE=10	SIZE=50
F	0.275/0.274/0.246/0.406	0.337/0.350/0.325/0.378	0.401/0.415/0.393/0.425
TF	0.305/0.388/0.281/0.430	0.386/0.406/0.376/0.435	0.454/0.462/0.436/0.477
DF	0.150/0.173/0.076/0.256	0.237/0.253/0.234/0.294	0.337/0.357/0.332/0.378
LR	0.192/0.370/0.194/0.378	0.255/0.280/0.254/0.317	0.303/0.302/0.273/0.320
MC-Val	0.218/0.296/0.240/0.388	0.317/0.334/0.307/0.365	0.399/0.400/0.369/0.420
FLR	0.305/0.410/0.298/0.469	0.361/0.397/0.364/0.429	0.423/0.435/0.404/0.455
TF-IDF	0.150/0.173/0.076/0.256	0.388/0.407/0.376/0.437	0.457/0.465/0.438/0.479
PP	0.223/0.327/0.285/0.514	0.285/0.299/0.282/0.331	0.329/0.317/0.279/0.331
FPP'	0.320/0.457/0.380/0.561	0.407/0.444/0.409/0.471	0.487/0.480/0.448/0.493

6 Results and Discussion

Table 2 shows the results on the corpus of 1, 10, and 50 articles in all the genres. Figure 3 plots the average precision for each corpus size (from 1 to 50) in the economy category.[6] In some cases, results on one article were better than those on 10 and 50 articles. This was mainly caused by the fact that the average precision is tend to be high on articles of short length, and the average length for one article was much shorter than that of ten articles in some genres. PP outperformed LR in most cases. We think the reason was that PP could provide more precious information about connections among term units. We observed that PP depended less on the size of the corpus than frequency-based methods like TF and MC-Val. FPP' had the best performance of all methods in all genres.

[6] We only show a graph in the economy genre, but the results in other genres were similar to this.

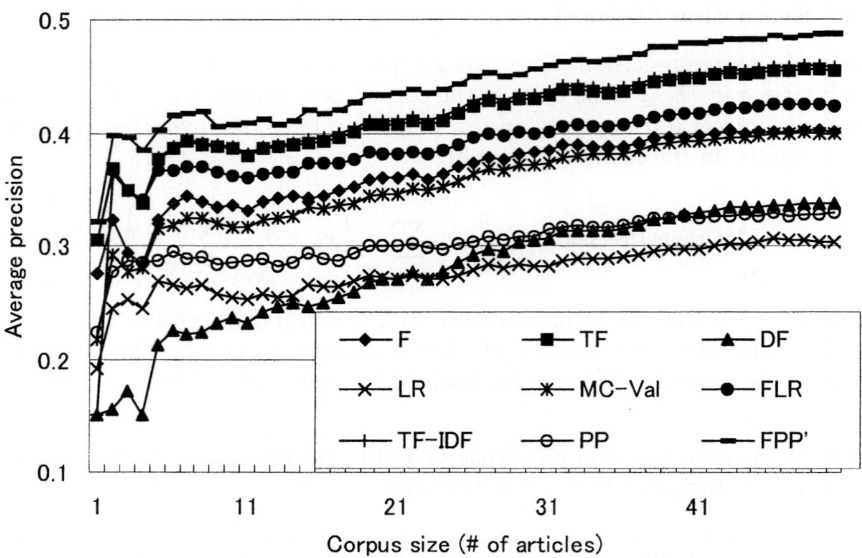

Fig. 3. Results in economy genre

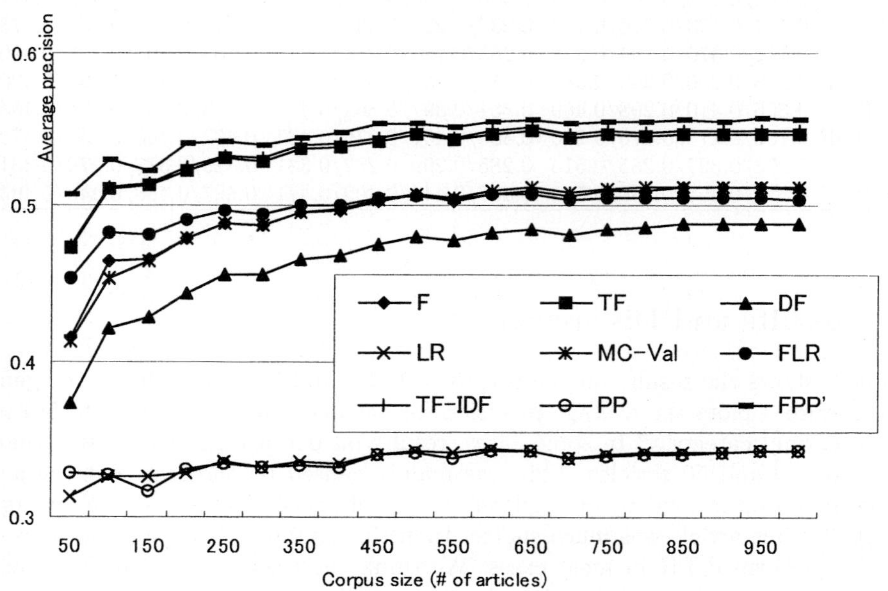

Fig. 4. Results on 50 – 1000 articles

Figure 4 plots the results in the economy genre when the corpus size was increased to 1,000 in increments of 50 articles. We observed that the performance of PP and LR got close with the increase in corpus size, especially with 200 articles and more. FPP' once again outperformed all the other methods in this experiment. The FPP' method exhibited the best performance regardless of corpus size.

7 Conclusion and Future Work

We proposed a new method for extracting terms. It involved the combination of two LR methods: Token-LR and Type-LR. We showed that these two could be combined by using the idea of perplexity, and gave a definition for the combined method. This new method was then combined with TF and experimental results on the test corpus consisting of news articles and their summaries revealed that the new method (FPP') outperformed existing methods including TF, TF-IDF, MC-Value, and FLR.

In future work, we would like to improve the performance of the method by, for example, adding preprocessing rules, such as the appropriate treatment of numerical characters, and developing more sophisticated methods for combining TF and PP. We also plan to extend our experiments to include other test collections like TMREC [6].

References

1. Ananiadou, S.: A methodology for automatic term recognition. In Proceedings of the 15th InternationalConference on Computational Linguistcs (COLING) (1994), pp. 1034–1038.
2. Asahara, M., Matsumoto, Y.: Extended Models and Tools for High-performance Part-of-Speech Tagger. Proceedings of COLING 2000. (2000).
3. COMPUTERM'98 First Workshop on Computational Terminology. (1998).
4. COMPUTERM'02 Second Workshop on Computational Terminology. (2002).
5. Frantzi, K. and Ananiadou, S.: The C-value/NC-value method for ATR. Journal of NLP, Vol. 6, No. 3, (1999). pp.145–179.
6. Kageura, K.: TMREC Task: Overview and Evaluation. Proc. of the First NTCIR Workshop on Research in Japanese Text Retrieval and Term Recognition, (1999). pp. 411–440.
7. Kageura, K and Umino, B.: Methods of automatic term recognition: A review. Terminology, Vol. 3, No. 2, (1996). pp. 259–289.
8. Manning, C.D., and Schutze, H..: Foundations of Statistical Natural Language Processing. (1999). The MIT Press.
9. Nakagawa, H. and Mori, T.: Automatic Term Recognition based on Statistics of Compound Nouns and their Components. Terminology, Vol. 9, No. 2, (2003). pp. 201–219.

Document Clustering with Grouping and Chaining Algorithms

Yllias Chali and Soufiane Noureddine

Department of Computer Science,
University of Lethbridge

Abstract. Document clustering has many uses in natural language tools and applications. For instance, summarizing sets of documents that all describe the same event requires first identifying and grouping those documents talking about the same event. Document clustering involves dividing a set of documents into non-overlapping clusters. In this paper, we present two document clustering algorithms: *grouping algorithm*, and *chaining algorithm*. We compared them with k-means and the EM algorithms. The evaluation results showed that our two algorithms perform better than the k-means and EM algorithms in different experiments.

1 Introduction

Document clustering has many uses in natural language tools and applications. For instance, summarizing sets of documents that all describe the same event requires first identifying and grouping those documents talking about the same event. Document clustering involves dividing a set of texts into non-overlapping clusters, where documents in a cluster are more similar to one another than to documents in other clusters. The term more *similar*, when applied to clustered documents, usually means closer by some measure of proximity or similarity.

According to Manning and Schutze [1], there are two types of structures produced by clustering algorithms, hierarchical clustering and flat or non-hierarchical clustering. Flat clustering are simply groupings of similar objects. Hierarchical clustering is a tree of subclasses which represent the cluster that contains all the objects of its descendants. The leaves of the tree are the individual objects of the clustered set. In our experiments, we used the non-hierarchical clustering k-means and EM [2] and our own clustering algorithms.

There are several similarity measures to help find out groups of related documents in a set of documents [3]. We use identical word method and semantic relation method to assign a similarity score to each pair of compared texts. For the identical word method, we use k-means algorithm, the EM algorithm, and our own *grouping algorithm* to cluster the documents. For the semantic relation method, we use our own *grouping algorithm* and *chaining algorithm* to do the clustering job. We choose WordNet 1.6 as our background knowledge. WordNet consists of synsets gathered in a hypernym/hyponym hierarchy [4]. We use it to get word senses and to evaluate the semantic relations between word senses.

R. Dale et al. (Eds.): IJCNLP 2005, LNAI 3651, pp. 280–291, 2005.

2 Identical Word Similarity

To prepare the texts for the clustering process using identical word similarity, we perform the following steps on each of the selected raw texts:

1. Preprocessing which consists in extracting file contents from the raw texts, stripping special characters and numbers, converting all words to lower cases and removing stopwords, and converting all plural forms to singular forms.
2. Create document word vectors: each document was processed to record the unique words and their frequencies. We built the local word vector for each document, each vector entry will record a single word and its frequency. We also keep track of the unique words in the whole texts to be tested. After processing all the documents, we convert each local vector to a global vector using the overall unique words.
3. Compute the identical word similarity score among documents: given any two documents, if we have their global vectors $\boldsymbol{x}$, $\boldsymbol{y}$, we can use the cosine measure [5] to calculate the identical word similarity score between these two texts.

$$cos(\boldsymbol{x}, \boldsymbol{y}) = \frac{\sum_{i=1}^{n} x_i y_i}{\sqrt{\sum_{i=1}^{n} x_i^2}\sqrt{\sum_{i=1}^{n} y_i^2}} \tag{1}$$

where $\boldsymbol{x}$ and $\boldsymbol{y}$ are n-dimensional vectors in a real-valued space.

Now, we determined a global vector for each text. We also have the identical word similarity scores among all texts. We can directly use these global vectors to run the k-means or the EM algorithms to cluster the texts. We can also use the identical word similarity scores to run *grouping algorithm* (defined later) to do the clustering via a different approach.

3 Semantic Relation Similarity

To prepare the texts for clustering process using semantic relation similarity, the following steps are performed on each raw texts:

1. Preprocessing which consists in extracting file contents, and removing special characters and numbers.
2. Extract all the nouns from the text using part-of-speech tagger (i.e. UPennsylvania tagger). The tagger parses each sentence of the input text into several forms with specific tags. We get four kinds of nouns as the results of running the tagger: NN, NNS, NNP and NNPS. We then run a process to group all the nouns into meaningful nouns and non-meaningful nouns. The basic idea is to construct the largest compound words using the possible adjective and following nouns, then check whether or not the compound words have a meaning in WordNet. If not, we break the compound words into possible smaller ones, then check again until we find the ones with meanings in

Wordnet. When we get a noun (or a compound noun) existing in WordNet, we insert it into the meaningful word set, which we call set of regular nouns, otherwise we insert it into the non-meaningful word set, which we call set of proper nouns.

During the processing of each document, we save the over-all unique meaningful nouns in an over-all regular nouns set. Because of the big overhead related to accessing WordNet, we try to reduce the overall access times to a minimal level. Our approach is to use these over-all unique nouns to retrieve the relevant information from WordNet and save them in a global file. For each sense of each unique noun, we save its synonyms, two level hypernyms, and one level hyponyms. If any process frequently needs the WordNet information, it can use the global file to store the information in a hash and thus provides fast access to its members.

3. Word sense disambiguation.

   Similarly to Galley and McKeown [6], we use lexical chain approach to disambiguate the nouns in the regular nouns for each document [7,8]. A lexical chain is a sequence of related words in the text, spanning short (adjacent words or sentences) or long distances (entire text). WordNet is one lexical resource that may be used for the identification of lexical chains. Lexical chains can be constructed in a source text by grouping (chaining) sets of word-senses that are semantically related. We designate the following nine semantic relations between two senses:

   (a) Two noun instances are identical, and used in the same sense;
   (b) Two noun instances are used in the same sense (i.e., are synonyms);
   (c) The senses of two noun instances have a hypernym/hyponym relation between them;
   (d) The senses of two noun instances are siblings in the hypernym/hyponym tree;
   (e) The senses of two noun instances have a grandparent/grandchild relation in the hypernym/hyponym tree;
   (f) The senses of two noun instances have a uncle/nephew relation in the hypernym/hyponym tree;
   (g) The senses of two noun instances are cousins in the hypernym/hyponym tree (i.e., two senses share the same grandparent in the hypernym tree of WordNet);
   (h) The senses of two noun instances have a great-grandparent/great-grandchild relation in the hypernym/hyponym tree (i.e., one sense's grandparent is another sense's hyponym's great-grandparent in the hypernym tree of WordNet).
   (i) The senses of two noun instances do not have any semantic relation.

   To disambiguate all the nouns in the regular nouns of a text, we proceed with the following major steps:

   (a) Evaluate the semantic relation between any two possible senses according to the hypernym/hyponym tree in WordNet. For our experiments, we use the following scoring scheme for the relations defined above as shown in Table 1. The score between A_i (sense i of word A) and B_j (sense j of word B) is denoted as $score(A_i, B_j)$. These scores are established empirically and give more weight to closer words according to WordNet hierarchy.

Table 1. Scoring Scheme for Relations

Relation	$Score(A_i, B_j)$
Identical	log(16)
Synonyms	log(15)
Hypernyms/hyponyms	log(14)
Siblings	log(13)
Grandparent/grandchild	log(12)
Uncle/nephew	log(11)
Cousins	log(10)
Great-grandparent/great-grandchild	log(9)
No relation	0

(b) Build the lexical chains using all possible senses of all nouns. To build the lexical chains, we assume each noun possesses all the possible senses from WordNet. For each sense of each noun in a text, if it is related to all the senses of any existing chain, then we put this sense into this chain, else we create a new chain and push this sense into the new empty chain. After this, we will have several lexical chains with their own scores.

(c) Using the lexical chain, try to assign a specific sense to each nouns. We sort the chains by their scores in a non-increasing order. We select the chain with the highest score and assign the senses in that chain to the corresponding words. These words are disambiguated now. Next, we process the next chain with the next highest score. If it contains a different sense of any disambiguated words, we skip it to process the next chain until we reach the chains with a single entry. We mark the chains which we used to assign senses to words as selected. For the single entry chains, if the sense is the only sense of the word, we mark it as disambiguated. For each undisambiguated word, we check each of its senses against all the selected chains. If it has a relation with all the senses in a selected chain, we will then remember which sense-chain pair has the highest relation score, then we assign that sense to the corresponding word.

After these steps, the leftover nouns will be the undisambiguated words. We save the disambiguated words and the undisambiguated words with their frequencies for calculating the semantic relation scores between texts.

4. Compute the similarity score for each pair of texts.

Now, we should have three parts of nouns for each text: disambiguated nouns, undisambiguated nouns and the non-meaningful nouns (proper nouns). We will use all of them to calculate the semantic similarity scores between each pair of texts. For the purpose of calculating the semantic similarity scores among texts, we use only the first three relations (a), (b), and (c) and the last relation (i) and their corresponding scores defined in *Table 1*. For a given text pair, we proceed as in the following steps to calculate the similarity scores:

- Using the disambiguated nouns, the score $score_1$ of the similarity between two texts T_1 and T_2 is computed as follows:

$$score_1 = \frac{\sum_{i=1}^{n} \sum_{j=1}^{m} score(A_i, B_j) \times freq(A_i) \times freq(B_j)}{\sqrt{\sum_{i=1}^{n} freq^2(A_i)} \sqrt{\sum_{j=1}^{m} freq^2(B_j)}} \tag{2}$$

  where A_i is a word sense from T_1 and B_j is a word sense from T_2; $score(A_i, B_j)$ is a semantic relation score defined in *Table 1*; n and m are the numbers of disambiguated nouns in T_1 and T_2; $freq(x)$ is the frequency of a word sense x.
- For the undisambiguated nouns, if two nouns are identical in their word formats, then the probability that they take the same sense in both texts is $1/s$, where s is the number of their total possible senses. The similarity score $score_2$ between two texts T_1 and T_2 according to the undisambiguated nouns is computed as follows:

$$score_2 = \frac{\sum_{i=1}^{n} \frac{log(16) \times freq_1(A_i) \times freq_2(A_i)}{s_i}}{\sqrt{\sum_{i=1}^{n} freq_1^2(A_i)} \sqrt{\sum_{j=1}^{n} freq_2^2(A_j)}} \tag{3}$$

  where A_i is a word common to T_1 and T_2; n is the number of common words to T_1 and T_2; $freq_1(A_i)$ is the frequency of A_i in T_1; $freq_2(A_i)$ is the frequency of A_i in T_2; s_i is the number of senses of A_i.
- The proper nouns are playing an important role in relating texts to each other. So, we use a higher score (i.e., $log(30)$) for the identical proper nouns. The similarity score $score_3$ between two texts T_1 and T_2 among the proper nouns between is computed as follows:

$$score_3 = \frac{\sum_{i=1}^{n} log(30) \times freq_1(A_i) \times freq_2(A_i)}{\sqrt{\sum_{i=1}^{n} freq_1^2(A_i)} \sqrt{\sum_{j=1}^{n} freq_2^2(A_j)}} \tag{4}$$

  where A_i is a proper noun common to T_1 and T_2; n is the number of common proper nouns to T_1 and T_2; $freq_1(A_i)$ is the frequency of A_i in T_1; $freq_2(A_i)$ is the frequency of A_i in T_2.
- Adding all the scores together as the total similarity score of the text pair:

$$score = score_1 + score_2 + score_3 \tag{5}$$

Now we make it ready to use the *grouping algorithm* or *chaining algorithm* defined shortly to cluster the texts.

4 Clustering Algorithms

Generally, every text should have a higher semantic similarity score with the texts from its group than the texts from a different groups [9]. There are a few rare cases where this assumption could fail. One case is that the semantic similarity score does not reflect the relationships among the texts. Another case is that the groups are not well grouped by common used criteria or the topic is too broad in that group.By all means, the texts of any well formed clusters should have stronger relations among its members than the texts in other clusters. Based on this idea, we developed two text clustering algorithms: *grouping algorithm* and *chaining algorithm* . They share some common features but with different approaches.

One major issue in partitioning texts into different clusters is choosing the cutoff on the relation scores. Virtually, all texts are related with each other to some extent. The problem here is how similar (or close) they should be so that we can put them into one cluster and how dissimilar (or far away) they should be so that we can group them into different clusters. Unless the similarity scores among all the texts can be represented as binary values, we will always face this problem with any kind of texts. In order to address this problem, we introduce two reference values in our text clustering algorithms: *high-threshold* and *low-threshold*. The high-threshold means the high standard for bringing two texts into the same cluster. The low-threshold means the minimal standard for possibly bringing two texts into the same cluster. If the score between any two texts reaches or surpasses the high-threshold, then they will go to the same cluster. If the score reaches the low-threshold but is lower than the high-threshold, then we will carry out further checking to decide if we should bring two texts into the same cluster or not, else, the two texts will not go to the same cluster.

We get our high-threshold and low-threshold for our different algorithms by running some experiments using the grouped text data. The high-threshold we used for our two algorithms is 1.0 and the low-threshold we used is 0.6. For our experiment, we always take a number of grouped texts and mix them up to make a testing text set. So, each text must belong to one cluster with certain number of texts.

4.1 Grouping Algorithm

The basic idea is that each text could gather its most related texts to form an initial group, then we decide which groups have more strength over other groups, make the stronger groups as final clusters, and use them to bring any possible texts to their clusters. First, we use each text as a leading text (T_l) to form a cluster. To do this, we put all the texts which have a score greater than the high-threshold with T_l into one group and add each score to the group's total score. By doing this for all texts, we will have N possible different groups with different entries and group scores, where N is the number of the total texts in the set. Next, we select the final clusters from those N groups. We arrange all the groups by their scores in a non-increasing order. We choose the group with the highest score and check if any text in this group has been clustered to the existing final clusters or not. If not more than 2 texts are overlapping with the final clusters, then we take this group as a final cluster, and remove the overlapping texts from other final clusters. We process the group with the next highest score in the same way until the groups' entries are less than 4. For those groups, we would first try to insert their texts into the existing final clusters if they can fit in one of them. Otherwise, we will let them go to the leftover cluster which holds all the texts that do not belong to any final clusters. The following is the pseudocode for the grouping algorithm:

```
Grouping Algorithm
// Get the initial clusters
for each text t_i
  construct a text cluster including all the texts(t_j)
  which score(t_i, t_j) >= high-threshold;
  compute the total score of the text cluster;
  find out its neighbor with maximum relation score;
end for

// Build the final clusters
sort the clusters by their total score in non-increasing order;
for each cluster g_i in the sorted clusters
  if member(g_i) > 3 and overlap-mem(g_i) <= 2
    take g_i as a final cluster c_i;
    mark all the texts in c_i as clustered;
  else
    skip to process next cluster;
  end if
end for

// Process the leftover texts and insert them into one of the final clusters
for each text t_j
  if t_j has not been clustered
    find cluster c_i with the highest score(c_i, t_j);
    if the average-score(c_i, t_j) >= low-threshold
      put t_j into the cluster c_i;
    else if the max score neighbor t_m of t_j is in c_k
      put t_j into cluster c_k;
    else
      put t_j into the final leftover cluster;
    end if
  end if
end for

output the final clusters and the final leftover cluster;
```

where: member(g_i) is the number of members in group g_i; overlap-mem(g_i) is the number of members that are overlapped with any final clusters; score(c_i, t_j) is the sum of scores between t_j and each text in c_i; average-score(c_i, t_j) is score(c_i, t_j) divide by the number of texts in c_i.

4.2 Chaining Algorithm

This algorithm is based on the observation of the similarities among the texts in groups. Within a text group, not all texts are always strongly related with any other texts. Sometimes there are several subgroups existing in a single group, i.e., certain texts have stronger relations with their subgroup members and have a weaker relation with other subgroup members. Usually one or more texts have stronger relation crossing different subgroups to connect them together, otherwise all the texts in the group could not be grouped together. So, there is a chaining effect in each group connecting subgroups together to form one entire group.

We use this chaining idea in the *chaining algorithm*. First, for each text T_j, we find all the texts which have similarity scores that are greater or equal than the high-threshold with T_j and use them to form a closer-text-set. All the texts in that set are called closer-text of T_j.

Next, for each text which has not been assigned to a final chain, we use its initial closer-text-set members to form a new chain. For each of the texts in the chain, if any of its closer-texts are relatively related (i.e., the score >= low-threshold) to all the texts in the chain, then we add it into the current chain. One thing needs to be noticed here is that we do not want to simply bring all the closer-texts of each current chain's members into the chain. The reason is to eliminate the unwanted over-chaining effect that could bring many other texts which are only related to one text in the existing chain. So, we check each candidate text against all the texts in the chain to prevent the over-chaining effect. We repeat this until the chain's size are not increasing. If the chain has less than 4 members, we will not use this chain for a final cluster and try to re-assign the chain members to other chains.

After the above process, if any text has not been assigned to a chain we check it against all existing chains and find the chain which has highest similarity score between the chain and this text. If the average similarity score with each chain members is over low-threshold, we insert this text into that chain, else we put it into the final leftover chain. The following is the pseudocode for the chaining algorithm:

5 Application

We chose as our input data the documents sets used in the Document Understanding Conferences [10,11], organized by NIST. We collected 60 test document directories for our experiments. Each directory is about a specific topic and has about 10 texts and each text has about 1000 words. Our experiment is to mix up the 60 directories and try to reconstitute them using one of our clustering

```
Chaining Algorithm
// construct a closer-text-set for each text
for each text t_i 0 < i <= N
  for each text t_j 0 < j <= N
    if score(t_i, t_j) >= high-threshold
      put t_j into closer-text-set s_i;
    end if
  end for
end for

// Build the chains
c = 0;
for each text t_i of all the texts
  if it has not been chained in
    put text t_i into chain c and mark it as been chained;
    bring all the text in closer_text-set s_i into the new chain c;
    mark s_i as processed;
    while (the size of chain c is changing)
      for each text t_k in chain c
        for each text t_m in s_k of t_k
          if the score between t_m and any text in chain c >= low-threshold
            put t_m into chain c;
            mark t_m as been chained to chain c;
          end if
        end for
      end for
    end while
    if the size of chain c < 4
      discard chain c;
      remark the texts in chain c as unchained;
    end if
    c++;
  end if
end for

// Process the leftover texts and insert them into one of the existing chains
for each unchained text t_j
  find chain c_i with the highest score(c_i, t_j);
  if the average-score(c_i, t_j) >= low-threshold
    put t_j into the chain c_i;
  else
    put t_j into the final leftover chain;
  end if
end for

output the valid chains and the final leftover chain.
```

algorithm. Then, we measure how successful are these algorithms in reconstituting the original directories. We implemented the *k-means algorithm* and the *EM algorithm* to compare them with our algorithms.

In our test, we found out that the chaining algorithm did not work well for identical method. We tested grouping algorithm, chaining algorithm, and EM algorithm with semantic method, and k-means algorithm, EM algorithm, and grouping algorithm with identical methods. We run the k-means and the EM algorithms 4 times with each experiment texts set and take the average performance. As we described before, semantic method represents text relations with scores, so k-means algorithm which needs input data in vector format will not be applied to semantic method.

6 Evaluation

For our testing, we need to compare the system clusters with the testing clusters (original text directories) to evaluate the performance of each system. We first compare each system cluster with all of the testing clusters to find the best matched cluster pair with the maximum number of identical texts. We then use recall, precision, and F-value to evaluate each matching pair. Finally, we use the average F-value to evaluate the whole system performance. For a best matched pair TC_j (testing cluster) and SC_i (system cluster), the recall (R), precision (P), and F-value (F) are defined as follows:

$$R = \frac{m}{t} \tag{6}$$

$$P = \frac{m}{m+n} \tag{7}$$

$$F(TC_j, SC_i) = \frac{2PR}{P+R} \tag{8}$$

where m is the number of the overlapping texts between TC_j and SC_i; n is the number of the non-overlapping texts in SC_i; t is the total number of texts in TC_j.

For the whole system evaluation, we use the *Average_F* which is calculated using the F-values of each matched pair of clusters.

$$Average\_F = \frac{\sum_{i,j} max(F(SCi, TCj))}{max(m, n)} \tag{9}$$

Where $i <= min(m, n)$, $j <= m$, m is the number of testing clusters, and n is the number of system clusters.

7 Results

The performance of grouping algorithm and chaining algorithm are very close using the semantic relation approach and most of their *Average_F* are over 90%. For the identical word approach, the grouping algorithm performance is much better than the performances of the k-means algorithm and the EM algorithm. The poor performance of the k-means algorithm results from randomly selected k initial values. Those initial N-dimensional values usually do not represent the whole data very well. For the semantic relation approach, both grouping and chaining algorithms performed better than the EM algorithm.

Table 2 and 3 are the system *Average_F* values for the different algorithms. The identical word similarity method used grouping algorithm, k-means algorithm, and EM algorithm. The semantic similarity method used grouping algorithm, chaining algorithm and EM algorithm.

Table 2. Comparisons of F-value using Identical Word Similarity

Identical Word Similarity		
Grouping	EM	k-means
0.98	0.81	0.66

Table 3. Comparisons of F-value using Semantic Relation Similarity

Semantic Relation Similarity		
Grouping	Chaining	EM
0.92	0.91	0.76

8 Conclusion

Document clustering is an important tool for natural language applications. We presented two novel algorithms grouping algorithm and chaining algorithm for clustering sets of documents, and which can handle a large set of documents and clusters. The two algorithms use semantic similarity and identical word measure, and their performance is much better than the performance of the K-means algorithm and the performance of the EM algorithm, used as a baseline for our evaluation.

Evaluating the system quality has been always a difficult issue. We presented an evaluation methodology to assess how the system clusters are related to the manually generated clusters using precision and recall measures.

The grouping and the chaining algorithm may be used in several natural language processing applications requiring clustering tasks such as summarizing set of documents relating the same event.

Acknowledgments

This work was supported by the Natural Sciences and Engineering Research Council (NSERC) research grant.

References

1. Manning, C.D., Schutze, H.: Foundations of Statistical Natural Language Processing. MIT Press (2000)
2. Berkhin, P.: Survey of clustering data mining techniques. Technical report, Accrue Software, San Jose, CA (2002)
3. Duda, R., Hart, P.: Pattern Classification and Scene Analysis. John Wiley & Sons, New York, NY (1973)
4. Miller, G.A., Beckwith, R., Fellbaum, C., Gross, D., Miller, K.: Five papers on wordnet. CSL Report 43, Cognitive Science Laboratory, Princeton University (1993)
5. Salton, G.: Automatic Text Processing: The Transformation, Analysis, and Retrieval of Information by Computer. Addison-Wesley Series in Computer Sciences (1989)
6. Galley, M., McKeown, K.: Improving word sense disambiguation in lexical chaining. In: Proceedings of the 18th International Joint Conference on Artificial Intelligence, Acapulco, Mexico. (2003)
7. Barzilay, R., Elhadad, M.: Using lexical chains for text summarization. In: Proceedings of the 35th Annual Meeting of the Association for Computational Linguistics and the 8th European Chapter Meeting of the Association for Computational Linguistics, Workshop on Intelligent Scalable Text Summarization, Madrid (1997) 10-17
8. Silber, H.G., McCoy, K.F.: Efficiently computed lexical chains as an intermediate representation for automatic text summarization. Computational Linguistics **28** (2002) 487–496
9. Pantel, P., Lin, D.: Document clustering with committees. In: Proceedings of the ACM SIGIR'02, Finland (2002)
10. Over, P., ed.: Proceedings of the Document Understanding Conference, NIST (2003)
11. Over, P., ed.: Proceedings of the Document Understanding Conference, NIST (2004)

Using Multiple Discriminant Analysis Approach for Linear Text Segmentation

Zhu Jingbo[1], Ye Na [1], Chang Xinzhi [1], Chen Wenliang [1], and Benjamin K Tsou[2]

[1] Natural Language Processing Laboratory,
Institute of Computer Software and Theory, Northeastern University, Shenyang, P.R. China
{zhujingbo, chenwl}@mail.neu.edu.cn
{yena, changxz}@ics.neu.edu.cn
[2] Language Information Sciences Research Centre,
City University of Hong Kong, HK
rlbtsou@cityu.edu.hk

Abstract. Research on linear text segmentation has been an on-going focus in NLP for the last decade, and it has great potential for a wide range of applications such as document summarization, information retrieval and text understanding. However, for linear text segmentation, there are two critical problems involving automatic boundary detection and automatic determination of the number of segments in a document. In this paper, we propose a new domain-independent statistical model for linear text segmentation. In our model, Multiple Discriminant Analysis (MDA) criterion function is used to achieve global optimization in finding the best segmentation by means of the largest word similarity within a segment and the smallest word similarity between segments. To alleviate the high computational complexity problem introduced by the model, genetic algorithms (GAs) are used. Comparative experimental results show that our method based on MDA criterion functions has achieved higher P_k measure (Beeferman) than that of the baseline system using TextTiling algorithm.

1 Introduction

Typically a document is concerned with more than one subject, and most texts consist of long sequences of paragraphs with very little structural demarcation. The goal of linear text segmentation is to divide a document into topically-coherent sections, each corresponding to a relevant subject. Linear text segmentation has been applied in document summarization, information retrieval, and text understanding. For example, in recent years, passage-retrieval techniques based on linear text segmentation, are becoming increasingly popular in information retrieval as relevant text passages often provide better answers than complete document texts in response to user queries[1].

In recent years, many techniques have been applied to linear text segmentation. Some have used linguistic information[2,3,4,5,6,9] such as cue phrases, punctuation marks, prosodic features, reference, and new words occurrence. Others have used statistical methods[7,8,10,11,12,13,14,15] such as those based on word co-occurrence, lexical cohesion relations, semantic network, similarity between adjacent parts of texts, similarity between all parts of a text, dynamic programming algorithm, and HMM model.

R. Dale et al. (Eds.): IJCNLP 2005, LNAI 3651, pp. 292 – 301, 2005.

In linear text segmentation study, there are two critical problems involving automatic boundary detection and automatic determination of the number of segments in a document. Some efforts have focused on using similarity between adjacent parts of a text to solve topic boundary detection. In fact, the similarity threshold is very hard to set, and it is very difficult to identify exactly topic boundaries only according to similarity between adjacent parts of a text. Other works have focused on the similarity between all parts of a text. Reynar[7] and Choi[13] used *dotplots* technique to perform linear text segmentation which can be seen as a form of approximate and local optimization. Yaari[16] has used agglomerative clustering to perform hierarchical segmentation. Others[10,17,18,19] used dynamic programming to perform exact and global optimization in which some prior parameters are needed. These parameters can be obtained via uninformative prior probabilities[18], or estimated from training data[19].

In this paper, we propose a new statistical model for linear text segmentation, which uses Multiple Discriminant Analysis (MDA) method to define a global criterion function for document segmentation. Our method focuses on within-segment word similarity and between-segment word similarity. This process can achieve global optimization in addressing the two aforementioned problems of linear text segmentation. Our method is domain-independent and does not use any training data.

In section 2, we introduce Multiple Discriminant Analysis (MDA) criterion functions in detail. In section 3, our statistical model of linear text segmentation is proposed. A new MDA criterion function revised by adding penalty factor is further discussed in section 4. Comparative experimental results are given in Section 5. At last, we address conclusions and future work in section 6.

2 MDA Criterion Function

In statistical pattern classification, MDA approach is commonly used to find effective linear transformations[20,21]. The MDA approach seeks a projection that best separates the data in a least-squares sense. As shown in Figure 1, using MDA method we could get the greatest separation over data space when average within-class distance is the smallest, and average between-class distance is the largest.

Similarly, if we consider a document as data space, and a segment as a class, the basic idea of our approach for linear text segmentation is to find best segmentation of a document(greatest separation over data space) by focusing on within-segment word similarity and between-segment word similarity. It is clear that the smaller the average within-class distance or the average between-class distance, the larger the within-segment word similarity or the between-segment word similarity, and vice versa. In other words, we want to find the best segmentation of a document in which within-segment word similarity is the largest, and between-segment word similarity is the smallest. To achieve this goal, we introduce a criterion function to evaluate the segmentation of a document and assign a score to it. In this paper, we adopt the MDA approach to define a global criterion function of document segmentation, and called as MDA criterion function, which is described below.

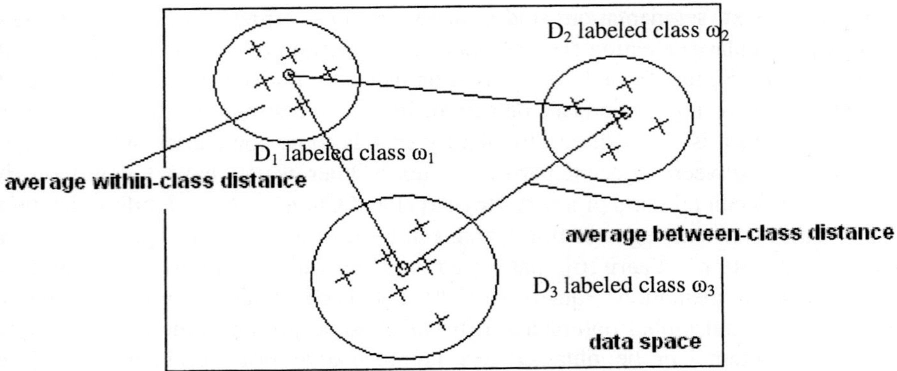

Fig. 1. When average within-class distance is the smallest, and average between-class distance is the largest, the greatest separation over data space is shown

Let $W=w_1w_2\ldots w_t$ be a text consisting of *t* words, and let $S=s_1s_2\ldots s_c$ be a segmentation of W consisting of *c* segments. We define W as data space, S as segmentation distribution over data space W. Because the lengths of paragraphs or sentences can be highly irregular, unbalanced comparisons can result in text segmentation process. Thus we adopt the *block* method that is used in the TextTiling algorithm[2,3], but we replace lexical word with block. In our model, we group *blocksize* words into a block which can be represented by a d-dimensional vector. In practice, we find that the value of *blocksize*=100 works well for many Chinese documents. Then $W=w_1w_2\ldots w_t$ can be redefined as $B=b_1b_2\ldots b_k$. As illustrated in Figure 1, a cross point can be defined as a d-dimensional block vector.

In this paper, we introduce MDA criterion function J_d in the following form[20]

$$J_d(s)=\frac{tr(S_B)}{tr(S_W)} \tag{1}$$

Where *tr(A)* is the trace of matrix A. S_W and S_B are within-segment scatter matrix and between-segment scatter matrix, respectively. S_W is defined by

$$S_W=\sum_{i=1}^{c}P_i\frac{1}{n_i}\sum_{b\in s_i}(b-m_i)(b-m_i)^t \tag{2}$$

Where b stands for blocks belonging to segment s_i, P_i is the a priori probability of segment s_i, and is defined to be the ratio of blocks in segment s_i divided by the total number of blocks of the document, n_i is the number of blocks in the segment s_i, m_i is the d-dimensional block mean of the segment s_i given by

$$m_i=\frac{1}{n_i}\sum_{b\in s_i}b. \tag{3}$$

Suppose that a total mean vector m is defined by

$$m = \frac{1}{n}\sum_{B} b = \frac{1}{n}\sum_{i=1}^{c} n_i m_i \tag{4}$$

In equation (1), between-segment scatter matrix S_B is defined by

$$S_B = \sum_{i=1}^{c} P_i (m_i - m)(m_i - m)^t \tag{5}$$

3 Statistical Model for Linear Text Segmentation

Using the same definitions of text W, segmentation S and blocks B in section 2, we first discuss the statistical model for linear text segmentation. The key of statistical model for text segmentation is to find the segmentation with maximum-probability. This can be turned into another task of finding segmentation with highest J_d score equally. The most likely segmentation is given by

$$\hat{S} = \arg\max_{S} \mathrm{P}(S \mid W) \overset{def}{=} \arg\max_{S} J_d(W, S) \tag{6}$$

As mentioned above, because paragraph or sentence length can be highly irregular, it leads to unbalanced comparisons in text segmentation process. So $W = w_1 w_2 \ldots w_n$ could be redefined as $B = b_1 b_2 \ldots b_k$, and the most likely segmentation is given by

$$\hat{S} = \arg\max_{S} \mathrm{P}(S \mid B) \overset{def}{=} \arg\max_{S} J_d(B, S) \tag{7}$$

The computational complexity for achieving the above solution is $O(2^k)$, where k is the number of blocks in a document. To alleviate the high computational complexity problem, we adopt the genetic algorithms (GAs)[22]. GAs provides a learning method motivated by an analogy to biological evolution. Rather than searching from general-to-specific hypotheses, or from simple-to-complex, GAs generate successor hypotheses by repeatedly mutating and recombining parts of the best currently known hypotheses. GAs have most commonly been applied to optimization problems outside machine learning, and are especially suited to tasks in which hypotheses are complex.

By adopting this methodology, we derive the following text segmentation algorithm, as illustrated in Figure 2. In this paper, we focus our study on paragraph-level linear text segmentation, in which the potential boundary mark between segments can be placed only between adjacent paragraphs.

Given a text W and blocks B, K_{max} is the total number of paragraphs in the text.
Initialization: $S_{best} = \{\}$, $J_d(B,S_{best})=0.0$
Segmentation:
For k = 2 **to** K_{max}
Begin
1) Use genetic algorithms and equation (7) to find the best segmentation S of k segments.
2) **If** $J_d(B,S_{best}) < J_d(B,S)$ **Then**
Begin
$S_{best} = S$ and $J_d(B,S_{best}) = J_d(B,S)$.
Endif
Endfor
Output the best segmentation S_{best}.

Fig. 2. MDA-based text segmentation algorithm

4 Penalty Factor

In the text segmentation process, adjacent boundary adjustment should be considered in cases when there are some very close adjacent but incorrect segment boundaries. In experiments we find that in these cases some single-sentence paragraphs are wrongly recognized as isolated segments. To solve the problem, we propose a penalty factor (PF) to prevent assignment of very short segment boundaries (such as a single-sentence segment) by adjusting very close adjacent boundaries, and therefore improve the performance of linear text segmentation system.

Suppose that we get a segmentation $S=s_1s_2...s_c$ of the input document, let L be the length of the document, L_i be the length of the segment s_i. We know $L=L_1+L_2+...+L_c$. We define penalty factor as

$$PF = \prod_{i=1}^{c} \frac{L_i}{L} \tag{8}$$

As can be seen, short-length segments would result in smaller penalty factor. We use penalty factor to revise the J_d scores of segmentations. To incorporate the penalty factor PF, our MDA criterion function J_d can be rewritten as

$$J_{d-PF}(x) = PF \times J_d(x) = \prod_{i=1}^{c} \frac{L_i}{L} \times \frac{tr(S_B)}{tr(S_W)} \tag{9}$$

In the following experiments, we will evaluate effectiveness of using the two MDA criterion functions J_d and $J_{d\text{-}PF}$ for linear text segmentation.

5 Experimental Results

5.1 Evaluation Methods

Precision and *recall* statistics are conventional means of evaluating the performance of classification algorithms. For the segmentation task, *recall* measures the fraction of actual boundaries that an automatic segmenter correctly identifies, and *precision* measures the fraction of boundaries identified by an automatic segmenter that are actual boundaries. The shortcoming is that every inaccurately estimated segment boundary is penalized equally whether it is near or far from a true segment boundary.

To overcome the shortcoming of *precision* and *recall*, we use a measure called P_k, proposed by Beeferman *et al.*[8]. P_k method measures the proportion of sentences which are wrongly predicted to belong in the same segment or sentences which are wrongly predicted to belong in different segments. More formally, given two segmentations *ref*(true segmentation) and *hyp*(hypothetical segmentation) for a document of n sentences, P_k is formally defined by

$$P_k(ref, hyp) = \sum_{1 \le i \le j \le n} D_\mu(i,j)(\delta_{ref}(i,j) \overline{\oplus} \delta_{hyp}(i,j)) \quad (10)$$

Where $\delta_{ref}(i,j)$ is an indicator function whose value is 1 if sentences i and j belong in the same segment in the true segmentation, and 0 otherwise. Similarly, $\delta_{hyp}(i,j)$ is an indicator function which evaluates to 1 if sentences i and j belong in the same segment in the hypothetical segmentation, and 0 otherwise. The operator between $\delta_{ref}(i,j)$ and $\delta_{hyp}(i,j)$ in the above formula is the *XNOR* function on its two operands. The function D_μ is a distance probability distribution over the set of possible distances between sentences chosen randomly from the document, and will in general depend on certain parameters μ such as the average spacing between sentences. In equation (10), $D_\mu$was defined as an exponential distribution with mean $1/\mu$, a parameter that we fix at the approximate mean document length for the domain[8].

$$D_\mu(i,j) = \gamma_\mu e^{-\mu|i-j|} \quad (11)$$

Where $\Upsilon_\mu$is a normalization chosen so that D_μ is a probability distribution over the range of distance it can accept. From the above formulation, we could find one weakness of the metric: there is no principled way of specifying the distance distribution D_μ. In the following experiments, we use P_k as performance measure, where the mean segment length in the test data was $1/\mu=11$ sentences.

5.2 Quantitative Results

We mainly focus our work on paragraph-level linear text segmentation techniques. The Hearst's TextTiling algorithm[2,3] is a simple and domain-independent technique for linear text segmentation, which segments at the paragraph level. Topic boundaries are determined by changes in the sequence of similarity scores. This algorithm uses a simple cutoff function to determine automatically the number of boundaries.

In our experiments, we use the TextTiling algorithm to provide the baseline system, and use the P_k measure to evaluate and compare the performance of the TextTiling and our method. Our data set - NEU_TS, is collected manually, and it consists of 100 Chinese documents, all from *2004-2005 Chinese People's Daily newspaper*. The number of segments per document varies from five to eight. The average number of paragraphs per document is 25.8 paragraphs. To build the ground truth for NEU_TS data set, five trained graduate students in our laboratory who are working on the analysis of Chinese document are asked to provide judgment on the segmentation of every Chinese document. We first use the toolkit CipSegSDK[23] for document preprocessing, including word segmentation, but with the removal of stopwords from all documents.

1) Experiment 1

In the first experiment, we assume the number of segments of an input document is known in advance. We use the NEU_TS data set and the P_k measure to evaluate and compare the performance of TextTiling and our method. The purpose of this experiment is to compare the performance of boundary detection techniques of TextTiling algorithm and our model using MDA criterion functions.

Table 1. P_k value with known number of document segments

Measure	TextTiling algorithm	MDA method using J_d	MDA method using $J_{d\text{-}PF}$
P_k value	0.825	0.869	0.905

In the TextTiling algorithm, topic boundaries are determined by changes in the sequence of similarity scores. The boundaries are determined by locating the lowermost portions of valleys in the resulting plot. Therefore, it is not a global evaluation method. However, in our model, MDA criterion function provides a global evaluation method to text segmentation; it selects the best segmentation with the largest within-segment word similarity and the smallest between-segment word similarity. Results shown in Table 1 indicated that our boundary detection techniques based on two MDA criterion functions perform better than the TextTiling algorithm, and MDA criterion function $J_{d\text{-}PF}$ works the best.

Table 2. P_k value with unknown number of document segments

Measure	TextTiling algorithm	MDA method using J_d	MDA method using $J_{d\text{-}PF}$
P_k value	0.808	0.831	0.87

2) Experiment 2

In this experiment, we assume the number of segments of a document is unknown in advance. In other words, Texttiling algorithm and our model should determine the number of segments of a document automatically. Similar to Experiment 1, the same data set is used and the P_k measure is calculated for both TextTiling and our method using MDA criterion functions J_d and $J_{d\text{-}PF}$. The comparative results are shown in Table 2.

As mentioned above, how to determine the number of segments to be assigned to a document is a difficult problem. Texttiling algorithm uses a simple cutoff function method to determine the number of segments and it is sensitive to the patterns of similarity scores[2,3]. The cutoff function is defined as a function of the average and standard deviations of the depth scores for the text under analysis. A boundary is drawn only if the depth score exceeds the cutoff value. We think that the simple cutoff function method is hard to achieve global optimization when solving these two key problems of linear text segmentation process. In our model, two MDA criterion functions J_d and $J_{d\text{-}PF}$ are used to determine the number of segments and boundary detection by maximizing J_d score of segmentations. Once the maximum-score segmentation is found, the number of segments of the document is produced automatically. Experimental results show that our MDA criterion functions are superior to the TextTiling's cutoff function in terms of automatic determination of the number of segments. It is also shown that the MDA criterion function $J_{d\text{-}PF}$ revised with Penalty Factor works better than J_d. In implementation, we have adopted genetic algorithms (GAs) to alleviate the computational complexity of MDA, and have obtained good results.

6 Conclusions and Future Work

In this paper, we studied and proposed a new domain-independent statistical model for linear text segmentation in which multiple discriminant analysis(MDA) approach is used as global criterion function for document segmentation. We attempted to achieve global optimization in solving the two fundamental problems of text segmentation involving automatic boundary detection and automatic determination of number of segments of a document, by focusing on within-segment word similarity and between-segment word similarity. We also applied genetic algorithms(GAs) to reduce the high computational complexity of MDA based method. Experimental results show that our method based on MDA criterion functions outperforms the TextTiling algorithm.

The solution to the high computational complexity problem will continue to be studied by using other effective optimization algorithm or near optimal solutions. In the next stage we plan to combine MDA criterion functions with other algorithms such as clustering to improve the performance of our text segmentation system, and apply the text segmentation technique to other text processing task, such as information retrieval and document summarization.

Acknowledgements

We thank Keh-Yih Su and Matthew Ma for discussions related to this work. This research was supported in part by the National Natural Science Foundation of China & Microsoft Asia Research Centre(No. 60203019), the Key Project of Chinese Ministry of Education(No. 104065), and the National Natural Science Foundation of China(No. 60473140).

References

1. Gerard Salton, Amit Singhal, Chris Buckley, and Mandar Mitra.: Automatic text decomposition using text segments and text themes. In proceedings of the seventh ACM conference on Hypertext, Bethesda, Maryland, United States (1996) 53-65
2. Hearst, M.A.: Multi-paragraph segmentation of expository text. In proceedings of the 32th Annual Meeting of the Association for Computational Linguistics, Las Cruces, New Mexico (1994) 9-16
3. Hearst, M.A.: TextTiling: segmenting text into multi-paragraph subtopic passages. Computational Linguistics, Vol.23, No.1 (1997) 33-64
4. Youmans, G.: A new tool for discourse analysis: The vocabulary management profile. Language, Vol.67, No.4 (1991) 763-789
5. Morris, J. and Hirst, G.: Lexical cohesion computed by thesauri relations as an indicator of the structure of text. Computational Linguistics, Vol.17, No.1 (1991) 21-42
6. Kozima, H.: Text segmentation based on similarity between words. In proceedings of the 31th Annual Meeting of the Association for Computational Linguistics, Student Session (1993) 286-288
7. Reynar, J.C.: An automatic method of finding topic boundaries. In proceedings of the 32 nd Annual Meeting of the Association for Computational Linguistics, Student Session, Las Cruces, New Mexico (1994) 331-333
8. Beeferman, D., Berger, A., and Lafferty, J.: Text segmentation using exponential models. In proceedings of the Second Conference on Empirical Methods in Natural Language Processing, pages, Providence, Rhode Island (1997) 35-46
9. Passoneau, R. and Litman, D.J.: Intention-based segmentation: Human reliability and correlation with linguistic cues. In proceedings of the 31st Meeting of the Association for Computational Linguistics (1993) 148-155
10. Jay M. Ponte and Bruce W. Croft.: Text segmentation by topic. In proceeding of the first European conference on research and advanced technology for digital libraries. U.Mass. Computer Science Technical Report TR97-18 (1997)
11. Reynar, J.C.: Statistical models for topic segmentation. In proceedings of the 37th Annual Meeting of the Association for Computational Linguistics (1999) 357-364
12. Hirschberg, J. and Grosz, B.: Intentional features of local and global discourse. In proceedings of the Workshop on Spoken Language Systems (1992) 441-446
13. Freddy Y. Y. Choi.: Advances in domain independent linear text segmentation. In Proc. of NAACL-2000 (2000)
14. Choi, F.Y.Y., Wiemer-Hastings, P. & Moore, J.: Latent semantic analysis for text segmentation. In proceedings of the 6th Conference on Empirical Methods in Natural Language Processing (2001) 109-117.
15. Blei, D.M. and Moreno, P.J.: Topic segmentation with an aspect hidden Markov model. Tech. Rep. CRL 2001-07, COMPAQ Cambridge Research Lab (2001)
16. Yaari, Y.: Segmentation of expository texts by hierarchical agglomerative clustering. In proceedings of the conference on recent advances in natural language processing (1997) 59-65
17. Heinonen, O.: Optimal multi-paragraph text segmentation by dynamic programming. In proceedings of 17th international conference on computational linguistics (1998) 1484-1486.
18. Utiyama, M., and Isahara, H.: A statistical model for domain-independent text segmentation. In proceedings of the 9th conference of the European chapter of the association for computational linguistics (2001) 491-498

19. A Kehagias, P Fragkou, V Petridis.: Linear Text Segmentation using a Dynamic Programming Algorithm. In proceedings of 10th Conference of European chapter of the association for computational linguistics (2003)
20. R. Duda, P. Hart, and D. Stork.: Pattern Classification. Second Edition, John Wiley & Sons (2001)
21. Julius T.Tol and Rafael C. Gonzaiez.: Pattern recognition principles. Addison-Wesley Publishing Company (1974)
22. Tom M.Mitchell.: Machine Learning. McGraw-Hill (1997)
23. Yao Tianshun, Zhu Jingbo, Zhang li, and Yang Ying.: Natural language processing-research on making computers understand human languages. Tsinghua university press (2002)

Classifying Chinese Texts in Two Steps

Xinghua Fan[1, 2, 3], Maosong Sun[1], Key-sun Choi[3], and Qin Zhang[2]

[1] State Key Laboratory of Intelligent Technology and Systems, Tsinghua University, Beijing 100084, China
fanxh@tsinghua.org.cn, sms@tsinghua.edu.cn
[2] State Intellectual Property Office of P.R. China, Beijing, 100088, China
zhangqin@sipo.gov.cn
[3] Computer Science Division, Korterm, KAIST, 373-1 Guseong-dong Yuseong-gu, Daejeon 305-701, Korea
kschoi@cs.kaist.ac.kr

Abstract. This paper proposes a two-step method for Chinese text categorization (TC). In the first step, a Naïve Bayesian classifier is used to fix the fuzzy area between two categories, and, in the second step, the classifier with more subtle and powerful features is used to deal with documents in the fuzzy area, which are thought of being unreliable in the first step. The preliminary experiment validated the soundness of this method. Then, the method is extended from two-class TC to multi-class TC. In this two-step framework, we try to further improve the classifier by taking the dependences among features into consideration in the second step, resulting in a Causality Naïve Bayesian Classifier.

1 Introduction

Text categorization (TC) is a task of assigning one or multiple predefined category labels to natural language texts. To deal with this sophisticated task, a variety of statistical classification methods and machine learning techniques have been exploited intensively[1], including the Naïve Bayesian (NB) classifier [2], the Vector Space Model (VSM)-based classifier [3], the example-based classifier [4], and the Support Vector Machine [5].

Text filtering is a basic type of text categorization (two-class TC). It can find many real-life applications [6], a typical one is the ill information filtering, such as erotic information and garbage information filtering on the web, in e-mails and in short messages of mobile phone. It is obvious that this sort of information should be carefully controlled. On the other hand, the filtering performance using the existing methodologies is still not satisfactory in general. The reason lies in that there exist a number of documents with high degree of ambiguity, from the TC point of view, in a document collection, that is, there is a fuzzy area across the border of two classes (for the sake of expression, we call the class consisting of the ill information-related texts, or, the negative samples, the category of TARGET, and, the class consisting of the ill information-not-related texts, or, the positive samples, the category of Non-TARGET). Some documents in one category may have great similarities with some other documents in the other category, for example, a lot of words concerning love

R. Dale et al. (Eds.): IJCNLP 2005, LNAI 3651, pp. 302 – 313, 2005.

story and sex are likely appear in both negative samples and positive samples if the filtering target is erotic information. We observe that most of the classification errors come from the documents falling into the fuzzy area between two categories.

The idea of this paper is inspired by the fuzzy area between categories. A two-step TC method is thus proposed: in the first step, a classifier is used to fix the fuzzy area between categories; in the second step, a classifier (probably the same as that in the first step) with more subtle and powerful features is used to deal with documents in the fuzzy area which are thought of being unreliable in the first step. Experimental results validate the soundness of this method. Then we extend it from two-class TC to multi-class TC. Furthermore, in this two-step framework, we try to improve the classifier by taking the dependences among features into consideration in the second step, resulting in a Causality Naïve Bayesian Classifier.

This paper is organized as follows: Section 2 describes the two-step method in the context of two-class Chinese TC; Section 3 extends it to multi-class TC; Section 4 introduces the Causality Naïve Bayesian Classifier; and Section 5 is conclusions.

2 Basic Idea: A Two-Step Approach to Text Categorization

2.1 Fix the Fuzzy Area Between Categories by the Naïve Bayesian Classifier

We use the Naïve Bayesian Classifier to fix the fuzzy area in the first step. For a document represented by a binary-valued vector $d = (W_1, W_2, \ldots, W_{|D|})$, the two-class Naïve Bayesian Classifier is given as follows:

$$\begin{aligned} f(d) &= \log \frac{\Pr\{c_1|d\}}{\Pr\{c_2|d\}} \\ &= \log \frac{\Pr\{c_1\}}{\Pr\{c_2\}} + \sum_{k=1}^{|D|} \log \frac{1\text{-}p_{k1}}{1\text{-}p_{k2}} + \sum_{k=1}^{|D|} W_k \log \frac{p_{k1}}{1\text{-}p_{k1}} - \sum_{k=1}^{|D|} W_k \log \frac{p_{k2}}{1\text{-}p_{k2}} \end{aligned} \quad (1)$$

where $\Pr\{\bullet\}$ is the probability that event $\{\bullet\}$ occurs, c_i is category i, and $p_{ki}=\Pr\{W_k=1|c_i\}$ (i=1,2). If $f(d) \geq 0$, the document d will be assigned the category label c_1, otherwise, c_2.

Let:

$$Con = \log \frac{\Pr\{c_1\}}{\Pr\{c_2\}} + \sum_{k=1}^{|D|} \log \frac{1\text{-}p_{k1}}{1\text{-}p_{k2}} \quad (2)$$

$$X = \sum_{k=1}^{|D|} W_k \log \frac{p_{k1}}{1\text{-}p_{k1}} \quad (3)$$

$$Y = \sum_{k=1}^{|D|} W_k \log \frac{p_{k2}}{1\text{-}p_{k2}} \quad (4)$$

where *Con* is a constant relevant only to the training set, X and Y are the measures that the document *d* belongs to categories c_1 and c_2 respectively.

We rewrite (1) as:

$$f(d) = X - Y + Con \tag{5}$$

Apparently, *f(d)*=0 is the separate line in a two-dimensional space with X and Y being X-coordinate and Y-coordinate. In this space, a given document *d* can be viewed as a point (x, y), in which the values of x and y are calculated according to (3) and (4).

As shown in Fig.1, the distance from the point (x, y) to the separate line will be:

$$Dist = \frac{1}{\sqrt{2}}(x - y + Con) \tag{6}$$

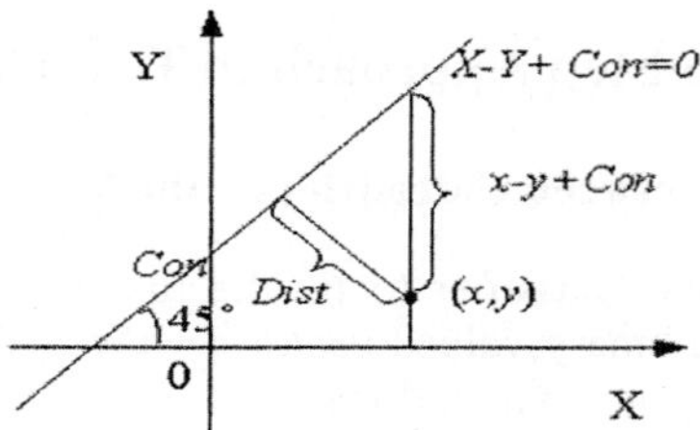

Fig. 1. Distance from point (x, y) to the separate line

Fig. 2 illustrates the distribution of a training set (refer to Section 2.2) regarding *Dist* in the two-dimensional space, with the curve on the left for the negative samples, and the curve on the right for the positive samples. As can be seen in the figure, most of the misclassified documents, which unexpectedly across the separate line, are near the line. The error rate of the classifier is heavily influenced by this area, though the documents falling into this area only constitute a small portion of the training set.

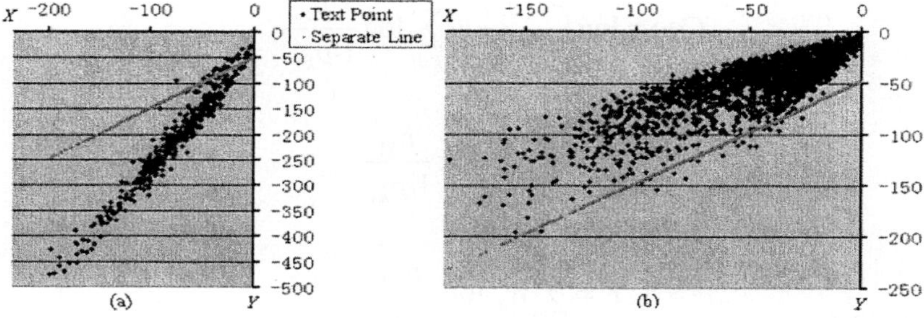

Fig. 2. Distribution of the training set in the two-dimensional space

Thus, the space can be partitioned into reliable area and unreliable area:

$$\begin{cases} Dist_2 \le Dist \le Dist_1, & \text{Decision for } d \text{ is unreliable} \\ Dist > Dist_1, & \text{Assigning the label } c_1 \text{ to } d \text{ is reliable} \\ Dist < Dist_2, & \text{Assigning the label } c_2 \text{ to } d \text{ is reliable} \end{cases} \tag{7}$$

where $Dist_1$ and $Dist_2$ are constants determined by experiments, $Dist_1$ is positive real number and $Dist_2$ is negative real number.

In the second step, more subtle and powerful features will be designed in particular to tackle the unreliable area identified in the first step.

2.2 Experiments on the Two-Class TC

The dataset used here is composed of 12,600 documents with 1,800 negative samples of TARGET and 10,800 positive samples of Non-TARGET. It is split into 4 parts randomly, with three parts as training set and one part as test set. All experiments in this section are performed in 4-fold cross validation.

CSeg&Tag3.0, a Chinese word segmentation and POS tagging system developed by Tsinghua University, is used to perform the morphological analysis for Chinese texts. In the first step, Chinese words with parts-of-speech verb, noun, adjective and adverb are considered as features. The original feature set is further reduced to a much smaller one according to formula (8) or (9). A Naïve Bayesian Classifier is then applied to the test set. In the second step, only the documents that are identified unreliable in terms of (7) in the first step are concerned. This time, bigrams of Chinese words with parts-of-speech verb and noun are used as features, and the Naïve Bayesian Classifier is re-trained and applied again.

$$MI_1(t_k, c) = \sum_{i=1}^{n} \Pr\{t_k, c_i\} \log \frac{\Pr\{t_k, c_i\}}{\Pr\{t_k\}\Pr\{c_i\}} \tag{8}$$

$$MI_2(t_k, c) = \sum_{i=1}^{n} \log \frac{\Pr\{t_k, c_i\}}{\Pr\{t_k\}\Pr\{c_i\}} \tag{9}$$

where t_k stands for the kth feature, which may be a Chinese word or a word bigram, and c_i is the ith predefined category.

We try five methods as follows.

Method-1: Use Chinese words as features, reduce features with (9), and classify documents directly without exploring the two-step strategy.

Method-2: same as Method-1 except feature reduction with (8).

Method-3: same as Method-1 except Chinese word bigrams as features.

Method-4: Use the mixture of Chinese words and Chinese word bigrams as features, reduce features with (8), and classify documents directly.

Method-5: (i.e., the proposed method): Use Chinese words as features in the first step and then use word bigrams as features in the second step, reduce features with (8), and classify the documents in two steps.

Note that the proportion of negative samples and positive samples is 1:6. Thus if all the documents in the test set is arbitrarily set to positive, the precision will reach 85.7%. For this reason, only the experimental results for negative samples are considered in evaluation, as given in Table 1. For each method, the number of features is set by the highest point in the curve of the classifier performance with respect to the number of features (For the limitation of space, we omit all the curves here). The numbers of features set in five methods are 4000, 500, 15000, 800 and 500+3000 (the first step + the second step) respectively.

Table 1. Performance comparisons of the five methods in two-class TC

Method used / Performance	Method-1	Method-2	Method-3	Method-4	Method-5
Precision	78.04%	93.35%	93.15%	95.86%	97.19%
Recall	88.72%	88.78%	94.17%	91.11%	93.94%
F_1	82.67%	91.00%	93.65%	93.42%	95.54%

Comparing Method-1 and Method-2, we can see that feature reduction formula (8) is superior to (9). Moreover, the number of features determined in the former is less than that in the latter (500 vs. 4000). Comparing Method-2, Method-3 and Method-4, we can see that Chinese word bigrams as features have better discriminating capability meanwhile with more serious data sparseness: the performances of Method-3 and Method-4 are higher than that of Method-2, but the number of features used in Method-3 is more than those used in Method-2 and Method-4 (15000 vs. 500 and 800). Table 1 shows that the proposed method (Methond-5) has the best performance (95.54% F1) and good efficiency. It integrates the merit of words and word bigrams. Using words as features in the first step aims at its better statistical coverage, -- the 500 selected features in the first step can treat a majority of documents, constituting 63.13% of the test set. On the other hand, using word bigrams as features in the second step aims at its better discriminating capability, although the number of features becomes comparatively large (3000). Comparing Method-5 with Method-2, Method-3 and Method-4, we find that the two-step approach is superior to either using only one kind of features (word or word bigram) in the classifier, or using the mixture of two kinds of features in one step.

3 Extending the Two-Step Approach to the Multi-class TC

We extend the two-step method presented in Section 2 to handle the multi-class TC now. The idea is to transfer the multi-class TC to the two-class TC. Similar to two-class TC, the emphasis is still on the misclassified documents given by a classifier, though we use a modified multi-class Naïve Bayesian Classifier here.

3.1 Fix the Fuzzy Area Between Categories by the Multi-class Bayesian Classifier

For a document represented by a binary-valued vector $d = (W_1, W_2, \ldots, W_{|D|})$, the multi-class Naïve Bayesian Classifier can be re-written as:

$$c^* = \arg\max_{c_i \in C}(\log \Pr\{c_i\} + \sum_{k=1}^{|D|} \log\ (1\text{-}p_{ki}) + \sum_{k=1}^{|D|} W_k \log\ \frac{p_{ki}}{1\text{-}p_{ki}}) \tag{10}$$

where $\Pr\{\bullet\}$ is the probability that event $\{\bullet\}$ occurs, $p_{ki}=\Pr\{W_k=1|c_i\}$, $(i=1,2, \ldots, |C|)$, C is the number of predefined categories. Let:

$$MV_i = \log \Pr\{c_i\} + \sum_{k=1}^{|D|} \log\ (1\text{-}p_{ki}) + \sum_{k=1}^{|D|} W_k \log\ \frac{p_{ki}}{1\text{-}p_{ki}} \tag{11}$$

$$MV_{\max\_F} = \underset{c_i \in C}{\text{maximum}}(MV_i) \tag{12}$$

$$MV_{\max\_S} = \underset{c_i \in C}{\text{second\_maximum}}(MV_i) \tag{13}$$

where MV_i stands for the likelihood of assigning a label $c_i \in C$ to the document d, MV_{max_F} and MV_{max_S} are the maximum and the second maximum over all MV_i $(i \in |C|)$ respectively. We approximately rewrite (10) as:

$$f(d) = MV_{\max\_F} - MV_{\max\_S} \tag{14}$$

We try to transfer the multi-class TC described by (10) into a two-class TC described by (14). Formula (14) means that the binary-valued multi-class Naïve Bayesian Classifier can be approximately regarded as searching a separate line in a two-dimensional space with MV_{max_F} being the X-coordinate and MV_{max_S} being the Y-coordinate. The distance from a given document, represented as a point (x, y) with the values of x and y calculated according to (12) and (13) respectively, to the separate line in this two-dimensional space will be:

$$Dist = \frac{1}{\sqrt{2}}(x - y) \tag{15}$$

The value of *Dist* directly reflects the degree of confidence of assigning the label c^* to the document d.

The distribution of a training set (refer to Section 3.2) regarding *Dist* in this two-dimensional space, and, consequently, the fuzzy area for the Naïve Bayesian Classifier, are observed and identified, similar to its counterpart in Section 2.2.

3.2 Experiments on the Multi-class TC

We construct a dataset, including 5 categories and the total of 17756 Chinese documents. The document numbers of five categories are 4192, 6968, 2080, 3175 and

1800 respectively, among which the last three categories have the high degree of ambiguity each other. The dataset is split into four parts randomly, one as the test set and the other three as the training set. We again run the five methods described in Section 2.2 on this dataset. The strategy of determining the number of features also follows that used in Section 2.2. The experimentally determined numbers of features regarding the five methods are 8000, 400, 5000, 800 and 400 + 9000 (the first step + the second step) respectively.

The average precision, average recall and average F_1 over the five categories are used to evaluate the experimental results, as shown in Table 2.

Table 2. Performance comparisons of the five methods in multi-class TC

Performance \ Method	Method-1	Method-2	Method-3	Method-4	Method-5
Average Precision	92.14%	97.03%	98.36%	97.99%	98.58%
Average Recall	91.13%	97.38%	98.17%	98.03%	98.55%
Average F_1	91.48%	97.20%	98.26%	98.01%	98.56%

We can see from Table 2 that the very similar conclusions as that in the two-class TC in Section 2.2 can be obtained here:

1) Formula (8) is superior to (9) in feature reduction. This comes from the performance comparison between Method-2 and Method-1: the former has higher performance and higher efficiency that the latter (the average F_1, 97.20% vs. 91.48%, and the number of features used, 400 vs. 8000).

2) Word bigrams as features have better discriminating capability than words as features, along with more serious data sparseness. The performances of Method-3 and Method-4, which use Chinese word bigrams and the mixture of words and word bigrams as features respectively, are higher than that of Method-2, which only uses Chinese words as features. But the number of features used in Method-3 is much more than those used in Method-2 and Method-4 (5000 vs. 400 and 800).

3) The proposed method (Methond-5) has the best performances and acceptable efficiency. In term of the average F_1, the performance is improved from the baseline 91.48% (Method-1) to 98.56% (Method-5). In the first step in Method-5, the number of feature set is small (only 400), but a majority of documents can be treated by it. The number of features exploited in Method-5 is the highest among the five methods (9000), but it is still acceptable.

4 Using Dependences Among Features in Two-Step Categorization

In this section, a two-step text categorization method taking the dependences among features into account is presented. We do the same task with the Naïve Bayesian Classifier in the first step, exactly same as what we did in Section 2 and Section 3. In the second step, each document identified unreliable in the first step are further processed by exploring the dependences among features. This is realized by a model named the Causality Naïve Bayesian Classifier.

4.1 The Causality Naïve Bayesian Classifier (CNB)

The Causality Naïve Bayesian Classifier (CNB) is an improved Naïve Bayesian Classifier. It contains two additional parts, i.e., the k-dependence feature list and the feature causality diagram. The former is used to represent the dependence relation among features, and the latter is used to estimate the probability distribution of a feature dynamically while taking its dependences into account.

K-Dependence Feature List (K-DFL): CNB allows each feature node Y to have a maximum of k features nodes as parents that constitute the k-dependence feature list representing the dependences among features. In other words, $\prod(Y) = \{Y_d, C\}$, where Y_d is the set of at most k features nodes, C is the category node, and $\prod(C) = \Phi$.

Note that we can build a K-DFL for each feature under each class c_t, which represents different dependence relations under different class.

Obviously, there exists a 0-dependence feature list for every feature in the Naïve Bayesian Classifier, from the definition of K-DFL.

The algorithm of constructing K-DFL is as follows: Given the maximum dependence number k, mutual information threshold θ and the class c_t. For each feature Y, repeat the follow steps. 1) Compute class conditional mutual information $MI(Y_i, Y_j| c_t)$, for every pair of features Y_i and Y_j, where $i \neq j$. 2) Construct the set $Si=\{ Y_j \mid MI(Y_i, Y_j| c_t) > \theta\}$. 3) Let $m= \min (k, | S_i|)$, select the top m features as K-DFL from S_i.

Feature Causality Diagram (FCD): CNB allows each feature Y, which occurs in a given document, to have a Feature Causality Diagram (FCD). FCD is a double-layer directed diagram, in which the first layer has only the feature node Y, and the second layer allows to have multiple nodes that include the class node C and the corresponding dependence node set S of Y. Here, $S=S_d \cap S_F$, S_d is the K-DFL node set of Y and $S_F=\{X_i | X_i$ is a feature node that occurs in the given document. There exists a directed arc from every node X_i at the second layer to the node Y at the first layer. The arc is called causality link event L_i which represents the causality intensity between node Y and X_i, and the probability of L_i is $p_i=\Pr\{L_i\}=\Pr\{Y=1|X_i=1\}$. The relation among all arcs is logical OR. The Feature Causality Diagram can be considered as a sort of simplified causality diagram [9][10].

Suppose feature Y's FCD is G, and it parent node set $S=\{X_1, X_2,\ldots,X_m\}$ $(m\geq 1)$ in G, we can estimate the conditional probability as follows while considering the dependences among features:

$$\Pr\{Y=1 | X_1=1,\cdots,X_m=1\} \cong \Pr\{Y=1 | G\} = \Pr\{\bigcup_{i=1}^{m} L_i\} = p_1 + \sum_{i=2}^{m} p_i \prod_{j=1}^{i-1}(1-p_j) \quad (16)$$

Note that when m=1, $\Pr\{Y=1 | X_1=1\} = \Pr\{Y=1 | G\} = \Pr\{Y=1 | C\}$.

Causality Naïve Bayesian Classifier (CNB): For a document represented by a binary-valued vector d=(X_1 ,X_2 , …,$X_{|d|}$), divide the features into two sets X_1 and X_2, X_1= {X_i| X_i=1} and X_2= {X_j| X_j=0}. The Causality Naïve Bayesian Classifier can be written as:

$$c^* = \arg\max_{c_t \in C}(\log\Pr\{c_t\} + \sum_{i=1}^{|X^1|}\log\Pr\{X_i \mid G_i\} + \sum_{j=1}^{|X^2|}\log(1-\Pr\{X_j \mid c_t\})) \tag{17}$$

4.2 Experiments on CNB

As mentioned earlier, the first step remains unchanged as that in Section 2 and Section 3. The difference is in the second step: for the documents identified unreliable in the first step, we apply the Causality Naïve Bayesian Classifier to handle them.

We use two datasets in the experiments. one is the two-class dataset described in Section 2.2, called Dataset-I, and the other one is the multi-class dataset described in Section 3.2, called Dataset-I.

To evaluate CNB and compare all methods presented in this paper, we experiment the following methods:

1) Naïve Bayesian Classifier (NB), i.e., the method-2 in Section 2.2;
2) CNB without exploring the two-step strategy;
3) The two-step strategy: NB and CNB in the first and second step (TS-CNB);
4) Limited Dependence Bayesian Classifier (DNB) [11];
5) Method-5 in Section 2.2 and Section 3.2 (denoted TS-DF here).

Experimental results for two-class Dataset-I and multi-class Dataset-II are listed in Table3 and Table 4. The data for NB and TS-DF are derived from the corresponding columns of Table 1 and Table 2. The parameters in CNB and TS-CNB are that the dependence number k=1 and 5, the thresholdθ= 0.0545 and 0.0045 for Dataset-I and Dataset-II respectively. The parameters in DNB are that dependence number k=1and 3, the thresholdθ= 0.0545 and 0.0045 for Dataset-I and Dataset-II respectively.

Table 3. Performance comparisons in two-class Dataset-I

Performance \ Method	NB	CNB	TS-CNB	DNB	TS-DF
Precision	93.95%	94.08%	94.08%	93.31%	97.19%
Recall	88.78%	89.00%	89.00%	90.61%	93.94%
F_1	91.00%	91.46%	91.46%	91.93%	95.54%

Table 3 and Table 4 demonstrate that 1) The performance of the Naïve Bayesian Classifier can be improved by taking the dependences among features into account, as evidenced by the fact that CNB, TS-CNB and DNB outperform NB. By tracing the experiment, we find an interesting phenomenon, as expected: for the documents identified reliable by NB, CNB cannot improve it, but for those identified unreliable by NB, CNB can improve it. The reason should be even though NB and CNB use the same features, but CNB uses the dependences among features additionally. 2) CNB and TS-CNB have the same capability in effectiveness, but TS-CNB has a higher computational efficiency. As stated earlier, TS-CNB uses NB to classify documents in the reliable area and then uses CNB to classify documents in the unreliable area. At the first glance, the efficiency of TS-CNB seems lower than that of using CNB only because the former additionally uses NB in the first step, but in fact, a majority of documents (e.g., 63.13% of the total documents in dataset-I) fall into the reliable area and are then treated by NB successfully (obviously, NB is higher than CNB in efficiency) in the first step, so they will never go to the second step, resulting in a higher computational efficiency of TS-CNB than CNB. 3) The performances of CNB, TS-CNB and DNB are almost identical, among which, the efficiency of TS-CNB is the highest. And, the efficiency of CNB is higher than that of DNB, because CNB uses a simpler network structure than DNB, with the same learning and inference formalism. 4) TS-DF has the highest performance among the all. Meanwhile, the ranking of computational efficiency (in descending order) is NB, TS-DF, TS-CNB, CNB, and DNB.

Table 4. Performance comparisons in multi-class Dataset-II

Performance \ Method	NB	CNB	TS-CNB	DNB	TS-DF
Average Precision	97.03%	97.95%	97.95%	98.18%	98.58%
Average Recall	97.38%	98.35%	98.35%	97.91%	98.55%
Average F_1	97.20%	98.15%	98.15%	98.04%	98.56%

5 Related Works

Combining multiple methodologies or representations has been studied in several areas of information retrieval so far, for example, retrieval effectiveness can be improved by using multiple representations [12]. In the area of text categorization in particular, many methods of combining different classifiers have been developed. For example, Yang et al. [13] used simple equal weights for normalized score of each classifier output so as to integrate multiple classifiers linearly in the domain of Topic Detection and Tracking; Hull at al. [14] used linear combination for probabilities or log odds scores of multiple classifier output in the context of document filtering. Larkey et al. [15] used weighted linear combination for system ranks and scores of multiple classifier output in the medical document domain; Li and Jain [16] used voting and classifier selection technique including dynamic classifier selection and adaptive classifier. Lam and Lai [17] automatically selected a classifier for each category based on the category-specific statistical characteristics. Bennett et al. [18] used voting, classifier-selection techniques and a hierarchical combination method with reliability indicators.

6 Conclusions

The issue of how to classify Chinese documents characterized by high degree ambiguity from text categorization's point of view is a challenge. For this issue, this paper presents two solutions in a uniform two-step framework, which makes use of the distributional characteristics of misclassified documents, that is, most of the misclassified documents are near to the separate line between categories. The first solution is a two-step TC approach based on the Naïve Bayesian Classifier. The second solution is to further introduce the dependences among features into the model, resulting in a two-step approach based on the so-called Causality Naïve Bayesian Classifier. Experiments show that the second solution is superior to the Naïve Bayesian Classifier, and is equal to CNB without exploring two-step strategy in performance, but has a higher computational efficiency than the latter. The first solution has the best performance in all the experiments, outperforming all other methods (including the second solution): in the two-class experiments, its F_1 increases from the baseline 82.67% to the final 95.54%, and in the multi-class experiments, its average F_1 increases from the baseline 91.48% to the final 98.56%.

In addition, the other two conclusions can be drawn from the experiments: 1) Using Chinese word bigrams as features has a better discriminating capability than using words as features, but more serious data sparseness will be faced; 2) formula (8) is superior to (9) in feature reduction in both the two-class and multi-class Chinese text categorization.

It is worth point out that we believe the proposed method is in principle language independent, though all the experiments are performed on Chinese datasets.

Acknowledgements

The research is supported in part by the National 863 Project of China under grant number 2001AA114210-03, 2003 Korea-China Young Scientists Exchange Program, the Tsinghua-ALVIS Project co-sponsored by the National Natural Science Foundation of China under grant number 60520130299 and EU FP6, and the National Natural Science Foundation of China under grant number 60321002.

References

1. Sebastiani, F. Machine Learning in Automated Text Categorization. ACM Computing Surveys, 34(1):1-47, 2002.
2. Lewis, D. Naive Bayes at Forty: The Independence Assumption in Information Retrieval. In Proceedings of ECML-98, 4-15, 1998.
3. Salton, G. Automatic Text Processing: The Transformation, Analysis, and Retrieval of Information by Computer. Addison-Wesley, Reading, MA, 1989.
4. Mitchell, T.M. Machine Learning. McCraw Hill, New York, NY, 1996.
5. Yang, Y., and Liu, X. A Re-examination of Text Categorization Methods. In Proceedings of SIGIR-99, 42-49,1999.
6. Xinghua Fan. Causality Reasoning and Text Categorization, Postdoctoral Research Report of Tsinghua University, P.R. China, April 2004. (In Chinese)

7. Dumais, S.T., Platt, J., Hecherman, D., and Sahami, M. Inductive Learning Algorithms and Representation for Text Categorization. In Proceedings of CIKM-98, Bethesda, MD, 148-155, 1998.
8. Sahami, M., Dumais, S., Hecherman, D., and Horvitz, E. A. Bayesian Approach to Filtering Junk E-Mail. In Learning for Text Categorization: Papers from the AAAI Workshop, 55-62, Madison Wisconsin. AAAI Technical Report WS-98-05, 1998.
9. Xinghua Fan. Causality Diagram Theory Research and Applying It to Fault Diagnosis of Complexity System, Ph.D. Dissertation of Chongqing University, P.R. China, April 2002. (In Chinese)
10. Xinghua Fan, Zhang Qin, Sun Maosong, and Huang Xiyue. Reasoning Algorithm in Multi-Valued Causality Diagram, Chinese Journal of Computers, 26(3), 310-322, 2003. (In Chinese)
11. Sahami, M. Learning Limited Dependence Bayesian Classifiers. In Proceedings of the Second International Conference on Knowledge Discovery and Data Mining, Portland, 335-338, 1996.
12. Rajashekar, T. B. and Croft, W. B. Combining Automatic and Manual Index Representations in Probabilistic Retrieval. Journal of the American society for information science, 6(4): 272-283,1995.
13. Yang, Y., Ault, T. and Pierce, T. Combining Multiple Learning Strategies for Effective Cross Validation. In Proceedings of ICML 2000, 1167–1174, 2000.
14. Hull, D. A., Pedersen, J. O. and H. Schutze. Method Combination for Document Filtering. In Proceedings of SIGIR-96, 279–287, 1996.
15. Larkey, L. S. and Croft, W. B. Combining Classifiers in Text Categorization. In Proceedings of SIGIR-96, 289-297, 1996.
16. Li, Y. H., and Jain, A. K. Classification of Text Documents. The Computer Journal, 41(8): 537-546, 1998.
17. Lam, W., and Lai, K.Y A Meta-learning Approach for Text Categorization. In Proceedings of SIGIR-2001, 303-309, 2001.
18. Bennett, P. N., Dumais, S. T., and Horvitz, E. Probabilistic Combination of Text Classifiers Using Reliability Indicators: Models and Results. In Proceedings of SIGIR-2002, 11-15, 2002.

Assigning Polarity Scores to Reviews Using Machine Learning Techniques

Daisuke Okanohara[1] and Jun'ichi Tsujii[1,2,3]

[1] Department of Computer Science, University of Tokyo, Hongo, 7-3-1, Bunkyo-ku, Tokyo 113-0013

[2] CREST, JST, Honcho, 4-1-8, Kawaguchi-shi, Saitama 332-0012

[3] School of Informatics, University of Manchester, POBox 88, Sackville St, Manchester, M60 1QD, UK

{hillbig, tsujii}@is.s.u-tokyo.ac.jp

Abstract. We propose a novel type of document classification task that quantifies how much a given document (review) appreciates the target object using not binary polarity (*good* or *bad*) but a continuous measure called *sentiment polarity score* (sp-score). An sp-score gives a very concise summary of a review and provides more information than binary classification. The difficulty of this task lies in the quantification of polarity. In this paper we use support vector regression (SVR) to tackle the problem. Experiments on book reviews with five-point scales show that SVR outperforms a multi-class classification method using support vector machines and the results are close to human performance.

1 Introduction

In recent years, discussion groups, online shops, and blog systems on the Internet have gained popularity and the number of documents, such as reviews, is growing dramatically. *Sentiment classification* refers to classifying reviews not by their topics but by the polarity of their sentiment (e.g, positive or negative). It is useful for recommendation systems, fine-grained information retrieval systems, and business applications that collect opinions about a commercial product.

Recently, sentiment classification has been actively studied and experimental results have shown that machine learning approaches perform well [13,11,10,20]. We argue, however, that we can estimate the polarity of a review more finely. For example, both reviews A and B in Table 1 would be classified simply as *positive* in binary classification. Obviously, this classification loses the information about the difference in the degree of polarity apparent in the review text.

We propose a novel type of document classification task where we evaluate reviews with scores like five stars. We call this score the *sentiment polarity score* (sp-score). If, for example, the range of the score is from one to five, we could give five to review A and four to review B. This task, namely, ordered multi-class classification, is considered as an extension of binary sentiment classification.

In this paper, we describe a machine learning method for this task. Our system uses support vector regression (SVR) [21] to determine the sp-scores of

R. Dale et al. (Eds.): IJCNLP 2005, LNAI 3651, pp. 314–325, 2005.

Table 1. Examples of book reviews

	Example of Review	binary	sp-score (1,...,5)
Review A	I believe this is very good and a "must read" I can't wait to read the next book in the series.	plus	5
Review B	This book is not so bad. You may find some interesting points in the book.	plus	4

Table 2. Corpus A: reviews for Harry Potter series book. Corpus B: reviews for all kinds of books. The column of *word* shows the average number of words in a review, and the column of *sentences* shows the average number of sentences in a review.

sp-score	Corpus A			Corpus B		
	review	words	sentences	review	words	sentences
1	330	160.0	9.1	250	91.9	5.1
2	330	196.0	11.0	250	105.2	5.2
3	330	169.1	9.2	250	118.6	6.0
4	330	150.2	8.6	250	123.2	6.1
5	330	153.8	8.9	250	124.8	6.1

reviews. This method enables us to annotate sp-scores for arbitrary reviews such as comments in bulletin board systems or blog systems. We explore several types of features beyond a bag-of-words to capture key phrases to determine sp-scores: n-grams and references (the words around the reviewed object).

We conducted experiments with book reviews from *amazon.com* each of which had a five-point scale rating along with text. We compared pairwise support vector machines (pSVMs) and SVR and found that SVR outperformed better than pSVMs by about 30% in terms of the squared error, which is close to human performance.

2 Related Work

Recent studies on sentiment classification focused on machine learning approaches. Pang [13] represents a review as a feature vector and estimates the polarity with SVM, which is almost the same method as those for topic classification [1]. This paper basically follows this work, but we extend this task to a multi-order classification task.

There have been many attempts to analyze reviews deeply to improve accuracy. Mullen [10] used features from various information sources such as references to the "work" or "artist", which were annotated by hand, and showed that these features have the potential to improve the accuracy. We use reference features, which are the words around the fixed review target word (book), while Mullen annotated the references by hand.

Turney [20] used *semantic orientation*, which measures the distance from phrases to "excellent" or "poor" by using search engine results and gives the word polarity. Kudo [8] developed decision stumps, which can capture substructures embedded in text (such as word-based dependency), and suggested that subtree features are important for opinion/modality classification.

Independently of and in parallel with our work, two other papers consider the degree of polarity for sentiment classification. Koppel [6] exploited a neutral class and applied a regression method as ours. Pang [12] applied a metric labeling method for the task. Our work is different from their works in several respects. We exploited square errors instead of precision for the evaluation and used five distinct scores in our experiments while Koppel used three and Pang used three/four distinct scores in their experiments.

3 Analyzing Reviews with Polarity Scores

In this section we present a novel task setting where we predict the degree of sentiment polarity of a review. We first present the definition of sp-scores and the task of assigning them to review documents. We then explain an evaluation data set. Using this data set, we examined the human performance for this task to clarify the difficulty of quantifying polarity.

3.1 Sentiment Polarity Scores

We extend the sentiment classification task to the more challenging task of assigning rating scores to reviews. We call this score the sp-score. Examples of sp-scores include *five-star* and *scores out of 100*. Let sp-scores take discrete values[1] in a closed interval $[min...max]$. The task is to assign correct sp-scores to unseen reviews as accurately as possible. Let $\hat{y}$ be the predicted sp-score and y be the sp-score assigned by the reviewer. We measure the performance of an estimator with the mean square error:

$$\frac{1}{n}\sum_{i=1}^{n}(\hat{y}_i - y_i)^2, \tag{1}$$

where $(x_1, y_1), ..., (x_n, y_n)$ is the test set of reviews. This measure gives a large penalty for large mistakes, while ordered multi-class classification gives equal penalties to any types of mistakes.

3.2 Evaluation Data

We used book reviews on *amazon.com* for evaluation data[2] [3]. Each review has stars assigned by the reviewer. The number of stars ranges from one to five:

[1] We could allow sp-scores to have continuous values. However, in this paper we assume sp-scores take only discrete values since the evaluation data set was annotated by only discrete values.

[2] *http://www.amazon.com*

[3] These data were gathered from google cache using google API.

one indicates the worst and five indicates the best. We converted the number of stars into sp-scores $\{1, 2, 3, 4, 5\}$ [4]. Although each review may include several paragraphs, we did not exploit paragraph information.

From these data, we made two data sets. The first was a set of reviews for books in the *Harry Potter* series (Corpus A). The second was a set of reviews for books of arbitrary kinds (Corpus B). It was easier to predict sp-scores for Corpus A than Corpus B because Corpus A books have a smaller vocabulary and each review was about twice as large. To create a data set with a uniform score distribution (the effect of skewed class distributions is out of the scope of this paper), we selected 330 reviews per sp-score for Corpus A and 280 reviews per sp-score for Corpus B [5]. Table 2 shows the number of words and sentences in the corpora. There is no significant difference in the average number of words/sentences among different sp-scores.

Table 3. Human performance of sp-score estimation. Test data: 100 reviews of Corpus A with 1,2,3,4,5 sp-score.

	Square error
Human 1	0.77
Human 2	0.79
Human average	0.78
cf. Random	3.20
All3	2.00

Table 4. Results of sp-score estimation: Human 1 (left) and Human 2 (right)

	Assigned					
	1	2	3	4	5	Total
Correct						
1	12	7	0	1	0	20
2	7	8	4	1	0	20
3	1	1	13	5	0	20
4	0	0	4	10	6	20
5	0	1	2	7	10	20
Total	20	17	23	24	16	100

	Assigned					
	1	2	3	4	5	total
Correct						
1	16	3	0	1	0	20
2	11	5	3	1	0	20
3	2	5	7	4	2	20
4	0	1	2	1	16	20
5	0	0	0	2	18	20
Total	29	14	12	9	36	100

3.3 Preliminary Experiments: Human Performance for Assigning Sp-scores

We treat the sp-scores assigned by the reviewers as correct answers. However, the content of a review and its sp-score may not be related. Moreover, sp-scores may vary depending on the reviewers. We examined the universality of the sp-score.

[4] One must be aware that different scales may reflect the different reactions than just scales as Keller indicated [17].

[5] We actually corrected 25000 reviews. However, we used only 2900 reviews since the number of reviews with 1 star is very small. We examined the effect of the number of training data is discussed in 5.3.

We asked two researchers of computational linguistics independently to assign an sp-score to each review from Corpus A. We first had them learn the relationship between reviews and sp-scores using 20 reviews. We then gave them 100 reviews with uniform sp-score distribution as test data. Table 3 shows the results in terms of the square error. The *Random* row shows the performance achieved by random assignment, and the *All3* row shows the performance achieved by assigning 3 to all the reviews. These results suggest that sp-scores would be estimated with 0.78 square error from only the contents of reviews.

Table 4 shows the distribution of the estimated sp-scores and correct sp-scores. In the table we can observe the difficulty of this task: the precise quantification of sp-scores. For example, human B tended to overestimate the sp-score as 1 or 5. We should note that if we consider this task as binary classification by treating the reviews whose sp-scores are 4 and 5 as positive examples and those with 1 and 2 as negative examples (ignoring the reviews whose sp-scores are 3), the classification precisions by humans A and B are 95% and 96% respectively.

4 Assigning Sp-scores to Reviews

This section describes a machine learning approach to predict the sp-scores of review documents. Our method consists of the following two steps: extraction of feature vectors from reviews and estimation of sp-scores by the feature vectors. The first step basically uses existing techniques for document classification. On the other hand, the prediction of sp-scores is different from previous studies because we consider ordered multi-class classification, that is, each sp-score has its own class and the classes are ordered. Unlike usual multi-class classification, large mistakes in terms of the order should have large penalties. In this paper, we discuss two methods of estimating sp-scores: pSVMs and SVR.

4.1 Review Representation

We represent a review as a feature vector. Although this representation ignores the syntactic structure, word positions, and the order of words, it is known to work reasonably well for many tasks such as information retrieval and document classification. We use *binary*, *tf*, and *tf-idf* as feature weighting methods [15]. The feature vectors are normalized to have L^2 norm 1.

4.2 Support Vector Regression

Support vector regression (SVR) is a method of regression that shares the underlying idea with SVM [3,16]. SVR predicts the sp-score of a review by the following regression:

$$f : R^n \mapsto R, y = f(x) = \langle \boldsymbol{w} \cdot \boldsymbol{x} \rangle + b. \tag{2}$$

SVR uses an ϵ-*insensitive loss function.* This loss function means that all errors inside the ϵ cube are ignored. This allows SVR to use few support vectors and gives generalization ability. Given a training set, $(\boldsymbol{x_1}, y_1), ..., (\boldsymbol{x_n}, y_n)$, parameters $\boldsymbol{w}$ and b are determined by:

$$\begin{array}{llll} & \text{minimize } \frac{1}{2}\langle \boldsymbol{w} \cdot \boldsymbol{w}\rangle + C\sum_{i=1}^{n}(\xi_i + \xi_i^*) & & \\ & \text{subject to} \quad ((\langle \boldsymbol{w} \cdot \boldsymbol{x_i}\rangle + b) - y_i & \leq \epsilon + \xi_i & \\ & \qquad\qquad\qquad y_i - ((\langle \boldsymbol{w} \cdot \boldsymbol{x_i}\rangle + b) & \leq \epsilon + \xi_i^* & \\ & \xi_i^{(*)} \geq 0 \qquad i = 1, ..., n. & & \end{array} \tag{3}$$

The factor $C > 0$ is a parameter that controls the trade-off between training error minimization and margin maximization. The loss in training data increases as C becomes smaller, and the generalization is lost as C becomes larger. Moreover, we can apply a kernel-trick to SVR as in the case with SVMs by using a kernel function.

This approach captures the order of classes and does not suffer from data sparseness. We could use conventional linear regression instead of SVR [4]. But we use SVR because it can exploit the kernel-trick and avoid over-training. Another good characteristic of SVR is that we can identify the features contributing to determining the sp-scores by examining the coefficients ($\boldsymbol{w}$ in (2)), while pSVMs does not give such information because multiple classifiers are involved in determining final results. A problem in this approach is that SVR cannot learn non-linear regression. For example, when given training data are $(x = 1, y = 1), (x = 2, y = 2), (x = 3, y = 8)$, SVR cannot perform regression correctly without adjusting the feature values.

4.3 Pairwise Support Vector Machines

We apply a multi-class classification approach to estimating sp-scores. pSVMs [7] considers each sp-score as a unique class and ignores the order among the classes. Given reviews with sp-scores $\{1, 2, .., m\}$, we construct $m \cdot (m-1)/2$ SVM classifiers for all the pairs of the possible values of sp-scores. The classifier for a sp-score pair $(avsb)$ assigns the sp-score to a review with a or b. The class label of a document is determined by majority voting of the classifiers. Ties in the voting are broken by choosing the class that is closest to the neutral sp-score (i.e, $(1+m)/2$).

This approach ignores the fact that sp-scores are ordered, which causes the following two problems. First, it allows large mistakes. Second, when the number of possible values of the sp-score is large (e.g, $n > 100$), this approach suffers from the data sparseness problem. Because pSVMs cannot employ examples that have close sp-scores (e.g, sp-score $= 50$) for the classification of other sp-scores (e.g, the classifier for a sp-score pair $(51vs100)$).

4.4 Features Beyond Bag-of-Words

Previous studies [9,2] suggested that complex features do not work as expected because data become sparse when such features are used and a bag-of-words

Table 5. Feature list for experiments

Features	Description	Example in Fig.1 review 1
unigram	single word	(I) (believe) .. (series)
bigram	pair of two adjacent words	(I believe) ... (the series)
trigram	adjacent three words	(I believe this) ... (in the series)
inbook	words in a sentence including "book"	(I) (can't) ... (series)
aroundbook	words near "book" within two words.	(the) (next) (in) (the)

approach is enough to capture the information in most reviews. Nevertheless, we observed that reviews include many chunks of words such as "very good" or "must buy" that are useful for estimating the degree of polarity. We confirmed this observation by using n-grams. Since the words around the review target might be expected to influence the whole sp-score more than other words, we use these words as features. We call these features *reference.* We assume the review target is only the word "book", and we use "inbook" and "aroundbook" features. The "inbook" features are the words appear in the sentences which include the word "book". The "around book" are the words around the word "book" within two words. Table 5 summarizes the feature list for the experiments.

5 Experiments

We performed two series of experiments. First, we compared pSVMs and SVR. Second, we examined the performance of various features and weighting methods.

We used Corpus A/B introduced in Sec. 3.2 for experiment data. We removed all HTML tags and punctuation marks beforehand. We also applied the Porter stemming method [14] to the reviews.

We divided these data into ten disjoint subsets, maintaining the uniform class distribution. All the results reported below are the average of ten-fold cross-validation. In SVMs and SVR, we used *SVMlight*[6] with the quadratic polynomial kernel $K(x, z) = (\langle x \cdot z \rangle + 1)^2$ and set the control parameter C to 100 in all the experiments.

5.1 Comparison of pSVMs and SVR

We compared pSVMs and SVR to see differences in the properties of the regression approach compared with those of the classification approach. Both pSVMs and SVR used unigram/tf-idf to represent reviews. Table 6 shows the square error results for SVM, SVR and a simple regression (least square error) method for Corpus A/B. These results indicate that SVR outperformed SVM in terms of the square error and suggests that regression methods avoid large mistakes by taking account of the fact that sp-scores are ordered, while pSVMs does not. We also note that the result of a simple regression method is close to the result of SVR with a linear kernel.

[6] http://svmlight.joachims.org/

Table 6. Comparison of multi-class SVM and SVR. Both use unigram/tf-idf.

	Square error	
Methods	Corpus A	Corpus B
pSVMs	1.32	2.13
simple regression	1.05	1.49
SVR (linear kernel)	1.01	1.46
SVR (polynomial kernel $((x \cdot z) + 1)^2$)	**0.94**	**1.38**

Figure 1 shows the distribution of estimation results for humans (top left: human 1, top right: human 2), pSVMs (below left), and SVR (below right). The horizontal axis shows the estimated sp-scores and the vertical axis shows the correct sp-scores. Color density indicates the number of reviews. These figures suggest that pSVMs and SVR could capture the gradualness of sp-scores better than humans could. They also show that pSVMs cannot predict neutral sp-scores well, while SVR can do so well.

5.2 Comparison of Different Features

We compared the different features presented in Section 4.4 and feature weighting methods. First we compared different weighting methods. We used only unigram features for this comparison. We then compared different features. We used only tf-idf weighting methods for this comparison.

Table 7 summarizes the comparison results of different feature weighting methods. The results show that *tf-idf* performed well on both test corpora. We should note that simple representation methods, such as *binary* or *tf*, give comparable results to tf-idf, which indicates that we can add more complex features without considering the scale of feature values. For example, when we add word-based dependency features, we have some difficulty in adjusting these feature values to those of unigrams. But we could use these features together in binary weighting methods.

Table 8 summarizes the comparison results for different features. For Corpus A, *unigram + bigram* and *unigram + trigram* achieved high performance. The performance of *unigram + inbook* was not good, which is contrary to our intuition that the words that appear around the target object are more important than others. For Corpus B, the results was different, that is, n-gram features could not predict the sp-scores well. This is because the variety of words/phrases was much larger than in Corpus A and n-gram features may have suffered from the data sparseness problem. We should note that these feature settings are too simple, and we cannot accept the result of reference or target object (*inbook*/*aroundbook*) directly.

Note that the data used in the preliminary experiments described in Section 3.3 are a part of Corpus A. Therefore we can compare the results for humans with those for Corpus A in this experiment. The best result by the machine learning approach (0.89) was close to the human results (0.78).

To analyze the influence of n-gram features, we used the linear kernel $k(x, z) := \langle x \cdot z \rangle$ in SVR training. We used tf-idf as feature weighting. We then

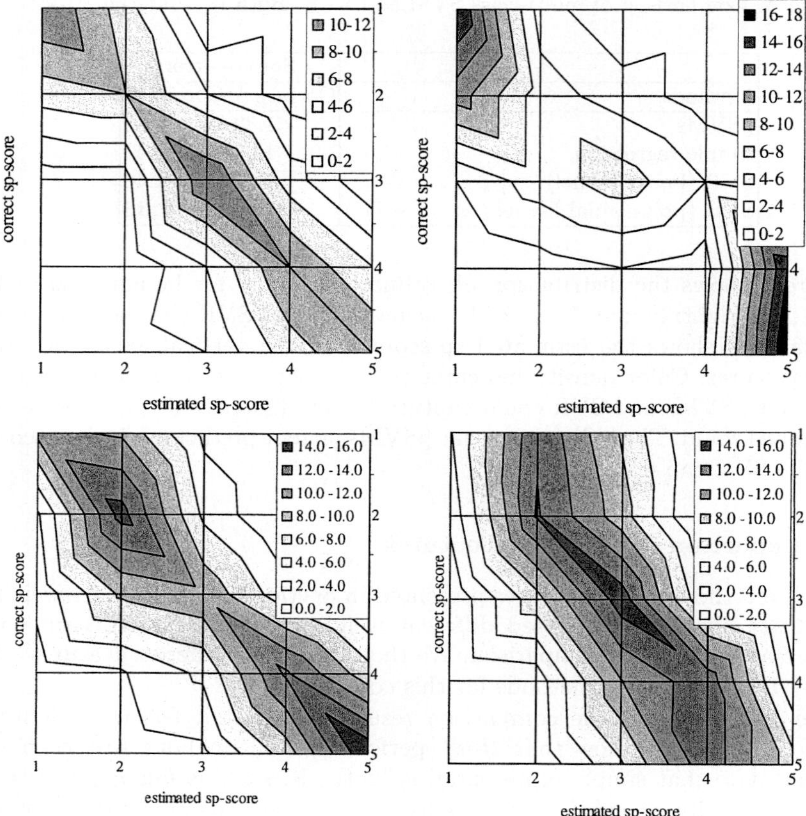

Fig. 1. Distribution of estimation results. Color density indicates the number of reviews. Top left: Human A, top right: Human B, below left: pSVMs, below right: SVR.

examined each coefficient of regression. Since we used the linear kernel, the coefficient value of SVR showed the polarity of a single feature, that is, this value expressed how much the occurrence of a feature affected the sp-score. Tables 9 shows the coefficients resulting from the training of SVR. These results show that neutral polarity words themselves, such as "all" and "age", will affect the overall sp-scores of reviews with other neutral polarity words, such as, "all ag (age)", "can't wait", "on (one) star", and "not interest".

5.3 Learning Curve

We generated learning curves to examine the effect of the size of training data on the performance. Figure 2 shows the results of a classification task using unigram /*tf-idf* to represent reviews. The results suggest that the performance can still be improved by increasing the training data.

Table 7. Comparison results of different feature weighting methods. We used unigrams as features of reviews.

	Square error	
Weighting methods (unigram)	Corpus A	Corpus B
tf	1.03	1.49
tf-idf	**0.94**	**1.38**
binary	1.04	1.47

Table 8. Comparison results of different features. For comparison of different features we tf-idf as weighting methods.

	Square error	
Feature (tf-idf)	Corpus A	Corpus B
unigram (baseline)	0.94	1.38
unigram + bigram	**0.89**	1.41
unigram + trigram	0.90	1.42
unigram + inbook	0.97	**1.36**
unigram + aroundbook	0.93	1.37

Table 9. List of bigram features that have ten best/worst polarity values estimated by SVR in Corpus A/B. The column of *pol* expresses the estimated sp-score of a feature, i.e., only this feature is fired in a feature vector. (word stemming was applied)

Corpus A (best)		Corpus B (best)		Corpus A (worst)		Corpus B (worst)	
pol	bigram	pol	bigram	pol	bigram	pol	bigram
1.73	best book	1.64	the best	-1.61	at all	-1.19	veri disappoint
1.69	is a	1.60	read it	-1.50	wast of	-1.13	wast of
1.49	read it	1.37	a great	-1.38	potter book	-0.98	the worst
1.44	all ag	1.34	on of	-1.36	out of	-0.97	is veri
1.30	can't wait	1.31	fast food	-1.28	not interest	-0.96	! !
1.20	it is	1.22	harri potter	-1.18	on star	-0.85	i am
1.14	the sorcer's	1.19	highli recommend	-1.14	the worst	-0.81	the exampl
1.14	great !	1.14	an excel	-1.13	first four	-0.79	bui it
1.13	sorcer's stone	1.12	to read	-1.11	a wast	-0.76	veri littl
1.11	come out	1.01	in the	-1.08	no on	-0.74	onli to

6 Conclusion

In this paper, we described a novel task setting in which we predicted sp-scores - degree of polarity - of reviews. We proposed a machine learning method using SVR to predict sp-scores.

We compared two methods for estimating sp-scores: pSVMs and SVR. Experimental results with book reviews showed that SVR performed better in terms of the square error than pSVMs by about 30%. This result agrees with our

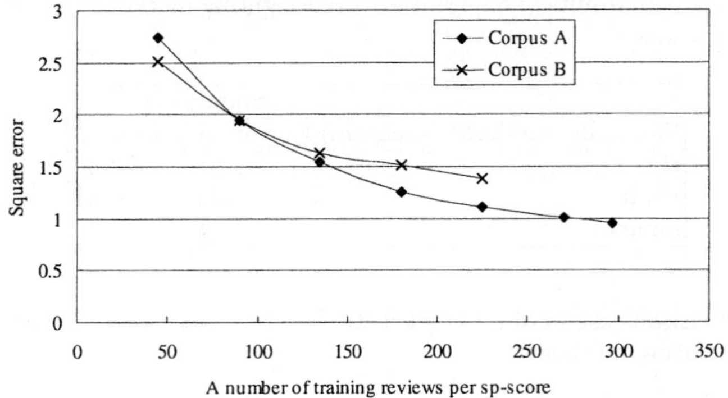

Fig. 2. Learning curve for our task setting for Corpus A and Corpus B. We used SVR as the classifier and unigram/*tf-idf* to represent of reviews.

intuition that pSVMs does not consider the order of sp-scores, while SVR captures the order of sp-scores and avoids high penalty mistakes. With SVR, sp-scores can be estimated with a square error of 0.89, which is very close to the square error achieved by human (0.78).

We examined the effectiveness of features beyond a bag-of-words and reference features (the words around the reviewed objects.) The results suggest that n-gram features and reference features contribute to improve the accuracy.

As the next step in our research, we plan to exploit parsing results such as predicate argument structures for detecting precise reference information. We will also capture other types of polarity than attitude, such as modality and writing position [8], and we will consider estimating these types of polarity.

We plan to develop a classifier specialized for ordered multi-class classification using recent studies on machine learning for structured output space [19,18] or ordinal regression [5] because our experiments suggest that both pSVMs and SVR have advantages and disadvantages. We will develop a more efficient classifier that outperforms pSVMs and SVR by combining these ideas.

References

1. T . Joachims. *Learning to Classify Text Using Support Vector Machines.* Kluwer, 2002.
2. C. Apte, F. Damerau, and S. Weiss. Automated learning of decision rules for text categorization. *Information Systems*, 12(3):233–251, 1994.
3. N. Cristianini and J. S. Taylor. *An Introduction to Support Vector Machines and other Kernel-based Learning Methods.* Cambridge University Press, 2000.
4. T. Hastie, R. Tibshirani, and J. Friedman. *The Elements of Statistical Learning.* Springer, 2001.
5. Ralf Herbrich, Thore Graepel, and Klaus Obermayer. Large margin rank boundaries for ordinal regression. In *Advances in Large Margin Classifiers*, pages 115–132. MIT press, 2000.

6. Moshe Koppel and Jonathan Schler. The importance of neutral examples for learning sentiment. In *In Workshop on the Analysis of Informal and Formal Information Exchange during Negotiations (FINEXIN)*, 2005.
7. U. Kresel. *Pairwise Classification and Support Vector Machines Methods.* MIT Press, 1999.
8. T. Kudo and Y. Matsumoto. A boosting algorithm for classification of semi-structured text. In *Proceedings of the 2004 Conference on Empirical Methods in Natural Language Processing (EMNLP)*, pages 301–308, 2004.
9. D. Lewis. An evaluation of phrasal and clustered representations on a text categorization task. In *Proceedings of SIGIR-92, 15th ACM International Conference on Research and Development in Information Retrieval*, pages 37–50, 1992.
10. A. Mullen and N. Collier. Sentiment analysis using Support Vector Machines with diverse information sources. In *Proceedings of the 42nd Meeting of the Association for Computational Linguistics (ACL)*, 2004.
11. B. Pang and L. Lee. A sentimental education: Sentiment analysis using subjectivity summarization based on minimum cuts. In *Proceedings of the 42nd Meeting of the Association for Computational Linguistics (ACL)*, pages 271–278, 2004.
12. B. Pang and L. Lee. Seeing stars: Exploiting class relationships for sentiment categorization with respect to rating scales. In *Proceedings of the 43nd Meeting of the Association for Computational Linguistics (ACL)*, 2005.
13. B. Pang, L. Lee, and S. Vaithyanathan. Thumbs up? sentiment classification using machine learning techniques. In *Proceedings of the 2002 Conference on Empirical Methods in Natural Language Processing (EMNLP)*, pages 79–86, 2002.
14. M.F. Porter. An algorithm for suffix stripping, program. *Program*, 14(3):130–137, 1980.
15. F. Sebastiani. Machine learning in automated text categorization. *ACM Computing Surveys*, 34(1):1–47, 2002.
16. A. Smola and B. Sch. A tutorial on Support Vector Regression. Technical report, NeuroCOLT2 Technical Report NC2-TR-1998-030, 1998.
17. Antonella Sorace and Frank Keller. Gradience in linguistic data. *Lingua*, 115(11):1497–1524, 2005.
18. B. Taskar. *Learning Structured Prediction Models: A Large Margin Approach.* PhD thesis, Stanford University, 2004.
19. I. Tsochantaridis, T. Hofmann, T. Joachims, and Y. Altun. Support vector machine learning for interdependent and structured output spaces. In *Machine Learning, Proceedings of the Twenty-first International Conference (ICML)*, 2004.
20. P. D. Turney. Thumbs up or thumbs down? semantic orientation applied to unsupervised classification of reviews. In *Proceedings of the 40th Meeting of the Association for Computational Linguistics (ACL)*, pages 417–424, 2002.
21. V. Vapnik. *The Nature of Statistical Learning Theory.* Springer, 1995.

Analogy as Functional Recategorization: Abstraction with HowNet Semantics

Tony Veale

Department of Computer Science, University College Dublin,
Belfield, D4, Dublin, Ireland
Tony.Veale@UCD.ie
http://www.cs.ucd.ie/staff/tveale.html

Abstract. One generally accepted hallmark of creative thinking is an ability to look beyond conventional labels and recategorize a concept based on its behaviour and functional potential. So while taxonomies are useful in any domain of reasoning, they typically represent the conventional label set that creative thinking attempts to look beyond. So if a linguistic taxonomy like WordNet [1] is to be useful in driving linguistic creativity, it must support some basis for recategorization, to allow an agent to reorganize its category structures in a way that unlocks the functional potential of objects, or that recognizes similarity between literally dissimilar ideas. In this paper we consider how recategorization can be used to generate analogies using the HowNet [2] ontology, a lexical resource like WordNet that in addition to being bilingual (Chinese/English) also provides explicit semantic definitions for each of the terms that it defines.

1 Introduction

Analogy is a knowledge-hungry process that exploits a conceptual system's ability to perform controlled generalization in one domain and re-specialization into another. The result is a taxonomic leap within an ontology that transfers semantic content from one term onto another. While all taxonomies allow vertical movement, a system must fully understand the effects of generalization on a given concept before any analogy or metaphor can be considered either deliberate or meaningful. So to properly support analogy, a taxonomy must provide a basis of abstracting not just to conventional categories, like *Person, Animal* or *Tool*, but to categories representing the specific causal behaviour of concepts such as *think-agent, pain-experiencer, cutting-instrument*, and so on. Thus, a surgeon can be meaningfully described as a repairman since both occupations have the function of restoring an object to an earlier and better state; a footballer can be meaningfully described as a gladiator or a warrior since each exhibits competitive behaviour; and a scalpel can be compared to a sabre, a sword or a cleaver since each has a cutting behaviour; and so on.

Theories of metaphor and analogy are typically based either on structure-mapping [3,4] or on abstraction e.g., [5,6,7,8,9,10]). While the former is most associated with analogy, the latter has been a near-constant in the computational treatment of metaphor. Structure-mapping assumes that the causal behaviour of a concept is expressed in an explicit, graph-theoretic form so that unifying sub-graph isomorphisms can be

R. Dale et al. (Eds.): IJCNLP 2005, LNAI 3651, pp. 326 – 333, 2005.

found between different representations. In contrast, abstraction theories assume that analogous concepts, even when far removed in ontological terms, will nonetheless share a common hypernym that captures their causal similarity. Thus, we should expect an analogous pairing like surgeon and butcher to have different immediate hypernyms but to ultimately share an abstraction like *cutting-agent* (see [8,9]).

However, the idea that a standard ontology will actually provide a hypernym like *cutting-agent* seems convenient almost to the point of incredulity. The problem is, of course, that as much as we want our ontologies to anticipate future analogies and metaphors with these pro-active categorizations, most ontologies simply do not possess terms as prescient as these. This is the question we address in this paper: if we assume that our ontologies lack these structures, can we nonetheless enable them to be added via automatic means? We argue that we can, by generalizing not on the basis of a concept's taxonomic position but on the basis of the specific relations that define its causal behaviour.

Clearly then, this approach to analogy requires a resource that is rich in causal relations. We find this richness in HowNet [2, 11], a bilingual lexical ontology for Chinese and English that employs an explicit propositional semantics to define each of its lexical concepts.

With this goal in mind, the paper observes the following structure: in section two we offer a concise survey of the considerable research that has, in the past, been dedicated to abstraction theories of analogy and metaphor. In section three we then compare and contrast WordNet [1] and HowNet as candidate resources for the current abstraction approach to analogical reasoning. In section four, having established an argument as to why HowNet is to be preferred, we indicate how HowNet's semantic definitions can be transformed in the service of analogical recategorization. The performance and competence of this recategorization ability is then evaluated in section five. Speculation about further possible contributions of HowNet to analogical research is reserved for the closing remarks of section six.

2 Abstraction Theories of Analogy

That analogy and metaphor operate across multiple levels of conceptual abstraction has been well known since classical times. Aristotle first provided a compelling taxonomic account of both in his Poetics (see [5], for a translation), and computationalists have been fascinated by this perspective ever since. While the core idea has survived relatively unchanged, one must discriminate theories that apparently presume a static type-hierarchy to be sufficient for all abstraction purposes (e.g., [6]), from theories that posit the need for a dynamic type hierarchy (e.g., [7, 8]). One must also differentiate theories that have actually been implemented (e.g., [6,8,9]) from those that are either notional or that seem to court computational intractability (e.g., [5,6]). Perhaps most meaningfully, one must differentiate theories and implementations that assume hand-crafted, purpose-built ontologies (e.g., [6]) from those that exploit an existing large-scale resource like WordNet (e.g., [8,9]). In the former, one has the flexibility to support as many functional abstractions like cutting-agent as are believed necessary, but at the cost of appearing to anticipate future analogies by hand-crafting them into the system.

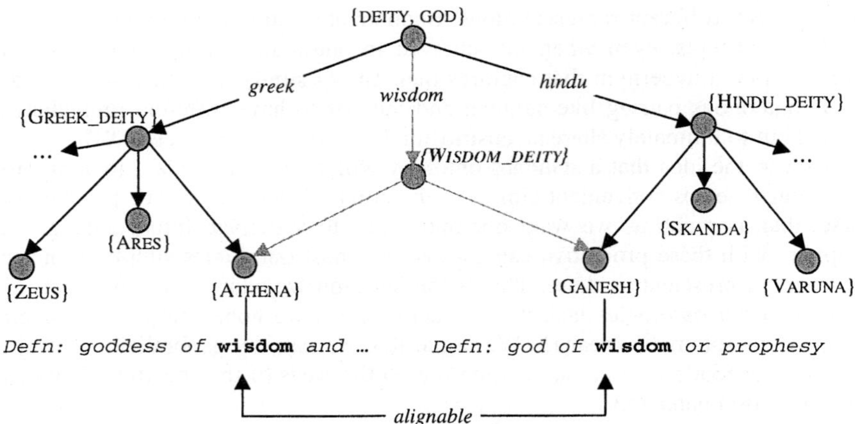

Fig. 1. Analysis of the WordNet gloss for {Athena} suggests that the word-form "wisdom" has analogical potential, since it is alignable with another use in {Ganesh}. This leads to the construction of the dynamic sense {Wisdom_deity} which can be used to make analogical leaps between these concepts.

This current work follows the latter course. We intend to automatically construct a new taxonomy of analogically-useful abstractions like *cutting-agent*, by analysing the semantic content of the definitions assigned to each word-sense in HowNet. Past work (e.g., [8]) has attempted this automatic construction of analogically-friendly taxonomies from WordNet, resulting in an approach that involves as much information-extraction from free text as it does semantic inference. This is because WordNet's glosses, unlike the semantic definitions of HowNet, are free-form sentences designed for human, rather than machine, consumption. For instance, Figure 1 above illustrates how features can be lifted from WordNet glosses to create new intermediate taxonyms, or dynamic types, from which subsequent abstraction-based analogies can be generated.

The explicitly-structured semantic forms that one finds in HowNet definitions will clearly make this lifting of features more logical and less heuristic. In general, this makes HowNet an ideal knowledge-source for a computational model of metaphor and analogy (e.g., see [10] for a topical perspective).

3 Comparing WordNet and HowNet

Generalization can be considered "controlled" if, when moving to a higher level of abstraction in a taxonomy, a conceptual system is able to precisely quantify that meaning which is lost. In this sense at least, most large-scale taxonomies do not provide a significant degree of control. Perhaps nowhere is this observation more keenly felt than in weak lexical ontologies like Princeton WordNet (PWN). In PWN [1], generalization of a concept/synset does not generally yield a functional or behavioural abstraction of the original concept. This is so because WordNet's taxonomy is designed not to capture common causality, function and behaviour, but to show how existing lexemes relate to each other. For example, the common abstraction that unites {surgeon, sawbones} and {tree_surgeon} is not a concept that captures a shared sense of repair, improvement or care, but {person, human}. To be fair, much the same must be said of other taxonomies, even that of HowNet [2,11], a Chinese/English semantic dictionary, and Cyc [12]. However, as we shall demonstrate, HowNet contains the necessary basis for such abstractions in its relational semantic definitions.

PWN and HowNet have each been designed according a different theory of semantic organization. PWN is differential is nature: rather than attempting to express the meaning of a word explicitly, PWN instead differentiates words with different meanings by placing them in different synsets, and further differentiates synsets from one another by assigning them to different positions in its ontology. In contrast, HowNet is constructive in nature, exploiting sememes from a less discriminating taxonomy than PWN's to compose a semantic representation of meaning for each word sense.

Nonetheless, HowNet compensates strongly with its constructive semantics. For example, HowNet assigns the concept surgeon|医生the following definition:

{human|人:HostOf={Occupation|职位},domain={medical|医},
{doctor|医治:agent={~}}}

which can be glossed thus: "a surgeon is a human with an occupation in the medical domain who acts as the agent of a doctoring activity." The {~} serves as a self-reference here, to mark the location of the concept being defined in the given semantic structure. The oblique reference offered by the tilde construct serves to make the definition more generic (thereby facilitating analogy), so that many different concepts can conceivably employ the same definition. Thus, HowNet uses the above definition not only for surgeon, but for medical workers in general, from orderlies to nurses to internists and neurologists.

4 Extracting Functional Structure

Our scheme for converting HowNet's constructive definitions into a more differential form hinges on the use of the tilde as a self-reference in relational structures. For instance, consider the semantic definition that HowNet gives to repairman|修理工:

{human|人:HostOf={Occupation|职位}, {repair|修理:agent={~}}}

Noting the position of {~} here, we can infer that a repairman is the agent of a repairing activity, or in differential terms, a repair-agent. Now, since HowNet defines repair|修理 as a specialization of the reinstatement activity resume|恢复, we can further establish repair-agent as a specialization of resume-agent.

	resume-agent	
repair-agent	**doctor-agent**	**amend-agent**
repairman|修理工	surgeon|医生	reviser|修订者
watchmaker|钟表匠	herbalist|药农	

Fig. 2. Portion of a three-level functional hierarchy derived from HowNet

This double layer of abstraction establishes a new taxonomy that organizes word-concepts according to their analogical potential, rather than their formal ontological properties. For instance, as shown in Figure 2, resume-agent encompasses not only repair-agent, but doctor-agent, since HowNet also defines the predicate doctor|医治 as a specialization of the predicate resume|恢复.

In general, given a semantic fragment F:role={~} in a HowNet definition, we create the new abstractions F-role and F'-role, where F' is the immediate hypernym of F. The role in question might be agent, instrument, location, patient, or any other role that HowNet supports. By way of example, Figure 3 illustrates a partial hierarchy derived from the HowNet semantics of various form-altering tools:

AlterForm- instrument

cut-instrument	**stab-instrument**	**split-instrument**	**dig-instrument**
knife|刀	sword|宝剑	grater|擦菜板	scissors|剪
razor|剃刀	lance|长矛	glasscutter|玻璃刀	chainsaw|油锯

Fig. 3. A hierarchy of instruments derived from instances of AlterForm|变形状

5 Evaluating Analogical Competence

We evaluate the analogical potential of the newly derived functional taxonomy using four criteria: topology – the branching structure of the new taxonomy dictates its ability to generate analogies; coverage – the percentage of unique HowNet definitions that can be functionally re-indexed in the new taxonomy; recall – the percentage of unique definitions for which at least one analogy can be found using the new taxonomy; and parsimony– the percentage of abstractions in the new taxonomy that can be used to generate analogies.

5.1 Topological Characteristics of the New Functional Taxonomy

The new functional taxonomy contains 1579 mid-level abstractions and 838 upper-level abstractions. In total, the taxonomy contains only 2219 unique abstractions, revealing that in 8% of cases, the upper-level abstraction of one concept serves as the upper-level abstraction of another.

Analogies will be generated only if two or more unique concept definitions are co-indexed under the same mid-level or upper-level abstraction in the new functional taxonomy. For example, knight|骑士 and gladiator.|打斗者 are both co-indexed directly under the mid-level abstraction fight-agent. Likewise, gladiator|打斗者 is indexed under HaveContest-agent via fight-agent, while footballer|足球运动员 is indexed under HaveContest-agent via compete-agent. The upper-level of abstraction, represented here by HaveContest-agent, is necessary to facilitate analogy between semantically distant concepts.

Nonetheless, we note that a certain degree of metaphoric licence has already been exercised by HowNet's designers in assigning semantic structures, so that even semantically distant concepts can still share the same mid-level abstraction. Creative analogies like "Death is an assassin" can, as shown in Figure 4, be understood via a single generalization.

MakeBad-agent

kill-agent	**attack-agent**
assassin | 刺客	intruder | 侵略者
Death | 死神	man-eater | 食人鲨

Fig. 4. Semantic diversity among concepts with the same mid-level abstraction

Furthermore, because HowNet contains 95,407 unique lexical concepts (excluding synonyms) but only 23,507 unique semantic definitions, these definitions must be under-specified to the extent that many are shared by non-identical concepts (e.g., cart | 板车 and bicycle | 单车, are simply defined as manual vehicles).

5.2 Analogical Coverage

Since this new taxonomy is derived from the use of {~} in HowNet definitions, both the coverage and recall of analogy generation crucially depend on the widespread use of this reflexive construct. However, of the 23,505 unique definitions in HowNet, just 6430 employ thus form of self-reference. The coverage of the new taxonomy is thus 27% of HowNet definitions.

5.3 Analogical Recall

A majority of the abstractions in the new taxonomy, 59%, serve to co-index two or more HowNet definitions. Overall, analogies are generated for 6184 unique HowNet definitions, though these individual definitions may have many different lexical realizations. The recall rate thus is 26% of HowNet's 23,507 unique definitions, or 96% of the 6430 HowNet definitions that make use of {~}. The most productive abstraction is control_agent, which serves to co-index 210 unique definitions.

5.4 Parsimony of Recall

Overall, 1,315 of the 2219 nodes in the new taxonomy prove useful in co-indexing two or more unique definitions, while 904 nodes serve to index just a single definition. The parsimony of the new taxonomy is thus 59%, which reveals a reasonable, if not ideal, level of representational uniformity across HowNet's semantic definitions.

6 Conclusions and Future Work

While just 27% of HowNet's definitions are sufficiently structured to support analogy, we are encouraged that almost all of this generative potential can be achieved with a new functional taxonomy that is straightforward and efficient to construct. Furthermore, though 27% may seem slim, these analogically-friendly {~} structures are concentrated in the areas of the HowNet taxonomy that can most benefit from analogical re-description. As revealed in Table 1 below, some areas of HowNet are clearly more amenable to analogical reasoning than others.

Table 1. Analogical coverage/recall for different areas of HowNet

	Humans	Artefacts	Animals	Overall
Coverage	.65	.68	.42	.27
Recall	.54	.58	.16	.26
Parsimony	.50	.54	.22	.59

But the analogical potential of HowNet resides not just in its explicit propositional semantics, but in its use of Chinese orthography. Consider that most Chinese entries in HowNet are multi-character terms, where each character is not so much a letter as a morpheme. . For instance, 手术刀, meaning "scalpel", is a composite not just of characters but of ideas, for 手术 means "surgery" and 刀 means "knife". This logographic compositionality affords a kind of semantic transparency on a scale that alphabetic writing systems (like that of English) simply can not match Thus, 哲学家, which translates as "philosopher", can be seen via HowNet as a composition of 哲学 ("philosophy") and 家 ("specialist" or "scientist"). In turn, philosophy|哲学 is organized by HowNet as a specialization of knowledge|知识, as is logic|辩学, mathematics|数学, lexicography|词典学 and even midwifery|产科学. By decomposing compound terms in this way and generalizing the extracted modifiers, yet another three-level taxonomy can be constructed. For instance, from these examples the partial taxonomy of Fig. 5 can be derived.

	Knowledge-human	
Mathematics-human	**philosophy-human**	**midwifery-human**
mathematician|数学家	philosopher|哲学家	midwife|产科

Fig. 5. Portion of a three-level hierarchy derived from compound Chinese terms

The analogical potential of this ontologization becomes clear when one notices that it supports the classical analogy of philosopher as midwife. Clearly, then, we have just scratched the surface of what can usefully be derived from the lexico-semantic content of HowNet. Our current investigations with HowNet suggest that the full semantic richness of Chinese orthography may yet play a considerable role in supporting creative reasoning at a linguistic level, if only because it opens a window onto a different cultural perspective on words and concepts.

References

1. Miller, G. A.: WordNet: A Lexical Database for English. Communications of the ACM, Vol. 38 No. 11 (1995)
2. Dong, Z.: Knowledge Description: What, How and Who? The Proceedings of the International Symposium on Electronic Dictionaries, Tokyo, Japan (1988)

3. Falkenhainer, B.; Forbus, K.; and Gentner, D.: Structure-Mapping Engine: Algorithm and Examples. Artificial Intelligence, 41, pages 1-63 (1989)
4. Veale, T., Keane, M. T.: The Competence of Sub-Optimal Structure Mapping on 'Hard' Analogies. The proceedings of IJCAI'97, the Int. Joint Conference on Artificial Intelligence, Nagoya, Japan. Morgan Kaufman, San Mateo California (1997)
5. Hutton, J.: Aristotle's Poetics. Norton, New York (1982)
6. Fass, D: An Account of Coherence, Semantic Relations, Metonymy, and Lexical Ambiguity Resolution. In: Small, S. I, Cottrell, G. W., Tanenhaus, M.K. (eds.): Lexical Ambiguity Resolution: Perspectives from Psycholinguistics, Neuropsychology and Artificial Intelligence. Morgan Kaufman, San Mateo California (1988)
7. Way, E. C.: Knowledge Representation and Metaphor. Studies in Cognitive systems, Kluwer Academic Publishers (1991)
8. Veale. T.: Dynamic Type Creation in Metaphor Interpretation and Analogical Reasoning: A Case-Study with WordNet. In the proceedings of ICCS2003, the 2003 International Conference on Conceptual Structures, Dresden, Germany (2003)
9. Veale, T.: WordNet sits the S.A.T.: A Knowledge-Based Approach to Lexical Analogy. The proceedings of ECAI'2004, the 16th European Conf. on Artificial Intelligence. John Wiley: London (2004)
10. Veale, T.: Analogy Generation in HowNet. In the proceedings of IJCAI'05, the 19th International Joint Conference on Artificial Intelligence. Morgan Kaufmann: CA.
11. Wong, S.H.S.: Fighting Arbitrariness in WordNet-like Lexical Databases – A Natural Language Motivated Remedy. The proceedings of GWC 2004, the 2nd Global WordNet conference. Edited by Sojka, Pala, Smrz, Fellbaum, Vossen (2004)
12. Lenat, D., Guha, R.V.: Building Large Knowledge-Based Systems. Addison Wesley (1990)

PLSI Utilization for Automatic Thesaurus Construction

Masato Hagiwara, Yasuhiro Ogawa, and Katsuhiko Toyama

Graduate School of Information Science, Nagoya University,
Furo-cho, Chikusa-ku, Nagoya, JAPAN 464-8603
{hagiwara, yasuhiro, toyama}@kl.i.is.nagoya-u.ac.jp

Abstract. When acquiring synonyms from large corpora, it is important to deal not only with such surface information as the context of the words but also their latent semantics. This paper describes how to utilize a latent semantic model PLSI to acquire synonyms automatically from large corpora. PLSI has been shown to achieve a better performance than conventional methods such as tf·idf and LSI, making it applicable to automatic thesaurus construction. Also, various PLSI techniques have been shown to be effective including: (1) use of Skew Divergence as a distance/similarity measure; (2) removal of words with low frequencies, and (3) multiple executions of PLSI and integration of the results.

1 Introduction

Thesauri, dictionaries in which words are arranged according to meaning, are one of the most useful linguistic sources, having a broad range of applications, such as information retrieval and natural language understanding. Various thesauri have been constructed so far, including *WordNet* [6] and *Bunruigoihyo* [14]. Conventional thesauri, however, have largely been compiled by groups of language experts, making the construction and maintenance cost very high. It is also difficult to build a domain-specific thesaurus flexibly. Thus it is necessary to construct thesauri automatically using computers.

Many studies have been done for automatic thesaurus construction. In doing so, synonym acquisition is one of the most important techniques, although a thesaurus generally includes other relationships than synonyms (e.g., hypernyms and hyponyms). To acquire synonyms automatically, contextual features of words, such as co-occurrence and modification are extracted from large corpora and often used. Hindle [7], for example, extracted verb-noun relationships of subjects/objects and their predicates from a corpus and proposed a method to calculate similarity of two words based on their mutual information. Although methods based on such raw co-occurrences are simple yet effective, in a naive implementation some problems arise: namely, noises and sparseness. Being a collection of raw linguistic data, a corpus generally contains meaningless information, i.e., noises. Also, co-occurrence data extracted from corpora are often very sparse, making them inappropriate for similarity calculation, which is also known as the "zero frequency problem." Therefore, not only surface information but also latent semantics should be considered when acquiring synonyms from large corpora.

Several latent semantic models have been proposed so far, mainly for information retrieval and document indexing. The most commonly used and prominent ones are Latent Semantic Indexing (LSI) [5] and Probabilistic LSI (PLSI) [8]. LSI is a geometric

R. Dale et al. (Eds.): IJCNLP 2005, LNAI 3651, pp. 334–345, 2005.

model based on the vector space model. It utilizes singular value decomposition of the co-occurrence matrix, an operation similar to principal component analysis, to automatically extract major components that contribute to the indexing of documents. It can alleviate the noise and sparseness problems by a dimensionality reduction operation, that is, by removing components with low contributions to the indexing. However, the model lacks firm, theoretical basis [9] and the optimality of inverse document frequency (idf) metric, which is commonly used to weight elements, has yet to be shown [13].

On the contrary, PLSI, proposed by Hofmann [8], is a probabilistic version of LSI, where it is formalized that documents and terms co-occur through a latent variable. PLSI puts no assumptions on distributions of documents or terms, while LSI performs optimal model fitting, assuming that documents and terms are under Gaussian distribution [9]. Moreover, ad hoc weighting such as idf is not necessary for PLSI, although it is for LSI, and it is shown experimentally to outperform the former model [8].

This study applies the PLSI model to the automatic acquisition of synonyms by estimating each word's latent meanings. First, a number of verb-noun pairs were collected from a large corpus using heuristic rules. This operation is based on the assumption that semantically similar words share similar contexts, which was also employed in Hindle's work [7] and has been shown to be considerably plausible. Secondly, the co-occurrences obtained in this way were fit into the PLSI model, and the probability distribution of latent classes was calculated for each noun. Finally, similarity for each pair of nouns can be calculated by measuring the distances or the similarity between two probability distributions using an appropriate distance/similarity measure. We then evaluated and discussed the results using two evaluation criteria, discrimination rates and scores.

This paper also discusses basic techniques when applying PLSI to the automatic acquisition of synonyms. In particular, the following are discussed from methodological and experimental views: (1) choice of distance/similarity measures between probability distributions; (2) filtering words according to their frequencies of occurrence; and (3) multiple executions of PLSI and integration of the results.

This paper is organized as follows: in Sect. 2 a brief explanation of the PLSI model and calculation is provided, and Sect. 3 outlines our approach. Sect. 4 shows the results of comparative experiments and basic techniques. Sect. 5 concludes this paper.

2 The PLSI Model

This section provides a brief explanation of the PLSI model in information retrieval settings. The PLSI model, which is based on the aspect model, assumes that document d and term w co-occur through latent class z, as shown in Fig. 1 (a).

The co-occurrence probability of documents and terms is given by:

$$P(d, w) = P(d) \sum_z P(z|d) P(w|z). \tag{1}$$

Note that this model can be equivalently rewritten as

$$P(d, w) = \sum_z P(z) P(d|z) P(w|z), \tag{2}$$

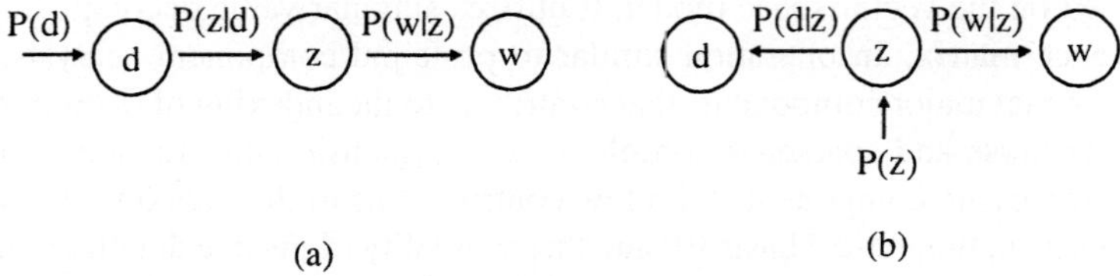

Fig. 1. PLSI model asymmetric (a) and symmetric (b) parameterization

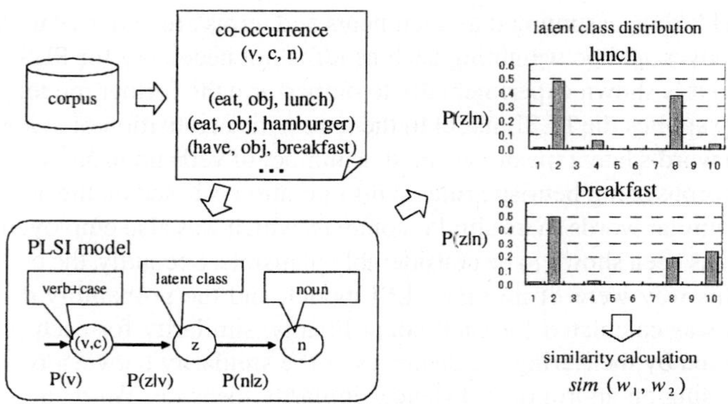

Fig. 2. Outline of our approach

whose graphical model representation is shown in Fig. 1 (b). This is a symmetric parameterization with respect to documents and terms. The latter parameterization is used in the experiment section because of its simple implementation.

Theoretically, probabilities $P(d)$, $P(z|d)$, $P(w|z)$ are determined by maximum likelihood estimation, that is, by maximizing the likelihood of document term co-occurrence:

$$L = \sum_{d,w} N(d,w) \log P(d,w), \tag{3}$$

where $N(d,w)$ is the frequency document d and term w co-occur.

While the co-occurrence of document d and term w in the corpora can be observed directly, the contribution of latent class z cannot be directly seen in this model. For the maximum likelihood estimation of this model, the EM algorithm [1], which is used for the estimation of systems with unobserved (latent) data, is used. The EM algorithm performs the estimation iteratively, similar to the steepest descent method.

3 Approach

The original PLSI model, as described above, deals with co-occurrences of documents and terms, but it can also be applied to verbs and nouns in the corpora. In this way, latent

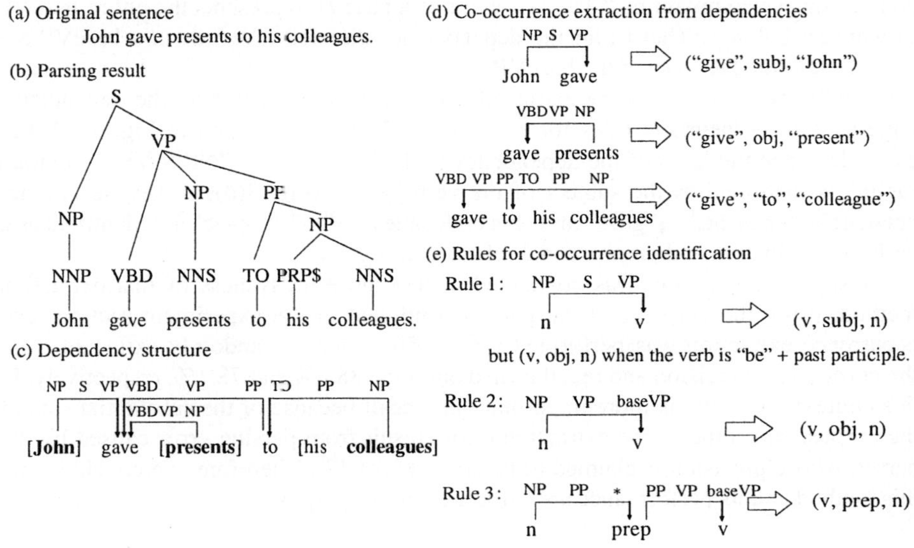

Fig. 3. Co-occurrence extraction

class distribution, which can be interpreted as latent "meaning" corresponding to each noun, is obtained. Semantically similar words are then obtained accordingly, because words with similar meaning have similar distributions. Fig. 2 outlines our approach, and the following subsections provide the details.

3.1 Extraction of Co-occurrence

We adopt triples (v, c, n) extracted from the corpora as co-occurrences fit into the PLSI model, where v, c, and n represent a verb, case/preposition, and a noun, respectively. The relationships between nouns and verbs, expressed by c, include case relation (subject and object) as well as what we call here "prepositional relation," that is, a co-occurrence through a preposition. Take the following sentence for example:

John gave presents to his colleagues.

First, the phrase structure (Fig. 3(b)) is obtained by parsing the original sentence (Fig. 3(a)). The resulting tree is then used to derive the dependency structure (Fig. 3(c)), using Collins' method [4]. Note that dependencies in baseNPs (i.e., noun phrases that do not contain NPs as their child constituents, shown as the groups of words enclosed by square brackets in Fig. 3(c)), are ignored. Also, we introduced baseVPs, that is, sequences of verbs [1], modals (MD), or adverbs (RB), of which the last word must be a verb. BaseVPs simplify the handling of sequences of verbs such as "might not be"

[1] Ones expressed as VB, VBD, VBG, VBN, VBP, and VBZ by the Penn Treebank POS tag set [15].

and "is always complaining." The last word of a baseVP represents the entire baseVP to which it belongs. That is, all the dependencies directed to words in a baseVP are redirected to the last verb of the baseVP.

Finally, co-occurrences are extracted and identified by matching the dependency patterns and the heuristic rules for extraction, which are all listed in Fig. 3 (e). For example, since the label of the dependency "John" →"gave" is "NP S VP", the noun "John" is identified as the subject of the verb "gave" (Fig. 3(d)). Likewise, the dependencies "presents"→"gave" and "his colleagues"→"to"→"gave" are identified as a verb-object relation and prepositional relation through "to".

A simple experiment was conducted to test the effectiveness of this extraction method, using the corpus and the parser mentioned in the experiment section. Co-occurrence extraction was performed for the 50 sentences randomly extracted from the corpus, and precision and recall turned out to be 88.6% and 78.1%, respectively. In this context, precision is more important than recall because of the substantial size of the corpus, and some of the extraction errors result from parsing error caused by the parser, whose precision is claimed to be around 90% [2]. Therefore, we conclude that this method and its performance are sufficient for our purpose.

3.2 Applying PLSI to Extracted Co-occurence Data

While the PLSI model deals with dyadic data (d, w) of document d and term w, the co-occurrences obtained by our method are triples (v, c, n) of a verb v, a case/preposition c, and a noun n. To convert these triples into dyadic data (pairs), verb v and case/preposition c are paired as (v, c) and considered a new "virtual" verb v. This enables it to handle the triples as the co-occurrence (v, n) of verb v and noun n to which the PLSI model becomes applicable. Pairing verb v and case/preposition c also has a benefit that such phrasal verbs as "look for" or "get to" can be naturally treated as a single verb.

After the application of PLSI, we obtain probabilities $P(z), P(v|z)$, and $P(n|z)$. Using Bayes theorem, we then obtain $P(z|n)$, which corresponds to the latent class distribution for each noun. In other words, distribution $P(z|n)$ represents the features of meaning possessed by noun n. Therefore, we can calculate the similarity between nouns n_1 and n_2 by measuring the distance or similarity between the two corresponding distribution, $P(z|n_1)$ and $P(z|n_2)$, using an appropriate measure. The choice of measure affects the synonym acquisition results and experiments on comparison of distance/similarity measures are detailed in Sect. 4.3.

4 Experiments

This section includes the results of comparison experiments and those on the basic PLSI techniques.

4.1 Conditions

The automatic acquisition of synonyms was conducted according to the method described in Sect. 3, using WordBank (190,000 sentences, 5 million words) [3] as a corpus. Charniak's parser [2] was used for parsing and TreeTagger [16] for stemming. A total of 702,879 co-occurrences was extracted by the method described in Sect. 3.1.

When using EM algorithm to implement PLSI, overfitting, which aggravates the performance of the resultant language model, occasionally occurs. We employed the tempered EM (TEM) [8] algorithm, instead of a naive one, to avoid this problem. TEM algorithm is closely related to the deterministic annealing EM (DAEM) algorithm [17], and helps avoid local extrema by introducing inverse temperature β. The parameter was set to $\beta = 0.86$, considering the results of the preliminary experiments.

As the similarity/distance measure and frequency threshold t_f, Skew Divergence ($\alpha = 0.99$) and $t_f = 15$ were employed in the following experiments in response to the results from the experiments described in Sects. 4.3 and 4.5. Also, because estimation by EM algorithm is started from the random parameters and consequently the PLSI results change every time it is executed, the average performance of the three executions was recorded, except in Sect. 4.6.

4.2 Measures for Performance

The following two measures, discrimination rate and scores, were employed for the evaluation of automated synonym acquisition.

Discrimination rate Discrimination rate, originally proposed by Kojima et al. [10], is the rate (percentage) of pairs (w_1, w_2) whose degree of association between two words w_1, w_2 is successfully discriminated by the similarity derived by a method. Kojima et al. dealt with three-level discrimination of a pair of words, that is, highly related (synonyms or nearly synonymous), moderately related (a certain degree of association), and unrelated (irrelevant). However, we omitted the moderately related level and limited the discrimination to two-level: high or none, because of the high cost of preparing a test set that consists of moderately related pairs.

The calculation of discrimination rate follows these steps: first, two test sets, one of which consists of highly related word pairs and the other of unrelated ones, were prepared, as shown in Fig. 4. The similarity between w_1 and w_2 is then calculated for each pair (w_1, w_2) in both test sets via the method under evaluation, and the pair is labeled highly related when similarity exceeds a given threshold t and unrelated when the similarity is lower than t. The number of pairs labeled highly related in the highly related test set and unrelated in the unrelated test set are denoted n_a and n_b, respectively. The discrimination rate is then given by:

$$\frac{1}{2}\left(\frac{n_a}{N_a} + \frac{n_b}{N_b}\right), \tag{4}$$

where N_a and N_b are the numbers of pairs in highly related and unrelated test sets, respectively. Since the discrimination rate changes depending on threshold t, maximum value is adopted by varying t.

We created a highly related test set using the synonyms in WordNet [6]. Pairs in a unrelated test set were prepared by first choosing two words randomly and then confirmed by hand whether the consisting two words are truly irrelevant. The numbers of pairs in the highly and unrelated test sets are 383 and 1,124, respectively.

highly related	unrelated
(answer, reply)	(animal, coffee)
(phone, telephone)	(him, technology)
(sign, signal)	(track, vote)
(concern, worry)	(path, youth)
⋮	⋮

Fig. 4. Test-sets for discrimination rate calculation

Table 5. Procedure for score calculation

base word: computer

rank	synonym	sim	sim^*	rel.(p)	$p \cdot sim^*$
1	equipment	0.6	0.3	B(0.5)	0.15
2	machine	0.4	0.2	A(1.0)	0.20
3	Internet	0.4	0.2	B(0.5)	0.10
4	spray	0.4	0.2	C(0.0)	0.00
5	PC	0.2	0.1	A(1.0)	0.10
total		2.0	1.0		0.55

Scores We propose a score which is similar to precision used for information retrieval evaluation, but different in that it considers the similarity of words. This extension is based on the notion that the more accurately the degrees of similarity are assigned to the results of synonym acquisition, the higher the score values should be.

Described in the following, along with Table 5, is the procedure for score calculation. Table 5 shows the obtained synonyms and their similarity with respect to the base word "computer." Results are obtained by calculating the similarity between the base word and each noun, and ranking all the nouns in descending order of similarity sim. The highest five are used for calculations in this example.

The range of similarity varies based on such factors as the employed distance/similarity measure, which unfavorably affects the score value. To avoid this, the values of similarity are normalized such that their sum equals one, as shown in the column sim^* in Fig. 5. Next, the relevance of each synonym to the base word is checked and evaluated manually, giving them three-level grades: highly related (A), moderately related (B), and unrelated (C), and relevance scores $p = 1.0, 0.5, 0.0$ are assigned for each grade, respectively ("rel.(p)" column in Fig. 5). Finally, each relevance score p is multiplied by corresponding similarity sim^* , and the products (the $p \cdot sim^*$ column in Fig. 5) are totaled and then multiplied by 100 to obtain a score, which is 55 in this case. In actual experiments, thirty words chosen randomly were adopted as base words, and the average of the scores of all base words was employed. Although this example considers only the top five words for simplicity, the top twenty words were used for evaluation in the following experiments.

4.3 Distance/Similarity Measures of Probability Distribution

The choice of distance measure between two latent class distributions $P(z|n_i)$, $P(z|n_j)$ affects the performance of synonym acquisition. Here we focus on the following seven distance/similarity measures and compare their performance.

- Kullback-Leibler (KL) divergence [12]: $KL(p \,||\, q) = \sum_x p(x) \log(p(x)/q(x))$
- Jensen-Shannon (JS) divergence [12]: $JS(p, q) = \{KL(p \,||\, m) + KL(q \,||\, m)\}/2$, $m = (p+q)/2$
- Skew Divergence [11]: $s_\alpha(p \,||\, q) = KL(p \,||\, \alpha q + (1-\alpha)p)$
- Euclidean distance: $\mathrm{euc}(p, q) = ||p - q||$
- L_1 distance: $L_1(p, q) = \sum_x |p(x) - q(x)|$

- Inner product: $p \cdot q = \sum_x p(x)q(x)$
- Cosine: $\cos(p, q) = (p \cdot q)/||p|| \cdot ||q||$

KL divergence is widely used for measuring the distance between two probability distributions. However, it has such disadvantages as asymmetricity and zero frequency problem, that is, if there exists x such that $p(x) \neq 0,\ q(x) = 0$, the distance is not defined. JS divergence, in contrast, is considered the symmetrized KL divergence and has some favorable properties: it is bounded [12] and does not cause the zero frequency problem. Skew Divergence, which has recently been receiving attention, has also solved the zero frequency problem by introducing parameter α and mixing the two distributions. It has shown that Skew Divergence achieves better performance than the other measures [11]. The other measures commonly used for calculation of the similarity/distance of two vectors, namely Euclidean distance, L_1 distance (also called Manhattan Distance), inner product, and cosine, are also included for comparison.

Notice that the first five measures are of distance (the more similar p and q, the lower value), whereas the others, inner product and cosine, are of similarity (the more similar p and q, the higher value). We converted distance measure D to a similarity measure sim by the following expression:

$$sim(p, q) = \exp\{-\lambda D(p, q)\}, \tag{5}$$

inspired by Mochihashi and Matsumoto [13]. Parameter λ was determined in such a way that the average of sim doesn't change with respect to D. Because KL divergence and Skew Divergence are asymmetric, the average of both directions (e.g. for KL divergence, $\frac{1}{2}(KL(p||q) + KL(q||p))$) is employed for the evaluation.

Figure 6 shows the performance (discrimination rate and score) for each measure. It can be seen that Skew Divergence with parameter $\alpha = 0.99$ shows the highest performance of the seven, with a slight difference to JS divergence. These results, along with several studies, also show the superiority of Skew Divergence. In contrast, measures for vectors such as Euclidean distance achieved relatively poor performance compared to those for probability distributions.

4.4 Word Filtering by Frequencies

It may be difficult to estimate the latent class distributions for words with low frequencies because of a lack of sufficient data. These words can be noises that may degregate the results of synonym acquisition. Therefore, we consider removing such words with low frequencies before the execution of PLSI improves the performance. More specifically, we introduced threshold t_f on the frequency, and removed nouns n_i such that $\sum_j \mathrm{tf}_j^i < t_f$ and verbs v_j such that $\sum_i \mathrm{tf}_j^i < t_f$ from the extracted co-occurrences.

The discrimination rate change on varying threshold t_f was measured and shown in Fig. 7 for $d = 100, 200$, and 300. In every case, the rate increases with a moderate increase of t_f, which shows the effectiveness of the removal of low frequency words. We consequently fixed $t_f = 15$ in other experiments, although this value may depend on the corpus size in use.

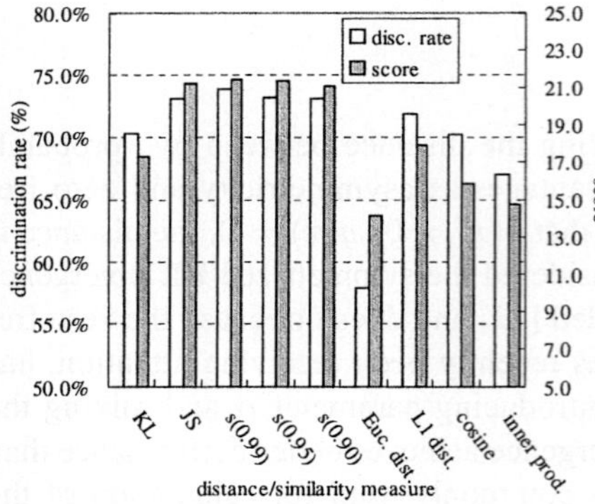

Fig. 6. Performances of distance/similarity measures

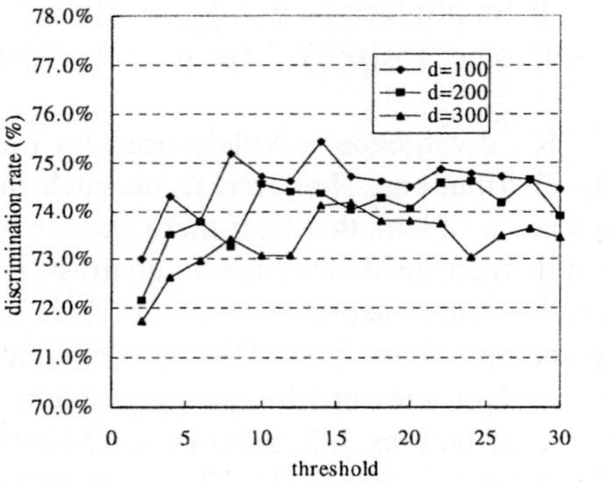

Fig. 7. Discrimination rate measured by varying threshold t_f

4.5 Comparison Experiments with Conventional Methods

Here the performances of PLSI and the following conventional methods are compared. In the following, N and M denote the numbers of nouns and verbs, respectively.

- tf: The number of co-occurrence tf_j^i of noun n_i and verb v_j is used directly for similarity calculation. The corresponding vector $\boldsymbol{n}_i$ to noun n_i is given by:

$$\boldsymbol{n}_i = {}^t[\mathrm{tf}_1^i \ \mathrm{tf}_2^i \ ... \ \mathrm{tf}_M^i]. \tag{6}$$

- tf·idf: The vectors given by tf method are weighted by idf. That is,

$$\boldsymbol{n}_i^* = {}^t[\mathrm{tf}_1^i \cdot \mathrm{idf}_1 \ \ \mathrm{tf}_2^i \cdot \mathrm{idf}_2 \ ... \ \mathrm{tf}_M^i \cdot \mathrm{idf}_M], \tag{7}$$

  where idf_j is given by

$$\mathrm{idf}_j = \frac{\log(N/\mathrm{df}_j)}{\max_k \log(N/\mathrm{df}_k)}, \tag{8}$$

  using df_j, the number of distinct nouns that co-occur with verb v_j.
- tf+LSI: A co-occurrence matrix X is created using vectors $\boldsymbol{n}_i$ defined by tf:

$$X = [\boldsymbol{n}_1 \ \boldsymbol{n}_2 \ ... \ \boldsymbol{n}_N], \tag{9}$$

  to which LSI is applied.
- tf·idf+LSI : A co-occurrence matrix X^* is created using vectors $\boldsymbol{n}_i^*$ defined by tf·idf:

$$X^* = [\boldsymbol{n}_1^* \ \boldsymbol{n}_2^* \ ... \ \boldsymbol{n}_N^*], \tag{10}$$

  to which LSI is applied.
- Hindle's method: The method described in [7] is used. Whereas he deals only with subjects and objects as verb-noun co-occurrence, we used all the kinds of co-occurrence mentioned in Sect. 3.1, including prepositional relations.

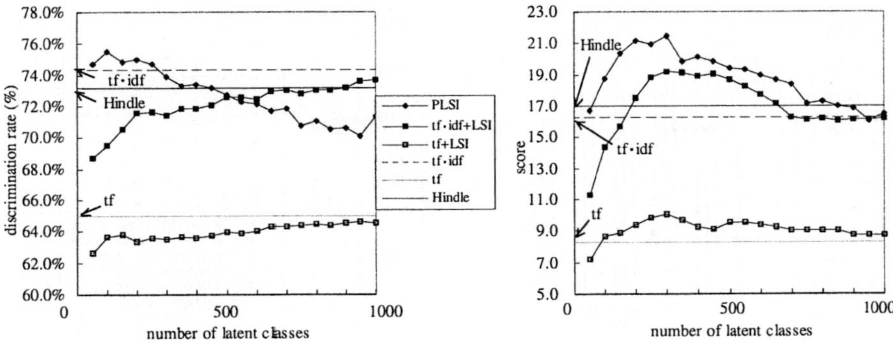

Fig. 8. Performances of PLSI and conventional methods

The values of discrimination rate and scores are calculated for PLSI as well as the methods described above, and the results are shown in Fig. 8. Because the number of latent classes d must be given beforehand for PLSI and LSI, the performances of the latent semantic models are measured varying d from 50 to 1,000 with a step of 50. The cosine measure is used for the similarity calculation of tf, tf·idf, tf+LSI, and tf·idf+LSI.

The results reveal that the highest discrimination rate is achieved by PLSI, with the latent class number of approximately 100, although LSI overtakes with an increase of d. As for the scores, the performance of PLSI stays on top for almost all the values of d, strongly suggesting the superiority of PLSI over the conventional method, especially when d is small, which is often.

The performances of tf and tf+LSI, which are not weighted by idf, are consistently low regardless of the value of d. PLSI and LSI distinctly behave with respect to d, especially in the discrimination rate, whose cause require examination and discussion.

4.6 Integration of PLSI Results

In maximum likelihood estimation by EM algorithm, the initial parameters are set to values chosen randomly, and likelihood is increased by an iterative process. Therefore, the results are generally local extrema, not global, and they vary every execution, which is unfavorable. To solve this problem, we propose to execute PLSI several times and integrate the results to obtain a single one.

To achieve this, PLSI is executed several times for the same co-occurrence data obtained via the method described in Sect. 3.1. This yields N values of similarity $sim_1(n_i, n_j), ..., sim_N(n_i, n_j)$ for each noun pair (n_i, n_j). These values are integrated using one of the following four schemes to obtain a single value of similarity $\overline{sim}(n_i, n_j)$.

- arithmetic mean: $\overline{sim}(n_i, n_j) = \frac{1}{N}\sum_{k=1}^{N} sim_k(n_i, n_j)$
- geometric mean: $\overline{sim}(n_i, n_j) = \sqrt[N]{\prod_{k=1}^{N} sim_k(n_i, n_j)}$
- maximum: $\overline{sim}(n_i, n_j) = \max_k sim_k(n_i, n_j)$
- minimum: $\overline{sim}(n_i, n_j) = \min_k sim_k(n_i, n_j)$

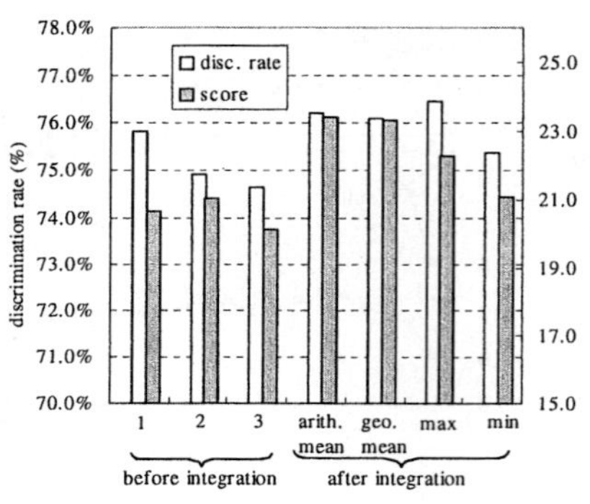

Fig. 9. Integration result for $N = 3$

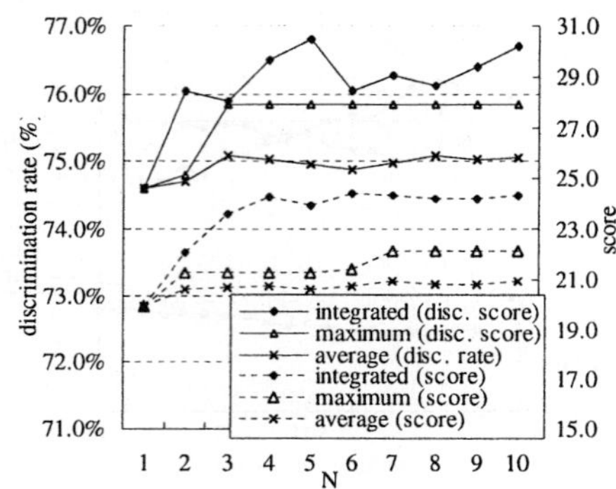

Fig. 10. Integration results varying N

Integration results are shown in Fig. 9, where the three sets of performance on the left are the results of single PLSI executions, i.e., before integration. On the right are the results after integration by the four schemes. It can be observed that integration improves the performance. More specifically, the results after integration are as good or better than any of the previous ones, except when using the minimum as a scheme.

An additional experiment was conducted that varied N from 1 to 10 to confirm that such performance improvement is always achieved by integration. Results are shown in Fig. 10, which includes the average and maximum of the N PLSI results (unintegrated) as well as the performance after integration using arithmetic average as the scheme. The results show that the integration consistently improves the performance for all $2 \leq N \leq 10$. An increase of the integration performance was observed for $N \leq 5$, whereas increases in the average and maximum of the unintegrated results were relatively low. It is also seen that using $N > 5$ has less effect for integration.

5 Conclusion

In this study, automatic synonym acquisition was performed using a latent semantic model PLSI by estimating the latent class distribution for each noun. For this purpose, co-occurrences of verbs and nouns extracted from a large corpus were utilized. Discrimination rates and scores were used to evaluate the current method, and it was found that PLSI outperformed such conventional methods as tf·idf and LSI. These results make PLSI applicable for automatic thesaurus construction. Moreover, the following techniques were found effective: (1) employing Skew Divergence as the distance/similarity measure between probability distributions; (2) removal of words with low frequencies, and (3) multiple executions of PLSI and integration of the results.

As future work, the automatic extraction of the hierarchical relationship of words also plays an important role in constructing thesauri, although only synonym relationships were extracted this time. Many studies have been conducted for this purpose, but extracted hyponymy/hypernymy relations must be integrated in the synonym relations to construct a single thesaurus based on tree structure. The characteristics of the latent class distributions obtained by the current method may also be used for this purpose.

In this study, similarity was calculated only for nouns, but one for verbs can be obtained using an identical method. This can be achieved by pairing noun n and case / preposition c of co-occurrence (v, c, n), not v and c as previously done, and executing PLSI for the dyadic data $(v, (c, n))$. By doing this, the latent class distributions for each verb v, and consequently the similarity between them, are obtained.

Moreover, although this study only deals with verb-noun co-occurrences, other information such as adjective-noun modifications or descriptions in dictionaries may be used and integrated. This will be an effective way to improve the performance of automatically constructed thesauri.

References

1. Bilmes, J. 1997. A gentle tutorial on the EM algorithm and its application to parameter estimation for gaussian mixture and hidden markov models. *Technical Report* ICSI-TR-97-021, International Computer Science Institute (ICSI), Berkeley, CA.
2. Charniak, E. 2000. A maximum-entropy-inspired parser. NAACL 1, 132–139.
3. Collins. 2002. Collins Cobuild Major New Edition CD-ROM. HarperCollins Publishers.
4. Collins, M. 1996. A new statistical parser based on bigram lexical dependencies. *Proc. of 34th ACL*, 184–191.
5. Deerwester, S., et al. 1990. Indexing by Latent Semantic Analysis. *Journal of the American Society for Information Science*, 41(6):391–407.
6. Fellbaum, C. 1998. *WordNet: an electronic lexical database.* MIT Press.
7. Hindle, D. 1990. Noun classification from predicate-argument structures. *Proc. of the 28th Annual Meeting of the ACL*, 268–275.
8. Hofmann, T. 1999. Probabilistic Latent Semantic Indexing. *Proc. of the 22nd International Conference on Research and Development in Information Retrieval (SIGIR '99)*, 50–57.
9. Hofmann, T. 2001. Unsupervised Learning by Probabilistic Latent Semantic Analysis. *Machine Learning*, 42:177–196.
10. Kojima, K., et. al. 2004. Existence and Application of Common Threshold of the Degree of Association. *Proc. of the Forum on Information Technology (FIT2004)* F-003.
11. Lee, L. 2001. On the Effectiveness of the Skew Divergence for Statistical Language Analysis. *Artificial Intelligence and Statistics 2001*, 65–72.
12. Lin, J. 1991. Divergence measures based on the shannon entropy. *IEEE Transactions on Information Theory*, 37(1):140–151.
13. Mochihashi, D., Matsumoto, Y. 2002. Probabilistic Representation of Meanings. *IPSJ SIG-Notes Natural Language*, 2002-NL-147:77–84.
14. The National Institute of Japanese Language. 2004. *Bunruigoihyo.* Dainippontosho.
15. Santorini, B. 1990. Part-of-Speech Tagging Guidelines for the Penn Treebank Project. ftp://ftp.cis.upenn.edu/pub/treebank/doc/tagguide.ps.gz
16. Schmid, H. 1994. Probabilistic Part-of-Speech Tagging Using Decision Trees. *Proc. of the First International Conference on New Methods in Natural Language Processing (NemLap-94)*, 44–49.
17. Ueda, N., Nakano, R. 1998. Deterministic annealing EM algorithm. *Neural Networks*, 11:271–282.

Analysis of an Iterative Algorithm for Term-Based Ontology Alignment

Shisanu Tongchim, Canasai Kruengkrai, Virach Sornlertlamvanich, Prapass Srichaivattana, and Hitoshi Isahara

Thai Computational Linguistics Laboratory,
National Institute of Information and Communications Technology,
112,Paholyothin Road, Klong 1, Klong Luang, Pathumthani 12120, Thailand
{shisanu, canasai, virach, prapass}@tcllab.org, isahara@nict.go.jp

Abstract. This paper analyzes the results of automatic concept alignment between two ontologies. We use an iterative algorithm to perform concept alignment. The algorithm uses the similarity of shared terms in order to find the most appropriate target concept for a particular source concept. The results show that the proposed algorithm not only finds the relation between the target concepts and the source concepts, but the algorithm also shows some flaws in the ontologies. These results can be used to improve the correctness of the ontologies.

1 Introduction

To date, several linguistic ontologies in different languages have been developed independently. The integration of these existing ontologies is useful for many applications. Aligning concepts between ontologies is often done by humans, which is an expensive and time-consuming process. This motivates us to find an automatic method to perform such task. However, the hierarchical structures of ontologies are quite different. The structural inconsistency is a common problem [1]. Developing a practical algorithm that is able to deal with this problem is a challenging issue.

The objective of this research is to investigate an automated technique for ontology alignment. The proposed algorithm links concepts between two ontologies, namely the MMT semantic hierarchy and the EDR concept dictionary. The algorithm finds the most appropriate target concept for a given source concept in the top-down manner. The experimental results show that the algorithm can find reasonable concept mapping between these ontologies. Moreover, the results also suggest that this algorithm is able to detect flaws and inconsistency in the ontologies. These results can be used for developing and improving the ontologies by lexicographers.

The rest of this paper is organized as follows: Section 2 discusses related work. Section 3 provides the description of the proposed algorithm. Section 4 presents experimental results and discussion. Finally, Section 5 concludes our work.

R. Dale et al. (Eds.): IJCNLP 2005, LNAI 3651, pp. 346–356, 2005.

2 Related Work

Daudé *et al.* [2] used a relaxation labeling algorithm – a constraint satisfaction algorithm – to map the verbal, adjectival and adverbial parts between two different WordNet versions, namely WordNet 1.5 and WordNet 1.6. The structural constraints are used by the algorithm to adjust the weights for the connections between WN1.5 and WN1.6. Later, some non-structural constraints are included in order to improve the performance [3].

Asanoma [4] presented an alignment technique between the noun part of WordNet and Goi-Taikei 's Ontology. The proposed technique utilizes sets of Japanese and/or English words and semantic classes from dictionaries in an MT system, namely ALT-J/E.

Chen and Fung [5] proposed an automatic technique to associate the English FrameNet lexical entries to the appropriate Chinese word senses. Each FrameNet lexical entry is linked to Chinese word senses of a Chinese ontology database called HowNet. In the beginning, each FrameNet lexical entry is associated with Chinese word senses whose part-of-speech is the same and Chinese word/phrase is one of the translations. In the second stage of the algorithm, some links are pruned out by analyzing contextual lexical entries from the same semantic frame. In the last stage, some pruned links are recovered if their scores are greater than the calculated threshold value.

Ngai *et al.* [6] also conducted some experiments by using HowNet. They presented a method for performing alignment between HowNet and WordNet. They used a word-vector based method which was adopted from techniques used in machine translation and information retrieval. Recently, Yeh *et al.* [7] constructed a bilingual ontology by aligning Chinese words in HowNet with corresponding synsets defined in WordNet. Their alignment approach utilized the co-occurrence of words in a parallel bilingual corpus.

Khan and Hovy [8] presented an algorithm to combine an Arabic-English dictionary with WordNet. Their algorithm also tries to find links from Arabic words to WordNet first. Then, the algorithm prunes out some links by trying to find a generalization concept.

Doan *et al.* [9] proposed a three steps approach for mapping between ontologies on the semantic web. The first step used machine learning techniques to determine the joint distribution of any concept pair. Then, a user-supplied similarity function is used to compute similarity of concept pairs based on the joint distribution from the first step. In the final step, a relaxation labeling algorithm is used to find the mapping configuration based on the similarity from the previous step.

3 Proposed Algorithm

In this section, we describe an approach for ontology alignment based on term distribution. To alleviate the structural computation problem, we assume that the considered ontology structure has only the hierarchical (or taxonomic) relation. One may simply think of this ontology structure as a general tree, where each node of the tree is equivalent to a concept.

Given two ontologies called the source ontology $\mathcal{T}_s$ and the target ontology $\mathcal{T}_t$, our objective is to align all concepts (or semantic classes) between these two ontologies. Each ontology consists of the concepts, denoted by $\mathcal{C}_1, \ldots, \mathcal{C}_k$. In general, the concepts and their corresponding relations of each ontology can be significantly different due to the theoretical background used in the construction process. However, for the lexical ontologies such as the MMT semantic hierarchy and the EDR concept dictionary, it is possible that the concepts may contain shared members in terms of English words. Thus, we can match the concepts between two ontologies using the similarity of the shared words.

In order to compute the similarity between two concepts, we must also consider their related child concepts. Given a root concept $\mathcal{C}_i$, if we flatten the hierarchy starting from $\mathcal{C}_i$, we obtain a nested cluster, whose largest cluster dominates all sub-clusters. As a result, we can represent the nested cluster with a feature vector $\mathbf{c}_i = (w_1, \ldots, w_{|\mathcal{V}|})^T$, where features are the set of unique English words $\mathcal{V}$ extracted from both ontologies, and w_j is the number of the word j occurring the nested cluster i. We note that a word can occur more than once, since it may be placed in several concepts on the lexical ontology according to its sense.

After concepts are represented with the feature vectors, the similarity between any two concepts can be easily computed. A variety of standard similarity measures exists, such as the *Dice coefficient*, the *Jaccard coefficient*, and the *cosine* similarity [10]. In our work, we require a similarity measure that can reflect the degree of the overlap between two concepts. Thus, the Jaccard coefficient is suitable for our task. Recently, Strehl and Ghosh [11] have proposed a version of the Jaccard coefficient called the *extended Jaccard similarity* that can work with continuous or discrete non-negative features. Let $\|\mathbf{x}_i\|$ be the L_2 norm of a given vector $\mathbf{x}_i$. The extended Jaccard similarity can be calculated as follows:

$$JaccardSim(\mathbf{x}_i, \mathbf{x}_j) = \frac{\mathbf{x}_i^T \mathbf{x}_j}{\|\mathbf{x}_i\|^2 + \|\mathbf{x}_j\|^2 - \mathbf{x}_i^T \mathbf{x}_j} . \quad (1)$$

We now describe an iterative algorithm for term-based ontology alignment. As mentioned earlier, we formulate that the ontology structure is in the form of the general tree. Our algorithm aligns the concepts on the source ontology $\mathcal{T}_s$ to the concepts on the target ontology $\mathcal{T}_t$ by performing search and comparison in the top-down manner.

Given a concept $\mathcal{C}_i \in \mathcal{T}_s$, the algorithm attempts to find the most appropriate concept $\mathcal{B}^* \in \mathcal{T}_t$, which is located on an arbitrary level of the hierarchy. The algorithm starts by constructing the feature vectors for the current root concept on the level l and its child concepts on the level $l+1$. It then calculates the similarity scores between a given source concept and candidate target concepts. If the similarity scores of the child concepts are not greater than the root concept, then the algorithm terminates. Otherwise, it selects a child concept having the maximum score to be the new root concept, and iterates the same searching procedure. Algorithms 1 and 2 outline our ontology alignment process.

Algorithm 1. ONTOLOGYALIGNMENT

input : The source ontology $\mathcal{T}_s$ and the target ontology $\mathcal{T}_t$.
output : The set of the aligned concepts $\mathcal{A}$.

begin
  Set the starting level, $l \leftarrow 0$;
  while $\mathcal{T}_s{}^{\langle l \rangle} \leq \mathcal{T}_s{}^{\langle max \rangle}$ **do**
    Find all child concepts on this level, $\{\mathcal{C}_i\}_{i=1}^{k} \in \mathcal{T}_s{}^{\langle l \rangle}$;
    Flatten $\{\mathcal{C}_i\}_{i=1}^{k}$ and build their corresponding feature vectors, $\{\mathbf{c}_i\}_{i=1}^{k}$;
    For each $\mathbf{c}_i$, find the best matched concepts on $\mathcal{T}_t$,
      $\mathcal{B} \leftarrow$ FINDBESTMATCHED($\mathbf{c}_i$);
      $\mathcal{A} \leftarrow \mathcal{A} \cup \{\mathcal{B}, \mathcal{C}_i\}$;
    Set $l \leftarrow l + 1$;
  end
end

Algorithm 2. FINDBESTMATCHED($\mathbf{c}_i$)

begin
  Set the starting level, $l \leftarrow 0$;
  BestConcept $\leftarrow \mathcal{T}_t$(root concept);
  repeat
    $s_{tmp} \leftarrow JaccardSim(\mathbf{c}_i, BestConcept)$;
    if $\mathcal{T}_t{}^{\langle l \rangle} > \mathcal{T}_t{}^{\langle max \rangle}$ **then**
      return *BestConcept;*
    Find all child concepts on this level, $\{\mathcal{B}\}_{j=1}^{h} \in \mathcal{T}_t{}^{\langle l \rangle}$;
    Flatten $\{\mathcal{B}_j\}_{j=1}^{h}$ and build corresponding feature vectors, $\{\mathbf{b}_j\}_{i=1}^{h}$;
    $s_{j^*} \leftarrow \text{argmax}_j JaccardSim(\mathbf{c}_i, \{\mathbf{b}_j\}_{j=1}^{h})$;
    if $s_{j^*} > s_{tmp}$ **then**
      BestConcept $\leftarrow \mathcal{B}_{j^*}$;
    Set $l \leftarrow l + 1$;
  until *BestConcept does not change*;
  return *BestConcept*;
end

Figure 1 shows a simple example that describes how the algorithm works. It begins with finding the most appropriate concept on $\mathcal{T}_t$ for the root concept $1 \in \mathcal{T}_s$. By flattening the hierarchy starting from given concepts ('1' on $\mathcal{T}_s$, and 'a', 'a-b', 'a-c' for $\mathcal{T}_t$), we can represent them with the feature vectors and measure their similarities. On the first iteration, the child concept 'a-c' obtains the maximum score, so it becomes the new root concept. Since the algorithm cannot find improvement on any child concepts in the second iteration, it stops the loop and the target concept 'a-c' is aligned with the source concept '1'. The algorithm proceeds with the same steps by finding the most appropriate concepts on $\mathcal{T}_t$ for the concepts '1-1' and '1-2'. It finally obtains the resulting concepts 'a-c-f' and 'a-c-g', respectively.

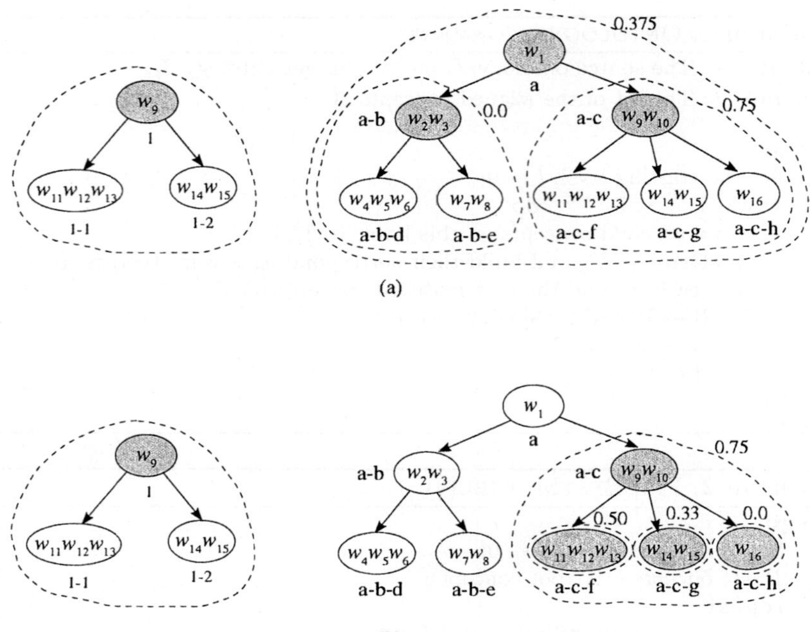

Fig. 1. An example of finding the most appropriate concept on $\mathcal{T}_t$ for the root concept $1 \in \mathcal{T}_s$

4 Experiments and Evaluation

4.1 Data Sets

Two dictionaries are used in our experiments. The first one is the EDR Electronic Dictionary [12]. The second one is the electronic dictionary of Multilingual Machine Translation (MMT) project [13].

The EDR Electronic Dictionary consists of lexical knowledge of Japanese and English divided into several sub-dictionaries (e.g., the word dictionary, the bilingual dictionary, the concept dictionary, and the co-occurrence dictionary) and the EDR corpus. In the revised version (version 1.5), the Japanese word dictionary contains 250,000 words, while the English word dictionary contains 190,000 words. The concept dictionary holds information on the 400,000 concepts that are listed in the word dictionary. Each concept is marked with a unique hexadecimal number.

For the MMT dictionary, we use the Thai-English Bilingual Dictionary that contains around 60,000 lexical entries. The Thai-English Bilingual Dictionary also contains semantic information about the case relations and the word concepts. The word concepts are organized in a manner of semantic hierarchy. Each word concept is a group of lexical entries classified and ordered in a hierarchical level of meanings. The MMT semantic hierarchy is composed of 160 concepts.

In our experiments, we used a portion of the MMT semantic hierarchy and the EDR concept dictionary as the source and the target ontologies, respectively. We considered the 'animal' concept as the root concepts and extracted its related concepts. In the EDR concept dictionary, however, the relations among concepts are very complex and organized in the form of the semantic network. Thus, we pruned some links to transform the network to a tree structure. Starting from the 'animal' concept, there are more than 200 sub-concepts (containing about 7,600 words) in the EDR concept dictionary, and 14 sub-concepts (containing about 400 words) in the MMT semantic hierarchy. It is important to note that these two ontologies are considerably different in terms of the number of concepts and words.

4.2 Experimental Results

The proposed algorithm is used to find appropriate EDR concepts for each one of 14 MMT concepts. The results are shown in Table 1. From the table, there are 6 relations (marked with the symbol '*') that are manually classified as *exact* mapping. This classification is done by inspecting the structures of both ontologies by hand. If the definition of a given MMT concept appears in the EDR concept and the algorithm seems to correctly match the most suitable EDR concept, this mapping will be classified as exact mapping. The remaining 8 MMT concepts, e.g. 'cold-blood' and 'amphibian', are mapped to closely related EDR concepts, although they are not considered to be exact mapping. The EDR concepts found by our algorithm for these 8 MMT concepts are considered to be only the subset of the source concepts. For example, the 'amphibian' concept of the MMT is mapped to the 'toad' concept of the EDR. The analysis in the later section will explain why some MMT concepts are mapped to specific sub-concepts.

Our algorithm works by flattening the hierarchy starting from the considered concept in order to construct a word list represented that concept. The word lists are then compared to match the concepts. In practice, only a portion of word list is intersected. Figure 2 illustrates what happens in general. Note that the EDR concept dictionary is much larger than the MMT semantic

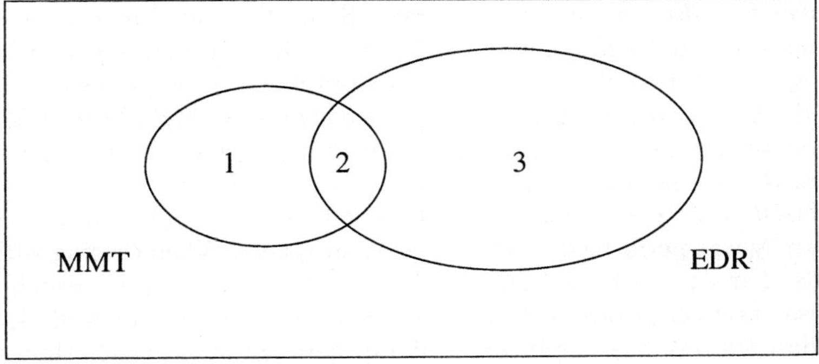

Fig. 2. A schematic of aligned concepts

Table 1. Results of aligned concepts between the MMT and the EDR

MMT concept	EDR concept
vertebrate	vertebrate *
| → warm-blood	mammal
| | → mammal	mammal *
| | → bird	bird *
| → cold-blood	reptile
| → fish	fish *
| → amphibian	toad
| → reptile	reptile *
| → snake	snake *
invertebrate	squid
| → worm	leech
| → insect	hornet
| → shellfish	crab
| → other sea creature	squid

* These concepts are manually classified as *exact* mapping.

hierarchy. Thus, it always has EDR words that are not matched with any MMT words. These words are located in the section 3 of the figure 2. The words in the section 1 are more important since they affects the performance of the algorithm. We assume that the EDR is much larger than the MMT. Therefore, most MMT words should be found in the EDR. The MMT words that cannot found any related EDR words may be results of incorrect spellings, specific words (i.e. only found in Thai language). In case of incorrect spelling and other similar problems, the results of the algorithm can be used to improve the MMT ontology.

By analyzing the results, we can classify the MMT words that cannot find any associated EDR words into 4 categories.

1. *Incorrect spelling or wrong grammar :* Some English words in the MMT semantic hierarchy are simply incorrect spelling, or they are written with wrong grammar. For example, one description of a tiger species is written as 'KIND A TIGER'. Actually, this instance should be 'KIND OF A TIGER'. The algorithm can be used to find words that possible have such a problem. Then, the words can be corrected by lexicographers.
2. *Inconsistency :* The English translation of Thai words in the MMT semantic hierarchy was performed by several lexicographers. When dealing with Thai words that do not have exact English words, lexicographers usually enter phrases as descriptions of these words. Since there is no standard of writing the descriptions, these is incompatibility between descriptions that explain the same concept. For example, the following phrases are used to describe fishes that their English names are not known.

- *Species of fish*
- *A kind of fish*
- *Species of fresh water fish*

3. *Thai specific words :* The words that we used in our experiments are animals. Several animals are region specific species. Therefore, they may not have any associated English words. In this case, some words are translated by using short phrases as English descriptions of these Thai words. Another way to translate these words is to use scientific names of species.

The problems mentioned earlier make it more difficult to match concepts by the algorithm. However, we can use the algorithm to identify where the problems occur. Then, we can use these results to improve the MMT ontology.

The proposed algorithm works in the top-down manner. That is, the algorithm attempts to find the most appropriate concept from the top level, and it will move down if the lower concepts yield better scores. In order to analyze the algorithm, we trace the algorithm during moving through the EDR concepts. The first example of the bird concept alignment is shown in Table 2. The concept alignment of this example is considered to be exact mapping. The first column indicates the level of EDR concepts. The second and third columns indicate the number of MMT words and the number of EDR words after flattening respectively. The fourth column shows the number of intersected words between the MMT and the EDR. From the table, the algorithm moves through the EDR concepts in order to find the most specific concept that still maintains shared terms. This example shows that the algorithm passes through 3 concepts until it stops at the 'bird' concept of the EDR. At the final step, the algorithm decides to trade few shared terms for a more specific EDR concept. Note that the MMT is not completely cleaned. When moving down to the EDR bird concept, three shared terms are lost. Our analysis shows that these terms are bat species. They are all wrongly classified to the MMT bird concept by some lexicographers. Thus, these shared terms will not intersect with any words in the EDR bird concept when the algorithm proceeds to the lower step. This result suggests that our algorithm is quite robust. The algorithm still finds an appropriate concept even the MMT ontology has some flaws.

Another analysis of exact mapping is shown in Table 3. The algorithm moves through 4 concepts until matching the EDR snake concept with the MMT snake concept. In this example, the number of members in the MMT snake concept is quite small. However, the number of shared terms is sufficient to correctly locate the EDR snake concept

Table 2. Concept alignment for the 'bird' concept

Level	MMT words	EDR words	Intersected words
1	67	2112	26
2	67	1288	26
3	67	373	23

Table 3. Concept alignment for the 'snake' concept

Level	MMT words	EDR words	Intersected words
1	17	2112	8
2	17	1288	8
3	17	71	8
4	17	26	8

The third example shown in Table 4 illustrates the case that is considered to be subset mapping. That is, the EDR concept selected by the algorithm is sub-concept of the MMT concept. This case happens several times since the EDR is more fine-grained than the MMT. If the members of MMT concept do not cover enough, the algorithm tends to return only sub-concepts. From the table, the MMT amphibian concept covers only toad and frog species (3 members). Thus, the algorithm moves down to a very specific concept, namely the EDR toad concept. Another example of subset mapping is shown in Table 5. This example also shows that the members of MMT concept do not cover enough. These results can be used to improve the MMT ontology. If the MMT concepts are extended enough, we expect that the correctness of alignment should be improved.

Table 4. Concept alignment for the 'amphibian' concept

Level	MMT words	EDR words	Intersected words
1	3	2112	2
2	3	1288	2
3	3	23	2
4	3	16	2
5	3	2	1

Table 5. Concept alignment for the 'other sea creature' concept

Level	MMT words	EDR words	Intersected words
1	17	2112	5
2	17	746	5
3	17	78	3
4	17	3	2

5 Conclusion

We have proposed an iterative algorithm to deal with the problem of automated ontology alignment. This algorithm works in the top-down manner by using the similarity of the terms from each ontology. We use two dictionaries in our experiment, namely the MMT semantic hierarchy and the EDR concept dictionary.

The results show that the algorithm can find reasonable EDR concepts for given MMT concepts. Moreover, the results also suggest that the algorithm can be used as a tool to locate flaws in the MMT ontology. These results can be used to improve the ontology.

There are several possible extensions to this study. The first one is to examine this algorithm with larger data sets or other ontologies. The second one is to improve and correct the ontologies by using the results from the algorithm. Then, we plan to apply this algorithm to the corrected ontologies, and examine the correctness of the results. The third one is to use structural information of ontologies in order to improve the correctness.

References

1. Ide, N. and Véronis, J.: Machine Readable Dictionaries: What have we learned, where do we go?. Proceedings of the International Workshop on the Future of Lexical Research, Beijing, China (1994) 137–146
2. Daudé, J., Padró, L. and Rigau, G.: Mapping WordNets Using Structural Information. Proceedings of the 38th Annual Meeting of the Association for Computational Linguistics, Hong Kong, (2000)
3. Daudé, J., Padró, L. and Rigau, G.: A Complete WN1.5 to WN1.6 Mapping. Proceedings of NAACL Workshop "WordNet and Other Lexical Resources: Applications, Extensions and Customizations", Pittsburg, PA, United States, (2001)
4. Asanoma, N.: Alignment of Ontologies: WordNet and Goi-Taikei. Proceedings of NAACL Workshop "WordNet and Other Lexical Resources: Applications, Extensions and Customizations", Pittsburg, PA, United States, (2001) 89–94
5. Chen, B. and Fung, P.: Automatic Construction of an English-Chinese Bilingual FrameNet. Proceedings of Human Language Technology conference, Boston, MA (2004) 29–32
6. Ngai, G., Carpuat , M. and Fung, P.: Identifying Concepts Across Languages: A First Step towards a Corpus-based Approach to Automatic Ontology Alignment. Proceedings of the 19th International Conference on Computational Linguistics, Taipei, Taiwan (2002)
7. Yeh, J.-F., Wu, C.-H., Chen, M.-J. and Yu, L.-C.: Automated Alignment and Extraction of a Bilingual Ontology for Cross-Language Domain-Specific Applications. International Journal of Computational Linguistics and Chinese Language Processing. **10** (2005) 35–52
8. Khan, L. and Hovy, E. Improving the Precision of Lexicon-to-Ontology Alignment Algorithms. Proceedings of AMTA/SIG-IL First Workshop on Interlinguas, San Diego, CA (1997)
9. Doan, A., Madhavan, J., Domingos, P., and Halevy, A.: Learning to Map Between Ontologies on the Semantic Web. Proceedings of the 11th international conference on World Wide Web, ACM Press (2002) 662–673
10. Manning, C. D., and Schütze, H.: Foundations of Statistical Natural Language Processing. MIT Press. Cambridge, MA (1999)

11. Strehl, A., Ghosh, J., and Mooney, R. J.: Impact of Similarity Measures on Web-page Clustering. Proceedings of AAAI Workshop on AI for Web Search (2000) 58–64
12. Miyoshi, H., Sugiyama, K., Kobayashi, M. and Ogino, T.: An Overview of the EDR Electronic Dictionary and the Current Status of Its Utilization. Proceedings of the 16th International Conference on Computational Linguistics (1996) 1090–1093
13. CICC: Thai Basic Dictionary. Center of the International Cooperation for Computerization, Technical Report 6-CICC-MT55 (1995)

Finding Taxonomical Relation from an MRD for Thesaurus Extension

SeonHwa Choi and HyukRo Park

Dept. of Computer Science,
Chonnam National University,
300 Youngbong-Dong, Puk-Ku Gwangju, 500-757, Korea
csh123@dreamwiz.com, hyukro@chonnam.ac.kr

Abstract. Building a thesaurus is very costly and time-consuming task. To alleviate this problem, this paper proposes a new method for extending a thesaurus by adding taxonomic information automatically extracted from an MRD. The proposed method adopts a machine learning algorithm in acquiring rules for identifying a taxonomic relationship to minimize human-intervention. The accuracy of our method in identifying hypernyms of a noun is 89.7%, and it shows that the proposed method can be successfully applied to the problem of extending a thesaurus.

1 Introduction

As the natural language processing (NLP) systems became large and applied to wide variety of application domains, the need for a broad-coverage lexical knowledge-base has increased more than ever before. A thesaurus, as one of these lexical knowledge-bases, mainly represents a taxonomic relationship between nouns. However, because building broad-coverage thesauri is a very costly and time-consuming job, they are not readily available and often too general to be applied to a specific domain.

The work presented here is an attempt to alleviate this problem by devising a new method for extending a thesaurus automatically using taxonomic information extracted from a machine readable dictionary (MRD).

Most of the previous approaches for extracting hypernyms of a noun from the definition in an MRD rely on the lexico-syntactic patterns compiled by human experts. Not only these methods require high cost for compiling lexico-syntactic patterns but also it is very difficult for human experts to compile a set of lexical-syntactic patterns with a broad-coverage because, in natural languages, there are various different expressions which represent the same concept. Accordingly the applicable scope of a set of lexico-syntactic patterns compiled by human is very limited.

To overcome the drawbacks of human-compiled lexico-syntactic patterns, we use part-of-speech (POS) patterns only and try to induce these patterns automatically using a small bootstrapping thesaurus and machine learning methods.

The rest of the paper is organized as follows. We introduce the related works in section 2. Section 3 deals with the problem of features selection. In section 4, our problem is formally defined as a machine learning method and discuss implementation details. Section 5 is devoted to experimenal result. Finally, we come to the conclusion of this paper in section 6.

R. Dale et al. (Eds.): IJCNLP 2005, LNAI 3651, pp. 357 – 365, 2005.

2 Related work

[3] introduced a method for the automatic acquisition of the hyponymy lexical relation from unrestricted text, and gave several examples of lexico-syntactic patterns for hyponymy that can be used to detect these relationships including those used here, along with an algorithm for identifying new patterns. Hearst's approach is complementary to statistically based approaches that find semantic relations between terms, in that hers requires a single specially expressed instance of a relation while the others require a statistically significant number of generally expressed relations. The hyponym-hypernym pairs found by Hearst's algorithm include some that she describes as "context and point-of-view dependent", such as "Washington/nationalist" and "aircraft/target". [4] was somewhat less sensitive to this kind of problem since only the most common hypernym of an entire cluster of nouns is reported, so much of the noise is filtered. [3] tried to discover new patterns for hyponymy by hand, nevertheless it is a costly and time-consuming job. In the case of [3] and [4], since the hierarchy was learned from text, it got to be domain-specific different from a general-purpose resource such as WordNet.

[2] proposed a method that combines a set of unsupervised algorithms in order to accurately build large taxonomies from any MRD, and a system that 1)performs fully automatic extraction of a taxonomic link from MRD entries and 2) ranks the extracted relations in a way that selective manual refinement is allowed. In this project, they introduced the idea of the hyponym-hypernym relationship appears between the entry word and the genus term. Thus, usually a dictionary definition is written to employ a genus term combined with differentia which distinguishes the word being defined from other words with the same genus term. They found the genus term by simple heuristic defined using several examples of lexico-syntactic patterns for hyponymy.

[1] presented the method to extract semantic information from standard dictionary definitions. Their automated mechanism for finding the genus terms is based on the observation that the genus term from verb and noun definitions is typically the head of the defining phrase. The syntax of the verb phrase used in verb definitions makes it possible to locate its head with a simple heuristic: the head is the single verb following the word *to*. He asserted that heads are bounded on the left and right by specific lexical defined by human intuition, and the substring after eliminating boundary words from definitions is regarded as a head.

By the similar idea to [2], [10] introduced six kinds of rule extracting a hypernym from Korean MRD according to a structure of a dictionary definition. In this work, Moon proposed that only a subset of the possible instances of the hypernym relation will appear in a particular form, and she divides a definition sentence into a head term combined with differentia and a functional term. For extracting a hypernym, Moon analyzed a definition of a noun by word list and the position of words, and then searched a pattern coinciding with the lexico-syntactic patterns made by human intuition in the definition of any noun, and then extracted a hypernym using an appropriate rule among 6 rules. For example, rule 2 states that if a word X occurs in front of a lexical pattern "*leul bu-leu-deon i-leum* (*the name to call*)",then X is extracted as a hypernym of the entry word.

Several approaches[11][12][13] have been researched for building a semantic hierarchy of Korean nouns adopting the method of [2].

3 Features for Hypernym Identification

Machine learning approaches require an example to be represented as a feature vector. How an example is represented or what features are used to represent the example has profound impact on the performance of the machine learning algorithms. This section deals with the problems of feature selection with respect to characteristics of Korean for successful identification of hypernyms.

Location of a word. In Korean, a head word usually appears after its modifying words. Therefore a head word has tendency to be located at the end of a sentence. In the definition sentences in a Korean MRD, this tendency becomes much stronger. In the training examples, we found that 11% of the hypernyms appeared at the start, 81% of them appeared at the end and 7% appeared at the middle of a definition sentence. Thus, the location of a noun in a definition sentences is an important feature for determining whether the word is a hypernym or not.

POS of a function word attached to a noun. Korean is an agglutinative language in which a word-phrase is generally a composition of a content word and some number of function words. A function word denotes the grammatical relationship between word-phrases, while a content word contains the central meaning of the word-phrase.

In the definition sentences, the function words which attached to hypernyms are confined to a small number of POSs. For example, nominalization endings, objective case postpositions come frequently after hypernyms but dative postpositions or locative postpositions never appear after hypernyms. A functional word is appropriate feature for identifying hypernyms.

Context of a noun. The context in which a word appears is valuable information and a wide variety of applications such as word clustering or word sense disambiguation make use of it. Like in many other applications, context of a noun is important in deciding hyperhyms too because hypernyms mainly appear in some limited context.

Although lexico-syntactic patterns can represent more specific contexts, building set of lexco-syntactic patterns requires enormous training data. So we confined ourselves only to syntactic patterns in which hypernyms appear.

We limited the context of a noun to be 4 word-phrases appearing around the noun. Because the relations between word-phrases are represented by the function words of these word-phrases, the context of a noun includes only POSs of the function words of the neighboring word-phrases. When a word-phrase has more than a functional morpheme, a representative functional morpheme is selected by an algorithm proposed by [8].

When a noun appears at the start or at the end of a sentence, it does not have right or left context respectively. In this case, two treatments are possible. The simplest approach is to treat the missing context as don't care terms. On the other hand, we could extend the range of available context to compensate the missing context. For example, the context of a noun at the start of a sentence includes 4 POSs of function words in its right-side neighboring word-phrases.

4 Learning Classification Rules

Decision tree learning is one of the most widely used and a practical methods for inductive inference such as ID3, ASSISTANT, and C4.5[14]. Because decision tree learning is a method for approximating discrete-valued functions that is robust to noisy data, it has therefore been applied to various classification problems successfully.

Our problem is to determine for each noun in definition sentences of a word whether it is a hypernym of the word or not. Thus our problem can be modeled as two-category classification problem. This observation leads us to use a decision tree learning algorithm C4.5.

Our learning problem can be formally defined as followings:

- Task T : determining whether a noun is a hypernym of an entry word or not .
- Performance measure P : percentage of nouns correctly classified.
- Training examples E : a set of nouns appearing in the definition sentences of the MRD with their feature vectors and target values.

To collect training examples, we used a Korean MRD provided by Korean TermBank Project[15] and a Korean thesaurus compiled by Electronic Communication Research Institute. The dictionary contains approximately 220,000 nouns with their definition sentences while the thesaurus has approximately 120,000 nouns and taxonomy relations between them. The fact that 46% of nouns in the dictionary are missing from the thesaurus shows that it is necessary to extend a thesaurus using an MRD.

Using the thesaurus and the MRD, we found that 107,000 nouns in the thesaurus have their hypernyms in the definition sentences in the MRD. We used 70% of these nouns as training data and the remaining 30% of them as evaluation data.

For each training pair of hypernym/hyponym nouns, we build a triple in the form of (hyponym definition-sentences hypernym) as follows.

<u>ga-gyeong</u>	[a-leum-da-un gyeong-chi *(a beautiful scene)*]	<u>gyeong-chi</u>
hyponym	definition sentence	hypernym

Morphological analysis and Part-Of-Speech tagging are applied to the definition sentences. After that, each noun appearing in the definition sentences is converted into a feature vector using features mentioned in section 3 along with a target value (i.e. whether this noun is a hypernym of the entry word or not).

Table 1 shows some of the training examples. In this table, the attribute *IsHypernym* which can have a value either Y or N is a target value for given noun. Hence the purpose of learning is to build a classifier which will predict this value for a noun unseen from the training examples.

In Table 1, *Location* denotes the location of a noun in a definition sentence. 0 indicates that the noun appears at the start of the sentence, 1 denotes at the middle of the sentence, and 2 denotes at the end of a sentence respectively. *FW of a hypernym* is the POS of a function word attachted to the noun and *context1,...,context4* denote the POSs of function words appearing to the right/left of the noun. "*" denotes a don't care condition. The meanings of POS tags are list in Appendix A.

Table 1. Some of training examples

Noun	*Location*	*FW of a hypernym*	*context1*	*context2*	*context3*	*context4*	*IsHypernym*
N1	1	jc	ecx	exm	nq	*	Y
N2	2	*	exm	ecx	jc	nq	Y
N3	2	*	exm	jc	nca	exm	Y
N4	1	exm	jc	jc	ecx	m	N
N5	1	jc	jc	ecx	m	jca	N
N6	1	jc	ecx	m	jca	exm	Y
N7	2	*	exm	exm	jca	exm	Y
N8	1	*	nc	jca	exm	jc	N
N9	1	jca	nc	nc	nc	jc	Y
N10	2	exn	a	nca	jc	nca	Y
..	..	..	..	..	..	..	..

Fig. 1 shows a part of decision tree learned by C4.5 algorithm. From this tree, we can easily find that the most discriminating attribute is *Location* while the least one is *Context*.

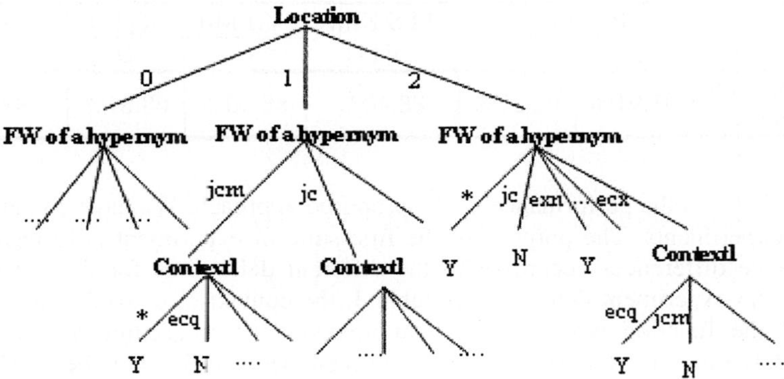

Fig. 1. A learned decision tree for task T

5 Experiment

To evaluate the proposed method, we measure classification accuracy as well as precision, recall, and F-measure which are defined as followings respectively.

$$classification\ accuracy = \frac{a+d}{a+b+c+d}$$

$$precision = \frac{a}{a+b}$$

$$recall = \frac{a}{a+c}$$

$$F-Measure = \frac{2 * precision * recall}{precision + recall}$$

Table 2. Contingency table for evaluating a binary classifier

	Yes is correct	No is correct
Yes was assigned	a	b
No was assigned	c	d

Table 3. Evaluation result

	Classification accuracy	Precesion	Recall	F-Measure
A	91.91%	95.62%	92.55%	94.06%
B	92.37%	93.67%	95.23%	94.44%
C	89.75%	83.83%	89.92%	86.20%

Table 4. Evaluation result

	Proposed		M.S.Kim 95[11]	Y.J.Moon 96[10]		Y.M.Choi 98[13]
	A	B		C	D	
Classification Accuracy	91.91%	92.37%	88.40%	88.40%	68.81%	89.40%

Table 3 shows the performance of the proposed approach. We have conducted two suite of experiments. The purpose of the first suite of experiment is to measure the performance differences according to the different definitions for the context of a word. In the experiment denoted A in table 3, the context of a word is defined as 4 POSs of the function words, 2 of them immediately proceeding and 2 of them immediately following the word. In the experiment denoted B, when the word appears at the beginning of a sentence or at the end of a sentence, we used only right or left context of the word respectively. Our experiement shows that the performance of B is slightly better than that of A.

In the second suite of experiment, we measure the performance of our system for nouns which do not appear in the thesaurus. This performance can give us a figure about how well our system can be applied to the problem of extending a thesaurus. The result is shown in Table 3 in the row labeled with C. As we expected, the performance is droped slightly, but the difference is very small. This fact convince us that the proposed method can be successfully applied to the problem of extending a thesuarus.

Table 4 compares the classification accuracy of the proposed method with those of the previous works. Our method outperforms the performance of the previous works reported in the literature[10] by 3.51%.

Because the performance of the previous works are measured with small data in a restricted domain, we reimplemented one of the those previous works[10] to compare the performances using same data. The result is shown in Table 4 under the column marked D. Column C is the performance of the [10] reported in the literature. This result shows that as the heuristic rules in [10] are dependent on lexical information, if the document collection is changed or the application domain is changed, the performance of the method degrades seriously.

6 Conclusion

To extend a thesaurus, it is necessary to identify hypernyms of a noun. There have been several works to build taxonomy of nouns from an MRD. However, most of them relied on the lexico-syntactic patterns compiled by human experts.

This paper has proposed a new method for extending a thesaurus by adding a taxonomic relationship extracted from an MRD. The taxonomic relationship is identified using nouns appearing in the definition sentences of a noun in the MRD and syntactic pattern rules compiled by a machine learning algorithm.

Our experiment shows that the classification accuracy of the proposed method is 89.7% for nouns not appearing in the thesaurus.

Throughout our research, we have found that machine learning approaches to the problems of identifying hypernyms from an MRD could be a competitive alternative to the methods using human-compiled lexico-syntactic patterns, and such taxonomy automatically extracted from an MRD can effectively supplement an existing thesaurus.

References

1. Martin S. Chodorow, Roy J. Byrd, George E. Heidorn. : Extracting Semantic Hierarchies From A Large On-Line Dictionary. In Proceedings of the 23rd Conference of the Association for Computational Linguistics (1985)
2. Rigau G., Rodriguez H., Agirre E. : Building Accurate Semantic Taxonomies from Mololingual MRDs. In Proceedings of the 36th Conference of the Association for Computational Linguistics (1998)
3. Marti A. Hearst. : Automatic acquisition of hyonyms from large text corpora. In Proceedings of the Fourteenth International Conference on Computational Linguistics (1992)
4. Sharon A. Caraballo. : Automatic construction of a hypernym-labled noun hierarchy from text. In Proceedings of the 37th Conference of the Association for Computational Linguistics (1999).
5. Fernando Pereira, Naftali Thishby, Lillian Lee. : Distributional clustering of English words. In Proceedings of the 31th Conference of the Association for Computational Linguistics (1993)
6. Brian Roark, Eugen Charniak. : Noun-phrase co-occurrence statistics for semi-automatic semantic lexicon construction. In Proceedings of the 36th Conference of the Association for Computational Linguistics and 17th International Conference on Computational Linguistics (1998)
7. Tom M. Mitchell.: Machine Learning. Carnegie Mellon University. McGraw-Hill (1997).
8. SeonHwa Choi, HyukRo Park. : A New Method for Inducing Korean Dependency Grammars reflecting the Characteristics of Korean Dependency Relations. In Proceedings of the 3rd Conterence on East-Asian Language Processing and Internet Information Technology (2003)
9. YooJin Moon, YeongTak Kim. :The Automatic Extraction of Hypernym in Korean. In Preceedings of Korea Information Science Society Vol. 21, NO. 2 (1994) 613-616

10. YooJin Moon. : The Design and Implementation of WordNet for Korean Nouns. In Proceedings of Korea Information Science Society (1996)
11. MinSoo Kim, TaeYeon Kim, BongNam Noh. : The Automatic Extraction of Hypernyms and the Development of WordNet Prototype for Korean Nouns using Koran MRD. In Proceedings of Korea Information Processing Society (1995)
12. PyongOk Jo, MiJeong An, CheolYung Ock, SooDong Lee. : A Semantic Hierarchy of Korean Nouns using the Definitions of Words in a Dictionary. In Proceedings of Korea Cognition Society (1999)
13. YuMi Choi and SaKong Chul. : Development of the Algorithm for the Automatic Extraction of Broad Term. In Proceedings of Korea Information Management Society (1998) 227-230
14. Quinlan J. R.: C4.5: Programs for Machine Learning. San Mateo, CA: Morgan Kaufman (1993) http://www.rulequest.com/Personal/
15. KORTERM. : KAIST language resources http://www.korterm.or.kr/

Appendix A. POS Tag Set

Table 5. POS tag set

CATEGORY		TAG	DESCRIPTION
noun	common	nn	common noun
		nca	active common noun
		ncs	statove common noun
		nct	time common noun
	proper	nq	proper noun
	bound	nb	bound noun
		nbu	unit bound noun
	numeral	nn	numeral
	pronoun	npp	personal pronoun
		npd	demonstrative pronoun
predicate	verb	pv	verb
	adjective	pa	adjective
		pad	demonstrative adjective
	auxiliary	px	auxiliary verb
modification	adnoun	m	adnoun
		md	demonstrative adnoun
		mn	numeral adnoun
	adverb	a	general adverb
		ajs	sentence conjunctive adverb
		ajw	word conjunctive adverb
		ad	demonstrative adverb
independence	interjection	ii	interjection
particle	case	jc	case
		jca	adverbial case particle
		jcm	adnominal case particle
		jj	conjunctive case particle
		jcv	vocative case particle

CATEGORY		TAG	DESCRIPTION
	auxiliary	jx	auxiliary
	predicative	jcp	predicative particle
ending	prefinal	efp	prefinal ending
	conjunctive	ecq ecs ecx	coordinate conjunctive ending subordinate conjunctive ending auxiliary conjunctive ending
	transform	exn exm exa	nominalizing ending adnominalizing ending adverbalizing ending
	final	ef	final ending
affix	prefix	xf	prefix
	suffix	xn xpv xpa	suffix verb-derivational suffix adjective-derivational suffix

Relation Extraction Using Support Vector Machine

Gumwon Hong

University of Michigan,
Ann Arbor, MI 48109
gwhong@umich.edu

Abstract. This paper presents a supervised approach for relation extraction. We apply Support Vector Machines to detect and classify the relations in Automatic Content Extraction (ACE) corpus. We use a set of features including lexical tokens, syntactic structures, and semantic entity types for relation detection and classification problem. Besides these linguistic features, we successfully utilize the distance between two entities to improve the performance. In relation detection, we filter out the negative relation candidates using entity distance threshold. In relation classification, we use the entity distance as a feature for Support Vector Classifier. The system is evaluated in terms of recall, precision, and F-measure, and errors of the system are analyzed with proposed solution.

1 Introduction

The goal of Information Extraction (IE) is to pull out pieces of information that are salient to the user's need from large volume of text. With the dramatic increase of World Wide Web, there has been growing interest in extracting relevant information from large textual documents. The IE tasks may vary in detail and reliability, but two subtasks are very common and closely related: named entity recognition and relation extraction. Named entity recognition identifies named objects of interest such as person, organizations or locations. Relation extraction involves the identification of appropriate relations among these entities. Examples of the specific relations are *employee-of* and *parent-of*. *Employee-of* relation holds between a particular person and a certain organization and *parent-of* holds between a father and his child. According to Message Understanding Conferences (MUC), while named entities can be extracted with 90% or more in F measure with a state of the art system, relation extraction was not so successful [8].

In this paper we propose a supervised machine learning approach for relation extraction. The goal of this paper is to investigate an empirical method to find out useful features and experimental procedure to increase the performance of relation extraction. We divide the extraction task into two individual subtasks: relation detection and relation classification. Relation detection is involved in identifying from every pair of entities positive examples of relations which can fall into one of many relation categories. In relation classification, we assign a specific class to each detected relation. To each task, we apply distinct linguistic features ranging from lexical tokens to syntactic structures as well as the semantic type information of the entities. We also applied the distance between two entities to make the detection problem easier and to increase the

R. Dale et al. (Eds.): IJCNLP 2005, LNAI 3651, pp. 366 – 377, 2005.

performance of both the relation detection and classification. We apply Support Vector Machines (SVMs) partly because it represents the state of the art performance for many classification tasks [3]. As we will discuss in section 3 about features, we are working on very high dimensional feature space, and this often leads to overfitting. Thus, the main reason to use SVMs is that this learning algorithm has a robust rationale for avoiding overfitting [11].

This paper is structured in the following manner. In section 2, we survey the previous work on relation extraction with emphasis on supervised machine learning approaches. In section 3, the problem formalization, the description of dataset and the feature extraction methods will be discussed. In section 4, we conduct a performance evaluation of the proposed approach and error analysis on ACE dataset. Finally, in section 5, a conclusion and discussion of future work will be followed.

2 Related Work

Relation extraction was formulated as part of Message Understanding Conferences (MUC) [8], which has focused on a series of information extraction tasks, including analyzing free text, recognizing named entities, and identifying relations of a specified type. Work on relation extraction over the last two decades has progressed from linguistically unsophisticated models to the adaptation of NLP techniques that use shallow parsers or full parsers and complicated machine learning methods.

[7] addressed the relation extraction problem by extending the statistical parsing model which simultaneously recovers syntactic structures, named entities, and relations. They first annotated sentences for entities, descriptors, coreference links and relation links, and trained the sentences from Penn Treebank. Then they applied to new training sentences and enhanced the parse trees to include the IE information. Finally they re-retrained the parser on newly enriched training data.

More recently, [12] introduced the kernel methods to extract relations from 200 news articles from different publications. The kernels are defined over shallow parse representations of text and computed through a dynamic programming fashion. They generated relation examples from shallow parses for two relations: person-affiliation and organization-location. Performance of the kernel methods was compared with feature-based methods and it showed that kernels have promising performance.

[4] extended work in [12] to estimate kernel functions between augmented dependency trees. Their experiment has two steps. Relations were first detected and then classified in cascading manner. However, the recall was relatively low because many positive examples of relations were dropped during detection phase. Detecting relations is hard job for kernel methods because, in detection, all negative examples are heterogeneous and it is difficult to use similarity function.

[13] proposed weakly supervised learning algorithm for classifying relations in ACE dataset. He introduced feature extraction methods for his supervised approach as well as a bootstrapping algorithm using random feature projection (called BootProject) on top of SVMs. He compared BootProject with supervised approach, and showed that BootProject algorithm reduced much work needed for labeling training data without decreasing the performance.

Our approach to relation extraction adapts some feature extraction methods from [13] but differs from [13] in two important aspects. First, instead of only classifying relations by assuming all candidate relations are detected, we perform relation detection before classifying relations by regarding every pair of entities in a sentence as a target of classification. Second, we used total 7652 (6140 for training and 1512 for development testing) relation examples in ACE dataset, but in [13] only 4238 relations were used for training and 1022 for testing. We increase the performance by using more training data and reducing errors in data processing stage.

3 Data Processing

3.1 Problem Definition

Our task is to extract relations from unstructured natural language text. Because we determine the relationship for every pair of entities in a sentence, our task is formalized with a standard classification problem as follows:

$$(e1, e2, s) \rightarrow r$$

where *e1* and *e2* are two entities existing in sentence *s*, and *r* is a label of the relation. Every pair of entities in a sentence can be a relation or not, so we call the triple *(e1, e2, s)* a relation candidate. With the possible set of values of *r*, there can be at least three tasks.

1. **Detection only:** For each relation candidate, we predict whether it constitutes an actual relation or not. In this task, a label *r* can be either +1 (two entities are related) or -1 (not related).
2. **Combined detection and classification:** For each relation candidate, we perform N+1 way classification, where N is the number of relation types. Five relation types are specified in next subsection. The additional class is -1 (two entities are not related).
3. **Classification only:** For each relation, we perform N way classification. In this task, we assume that all relation candidates in test data are manually labeled with N+1 way classification. We only consider the classifier's performance on the N relation types.

We use a supervised machine learning technique, specifically Support Vector Machine classifiers, and we empirically evaluate the performance in terms of recall, precision and F measure. To make the problem more precisely, we constrain the task of relation extraction with following assumptions:

1. Entities should be tagged beforehand so that all information regarding entities is available when relations are extracted.
2. Relations are binary, i.e., every relation takes exactly two primary arguments.
3. The two arguments of a relation, i.e., an entity pair, should explicitly occur within a sentence.
4. Evaluation is performed over five limited types of relations as in Table 1.

A relation is basically an ordered pair, thus "**Sam** was flown to **Canada**" contains the relation AT(Sam, Canada) but not AT(Canada, Sam). However, 7 relations in NEAR (relative location) and SOCIAL (associate, other-personal, other-professional, other-relative, sibling, and spouse) types are symmetric. For example, the sentences such as "**Bill** is the neighbor of **Sarah**." and "**The park** is two blocks from **Walnut Street**" do not distinguish the order of entities.

Table 1. Relation types and their subtypes in ACE 2 corpus

AT	BASED-IN, LOCATED, RESIDENCE
NEAR	RELATIVE-LOCATION
PART	OTHER, PART-OF, SUBSDIARY
ROLE	AFILIATE-PARTNER, CITIZEN-OF, CLIENT, FOUNDER, GENERAL-STAFF, MANAGEMENT, MEMBER, OTHER, OWNER
SOCIAL	ASSOCIATE, GRANDPARENT, OTHER-PERSONAL, OTHER-PROFESSIONAL, OTHER-RELATIVE, PARENT, SIBLING, SPOUSE

3.2 Data Set

We extract relations from the Automatic Content Extraction (ACE) corpus, specifically version 1.0 of the ACE 2 corpus, provided by the National Institute for Standards and Technology (NIST). ACE corpora consist of 519 annotated text documents assembled from a variety of sources selected from broadcast news programs, newspapers, and newswire reports [1].

According to the scope of the LDC ACE program 1, current research in information extraction has three main objectives: Entity Detection and Tracking (EDT), Relation Detection and Characterization (RDC), and Event Detection and Characterization (EDC). This paper focuses on the second sub-problem, RDC. For example, we want to determine whether a particular person is at certain location, based on the contextual evidence. According to the RDC guideline version 3.6, Entities are limited to 5 types (PERSON, ORGANIZATION, GEO-POLITICAL ENTITY (GPE), LOCATION, and FACILITY), and relations are also classified into 5 types:

Role: Role relations represent an affiliation between a Person entity and an Organization, Facility, or GPE entity.
Part: Part relations represent part-whole relationships between Organization, Facility and GPE entities.
At: At relations represent that a Person, Organization, GPE, or Facility entity is located at a Location entity.
Near: Near relations represent the fact that a Person, Organization, GPE or Facility entity is near (but not necessarily "at") a Location or GPE entity.
Social: Social relations represent personal and professional affiliations between Person entities.

Table 1 lists the 5 major relation types and their subtypes. The numbers in the bottom row indicate the number of instances in training data and development testing data. We do not classify the 24 subtypes of relations due to the sparse instances of many subtypes.

Table 2. Breakdown of the ACE dataset (#f and #r means number of files and number of relations respectively)

Training data		Held-out data		Test data	
#f	# r	#f	# r	#f	# r
325	4628	97	1512	97	1512

Table 2 shows the breakdown of the ACE dataset for our task. Training data takes about 60% of all ACE corpora, and each held-out data and test data contains about 20% of the whole distribution in the number of files as well as in the number of relations.[1]

3.3 Data Processing

We start with entity marked data and the first step is to detect the sentence boundary using the sentence segmenter provided by DUC competition[2]. Performance of the sentence segmentater is crucial for relation detection because the number of entity pairs combinatorially increases as a sentence grows in size. The original DUC segmenter fails to detect sentence boundary if the last word of a sentence is a named entity and annotated with brackets, i.e., '<' and '>'. We modified the DUC segmenter by adding simple rules where we mark sentence boundary if every bracket is followed by '?', '!', or '.'. At this step, we drop the sentences if the sentence has less than two entities.

Sentence parsing is then performed using Charniak parser [6] on these target sentences in order to obtain the necessary linguistic information. To facilitate the feature extraction, parse trees are converted into chunklink format [2]. Chunklink format contains the same information as the original parse tree, but it provides for each word the chunk to which it belongs, its grammatical function, grammatical structure hierarchy, and trace information.

3.4 Features

We are ready to introduce our feature sets. The following features include lexical tokens, part of speech, syntactic features, semantic entity types, and the distance between two entities (we will say "entity distance" to refer to distance between two entities in the remaining part of this paper). These features are selectively used for three tasks defined in section 3.1.

1. Words. Lexical token of both entity mentions[3] *as well as all the words between them. If two or more words constitute an entity, each individual word in an entity is a separate feature.*

2. Part of speech. Part of speech corresponding to each word feature described above.

---

[1] Training data and held-out data together are called "train", and test data is called "devtest" in the ACE distribution.

[2] http://duc.nist.gov/past_duc/duc2003/software/

[3] Entities are objects and they have a group of mentions, and the mentions are textual references to the objects.

3. Entity type. Entities have one of five types (person, location, organization, geo-political entity, or facility).

4. Entity mention type. An entity mention can be named, nominal, or pronominal. Entity mention type is also called the level of a mention.

5. Chunk tag. A word is inside (I), outside (O) or in the beginning (B) of a chunk. A chunk here stands for a standard phrase. Thus, the word "George" at the beginning of NP chunk "George Bush" has B-NP tag. Similarly, the word "named" has I-VP tag in VP chunk "was named".

6. Grammatical function tag. If a word is the head word of a chunk, it has function of whole chunk. The other words in a chunk that are not the head have "NOFUNC" as their function. For example, the word "task" is head of NP chunk "the task" and it has grammatical function tag "NP", while "the" has "NOFUNC".

7. IOB chain. The syntactic categories of all the constituents on the path from the root node to the leaf node of a parse tree. For example, a word's IOB chain I-S/I-NP/B-PP means that it is inside a sentence, inside a NP chunk, and in the beginning of PP chunk.

8. Head word Path. The head word sequence in the path between two entity mentions in the parse tree. This feature is used after removing duplicate elements.

9. Distance. The number of words between two entity mentions.

10. Order. Relative position of two relation arguments.

Two entities and all words between them have separate features of chunk tags (5), grammatical function tags (6), and IOB chains (7), and these three features are all automatically computed by chunklink.pl. See [2] for further description of these three terminologies. We use the same method as in [13] to use the features described in 3, 5, 6, 7, and 10. The concept of the head word path is adapted from [10].

Let us take a sentence "**Officials** in **New York** took the task" for an example. Two entity mentions, officials and New York, constitute a relation AT(officials, New York). For the noun phrase "officials in New York", the corresponding parse tree is shown in Fig 2.

To compute the head word path, we need to know what a head word is. At the terminal nodes, the head word is simply the word from the sentence the node represents. At non-terminal nodes in the parse tree, "The head of a phrase is the element inside the phrase whose properties determine the distribution of that phrase, i.e. the environments in which it can occur." [9]

The head word path is computed in the following way. The head words of the two entity mentions are officials and York respectively. The path between these two head words is the sequence officials-NP-PP-NP-York which is in bold in Fig. 1. Then we change each non-terminal into its head word, and we get officials-officials-in-York-York. If we remove the duplicate elements, we get officials-in-York. Finally, we replace the two entity mentions with their entity mention types, resulting in PERSON-in-GPE.

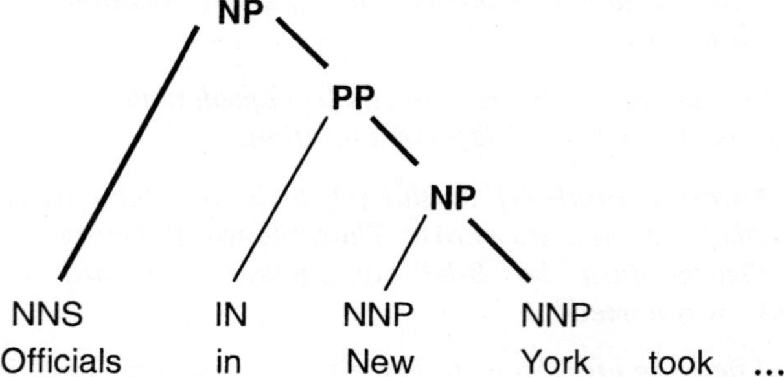

Fig. 1. Parse tree for the fragment "officials in New York". The path between two entity mentions is in bold.

Table 3 shows the features for the noun phrase "officials in New York". Note that all features are binary and they are assigned 1 or -1 depending on whether an example contains the feature or not. We could have *n*+1 possible distance features, where *n* is the entity distance threshold.

Table 3. Example of features for *Officials in New York.* e1 and e2 are two entities that constitute a relation AT(officials, New York).

Features	Example
Words	officials(e1), in, New(e2-1), York(e2-2)
Part-of-speech	NNS(e1), IN, NNP(e2-1), NNP(e2-2)
Entity type	officials: PERSON, New York: GPE
Entity mention type	officials: NOMINAL, New York: NAME
Chunk tag	B-NP, B-PP,B-NP, I-NP
Grammatical function tag	NP, PP, NOFUNC, NP
IOB chain	officials: B-S/B-NP/B-NP, in: I-S/I-NP/B-PP, New: I-S/I-NP/I-PP/B-NP York: I-S/I-NP/I-PP/I-NP
Head word path	PERSON-in-GPE
Distance	Distance=1
Order	e1 before e2

Besides the linguistic features, we apply entity distance to each task. When detecting actual relations, we use the entity distance to filter the unnecessary examples. To achieve the optimal performance, we set a threshold to keep the balance between recall and precision. We choose the threshold of entity distance based on the detection performance on held-out data. When classifying the individual relation types, the entity distance is also successfully used as a feature. We will discuss how the entity distance is utilized as a feature in the next section.

When performing combined detection and classification, we use two-staged extraction: we first detect relations in the same way as detection only task, and then perform classification on detected relations to predict the specific relation types. There are two important reasons that we choose this two-staged extraction.

First, we detect relations to increase the recall for whole extraction task. Because every combination of two entities in a sentence can construct a relation, we have far more negative examples of relation[4] in our training data. If we perform single-staged N+1 classification, the classifier is more likely to identify a testing instance as a non-relation because of the disproportionate size in samples which often decreases the performance. Thus in detection stage (or detection only task), we perform binary classification by enriching our training samples by assuming 5 types of relations to be one positive class.

Second, before performing relation classification, we can reduce a significant number of negative examples with only limited sacrifice of the detection performance by using a filtering technique with entity distance threshold. Fig. 2 shows the positive and negative examples distributed over the entity distances in training data. As we can see from the positive example curve (lower curve in the graph), the number of positive examples decreases as the entity distance exceeds 1. Positive examples do not exist where the entity distance is more than 32, while negative examples can have entity distances more than 60.

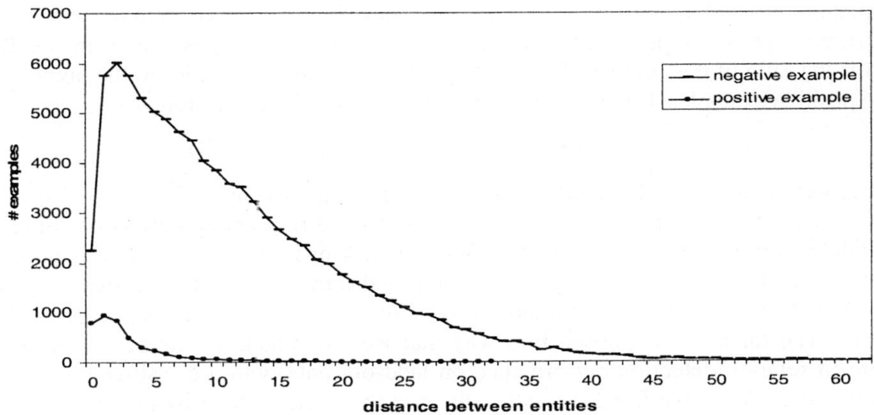

Fig. 2. Distribution of samples over entity distances in training data

We can also discover that almost 99% of the positive examples are distributed below the entity distance 20. If we restrict an entity distance threshold to 5, that is if we remove samples whose entity distances are more than 5, then whereas 71% of negative examples are dropped out, we can still maintain 80% of the positive examples. As can be seen in the graph, negative relations take more than 95% of whole entity pairs. This class imbalance makes the classifier less likely to identify a testing instance as a relation. The threshold makes relation detection easier because we can remove the large portion of negative examples, and we can get the result in reasonable time.

---

4 We have total 6551 positive relation examples out of 131510 entity pairs in training data.

In our experiment we tested the following 3 sets of features:

F1: words + entity type + entity mention type + order
F2: F1 + all syntactic features (2, 5, 6, 7 and 8)
F3: F2 + distance

F1 is the set of simple features that can be obtained directly from the ACE corpus without applying any NLP techniques. Features in F2 require sentence boundary detection and parsing to acquire the syntactic structure of a sentence. F3 is used to determine whether an entity distance can be successfully used for our task.

4 Experiments and Error Analysis

We applied Support Vector Machines (SVMs) classifier to the task. More specifically, we used LIBSVM with RBF (Radial Basis Function) kernel [3]. SVMs attempt to find a hyperplane that split the data points with maximum margin, i.e., the greatest distance between opposing classes [11].

The system performance is usually reflected using the performance measures of information retrieval: precision, recall, and F-measure. Precision is the ratio of the number of correctly predicted positive examples to the number predicted positive examples. Recall is the ratio of the number of correctly predicted positive examples to the number of true positive examples. F-measure combines precision and recall as follows:

$$\text{F-measure} = 2 * \text{precision} * \text{recall} / (\text{precision} + \text{recall})$$

We report precision, recall, and F-measure for each experiment.

We use different features for relation detection and relation classification. In relation detection, which is either in detection only task or in the first stage of combined detection and classification, we do not use entity distance as a feature. Instead, we get rid of the negative examples of relations by setting a threshold value of the entity distances. The threshold is chosen in a way that we could achieve the best F-measure score of relation detection performance on held-out data with a classifier trained on training data. We have fixed the entity distance threshold to be 7 by this experiment, and this threshold enables us to remove 67% of the negative examples and keep 93% of the positive example. We will use this value in the remaining experiments.

In relation classification, which is either in the second stage of combined extraction or in classification only task, we use all the features described in Table 3. Entity distance is successfully used as a feature to classify the individual relation types. Let us take a relation type NEAR for an example to see why entity distance is useful. As shown in table 4, the average entity distance of NEAR relations is relatively greater than the average distances of any other types of relations.

Table 4. Average entity distance for 5 relation types in training data. The first row indicates the average entity distances over the relations whose entity distances are less than or equal to 7.

Relation	ROLE	PART	AT	NEAR	SOCIAL	ALL
Avg Entity distance (<= 7)	1.95	1.63	2.79	3.23	1.55	2.13
Avg Entity distance (all)	2.89	2.2	4.38	5.55	2.42	3.26

Table 5. Frequency of misclassification of relations (R: ROLE, A: AT, S: SOCIAL, N: NEAR, P: PART). Model was trained on training data with F2 features and tested on held-out data.

System	R	A	S	P	**P**	A	P	P	A	R	N	R	N
Gold	A	R	R	R	**N**	P	P	A	N	S	A	N	P
Frequency	46	34	29	23	**21**	19	12	11	7	6	1	1	1

This does not necessarily mean that we can choose NEAR when the entity distance in an example is close to 3.23. However, there is an interesting result about NEAR when we apply the classifier trained on training data to held-out data. Table 5 shows classification errors discovered after testing on held-out data. As shown in table 5, NEAR is misclassified as PART relatively often (almost 60% of the times). We also find by looking at samples in training data that only a small portion (about 5%) of the PART relations have entity distance more than 4, while more than 50% of NEAR relations have entity distance more than 4. This discovery suggests that we can prevent the misclassification by adding the distance features to original feature set to increase the performance.

Table 6. Detection only performance trained on training + held-out data and applied on test data (P: preprocessed with distance threshold = 7, N: no threshold is used)

Features	Precision	Recall	F-measure
F1 (N)	82.6	43.2	56.7
F2 (N)	69.4	62.1	65.5
F1 (P)	92.3	44.1	59.6
F2 (P)	77.8	69.3	73.3

Table 6 shows the performance of detection only task. The filtering process with distance threshold resulted in performance increase in all measurements.

As described in previous section, we divide the corpus into three different sets: training data, held-out data, and test data. We first build the classifier on training data, and applied the classifier to held-out data. In this experiment, we choose the threshold of entity distance until we get the optimal performance of relation detection on held-out data. We also count the misclassification of relations on held-out data. Next, we retrained the data on whole training set, i.e., training data plus held-out data, and then applied to the test data.

Table 7 shows the performance of combined detection and classification task on test data. We can see in table 7 that the system using all features achieved the highest performance. We can also find that the system using all syntactic features performs better in F-measure than the system without syntactic features. However, the features which do not require any language processing (F1) achieved relatively high precision compared to F2 and F3. When entities are very close, sometimes syntactic features would not be of much help. For example, relations such as "a **town** west of **Jerusalem**", "**park** outside **Paris**", "**his friend/wife/brother**" are highly dependent on the lexical feature, i.e., "west of", "outside", and "friend/wife/brother" are the most important clue to determine the class of the relations. Finally, as we previously discussed, F3 is always better, in all kinds of measurements, than F1 and F2. This proves that our system certainly benefits from the distance feature.

Table 7. Combined detection and classification performance. Model is trained on training data + held-out data and tested on test data (trained over 6140 relations and tested on 1512 relations)

Features	Precision	Recall	F-measure
F1	76.2	38.3	50.9
F2	65.2	49.7	56.4
F3	**68.8**	**51.4**	**58.8**

Table 8. Classification only performance. Model is trained on training data + held-out data and tested on test data (trained over 6140 relations and tested on 1512 relations).

Relation Type	Precision	Recall	F-measure
ROLE	85.7	84.3	85.0
PART	67.8	73.6	70.6
AT	81.5	82.9	82.2
NEAR	43.2	62.6	51.1
SOCIAL	74.9	88.2	81.0

We perform classification only task to compare the result with [13]. Table 8 shows the performance evaluation on 5 types of relation in test data. Direct comparison with [13] at each relation type is not a relevant process because the published result in [13] regarded a reduced set of relations (5,260 relations) as total relations tagged in the ACE data set. Nevertheless, our system performs better in F-measure in all relation types by capable of using much more relation examples and by utilizing entity distance feature.

5 Conclusion

We have presented a supervised approach for relation extraction where we apply Support Vector Machines to detect actual relations and to classify the specific types of those relations. We combine diverse lexical, syntactic and semantic features as well as entity distance.

Our system benefits from performing two-staged extraction as well as using the entity distance. In detection, we use binary classification to use more positive examples, and entity distance threshold also helps to remove large part of negative candidates for relations in reasonable time. Furthermore, entity distance is successfully used as a feature in classifying specific relations to increase the performance of the system.

The most immediate extension is to include semantic information such as semantic indexing and disambiguating the sense of entities. For example, as in table 5, SOCIAL relations are always confused with ROLE relations which often have similar lexical pattern. Moreover, NEAR and AT relations often have very similar syntactic structures. These examples do not benefit from lexical or syntactic features alone.

The next goal in this research will be to develop a classifier to apply other tasks of information extraction problem. We plan to integrate the entity recognition and relation extraction.

References

1. ACE. 2004. The NIST ACE evaluation website. http://www.nist.gov/speech/tests/ace/.
2. Buchholz, S.: The chunklink script (2000) http://ilk.uvt.nl/~sabine/chunklink/
3. Chang, C.-C. and Lin, C.-J.: LIBSVM: a library for support vector machines (2001) Software available at. http://www.csie.ntu.edu.tw/~cjlin/libsvm.
4. Culotta, A. and Sorensen, J.: Dependency tree kernels for relation extraction. Proceedings of the 42nd Annual Meeting of the Association for Computational Linguistics, Barcelona (2004)
5. Cortes, C. and Vapnik, V.: Supportvector networks. Machine Learning, (1995) 20(3):273–297
6. Charniak, E.: A maximum-entropy-inspired parser. Technical Report CS-99-12, Computer Scicence Department, Brown University (1999)
7. Miller, S., Crystal, M., Fox, H., Ramshaw, L., Schwartz, R., Stone, R., Weischedel, R., and The Annotation Group.: Algorithms that learn to extract information, bbn: Description of the sift system as used for muc-7. Technical report, BBN Technologies (2000)
8. National Institute of Standars and Technology. Proceedings of the 6th Message Undertanding Conference (MUC-7) (1998)
9. Sag, I., Wasow, T., and Bender, E.: Syntactic Theory: A Formal Introduction, volume 152 of CSLI Lecture Notes. CSLI Publications, Stanford, California, 2 edition (2003)
10. Singh, Natasha.: Syntactic features in relation extraction. MEng thesis. MIT. (2004)
11. Vapnik, V.: Statistical Learning Theory. John Wiley, (1998)
12. Zelenko, D., Aone, C., and Richardella, A.: Kernel methods for relation extraction. Journal of Machine Learning Research (2003) 1083–1106
13. Zhang, Z.: Weakly-supervised relation classification for information extraction. Proceedings of the Thirteenth ACM conference on Information and knowledge management. Washington D.C. (2004)

Discovering Relations Between Named Entities from a Large Raw Corpus Using Tree Similarity-Based Clustering

Min Zhang[1], Jian Su[1], Danmei Wang[1,2], Guodong Zhou[1], and Chew Lim Tan[2]

[1] Institute for Infocomm Research,
21 Heng Mui Keng Terrace, Singapore 119613
{mzhang, sujian, stuwang, zhougd}@i2r.a-star.edu.sg
[2] Department of Computer Science,
National University of Singapore,
Singapore, 117543
tancl@comp.nus.edu.sg

Abstract. We propose a tree-similarity-based unsupervised learning method to extract relations between Named Entities from a large raw corpus. Our method regards relation extraction as a clustering problem on shallow parse trees. First, we modify previous tree kernels on relation extraction to estimate the similarity between parse trees more efficiently. Then, the similarity between parse trees is used in a hierarchical clustering algorithm to group entity pairs into different clusters. Finally, each cluster is labeled by an indicative word and unreliable clusters are pruned out. Evaluation on the New York Times (1995) corpus shows that our method outperforms the only previous work by 5 in F-measure. It also shows that our method performs well on both high-frequent and less-frequent entity pairs. To the best of our knowledge, this is the first work to use a tree similarity metric in relation clustering.

1 Introduction

The relation extraction task identifies various semantic relations such as location, affiliation, revival and so on between entities from text. For example, the sentence "George Bush is the president of the United States." conveys the semantic relation "President", between the entities "George Bush" (*PERSON*) and "the United States" (*GPE*[1]). The task of relation extraction was first introduced as part of the Template Element task in MUC6 and formulated as the Template Relation task in MUC7 [1]. Most work at MUC [1] was rule-based, which tried to use syntactic and semantic patterns to capture the corresponding relations by means of manually written linguistic rules. The major drawback of this method is the poor adaptability and the poor robustness in handling large-scale or new domain data due to two reasons. First, rules have to be rewritten for different tasks or when porting to different domains. Second, generating rules manually is quite labor- and time-consuming.

[1] GPE is an acronym introduced by the ACE (2004) program to represent a Geo-Political Entity --- an entity with land and a government.

R. Dale et al. (Eds.): IJCNLP 2005, LNAI 3651, pp. 378 – 389, 2005.

Since then, various supervised learning approaches [2,3,4,5] have been explored extensively in relation extraction. These approaches automatically learn relation patterns or models from a large annotated corpus. To decrease the corpus annotation requirement, some researchers turned to weakly supervised learning approaches [6,7], which rely on a small set of initial seeds instead of a large annotated corpus. However, there is no systematic way in selecting initial seeds and deciding an "optimal" number of them.

Alternatively, Hasegawa et al. [8] proposed a cosine similarity-based unsupervised learning approach for extracting relations from a large raw corpus. The context words in between the same entity pairs in different sentences are used to form word vectors, which are then clustered according to the cosine similarity. This approach does not rely on any annotated corpus and works effectively on high-frequent entity pairs [8]. However, there are two problems in this approach:

- The assumption that the same entity pairs in different sentences have the same relation.
- The cosine similarity measure between the flat feature vectors, which only consider the words between entities.

In this paper, we propose a tree similarity-based unsupervised learning approach for relation extraction. In order to resolve the above two problems in Hasegawa et al. [8], we assume that the same entity pairs in different sentences can have different relation types. Moreover, rather than the cosine similarity measure, a similarity function over parse trees is proposed to capture much larger feature spaces instead of the simple word features.

The rest of the paper is organized as follows. In Section 2, we discuss the proposed tree-similarity-based clustering algorithm. Section 3 shows the experimental result. Section 4 compares our work with the previous work. We conclude our work with a summary and an outline of the future direction in Section 5.

2 Tree Similarity-Based Unsupervised Learning

We use the shallow parse tree as the representation of relation instances, and regard relation extraction as a clustering problem on shallow parse trees. Our method consists of three steps:

1) Calculating the similarity between two parse trees using a tree similarity function;
2) Clustering relation instances based on the similarities using a hierarchical clustering algorithm;
3) Labeling each cluster using indicative words as its relation type, and pruning out unreliable clusters.

In this section, we introduce the parse tree representation for a relation instance, define the tree similarity function, and describe the clustering algorithm.

2.1 Parse Tree Representation for Relation Instance

A parse tree T is a set of node $\{p_1 \ldots p_n\}$, which are connected hierarchically. Here, a node p_i includes a set of features $\{f_1, \ldots, f_4\}$ as follows:

- **Head Word** (f_1)**:** for a leaf (or terminal) node, it is the word itself of the leaf node; for a non-terminal node, it is a "**Head Word**" propagated from a leaf node. This feature defines the main meaning of the phrase or the sub-tree rooted by the current node.
- **Node Tag** (f_2)**:** for a leaf node, it is the part-of-speech of this node; for a non-terminal node, it is a phrase name, such as Noun Phrase (NP), Verb Phrase (VP). This feature defines the linguistic category of this node.
- **Entity Type** (f_3)[2]**:**it indicates the entity type which can be PER, COM or GPE if the current node refers to a Named Entity.
- **Relation Order** (f_4)**:** it is used to differentiate asymmetric relations, e.g., "A belongs to B" or "B belongs to A".

These features are widely-adopted in Relation Extraction task. In the parse tree representation, we denote by $p_i.f_j$ the jth feature of node p_i, by $p_i[j]$ the jth child of node p_i, and by $p_i[\mathbf{C}]$ the set of all children of node p_i, *i.e.*, $p_i[j] \in p_i[\mathbf{C}]$.

2.2 Tree Similarity Function

Inspired by the special property of kernel-based methods[3], we extend the tree kernels in Zelenko et al. [3] to a novel tree similarity measure function, and apply the above tree similarity function to unsupervised learning for relation extraction. Mostly, in previous work, kernels are used in supervised learning algorithms such as SVM, Perceptron and PCA (Collins and Duffy, 2001). In our approach, the hierarchical clustering algorithm is adopted, this allows us to explore more robust and powerful similarity functions, other than a proper kernel function[4].

A similarity function returns a normalized, symmetric similarity score in the range [0, 1]. Especially, our tree similarity function $K(T_1, T_2)$ over two trees T_1 and T_2, with the root nodes r_1 and r_2, is defined as follows:

$$K(T_1, T_2) = m(r_1, r_2) * \{s(r_1, r_2) + K_C(r_1[\mathbf{c}], r_2[\mathbf{c}])\} \quad (1)$$

where,

---

[2] For the features of "**Entity Type**", please refer to the literature ACE [22] for details.

[3] As an alternative to the feature-based method [5], the advantage of kernels [9] is that they can replace any dot product between input points in a high dimensional feature space. Compared with the feature-based method, the kernel method displays several unique characteristics, such as implicitly mapping the feature space from low-dimension to high-dimension, and effectively modeling structure data. A few kernels over structured data have been proposed in NLP study [10-16]. Zelenko et al. [3] and Culotta et al. [4] explored tree kernels with SVM [9] for relation extraction. We study the tree kernels from similarity measure viewpoints.

[4] A function is a kernel function if and only if the function is *symmetric* and *positive semi-definite* [3, 9].

- $m(p_i, p_j)$ is a matching function over the features of two tree nodes p_i and p_j. In this paper, only the node tag feature (f_2) is considered:

$$m(p_i, p_j) = \begin{cases} 1 & \text{if } p_i.f_2 = p_j.f_2 \\ 0 & \text{otherwise} \end{cases} \quad (2)$$

  The binary function (1) means that two nodes are matched only if they share the same **Node Tag**.

- $s(p_1, p_2)$ is a similarity function between two nodes p_i and p_j:

$$s(p_i, p_j) = \begin{cases} 1 & \text{if } \begin{cases} p_i.f_1 = p_j.f_1 \\ \& \ p_i.f_3 = p_j.f_3 \end{cases} \\ 0.5 & \text{else if } p_i.f_1 = p_j.f_1 \\ 0.25 & \text{other features match} \\ 0 & \text{no match} \end{cases} \quad (3)$$

where the values of the weights are assigned empirically according to the discriminative ability of the feature types. Function (3) measures the similarity between two nodes according to the weights of matched features.

- K_C is the similarity function over the two children node sequences $p_1[\boldsymbol{c}]$ and $p_2[\boldsymbol{c}]$:

$$K_C(p_1[\boldsymbol{c}], p_2[\boldsymbol{c}]) = \underset{\boldsymbol{a},\boldsymbol{b},\, l(\boldsymbol{a})=l(\boldsymbol{b})}{\operatorname{argmax}} \{K(p_1[\boldsymbol{a}], p_2[\boldsymbol{b}])\} \quad (4)$$

$$K(p_1[\boldsymbol{a}], p_2[\boldsymbol{b}]) = \sum_{i=1}^{l(\boldsymbol{a})} K(p_1[\boldsymbol{a}_i], p_2[\boldsymbol{b}_i]) \quad (5)$$

where $\boldsymbol{a}$ and $\boldsymbol{b}$ are two index sequences, *i.e.*, $\boldsymbol{a}$ is a sequence $0<a_1...<a_m \le |p_1[C]|$ and $l(\boldsymbol{a})$ is the length of sequence $\boldsymbol{a}$, and likewise for $\boldsymbol{b}$. The node set $p_1[\boldsymbol{a}] = \{p_1[\boldsymbol{a}_1], ..., p_1[\boldsymbol{a}_m]\}$ is the subset of $p_1[\boldsymbol{c}]$, $p_1[\boldsymbol{a}] \subseteq p_1[\boldsymbol{c}]$, $p_1[a_i]$ is the ith node of $p_1[\boldsymbol{a}]$, and likewise for p_2.

We define $K(T_1, T_2)$ in terms of the similarity function $s(r_1, r_2)$ between the parent nodes and the similarity function K_C over the two children node sequences $r_1[\boldsymbol{c}]$ and $r_2[\boldsymbol{c}]$. Formula (5) defines the similarity between two node sequences by summing up the similarity of each corresponding node pair. K_C in Formula (4) searches out such two children node subsequences $p_1[\boldsymbol{a}]$ and $p_2[\boldsymbol{b}]$, which has the maximum node sequence similarity among all the possible combining pairs of node subsequences. Given the similarity scores of all children node pairs, Formula (4) can be easily resolved by the dynamic programming (DP) algorithm[5]. By traversing the two trees from top to down and applying the DP algorithm layer by layer, the parse tree similarity $K(T_1, T_2)$ defined by Formula (1) is obtained. Due to the DP algorithm, the defined tree similarity function is computable in O(mn), where m and n are the number of nodes in the two trees, respectively. The matching function $m(p_i, p_j)$ in Formula (2) can narrow down the search space during similarity calculation, since the sub-trees with unmatched root nodes are unnecessary to be further explored.

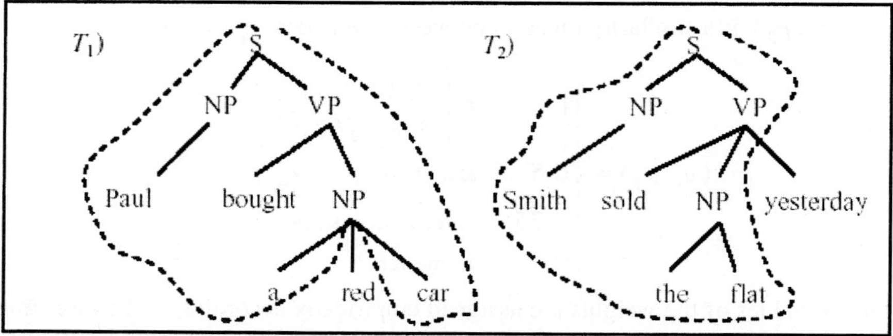

Fig. 1. Sub-structure with maximum similarity

From the above discussion, we can see that our defined tree similarity function is trying to detect the two trees' maximum isomorphic sub-structures. The similarity score between the maximum isomorphic sub-structures is returned as the value of the similarity function. Fig. 1 illustrates the sub-structures with the maximum similarity between two trees. Among the all matched sub-structures, only the sub-structures circled by the dashed lines are the isomorphic sub-structures with the maximum similarity. The similarity score between the sub-structures is obtained by summing up the similarity score between the corresponding matched nodes.

Finally, since the size of the input parse tree is not constant, the similarity score is normalized as follows:

$$\hat{K}(T_1, T_2) = \frac{K(T_1, T_2)}{\sqrt{K(T_1, T_1) * K(T_2, T_2)}} \tag{6}$$

The value of $\hat{K}(T_1, T_2)$ ranges from 0 to 1. In particular, $\hat{K}(T_1, T_2) = 1$ if and only if $T_1 = T_2$. For example, given two parse trees A and B, and A is a subtree of B, then under Formula (1), $K(A, B) = K(A, A)$. However, after the normalization through

[5] A well-known application of Dynamic Programming is to compute the edit distance between two character strings. Let us regard a node as a character and a node sequence as a character string. Then given the similarity score between nodes, Formula (4) can be resolved using DP algorithm in the same way as that of strings. Due to space limitation, the implementation deatils are not discussed here.

Equation (6), we can get $\hat{K}(A,B) < \hat{K}(A,A) = 1$. In this way, we can differentiate such two cases.

According to the Formula (1) to (5), the similarity function $K(T_1, T_2)$ over the two trees in Fig. 1 is computed as follows:

$$
\begin{aligned}
K(T_1,T_2) &= m(\mathrm{S},\mathrm{S}) * \{s(\mathrm{S},\mathrm{S}) + K_C([\mathrm{NP},\ \mathrm{VP}],[\mathrm{NP},\ \mathrm{VP}])\} \\
&= 0.25 + K(\mathrm{NP},\ \mathrm{NP}) + K(\mathrm{VP},\ \mathrm{VP}) \\
&= 0.25 + 0.25 + K(\mathrm{Paul},\ \mathrm{Smith}) + 0.25 \\
&\quad + K_C([\mathrm{bought},\ \mathrm{NP}],[\mathrm{sold},\ \mathrm{NP},\ \mathrm{yesterday}]) \\
&= 1 + K(\mathrm{bought},\ \mathrm{sold}) + K(\mathrm{NP},\ \mathrm{NP}) \\
&= 1 + 0.25 + 0.25 + K_C([\mathrm{a},\ \mathrm{red},\ \mathrm{car}],[\mathrm{the},\ \mathrm{flat}]) \\
&= 1.5 + K(\mathrm{a},\ \mathrm{the}) + K(\mathrm{car},\ \mathrm{flat}) \\
&= 2
\end{aligned}
$$

The above similarity score is more than one. This is because we did not normalize the score using Formula (6).

2.3 Tree Similarity Based Unsupervised Learning

Our method consists of five steps:

1) Named Entity (NE) tagging and sentence parsing: Detailed and accurate NE types provide more effective information for relation discovery. Here we use Sekine's NE tagger [20], where 150 hierarchical types and subtypes of Named Entities are defined [21]. This NE tagger has also been adopted by Hasegawa et al. [8]. Besides, Collin's parser [18] is adopted to generate shallow parse trees.

2) Similarity calculation: The similarity between two relation instances is defined between two parse trees. However, the state-of-the-art of parser is always error-prone. Therefore, we only use the minimum span parse tree including the NE pairs when calculating the similarity function [4]. Please note that the two entities may not be the leftmost or rightmost node in the sub-tree.

3) NE pairs clustering: Clustering of NE pairs is based on the similarity score generated by the tree similarity function. Rather than k-means [17], we used a bottom-up hierarchical clustering method so that there is no need to determine the number of clusters in advance. This means that we are not restricted to the limited types of relations defined in MUC [1] or ACE [22]. Therefore, more substantial existing relations can be discovered. We adopt the group-average clustering algorithm [17] since it produces the best performance compared with the complete-link and single-link algorithms in our study.

4) Cluster labeling: In our study, we label each cluster by the most frequent "**Head Word**" in this cluster. As indicated in subsection 2.1, the "**Head Word**" of root node defines the main meaning of a parse tree. This way, the "**Head Word**" of the root node of the minimum span tree naturally characterizes the relation between this NE pair in this tree. Thus, we simply count the frequency of the "**Head Word**" of the root node in the cluster, and then chose the most frequent "**Head Word**" as the relation type of the cluster.

5) Cluster pruning: Unreliable clusters may be generated due to various reasons such as divergent relation type distributions and the fact that most of the entity pairs inside this cluster are totally unrelated. Therefore, pruning is necessary and done in our approach using two criteria. Firstly, if the most frequent "**Head Word**" occurs less than a predefined percentage in this cluster, which means that the relation type defined by this "**Head Word**" is not significant statistically, the cluster is pruned out. Secondly, we prune out the clusters whose NE pair number is below a predefined threshold because such clusters may not be representative enough for this relation.

3 Experiments

3.1 Experimental Setting

To verify our proposed method and establish proper comparison with Hasegawa et al. [8], we use the same corpus "The New York Times (1995)", and evaluate our work on the same two kinds of NE pairs: COMPANY-COMPANY (COM-COM) and PERSON-GPE (PER-GPE) as Hasegawa et al. in [8]. First, we iterate over all pairs of Named Entities occurring in the same sentence to generate potential relation instances. Then, according to the co-occurrence frequency of NE pairs, all the relation instances are grouped into three categories:

1) High frequent instances with the co-occurrence frequency not less than 30. In this category, only the relation instances, which satisfy the all criteria of Hasegawa et al. [8][6], are kept for final experiment. By doing so, this category data is the same as the entire experimental set used by Hasegawa et al. [8].
2) Intermediate frequent instances with the co-occurrence frequency between 5 and 30. In this category, only two distinct NE pairs are randomly picked at each frequency for final evaluation due to the large number of such NE pairs.
3) Less frequent instances with the co-occurrence frequency not more than 5. In this category, twenty distinct NE pairs are randomly picked at each frequency for final evaluation due to the similar reason as 2).

Table 1 reports the statistics of the entire evaluation corpus[7] which is manually tagged. Table 2 reports the percentage of the NE pairs which carry more than one relation types when occurring at different relation instances. The numbers inside parentheses in Table 1 and Table 2 correspond to the statistical values of the NE pair "PER-GPE", while the numbers outside parentheses are related to the NE pair "COM-COM". Table 2 shows that at least 9.88% of distinct NE pairs have more than one

[6] To discover reliable relations, Hasegawa et al. [8] sets five conditions to generate relation instance set. NE pair co-occurrence more than 30 times is one of the five conditions.

[7] Due to the parsing errors and NE tagging errors, the actual number of relation instances is less than the theory number that we should pick up.

relation types in the test corpus. Thus it is reasonable and necessary to assume that each occurrence of NE pairs forms one individual relation instance.

Table 1. Statistics on the manually annotated evaluation data

Category by frequency	# of instances	# of distinct NE pairs	# of relation types
High	8931 (13205)	65 (177)	10 (38)
Intermediate	672 (783)	38 (41)	6 (7)
Less	276 (215)	76 (81)	5 (8)

Table 2. % of distinct NE pairs with more than one relation types on the evaluation data

Category by frequency	% of NE pairs have more than one relations
High	15.4 (12.99)
Intermediate	28.9 (24.4)
Less	11.8 (9.88)

3.2 Evaluation Measures

All the experiments are carried out against the manually annotated evaluation corpus. We adopt the same criteria as Hasegawa et al. [8] to evaluate the performance of our method. Grouping and labeling are evaluated separately. For grouping evaluation, all the single NE pair clusters are labeled as non-relation while all the other clusters are labeled as the most frequent relation type counted in this cluster. For each individual relation instance, if the manually assigned relation type is the same as its cluster label, the grouping of this relation instance is counted as correct, otherwise, are counted as incorrect. Recall (**R**), Precision (**P**) and F-measure (**F**) are adopted as the main performance measure for grouping [8]. For labeling evaluation, a cluster is labeled correctly only if the labeling relation type, represented by most frequent "**Head Word**" of the root node of the minimal-span subtree, is the same as the cluster label gotten in the grouping process.

3.3 Experimental Results

Like other applications using clustering algorithms, the performance of the proposed method also depends on the threshold of the clustering similarity. Here this threshold is used to truncate the hierarchical tree, so that the different clusters are generated. When the threshold is set to 1, then each individual relation instance forms one unique group; when the threshold is set to 0, then the all relation instance form one big group. Table 3 reports the evaluation results of grouping, where the best F-measures and the corresponding similarity thresholds are listed. We can see that our method not only achieves good performance on the high-frequent data, but also performs well on the intermediate and less-frequent data. The higher frequency, the higher performance. Since the best thresholds of the two NE cases are the almost same, we just fix the universal threshold as the one used in "PER-GPE" case in each category.

Table 3. Performance evaluation of Grouping phase, the numbers inside parentheses correspond to the evaluation score of "PER-GPE" while the numbers outside parentheses are related to "COM-COM".

Category by frequency	Performance			Threshold
	F	**P** (%)	**R** (%)	
High	80 (87)	82 (90)	78 (84)	0.28 (0.29)
Intermediate	74 (76)	87 (84)	64 (69)	0.32 (0.30)
Less	62 (65)	75 (77)	53 (56)	0.36 (0.35)

Table 4. Best performance comparison in the high-frequent data (**F**)

	Our approach	Hasegawa et al. [8]
PER-GPE	87	82
COM-COM	80	77

Table 4 compares the performances of the proposed method and Hasegawa et al. [8], where the best F-measures on the same high-frequent data are reported. Table 4 shows that our method outperforms the previous approach by 5 and 3 F-measures in clustering NE pairs of "PER-GPE" and "COM-COM", respectively.

An interesting phenomenon is that the best threshold is set to be just above 0 for the cosine similarity in Hasegawa et al. [8]. This means that each word feature vector of each combination of NE pairs in the same cluster shares at least one word in common --- and most of these common words were pertinent to the relations [8]. This also prevents them from working well on less-frequent data [8]. In contrast, for the similarity function in our approach, the best threshold is much greater than 0. The difference between the two thresholds implies that the similarity function over the parse trees can capture more common structured features than the word feature vectors can. This is also the reason why our method is effective on both high and less-frequent data.

It is not surprising that we do have that a few identical NE pairs, occurring in different relation instances, are grouped into different relation sets. For example, the NE pairs "*General Electric Co.* and *NBC*", in one sentence "*General Electric Co.*, which bought *NBC* in 1986, will announce a new marketing plan.", is grouped into the relation set "*M&A*", but in another sentence "Prime Star Partners and *General Electric Co.*, parent of *NBC*, has signed up 430,000 subscribers.", is grouped into another relation set "*parent*". Among all the NE pairs that carry more than one relation types, 41.8% of them are grouped correctly using our tree similarity function.

The performance of grouping is the upper bound of the performances of labeling and pruning. In the final, there are 146 PER-GPE clusters and 95 COM-COM clusters are generated after grouping. Out of which, only 57 PER-GPE clusters and 42 COM-COM clusters are labeled correctly before pruning. This is because that a large portion of the non-relation clusters are labeled as one kind of true relations. After pruning, 117 PER-GPE clusters and 84 COM-COM clusters are labeled correctly. This is because lots of the non-relation clusters are labeled correctly by the pruning process, so we can say that pruning is a non-relation labeling process, which greatly improves the performance of labeling.

The experimental results discussed above suggest that our proposed method is an effective solution for discovering relation from a large raw corpus.

4 Discussions

It would be interesting to review and summarize how the proposed method deals with the relation extraction issue differently from other related works. Table 5 in the next page summarizes the differences between our method and Hasegawa et al. [8].

Table 5. The differences between our method and Hasegawa et al. [8]

	Our approach	Hasegawa et al. [8]
Similarity Measure	tree similarity over parse tree structures	cosine similarity between the context word feature vectors
Assumption	No	Yes (The same entity pairs in different sentences have the same relation)
Labeling	the most frequent "**Head Word**" of the root node of sub-tree	the most frequent context word
Pruning	Yes (We present two pruning criterion)	No
Data Frequency	effective on both high and less-frequent data	effective only on high-frequent data

In addition, since our tree similarity function has benefited from the relation tree kernels of Zelenko et al. [3], let us compare our similarity measure function with their relation kernel function [3] from the viewpoint of computational efficiency. Zelenko et al. [3] defined the first parse tree kernels for relation extraction, and then this relation tree kernels were extended to dependency tree kernels by Culotta et al. [4]. Their tree kernels sum up the similarity scores among all possible subsequences of children nodes with matching parents, and give a penalty to longer sequences. Their tree kernels are closely related to the convolution kernels [12]. But, by doing so, lots of sub-trees will be considered again and again. An extreme case occurs when two tree structures are identical. In that situation all the sub-trees will be considered exhaustedly, even if the sub-tree is a part of other bigger sub-trees. We use the maximum score in Formula (4) instead of the summation in our approach. With our approach, the entire tree is only considered once. The replacement of summation with maximization reduces the computational time greatly.

5 Conclusions and Future Directions

We modified the relation tree kernels [3] to be a tree similarity measure function by replacing the summation over all possible subsequences of children nodes with maximization, and used it in clustering for relation extraction. The experimental result showed much improvement over the previous best result [8] on the same test corpus. It also showed that our method is high effective on both high-frequent and less-frequent data. Our work demonstrated the effectiveness of combining the tree similarity measure with unsupervised learning for relation extraction.

Although our method shows good performance, there are still other aspects of the proposed method worth discussing here. Without additional knowledge, relation detecting and relation labeling are still not easy to be resolved, especially in less-frequent data. We expect that using additional easily-acquired knowledge can improve the performance of the proposed method. For example, we can introduce the WordNet [19] thesaurus information into Formula (3) to obtain more accurate node similarities and resolve data sparse problem. We can also use the same resource to improve the labeling scheme and find more abstract relation types like the definitions used in ACE program [22].

References

1. MUC. 1987-1998. The nist MUC website: http://www.itl.nist.gov/iaui/894.02/related_projects/muc/
2. Miller, S., Fox, H., Ramshaw, L. and Weischedel, R. 2000. A novel use of statistical parsing to extract information from text. Proceedings of NAACL-00
3. Zelenko, D., Aone, C. and Richardella, A. 2003. Kernel Methods for Relation Extraction. Journal of Machine Learning Research. 2003(2):1083-1106
4. Culotta, A. and Sorensen, J. 2004. Dependency Tree Kernel for Relation Extraction. Proceeding of ACL-04
5. Kambhatla, N. 2004. Combining Lexical, Syntactic, and Semantic Features with Maximum Entropy Models for Extracting Relations. Proceeding of ACL-04, Poster paper.
6. Agichtein, E. and Gravano, L. 2000. Snow-ball: Extracting Relations from Large Plain-text Collections. Proceedings of the Fifth ACM International Conference on Digital Libraries.
7. Stevenson, M. 2004. An Unsupervised WordNet-based Algorithm for Relation Extraction. Proceedings of the 4th LREC workshop "Beyond Named Entity: Semantic Labeling for NLP tasks"

8. Hasegawa, T., Sekine, S. and Grishman, R. 2004. Discovering Relations among Named Entities from Large Corpora. Proceeding of ACL-04
9. Vapnik, V. 1998. Statistical Learning Theory. John Wiley
10. Collins, M. and Duffy, N. 2001. Convolution Kernels for Natural Language. Proceeding of NIPS-01
11. Collins, M. and Duffy, N. 2002. New Ranking Algorithm for Parsing and Tagging: Kernel over Discrete Structure, and the Voted Perceptron. Proceeding of ACL-02.
12. Haussler, D. 1999. Convolution Kernels on Discrete Structures. Technical Report UCS-CRL-99-10, University of California
13. Lodhi, H., Saunders, C., Shawe-Taylor, J., Cristianini, N. and Watkins, C. 2002. Text classification using string kernel. Journal of Machine Learning Research, 2002(2):419-444
14. Suzuki, J., Hirao, T., Sasaki Y. and Maeda, E. 2003. Hierarchical Directed Acyclic Graph Kernel: Methods for Structured Natural Language Data. Proceedings of ACL-03
15. Suzuki, J., Isozaki, H. and Maeda, E. 2003. Convolution Kernels with Feature Selection for Natural Language Processing Tasks. Proceedings of ACL-04
16. Moschitti, A. 2004. A study on Convolution Kernels for Shallow Semantic Parsing. Proceedings of ACL-04
17. Manning, C. and Schutze, H. 1999. Foundations of Statistical Natural Language Processing. The MIT Press: 500-527
18. Collins, M. 1999. Head-Driven Statistical Models for Natural Language Parsing. Ph.D. Thesis. University of Pennsylvania
19. Fellbaum, C. 1998. WordNet: An Electronic Lexical Database and some of its Applications. Cambridge, MA: MIT Press.
20. Sekine, S. 2001. OAK System (English Sentence Analysis). Http://nlp.cs.nyu.edu/oak
21. Sekine, S., Sudo, K. and Nobata, C. 2002. Extended named entity hierarchy. Proceedings of LREC-02
22. ACE. 2004. The Automatic Content Extraction (ACE) Projects. http://www.ldc.upenn.edu/Projects/ACE/

Automatic Relation Extraction with Model Order Selection and Discriminative Label Identification

Chen Jinxiu[1], Ji Donghong[1], Tan Chew Lim[2], and Niu Zhengyu[1]

[1] Institute of Infocomm Research,
21 Heng Mui Keng Terrace, Singapore, 119613
{jinxiu, dhji, zniu}@i2r.a-star.edu.sg
[2] Department of Computer Science,
National University of Singapore, Singapore, 117543
tancl@comp.nus.edu.sg

Abstract. In this paper, we study the problem of unsupervised relation extraction based on model order identification and discriminative feature analysis. The model order identification is achieved by stability-based clustering and used to infer the number of the relation types between entity pairs automatically. The discriminative feature analysis is used to find discriminative feature words to name the relation types. Experiments on ACE corpus show that the method is promising.

1 Introduction

Relation extraction is the task of finding relationships between two entities from text contents. Recently, it has received more and more attention in many areas, e.g., information extraction , ontology construction, and bioinformatics, etc. In this paper, we propose an unsupervised method for relation extraction from corpus.

Since the concept of relation extraction was introduced in MUC 6 [1], there has been considerable work on supervised learning of relation patterns, using corpora which have been annotated to indicate the information to be extracted [2,9,8]. A range of extraction models have been used, including both symbolic rules and statistical rules such as HMMs or Kernels. These methods have been particularly successful in some specific domains. However, manually tagging of large amounts of training data is very time-consuming; furthermore, it is difficult for one extraction system to be ported across different domains.

Due to the limitation of supervised methods, some weakly (semi-) supervised approaches have been suggested [3,6,5,4]. One common feature of these algorithms is that they need to pre-define some initial seeds for any particular relation, then bootstrap from the seeds to acquire the relation. However, to determine how to select these seeds and how many seeds to be selected tends to be very subjective.

Hasegawa, et al. put forward an unsupervised approach for relation extraction from large text corpora [7]. Their assumption is that pairs of entities with

R. Dale et al. (Eds.): IJCNLP 2005, LNAI 3651, pp. 390–401, 2005.

same relation between them tend to occur in similar contexts, and the representative words in the contexts can be regarded as somewhat characterization of the relation.Thus their method contains two key steps, the first is to cluster the contexts in which the pairs of entities occur, and the second is to extract the representative words from the contexts.

For the unsupervised approach, we noticed some limitations. First, they adopted a hierarchical clustering method to cluster the contexts. However, the similarity threshold for the clusters, like the appropriate number of clusters, is somewhat difficult to pre-define. Second, after context clustering, they selected the most frequent words in the contexts to represent the relation that holds between the entities. However, such words may occur frequently in any other clusters too. Hence, they may not have quality to discriminate between clusters.

In this paper, we try to resolve the above limitations of the unsupervised approach by model order selection and discriminative label identification. First, we adopt a stability-based method to cluster the contexts, which can infer the number of the appropriate clusters automatically. Second, we propose a feature weighting method and try to extract more discriminative words from the contexts to represent the relations.

The rest of this paper is organized as follows. In section 2 we overview the main phases in our proposed method. In section 3 we present the stability based model analysis algorithm to estimate the "correct" number of relation types. In section 4 we talk about how to identify discriminative labels for each relation type. Then we describe experiments and evaluations in section 5. In section 6 we give some discussions about our approach. Finally, the conclusions and future work are given in section 7.

2 Overview

For each pair of entities (E_1 and E_2)[1] with at least one known relation, we propose a method to cluster these relations into similar types. To discover such relationships, our proposed approach consists of the following three phases.

- to collect the contexts in which the entities co-occur;
- to cluster the contexts using stability-based method;
- to select discriminative features and label the clusters.

In phase 1, we assume that for any two particulate entities $e_1 \in E_1$, and $e_2 \in E_2$, they may hold more than one kind of relations. So, we collect the contexts from a corpus in which e_1 and e_2 co-occur within a context window of d words. Here,the context includes the words between, before and after them (In this paper, we use only words as the features of context vectors.). In fact, the approach also applies to the cases that e_1 and e_2 hold only one kind of relations, in such cases, we need to collect and accumulate the contexts.

[1] Entities refer to names, location, proper nouns, etc.

In phase 2, we cluster each context by the type of relation it represents. For a cluster c with a relation r, the entities e_1 and e_2 whose context belongs to c can be regarded as holding the relation r. In our experiments, cosine-similarity measure is used to compare contexts.

In phase 3, we select feature words from the contexts for each cluster as the label of the cluster, and it can also be seen as the name of the relation type. So the feature word should be discriminative among the clusters.

3 Context Clustering

Since we do not know how many relation types in advance and do not have any labelled relation training examples at hand, the problem of model order selection arises, i.e. estimating the "correct" number of clusters. In this paper, the model selection capability is achieved by resampling based stability analysis, which has been successfully applied to several unsupervised learning problems (e.g. [11], [10], [13], [12]).

To estimate the number of the clusters, we need a criterion to evaluate the merit for each possible number of clusters, and select the model order which maximizes the criterion. Formally, let k be the model order, we need to find k in Equation: $k = \arg\max_k\{criterion(k)\}$. Here, the criterion is set up based on resampling-based stability.

Let P^μ be a subset sampled from full entity pairs set P with size $\alpha|P|$ (α set as 0.9 in this paper.), $C(C^\mu)$ be $|P| \times |P|(|P^\mu| \times |P^\mu|)$ connectivity matrix based on the clustering results on $P(P^\mu)$. Each entry $c_{ij}(c^\mu_{ij})$ of $C(C^\mu)$ is calculated in the following: if the entity pair $p_i \in P(P^\mu)$, $p_j \in P(P^\mu)$ belong to the same cluster, then $c_{ij}(c^\mu_{ij})$ equals 1, else 0. Then the stability is defined in Equation 1:

$$M(C^\mu, C) = \frac{\sum_{i,j} 1\{C^\mu_{i,j} = C_{i,j} = 1, p_i \in P^\mu, p_j \in P^\mu\}}{\sum_{i,j} 1\{C_{i,j} = 1, p_i \in P^\mu, p_j \in P^\mu\}} \quad (1)$$

Intuitively, $M(C^\mu, C)$ denotes the consistency between the clustering results on C^μ and C. The assumption is that if the cluster number k is actually the "natural" number of relation types, then clustering results on subsets P^μ generated by sampling should be similar to the clustering result on full entity pair set P. Obviously, the above function satisfies $0 \leq M \leq 1$.

It is noticed that $M(C^\mu, C)$ tends to decrease when increasing the value of k. Therefore for avoiding the bias that small value of k is to be selected as cluster number, we use the cluster validity of a random predictor ρ_k to normalize $M(C^\mu, C)$. The random predictor ρ_k achieved the stability value by assigning uniformly drawn labels to objects, that is, splitting the data into k clusters randomly. Furthermore, for each k, we tried q times. So, the normalized object function can be defined as equations 2:

$$M_k^{norm} = \frac{1}{q}\sum_{i=1}^{q} M(C_k^{\mu_i}, C_k) - \frac{1}{q}\sum_{i=1}^{q} M(C_{\rho_k}^{\mu_i}, C_{\rho_k}) \quad (2)$$

Normalizing $M(C^{\mu}, C)$ by the stability of the random predictor can yield values independent of k. The effect of such normalization can be observed from the experimental results (See Table 5). The overall algorithm is in Table 1. Table 2 shows the evaluation procedure of model order selection.

Table 1. Model Selection Algorithm for Relation Extraction

Input: Corpus D tagged with Entities(E_1, E_2);
Output: Model Order (number of relation types);

1. Collect the contexts of all entity pairs in the document corpus D, namely P;
2. Set the range (K_l, K_h) for the possible number of relation clusters;
3. Set estimated model order $k = K_l$;
4. Cluster all entity pairs set P into k clusters using stability analysis method;
5. Record k and the score of the merit of k, namely M_k;
6. If $k < K_h$, $k = k + 1$, go to step 4; otherwise, go to Step 7;
7. Select k which maximizes the score of the merit M_k;

Table 2. Unsupervised Algorithm for Evaluation of Model Order Selection

Function: criterion(k, P, q)
Input: cluster number k, entity pairs set P, and sampling frequency q;
Output: the score of the merit of k;

1. With k as input, perform k-means clustering analysis on pairs set P;
2. Construct connectivity matrix C_k based on above clustering solution on P;
3. Use random predictor ρ_k to assign uniformly drawn labels to each object in P;
4. Construct connectivity matrix C_{ρ_k} based on above clustering solution on P;
5. Construct q subsets of the full pairs set, by randomly selecting αN of the N original pairs, $0 \leq \alpha \leq 1$;
6. For each subset, perform the clustering analysis in Step $2, 3, 4$, and result C_k^{μ}, $C_{\rho_k}^{\mu}$;
7. Compute M_k to evaluate the merit of k using Equation 2;
8. Return M_k;

Table 3. Some Context examples in two clusters of the output in the domain PER-ORG

Cluster 1:
[PER] vice president of the [ORG]
[PER] president and chief operating officer of [ORG]
[PER] senior vice president of [ORG]
⋮

Cluster 2:
[PER] joined the communist -backed [ORG]
[PER] and joined a laborer's [ORG]
[PER] a partner in Blackstone, will join Host Marriott's [ORG]
⋮

After the number of optimal clusters has been chosen, we adopted the kmeans algorithm for the clustering phase. The output of context clustering is a set of context clusters, each of them is supposed to denote one relation type. As an example, Table 3 lists two clusters with some context examples.

4 Relation Labelling

For labelling each relation type, we use DCM (discriminative category matching) scheme to identify discriminative label, which is also used in document classification [14] and weights the importance of a feature based on their distribution. In this scheme, a feature is not important if the feature appears in many clusters and is evenly distributed in these clusters, otherwise it will be assigned higher importance.

To weight a feature f_i within a category, we take into account the following information to ensure the selected features have the discrimination power:

- The relative importance of f_i within a cluster:

$$WC_{i,k} = \frac{\log_2(pf_{i,k} + 1)}{\log_2(N_k + 1)}. \tag{3}$$

  where $pf_{i,k}$ is the number of those term pairs which contain feature f_i in cluster k. N_k is the total number of term pairs in cluster k.
- The relative importance of f_i across clusters:

$$CC_i = \log \frac{N \cdot \max_{k \in C_i}\{WC_{i,k}\}}{\sum_{k=1}^{N} WC_{i,k}} \cdot \frac{1}{\log N} \tag{4}$$

  where C_i is the set of clusters which contain feature f_i. N is the total number of clusters.

In Equation 3, both numerator and denominator are logarithmic, which is based on the observation that the frequency of a feature appearing over many pairs is rare.

In Equation 4, the summation is used for gathering the total importance of a feature across all categories, while the maximum is used for averaging the summation value. If a feature is regarded as important in many clusters, then this feature is obviously not important for relation labelling. In other words, the higher the value of the numerator, the smaller the discriminative power is. The term, $1/\log(N)$, is used for normalization such that $0 \leq CC_i \leq 1$.

Here, $WC_{i,k}$ and CC_i are designed to capture the local information within a cluster and global information about the feature distribution across clusters respectively. It is insufficient to describe the importance and discrimination power of a feature by examining any one information only. As a result, combining both $WC_{i,k}$ and CC_i we define the weight $W_{i,k}$ of f_i in cluster k as:

$$W_{i,k} = \frac{WC_{i,k}^2 \cdot CC_i^2}{\sqrt{WC_{i,k}^2 + CC_i^2}} \cdot \sqrt{2} \tag{5}$$

Where $\sqrt{2}$ is used for normalization such that $0 \leq W_{i,k} \leq 1$.

As an example, we list some features with their weighting score for the two clusters in Table 3.

Cluster 1: (president, 0.629374), (chairman, 0.188562), (ceo, 0.155908), (chief, 0.147443), ...;

Cluster 2: (join, 0.272382), (serve, 0.114423), (communist, 0.049031), (bond, 0.044387), (aid, 0.044387), ...

5 Experimental Evaluations

5.1 Data

We constructed three subsets from ACE corpus[2] for domains PER-ORG (person-organization), ORG-GPE (organization-gpe) and ORG-ORG (organization - organization) respectively. The details of these subsets are given in Table 4, which are broken down by different relation types.

Table 4. Three domains of entity pairs: frequency distribution for different relation types

PER-ORG	num:786	ORG-GPE	num:262	ORG-ORG	num:580
Relation types	Percentage	Relation types	Percentage	Relation types	Percentage
Management	36.39%	Based-In	46.56%	Member	27.76%
General-staff	29.90%	Located	35.11%	Subsidiary	19.83%
Member	19.34%	Member	11.07%	Part-Of	18.79%
Owner	4.45%	Affiliate-Partner	3.44%	Affiliate-Partner	17.93%
Located	3.28%	Part-Of	2.29%	Owner	8.79%
Client	1.91%	Owner	1.53%	Client	2.59%
Other	1.91%			Management	2.59%
Affiliate-Partner	1.53%			Other	1.21%
Founder	0.76%			Other	0.52%

The ACE corpus contains about 519 files from sources including broadcast, newswire, and newspaper. To verify our proposed method, we only extracted those pairs of entity mentions which have been tagged relation types in the given corpus. Then the relation type tags were removed to test the unsupervised relation disambiguation. During the evaluation procedure, the relation type tags were used as ground truth classes.

The data preprocessing involves lowering the upper case characters, ignoring all words that contain digits or non alpha-numeric characters, removing words from a stop word list, stemming and filtering out low frequency words which appeared only once in the entire set.

---

[2] http://www.ldc.upenn.edu/Projects/ACE/, RDC(Relation Detection and Characterization) is one of the tasks of ACE program. There are five entity types in the ACE corpus, that is, ORGANIZATION, PERSON, GPE, LOCATION and FACILITY.

5.2 Evaluation Method for Clustering Result

When assessing the agreement between clustering result and hand-tagged relation types (ground truth classes), we would encounter the problem that there was no relation type tags for each cluster in our clustering results.

To resolve the problem, we adopted a permutation procedure to assign different relation type tags to only $min(|EC|,|TC|)$ clusters, where $|EC|$ is the estimated number of clusters, and $|TC|$ is the number of ground truth classes (relation types). This procedure aims to find an one-to-one mapping function Ω from the TC to EC which is based on the assumption that for any two clusters, they do not share the same class labels. Under this assumption, there are at most $|TC|$ clusters which are assigned relation type tags. If the number of the estimated clusters is less than the number of the ground truth clusters, empty clusters should be added so that $|EC| = |TC|$ and the one-to-one mapping can be performed.

With the estimated clusters and the ground truth classes, we construct a contingency table T, where each entry $t_{i,j}$ gives the number of the instances that belong to both the i-th cluster and j-th ground truth class. The mapping procedure can be formulated as the function: $\hat{\Omega} = \arg\max_{\Omega} \sum_{j=1}^{|TC|} t_{\Omega(j),j}$, where $\Omega(j)$ is the index of the estimated cluster associated with the j-th class.

Given the result of one-to-one mapping, we can define the evaluation measure as follows:

$$Accuracy(P) = \frac{\sum_j t_{\hat{\Omega}(j),j}}{\sum_{i,j} t_{i,j}}. \tag{6}$$

Intuitively, it reflects the accuracy of the clustering result.

5.3 Evaluation Method for Relation Labelling

For evaluation of the relation labeling, we need to explore the relatedness between the identified labels and the pre-defined relation names. To do this, we use one information-content based measure [16,15], which is provided in Wordnet-Similarity package [17] to evaluate the similarity between two concepts in Wordnet. Intuitively, the relatedness between two concepts in Wordnet is captured by the information content of their lowest common subsumer (lcs) and the information content of the two concepts themselves. This can be viewed as taking the information content of the intersection, which can be formalized as follows:

$$Relatedness_{lin}(c_1, c_2) = \frac{2 \times IC(lcs(c_1, c_2))}{IC(c_1) + IC(c_2)} \tag{7}$$

This measure depends upon the corpus to estimate information content. Information content of a concept is estimated by counting the frequency of that concept in a large corpus and thereby determining its probability via a maximum likelihood estimate. We carried out the experiments using the British National Corpus (BNC) as the source of information content.

5.4 Experiments and Results

For comparison of the effect of the outer and within context of entity pairs, we conducted five different settings of context window size (WIN$_{pre}$-WIN$_{mid}$-WIN$_{post}$) for each domain. For example, the setting of "2-5-2" means that the intervening words between an entity pair should not exceed 5 words and these intervening words together with the two words before the first entity and two words following the second entity constitute the context of an entity pair. Table 5 shows the results of model order identification with unnormalized and normalized objective functions. The results show that the model order identification algorithm with M_k^{unnorm} fail to identify the real number of relation types since the score of M_k^{unnorm} decreased when increasing the cluster number k and finally resulted in 2 clusters over all domains. From Table 5, we can find that with the context setting, 0-10-0, the estimated number of the clusters equals or very closes to the number of classes. It demonstrates that the intervening words less than 10 are appropriate features to reflect the structure behind the contexts, while the intervening words less than 5 is not enough to infer the structure. For the contextual words beyond (before or after) the entities, they tend to be noisy features for the relation estimation, as can be seen that the performance deteriorates when taking them into consideration.

Table 6 shows the accuracy result of the clustering algorithm over three domains with different context window size settings. In this table,we compared

Table 5. Automatically determined the number of relation types using different evaluation functions

	PER-ORG			ORG-GPE			ORG-ORG		
Context Window	Real #	M_k^{unnorm}	M_k^{norm}	Real #	M_k^{unnorm}	M_k^{norm}	Real #	M_k^{unnorm}	M_k^{norm}
0-5-0	9	2	7	6	2	3	9	2	7
2-5-2	9	2	8	6	2	2	9	2	7
0-10-0	9	2	8	6	2	6	9	2	9
2-10-2	9	2	6	6	2	4	9	2	6
5-10-5	9	2	5	6	2	2	9	2	8

Table 6. Performance of the clustering algorithm with various context window size settings over three domains

	PER-ORG		ORG-GPE		ORG-ORG	
Context Window size	Accuracy1 (our method)	Accuracy2 (Hasegawa's method)	Accuracy1 (our method)	Accuracy2 (Hasegawa's method)	Accuracy1 (our method)	Accuracy2 (Hasegawa's method)
0-5-0	33.8%	30.6%	47.4%	47.9%	**40.7%**	27.2%
2-5-2	35.7%	33.5%	45.2%	43.1%	37.3%	27.6%
0-10-0	**39.3%**	36.6%	**50.9%**	42.3%	37.2%	26.3%
2-10-2	32.5%	33.5%	47.8%	43.1%	33.5%	25.3%
5-10-5	30.2%	27.6%	45.7%	42.3%	32.4%	26.0%

our clustering results with the Hasegawa's clustering algorithm provided in the paper [7], where we specify the cluster number as the number of ground truth classes. Comparing the accuracy of two clustering methods, we can find that our proposed method can achieve better or comparable performance. In addition, in three domains, from the column of accuracy1 with different setting of context window size: $(0-5-0, 2-5-2)$, $(0-10-0, 2-10-2$, and $5-10-5)$, we can see that the performance does not improve or even becomes worse when extending the context window. The reason is that extending the context may include more features, but at the same time, the noise also increases.

The automatically estimated labels for relation types over 3 domains from estimated clusters are given in Table 7. In each domain, we select two features as labels of each relation type according to their DCM weight scores and calculate the average relatedness between our selected labels (E) and the predefined labels (H). Following the same strategy, we also extracted relation labels (T) from the ground truth classes and provided the average relatedness between T and H. From the column of relatedness (E-H), we can see that it is not easy to find the hand-tagged relation labels exactly, furthermore, the identified labels from the

Table 7. Result for Relation Labelling using DCM strategy. Here, (H) denotes the hand-tagged relation label. (T) denotes the identified relation labels from ground truth classes. (E) is the identified relation labels from our estimated clusters.

Domain	Hand-tagged Label (H)	Identified Label(T)	Identified Label(E)	Relatedness: Ave (T-H)	Relatedness: Ave (E-H)	Relatedness: Ave (E-T)
PER-ORG	management	head,president	president,chairman	0.3703	0.1445	0.8639
	general-staff	work,fire	work,charge	0.6254	0.6411	0.6900
	member	join,communist	join,serve	0.394	0.1681	0.5306
	owner	bond,bought	control,house	0.1351	0.1578	0.4308
	located	appear,include	lobby,appear	0.0000	0.1606	0.2500
	client	hire,reader	bought,consult	0.4378	0.0000	0.1417
	affiliate	affiliate,associate	affiliate,director	0.9118	0.8002	0.8615
	founder	form,found	state,party	0.1516	0.2846	0.3909
ORG-GPE	based-in	base,unit	unit,base	0.7938	0.7938	0.7938
	located	northwest,travel	travel,bank	0.0000	0.1832	0.4734
	member	federal,led	construct,federal	0.2155	0.1408	0.2500
	affiliate	fund,sell	fund,have	0.4779	0.4505	0.6886
	part-of	include,involve	hold,assembly	0.1905	0.6049	0.8893
	owner	represent,mountain	represent,detain	0.0694	0.0000	0.3314
ORG-ORG	member	communist,join	communist,family	0.3141	0.4589	0.6243
	subsidiary	hire,joint	agree,form	0.1446	0.1746	0.2406
	part-of	part,include	hold,include	0.6905	0.6137	0.7959
	affiliate	work,affiliate	affiliate,joint	0.6719	0.7536	0.6719
	owner	have,asset	asset,deal	0.1782	0.0698	0.7204
	client	service,buy	import,consume	0.1633	0.1377	0.2926
	management	share,control	lead,control	0.3364	0.3146	0.7189

Table 8. Result for Relation Labelling using the frequency strategy in [7] for the domain PER-ORG

Hand-tagged Relation Label (H)	Identified Relation Label from ground truth classes (T)	Identified Relation Label from estimated clusters (E)
management	said,chief	two,head
general-staff	said,work	work,said
member	said,two	say,join
owner	bond,bought	are,become
located	said,apppear	are,appear
client	hire,reader	said,bought
affiliate-partner	affiliate,associate	affiliate,three
founder	form,found	work,said

ground-truth classes are either non-comparable to the pre-defined labels in most cases (T-H). The reason may be that the pre-defined relation names tend to be some abstract labels over the features, e.g., 'management' vs. 'president', 'head' or 'chairman'; 'member' vs. 'join', 'serve', etc., while the abstract words and the features are located far away in Wordnet.

Table 7 also lists the relatedness between the labels identified from the clusters and those from ground truth classes (E-T). We can see that the labels are comparable by their average relatedness.

Table 8 shows the result for relation labelling using frequency strategy in [7] for the domain PER-ORG. From this table, we can see that the frequency strategy is likely to select those common words as the relation labels, which may occur in more than one clusters, and can not discriminate between clusters.

6 Discussion

In this paper, we try to resolve the relation extraction task in an unsupervised manner. Compared with the existing unsupervised method [7], there are several advantages in our approach.

Relation Types. In [7], each term pair is treated as having one and only one relation type, so they accumulated contexts of all occurrences of a term pair. That is, only one context vector was generated for a term pair. However, our proposed method is based on a more reasonable assumption that there may exist several relation types among different occurrences of a term pair, so, we collect all instances of the occurrences of a term pair, and represent each instance using a context vector. Then our task turns to disambiguate the relation types among the context occurrences of all term pairs.

Context Clustering. [7] adopted a hierarchical clustering method to cluster the contexts. It is very difficult to determine the threshold for the similarity between clusters, like the appropriate number of clusters. In contrast, through model order selection we can estimate the "nature" number of relation types so that we don't need to manually pre-define any parameters during the clustering process.

Relation Label. In [7], the author labelled each relation type simply by choosing the most frequent words in a cluster. This method can not ensure that the label of the cluster has the discriminative power since it only considered the frequency of the words. In this paper, we try to discover the feature distribution within a collection, not only in the same cluster but also across the clusters. The features produced by this weighting scheme will provide more valuable characteristics for relation labelling.

Evaluation method. In [7], each cluster is mapped to one ground truth class simply by choosing the one which has the most overlap with it. But two clusters may be mapped to the same relation class, to avoid this bias, we try to find a one to one mapping from estimated cluster to the ground truth classes. Furthermore, we utilize the WordNet to compare the relatedness of our identified labels and the predefined relation labels.

7 Conclusion and Future Work

In this paper, we proposed a method of using model order identification and discriminative feature analysis to improve the unsupervised approach for relation extraction from corpus. The advantages of the proposed approach includes that it doesn't need any manual labelling of the relation instances, it doesn't need to pre-define the number of the context clusters, or pre-specify the similarity threshold for the clusters, and it can avoid extracting those common words as characterization of the relations.

One future work is to use some feature selection techniques to acquire good features and incorporate second-order context information to enrich the context information of the entity pairs. Future work also includes using the concepts in Wordnet and other discriminative feature weighting, e.g. information gain, to improve the labelling of the relation types, and applying this technique in ontology construction to acquire the relations between concepts in ontology.

References

1. Defense Advanced Research Projects Agency.: Proceedings of the Sixth Message Understanding Conference (MUC-6). Morgan Kaufmann Publishers, Inc.(1995)
2. Mary Elaine Califf and Raymond J.Mooney.: Relational Learning of Pattern-Match Rules for Information Extraction, AAAI(1999)
3. Sergey Brin.: Extracting patterns and relations from world wide web. In Proc. of WebDB Workshop at 6th International Conference on Extending Database Technology, pages 172-183 (1998)

4. Kiyoshi Sudo, Satoshi Sekine and Ralph Grishman.: An Improved Extraction Pattern Representation Model for Automatic IE Pattern Acquisition. Proceedings of ACL, Sapporo, Japan.(2003)
5. Yangarber,R., R.Grishman, P.Tapanainen, and S.Huttunen.: Unsupervised discovery of scenario-level patterns for information extraction. In proceedings of the Applied Natural Language Processing Conference, Seattle, WA (2000)
6. Eugene Agichtein and Luis Gravano.: Snowball: Extracting Relations from large Plain-Text Collections. In Proc. of the 5th ACM International Conference on Digital Libraries (2000)
7. Takaaki Hasegawa, Satoshi Sekine and Ralph Grishman.: Discovering Relations among Named Entities from Large Corpora. Proceeding of Conference ACL, Barcelona, Spain (2004)
8. Dmitry Zelenko, Chinatsu Aone and Anthony Richardella.: Kernel Methods for Relation Extraction. Proceedings of the Conference on Empirical Methods in Natural Language Processing (EMNLP), Philadelphia (2002)
9. S.Soderland.: Learning information extraction rules for semi-structured and free text. Machine Learning, 31(1-3):233-272 (1999)
10. Lange,T., Braun,M.,Roth, V., and Buhmann,J.M..: Stability-Based Model Selection. Advances in Neural Information Processing Systems 15 (2002)
11. Levine,E. and Domany,E..: Resampling Method for Unsupervised Estimation of Cluster Calidity. Neural Computation, Vol.13, 2573-2593 (2001)
12. Zhengyu Niu, Donghong Ji and Chew Lim Tan.: Document Clustering Based on Cluster Validation. CIKM'04, Washington, DC, USA, November 8-13 (2004)
13. Volker Roth and Tilman Lange.: Feature Selection in Clustering Problems. NIPS2003 workshop (2003)
14. Gabriel Pui Cheong Fung, Jeffrey Xu Yu and Hongjun Lu.: Discriminative Category Matching: Efficient Text Classification for Huge Document Collections. Proceedings of the IEEE International Conference on Data Mining (ICDM), Maebashi City, Japan, December 09-12 (2002)
15. D.Lin.: Using syntactic dependency as a local context to resolve word sense ambiguity. In Proceedings of the 35th Annual Meeting of the Association for Computational Linguistics, pages 64-71,Madrid, July (1997)
16. P.Resnik.: Using information content to evaluate semantic similarity in a taxonomy. In proceedings of the 14th International Joint Conference on Artificial Intelligence, Montreal, August (1995)
17. Ted Pedersen, Siddharth Patwardhan and Jason Michelizzi.: WordNet::Similarity-Measuring the Relatedness of Concepts. AAAI (2004)

Mining Inter-Entity Semantic Relations Using Improved Transductive Learning

Zhu Zhang

School of Information and Department of EECS,
University of Michigan, Ann Arbor, MI 48105, U.S.A

Abstract. This paper studies the problem of mining relational data hidden in natural language text. In particular, it approaches the relation classification problem with the strategy of transductive learning. Different algorithms are presented and empirically evaluated on the ACE corpus. We show that transductive learners exploiting various lexical and syntactic features can achieve promising classification performance. More importantly, transductive learning performance can be significantly improved by using an induced similarity function.

1 Introduction

The world today is full of various information sources, with different ways of representing the same information. One common problem that arises in the data management community is that data existing in one format may be needed in a different format for another purpose. An instance of this general problem is that relational data don't always exist in the form of relational tables; lots of them are hidden in natural language text. For example, `(author, book)` pairs can be instantiated as "...*Shakespeare*'s famous work *Hamlet* ..." or "...*A Brief History of Time* was written by *Stephen Hawking* ..." in text.

On the other hand, within the information retrieval and natural language processing community, Information Extraction (IE) systems are understood as techniques for automatically extracting information from text, specifically, identifying relevant information (usually of pre-defined types) from text documents in a certain domain. Once extracted, the information can be used for purposes such as database population and text indexing. While significant progress has been made in IE research, stimulated in particular by the Message Understanding Conferences (MUC) [1] and the recent ACE (Automatic Content Extraction) program [2] organized by the LDC (Linguistic Data Consortium), it is generally agreed that many barriers exist to the wider use of IE technologies due to the difficulties in adapting systems to new applications and domains. Keeping track of dynamic information sources (e.g., web pages) is challenging as well.

To address these challenges, there has been a recent trend shift in the research community from knowledge-based approaches to machine learning techniques. Moreover, due to the cost related to acquiring large amount of labeled training

[1] http://www.itl.nist.gov/iaui/894.02/related_projects/muc/
[2] http://www.ldc.upenn.edu/Projects/ACE/

R. Dale et al. (Eds.): IJCNLP 2005, LNAI 3651, pp. 402–413, 2005.

data, researchers have been looking at various learning algorithms exploiting cheaply available unlabeled data (usually in much larger amounts), which aim at minimizing the need for labeled data while still achieving comparable results.

According to the scope of ACE, current IE research has three main objectives: Entity Detection and Tracking (EDT), Relation Detection and Characterization (RDC), and Event Detection and Characterization (EDC). This study focuses on the second subproblem, RDC. In particular, the goal is to automatically classify binary relations between entities, i.e., to decide in which relational table to put each entity pair, using transductive learning algorithms. We propose an improved transductive learner and empirically compare it with the baseline learner on the ACE corpus.

2 Related Work

The current paper draws upon previous work in NLP and machine learning.

2.1 Relation Extraction and Classification

Within the realm of information extraction, there are several representative systems that use machine learning for extracting relations.

Snowball [1] is a bootstrapping-based system that requires only a handful of training examples of tuples of interest. These examples are used to generate extraction patterns, which in turn result in new tuples being extracted from the document collection. At each iteration of the extraction process, Snowball evaluates the quality of these patterns and tuples without human intervention, and keeps only the most reliable ones for the next iteration. A scalable evaluation methodology is also developed for the task. The approach was illustrated on the problem of extracting `(organization, headquarter location)` pairs from a collection of more than 300, 000 newspaper documents.

DIPRE (Dual Iterative Pattern Relation Expansion) [2] is another technique that exploits the duality between sets of patterns and relations to grow the target relation starting from a small sample. The technique was used to extract `(author, title)` pairs from the World Wide Web.

In [3], an application of kernel methods to extracting relations from natural language text is presented. The authors introduce kernels defined over shallow parse representations of text, and design efficient algorithms for computing the kernels. The devised kernels are used in conjunction with SVM and Voted Perceptron learning algorithms for the task of extracting `person-affiliation` and `organization-location` relations from text. The proposed methods are compared with feature-based learning algorithms, with promising results.

More recently, Zhang [4] investigates the relation classification problem by bootstrapping from a small amount of labeled data. Bootstrapping procedures are built on top of SVM classifiers and evaluated on the ACE corpus.

Rosario and Hearst [5] examine the problem of distinguishing among seven relation types that can occur between the entities "treatment" and "disease" in bioscience text, and the problem of identifying such entities. Five different generative graphical models and a neural network model using lexical, syntactic, and semantic features are compared. The authors find that the neural network helps achieve high classification accuracy.

2.2 Transductive Learning

Almost all work above falls into the realm of "inductive learning", in the sense that a "model" is first induced from the labeled (training) data and then used to predict unseen data. The beauty of this approach is that once the classification function (model) is generalized (assuming a "good" generalization algorithm), it can be used for prediction independently of the labeled data on which it was trained.

In many domains, including NLP, there is usually a large amount of unlabeled data but only limited amount of labeled training data. If a generalized model is preferred, one can still follow the inductive learning paradigm, which entails work such as bootstrapping [6]. On the other hand, we might encounter the following situation:

- we are only concerned about performance on a particular pool of data,
- and we don't care about generalizability,
- and data points can be effectively queried/accessed

If all the conditions above are true, the learner can observe the test data and potentially exploit structures in their distribution. In other words, there is really no difference between "unlabeled data" and "test data", and the research question is: "given some labeled data and a large set of (unlabeled) test data, can properties of the entire data set be used to make predictions?" This is the motivation behind transductive learning. The setting itself, specifically, transductive SVMs, was first introduced by Vapnik [7], and then later refined by [8] and [9]. Other approaches are based on $s-t$ cuts [10,11] or multi-way cuts [12]. Joachims [13] presents Spectral Graph Transducer (SGT), which is a transductive version of the k nearest-neighbor classifier.

3 Problem Definition

The research problem of this paper is classification of relations between entities. In other words, the task is to determine the appropriate relational table into which one should put a given pair of related entities. To be more precise,

- We only focus on binary relations, i.e., ones between pairs of entities.
- We only deal with intra-sentence explicit relations in this study. In other words, the (two) EDT mentions of the entity arguments of a relation must occur within a common syntactic construction, in this case a sentence. The relations also have to be "explicit" in the sense that they should have explicit textual support and don't require further reasoning based on understanding of the context's meaning.
- We don't actually "detect" relations. Rather, the goal is to classify the type of relation between two entities (or, in other words, to put the entity pair into the correct relational table), given that they are known to be related.

- It is also assumed that entity recognition already takes place beforehand, hence all entity-related information is available.

We use the five high-level relations defined in ACE RDC Annotation Guidelines V3.6 as the target set of classes of the classification task (in other words, they define the five candidate relational tables into which the entity pairs will be dispatched). These are:

ROLE affiliation between people and organizations, facilities, and GPEs (Geo-Political Entities). This includes employment, office holder, ownership, founder, member, and nationality relationships, etc.

PART part-whole relationships between organizations, facilities and GPEs.

AT location of a Person, Organization, GPE, or Facility entity. For example, a person is at a Location, GPE or Facility if the context indicates that the person was, is or will be there. An Organization is in a Location/GPE if it has a branch there.

NEAR indicates that an entity is explicitly near a location, but not actually in that location or part of that location.

SOC personal or professional relationships between people, such as relative, associate, etc.

First, for each relation r in the list above, we learn the following classifier:

$$C_r : (c_{pr}, e_1, c_m, e_2, c_{pt}) \rightarrow l$$

where a sentence is a concatenation of five parts, with e_1 and e_2 representing the entities, and c_{pr}, c_m, and c_{pt} representing the pre-, mid-, and post-context respectively. A label $l \in \{0, 1\}$ is assigned to the five-tuple. For example, in the following sentence,

`Shares of Disney, parent company of ABC, are up five eighths.`

"Disney" and "ABC" are the two "ORGANIZATION" entities, and they divide the whole sentence into three context windows (the pre-context before "Disney", the post-context after "ABC", and the mid-context between the two entities). With regard to the "PART" relation, the label is "1", and "0" for other relations.

Then we combine the multiple binary classifiers and get a single classifier

$$C(c_{pr}, e_1, c_m, e_2, c_{pt}) = \arg\max_{r_i} C_{r_i}(c_{pr}, e_1, c_m, e_2, c_{pt})$$

In the example above, a label "PART" is eventually assigned to the tuple.

4 Approach: Learning Similarity Functions for Transductive Learning

4.1 Formalization of Different Learning Paradigms

Assuming we have

- Input (instance) space X and output (label) space Y

– Labeled data set L and unlabeled data set U (as mentioned before, no distinction is made between "unlabeled" and "test" data in the transductive learning setting)

One could distinguish three types of learning paradigms:

– *Induction*

$$(X_L, Y_L) \mapsto f \tag{1}$$

where f represents the induced model

– *Induction with unlabeled data*

$$(X_L, Y_L) \cup X_U \mapsto f \tag{2}$$

– *Transduction*

$$(X_L, Y_L) \cup X_U \mapsto Y_U \tag{3}$$

The three learning paradigms clearly have different advantages and different application scenarios. However, when it comes to exploiting unlabeled data, the tradeoff between the last two is not yet well understood. In this paper, we focus on the last learning paradigm, i.e., transductive learning.

4.2 Transductive Learning with Learned Similarity Function

A general approach to transductive learning is to construct a graph of all data points based on distance or similarity among them, and then to use the "known" labels to perform some type of graph partitioning or label propagation.

In this study, we use the Spectral Graph Transducer (implemented in SGT-light) [13] as our baseline transductive learner, which exactly follows the transducitve learning paradigm defined by Equation (3). The basic idea of SGT is to construct a similarity weighted undirected k nearest-neighbor (kNN) graph G on X with adjacency matrix A (defined below), and then run spectral partitioning on it.

$$A_{ij} = \begin{cases} \frac{similarity(x_i, x_j)}{\sum_{x_k \in knn(x_i)} similarity(x_i, x_k)} & x_j \in knn(x_i) \\ 0 & otherwise \end{cases} \tag{4}$$

Notice that what takes a crucial role in shaping the structure of graph is the similarity function, as which SGT uses the cosine value between feature vectors. However, there might exist other choices for similarity functions. Our hypothesis is:

If we can **learn (induce)** *a similarity function from part of the labeled data and use it to construct a new weighted graph G' over the unlabeled data and the remaining labeled data, a transductive learner on G' will outperform the baseline transductive learner that works on G.*

This defines the following modified version of the transductive learning paradigm:

$$\begin{aligned} (X_{L_1}, Y_{L_1}) &\mapsto f_{L_1} \\ f_{L_1}(X_{L_2} \cup X_U) &\mapsto G' \\ ((X_{L_2}, Y_{L_2}) \cup X_U)^{G'} &\mapsto Y_U \end{aligned} \tag{5}$$

in which $L_1 \cup L_2 = L$ and $L_1 \cap L_2 = \phi$.

Below is a very straightforward (yet effective, as the readers will see from experimental results) way of defining the "learned" similarity function. Suppose the induced model f_{L_1} assigns a confidence score $confidence_{f_{L_1}}(x_i)$ to each data points based on its model trained on the the labeled data, then the similarity function in G' can be defined as:

$$similarity(x_i, x_j) = e^{-distance(x_i, x_j)} \tag{6}$$

where the "distance" between two data points is defined as

$$distance(x_i, x_j) = |confidence_{f_{L_1}}(x_i) - confidence_{f_{L_1}}(x_j)| \tag{7}$$

Simply put: the more different the confidence scores, the further away two instances are from each other; the further away, the less similar they are.

4.3 Features

We extract the following lexical and syntactic features (all categorical features are binarized) from the linguistic context in which the two entities co-occur:

Lexical features. Surface tokens of the two entities and three context windows.

Shallow-syntactic features. Part-Of-Speech tags (e.g., "noun", etc.) corresponding to all tokens in the two entities and three context windows.

Deep-syntactic features. To capture the syntactic dependencies between entities, the following features are extracted from the chunklink representation (flattened parse trees):

- *Chunk tags* of the two entities and three context windows. This information is not explicitly present in the treebank format. For example, the "O" tag means that the current word is outside of any chunk; the "I-XP" tag means that this word is inside an XP chunk; the "B-XP" by default means that the word is at the beginning of an XP chunk.
- *Grammatical function tags* of the two entities and three context windows. The last word in each chunk is its head, and the function of the head is the function of the whole chunk. For example, "NP-SBJ" means an NP chunk as the subject of the sentence. The other words in a chunk that are not the head have "NOFUNC" as their function.
- *IOB-chains* of the heads of the two entities, each of which is a lexicalized path, in other words, a concatenation of the syntactic categories of all

the constituents on the path from the root node to this leaf node of the tree (e.g., "S/VP/NP/NN").

Other features. Miscellaneous information including:

- An *ordering flag* that indicates the relative position of the two entity arguments of a relation.
- *Types* of the two entities, such as "PERSON" or "GPE".

The context windows are defined as the following:

- Mid-context: everything between the two entities.
- Pre- (post-) context: up to two words before (after) the corresponding entity.

5 Experiments and Results

5.1 Data

We use the ACE corpus for our task. Specifically, ACE-2 version 1.0 is used, which contains 519 files from sources including broadcast, newswire, and newspaper. The corpus contains 5,260 manually tagged relations (a small number of additional relations are dropped out due to data preprocessing errors). A breakdown of the data by different relation type is given in Table 1. We treat the "training" and "devtest" portions of the corpus as a whole and perform our split on the data in the experiments.

Table 1. Number of relations: break-down by relation type

Relation type	Training	Devtest
ROLE	1964	472
PART	549	123
AT	1249	328
NEAR	78	31
SOC	398	68
Total	4238	1022

The following steps are taken to process the data:

1. Parse the ACE data in XML format; extract and index entities and relations.
2. Segment the text into sentences using the sentence segmenter provided by the DUC competition [3].
3. Parse the sentences using the Charniak parser [14].
4. Convert the parse trees into chunklink format using chunklink.pl [15].
5. Extract and compute features from the chunklink format.

[3] http://duc.nist.gov/past_duc/duc2003/software/

5.2 Experimental Setup and Evaluation Metrics

To test the superiority of the learned similarity function in the transductive setting, we experiment the following three scenarios:

- A vanilla SGT learner that uses a labeled set of size 2,000 and an unlabeled set (by hiding the labels) of size 3,260.
- A modified SGT learner (SVM-SGT) that uses SVM-light [16] as the inductive learner for similarity functions. (In this case, the confidence score for each data point is the value of the decision function.)
- Another modified SGT learner (SNoW-SGT) that uses SNoW [17] with the Winnow updating rule [18] as the inductive learner for similarity functions. (In this case, the confidence score for each data point is the softmax normalized activation for the positive label.)

For both the SVM-SGT and SNoW-SGT learners, we use the same amount of labeled and unlabeled data as for the vanilla SGT learner, with half of the labeled data (1,000 data points) used for inducing the similarity function, and the other half used for SGT learning on the modified graph/matrix. All three experiments are run with 10 random splits of the whole data set, which contains 5,260 data points.

In all three scenarios, the final combination of multiple classifiers is done by assigning the label for which the corresponding binary classifier has the highest confidence score (i.e., the solution of the spectral optimization problem in SGT).

To evaluate the performance of learning algorithms, we compute overall classification accuracy, and for each class, the precision, recall, and F-measure.

5.3 Experimental Results: Effect of Induced Similarity Measure

We experimented different values of k, ranging from 20 to 120, for kNN graph. Empirically, they do not seem to make a lot of difference. All the performance numbers reported below are based on 100-NN graphs.

With the vanilla SGT learner, we get a 70.34% accuracy, and the class-specific performance is summarized in Table 2.

With the SVM-SGT learner, we get a 78.04% accuracy, and the class-specific performance is summarized in Table 3.

With the SNoW-SGT learner, we get a 76.02% accuracy, and the class-specific performance is summarized in Table 4.

Table 2. Performance of vanilla SGT learner (full)

Relation type	Precision	Recall	F-measure
ROLE	73.72%	83.31%	78.19%
PART	63.34%	42.32%	49.93%
AT	67.43%	72.88%	69.95%
NEAR	65.92%	7.36%	12.71%
SOC	71.87%	47.81%	56.96%

Table 3. Performance of SVM-SGT learner (full)

Relation type	Precision	Recall	F-measure
ROLE	82.87%	84.01%	83.41%
PART	63.31%	57.49%	60.13%
AT	77.16%	79.69%	78.36%
NEAR	4.81%	0.62%	5.32%
SOC	76.23%	88.88%	81.93%

Table 4. Performance of SNow-SGT learner (full)

Relation type	Precision	Recall	F-measure
ROLE	81.47%	79.61%	80.44%
PART	62.72%	62.34%	62.35%
AT	74.57%	81.15%	77.64%
NEAR	0.59%	0.13%	NA
SOC	73.73%	77.92%	75.96%

The most important result of interest is that both modified SGT learners consistently outperforms the vanilla SGT learner across all random runs, and the differences are statically significant ($p << 0.01$). This justifies our hypothesis that a learned similarity function between data points, as opposed to naive cosine similarity, can significantly improve the performance of transductive learners.

5.4 Experimental Results: Comparison with Supervised Inductive Learners

To get a sense of the empirical difference between transductive, improved transductive, and inductive learning algorithms, we also present the performance of a few supervised inducitve learners on the same number of training examples (2,000). Results are also averaged over 10 random runs.

With the supervised SVM learner, we get a 82.31% accuracy, and the class-specific performance is summarized in Table 5.

With the supervised SNoW learner, we get a 77.37% accuracy, and the class-specific performance is summarized in Table 6.

Table 5. Performance of supervised SVM learner (full)

Relation type	Precision	Recall	F-measure
ROLE	86.27%	85.96%	86.11%
PART	75.90%	58.36%	65.89%
AT	78.87%	88.65%	83.46%
NEAR	83.96%	3.57%	8.41%
SOC	82.13%	94.29%	87.74%

Table 6. Performance of supervised SNoW learner (full)

Relation type	Precision	Recall	F-measure
ROLE	85.46%	80.30%	82.19%
PART	64.93%	64.40%	64.50%
AT	77.07%	79.77%	77.77%
NEAR	28.94%	27.95%	24.56%
SOC	79.69%	84.32%	81.21%

Table 7. Performance of supervised naive bayes learner (full)

Relation type	Precision	Recall	F-measure
ROLE	52.63%	97.56%	68.37%
PART	0%	0%	0%
AT	78.13%	35.83%	48.82%
NEAR	0%	0%	0%
SOC	0%	0%	0%

With the supervised Naive Bayes learner, we get a 56.10% accuracy, and the class-specific performance is summarized in Table 7.

If we compare the performance presented in this subsection with those of the corresponding transductive learners in the previous subsection, we observe the following pattern:

$$\text{NB} < \text{SGT} < \text{SNoW-SGT} < \text{SNoW} < \text{SVM-SGT} < \text{SVM}$$

With regard to the purpose of this study, again, it is most important to notice that the induction-aided transductive learners significantly outperform the "pure" transductive learner. On the other hand, it is reasonable to expect that with improvement of the fundamental algorithm (e.g., spectral partioning), the transductive learners (with or without induced similarity measures) may outperform the best inductive learners.

6 Conclusions and Future Work

This paper approaches the relation classification problem with improved transductive learning. Specifically, we learned the following:

- Application of transductive learning on NLP problems, including information extraction, has been under-explored. This paper makes the attempt to show that binary relations hidden in natural language text can be effectively classified by using transductive learning.
- It is shown that an improved transductive learner using similarity functions induced from a small amount of labeled data outperforms its naive transductive counterpart.

- Further more, the general idea of inducing similarity functions for transductive learning are potentially applicable to other classification problems, since it doesn't have any specific characteristics tied to the current relation classification problem.

In the future, we are interested in pursuing the following directions:

- The current work only deals with binary relations. The algorithms presented should be generalized so that they can work on higher-order relations.
- In this study, we only used a randomly selected portion of the labeled data available as the seed labeled set for inducing similarity functions. It is conceivable that if we anchor the seed data points more intelligently (e.g., using clustering or in other unsupervised fashion), better classification performance of the modified transductive learner can be expected.
- This chapter presents one particular way of inducing the similarity function for transductive learning, which is simple yet effective. However, it may be worth the effort to investigate other alternatives.
- In the machine learning community, how to exploit unlabeled data remains largely an open question. In the long run, it would be very interesting and useful to investigate, both theoretically and empirically, the tradeoff between induction with unlabeled data vs. transduction (including "induction-aided" transduction discussed in this paper).

References

1. Agichtein, E., Gravano, L.: Snowball: Extracting relations from large plain-text collections. In: Proceedings of the Fifth ACM International Conference on Digital Libraries. (2000)
2. Brin, S.: Extracting patterns and relations from the world wide web. In: WebDB Workshop at 6th International Conference on Extending Database Technology, EDBT'98. (1998)
3. Zelenko, D., Aone, C., Richardella, A.: Kernel methods for relation extraction. J. Mach. Learn. Res. **3** (2003) 1083–1106
4. Zhang, Z.: Weakly-supervised relation classification for information extraction. In: Proceedings of the 13th International Conference on Information and Knowledge Management CIKM 2004, Washington DC (2004)
5. Rosario, B., Hearst, M.: Classifying semantic relations in bioscience text. In: Proceedings of the 42nd Annual Meeting of the Association for Computational Linguistics. (2004)
6. Abney, S.: Understanding the Yarowsky algorithm. Computational Linguistics **30** (2004)
7. Vapnik, V.N.: Statistical learning theory. John Wiley, NY (1998)
8. Joachims, T.: Transductive inference for text classification using support vector machines. In Bratko, I., Dzeroski, S., eds.: Proceedings of ICML-99, 16th International Conference on Machine Learning, Bled, SL, Morgan Kaufmann Publishers, San Francisco, US (1999) 200–209
9. Bennett, K.: Combining support vector and mathematical programming methods for classification. In Sch?lkopf, B., Burges, C., Smola, A., eds.: Advances in Kernel Methods - Support Vector Learning. MIT-Press (1999)

10. Blum, A., Chawla, S.: Learning from labeled and unlabeled data using graph mincuts. In: ICML '01: Proceedings of the Eighteenth International Conference on Machine Learning, San Francisco, CA, USA, Morgan Kaufmann Publishers Inc. (2001) 19–26
11. Blum, A., Lafferty, J., Rwebangira, M.R., Reddy, R.: Semi-supervised learning using randomized mincuts. In: ICML '04: Twenty-first international conference on Machine learning, New York, NY, USA, ACM Press (2004)
12. Kleinberg, J., Tardos, E.: Approximation algorithms for classification problems with pairwise relationships: metric labeling and Markov random fields. In: Proceedings of the 40th Annual Symposium on Foundations of Computer Science. (1999) 14–23
13. Joachims, T.: Transductive learning via spectral graph partitioning. In: Proceedings of The Twentieth International Conference on Machine Learning (ICML). (2003)
14. Charniak, E.: A maximum-entropy-inspired parser. Technical Report CS-99-12, Computer Scicence Department, Brown University (1999)
15. Buchholz, S.: The chunklink script. (2000) Software available at `http://ilk.uvt.nl/~sabine/chunklink/`.
16. Joachims, T.: Making large-scale support vector machine learning practical. In: Advances in kernel methods: support vector learning. MIT Press, Cambridge, MA, USA (1999) 169–184
17. Carlson, A., Cumby, C., Rosen, J., Roth, D.: The SNoW learning architecture. Technical Report UIUCDCS-R-99-2101, UIUC Computer Science Department (1999)
18. Littlestone, N.: Learning quickly when irrelevant attributes abound: A new linear-threshold algorithm. Mach. Learn. **2** (1988) 285–318

A Preliminary Work on Classifying Time Granularities of Temporal Questions

Wei Li[1], Wenjie Li[1], Qin Lu[1], and Kam-Fai Wong[2]

[1] Department of Computing, The Hong Kong Polytechnic University, Hung Hom, Hong Kong
{cswli, cswjli, csluqin}@comp.polyu.edu.hk
[2] Department of Systems Engineering, the Chinese University of Hong Kong, Shatin, Hong Kong
kfwong@se.cuhk.edu.hk

Abstract. Temporal question classification assigns time granularities to temporal questions ac-cording to their anticipated answers. It is very important for answer extraction and verification in the literature of temporal question answering. Other than simply distinguishing between "date" and "period", a more fine-grained classification hierarchy scaling down from "millions of years" to "second" is proposed in this paper. Based on it, a SNoW-based classifier, combining user preference, word N-grams, granularity of time expressions, special patterns as well as event types, is built to choose appropriate time granularities for the ambiguous temporal questions, such as When- and How long-like questions. Evaluation on 194 such questions achieves 83.5% accuracy, almost close to manually tagging accuracy 86.2%. Experiments reveal that user preferences make significant contributions to time granularity classification.

1 Introduction

Temporal questions, such as the questions with the interrogatives “when”, “how long” and “which year”, seek for the occurrence time of the events or the temporal attributes of the entities. Temporal question classification plays an important role in the literature of question answering and temporal information processing. In the evaluation of TREC 10 Question-Answering (QA) track [1], more than 10% of questions in the test question corpus are temporal questions. Different from TREC QA track, Workshop TERQAS (*http://www.timeml.org/terqas/*) particularly investigated on temporal question answering instead of a general one. It focused on temporal and event recognition in question answering systems and paid great attention to temporal relations among states, events and time expressions in temporal questions. TimeML (*http://www.timeml.org*), a temporal information (e.g. time expression, tense & aspect) annotation standard, has also been used for temporal question answering in this workshop [2]. Correct understanding of a temporal question will greatly help extracting and verifying its answers and certainly improve the performance of any question answering system. Look at the following examples.

[Ea]. What is the birthday of Abraham Lincoln?
[Eb]. When did the Neanderthal man live?

R. Dale et al. (Eds.): IJCNLP 2005, LNAI 3651, pp. 414 – 425, 2005.

In a general question answering system, the question classifier commonly classifies temporal questions into two classes, i.e. "date" and "period". With such a system, the above two questions are both assigned a "date". Whereas it is natural for the question [Ea] to be answered with a particular data (e.g. "12/02/1809"), it is not the case for question [Eb], because a proper answer could be "35,000 years ago". However, if it is known that the time granularity concerned is "thousands of years", answer extraction turn to be more targeted. The need for a more fine-grained classification is obvious. Although there were different question classification hierarchies, as reported [3,4,12,13,14], few inclined to introducing the classification hierarchy (e.g. "year", "month" and "day") which could give a clearer direction to guide answer extraction and verification of temporal questions. In the following, we try to find out whether temporal questions can be further classified into finer time granularity and how to classify them.

By examining a temporal question corpus consisting of 348 questions, 293 of which are gathered from UIUC question answering labelled data (*http://l2r.cs.uiuc.edu/~cogcomp/Data/QA/QC*), and the rest 55 from TREC 10 test corpus, we find two different cases. On the one hand, some questions are very straightforward in expressing the time granularities of the answers expected, e.g. the questions beginning with "which year" or "for how many years". On the other hand, some questions are not so obvious, e.g. the questions headed by "when" or "for how long". We call such questions ambiguous questions. Not surprisingly, the ambiguous *When*- and *How long*-like questions account for a large proportion in this temporal question corpus, i.e. 197 from 348 in total.

We further investigate on those 197 ambiguous questions in order to find out whether they can be classified into finer time granularity. Three experimenters are requested to tag a time granularity to each question independently[1]. Answers are not provided. The tag with two agreements is taken as the time granularity class of the corresponding temporal question. Otherwise the tag "UNKNOWN" is assigned. Reference answers for the questions are extracted from AltaVista Web Search *(http://www.altavista.com)*. Comparing the time granularities tagged manually with those provided by the reference answers, we find that only 27 out of 197 questions are incorrectly tagged, in other words, the manually tagging accuracy is 86.2%. Errors exist though, the relatively high agreement between users' tagging and reference answers lights the hope of automatically determining the time granularities of temporal questions.

Analysing the tagging results, it is revealed that the tagging errors arouse from three sources: insufficient world knowledge, different speaking habits and different expected information granularity among human. See the following examples:

[Ec]. When did the Neanderthal man live?
User: year; Ref.: thousands of years

[Ed]. How long is human gestation?
User: month; Ref.: week

[Ee]. When was the first Wall Street Journal published?
User: year; Ref.: day

[1] The granularity hierarchy and the tagging principle will be detailed later.

For question [Ec], the time granularity should be "thousands of years", rather than "year". This error could be corrected if one knows that Neanderthal man existed 35,000 years ago. The time granularity of question [Ed] should be "week", but not "month" in accordance with the habit. For question [Ee], users' tag is "year", different from the reference answer's tag "day". However, both granularities are acceptable in commonsense, because the different users may want coarser or finer information. This observation suggests that incorporating question context, world knowledge, and speaking habits would help determine the time granularities of temporal questions.

In this paper, we propose a fine-grained temporal question classification scheme, i.e. time granularity hierarchy, consisting of sixteen non-exclusive classes and scaling down from "millions of years" to "second". The SNoW-based classifier is then built to combine linguistic features (including word *N*-grams, granularity of time expressions and special patterns), user preferences and event types, and assign one of the sixteen classes to each temporal question. In our work, user preference, which characterizes world knowledge and speaking habits, is estimated by means of the time granularities of the entities and/or events involved. The SNoW-based classifier achieves 83.5% accuracy, almost close to 86.2% of manually tagging accuracy. Experiments also show that user preference makes a great contribution to time granularity classification.

The rest of this paper is organized as follows. In the next section various related works in this literature are introduced. In Sect. 3, we demonstrate the time granularity hierarchy and principles. User preference is fully investigated in Sect. 4. Feature design is depicted in Sect. 5. Time granularity classifiers are introduced in Sect. 6 and the experiment results are presented in Sect. 7. We finally conclude this paper in the last section.

2 Related Works

In TREC QA track, almost every QA system joining in the evaluation has a question classification module. This makes question classification a hot topic. Questions can be classified from several aspects. Most classification hierarchies [3,4,12,13,14] adopt the anticipated answer types as its classification criteria. Abney et al. [4] gave a coarse classification hierarchy with seven classes (person, location, etc.). Hovy et al. [13] introduced a finer classification with forty-seven classes manually constructed from 17,000 practical questions. Li et al. [3] proposed a two-level classification hierarchy, a coarser one with six classes and a finer one with fifty classes. In all these classification hierarchies, temporal questions are simply classified into two classes, i.e. "date" and "period". Some works classified temporal questions from other aspects. In [2], a temporal question classification hierarchy is proposed according to the temporal relation among state, event and time expression. In [5], temporal questions are classified into three types with regard to question structure: non-temporal, simple and complex. Diaz F. et al. [6] did an interesting work on the statistics of the number of topics along timeline. According to whether questions or topics have a clear distribution along timeline, they can be classified into three types: atemporal, temporal clear and temporal ambiguous. Focusing on ambiguous temporal questions, e.g. *when* and *how long*-like questions, we introduce a classification hierarchy in terms of the anticipated answer types.

It is an extension of two classes "date" and "period" and includes sixteen non-exclusive classes scaling down from "millions of years" to "second".

Related to the work of features design, Li et al. [3] built the question classifier based on three types of features, including surface text (e.g. N-grams), syntactic features (e.g. part-of-speech and name entity tags), and semantic related words (words that often occur with a specific question class). Later works of Li et al. [10] introduced semantic information and world knowledge from external resources such as WordNet. In this paper, we introduce a new feature, user preference, which is expected to imply the world knowledge in time granularity in the experiment. User preference is estimated from statistics with which Diaz F. et al. [6] determine whether a question is temporal ambiguous or not. E. Saquete et al. [5] suggested that questions had different structures, i.e. non-temporal, simple and complex, which is helpful to handle questions more orderly. It gives us inspiration to use question focus, i.e. whether a question is event-based or entity-based.

Many machine-learning methods have been used in question classification, such as language model [7], SNoW [3,10], maximum entropy [15] and support vector machine [8,9]. In our experiments, language model is selected as the baseline model, and SNoW is selected to tackle to the large feature space and build the classifier. In fact, SNoW has already been used in many other fields, such as text categorization, word sense disambiguation and even facial feature detection.

3 Time Granularity Hierarchy and Tagging Principles

In traditional question answering systems, only two question types are time-related, i.e. "date" and "period". For the reasons explained in Sect. 1, we propose a more detailed temporal question classification scheme, namely time granularity hierarchy scaling down from "millions of years" to "second" in order to facilitate answer extraction and verification. The initial time granularity hierarchy includes the following twelve classes: "second", "minute", "hour", "day", "week", "month", "season", "year", "decade", "century", "thousands of years" and "millions of years".

Granularity "weekday" is added to the initial hierarchy because some temporal questions favor "weekday" instead of "day", although both of them indicate one day. Some questions favour a region of time granularity. Look at the following examples.

[Ef]. What time of year has the most air travel?
[Eg]. What time of day did Emperor Hirohito die?

For [Ef] question, its time granularity could be "season", "month" or even "day"; and for question [Eg], the time granularity could be "hour" or "minute". We can only determine that their time granularities are less than "year" or "day" respectively, but cannot go any further. Such situations only occur to time granularity "year" and "day", so we expand the original classification hierarchy by adding another two types: "less than day", "less than year". Besides, the questions asking for festivals are classified into "special date".

Up to now, the time granularity hierarchy has sixteen classes. The less frequent temporal measures, such as "microsecond" and "billions of years" are ignored. As mentioned above, the class "less than day" overlaps several granularities, e.g. "hour" and "minute", so the time granularity hierarchy we proposed is non-exclusive.

In reality, some temporal questions can be answered in several different time granularities. For example, question "when was Abraham Lincoln born?", its answers can be a "day" ("12/02/1809") or a "year" ("1809"). To resolve this confliction, we adopt two principles for time granularity annotation.

[Pa]. Assign the minimum time granularity we can determine to a given temporal question if several time granularities are applicable.
[Pb]. Select the time granularity with regard to speaking habits or user preferences.

When the two principles conflict to each other, principle [Pb] takes the priority. With principle [Pa], time granularity of the above question can only be "day".

4 User Preference

In general, temporal questions have two different focuses: entity-based and event-based.

[a]. Entity-based question: temporal interrogative words + (be) + entity, e.g. "When was the World War II?"
[b]. Event-based question: temporal interrogatives + event, e.g. "When did Mount St. Helen last have a significant eruption?"

Time granularities of entities (or events) have great significance to those of entity-based (or event-based) temporal questions. So, in the following, we make estimation of the time granularities of entities and events from statistics, based on the intuition that some entities or events may favor certain types of time granularities, which is called user preference here.

4.1 Estimation of Time Granularities of Entities and Events

4.1.1 Time Granularity of Entities

The time granularity of the entity is derived by counting the co-occurrences of the entity and time granularities. The statistics is gathered from AltaVista Web Search. The sentences containing both the entity and time expressions are extracted from the first one hundred results returned by AltaVista with the entity as the searching keyword. The probability P of a time granularity class tg_i on the occurrence of the entity is calculated as the following Equation (1).

$$P(tg_i \mid entity) = \frac{\#(tg_i \cap entity)}{\#(entity)} \quad TG(entity) = Arg\max_{tg_i} P(tg_i \mid entity) \qquad (1)$$

#( ) is the number of the sentences containing the expressions between the parenthesis. *TG(entity)* represents the time granularity of the entity.

4.1.2 Time Granularity of Events

The time granularities of the events are not directly extracted as what is done to the entities, because they have little chance to be reused on the observation that there are rarely two identical events in a question corpus. As an alternative, the time granularity of an event is estimated from a sequence of entity-verb-entity' approximating the event. The time granularity of the verb is determined as Equation (1) by substituting "*verb*" for "*entity*". We choose two strategies for the estimation: maximum product and one-win-all.

Maximum product: $P(tg_i \mid event) = \frac{1}{Z} P(tg_i \mid entity) P(tg_i \mid verb) P(tg_i \mid entity')$

$$TG(event) = Arg\max_{tg_i} P(tg_i \mid event) \tag{2}$$

TG(event) represents time granularity of event. *Z* is used for normalization.

One-win-all: $TG(event) = Arg\max_{tg_i} \{P(tg_i \mid entity), P(tg_i \mid verb), P(tg_i \mid entity')\}$ (3)

Equation (1) is smoothed in order to avoid 0 values in Equation (2).

$$P(tg_i \mid w) = \frac{\#(tg_i \cap w) + 1}{\#(w) + t} \qquad t = |tg_i| \tag{4}$$

t is the number of the time granularity classes, *w* is either an entity or a verb.

4.1.3 Experiment: Evaluating the Estimation

In the 197 ambiguous questions, 12 questions are entity-based, and the rest 185 questions are event-based. If all the 197 questions are arbitrarily assigned a tag "year", the tagging accuracy is 48.2%.

For each entity-based or event-based question, the time granularity of the entity or event within it are assumed as the time granularity of the question. Compared with the time granularity of the reference answer, for the entity-based questions, we achieve 75% accuracy; for the event-based question, the accuracy of maximum product strategy and one-win-all strategy are 67.0% and 64.3% respectively. It seems that maximum product strategy is more effective than one-win-all strategy in this application. With maximum product strategy, the overall accuracy on all the 197 ambiguous questions is 67.4%. Notice that the accuracy of arbitrarily tagging is only 48.2%, so the estimation of the time granularities of the entities and the events is useful for determining the time granularities of temporal questions.

4.2 Distribution of the Time Granularity of Entities and Events

4.2.1 Observation of Distribution

In the experiments of estimation, we find that some entities or events tend to favor only one certain time granularity, some others tend to favor several time granularities, and the rest may have a uniform distribution almost on every time granularity.

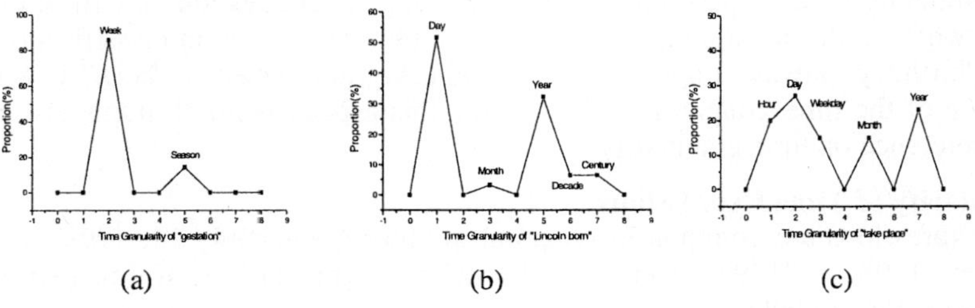

Fig. 1. Distribution of the time granularities of the entities and events

In Fig. 1(a), time granularity "day" takes a preponderant proportion, i.e. more than 80%, in the distribution of "gestation", which is called single-peak-distribution. In Fig. 1(b), both "day" and "year" take a large proportion, so "Lincoln born" is multi-peak-distributed. In Fig. 1(c), for "take place", all the time granularities almost take a similar proportion and it is a uniform distribution.

4.2.2 Experiments on Distribution

Assume an entity (or event) *E*, its possible time granularities $\{tg_i, i=1,\ldots t\}$ and the corresponding probabilities $\{P_i, i=1,\ldots t\}$ (calculated by Equation 1 and 2).

$$\mu = \frac{1}{t}\sum_i P_i \; ; \; d = \sum_i I(P_i, \mu) \; ; \; I(P_i, \mu) = \begin{cases} 1 & P_i > \mu \\ 0 & P_i \leq \mu \end{cases} \tag{5}$$

d is the number of time granularities tg_i with higher probability P_i than average probability μ. For simplicity, distribution D_E of the time granularity of *E* is determined as follows,

$$D_E = \begin{cases} Single & d = 1 \\ Multi & 1 < d \leq 3 \\ Uniform & d > 3 \end{cases} \tag{6}$$

Observing the experiment results in Sect. 4.1.3, 88.7%, 56.3% and 18.9% accuracy are achieved on the questions within which the time granularities of the entities or events are estimated to be single-peak-, multi-peak-, and uniform-distributed respectively. So whether the estimated time granularity of the entity or event is single-peak-, multi-peak-, or uniform-distributed highlights the confidence on the estimation, which can be taken as a feature associated with the estimation of the time granularities.

5 Feature Design

As described in the above section, estimation of the time granularities of the entities and the events is useful for determining the time granularities of temporal questions; whether a question is entity-based or not and the distribution of time granularities of the entities and events within the questions will also be taken as associated features. These three features are named user preference feature in total. Besides, another four types of features are considered.

Word N-grams

Word N-grams feature, e.g. unigram and bigram is the most straightforward feature and commonly used in question classification. In general question classification, unigram "when" indicates a temporal question. In temporal question classification, unigram "birthday" always implies a "day" while bigram "when … born" is a strong evidence of the time granularity "day". From this aspect, word N-grams also reflect user preference on time granularity.

Granularity of Time Expressions

Time expressions are common in temporal questions, e.g. "July 11, 1998" and date modifier "1998" in "1998 Superbowl". We take the granularities of time expressions as features, for example,

TG("in 1998") = "year" TG("July 11, 1998") = "day"

Granularities of time expressions impose the constraints on the time granularities of temporal questions. If there is a time expression whose time granularity is *tg* in a temporal question, time granularity of this question can not be *tg*. For example, question "When is the 1998 SuperBowl?", its time granularity can not be "Year", i.e. the time granularity of "1998".

Special Patterns
In word N-gram features, words are equally processed, however, some special words combining with the verbs or the temporal connectives (e.g. "when", "before" and "since") will produce special patterns and affect the time granularities of temporal questions. Look at the following examples.

[Eh]. Since when hasn't John Sununu been able to fly on government planes for personal business?

[Ei]. What time of the day does Michael Milken typically wake up?

For question [Eh], the temporal preposition "since" combined with "when" highlights that this question is seeking for a beginning point time, which implies a finer time granularity; for question [Ei], "typically" combined with verb "wake up" indicates a generally occurred event, and implies that its time granularity could be "less than day" or "less than year".

Event Types
In general, there are four event types: states, activities, accomplishments, and achievements. States and activities favour larger time granularities, while accomplishments and achievements favour smaller ones. For example, the activity "stay" will favour larger time granularity than the accomplishment event "take place".

6 Classifier Building

In this work, we choose the Sparse Network of Winnow (SNoW) model as the time granularity classifier and compare it with a commonly used Language Model (LM) classifier.

6.1 Language Model (LM)

As language model has already been used in question classification [7], it is taken as the baseline model in the experiments. Language model mainly combines two types of features, i.e. unigram and bigram. Given a temporal question *Q*, its time granularity *TG(Q)* is calculated by Equation (7).

$$TG(Q) = Argmax_{tg_i} \lambda \prod_{j=1}^{j=m} P(tg_i \mid w_j) + (1-\lambda) \prod_{j=1}^{j=n} P(tg_i \mid w_j w_{j+1}) \quad (7)$$

w represents words. m and n are the numbers of unigrams and bigrams in questions respectively. λ assigns different weights to unigrams and bigrams. In the experiment, best accuracy is achieved when $\lambda = 0.7$ (see Sect. 7.3.1).

6.2 Sparse Network of Winnow (SNoW)

SNoW is a learning framework and applicable to the tasks with a very large number of features. It selects active features by updating weights of features, and learns a linear function from a corpus consisting of positive and negative examples. Let $Ac=\{i_1, ..., i_m\}$ be the set of features that are active and linked to target class c. Let s_i be the real valued strength associated with feature in the example. Then the example's class is c if and only if,

$$\sum_{i\in Ac} w_{c,i} s_i \geq \theta_c \tag{8}$$

$w_{c,i}$ is weight of feature i connected with class c, which is learned from the training corpus. SNoW has already been used in question classification [3,10] and good results are reported. As mentioned in Sect. 5, five types of features are selected for our task. They are altogether counted to more than ten thousand features. Since it is a large feature set, SNoW is a good choice.

7 Experiments

7.1 Setup

In this 348-question-corpus (see Sect. 1), time granularities of 151 questions are straightforward, while those of the rest 197 questions are ambiguous. For the sixteen time granularity classes, we only consider ten classes including more than four questions. Questions with unconsidered time granularity classes excluded, the question corpus has 339 questions in total, 145 for training and 194 for testing. As a result, the task is to learn a model from the 145-question training corpus and classify questions in the 194-question test corpus into ten classes: "second", "minute", "hour", "day", "weekday", "week", "month", "season", "year" and "century". The SNoW classifier is downloaded from UIUC *(http://l2r.cs.uiuc.edu/~cogcomp/download.php?key=SNOW).*

7.2 Evaluation Criteria

The primary evaluation standard is accuracy$_1$, i.e. the proportion of the correct classified questions out of the test questions (see Equation 9). However, if a question seeking for a finer time granularity, e.g. "day", has been incorrectly determined as a coarser one, e.g. "year", it should also be taken as partly correct, which is reflected in accuracy$_2$ (see Equation 10).

$$Accuracy_1 = \frac{\#(correct)}{\#(test)} \tag{9}$$

#( ) is number of questions.

$$Accuracy_2 = \frac{\sum_i RR(Q_i)}{\#(test)} \qquad RR(Q) = \begin{cases} 1 & R(tg_Q') = R(tg_Q) \\ 0 & R(tg_Q') < R(tg_Q) \\ 1/(R(tg_Q') - R(tg_Q) + 1) & R(tg_Q') > R(tg_Q) \end{cases} \tag{10}$$

tg_Q and tg_Q' are the reference and classification result respectively. $R(tg_Q)$ is the rank of the time granularity class tg_Q, scaling down from "millions of years" to "second". Rank of "second" is 1, while rank of "year" is 9. The ranks of the last three time granularities, i.e. “special date”, “less than day” and “less than year” are 14, 15 and 16 respectively. Likewise, $R(tg_Q')$ is the rank of tg_Q'.

7.3 Experimental Results and Analysis

In the experiments, language model is taken as the baseline model. Performance of SNoW-based classifier will be compared with that of language model. Different combinations of features are tested in SNoW-based classifier and their performances are investigated.

7.3.1 LM Classifier

The LM classifier takes two types of features: unigram and bigram. Experiment results are presented in Fig. 2.

Accuracy varies with different feature weight λ and best accuracy (accuracy$_1$ 68.0% and accuracy$_2$ 68.9%) achieves when λ=0.7. Accuracy when λ=1.0 is higher than that when λ=0. It indicates that, in the framework of language model, unigrams achieves better performance than bigrams, which accounts from the sparseness of bigram features.

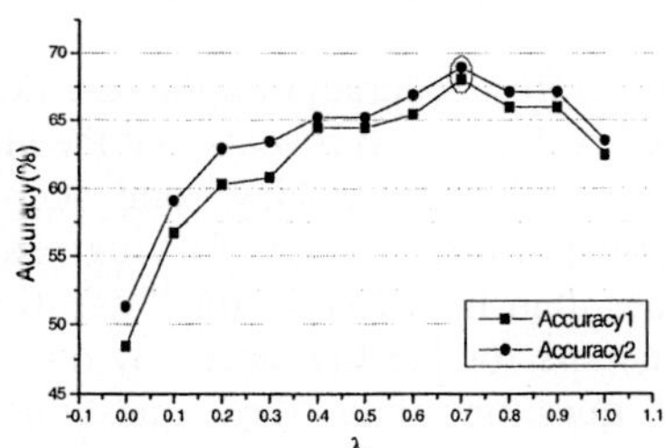

Fig. 2. Accuracy of LM classifier. Data in circle is the best performance achieved.

7.3.2 SNOW Classifier

Our SNoW classifier requires binary features. We then encode each feature with an integer label. When a feature is observed in a question, its label will appear in the extracted feature set of this question. There are six types of features: 15 user preferences (10 for the estimation of time granularities, 3 for the estimation distributions, and 2 for question focuses) (F_1), 951 unigrams (F_2), 9277 bigrams (F_3), 10 granularity of time expressions (F_4), 14 special patterns (F_5), and 4 event types (F_6). Although the number of all features is more than ten thousand, the features in one question are no more than twenty in general. Accuracies of SNoW classifier on 194 test questions are presented in Table 1. It shows that simply using unigram features, SNoW classifier has already achieved better accuracy than LM classifier (accuracy$_1$: 69.5% vs. 68.0%; accuracy$_2$: 70.3% vs. 68.9%). From this view, SNoW classifier outperforms LM classifier in handling sparse features. When all the six types of features are used, SNoW classifier achieves 83.5% in accuracy$_1$ and 83.9% in accuracy$_2$, almost close to the accuracy of user tagging, i.e. 86.2%.

Table 1. Accuracy (%) of SNoW classifier

Feature Set	F_2	$F_{2,3}$	$F_{1\sim6}$
$Accuracy_1$	69.5	72.1	83.5
$Accuracy_2$	70.3	72.7	83.9

Table 2. $Accuracy_1$ (%) on different types of time granularities

TG	second	minute	hour	day	weekday
$Accuracy_1$	100	100	100	64.2	100
TG	week	month	season	year	century
$Accuracy_1$	100	60	100	90.5	66.7

Table 3. Accuracy (%) on combination of different types of features

Feature Set	$F_{2,3}$	$F_{1,2,3}$	$F_{2,3,4}$	$F_{2,3,5}$	$F_{2,3,6}$
$Accuracy_1$	72.1	79.8	73.7	74.7	72.6
$Accuracy_2$	72.7	80.6	74.7	75.2	73.1

With all the six types of features, $accuracy_1$ on the questions with different types of time granularity is illustrated in Table 2. It reveals that the classification errors mainly come from time granularity of "month", "day" and "century". Low accuracy on "month" and "century" accounts from absence of enough examples, i.e. examples for training and testing both less than five. Many "day" questions are incorrectly classified into "year", which accounts for the low accuracy on "day". The reason lies in that there are more "year" questions than "day" questions in the training question corpus (116 vs. 56).

In general, we can extract three F_1 features, one F_4 feature, less than two F_5 features, and one F_6 feature from one question. It is hard for SNoW classifier to train and test independently on each of these types of the features because of the small feature number in one example question. However, the numbers of F_2 and F_3 features in a question are normally more than ten. So we take unigrams (F_2) and bigrams (F_3) as the basic feature set. Table 3 presents the accuracy when the rest four types of features are added into the basic feature set respectively. As expected user preference makes the most significant improvement, 7.82% in $accuracy_1$ and 7.90% in $accuracy_2$. Special patterns also play an important role, which makes 2.6% $accuracy_1$ improvement. It is strange that event type makes such a modest improvement (0.5%). After analyzing the experimental results, we find that as there are only four event types, it makes limited contribution to 10-class time granularity classification.

8 Conclusion

Various features for time granularity classification of temporal questions are investigated in this paper. User preference is shown to make a significant contribution to classification performance. SNoW classifier, combining user preference, word

N-grams, granularity of time expressions, special patterns and event types, achieves 83.5% accuracy in classification, close to manually tagging accuracy 86.2%.

Acknowledgement

This project is partially supported by Hong Kong RGC CERG (Grant No: PolyU5181/03E), and partially by CUHK Direct Grant (No: 2050330).

References

1) TREC (ed.): The TREC-8 Question Answering Track Evaluation. Text Retrieval Conference TREC-8, Gaithersburg, MD (1999)
2) Radev D. and Sundheim B.: Using TimeML in Question Answering. http://www.cs.brandeis.edu/~jamesp/arda/time/documentation/TimeML-use-in-qa-v1.0.pdf, (2002)
3) Li, X. and Roth, D.: Learning Question Classifiers. Proceedings of the 19th International Conference on Computational Linguistics (2002) 556-562
4) S. Abney, M. Collins, and A. Singhal: Answer Extraction. Proceedings of the 6th ANLP Conference (2000) 296-301
5) Saquete E., Martínez-Barco P., Muñoz R.: Splitting Complex Temporal Questions for Question Answering Systems. Proceedings of the 42nd Annual Meeting of the Association for Computational Linguistics (2004) 567-574
6) Diaz, F. and Jones, R.: Temporal Profiles of Queries. Yahoo! Research Labs Technical Report YRL-2004-022 (2004)
7) Wei Li: Question Classification Using Language Modeling. CIIR Technical Report (2002)
8) Dell Zhang and Wee Sun Lee: Question Classification Using Support Vector Machines. Proceedings of the 26th Annual International ACM SIGIR Conference on Research and Development in Information Retrieval (2003) 26-32
9) Jun Suzuki, Hirotoshi Taira, Yutaka Sasaki, and Eisaku Maeda: Question Classification Using HDAG Kernel. Proceedings of Workshop on Multilingual Summarization and Question Answering (2003) 61-68
10) Li X., Roth D., and Small K.: The Role of Semantic Information in Learning Question Classifiers. Proceedings of the International Joint Conference on Natural Language Processing (2004)
11) Schilder, Frank & Habel, Christopher: Temporal Information Extraction for Temporal Question Answering. In New Directions in Question Answering. Papers from the 2003 AAAI Spring Symposium TR SS-03-07 (2003) 34-44
12) Rohini K. Srihari, Wei Li: A Question Answering System Supported by Information Extraction. Proceedings of Association for Computational Linguistics (2000) 166-172
13) Eduard Hovy, Laurie Geber, Ulf Hermjakob, Chin-Yew Lin, and Deepak Ravichandran: Towards Semantics-Based Answer Pinpointing. Proceedings of the DARPA Human Language Technology Conference (2001)
14) Hermjacob U.: Parsing and Question Classification for Question Answering. Proceedings of the Association for Computational Linguists Workshop on Open-Domain Question Answering (2001) 17-22
15) Ittycheriah, Franz M., Zhu W., Ratnaparki A. and Mammone R.: Question Answering Using Maximum Entropy Components. Proceedings of the North American chapter of the Association for Computational Linguistics (2001) 33-39

Classification of Multiple-Sentence Questions

Akihiro Tamura, Hiroya Takamura, and Manabu Okumura

Precision and Intelligence Laboratory,
Tokyo Institute of Technology, Japan
aki@lr.pi.titech.ac.jp
{takamura, oku}@pi.titech.ac.jp

Abstract. Conventional QA systems cannot answer to the questions composed of two or more sentences. Therefore, we aim to construct a QA system that can answer such multiple-sentence questions. As the first stage, we propose a method for classifying multiple-sentence questions into question types. Specifically, we first extract the core sentence from a given question text. We use the core sentence and its question focus in question classification. The result of experiments shows that the proposed method improves F-measure by 8.8% and accuracy by 4.4%.

1 Introduction

Question-Answering (QA) systems are useful in that QA systems return the answer itself, while most information retrieval systems return documents that may contain the answer.

QA systems have been evaluated at TREC QA-Track[1] in U.S. and QAC (Question & Answering Challenge)[2] in Japan. In these workshops, the inputs to systems are only *single-sentence questions*, which are defined as the questions composed of one sentence. On the other hand, on the web there are a lot of *multiple-sentence questions* (e.g., answer bank[3], AskAnOwner[4]), which are defined as the questions composed of two or more sentences: For example, *"My computer reboots as soon as it gets started. OS is Windows XP. Is there any homepage that tells why it happens?"*. For conventional QA systems, these questions are not expected and existing techniques are not applicable or work poorly to these questions. Therefore, constructing QA systems that can handle multiple-sentence questions is desirable.

An usual QA system is composed of three components: question processing, document retrieval, and answer extraction. In question processing, a given question is analyzed, and its question type is determined. This process is called "question classification". Depending on the question type, the process in the answer extraction component usually changes. Consequently, the accuracy and the efficiency of answer extraction depend on the accuracy of question classification.

[1] http://trec.nist.gov/tracks.htm
[2] http://www.nlp.is.ritsumei.ac.jp/qac/
[3] http://www.theanswerbank.co.uk/
[4] http://www.askanowner.com/

R. Dale et al. (Eds.): IJCNLP 2005, LNAI 3651, pp. 426–437, 2005.

Therefore, as a first step towards developing a QA system that can handle multiple-sentence questions, we propose a method for classifying multiple-sentence questions. Specifically, in this work, we treat only questions which require one answer. For example, if the question *"The icon to return to desktop has been deleted. Please tell me how to recover it."* is given, we would like "WAY" to be selected as the question type. We thus introduce core sentence extraction component, which extracts the most important sentence for question classification. This is because there are unnecessary sentences for question classification in a multiple-sentence question, and we hope noisy features should be eliminated before question classification with the component. If a multiple-sentence question is given, we first extract the most important sentence for question classification and then classify the question using the only information in the sentence.

In Section 2, we present the related work. In Section 3, we explain our proposed method. In Section 4, we describe our experiments and results, where we can confirm the effectiveness of the proposed method. Finally, in Section 5, we describe the summary of this paper and the future work.

2 Related Work

This section presents some existing methods for question classification. The methods are roughly divided into two groups: the ones based on hand-crafted rules and the ones based on machine learning. The system "SAIQA" [1], Xu et al. [2] used hand-crafted rules for question classification. However, methods based on pattern matching have the following two drawbacks: high cost of making rules or patterns by hand and low coverage.

Machine learning can be considered to solve these problems. Li et al. [3] used SNoW for question classification. The SNoW is a multi-class classifier that is specifically tailored for learning in the presence of a very large number of features. Zukerman et al. [4] used decision tree. Ittycheriah et al. [5] used maximum entropy. Suzuki [6] used Support Vector Machines (SVMs). Suzuki [6] compared question classification using machine learning methods (decision tree, maximum entropy, SVM) with a rule-based method. The result showed that the accuracy of question classification with SVM is the highest of all. According to Suzuki [6], a lot of information is needed to improve the accuracy of question classification and SVM is suitable for question classification, because SVM can classify questions with high accuracy even when the dimension of the feature space is large. Moreover, Zhang et al. [7] compared question classification with five machine learning algorithms and showed that SVM outperforms the other four methods as Suzuki [6] showed. Therefore, we also use SVM in classifying questions, as we will explain later.

However, please note that we treat not only usual single-sentence questions, but also multiple-sentence questions. Furthermore, our work differs from previous work in that we treat real data on the web, not artificial data prepared for the QA task. From these points, the results in this paper cannot be compared with the ones in the previous work.

3 Two-Step Approach to Multiple-Sentence Question Classification

This section describes our method for classifying multiple-sentence questions. We first explain the entire flow of our question classification. Figure 1 shows the proposed method.

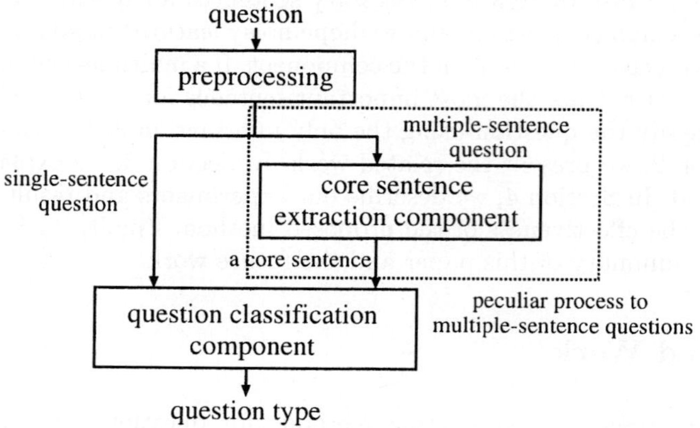

Fig. 1. The entire flow of question classification

An input question consisting of possibly multiple sentences is first preprocessed. Parentheses parts are excluded in order to avoid errors in syntactic parsing. The question is divided into sentences by punctuation marks.

The next process changes depending on whether the given question is a single-sentence question or a multiple-sentence question. If the question consists of a single sentence, the question is sent directly to question classification component. If the question consists of multiple sentences, the question is sent to core sentence extraction component. In the component, *a core sentence*, which is defined as the most important sentence for question classification, is extracted. Then, the core sentence is sent to the question classification component and the question is classified using the information in the core sentence. In Figure 1, "core sentence extraction" is peculiar to multiple-sentence questions.

3.1 Core Sentence Extraction

When a multiple-sentence question is given, the core sentence of the question is extracted. For example, if the question *"I have studied the US history. Therefore, I am looking for the web page that tells me what day Independence Day is."* is given, the sentence *"Therefore, I am looking for the web page that tells me what day Independence Day is."* is extracted as the core sentence.

With the core sentence extraction, we can eliminate noisy information before question classification. In the above example, the occurrence of the sentence

"I have studied the US history." would be a misleading information in terms of question classification.

Here, we have based our work on the following assumption: a multiple-sentence question can be classified using only the core sentence. Please note that we treat only questions which require one answer.

We explain the method for extracting a core sentence. Suppose we have a classifier, which returns $Score(S_i)$ for each sentence S_i of $Question$. $Question$ is the set of sentences composing a given question. $Score(S_i)$ indicates the likeliness of S_i being the core sentence. The sentence with the largest value is selected as the core sentence:

$$\text{Core sentence} = \text{argmax}_{S_i \in Question} Score(S_i). \tag{1}$$

We then extract features for constructing a classifier which returns $Score(S_i)$. We use the information on the words as features. Only the features from the target sentence would not be enough for accurate classification. This issue is exemplified by the following questions (core sentences are underlined).

- Question 1:
  Please advise a medication effective for hay fever. **I want to relieve my headache and stuffy nose.** Especially my headache is severe.
- Question 2:
  I want to relieve my headache and stuffy nose. Especially my headache is severe.

While the sentence *"I want to relieve my headache and stuffy nose."* written in bold-faced type is the core sentence in Question 2, the sentence is not suitable as the core sentence in Question 1. These examples show that the target sentence alone is sometimes not a sufficient evidence for core sentence extraction.

Thus, in classification of a sentence, we use its preceding and following sentences. For that purpose, we introduce a notion of *window size.* "Window size is n" means "the preceding n sentences and the following n sentences in addition to the target sentence are used to make a feature vector". For example, if window size is 0, we use only the target sentence. If window size is ∞, we use all the sentences in the question.

We use SVM as a classifier. We regard the functional distance from the separating hyperplane (i.e., the output of the separating function) as $Score(S_i)$. Word unigrams and word bigrams of the target sentence and the sentences in the window are used as features. A word in the target sentence and the same word in the other sentences are regarded as two different features.

3.2 Question Classification

As discussed in Section 2, we use SVM in the classification of questions. We use five sets of features: word unigrams, word bigrams, semantic categories of nouns, question focuses, and semantic categories of question focuses. The semantic categories are obtained from a thesaurus (e.g., *SHOP*, *STATION*, *CITY*).

"Question focus" is the word that determines the answer class of the question. The notion of question focus was described by Moldovan et al. [8]. For instance, in the question "What country is —?", the question focus is "country". In many researches, question focuses are extracted with hand-crafted rules. However, since we treat all kinds of questions including the questions which are not in an interrogative form, such as "Please teach me –" and "I don't know –", it is difficult to manually create a comprehensive set of rules. Therefore, in this paper, we automatically find the question focus in a core sentence according to the following steps :

step 1 find the phrase[5] including the last verb of the sentence or the phrase with "?" at the end.
step 2 find the phrase that modifies the phrase found in step 1.
step 3 output the nouns and the unknown words in the phrase found in step 2.

The output of this procedure is regarded as a question focus. Although this procedure itself is specific to Japanese, we suppose that we can extract question focus for other languages with a similar simple procedure.

4 Experiments

We designed experiments to confirm the effectiveness of the proposed method.

In the experiments, we use data in Japanese. We use a package for SVM computation, TinySVM [6], and a Japanese morphological analyzer, ChaSen [7] for word segmentation of Japanese text. We use CaboCha [8] to obtain dependency relations, when a question focus is extracted from a question. Semantic categories are obtained from a thesaurus "Goitaikei" [9].

4.1 Experimental Settings

We collect questions from two Japanese Q&A sites: hatena[9] and Yahoo!tiebukuro[10]. 2000 questions are extracted from each site and experimental data consist of 4000 questions in total. A Q&A site is the site where a user puts a question on the site and other users answer the question on the site. Such Q&A sites include many multiple-sentence questions in various forms. Therefore, those questions are appropriate for our experiments where non-artificial questions are required.

Here, we manually exclude the following three kinds of questions from the dataset: questions whose answers are only Yes or No, questions which require two

[5] Phrase here is actually Japanese *bunsetsu* phrase, which is the smallest meaningful sequence consisting of an independent word and accompanying words.
[6] `http://chasen.org/~taku/software/TinySVM/`
[7] `http://chasen.naist.jp/hiki/ChaSen/`
[8] `http://chasen.org/~taku/software/cabocha/`
[9] `http://www.hatena.ne.jp/`
[10] `http://knowledge.yahoo.co.jp/`

Table 1. The types and the distribution of 2376 questions

Nominal Answer		Non-nominal Answer	
Question Type	Number	Question Type	Number
PERSON	64	REASON	132
PRODUCT	238	WAY	500
FACILITY	139	DEFINITION	73
LOCATION	393	DESCRIPTION	228
TIME	108	OPINION	173
NUMBER	53	OTHERS (TEXT)	131
OTHERS (NOUN)	144		
	1139		1237
TOTAL 2376			

or more answers, and questions which are not actually questions. This deletion left us 2376 questions. The question types that we used and their numbers are shown in Table 1[11]. Question types requiring nominal answers are determined referring to the categories used by Sasaki et al. [1].

Of the 2376 questions, 818 are single-sentence questions and 1558 are multiple-sentence questions. The average number of sentences in a multiple-sentence question is 3.49. Therefore, the task of core sentence extraction in our setting is to decide a core sentence from 3.49 sentences on the average. As an evaluation measure for core sentence extraction, we use accuracy, which is defined as the number of multiple-sentence questions whose core sentence is correctly identified over the number of all the multiple-sentence questions. To calculate the accuracy, correct core sentence of the 2376 questions is manually tagged in the preparation of the experiments.

As an evaluation measure for question classification, we use F-measure, which is defined as $2 \times \text{Recall} \times \text{Precision} / (\text{Recall} + \text{Precision})$. As another evaluation measure for question classification, we use also accuracy, which is defined as the number of questions whose type is correctly classified over the number of the questions. All experimental results are obtained with two-fold cross-validation.

4.2 Core Sentence Extraction

We conduct experiments of core sentence extraction with four different window sizes (0, 1, 2, and ∞) and three different feature sets (unigram, bigram, and unigram+bigram). Table 2 shows the result.

As this result shows, we obtained a high accuracy, more than 90% for this task. The accuracy is so good that we can use this result for the succeeding task of question classification, which is our main target. This result also shows that large widow sizes are better for core sentence extraction. This shows that good clues for core sentence extraction are scattered all over the question.

[11] Although Sasaki et al. [1] includes ORGANIZATION in question types, ORGANIZATION is integrated into OTHERS (NOUN) in our work because the size of ORGANIZATION is small.

Table 2. Accuracy of core sentence extraction with different window sizes and features

Window Size\ Features	Unigram	Bigram	Unigram+Bigram
0	1350/1558= 0.866	1378/1558= 0.884	1385/1558= 0.889
1	1357/1558= 0.871	1386/1558= 0.890	1396/1558= 0.896
2	1364/1558= 0.875	1397/1558= 0.897	1405/1558= 0.902
∞	1376/1558= 0.883	1407/1558= 0.903	**1416/1558= 0.909**

Table 3. Accuracy of core sentence extraction with simple methodologies

Methodology	Accuracy
First Sentence	743/1558= 0.477
Last Sentence	471/1558= 0.302
Interrogative Sentence	1077/1558= 0.691

The result in Table 2 also shows that unigram+bigram features are most effective for any window size in core sentence extraction.

To confirm the validity of our proposed method, we extract core sentences with three simple methodologies, which respectively extract one of the following sentences as the core sentence : (1) the first sentence, (2) the last sentence, and (3) the last interrogative sentence (or the first sentence). Table 3 shows the result. The result shows that such simple methodologies would not work in core sentence extraction.

4.3 Question Classification: The Effectiveness of Core Sentence Extraction

We conduct experiments to examine whether the core sentence extraction is effective for question classification or not. For that purpose, we construct the following three models:

Plain question. The given question is the input of question classification component without core sentence extraction process.

Predicted core sentence. The core sentence extracted by the proposed method in Section 3.1 is the input of question classification component. The accuracy of core sentence extraction process is 90.9% as mentioned in Section 4.2.

Correct core sentence. The correct core sentence tagged by hand is the input of question classification component. This case corresponds to the case when the accuracy of core sentence extraction process is 100%.

Word unigrams, word bigrams, and semantic categories of nouns are used as features. The features concerning question focus cannot be used for the plain question model, because the method for identifying the question focus requires that the input be one sentence. Therefore, in order to clarify the effectiveness of core sentence extraction itself, through fair comparison we do not use question focus for each of the three models in these experiments.

Table 4. F-measure and Accuracy of the three models for question classification

Model	Plain Question	Predicted Core Sentence	Correct Core Sentence
Accuracy Of Core Sentence Extraction	–	0.909	1.000
PERSON	0.462	0.434	0.505
PRODUCT	0.381	0.467	0.480
FACILITY	0.584	0.569	0.586
LOCATION	0.758	0.780	0.824
TIME	0.340	0.508	0.524
NUMBER	0.262	0.442	0.421
OTHERS (NOUN)	0.049	0.144	0.145
REASON	0.280	0.539	0.579
WAY	0.756	0.778	0.798
DEFINITION	0.643	0.624	0.656
DESCRIPTION	0.296	0.315	0.317
OPINION	0.591	0.675	0.659
OTHERS (TEXT)	0.090	0.179	0.186
Average	0.423	0.496	0.514
Accuracy	0.617	0.621	0.652

Table 4 shows the result. For most question types, the proposed method with a predicted core sentence improves F-measure. This result shows that the core sentence extraction is effective in question classification. We can still expect some more improvement of performance, by boosting accuracy of core sentence extraction.

In order to further clarify the importance of core sentence extraction, we examine the accuracy for the questions whose core sentences are not correctly extracted. Of 142 such questions, 54 questions are correctly classified. In short, the accuracy is 38% and very low. Therefore, we can claim that without accurate core sentence extraction, accurate question classification is quite hard.

4.4 Question Classification: More Detailed Investigation of Features

Here we investigate the effectiveness of each set of features and the influence of the preceding and the following sentences of the core sentence. After that, we conduct concluding experiments. In the first two experiments of this section, we use only the correct core sentence tagged by hand as the input of question classification.

The Effectiveness of Each Feature Set

First, to examine which feature set is effective in question classification, we exclude a feature set one by one from the five feature sets described in Section 3.2 and conduct experiments of question classification. Please note that the five feature sets can be used unlike the last experiment (Table 4), because the input of question classification is one sentence.

Table 5. Experiments with each feature set being excluded. Here "sem. noun" means semantic categories of nouns. "sem. qf" means semantic categories of question focuses.

		Excluded Feature Set				
	All	Unigram	Bigram	Sem. noun	Qf	Sem. Qf
PERSON	0.574	0.571 (-0.003)	0.620 (+0.046)	0.536 (-0.038)	0.505 (-0.069)	0.505 (-0.069)
PRODUCT	0.506	0.489 (-0.017)	0.579 (+0.073)	0.483 (-0.023)	0.512 (+0.006)	0.502 (-0.004)
FACILITY	0.612	0.599 (-0.013)	0.642 (+0.03)	0.549 (-0.063)	0.615 (+0.003)	0.576 (-0.036)
LOCATION	0.832	0.826 (-0.006)	0.841 (+0.009)	0.844 (+0.012)	0.825 (-0.007)	0.833 (+0.001)
TIME	0.475	0.506 (+0.031)	0.548 (+0.073)	0.420 (-0.055)	0.502 (+0.027)	0.517 (+0.042)
NUMBER	0.442	0.362 (-0.080)	0.475 (+0.033)	0.440 (-0.002)	0.466 (+0.024)	0.413 (-0.029)
OTHERS (NOUN)	0.210	0.182 (-0.028)	0.267 (+0.057)	0.204 (-0.006)	0.198 (-0.012)	0.156 (-0.054)
REASON	0.564	0.349 (-0.215)	0.622 (+0.058)	0.603 (+0.039)	0.576 (+0.012)	0.582 (+0.018)
WAY	0.817	0.803 (-0.014)	0.787 (-0.030)	0.820 (+0.003)	0.817 (±0.000)	0.807 (-0.010)
DEFINITION	0.652	0.659 (+0.007)	0.603 (-0.049)	0.640 (-0.012)	0.647 (-0.005)	0.633 (-0.019)
DESCRIPTION	0.355	0.308 (-0.047)	0.355 (±0.000)	0.363 (+0.008)	0.357 (+0.002)	0.334 (-0.021)
OPINION	0.696	0.670 (-0.026)	0.650 (-0.046)	0.703 (+0.007)	0.676 (-0.020)	0.685 (-0.011)
OTHERS (TEXT)	0.183	0.176 (-0.007)	0.179 (-0.004)	0.154 (-0.029)	0.190 (+0.007)	0.198 (+0.015)
Average	0.532	0.500 (-0.032)	0.551 (+0.019)	0.520 (-0.012)	0.530 (-0.002)	0.518 (-0.014)
Accuracy	0.674	0.632	0.638	0.668	0.661	0.661

Table 5 shows the result. The numbers in parentheses are differences of F-measure compared with its original value. The decrease of F-measure suggests the effectiveness of the excluded feature set.

We first discuss the difference of F-measure values in Table 5, by taking PRODUCT and WAY as examples. The F-measure of PRODUCT is much smaller than that of WAY. This difference is due to whether characteristic expressions are present in the type or not. In WAY, words and phrases such as "*method*" and "*How do I - ?*" are often used. Such words and phrases work as good clues for classification. However, there is no such characteristic expressions for PRODUCT. Although there is a frequently-used expression "*What is [noun] - ?*", this expression is often used also in other types such as LOCATION and FACILITY. We have to rely on currently-unavailable world knowledge of whether the noun is a product name or not. This is the reason of the low F-measure for PRODUCT.

We next discuss the difference of effective feature sets according to question types. We again take PRODUCT and WAY as examples. The most effective

Table 6. Experiments with different window sizes

	Window Size			
	0	1	2	∞
PERSON	**0.574**	0.558	0.565	0.570
PRODUCT	**0.506**	0.449	0.441	0.419
FACILITY	**0.612**	0.607	0.596	0.578
LOCATION	**0.832**	0.827	0.817	0.815
TIME	**0.475**	0.312	0.288	0.302
NUMBER	**0.442**	0.322	0.296	0.311
OTHERS (NOUN)	**0.210**	0.123	0.120	0.050
REASON	**0.564**	0.486	0.472	0.439
WAY	**0.817**	0.808	0.809	0.792
DEFINITION	0.652	**0.658**	0.658	0.641
DESCRIPTION	0.355	**0.358**	0.357	0.340
OPINION	**0.696**	0.670	0.658	0.635
OTHERS (TEXT)	**0.183**	0.140	0.129	0.133
Average	**0.532**	0.486	0.477	0.463
Accuracy	**0.674**	0.656	0.658	0.653

feature set is semantic categories of nouns for "PRODUCT" and bigrams for "WAY". Since whether a noun is a product name or not is important for PRODUCT as discussed before, semantic categories of nouns are crucial to PRODUCT. On the other hand, important clues for WAY are phrases such as "*How do I*". Therefore, bigrams are crucial to WAY.

Finally, we discuss the effectiveness of a question focus. The result in Table 5 shows that the F-measure does not change so much even if question focuses or their semantic categories are excluded. This is because both question focuses and their semantic categories are redundantly put in the feature sets. By comparing Tables 4 and 5, we can confirm that question focuses improve question classification performance (F-measure increases from 0.514 to 0.532). Please note again that question focuses are not used in Table 4 for fair comparison.

The Influence of Window Size

Next, we clarify the influence of *window size.* As in core sentence extraction, "Window size is n" means that "the preceding n sentences and the following n sentences in addition to the core sentence are used to make a feature vector". We construct four models with different window sizes (0, 1, 2, and ∞) and compare their experimental results. In this experiment, we use five sets of features and correct core sentence as the input of question classification like the last experiment (Table 5).

Table 6 shows the result of the experiment. The result in Table 6 shows that the model with the core sentence alone is best. Therefore, the sentences other than the core sentence are considered to be noisy for classification and would not contain effective information for question classification. This result suggests that the assumption (a multiple-sentence question can be classified using only the core sentence) described in Section 3.1 be correct.

Table 7. The result of concluding experiments

	Plain Question	The Proposed Method
core sentence extraction	No	Yes
feature sets	unigram, bigram sem. noun	unigram,bigram,qf sem. noun,sem. qf
PERSON	0.462	0.492
PRODUCT	0.381	0.504
FACILITY	0.584	0.575
LOCATION	0.758	0.792
TIME	0.340	0.495
NUMBER	0.262	0.456
OTHERS (NOUN)	0.049	0.189
REASON	0.280	0.537
WAY	0.756	0.789
DEFINITION	0.643	0.626
DESCRIPTION	0.296	0.321
OPINION	0.591	0.677
OTHERS (TEXT)	0.090	0.189
Average	0.423	0.511
Accuracy	0.617	0.661

Concluding Experiments

We have so far shown that core sentence extraction and question focuses work well for question classification. In this section, we conduct concluding experiments which show that our method significantly improves the classification performance. In the discussion on effective features, we used correct core sentences. Here we use predicted core sentences.

The result is shown in Table 7. For comparison, we add to this table the values of F-measure in Table 4, which correspond to plain question (i.e., without core sentence extraction). The result shows that F-measure of most categories increase, except for FACILITY and DEFINITION. From comparison of "All" in Table 5 with Table 7, the reason of decrease would be the low accuracies of core sentence extraction for these categories. As shown in this table, in conclusion, we obtained 8.8% increase of average F-measure of all and 4.4% increase of accuracy, which is statistically significant in the sign-test with 1% significance-level.

Someone may consider that the type of multiple-sentence questions can be identified by "one-step" approach without core sentence extraction. In a word, the question type of each sentence in the given multiple-sentence question is first identified by a classifier, and then the type of the sentence for which the classifier outputs the largest score is selected as the type of the given question. The classifier's output indicates the likeliness of being the question type of a given question. Therefore, we compared the proposed model with this model in the preliminary experiment. The accuracy of question classification with the proposed model is 66.1% (1570/2376), and that of the one-step approach is 61.7% (1467/2376). This result shows that our two-step approach is effective for classification of multiple-sentence questions.

5 Conclusions

In this paper, we proposed a method for identifying the types of multiple-sentence questions. In our method, the core sentence is first extracted from a given multiple-sentence question and then used for question classification.

We obtained accuracy of 90.9% in core sentence extraction and empirically showed that larger window sizes are more effective in core sentence extraction.

We also showed that the extracted core sentences and the question focuses are good for question classification. Core sentence extraction is quite important also in the sense that question focuses could not be introduced without core sentences. With the proposed method, we obtained the 8.8% increase of F-measure and 4.4% increase of accuracy.

Future work includes the following. The question focuses extracted in the proposed method include nouns which might not be appropriate for question classification. Therefore, we regard the improvement on the question focus detection as future work. To construct a QA system that can handle multiple-sentence question, we are also planning to work on the other components: document retrieval, answer extraction.

References

1. Yutaka Sasaki, Hideki Isozaki, Tsutomu Hirao, Koji Kokuryou, and Eisaku Maeda: NTT's QA Systems for NTCIR QAC-1. Working Notes, NTCIR Workshop 3, Tokyo, pp. 63–70, 2002.
2. Jinxi Xu, Ana Licuanan, and Ralph M.Weischedel: TREC 2003 QA at BBN: Answering Definitional Questions. TREC 2003, pp. 98–106, 2003.
3. Xin Li and Dan Roth: Learning Question Classifiers. COLING 2002, Taipei, Taiwan, pp. 556–562, 2002.
4. Ingrid Zukerman and Eric Horvitz: Using Machine Learning Techniques to Interpret WH-questions. ACL 2001, Toulouse, France, pp. 547–554, 2001.
5. Abraham Ittycheriah, Martin Franz, Wei-Jing Zhu, and Adwait Ratnaparkhi: Question Answering Using Maximum Entropy Components. NAACL 2001, pp. 33–39, 2001.
6. Jun Suzuki: Kernels for Structured Data in Natural Language Processing, Doctor Thesis, Nara Institute of Science and Technology, 2005.
7. Dell Zhang and Wee Sun Lee: Question Classification using Support Vector Machines. SIGIR, Toronto, Canada, pp. 26–32, 2003.
8. Dan Moldovan, Sanda Harabagiu, Marius Pasca, Rada Mihalcea, Richard Goodrum, Roxana Girju, and Vasile Rus: Lasso: A Tool for Surfing the Answer Net. TREC-8, pp. 175–184, 1999.
9. Satoru Ikehara, Masahiro Miyazaki, Satoshi Shirai, Akio Yokoo, Hiromi Nakaiwa, Kentaro Ogura, Yoshifumi Oyama, and Yoshihiko Hayashi, editors: *The Semantic System, volume 1 of Goi-Taikei – A Japanese Lexicon*. Iwanami Shoten, 1997 (in Japanese).

A Rule Based Syllabification Algorithm for Sinhala

Ruvan Weerasinghe, Asanka Wasala, and Kumudu Gamage

Language Technology Research Laboratory, University of Colombo School of Computing, 35, Reid Avenue, Colombo 7, Sri Lanka
arw@ucsc.cmb.ac.lk, {awasala, kgamage}@webmail.cmb.ac.lk

Abstract. This paper presents a study of Sinhala syllable structure and an algorithm for identifying syllables in Sinhala words. After a thorough study of the Syllable structure and linguistic rules for syllabification of Sinhala words and a survey of the relevant literature, a set of rules was identified and implemented as a simple, easy-to-implement algorithm. The algorithm was tested using 30,000 distinct words obtained from a corpus and compared with the same words manually syllabified. The algorithm performs with 99.95 % accuracy.

1 Introduction

Syllabification algorithms are mainly used in text-to-speech (TTS) systems in producing natural sounding speech, and in speech recognizers in detecting out-of-vocabulary words. The key objectives of this study are to identify the syllable structures in modern Sinhala language and to define an algorithm to syllabify a given Sinhala word to be used in our TTS system. Syllabification algorithms have been proposed for different languages including English, German, Spanish and Hindi, among others. Although a few researchers have documented attempts at syllabifying modern Sinhala words in the Linguistics literature, this is the first known documented *algorithm* for Sinhala syllabification and certainly the first *evaluation* of any syllabification scheme for Sinhala.

Languages differ considerably in the syllable structures that they permit. For most languages, syllabification can be achieved by writing a set of declarative grammatical rules which explain the location of syllable boundaries of words step-by-step. It has been identified that most of these rules adhere to well known theories such as the *Maximum Onset Principle* and the *Sonority Profile*. The association of consonants with the syllable nucleus is derived by the Maximum Onset Principle (MOP).

Maximum Onset Principal: First make the onset as long as it legitimately can be; then form a legitimate coda [2].

Sonority Profile: The sonority of a syllable increases from the beginning of the syllable onward, and decreases from the beginning of the peak onwards [2].

Sonority is related to the acoustic intensity of a sound. Thus, by measuring the acoustic intensities of sounds, the sonority of a sound can be estimated [1]. The classes of vowel and consonant sounds (segments) that are usually distinguished along this dimension are listed in the order of increasing sonority, and this list is referred to as the Sonority Scale [2].

R. Dale et al. (Eds.): IJCNLP 2005, LNAI 3651, pp. 438 – 449, 2005.

Sonority Scale:
Obstruents – Nasals – Liquids ([l, r] etc.) – Glides ([w, j]) etc.) – Vowels

Many syllabification algorithms have been developed based on these two theories. For example, the Festival Speech Synthesis System (the framework we use in our Sinhala TTS) by default syllabifies words by finding the minimum sonorant position between vowels [3]. Another sonority scale based syllabification algorithm is presented in detail in [4]. The sonority theory of the syllable does not, however, account for all the phenomena observed in language. Many examples have been provided in the literature to demonstrate this [1], [2]. To avoid the difficulties encountered when using the sonority profile, most of the language specific syllabication schemes are modeled by using finite state machines or neural networks. A multilingual syllabification algorithm using weighted finite-state transducers has been proposed in [5].

In this research, an algorithm to divide Sinhala words into syllables is proposed. The algorithm was tested by using a text corpus containing representative words for each grammatical rule, and its performance was then measured in terms of the percentage of correctly syllabified words. The rest of this paper is organized as follows: Section 2 gives an overview of the Sinhala Phonemic Inventory and Section 3 briefly reviews the linguistic background of modern Sinhala word syllabification including issues we identified and our proposed solutions. Section 4 describes the implementation of the algorithm. The paper concludes with the results & discussion in Section 5.

2 The Sinhala Phonemic Inventory

Sinhala is one of the official languages of Sri Lanka and the mother tongue of the majority (about 74%) of its population. Spoken Sinhala contains 40 segmental phonemes; 14 vowels and 26 consonants as classified below in Table 1 and Table 2 [6].

There are two nasalized vowels occurring in two or three words in Sinhala. They are /ã/, /ã:/, /æ̃/, and /æ̃:/ [6]. Spoken Sinhala also contains the following Diphthongs, /iu/, /eu/, /æu/, /ou/, /au/, /ui/, /ei/, /æi/, /oi/, and /ai/ [7].

A separate letter for vowel /ə/ has not been provided by the Sinhala writing system. In terms of distribution, the vowel /ə/ does not occur at the beginning of a syllable except in the conjugational variants of verbs formed from the verbal stem /kərə/ *(to do.)*. In contrast to this, though the letter "ඦ" exists in Sinhala writing system (corresponding to the consonant sound /ʝ/), it is not considered a phoneme in Sinhala.

Table 1. Spoken Sinhala vowel classification

	Front		Central		Back	
	Short	Long	Short	Long	Short	Long
High	i	i:			u	u:
Mid	e	e:	ə	ə:	o	o:
Low	æ	æ:	a	a:		

Table 2. Spoken Sinhala consonant classification

		Labial	Dental	Alveolar	Retroflex	Palatal	Velar	Glottal
Stops	Voiceless	p	t		ʈ		k	
	Voiced	b	d		ɖ		g	
Affricates	Voiceless					c		
	Voiced					j		
Pre-nasalized voiced stops		b̆	d̆		ɖ̆		g̃	
Nasals		m		n		ɲ	ŋ	
Trill				r				
Lateral				l				
Spirants		f	s			ś		h
Semivowels		v				y		

3 Syllable Structure

3.1 Methodology

The methodology adopted in this study was to first examine the Sinhala syllable structure from the Linguistics literature to gather the views of scholars from the various linguistic traditions. It was expected that this study would reveal the main issues related to the syllabification of Sinhala and how these issues are addressed by scholars in the literature. This was then subjected to the scrutiny of an algorithm in order to select from among alternative theories.

3.2 Sinhala Syllable Structure

3.2.1 Background

Words in the Sinhala language can be divided in to three groups namely *Nishpanna*, *Thadbhava* and *Thathsama* as described below:

Nishpanna: Words that are of local origin.
Thathsama: Words borrowed from other languages *in their (near) original form.*
Thadbhava: Words derived from other languages but modified to be incorporated to Sinhala (mainly from Sanskrit and Pali).

The high impact of Sanskrit in Sinhala vocabulary formation is due to the fact that, Sinhala and Sanskrit belong to the same Indo-Aryan language family. Further, as the vehicle of Buddhism to Sri Lanka, the Pali (spoken) language has also significantly influenced the vocabulary of Sinhala. Due to various cultural, historical and socio-linguistic factors, other languages such as Tamil, Portuguese, Dutch and English have also impacted the structure and vocabulary of Sinhala.

It is important to note that the *Thathsama*, and *Thadbhava*, categories of words are available in modern Sinhala and are indistinguishable to the layman from words in the *Nishpanna* Category. While no documented evidence exists, it is thought that the percentage of words in the *Nispanna* category is less than 5%, while the percentage of words in the *Thathsama* and *Thadbhava* categories in Sinhala (the remaining > 95%), are more or less equal. However, for words in the *Thathsama* and *Thadbhava* categories, no official syllable structures were found in literature. This puts the onus on any TTS researcher dealing with Sinhala syllabification to pay urgent attention to the study of the *Thathsama* and *Thadbhava* categories of words.

3.2.2 Syllabification of Words Belonging to the *Nishpanna* Category

It has been identified that there are four legal syllable structures in Sinhala, namely V, VC, CV and CVC for words which belong to the *Nishpanna* category [7]. This can also be represented using the expression: (C)V(C). Though a large number of examples for syllabified words belonging to each of the above structures are presented in the literature [7], the methodology or grammatical rules describing how to syllabify a given word has not been presented. A word can be syllabified in many ways retaining the permitted structures, but only a single correct combination of structures is accepted in a properly syllabified word.

For example, a word having the consonant-vowel structure VCVCVC can be syllabified in the following different ways, retaining the valid syllable structures described in the literature: (V)(CVC)(VC), (VC)(VC)(VC), (VC)(V)(CVC). However, only one of these forms represents the properly syllabified word.

The determination of a proper mechanism leading to the identification of the correct combination and sequence of syllable structures in syllabifying a given word became the major challenge in this research.

Further review of the literature and empirical observation led to the following model with regard to Sinhala syllabification;

1. A fundamental assumption that the accurately syllabified form of a word can be uniquely obtained by formulating a set of rules.
2. That the following set of rules can be empirically shown to be effective.

Syllabification Procedure for the Nishpanna Category

a. Reach the first vowel of the given word and then,

1. If the phoneme next to this vowel is a consonant followed by another vowel, then mark the syllable boundary just after the first vowel. (Rule #1)
   i.e. a word having a consonant-vowel structure xVCV... Should be syllabified as (xV)(CV...), where x denotes either a single consonant or zero consonant.
2. If the phoneme next to this vowel is a consonant followed by another consonant and a vowel, then mark the syllable boundary just after the first consonant. (Rule #2)
   i.e. a word having a consonant-vowel structure xVCCV... should be syllabified as (xVC)(CV...), where x denotes either a single consonant or zero consonant.
3. If the phoneme next to this vowel is another vowel, then mark the syllable boundary just after the first vowel. (Rule #3)
   i.e. a word having a consonant-vowel structure xVV... should be syllabified as (xV)(V...), where x denotes either a single consonant or zero consonant. Only a few words were found in Sinhala having two consecutive vowels in a single word. e.g. “giriulltə” *(Name of city.)*, “aa:və” *(Alphabet)*. The syllable structure (V) mostly occurs at the beginning of the word, except for this type of rare word.

b. Having marked the first syllable boundary, continue the same procedure for the rest of the phonemes as in the case of a new word.
   i.e. Repeat the step (a) for the rest of the word, until the whole word is syllabified.

The accuracy of this model was first tested by calculating the syllable boundaries using the examples given in the literature. Convinced that the results were consistent with the *descriptive treatment* of the subject in the literature, it was concluded that the above set of rules could describe an accurate *syllabification algorithm* for words belonging to the *Nishpanna* category.

3.2.3 Syllabification of Words of the *Thathsama* and *Thadbhava* Categories

In the syllabification of foreign words, it has been observed that words borrowed from Sanskrit play a major role compared to those borrowed from other languages. The reason behind this is the presence of a large number of Sanskrit words in Sinhala (about 75% of the *Thathsama* category [8]), and the complexity of codas and onsets of these words when they intermix with the Sinhala phonetic inventory. Defining proper syllabic structures for words borrowed or derived from Sanskrit therefore became a primary focus in this study due to this reason. For this purpose, a carefully chosen list of words in this category (see Appendix A) was presented to recognized scholars of Sinhala and Sanskrit for syllabification and recommendations. A careful analysis of the information and views gathered, led to the identification of a new set of rules distinct from those defined in previous section, on how to syllabify these *borrowed* Sanskrit words. It is proposed that Syllabic structures for words originating from Sanskrit can be represented using the consonant-vowel pattern (C)(C)(C)V(C)(C)(C). It is also noteworthy to mention that the syllabic structures for words belong to the category of *Nishpanna* i.e. (C)V(C) is in fact a subset of this structure.

Languages are unique in syllable structures. Syllabification of words belonging to the categories of *Thathsama* and *Thadbhava* do not completely adhere to the syllabification rules imposed in the language from which the word originated. Syllabification of such words will naturally be altered according to the phonetic inventory and existing syllable structures of the host language, Sinhala in this case. This view was expressed by all of the scholars whom we consulted regarding the syllabification of foreign words. In support of this observation, it was evident that the syllabification of almost all the words borrowed from languages other than Sanskrit (e.g. Pali, Tamil and English) are also consistent with the above set of syllabification rules and syllabic structures produced by them. An algorithm to capture this feature of the language is presented below:

Syllabification Procedure for Thathsama and Thadbhava Category
a. Reach the first vowel of the given word and then,
   1. If the vowel is preceded by a consonant cluster of 3, followed by a vowel,
      - If the consonant preceded by the last vowel is /r/ or /y/ then mark the syllable boundary after the first consonant of the consonant cluster. (Rule #4)
        i.e. a word having a consonant-vowel structure xVCC[/r/ or /y/]V.., should be syllabified as (xVC)(C[/r/ or /y/]V...), where x denotes zero or any number of consonants.

- In the above rule, if the consonant preceded by the last vowel is a phoneme other than /r/ or /y/ then,
  - If the first two consonants in the consonant cluster are both stop consonants, then mark the syllable boundary after the first consonant of the consonant cluster. (Rule #5)

  i.e. a word having a consonant-vowel structure xV[C-Stop][C-Stop]CV..., should be syllabified as (xVC)(CCV...), where x denotes zero or any number of consonants.
  - In other situations, mark the syllable boundary after the second consonant of the consonant cluster. (Rule #6)

  i.e. a word having a consonant-vowel structure xVCCCV..., should be syllabified as (xVCC)(CV...), where x denotes zero or any number of consonants.

2. If this vowel is preceded by a consonant cluster of more than 3 consonants ,
   - If the consonant just before the last vowel is /r/ or /y/ then, mark the syllable boundary before 2 consonants from the last vowel. (Rule #7)
   i.e. a word having a consonant-vowel structure xVCCC...[/r/ or /y/]V... should be syllabified as (xVCCC...)(C[/r/ or /y/]V..), where x denotes zero or any number of consonants.
   - In other situations, mark the syllable boundary just after the minimum sonorant consonant phoneme of the consonant cluster. (Rule #8)
   i.e. a word having a consonant-vowel structure xVCCC...CV..., should be syllabified just next to the minimum sonorant consonant in the consonant cluster.

b. Having marked the first syllable boundary, continue the same procedure for the rest of the phonemes as in a new word.
i.e. Repeat the step (a) for the rest of the word, until the whole word is syllabified.

The words with consonant clusters of more than 3 consonants are rarely found in Sinhala, and to avoid the confusion of syllabification of words in such situations, the algorithm makes use of the universal sonority hierarchy in deciding the proper position to mark the syllable boundary. In these situations, the syllable boundary is marked next to the first occurrence of a minimum sonorant consonant.

3.2.4 Ambisyllabic Words in Sinhala

Some ambisyllabic words are also found in Sinhala. This situation arises due to the fact that some words with complex coda or onset can be syllabified in several ways.

For example, a word such as /sampre:kʃənə/ (transmit) the /p/ can be interpreted as a coda with respect to the preceding vowel, as in /samp/re:k/ʃə/nə/or as an onset with respect to the following vowel, as in /sam/pre:k/ʃə/nə/.

More examples for this kind of word include, /mats/yə/, /mat/syə/ *(fish);* /sank/ya:/, /san/kya:/ *(number)* and /lakʃ/yə/,/lak/ʃyə/*(point).*

Some Sanskrit loan words in Sinhala (including word internal clusters ending in /r/ and preceding a vowel) can either be syllabified by reduplicating the first consonant sound of the cluster or by retaining the original word as in the following examples.

/krə/mak/rə/mə/yə/→ /krə/mak/krə/mə/yə/ *(gradually)*
/ap/rə/ma:/nə/→ /ap/prə/ma:/nə/ *(unlimited)*
/ja/yag/ra:/hi:/→ /ja/yag/gra:/hi:/ *(victory)*

This description demonstrates that the rules and procedures determined above are complied with even by ambisyllabic words. It is important to note that while both forms are acceptable, *one* of these will be provided by the algorithm stated above.

4 The Syllabification Algorithm

The rules identified in sections 3.2.2 and 3.2.3 are sensitive to the sequence since they interact with each other. In this section, the Sinhala syllabification rules identified above are presented in the form of a formal *algorithm*. The function *syllabify()* accepts an array of phonemes generated by our *Letter-To-Sound* module[1] for a particular word, along with a variable called *current_position* which is used to determine the position of the given array currently being processed by the algorithm.

Initially the *current_position* variable will be initialized to 0. The *syllabify()* function is called recursively until all phonemes in the array are processed. The function *mark_syllable_boundary(postion)* will mark the syllable boundaries of an accepted array of phonemes. The other functions used within the *syllabify()* function are described below.

- *no_of_vowels(phonemes):* accepts an array of phonemes and returns the number of vowels contained in that array.
- *is_a_vowel(phoneme):* accepts a phoneme and returns true if the given phoneme is a vowel.
- *count_no_of_consonants_upto_next_vowel(phonemes, position):* accepts an array of phonemes and a starting position; and returns the count of consonants from the starting position of the given array until the next vowel is found.
- *is_a_stop(phoneme):* returns true if the accepted phoneme is a stop consonant.
- *find_min_sonority_position(phonemes, position):* returns the minimum sonorant position of a given array of phonemes, by starting the search from the given position.

A complete listing of the algorithm is provided in Appendix B.

5 Results and Discussion

Our algorithm was tested on 30,000 distinct words extracted from the (unbalanced) *UCSC Sinhala Corpus BETA*, and compared with correctly hand syllabified words. Text obtained from the category "*News Paper > Feature Auricles > Other*" was chosen for testing the algorithm due to the heterogeneous nature of these texts and hence the perceived better representation of the language in this section of the corpus[2]. A list

---

[1] Discussed in another paper in preparation.

[2] This accounts for almost two-thirds of the size of this version of the corpus.

of distinct words was first extracted, and the 30,000 most frequently occurring words chosen for testing our algorithm.

The 30,000 words yielded some 78,775 syllables which were distributed as follows among the 8 rules of the algorithm given: Rule #1: 67,350; Rule #2: 10,899; Rule #3: 71; Rule #4: 324; Rule #5: 28; Rule #6: 77; Rule #7: 21 and Rule #*: 5. Note however that owing to the syllable structure of words in the *Nishpanna* category being a subset of those of the *Thathsama* and *Thadbhava* categories, nothing can be inferred about the actual percentages of words in each category from this analysis alone.

The algorithm achieves an overall accuracy of 99.95% when compared with the same words manually syllabified by an expert. An error analysis revealed the following two types of errors:

1. Words composed by joining two or more words (i.e. Single words formed by combining 2 or more distinct words; such as in the case of the English word *"thereafter"*). In this case, syllabification needs to be carried out separately for each word of the compound word, and then concatenated to form a single syllabified word.
2. Foreign (mainly English) words directly encoded in Sinhala.

A detailed study of Sinhala syllabification is presented in the research above. Though a great number of diverse algorithms have been proposed for syllabification in different languages, to the best of our knowledge this is the first such study for Sinhala syllabification proposing a formal algorithm describing the process. The initial study of the literature revealed certain unresolved issues which this study resolved with the aid of scholars. A significant task was carried out in identifying valid syllable structures for words borrowed from Sanskrit. A major effort was also made in identifying and defining a formal set of linguistic rules for syllabification, and then translating same into a simple and easy-to-implement algorithm. Finally, the effectiveness of the proposed algorithm was demonstrated using a set of words extracted from a Sinhala corpus.

Syllabification is an important component of many speech and language processing systems, and this algorithm is expected to be a significant contribution to the field, and especially to researchers working on various aspects of the Sinhala language.

Acknowledgement

This work has been supported through the PAN Localization Project, (*http://www.PANL10n.net*) grant from the International Development Research Center (IDRC), Ottawa, Canada, administered through the Center for Research in Urdu Language Processing, National University of Computer and Emerging Sciences, Pakistan. The authors are indebted to Sinhala Language scholars, Prof. Wimal G. Balagalle, Prof. S.A.G. Wijesinghe, Prof. R.M.W. Rajapaksha, and Prof. J.B. Dissanayake for their invaluable support and advice throughout the study. We also wish to acknowledge the contribution of Mr. Viraj Welgama, Mr. Dulip Herath, and Mr. Nishantha Medagoda of Language Technology Research Laboratory of the University of Colombo School of Computing, Sri Lanka.

References

1. Ladeforged, P., A Course In Phonetics, 3rd edn., Harcourt Brace Jovanovich College Publishers, 301, Commerce Street, Suite 3700, Fort Worth TX 76102 (1993)
2. Gussenhoven, C., Jacobs, H., Understanding Phonology, Oxford University Press Inc, 198, Madison Avenue, New York, NY 10016 (1998)
3. Black, A.W., Taylor, P., Caley R., The Festival Speech Synthesis System: System Documentation, University of Edinburgh, Edinburgh (1999)
4. Brasington, R., "A simple syllabifier", (LOGO and natural language), Available: http://www.personal.rdg.ac.uk/~llsling1/Logo.WWW/Sound.patterns/Simple.syllabifier.html,(Accessed: 2005, February, 02)
5. Kiraz, G.A., Mobius, B., "Multilingual Syllabification Using Weighted Finite-State Transducers", Bell Labs – Lucent Technologies, Murray Hill, NJ 07974, USA, In Proceedings of the Third ESCA Workshop on Speech Synthesis (Jenolan Caves, Australia, 1998) (1998)
6. Karunatillake, W.S., An introduction to spoken Sinhala, 3rd edn., M.D. Gunasena & Co. ltd., 217, Olcott Mawatha, Colombo 11 (2004)
7. Disanayaka, J.B., The structure of spoken Sinhala, National Institute of Education, Maharagama (1991)
8. Jayathilake, K., *Nuthana Sinhala Vyakaranaye Mul Potha*, Pradeepa Publications, 34/34, Lawyers' Office Complex, Colombo 12, (1991)

Appendix A: Word-List

කූටෝපක්‍රම	ku: to: p a k k r ə m ə
පෘතග්ජන	p r u t a g j a n ə
ක්‍රමක්‍රමයෙන්	k r ə m a k k r ə m ə y e n
ස්ත්‍රීන්	s t r i: n
විද්‍යාඥයා	v i d y a: j ɲ ə y a:
කෘමියා	k r u m i y a:
පීතෘන්	p i: t t r u: n
සෞභාග්‍ය	s a u b a: g y ə
කාව්‍යෝපදේශය	k a: v y o: p ə d e: ʃ ə y ə
අවිද්‍යාව	a v i d y a: v ə
ප්‍රඥාව	p r a j ɲ a: v ə
කොන්ස්තන්තිනෝපලය	k o ŋ s t a n t i n o: p ə l ə y ə
ස්වප්න	s v a p n ə
ශල්‍යකර්ම	ʃ a l y ə k a r m ə
පාර්ලිමේන්තුව	p a: r l i m e: n t u w ə
ද්වන්ද්ව	d v a n d v ə
හෘදස්පන්දනය	h ə r d ə s p a n d ə n ə y ə
සම්ප්‍රේක්ෂණ	s a m p r e: k ʃ ə n ə
ක්ෂේත්‍ර	ʃ e: ʃ t r ə
ප්‍රවෘත්ති	p r ə v u r t i
ප්‍රව්‍රජ්‍යා	p r ə v u r j ya:

ප්‍රශ්‍රබ්ධිය	p r ə ʃ r a b d i y ə
සංස්කෘත	s a n s k r u tə
springs	s p r i ŋ g s
scratched	s k r æ c ɖ
straights	s t r e: i t s
strength	s t r e n t s
postscript	p o: s t s k r i p t
area	e: r i a:

Appendix B: Syllabification Algorithm

```
function syllabify (phonemes, current_position)
 if no_of_vowels(phonemes) is 1 then
  mark_syllable_boundary(at_the_end_of_phonemes)
 else
  if is_a_vowel(phonemes[current_position]) is true
  then
   no_of_consonants=
   count_no_of_consonants_upto_next_vowel
   (phonemes,current_position)
   if no_of_consonants is 0 then
    if is_a_vowel(phonemes[current_position+1]) is
    true then
     mark_syllable_boundary(current_position) % Rule#3
     syllabify(phonemes, current_position+1)
    end if
   else
    if no_of_consonants is 1 then
     mark_syllable_boundary(current_position) % Rule#1
     syllabify(phonemes, current_position+2)
    end if
    if no_of_consonants are 2 then
     mark_syllable_boundary(current_position+1)
     syllabify(phonemes, current_position+3) % Rule#2
    end if
    if no_of_consonants are 3 then
```

```
if phonemes[current_position+3] is
( "r" or "y") then
  mark_syllable_boundary(current_position+1)
  % Rule#4
  syllabify(phonemes, current_position+4)
else
  if is_a_stop(phonemes[current_posi+1]) is
  true and is_a_stop(phonemes[current_posi+2])) is
  true then
      mark_syllable_boundary(current_position+1)
     % Rule#5
      syllabify(phonemes, current_position+4)
     else
      mark_syllable_boundary(current_position+2)
      % Rule#6
       syllabify(phonemes, current_position+4)
       end if
     end if
    end if
  if no_of_consonants are greater than 3 then
   if phonemes[current_position+no_of_consonants]
   is( "r" or "y") then
     mark_syllable_boundary
     (current_position+no_of_consonants-2) % Rule#7
     Syllabify
     (phonemes, current_position
     +no_of_consonants-1)         else
    syllable_boundary=find_min_sonority_position
                    (phonemes,current_postion)
     mark_syllable_boundary(syllable_boundary)
    % Rule#8
     Syllabify
     (phonemes, syllable_boundary+1)
   end if
  end if
```

```
        end if
      else
        temp=current_postion
        repeat
          temp = temp + 1;
        until(is_a_vowel(phonemes[temp]) is true
        syllabify(phonemes,temp)
      end if
end if
```

An Ensemble of Grapheme and Phoneme for Machine Transliteration

Jong-Hoon Oh and Key-Sun Choi

Department of Computer Science, KAIST/KORTERM/BOLA,
373-1 Guseong-dong, Yuseong-gu, Daejeon, 305-701, Republic of Korea
{rovellia, kschoi}@world.kaist.ac.kr

Abstract. Machine transliteration is an automatic method to generate characters or words in one alphabetical system for the corresponding characters in another alphabetical system. There has been increasing concern on machine transliteration as an assistant of machine translation and information retrieval. Three machine transliteration models, including "grapheme-based model", "phoneme-based model", and "hybrid model", have been proposed. However, there are few works trying to make use of correspondence between source grapheme and phoneme, although the correspondence plays an important role in machine transliteration. Furthermore there are few works, which dynamically handle source grapheme and phoneme. In this paper, we propose a new transliteration model based on an ensemble of grapheme and phoneme. Our model makes use of the correspondence and dynamically uses source grapheme and phoneme. Our method shows better performance than the previous works about 15~23% in English-to-Korean transliteration and about 15~43% in English-to-Japanese transliteration.

1 Introduction

Machine transliteration is an automatic method to generate characters or words in one alphabetical system for the corresponding characters in another alphabetical system. For example, English word *data* is transliterated into Korean 'deita' [1] and Japanese 'deeta'. Transliteration is used to phonetically translate proper names and technical terms especially from languages in Roman alphabets to languages in non-Roman alphabets such as from English to Korean, Japanese, and Chinese and so on. There has been increasing concern on machine transliteration as an assistant of Machine Translation (MT) [2], [10], mono-lingual information retrieval (MLIR) [8], [11] and cross-lingual information retrieval (CLIR) [6]. In the area of MLIR and CLIR, machine transliteration bridges the gap between a transliterated localized form and its original form by generating all possible transliterated forms from each original form. Especially for CLIR, machine transliteration gives a help to query translation where proper names and technical terms frequently appear in source language queries. In the area of MT, machine transliteration prevents translation failure when translations of

[1] In this paper, target language transliterations are represented with their Romanization form in a quotation mark ('') .

R. Dale et al. (Eds.): IJCNLP 2005, LNAI 3651, pp. 450–461, 2005.

proper names and technical terms are not registered in a translation dictionary. A machine transliteration system, therefore, may affect the performance of MT, MLIR, and CLIR system.

Three machine transliteration models have been studied: called "**grapheme[2]-based transliteration model (ψ_G)**" [7], [8], [9], [11], [12], [13], "**phoneme[3]-based transliteration model (ψ_P)**" [10], [12], and "**hybrid transliteration model (ψ_H)**" [2], [4], [12]. ψ_G and ψ_P are classified in terms of units to be transliterated. ψ_G is referred to the direct model because it directly transforms source language graphemes to target language graphemes without any phonetic knowledge of source language words. ψ_P is called the pivot model because it makes use of phonemes as a pivot during a transliteration process. Therefore ψ_P usually needs two steps; the first step is to produce phonemes from source language graphemes, and the second step is to produce target language graphemes from phonemes. ψ_H combines ψ_G and ψ_P with the linear interpolation style. Hereafter, we will use a source grapheme for a source language grapheme and a target grapheme for a target language grapheme.

Though transliteration is the phonetic process (ψ_P) rather than the orthographic one (ψ_G) [10], we should consider both source grapheme and phoneme to achieve high performance in machine transliteration because the standard transliterations are not restricted to phoneme-based transliterations[4]. However, many previous works make use of either source grapheme or phoneme. They simplify a machine transliteration problem into either ψ_G or ψ_P assuming that one of ψ_G and ψ_P is able to cover all transliteration behaviors. However, transliteration is a complex process, which does not rely on either source grapheme or phoneme. For example, the standard Korean transliterations of *amylase* and *data* are grapheme-based transliteration 'amillaaje' and phoneme-based transliteration 'deiteo', respectively. A machine transliteration model, therefore, should reflect the dynamic transliteration behaviors in order to produce the correct transliterations.

ψ_H has the limited power for producing the correct transliterations because it just combines ψ_G and ψ_P with the linear interpolation style. ψ_H does not consider correspondence between source grapheme and phoneme during the transliteration process. However the correspondence plays important roles in machine transliteration. For example, phoneme /AH/[5] produces high ambiguities since it can be mapped to almost every single vowels in source language and target language (the underlined grapheme corresponds to /AH/: cinem**a**, host**e**l, hol**o**caust in English, 'sinem**a**', 'host**e**l', 'hol**o**koseuteu' in their Korean counterparts, and 'sinem**a**', 'hoseut**e**ru', 'hor**o**koosuto' in

[2] *Graphemes* refer to the basic units (or the smallest contrastive units) of written language: for example, English has 26 graphemes or letters, Korean has 24, and German has 30.

[3] *Phonemes* are the simplest significant unit of sound (or the smallest contrastive units of the spoken language): for example, the /M/, /AE/, and /TH/ in *math*.

[4] In an English-to-Korean transliteration test set [14], we find that about 60% are phoneme-based transliterations, while about 30% are grapheme-based ones. The others are transliterations generated by combining ψ_G and ψ_P.

[5] ARPAbet symbol will be used for representing phonemes. ARPAbet is one of the methods used for coding phonemes into ASCII characters (*www.cs.cmu.edu/~laura/pages/arpabet.ps*). In this paper, we will denote phonemes and pronunciation with two slashes like so : /AH/. Pronunciation represented in this paper is based on *The CMU Pronunciation Dictionary* and *The American Heritage(r) Dictionary of the English Language.*

their Japanese counterparts). If we know the correspondence between source grapheme and phoneme in this context, then we can more easily infer the correct transliteration of /AH/, since a target grapheme of /AH/ usually depends on a source grapheme corresponding to /AH/. Korean transliterations of source grapheme *a* is various such as 'a', 'ei', 'o', 'eo' and so on. Like the previous example, correspondence makes it possible to reduce transliteration ambiguities like Table 1. In Table 1, the underlined source grapheme *a* in the example column is pronounced as the phoneme in the phoneme column. The correct Korean transliterations of source grapheme *a* can be more easily found, like in the Korean grapheme column, by means of phonemes in the phoneme column.

Table 1. Examples of Korean graphemes derived from source grapheme *a* and its corresponding phoneme: the underline indicates source graphemes corresponding to each phoneme in the phoneme column

Korean grapheme	Phoneme	Example
'a'	/AA/	ad**a**gio, saf**a**ri, viv**a**ce
'ae'	/AE/	adv**a**ntage, **a**lab**a**ster, tr**a**vertine
'ei'	/EY/	ch**a**mber, champ**a**gne, ch**a**os
'i'	/IH/	advant**a**ge, average, sil**a**ge
'o'	/AO/	**a**llspice, b**a**ll, ch**a**lk

In this paper, we propose a new machine transliteration model based on an ensemble of source grapheme and phoneme, symbolized as ψ_C (**"correspondence-based transliteration model"**). ψ_C has two strong points over ψ_G, ψ_P, and ψ_H. First, ψ_C can produce transliterations by considering correspondence between source grapheme and phoneme. As described above, correspondence is very useful for reducing transliteration ambiguities. From the viewpoint of reducing the ambiguities, ψ_C has an advantage over ψ_G, ψ_P, and ψ_H because ψ_C can more easily reduce the ambiguities by considering the correspondence. Second, ψ_C can dynamically handle source grapheme and phoneme according to their contexts. Because of this property, ψ_C can produce grapheme-based transliterations as well as phoneme-based transliterations. It can also produce a transliteration, where one part is a grapheme-based transliteration and the other part is a phoneme-based transliteration. For example, the Korean transliteration of *neomycin*, 'neomaisin', where 'neo' is a grapheme-based transliteration and 'maisin' is a phoneme-based transliteration.

2 Correspondence-Based Machine Transliteration Model

Correspondence-based transliteration model (ψ_C) is composed of two component functions (ψ_C: $\delta_p \times \delta_t$). In this paper, we refer to δ_p as a function for **"producing pronunciation"** and δ_t as a function for **"producing target grapheme"**. First, δ_p produces pronunciation and then δ_t produces target graphemes with correspondence between source grapheme and phoneme produced by δ_p. The goal of the δ_p is to produce the most probable sequence of phonemes corresponding to source graphemes. For example, δ_p produces /B/, /AO/, /~/[6], /R/, and /D/ for each source grapheme, *b, o, a, r,* and *d* in *board* (see "The result of δ_p" in the right side of Fig 1). In this step, pronunciation is generated through two ways; **pronunciation dictionary search** and **pronunciation estimation**. A pronunciation dictionary contains the correct pronunciation corresponding to English words. Therefore, English words are first investigated whether they are registered in the dictionary otherwise their pronunciation is estimated by pronunciation estimation. The goal of δ_t is to produce the most probable sequence of target graphemes with correspondence between source grapheme and phoneme, which is the result of δ_p. For example, δ_t produces 'b', 'o', '~', '~', and 'deu' using the result of δ_p, *b-/B/, o-/AO/, a-/~/, r-/R/,* and *d-/D/* (see "The result of δ_t" in the right side of Fig 1). Finally, the target language transliteration, such as the Korean transliteration 'bodeu' for *board*, can be acquired by concatenating the sequence of target graphemes in the result of δ_t.

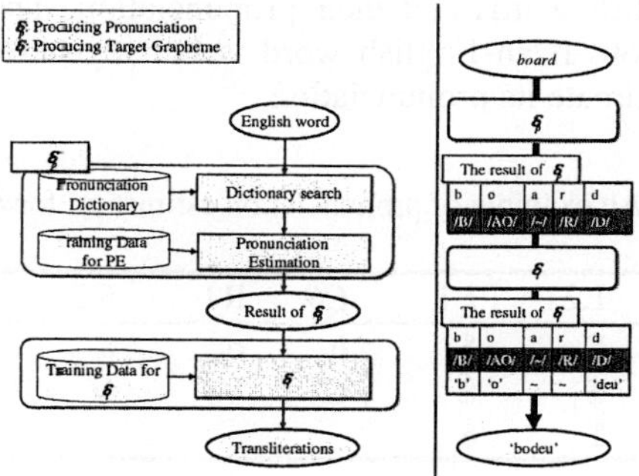

Fig. 1. The overall system architecture

Table 2. Feature types used for correspondence-based transliteration model: where *S* is a set of source graphemes (e.g. English alphabets), *P* is a set of phonemes defined in ARPABET, *T* is a set of target graphemes. Note that $f_{S,GS}$ is a symbol for indicating both f_S and f_{GS}. $f_{P,GP}$ is a symbol for indicating both f_P and f_{GP}.

Feature	Type	Description	Possible feature values
$f_{S,GS}$	f_S	Source graphemes	Source grapheme in S; 26 alphabets for English
	f_{GS}	Source grapheme type	Consonant (C), and Vowel (V)
$f_{P,GP}$	f_P	Phonemes	Phonemes in *P* (/AA/, /AE/, etc.)
	f_{GP}	Phoneme type	Consonant (C), Vowel (V), Semi-vowel (SV) and silence (/~/)
	f_T	Target graphemes	Target graphemes in *T*

Pronunciation estimation in δ_p and δ_t are trained by machine learning algorithms. To train each component function, we need features that represent training instance

[6] In this paper, '/~/' represents silence and '~' represents null target grapheme.

and data. Table 2 shows five feature types, f_S, f_P, f_{GS}, f_{GP}, and f_T that our model uses. Depending on component functions, different feature types are used. For example, $\delta_p(s_i)$ uses (f_S, f_{GS}, f_P) and $\delta_t(s_i, \delta_p(s_i))$ does (f_S, f_P, f_{GS}, f_{GP}, f_T).

2.1 Producing Pronunciation (δ_p)

Producing pronunciation (δ_p:$S \rightarrow P$) is a function that finds phonemes in a set P for each source grapheme, where P is a set of phonemes defined in ARPABET, and S is a set of source graphemes (e.g. English alphabets). The results of this step can be represented as a sequence of correspondences between source grapheme and phoneme. We will denote it as $GP=\{gp_1,gp_2,...,gp_n; gp_i=(s_i, \delta_p(s_i))\}$ where s_i is the ith source grapheme of $SW=s_1,s_2,...,s_n$. Producing pronunciation is composed of two steps. The first step involves a search in the pronunciation dictionary, which contains English words and their pronunciation. This paper uses *The CMU Pronouncing Dictionary*[7], which contains 120,000 English words and their pronunciation. The second step involves pronunciation estimation. If an English word is not registered in the pronunciation dictionary, we must estimate its pronunciation.

Table 3. An example of pronunciation estimation for *b* in *board*

Feature type	L3	L2	L1	***C0***	R1	R2	R3	$\delta_p(C0)$
f_S	$	$	$	***b***	o	a	r	***/B/***
f_{GS}	$	$	$	***C***	V	V	C	
f_P	$	$	$					

Let $SW=s_1,s_2,...,s_n$ be an English word, and $P_{SW}= p_1,p_2,...,p_n$ be SW's pronunciation, where s_i represents the ith grapheme and $p_i=\delta_p(s_i)$. Pronunciation estimation is a task to find the most relevant phoneme among a set of all possible phonemes, which can be derived from source grapheme s_i. Table 3 shows an example of pronunciation estimation for *b* in *board.* In Table 3, L1~L3 and R1~R3 represent the left contexts and right contexts, respectively. C0 means the current context (or focus). δ_p(C0) means the estimated phoneme of C0. $ is a symbol for representing the start of words. The result can be interpreted as follows. The most relevant phoneme of *b*, /B/, can be produced with the context, f_S, f_{GS}, and f_P in contexts of L1~L3, C0, and R1~R3. Other phonemes for *o*, *a*, *r*, and *d* in *board* are produced in the same manner. Thus, we can get the pronunciation of *board* as /B AO R D/ by concatenating the phoneme sequence.

2.2 Producing Target Graphemes (δ_t)

Producing target graphemes (δ_t:$S \times P \rightarrow T$) is a function that finds the target grapheme in T for each gp_i that is a result of δ_p. A result of this step, GT, is represented by a sequence of gp_i and its corresponding target graphemes generated by δ_t, like $GT=\{gt_1, gt_2 ,..., gt_n; gt_i=(gp_i, \delta_t(gp_i))\}$.

[7] Available at http://www.speech.cs.cmu.edu/cgi-bin/cmudict

Table 4. An example of δ_t for *b* in *board*

Feature type	L3	L2	L1	***C0***	R1	R2	R3	***δ_t(C0)***
f_S	\$	\$	\$	***b***	o	a	r	**'b'**
f_P	\$	\$	\$	***/B/***	/AO/	/~/	/R/	
f_{GS}	\$	\$	\$	***C***	V	V	C	
f_{GP}	\$	\$	\$	***C***	V	/~/	C	
f_T	\$	\$	\$					

Let $SW=s_1,s_2,...,s_n$ be a source language word, $P_{SW}= p_1,p_2,...,p_n$ be *SW*'s pronunciation and $T_{SW}= t_1, t_2,...,t_n$ be a target language word of *SW*, where s_i, $\delta_p(s_i)=p_i$ and $\delta_t(gp_i) = t_i$ represent the ith source grapheme, phoneme corresponding to s_i, and target grapheme corresponding to gp_i, respectively. δ_t finds the most probable target grapheme among a set of all possible target graphemes, which can be derived from gp_i. δ_t produces target graphemes with source grapheme (f_S), phoneme (f_P), source grapheme type (f_{GS}), phoneme type (f_{GP}) and δ_t's previous output (f_T) in the context window. Table 4 shows an example of δ_t for *b* in *board*. δ_t produces the most probable sequence of target graphemes (e.g. Korean), like $\delta_t(gp_1)$= 'b', $\delta_t(gp_2)$= 'o', $\delta_t(gp_3)$='~', $\delta_t(gp_4)$='~', and $\delta_t(gp_5)$='deu' for *board*. Finally, the target language transliteration of *board* as 'bodeu' can be acquired by concatenating the sequence of produced target graphemes.

3 Machine Learning Algorithms for Each Component Function

In this section we will describe a way of modeling component functions using three machine learning algorithms (maximum entropy model, decision tree, and memory-based learning).

3.1 Maximum Entropy Model

The maximum entropy model (MEM) is a widely used probability model that can incorporate heterogeneous information effectively [3]. In the maximum entropy model, an event *ev* is usually composed of a target event (*te*) and a history event (*he*), say *ev*=<*te, he*>. Event *ev* is represented by a bundle of feature functions, $fe_i(ev)$, which represent the existence of a certain characteristic in event *ev*. A feature function is a binary valued function. It is activated ($fe_i(ev)=1$) when it meets its activating condition, otherwise it is deactivated ($fe_i(ev)=0$) [3].

δ_p and δ_t based on the maximum entropy model can be represented as formula (1). History events in each component function are made from the left, right and current context. For example, history events for δ_t are composed of $f_{S,GS\,(i-3,i+3)}$, $f_{P,GP\,(i-3,i+3)}$, and $f_{T\,(i-3,i-1)}$ where i is a index of the current source grapheme and phoneme to be transliterated and $f_{X(l,m)}$ represents features of feature type f_X located from position l to position m. Target events are a set of target graphemes (phonemes) derived from history events of δ_t (δ_p). Given history events, δ_t (δ_p) finds the most probable target grapheme (phoneme), which maximizes formula (1). One important thing in designing a model based on the maximum entropy model is to determine feature functions which effectively support certain decision of the model. Our basic philosophy of feature function design for each component function is that context information collocated with the unit of interest is an important factor. With the philosophy, we determined the history events (or activating conditions) of the feature functions by combinations of features in feature types. Possible feature combinations for history events are between features in the same feature type and between features in different feature types. The used feature combinations in each component function are listed in Table 5.

Table 5. Used feature combinations for history events

δ_p	δ_t
Between features in the same feature type	Between features in the same feature type
Between features in different feature types	Between features in different feature types
• $f_{S,GS}$ and f_P	• $f_{S,GS}$ and $f_{P,GP}$ • $f_{S,GS}$ and f_T • $f_{P,GP}$ and f_T

In formula (1), history events of δ_p and δ_t are defined by the conditions described in Table 5. Target events of δ_t are all possible target graphemes derived from its history events; while those of δ_p are all possible phonemes derived from its history events. In order to model each component function based on MEM, Zhang's maximum entropy modeling tool is used [16].

$$\begin{aligned} \delta_t(s_i, \delta_p(s_i)) &= \arg\max p(t_i \mid f_{T\,i-3,i-1}, f_{S,GS\,i-3,i+3}, f_{P,GP\,i-3,i+3}) \\ \delta_p(s_i) &= \arg\max p(p_i \mid f_{P\,i-3,i-1}, f_{S,GS\,i-3,i+3}) \end{aligned} \quad (1)$$

3.2 Decision Tree

Decision tree learning is one of the most widely used and well-known methods for inductive inference [15]. ID3, which is a greedy algorithm and constructs decision trees in a top-down manner, adopts a statistical measure called *information gain* that measures how well a given feature (or attribute) separates training examples according to their target class [15]. We use C4.5 [15], which is a well-known tool for decision tree learning and implementation of Quinlan's ID3 algorithm.

Training data for each component function is represented by features of feature types in the context of L3~L1, C0, and R1~R3 as described in Table 3. Fig. 2 shows a fraction of our decision trees for δ_p and δ_t in English-to-Korean transliteration (note that the left side represents the decision tree for δ_p and the right side represents the decision tree for δ_t). A set of the target classes in the decision tree for δ_p will be a set of phonemes and that for δ_t will be a set of target graphemes. In Fig. 2, rectangles indicate a leaf node and circles indicate a decision node. In order to simplify our examples, we just use f_S and f_P in Fig. 2. Intuitively, the most effective feature for δ_p and δ_t may be located in C0 among L3~L1, C0, and R1~R3 because the correct outputs of δ_p and δ_t strongly depend on source grapheme or phoneme in the C0 position. As we expected, the most effective feature in the decision trees is located in the C0 position like C0(f_S) for δ_p and C0(f_P) for δ_t (Note that the first feature to be tested is the most effective feature). In Fig. 2, the decision tree for δ_p outputs phoneme /AO/ for the instance *x(SP)* by retrieving the decision nodes C(f_S)=*o*, R1(f_S)=*a*, and R2(f_S)=*r* represented with '*'. With the similar manner, the decision tree for δ_t produces target grapheme (Korean grapheme) 'o' for the instance *x(SPT)* by retrieving the decision nodes from C0(f_P)=/AO/ to R1(f_P)=/~/ represented with '*'.

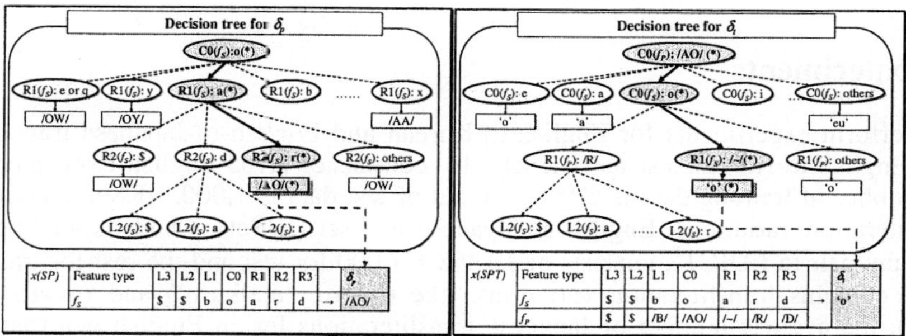

Fig. 2. Decision tree for δ_p and δ_t

3.3 Memory-Based Learning

Memory-based learning (MBL) is an example-based learning method. It is also called instance-based learning and case-based learning method. It is based on a *k*-nearest neighborhood algorithm [1], [5]. MBL represents a training data as a vector. In the training phase, MBL puts all training data as examples in memory, and clusters some examples with a *k-nearest neighborhood* principle. It then outputs a target class using similarity-based reasoning between test data and examples in the memory. Let test data be x and a set of examples in a memory be Y, the similarity between x and Y is estimated by a distance function, $\Delta(x,Y)$. MBL selects an example y_i or a cluster of examples that are most similar to x, then assign a target class of the example to x's class. We use a memory-based learning tool called TiMBL (Tilburg memory-based learner) version 5.0 [5].

Training data for each component function is represented by features of feature types in the context of L3~L1, C0, and R1~R3 as described in Table 4. Fig. 3 shows examples of δ_p and δ_t based on MBL in English-to-Korean transliteration. In order to simplify our examples, we just use f_S and f_P in Fig. 3. All training data are represented with their features in the context of L3~L1, C0, and R1~R3 and their target classes for δ_p and δ_t. They are stored in the memory through a training phase. Feature weighting for dealing with features of differing importance is also performed in the training phase. In Fig. 3, δ_p based on MBL outputs the phoneme /AO/ for *x(SP)* by comparing the similarities between *x(SP)* and Y using distance metric $\Delta(x(SP),Y)$. With the similar manner, δ_t based on MBL outputs the target grapheme 'o'.

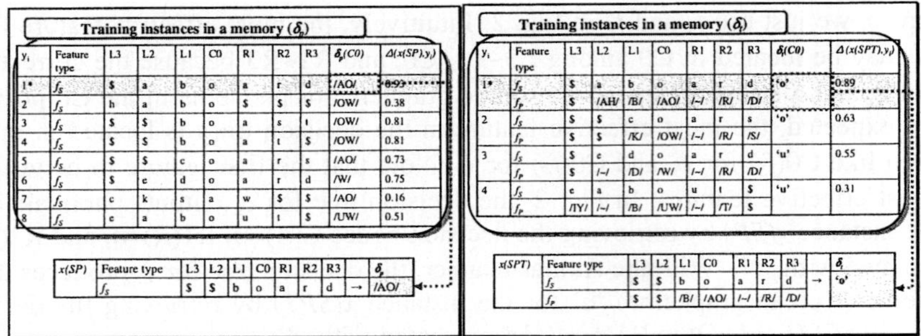

Fig. 3. Memory-based learning for δ_p and δ_t

4 Experiments

We perform experiments for English-to-Korean and English-to-Japanese transliteration. English-to-Korean test set (EKSet) [14] consists of 7,185 English-Korean pairs – the number of training data is 6,185 and that of test data is 1,000. EKSet contains no transliteration variations. English-to-Japanese test set (EJSet), which is an English-katakana pair in EDICT[8], consists of 10,398 – 1,000 for test and the rest for training. EJSet contains transliteration variations, like (micro, 'maikuro') and (micro, 'mi-kuro'); the average number of Japanese transliterations for an English word is 1.15. Evaluation is performed by word accuracy (W. A.) in formula (2).

$$W.A. = \frac{\#\,of\ correct\ words}{\#\,of\ generated\ words} \quad (2)$$

We perform two experiments called "**Comparison test**" and "**Context window size test**". In the "Comparison test", we compare our ψ_C with the previous works. In "Context window size test", we evaluate the performance of our transliteration model depending on context window size.

4.1 Experimental Results

Table 6 shows results of "**Comparison test**". MEM, DT, and MBL represent ψ_C based on maximum entropy model, decision tree, and memory-based learning, respectively. GDT [8], GPC [9], GMEM [7] and HWFST [4], which are one of the best machine transliteration methods in English-to-Korean transliteration and English-to-Japanese transliteration, are compared with ψ_C. Table 7 shows the key feature of each method in the viewpoint of **information type** (SG, PH, COR) and **information usage** (Context size, POut). Information type indicates that each transliteration method belongs to which transliteration model. For example, GDT, GPC, and GMEM will belong to ψ_G because they use only the source grapheme; while HWFST belongs to ψ_H. Information usage gives information about what kinds of information each transliteration method can deal with. From the viewpoint of information type, phoneme and correspondence, which most previous works do not consider, is the key point of the performance gap between our method and the previous works.

[8] http://www.csse.monash.edu.au/~jwb/j_edict.html

Table 6. Evaluation results of "Comparison test"

Method	EKSet		EJSet	
	W.A	Chg %	W.A	Chg %
GDT	51.4%	23.2%	50.3%	43.5%
GPC	55.1%	17.6%	53.2%	35.7%
GMEM	55.9%	16.4%	56.2%	28.5%
HWFST	58.3%	14.7%	62.5%	15.5%
DT	62.0%	7.3%	66.8%	8.1%
MEM	63.3%	5.4%	67.0%	7.8%
MBL	66.9%	0%	72.2%	0%

Table 7. Key features of our machine transliteration model and the previous works: SG, PH, COR and POut represent source grapheme, phoneme, correspondence and previous output, respectively

Method	SG	PH	COR	Context size	POut
GDT	O	X	X	<-3, +3>	X
GPC	O	X	X	Unbounded	O
GMEM	O	X	X	<-3, +3>	O
HWFST	O	O	X	-	-
Ours	O	O	O	<-3, +3>	O

From the viewpoint of information usage, if a transliteration model adopts wide context window and considers previous outputs, it tends to show better performance. For example, GMEM that satisfies the conditions gives more accurate results than GDT which does not satisfy one of them. Because machine transliteration is sensitive to context, wider contexts give more powerful transliteration ability to machine transliteration systems. Note that the previous works, however, limit their context window size to 3, because the context window size over 3 degrades the performance [8] or does not change the performance of their transliteration model [9]. Determining reasonable context window size, therefore, is very important for machine transliteration.

For "**Context window size test**", we use ψ_C based on MBL, which shows the best performance among three machine learning algorithms in Table 6. Experiments are performed by changing the context window size from 1 to 5. Table 8 shows results of context window size test. The results indicate that the best performance is shown when the context window size is 3. When the context window size is 1, there are many cases where the correct transliterations are not produced due to lack of information. For example, in order to produce the correct target grapheme of *t* in *-tion*, we need the right three graphemes of *t*, *-ion*. When the context window size is over 3, it is difficult to generalize the training data because of increase of variety of the training data. With the two reasons, our system shows the best performance when the context window size is 3. Table 8 also shows that context size should be at least 2 to avoid significant decrease of performance due to lack of contextual information.

Table 8. Evaluation results of "Context window size test"

Context Size	EKSet	EJSet
1	54.5%	62.7%
2	63.3%	70.0%
3	66.9%	72.2%
4	63.9%	70.7%
5	63.8%	69.3%

In summary, our method shows significant performance improvement, about 15%~23%, in English-to-Korean transliteration, and about 15%~ 43% in English-to-Japanese transliteration. Experiments show that a good transliteration system should consider; 1) source grapheme and phoneme along with their correspondence simultaneously and 2) reasonable context size and previous output. Our transliteration model satisfies the two conditions, thus it shows higher performance than the previous works.

5 Conclusion

This paper has described a correspondence-based machine transliteration model (ψ_C). Unlike the previous transliteration models, ψ_C uses correspondence between source grapheme and phoneme. The correspondence makes it possible for ψ_C to effectively produce both grapheme-based transliterations and phoneme-based transliterations. Moreover, the correspondence helps ψ_C to reduce transliteration ambiguities more easily. Experiments show that ψ_C is more powerful transliteration model than the previous transliteration models (ψ_C shows significant performance improvement, about 15%~23%, in English-to-Korean transliteration, and about 15%~ 43% in English-to-Japanese transliteration).

In future work, we will apply our transliteration model to English-to-Chinese transliteration model. In order to prove usefulness of our method in NLP applications, we need to apply our system to applications such as automatic bi-lingual dictionary construction, information retrieval, machine translation, speech recognition and so on.

Acknowledgement

This work was supported by the Korea Ministry of Science and Technology, the Korea Ministry of Commerce, Industry and Energy, and the Korea Science and Engineering Foundation (KOSEF).

References

1. Aha, D. W. Lazy learning: Special issue editorial. Artificial Intelligence Review, 11:710, (1997).
2. Al-Onaizan Y. and Kevin Knight, "Translating Named Entities Using Monolingual and Bilingual Resources", In the Proceedings of ACL 2002, (2002)

3. Berger, A., S. Della Pietra, and V. Della Pietra. , A maximum entropy approach to natural language processing. Computational Linguistics, 22(1), (1996), 39—71
4. Bilac Slaven and Hozumi Tanaka. "Improving Back-Transliteration by Combining Information Sources". In Proc. of IJC-NLP2004, (2004) 542—547
5. Daelemans, W., Jakub Zavrel, Ko van der Sloot, and Antal van den Bosch, 2002, Timble TiMBL: Tilburg Memory Based Learner, version 4.3, Reference Guide, ILK Technical Report 02-10, (2002).
6. Fujii, Atsushi and Tetsuya, Ishikawa. Japanese/English Cross-Language Information Retrieval: Exploration of Query Translation and Transliteration. Computers and the Humanities, Vol.35, No.4, (2001) 389—420
7. Goto, I., N. Kato, N. Uratani and T. Ehara, Transliteration Considering Context Information Based on the Maximum Entropy Method, In Proceedings of MT-Summit IX, (2003)
8. Kang B.J. and K-S. Choi, "Automatic Transliteration and Back-transliteration by Decision Tree Learning", In Proceedings of the 2nd International Conference on Language Resources and Evaluation, (2000)
9. Kang, I.H. and G.C. Kim, "English-to-Korean Transliteration using Multiple Unbounded Overlapping Phoneme Chunks", In Proceedings of the 18th International Conference on Computational Linguistics, (2000).
10. Knight, K. and J. Graehl, "Machine Transliteration". In Proceedings. of the 35th Annual Meetings of the Association for Computational Linguistics (ACL), (1997)
11. Lee, J. S. and K. S. Choi, English to Korean Statistical transliteration for information retrieval. Computer Processing of Oriental Languages, 12(1), (1998), 17-37.
12. Lee, J.S., An English-Korean transliteration and Retransliteration model for Cross-lingual information retrieval, PhD Thesis, Computer Science Dept., KAIST, (1999)
13. Li Haizhou, Min Zhang and Jian Su , A Joint Source-Channel Model for Machine Transliteration , ACL 2004, (2004), 159—166
14. Nam, Y.S., Foreign dictionary, Sung-An-Dang publisher, (1997)
15. Quinlan, J.R., "C4.5: Programs for Machine Learning", Morgan Kauffman, (1993)
16. Zhang, Le. Maximum Entropy Modeling Toolkit for Python and C++. http://www.nlplab.cn/zhangle/, (2004)

Improving Statistical Word Alignment with Ensemble Methods

Hua Wu and Haifeng Wang

Toshiba (China) Research and Development Center, 5/F., Tower W2, Oriental Plaza, No.1, East Chang An Ave., Dong Cheng District, Beijing, 100738, China
{wuhua, wanghaifeng}@rdc.toshiba.com.cn

Abstract. This paper proposes an approach to improve statistical word alignment with ensemble methods. Two ensemble methods are investigated: bagging and cross-validation committees. On these two methods, both weighted voting and unweighted voting are compared under the word alignment task. In addition, we analyze the effect of different sizes of training sets on the bagging method. Experimental results indicate that both bagging and cross-validation committees improve the word alignment results regardless of weighted voting or unweighted voting. Weighted voting performs consistently better than unweighted voting on different sizes of training sets.

1 Introduction

Bilingual word alignment is first introduced as an intermediate result in statistical machine translation (SMT) [3]. Besides being used in SMT, it is also used in translation lexicon building [9], transfer rule learning [10], example-based machine translation [14], etc. In previous alignment methods, some researchers employed statistical word alignment models to build alignment links [3], [4], [8], [11], [16]. Some researchers used similarity and association measures to build alignment links [1], [15].

One issue about word alignment is how to improve the performance of a word aligner when the training data are fixed. One possible solution is to use ensemble methods [5], [6]. The ensemble methods were proposed to improve the performance of classifiers. An ensemble of classifiers is a set of classifiers whose individual decisions are combined in some way (weighted or unweighted voting) to classify new examples. Many methods for constructing ensembles have been developed [5]. One kind of methods is to resample the training examples. These methods include bagging [2], cross-validation committees [12] and boosting [7]. The two former methods generate the classifiers in parallel while boosting generates the classifiers sequentially. In addition, boosting changes the weights of the training instance that is provided as input to each inducer based on the previously built classifiers.

In this paper, we propose an approach to improve word alignment with ensemble methods. Although word alignment is not a classification problem, we can still build different word aligners by resampling the training data. If these aligners perform accurately and diversely on the corpus [6], they can be employed to improve the word alignment results. Here, we investigate two ensemble methods: bagging and

R. Dale et al. (Eds.): IJCNLP 2005, LNAI 3651, pp. 462 – 473, 2005.

cross-validation committees. For both of the ensemble methods, we employ weighted and unweighted voting to build different ensembles. Experimental results indicate that both bagging and cross-validation committees improve the word alignment results. The weighted ensembles perform much better than the unweighted ensembles according to our word alignment results. In addition, we analyze the effect of different sizes of training data on the bagging algorithm. Experimental results also show that the weighted bagging ensembles perform consistently better than the unweighted bagging ensembles on different sizes of training sets.

The remainder of the paper is organized as follows. Section 2 describes statistical word alignment. Section 3 describes the bagging algorithm. Section 4 describes the cross-validation committees. Section 5 describes how to calculate the weights used for voting. Section 6 presents the evaluation results. Section 7 discusses why the ensemble methods used in this paper are effective for the word alignment task. The last section concludes this paper and presents the future work.

2 Statistical Word Alignment

In this paper, we use the IBM model 4 as our statistical word alignment model [3]. This model only allows word to word and multi-word to word alignments. Thus, some multi-word units cannot be correctly aligned. In order to tackle this problem, we perform word alignment in two directions (source to target and target to source) as described in [11]. In this paper, we call these two aligners *bi-directional* aligners.[1] Thus, for each sentence pair, we can get two alignment results. We use S_1 and S_2 to represent the bi-directional alignment sets. For alignment links in both sets, we use i for source words and j for target words.

$$S_1 = \{(A_j, j) \mid A_j = \{i \mid i = a_j,\ a_j \geq 0\}\} \tag{1}$$

$$S_2 = \{(i, A_i) \mid A_i = \{j \mid a_j = i,\ a_j \geq 0\}\} \tag{2}$$

Where, a_j represents the index position of the source word aligned to the target word in position j. For example, if a target word in position j is connected to a source word in position i, then $a_j=i$. If a target word in position j is connected to source words in positions i_1 and i_2, then $A_j=\{i_1,i_2\}$. We name an element in the alignment set an *alignment link*.[2]

3 Bagging

The *bagging* algorithm (derived from *b*ootstrap *agg*regat*ing*) votes classifiers generated by different bootstrap replicates [2]. A bootstrap replicate is generated by uniformly sampling m instances from the training set with replacement. In general, T

[1] The GIZA++ toolkit is used to perform statistical alignment. It is located at http://www.fjoch.com/GIZA++.html.

[2] Our definition of alignment link is different from that in [11]. In [11], alignment links are classified into possible links and sure links. In our paper, both one-to-one and non one-to-one links are taken as sure links.

bootstrap replicates are built in the sampling process. And T different classifiers are built based on the bootstrap replicates. A final classifier is built from these T sub-classifiers using weighted voting or unweighted voting. The original unweighted bagging algorithm is shown in Figure 1.

Input: a training set $S = \{(y_i, x_i), i \in \{1, ..., m\}\}$
an induction algorithm Ψ

(1) For $j = 1$ to T {
(2) S_j = bootstrap replicate of S by sampling m items from S with replacement
(3) $C_j = \Psi(S_j)$
(4) }
(5) Create a final classifier with majority voting:
$$C^*(x) = \arg\max_{y \in Y} \sum_j \delta(C_j(x), y)$$
Where, $\delta(x, y) = 1$ if $x = y$; else $\delta(x, y) = 0$.

Output: Classifier C^*

Fig. 1. The Unweighted Bagging Algorithm

3.1 Bagging the Statistical Word Aligner

In this section, we apply the technique of bagging to word alignment, the detailed algorithm is shown in Figure 2. In the algorithm, we first resample the training data to train the word aligners. We choose to resample the training set in the same way as the original bagging algorithm. With these different bootstrap replicates, we build the different word aligners. As described in Section 2, we perform word alignment in two directions to improve multiword alignment. Thus, on each bootstrap replicate, we train a word aligner in the source to target direction and another word aligner in the target to source direction, which is described in b) of step (1).

After building the different word aligners, we combine or aggregate the alignments generated by the individual alignment models to create the final alignments for each sentence pair. In this paper, the final alignment link for each word is chosen by performing a majority voting on the alignments provided by each instance of the model. The majority voting can be weighted or unweighted. For weighted voting, the weights of word alignment links produced by the bi-directional word aligners are trained from the training data, which will be further described in section 5. For unweighted voting, the best alignment link for a specific word or unit is voted by more than half of the word aligners in the ensemble. For those words that have no majority choice, the system simply does not align them.

Input: a training set $S = \{(y_i, x_i), i \in \{1...m\}\}$
a word alignment model M

(1) For $j = 1$ to T

a) S_j = bootstrap replicate of S by sampling m items from S with replacement

b) Train the bi-directional alignment models M_j^{st} and M_j^{ts} with the bootstrap replicate S_j

(2) For $k = 1$ to N (N is the number of sentence pairs)
For each word s:

a) For weighted voting

$$M^*(s,k) = \arg\max_t \sum_j W_j(s,t) * (\delta(M_j^{st}(s,k),t) + \delta(M_j^{ts}(s,k),t))$$

t is the word or phrase in the target sentence;
$W_j(s,t)$ is the weight for the alignment link (s, t) produced by the aligner M_j^{st} or M_j^{ts};
$\delta(x, y) = 1$ if $x = y$; else $\delta(x, y) = 0$.

b) For unweighted voting

$$M^*(s,k) = \arg\max_{t:n(t)>\frac{T}{2}} \sum_{j=1}^{T} (\delta(M_j^{st}(s,k),t) + \delta(M_j^{ts}(s,k),t))$$

where, $n(t) = \sum_{j=1}^{T} (\delta(M_j^{st}(s,k),t) + \delta(M_j^{ts}(s,k),t))$

Output: The final word alignment results

Fig. 2. The Bagging Algorithm for Word Alignment

4 Cross-Validation Committee

The difference between bagging and cross-validation committees lies in the way to resample the training set. The cross-validation committees construct the training sets by leaving out disjoint subsets of the training data. For example, the training set can be randomly and evenly divided into *N* disjoint subsets. Then *N* overlapping training sets can be constructed by dropping out a different one of these *N* subsets. This procedure is the same as the one to construct training sets for N-fold cross-validation. Thus, ensembles constructed in this way are called cross-validation committees.

For word alignment, we also divide the training set into *N* even parts and build *N* overlapping training sets. With the *N* sets, we build *N* alignment models as described above. Since the training sets are different, the word alignment results may be different for individual words. Using the same majority voting as described in Figure 2, we get the final word alignment results.

5 Weight Calculation

In this paper, we compare both weighted voting and unweighted voting under our word alignment task. The algorithm in Figure 2 shows that the weights are related with the specific word alignment links and the specific word aligner. We calculate the weights based on the word alignment results on the training data.

As described in Section 3.1, on each bootstrap replicate *j*, we train a word aligner M_j^{st} in the source to target direction and a word aligner M_j^{ts} in the target to source direction. That is to say, we obtain two different word alignment sets S_j^{st} and S_j^{ts} for each of the bootstrap replicate. For each word alignment link $(s,\ t)$ produced by M_j^{st} or M_j^{ts}, we calculate its weight as shown in (3). This weight measures the association of the source part and the target part in an alignment link. This measure is like the Dice Coefficient. Smadja et al. [13] showed that the Dice Coefficient is a good indicator of translation association.

$$W_i(s,t) = \frac{2 * count(s,t)}{\sum_{t'} count(s,t') + \sum_{s'} count(s',t)} \tag{3}$$

Where, $count(s,t)$ is the occurring frequency of the alignment link $(s,\ t) \in S_j^{st} \cup S_j^{ts}$.

6 Experiments

6.1 Training and Testing Set

We perform experiments on a sentence aligned English-Chinese bilingual corpus in general domain. There are about 320,000 bilingual sentence pairs in the corpus, from which, we randomly select 1,000 sentence pairs as testing data. The remainder is used as training data. In the sentence pairs, the average length of the English sentences is 13.6 words while the average length of the Chinese sentences is 14.2 words.

The Chinese sentences in both the training set and the testing set are automatically segmented into words. The segmentation errors in the testing set are post-corrected. The testing set is manually annotated. It has totally 8,651 alignment links. Among them, 866 alignment links include multiword units, which accounts for about 10% of the total links.

6.2 Evaluation Metrics

We use the same evaluation metrics as in [17]. If we use S_G to represent the set of alignment links identified by the proposed methods and S_R to denote the reference alignment set, the methods to calculate the precision, recall, f-measure, and alignment error rate (AER) are shown in Equation (4), (5), (6), and (7). In addition, t-test is used for testing statistical significance. From the evaluation metrics, it can be seen that the higher the f-measure is, the lower the alignment error rate is. Thus, we will only show precision, recall and AER scores in the experimental results.

$$precision = \frac{|S_G \cap S_R|}{|S_G|} \tag{4}$$

$$recall = \frac{|S_G \cap S_R|}{|S_R|} \tag{5}$$

$$fmeasure = \frac{2*|S_G \cap S_R|}{|S_G|+|S_R|} \tag{6}$$

$$AER = 1 - \frac{2*|S_G \cap S_R|}{|S_G|+|S_R|} = 1 - fmeasure \tag{7}$$

6.3 Evaluation Results for Bagging

For the bagging method, we use ten word aligners trained on five different bootstrap replicates. Among them, five aligners are trained in the source to target direction. The other five aligners are trained in the target to source direction. The bagging method will be compared with a *baseline* method using the entire training data. For this baseline method, we also train bi-directional models. Based on the alignment results on the entire training data, we calculate the alignment weights for the two word aligners as described in Section 5.

The results using weighted voting are shown in Table 1. The number in brackets of the first column describes the number of word aligners used in the ensembles. For example, in the ensemble "bagging (4)", two word aligners are trained in the source to target direction and the other two are trained in the target to source direction.

From the results, it can be seen that the bagging methods obtain significantly better results than the baseline. The best ensemble achieves an error rate reduction of 7.34% as compared with the baseline. The results show that increasing the number of word aligner does not greatly reduce the word alignment error rate. The reduction is even smaller when the number increases from 8 to 10.

Table 1. Weighted Bagging Results

Method	Precision	Recall	AER
Bagging (4)	0.8035	0.7898	0.2034
Bagging (6)	0.8048	0.7922	0.2015
Bagging (8)	0.8061	0.7948	0.1996
Bagging (10)	0.8064	0.7948	0.1994
Baseline	0.7870	0.7826	0.2152

In order to further analyze the effect of the weights on the word alignment results, we also use unweighted voting in the ensembles. The results are shown in Table 2. The *baseline* method also trains bi-directional aligners with the entire training data. The final word alignment results are obtained by taking an unweighted voting on the two alignment results produced by the bi-directional aligners. That is the same as that by taking the intersection of the two word alignment results.

Table 2. Unweighted Bagging Results

Method	Precision	Recall	AER
Bagging (4)	0.9230	0.6073	0.2674
Bagging (6)	0.9181	0.6200	0.2598
Bagging (8)	0.9167	0.6307	0.2527
Bagging (10)	0.9132	0.6347	0.2511
Baseline	0.9294	0.5756	0.2810

Increasing the number of word aligners in the ensembles, the unweighted bagging method does not greatly reduce AER. However, the ensembles obtain much lower error rate as compared with the baseline. The best ensemble achieves a relative error rate reduction of 10.64%, indicating a significant improvement. From the experimental results, we find that there are no multiword alignment links selected in the ensembles. This is because unweighted voting in this paper requires more than half of the word aligners in the ensembles to vote for the same link. Thus, there should be bi-directional word aligners voting for the target alignment link. The intersection of bi-directional word alignment results produced by the IBM models only creates single word alignments. It can also be seen from the Equations (1) and (2) in Section 2.

Comparing the results obtained using weighted voting in Table 1 and those obtained using unweighted voting in Table 2, we find that (1) the weighted bagging methods are much better than the unweighted bagging methods; (2) the ensembles using unweighted voting obtain higher precision but lower recall than those using weighted voting. For example, the weighted voting "bagging (10)" achieves a relative error rate reduction of 20.59% as compared with the corresponding unweighted voting. This indicates that the method used to calculate voting weights described in section 5 is very effective.

6.4 Evaluation Results for Cross-Validation Committees

For the cross-validation committees, we divide the entire training data into five disjoint subsets. For each bootstrap replicate, we leave one out. Thus, each replicate includes 80% sentence pairs of the full training data. For each replicate, we train bi-directional word alignment models. Thus, we totally obtain ten individual word aligners. The baseline is the same as shown in Table 1. The results obtained using weighted voting are shown in Table 3. The number in the brackets of the first column describes the number of word aligners used in the ensembles.

Table 3. Evaluation Results for Weighted Cross-Validation Committees

Method	Precision	Recall	AER
Validation (4)	0.8059	0.7913	0.2015
Validation (6)	0.8070	0.7928	0.2002
Validation (8)	0.8063	0.7933	0.2002
Validation (10)	0.8068	0.7947	0.1993
Baseline	0.7870	0.7826	0.2152

From the results, it can be seen that the cross-validation committees perform better than the baseline. The best ensemble "validation (10)" achieves an error rate reduction of 7.39% as compared with the baseline, indicating a significant improvement. The results also show that increasing the number of word aligner does not greatly reduce the word alignment error rate.

As described in section 6.3, we also use unweighted voting for the cross-validation committees. The results are shown in Table 4. The baseline is the same as described in Table 2.

Table 4. Evaluation Results for Unweighted Cross-Validation Committees

Method	Precision	Recall	AER
Validation (4)	0.9199	0.5943	0.2779
Validation (6)	0.9174	0.6124	0.2655
Validation (8)	0.9154	0.6196	0.2610
Validation (10)	0.9127	0.6245	0.2584
Baseline	0.9294	0.5756	0.2810

From the results, it can be seen that increasing the number of word aligners in the ensembles, the alignment error rate is reduced. The best ensemble achieves a relative error rate reduction of 8.04% as compared with the baseline, indicating a significant improvement. Comparing the results in Table 3 and Table 4, we find that the weighted methods are also much better than the unweighted ones. For example, the weighted method "Validation (10)" achieves an error rate reduction of 22.87% as compared with the corresponding unweighted method.

6.5 Bagging vs. Cross-Validation Committees

According to the evaluation results, bagging and cross-validation committees achieve comparable results. In order to further compare bagging and cross-validation committees, we classify the alignment links in the weighted ensembles into two classes: single word alignment links (SWA) and multiword alignment links (MWA). SWA links only include one-to-one alignments. MWA links refer to those including multiword units in the source language or/and in the target language. The SWA and MWA for the bagging ensembles are shown in Table 5 and Table 6. The SWA and MWA for the cross-validation committees are shown in Table 7 and Table 8. The AERs of the baselines for SWA and MWA are 0.1531 and 0.8469, respectively.

Table 5. Single Word Alignment Results for the Weighted Bagging Methods

Method	Precision	Recall	AER
Bagging (4)	0.8263	0.8829	0.1463
Bagging (6)	0.8270	0.8845	0.1452
Bagging (8)	0.8270	0.8877	0.1437
Bagging (10)	0.8265	0.8876	0.1440

Table 6. Multiword Alignment Results for the Weighted Bagging Methods

Method	Precision	Recall	AER
Bagging (4)	0.4278	0.1815	0.7451
Bagging (6)	0.4432	0.1896	0.7344
Bagging (8)	0.4540	0.1884	0.7336
Bagging (10)	0.4620	0.1896	0.7311

Table 7. Single Word Alignment Results for Weighted Cross-Validation Committees

Method	Precision	Recall	AER
Validation (4)	0.8282	0.8833	0.1452
Validation (6)	0.8285	0.8847	0.1443
Validation (8)	0.8275	0.8851	0.1447
Validation (10)	0.8277	0.8867	0.1438

Table 8. Multiword Alignment Results for Weighted Cross-Validation Committees

Method	Precision	Recall	AER
Validation (4)	0.4447	0.1908	0.7330
Validation (6)	0.4538	0.1931	0.7291
Validation (8)	0.4578	0.1942	0.7273
Validation (10)	0.4603	0.1942	0.7268

From the results, it can be seen that the single word alignment results are much better than the multiword alignment results for both of the two methods. This indicates that it is more difficult to align the multiword units than to align single words.

Comparing the bagging methods and validation committees, we find that these two methods obtain comparable results on both the single word alignment links and multiword alignment links. This indicates that the different resampling methods in these two ensemble methods do not much affect the results on our word alignment task.

6.6 Different Sizes of Training Data

In this section, we investigate the effect of the size of training data on the ensemble methods. Since the difference between bagging and cross-validation committees is very small, we only investigate the effect on the bagging ensembles.

We randomly select training data from the original training set described in Section 6.1 to construct different training sets. We construct three training sets, which include 1/4, 1/2 and 3/4 of sentence pairs of the original training set, respectively.

For each of the training set, we obtain five bootstrap replicates and train ten word aligners. The results of ensembles consisting of ten word aligners are shown in Table 9 and Table 10. Table 9 and Table 10 show the weighted and unweighted bagging results, respectively. The methods to construct the baselines for different training sets in Table 9 and Table 10 are the same as those in Table 1 and Table 2, respectively. For convenience, we also list the results using the original training set in the tables. The first column describes the size of the training sets used for the ensembles. The last column presents the relative error rate reduction (RERR) of the ensembles as compared with the corresponding baselines. From the results, it can be seen that both weighted and unweighted bagging ensembles are effective to improve word alignment results. The weighted ensembles perform consistently better than the unweigted ensembles on different sizes of training sets.

Table 9. Weighted Bagging Results on Different Sizes of Training Sets

Data	Precision	Recall	AER	Baseline (AER)	RERR
1/4	0.7684	0.7517	0.2316	0.2464	6.00%
1/2	0.7977	0.7775	0.2125	0.2293	7.33%
3/4	0.8023	0.7869	0.2055	0.2184	5.89%
All	0.8064	0.7948	0.1994	0.2152	7.34%

Table 10. Unweighted Bagging Results on Different Sizes of Training Sets

Data	Precision	Recall	AER	Baseline (AER)	RERR
1/4	0.8960	0.6033	0.2789	0.3310	15.72%
1/2	0.9077	0.6158	0.2662	0.3050	12.72%
3/4	0.9140	0.6270	0.2562	0.2943	12.95%
All	0.9132	0.6347	0.2511	0.2810	10.64%

7 Discussion

Both bagging and cross-validation committees utilize multiple classifiers to make different assumptions about the learning system. Bagging requires that the learning system should not be stable, so that small changes to the training set would lead to different classifiers. Breiman [2] also noted that poor predicators could be transformed into worse ones by bagging.

In this paper, the learning system is the word alignment model described in Section 2. The classifiers refer to the different word aligners trained on different bootstrap replicates. In our experiments, although word alignment models do not belong to unstable learning systems, bagging obtains better results on all of the datasets. This is because the training data is insufficient or subject to data sparseness problem. Thus, changing the training data or resampling the training data causes the alternation of the trained parameters of the alignment model. The word aligners trained on a different bootstrap replicate produce different word alignment links for individual words. Using majority voting, the ensembles can improve the alignment precision and recall, resulting in lower alignment error rates.

The experiments also show that weighted voting is better than unweighted voting. The advantage of weighted voting is that it can select the good word alignment link even if only one aligner votes for it in the ensembles. This is because the selected alignment link gets much higher weight than the other links.

8 Conclusion and Future Work

Two ensemble methods are employed in this paper to improve word alignment results: bagging and cross-validation committees. Both of these two methods obtain better results than the original word aligner without increasing any training data. In this paper, we use two different voting methods: weighted voting and unweighted voting. Experimental results show that the weighted bagging method and weighted cross-validation committees achieve an error rate reduction of 7.34% and 7.39% respectively, as compared with the original word aligner. Results also show that weighted voting is much better than unweighted voting on the word alignment task. Unweighted voting obtains higher precision but lower recall than weighted voting. In addition, the weighted voting used in this paper obtains multiword alignment links while the unweighted voting cannot.

We also compare the two ensemble methods on the same training data and testing data. Bagging and cross-validation committees obtain comparable results on both single word alignment links and multiword alignment links. This indicates that the different resampling methods in these two ensemble methods do not much affect the results under our word alignment task.

We also investigate the bagging method on different sizes of training sets. The results show that both weighted voting and unweighted voting are effective to improve word alignment results. Weighted voting performs consistently better than unweigted voting on different sizes of training sets.

In future work, we will investigate more ensemble methods on the word alignment task such as the boosting algorithm. In addition, we will do more research on the weighting schemes in voting.

References

1. Ahrenberg, L., Merkel, M., Andersson, M.: A Simple Hybrid Aligner for Generating Lexical Correspondences in Parallel Texts. In Proc. of the 36th Annual Meeting of the Association for Computational Linguistics and the 17th Int. Conf. on Computational Linguistics (ACL/COLING-1998), 29-35
2. Breiman, L.: Bagging Predicators. Machine Learning (1996), 24(1): 123-140
3. Brown, P. F., Pietra, S. D., Pietra, V. D., Mercer, R.: The Mathematics of Statistical Machine Translation: Parameter Estimation. Computational Linguistics (1993), 19(2): 263-311

4. Cherry, C., Lin, D.: A Probability Model to Improve Word Alignment. In Proc. of the 41st Annual Meeting of the Association for Computational Linguistics (ACL-2003), pp. 88-95
5. Dietterich, T.: Machine Learning Research: Four Current Directions. AI Magazine (1997), 18 (4): 97-136
6. Dietterich, T.: Ensemble Methods in Machine Learning. In Proc. of the First Int. Workshop on Multiple Classifier Systems (2000), 1-15
7. Freund, Y., Schapire, R.: Experiments with a new boosting algorithm. In Machine Learning: Proc. of the Thirteenth International Conference (1996), 148-156
8. Matusov, E., Zens, R., Ney H.: Symmetric Word Alignments for Statistical Machine Translation. In Proc. of the 20th Int. Conf. on Computational Linguistics (COLING-2004), 219-225
9. Melamed, I. D.: Automatic Construction of Clean Broad-Coverage Translation Lexicons. In Proc. of the 2nd Conf. of the Association for Machine Translation in the Americas (AMTA-1996), 125-134
10. Menezes, A., Richardson, S.D.: A Best-first Alignment Algorithm for Automatic Extraction of Transfer Mappings from Bilingual Corpora. In Proc. of the ACL 2001 Workshop on Data-Driven Methods in Machine Translation (2001), 39-46
11. Och, F. J., Ney, H.: Improved Statistical Alignment Models. In Proc. of the 38th Annual Meeting of the Association for Computational Linguistics (ACL-2000), 440-447
12. Parmanto, B., Munro, P., Doyle, H.: Improving Committee Diagnosis with Resampling Techniques. In Touretzky, D., Mozer, M., Hasselmo, M. (Ed..): Advances in Neural Information Processing Systems (1996), Vol. 8, 882-888
13. Smadja, F. A., McKeown, K. R., Hatzivassiloglou, V.: Translating Collocations for Bilingual Lexicons: a Statistical Approach. Computational Linguistics (1996), 22 (1):1-38
14. Somers, H.: Review Article: Example-Based Machine Translation. Machine Translation (1999), 14: 113-157
15. Tufis, D., Barbu, M.: Lexical Token Alignment: Experiments, Results and Application. In Proc. of the 3rd Int. Conf. on Language Resources and Evaluation (LREC-2002), 458-465
16. Wu, D.: Stochastic Inversion Transduction Grammars and Bilingual Parsing of Parallel Corpora. Computational Linguistics (1997), 23(3): 377-403
17. Wu, H., Wang, H.: Improving Domain-Specific Word Alignment with a General Bilingual Corpus. In Frederking R., Taylor, K. (Eds.): Machine Translation: From Real Users to Research: 6th Conf. of the Association for Machine Translation in the Americas (AMTA-2004), 262-271

Empirical Study of Utilizing Morph-Syntactic Information in SMT

Young-Sook Hwang, Taro Watanabe, and Yutaka Sasaki

ATR SLT Research Labs, 2-2-2 Hikaridai Seika-cho,
Soraku-gun Kyoto, 619-0288, Japan
{youngsook.hwang, taro.watanabe, yutaka.sasaki}@atr.jp

Abstract. In this paper, we present an empirical study that utilizes morph-syntactical information to improve translation quality. With three kinds of language pairs matched according to morph-syntactical similarity or difference, we investigate the effects of various morpho-syntactical information, such as base form, part-of-speech, and the relative positional information of a word in a statistical machine translation framework. We learn not only translation models but also word-based/class-based language models by manipulating morphological and relative positional information. And we integrate the models into a log-linear model. Experiments on multilingual translations showed that such morphological information as part-of-speech and base form are effective for improving performance in morphologically rich language pairs and that the relative positional features in a word group are useful for reordering the local word orders. Moreover, the use of a class-based n-gram language model improves performance by alleviating the data sparseness problem in a word-based language model.

1 Introduction

For decades, many research efforts have contributed to the advance of statistical machine translation. Such an approach to machine translation has proven successful in various comparative evaluations. Recently, various works have improved the quality of statistical machine translation systems by using phrase translation [1,2,3,4] or using morpho-syntactic information [6,8]. But most statistical machine translation systems still consider surface forms and rarely use linguistic knowledge about the structure of the languages involved[8]. In this paper, we address the question of the effectiveness of morpho-syntactic features such as parts-of-speech, base forms, and relative positions in a chunk or an agglutinated word for improving the quality of statistical machine translations.

Basically, we take a statistical machine translation model based on an IBM model that consists of a language model and a separate translation model [5]:

$$e_1^I = argmax_{e_1^I} Pr(f_1^J|e_1^I)Pr(e_1^I) \tag{1}$$

The translation model links the source language sentence to the target language sentence. The target language model describes the well-formedness of the target language sentence.

R. Dale et al. (Eds.): IJCNLP 2005, LNAI 3651, pp. 474–485, 2005.

One of the main problems in statistical machine translation is to learn the less ambiguous correspondences between the words in the source and target languages from the bilingual training data. When translating one source language(which may be inflectional or non-inflectional) into the morphologically rich language such like Japanese or Korean, the bilingual training data can be exploited better by explicitly taking into account the interdependencies of related inflected or agglutinated forms. In this study, we represent a word with its morphological features in both sides of the source and the target language to learn less ambiguous correspondences between the source and the target language words or phrases. In addition, we utilize the relative positional information of a word in its word group to consider the word order in an agglutinated word or a chunk.

Another problem is to produce a correct target sentence. To produce more correct target sentence, we should consider the following problems: word reordering in a language pair with different word order, production of correct inflected and agglutinated words in an inflectional or agglutinative target language. In this study, we tackle the problem with language models. For learning language model that can treat morphological and word-order problem, we represent a word with its morphological and positional information. However, a word-based language model with enriched word is likely to suffer from a severe data sparseness problem. To alleviate the problem, we interpolate the word-based language model with a class-based n-gram model.

In the next section, we briefly discuss related works. Then, we describe the method that utilizes morpho-syntactic information under consideration for improving the quality of translations. Then we report the experimental results with some analysis and conclude our study.

2 Related Work

Few papers deal with the integration of linguistic information into the process of statistical machine translation. [8] introduced hierarchical lexicon models including base-form and POS information for translation from German into English. Irrelevant information contained in the German entries for the generation of the English translation were omitted. They trained the lexicon model using maximum entropy. [6] enriched English with knowledge to help select the correct full-form from morphologically richer languages such as Spanish and Catalan. In other words, they introduced a splicing operation that merged the pronouns/modals and verbs for treating differences in verbal expressions. To treat the unknown entries in the lexicon resulting from the splicing operation, they trained the lexicon model using maximum entropy and used linguistic knowledge just in the source language part and not in the target language. They don't use any linguistic knowledge in the target language and use full-form words during training.

In addition, [6] and [8] proposed re-ordering operations to make similar word orders in the source and target language sentences. In other words, for the interrogative phrases with different word order from the declarative sentences, they introduced techniques of question inversion and removed unnecessary auxiliary verbs. But, such inversion techniques require additional preprocessing with heuristics.

Unlike them, we investigate methods for utilizing linguistic knowledge in both of the source and the target language at the morpheme level. To generate a correct full-form word in a target language, we consider not only both the surface and base form of a morpheme but also the relative positional information in a full-form word. We strongly utilize the combined features in language modeling. By training alignments and language models with morphological and positional features at the morpheme-level, the severe data sparseness problem can be alleviated with the combined linguistic features. And the correspondence ambiguities between the source and target words can be decreased.

3 Utilization of Morpho-Syntactic Information in SMT

Generally, the probabilistic lexicon resulting from training a translation model contains all word forms occurring in the training corpus as separate entries, not taking into account whether they are inflected forms. A language model is also composed of the words in the training corpus. However, the use of a full-form word itself may cause severe data sparseness problem, especially relevant for more inflectional/agglutinative languages like Japanese and Korean. One alternative is to utilize the results of morphological analysis such as base form, part-of-speech and other information at the morpheme level. We address the usefulness of morphological information to improve the quality of statistical machine translation.

3.1 Available Morpho-Syntactic Information

A prerequisite for methods that improve the quality of statistical machine translation is the availability of various kinds of morphological and syntactic information. In this section, we examine the morpho-syntactic information available from the morphological analyzers of Korean, Japanese, English and Chinese and describe a method of utilizing the information.

Japanese and Korean are highly inflectional and agglutinative languages, and in English inflection has only a marginal role; whereas Chinese usually is regarded as an isolating language since it has almost no inflectional morphology. As the syntactic role of each word within Japanese and Korean sentences are often marked, word order in a sentence plays a relatively small role in characterizing the syntactic function of each word than in English or Chinese sentences. Thus, Korean and Japanese sentences have a relatively free word order; whereas words within Chinese and English sentences adhere to a rigid order. The treatment of inflection, and not word order, plays the most important role in processing Japanese and Korean, while word order has a central role in Chinese and English.

Figure 1 shows some examples of morphological information by Chinese, Japanese, English and Korean morphological analyzers and Figure 2 the correspondences among the words. Note that Korean and Japanese are very similar:

<table>
<tr><td>请告诉我车站在哪里</td><td>駅はどこか教えて下さい</td><td>Please tell me where the station is</td><td>역은 어디인지 알려 주세요</td></tr>
<tr><td>请||请|v|
告诉||告诉|v|
我||我|r|
车站||车站|ns|
在||在|v|
哪里||哪里|r|</td><td>駅|エキ|駅|普通名詞
は|ハ|は|係助詞|
どこ|ドコ|どこ|代名詞
か|カ|か|副助詞
教え|オシエ|教える|本動詞
て下さい|テクダサイ|て下さる|助動詞</td><td>please||please|ADV
tell||tell|V
me||me|PRON
where||where|WHADV
the||the|DET
station||station|CN
is||be|BEV</td><td>역||역|NNCG|0-0
은||은|PX|1-1
어디||어디|NNCG|0-1
인||이|II|2-2
인지||ㄴ지|EFC|2-3
알려||알리|VV|0-1
려||어|EFC|1-1
주||주|VV|0-0
세||시|EP|1-1
세요||어요|EFF|1-2</td></tr>
</table>

Notation of representation of morphological information: 1|2|3|4|5
(1. surface form 2. pronunciation 3. part-of-speech 4. Base form 5. relative position in a spacing word)

Fig. 1. Examples of linguistic information from Chinese, Japanese, English, and Korean morphological analyzers

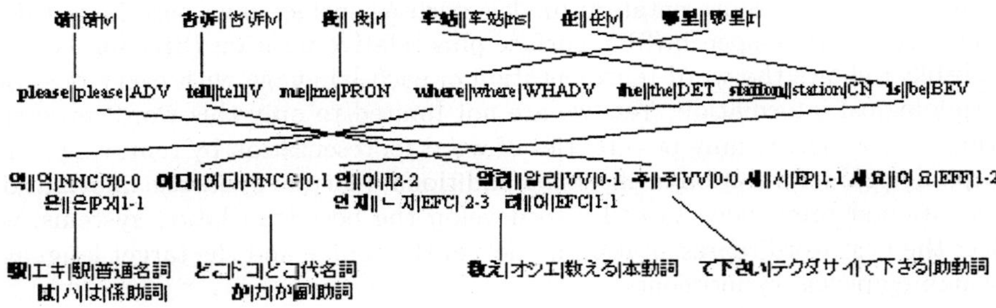

Fig. 2. Correspondences among the words in parallel sentences

highly inflected and agglutinated. One difference in Korean from Japanese is that a Korean sentence consists of spacing units, *eojeols*,[1] while there are no space in a Japanese sentence. Especially, a spacing unit(i.e., *eojeol*) in Korean often becomes a base phrase that contains such syntactic information as subject, object, and the mood/tense of a verb in a given sentence. The treatment of such a Korean spacing unit may contribute to the improvement of translation quality because a morpheme can be represented with its relative positional information within an eojeol. The relative positional information is obtained by calculating the distance between the beginning syllable of a given eojeol and the beginning of each morpheme within the eojeol. The relative positional information is represented with indexes of the beginning and the ending syllables (See Figure 1).

3.2 Word Representation

A word(i.e. morpheme) is represented by the combination of the information provided by a morphological analyzer including the surface form, base form, part-of-speech or other information such as relative position within an eojeol. The word

[1] An eojeol is composed of no less than one morpheme by agglutination principle.

Table 1. Word Representation According to Morpho-Syntactic Characteristics (S: surface form, B:base form, P:part-of-speech, L:RelativePosition)

	Chinese	English	Japanese	Korean
Morph-Syntactic Characteristics	no inflection	Inflectional	Inflectional, Agglutinative	Inflectional Agglutinative Spacing Unit
(Word-Order)	Rigid	Rigid	Partial Free	Partial Free
Word Representation	S‖P	S‖B‖P S‖B, S‖P	S‖B‖P S‖B, S‖P	S‖B‖P‖L S‖B‖P, S‖B‖L, S‖P‖L S‖B, S‖P, S‖L

enriched by the combination of morph-syntactic information must alway include the surface form of a given word for the direct generation of target sentence without any post-processing. Other different morphological information is combined according to representation models such as surface plus base form (SB), surface plus part-of-speech (SP), surface plus relative position (SL), and so on.

Table 1 shows the word representation of each language with every possible morphological information. Yet, we are not limited to only this word representation, but we have many possibilities of word representation by removing some morphological information or inserting additional morpho-syntactic information as mentioned previously. In order to develop the best translation systems, we select the best word representation models of the source and the target language through empirical experiments.

The inherent in the original word forms is augmented by a morphological analyzer. Of course, this results in an enlarged vocabulary while it may provide useful disambiguation clues. However, since we regard a morpheme as a word in a corpus(henceforth, we call a morpheme a word), the enlarged vocabulary does not make more severe data sparseness problem than using the inflected or agglutinated word. By taking the approch of morpheme-level alignment, we may obtain more accurate correspondences among words as illustrated in Figure 2. Moreover, by learning the language model with rich morph-syntactic information, we can generate more syntactically fluent and correct sentence.

3.3 Log-Linear Model for Statistical Machine Translation

In order to improve translation quality, we evaluate the translation candidates by using the relevant features in a log-linear model framework[11]. The log-linear model used in our statistical translation process, $Pr(e_1^I|f_1^J)$, is:

$$Pr(e_1^I|f_1^I) = \frac{exp(\sum_m \lambda_m h_m(e_1^I, f_1^J, a_1^J))}{\sum_{e_1'^I, f_1^I, a_1^I} exp(\sum_m \lambda_m h_m(e_1'^I, f_1^J, a_1^J))} \quad (2)$$

where $h_m(e_1^I, f_1^J, a_1^J)$ is the logarithm value of the m-th feature; λ_m is the weight of the m-th feature. Integrating different features in the equation results in different models.

The statistical machine translation process in IBM models is as follows; a given source string $f_1^J = f_1 \cdots f_J$ is to be translated into $e_1^I = e_1 \cdots e_I$. According to the Bayes' decision rule, we choose the optimal translation for given string f_1^J that maximizes the product of target language model $Pr(e_1^I)$ and translation model $Pr(f_1^J|e_1^I)$

$$e_1^I = argmax_{e_1^I} Pr(f_1^J|e_1^I)Pr(e_1^I) \tag{3}$$

In IBM model 4, translation model $P(f_1^J|e_1^I)$ is further decomposed into four submodels:

- Lexicon Model, $t(f|e)$: probability of word f in the source language being translated into word e in the target language.
- Fertility model, $n(\phi|e)$: probability of target language word e generating ϕ words.
- Distortion model d: probability of distortion, which is decomposed into the distortion probabilities of head words and non-head words.
- NULL translation model p_1: a fixed probability of inserting a NULL word after determining each target word.

In addition to the five features ($Pr(e_1^I)$, $t(f|e)$, $n(\phi|e)$, d, p_1) from IBM model 4, we incorporate the following features into the log-linear translation model:

- Class-based n-gram model $Pr(e_1^I) = \prod_i Pr(e_i|c_i)Pr(c_i|c_1^{i-1})$: Grouping of words into C classes is done according to the statistical similarity of their surroundings. Target word e_i is mapped into its class, c_i, which is one of C classes[13].
- Length model $Pr(l|e_1^I, f_i^J)$: l is the length (number of words) of a translated target sentence.
- Example matching score: The translated target sentence is matched with phrase translation examples. A score is derived based on the number of matches [10]. To extract phrase translation examples, we compute the intersection of word alignment of both directions and derive the union. Then we grab the phrase translation pairs that contain at least one intersected word alignment and some unioned word alignments[1].

Under the framework of log-linear models, we investigate the effects of morpho-syntactic information with word representation. The overall training and testing process with morphological and positional information is depicted in Figure 3. In the training step, we train the word- and class-based language models with various word representation methods[12]. Also, we make word alignments through the learning of IBM models by using GIZA++ toolkit[3]: we learn the translation model toward IBM model 4, initiating translation iterations from IBM model 1 with intermediate HMM model iterations. Then, we extract example phrases and translation model features from the alignment results.

Then in the test step, we perform morphological anlysis of a given sentence for word representation corresponding to training corpus representation. We decode the best translation of a given test sentence by generating word graphs and searching for the best hypothesis in a log-linear model[7].

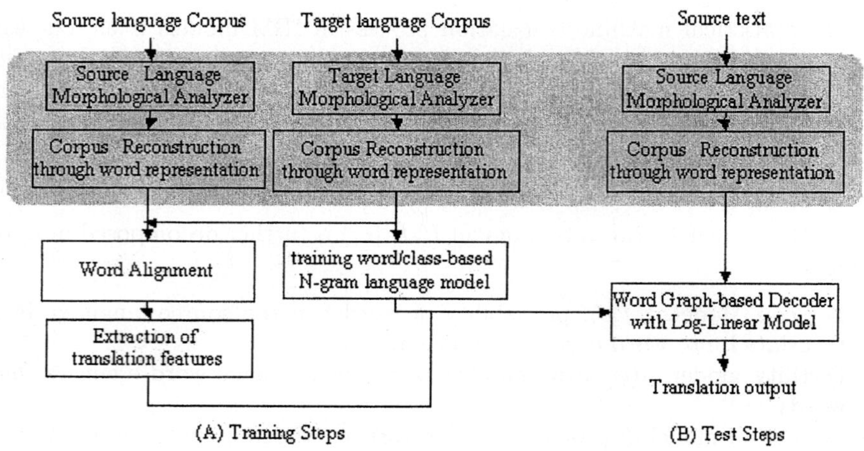

Fig. 3. Overview of training and test of statistical machine translation system with linguistic information

4 Experiments

4.1 Experimental Environments

The corpus for the experiment was extracted from the Basic Travel Expression Corpus (BTEC), a collection of conversational travel phrases for Chinese, English, Japanese and Korean[15]. The entire corpus was split into three parts: 152,169 sentences in parallel for training, 10,150 sentences for testing and the remaining 10,148 sentences for parameter tuning, such as termination criteria for training iteration and parameter tuning for decoders. For the reconstruction of each corpus with morphological information, we used in-house morphological

Table 2. Statistics of Basic Travel Expression Corpus

	Chinese	English	Japanese	Korean
# of sentences	167,163			
# of words(morph)	1,006,838	1,128,151	1,226,774	1,313,407
Vocabulary size(S)	17,472	11,737	19,485	17,600
Vocabulary size(B)	17,472	9172	15,939	15,410
Vocabulary size(SB)	17,472	13,385	20,197	18,259
Vocabulary size(SP)	18,505	13,467	20,118	20,249
Vocabulary size(SBP(L))	18,505	14,408	20,444	20,369(26,668)
# of singletons(S)	7,137	4,046	8,107	7,045
# of singletons(B)	7,137	3,025	6,497	6,303
# of singletons(SB)	7,137	4,802	9,453	7,262
# of singletons(SP)	7,601	4,693	8,343	7,921
# of singletons(SBP(L))	7,601	5,140	8,525	7,983(11,319)

Table 3. Perplexities of tri-gram language model trained on the training corpora with S, SB, SP SBP, SBL, and SBPL morpho-syntactic representation: word-based 3-gram/class-based 5-gram

	S	SB	SP	SBP	SBL	SBPL
Chinese	31.57/24.09	N/S	35.83/26.28	N/A	N/A	N/A
English	22.35/18.82	22.19/18.54	22.24/18.12	22.08/18.03	N/A	N/A
Japanese	17.89/ 13.44	17.92/13.29	17.82/13.13	17.83/13.06	N/A	N/A
Korean	15.54/12.42	15.41/12.09	16.04/11.89	16.03/11.88	16.48/12.24	17.13/11.99

analyzers for four languages: Chinese morphological analyzer with 31 parts-of-speech tags, English morphological analyzer with 34 tags, Japanese morphological analyzer with 34 tags, and Korean morphological analyzer with 49 tags. The accuracies of Chinese, English, Japanese and Korean morphological analyzers including segmentation and POS tagging are 95.82% , 99.25%, 98.95%, and 98.5% respectively. Table 2 summarizes the morph-syntactic statistics of the Chinese, English, Japanese, and Korean.

For the four languages, word-based and class-based n-gram language models were trained on the training set by using SRILM toolkit[12]. The perplexity of each language model is shown in Table 3.

For the four languages, we chose three kinds of language pairs according to the linguistic characteristics of morphology and word order, Chinese-Korean, Japanese-Korean, and English-Korean. 42 translation models based on word representation methods(S, SB, SP, SBP, SBL, SPL,SBPL) were trained by using GIZA++[3].

4.2 Evaluation

Translation evaluations were carried out on 510 sentences selected randomly from the test set. The metrics for the evaluations are as follows:

mWER(multi-reference Word Error Rate), which is based on the minimum edit distance between the target sentence and the sentences in the reference set [9].

BLEU, which is the ratio of the n-gram for the translation results found in the reference translations with a penalty for too short sentences [14].

NIST which is a weighted n-gram precision in combination with a penalty for too short sentences.

For this evaluation, we made 16 multiple references available. We computed all of the above criteria with respect to these multiple references.

Table 4, 5 and 6 show the evaluation results on three kinds of language pairs. The effects of morpho-syntactic information and class-based n-gram language models on multi-lingual machine translation are shown: The combined morphological information was useful for improving the translation quality in the NIST, BLEU and mWER evaluations. Moreover, the class-based n-gram language models were effective in the BLEU and the mWER scores.

Table 4. Evaluation results of Japanese to Korean and Korean to Japaneses translations(with class-based n-gram/word-based n-gram language model)

	J to K			K to J		
	NIST	BLEU	WER	NIST	BLEU	WER
S	8.46/8.64	0.694/0.682	26.33/26.73	8.21/8.39	0.666/0.649	25.00/25.81
SB	8.05/8.32	0.705/0.695	26.82/26.97	7.67/8.17	0.690/0.672	23.77/24.68
SP	9.15/9.25	0.755/0.747	21.71/22.22	9.02/9.13	0.720/0.703	21.94/23.50
SL	8.37/8.47	0.699/0.667	25.49/27.76	8.48/8.74	0.671/0.629	25.14/27.88
SBL	8.92/9.12	0.748/0.730	22.66/23.36	8.85/8.92	0.712/0.691	21.88/23.37
SBP	8.19/8.57	0.713/0.696	26.17/27.09	8.21/8.39	0.698/0.669	22.94/24.88
SBPL	8.41/8.85	0.772/0.757	22.30/21.74	7.77/7.83	0.626/0.619	25.19/25.57

Table 5. Evaluation results of English to Korean and Korean to English translations(with class-based n-gram/word-based n-gram language model)

	E to K			K to E		
	NIST	BLEU	WER	NIST	BLEU	WER
S	5.12/5.79	0.353/0.301	51.12/58.52	5.76/6.05	0.300/0.255	52.54/61.23
SB	6.71/6.87	0.533/0.474	39.10/47.18	7.72/8.15	0.482/0.446	37.86/42.71
SP	6.88/7.19	0.552/0.502	37.63/42.34	8.01/8.46	0.512/0.460	35.13/40.91
SL	6.66/6.96	0.546/0.516	38.20/40.67	7.71/8.02	0.484/0.436	36.79/42.88
SPL	6.16/7.01	0.542/0.519	38.21/39.85	7.83/8.22	0.482/0.443	37.52/41.63
SBL	6.52/6.93	0.547/0.504	37.76/42.23	7.64/8.08	0.479/0.439	37.10/42.30
SBP	7.42/7.60	0.612/0.573	32.17/35.96	8.86/9.05	0.551/0.523	33.13/37.07
SBPL	6.29/6.59	0.580/0.561	36.73/38.36	8.08/8.36	0.528/0.515	36.46/38.21

Table 6. Evaluation results of Chinese to Korean and Korean to Chinese translations(with class-based n-gram/word-based n-gram language model)

	C to K			K to C		
	NIST	BLEU	WER	NIST	BLEU	WER
S	7.62/7.82	0.640/0.606	30.01/32.79	7.85/7.69	0.380/0.365	53.65/58.46
SB	7.73/7.98	0.643/0.632	29.26/30.08	7.68/7.50	0.366/0.349	54.48/60.49
SP	7.71/7.98	0.651/0.643	28.26/28.60	8.00/7.77	0.383/0.362	54.15/58.30
SL	7.64/7.97	0.656/0.635	28.94/30.33	7.84/7.65	0.373/0.350	54.53/58.38
SPL	7.69/7.93	0.665/0.659	28.43/28.88	7.78/7.62	0.373/0.351	56.14/59.54
SBL	7.65/7.94	0.659/0.635	28.76/30.87	7.85/7.64	0.377/0.354	55.01/58.39
SBP	7.81/7.98	0.660/0.643	28.85/29.61	7.94/7.68	0.386/0.360	53.99/58.94
SBPL	7.64/7.90	0.652/0.634	29.54/30.46	7.82/7.66	0.376/0.358	55.64/58.79

In detail, Table 4 shows the effects of the morphological and relative positional information on Japanese-to-Korean and Korean-to-Japanese translation. In almost of the evaluation metrics, the SP model in which a word is represented by a combination of its surface form and part-of-speech showed the best performance. The SBL model utilizing the base form and relative positional information only in Korean showed the second best performance. In Korean-to-Japanese translation, the SBPL model showed the best score in BLEU and mWER. In this language pair of highly inflectional and agglutinative languages, the part-of-speech information combined with surface form was the most effective in improving the performance. The base form and relative positional information were less effective than part-of-speech. It could be explained in several points: Japanese and Korean are very similar languages in the word order of SOVs and the ambiguities of translation correspondences in both directions were converged into 1.0 by combining the distinctive morphological information with the surface form. When refering to the vocabulay size of SP model in Table 2, it makes it more clear. The Japanese-to-Korean translation outperforms the Korean-to-Japanese. It might be closely related to the language model: the perplexity of the Korean language model is lower than Japanese according to our corpus statistics.

Table 5 shows the performance of the English-to-Korean and Korean-to-English translation: a pair of highly inflectional and agglutinative language with partially free word-order and an inflectional language with rigid word order. In this language pair, the combined word representation models improved the translation performance into significantly higher BLEU and mWER scores in both directions. The part-of-speech and the base form information were distinctive features. When comparing the performance of SP, SB and SL models, part-of-speech might be more effective than base form or relative positional information, and the relative positional information in Korean might play a role not only in controlling word order in the language models but also in discriminating word correspondences during alignment.

When the target language was Korean, we had higher BLEU scores in all the morpho-syntactic models but lower NIST scores. In other words, we took advantage of generating more accurate full-form eojeol with positional information, i.e. local word ordering.

Table 6 shows the performance of the Chinese-to-Korean and Korean-to-Chinese translation: a pair of a highly inflectional and agglutinative language with partially free word order and a non-inflectional language with rigid word order. This language pair is a quite morpho-syntactically different. When a non-inflectional language is a target language(i.e. Korean-to-Chinese translation), the performance was the worst compared with other language pairs and directions in BLEU and mWER. On the other hand, the performance of Chinese-to-Korean was much better than Korean-to-Chinese, meaning that it is easier to generate Korean sentence from Chinese the same as in Japanese-to-Korean and English-to-Korean. In this language pair, we had gradual improvements according to the use of combined morpho-syntactic information, but there was no significant difference from the use of only the surface form. There was scant contribution of Chinese morphological information such as part-of-speech. On the other hand, we could get some advantageous Korean morpho-syntactic information in the Chinese-to-Korean translation, i.e., the advantage of language and translation models using morpho-syntactic information.

5 Conclusion and Future Works

In this paper, we described an empirical study of utilizing morpho-syntactic information in a statistical machine translation framework. We empirically investigated the effects of morphological information with several language pairs: Japanese and Korean with the same word order and high inflection/agglutination, English and Korean, a pair of a highly inflecting and agglutinating language with partial free word order and an inflecting language with rigid word order, and Chinese-Korean, a pair of a highly inflecting and agglutinating language with partially free word order and a non-inflectional language with rigid word order. As the results of experiments, we found that combined morphological information is useful for improving the translation quality in BLEU and mWER evaluations. According to the language pair and the direction, we had different combinations of morpho-syntactic information that are the best for improving the translation quality: SP(surface form and part-of-speech) for translating J-to-K or K-to-J, SBP(surface form, base form and part-of-speech) for E-to-K or K-to-E, SPL(surface form, part-of-speech and relative position) for C-to-K. The utilization of morpho-syntactic information in the target language was the most effective. Language models based on morpho-syntactic information were very effective for performance improvement. The class-based n-gram models improved the performance with smoothing effects in the statistical language model. However, when translating an inflectional language, Korean into a non-inflectional language, Chinese with quite different word order, we found very few advantages using morphological information. One of the main reasons might be the relatively low performance of the Chinese morphological analyzer. The other might come from the linguistic difference. For the latter case, we need to adopt approaches to reflect the structural characteristics such like using a chunker/parser, context-dependent translation modeling.

Acknowledgments

The research reported here was supported in part by a contract with the National Institute of Information and Communications Technology entitled "A study of speech dialogue translation technology based on a large corpus".

References

1. Koehn P., Och F.J., and Marcu D.: Statistical Phrase-Based Translation, Proc. of the Human Language Technology Conference(HLT/NAACL) (2003)
2. Och F. J., Tillmann C., Ney H.: Improved alignment models for statistical machine translation, Proc. of EMNLP/WVLC (1999).
3. Och F.J. and Ney H. Improved Statistical Alignment Models, Proc. of the 38th Annual Meeting of the Association for Computational Linguistics (2000) pp. 440-447.
4. Zens R. and Ney H.: Improvements in Phrase-Based Statistical Machine Translation, Proc. of the Human Language Technology Conference (HLT-NAACL) (2004) pp. 257-264

5. Brown P. F., Della Pietra S. A., Della Pietra V. J., and Mercer R. L.: The mathematics of statistical machine translation: Parameter estimation, Computational Linguistics, (1993) 19(2):263-311
6. Ueffing N., Ney H.: Using POS Information for Statistical Machine Translation into Morphologically Rich Languages, In Proc. 10th Conference of the European Chapter of the Association for Computational Linguistics (EACL), (2003) pp. 347-354
7. Ueffing N., Och F.J., Ney H.: Generation of Word Graphs in Statistical Machine Translation In Proc. Conference on Empirical Methods for Natural Language Processing, (2002) pp. 156-163
8. Niesen S., Ney H.: Statistical Machine Translation with Scarce Resources using Morpho-syntactic Information, Computational Linguistics, (2004) 30(2):181-204
9. Niesen S., Och F.J., Leusch G., Ney H: An Evaluation Tool for Machine Translation: Fast Evaluation for MT Research, Proc. of the 2nd International Conference on Language Resources and Evaluation, (2000) pp. 39-45
10. Watanabe T. and Sumita E.: Example-based Decoding for Statistical Machine Translation, Proc. of MT Summit IX (2003) pp. 410–417
11. Och F. J. Och and Ney H.: Discriminative Training and Maximum Entropy Models for Statistical Machine Translation, Proc. of ACL (2002)
12. Stolcke, A.: SRILM - an extensible language modeling toolkit. In Proc. Intl. Conf. Spoken Language Processing, (2002) Denver.
13. Brown P. F., Della Pietra V. J. and deSouza P. V. and Lai J. C. and Mercer R.L.: Class-Based n-gram Models of Natural Language, Computational Linguistics (1992) 18(4) pp. 467-479
14. Papineni K., Roukos S., Ward T., and Zhu W.-J.: Bleu: a method for automatic evaluation of machine translation, IBM Research Report,(2001) RC22176.
15. Takezawa T., Sumita E., Sugaya F., Yamamoto H., and Yamamoto S.: Toward a broad-coverage bilingual corpus for speech translation of travel conversations in the real world, Proc. of LREC (2002), pp. 147-152.

Instance-Based Generation for Interactive Restricted Domain Question Answering Systems

Matthias Denecke and Hajime Tsukada

NTT Communication Science Laboratories,
2-4 Hikaridai, Seika-Cho, Soraku-gun, Kyoto
{denecke, tsukada}@cslab.kecl.ntt.co.jp

Abstract. One important component of interactive systems is the generation component. While template-based generation is appropriate in many cases (for example, task oriented spoken dialogue systems), interactive question answering systems require a more sophisticated approach. In this paper, we propose and compare two example-based methods for generation of information seeking questions.

1 Introduction

Question answering is the task of providing natural language answers to natural language questions using an information retrieval engine. Due to the unrestricted nature of the problem, shallow and statistical methods are paramount.

Spoken dialogue systems address the problem of accessing information from a structured database (such as time table information) or controlling appliances by voice. Due to the fact that the scope of the application defined by the back-end, the domain of the system is well-defined. Therefore, in the presence of vague, ill-defined or misrecognized input from the user, dialogue management, relying on the domain restrictions as given by the application, can interactively request more information from the user until the users' intent has been determined. In this paper, we are interested in generation of information seeking questions in interactive question-answering systems.

1.1 Our System

We implemented a system that combines features of question answering systems with those of spoken dialogue systems. We integrated the following two features in an interactive restricted domain question answering system: (1) As in question answering systems, the system draws its knowledge from a database of unstructured text. (2) As in spoken dialogue systems, the system can interactively query for more information in the case of vague or ill-defined user queries.

1.2 Problem Addressed in This Paper

Restricted domain question answering systems can be deployed in interactive problem solving solutions, for example, software trouble shooting. In these scenarios, interactivity becomes a necessity. This is because it is highly unlikely that all facts relevant to retrieving the appropriate response are stated in the query. For example, in the software trouble shooting task described in [5], a frequent system generated information seeking question is for the version of the software. Therefore,

R. Dale et al. (Eds.): IJCNLP 2005, LNAI 3651, pp. 486–497, 2005.

there is a need to inquire additional problem relevant information from the user, depending on the interaction history and the problem to be solved.

In this paper, we specifically address the problem of how to generate information seeking questions in the case of ambiguous, vague or ill-defined user questions. We assume that the decision of whether an information seeking question is needed is made outside of the module described here. More formally, the problem we address can be described as follows:

Given 1. A representation of the previous interaction history, consisting of user and system utterances, and retrieval results from the IR subsystem,
2. A decision for a information seeking question

Produce An information seeking question.

Problems of this kind have appeared traditionally in task oriented spoken dialogue systems, where missing information needs to be prompted. However, in the case of spoken dialogue systems, question generation is typically not a substantial problem: the fact that the back-end is well-structured allows for simple template-based generation in many cases. For example, missing values for database queries or remote method invocations can be queried that way. (But see also Oh and Rudnicky [7] or Walker *et al* [12] for more elaborated approaches to generation for spoken dialogue systems).

In our case, however, a template-based approach is unrealistic. This is due to the unstructured back-end application. Unlike as spoken dialogue systems, we cannot make assumptions over what kind of questions to ask as this is determined by the result set of articles as returned by the information retrieval engine. Existing interactive question-answering systems (see section 7.1 for a more detailed description) either use canned text on dialogue cards [5], break down the dialogue representation into frames and then techniques from spoken dialogue systems [8], or make simplifying assumptions to the extent that generation essentially becomes equivalent to template-based generation.

1.3 Proposed Solution

For reasons discussed above, we propose an example-based approach to generation. More specifically, we use an existing dialogue corpus to retrieve appropriate questions and modify in order to fit the situation at hand. We describe two algorithms for instance-based natural language questions generation by first selecting appropriate candidates from the corpus, then modifying the candidates to fit the situation at hand, and finally re-rank the candidates. This is an example of a memory-based learning approach, which in turn is a kind of a case-based reasoning. To the best of our knowledge, this is the first work addressing the problem of example-based generation information seeking questions in the absence of a structured back-end application.

2 Instance Based Natural Language Generation

In this section, we review the background in memory-based learning and its application in natural language generation.

2.1 Memory-Based Reasoning

Memory-based reasoning (MBR) is often considered a subtype of *Case-based reasoning*. Case-based reasoning was proposed in the 80's as an alternative to rule-based approaches. Instead of expressing regularities about the domain to be modeled in rules, the primary knowledge source in case-based reasoning is a memory of cases representing episodes of encountered problems. Generating a solution to a given problem consists of retrieving an appropriate case from memory and adapting it to the problem at hand.

MBR solves problems by retrieving stored precedents as a starting point for new problem-solving (e.g., [9]). However, its primary focus is on the retrieval process, and in particular on the use of parallel retrieval schemes to enable retrieval without conventional index selection. One aspect of memory-based systems is to choose a distance that appropriately selects candidate exemplars.

Memory-based reasoning has been applied to machine translation, parsing, unit selection text-to-speech synthesis, part-of-speech tagging, and others. An overview of memory-based approaches to natural language processing can be found in the introduction to the special issue [2].

2.2 Statistical and Instance-Based Generation

The most prominent example for statistical generation is NITROGEN [6]. This system has been designed to allows large scale generation while requiring only a minimal knowledge base. An abstract meaning representation is turned into a lattice of surface sentences using a simple keyword based grammar. Using statistical information acquired from a corpus, the sentences in the lattices are re-ranked to determine the optimal surface string.

More recently, example-based natural language generation using a corpus was proposed [11]. It is assumed in this work that content determination has already taken place and the input has been broken down to sentence-size pieces. The approach is to use a learned grammar to generate a list of candidates using a traditional chart based generation algorithm. The grammar is learned using statistical methods. During generation, edges that are added to the chart are ranked depending on their distance to the closest instance in the example base. This is where the memory-based approach comes into play. In order to allow for careful generalization in the instance base, the authors propose to add a list of tag ("slots") with which the corpus is annotated. Based on this annotated corpus, a semantic grammar is learned. For ranking the edge based on the instances, the authors propose the well-known *tf-idf* scheme with the difference that those words that are annotated with a semantic tag are replaced by their tag.

3 Kernels

Memory-based learning requires a distance metric in order to identify instances similar to the problem at hand. We propose to use *convolution kernels* as distance metric. A kernel K can be seen as a generalized form of a distance metric that performs the following calculation

$$K(x, y) = \langle \phi(x), \phi(y) \rangle,$$

where ϕ is a non-linear mapping from the input space into some higher dimensional feature space, and $\langle \cdot, \cdot \rangle$ is the inner product in the feature space. Calculating the inner product in some space of higher dimension than the input space is desirable for classifiers because non linearly separable sets can be linearly separated in the higher dimensional feature space. Kernel methods are computationally attractive because the kernel can calculate the mapping and the inner product implicitly rather than explicitly determining the image under ϕ of the input.

While *Bag-of-Words* techniques can be employed as an approximation to derive feature vectors for classifiers, the loss of structure is not desirable. To address this problem, Haussler [3] proposed *Convolution Kernels* that are capable of processing structured objects x and y. The structured objects x and y consist of components $x_1, \ldots, x_m$ and $y_1, \ldots, y_n$. The convolution kernel of x and y is given by the sum of the products of the components' convolution kernels. This approach can be applied to structured objects of various kinds, and results have been reported for string kernels and tree kernels.

3.1 Hierarchical Tree Kernel

The idea behind Convolution Kernels is that the kernel of two structures is defined as the sum of the kernels of their parts. Formally, let D be a positive integer and $X, X_1, \ldots, X_D$ separable metric spaces. Furthermore, let x and y be two structured objects, and $\mathbf{x} = x_1, \ldots, x_D$ and $\mathbf{y} = y_1, \ldots, y_D$ their parts. The relation $R \subseteq X_1 \times \ldots \times X_D \times X$ holds for $\mathbf{x}$ and x if $\mathbf{x}$ are the parts of x. The inverse R^{-1} maps each structured object onto its parts, i.e. $R^{-1}(x) = \{\mathbf{x} : R(\mathbf{x}, x)\}$. Then the kernel of x and y is given by the following generalized convolution:

$$K(x,y) = \sum_{\mathbf{x} \in R^{-1}(x)} \sum_{\mathbf{y} \in R^{-1}(y)} \prod_{1}^{D} K_d(x_d, y_d)$$

Informally, the value of a convolution kernel for two objects X and Y is given by the sum of the kernel value for each of the substructures, i.e. their convolution.

Suzuki et al [10] proposed *Hierarchical Directed Acyclic Graph* kernels in which the substructures contain nodes which can contain graphs themselves. The hierarchy of graphs allows extended information from multiple components to be represented and used in classification. In addition, nodes may be annotated with attributes, such as part of speech tags, in order to add information. For example, in a Question-Answering system, components such as Named Entity Extraction, Question Classification, Chunking and so on may each add to the graph.

4 Corpus

We collected a corpus for our instance based generation system as follows. We set up communications between a wizard and users. The wizard was instructed to "act like the system" we intend to build, that is, she was required to interact with the user either by prompting for more information or give the user the information she thought he wanted. Altogether, 20 users participated in the

W: こちらは旅行ガイドです
This is the travel guide.
U: 京、京都で１日ゆったりとお寺巡りをしようと思っているんですが、京都駅から、お寺を、
お寺巡りをする、効率的というか、こうしたらいいんじゃないかっていうコースはありますか
I was thinking to take a small trip to Kyoto to see some temples. starting
from Kyoto station. is there something like an efficient course to do this?
W: はい、それでは京都駅周辺でお調べ致します
京都駅周辺をゆったりと回る、でよろしいですか
Yes then I will look for something around Kyoto station.
A quiet trip around Kyoto station. would that be okay?
U: はい
Yes.
W: それではJR京都駅から東寺、梅小路蒸気機関車館、門屋もてなしの文化美術館、西本願寺、
コウセイジ、京都タワー、そしてJR京都駅に戻ってくるというコースはいかがでしょうか
Then starting from Kyoto station. going to the Touji temple. to a steam train museum.
Kadoya museum. Nishi-Hongan temple. Kousei temple. Kyoto tower and back to Kyoto station.
would that be okay?

Fig. 1. Extract from the dialogue corpus

data collection effort. Each user contributed to 8 to 15 dialogues. The length of the dialogues varies between 11 and 84 turns, the median being 34 turns. Altogether, the corpus consists of 201 dialogues. The corpus consists of 6785 turns, 3299 of which are user turns and the remaining 3486 are wizard turns. Due to the strict dialogue regiment prescribed in the onset of the data collection, each dialogue consists either of an equal number of user and wizard turns (in case the user ends the dialogue; 14 cases) or one wizard turn more than user turn in case the wizard ends the dialogue (187 cases). Figure 1 shows the first part of a dialogue from the corpus.

5 Generation Algorithm

5.1 Overview of the Algorithm

We now describe our algorithm informally. Given the dialogue history up until now, the last user utterance and the result list as a response to the last user utterance, it is the task of the algorithm to generate an appropriate question to elicit more information from the user. Recall an external dialogue module (not described in this paper) decides whether an information seeking question should be generated (as opposed to, say, turning the information found in the highest ranking article into an answer).

Informally, the algorithm works as follows. Initially, the dialogue corpus is preprocessed, including word segmentation and part-of-speech labeling (see section 5.2). In step 1, a ranked list of question candidates is generated (see section 5.3). In step 2, for each of the candidates, a list of change positions is determined (see section 5.4). These indicate the part of the questions that need to be adapted to the current situation. Subsequently, the portions indicated by the change positions are replaced by appropriate constituents. In the step 3, the candidates generated in the previous step are re-ranked (see section 5.5). Re-ranking takes place by using the same distance as the one in step 1. The highest ranking candidate is then presented to the user.

5.2 Corpus Preprocessing

Since Japanese does not provide word segmentation, we need to preprocess the corpus. The corpus consists of a set of dialogues. Each dialogue consists of a set of utterances. Each utterance is annotated for speaker and utterance type. In a dialogue, wizard and user utterance strictly alternate, with no interjections.

Preprocessing is done as follows. Each utterance is stripped of its annotations and presented to the part-of-speech tagger *Chasen* [1]. Chasen segments the input sentence, reduces inflected words to their base forms and assigns part of speech tags to the base forms. We use the notation $cw(u)$ to designate the content words in utterance, sentence or newspaper article u. For our purposes, content words are adjectives, nouns and verbs, de-inflected to their base form, if necessary. A subsequent processing step assigns semantic labels and named entity classes to the de-inflected word forms.

5.3 Sentence Selection

In order to understand the motivation for our approaches to sentence selection, it is necessary to recall the context in which sentences are selected. We would like to find a information seeking question similar to the one we want to generate. The question to be generated is determined by the dialogue context. A natural approach is to choose a bag-of-word distance measure for sentences, define a distance for partial dialogues based on this distance and then choose the dialogue, and a sentence from that dialogue with the lowest distance.

It turns out, however, that this approach does not work too well. One problem is that in the beginning of a dialogue not many informative words are contained in the utterances, therefore making an informed selection of utterances difficult. The point of this paper is to determine how to overcome this problem. In the following two sections, we propose two approaches. The first uses additional information in the retrieved documents, and the second uses additional syntactic and semantic information when calculating the distance between sentences. Both methods consists of calculating a score for candidate sentences and selecting the highest ranking one.

Method 1. Information retrieval over large corpora works well due to the redundancy in the document data, a fact that for example Latent Semantic Indexing exploits. The principal idea of the first method is to use the redundancy in the unrestricted document corpus when scoring sentence candidates. Instead of determining the bag-of-word score between a candidate sentence and the query sentence, we submit the information extracted from the candidate dialogue and the current dialogue to the information retrieval engine, resulting in two n best lists of articles L and L'. In order to score the degree of similarity, we determine the the intersection of content words in the retrieved articles. The larger the intersection, the higher the score is to be ranked. In order to take relevance in the result set into account, the scores are discounted by the position of the article in the n best list. More specifically, we calculate the similarity score between the current dialogue and an example dialogue as follows. Let d be the currently developing dialogue consisting of t user utterances and $u_1, \ldots u_t$ be the user utterances in the current dialogue up until now. Furthermore, let d' be an example dialogue from the corpus and let $u'_1, \ldots u'_{t'}$ be the first t' user utterances in the example dialogue. Then:

1. Form the union of content words $CW = \bigcup_t cw(u_t)$, $CW' = \bigcup_{t'} cw(u'_{t'})$
2. Submit two queries to the information retrieval engine consisting of CW and CW', respectively and obtain two article n best lists L and L'.
3. Calculate the similarity score according to

$$sim(u_t, u'_{t'}) = \sum_{l \in L} \sum_{l' \in L'} \frac{cw(l) \cap cw(l')}{rank(l) + rank(l')}$$

Method 2. In the first method described above, we seek to overcome poor scoring function by adding redundancy from the information retrieval engine. The second method we propose attempts to improve scoring by adding syntactic and semantic structure to the distance metric. More specifically, we directly compare the last user utterance in the current dialogue with the last utterance in the example dialogue, but do so in a more detailed manner. To this end, we determine the similarity score as the output of the hierarchical directed acyclic graph kernel. The similarity is thus defined as $sim(u_t, u'_{t'}) = K(u_t, u'_{t'})$.

5.4 Sentence Adaptation

The adaptation of the highest ranking question to the current dialogue consists of four steps. First, we determine the location(s) where change should take place. Second, we determine constraints for the substituting constituent. Third, we determine a list of substituents for each location of change. Fourth, we replace the phrase(s) at the location(s) of change with the highest ranking element from the corresponding list of substituents.

Determining Locations of Change. After the example sentences have been retrieved from the corpus, we need to determine where and how the questions need to be adapted to the current dialogue. We determine the locations of change l_i by identifying suitable head words of phrase to be exchanged. What are the criteria for suitable head words? Recall that the example sentences are drawn from dialogue similar in topics but in which the content words are exchanged. This limits the part-of-speech of the words to be exchanged to nouns and verbs. Therefore, we construct a list l of nouns and verbs that are part of the retrieved sentence but cannot be found in the current user query. Second, since we are interested in replacing those content words that are specific to the retrieved dialogue with those specific to the current dialogue, we would like to incorporate some measure of informativeness. For that reason, we determine the unigram count for all content words in l. High ranking candidates for change are those words that are specific (i.e., have a low unigram count above a certain threshold).

Constraints for Substituents. The constraints for the substituents are given by the semantic and syntactic information of the phrase at the change location. More specifically, the constraints include the following features: Part of speech, type of named entity, if applicable (the type includes location, state, person name and so on), and semantic class.

Determining Substituents. After having determined the change locations and constraints of the substituents, we proceed to determine the substituents.

The primary source for substituents are the retrieved newspaper articles. However, since we wish to apply the generation component in a dialogue system, we need to take implicit confirmation into account as well. For this reason, we determine whether a phrase matching the phrase at change location l_i occurs before l_i previously in the dialogue. If this is the case, the source for the substituent is to be the current dialogue.

Given the constraints for a change location determined in the previous step, we add all content words from the highest ranking article to the candidate list for that change location. The score for a content word is given by the number of constraints it fulfills. Ties are broken by unigram counts so that rare words get a higher score due to their informativeness.

Application of Change. Applying the change simply consists of removing the phrase whose head word is located at the change location and replacing it with the highest ranking word from the candidate list for that score.

5.5 Reranking

The previous steps produce a list of sentence candidates. For each of the sentence candidates, we calculate the similarity between the generated sentence with the sentences from a small corpus of desirable sentences. Finally, the sentence with the highest score is presented to the user. Examples of generated sentences are shown in figure 2. The complete algorithm is given in figure 3.

U : 横浜の観光施設を教えてください
: Please tell me about sightseeing attractions in Yokohama.
S : どういった観光施設をお期待するんですか
: What kind of sightseeing attractions are you looking for?
U : 家族で楽しめるところを
: Something to enjoy with my family.
S : それではシルク市場や、横浜開港資料館はいかがでしょうか
: In that case, how about silk market or Yokohama Port Museum?

Fig. 2. Generated questions. The substituent in the first question comes from the dialogue context, while the other substituents come from retrieved articles.

6 Evaluation

The evaluation was done as follows. We divided the corpus in a example base and a test set. The example base consists of 151 randomly selected dialogues, the test set consists of the remaining 50 dialogues. From each of the test examples, we supplied the initial wizard greeting and the initial user utterance as context for the dialogue. Given this context, each method generated an n best list consisting of 3 information seeking questions.

The generated lists were labeled by three annotators according to the following criteria. For each of the three questions in the n best lists, the annotators had to determine a syntactic, a semantic and an overall score. The scores range over the labels *poor, acceptable, good.* The same score could be assigned more

Input: Preprocessed dialogue corpus $C = \{d'_1, \ldots, d'_n\}$
Current dialogue d with user utterances $u_1, \ldots, u_t$

Output: Information seeking question

Step 1: Determine $sim(u_t, u'_{t'})$ for all user utterances $u'_{t'}$ from the dialogue corpus
Select the $w'_1, \ldots w'_k$ wizard utterances directly following the k highest ranking utterances

Step 2: **for each** $w'_i \in \{w'_1, \ldots, w'_k\}$:
Determine change locations $l_1, \ldots, l_l$
for each $l_j \in \{l_1, \ldots, l_l\}$
Determine list of substituents $s^1_{ij}, \ldots, s^p_{ij}$

Generate modified sentence list $v_1, \ldots, v_m$ by replacing substituents at change locations

Step 3: Determine and return highest ranking v_{i^*}.

Fig. 3. Generation algorithm

than once, for example, in case the sentence selection algorithm produced an unreliable candidate, the overall score for all three sentence candidates could be *bad*. Furthermore, the evaluators had to re-arrange the 3 best list according to the quality of the generated questions. Finally, the annotators had provide a sentence they consider good. For easy comparison, the symbolic scores *poor, acceptable, good* translate to 0,0.5 and 1, respectively, in the tables below.

6.1 Scoring Results

The results of the three best syntactic and semantic sentence scoring are shown in table 1 (a) and 1 (b). The inter-annotator agreement is given by their kappa scores for each method separately. Table 1 (c) shows the average of syntactic and semantic scores. The kappa coefficient for the inter-annotator agreement for these scores are 0.68, 0.72, and 0.71, respectively.

The syntactic scores rank higher than the semantic scores. This is explained by the fact that the corpus contains syntactically relatively well-formed example sentences, and the replacement operator, in addition to being constrained by

Table 1. Average of syntactic and semantic scores

	Method 1	Method 2
1	0.796	0.800
2	0.657	0.790
3	0.787	0.780

(a)

	Method 1	Method 2
1	0.573	0.393
2	0.393	0.426
3	0.416	0.376

(b)

	Method 1	Method 2
1	0.685	0.596
2	0.525	0.608
3	0.602	0.578

(c)

part-of-speech as well as semantic information, does not have much opportunity to create a syntactically malformed sentence. Furthermore, method 1 produces sentences that are semantically more accurate than method 2.

6.2 Ranking Results

In order to determine the quality of the ranking, the annotators had to rerank the generated questions. We determine the distance between two rankings according to the Edit distance. Since the generated lists are only of length 3, there are only three possibilties: the lists are equal (edit distance 0), one element in both lists is the same (edit distance 2), and no element in the lists is the same, (edit distance 3). In order to allow easy comparison with the table above, we award scores of 1, 0.5 and 0 for edit distances of 0, 2 and 3, respectively (i.e., 1 is best, 0 is worst). The annotators were asked to rank the questions according to syntactic criteria alone, semantic criteria alone and all criteria. The results are shown in Table 2.

Table 2. Comparison of ranking: Syntactic, semantic and overall

	Method 1	Method 2
1	0.493	0.893
2	0.813	0.860
3	0.767	0.227

(a)

	Method 1	Method 2
1	0.720	0.873
2	0.760	0.780
3	0.567	0.353

(b)

	Method 1	Method 2
1	0.766	0.853
2	0.740	0.726
3	0.573	0.213

(c)

It can be seen that method 2 ranks the example sentences in a way that is more in line with the choices of the annotators than method 1.

6.3 Quality of Ranking

We hypothesize that the differences in the performance of the algorithms is due to the different selection mechanisms. In order to validate this point, we asked the three annotators to each provide one utterance they would rank highest for each system question (called *gold standard*). Then, we formed a list of 6 sentences $u'_1, \ldots u'_6$ (3 generated by the generation algorithm and 3 by the annotators) and compared for each dialogue context the scores $sim(u_t, u'_i)$ for those 6 sentences where u_t is the user utterance from the corresponding test case. We expect a perfect ranking algorithm to value the gold standard as least as high as any sentence from the corpus, and to value the gold standard higher every time the annotators found the generated sentences faulty. It turns out that method 1 places the sentences of the gold standard in the top 3 in 42.3% of the cases while method 2 does this in 59.3% of the cases.

7 Discussion

It can be seen that in general, method 1 produces higher quality sentences while method 2 ranks the sentences better. We interpret this as follows. For sentence selection, the redundancy as provided by the IR engine is helpful, whereas for ranking of example sentences, the additional structure as expressed in the kernel helps.

7.1 Related Work

Kiyota and colleagues [5] describe an interactive restricted domain question answering system where users can interactively retrieve causes for problems with a computers' operating system. Here, the problem of missing structure is solved by providing so-called *dialogue cards* which provide the knowledge necessary for dialogue processing. A dialogue card contains keywords, a question as asked by the user in natural language (for example "Windows does not boot"), an information seeking question to be issued by the system (for example "Which version of Windows do you use") and a list of options associated with actions. The actions are executed in function of the users' answer to the question. Dialogue processing takes place by retrieving relevant dialogue cards, where relevance is determined by matching the users' question and keywords with the question and keywords noted on the dialogue card. Compared to our method, this method requires substantially more structure to be represented in the dialogue cards and is therefore more expensive to develop. Furthermore, the absence of any sort of change operators to adapt the question from the dialogue card to the current situation does not provide as much flexibility as our method. On the other hand, the highly structured dialogue cards give the developers more control (at the price of a higher development cost) over the systems behavior than our method and is therefore less risky in situations where failure is expensive.

In Small *et al* [8], retrieved documents are forced into frame structures. Mismatches or between the fillers of the frame structures or missing fillers trigger information seeking questions to the user. While the generation as it is actually used is not described in the paper, we believe that the frames provide sufficient structure for template-based approaches.

Hori and coworkers [4] developed an interactive question answering system based on a Japanese newspaper corpus. The purpose of information seeking questions is to prompt the user for missing or disambiguating information. From a generation point of view, strong assumptions are made on the surface form of the generated information seeking question. More specifically, ambiguous keywords are combined with disambiguating options by means of the Japanese particle 'no'.

7.2 Summary

To summarize, the presented approaches attempt in different ways to compensate for the lack of structure in an question answering system. Structure can be provided explicitly as in the case of the dialogue cards, can be introduced during processing as in the case of the frame-based document representations, and can be assumed in the target expression as in the case of the generation templates. In contrast to the described methods, our method does not require an explicit representation of structure. Rather, the structure is given by whatever structure the kernel and the change operators construct during generation. In other words, the structure our approach uses is (1) restricted to the question to be generated and does not apply to the document level, and (2) in tradition with the lazy learning characteristics of memory-based approaches is generated on the fly on an as-needed basis, as opposed to being dictated from the outset at design time.

Acknowledgements

We acknowledge the help of Takuya Suzuki with the implementation. Jun Suzuki provided the implementation of the HDAG kernel. We would like to thank Hideki Isozaki and our colleagues at NTT CS labs for discussion and encouragement.

References

1. M. Asahara and Y. Matsumoto. 2000. Extended Models and Tools for High-Performance Part-of-Speech Tagger. In *Proceedings of The 18th International Conference on Computational Linguistics, Coling 2000, Saarbrücken, Germany.*
2. W. Daelemans. 1999. Introduction to the Special Issue on Memory-Based Language Processing. *Journal of Experimental and Theoretical Artificial Intelligence.*
3. D. Haussler. 1999. Convolution kernels on discrete structures. Technical report, UC Santa Cruz.
4. C. Hori, T. Hori, H. Tsukada, H. Isozaki, Y. Sasaki, and E. Maeda. 2003. Spoken interactive odqa system: Spiqa. In *Proc. of the 41th Annual Meeting of Association for Computational Linguistics (ACL-2003), Sapporo, Japan.*
5. K. Kiyota, S. Kurohashi, and F. Kido. 2002. "Dialog Navigator": A Question Answering System based on Large Text Knowledge Base. In *Proceedings of The 19th International Conference on Computational Linguistics, Coling 2002, Taipei, Taiwan.*
6. I. Langkilde and K. Knight. 1998. Generation that exploits Corpus-Based Statistical Knowledge. In *Proceedings of the Conference of the Association for Computational Linguistics (COLING/ACL).*
7. A.H. Oh and A. Rudnicky. 2000. Stochastic Language Generation for Spoken Dialogue Systems. In *ANLP/NAACL 2000 Workshop on Conversational Systems*, pages 27–32.
8. S. Small and T. Strzalkowski. 2004. Hitiqa: Towards analytical question answering. In *Proceedings of The 20th International Conference on Computational Linguistics, Coling 2004, Geneva Switzerland.*
9. C. Stanfill and D. Waltz. 1986. Toward Memory-based Reasoning. Communications of the ACM, vol. 29, pages 1213-1228.
10. J. Suzuki, T. Hirao, Y. Sasaki, and E. Maeda. 2003. Hierarchical directed acyclic graph kernel: Methods for structured natural language data. In *Proc. of the 41th Annual Meeting of Association for Computational Linguistics (ACL-2003), Sapporo, Japan*, pages 32–39.
11. S. Varges and C. Mellish. 2001. Instance-based natural language generation. In *Proceedings of the 2nd Meeting of the North American Chapter of the Association for Computational Linguistics*, pages 1–8.
12. M. Walker, O. Rambow, and M. Rogati. 2001. SPoT: A Trainable Sentence Planner. In *Proceedings of the North American Meeting of the Association for Computational Linguistics.*

Answering Definition Questions Using Web Knowledge Bases

Zhushuo Zhang, Yaqian Zhou, Xuanjing Huang, and Lide Wu

Department of Computer Science and Engineering, Fudan University, Shanghai, China, 200433
{zs_zhang, zhouyaqian, xjhuang, ldwu}@fudan.edu.cn

Abstract. This paper presents a definition question answering approach, which is capable of mining textual definitions from large collections of documents. In order to automatically identify definition sentences from a large collection of documents, we utilize the existing definitions in the Web knowledge bases instead of hand-crafted rules or annotated corpus. Effective methods are adopted to make full use of Web knowledge bases, and they promise high quality response to definition questions. We applied our system in the TREC 2004 definition question-answering task and achieved an encouraging performance with the F-measure score of 0.404, which was ranked second among all the submitted runs.

1 Introduction

When people want to learn an unknown concept from a large collection of documents, the most commonly used tools are the search engines. They submit a query to a search engine system, and the search engine returns a number of pages related to the query terms. Usually, the pages returned are ranked mainly based on keywords matching rather than their relevance to the query terms. The users have to read a lot of returned pages to organize the information they wanted by themselves. This procedure is time-consuming, and the information acquired is not concentrative. The research of Question Answering (QA) intends to resolve this problem by answering user's questions with exact answers.

Questions like "Who is Colin Powell?" or "What is mold?" are definition questions [3]. Their relatively frequent occurrences in logs of Web search engines [2] indicate that they are an important type of question. The Text REtrieval Conference (TREC) provides an entire evaluation for definition question answering from TREC2003. A typical definition QA system extracts definition nuggets that contain the most descriptive information about the question target (the concept for which information is being sought is called the target term, or simply, the target) from multiple documents.

Until recently, definition questions remained a largely unexplored area of question answering. Standard factoid question answering technology, designed to extract single answers, cannot be directly applied to this task. The solution to this interesting research challenge will involve the techniques in related fields such as information extraction, multi-document summarization, and answer fusion.

In order to extract definitional nuggets/sentences, most systems use various pattern matching approaches. Kouylekov *et al.* [10] relied on a set of hand-crafted rules to

R. Dale et al. (Eds.): IJCNLP 2005, LNAI 3651, pp. 498 – 506, 2005.

find definitional sentences. Sasha *et al.* [12] proposed to combine data-driven statistical method and machine learned rules to generate definitions. Cui *et al.* [7] used soft patterns, which were generated by unsupervised learning. Such methods require human labor to construct patterns or to annotate corpus more or less.

Prager *et al.* [8] try to solve this problem through existing technology. They decompose a definition question into a series of factoid questions. The answers to the factoid questions are merged to form the answer to the original question. However, the performance of their system on the TREC definition QA task is unsatisfactory. They need a more proper framework to determine how to generate these follow-up questions [8].

Some systems [1] [7] [9] statistically rank the candidate answers based on the external knowledge. They all adopt a centroid-based ranking method. For each question, they form one centroid (i.e., vector of words and frequencies) of the information in the external knowledge, and then calculate the similarity between the candidate answer and this centroid. The ones that have large similarity are extracted as the answers to this question.

Among the abundant information on the Web, Web knowledge bases (KBs) are one kind of most useful resource to acquire information. Dictionary definitions often supply knowledge that can be exploited directly. The information from them can model the interests of a typical user more reliably than other information. So we go further in identifying and selecting definition sentences from document collection using Web knowledge bases.

Our work differs from the above in that we make use of the Web knowledge bases in a novel and effective way. Instead of using centroid-based ranking, we try to find out more effective methods in ranking the candidate sentences. We consider the relationship and the difference between the definitions from different knowledge sources. In our first algorithm, we calculate the similarity scores between the candidate sentence and the definitions from different knowledge bases respectively, and merge these scores to generate the weight of this candidate sentence. In another algorithm, we first summarize the definitions from different KBs in order to eliminate the redundant information, and then use this summary to rank the candidate sentences. We have applied our approaches to the TREC 2004 definition question-answering task. The results reveal that these procedures can make better use of the knowledge in the Web KBs, and the extracted sentences contain the most descriptive information about the question target.

The remainder of the paper is organized as follows. In Section 2, we describe the system architecture. Then in Section 3 we give the details of our definition extraction methods. The evaluation of our system and the concluding remarks are given in Section 4 and Section 5 respectively.

2 System Architecture

We adopt a general architecture for definition QA. The system consists of five modules: question processing, document processing, Web knowledge acquisition, definition extraction, and an optional module corpus information acquisition. The process of answering a definition question is briefly described as follows.

Firstly, a definition question is input, and the question processing module identifies the question target from this question. The so called target or target term is a term for which information is being sought (e.g., the target of the question "What is Hale Bopp comet?" is "Hale Bopp comet".) The target term is the input for document processing module and knowledge acquisition module.

Secondly, the document processing module generates the candidate sentence set according to this target term. This module has three steps, document retrieval, relevant sentence extraction and redundancy removal. In the first step, the documents that relevant to the target are retrieved from the corpus. In the second step, the sentences that relevant to the target are extracted from these documents. We first cut the documents into sentences, and delete the irrelevant sentences by a few heuristic rules. In the third step, the redundant sentences are deleted by calculating the percentage of shared content words between sentences. After these three steps, we get the candidate sentence set.

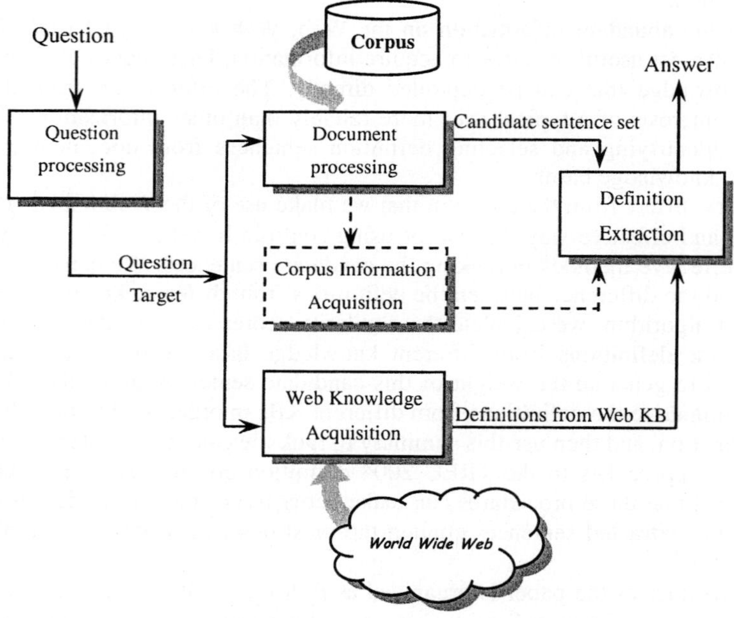

Fig. 1. System architecture

Thirdly, the Web knowledge acquisition module acquires the definitions of the target term from the Web knowledge base. If we can find definitions from these sources (the Web KBs we used will be described in Section 3.1), we use them to rank the candidate sentences set.

At last, the definition extraction module extracts the definition from the candidate sentence set based on the knowledge which is got from the Web knowledge base.

In very few situations, no definitions can be found from the Web KBs, and the module named "corpus information acquisition" is adopted to form the centroid of the candidate sentence set. We rank candidate sentences based on this centroid. The sentences that have high similarity with this centroid are extracted as the answers to the question. The assumption is that words co-occurring frequently with the target in the corpus are more important ones for answering the question.

The system architecture is illustrated in Fig.1.

In this paper, we focus on how to make use of the Web KBs in extracting definition sentences, so we will describe the detail of the definition extraction module below.

3 Definition Extraction Based on Web Knowledge Bases

3.1 Web Knowledge Base

There are lots of specific websites on the Web, such as online biography dictionaries or online cyclopaedias. We can get biography of a person, the profile of an organization or the definition of a generic term from them. We call this kind of website Web knowledge base (KB). The definitions from them often supply knowledge that can be exploited directly. So we answer definition questions by utilizing the existing definitions in the Web knowledge bases. The results of our system reveal that the Web knowledge bases are quite helpful to answering definition questions.

Usually, different knowledge bases may pay attention to different kind of concept, and they may have different kind of entries. For example, the biography dictionary (www.s9.com) is a dictionary that covers widely on biography of people, and other KBs may pay attention to other kinds of concept. We choose several authoritative KBs that cover different kinds of concept to achieve our goal.

The Web knowledge bases we used are the Encyclopedia(www.encyclopedia.com), the Wikipedia(www.wikipedia.com), the Merriam-Webster dictionary (www.mw.com), the WordNetglossaries (www.cogsci.princeton.edu/cgi-bin/webwn) and a biographies dictionary (www.s9.com).

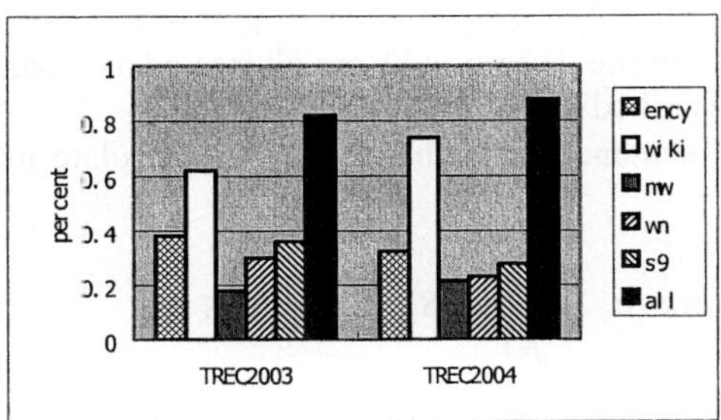

Fig. 2. The Web KBs' coverage of TREC data

These Web KBs can cover most of the target terms, and the definitions in them are exact and concise.This can be confirmed from the experiment on TREC's data set. Fig.2 gives our experiment results on the TREC 2003 and TREC 2004's definition question sets, which have 50 and 65 target terms respectively. The "ency", "wiki", "mw", "wn" and "s9" stand for the five online KBs we have used. Each column represents the percent of the target terms that can be found in the corresponding online knowledge base. The column marked "all" represents the percent of the target terms that can be found in at least one of these five online knowledge bases.

It is easy to see that a high coverage can be got by using these Web knowledge bases. In the Section 3.2 and Section 3.3 we will show how to use these KBs, and in Section 4 we can see that it boosts the performance of the system significantly.

3.2 Definition Extraction Based on *GDS*

As mentioned above, we may get most of the submitted target terms' definitions by utilizing multiple Web KBs. One target may find its definitions in more than one knowledge base. Are all of them useful? The experimental data tells that, the different definitions belonging to one target differ from each other in some degree. They are short or long, concise or detailed.

Considering the above factor, we try to utilize all of the definitions from different Web KBs to accomplish our task. For one target term, the definitions from all Web knowledge bases compose its "general definition set", which is abbreviated to ***GDS***. Each element of this set is a definition from one Web knowledge base, so the number of the elements in this set is the same as the number of the Web KBs we used. When we cannot find its entry in a certain Web KB, its corresponding element will be an empty string.

For each target, its candidate sentence set is expressed as $S_A = \{A_1, A_2,\ldots, A_m\}$, where A_k (k=1..m) is a candidate sentence in the set and *m* is the total number of the candidate sentences.

GDS is expressed as $S_{GD} = \{D_1, D_2,\ldots, D_n\}$, where D_k (k=1..n) is the definition of the target from the *k*th knowledge base, and *n* is the number of the knowledge bases. D_k may be an empty string when the target has no definition in the knowledge base *k*. In this algorithm, we rank the candidate sentences set $S_A = \{A_1, A_2,\ldots, A_m\}$ using S_{GD}.

Let S_{ij} be the similarity of A_i and D_j. The similarity is the tf.idf score, where the candidate sentence A_i and the definition D_j are all treated as a bag of words. The tf.idf function we used is described in [5].

For each candidate sentence A_i in the set S_A, we calculate its score based on the ***GDS*** as follows:

$$score_i = \sum_{j=1}^{n} w_j S_{ij} \quad (\sum_{j=1}^{n} w_j = 1)\,. \tag{1}$$

The weights w_j are fixed based on experiment, considering the authoritativeness of the knowledge base from which D_j comes. The sentences of set S_A are ranked based on this score, and the top ones are chosen as the definition of the target term.

3.3 Definition Extraction Based on *EDS*

As we have seen, for a target term, different definitions in its "general definition set" may overlap in some degree. We intent to modify this set by merging its elements into one concise definition. We extract the essential information from the "general definition set" to form the "essential definition set", which is abbreviated to ***EDS***.

EDS is expressed as $S_{ED} = \{d_1, d_2, \ldots, d_l\}$, where each element d_k (k=1..*l*) is an essential definition sentence about the target, and *l* is the number of the essential definition sentences. We hope that each element can tell one important aspect of the target term, and the whole "essential definition set" may contain as much information as ***GDS*** but no redundant information.

We try to use an automatic text summary technique [11] to get ***EDS***. This technique is based on sentence's weight and similarity between sentences. Firstly, calculate the weights of all sentences and similarities between any two sentences, and then extract sentence based on these weights. After one sentence has been extracted, calculate the new weights of the remained sentences based on their similarities. Iterate the above procedure until the extracted sentences reach the required length. More detail of this technique can be found in [11]. In this section we will try to use the "essential definition set" to extract definitions from the candidate sentence set.

---

1. Initially set the result set A={ }, and *i*=1.
2. For the element d_i in the set S_{ED}:
First get the similarity between d_i and A_j (j=1..m), which is expressed as S_{ij}.
Then let $S_{ik} = \max\{S_{i1}, S_{i2}, \ldots, S_{im}\}$. If $S_{ik} > minsim$, then add A_k to the set A and delete A_k from the set S_A.
3. If $\sum_{k=1}^{m'} L(A_k) > max\_length$ or *i* equals to *l*, the algorithm ends; otherwise, $i = i + 1$, go to step2.

Fig. 3. Definition extraction using *EDS*

The algorithm was showed in Fig.3. The candidate sentence set is also expressed as $S_A = \{A_1, A_2, \ldots, A_m\}$, where A_k (k=1..m) is a candidate sentence in the set and *m* is the total number of the candidate sentences. The similarity S_{ij} is calculated as the same as in Section 3.2. $L(A_k)$ represents the length of string A_k in character and m' is the number of elements in set A. The parameters *max_length* and *minsim* were empirically set based on TREC's definition question set. The last result is set A, where $A=\{A_1, A_2, \ldots, A_{m'}\}$.

4 Evaluation

In order to get comparable evaluation, we apply our approach to TREC2004 definition QA task. We can see that our approach is an effective one compared with peer systems in this competitive evaluation.

In this section we present the evaluation criterion and system performance on TREC task, and discuss the effectiveness of our approach.

4.1 Evaluation Criterion

The TREC evaluation criterion [3] is summarized here for the purpose of discussing the evaluation results.

For an individual definition question, there is a list of essential nuggets and acceptable nuggets provided by TREC. These given nuggets are used to score the definition generated by the system.

An individual definition question will be scored using nugget recall (R) and an approximation to nugget precision (P) based on length. In particular,

R = # essential nuggets returned in response/# essential nuggets

P is defined as: if length < allowance, P = 1

else P=1-[(length-allowance)/length]

where allowance = 100*(# essential+acceptable nuggets returned)

length = total # non-white-space characters in answer strings

The F measure is:

$$F = \frac{(\beta^2 + 1)PR}{\beta^2 P + R} . \quad (2)$$

where β value is fixed three in TREC 2004, and we also use three to get comparable result.

The score of a system is the arithmetic mean of F-measure scores of all the definition questions output by the system.

4.2 Effectiveness of Web Knowledge Bases

To compare the effectiveness of the Web knowledge bases, we experimented on the TREC 2004 definition question set. The result can be seen in Table1.

Table 1 shows the F-measure scores of our two algorithms and the baseline method. It also shows the median of the scores of all participating systems in TREC 2004. The baseline method is: for an input question, form the candidate sentence set by using the approach described in Section 2. Then put the sentence of this set into the answer set one by one until all the sentences in the candidate sentence set are considered or the answer length is greater than a pre-fixed length (we set the length 3000 characters in our experiment).

We can see that our two algorithms all outperform the median and the baseline method which does not use Web knowledge bases. In conclusion, the Web knowledge bases are effective resources to definition question answering.

Table 1. The F- measure score of the baseline method, the median system in TREC2004, and our two methods on TREC 2004 data set

	Baseline method	Median	Ranking using ***GDS***	Ranking using ***EDS***
F-measure score (β=3)	0.231	0.184	0.404	0.367

4.3 Definition Extraction Based on *GDS* vs. Based on *EDS*

As we have mentioned, we have tried two algorithms in the definition extraction module, which are based on ***GDS*** and ***EDS*** respectively. The performance of these algorithms is shown in Table 2.

Table 2. Performance of our three runs on the three types of quesitions and on the whole 64 questions of TREC 2004

	Num Q	Run A	Run B	Run C
all	64	0.404	0.389	0.367
PERSON	23	0.366	0.372	**0.404**
ORG	25	**0.413**	0.389	0.326
THING	16	**0.446**	0.415	0.379

We have submitted three runs in TREC2004, which were generated by using different algorithm in the definition extraction module. Run A and run B were generated by using ***GDS*** with slightly different weights in formula (1), and run C was generated by using ***EDS***. All the 64 questions are divided into three classes based on the entity types of the targets, which are person, organization and other thing. Table 2 shows the three runs' F-measure scores on these three types and their overall score on the whole 64 questions.

Two algorithms' F-measure scores are all among the best of total 63 runs. Run C's score on the "PERSON", 0.404 is the highest of our three runs on this type. Run A does better on the types named "ORG" and "THING". We can say that these two algorithms contribute to different kinds of target terms. Dividing definition questions into different subclass and processing them with different methods could be a proper direction.

Considering the score on all the 64 questions, the former algorithm is slightly higher than the latter one. However, the result of the latter one is also encouraging. Since the "essential definition set" contain the important information and less redundancy, it has the potential to get the answers, which are not only concise but also have wide coverage about the target. We believe it is an appropriate way to extract the high quality definitions. A preliminary analysis shows that the major problem is how to improve the quality and the coverage of the essential definition set. We believe that the performance could be boosted through improving this technique.

In conclusion, we can say that our methods can make better use of the external knowledge in answering definition question.

5 Conclusions

This paper proposes a definition QA approach, which makes use of Web knowledge bases and several complementary technology components. The experiments reveal that the Web knowledge bases are effective resources to definition question answering, and the presented method gives an appropriate framework for answering this kind of question. Our approach has achieved an encouraging performance with the F-measure score of 0.404, which is ranked second among all the submitted runs in TREC2004.

Since definitional patterns can not only filter out those statistically highly-ranked sentences that are not definitional, but also bring those definition sentences that are written in certain styles for definitions but are not statistically significant into the answer set. [6] In the future work, we will employ some pattern matching methods to reinforce our existing method.

Acknowledgements

This research was partly supported by NSF (Beijing, China) under contract of 60435020, and Key Project of Science and Technology Committee of Shanghai under contract of 035115028.

References

1. Abdessamad Echihabi, Ulf Hermjakob, Eduard Hovy: Multiple-Engine Question Answering in TextMap. In Proceedings of the Twelfth Text REtreival Conference. NIST, Gathersburg, MD (2003) 772–781
2. Ellen M. Voorhees: Overview of the TREC 2001 question answering track. In Proceedings of the Tenth Text REtreival Conference. NIST, Gathersburg, MD (2001) 42–51
3. Ellen M. Voorhees: Overview of the TREC 2003 Question Answering Track. In Proceedings of the Twelfth Text REtreival Conference. NIST, Gathersburg, MD (2003) 54–68
4. Ellen M. Voorhees: Evaluating answers to definition questions. In Proceedings of the 2003 Human Language Technology Conference of the North American Chapter of the Association for Computational Linguistics (2003) Volume 2: 109–111
5. G.Salton, C. Buckley: Term weighting approaches in automatic text retrieval. Information Processing and Management (1988) 24(5): 513–523
6. Hang Cui, Min-Yen Kan, Tat-Seng Chua, Jing Xiao: A comparative Study o Sentence Retrieval for Definitional Question Answering. In Proceedings of the 27th Annual International ACM SIGIR Conference (2004)
7. Hang Cui, Keya Li, Renxu Sun, Tat-Seng Chua, Min-Yen kan: National University of Singapore the TREC-13 Question Answering Main Task. In Proceedings of the Thirteenth Text REtreival Conference. NIST, Gathersburg, MD (2004)
8. J. M. Prager, Jennifer Chu-Carroll, Krzysztof Czuba, Christopher Welty, Abraham Ittycheiach, Ruchi Mahindru: IBM's PIQUANT in TREC2003. In Proceedings of the Twelfth Text REtreival Conference. NIST, Gathersburg, MD (2003) 283–292
9. Jinxi Xu, Ana Licuanan, Ralph Weischedel: TREC2003 QA at BBN: Answering definitional Questions. In Proceedings of the Twelfth Text REtreival Conference. NIST, Gathersburg, MD (2003) 98~106
10. Milen Kouylekov, Bernardo Magnini, Matteo Negri, Hristo Tanev: ITC-irst at TREC-2003: the DIOGENE QA system. In Proceedings of the Twelfth Text REtreival Conference. NIST, Gathersburg, MD (2003) 349–357
11. Qi Zhang, Xuanjing Huang, Lide Wu: A New Method for Calculating Similarity between Sentences and Application on Automatic Text Summarization. In Proceedings of the first National Conference on Information Retrieval and Content Security (2004)
12. Sasha Blair-Goldensohn, Kathleen R. McKeown, Andrew Hazen Schlaikjer: A hybrid approach for QA track definitional questions. In Proceedings of the Twelfth Text REtreival Conference. NIST, Gathersburg, MD (2003) 185–192

Exploring Syntactic Relation Patterns for Question Answering

Dan Shen[1,2], Geert-Jan M. Kruijff [1], and Dietrich Klakow[2]

[1] Department of Computational Linguistics, Saarland University,
Building 17, Postfach 15 11 50, 66041 Saarbruecken, Germany
{dshen, gj}@coli.uni-sb.de
[2] Lehrstuhl Sprach Signal Verarbeitung,Saarland University,
Building 17, Postfach 15 11 50, 66041 Saarbruecken, Germany
{dietrich.klakow}@lsv.uni-saarland.de

Abstract. In this paper, we explore the syntactic relation patterns for open-domain factoid question answering. We propose a pattern extraction method to extract the various relations between the proper answers and different types of question words, including target words, head words, subject words and verbs, from syntactic trees. We further propose a QA-specific tree kernel to partially match the syntactic relation patterns. It makes the more tolerant matching between two patterns and helps to solve the data sparseness problem. Lastly, we incorporate the patterns into a Maximum Entropy Model to rank the answer candidates. The experiment on TREC questions shows that the syntactic relation patterns help to improve the performance by 6.91 MRR based on the common features.

1 Introduction

Question answering is to find answers for open-domain natural language questions in a large document collection. A typical QA system usually consists of three basic modules: 1. Question Processing (QP) Module, which finds some useful information from questions, such as expected answer type and key words; 2. Information Retrieval (IR) Module, which searches a document collection to retrieve a set of relevant sentences using the key words; 3. Answer Extraction (AE) Module, which analyzes the relevant sentences using the information provided by the QP module and identify the proper answer. In this paper, we will focus on the AE module.

In order to find the answers, some evidences, such as expected answer types and surface text patterns, are extracted from answer sentences and incorporated in the AE module using a pipelined structure, a scoring function or some statistical-based methods. However, the evidences extracted from plain texts are not sufficient to identify a proper answer. For examples, for "*Q1910: What are pennies made of?*", the expected answer type is unknown; for "*Q21: Who was the first American in space?*", the surface patterns may not detect the long-distance relations between the question key phrase "*the first American in space*" and the answer "*Alan Shepard*" in "*… that carried Alan Shepard on a 15 - minute suborbital flight in 1961 , making him the first*

R. Dale et al. (Eds.): IJCNLP 2005, LNAI 3651, pp. 507 – 518, 2005.

American in space." To solve these problems, more evidences need to be extracted from the more complex data representations, such as parse trees.

In this paper, we explore the syntactic relation patterns (SRP) for the AE module. An SRP is defined as a kind of relation between a question word and an answer candidate in the syntactic tree. Different from the textual patterns, the SRPs capture the relations based on the sentence syntactic structure rather than the sentence surface. Therefore, they may get the deeper understanding of the relations and capture the long range dependency between words regardless of their ordering and distance in the surface text. Based on the observation of the task, we find that the syntactic relations between different types of question words and answers vary a lot with each other. We classify the question words into four classes, including target words, head words, subject phrases and verbs, and generate the SRPs for them respectively. Firstly, we generate the SRPs from the training data and score them based on the support and confidence measures. Next, we propose a QA-specific tree kernel to calculate the similarity between two SRPs in order to match the patterns from the unseen data into the pattern set. The tree kernel makes the partial matching between two patterns and helps to solve the data sparseness problem. Lastly, we incorporate the SRPs into a Maximum Entropy Model along with some common features to classify the answer candidates. The experiment on TREC questions shows that the syntactic relation patterns improve the performance by 6.91 MRR based on the common features.

Although several syntactic relations, such as subject-verb and verb-object, have been also considered in some other systems, they are basically extracted using a small number of hand-built rules. As a result, they are limited and costly. In our task, we automatically extract the various relations between different question words and answers and more tolerantly match the relation patterns using the tree kernel.

2 Related Work

The relations between answers and question words have been explored by many successful QA systems based on certain sentence representations, such as word sequence, logic form, parse tree, etc.

In the simplest case, a sentence is represented as a sequence of words. It is assumed that, for certain type of questions, the proper answers always have certain surface relations with the question words. For example, "*Q: When was X born?*", the proper answers often have such relation "*<X> (<Answer>--*" with the question phrase *X* . [14] first used a predefined pattern set in QA and achieved a good performance at TREC10. [13] further developed a bootstrapping method to learn the surface patterns automatically. When testing, most of them make the partial matching using regular expression. However, such surface patterns strongly depend on the word ordering and distance in the text and are too specific to the question type.

LCC [9] explored the syntactic relations, such as subject, object, prepositional attachment and adjectival/adverbial adjuncts, based on the logic form transformation. Furthermore they used a logic prover to justify the answer candidates. The prover is accurate but costly.

Most of the QA systems explored the syntactic relations on the parse tree. Since such relations do not depend on the word ordering and distance in the sentence, they may cope with the various surface expressions of the sentence. ISI [7] extracted the relations, such as "subject-verb" and "verb-object", in the answer sentence tree and compared with those in the question tree. IBM's Maximum Entropy-based model [10] integrated a rich feature set, including words co-occurrence scores, named entity, dependency relations, etc. For the dependency relations, they considered some predefined relations in trees by partial matching. BBN [15] also considered the verb-argument relations.

However, most of the current QA systems only focus on certain relation types, such as verb-argument relations, and extract them from the syntactic tree using some heuristic rules. Therefore, extracting such relations is limited in a very local context of the answer node, such as its parent or sibling nodes, and does not involve long range dependencies. Furthermore, most of the current systems only concern the relations to certain type of question words, such as verb. In fact, different types of question words may have different indicative relations with the proper answers. In this paper, we will automatically extract more comprehensive syntactic relation patterns for all types of question words, partially match them using a QA-specific tree kernel and evaluate their contributions by integrating them into a Maximum Entropy Model.

3 Syntactic Relation Pattern Generating

In this section, we will discuss how to extract the syntactic relation patterns. Firstly, we briefly introduce the question processing module which provides some necessary information to the answer extraction module. Secondly, we generate the dependency tree of the answer sentence and map the question words into the tree using a Modified Edit Distance (MED) algorithm. Thirdly, we define and extract the syntactic relation patterns in the mapped dependency tree. Lastly, we score and filter the patterns.

3.1 Question Processing Module

The key words are extracted from the questions. Considering that different key words may have different syntactic relations with the answers, we divide the key words into the following four types:

1. Target Words, which are extracted from *what / which* questions. Such words indicate the expected answer types, such as "*party*" in "*Q1967: What party led …?*".
2. Head Words, which are extracted from *how* questions. Such words indicate the expected answer heads, such as "*dog*" in the "*Q210: How many dogs pull …?*"
3. Subject Phrases, which are extracted from all types of questions. They are the base noun phrases of the questions except the target words and the head words.
4. Verbs, which are the main verbs extracted from non-definition questions.

The key words described above are identified and classified based on the question parse tree. We employ the Collins Parser [2] to parse the questions and the answer sentences.

3.2 Question Key Words Mapping

From this section, we start to introduce the AE module. Firstly, the answer sentences are tagged with named entities and parsed. Secondly, the parse trees are transformed to the dependency trees based on a set of rules. To simplify a dependency tree, some special rules are used to remove the non-useful nodes and dependency information. The rules include

1. Since the question key words are always NPs and verbs, only the syntactic relations between NP and NP / NP and verb are considered.
2. The original form of Base Noun Phrase (BNP) is kept and the dependency relations within the BNPs are not considered, such as adjective-noun. A base noun phrase is defined as the smallest noun phrase in which there are no noun phrases embedded.

An example of the dependency tree is shown in Figure 1. We regard all BNP nodes and leaf nodes as answer candidates.

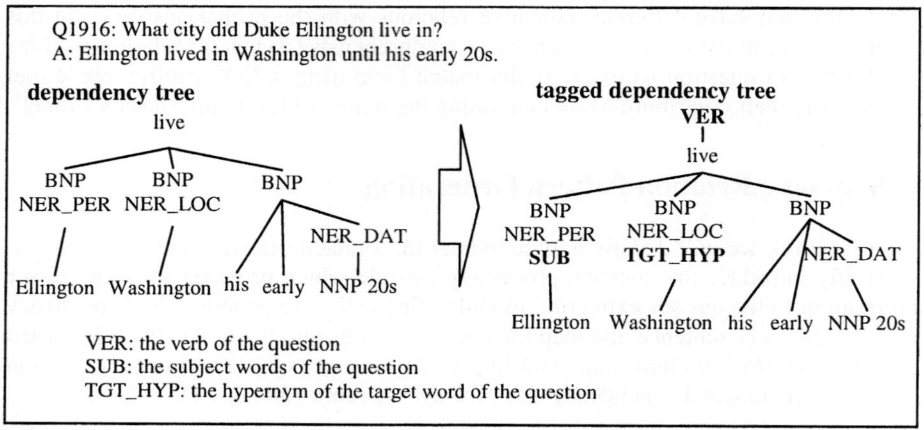

Fig. 1. Dependency tree and Tagged dependency tree

Next, we map the question key words into the simplified dependency trees. We propose a weighted edit distance (WED) algorithm, which is to find the similarity between two phrases by computing the minimal cost of operations needed to transform one phrase into the other, where an operation is an insertion, deletion, or substitution.

Different from the commonly-used edit distance algorithm [11], the WED defines the more flexible cost function which incorporates the morphological and semantic alternations of the words. The morphological alternations indicate the inflections of noun/verb. For example, for *Q2149: How many Olympic gold medals did Carl Lewis win?* We map the verb *win* to the nominal *winner* in the answer sentence "*Carl Lewis, winner of nine Olympic gold medals, thinks that ...*". The morphological alternations are found based on a stemming algorithm and the "derivationally related forms" in WordNet [8]. The semantic alternations consider the synonyms of the words. Some types of the semantic relations in WordNet enable the retrieval of synonyms, such as hypernym, hyponym, etc. For example, for *Q212: Who invented the electric guitar?* We may map the verb *invent* to its direct hypernym *create* in answer sentences. Based on the observation of the task, we set the substitution costs of the alternations as follows: Identical words have cost 0; Words with the same morphological root have cost 0.2; Words with the hypernym or hyponym relations have cost

0.4; Words in the same SynSet have cost 0.6; Words with subsequence relations have cost 0.8; otherwise, words have cost 1. Figure 1 also shows an example of the tagged dependency tree.

3.3 Syntactic Relation Pattern Extraction

A syntactic relation pattern is defined as the smallest subtree which covers an answer candidate node and one question key word node in the dependency tree. To capture different relations between answer candidates and different types of question words, we generate four pattern sets, called *PSet_target*, *PSet_head*, *PSet_subject* and *PSet_verb*, for the answer candidates. The patterns are extracted from the training data. Some pattern examples are shown in Table 1. For a question *Q*, there are a set of relevant sentences *SentSet*. The extraction process is as follows:

1. for each question *Q* in the training data
2. question processing model extract the key words of Q
3. for each sentence *s* in *SentSet*
    a) parse *s*
    b) map the question key words into the parse tree
    c) tag all BNP nodes in the parse tree as answer candidates.
    d) for each answer candidate (*ac*) node
        for each question word (*qw*) node
            extract the syntactic relation pattern (*srp*) for *ac* and *qw*
            add *srp* to *PSet_target*, *PSet_head*, *PSet_subject* or *PSet_verb* based on the types of *qw*.

Table 1. Examples of the patterns in the four pattern sets

PatternSet	Patterns	Sup.	Conf.
PSet_target	(NPB~AC~TGT)	0.55	0.22
	(NPB~AC~null (NPB~null~TGT))	0.08	0.06
	(NPB~null~null (NPB~AC~null) (NPB~null~TGT))	0.02	0.09
PSet_head	(NPB~null~null (CD~AC~null) (NPB~null~HEAD))	0.59	0.67
PSet_subject	(VP~null~null (NPB~null~SUB) (NPB~null~null (NPB~AC~null)))	0.04	0.33
	(NPB~null~null (NPB~null~SUB) (NPB~AC~null))	0.02	0.18
PSet_verb	(VP~null~VERB (NPB~AC~null))	0.18	0.16

3.4 Syntactic Relation Pattern Scoring

The patterns extracted in section 3.3 are scored by support and confidence measures. Support and confidence measures are most commonly used to evaluate the association rules in the data mining area. The support of a rule is the proportion of times the rule applies. The confidence of a rule is the proportion of times the rule is correct. In our task, we score a pattern by measuring the strength of the association rule from the pattern to the proper answer (the pattern is matched => the answer is correct). Let p_i be any pattern in the pattern set $PSet$,

$$\text{support}(p_i) = \frac{\text{the number of } p_i \text{ in which } ac \text{ is correct}}{\text{the size of } PSet}$$

$$\text{confidence}(p_i) = \frac{\text{the number of } p_i \text{ in which } ac \text{ is correct}}{\text{the number of } p_i}$$

We score the patterns in the *PSet_target, PSet_head, PSet_subject* and *PSet_verb* respectively. If the support value is less than the threshold t_{sup} or the confidence value is less than the threshold t_{conf}, the pattern is removed from the set. In the experiment, we set t_{sup} 0.01 and t_{conf} 0.5. Table 1 lists the support and confidence of the patterns.

4 Syntactic Relation Pattern Matching

Since we build the pattern sets based on the training data in the current experiment, the pattern sets may not be large enough to cover all of the unseen cases. If we make the exact match between two patterns, we will suffer from the data sparseness problem. So a partial matching method is required. In this section, we will propose a QA-specific tree kernel to match the patterns.

A kernel function $K(x_1, x_2): \mathbf{X} \times \mathbf{X} \rightarrow [0, \boldsymbol{R}]$, is a similarity measure between two objects x_1 and x_2 with some constraints. It is the most important component of kernel methods [16]. Tree kernels are the structure-driven kernels used to calculate the similarity between two trees. They have been successfully accepted in the natural language processing applications, such as parsing [4], part of speech tagging and named entity extraction [3], and information extraction [5, 17]. To our knowledge, tree kernels have not been explored in answer extraction.

Suppose that a pattern is defined as a tree T with nodes $\{t_0, t_1, ..., t_n\}$ and each node t_i is attached with a set of attributes $\{a_0, a_1, ..., a_m\}$, which represent the local characteristics of t_i. In our task, the set of the attributes include Type attributes, Orthographic attributes and Relation Role attributes, as shown in Table 2. Figure 2 shows an example of the pattern tree *T_ac#target.*

The core idea of the tree kernel $K(T_1, T_2)$ is that the similarity between two trees T_1 and T_2 is the sum of the similarity between their subtrees. It can be calculated by dynamic programming and can capture the long-range relations between two nodes. The kernel we use is similar to [17] except that we define a task-specific matching function and similarity function, which are two primitive functions to calculate the similarity between two nodes in terms of their attributes.

Matching function $$m(t_i, t_j) = \begin{cases} 1 & \text{if } t_i.type = t_j.type \text{ and } t_i.role = t_j.role \\ 0 & \text{otherwise} \end{cases}$$

Similarity function $s(t_i, t_j) = \sum_{a \in \{a_0,\ldots,a_m\}} f(t_i.a, t_j.a)$

where, $f(t_i.a, t_j.a)$ is a compatibility function between two feature values

$$f(t_i.a, t_j.a) = \begin{cases} 1 & \text{if } t_i.a = t_j.a \\ 0 & \text{otherwise} \end{cases}$$

Table 2. Attributes of the nodes

Attributes		Examples
Type	POS tag	CD, NNP, NN…
	syntactic tag	NP, VP, …
Orthographic	Is Digit?	DIG, DIGALL
	Is Capitalized?	CAP, CAPALL
	length of phrase	LNG1, LNG2#3, LNGgt3
Role1	Is answer candidate?	true, false
Role2	Is question key words?	true, false

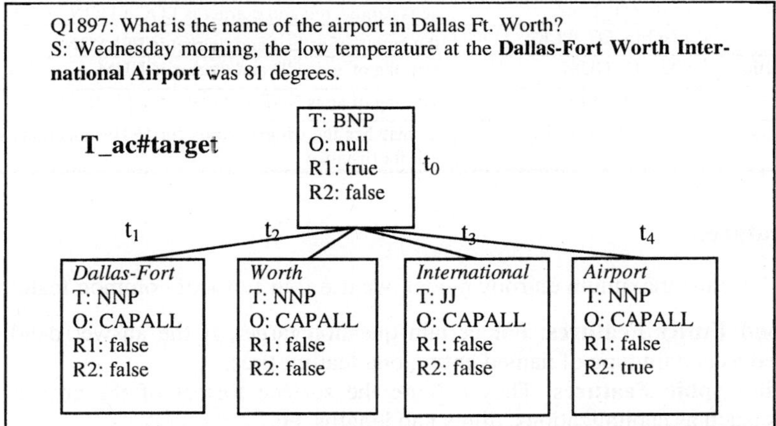

Fig. 2. An example of the pattern tree T_ac#target

5 ME-Based Answer Extraction

In addition to the syntactic relation patterns, many other evidences, such as named entity tags, may help to detect the proper answers. Therefore, we use maximum entropy to integrate the syntactic relation patterns and the common features.

5.1 Maximum Entropy Model

[1] gave a good description of the core idea of maximum entropy model. In our task, we use the maximum entropy model to rank the answer candidates for a question,

which is similar to [12]. Given a question q and a set of possible answer candidates $\{ac_1, ac_2...ac_n\}$, the model outputs the answer $ac \in \{ac_1, ac_2...ac_n\}$ with the maximal probability from the answer candidate set. We define M feature functions $f_m(ac, \{ac_1, ac_2...ac_n\}, q)$, m=1,...,M. The probability is modeled as

$$P(ac \mid \{ac_1, ac_2...ac_n\}, q) = \frac{\exp[\sum_{m=1}^{M} \lambda_m f_m(ac, \{ac_1, ac_2...ac_n\}, q))]}{\sum_{ac'} \exp[\sum_{m=1}^{M} \lambda_m f_m(ac', \{ac_1, ac_2...ac_n\}, q)]}$$

where, λ_m (m=1,...,M) are the model parameters, which are trained with Generalized Iterative Scaling [6]. A Gaussian Prior is used to smooth the ME model.

Table 3. Examples of the common features

Features	Examples	Explanation
NE	NE#DAT_QT_DAT	ac is NE (DATE) and qtarget is DATE
	NE#PER_QW_WHO	ac is NE (PERSON) and qword is WHO
Ortho-graphic	SSEQ_Q	ac is a subsequence of question
	CAP_QT_LOC	ac is capitalized and qtarget is LOCATION
	LNGlt3_QT_PER	the length of ac $\leq$ 3 and qtarget is PERSON
Syntactic Tag	CD_QT_NUM	syn. tag of ac is CD and qtarget is NUM
	NNP_QT_PER	syn. tag of ac is NNP and qtarget is PERSON
Triggers	TRG_HOW_DIST	ac matches the trigger words for HOW questions which ask for distance

5.2 Features

For the baseline maximum entropy model, we use four types of common features:

1. **Named Entity Features**: For certain question target, if the answer candidate is tagged as certain type of named entity, one feature fires.
2. **Orthographic Features**: They capture the surface format of the answer candidates, such as capitalizations, digits and lengths, etc.
3. **Syntactic Tag Features**: For certain question target, if the word in the answer candidate belongs to a certain syntactic / POS type, one feature fires.
4. **Triggers**: For some *how* questions, there are always some trigger words which are indicative for the answers. For example, for "*Q2156: How fast does Randy Johnson throw?*", the word "*mph*" may help to identify the answer "*98-mph*" in "*Johnson throws a 98-mph fastball.*"

Table 3 shows some examples of the common features. All of the features are the binary features. In addition, many other features, such as the answer candidate frequency, can be extracted based on the IR output and are thought as the indicative evidences for the answer extraction [10]. However, in this paper, we are to evaluate the answer extraction module independently, so we do not incorporate such features in the current model.

In order to evaluate the effectiveness of the automatically generated syntactic relation patterns, we also manually build some heuristic rules to extract the relation features from the trees and incorporate them into the baseline model. The baseline model uses 20 rules. Some examples of the **hand-extracted relation features** are listed as follows,

- If the ac node is the same of the qtarget node, one feature fires.
- If the ac node is the sibling of the qtarget node, one feature fires.
- If the ac node is the child of the qsubject node, one feature fires.
- ...

Next, we will discuss the use of the **syntactic relation features**. Firstly, for each answer candidate, we extract the syntactic relations between it and all mapped question key words in the sentence tree. Then for each extracted relation, we match it in the pattern set *PSet_target*, *PSet_head*, *PSet_subject* or *PSet_verb*. A tree kernel discussed in Section 4 is used to calculate the similarity between two patterns. Finally, if the maximal similarity is above a threshold λ, the pattern with the maximal similarity is chosen and the corresponding feature fires. The experiments will evaluate the performance and the coverage of the pattern sets based on different λ values.

6 Experiment

We apply the AE module to the TREC QA task. Since this paper focuses on the AE module alone, we only present those sentences containing the proper answers to the AE module based on the assumption that the IR module has got 100% precision. The AE module is to identify the proper answers from the given sentence collection.

We use the questions of TREC8, 9, 2001 and 2002 for training and the questions of TREC2003 for testing. The following steps are used to generate the data:

1. Retrieve the relevant documents for each question based on the TREC judgments.
2. Extract the sentences, which match both the proper answer and at least one question key word, from these documents.
3. Tag the proper answer in the sentences based on the TREC answer patterns.

In TREC 2003, there are 413 factoid questions in which 51 questions (NIL questions) are not returned with the proper answers by TREC. According to our data generation process, we cannot provide data for those NIL questions because we cannot get the sentence collections. Therefore, the AE module will fail on all of the NIL questions and the number of the valid questions should be 362 (413 – 51). In the experiment, we still test the module on the whole question set (413 questions) to keep consistent with the other's work. The training set contains 1252 questions. The performance of our system is evaluated using the mean reciprocal rank (MRR). Furthermore, we also list the percentages of the correct answers respectively in terms of the top 5 answers and the top 1 answer returned. No post-processes are used to adjust the answers in the experiments.

In order to evaluate the effectiveness of the syntactic relation patterns in the answer extraction, we compare the modules based on different feature sets. The first ME module *ME1* uses the common features including NE features, Orthographic features,

Syntactic Tag features and Triggers. The second ME module *ME2* uses the common features and some hand-extracted relation features, described in Section 5.2. The third module *ME3* uses the common features and the syntactic relation patterns which are automatically extracted and partial matched with the methods proposed in Section 3 and 4. Table 4 shows the overall performance of the modules. Both *ME2* and *ME3* outperform *ME1* by 3.15 MRR and 6.91 MRR respectively. This may indicate that the syntactic relations between the question words and the answers are useful for the answer extraction. Furthermore, *ME3* got the higher performance (+3.76 MRR) than *ME2*. The probable reason may be that the relations extracted by some heuristic rules in *ME2* are limited in the very local contexts of the nodes and they may not be sufficient. On the contrary, the pattern extraction methods we proposed can explore the larger relation space in the dependency trees.

Table 4. Overall performance

	ME1	ME2	ME3
Top1	44.06	47.70	51.81
Top5	53.27	55.45	58.85
MRR	47.75	50.90	54.66

Table 5. Performances for two pattern matching methods

	ExactMatch	PartialMatch				
	(λ=1)	λ=0.8	λ=0.6	λ=0.4	λ=0.2	λ=0
Top1	50.12	51.33	**51.81**	51.57	50.12	50.12
Top5	57.87	58.37	**58.85**	58.60	57.16	57.16
MRR	53.18	54.18	**54.66**	54.41	52.97	52.97

Furthermore, we evaluate the effectiveness of the pattern matching method in Section 4. We compare two pattern matching methods: the exact matching (*ExactMatch*) and the partial matching (*PartialMatch*) using the tree kernel. Table 5 shows the performances for the two pattern matching methods. For *PartialMatch*, we also evaluate the effect of the parameter λ (described in Section 5.2) on the performance. In Table 5, the best *PartialMatch* (λ = 0.6) outperforms *ExactMatch* by 1.48 MRR. Since the pattern sets extracted from the training data is not large enough to cover the unseen cases, *ExactMatch* may have too low coverage and suffer with the data sparseness problem when testing, especially for *PSet_subject* (24.32% coverage using *ExactMatch* vs. 49.94% coverage using *PartialMatch*). In addition, even the model with *ExactMatch* is better than *ME2* (common features + hand-extracted relations) by 2.28 MRR. It indicates that the relation patterns explored with the method proposed in Section 3 are more effective than the relations extracted by the heuristic rules.

Table 6 shows the size of the pattern sets *PSet_target*, *PSet_head*, *PSet_subject* and *PSet_verb* and their coverage for the test data based on different λ values. *PSet_verb* gets the low coverage (<5% coverage). The probable reason is that the verbs in the answer sentences are often different from those in the questions, therefore only a few question verbs can be matched in the answer sentences. *PSet_head* also gets the relatively low coverage since the head words are only exacted from *how* questions and there are only 49/413 *how* questions with head words in the test data.

Table 6. Size and coverage of the pattern sets

	size	coverage (*%)					
		λ =1	λ =0.8	λ =0.6	λ =0.4	λ =0.2	λ =0
PSet_target	45	49.85	53.73	57.01	58.14	58.46	58.46
PSet_head	42	5.82	6.48	6.69	6.80	6.80	6.80
PSet_subject	123	24.32	44.82	49.94	51.29	51.84	51.84
PSet_verb	125	2.21	3.49	3.58	3.58	3.58	3.58

We further evaluate the contributions of different types of patterns. We respectively combine the pattern features in different pattern set and the common features. Some findings can be concluded from Table 7: All of the patterns have the positive effects based on the common features, which indicates that all of the four types of the relations are helpful for answer extraction. Furthermore, *P_target* (+4.21 MRR) and *P_subject* (+2.47 MRR) are more beneficial than *P_head* (+1.25 MRR) and *P_verb* (+0.19 MRR). This may be explained that the target and subject patterns may have the effect on the more test data than the head and verb patterns since *PSet_target* and *PSet_subject* have the higher coverage for the test data than *PSet_head* and *PSet_verb*, as shown in Table 6.

Table 7. Performance on feature combination

Combination of features	MRR
common features	47.75
common features + P_target	51.96
common features + P_head	49.00
common features + P_subject	50.22
common features + P_verb	47.94

7 Conclusion

In this paper, we study the syntactic relation patterns for question answering. We extract the various syntactic relations between the answers and different types of question words, including target words, head words, subject words and verbs and score the extracted relations based on support and confidence measures. We further propose a QA-specific tree kernel to partially match the relation patterns from the unseen data to the pattern sets. Lastly, we incorporate the patterns and some common features into a Maximum Entropy Model to rank the answer candidates. The experiment shows that the syntactic relation patterns improve the performance by 6.91 MRR based on the common features. Moreover, the contributions of the pattern matching methods are evaluated. The results show that the tree kernel-based partial matching outperforms the exact matching by 1.48 MRR. In the future, we are to further explore the syntactic relations using the web data rather than the training data.

References

1. Berger, A., Della Pietra, S., Della Pietra, V.: A maximum entropy approach to natural language processing. Computational Linguistics (1996), vol. 22, no. 1, pp. 39-71
2. Collins, M.: A New Statistical Parser Based on Bigram Lexical Dependencies. In: Proceedings of ACL-96 (1996) 184-191
3. Collins, M.: New Ranking Algorithms for Parsing and Tagging: Kernel over Discrete Structures, and the Voted Perceptron. In: Proceeings of ACL-2002 (2002).
4. Collins, M., Duffy, N.: Convolution Kernels for Natural Language. Advances in Neural Information Processing Systems 14, Cambridge, MA. MIT Press (2002)
5. Culotta, A., Sorensen, J.: Dependency Tree Kernels for Relation Extraction. In: Proceedings of ACL-2004 (2004)
6. Darroch, J., Ratcliff, D.: Generalized iterative scaling for log-linear models. The annuals of Mathematical Statistics (1972), vol. 43, pp. 1470-1480
7. Echihabi, A., Hermjakob, U., Hovy, E., Marcu, D., Melz, E., Ravichandran, D.: Multiple-Engine Question Answering in TextMap. In: Proceedings of the TREC-2003 Conference, NIST (2003)
8. Fellbaum, C.: WordNet - An Electronic Lexical Database. MIT Press, Cambridge, MA (1998)
9. Harabagiu, S., Moldovan, D., Clark, C., Bowden, M., Williams, J., Bensley, J.: Answer Mining by Combining Extraction Techniques with Abductive Reasoning. In: Proceedings of the TREC-2003 Conference, NIST (2003)
10. Ittycheriah, A., Roukos, S.: IBM's Statistical Question Answering System - TREC 11. In: Proceedings of the TREC-2002 Conference, NIST (2002)
11. Levenshtein, V. I.: Binary Codes Capable of Correcting Deletions, Insertions and Reversals. Doklady Akademii Nauk SSSR 163(4) (1965) 845-848
12. Ravichandran, D., Hovy, E., Och, F. J.: Statistical QA - Classifier vs. Re-ranker: What's the difference? In: Proceedings of Workshop on Multilingual Summarization and Question Answering, ACL (2003)
13. Ravichandran, D., Hovy, E.: Learning Surface Text Patterns for a Question Answering System. In: Proceedings of ACL-2002 (2002) 41-47
14. Soubbotin, M. M., Soubbotin, S. M.: Patterns of Potential Answer Expressions as Clues to the Right Answer. In: Proceedings of the TREC-10 Conference, NIST (2001)
15. Xu, J., Licuanan, A., May, J., Miller, S., Weischedel, R.: TREC 2002 QA at BBN: Answer Selection and Confidence Estimation. In: Proceedings of the TREC-2002 Conference, NIST (2002)
16. Vapnik, V.: Statistical Learning Theory, John Wiley, NY, (1998) 732.
17. Zelenko, D., Aone, C., Richardella, A.: Kernel Methods for Relation Extraction. Journal of Machine Learning Research (2003) 1083-1106.

Web-Based Unsupervised Learning for Query Formulation in Question Answering

Yi-Chia Wang[1], Jian-Cheng Wu[2], Tyne Liang[1], and Jason S. Chang[2]

[1] Dep. of Computer and Information Science, National Chiao Tung University, 1001 Ta Hsueh Rd., Hsinchu, Taiwan 300, R.O.C.
rhyme.cis92g@nctu.edu.tw, tliang@cis.nctu.edu.tw
[2] Dep. of Computer Science, National Tsing Hua University, 101, Section 2 Kuang Fu Road, Hsinchu, Taiwan 300, R.O.C.
d928322@oz.nthu.edu.tw, jschang@cs.nthu.edu.tw

Abstract. Converting questions to effective queries is crucial to open-domain question answering systems. In this paper, we present a web-based unsupervised learning approach for transforming a given natural-language question to an effective query. The method involves querying a search engine for Web passages that contain the answer to the question, extracting patterns that characterize fine-grained classification for answers, and linking these patterns with n-grams in answer passages. Independent evaluation on a set of questions shows that the proposed approach outperforms a naive keyword-based approach in terms of mean reciprocal rank and human effort.

1 Introduction

An automated *question answering* (QA) system receives a user's natural-language question and returns exact answers by analyzing the question and consulting a large text collection [1, 2]. As Moldovan et al. [3] pointed out, over 60% of the QA errors can be attributed to ineffective question processing, including query formulation and query expansion.

A naive solution to query formulation is using the keywords in an input question as the query to a search engine. However, it is possible that the keywords may not appear in those answer passages which contain answers to the given question. For example, submitting the keywords in "*Who invented washing machine?*" to a search engine like Google may not lead to retrieval of answer passages like "*The inventor of the automatic washer was John Chamberlain.*" In fact, by expanding the keyword set ("*invented*", "*washing*", "*machine*") with "*inventor of,*" the query to a search engine is effective in retrieving such answer passages as the top-ranking pages. Hence, if we can learn how to associate a set of questions (e.g. ("*who invented …?*") with effective keywords or phrases (e.g. "*inventor of*") which are likely to appear in answer passages, the search engine will have a better chance of retrieving pages containing the answer.

In this paper, we present a novel Web-based unsupervised learning approach to handling question analysis for QA systems. In our approach, training-data questions are first analyzed and classified into a set of fine-grained categories of question

R. Dale et al. (Eds.): IJCNLP 2005, LNAI 3651, pp. 519 – 529, 2005.

patterns. Then, the relationships between the question patterns and n-grams in answer passages are discovered by employing a word alignment technique. Finally, the best query transforms are derived by ranking the n-grams which are associated with a specific question pattern. At runtime, the keywords in a given question are extracted and the question is categorized. Then the keywords are expanded according the category of the question. The expanded query is the submitted to a search engine in order to bias the search engine to return passages that are more likely to contain answers to the question. Experimental results indicate the expanded query indeed outperforms the approach of directly using the keywords in the question.

2 Related Work

Recent work in Question Answering has attempted to convert the original input question into a query that is more likely to retrieve the answers. Hovy et al. [2] utilized WordNet hypernyms and synonyms to expand queries to increase recall. Hildebrandt et al. [4] looked up in a pre-compiled knowledge base and a dictionary to expand a definition question. However, blindly expanding a word using its synonyms or dictionary gloss may cause undesirable effects. Furthermore, it is difficult to determine which of many related word senses should be considered when expanding the query.

Radev et al. [5] proposed a probabilistic algorithm called *QASM* that learns the best query expansion from a natural language question. The query expansion takes the form of a series of operators, including INSERT, DELETE, REPLACE, etc., to paraphrase a factual question into the best search engine query by applying Expectation Maximization algorithm. On the other hand, Hermjakob et al. [6] described an experiment to observe and learn from human subjects who were given a question and asked to write queries which are most effective in retrieving the answer to the question. First, several randomly selected questions are given to users to "manually" generate effective queries that can bias Web search engines to return answers. The questions, queries, and search results are then examined to derive seven query reformulation techniques that can be used to produce queries similar to the ones issued by human subjects.

In a study closely related to our work, Agichtein et al. [7] presented *Tritus* system that automatically learns transforms of wh-phrases (e.g. expanding "*what is*" to "*refers to*") by using FAQ data. The wh-phrases are restricted to sequences of function word beginning with an interrogative, (i.e. who, what, when, where, why, and how). These wh-phrases tend to coarsely classify questions into a few types. *Tritus* uses heuristic rules and thresholds of term frequencies to learn transforms.

In contrast to previous work, we rely on a mathematical model trained on a set of questions and answers to learn how to transform the question into an effective query. Transformations are learned based on a more fine-grained question classification involving the interrogative and one or more content words.

3 Transforming Question to Query

The method is aimed at automatically learning of the best transforms that turn a given natural language question into an effective query by using the Web as corpus. To that end, we first automatically obtain a collection of answer passages (*AP*s) as the training corpus from the Web by using a set of (*Q*, *A*) pairs. Then we identify the question pattern for each *Q* by using statistical and linguistic information. Here, a question pattern Q_p is defined as a question word plus one or two keywords that are related to the question word. Q_p represents the question intention and it can be treated as a preference indicative for fine-grained type of named entities. Finally, we decide the transforms *T*s for each Q_p by choosing those phrases in the *AP*s that are statistically associated with Q_p and adjacent to the answer *A*.

Table 1. An example of converting a question (*Q*) with its answer (*A*) to a *SE* query and retrieving answer passages (*AP*)

(*Q*, *A*)	***AP***
What is the capital of Pakistan? Answer:(*Islamabad*)	Bungalow For Rent in *Islamabad*, Capital Pakistan. Beautiful Big House For …
(k_1, k_2,…, k_n, *A*)	*Islamabad* is the capital of Pakistan. Current time, …
capital, Pakistan, Islamabad	…the airport which serves Pakistan's capital *Islamabad*, …

3.1 Search the Web for Relevant Answer Passages

For training purpose, a large amount of question/answer passage pairs are mined from the Web by using a set of question/answer pairs as seeds.

More formally, we attempt to retrieve a set of (*Q*, *AP*) pairs on the Web for training purpose, where *Q* stands for a natural language question, and *AP* is a passage containing at least one keyword in *Q* and *A* (the answer to *Q*). The seed data (*Q*, *A*) pairs can be acquired from many sources, including trivia game Websites, TREC QA Track benchmarks, and files of Frequently Asked Questions (FAQ). The output of this training-data gathering process is a large collection of (*Q*, *AP*) pairs. We describe the procedure in details as follows:

1. For each (*Q*, *A*) pair, the keywords k_1, k_2,…, k_n are extracted from *Q* by removing stopwords.
2. Submit (k_1, k_2,…, k_n, *A*) as a query to a search engine *SE*.
3. Download the top *n* summaries returned by *SE*.
4. Separate sentences in the summaries, and remove HTML tags, URL, special character references (e.g., "<").
5. Retain only those sentences which contain *A* and some k_i.

Consider the example of gathering answer passages from the Web for the (*Q*, *A*) pair where *Q* = "*What is the capital of Pakistan?*" and *A* = "*Islamabad*." See Table 1 for the query submitted to a search engine and potential answer passages returned.

3.2 Question Analysis

This subsection describes the presented identification of the so-called "question pattern" which is critical in categorizing a given question and transforming the question into a query.

Formally, a "question pattern" for any question is defined as following form:

question-word head-word+

where "question-word" is one of the interrogatives (Who/What/Where/When/How) and the "head-word" represents the headwords in the subsequent chunks that tend to reflect the intended answer more precisely. If the first headword is a light verb, an additional headword is needed. For instance, "*who had hit*" is a reasonable question pattern for "*Who had a number one hit in 1984 with 'Hello'?*", while "*who had*" seems to be too coarse.

In order to determine the appropriate question pattern for each question, we examined and analyzed a set of questions which are part-of-speech (POS) tagged and phrase-chunked. With the help of a set of simple heuristic rules based on POS and chunk information, fine-grained classification of questions can be carried out effectively.

Question Pattern Extraction

After analyzing recurring patterns and regularity in quizzes on the Web, we designed a simple procedure to recognize question patterns. The procedure is based on a small set of prioritized rules.

The question word which is one of the wh-words ("*who,*" "*what,*" "*when,*" "*where,*" "*how,*" or "*why*") tagged as determiner or adverbial question word. According to the result of POS tagging and phrase chunking, we further decide the main verb and the voice of the question. Then, we apply the following expanded rules to extract words to form question patterns:

Rule 1: *Question word in a chunk of length more than one (see Example (1) in Table 2).*
Qp = question word + headword in the same chunk

Rule 2: *Question word followed by a light verb and Noun Phrase(NP) or Prepositional Phrase(PP) chunk (Example (2)).*
Qp = question word + light verb +headword in the following NP or PP chunk

Rule 3: *Question word followed immediately by a verb (Example (3)).*
Qp = question word + headword in the following Verb Phrase(VP) or NP chunk

Rule 4: *Question word followed by a passive VP (Example (4)).*
Qp = Question word + "to be" + headword in the passive VP chunk

Rule 5: *Question word followed by the copulate "to be" and an NP (Example (5)).*
Qp = Question word + "to be" + headword in the next NP chunk

Rule 6: *If none of the above rules are applicable, the question pattern is the question word.*

By exploiting linguistic information of POS and chunks, we can easily form the question pattern. These heuristic rules are intuitive and easy to understand. Moreover, the fact that these patterns which tend to recur imply that they are general and it is easy to gather training data accordingly. These question patterns also indicate a preference for the answer to be classified with a fine-grained type of proper nouns. In the next section, we describe how we exploit these patterns to learn the best question-to-query transforms.

Table 2. Example questions and question patterns (of words shown in bold)

(1)	**Which** female **singer** performed the first song on Top of the Pops?
(2)	**Who** in 1961 **made** the first space **flight**?
(3)	**Who painted** "The Laughing Cavalier"?
(4)	**What is** a group of geese **called**?
(5)	**What** is the second longest **river** in the world?

3.3 Learning Best Transforms

This section describes the procedure for learning transforms *T*s which convert the question pattern Q_p into bigrams in relevant *AP*s.

Word Alignment Across *Q* and *AP*

We use word alignment techniques developed for statistical machine translation to find out the association between question patterns in *Q* and bigrams in *AP*. The reason why we use bigrams in *AP*s instead of unigrams is that bigrams tend to have more unique meaning than single words and are more effective in retrieving relevant passages.

We use Competitive Linking Algorithm [8] to align a set of (*Q*, *AP*) pairs. The method involves preprocessing steps for each (*Q*, *AP*) pair so as to filter useless information:

1. Perform part-of-speech tagging on *Q* and *AP*.
2. Replace all instances of *A* with the tag <ANS> in *AP*s to indicate the location of the answers.
3. Identify the question pattern, Q_p and keywords which are *not* a named entity. We denote the question pattern and keywords as $q_1, q_2, ..., q_n$.
4. Convert *AP* into bigrams and eliminate bigrams with low term frequency (tf) or high document frequency (df). Bigrams composed of two function words are also removed, resulting in bigrams $a_1, a_2, ..., a_m$.

We then align *q*'s and *a*'s via Competitive Linking Algorithm (CLA) procedure as follows:

Input: A collection *C* of (*Q*; *A*) pairs, where $(Q; A) = (q_1 = Q_p, q_2, q_3, ..., q_n ; a_1, a_2, ..., a_m)$

Output: Best alignment counterpart *a*'s for all *q*'s in *C*

1. For each pair of (*Q*; *A*) in *C* and for all q_i and a_j in each pair of C, calculate LLR(q_i, a_j), logarithmic likelihood ratio (LLR) between q_i and a_j, which reflects their statistical association.
2. Discard (*q*, *a*) pairs with a LLR value lower than a threshold.

3. For each pair of (Q; A) in C and for all q_i and a_j therein, carry out Steps 4-7:
4. Sort list of (q_i, a_j) in each pair of (Q ; A) by decreasing LLR value.
5. Go down the list and select a pair if it does not conflict with previous selection.
6. Stop when running out of pairs in the list.
7. Produce the list of aligned pairs for all Qs and APs.
8. Tally the counts of aligning (q, a).
9. Select top k bigrams, t_1, t_2, ..., t_k, for every question pattern or keyword q.

The LLR statistics is generally effective in distinguishing related terms from unrelated ones. However, if two terms occur frequently in questions, their alignment counterparts will also occur frequently, leading to erroneous alignment due to indirect association. CLA is designed to tackle the problem caused by indirect association. Therefore, if we only make use of the alignment counterpart of the question pattern, we can keep the question keywords in Q so as to reduce the errors caused by indirect association. For instance, the question "*How old was Bruce Lee when he died?*" Our goal is to learn the best transforms for the question pattern "*how old.*" In other words, we want to find out what terms are associated with "*how old*" in the answer passages. However, if we consider the alignment counterparts of "*how old*" without considering those keyword like "*died,*" we run the risk of getting "*died in*" or "*is dead*" rather than "*years old*" and "*age of.*" If we have sufficient data for a specific question pattern like "*how long,*" we will have more chances to obtain alignment counterparts that are effective terms for query expansion.

Distance Constraint and Proximity Ranks

In addition to the association strength implied with alignment counts and co-occurrence, the distance of the bigrams to the answer should also be considered. We observe that terms in the answer passages close to the answers intuitively tend to be useful in retrieving answers. Thus, we calculate the bigrams appearing in a window of three words appearing on both sides of the answers to provide additional constraints for query expansion.

Combing Alignment and Proximity Ranks

The selection of the best bigrams as the transforms for a specific question pattern is based on a combined rank of alignment count and proximity count. It takes the average of these two counts to re-rank bigrams. The average rank of a bigram b is

$$Rank_{avg}(b) = (Rank_{align}(b) + Rank_{prox}(b))/2,$$

where $Rank_{align}(b)$ is the rank of b's alignment count and $Rank_{prox}(b)$ is the rank of b's proximity count. The n top-ranking bigrams for a specific type of question will be chosen to transform the question pattern into query terms. For the question pattern "*how old,*" the candidate bigrams with alignment ranks, co-occurring ranks, and average ranks are shown in Table 3.

Table 3. Average rank calculated from for the bigram counterparts of "*how old*"

Bigrams	Alignment Rank	Proximity Rank	Avg. Rank	Final Rank
age of	1	1	1	1
years old	2	2	2	2
ascend the	3	-	-	-
throne in	4	3	3.5	3
the youngest	3	-	-	-
…	…	…	…	…

3.4 Runtime Transformation of Questions

At runtime, a given question Q submitted by a user is converted into one or more keywords and a question pattern, which is subsequently expanded in to a sequence of query terms based on the transforms obtained at training.

We follow the common practice of keyword selection in formulating Q into a query:

- Function words are identified and discarded.
- Proper nouns that are capitalized or quoted are treated as a single search term with quotes.

Additionally, we expand the question patterns based on alignment and proximity considerations:

- The question pattern Q_p is identified according to the rules (in Section 3.2) and is expanded to be a disjunction (sequence of ORs) of Q_p's headword and n top-ranking bigrams (in section 3.3)
- The query will be a conjunction (sequence of ANDs) of expanded Q_p, proper names, and remaining keywords. Except for the expanded Q_p, all other proper names and keywords will be in the original order in the given question for the best results.

Table 4. An example of transformation from question into query

<table>
<tr><th colspan="3">Question</th></tr>
<tr><td colspan="3">How old was Bruce Lee when he died?</td></tr>
<tr><th>Question pattern</th><th>Proper noun</th><th>Keyword</th></tr>
<tr><td>how old</td><td rowspan="3">"Bruce Lee"</td><td rowspan="3">died</td></tr>
<tr><th>Transformation</th></tr>
<tr><td>age of, years old</td></tr>
<tr><th colspan="3">Expanded query</th></tr>
<tr><td colspan="3">Boolean query: ("old" OR "age of" OR "years old") AND "Bruce Lee" AND "died"</td></tr>
<tr><td colspan="3">Equivalent Google query: (old || "age of" || "years old") "Bruce Lee" died</td></tr>
</table>

For example, formulating a query for the question "*How old was Bruce Lee when he died?*" will result in a question pattern "*how old.*" Because there is a proper noun "*Bruce Lee*" in the question and a remaining keyword "*died,*" the query becomes "('*old*' OR '*age of*' OR '*years old*') AND '*Bruce Lee*' AND '*died.*'" Table 4 lists the query formulating for the example question.

4 Experiments and Evaluation

The proposed method is implemented by using the Web search engine, Google, as the underlying information retrieval system. The experimental results are also justified with assessing the effectiveness of question classification and query expansion.

We used a POS tagger and chunker to perform shallow parsing of the questions and answer passages. The tagger was developed using the Brown corpus and WordNet. The chunker is built from the shared CoNLL-2000 data provided by CoNLL-2000. The shared task CoNLL-2000 provides a set of training and test data for chunks. The chunker we used produces chunks with an average precision rate of about 94%.

4.1 Evaluation of Question Patterns

The 200 questions from TREC-8 QA Track provide an independent evaluation of how well the proposed method works for question pattern extraction works. We will also give an error analysis.

Table 5. Evaluation results of question pattern extraction

	Two "good" labels	At least one "good" label
Precision (%)	86	96

Table 6. The first five questions with question patterns and judgment

Question	Question pattern	Judgment
Who is the author of the book, "The Iron Lady: A Biography of Margaret Thatcher"?	Who-author	good
What was the monetary value of the Nobel Peace Prize in 1989?	What value	good
What does the Peugeot company manufacture?	What do manufacture	good
How much did Mercury spend on advertising in 1993?	How much	good
What is the name of the managing director of Apricot Computer?	What name	bad

Two human judges both majoring in Foreign Languages were asked to assess the results of question pattern extraction and give a label to each extracted question pattern. A pattern will be judged as "good" if it clearly expresses the answer preference of the question; otherwise, it is tagged as "bad." The precision rate of extraction for these 200 questions is shown in Table 5. The second column indicates the precision rate when both of two judges agree that an extracted question pattern is "good." In addition, the third column indicates the rate of those question patterns that are found to be "good" by either judge. The results imply that the proposed pattern extraction rules are general, since they are effective even for questions independent of the training and development data. Table 6 shows evaluation results for "two 'good' labels" of the first five questions.

We summarize the reasons behind these bad patterns:

- Incorrect part-of-speech tagging and chunking
- Imperative questions such as "*Name the first private citizen to fly in space.*"
- Question patterns that are not specific enough

For instance, the system produces "*what name*" for "*What is the name of the chronic neurological autoimmune disease which ...* ?", while the judges suggested that "*what disease*.". Indeed, some of the patterns extracted can be modified to meet the goal of being more fine-grained and indicative of a preference to a specific type of proper nouns or terminology.

4.2 Evaluation of Query Expansion

We implemented a prototype of the proposed method called *Atlas* (Automatic Transform Learning by Aligning Sentences of question and answer). To develop the system of *Atlas,* we gathered seed training data of questions and answers from a trivia game website, called QuizZone[1]. We collected the questions posted in June, 2004 on QuizZone and obtained 3,851 distinct question-answer pairs. We set aside the first 45 questions for testing and used the rest for training. For each question, we form a query with question keywords and the answer and submitted the query to Google to retrieve top 100 summaries as the answer passages. In all, we collected 95,926 answer passages.

At training time, we extracted a total of 338 distinct question patterns from 3,806 questions. We aligned these patterns and keywords with bigrams in the 95,926 answer passages, identified the locations of the answers, and obtained the bigrams appearing within a distance of 3 of the answers. At runtime, we use the top-ranking bigram to expand each question pattern. If no such bigrams are found, we use only the keyword in the question patterns. The expanded terms for question pattern are placed at the beginning of the query.

We submitted forty-five keyword queries and the same number of expanded queries generated by *Atlas* for the test questions to Google and obtained ten returned summaries for evaluation. For the evaluation, we use three indicators to measure the performance. The first indicator is the mean reciprocal rank (*MRR*) of the first relevant document (or summary) returned. If the *r*-th document (summary) returned is the one with the answer, then the reciprocal rank of the document (summary) is *1/r*.

[1] QuizZone (http://www.quiz-zone.co.uk)

The mean reciprocal rank is the average reciprocal rank of all test questions. The second indicator of effective query is the recall at *R* document retrieved (Recall at *R*). The last indicator measures the human effort (*HE*) in finding the answer. *HE* is defined as the least number of passages needed to be viewed for covering all the answers to be returned from the system.

The average length of these test questions is short. We believe the proposed question expansion scheme helps those short sentences, which tend to be less effective in retrieving answers. We evaluated the expanded queries against the same measures for summaries returned by simple keyword queries. Both batches of returned summaries for the forty-five questions were verified by two human judges.

As shown in Table 7, the MRR produced by keyword-based scheme is slightly lower than the one yielded by the presented query expansion scheme. Nevertheless, such improvement is encouraging by indicating the effectiveness of the proposed method.

Table 8 lists the comparisons in more details. It is found that our method is effective in bringing the answers to the top 1 and top 2 summaries as indicated by the high Recall of 0.8 at $R = 2$. In addition, Table 8 also shows that less user's efforts are needed by using our approach. That is, for each question, the average of summaries required to be viewed by human beings goes down from 2.7 to 2.3.

In the end, we found that those bigrams containing a content word and a function word turn out to be very effective. For instance, our method tends to favor transforms

Table 7. Evaluation results of MRR

Performances	MRR
GO (Direct keyword query for Google)	0.64
AT+GO (Atlas expanded query for Google)	0.69

Table 8. Evaluation Result of Recall at R and Human Effort

Rank	Rank count		Recall at *R*	
	GO	AT+GO	GO	AT+GO
1	25	26	0.56	0.58
2	6	10	0.69	0.80
3	5	3	0.80	0.87
4	0	1	0.80	0.89
5	1	1	0.82	0.91
6	2	0	0.87	0.91
7	1	0	0.89	0.91
8	2	0	0.93	0.91
9	0	1	0.93	0.93
10	0	0	0.93	0.93
No answers	3	3		
Human Effort	122	105		
# of questions	45	45		
HE per question	2.7	2.3		

such as "*who invented*" to bigrams such as "*invented by,*" "*invent the,*" and "*inventor of.*" This contrasts to conventional wisdom of using a stoplist of mostly function words and excluding them from consideration in a query. Our experiment also shows a function word as part of a phrasal term seems to be very effective, for it indicate an implied relation with the answer.

5 Conclusion and Future Work

In this paper, we introduce a method for learning query transformations that improves the ability to retrieve passages with answers using the Web as corpus. The method involves question classification and query transformations using a learning-based approach. We also describe the experiment with over 3,000 questions indicates that satisfactory results were achieved. The experimental results show that the proposed method provides effective query expansion that potentially can lead to performance improvement for a question answering system.

A number of future directions present themselves. First, the patterns learned from answer passages acquired on the Web can be refined and clustered to derive a hierarchical classification of questions for more effective question classification. Second, different question patterns, like "*who wrote*" and "*which author*", should be treated as the same in order to cope with data sparseness and improve system performance. On the other hand, an interesting direction is the generating pattern transformations that contain the answer extraction patterns for different types of questions.

References

1. Ittycheriah, A., Franz, M., Zhu, W.-J., and Rathaparkhi, A. 2000. IBM's statistical question answering system. In Proceedings of the TREC-9 Question Answering Track, Gaithersburg, Maryland.
2. Hovy, E., Gerber, L., Hermjakob, U., Junk, M., and Lin, C.-Y. 2000. Question answering in Webclopedia. In Proceedings of the TREC-9 Question Answering Track, Gaithersburg, Maryland.
3. Moldovan D., Pasca M., Harabagiu S., & Surdeanu M. 2002. Performance Issues and error Analysis in an Open-Domain Question Answering System. In Proceedings of the 40th Annual Meeting of ACL, Philadelphia, Pennsylvania.
4. Hildebrandt, W., Katz, B., & Lin, J. 2004. Answering definition questions with multiple knowledge sources. In Proceedings of the 2004 Human Language Technology Conference and the North American Chapter of the Association for Computational.
5. Radev, D. R., Qi, H., Zheng, Z., Blair-Goldensohn, S., Fan, Z. Z. W., and Prager, J. M. 2001. Mining the web for answers to natural language questions. In Proceedings of the International Conference on Knowledge Management (CIKM-2001), Atlanta, Georgia.
6. Hermjakob, U., Echihabi, A., and Marcu, D. 2002. Natural Language Based Reformulation Resource and Web Exploitation for Question Answering. In Proceeding of TREC-2002, Gaithersburg, Maryland.
7. Agichtein, E., Lawrence, S., and Gravano, L. Learning to find answers to questions on the Web. 2003. In ACM Transactions on Internet Technology (TOIT), 4(2):129-162.
8. Melamed, I. D. 1997. A Word-to-Word Model of Translational Equivalence. In Proceedings of the 35st Annual Meeting of ACL, Madrid, Spain.
9. Yi-Chia Wang, Jian-Cheng Wu, Tyne Liang, and Jason S. Chang. 2004. Using the Web as Corpus for Un-supervised Learning in Question Answering, Proceedings of Rocling 2004, Taiwan.

A Chunking Strategy Towards Unknown Word Detection in Chinese Word Segmentation

Zhou GuoDong

Institute for Infocomm Research, 21 Heng Mui Keng Terrace, Singapore 119613
zhougd@i2r.a-star.edu.sg

Abstract. This paper proposes a chunking strategy to detect unknown words in Chinese word segmentation. First, a raw sentence is pre-segmented into a sequence of word atoms [1] using a maximum matching algorithm. Then a chunking model is applied to detect unknown words by chunking one or more word atoms together according to the word formation patterns of the word atoms. In this paper, a discriminative Markov model, named Mutual Information Independence Model (MIIM), is adopted in chunking. Besides, a maximum entropy model is applied to integrate various types of contexts and resolve the data sparseness problem in MIIM. Moreover, an error-driven learning approach is proposed to learn useful contexts in the maximum entropy model. In this way, the number of contexts in the maximum entropy model can be significantly reduced without performance decrease. This makes it possible for further improving the performance by considering more various types of contexts. Evaluation on the PK and CTB corpora in the First SIGHAN Chinese word segmentation bakeoff shows that our chunking approach successfully detects about 80% of unknown words on both of the corpora and outperforms the best-reported systems by 8.1% and 7.1% in unknown word detection on them respectively.

1 Introduction

Prior to any linguistic analysis of Chinese text, Chinese word segmentation is the necessary first step and one of major bottlenecks in Chinese information processing since a Chinese sentence is written in a continuous string of characters without obvious separators (such as blanks) between the words. During the past two decades, this research has been a hot topic in Chinese information processing [1-10].

There exist two major problems in Chinese word segmentation: ambiguity resolution and unknown word detection. While n-gram modeling and/or word co-occurrence has been successfully applied to deal with the ambiguity problems [3, 5, 10, 12, 13], unknown word detection has become the major bottleneck in Chinese

[1] In this paper, word atoms refer to basic building units in words. For example, the word "计算机" (computer) consists of two word atoms: "计算"(computing) and "机"(machine). Generally, word atoms can either occur independently, e.g. "计算"(computing), or only become a part of a word, e.g. "机"(machine) in the word "计算机" (computer).

R. Dale et al. (Eds.): IJCNLP 2005, LNAI 3651, pp. 530 – 541, 2005.

word segmentation. Currently, almost all Chinese word segmentation systems rely on a word dictionary. The problem is that when the words stored in the dictionary are insufficient, the system's performance will be greatly deteriorated by the presence of words that are unknown to the system. Moreover, manual maintenance of a dictionary is very tedious and time consuming. It is therefore important for a Chinese word segmentation system to identify unknown words from the text automatically.

In literature, two categories of competing approaches are widely used to detect unknown words[2]: statistical approaches [5, 11, 12, 13, 14, 15] and rule-based approaches [5, 11, 14, 15]. Although rule-based approaches have the advantage of being simple, the complexity and domain dependency of how the unknown words are produced greatly reduce the efficiency of these approaches. On the other hand, statistical approaches have the advantage of being domain-independent [16]. It is interesting to note that many systems apply a hybrid approach [5, 11, 14, 15]. Regardless of the choice of different approaches, finding a way to automatically detect unknown words has become a crucial issue in Chinese word segmentation and Chinese information processing in general.

Input raw sentence: 张杰毕业自交通大学
MMA pre-segmentation: 张 杰 毕业 自 交通 大学 .
Unknown word detection: 张杰 毕业 自 交通大学 .
Zhang Jie graduate from JiaoTong University.

Fig. 1. MMA and unknown word detection by chunking: an example

This paper proposes a chunking strategy to cope with unknown words in Chinese word segmentation. First, a raw sentence is pre-segmented into a sequence of word atoms (i.e. single-character words and multi-character words) using a maximum matching algorithm (MMA)[3]. Then a chunking model is applied to detect unknown words by chunking one or more word atoms together according to the word formation patterns of the word atoms. Figure 1 gives an example. Here, the problem of unknown word detection is re-cast as chunking one or more word atoms together to form a new word and a discriminative Markov model, named Mutual Information Independence Model (MIIM), is adopted in chunking. Besides, a maximum entropy model is applied to integrate various types of contexts and resolve the data sparseness problem in MIIM. Moreover, an error-driven learning approach is proposed to learn useful

[2] Some systems [13,14] focus on proper names due to their importance in Chinese information processing.

[3] A typical MMA identifies all character sequences which are found in the word dictionary and marks them as words. These character sequences, which can be segmented in more than one way, are marked as ambiguous and a word unigram model is applied to choose the most likely segmentation sequence. The remaining sequences, i.e. those not found in the dictionary, are called fragments and segmented into single characters. In this way, each Chinese sentence is pre-segmented into a sequence of single-character words and multi-character words. For convenience, we call these single-character words and multi-character words in the output of the MMA algorithm as word atoms.

contexts in the maximum entropy model. In this way, the number of contexts in the maximum entropy model can be significantly reduced without performance decrease. This makes it possible for further improving the performance by considering more various types of contexts in the future. Evaluation on the PK and CTB corpora in the First SIGHAN Chinese word segmentation bakeoff shows that our chunking strategy performs best in unknown word detection on both of the corpora.

The rest of the paper is as follows: In Section 2, we will discuss in details about our chunking strategy in unknown word detection. Experimental results are given in Section 3. Finally, some remarks and conclusions are made in Section 4.

2 Unknown Word Detection by Chunking

In this section, we will first describe the chunking strategy in unknown word detection of Chinese word segmentation using a discriminative Markov model, called Mutual Information Independence Model (MIIM). Then a maximum entropy model is applied to integrate various types of contexts and resolve the data sparseness problem in MIIM. Finally, an error-driven learning approach is proposed to select useful contexts and reduce the context feature vector dimension.

2.1 Mutual Information Independence Model and Unknown Word Detection

Mutual Information Independence Model

In this paper, we use a discriminative Markov model, called Mutual Information Independence Model (MIIM) proposed by Zhou et al [17][4], in unknown word detection by chunking. MIIM is derived from a conditional probability model. Given an observation sequence $O_1^n = o_1 o_2 \cdots o_n$, the goal of a conditional probability model is to find a stochastic optimal state(tag) sequence $S_1^n = s_1 s_2 \cdots s_n$ that maximizes:

$$\log P(S_1^n \mid O_1^n) = \log P(S_1^n) + \log \frac{P(S_1^n, O_1^n)}{P(S_1^n) \cdot P(O_1^n)} \tag{1}$$

The second term in Equation (1) is the pair-wise mutual information (PMI) between S_1^n and O_1^n. In order to simplify the computation of this term, we assume a pair-wise mutual information independence (2):

$$PMI(S_1^n, O_1^n) = \sum_{i=1}^{n} PMI(s_i, O_1^n) \quad \text{or}$$

$$\log \frac{P(S_1^n, O_1^n)}{P(S_1^n) \cdot P(O_1^n)} = \sum_{i=1}^{n} \log \frac{P(s_i, O_1^n)}{P(s_i) \cdot P(O_1^n)} \tag{2}$$

[4] We have renamed the discriminative Markov model in [17] as the Mutual Information Independence Model according to the novel pair-wise mutual information independence assumption in the model. Another reason is to distinguish it from the traditional Hidden Markov Model [18] and avoid misleading.

That is, an individual state is only dependent on the observation sequence O_1^n and independent on other states in the state sequence S_1^n. This assumption is reasonable because the dependence among the states in the state sequence S_1^n has already been captured by the first term in Equation (1). Applying Equation (2) to Equation (1), we have Equation (3)[5]:

$$\log P(S_1^n \mid O_1^n) = \sum_{i=2}^{n} PMI(s_i, S_1^{i-1}) + \sum_{i=1}^{n} \log P(s_i \mid O_1^n) \tag{3}$$

We call the above model as shown in Equation (3) the Mutual Information Independence Model due to its pair-wise mutual information assumption as shown in Equation (2). The above model consists of two sub-models: the state transition model $\sum_{i=2}^{n} PMI(s_i, S_1^{i-1})$ as the first term in Equation (3) and the output model $\sum_{i=1}^{n} \log P(s_i \mid O_1^n)$ as the second term in Equation (3). Here, a variant of the Viterbi algorithm [19] in decoding the standard Hidden Markov Model (HMM) [18] is implemented to find the most likely state sequence by replacing the state transition model and the output model of the standard HMM with the state transition model and the output model of the MIIM, respectively.

Unknown Word Detection

For unknown word detection by chunking, a word (known word or unknown word) is regarded as a chunk of one or more word atoms and we have:

- $o_i =< p_i, w_i >$; w_i is the $i-th$ word atom in the sequence of word atoms $W_1^n = w_1 w_2 \cdots w_n$; p_i is the word formation pattern of the word atom w_i. Here p_i measures the word formation power of the word atom w_i and consists of:
  - o The percentage of w_i occurring as a whole word (round to 10%)
  - o The percentage of w_i occurring at the beginning of other words (round to 10%)
  - o The percentage of w_i occurring at the end of other words (round to 10%)
  - o The length of w_i
  - o The occurring frequency feature of w_i, which is mapped to max(log(Frequency), 9).
- s_i : the states are used to bracket and differentiate various types of words. In this way, Chinese unknown word detection can be regarded as a bracketing process while differentiation of different word types can help the bracketing process. s_i is structural and consists of three parts:

[5] Details about the derivation are omitted due to space limitation. Please see [17] for more.

- **Boundary Category (B):** it includes four values: {O, B, M, E}, where O means that current word atom is a whOle word and B/M/E means that current word atom is at the Beginning/in the Middle/at the End of a word.
- **Word Category (W):** It is used to denote the class of the word. In our system, words are classified into two types: pure Chinese word type and mixed word type (i.e. including English characters and Chinese digits/numbers/symbols).
- **Word Atom Formation Pattern (P):** Because of the limited number of boundary and word categories, the word atom formation pattern described above is added into the structural state to represent a more accurate state transition model in MIIM while keeping its output model.

Problem with Unknown Word Detection Using MIIM
From Equation (3), we can see that the state transition model of MIIM can be computed by using ngram modeling [20, 21, 22], where each tag is assumed to be dependent on the N-1 previous tags (e.g. 2). The problem with the above MIIM lies in the data sparseness problem raised by its output model: $\sum_{i=1}^{n} \log P(s_i \mid O_1^n)$. Ideally, we would have sufficient training data for every event whose conditional probability we wish to calculate. Unfortunately, there is rarely enough training data to compute accurate probabilities when decoding on new data. Generally, two smoothing approaches [21, 22, 23] are applied to resolve this problem: linear interpolation and back-off. However, these two approaches only work well when the number of different information sources is very limited. When a few features and/or a long context are considered, the number of different information sources is exponential. This makes smoothing approaches inappropriate in our system. In this paper, the maximum entropy model [24] is proposed to integrate various context information sources and resolve the data sparseness problem in our system. The reason that we choose the maximum entropy model for this purpose is that it represents the state-of–the-art in the machine learning research community and there are good implementations of the algorithm available. Here, we use the open NLP maximum entropy package[6] in our system.

2.2 Maximum Entropy

The maximum entropy model is a probability distribution estimation technique widely used in recent years for natural language processing tasks. The principle of the maximum entropy model in estimating probabilities is to include as much information as is known from the data while making no additional assumptions. The maximum entropy model returns the probability distribution that satisfies the above property with the highest entropy. Formally, the decision function of the maximum entropy model can be represented as:

$$P(o,h) = \frac{1}{Z(h)} \prod_{j=1}^{k} \alpha_j^{f_j(h,o)} \tag{4}$$

[6] http://maxent.sourceforge.net

where o is the outcome, h is the history (context feature vector in this paper), $Z(h)$ is a normalization function, $\{f_1, f_2, ..., f_k\}$ are feature functions and $\{\alpha_1, \alpha_2, \ldots, \alpha_k\}$ are the model parameters. Each model parameter corresponds to exactly one feature and can be viewed as a "weight" for that feature. All features used in the maximum entropy model are binary, e.g.

$$f_j(h,o) = \begin{cases} 1, & \text{if} \quad o = IndependentWord, \quad CurrentWordAtom = \text{我们}\,(we); \\ 0, & otherwise. \end{cases} \tag{5}$$

In order to reliably estimate $P(s_i \mid O_1^n)$ in the output model of MIIM using the maximum entropy model, various context information sources are included in the context feature vector:

- p_i: current word atom formation pattern
- $p_{i-1}p_i$: previous word atom formation pattern and current word atom formation pattern
- $p_i p_{i+1}$: current word atom formation pattern and next word atom formation pattern
- $p_i w_i$: current word atom formation pattern and current word atom
- $p_{i-1}w_{i-1}p_i$: previous word atom formation pattern, previous word atom and current word atom formation pattern
- $p_i p_{i+1} w_{i+1}$: current word atom formation pattern, next word atom formation pattern and next word atom
- $p_{i-1}p_i w_i$: previous word atom formation pattern, current word atom formation pattern and current word atom
- $p_i w_i p_{i+1}$: current word atom formation pattern, current word atom and next word atom formation pattern
- $p_{i-1}w_{i-1}p_i w_i$: previous word atom formation pattern, previous word atom, current word atom formation pattern and current word atom
- $p_i w_i p_{i+1} w_{i+1}$: current word atom formation pattern, current word atom, next word atom formation pattern and next word atom

However, there exists a problem when we include above various context information in the maximum entropy model: the context feature vector dimension easily becomes too large for the model to handle. One easy solution to this problem is to only keep those frequently occurring contexts in the model. Although this frequency filtering approach is simple, many useful contexts may not occur frequently and be filtered out while those kept may not be useful. To resolve this problem, we propose an alternative error-driven learning approach to only keep useful contexts in the model.

2.3 Context Feature Selection Using Error-Driven Learning

Here, we propose an error-driven learning approach to examine the effectiveness of various contexts and select useful contexts to reduce the size of the context feature vector used in the maximum entropy model for estimating $P(s_i \mid O_1^n)$ in the output model of MIIM. This makes it possible to further improve the performance by incorporating more various types of contexts in the future.

Assume Φ is the container for useful contexts. Given a set of existing useful contexts Φ and a set of new contexts $\Delta\Phi$, the effectiveness of a new context $C_i \in \Delta\Phi$, $E(\Phi, C_i)$, is measured by the C_i-related reduction in errors which results from adding the new context set $\Delta\Phi$ to the useful context set Φ:

$$E(\Phi, C_i) = \#Error(\Phi, C_i) - \#Error(\Phi + \Delta\Phi, C_i) \tag{6}$$

Here, $\#Error(\Phi, C_i)$ is the number of C_i-related chunking errors before $\Delta\Phi$ is added to Φ and $\#Error(\Phi + \Delta\Phi, C_i)$ is the number of C_i-related chunking errors after $\Delta\Phi$ is added to Φ. That is, $E(\Phi, C_i)$ is the number of the chunking error corrections made on the context $C_i \in \Delta\Phi$ when $\Delta\Phi$ is added to Φ. If $E(\Phi, C_i) > 0$, we declare that the new context C_i is a useful context and should be added to Φ. Otherwise, the new context C_i is considered useless and discarded.

Given the above error-driven learning approach, we initialize $\Phi = \{p_i\}$ (i.e. we assume all the current word atom formation patterns are useful contexts) and choose one of the other context types as the new context set $\Delta\Phi$, e.g. $\Phi = \{p_i w_i\}$. Then, we can train two MIIMs with different output models using Φ and $\Phi + \Delta\Phi$ respectively. Moreover, useful contexts are learnt on the training data in a two-fold way. For each fold, two MIIMs are trained on 50% of the training data and for each new context C_i in $\Delta\Phi$, evaluate its effectiveness $E(\Phi, C_i)$ on the remaining 50% of the training data according to the context effectiveness measure as shown in Equation (6). If $E(\Phi, C_i) > 0$, C_i is marked as a useful context and added to Φ. In this way, all the useful contexts in $\Delta\Phi$ are incorporated into the useful context set Φ. Similarly, we can include useful contexts of other context types into the useful context set Φ one by one. In this paper, various types of contexts are learnt one by one in the exact same order as shown in Section 2.2. Finally, since different types of contexts may have cross-effects, the above process is iterated with the renewed useful context set Φ until very few useful contexts can be found at each loop. Our experiments show that iteration converges within four loops.

3 Experimental Results

All of our experiments are evaluated on the PK and CTB benchmark corpora used in the First SIGHAN Chinese word segmentation bakeoff[7] with the closed configuration. That is, only the training data from the particular corpus is used during training. For unknown word detection, the chunking training data is derived by using the same Maximum Matching Algorithm (MMA) to segment each word in the original training data as a chunk of word atoms. This is done in a two-fold way. For each fold, the

[7] http://www.sighan.org/bakeoff2003/

MMA is trained on 50% of the original training data and then used to segment the remaining 50% of the original training data. Then the MIIM is used to train a chunking model for unknown word detection on the chunking training data. Table 1 shows the details of the two corpora. Here, OOV is defined as the percentage of words in the test corpus not occurring in the training corpus and indicates the out-of-vocabulary rate in the test corpus.

Table 1. Statistics of the corpora used in our evaluation

Corpus	Abbreviation	OOV	Training Data	Test Data
Beijing University	PK	6.9%	1100K words	17K words
UPENN Chinese Treebank	CTB	18.1%	250K words	40K words

Table 2 shows the detailed performance of our system in unknown word detection and Chinese word segmentation as a whole using the standard scoring script[8] on the test data. In this and subsequent tables, various evaluation measures are provided: precision (P), recall (R), F-measure, recall on out-of-vocabulary words (R_{OOV}) and recall on in-vocabulary words (R_{IV}). It shows that our system achieves precision/recall/F-measure of 93.5%/96.1%/94.8 and 90.5%/90.1%/90.3 on the PK and CTB corpora respectively. Especially, our chunking approach can successfully detect 80.5% and 77.6% of unknown words on the PK and CTB corpora respectively.

Table 2. Detailed performance of our system on the 1st SIGHAN Chinese word segmentation benchmark data

Corpus	P	R	F	R_{OOV}	R_{IV}
PK	93.5	96.1	94.8	80.5	97.3
CTB	90.5	90.1	90.3	77.6	92.9

Table 3 and Table 4 compare our system with other best-reported systems on the PK and CTB corpora respectively. Table 3 shows that our chunking approach in unknown word detection outperforms others by more than 8% on the PK corpus. It also shows that our system performs comparably with the best reported systems on the PK corpus when the out-of-vocabulary rate is moderate(6.9%). Our performance in Chinese word segmentation as a whole is somewhat pulled down by the lower performance in recalling in-vocabulary words. This may be due to the preference of our chunking strategy in detecting unknown words by wrongly combining some of in-vocabulary words into unknown words. Such preference may cause negative effect in Chinese word segmentation as a whole when the gain in unknown word detection fails to compensate the loss in wrongly combining some of in-vocabulary words into unknown words. This happens when the out-of-vocabulary rate is not high, e.g. on the

[8] http://www.sighan.org/bakeoff2003/score

PK corpus. Table 4 shows that our chunking approach in unknown word detection outperforms others by more than 7% on the CTB corpus. It also shows that our system outperforms the other best-reported systems by more than 2% in Chinese word segmentation as a whole on the CTB corpus. This is largely due to the huge gain in unknown word detection when the out-of-vocabulary rate is high (e.g. 18.1% in the CTB corpus), even though our system performs worse on recalling in-vocabulary words than others. Evaluation on both the PK and CTB corpora shows that our chunking approach can successfully detect about 80% of unknown words on corpora with a large range of the out-of-vocabulary rates. This suggests the powerfulness of using various word formation patterns of word atoms in detecting unknown words. This also demonstrates the effectiveness and robustness of our chunking approach in unknown word detection of Chinese word segmentation and its portability to different genres.

Table 3. Comparison of our system with other best-reported systems on the PK corpus

Corpus	P	R	F	R_{OOV}	R_{IV}
Ours	93.5	96.1	94.8	80.5	97.3
Zhang et al [25]	94.0	96.2	95.1	72.4	97.9
Wu [26]	93.8	95.5	94.7	68.0	97.6
Chen [27]	93.8	95.5	94.6	64.7	97.7

Table 4. Comparison of our system with other best-reported systems on the CTB corpus

Corpus	P	R	F	R_{OOV}	R_{IV}
Ours	90.5	90.1	90.3	77.6	92.9
Zhang et al [25]	87.5	88.6	88.1	70.5	92.7
Duan et al [28]	85.6	89.2	87.4	64.4	94.7

Finally, Table 5 and Table 6 compare our error-driven learning approach with the frequency filtering approach in learning useful contexts for the output model of MIIM on the PK and CTB corpora respectively. Due to memory limitation, at most 400K useful contexts are considered in the frequency filtering approach. First, they show that the error-driven learning approach is much more effective than the simple frequency filtering approach. With the same number of useful contexts, the error-driven learning approach outperforms the frequency filtering approach by 7.8%/0.6% and 5.5%/0.8% in R_{OOV} (unknown word detection)/F-measure(Chinese word segmentation as a whole) on the PK and CTB corpora respectively. Moreover, the error-driven learning approach slightly outperforms the frequency filtering approach with the best configuration of 2.5 and 3.5 times of useful contexts. Second, they show that increasing the number of frequently occurring contexts using the frequency filtering approach may not increase the performance. This may be due to that some of frequently occurring contexts are noisy or useless and including them may have negative effect. Third, they show that the error-driven learning approach is effective in learning useful contexts by reducing 96-98% of possible contexts. Finally, the figures inside parentheses show the number of useful patterns shared between the error-driven learning approach and the frequency filtering approach. They show that about 40-50% of useful contexts selected using the error-driven learning approach do not occur frequently in the useful contexts selected using the frequency filtering approach.

Table 5. Comparison of the error-driven learning approach with the frequency filtering approach in learning useful contexts for the output model of MIIM on the PK corpus (Total number of possible contexts: 4836K)

Approach	#useful contexts	F	R_{OOV}	R_{IV}
Error-Driven Learning	98K	94.8	80.5	97.3
Frequency Filtering	98K (63K)	94.2	72.7	97.4
Frequency Filtering (best performance)	250K (90K)	94.7	80.2	97.3
Frequency Filtering	400K (94K)	94.6	79.1	97.1

Table 6. Comparison of the error-driven learning approach with the frequency filtering approach in learning useful contexts for the output model of MIIM on the CTB corpus (Total number of possible contexts: 1038K)

Approach	#useful contexts	F	R_{OOV}	R_{IV}
Error-Driven Learning	43K	90.3	77.6	92.9
Frequency Filtering	43K (21K)	89.5	72.1	92.8
Frequency Filtering (best performance)	150K	90.1	76.1	93.0
Frequency Filtering	400K (40K)	89.9	75.8	92.9

4 Conclusion

In this paper, a chunking strategy is presented to detect unknown words in Chinese word segmentation by chunking one or more word atoms together according to the various word formation patterns of the word atoms. Besides, a maximum entropy model is applied to integrate various types of contexts and resolve the data sparseness problem in our strategy. Finally, an error-driven learning approach is proposed to learn useful contexts in the maximum entropy model. In this way, the number of contexts in the maximum entropy model can be significantly reduced without performance decrease. This makes it possible for further improving the performance by considering more various types of contexts. Evaluation on the PK and CTB corpora in the First SIGHAN Chinese word segmentation bakeoff shows that our chunking strategy can detect about 80% of unknown words on both of the corpora and outperforms the best-reported systems by 8.1% and 7.1% in unknown word detection on them respectively. While our Chinese word segmentation system with chunking-based unknown word detection performs comparably with the best systems on the PK corpus when the out-of-vocabulary rate is moderate(6.9%), our system significantly outperforms others by more than 2% when the out-of-vocabulary rate is high(18.1%). This demonstrates the effectiveness and robustness of our chunking strategy in unknown word detection of Chinese word segmentation and its portability to different genres.

References

1. Jie CY, Liu Y and Liang NY. (1989). On methods of Chinese automatic segmentation, *Journal of Chinese Information Processing,* 3(1):1-9.
2. Li KC, Liu KY and Zhang YK. (1988). Segmenting Chinese word and processing different meanings structure, *Journal of Chinese Information Processing,* 2(3):27-33.
3. Liang NY, (1990). The knowledge of Chinese word segmentation, *Journal of Chinese Information Processing,* 4(2):29-33.
4. Lua KT, (1990). From character to word - An application of information theory, *Computer Processing of Chinese & Oriental Languages,* 4(4):304-313.
5. Lua KT and Gan GW. (1994). An application of information theory in Chinese word segmentation. *Computer Processing of Chinese & Oriental Languages*, 8(1):115-124.
6. Wang YC, SU HJ and Mo Y. (1990). Automatic processing of Chinese words. *Journal of Chinese Information Processing.* 4(4):1-11.
7. Wu JM and Tseng G. (1993). Chinese text segmentation for text retrieval: achievements and problems. *Journal of the American Society for Information Science.* 44(9):532-542.
8. Xu H, He KK and Sun B. (1991) The implementation of a written Chinese automatic segmentation expert system, *Journal of Chinese Information Processing,* 5(3):38-47.
9. Yao TS, Zhang GP and Wu YM. (1990). A rule-based Chinese automatic segmentation system, *Journal of Chinese Information Processing,* 4(1):37-43.
10. Yeh CL and Lee HJ. (1995). Rule-based word identification for Mandarin Chinese sentences - A unification approach, *Computer Processing of Chinese & Oriental Languages,* 9(2):97-118.
11. Nie JY, Jin WY and Marie-Louise Hannan. (1997). A hybrid approach to unknown word detection and segmentation of Chinese, *Chinese Processing of Chinese and Oriental Languages*, 11(4): pp326-335.
12. Tung CH and Lee HJ. (1994). Identification of unknown word from a corpus, *computer Processing of Chinese & Oriental Languages,* 8(Supplement):131-146.
13. Chang JS et al. (1994). A multi-corpus approach to recognition of proper names in Chinese Text, *Computer Processing of Chinese & Oriental Languages,* 8(1):75-86
14. Sun MS, Huang CN, Gao HY and Fang J. (1994). Identifying Chinese Names In Unrestricted Texts, *Communications of Chinese and Oriental Languages Information Processing Society*, 4(2):113-122.
15. Zhou GD and Lua KT, (1997). Detection of Unknown Chinese Words Using a Hybrid Approach, *Computer Processing of Chinese & Oriental Language*, 11(1):63-75.
16. Eugene Charniak, *Statistical language learning,* The MIT Press, ISBN 0-262-03216-3
17. Zhou GDong and Su J. (2002). Named Entity Recognition Using a HMM-based Chunk Tagger, *Proceedings of the Conference on Annual Meeting for Computational Linguistics (ACL'2002).* 473-480, Philadelphia.

18. Rabiner L. 1989. A Tutorial on Hidden Markov Models and Selected Applications in Speech Recognition. *IEEE 77(*2), pages257-285.
19. Viterbi A.J. 1967. Error Bounds for Convolutional Codes and an Asymptotically Optimum Decoding Algorithm. *IEEE Transactions on Information Theory,* IT 13(2), 260-269.
20. Gale W.A. and Sampson G. 1995. Good-Turing frequency estimation without tears. *Journal of Quantitative Linguistics*. 2:217-237.
21. Jelinek F. (1989). Self-Organized Language Modeling for Speech Recognition. In Alex Waibel and Kai-Fu Lee(Editors). *Readings in Speech Recognitiopn*. Morgan Kaufmann. 450-506.
22. Katz S.M. (1987). Estimation of Probabilities from Sparse Data for the Language Model Component of a Speech Recognizer. *IEEE Transactions on Acoustics. Speech and Signal Processing*. 35: 400-401.
23. Chen and Goodman. (1996). An Empirical Study of Smoothing Technniques for Language Modeling. In *Proceedings of the 34th Annual Meeting of the Association of Computational Linguistics (ACL'1996)*. pp310-318. Santa Cruz, California, USA.
24. Ratnaparkhi A. (1996). A Maximum Entropy Model for Part-of-Speech Tagging. *Proceedings of the Conference on Empirical Methods in Natural Language Processing.*, 133-142.
25. Zhang HP, Yu HK, Xiong DY and Liu Q. (2003). HHMM-based Chinese Lexical Analyzer ICTCLAS. *Proceedings of 2nd SIGHAN Workshop on Chinese Language Processing*. 184-187. Sapporo, Japan.
26. Wu AD. (2003). Chinese Word Segmentation in MSR-NLP. *Proceedings of 2nd SIGHAN Workshop on Chinese Language Processing*. 172-175. Sapporo, Japan.
27. Chen AT. (2003). Chinese Word Segmentation Using Minimal Linguistic Knowledge. *Proceedings of 2nd SIGHAN Workshop on Chinese Language Processing.* 148-151. Sapporo, Japan.
28. Duan HM, Bai XJ, Chang BB and Yu SW. (2003). Chinese Word Segmentation at Peking University. *Proceedings of 2nd SIGHAN Workshop on Chinese Language Processing*. 152-155. Sapporo, Japan.

A Lexicon-Constrained Character Model for Chinese Morphological Analysis

Yao Meng, Hao Yu, and Fumihito Nishino

Fujitsu R&D Center Co., Ltd, Room B1003, Eagle Run Plaza, No. 26 Xiaoyun Road, Chaoyang District, Bejing, 100016, P. R. China
{Mengyao, Yu, Nishino}@frdc.fujitsu.com

Abstract. This paper proposes a lexicon-constrained character model that combines both word and character features to solve complicated issues in Chinese morphological analysis. A Chinese character-based model constrained by a lexicon is built to acquire word building rules. Each character in a Chinese sentence is assigned a tag by the proposed model. The word segmentation and part-of-speech tagging results are then generated based on the character tags. The proposed method solves such problems as unknown word identification, data sparseness, and estimation bias in an integrated, unified framework. Preliminary experiments indicate that the proposed method outperforms the best SIGHAN word segmentation systems in the open track on 3 out of the 4 test corpora. Additionally, our method can be conveniently integrated with any other Chinese morphological systems as a post-processing module leading to significant improvement in performance.

1 Introduction

Chinese morphological analysis is a fundamental problem that has been studied extensively [1], [2], [3], [4], [5], [6], [7], [8]. Researchers make use of word or character features to cope with this problem. However, neither of them seems completely satisfactory.

In general, a simple word-based approach can achieve about 90% accuracy for segmentation with a medium-size dictionary. However, since no dictionary includes every Chinese word, the unknown word (or Out Of Vocabulary, OOV) problem [9], [10] can severely affect the performance of word-based approaches. Furthermore, word-based models have an estimation bias when faced with segmentation candidates with different numbers of words. For example, in the standard hidden Markov model, the best result, $T^* = \underset{T}{\operatorname{argmax}}\, p(T \mid W) = \underset{T}{\operatorname{argmax}} \prod_{i=1}^{n} p(w_i \mid t_i) p(t_i \mid t_1..t_{i-1})$, is related to the number of the words in the segmentation candidates. As such, a candidate with fewer words is preferred over those with more words in the selection process. Therefore, most word-based models are likely to fail when a combinational ambiguity[1] sequence is separated into multiple words.

[1] A typical segmentation ambiguity, it refers to a situation in which the same Chinese sequence may be one word or several words in different contexts.

R. Dale et al. (Eds.): IJCNLP 2005, LNAI 3651, pp. 542 – 552, 2005.

Compared with Chinese words, Chinese characters are relatively less unambiguous. The Chinese character set is very limited. Therefore, unknown characters occur rarely in a sentence. The grammatical advantages of characters have inspired researchers to adopt character features in Chinese morphology and parsing [5], [6], [11], [12]. However, it is difficult to incorporate necessary word features, such as the form of a Chinese word and its fixed part-of-speech tags, in most character-based approaches. For this reason, character-based approaches have not achieved satisfactory performance in large-scale open tests.

In this paper, we propose a lexicon-constrained character model to combine the merits of both approaches. We explore how to capture the Chinese word building rules using a statistical method, which reflects the regularities in the word formation process. First, a character hidden Markov method assigns the candidate tags to each character. Next, a large-size word list combined with linguistic information is used to filter out erroneous candidates. Finally, segmentation and part-of-speech tagging for the sentence are provided based on the character tags.

The proposed model solves the problems of unknown word detection, word segmentation and part-of-speech tagging using both word and character features. Additionally, our module is a post-processing module, which can be coupled to any existing Chinese morphological system; and it can readily recall some of the unknown words omitted by the system, and as a result, significantly improves the overall performance. Evaluations of the proposed system on SIGHAN open test sets indicate that our method outperforms the best bakeoff results on 3 test sets, and ranks 2nd in the 4th test set [9].

2 A Lexicon-Constrained Character Model for Chinese Morphology

2.1 An Elementary Model to Describe Chinese Word Building Rules

It is recognized that there are some regularities in the process of forming words from Chinese characters. This in general can be captured by word building rules. In this paper, we explore a statistical model to acquire such rules. The following are some definitions used in the proposed model.

[Def. 1] character position feature

We use four notations to denote the position of a character in a Chinese word. 'F' means the first character of the word, 'L' the last character, 'M' is a character within it and 'S' the word itself.

[Def. 2] character tag set

It is the product of the set of character position features and the set of part-of-speech tags.

Character tag set $=\{xy | x \in word$ POS $set, y \in \{S, F, M, L\}\}$, where, x denotes one part-of-speech (POS) tag and y a character position feature. Together they are used to define the rules of Chinese word formation.

[Def. 3] character tagging

Given a Chinese sentence; character tagging is the process for assigning a character tag to each character in the sentence.

Word building rules are acquired based on the relation between the character and the corresponding character tag. Word segmentation and part-of-speech tagging can be achieved easily based on the result of character tagging. For example, a character with '*x*S' is a single character word with the part-of-speech tag '*x*'; a character sequence starting with '*x*F' and ending with '*x*L' is a multiple character word with the part-of-speech tag '*x*'.

The elementary model adopts the character bi-gram hidden Markov model. In hidden Markov model, given the sentence, $s : c_1 c_2 ... c_{n-1} c_n$, and character tagging result $t : xy_1 xy_2 ... xy_{n-1} xy_n$, the probability of result t of s is estimated as:

$$p(t \mid s) = \prod_{i=1,n} p(xy_i \mid xy_{i-2}\, xy_{i-1}) \times p(c_i \mid xy_i) \tag{1}$$

The best character tagging result for the sentences is given by equation (2):

$$t^* = \arg\max_t \prod_{i=1,n} p(xy_i \mid xy_{i-2} xy_{i-1}) \times p(c_i \mid xy_i) \tag{2}$$

We used the People's Daily Corpus of 1998 [13] to train this model. Also we adopted a 100,000-word dictionary listing all valid part-of-speech tags for each Chinese word in the training phase to solve the data sparseness problem. The training data are converted into character tagging data through the following steps: a single character word with '*x*' is converted into the character marked with tag '*x*S'; a two-character word with '*x*' is converted into a first character with '*x*F' and a second character with '*x*L'; a word with more than two characters with '*x*' are converted into a first character with '*x*F', middle characters with '*x*M' and last character with '*x*L'. We adopt the POS tag set from the People's Daily Corpus, which consists of 46 tags. Taking into account of the four position features, the final character tag set is comprised of 184 tags.

The emitted probability and transition probability of the model are estimated by the maximum likelihood method. The emitted probability is counted by the training Corpus and the dictionary, where the Chinese words in the dictionary are counted one time. The transition probability is trained from the training Corpus only.

2.2 An Improved Character-Based Model Using Lexicon Constraints

We tested the above model based on the SIGHAN open test set [9]. The average precision for word segmentation was more than 88%. This means that most of the word building rules in Chinese have been obtained by the elementary model. However, the performance was relatively inferior to other word segmentation systems. It indicated that the model needed more features to learn word building rules. In error analysis, we found that the elementary model was so flexible that it produced many pseudo-words and invalid part-of-speech tags. In practice, a Chinese word is a stable sequence of Chinese characters, whose formation and part-of-speech tags are fixed by long-term usage. It seemed that only character position and meaning cannot describe a word building rule effectively.

We also observed that word segmentation systems based on a simple dictionary matching algorithm and a few linguistic rules could achieve about 90% accuracy [14]. This suggested that a lexicon may have contribution to word building rules. Thus, we tried to incorporate a lexicon to the model to improve the performance.

The major errors in the elementary model were pseudo words and invalid part-of-speech (POS) tags. We proposed two constraints based on the lexicon to deal with these errors:

1. If a possible word produced from the elementary model is in the word-dictionary, the character tag of the characters forming this word should be consistent with the part-of-speech tag of the word in the dictionary.
2. If a possible word produced is not in the dictionary, it must include one or more single characters, and none of which may be subsumed by any word in the dictionary in the current context.

The first constraint eliminates invalid character tags. For example, the character '明' has six character tags: '*aF*' (first in adjective) , '*dF*' (first in adverb), '*nF*' (first in noun), '*nrF*' (first in person name), '*tF*' (first in time), and '*vF*' (first in verb). The character '天' has five character tags: '*dL*', '*nL*', '*nrL*', '*tL*', and '*vL*'. The combination of the two characters produces the possible word '明天', which includes five possible word part-of-speech tags: '*d*', '*n*', '*nr*', '*t*', and '*v*' based on these character tags. But '明天' is a word in the dictionary, which only has two valid part-of-speech tags, namely, 'time' and 'person name'. Obviously, the part-of-speech tags: '*d*', '*n*' and '*v*' of '明天' are invalid. Accordingly, the tags '*aF*', '*dF*', '*nF*' , '*vF*' on '明' and the tags '*dL*', '*nL*', '*vL*' on '天' are also invalid. So they should be pruned from the candidates of the character tagging.

The second constraint prunes pseudo words in the elementary model. Many studies in dictionary-based segmentation treat unknown words as sequences of single characters [1], [14]. The second constraint ensures that the new word produced by the elementary model must have one or more 'unattached' single characters (not subsumed by any other words). For example, the sequence '程序错误' (program error) will combine the pseudo word '序错' because of the tag '*nF*' on '序' and the tag '*nL*' on '错'. The second constraint will prune '序错' since '程序' (program) and '错误' (error) are already in the dictionary and there is no "unattached" single character in it. Accordingly, the tag '*nF*' on '序' and the tag '*nL*' on '错' will be deleted from the candidates of character tagging.

The following experiments show the lexicon-based constraints are very effective in eliminating error cases. The elementary model faces an average of 9.3 character tags for each character. The constraints will prune 70% of these error tags from it. As a result, the performance of character tagging is improved.

It is worth noting that the lexicon in the elementary model cannot distort the probability of the character tagging results in the model. The pruned cases are invalid cases which cannot occur in the training data because all the words and POS tags in the training data are valid. Thus, the model built from the training data is not affected by the pruning process.

2.3 Case Study

In this subsection, we illustrate the advantages of the proposed method for Chinese morphology with an example.

Example: 小明明天将就程序错误进行分析
(Xiaoming will analyze the program errors tomorrow).

Where, '*小明*' is an unknown word (person name), and the sequence '*将就*' is a combinational ambiguity (either '*将就*' (put up with) or '*将*+ '*就*' (will)). Here is how our approach works.

Step 1: List all the character tags for each character. Figure 1 shows the character tags in the sequence '*小明明天*'.

小	aF	dF	nF	nrF	nM	nrM	nsM	qM	vM	aL	dL	vL	aS
明	aF	dF	nF	nrF	vF	tF	nM	lM	tM	aL	dL	nrL	aS
明	aF	dF	nF	nrF	vF	tF	nM	lM	tM	aL	dL	nrL	aS
天	nF	tF	nrM	dL	nL	nrL	tL	vL					

Fig. 1. Candidates for the sequence '小明明天'

In this step we are able to find possible unknown words based on character position features. For example, the character tags in '*小明明天*' combine four possible unknown words: '*小明*', '*小明明*', '***明明天***', and '*小明明天*'.

Step 2: Prune the invalid candidates using constraints.

The first constraint prunes some invalid character tags. For example, '*明明*' can be either an adverb (d) or a personal name (nr); '*明天*' is a time (t) word. The other part-of-speech tags of these two words will be deleted. With the second constraint, we can delete '*明明天*' because '*明明*' and '*明天*' are words in the dictionary. However, '*小明*', '*小明明*', and '*小明明天*' will be kept because '*小*' is a "unattached" single character. The remaining candidates are shown in figure 2.

小	aF	dF	nF	nrF	nM	nrM	nsM	qM	vM	aL	dL	vL	aS
明		dF		nrF			nM	lM	tM				aS
明						tF	nM	lM	tM		dL	nrL	aS
天	nF	tF	nrM			nrL	tL						

Fig. 2. Remaining Candidates for the sequence '小明明天'

Step 3: Choose the best character tagging result based on the proposed character hidden Markov model.

The best character tagging result is chosen using equation 2 in Section 2.1. The ambiguities in segmentation and word POS tagging are solved in the character tagging process.

Consider the combinational ambiguity '*将就*' in the following 2 candidates:

Candidate 1: '*小明/nr 明天/t 将/d 就/d 程序/n 错误/n 进行/v 分析/v*'
Candidate 2: '*小明/nr 明天/t 将就/v 程序/n 错误/n 进行/v 分析/v*'

In word-based linear model, the erroneous candidate 2 will be prior to the correct candidate 1 since the model counts 9 nodes in candidate 1 but 8 nodes in candidate 2. However, there is no such bias in the character model because the number of characters does not change. The combinational ambiguity '*将就*' will be denoted as '*将/dS 就/dS*' or '*将/vF 就/vL*'. The number of nodes in all candidates of character tagging is the same.

At last, the correct result '小/*nr*F 明/*nr*L 明/*t*F 天/*t*L 将/*dS* 就/*dS*程/*n*F 序/*n*L 错/*n*F 误/*n*L 进/*v*F 行/*v*L 分/*v*F 析/*v*L' is selected, and the corresponding morphological result is: '小明/*nr* 明天/*t* 将/*d* 就/*d* 程序/*n* 错误/*n* 进行/*v* 分析/*v* '.

The above steps show the proposed approach solves the various issues related to Chinese morphology by a concise character tagging process where word building is revealed.

3 Experiments and Discussion

We evaluated the proposed character method using the SIGHAN Backoff data, i.e. the one-month People's Daily Corpus of 1998, and the first version of Penn Chinese Treebank [15]. We compared our approach against two state-of-the-art systems: one is based on a bi-gram word segmentation model [7], and the other based on a word-based hidden Markov model [3]. For simplicity, we only considered three kinds of unknown words (personal name, location name, and organization name) in the all methods.

The same corpus and word-dictionary were used to train the above three systems. The training data set was the 5-month People's Daily Corpus of 1998, which contained approximately 6,300,000 words and 46 word part-of-speech tags. The system dictionary contained 100,000 words and the valid part-of-speech tag(s) of each word. On average, there were 1.3 part-of-speech tags for a word in the dictionary.

In the following, chr-HMM refers to the proposed elementary model; chr-HMM+Dic refers to the character model improved by integrating linguistic information. W-Bigram is the word-based bi-gram system, and W-HMM is the word-based hidden Markov system.

3.1 Morphological Experimental Results

We examined the performance of our model in comparison against W-Bigram and W-HMM. Table 1 compares the segmentation performance of our model against that of other models. Table 2 shows the accuracy in unknown word identification. Table 3 illustrates the performance of the part-of-speech tagging. The experiments in Table 1 and Table 2 were examined using the SIGHAN open test corpora. The experiments in Table 3 were performed again on the one-month People's Daily Corpus (PD corpus) and 4,000 sentences in the Penn Chinese Treebank (Penn CTB). We only examined 4 major word categories in the Penn Chinese Treebank due to inconsistency in the part-of-speech tag sets between the two corpora. The 4 major word categories were: noun (shown as NN, NR in Penn CTB; n, nr, ns, nz in PD corpus), verb (VV in Penn CTB; v, vd, vn in PD corpus), adjective (JJ in Penn CTB; a, ad, an in PD corpus) and adverb (AD in Penn CTB; d in PD corpus).

Segmentation and word POS tagging performance is measured in precision (P%), recall (R%) and F-score (F). Unknown words (NW) are those words not found in our word-dictionary, which include named entities and other new words. The unknown word rate (NW-Rate), the precision on unknown words (NW-Precision) and recall on total unknown words (NW-Recall) are given by:

$$\text{NW-Rate}=\frac{\text{\# of unknown words}}{\text{total \# of NW identified}} \qquad \text{NW-Precision}=\frac{\text{\# of valid unknown words}}{\text{total \# of NW identified}}$$

$$\text{NW-Recall}=\frac{\text{\# of valid unknown word}}{\text{total \# of NW in testing data}}$$

Table 1 shows that the above three systems achieve similar performances on the PK testing corpus. All of them were trained by the People's Daily corpus. For this reason, their performances were similar when the testing data had similar styles. But for other texts, the proposed character model performed much better than the word-based models in both recall and precision. This indicated that our approach performed better for unseen data.

Table 2 shows that our method for unknown word identification also outperforms the word-based method. We notice that word-based approaches and character-based approaches have similar precision on unknown word identification, however word-based approaches have much lower recall than character-based ones. The main reason for this is that word-based systems focus only on unknown words with proper word structures, but cannot recognize newly generated words, rare words, and other new words unlisted in the dictionary. A very high proportion of these types of unknown word in the SIGHAN testing data affects the recall of the word-based methods on unknown words. The experiments reveal that our method could effectively identify all kinds of new words. This is because our model has defined word building rules for all kinds of words.

Without a widely recognized testing standard, it is very hard to evaluate the performance on part-of-speech tagging. The results in Penn Chinese Treebank was better than that in the People's Daily Corpus since we examined all 42 POS tags in the People's Daily Corpus, but we only tested four major POS tags in Penn Chinese Treebank. Our approach is better than the word-based method for two test data sets. However, we could not conclude that our method was superior to the word-based method because of the limited testing approaches and testing data. A thorough empirical comparison among different approaches should be investigated in the future.

Table 1. Comparison of word segmentation based on SIGHAN open test sets

	PK		CTB		HK		AS	
	R%/ P%	F	R%/ P%	F	R%/ P%	F	R%/ P%	F
Chr-HMM	91.9/91.8	91.8	86.9/87.3	87.1	87.7/86.7	87.2	89.9/89.1	89.5
Chr-HMM+Dic	**95.9/96.7**	**96.3**	**92.7/93.5**	**93.1**	**91.1/91.9**	**91.5**	**92.3/93.9**	**93.1**
W-Bigram	94.7/95.4	95.1	87.4/86.8	87.1	88.7/83.7	86.3	87.9/85.1	86.5
W-HMM	94.6/95.1	94.9	88.6/89.2	88.9	90.7/89.1	89.9	90.7/87.2	89.0
Rank 1 in SIG	96.3/95.6	96.0	91.6/90.7	91.2	95.8/95.4	95.6	91.5/89.4	90.5
Rank 2 in SIG	96.3/94.3	95.3	91.1/89.1	90.1	90.9/86.3	88.6	89.2/85.3	87.3

Table 2. Accuracy of unknown word identification for SIGHAN open test sets

	PK			CTB			HK			AS		
Chr-HMM	UWR%	P%	R%	UWR%	P%	R%	UWR%	P%	R%	UWR%	P%	R%
Chr-HMM+Dic	2.3	56.2	54.8	10.4	68.8	64.4	9.7	61.4	58.4	8	65.4	62.9
W-Bigram	2.3	54.7	53.6	10.4	53.9	23.8	9.7	53.0	29.6	8	64.6	35.3
W-HMM	2.3	58.1	51.3	10.4	68.3	37.2	9.7	62.3	40.7	8	68.4	41.1

Table 3. Comparison of word part-of-speech tagging

	People Daily			Penn CTB		
	P%	R%	F-score	P%	R%	F-score
Chr-HMM	82.4%	82.5%	82.5	89.7%	88.5%	89.1
Chr-HMM+Dic	89.3	87.8	88.6	92.5	91.5	92.0
W-HMM	86.2%	85.4%	85.7	91.1%	90.8%	91.0

From Table 1 and Table 3, we notice that chr-HMM achieved 88% accuracy in word segmentation and 80% in part-of-speech tagging without a word-dictionary. Chr-HMM is a state-of-the-art Chinese morphology system without a word-dictionary. Its performance is comparable to some dictionary-based approaches (e.g., forward-maximum). This result indicates that our model has effectively captured most of the Chinese word building rules.

The results also show that chr-HMM+Dic outperformed the best SIGHAN word segmentation system on 3 out of the 4 SIGHAN open track test corpora, and achieved top 2 in the case of HK testing corpus.

3.2 Incorporation with Other Systems

The advantage of the proposed model is proficiency in describing word building rules and since many existing NLP application systems are weak in identifying new words, it is intuitive to integrate our model to existing systems and serves as a post-processing subsystem. In this subsection, we show how existing word segmentation systems could be improved using chr-HMM.

Given a segmentation result, we assume that unidentified new words may be a sequence of unattached characters. That is, all multiple-character words in the given result are considered correct, while single words, which might include unidentified new words will be rechecked by the chr-HMM. The entire process involves 3 steps:

1. Only character tags that are consistent with the position of the character in the word are listed for multi-character words.
2. The unattached characters are tagged with all possible character tags. In this way, the original segmentation result is converted into a group of character tagging candidates.
3. We then input these character tagging candidates into the chr-HMM to select the best one.

Consider an original result:

乔丹 [昨 日 从 谷 底] 强力 [反 弹] (Jordan bounced back strongly from the bottom yesterday)

The parts in brackets are the sequence of single characters where the new words may appear. The chr-HMM will list all possible character tags for these "unattached" characters. The parts outside the brackets are multiple-character words identified by the original system. They are assumed correct and maintain also positional information. Only the character tags, which are consistent with the positions of the character in the word are listed. The character tagging candidates for the above sample is given in Figure 3:

			…		…	…				
			vL	…	nL	nsL			…	
			tL	vL	nM	nrL			vM	
		…	nL	lM	nsF	nL			nM	…
nrF	nrL	tL	nM	vF	nrF	nM	vF	vL	vF	vL
nF	nL	nL	aM	pS	nF	vF	nF	nL	aF	nL
aF	aL	tS	tS	dS	nS	nS	aF	aL	aS	vS
乔	丹	昨	日	从	谷	底	强	力	反	弹

Fig. 3. Character tagging candidates for rechecking

Chr-HMM is then applied to the character tagging candidates and the best character tagging selected based on the probability of the candidates is output as the result. In this example, the result is: *'乔丹 (Jordan)* ***昨日*** *(yesterday)* ***从*** *(from)* ***谷底*** *(earth) 强力 (strongly)* ***反弹*** *(bound)'*. The three missing new words in the original system are identified by this post-processing subsystem.

We re-assigned the word segmentation results for all participants who have given permission to release data from the SIGHAN site (available for download from http://www.sighan.org/bakeoff2003). Table 4 enlists the performance of SIGHAN open test with and without chr-HMM. The participant numbers correspond to the sites listed in [9].

Table 4. Comparison of results with and without chr-HMM

Corpus	Site		R%	P%	F
AS	03	Before	89.2	85.3	87.2
		After	90.8	92.0	91.4
CTB	01	Before	88.7	87.6	88.1
		After	90.1	91.8	90.9
	03	Before	85.3	80.6	82.9
		After	86.4	87.8	87.1
	10	Before	91.1	89.1	90.1
		After	91.0	93.5	92.3
HK	03	Before	90.9	86.3	88.6
		After	89.4	91.0	90.2
PK	03	Before	94.1	91.1	92.5
		After	94.4	95.3	94.9
	10	Before	96.3	95.6	95.9
		After	95.6	97.7	96.7

From Table 4, it is obvious that word segmentation precision increases significantly, and at the same time, the corresponding recall remains the same or slightly declined. This implies that the chr-HMM retains the correct words by the original system and concurrently decreases significantly its errors.

4 Related Work

Although character features are very important in Chinese morphology, research in character-based approach is unpopular. Chooi-Ling Goh et al. [16], Jianfeng Gao et al. [8] and Huaping Zhang [3] adopted character information to handle unknown words; X. Luo [11], Yao Meng [12] and Shengfen Luo [17] each presented character-based parsing models for Chinese parsing or new-word extraction. T. Nakagawa used word-level information and character-level information for word segmentation [6]. Hwee Tou Ng et al. [5] investigated word-based and character-based approaches and proposed a maximum entropy character-based POS analyzer. Although the character tags proposed in this paper are essentially similar to some of the previous work mentioned above, here our focus is to integrate various word features with the character-based model in such a way that the probability of the model is undistorted. The proposed model is effective in acquiring word building rules. To our knowledge, our work is the first character-based approach, which outperforms the word-based approaches for SIGHAN open test. Also, our approach is versatile and can be easily integrated with existing morphological systems to achieve improved performance.

5 Conclusion and Future Works

A lexicon-constrained character model is proposed to capture word building rules using word features and character features. The combination of word and character features improves the performance of word segmentation and part-of-speech tagging. The proposed model can solve complicated issues in Chinese morphological analysis. The Chinese morphological analysis is generalized into a process of specific character tagging and word filtering. A lexicon supervises the character-based model to eliminate invalid character tagging candidates.

Our system outperformed the best SIGHAN word segmentation system in 3 out of the 4 SIGHAN open test sets. To our knowledge, our work is the first character-based approach, which performs better than word-based approaches for SIGHAN open test. In addition, the proposed method is versatile and can be easily integrated to any existing Chinese morphological system as a post-processing subsystem leading to enhanced performance.

In this paper, we focused on word features in character-based mode, and adopted HMM as the statistical model to identify the rules. Other statistical models, such as maximum entropy, boosting, support vector machine, etc., may also be suitable for this application. They are worth investigating. The data sparseness problem is practically non-existent in the character-based model for the Chinese character set is limited. However, odd characters are occasionally found in Chinese personal or place names. Some rules using named entity identification technique may help smoothen this. In a broader view, the word building rules proposed in our model is simple enough for linguistic studies to better understand for example formation of Chinese words or even the Chinese language itself.

References

1. Andi Wu. Chinese Word Segmentation in MSR-NLP. In Proc. of SIGHAN Workshop, Sapporo, Japan, (2003) 127-175
2. GuoDong Zhou and Jian Su. A Chinese Efficient Analyzer Integrating Word Segmentation, Part-Of-Speech Tagging, Partial Parsing and Full Parsing. In Proc. Of SIGHAN Workshop, Sapporo, Japan, (2003) 78-83
3. Huaping Zhang, Hong-Kui Yu et al.. HHMM-based Chinese Lexical Analyzer ICTCLAS. In Proc. Of SIGHAN Workshop, Sapporo, Japan, (2003) 184-187
4. Nianwen Xue and Libin Shen. Chinese Word Segmentation as LMR Tagging. In Proc. Of SIGHAN Workshop, Sapporo, Japan, (2003) 176-179
5. Hwee Tou Ng, Low, Jin Kiat. *Chinese Part-of-Speech Tagging: One-at-a-Time or All-at-Once? Word-Based or Character-Based?* In Proc. of EMNLP, Barcelona, Spain, (2004) 277-284
6. Tetsuji Nakagawa. Chinese and Japanese Word Segmentation Using Word-level and Character-level Information, In Proc. of the 20th COLING, Geneva, Switzerland, (2004) 466-472
7. Guohong Fu and Kang-Kwong Luke. *A Two-stage Statistical Word Segmentation System for Chinese.* In Proc. Of SIGHAN Workshop, Sapporo, Japan, (2003) 156-157
8. Jianfeng Gao, Andi Wu, Chang-Ning Huang et al. *Adaptive Chinese Word Segmentation.* In Proc. of 42nd ACL. Barcelona, Spain, (2004) 462-469
9. Richard Sproat and Thomas Emerson. *The First International Chinese Word Segmentation Bakeoff.* In Proc. Of SIGHAN Workshop, Sapporo, Japan, (2003) 133-143
10. X. Luo. A Maximum Entropy Chinese Character-based Parser. In Proc. of EMNLP. Sapporo, Japan, (2003) 192-199
11. Honglan Jin, Kam-Fai Wong, "A Chinese Dictionary Construction Algorithm for Information Retrieval", ACM Transactions on Asian Language Information Processing, 1(4):281-296, Dec. 2002.
12. Yao Meng, Hao Yu and Fumihito Nishino. 2004. *Chinese New Word Identification Based on Character Parsing Model.* In Proc. of 1st IJCNLP, Hainan, China, (2004) 489-496
13. Shiwen Yu, Huiming Duan, etal. 北京大学现代汉语语料库基本加工规范. 中文信息学报v(5), (2002) 49-64, 58-65
14. Maosong Sun and Benjamin K. T' Sou. *Ambiguity Resolution in Chinese Word Segmentation.* In Proc. of 10th Pacific Asia Conference on Language, Information & Computation, (1995) 121-126
15. Nianwen Xue, Fu-Dong Chiou and Martha Palmer. *Building a Large-scale Annotated Chinese Corpus.* In Proc. of the 19th COLING. Taibei, Taiwan, (2002)
16. Chooi-Ling GOH, Masayuki Asahara, Yuji Matsumoto. *Chinese Unknown Word Identification Using Character-based Tagging and Chunking.* In Proc. of the 41st ACL, Interactive Poster/Demo Sessions, Sapporo, Japan, (2003) 197-200
17. Shengfen Luo, Maosong Sun. 2003, *Two-character Chinese Word Extraction Based on Hybrid of Internal and Contextual Measure*, In Proc. of the 2nd SIGHAN Workshop, Sapporo, Japan, (2003) 20-30

Relative Compositionality of Multi-word Expressions: A Study of Verb-Noun (V-N) Collocations

Sriram Venkatapathy[1,*] and Aravind K. Joshi[2]

[1] Language Technologies Research Center,
International Institute of Information Technology - Hyderabad, Hyderabad, India
sriram@research.iiit.ac.in

[2] Department of Computer and Information Science
and Institute of Research in Cognitive Science,
University of Pennsylvania, Philadelphia, PA, USA
joshi@linc.cis.upenn.edu

Abstract. Recognition of Multi-word Expressions (MWEs) and their relative compositionality are crucial to Natural Language Processing. Various statistical techniques have been proposed to recognize MWEs. In this paper, we integrate all the existing statistical features and investigate a range of classifiers for their suitability for recognizing the non-compositional Verb-Noun (V-N) collocations. In the task of ranking the V-N collocations based on their relative compositionality, we show that the correlation between the ranks computed by the classifier and human ranking is significantly better than the correlation between ranking of individual features and human ranking. We also show that the properties 'Distributed frequency of object' (as defined in [27]) and 'Nearest Mutual Information' (as adapted from [18]) contribute greatly to the recognition of the non-compositional MWEs of the V-N type and to the ranking of the V-N collocations based on their relative compositionality.

1 Introduction

The main goals of the work presented in this paper are **(1)** To investigate a range of classifiers for their suitability in recognizing the non-compositional V-N collocations, and **(2)** To examine the relative compositionality of collocations of V-N type. Measuring the relative compositionality of V-N collocations is extremely helpful in applications such as machine translation where the collocations that are highly non-compositional can be handled in a special way.

Multi-word expressions (MWEs) are those whose structure and meaning cannot be derived from their component words, as they occur independently. Examples include conjunctions like 'as well as' (meaning 'including'), idioms like

* Part of the work was done at Institute for Research in Cognitive Science, University of Pennsylvania, Philadelphia, PA 19104, USA, when he was visiting IRCS as a visiting Scholar, February to December, 2004.

R. Dale et al. (Eds.): IJCNLP 2005, LNAI 3651, pp. 553–564, 2005.

'kick the bucket' (meaning 'die'), phrasal verbs like 'find out' (meaning 'search') and compounds like 'village community'. A typical natural language system assumes each word to be a lexical unit, but this assumption does not hold in case of MWEs [6] [12]. They have idiosyncratic interpretations which cross word boundaries and hence are a 'pain in the neck' [23]. They account for a large portion of the language used in day-to-day interactions [25] and so, handling them becomes an important task.

A large number of MWEs have a standard syntactic structure but are non-compositional semantically. An example of such a subset is the class of non-compositional verb-noun collocations (V-N collocations). The class of V-N collocations which are non-compositional is important because they are used very frequently. These include verbal idioms [22], support-verb constructions [1] [2] etc. The expression 'take place' is a MWE whereas 'take a gift' is not a MWE.

It is well known that one cannot really make a binary distinction between compositional and non-compositional MWEs. They do not fall cleanly into mutually exclusive classes, but populate the continuum between the two extremes [4]. So, we rate the MWEs (V-N collocations in this paper) on a scale from 1 to 6 where 6 denotes a completely compositional expression, while 1 denotes a completely opaque expression. But, to address the problem of identification, we still need to do an approximate binary distinction. We call the expressions with a rating of 4 to 6 compositional and the expressions with rating of 1 to 3 as non-compositional. (See Section 4 for further details).

Various statistical measures have been suggested for identification of MWEs and ranking expressions based on their compositionality. Some of these are Frequency, Mutual Information [9], Log-Likelihood [10] and Pearson's χ^2 [8]. Integrating all the statistical measures should provide better evidence for recognizing MWEs and ranking the expressions. We use various Machine Learning Techniques (classifiers) to integrate these statistical features and classify the V-N collocations as MWEs or Non-MWEs. We also use a classifier to rank the V-N collocations according to their compositionality. We then compare these ranks with the ranks provided by the human judge. A similar comparison between the ranks according to Latent-Semantic Analysis (LSA) based features and the ranks of human judges has been done by McCarthy, Keller and Caroll [19] for verb-particle constructions. (See Section 3 for more details). Some preliminary work on recognition of V-N collocations was presented in [28].

In the task of classification, we show that the technique of weighted features in distance-weighted nearest-neighbour algorithm performs slightly better than other machine learning techniques. We also find that the 'distributed frequency of object (as defined by [27])' and 'nearest mutual information (as adapted from [18])' are important indicators of the non-compositionality of MWEs. In the task of ranking, we show that the ranks assigned by the classifier correlated much better with the human judgement than the ranks assigned by individual statistical measures.

This paper is organised in the following sections **(2)** Basic Architecture, **(3)** Related work, **(4)** Data used for the experiments, **(5)** Agreement between the Judges, **(6)** Features, **(7)** Experiments - Classification, **(8)** Experiments - Ranking and **(9)** Conclusion.

2 Basic Architecture

Recognition of MWEs can be regarded as a classification task where every V-N collocation can be classified either as a MWE or as a Non-MWE. Every V-N collocation is represented as a vector of features which are composed largely of various statistical measures. The values of these features for the V-N collocations are extracted from the British National Corpus. For example, the V-N collocation 'raise an eyebrow' can be represented as
[Frequency = 271, Mutual Information = 8.43, Log-Likelihood = 1456.29, etc.].

Now, to recognise the MWEs, the classifier has to do a binary classification of this vector. So, ideally, the classifier should take the above information and classify 'raise an eyebrow' as an MWE. The classifier can also be used to rank these vectors according to their relative compositionality.

3 Related Work

Church and Hanks (1989) proposed a measure of association called Mutual Information [9]. Mutual Information (MI) is the logarithm of the ratio between the probability of the two words occurring together and the product of the probability of each word occurring individually. The higher the MI, the more likely are the words to be associated with each other. The usefulness of the statistical approach suggested by Church and Hanks [9] is evaluated for the extraction of V-N collocations from German text Corpora [7]. Several other measures like Log-Likelihood [10], Pearson's χ^2 [8], Z-Score [8] , Cubic Association Ratio (MI3), Log-Log [17], etc., have been proposed. These measures try to quantify the association of the two words but do not talk about quantifying the non-compositionality of MWEs. Dekang Lin proposes a way to automatically identify the non-compositionality of MWEs [18]. He suggests that a possible way to separate compositional phrases from non-compositional ones is to check the existence and mutual-information values of phrases obtained by replacing one of the words with a similar word. According to Lin, a phrase is probably non-compositional if such substitutions are not found in the collocations database or their mutual information values are significantly different from that of the phrase. Another way of determining the non-compositionality of V-N collocations is by using 'distributed frequency of object'(DFO) in V-N collocations [27]. The basic idea in there is that "if an object appears only with one verb (or few verbs) in a large corpus we expect that it has an idiomatic nature" [27].

Schone and Jurafsky [24] applied Latent-Semantic Analysis (LSA) to the analysis of MWEs in the task of MWE discovery, by way of rescoring MWEs extracted from the corpus. An interesting way of quantifying the relative compositionality of a MWE is proposed by Baldwin, Bannard, Tanaka and Widdows [3]. They use latent semantic analysis (LSA) to determine the similarity between an MWE and its constituent words, and claim that higher similarity indicates great decomposability. In terms of compositionality, an expression is likely to be relatively more compositional if it is decomposable. They evaluate their model on English NN compounds and verb-particles, and showed that the model correlated moderately well with the Wordnet based decomposibility theory [3].

Evert and Krenn [11] compare some of the existing statistical features for the recognition of MWEs of adjective-noun and preposition-noun-verb types. Galiano, Valdivia, Santiago and Lopez [14] use five statistical measures to classify generic MWEs using the LVQ (Learning Vector Quantization) algorithm. In contrast, we do a more detailed and focussed study of V-N collocations and the ability of various classifiers in recognizing MWEs. We also compare the roles of various features in this task.

McCarthy, Keller and Caroll [19] judge compositionality according to the degree of overlap in the set of most similar words to the verb-particle and head verb. They showed that the correlation between their measures and the human ranking was better than the correlation between the statistical features and the human ranking. We have done similar experiments in this paper where we compare the correlation value of the ranks provided by the classifier with the ranks of the individual features for the V-N collocations. We show that the ranks given by the classifier which integrates all the features provides a significantly better correlation than the individual features.

4 Data Used for the Experiments

The data used for the experiments is British National Corpus of 81 million words. The corpus is parsed using Bikel's parser [5] and the Verb-Object Collocations are extracted. There are 4,775,697 V-N of which 1.2 million were unique. All the V-N collocations above the frequency of 100 (n=4405) are taken to conduct the experiments so that the evaluation of the system is feasible. These 4405 V-N collocations were searched in Wordnet, American Heritage Dictionary and SAID dictionary (LDC,2003). Around 400 were found in at least one of the dictionaries. Another 400 were extracted from the rest so that the evaluation set has roughly equal number of compositional and non-compositional expressions. These 800 expressions were annotated with a rating from 1 to 6 by using guidelines independently developed by the authors. 1 denotes the expressions which are totally non-compositional while 6 denotes the expressions which are totally compositional. The brief explanation of the various rating are **(1)** No word in the expression has any relation to the actual meaning of the expression. Example: "**leave a mark**". **(2)** Can be replaced by a single verb. Example : "**take a look**". **(3)** Although meanings of both words are involved, at least one of the words is not used in the usual sense. Example : "**break news**". **(4)** Relatively more compositional than (3). Example : "**prove a point**". **(5)** Relatively less compositional than (6). Example : "**feel safe**". **(6)** Completely compositional. Example : "**drink coffee**". For the experiments on classification (Section 7), we call the expressions with ratings of 4 to 6 as compositional and the expressions with rating of 1 to 3 as non-compositional. For the experiments on ranking the expressions based on their relative compositionality, we use all the 6 ratings to represent the relative compositionality of these expressions.

5 Agreement Between the Judges

The data was annotated by two fluent speakers of English. For 765 collocations out of 800, both the annotators gave a rating. For the rest, atleast one of the annotators marked the collocations as "don't know". Table 1 illustrates the details of the annotations provided by the two judges.

Table 1. Details of the annotations of the two annotators

Ratings	6	5	4	3	2	1	Compositional (4 to 6)	Non-Compositional (1 to 3)
Annotator1	141	122	127	119	161	95	390	375
Annotator2	303	88	79	101	118	76	470	195

From the table we see that annotator1 distributed the rating more uniformly among all the collocations while annotator2 observed that a significant proportion of the collocations were completely compositional. To measure the agreement between the two annotators, we used the Kendall's TAU (τ). τ is the correlation between the rankings[1] of collocations given by the two annotators. W ranges between 0 (little agreement) and 1 (full agreement). W is calculated as below,

$$\tau = \frac{\sum_{i<j} sgn(x_i - x_j) sgn(y_i - y_j)}{\sqrt{(T_0 - T_1)(T_0 - T_2)}}$$

where $T_0 = n(n-1)/2$, $T_1 = \sum t_i(t_i - 1)/2$, $T_2 = \sum u_i(u_i - 1)/2$ and where, n is the number of collocations, t_i is the number of tied x values of ith group of tied x values and u_i is the number of tied y values of ith group of tied y values.

We obtained a τ score of **0.61** which is highly significant. This shows that the annotators were in a good agreement with each other in deciding the rating to be given to the collocations. We also compare the ranking of the two annotators using Spearman's Rank-Correlation coefficient (r_s) (more details in section 8). We obtained a r_s score of **0.71** indicating a good agreement between the annotators. A couple of examples where the annotators differed are **(1)** "perform a task" was rated 3 by annotator1 while it was rated 6 by annotator2 and **(2)** "pay tribute" was rated 1 by annotator1 while it was rated 4 by annotator2.

The 765 samples annotated by both the annotators were then divided into a training set and a testing set in several possible ways to cross-validate the results of classification and ranking.

[1] Computed from the ratings.

6 Features

Each collocation is represented by a vector whose dimensions are the statistical features obtained from the British National Corpus. This list of features are given in Table 2.[2] While conducting the experiments, all features are scaled from 0 to 1 to ensure that all features are represented uniformly.

Table 2. List of features and their top-3 example collocations

Feature	Top-3		Feature	Top-3
Frequency	take place have effect have time		Mutual Information [9]	shrug shoulder bridge gap plead guilty
Cubic Association Measure (Oakes, 1998)	take place shake head play role		Log-Log [17]	shake head commit suicide fall asleep
Log-Likelihood [10]	take place shake head play role		Pearson's χ^2 [8]	shake head commit suicide fall asleep
T-Score [9]	take place have effect shake head		Z-Score [26]	shake head commit suicide fall asleep
ϕ-coefficient	bridge gap shrug shoulder press button		Distributed freq. of object (DFO) [27]	come true become difficult make sure
Nearest MI (NMI) [18]	Collocations with no neigh. MI		Whether object can occur as a verb	(Binary feature)
Whether object is a nomin. of some verb	(Binary feature)			

7 Experiments - Classification

The evaluation data (765 vectors) is divided randomly into training and testing vectors in 10 ways for cross-validation. The training data consists of 90% of 786 vectors and the testing data consists of the remaining.

We used various Machine Learning techinques to classify the V-N collocations into MWEs and non-MWEs. For every classifier, we calculated the average accuracy of all the test sets of each of the annotators. We then compare the average accuracies of all the classifiers. We found that the classifier that we used, the technique of weighted features in distance-weighted nearest-algorithm, performs somewhat better than other machine learning techniques.

The following are brief descriptions of the classifiers that we used in this paper.

[2] The formulas of features are not given due to lack of space.

7.1 Nearest-Neighbour Algorithm

This is an instance-based learning technique where the test vector is classified based on its nearest vectors in the training data. The simple distance between two vectors x_i and x_j is defined as d(x_i,x_j), where

$$d(x_i, x_j) = \sqrt{\sum_{r=1}^{n} (a_r(x_i) - a_r(x_j))^2}.$$

Here, x is an instance of a vector and $a_r(x)$ is the value of the rth feature.

One can use K neighbours to judge the class of the test vector. The test vector is assigned the class of maximum number of neighbours. This can be furthur modified by calculating the inverse weighted distance between the test vector and the neighbouring training vectors in each of the classes. The test vector is then assigned the class which has the higher inverse-weighted distance. One can also use all the training vectors and the weighted-distance principle to classify the test vector.

The average classification accuracy of each of the above methods on the test sets of each of the annotators is shown in Table 3.

Table 3. Average accuracies of MWE recognition using simple nearest-neighbour algorithms and weighted distance nearest neighbour algorithms

	Simple K-Nearest neighbour				Weighted-distance Nearest neighbour			
Type	K=1	K=2	K=3		K=1	K=2	K=3	K=All
Annot.1	62.35	61.31	62.48		62.35	62.35	62.61	66.66
Annot.2	57.64	54.10	60.89		57.64	57.64	60.37	63.52

7.2 SVM-Based Classifiers

SVMs [15] have been very successful in attaining high accuracy for various machine-learning tasks. Unlike the error-driven algorithms (Perceptron etc.), SVM searches for the two distinct classes and maximizes the margin between two classes. Data of higher dimension can also be classified using the appropriate Kernel. We used Linear and Polynomial Kernel (degree=2) to test the evaluation data. We also used the radial-basis network in SVMs to compare the results because of their proximity to the nearest-neigbour algorithms.

Table 4. Average accuracies of MWE recognition using SVMs (Linear, Polynomial and Radial Basis Function Kernel)

	Linear Ker.	Polynomial Ker.		Radial Basis networks			
Parameters				$\sigma = 0.5$	$\sigma = 1.0$	$\sigma = 1.5$	$\sigma = 2.0$
Annot.1	65.89	65.75		67.06	66.66	66.93	67.06
Annot.2	62.61	65.09		64.17	63.51	62.99	62.99

The average classification accuracy of each of the above methods on the test sets of each of the annotators is shown in Table 4.

7.3 Weighted Features in Distance-Weighted Nearest-Neighbour Algorithm

Among all the features used, only a few might be very relevant to recognizing the non-compositionality of the MWE. As a result, the distance metric used by the nearest-neighbour algorithm which depends on all the features might be misleading. The distance between the neighbour will be dominated by large number of irrelevant features.

A way of overcoming this problem is to weight each feature differently when calculating the distance between the two instances. This also gives us an insight into which features are mainly responsible for recognizing the non-compositionality of MWEs. The jth feature can be multiplied by the weight z_j, where the values of $z_1...z_n$ are chosen to minimize the true classification error of the learning algorithm [20]. The distance using these weights is represented as

$$d(x_i, x_j) = \sqrt{\sum_{r=1}^{n} (z_r * (a_r(x_i) - a_r(x_j)))^2},$$

where z_r is the weight of the rth feature.

The values of $z_1...z_n$ can be determined by cross-validation of the training data. We use leave-one-out cross-validation [21], in which the set of m training vectors are repeatedly divided into a training set of m-1 and a test set of 1, in all possible ways. So, each vector in the training data is classified using the remaining vectors. The classification accuracy is defined as

$$Clacc = 100 * (\sum_{1}^{m} classify(i)/m)$$

where classify(i)=1, if the ith training example is classified correctly using the distance-weighted nearest neighbour algorithm, otherwise classify(i)=0.

Now, we try to maximize the classification accuracy in the following way,

- In every iteration, vary the weights of the features one by one.
- Choose the feature and its weight which brings the maximum increase in the value of *Clacc*. One can also choose the feature and its weight such that it brings the minimum increase in the value of *Clacc*.
- Update the weight of this particular feature and go for the next iteration.
- If there is no increase in classification accuracy, stop.

When the weights are updated such that there is maximum increase in classification accuracy in every step, the average accuracies are **66.92%** and **64.30%** on the test sets of the two annotators respectively. But when the weights are updated such there is a minimum increase in classification accuracy at every

Table 5. The top three features according to the average weight when there is maximum increase in Clacc at every step

Annotator1	Weight	Annotator2	Weight
DFO	1.09	MI	1.17
T-Score	1.0	T-Score	1.1
Z-Score	1.0	ϕ-coefficient	1.0

Table 6. The top three features according to the average weight calculated when there is minimum increase in Clacc at every step

Annot.1	Weight	Annot.2	Weight
DFO	1.07	MI	2.06
NMI	1.02	T-Score	1.0
Log-Like.	0.97	ϕ-coefficient	1.0

step, the average accuracies are **66.13%** and **64.04%** on the test sets of the two annotators respectively, which are slightly better than that obtained by the other Machine Learning Techniques.

In the above two methods (Updating weights such that there is maximum or minimum increase in classification accuracy), we add the weights of the features of each of the evaluation sets. According to the average weights, the top three features (having high average weight) are shown in Tables 5 and 6.

In both the above cases, we find that the properties 'Mutual-Information' and the compositionality oriented feature 'Distributed Frequency of an Object' performed significantly better than the other features.

8 Experiments - Ranking

All the statistical measures show that the expressions ranked higher according to their decreasing values are more likely to be non-compositional. We compare these ranks with the average of the ranks given by the annotator (obtained from his rating). To compare, we use Spearman Rank-Order Correlation Coefficient (r_s), defined as

$$r_s = \frac{(R_i - \bar{R})(S_i - \bar{S})}{\sqrt{\sum(R_i - \bar{R})^2 \sum(S_i - \bar{S})^2}}$$

where R_i is the rank of ith x value, S_i is the rank of ith y value, $\bar{R}$ is the mean of the R_i values and $\bar{S}$ is the mean of S_i values.

We use an SVM-based ranking system [16] for our training. Here, we use 10% of the 765 vectors for training and the remaining for testing. The SVM-based ranking system builds a preference matrix of the training vectors to learn. It then ranks the test vectors. The ranking system takes a lot of time to train itself, and hence, we decided to use only a small proportion of the evaluation set for training.

Table 7. The correlation values of the ranking of individual features and the ranking of classifier with the ranking of human judgements

MI	**-0.125**	Z-Score	-0.059
MI3	0.001	ϕ-coeff	-0.102
Log-Log	-0.086	DFO	**-0.113**
Log-Likelihood	0.005	NMI	**-0.167**
χ^2	-0.056	**Class.**	**0.388**
T-Score	0.045		

We also compare our ranks (the average of the ranks suggested by the classifier) with the gold standard using the Spearman Rank-Order Correlation Coefficient. The results are shown in Table 7.

In Table 7, we observe that the correlation between the ranks computed by the classifier and human ranking is better than the correlation between ranking of individual statistical features and human ranking.

We observe that among all the statistical features the ranks based on the properties 'Mutual Information', 'Distributed Frequency of an Object' [27] and 'Nearest mutual information' [18] correlated better with the ranks provided by the annotator. This is in accordance with the observation we made while describing the classification experiments, where we observed that the properties 'Distributed Frequency of an Object' and 'Mutual Information' contributed much to the classification of the expressions. When we compare the correlation values of MI, Log-likelihood and χ^2, we see that the Mutual-Information values correlated better. This result is similar to the observation made by McCarthy, Keller and Caroll [19] for phrasal verbs.

9 Conclusion

In this paper, we integrated the statistical features using various classifiers and investigated their suitability for recognising non-compositional MWEs of the V-N type. We also used a classifier to rank the V-N collocations according to their relative compositionality. This type of MWEs constitutes a very large percentage of all MWEs and are crucial for NLP applications, especially for Machine Translation. Our main results are as follows.

- The technique of weighted features in distance-weighted nearest neighbour algorithm performs better than other Machine Learning Techniques in the task of recognition of MWEs of V-N type.
- We show that the correlation between the ranks computed by the classifier and human ranking is significantly better than the correlation between ranking of individual features and human ranking.
- The properties 'Distributed frequency of object' and 'Nearest MI' contribute greatly to the recognition of the non-compositional MWEs of the V-N type and to the ranking of the V-N collocations based on their relative compositionality.

Our future work will consist of the following tasks

- Evaluate the effectiveness of the techniques developed in this paper for applications like Machine Translation.
- Improve our annotation guidelines and create more annotated data.
- Extend our approach to other types of MWEs.

Acknowledgements

We want to thank Libin Shen and Nikhil Dinesh for their help in clarifying various aspects of Machine Learning Techniques. We would like to thank Roderick Saxey and Pranesh Bhargava for annotating the data and Mark Mandel for considerable editorial help.

References

1. Abeille, Anne . Light verb constuctions and extraction out of NP in a tree adjoining grammar. Papers of the 24th Regional Meeting of the Chicago Linguistics Society. (1988)
2. Akimoto, Monoji . Papers of the 24th Regional Meeting of the Chicago Linguistics Society. Shinozaki Shorin . (1989)
3. Baldwin, Timothy and Bannard, Colin and Tanaka, Takaaki and Widdows, Dominic . An Empirical Model of Multiword Expression . Proceedings of the ACL-2003 Workshop on Multiword Expressions: Analysis, Acquisition and Treatment. (2003)
4. Bannard, Colin and Baldwin, Timothy and Lascarides, Alex . A Statistical Approach to the Semantics of Verb-Particles . Proceedings of the ACL-2003 Workshop on Multiword Expressions: Analysis, Acquisition and Treatment. (2003)
5. Bikel, Daniel M. . A Distributional Analysis of a Lexicalized Statistical Parsing Model . Proceedings of EMNLP . (2004)
6. Becker, Joseph D. . The Phrasal Lexicon . Theoritical Issues of NLP, Workshop in CL, Linguistics, Psychology and AI, Cambridge, MA. (1975)
7. Breidt, Elisabeth . Extraction of V-N-Collocations from Text Corpora: A Feasibility Study for German . CoRR-1996 . (1995)
8. Church, K. and Gale, W. and Hanks, P. and Hindle, D. . Parsing, word associations and typical predicate-argument relations . Current Issues in Parsing Technology. Kluwer Academic, Dordrecht, Netherlands, 1991 . (1991)
9. Church, K. and Patrick Hanks . Word Association Norms, Mutual Information, and Lexicography . Proceedings of the 27th. Annual Meeting of the Association for Computational Linguistics, 1990 . (1989)
10. Dunning, Ted . Accurate Methods for the Statistics of Surprise and Coincidence . Computational Linguistics - 1993 . (1993)
11. Stefan Evert and Brigitte Krenn . Methods for the Qualitative Evaluation of Lexical Association Measures . Proceedings of the ACL - 2001 . (2001)
12. Charles Fillmore . An extremist approach to multi-word expressions . A talk given at IRCS, University of Pennsylvania, 2003. (2003)
13. Fontenelle and Bruls, Th. W. and Thomas, L. and Vanallemeersch, T. and Jansen, J. . Survey of collocation extraction tools . Deliverable D-1a, MLAP-Project 93-19 DECIDE, University of Liege, Belgium. (1994)

14. Diaz-Galiano, M.C. and Martin-Valdivia, M.T. and Martinez-Santiago, F. and Urena-Lopez, L. A. . Multi-word Expressions Recognition with the LVQ Algorithm. Proceedings of Methodologies and Evaluation of Multiword Unit in Real-world Applications, LREC, 2004 . (2004)
15. Joachims, T. . Making large-Scale SVM Learning Practical . Advances in Kernel Methods - Support Vector Learning . (1999)
16. Joachims, T. . Optimizing Search Engines Using Clickthrough Data. Advances in Kernel Methods - Support Vector Learning edings of the ACM Conference on Knowledge Discovery and Data Mining (KDD), ACM, 2002. (2002)
17. Kilgariff, A. and Rosenzweig, J. . Framework and Results for English Senseval . Computers and the Humanities, 2000 . (2000)
18. Dekang Lin . Automatic Identification of non-compositonal phrases. Proceedings of ACL- 99, College Park, USA . (1999)
19. McCarthy, D. and Keller, B. and Carroll, J. . Detecting a Continuum of Compositionality in Phrasal Verbs . Proceedings of the ACL-2003 Workshop on Multi-word Expressions: Analysis, Acquisition and Treatment, 2003. (2003)
20. Mitchell, T. Instance-Based Learning . Machine Learning, McGraw-Hill Series in Computer Science, 1997 . (1997)
21. Moore, A. W. and Lee, M.S. . Proceedings of the 11 International Conference on Machine Learning, 1994. (1994)
22. Nunberg, G. and Sag, I. A. and Wasow, T. . Idioms . Language, 1994 . (1994)
23. Sag, I. A. and Baldwin, Timothy and Bond, Francis and Copestake, Ann and Flickinger, Dan. . Multi-word expressions: a pain in the neck for nlp . Proceedings of CICLing , 2002 . (2002)
24. Schone, Patrick and Jurafsky, Dan. Is Knowledge-Free Induction of Multiword Unit Dictionary Headwords a Solved Problem? . Proceedings of EMNLP , 2001 . (2001)
25. Schuler, William and Joshi, Aravind K. Relevance of tree rewriting systems for multi-word expressions. To be published. (2005)
26. Smadja, F. . Retrieving Collocations from Text : Xtract . Computational Linguistics - 1993 . (1993)
27. Tapanainen, Pasi and Piitulaine, Jussi and Jarvinen, Timo Idiomatic object usage and support verbs . 36th Annual Meeting of the Association for Computational Linguistics . (1998)
28. Venkatapathy, Sriram and Joshi, Aravind K. Recognition of Multi-word Expressions: A Study of Verb-Noun (V-N) Collocations. Proceedings of the International Conference on Natural Language Processing, 2004. (2004)

Automatic Extraction of Fixed Multiword Expressions

Campbell Hore*, Masayuki Asahara, and Yūji Matsumoto

Graduate School of Information Science,
Nara Institute of Science and Technology,
8916-5 Takayama, Ikoma, Nara 630-0192, Japan
{campbe-h, masayu-a, matsu}@is.naist.jp
http://cl.naist.jp

Abstract. Fixed multiword expressions are strings of words which together behave like a single word. This research establishes a method for the automatic extraction of such expressions. Our method involves three stages. In the first, a statistical measure is used to extract candidate bigrams. In the second, we use this list to select occurrences of candidate expressions in a corpus, together with their surrounding contexts. These examples are used as training data for supervised machine learning, resulting in a classifier which can identify target multiword expressions. The final stage is the estimation of the part of speech of each extracted expression based on its context of occurence. Evaluation demonstrated that collocation measures alone are not effective in identifying target expressions. However, when trained on one million examples, the classifier identified target multiword expressions with precision greater than 90%. Part of speech estimation had precision and recall of over 95%.

1 Introduction

1.1 Multiword Expressions

For natural language processing purposes, a naive definition of a word in English is '*a sequence of letters delimited by spaces*'. By this definition, the expression *ad hoc*, which originally came from Latin, consists of two "words", *ad* and *hoc*. However, in isolation *hoc* is not a meaningful English word. It is always preceded by *ad*. This suggests that treating these two words as if they together form a single "word with spaces" more closely models their behaviour in text. A sequence of words which for one reason or another is more sensibly treated as a single lexical item, rather than as individual words, is known as a multiword expression (MWE). In other words, an MWE is a sequence of words which together behave as though they were a single word.

MWEs are not limited to imported foreign phrases such as *ad hoc*. They cover a large range of expression types including proper nouns such as *New York*, verb-particle constructions such as *to call up* (i.e. to telephone someone), and light

* Supported by the Japanese government's MEXT scholarship programme.

R. Dale et al. (Eds.): IJCNLP 2005, LNAI 3651, pp. 565–575, 2005.

verbs such as *to make a mistake*. The justification for treating such expressions as MWEs is that their linguistic properties are odd in some way as compared to "normal" expressions: either their part of speech or their meaning is unpredictable despite full knowledge about the parts of speech or meanings of their constituent words.

1.2 Fixed Multiword Expressions

By *fixed*, we mean that this particular type of MWE consists of a contiguous sequence of words. Other MWE types can consist of discontinuous word sequences. For example, the verb-particle construction *to call up* takes an indirect object, the person who receives the telephone call. This person can appear after the verb-particle construction (e.g. "I called up *Mohammad*") but it can also appear in the *middle* of the verb-particle construction, (e.g. "I called *Mohammad* up"). In contrast, fixed MWEs consist of contiguous word sequences. For example, *by and large* cannot be modified by insertion of other words (e.g. *"by and *very* large").

1.3 Multiword Expressions in Parsing

The aim of our research is the development of a method for the automatic extraction and part of speech estimation of fixed MWEs. The ability to identify this type of MWE in texts is of potential use in a wide variety of natural language processing tasks because it should enable an improvement in the precision of sentence parsing. Sentence parsing is frequently the first step in more sophisticated language processing tasks, so an increase in parsing precision should improve results in a large number of natural language processing applications.

A parser generally takes a sentence as input, together with the parts of speech of the tokens[1] in the sentence. The parser then attempts to estimate the most probable syntactic structure for the sentence. Some kinds of MWE have the potential to disrupt this process because the part of speech of the MWE as a whole, cannot be predicted on the basis of the parts of speech of its constituent words. For example, the part of speech sequence for the expression *by and large* is Preposition + Conjunction + Adjective, which is a sequence almost certainly unique to this expression. A parser which is not explicitly informed about *by and large* will therefore struggle to cope with this part of speech sequence, and may incorrectly try to group one or more parts of the expression with words in the surrounding context.

The solution to this problem of syntactically unpredictable MWEs is to add them to the dictionary used by the parser. When the parser comes across a sequence of words that matches an MWE in its dictionary, it can use the MWE's part of speech to parse the sentence treating the MWE as a single lexical item.

[1] We use the term *tokens* here rather than *words* because texts actually contain many space delimited character strings which are not normally thought of as words, such as numbers and punctuation. In addition, some purely alphabetic character strings are not words in their own right, as is the case for *hoc*, mentioned above.

In reality, some sequences of words are an MWE only in specific contexts. For example, *in the main* is an MWE when it means "overall" or "mostly" as seen in the sentence "*In the main, the biggest improvements have been in child health*". In contrast, in a sentence such as "*Village hotels ought to be in the main square, not at the outskirts of a village*" the word sequence *in the main* is not an MWE, and can therefore be treated normally by the parser as separate words.

1.4 Target Problems

We approach the task of extracting fixed MWEs by decomposing it into three sub-problems, as illustrated in Fig. 1. The first (§3.1, described in Section 3.1) is simple collocation extraction. We use a standard collocation measure to extract as many candidate bigram MWEs from the corpus as possible.

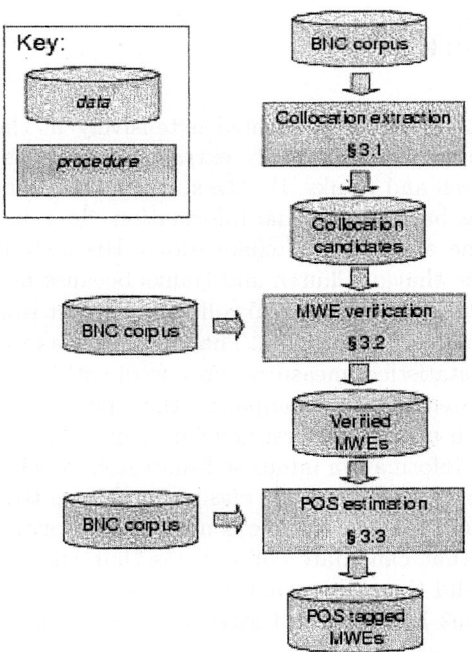

Fig. 1. Flowchart of processing

The second problem (§3.2) is refinement of the list of candidate MWEs. Many of the candidates are *not* target multiword expressions. Distinguishing between word sequences that are MWEs, and those that *never* are, represents one sub-task. Hereafter, we refer to word sequences which are never MWEs as *non-MWEs*. Some word sequences have dual identities. In one context a word sequence may be an MWE, but in another, it may be just a normal, literal word sequence. For example, a child forced to help wash the family car, and acting petulantly, might be scolded "Don't kick the bucket!". In this case *kick the bucket* is a normal, compositional phrase; its meaning can be understood based on the literal meaning of its constituent words. When *kick the bucket* is used as a euphemism for "to die" however, its meaning is non-compositional, and thus in this context it *is* an MWE. In this paper we refer to occurrences of literal word sequences which have the *appearance* of being an MWE as *pseudo-MWEs*. We deal with these two sub-tasks simultaneously, using supervised machine learning.

The third problem we tackle (§3.3) is estimation of the part of speech of MWEs. This problem is also solved using supervised machine learning. In this research we limit ourselves to MWEs containing only two words (i.e. bigrams). In the future, we plan to generalize the method so that it works with MWEs of arbitrary length.

2 Related Work

Collocation extraction has been covered extensively in the literature. One of the earliest attempts to automatically extract collocations from a corpus was undertaken by Church and Hanks [1]. The statistical measure they used to identify collocations was based on mutual information. Smadja [2] developed a tool called Xtract for the extraction of collocations. His definition of a collocation differed slightly from that of Church and Hanks because he claimed expressions such as *doctors and nurses* are not real collocations, just words related by virtue of their shared domain or semantics. Thanopoulos, Fakotakis and Kokkinakis in [3] reviewed the statistical measures most frequently used for collocation extraction, and evaluated them by comparing their performance with that of two new measures of their own. Their first novel measure, Mutual Dependency (MD) is pointwise mutual information minus self-information. The second measure attempts to introduce a slight frequency bias by combining the t-score with mutual dependency. Although frequency alone is not sufficient evidence of collocational status, they argue that candidate collocations that have a high frequency are more likely to be valid than those that are very rare.

While collocations have received attention over a number of years, MWEs have only relatively recently emerged as a research topic within natural language processing. In consequence, there are relatively few articles specifically about MWEs. Sag et al. in [4] gave a linguistic categorisation of the different types of MWE, and described ways of representing them efficiently within a computational framework[2]. Although MWEs as a whole have yet to receive widespread investigation, attention has been paid to specific types of MWE. For example, verb-particle constructions have been the subject of several studies (see for example [5] and [6]).

[2] Head-driven Phrase Structure Grammar (HPSG).

3 Method

In order to extract information about fixed MWEs from a corpus, we use a three stage process. In the first stage we identify a list of candidate MWEs based on the statistical behaviour of the tokens in the corpus. Two words whose probability of appearing together is greater than that which would be expected based on their individual frequencies, are considered to constitute a potential MWE and are extracted for later processing. In other words, stage one is collocation extraction.

In the second stage, we use this list of candidate MWEs as the basis for extracting from the corpus examples of candidates together with their contexts. These examples are then used as training data for supervised machine learning resulting in a classifier capable of distinguishing between, on the one hand, true MWEs, and on the other, non-MWEs and pseudo-MWEs.

In the final stage we use supervised machine learning to train a classifier to perform MWE part of speech assignment. By examining the context surrounding an MWE, it is possible for the classifier to determine the most likely part of speech for the MWE in that context.

3.1 Collocation Extraction

Collocation extraction was performed using one of the statistical measures discussed in [3]. The measures we experimented with were: frequency, χ-square [7], log-likelihood ratio [8], t-score [7], mutual information (MI) [1], mutual dependency (MD – mutual information minus self-information) [3], and log-frequency biased mutual dependency (LFMD – a combination of the t-score and mutual dependency) [3]. The equations of these measures are shown in Fig. 2.

We compared the resulting ranked lists of bigrams with a list of target MWEs extracted from the British National Corpus (BNC)[3]. The target list was produced by starting with a list of all MWEs tagged as such in the BNC, and removing MWEs with a frequency of less than five, and MWEs with a part of speech of noun, or adjective. This reduction was performed for two reasons. Firstly, many MWE instances in the BNC can be considered noise in that they contain spelling variants, and features of spoken language. Secondly, a collocation consisting entirely of a combination of one or more nouns and adjectives is almost certainly a noun phrase, or part of a noun phrase. Noun phrases tend to be easily identifiable as such by parsers, and so are not relevant to our research aim. By removing the above MWEs we were able to reduce computational costs at later stages of processing.

3.2 Verification

Verification was performed with the aim of extracting a much higher quality list of candidate MWEs from the list of candidate MWEs produced in the collocation stage.

---

[3] http://www.natcorp.ox.ac.uk/

t-score

$$t = \frac{\overline{x} - \mu}{\sqrt{\frac{s^2}{N}}}$$

Where $\overline{x}$ is the sample mean, s^2 is the sample variance, N is the sample size and μ is the distribution's mean.

χ-square

$$\chi^2 = \frac{(f_{w_1 w_2} - f_{w_1} f_{w_2})^2}{f_{w_1} f_{w_2}} + \frac{(f_{w_1 \overline{w_2}} - f_{w_1} f_{\overline{w_2}})^2}{f_{w_1} f_{\overline{w_2}}} + \frac{(f_{\overline{w_1} w_2} - f_{\overline{w_1}} f_{w_2})^2}{f_{\overline{w_1}} f_{w_2}} + \frac{(f_{\overline{w_1 w_2}} - f_{\overline{w_1}} f_{\overline{w_2}})^2}{f_{\overline{w_1}} f_{\overline{w_2}}}$$

Where f is the frequency of an event, $w_1 w_2$ is the sequence of events (in this case words) w_1 then w_2, and $\overline{w_1}$ is the negation of the event w_1.

log-likelihood ratio

$$-2 \log \lambda = 2 \cdot \log \frac{L(H_1)}{L(H_0)}$$

Where $L(H)$ is the likelihood of hypothesis H assuming a binomial distribution.

pointwise mutual information (PMI)

$$I(w_1, w_2) = log_2 \frac{P(w_1 w_2)}{P(w_1) \cdot P(w_2)}$$

Where $P(w)$ is the probability of a given word.

mutual dependency (MD)

$$D(w_1, w_2) = log_2 \frac{P^2(w_1 w_2)}{P(w_1) \cdot P(w_2)}$$

Where $P(w)$ is the probability of a given word.

log-frequency biased mutual dependency (LFMD)

$$D_{LF}(w_1, w_2) = D(w_1, w_2) + log_2 P(w_1 w_2)$$

Where $P(w)$ is the probability of a given word.

Fig. 2. Collocation measures

Features. In order to train a classifier, a decision must be made about which features to include in the training data. We decided to use the tokens and their parts of speech from a context window of three tokens to the left and three tokens to the right of each candidate MWE. We also used the tokens in the candidate MWE itself and their parts of speech. The cutoff value of three is somewhat arbitrary, but most lexical dependencies can be assumed to be relatively local, so we can assume that it is large enough to capture the most useful information available from the context.

Contexts were not allowed to cross sentence boundaries. In cases where the available context surrounding a candidate MWE was shorter than the three token window, we inserted the appropriate number of dummy tokens and dummy parts of speech to fill up the deficit: "BOS" (Beginning Of Sentence) tokens in the left context, and "EOS" (End Of Sentence) tokens in the right context.

Part of Speech Tagging. The part of speech information was provided by tagging the corpus using the part of speech tagger TnT[4]. The BNC is a part of speech tagged corpus, but retagging was necessary because although each MWE in the BNC is tagged with a part of speech, its constituent tokens are not. The tokens which make up each MWE must therefore be tagged with individual parts of speech. It might be argued that combining the original BNC tagging with the TnT tagging of the words in the MWEs would have produced more accurate training data, but in a real world application, the part of speech information in the classifier's input data will be produced entirely using a tagger such as TnT. By using the same part of speech tagger at both the training, and application stages, any systematic tagging mistakes will hopefully (at least in part) be learnt and compensated for by the classifier. The tagger was trained on a subset of BNC files containing just under 5.5 million tokens. It was then tested on a different set of files, containing approximately 5.3 million tokens. The tagger's precision when tested on this data was 94.7%.

Training. The corpus used for training the classifier was a sub-corpus of the BNC containing approximately ninety million tokens covering all domains in the corpus. Examples used for training were the occurrences in the training corpus of the top 10,000 bigrams identified using the t-score and LFMD collocation measures. Most of the bigrams in the corpus were negative examples, either non-MWEs, or pseudo-MWEs.

We used TinySVM[5] to create a binary classifier. Training was performed (using the software's default settings) on the training corpus. Several training runs were performed using different amounts of data in order to investigate the relationship between volume of training data and the resulting model's performance.

Testing. Another sub-corpus of the BNC, independent of that used in training, was used for testing the classifier. This testing corpus contained approximately six million tokens and included texts from each domain in the corpus.

3.3 Part of Speech Estimation of Multiword Expressions

We treated the estimation of the part of speech of a given MWE as a classification task using the same approach as we used for the classification of true and false MWEs. We trained a separate classifier for each target part of speech. A positive

[4] http://www.coli.uni-sb.de/~thorsten/tnt/

[5] http://chasen.org/~taku/software/TinySVM/

training example was an occurrence of an MWE with the target part of speech. A negative example was an occurrence of any MWE with a non-target part of speech. The features used were the token and part of speech of three tokens to the left and to the right of the target MWE, as well as the tokens and parts of speech of the words in the MWE itself. The training and testing corpora were the same as used at the verification stage described above (Section 3.2). This was acceptable because the two tasks are independent of each other.

We chose the target parts of speech (adverbs, prepositions and conjunctions) because these relatively closed class, high frequency types are expected to be most useful in applications like parsing. We also experimented with an open class type (nouns) for comparison. Verbs could not be tested because there were insufficient numbers of them in the testing corpus. There are few fixed MWE verbs, so a scarcity of data was not surprising.

4 Results and Discussion

4.1 Collocation Extraction

Results for collocation extraction (Table 1) show that standard collocation measures perform poorly in the task of extracting the target MWEs. Even when

Table 1. Precision and recall for top 100, 1,000 and 10,000 candidate multiword expressions extracted using different collocation measures

Measure	Cutoff	Precision	Recall	F-measure
	10,000	0.009	0.251	0.017
freq	1,000	0.032	0.091	0.047
	100	0.010	0.003	0.004
	10,000	0.009	**0.257**	0.017
t-score	1,000	0.037	0.106	0.055
	100	0.030	0.009	0.013
	10,000	0.006	0.169	0.011
χ^2	1,000	0.013	0.037	0.019
	100	0.020	0.006	0.009
	10,000	0.004	0.117	0.008
log-like	1,000	0.008	0.023	0.012
	100	0.000	0.000	0.000
	10,000	0.003	0.083	0.006
MI	1,000	0.002	0.006	0.003
	100	0.000	0.000	0.000
	10,000	0.003	0.091	0.006
MD	1,000	0.003	0.009	0.004
	100	0.000	0.000	0.000
	10,000	0.008	**0.229**	0.015
LFMD	1,000	0.017	0.049	0.025
	100	0.080	0.023	0.036

calculated based on the top 10,000 candidate collocations, recall is only 26% (using the t-score).

A limitation in our approach to measuring collocation extraction may be partly to blame for the poor results in this task. Our target list consisted of *all* target MWEs, irrespective of their length. Since the collocations extracted were limited to bigrams, some of these may in fact be only *part* of a larger MWE in our target list.

Nevertheless, it may be that collocation measures are relatively ineffective at extracting fixed MWEs. Collocation measures are most effective when applied to expressions such as noun compounds. Many of the target MWEs contain high frequency function words such as prepositions, and thus are atypical of the types of expressions for which collocation measures were originally developed.

4.2 Verification

Verification of candidate MWEs produced better results (Table 2). For example, a classifier trained using one million examples, had precision of 96.56%, and recall of 89.11% giving an F-measure of 92.69.

Table 2. Performance of verifier using models trained on different quantities of data

Measure	Examples	Precision (%)	Recall (%)	F-measure
LFMD	1,000,000	96.56	89.11	92.69
	100,000	96.35	79.87	87.34
	10,000	93.66	56.04	70.12
	1,000	92.83	11.56	20.56

Initial review of classification results suggests a number of sources of error. Tagging errors seem to cause many of the false negative results. Proper nouns tend to be tagged as "unclassified words" which is intelligent in as much as it bundles all unusual words the tagger is unsure of together, but it results in incorrect tagging which prevents the classifier identifying true MWEs. Similarly, capitalisation of words in titles results in incorrect tagging of ordinary words as proper nouns. One title in particular *Sport in Short* occurs multiple times in the corpus, resulting in numerous errors.

False positives seem to be caused by proper nouns (e.g. *Kuala Lumpur*) and foreign words (e.g. *Vive L'Empereur*). Both false positives and false negatives seem to occur often in the context of punctuation, suggesting that this presents a particular difficulty for the classifier.

Interestingly, some false positives are in fact substrings of longer MWEs. Because we focused on bigrams in this paper, MWEs of longer than two tokens were ignored when assessing whether a candidate MWE was a true or false MWE. However, some of these candidate MWEs were in fact substrings of a longer MWE. The classifier may therefore be recognising that a given substring occurs in a context typical of MWEs, and is identifying the MWE substring as being a MWE in its own right. A fuller implementation which extracts MWEs longer than two tokens might therefore be expected to eliminate this source of error.

In spite of the occasional error, applying a classifier to the context surrounding a candidate MWE seems to offer an effective means of distinguishing true MWEs from non-MWEs and pseudo-MWEs.

4.3 Part of Speech Estimation

Evaluation of the part of speech classifiers shows them to be an effective means of estimating an MWE's part of speech based on its context of occurrence (Table 3). As we might expect, the classifier for nouns performed best, with near perfect recall and high precision. The conjunctions classifier performed least well with recall in particular being lower than that achieved for other parts of speech. This may reflect a greater variability in the contexts surrounding conjunctive MWEs. Conjunctions often play a discursive role in sentences, so evidence of an expression being a conjunction or not might be found at a higher level of linguistic analysis than the immediate lexical context used in our experiment.

Table 3. Part of speech estimation results

Part of speech	Precision (%)	Recall (%)	F-measure
Prepositions	98.06	98.40	98.23
Conjunctions	97.10	95.37	96.23
Adverbs	98.73	98.72	98.72
Nouns	98.88	99.25	99.07

5 Future Work

In this work we have focused on bigrams. We hope to generalise our approach, so that MWEs of length greater than two can be extracted and assigned a part of speech.

We plan to evaluate the performance of the BNC models described above on another corpus to determine their flexibility. Specifically, we plan to use a corpus of North American English such as the Penn Treebank, in the hope of demonstrating the models' ability to handle American as well as British English.

We also plan to check the effect on parsing accuracy of using the extracted multiword expressions in the input to a parser such as Collins' [9] or Yamada's [10].

6 Conclusion

In this research we aimed to identify a method for the automatic extraction and part of speech estimation of fixed MWEs. Knowledge about fixed MWEs has the potential to improve the accuracy of numerous natural language processing applications. Generating such a list therefore represents an important natural language processing task.

Our method uses a collocation measure to produce a list of candidate bigrams. These candidates are then used to select training data for a classifier. The trained classifier was successfully able to distinguish between contexts containing a true MWE, from contexts containing a pseudo-MWE or no MWE at all. The classifier trained on one million example candidates identified using LFMD had precision of 96.56%, and recall of 89.11%, giving an F-measure of 92.69%. Part of speech classifiers were then trained and tested. The classifiers were able to identify the correct part of speech for an MWE with a precision and recall of over 95%.

These results show that the local context surrounding an MWE contains sufficient information to identify its presence, and estimate its part of speech. If this information is detailed enough, we may be able to perform additional processing steps. For example, it may be possible to distinguish between specific sub-types of fixed MWE. The present method needs to be generalised so it can deal with MWEs of any length, not just bigrams. We plan to explore these issues in future research.

References

1. Church, K., Hanks, P.: Word association norms, mutual information, and lexicography. Computational Linguistics **16** (1990) 22–29
2. Smadja, F.: Retrieving collocations from text: Xtract. Computational Linguistics **19** (1993) 143–177 *Special Issue on Using Large Corpora: I.
3. Thanopoulos, A., Fakotakis, N., Kokkinakis, G.: Comparative evaluation of collocation extraction metrics. In: International Conference on Language Resources and Evaluation (LREC-2002). (2002) 620–625
4. Sag, I., Baldwin, T., Bond, F., Copestake, A., Flickinger, D.: Multiword expressions: A pain in the neck for NLP. In: Proceedings of the Third International Conference on Intelligent Text Processing and Computational Linguistics (CICLING 2002), Mexico City, Mexico, CICLING (2002) 1–15
5. Baldwin, T., Villavicencio, A.: Extracting the unextractable: A case study on verb-particles. In Roth, D., van den Bosch, A., eds.: Proceedings of the 6th Conference on Natural Language Learning (CoNLL-2002), Taipei, Taiwan (2002) 98–104
6. Villavicencio, A.: Verb-particle constructions and lexical resources. In Bond, F., Korhonen, A., McCarthy, D., Villavicencio, A., eds.: Proceedings of the ACL 2003 Workshop on Multiword Expressions: Analysis, Acquisition and Treatment, ACL (2003) 57–64
7. Manning, C.D., Schütze, H.: Foundations of Statistical Natural Language Processing. The MIT Press, Cambridge, Massachusetts (1999)
8. Dunning, T.: Accurate methods for the statistics of surprise and coincidence. Computational Linguistics **19** (1993) 61–74
9. Collins, M.: Head-Driven Statistical Models for Natural Language Parsing. PhD thesis, University of Pennsylvania (1999)
10. Yamada, H., Matsumoto, Y.: Statistical dependency analysis with support vector machines. In: IWPT 2003: 8th International Workshop on Parsing Technologies. (2003) 195–206

Phrase-Based Statistical Machine Translation: A Level of Detail Approach

Hendra Setiawan[1,2], Haizhou Li[1], Min Zhang[1], and Beng Chin Ooi[2]

[1] Institute for Infocomm Research,
21 Heng Mui Keng Terrace,
Singapore 119613
{stuhs, hli, mzhang}@i2r.a-star.edu.sg
[2] School of Computing,
National University of Singapore,
Singapore 117543
{hendrase, ooibc}@comp.nus.edu.sg

Abstract. The merit of phrase-based statistical machine translation is often reduced by the complexity to construct it. In this paper, we address some issues in phrase-based statistical machine translation, namely: the size of the phrase translation table, the use of underlying translation model probability and the length of the phrase unit. We present Level-Of-Detail (LOD) approach, an agglomerative approach for learning phrase-level alignment. Our experiments show that LOD approach significantly improves the performance of the word-based approach. LOD demonstrates a clear advantage that the phrase translation table grows only sub-linearly over the maximum phrase length, while having a performance comparable to those of other phrase-based approaches.

1 Introduction

Early approach to statistical machine translation relies on the word-based translation model to describe the translation process [1]. However, the underlying assumption of word-to-word translation often fails to capture all properties of the language, i.e. the existence of the phrase where a group of words often function together as a unit. Many researchers have proposed to move from the word-based to the phrase-based translation model [2] [3] [4]. A phrase-based approach offers many advantages as a phrase translation captures word context and local reordering inherently [3]. It has become popular in statistical machine translation applications.

There are typically two groups of approaches to constructing the phrase-based model. The first group learns phrase translation directly from the sentence pair. It learns both word and phrase units simultaneously. Although these approaches appear intuitive, it usually suffers from a prohibitive computational cost. It might have to consider all possible multi-word sequences as phrase candidates and all possible pairings as phrase translations at the same time.

R. Dale et al. (Eds.): IJCNLP 2005, LNAI 3651, pp. 576–587, 2005.

The second group of approaches learns phrase translations through word-level alignment: alignment template [2] and projection extension [6], just to name a few. In general, these approaches take the word-level alignment, a by-product of the word-based translation model, as their input and then utilize a heuristic measurement to learn the phrase translation. The heuristic measurement contains all possible configurations of word-level alignment on a phrase translation.

It is noted that the underlying word-level alignment is just an approximation to the exact alignment. The approximation is reflected by a probability produced by the word-based translation model. The majority of approaches do not make use of this probability, whereas it may provide a valuable clue leading to a better phrase translation from a statistical point of view. Koehn, et. al [8] compared the representative of both groups and reported that learning phrase translation using a simple heuristic from word alignment yields a better translation performance than learning phrase translation directly from the sentence pair.

Many approaches try to learn all phrase translations in one step, either directly from the sentence pair or through word alignment. As a result, they may encounter a huge amount of phrase translation candidates at once. Usually, they limit the maximum phrase length to reduce the choice of candidates. Although this method is sufficient to satisfy the computational requirement, it comes with the cost of not finding the good phrases longer than the imposed limit. Additionally, to reduce the candidates, those approaches use a threshold to separate good phrase translation from the rest. The threshold is ad-hoc and often not capable of making a clear separation. Therefore, the use of threshold often comes with the cost of the inclusion of undesired phrase translations and the absence of good phrase translations in the phrase translation table. The cost may be reflected from the size of the phrase translation table that often grows almost linearly over the phrase length limit [6][8]. The growth implies a non-intuitive behavior: two phrases with different length introduce an equal number of additional entries to the phrase translation table. As longer phrases occur less often, there should be fewer entries introduced into the phrase translation table.

We propose an agglomerative approach to learn phrase translations. Our approach is motivated by the second group, which is to learn phrase translation through word-alignment, while addressing the common issues: the size of the phrase translation table, the use of underlying translation model probability and the length of the phrase unit.

Only a few approaches move away from one-step learning. Melamed [13] presented an agglomerative approach to learn the phrases progressively from a parallel corpus by using sub-phrase bigram statistics. Moore [14] proposed a similar approach which identifies the phrase candidates by parsing the raw training data. Our idea differs from these approaches in that we look into the association of the alignments rather than the association of the words to discover the phrases.

In this paper, we propose the Level of Detail (LOD) approach for learning of phrase translations in phrase-based statistical machine translation. Section 2 discusses the background and motivation and then formulates the LOD approach while section 3 describes the learning process in details. Section 4 describes the experimental results. In this section, we compare LOD with state-of-the-art word-based approach in translation tasks. Finally, section 5 concludes this paper by providing some discussion in comparison with other related works.

2 Statistical Machine Translation: A Level of Detail

2.1 Motivation and Background

It is often not intuitive to model the translation of a phrase using the word-based translation model. First, the literal translation of phrase constituents is often inappropriate from a linguistic point of view. The word-based translation model treats a phrase as a multi-word. One such example is the case where a phrase appears as an idiom. The translation of an idiom cannot be synthesized from the literal translation of its constituents but rather from the semantic translation of the whole. Besides, the literal translation of an idiom detracts from the intended meaning. In one such example, the literal translation of French "*manger sur le pouce*" is "*to eat on the thumb*". This detracts from the correct translation "*to grab a bite to eat* ". In addition, to produce the correct translation, the word-based translation model might have to learn that "*manger*" is translated as "*eat*" or "*pouce*" is translated as "*thumb*". Although it may serve the translation purpose, it will introduce many non-intuitive entries to the dictionary.

Second, even if it is possible to translate a phrase verbatim, modeling phrase translation using the word-based translation model suffers from a disadvantage: the number of word alignments required to synthesize the phrase translation is large. It requires four word alignments to model the translation between "*une minute de silence*" and "*one minute of silence*", whereas one phrase alignment is adequate. The introduction of more alignments also implies the requirement to estimate more parameters for the translation model. The implication often comes with the cost of learning wrong word alignments.

Third, a phrase often constitutes some spurious words. The word-based translation model often has trouble in modeling spurious words, such as function words. Function words may appear freely in any position and often may not be translated to any word. We observe that many of these function words appear inside a phrase. It is beneficial to realize these spurious words inside a phrase unit so as to improve statistical machine translation performance and also to remove the necessity to model them explicitly. All these suggest that, ideally, a phrase translation should be realized as a phrase alignment, where the lexical correspondence is established on phrase level rather than on its word constituents.

The discussion above suggests that phrase-based translation is a wise choice. Practically, as a phrase is not a well defined lexical entry, a mechanism is needed to judge what constitutes a phrase in the context of statistical machine translation. In this paper, we advocate an approach to look into the phrase discovery process at different level of details. The level of detail refers to the size of a phrase unit. At its finest level of detail, a phrase translation uses the word-based translation model where a phrase is modeled through its word constituent. At a coarser level of detail, a sub-phrase unit is introduced as a sequence of words, making it a constituent of the phrase. The coarsest level of detail refers to the status of a phrase where all word constituents converge into a whole unit.

Our Level-Of-Detail (LOD) approach views the problem of phrase-based translation modeling through a LOD process. It starts from the finest word-level alignment and transforms the phrase translation into its coarsest level of detail.

2.2 Formulation

Let $< \mathbf{e}, \mathbf{f} >$ be a sentence pair of two sequences of words with $\mathbf{e}$ as an English sentence and $\mathbf{f}$ as its translation in French[1]. Let $< \tilde{\mathbf{e}}, \tilde{\mathbf{f}} >$ represents the same sentence pair but with the phrase as its atomic unit rather than the word. To generalize the notation, we treat word and phrase unit similarly by considering a word as a phrase of length one. Therefore, $< \mathbf{e}, \mathbf{f} >$ hereafter will be referred as $< \tilde{\mathbf{e}}, \tilde{\mathbf{f}} >^{(0)}$, which represents the finest level of detail, and $< \tilde{\mathbf{e}}, \tilde{\mathbf{f}} >$ as $< \tilde{\mathbf{e}}, \tilde{\mathbf{f}} >^{(N)}$, which represents the coarsest level of detail. Let each tuple in the sentence pair of any level of detail n, $< \tilde{\mathbf{e}}, \tilde{\mathbf{f}} >^{(n)}$ be $\tilde{\mathbf{e}}^{(n)} = \{\tilde{e}_0^{(n)}, \tilde{e}_1^{(n)}, \ldots, \tilde{e}_i^{(n)}, \ldots, \tilde{e}_{l^{(n)}}^{(n)}\}$ and $\tilde{\mathbf{f}}^{(n)} = \{\tilde{f}_0^{(n)}, \tilde{f}_1^{(n)}, \ldots, \tilde{f}_j^{(n)}, \ldots, \tilde{f}_{m^{(n)}}^{(n)}\}$ where $\tilde{e}_0^{(n)}, \tilde{f}_0^{(n)}$ represent the special token $NULL$ as suggested in [1] and $l^{(n)}, m^{(n)}$ represent the length of the corresponding sentence. Let $T^{(n)}$ be a set of alignment defined over the sentence pair $< \tilde{e}, \tilde{f} >^{(n)}$ with $t_{ij}^{(n)} = [\tilde{e}_i^{(n)}, \tilde{f}_j^{(n)}]$ as its member. The superscript in all notations denotes the level of detail where 0 represents the finest and N represents the coarsest level of detail.

LOD algorithm iteratively transforms $< \tilde{\mathbf{e}}, \tilde{\mathbf{f}} >^{(0)}$ to $< \tilde{\mathbf{e}}, \tilde{\mathbf{f}} >^{(N)}$ through re-alignment of phrases and re-estimation of phrase translation probability. At n-th iteration, LOD harvests all bi-directional alignments from the sentence pair $< \tilde{\mathbf{e}}, \tilde{\mathbf{f}} >^{(n)}$. The alignment is obtained by a typical word-based translation model, such as the IBM model, while treating a sub-phrase at n-th iteration as a word. We refer to those alignments as $\mathcal{B}^{(n)}$, a pool of sub-phrase alignments unique to the particular iteration. Afterwards, LOD generates all possible phrase alignment candidates $\mathcal{C}^{(n)}$ for a coarser level of detail from these sub-phrase alignments. A resulting phrase alignment candidate is basically a joining of two adjacent sub-phrase alignments subject to a certain criterion. It represents the future coarser level alignment. Up to this point, two sets of alignment are obtained over$< \tilde{\mathbf{e}}, \tilde{\mathbf{f}} >^{(n)}$: a pool of sub-phrase alignments $\mathcal{B}^{(n)}$ at the current level and a pool of phrase alignment candidates $\mathcal{C}^{(n)}$ at a coarser level. From these two sets of alignments $\mathcal{B}^{(n)} \cup \mathcal{C}^{(n)}$, we would like to derive a new set of alignments $T^{(n+1)}$ that best describes the training corpus with the re-estimated statistics obtained at n-th iteration. LOD constructs $< \tilde{\mathbf{e}}, \tilde{\mathbf{f}} >^{(n+1)}$ from the new set of alignment. Algorithm 1 provides the general overview of LOD algorithm.

[1] Subsequently, we will refer $\mathbf{e}$ as source sentence and $\mathbf{f}$ as target sentence, but the term does not always reflect the translation direction.

Algorithm 1. An overview of LOD approach in learning phrase translation. The LOD approach takes a sentence pair at its finest level of detail as its input, learns the phrase-level alignment iteratively and outputs the same sentence pair at its coarsest level of detail along with its phrase translation table.

input $\langle \tilde{\mathbf{e}}, \tilde{\mathbf{f}} \rangle^{(0)}$
for $n = 0$ **to** $(N-1)$ **do**
- Generate bi-directional sub-phrase level alignments $\mathcal{B}^{(n)}$ from $\langle \tilde{\mathbf{e}}, \tilde{\mathbf{f}} \rangle^{(n)}$
- Identify phrase-level alignment candidates $\mathcal{C}^{(n)}$ from $\mathcal{B}^{(n)}$
- Estimate the alignment probability in $\mathcal{B}^{(n)}$ and $\mathcal{C}^{(n)}$
- Learn coarser level alignment $T^{(n+1)}$ from $\mathcal{B}^{(n)} \cup \mathcal{C}^{(n)}$ and construct $\langle \tilde{\mathbf{e}}, \tilde{\mathbf{f}} \rangle^{(n+1)}$

output $\langle \tilde{\mathbf{e}}, \tilde{\mathbf{f}} \rangle^{(N)}$ and $T^{(N)}$

3 Learning Phrase Translation

In this section, we discuss the steps of LOD algorithm in detail. As presented in Algorithm 1, moving from one level of alignment to its coarser level, LOD follows four simple steps:

1. Generation of bi-directional sub-phrase level alignments [2]
2. Identification of phrase level alignment candidates
3. Estimation of alignment probability
4. Learning coarser level alignment

3.1 Generation of Bi-directional Sub-phrase Level Alignments

LOD follows the common practice to utilize the IBM translation model for learning the phrase translation. That is to harvest all alignments from both translation directions. For the sake of clarity, LOD defines the following notation for these alignments, as follows:

Let $\Gamma_{ef}^{(n)} : \tilde{e}_i^{(n)} \longrightarrow \tilde{f}_j^{(n)}$ be an alignment function represents all alignments from translating the source English sentence to the target French sentence, and $\Gamma_{fe}^{(n)} : \tilde{f}_j^{(n)} \longrightarrow \tilde{e}_i^{(n)}$ be the reversed translation direction. Then, bi-directional sub-phrase alignment $\mathcal{B}^{(n)}$ includes all possible alignment by both functions:

$$\mathcal{B}^{(n)} = \{t_{ij}^{(n)} = [\tilde{e}_i^{(n)}, \tilde{f}_j^{(n)}] | (\Gamma_{ef}^{(n)}(\tilde{e}_i^{(n)}) = \tilde{f}_j^{(n)}) \cup (\Gamma_{fe}^{(n)}(\tilde{f}_j^{(n)}) = \tilde{e}_i^{(n)})\}$$

Let us denote $NULL$ alignments, $\mathcal{N}^{(n)}$, a subset of alignments in $\mathcal{B}^{(n)}$ in which the special token $NULL$ is involved.

[2] The process starts with word level alignment. A word here is also referred to as a sub-phrase.

3.2 Identification of Phrase Alignment Candidates

LOD applies a simple heuristic to identify a phrase alignment candidate. First, LOD considers every combination of two distinct sub-phrase alignments and assesses its candidacy. Here, we define a phrase alignment candidate $< t_{ij}^{(n)}, t_{i'j'}^{(n)} > \in \mathcal{C}^{(n)}$ as follows:

Let $< t_{ij}^{(n)}, t_{i'j'}^{(n)} >$ be a set of two tuples, where $t_{ij}^{(n)} \in \mathcal{B}^{(n)}$ and $t_{i'j'}^{(n)} \in \mathcal{B}^{(n)}$. Then $< t_{ij}^{(n)}, t_{i'j'}^{(n)} >$ is a phrase aligment candidate **if and only if**

1. **not** $((i, i') \neq 0)$ **or** $(|i - i'| = 1)$
2. **not** $((t_{ij}^{(n)} \in \mathcal{N}^{(n)})$ **and** $(t_{i'j'}^{(n)} \in \mathcal{N}^{(n)}))$

In the definition above, the first clause defines a candidate as a set of two whose source sub-phrases are adjacent. The second clause forbids the consideration of two $NULL$ alignments.

As LOD considers only two alignments for each phrase alignment candidate, it implies that, at the n-th iteration, the length of the longest possible phrase is bounded by 2^n. Apparently, we do not have to examine sub-phrase alignment trunks of more than two sub-phrases because the iteration process guarantees LOD to explore phrases of any length given sufficient iteration. This way, the search space at each iteration can be manageable at each iteration.

3.3 Estimation of Alignment Probability

Joining the alignment set $\mathcal{B}^{(n)}$ derived in Section 3.1 and the coarser level alignment $\mathcal{C}^{(n)}$ derived in Section 3.2, we form a candidate alignment set $\mathcal{B}^{(n)} \cup \mathcal{C}^{(n)}$. Assuming that there are two alignments $x \in \mathcal{B}^{(n)}$, $y \in \mathcal{B}^{(n)}$, and a candidate alignment $< x, y > \in \mathcal{C}^{(n)}$, we derive the probability $p(x)$ and $p(y)$ from the statistics as the count of x and y normalized by the number of alignments in the corpus, and we derive the joint probability $p(< x, y >)$ in a similar way.

If there is a genuine association between the two alignments, x and y, then we expect that $p(< x, y >) \gg p(x)p(y)$. If there is no interesting relationship between x and y, then $p(< x, y >) \approx p(x)p(y)$ where we say that x and y are independent. If x and y are in a complementary relationship, then we expect to see that $p(< x, y >) \ll p(x)p(y)$. These statistics allow us to discover a genuine sub-phrase association.

The probability is estimated by the count of observed events normalized by the corpus size. Note that the alignment from the IBM translation model is derived using a Viterbi-like decoding scheme. Each observed event is counted as one. This is referred to as hard-counting. As the alignment is done according to probability distribution, another way of counting the event is to use the fractional count that can be derived from the translation model. We refer to it as soft-counting.

3.4 Learning a Coarser Level Alignment

From section 3.1 to 3.3, we have prepared all the necessary alignments with their probability estimates. The next step is to re-align $< \tilde{\mathbf{e}}, \tilde{\mathbf{f}} >^{(n)}$ into $< \tilde{\mathbf{e}}, \tilde{\mathbf{f}} >^{(n+1)}$

using alignment phrases in $\mathcal{B}^{(n)} \cup \mathcal{C}^{(n)}$ with their newly estimated probability distribution. The re-alignment is considered as a constrained search process. Let $p(t_{ij}^{(n)})$ be the probability of a phrase alignment $t_{ij}^{(n)} \in (\mathcal{B}^{(n)} \cup \mathcal{C}^{(n)})$ as defined in Section 3.3, $T^{(n)}$ be the potential new alignment sequence for $< \tilde{\mathbf{e}}, \tilde{\mathbf{f}} >^{(n)}$, we have the likelihood for $T^{(n)}$ as

$$\log P(< \tilde{\mathbf{e}}, \tilde{\mathbf{f}} >^{(n)} |T^{(n)}) = \sum_{t_{ij}^{(n)} \in T^{(n)}} \log p(t_{ij}^{(n)}) \quad (1)$$

The constrained search is to decode an alignment sequence that produces the highest likelihood possible in the current iteration, subject to the following constraints:

1. to preserve the phrase ordering of the source and target languages
2. to preserve the completeness of word or phrase coverage in the sentence pair
3. to ensure the mutual exclusion between alignments (except for the special *NULL* tokens)

The constrained search can be formulated as follows:

$$T^{(n+1)} = \underset{\forall T^{(n)}}{\text{argmax}} \log P(< \tilde{\mathbf{e}}, \tilde{\mathbf{f}} >^{(n)} |T^{(n)}) \quad (2)$$

In Eq.(2), we have $T^{(n+1)}$ as the best alignment sequence to re-align sentence pair $< \tilde{\mathbf{e}}, \tilde{\mathbf{f}} >^{(n)}$ to $< \tilde{\mathbf{e}}, \tilde{\mathbf{f}} >^{(n+1)}$.

The constraints are to ensure that the search leads to a valid alignment result. The search is essentially a decoding process, which traverses the sentence pair along the source language and explores all the possible phrase alignments with the target language. In practice, LOD tries to find a phrase translation table that maximizes Eq.(2) as formulated in Algorithm 2. As the existing alignment for $< \tilde{\mathbf{e}}, \tilde{\mathbf{f}} >^{(n)}$ in the n-th iteration is a valid alignment subject to three

---

Algorithm 2. A stack decoding algorithm to explore the best alignment path between source and target languages by considering all alignment candidates in $\mathcal{B}^{(n)} \cup \mathcal{C}^{(n)}$ at n-th iteration.

---

1. Initialize a lattice of $l^{(n)}$ slots for $l^{(n)}$ sub-phrase in source language.
2. Starting from i=1, for all phrases in source language e_i;
   1) Register all the alignments $t_{ij}^{(n)}$ that map source phrases ending with e_i, including e_i itself, into slot i in the lattice;
   2) Register the probability of alignment $p(t_{ij}^{(n)})$ together with the alignment entry $t_{ij}^{(n)}$
   3) Repeat 1) and 2) until i=$l^{(n)}$
3. Apply stack decoding [15] process to find the top n-best paths subject to the three constraints. During the decoding processing, the extension of partial path is subject to a connectivity test to enforce the three constraints.
4. Output the top best alignment result as the final result.

---

constraints, it also serves as one resolution to the search. In the worst case, if the constrained search can not discover any new alignment other than the existing one, then the existing alignment in the current iteration will stand through the next iteration.

In Algorithm 2, we establish the lattice along the source language. In the case of English to French translation, we follow the phrases in the English order. However, it can be done along the target language as well since our approach follows a symmetric many-to-many word alignment strategy.

This step ends with the promotion of all phrase alignment candidates in the best alignment sequence $T^{(n+1)}$. The promotion includes the merging of the two sub-phrase alignments and the concerning sub-phrases. The merged unit will be considered as a unit in the next iteration.

4 Experiments

The objective of our experiments is to validate our LOD approach in machine translation task. Additionally, we are interested in investigating the following: the effect of soft-counting in probability estimation, and the behavior of LOD approach in every iteration, in terms of the length of the phrase unit and the size of the phrase translation table. We report all our experiments using BLEU metrics [10]. Furthermore, we report confidence intervals with 95% statistical significance level of each experiments, as suggested by Koehn [16].

We validate our approach through several experiments using English and French language pairs from the Hansard corpus. We restrict the sentence length to at most 20 words to obtain around 110 thousands sentence pairs. Then we randomly select around 10 thousands sentence pair as our own testing set. In total, the French corpus consists of 994,564 words and 29,360 unique words; while the English corpus consists of 1,055,167 words and 20,138 unique words. Our experiment is conducted on both English-to-French (e2f) and French-to-English (f2e) tasks under open testing set-up. We use these available tools: GIZA++[3] for word-based IBM 4 model training and ISI ReWrite[4] for translation test. For measuring the BLEU score and deriving the confidence intervals, we use the publicly available tools[5].

4.1 Soft-Counting vs. Hard-Counting

Table 1 summarizes our experiments in analyzing the effect of soft-counting and hard-counting in the probability estimation on the BLEU score. Case I demonstrates the BLEU score of the experiment using the underlying translation model probability or soft-counting, while Case II demonstrates the score of

[3] http://www.fjoch.com/

[4] http://www.isi.edu/licensed-sw/rewrite-decoder/

[5] http://www.nist.gov/speech/tests/mt/resources/scoring.htm and http://projectile.is.cs.cmu.edu/research/public/tools/bootStrap/tutorial.htm

Table 1. Summary of experiment showing the contribution of using the translation model probability. The experiments are conducted on English-to-French task. Case I indicates the BLEU score of the LOD approach using soft-counting whereas Case II indicates the BLEU score of hard-counting. The value in the column indicates the BLEU score. The range inside the bracket indicates the confidence intervals with 95% statistical significance level.

iteration	Case I	Case II
1	29.60 (29.01-30.14)	28.80 (28.20-29.38)
2	30.72 (30.09-31.29)	30.11 (29.48-30.67)
3	31.52 (30.87-32.06)	30.70 (30.05-31.32)
4	31.93 (31.28-32.50)	30.93 (30.30-31.51)
5	31.90 (31.45-32.68)	31.07 (30.39-31.62)

hard-counting. The experimental results suggest that the use of the underlying translation model probability is beneficial as it gives consistently higher BLEU scores in all the iterations. The comparison using paired bootstrap resampling [16] also confirms the conclusion.

4.2 LOD Behavior over Iteration

Table 2 summarizes the performance of our LOD approach for the first 10 iterations in comparison with the baseline IBM 4 word-based approach. The results show that the LOD approach produces a significant improvement over IBM 4 consistently. The first iteration yields the biggest improvement. We achieve an absolute BLEU score improvement of 5.01 for the English-to-French task and 5.48 for the French-to-English task from the first iteration. The subsequent improvement is obtained by performing more iterations and capturing longer phrase translation, however, the improvement gained is less significant compared to that of the first iteration.

Table 2 also summarizes the maximum phrase length and the behavior of the phrase translation table: its size and its increment over iteration. It shows that the phrase length is soft-constrained by the maximum likelihood criterion in Eq. (2) rather than limited. As iteration goes on, longer phrases are learnt but their probabilities are less probable than shorter one. Consequently, longer phrases introduce fewer entries to the phrase translation table. Table 2 captures the behavior of the phrase translation table. The first iteration contributes the highest increment of 12.5 % to the phrase translation table while the accumulated increment of table size up to 10th iteration only contributes 27.5% increment over the original size. It suggests that as iteration goes and longer phrases are captured, fewer additional entries are introduced to the phrase translation table. The results also show the growth of the size of the phrase translation table is sub-linear and it converges after reasonable number of iterations. This represents a clear advantage of LOD over other related work [6][8].

Table 2. Summary of experiments showing the behavior of LOD approach and the characteristics of the phrase translation table in each iteration. The table shows the translation performance of the word-based IBM 4 approach and the first 10 iteration of LOD approach in BLEU score. The value in the columns indicate the BLEU score while the range inside the bracket represents the confidence intervals with 95% statistical significance level. The table also shows the trend of the phrase translation table: the maximum phrase length, its size, and its increase over iterations.

Iteration	Max Phrase Length	Table Size	Increase	BLEU with confidence intervals e2f	f2e
IBM 4	1	216,352	-	24.59 (24.12-25.21)	26.76 (26.15-27.33)
1	2	244,097	27,245	29.60 (29.01-30.14)	32.24 (31.58-32.83)
2	4	258,734	14,637	30.72 (30.09-31.29)	32.93 (32.28-33.57)
3	7	266,209	7,475	31.52 (30.87-32.06)	33.88 (33.22-34.49)
4	7	270,531	4,322	31.93 (31.28-32.50)	34.14 (33.46-34.76)
5	10	271,793	1,262	31.90 (31.45-32.68)	34.26 (33.56-34.93)
6	11	273,589	1,796	32.14 (31.48-32.72)	34.50 (33.78-35.16)
7	12	274,641	1,052	32.09 (31.43-32.68)	34.55 (33.81-35.18)
8	12	275,399	758	32.07 (31.39-32.60)	34.43 (33.71-35.09)
9	13	275,595	196	31.98 (31.32-32.55)	34.65 (33.93-35.29)
10	14	276,508	913	32.22 (31.55-32.79)	34.61 (33.91-35.26)

5 Discussion

In this paper, we propose LOD approach to phrase-based statistical machine translation. The LOD approach addresses three issues in the phrase-based translation framework: the size of phrase translation table, the use of underlying translation model probability and the length of the phrase unit.

In terms of the size of the phrase translation table, our LOD approach presents a sub-linear growth of the phrase translation table. It demonstrates a clear advantage over other reported attempts, such as in [6][8] where the phrase translation table grows almost linearly over the phrase length limit. The LOD approach manages the phrase translation table size in a systematic way as a result of the incorporation of maximum likelihood criterion into the phrase discovery process.

In terms of the use of underlying translation model probability, we propose to use soft-counting instead of hard-counting in the re-estimation processing of probability estimation. In the projection extension algorithm [6], the phrases are learnt based on the presence of alignment in certain configurations. In alignment template[2], two phrases are considered to be translation of each other, if the word alignments exist within the phrases and not to the words outside. Both methods are based on hard-counting of translation event. Our experiment results suggest the use of soft-counting.

In terms of the length of the phrase unit, we move away from the window-like limit for phrase candidacy [4][9]. The LOD approach is shown to be more flexible in capturing phrases of different length. It gradually explores longer phrases as iteration goes, leading any reasonable length given sufficient iteration as long as they are statistically credible.

It is known that statistical machine translation relies very much on the training corpus. A larger phrase translation table means more training data are needed for the translation model to be statistically significant. In this paper, we successfully introduce the LOD approach to control the process of new phrase discovery process. The results are encouraging.

References

1. Peter F. Brown, Stephen A. Della Pietra, Vincent J. Della Pietra, and Robert L. Mercer. 1993. The mathematics of statistical machine translation: parameter estimation. Computational Linguistics, 19(2), pp. 263-311.
2. Franz Josef Och, Christoph Tillmann, and Hermann Ney. 1999. Improved alignment models for statistical machine translation. In Proc of the Joint SIGDAT Conference on Empirical Methods in Natural Language Processing and Very Large Corpora, pp. 20-28, University of Maryland, College Park, MD, June.
3. Franz Josef Och and Hermann Ney. 2000. A Comparison of alignment models for statistical machine translation. In Proc of the 18th International Conference of Computational Linguistics, Saarbruken, Germany, July.
4. Daniel Marcu and William Wong. 2002. A phrase-Based, joint probability model for statistical machine translation. In Proc. of the Conference on Empirical Methods in Natural Language Processing, pp. 133-139, Philadelphia, PA, July.
5. Stephan Vogel, Hermann Ney, and Christoph Tillmann. 1996. HMM-based word alignment in statistical translation, Proc. of COLING '96: The 16th International Conference of Computational Linguistics. pp. 836-841. Copenhagen, Denmark.
6. Christoph Tillmann. 2003. A projection extension algorithm for statistical machine translation. in Proc. of the Conference on Empirical Methods in Natural Language Processing, Sapporo, Japan.
7. Ying Zhang, Stephan Vogel, Alex Waibel. 2003. Integrated phrase segmentation and alignment algorithm for statistical machine translation. in Proc. of the Conference on Natural Language Processing and Knowledge Engineering, Beijing, China.
8. Philipp Koehn, Franz Josef Och, Daniel Marcu. 2003. Statistical Phrase-based Translation. In Proc. of the Human Language Technology Conference, pp. 127-133, Edmonton, Canada, May/June.
9. Ashish Venugopal, Stephan Vogel, Alex Waibel. 2004. Effective phrase translation extraction from alignment models. in Proc. of 41st Annual Meeting of Association of Computational Linguistics, pp. 319-326, Sapporo, Japan, July.
10. K. Papineni, S. Roukos, T. Ward and W. J. Zhu. 2001. BLEU: A method for automatic evaluation of machine translation. Technical Report RC22176 (W0109-022), IBM Research Report.
11. G. Doddington. 2002. Automatic evaluation of machine translation quality using N-gram co-occurence statistics. In Proc. of the Conference on Human Language Technology, pp. 138-135, San Diego, CA, USA.

12. Richard Zens, Hermann Ney. 2004. Improvements in phrase-Based statistical machine translation. in Proc. of Conference on Human Language Technology, pp. 257-264, Boston, MA, USA.
13. I. D. Melamed. 1997. Automatic discovery of non-compositional compounds in parallel data. In Proc. of 2nd Conference on Empirical Methods in Natural Language Processing, Provicence, RI.
14. Robert C Moore. 2001. Towards a simple and accurate statistical approach to learning translation relationships among words. In Proc of Workshop on Data-driven Machine Translation, 39th Annual Meeting and 10th Conference of the European Chapter, Association for Computational Linguistics, pp. 79-86, Toulouse, France.
15. R Schwartz and Y. L. Chow . 1990. The N-best algorithm: An efficient and exact procedure for finding the N most likely sentence hypothesis. In Proc. of ICASSP 1990, pp. 81-84. Albuquerque, CA.
16. Philipp Koehn. 2004. Statistical significance tests for machine translation evaluation. In Proc. of the 2004 Conference on Empirical Methods in Natural Language Processing, pp. 388-395.

Why Is Zero Marking Important in Korean?

Sun-Hee Lee[1,*], Donna K. Byron[2], and Seok Bae Jang[3]

[1,2] 395, Dreese Lab., 2015, Neil Avenue,Columbus, OH 43210
shlee@ling.ohio-state edu
dbyron@cse.ohio-state.edu
[3] 37th and O Sts., NW, Washington, D.C, 20057
sbj3@georgetown.edu

Abstract. This paper argues for the necessity of zero pronoun annotations in Korean treebanks and provides an annotation scheme that can be used to develop a gold standard for testing different anaphor resolution algorithms. Relevant issues of pronoun annotation will be discussed by comparing the Penn Korean Treebank with zero pronoun mark-up and the newly developing Sejong Teebank without zero pronoun mark-up. In addition to supportive evidence for zero marking, necessary morphosyntactic and semantic features will be suggested for zero annotation in Korean treebanks.

1 Introduction

This paper discusses the importance of zero pronoun marking in treebanks and investigates what kind of linguistic features are needed for treebank annotation in order to increase the usability of annotated corpora. Zero pronouns refer to empty pronouns without phonological realization, which work in a similar manner as English pronouns.

In the recent decade, there has been remarkable progress in the realm of building large corpora in Korean and applying them for linguistic research and natural language processing. Based on the broad acknowledgement of the importance of corpus and applicative tools, the 21st century Sejong project was launched in 1998 and has been developing various database and relevant computational tools including electronic dictionaries, annotation tools, morphological analyzers, parsers, etc. As a part of the Sejong project, the syntactically annotated treebank of Korean has been under construction. In addition to the Sejong Treebank (henceforth, ST), the Penn Korean Treebank (Han et al.[4] henceforth, PKT) has already been released and continues to be expanded. These treebanks with abundant linguistic information are expected to fulfill a function as informative databases in broad domains of theoretical linguistics and computational linguistics such as statistical approaches, machine learning, etc.

A notable point is that there is a critical difference between annotations of ST and PKT with respect to marking zero elements including traces, zero pronouns, etc. The most current guidelines of ST specify that zeros are dropped in order to maintain the

* This work was supported by the Korea Research Foundation Grant (KRF-2004-037-A00098) for the author.

R. Dale et al. (Eds.): IJCNLP 2005, LNAI 3651, pp. 588 – 599, 2005.

consistency and efficiency of the treebank. In contrast, PKT advocates for representing zero elements. According to different approaches to zero marking, the structure of the following sentence (1a) is differently analyzed as in (1b) and (1c); in (1b) ST does not contain any missing subject while PKT marks the missing subject and object as *pros* in (1c)[1]

```
(1) a. 어제밤        12시-에      받-았-습니다.
       eceypam      12 si-ey      pat-ass-supnita.
       last night     12 o'clock-at  receive-Past-E
      'Last night at 12 o'clock, (I/(s)he/they) received (it)'.
    b. ST: (VP  (AP   어젯밤/MAG)
                (VP  (NP_AJT 12/SN + 시/NNB + 에/JKB)
                     (VP 받/VV+았/EP+습니다/EF.+ ./SF )))
    c. PKT :(S  (NP-SUBJ  *pro*)
                (VP  (NP-ADV 어젯밤/NNC)
                     (NP-ADV 12/NNU 시/NNX+에/PAD)
                     (VP  (NP-OBJ  *pro*)
                          받/VV+았/EPF+습니다/EFN))) ./SFN).
```

The sentence representation of (1b) does not fully present the subject-predicate relation in contrast with (1c). In this paper, we argue that failure to mark zeros may cause a loss of valuable linguistic information such as filler-gap dependencies, argument-predication relations, semantic and discourse interpretations of sentences, etc. The ST style zero-less annotation will impose the burden of zero marking on the post-annotation tasks, which utilize treebank resources for developing computational tools. This, however, is inconsistent with the purpose of developing treebanks. As pointed out in Dickinson & Meurers [3], treebanks have major usage for two types of linguists; one is for theoretical linguists who search through the corpora in order to identify certain linguistic patterns. The other is for computational linguists who use computational technology and develop statistical models from the annotated corpora in order to develop parsers and question-answer systems and to extract information such as subcategorization frames of predicates, event nouns, complex predicates, etc. In general, treebanks are manually or semi-manually annotated by humans. This guarantees more sophisticated representations of sentence structure and reliable mark-ups for ambiguous morphosyntactic units. While focusing on the usability of treebanks, we propose an argument against dropping zero mark-ups in treebanks and investigate the empirical necessity of zero annotation in Korean treebanks.

In this paper, we will discuss some significant problems of zero-less treebank annotation and explain why zero annotation is important in languages like Korean. Then we will present a general annotation scheme and features of zero pronouns that can be used to develop a gold standard for testing an anaphor resolution algorithm. Adding zero mark-up will solidify accurate syntactic representation and increase the usability of treebanks even though it takes strenuous efforts and time for development.

---

[1] The tagsets of ST and PKT are somewhat different (i.e., MAG represents an adverb, AP, an adverbial phrase, and NP-ADV , a nominal functioning as an adverbial modifier in ST).

2 Necessity of Zero Annotation in Korean Treebank

In contrast with English where a repeated element tends to appear as a pronoun, in topic prominent languages like Korean, a repeated element has no surface realization. Thus, Korean zero elements are often called zero pronouns.

(2) a. John met Mary yesterday.
    b. Kim met her, too.
(3) a. John-i eycey Mary-lul mannassta.
    John-Nom yesterday Mary-Acc met
    'John met with Mary yesterday. .
    b. Kim-to Ø ,mannaassta.
    Kim also OBJ met
    'Kim also met (zero=her).'

The discrepancy between ST and PKT with respect to zero annotation brings us two different values with respect to corpus annotation; economy vs. usability. At the stage of annotating corpora, excluding all the missing subjects from the Korean treebanks may reduce the burden of annotation tasks such as classifying zeros, sorting markable zeros, training annotators and maintaining the legitimate level of inter-annotator agreement. However, at the later stage zero marked treebanks have higher usability by higher level processing including anaphor resolution, extracting subcategorization frames of predicates, discourse analysis, etc.

More specifically, our arguments against zero-less treebanks can be presented as follows. First, zero-less treebanks may provide misleading representations with respect to the general patterns of sentence realization. In so-called pro-drop languages such as Korean, Japanese, Spanish and Portuguese, basic units of sentence structure, such as subjects of matrix clauses, are frequently unrealized. Although missing subject information in languages like Spanish and Portuguese is recoverable from verb morphology, interpretations of missing arguments do not correspond to specific verb morphology in Korean. Thus, marking the place of a zero element is an inevitable process not only for structural representation but for processing the meaning of a sentence. Zero-less treebanks license various VP or S nodes without capturing correct argument-predicate relations. For example, the following sentence is simply represented as VP, which is inconsistent with the subcategorization frame of the main verb.

(4) 그냥 잠자코 운동장-만 내다보-고 있-었-습니다.
    kunyang camcakho wuntongcang-man naytapo-ko iss-ess-supnita.
    just silently playground-only look down-PreP-Past-E
    '(I/you/he/she/they) was only looking down the playground just silently.'

```
(VP (AP 그냥/MAG)
    (VP (AP 잠자코/MAG)
        (VP (NP_OBJ 운동장/NNG + 만/JX)
            (VP (VP 내다보/VV + 고/EC)
                (VP 있/VX + 었/EP + 습니다/EF + ./SF)))))
```

According to Hong [6], the rate of subject drop is 57% in spoken Korean, which is higher than other elements. In particular, when the subject refers to a nominal entity mentioned in the previous utterance, it naturally disappears in speech rather than appearing as a pronoun. This suggests that the number of VPs lacking subjects will be significantly high in the spoken corpora. We extracted only 100 sentences from the ST corpus containing natural spoken conversations and found that 81 sentences are represented as VPs or VNPs (predicate nominal phrases). However, it may derive a misleading generalization such that canonical sentence patterns in the given corpus are VPs or VNPs. In line with this, semantic interpretations of those incomplete VPs or VNPs subsume the meaning of the zero pronouns whose antecedents appear in the previous utterances. However, zero-less mark-up poses a difficulty in retrieving the complete sentential meaning from the given phrasal categories of VPs or VNPs.

Second, zero-less treebanks make it difficult to extract certain constructions that linguists want to identify. For example, one of the most frequently discussed topics in Korean grammar is formation of Double Subject Constructions (DSCs), which license two subjects. However, zero-less treebanks do not correctly represent Double Subject Constructions and represent (5) and (6) differently in spite of their similarity in argument realization.

(5) 햇밤-이 맛-이 썩 좋-았-습니다.
hayspam-i mas-i ssek choh-ass-supnita.
new chestnut-Nom taste-Nom quite good-Past-End
'New chestnuts had pretty good taste.'
(S (NP_SUB 햇밤/NNG + 이/JKS)
(S (NP_SBJ 맛/NNG + 이/JKS)
(VP (AP 썩/MAG)
(VP 좋/VA + 았/EP + 습니다/EF + ./SF))))

(6) 유난히 맛-이 썩 좋-았-습니다.
yunanhi mas-i ssek choh-ass-supnita.
particularly taste-Nom quite good-Past-End
'Particularly, the taste of (it) was pretty good.'
(S (AP 유난히/MAG)
(S (NP_SBJ 맛/NNG + 이/JKS)
(VP (AP 썩/MAG)
(VP 좋/VA + 았/EP + 습니다/EF + ./SF))))

According to the analysis of ST, (5) is represented as a DSC that licenses two subjects, *hayspam* and *mas*. In contrast, (6) is represented as a complex clause that only licenses a single matrix subject, *mas* and the first zero subject referring to the same nominal entity in the preceding phrase has been ignored in the sentential representation. It is difficult to extract certain syntactic patterns from the zero-less treebanks because their structural representations do not reflex the accurate argument-predicate realization. It is because they focus on surface realization of arguments instead of considering lexical constraints of argument-predicate relations.

The third critical problem of zero-less treebanks is related to discourse analysis. Unrealized arguments are important for tracking the attentional state of a discourse in topic-oriented languages like Korean and Japanese. Within the framework of centering theory, e.g. Walker et al. [9], Iida [7]), Hong [6], etc. it has been shown that a salient entity recoverable by inference from the context is frequently omitted, and therefore interpreting these zero pronouns allows one to follow the center of the attentional state. Walker et al. [9] applied the centering model, developed for pronoun resolution in English, to zero pronoun resolution in Japanese. They argue that interpretation of a zero pronoun is determined by discourse factors. This suggests that identifying occurrences of zero pronouns and retrieving their antecedents are important in developing a computational model of discourse interpretations as well as syntactic and semantic analyses. When it comes to topic information retrieval, the salient element under the discussion of the given discourse is realized as a zero. Grammatical roles and semantic restrictions provide crucial cues for the interpretations of them. However, without specifying the argument positions of these zeros, discourse processing of the given utterances is impossible.

3 Relevant Issues of Zero Annotation

Zero marked treebanks function as useful resource for researchers, especially the anaphora resolution community. For developing computational tools of anaphor resolution, it is necessary to determine the distribution of zero pronouns and their link to other discourse properties. There has historically been a lack of annotated material available to the wider research community that would allow us to investigate these questions. Researchers in the past worked mainly with small amounts of hand-constructed data rather than being able to do large-scale corpus analysis. This lack has been recently pointed out by Lee et al. [8] evaluating the Penn Korean Treebank (Han et. al. [4]), which includes annotations indicating the position of zero pronouns. In PKT, annotations of zeros are problematic due to inconsistent mark-up for zero pronouns and structural representation of trees. Inconsistent annotation of zero pronouns in PTK brings an imminent issue for developers of Treebanks and other annotated language resources; when and how should these unrealized elements be explicitly introduced into the linguistic material being developed? Unless these questions are resolved, treebanks cannot fulfill their potential as a source of linguistic knowledge about zero pronouns. Also, the same question should be taken into consideration by other teams developing similar resources in other languages.

3.1 Argument vs. Adjunct

Previous authors have pointed out that the antecedents of zero pronouns can often be determined by using various grammatical properties such as topicality, agreement, tense, and aspect as well as subcategorization information (Walker et al. [9]; Iida [7]; Hong [6], etc.). However, in order for these factors to be useful in developing anaphora resolution algorithms, they must be reliably and consistently annotated into the source data. Thus, the first crucial step for zero pronoun resolution is identifying the exact positions of zero pronouns. Determining the positions of invisible zeros is a difficult task. This process needs to refer to the argument realization in a given utterance and the previous utterances of the same discourse unit. The argument realization of a sentence is based upon argument structure of a predicate.

(7) a. John-i . kesil-eyse swi-ko iss-ess-ta?
John-Nom living room-in rest-Pres Prog-Past-E
'John was resting in the living room.'
b. sakwa-lul mek-ess-ta.
apple-Acc eat-past-E
'(He) ate an apple.'

In (7b), the argument structure of *mekta* 'eat' suggests that the subject is missing in a sentence *sakwalul mekesse* 'ate an apple'. However, do we need to mark the adjunct *kesileyse* 'in the living room' in (7b)? In the given utterances, it seems to be possible for John to have eaten the apple in the living room but it is not necessarily true. The combinations of adjunct and predicate are not predictable by using argument structure of a predicate. With no specific guideline, identifying missing adjuncts complicates the annotation process. Thus, we argue that only missing arguments must be marked.

As for zero argument annotation, the current annotation in PKT is somewhat problematic due to unclear distinction of obligatory argument vs. optional argument. According to the guidelines of PKT, only a missing obligatory argument should be annotated as an empty element. Missing optional arguments and adjuncts are not. Thus, in PKT, missing subject or object elements were marked as zeros while missing locative arguments were not marked when they were omitted. However, the annotation method based on an obligatory vs. optional argument may result in the loss of crucial information needed at later stage of retrieving an antecedent of a zero element. For example, the locative argument, 'the 45th division-in' has not been marked up as a zero pronoun in the tagged sentence of (8b)

(8) a: 제 45 사단은 또 무엇-으로 구성되어 있는가 ?
the 45 division again what-with composed be
'What is the 45th Division composed of ?'
(S (NP-SBJ 제/XPF+45/NNU
사단/NNC+은/PAU)
(VP (VP (ADVP 또/ADV)
(VP (NP-COMP 무엇/NPN+으로/PAD)
(VV 구성/NNC+되/XSV+어/EAU)))
있/VX+는가/EFN) ?/SFN)
b: 사단 지희부-가 있습니다 .
division head-Nom exist
'The head division is (there).
(S (NP-SBJ 사단/NNC
지휘부/NNC+가/PCA)
(ADJP 있/VJ+습니다/EFN). /SFN)

In the given discourse segments, the adjective 있다 *issta* requires a locative argument which has been treated as an optional argument in PKT. Thus, the information of the missing locative has not been represented even though it is crucial for retrieving the meaning of the sentence. Another concern with respect to distinction of argument and adjunct is that ST classifies only subject and object as arguments and excludes other case-marked nominals as adjunct[2]. This classification may cause problems when zero pronouns are added in their treebanks.

In identifying missing zero arguments, maintaining consistency is crucial. For this task, we can rely on a dictionary containing constant argument structure of predicates. Dictionaries with specific argument structure information can be used here, such as

---

[2] In addition to subject and object, nominals in front of predicates, *toyta*, *anita* and quotation clause have been included as arguments.

the Yonsei Korean dictionary, where different subcategorization frames are listed according to semantically disambiguated senses for each predicate. For correct identification of a zero pronoun in the given utterance, annotators need to examine the relevant previous utterances in the same discourse unit and determine the exact verb sense of the relevant predicate by using the dictionary. In addition, checking inter-annotator agreement is also an essential task (Carletta [2]).

3.2 Language Specific Properties of Korean

Another notable point is that the developers need to pay attention to language specific properties of Korean. There are some notable morphosyntactic properties of Korean with respect to zero pronoun annotation. In order to maintain constant annotation of zero pronouns, it is important to carefully represent specific features related to zero pronouns. In this section, we will discuss specific properties that can be added for zero pronoun annotation. It will increase the applicability of the treebank to both theoretical research on anaphors and computational modeling of anaphor resolution.

[1] CASE MARKING

In determining an antecedent of a zero pronoun, the existence of topics plays an important role in Korean. In the previous theoretical literature, it has been commonly assumed that the topic marked elements appear at the higher phrasal level than the phrasal combination of subject-predicate. At the discourse level, Walker et al. [9] and Iida [7] provide evidence that topic marked elements function as antecedents of zero pronouns in Japanese. The similar property has been also observed with Korean by Hong [6]. As seen in the following examples, the sentence-initial topic functions as the antecedent of zero pronouns that appear in the latter utterances. This phenomenon suggests that the topic marker needs to be differentiated from other postpositions and that grammatical topics are to be differentiated from other grammatical arguments like subjects and objects.

(9) a **Seyho-nun** apeci-eykey chingchan-ul pat-ca ekkay-ka ussukhayci-pnita.
Seyho-Top father-to praise-Acc receive-E be proud of
'As for **Seyho**, he felt pride when he received praise from father.'
b. Ø 20 ilman-ey tut-nun chingchan-ila kippum-un hankyel tehaysssupnita
20days-in hear-Rel praise-since pleasure-Top far more
'Since it was the praise (he) heard for the first time in 20 days, his pleasure was much more.'
c. Ø emeni-eykey-nun nul kkwucilam-kwa cansoli-man tulesssupnita.
mother-to-Top always scolding-and lecture-only heard
'From his mother, (he) always heard only scolding and lecture.'

In general, while the marker *nun* functions as a topic marker in a sentence initial position, it also works as an auxiliary postposition in a non-initial position of a sentence in Korean. The first is classified as a grammatical topic marker while the latter is a contrastive topic marker in traditional Korean grammar. However, the current annotations of PKT and ST treat topic marker *nun* as the same auxiliary postposition, which is similar to other postpositions *man* 'only', *to* 'also', and *mace* 'even'. In particular, PKT and ST represent a subject NP with a topic marker as the subject, while an object with a topic marker is treated as a scrambled argument out of its canonical position. With respect to zero pronouns, the sentence initial topic marker needs to be distinctly marked from other postpositions. In addition, we claim that the structural position of a topicalized subject needs to be differentiated from a normal subject position in parallel with a topicalized object and other element, which leave zero traces in their original positions.

Another problem with case markers is subject marker *-eyse*, which only combines with nominals referring to a group or organization. In Korean, these group nominals do not take the nominative case *i/ka* but the case marker *-eyse* as in (12)

(10) wuli hakkyo-eyse wusung-ul hayssta.
our school-Nom winning-Acc did
'Our school won.'

Although *-eyse* has been treated as a nominative case marker in traditional Korean grammar, both PKT and ST do not treat *-eyse* as a nominative marker. Instead, group or organization nominals with the case marker-*eyse* are analyzed as NP adverbial phrases. This, however, mistakenly licenses a zero subject in the following example of PKT even though the subject with case marker *-eyse* exists. In order to eliminate redundant marking for the zero subjects, it is better to analyze the case marker, *-eyse* as a nominative case marker in Korean.

(11) 2 대대-에서 어떤 무전망-을 운용하-고 있-지?
2 taytay-eyse etten mwucenmang-ul wunyonha-ko iss-ci?
2 squadron-Nom which radio network-Acc use-PresP-Q
'What kind of radio network is the 2nd squadron using?'
(S (NP-ADV 2/NNU
대대/NNC+에서/PAD)
(S (NP-SBJ ***pro***)
(VP (VP (ADVP 또/ADV)
(VP (NP-OBJ 어떤/DAN
무전망/NNC+을/PCA)
(VV 운용/NNC+하/XSV+고/EAU)))
있/VX+지/EFN) ?/SFN)

[2] SUBJECTLESS CONSTRUCTIONS

Unlike English having expletive pronouns *it* or *there*, certain predicate constructions do not license subject positions at all in Korean. Some examples are presented in (12),which include incomplete predicates with few inflectional forms.

(12) *-ey tayhaye*, 'regarding on'*-ey kwanhaye*, 'about' *-ey uyhaye*, 'in terms of'
-lo inhayse 'due to~', *-wa tepwule* 'with ~' etc.

In addition, some modal auxiliary verbs like *sangkita*, *poita*, *toyta*, etc. do not license subject positions and have already been classified as subjectless constructions in Korean grammar. While ST treats these modal verbs to be included in the preceding verbal clusters, PKT separates them from the preceding verbs and assigns zero subjects for these verbs. Thus, the PKT approach redundantly assigns zero subjects for subjectless predicates.

[3] VERBAL MORPHOLOGY OF SPEECH ACT

As for zero pronoun resolution, verbal suffixes representing speech act can be a useful source. Thus, we argue for adding these morphosyntactic features in treebanks. It has been well known that in Korean certain speech acts such as declaration, request, question, promise, etc. are associated with verb morphology; five different types of verbal inflections are used to indicate declaratives, interrogatives, imperatives, propositives, and exclamatives. Information of a missing subject can be retrieved from verbal morphology. For example, the imperative verbal endings suggest that a missing subject refers to the hearer while promising verbal endings imply that a missing subject is the speaker. Thus, the missing subjects of the following examples are respectively interpreted as I, you and we based on the verbal suffixes representing a particular speech act.

(13) a. Ø ka-llay. (Question)
go-Q
'Do (you) want to go?'
b. Ø ka-llay. (Declaration)
go-will
'(I) will go.'
c. Ø ka-ca. (Request)
go-let's
'Let's go.'

Verbal endings of speech acts can be used to enhance the process of determining an antecedent of a zero pronoun subject. In the current annotations of PKT and ST, verbal suffixes do not subclassify the final endings. We argue that annotating the five classes of verbal suffixes differently will facilitate application of anaphor resolution algorithms on treebanks.

[4] WH-PRONOUN TAGGING

Wh-pronouns in Korean include *nwuka* 'who', *mwues* 'what', *encey* 'when', *etise* 'where', *way* 'why', *ettehkey* 'how', etc. Unfortunately, *wh*-pronouns are not distinctly tagged from other pronouns in the PKT and the ST. The information of *wh*-pronouns can be useful for resolving the meaning of zero pronouns in the next answering utterance As seen in (14b), a fragment directly related to a *wh*-pronoun necessarily appears in the answering utterance while non-*wh*-elements previously mentioned are easily dropped. This is because pairs of *wh*-question-answer tend to have the same predicates with the same argument structure. Therefore, answering utterances of the *wh*-questions generally contain zero pronouns, whose antecedents appear in the preceding questioning utterances.

(14) A: John-i Min-ul mwe-la-ko mitko iss-ni?
John-Nom Min-Acc what-Co-Comp believe being-Q
'What does John believe Min to be?'
B: Ø Ø kyoswu-la-ko mitko iss-nuntey.
SUBJ OBJ professor-Co-Comp believe being-END
'(He) believes (her) to be a professor.'

4 New Annotation Scheme of Korean Zero Pronouns

Once zeros are identified by argument structure information of predicates and the previous utterances in the given discourse, the additional reference information can be added in treebanks to support anaphor resolution. Zeros in Korean can be classified into different classes according to properties of their reference. Anaphor resolution algorithms can be applied for certain types of pronouns. For example, in order to retrieve the meaning of a zero pronoun referring to a nominal entity in the previous utterance, the resolution algorithm will search nominal entities that appear in the previous utterance by making a list of antecedent candidates and selecting the most appropriate candidate. In contrast, the searching algorithm does not need to apply for a zero element referring to an indefinite entity as in (15).

(15) Ø holangi kwul-ey ka-ya holangi-lul capnunta.
tiger den-to go-E tiger-Acc catch
(Lit.) 'One should go to the tiger's den in order to catch a tiger.
(Trans.) 'Don't hesitate but pursue what you need to do.'

According to reference relation between a zero pronoun and its antecedent, zero pronouns in Korean can be divided into three classes as in Table 1; discourse anaphoric zeros, deictic and indexical zeros, and indefinite zeros.

In the given classification, discourse anaphoric zeros take their reference from antecedents in the previous utterances in the given discourse. This class is the main one that anaphor resolution systems aim to handle. The discourse anaphoric zeros can be divided into three subclasses according to the semantic properties of their antecedents.

Table 1. Classification of Korean Zero Pronouns

Discourse Anaphoric Zeros	Individual Entities
	Propositions
	Eventualities
Deictic and Indexical Zeros	
Indefinite Zeros	

The first subclass of discourse anaphoric zeros refers to individual domain entities, the second, eventualities, and the third, propositions. The zeros of individual entities refer to entities that were introduced into the discourse via noun phrases. Most examples presented in the previous sections correspond to this class. The zeros of propositions refer to propositions introduced in the previous utterance as in (16).

(16) A: 108 yentay cihwipwu-nun hyencay eti-ey wichihako issnun-ka?
108 regiment headquarter-TOP now where-at locate being-Q
'Where is the headquarter of the 108th regiment located?'
B: Ø1 Ø2 molukeyss-supnita.
SUBJ OBJ not know-END
'I don't know.'
(Ø1 = 'B', Ø2= 'Where the headquarter of the 108th regiment is located')

The third class of zero anaphors referring to eventualities, i.e. action and event as in (17) (Asher [1]).

(17) A: Mary-ka cip-ey - ka-ko sipheha-ci anha.
Mary-Nom home-to go-E want-END don't
'Children don't want to go home.'
B: na-to Ø silhe.
I-also hate
'I also hate to go home.' (Ø = the action of going home)

The second class of zero pronouns includes deictic and indexical zeros that directly refer to entities that can be determined in the given spatiotemporal context, which generally include a speaker and an addressee. The third class includes indefinite zeros referring to general people, which corresponds to they, one, and you in English.

Given the classification of zero pronouns, different coding systems can be provided for each class for annotating these elements. According to different classes of zeros, the resolution process varies. Zero anaphors of discourse anaphoric entities will be marked the same as their antecedents in the previous utterances. Anaphor resolution algorithms determine the antecedent of a zero anaphor by searching through the antecedent candidates in different orders. Deictic and indexical zeros are dependent on discourse participants. In general, a zero anaphor can also refer to the speaker or the hearer. Overlapping mark-up for these zeros need to be allowed although resolution mechanisms for deictic and indexical zeros are different from those for anaphors. Indefinite zeros need to be marked but anaphor resolution algorithms do not need to be applied to them.

5 Conclusion

In this paper, we discussed why zero marking is necessary for Korean treebanks and how invisible zeros can be consistently marked in annotated corpora like treebanks. The importance of zero mark-up in Korean treebanks has been discussed with respect to correct linguistic analysis and efficient application of computational process. We also claimed that only missing arguments are marked as zeros and a dictionary like Yonsei Dictionary with full specification of argument-predicate relations can be a useful source for the annotation task. By examining PKT and the newly developing ST, we determined four linguistic features that are useful for anaphor resolution in Korean; case marking, subjectless construction, verb morphology of speech acts and *wh*-pronoun tagging. In addition, we provided a new annotation scheme that can be utilized for annotating treebanks and testing anaphor resolution algorithms with annotated corpora.

References

1. Asher, N.:. Reference to Abstract Objects in Discourse. Kluwer Academic Publishers. (1993).
2. Carletta, J. Assessing Agreement on Classification Tasks: the Kappa Statistic, Computational Linguistics 22(2) (1996) 249-254.
3. Dickinson, M. and Meurers, D.: Detecting Inconsistencies in Treebanks in Proceedings of the Second Workshop on Treebanks and Linguistics Theories.(TLT 2003)..Växjö. Sweden. (2003)

4. Han, C-H., Han, N-R., Ko, E-S.and Palmer, M.: Development and Evaluation of a Korean Treebank and Its Application to NLP.in Proceedings of the 3rd International Conference on Language Resources and Evaluation (LREC).(2002)
5. Han, N-R.: Korean Null Pronouns: Classification and Annotation in Proceedings of the ACL 2004 Workshop on Discourse Annotation. (2004) 33-40.
6. Hong M.: Centering Theory and Argument Deletion in Spoken Korean. The Korean Journal Cognitive Science. Vol. 11-1 (2000) 9-24.
7. Iida, M.: Discourse Coherence and Shifting Centers in Japanese texts in Walker, M., Joshi A.K., Prince E.F. (Eds.) Centering Theory in Discourse. Oxford University Press, Oxford: UK..(1998) 161-182.
8. Lee, S., Byron, D., and Gegg-Harrison, W.: Annotations of Zero Pronoun Resolution in Korean Using the Penn Korean Treebank in the 3rd Worksop on Treebanks and Linguistics Theories (TLT 2004). Tübingen. Germany. (2004) 75-88.
9. Walker, M., Iida, M., .Cotes, S.: Japanese Discourse and the Process of Centering in Computational Linguistics, Vol. 20-2.: (1994.) 193-232
10. 10. Dictionary Yonsei Korean Dictionary. (1999) Dong-A Publishing Co.
11. Guidelines of the Sejong Treebank. Korea University

A Phrase-Based Context-Dependent Joint Probability Model for Named Entity Translation

Min Zhang[1], Haizhou Li[1], Jian Su[1], and Hendra Setiawan[1,2]

[1] Institute for Infocomm Research,
21 Heng Mui Keng Terrace, Singapore 119613
{mzhang, hli, sujian, stuhs}@i2r.a-star.edu.sg
[2] Department of Computer Science,
National University of Singapore, Singapore, 117543
hendrase@comp.nus.edu.sg

Abstract. We propose a phrase-based context-dependent joint probability model for Named Entity (NE) translation. Our proposed model consists of a lexical mapping model and a permutation model. Target phrases are generated by the context-dependent lexical mapping model, and word reordering is performed by the permutation model at the phrase level. We also present a two-step search to decode the best result from the models. Our proposed model is evaluated on the LDC Chinese-English NE translation corpus. The experiment results show that our proposed model is high effective for NE translation.

1 Introduction

A Named Entity (NE) is essentially a proper noun phrase. Automatic NE translation is an indispensable component of cross-lingual applications such as machine translation and cross-lingual information retrieval and extraction.

NE is translated by a combination of meaning translation and/or phoneme transliteration [1]. NE transliteration has been given much attention in the literature. Many attempts, including phoneme and grapheme-based methods, various machine learning and rule-based algorithms [2,3] and Joint Source-Channel Model (JSCM) [4], have been made recently to tackle the issue of NE transliteration. However, only a few works have been reported in NE translation. Chen et al. [1] proposed a frequency-based approach to learn formulation and transformation rules for multilingual Named Entities (NEs). Al-Onaizan and Knight [5] investigated the translation of Arabic NEs to English using monolingual and bilingual resources. Huang et al. [6] described an approach to translate rarely occurring NEs by combining phonetic and semantic similarities. In this paper, we pay special attention to the issue of NE translation.

Although NE translation is less sophisticated than machine translation (MT) in general, to some extent, the issues in NE translation are similar to those in MT. Its challenges lie in not only the ambiguity in lexical mapping such as <副 (*Fu*) ,Deputy> and <副 (*Fu*),Vice> in Fig.1 in the next page, but also the position permutation and fertility of words. Fig.1 illustrates two excerpts of NE translation from the LDC corpus [7]:

R. Dale et al. (Eds.): IJCNLP 2005, LNAI 3651, pp. 600 – 611, 2005.

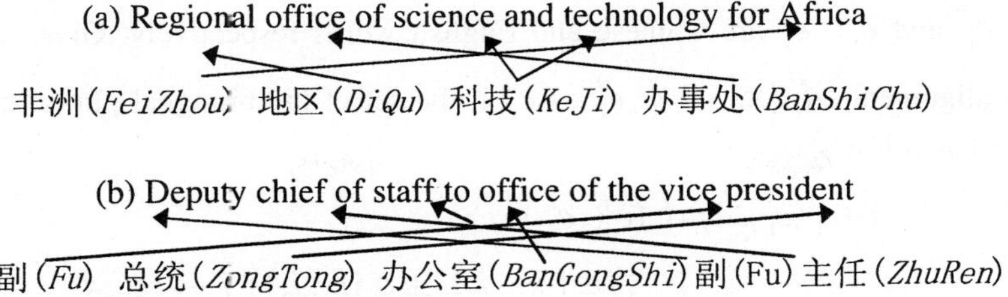

Fig. 1. Example bitexts with alignment

where the *italic* word is the Chinese *pinyin* transcription.

Inspired by the JSCM model for NE transliteration [4] and the success of statistical phrase-based MT research [8-12], in this paper we propose a phrase-based context-dependent joint probability model for NE translation. It decomposes the NE translation problem into two cascaded steps:

1) Lexical mapping step, using the phrase-based context-dependent joint probability model, where the appropriate lexical item in the target language is chosen for each lexical item in the source language;
2) Reordering step, using the phrase-based *n*-gram permutation model, where the chosen lexical items are re-arranged in a meaningful and grammatical order of target language.

A two-step decoding algorithm is also presented to allow for effective search of the best result in each of the steps.

The layout of the paper is as follows. Section 2 introduces the proposed model. In Section 3 and 4, the training and decoding algorithms are discussed. Section 5 reports the experimental results. In Section 6, we compare our model with the other relevant existing models. Finally, we conclude the study in Section 7.

2 The Proposed Model

We present our method by starting with a definition of translation unit in Section 2.1, followed by the formulation of the lexical mapping model and the permutation model in Section 2.2.

2.1 Defining Translation Unit

Phrase level translation models in statistical MT have demonstrated significant improvement in translation quality by addressing the problem of local re-ordering across language boundaries [8-12]. Thus we also adopt the same concept of phrase used in statistical phrase-based MT [9,11,12] as the basic NE translation unit to address the problems of word fertility and local re-ordering within phrase.

Suppose that we have Chinese as the source language $c_1^J = c_1 ... c_j ... c_J$ and English as the target language $e_1^I = e_1 ... e_i ... e_I$ in an NE translation (c_1^J, e_1^I), where

$c_j \in c_1^J$ and $e_i \in e_1^I$ are Chinese and English words respectively. Given a directed word alignment $\mathcal{A}:\{ c_1^J \rightarrow e_1^I, e_1^I \rightarrow c_1^J \}$, the set of the bilingual phrase pairs Λ is defined as follows:

$$\Lambda(c_1^J, e_1^I, \mathcal{A}) = \{ (c_{j_1}^{j_2}, e_{i_1}^{i_2}) : \forall j \in \{j_1 ... j_2\}, \exists i \in \{i_1 ... i_2\} : j \rightarrow i \in \mathcal{A} \wedge \textit{vice versa} \} \quad (1)$$

The above definition means that two phrases are considered to be translations of each other, if the words are aligned exclusively within the phrase pair, and not to the words outside [9,11,12]. The phrases have to be contiguous and a *null* phrase is not allowed.

Suppose that the NE pair (c_1^J, e_1^I) is segmented into X phrase pairs $(\tilde{c}_1^X, \tilde{e}_1^X)$ according to the phrase pair set Λ, where $\tilde{e}_1^X$ is reordered so that the phrase alignment is in monotone order, *i.e.*, $\tilde{c}_x$ is aligned $\tilde{c}_x \leftrightarrow \tilde{e}_x$ For simplicity, we denote by $\lambda_x =< \tilde{c}_x, \tilde{e}_x >$ the xth phrase pair in $(\tilde{c}_1^X, \tilde{e}_1^X) = \lambda_1 ... \lambda_x ... \lambda_X$, $\lambda_x \in \Lambda$.

2.2 Lexical Mapping Model and Permutation Model

Given the phrase pair set Λ, an NE pair (c_1^J, e_1^I) can be rewritten as $(\tilde{c}_1^X, \tilde{e}_1^X) = \lambda_1 ... \lambda_x ... \lambda_X = \lambda_1^X$. Let us describe a Chinese to English (C2E) bilingual training corpus as the output of a generative stochastic process:

---

(1) Initialize queue Q_c and Q_e as empty sequences;
(2) Select a phrase pair $\lambda_x =< \tilde{c}_x, \tilde{e}_x >$ according to the probability distribution $p(\lambda_x \mid \lambda_1^{x-1})$, remove λ_x from Λ;
(3) Append the phrase $\tilde{c}_x$ to Q_c and append the phrase $\tilde{e}_x$ to Q_e;
(4) Repeat steps 2) and 3) until Λ is empty;
(5) Reorder all phrases in Q_e according to the probability distribution of the permutation model;
(6) Output Q_e and Q_c .

As $p(\lambda_x \mid \lambda_1^{x-1})$ is typically obtained from a source-ordered aligned bilingual corpus, reordering is needed only for the target language. According to this generative story, the joint probability of the NE pair (c_1^J, e_1^I) can then be obtained by summing the probabilities over all possible ways of generating various sets of Λ and all possible permutations that can arrive at (c_1^J, e_1^I). This joint probability can be formulated in *Eq.*(2). Here we assume that the generation of the set Λ and the reordering process are modeled by *n*-order Markov models, and the reordering process is independent of the source word position.

$$
\begin{aligned}
p(c_1^J, e_1^I) &= \sum_{\Lambda} \{ p(\lambda_1^X) * p(e_1^I \mid \tilde{e}_1^X) \} \\
&\approx \sum_{\Lambda} \{ (\prod_{x=1}^{X} p(\lambda_x \mid \lambda_{x-n}^{x-1})) * p(\tilde{e}_{k_1}^{k_X} \mid \tilde{e}_1^X) \}
\end{aligned} \tag{2}
$$

$$
p(\tilde{e}_{k_1}^{k_X} \mid \tilde{e}_1^X) \approx \prod_{x=1}^{X} p(\tilde{e}_{k_x} \mid \tilde{e}_{k_{x-n}}^{k_{x-1}}) \tag{3}
$$

where $\tilde{e}_{k_1}^{k_X}$ stands for one of the permutational sequences of $\tilde{e}_1^X$ that can yield e_1^I by linearly joining all phrases, i.e., $e_1^I = \tilde{e}_{k_1}^{k_X}$ (). The generative process, as formulated above, does not try to capture how the source NE is mapped into the target NE, but rather how the source and target translation units can be generated simultaneously in the source order and how the target NE can be constructed by reordering the target phrases, $\tilde{e}_1^X$.

In essence, our proposed model consists of two sub-models: a **lexical mapping model (LMM)**, characterized by $p(\lambda_x \mid \lambda_{x-n}^{x-1})$, that models the monotonic generative process of phrase pairs; and **a permutation model (PM)**, characterized by $p(\tilde{e}_{k_x} \mid \tilde{e}_{k_{x-n}}^{k_{x-1}})$, that models the permutation process for reordering of the target language. The **LMM** in this paper is among the first attempts to introduce context-dependent lexical mapping into statistical MT (Och *et al.*, 2003). The **PM** here is also different from the widely used position-based distortion model in that it models phrase connectivity instead of position distortion. Although **PM** functions as an *n*-gram language model, it only models the ordering connectivity between target language phrases, i.e., it is not in charge of target word selection.

Since the proposed model is phrase-based and we use conditional joint probability in **LMM** and use context-dependent *n*-gram in **PM**, we call the proposed model a phrase-based context-dependent joint probability model.

3 Training

Following the modeling strategy discussed above, the training process consists of three steps: phrase alignment, reordering of corpus, and learning statistical parameters for lexical mapping and permutation models.

3.1 Acquiring Phrase Pairs

To reduce vocabulary size and avoid sparseness, we constrain the phrase length to up to three words and the lower-frequency phrase pairs are pruned out for accurate phrase-alignment[1]. Given a word alignment corpus which can be obtained by means of the publicly available GIZA++ toolkit [15], it is very straightforward to construct the phrase-alignment corpus by incrementally traversing the word-aligned NE from left to right[2]. The set of resulting phrase pairs forms a lexical mapping table.

3.2 Reordering Corpus

The context-dependent lexical mapping model assumes monotonic alignment in the bilingual training corpus. Thus, the phrase aligned corpus needs to be reordered so that it is in either source-ordered or target-ordered alignment. We choose to reorder the target phrases to follow the source order. Only in this way can we use the lexical mapping model to describe the monotonic generative process and leave the reordering of target translation units to the permutation model.

3.3 Training LMM and PM

According to *Eq.* (2), the **lexical mapping model (LMM)** and the **permutation model (PM)** can be interpreted as a kind of *n*-gram Markov model. The phrase pair is the basic token of **LMM** and the target phrase is the basic token of **PM**. A bilingual corpus aligned in the source language order is used to train **LMM**, and a target language corpus with phrase segmentation in their original word order is used to train **PM**. Given the two corpora, we use the SRILM Toolkit [13] to train the two *n*-gram models.

4 Decoding

The proposed modeling framework allows **LMM** and **PM** decoding to cascade as in Fig.2.

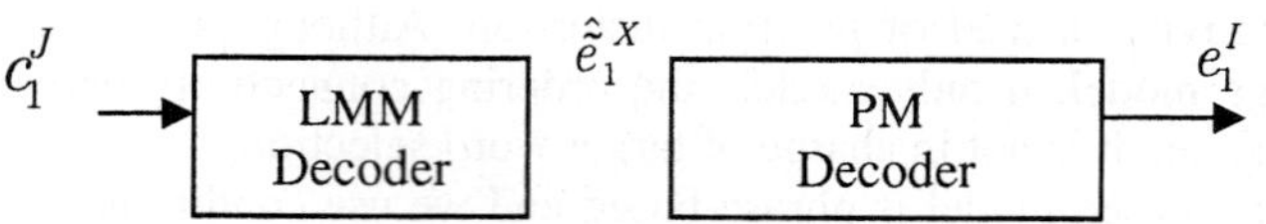

Fig. 2. A cascaded decoding strategy

The two-step operation is formulated by *Eq.*(4) and *Eq.*(5). Here, the probability summation as in *Eq.*(2) is replaced with maximization to reduce the computational complexity:

$$\hat{\tilde{e}}_1^X = \arg\max_{\Lambda}\{\prod_{x=1}^{X} p(\lambda_x \mid \lambda_{x-n}^{x-1})\} \tag{4}$$

[1] Koehn et. al. [12] found that that in MT learning phrases longer than three words and learning phrases from high-accuracy word-alignment does not have strong impact on performance.

[2] For the details of the algorithm to acquire phrase alignment from word alignment, please refer to the section 2.2 & 3.2 in [9] and the section 3.1 in [12].

$$\hat{e}_1^I = \arg\max_{\Omega}\{\prod_{x=1}^{X} p(\tilde{e}_{k_x} \mid \tilde{e}_{k_{x-n}}^{k_{x-1}})\} \tag{5}$$

LMM decoding: Given the input c_1^J, the **LMM** decoder searches for the most probable phrase pair set Λ in the source order using *Eq.*(4). Since this is a monotone search problem, we use a stack decoder [14,18] to arrive at the *n*-best results.

PM decoding: Given the translation phrase sequence $\hat{\tilde{e}}_1^X$ from the **LMM** decoder, the **PM** decoder searches for the best phrase order that gives the highest *n*-gram score by using *Eq.*(5) in the search space Ω, which is all the $X!$ permutations of the all phrases in $\hat{\tilde{e}}_1^X$. This is a non-monotone search problem.

The **PM** decoder conducts a time-synchronized search from left to right, where time clocking is synchronized over the number of phrases covered by the current partial path. To reduce the search space, we prune the partial paths along the way. Two partial paths are considered identical if they satisfy the following both conditions:

1) They cover the same set of phrases regardless of the phrase order;
2) The last *n*-1 phrases and their ordering are identical, where *n* is the order of the *n*-gram permutation model.

For any two identical partial paths, only the path with higher *n*-gram score is retained. According to *Eq.* (5), the above pruning strategy is risk-free because the two partial paths cover the exact same portion of input phrases and the *n*-gram histories for the next input phrases in the two partial paths are also identical.

It is also noteworthy that the decoder only needs to perform $X/2$ expansions as after $X/2$ expansions, all combinations of $X/2$ phrases would have been explored already. Therefore, after $X/2$ expansions, we only need to combine the corresponding two partial paths to make up the entire input phrases, then select the path with highest *n*-gram score as the best translation output.

Let us examine the number of paths that the **PM** decoder has to traverse. The pruning reduces the search space by a factor of $Z!$, from $P_X^Z = \frac{X!}{(X-Z)!}$ to $C_X^Z = \frac{X!}{Z! \bullet (X-Z)!}$, where Z is the number of phrases in a partial path. Since $C_X^Z = C_X^{X-Z}$, the maximum number of paths that we have to traverse is $C_X^{X/2}$. For instance, when $X=10$, the permutation decoder traverses $C_{10}^5 = 252$ paths instead of the $P_{10}^5 = 30,240$ in an exhausted search.

By cascading the translation and permutation steps, we greatly reduce the search space. In **LMM** decoding, the traditional stack decoder for monotone search is very fast. In **PM** decoding, since most of NE is less than 10 phrases, the permutation decoder only needs to explore at most $C_{10}^5 = 252$ living paths due to our risk-free pruning strategy.

5 Experiments

5.1 Experimental Setting and Modeling

All the experiments are conducted on the LDC Chinese-English NE translation corpus [7]. The LDC corpus consists of a large number of Chinese-Latin language NE entries. Table 1 reports the statistics of the entire corpus. Because person and place names in this corpus are translated via transliteration, we only extract the categories of organization, industry, press, international organization, and others to form a corpus subset for our NE translation experiment, as indicated in bold in Table 1. As the corpus is in its beta release, there are still many undesired entries in it. We performed a quick proofreading to correct some errors and remove the following types of entries:

1) The duplicate entry;
2) The entry of single Chinese or English word;
3) The entries whose English translation contains two or more non-English words.

We also segment the Chinese translation into a word sequence. Finally, we obtain a corpus of 74,606 unique bilingual entries, which are randomly partitioned into 10 equal parts for 10-fold cross validation.

Table 1. Statistics of the LDC Corpus

Category	# of Entries	
	C2E	E2C
Person	486,212	572,213
Place	276,382	298,993
Who-is-Who	30,028	36,881
Organization	**30,800**	**37,145**
Industry	**54,747**	**58,468**
Press	**29,757**	**32,922**
Int'l Org	**7,040**	**7,040**
Others	**13,007**	**14,066**

As indicated in Section 1, although MT is more difficult than NE translation, they both have many properties in common, such as lexical mapping ambiguity and permutation/distortion. Therefore, to establish a comparison, we use the publicly available statistical MT training and decoding tools, which can represent the state-of-the-art of statistical phrase-based MT research, to carry out the same NE translation experiments as reference cases. All the experiments conducted in this paper are listed as follow:

1) IBM method C: word-based IBM Model 4 trained by GIZA++[3] [15] and ISI Decoder[4] [14,16];

[3] http://www.fjoch.com/

[4] http://www.isi.edu/natural-language/software/decoder/manual.html

2) IBM method D: phrase-based IBM Model 4 trained by GIZA++ on phrase-aligned corpus and ISI Decoder working on phrase-segmented testing corpus.
3) Koehn method: Koehn et al.'s phrase-based model [12] and PHARAOH[5] decoder[6];
4) Our method: phrase-based bi-gram **LMM** and bi-gram **PM**, and our two-step decoder.

To make an accurate comparison, all the above three phrase-based models are trained on the same phrase-segmented and aligned corpus, and tested on the same phrase-segmented corpus. ISI Decoder carries out a greedy search, and PHARAOH is a beam-search stack decoder. To optimize their performances, the two decoders are allowed to do unlimited reordering without penalty. We train trigram language models in the first three experiments and bi-gram models in the forth experiment.

5.2 NE Translation

Table 2 and Table 3 report the performance of the four methods on the LDC NE translation corpus. The results are interpreted in different scoring measures, which allow us to compare the performances from different viewpoints.

- *ACC* reports the accuracy of the exact;
- *WER* reports the word error rate;
- *PER* is the position-independent, or "bag-of-words" word error rate;
- *BLEU* score measures *n*-gram precision [19]
- *NIST* score [20] is a weighted *n*-gram precision.

Please note that *WER* and *PER* are error rates, the lower numbers represent better results. For others, the higher numbers represents the better results.

Table 2. E2C NE translation performance (%)

			IBM method C	IBM method D	Koehn method	Our method
E2C	Open test	*ACC*	**24.5**	**36.3**	**47.1**	**51.5**
		WER	51.0	38.5	32.5	26.6
		PER	**48.5**	**36.2**	**26.8**	**16.3**
		BLEU	**29.9**	**41.8**	**51.2**	**56.1**
		NIST	7.2	8.6	9.3	10.2
	Closed test	*ACC*	51.1	78.9	88.2	90.9
		WER	34.1	12.8	6.3	4.3
		PER	31.5	9.5	4.1	2.7
		BLEU	54.7	80.9	89.1	91.9
		NIST	11.1	14.2	14.7	14.8

[5] http://www.isi.edu/licensed-sw/pharaoh/
[6] http://www.isi.edu/licensed-sw/pharaoh/manual-v1.2.ps

Table 3. C2E NE translation performance (%)

			IBM method C	IBM method D	Koehn method	Our method
C2E	open test	*ACC*	**13.4**	**21.8**	**31.2**	**36.1**
		WER	60.8	45.8	41.3	38.9
		PER	**49.6**	**38.2**	**32.6**	**26.6**
		BLEU	**25.1**	**49.8**	**52.9**	**54.1**
		NIST	5.94	8.21	8.91	9.25
	closed test	*ACC*	34.3	69.5	79.2	81.3
		WER	48.2	23.6	11.3	9.2
		PER	35.7	14.7	8.7	6.2
		BLEU	42.5	76.2	85.7	88.0
		NIST	8.7	12.7	13.8	14.4

Table 2 & 3 show that our method outperforms the other three methods consistently in all cases and by all scores. IBM method D gives better performance than IBM method C, simply because it uses phrase as the translation unit instead of single word. Koehn et al.'s phrase-based model [12] and IBM phrase-based Model 4 used in IBM method D are very similar in modeling. They both use context-independent lexical mapping model, distortion model and trigram target language model. The reason why Koehn method outperforms IBM method D may be due to the different decoding strategy. However, we still need further investigation to understand why Koehn method outperforms IBM method D significantly. It may also be due to the different LM training toolkits used in the two experiments.

Our method tops the performance among the four experiments. The significant position-independent word error rate (*PER*) reduction shows that our context-dependent joint probability lexical mapping model is quite effective in target word selection compared with the other context-free conditional probability lexical model together with target word *n*-gram language model.

Table 4. Step by step top-1 performance (%)

	LMM decoder	**LMM+PM** decoder
E2C	59.9	51.5
C2E	40.5	36.1

Table 4 studies the performance of the decoder by steps. The **LMM** decoder column reports the top-1 "bag-of-words" accuracy of the **LMM** decoder regardless of word order. This is the upper bound of accuracy that the PM decoder can achieve. The **LMM+PM** decoder column shows the combined performance of two steps, where we measure the top-1 **LMM+PM** accuracy by taking top-1 **LMM** decoding results as input. It is found that the **PM** decoder is surprisingly effective in that it perfectly reorders 85.9% (51.5/59.9) and 89.1% (36.1 /40.5) target languages in E2C and C2E translation respectively.

All the experiments above recommend that our method is an effective solution for NE translation.

6 Related Work

Since our method has benefited from the JSCM of Li *et al.* [4] and statistical MT research [8-12], let us compare our study with the previous related work.

The *n*-gram JSCM was proposed for machine transliteration by Li *et al.* [4]. It couples the source and channel constraints into a generative model to directly estimate the joint probability of source and target alignment using *n*-gram statistics. It was shown that JSCM captures rich contextual information that is present in a bilingual corpus to model the monotonic generative process of sequential data. In this point, our **LMM** model is the same as JSCM. The only difference is that in machine transliteration Li *et al.* [4] use phoneme unit as the basic modeling unit and our **LMM** is phrase-based.

In our study, we enhance the **LMM** with the **PM** to account for the word reordering issue in NE translation, so our model is capable of modeling the non-monotone problem. In contrast, JSCM only models the monotone problem.

Both rule-based [1] and statistical model-based [5,6] methods have been proposed to address the NE translation problem. The model-based methods mostly are based on conditional probability under the noisy-channel framework [8]. Now let's review the different modeling methods:

1) As far as lexical choice issue is concerned, the noisy-channel model, represented by IBM Model 1-5 [8], models lexical dependency using a context-free conditional probability. Marcu and Wong [10] proposed a phrase-based context-free joint probability model for lexical mapping. In contrast, our **LMM** models lexical dependency using *n*-order bilingual contextual information.
2) Another characteristic of our method lies in its modeling and search strategy. NE translation and MT are usually viewed as a non-monotone search problem and it is well-known that a non-monotone search is exponentially more complex than a monotone search. Thus, we propose the two separated models and the two-step search, so that the lexical mapping issue can be resolved by monotone search. This results in a large improvement on translation selection.
3) In addition, instead of the position-based distortion model [8-12], we use the *n*-gram permutation model to account for word reordering. A risk-free decoder is also proposed for the permutation model.

One may argue that our proposed model bears a strong resemblance to IBM Model 1: a position-independent translation model and a language model on target sentence without explicit distortion modeling. Let us discuss the major differences between them:

1) Our **LMM** models the lexical mapping and target word selection using a context-dependent joint probability while IBM Model 1 using a context-independent conditional probability and a target n-gram language model.
2) Our **LMM** carries out the target word selection and our **PM** only models the target word connectivity while the language model in IBM Model 1 performs the function of target word selection.

Alternatively, finite-state automata (FSA) for statistical MT were previous suggested for decoding using contextual information [21,22]. Bangalore and Riccardi [21] proposed a phrase-based variable length n-gram model followed by a reordering scheme for spoken language translation. However, their re-ordering scheme was not evaluated by empirical experiments.

7 Conclusions

In this paper, we propose a new model for NE translation. We present the training and decoding methods for the proposed model. We also compare the proposed method with related work. Empirical experiments show that our method outperforms the previous methods significantly in all test cases. We conclude that our method works more effectively and efficiently in NE translation than previous work does.

Our method does well in NE translation, which is relatively less sophisticated in terms of word distortion. We expect to improve its permutation model by integrating a distortion model to account for larger sentence structure and apply to machine translation study.

Acknowledgments

We would like to thank the anonymous reviews for their invaluable suggestions on our original manuscript.

References

1. Hsin-Hsi Chen, Changhua Yang and Ying Lin. 2003. Learning Formulation and Transformation Rules for Multilingual NEs. Proceedings of the ACL 2003 Workshop on MMLNER
2. K. Knight and J. Graehl. 1998. Machine Transliteration. Computational Linguistics, 24(4)
3. Jong-Hoon Oh and Key-Sun Choi, 2002. An English-Korean Transliteration Model Using Pronunciation and Contextual Rules. Proceedings of COLING 2002
4. Haizhou Li, Ming Zhang and Jian Su. 2004. A Joint Source-Channel Model for Machine Transliteration. Proceedings of the 42th ACL, Barcelona, 160-167
5. Y. Al-Onaizan and K. Knight, 2002. Translating named entities using monolingual and bilingual resources. Proceedings of the 40th ACL, Philadelphia, 400-408
6. Fei Huang, S. Vogel and A. Waibel, 2004. Improving NE Translation Combining Phonetic and Semantic Similarities. Proceedings of HLT-NAACL-2004
7. LDC2003E01, 2003. http://www.ldc.upenn.edu/

8. P.F. Brown, S.A.D. Pietra, V.J.D. Pietra and R.L. Mercer.1993. The mathematics of statistical machine translation. Computational Linguistics,19(2):263-313
9. Richard Zens and Hermann Ney. 2004. Improvements in Phrase-Based Statistical Machine Translation. Proceedings of HLT-NAACL-2004
10. D. Marcu and W. Wong. 2002. A Phrase-based, Joint Probability Model for Statistical Machine Translation. Proceedings of EMNLP-2002
11. Franz Joseh Och, C. Tillmann and H. Ney. 1999. Improved Alignment Models for Statistical Machine Translation. Proceedings of Joint Workshop on EMNLP and Very Large Corpus: 20-28
12. P. Koehn, F. J. Och and D. Marcu. 2003. Statistical Phrase-based Translation. Proceedings of HLT-2003
13. A. Stolcke. 2002. SRILM -- An Extensible Language Modeling Toolkit. Proceedings of ICSLP-2002, vol. 2, 901-904, Denver.
14. U. Germann, M. Jahr, K. Knight, D. Marcu and K. Yamada. 2001. Fast Decoding and Optimal Decoding for Machine Translation. Proceedings of ACL-2001
15. Franz Joseh Och and Hermann Ney. 2003. A Systematic Comparison of Various Statistical Alignment Models. Computational Linguistics, 29(1):19-51
16. U. Germann. 2003. Greedy Decoding for Statistical Machine Translation in Almost Linear Time. Proceedings of HLT-NAACL-2003
17. Christoph Tillmann and Hermann Ney. 2003. Word Reordering and a Dynamic Programming Beam Search Algorithm for Statistical Machine Translation. Computational Linguistics, 29(1):97-133
18. R. Schwartz and Y. L. Chow. 1990. The N-best algorithm: An efficient and Exact procedure for finding the N most likely sentence hypothesis, Proceedings of ICASSP 1990, 81-84
19. K. Papineni, S. Roukos, T. Ward and W. J. Zhu. 2001. BLEU: a method for automatic evaluation of machine translation. Technical Report RC22176 (W0109-022), IBM Research Report.
20. G. Doddington. 2002. Automatic evaluation of machine translation quality using n-gram co-occurrence statistics. Proceedings of ARPA Workshop on HLT
21. S. Bangalore and G. Riccardi, 2000, Stochastic Finite State Models for Spoken Language Machine Translation, Workshop on Embedded MT System
22. Stephan Kanthak and Hermann Hey, 2004. FSA: An Efficient and Flexiable C++ Tookkit for Finite State Automata Using On-Demand Computation, Proceedings of ACL-2004

Machine Translation Based on Constraint-Based Synchronous Grammar

Fai Wong[1], Dong-Cheng Hu[1], Yu-Hang Mao[1],
Ming-Chui Dong[2], and Yi-Ping Li[2]

[1] Speech and Language Processing Research Center,
Department of Automation, Tsinghua University, 100084 Beijing
huangh01@mails.tsinghua.edu.cn
{hudc, myh-dau}@mail.tsinghua.edu.cn
[2] Faculty of Science and Technology of University of Macao,
Av. Padre Tomás Pereira S.J., Taipa, Macao
{dmc, ypli}@umac.mo

Abstract. This paper proposes a variation of synchronous grammar based on the formalism of context-free grammar by generalizing the first component of productions that models the source text, named Constraint-based Synchronous Grammar (CSG). Unlike other synchronous grammars, CSG allows multiple target productions to be associated to a single source production rule, which can be used to guide a parser to infer different possible translational equivalences for a recognized input string according to the feature constraints of symbols in the pattern. Furthermore, CSG is augmented with independent rewriting that allows expressing discontinuous constituents in the inference rules. It turns out that such grammar is more expressive to model the translational equivalences of parallel texts for machine translation, and in this paper, we propose the use of CSG as a basis for building a machine translation (MT) system for Portuguese to Chinese translation.

1 Introduction

In machine translation, to analyze the structure deviations of languages pair hence to carry out the transformation from one language into another as the target translation is the kernel part in a translation system, and this requires a large amount of structural transformations in both grammatical and concept level. The problems of syntactic complexity and word sense ambiguity have been the major obstacles to produce promising quality of translation. In order to overcome the obstacles and hence to improve the quality of translation systems, several alternative approaches have been proposed.

As stated in [1], much of the theoretical linguistics can be formulated in a very natural manner as stating correspondences between layers of representations. In similar, many problems in natural language processing, in particular language translation and grammar rewriting systems, can be expressed as transduction through the use of synchronous formalisms [2,3,4,5,6]. Recently, synchronous grammars are becoming more and more popular for the formal description of parallel texts representing translations for the same document. The underlying idea of such formalisms is to combine two generative devices through a pairing of their productions in such a way that right

R. Dale et al. (Eds.): IJCNLP 2005, LNAI 3651, pp. 612–623, 2005.

hand side non-terminal symbols in the paired productions are linked. However, such formalisms are less expressive and unable to express mutual translations that have different lengths and crossing dependencies. Moreover, synchronous formalisms do not deal with unification and feature structures, as in unification-based formalisms, that give patterns additional power for describing constraints on features. For examples, Multiple Context-Free Grammar [4], where functions are engaged to the non-terminal symbols in the productions to further interpreting the symbols in target generation. In [7], Inversion Transduction Grammar (ITG) has been proposed for simultaneously bracketing parallel corpora as a variant of Syntax Directed translation schema [8]. But these formalisms are lacked of expressive to describe discontinuous constituents in linguistic expression. Generalized Multitext Grammar (GMTG) proposed by [5,9] is constructed by maintaining two sets of productions as components, one for each language, for modeling parallel texts. Although GMTG is more expressive and can be used to express as independent rewriting, the lack of flexibility in the way to describe constraints on the features associated with a non-terminal makes it difficult to the development of practical MT system.

In this paper, a variation of synchronous grammar, Constraint-Based Synchronous Grammar (CSG), is proposed based on the formalism of context-free grammar. Through the use of feature structures as that in unification-based grammar, the first component of productions in CSG, that describes the sentential patterns for source text, is generalized while the corresponding target rewriting rules for each production are grouped in a vector representing the possible translation patterns for source production. The choice of rule for target generation is based on the constraints on features of non-terminal symbols in pattern. Our motivation is three-fold. First, synchronous formalisms have been proposed for modeling of parallel text, and such algorithms can infer the synchronous structures of texts for two different languages through the grammar representation of their syntactic deviations. That is quite suitable for use in the analysis of languages pair in the development of MT system. Secondly, by augmented the synchronous models with feature structures can enhance the pattern with additional power in describing gender, number, agreement, etc. Since the descriptive power of unification-based grammars is considerably greater than that of classical CFG [10,11]. Finally, by retaining the notational and intuitive simplicity of CFG, we can enjoy both a grammar formalism with better descriptive power than CFG and more efficient parsing and generation algorithm controlled by the feature constraints of symbols hence to achieve the purposes of word sense and syntax disambiguation.

2 Constraint-Based Synchronous Grammars

Constraint-Based Synchronous Grammars (CSG) is defined by means of the syntax of context-free grammar (CFG) to the case of synchronous. The formalism consists of a set of generative productions and each production is constructed by a pair of CFG rules with zero and more syntactic head and link constraints for the non-terminal symbols in patterns. In a similar way, the first component (in right hand side of productions) represents the sentential patterns of source language, while the second component represents the translation patterns in target language, called source and target component respectively in CSG. Unlike other synchronous formalisms, the target component of production consists of one or more generative rules associated with zero or more controlled conditions based on the features of non-terminal symbols of source rule for describing the possible generation correspondences in target translation. In such a way, the source components in CSG are generalized by leaving the task of handling constraints on features in target component, so this also helps to reduce the grammar size. For example, following is one of the productions used in the MT system for Portuguese to Chinese translation:

$$S \rightarrow NP_1\ VP^*\ NP_2\ PP\ NP_3\ \{[NP_1\ VP^1\ NP_3\ VP^2\ NP_2; VP_{cate}=vb1, VP_{s:sem} = NP_{1sem}, VP_{io:sem}=NP_2sem, VP_{o:sem}=NP_{3sem}], [NP_1\ VP\ NP_3\ NP_2\ ; VP = vb0, VP_{s:sem} = NP_{1sem}, VP_{io:sem}=NP_{2sem}]\} \quad (1)$$

The production has two components beside the reduced syntactic symbol on left hand side, the first modeling Portuguese and the second Chinese. The target component in this production consists of two generative rules maintained in vector, and each of which is engaged with control conditions based on the features of symbols from the source component, and this is used as the selectional preferences in parsing. These constraints, in the parsing/generation algorithm, are used for inferring, not only, the structure of input to dedicate what structures are possible or probable, but also the structure of output text for target translation. For example, the condition expression: $VP_{cate}=vb1$, $VP_{s:sem}=NP_{1sem}$, $VP_{io:sem}=NP_{2sem}$, $VP_{o:sem}=NP_{3sem}$, specifies if the senses of the first, second and the third nouns (*NP*s) in the input strings matched to that of the subject, direct and indirect objects governed by the verb, *VP*, with the category type of *vb1*. Once the condition gets satisfied, the source structure is successfully recognized and the corresponding structure of target language, $NP_1\ VP^1\ NP_3\ VP^2\ NP_2$, is determined also.

Non-terminal symbols in source and target rules are linked if they are given the same index "*subscripts*" for case of multiple occurrences, such as *NP*s in the production: $S \rightarrow NP_1\ VP\ NP_2\ PP\ NP_3\ [NP_1\ VP^*\ NP_3\ NP_2]$, otherwise symbols that appear only once in both the source and target rules, such as *VP*s, are implicitly linked to give the synchronous rewriting. Linked non-terminal must be derived from a sequence of synchronized pairs. Consider the production: $S \rightarrow NP_1\ VP\ NP_2\ PP\ NP_3\ [NP_1\ VP^*\ NP_3\ NP_2]$, the second *NP* ($NP_2$) in the source rule corresponds to the third *NP* (NP_2) in the target rule, the third *NP* (NP_3) in source rule corresponds to the second *NP* (NP_3) in target pattern, while the first *NP* (NP_1) and *VP* correspond to each other in both source and target rules. The symbol marked by an "*" is designated as *head* element in pattern, this allows the features of designated head symbol propagate to the reduced non-terminal symbol in the left hand side of production rule, hence to achieve the property of features inheritance in CSG formalism. The use of features structures associated to non-terminal symbols will be discussed in the later section in this paper.

In modeling of natural language, in particular for the process of languages-pair, the treatment for non-standard linguistic phenomena, i.e. crossing dependencies, discontinuous constituents, etc., is very important due to the structure deviations of two different languages, in particular for languages from different families such as Portuguese and Chinese [12,13]. Linguistic expressions can vanish and appear in translation. For example, the preposition (*PP*) in the source rule does not show up in any of the target rules in Production (1). In contrast, Production (2) allows the Chinese characters of "本" and "輛" to appear in the target rules for purpose to modify the noun (*NP*) together with the quantifier (*num*) as the proper translation for the source text. This explicitly relaxes the synchronization constraint, so that the two components can be rewritten independently.

$$\text{NP} \rightarrow \text{num NP* } \{[\text{num 本 NP; NP}_{sem}\text{=SEM}_{\_book}], [\text{num 輛 NP; NP}_{sem}\text{=SEM}_{\_automobile}]\} \quad (2)$$

A remarkable strength of CSG is its expressive power to the description of discontinuous constituents. In Chinese, the use of combination words that discontinuously distributed in a sentence is very common. For example, take the sentences pair ["*Ele vendeu-me todas as uvas.* (He sell me all the grapes.)", "*他把所有的葡萄賣了給我* "]. The Chinese preposition "*把*" and the verb "*賣了給*" should be paired with the Portuguese verb "*vendeu*", and this causes a *fan-out*[1] and discontinuous constituent in the Chinese component. The following fragment of CSG productions represents such relationships.

$$\text{S} \rightarrow \text{NP}_1 \text{ VP* NP}_2 \text{ NP}_3 \{[\text{NP}_1 \text{ VP}^1 \text{ NP}_3 \text{ VP}^2 \text{ NP}_2; \text{VP}_{cate}\text{=vb0,...}],..\} \quad (3)$$

$$\text{VP} \rightarrow vendeu^* \{[把, 賣了給 ;\varnothing]\} \quad (4)$$

In Production (3), the corresponding discontinuous constituents of *VP* (from source rule) are represented by VP^1 and VP^2 respectively in the target rule, where the "*superscripts*" are added to indicate the pairing of the *VP* in target component. The corresponding translation constituents in the lexicalized production are separated by commas representing the discontinuity between constituents "*把*" and "*賣了給*" in target translation. During the rewriting phase, the corresponding constituents will be used to replace the syntactic symbols in pattern rule.

3 Definitions

Let *L* be a context-free language defined over *terminal* symbol V_T and generated by a context-free grammar *G* using non-terminal symbol V_N disjointed with V_T, starting symbol *S*, and productions of the form $A \rightarrow w$ where *A* is in V_N and *w* in $(V_N \cup V_T)^*$. Let *Z* as a set of integers, each non-terminal symbol in V_N is assigned with an integer, $\Gamma(V_N) = \{W_\omega \mid W \in V_N, \omega \in Z\}$. The elements of $\Gamma(V_N)$ are indexed non-terminal symbols. Now, we extend to include the set of *terminal* symbols $V_{T'}$ as the translation in target language, disjoint from V_T, $(V_T \bullet V_{T'} = \varnothing)$. Let $R = \{r_1, \ldots, r_n \mid r_i \in (\Gamma(V_N) \cup V_{T'}), 1 \leq i \leq n\}$ be a finite set of rules, and $C = \{c_1, \ldots, c_m\}$ be a finite set of constraints over the associated features of $(\Gamma(V_N) \cup V_{T'})$, where the features of non-terminal $\Gamma(V_N)$, the syntactic symbols, are inherited from the designated head element during rule reduction. A *target rule* is defined as pair $[r \in R^*, c \in C^*]$ in γ, where $\gamma = R^* \times C^*$ in form of $[r, c]$. Now, we define $\psi(\gamma_i)$ to denote the number of conjunct features being considered in

[1] We use this term for describing a word where its translation is paired of discontinuous words in target language, e.g. "*vendeu*[*-pro*] [*NP*]" in Portuguese gives similar English translation as "*sell* [*NP*] *to* [*pro*]", so "*vendeu*", in this case, is corresponding to "*sell*" and "*to*".

the associated constraint, hence to determine the degree of generalization for a constraint. Therefore, the rules, γ_i and γ_j, are orderable, $\gamma_i \prec \gamma_j$, if $\psi(\gamma_i) \geq \psi(\gamma_j)$ (or $\gamma_i \succ \gamma_j$, if $\psi(\gamma_i) < \psi(\gamma_j)$). For $\gamma_i \prec \gamma_j$ ($\psi(\gamma_i) \geq \psi(\gamma_j)$), we say, the constraint of the rule, γ_i, is more specific, while the constraint of γ_j is more general. In what follows, we consider a set of related target rules working over the symbols, w', on the RHS of production $A \rightarrow w'$, the source rule, where $w' \in \Pi(V_N) \cup V_T$. All of these non-terminals are co-indexed as *link*.

Definition 1: A *target component* is defined as a ordered vector of *target rules* in γ having the form $\sigma = \{\gamma_1, \ldots, \gamma_q\}$, where $1 \leq i \leq q$ to denote the i-th tuple of σ. The rules are being arranged in the order of $\gamma_1 \prec \gamma_2 \prec \ldots \prec \gamma_q$.

In rule reduction, the association conditions of the target rules are used for investigating the features of corresponding symbols in source rules, similar to that of feature unification, to determine if the active reduction successes or not. At the mean while, this helps in determining the proper structure as the target correspondence.

Definition 2: A *Constraint-Based Synchronous Grammar* (*CSG*) is defined to be 5-tuple $G = (V_N, V_T, P, C_T, S)$ which satisfies the following conditions:

- V_N is a finite set of *non-terminal* symbols;
- V_T is a finite set of *terminal* symbols which is disjoint with V_N;
- C_T is a finite set of *target components*;
- P is a finite set of *productions* of the form $A \rightarrow \alpha\ \beta$, where $\alpha \in (\Pi(V_N) \cup V_T)^*$ and, $\beta \in C_T$, the non-terminal symbols that occur from both the source and target rules are *linked* under the index given by $\Pi(V_N)$[2].
- $S \in V_N$ is the initial symbol.

For example, the following CSG productions can generate both of the parallel texts ["*Ele deu um livro ao José*. (He gave a book to José)", "*他給了若澤一本書*"] and ["*Ele comprou um livro ao José*. (He bought a book from José)", "*他向若澤買了一本書*"]:

$$S \rightarrow NP_1\ VP^*\ NP_2\ PP\ NP_3\ \{[NP_1\ VP^1\ NP_3\ VP^2\ NP_2; VP_{cate}=vb1, VP_{s:sem} = NP_{1sem}, P_{io:sem}=NP_2 sem, VP_{o:sem}=NP_{3sem}], [NP_1\ VP\ NP_3\ NP_2\ ; VP = vb0, VP_{s:sem} = NP_{1sem}, VP_{io:sem}=NP_{2sem}]\} \quad (5)$$

$$VP \rightarrow v^3\ \{[v\ ; \varnothing]\} \quad (6)$$

$$NP \rightarrow det\ NP^*\ \{[NP\ ; \varnothing]\} \quad (7)$$

$$NP \rightarrow num\ NP^*\ \{[num\ 本NP; NP_{sem}=SEM_{\_book}]\} \quad (8)$$

---

2 Link constraints are dedicated by the symbols indices, which is trivially for connecting the corresponding symbols between the source and target rules. Hence, we assume, without loss of generality, that index is only given to the non-terminal symbols that have multiple occurrences in the production rules. It is assumed that "$S \rightarrow NP_1\ VP_2\ PP_3\ NP_4\ \{NP_1\ VP_2^1\ NP_4\ VP_2^2\}$" implies "$S \rightarrow NP_1\ VP\ PP\ NP_2\ \{NP_1\ VP^1\ NP_2\ VP^2\}$".

3 Similar for the designation of head element in productions, the only symbol from the RHS of production will inherently be the head element. Thus, no head mark "*" is given for such rules, and we assume that "$VP \rightarrow v^*$" implies "$VP \rightarrow v$".

NP → n {[n ; ∅]} (9)
NP → pro {[pro ; ∅]} (10)
PP → p {[p ; ∅]} (11)
n → *José* {[*若澤* ; ∅]}| *livro* {[*書* ; ∅]} (12)
pro → *ele* {[*他* ; ∅]} (13)
v → *deu*{[*給了* ; ∅]} | *comprou* {[*向*, *買了* ;∅]} (14)
num → *um* {[一 ; ∅]} (15)
p → *a* {∅} (16)
det → *o* {∅} (17)

A set *P* of productions is said to *accept* an input string *s* iff there is a derivation sequence *Q* for *s* using source rules of *P*, and any of the constraint associated with every *target component* in *Q* is satisfied[4]. Similarly, *P* is said to *translate s* iff there is a synchronized derivation sequence *Q* for *s* such that *P* accepts *s*, and the link constraints of associated *target rules* in *Q* is satisfied. The derivation *Q* then produces a translation *t* as the resulting sequence of terminal symbols included in the determined target rules in *Q*. The translation of an input string *s* essentially consists of three steps. First, the input string is parsed by using the source rules of productions. Secondly, the link constraints are propagated from source rule to target component to determine and build a target derivation sequence. Finally, translation of input string is generated from the target derivation sequence.

3.1 Feature Representation

In CSG, linguistic entities are modeled as feature structures which give patterns additional power for describing gender, number, semantic, attributes and number of the arguments required by a verb, and so on. These information are encoded in the commonly used attribute value matrices (AVMs), attached to each of the lexical and syntactic symbols in CSG. This allows us to specify such as syntactic dependencies as agreement and sub-categorization in patterns. Unlike other unification-based grammars [11,14], we do not carry out the unification in full, only interested conditions that are explicitly expressed in the rule constraints are tested and unified. Such unification process can perform in constant time. The use of feature constraints has to be restricted to maintain the efficiency of parsing and generating algorithms, especially to the prevention from generating a large number of ambiguous structure candidates. The word selection in the target language can also be achieved by checking features. In the parsing and generating algorithm, the features information are propagated to the reduced symbol from the designated head element in pattern, hence to realize the mechanism of features inheritance. Features can either be put in lexical dictionary isolated from the formalism to make the work simpler to the construction of analytical grammar, or explicitly encoded in the pre-terminal rules as:

[4] If there is no any constraint associated to a target rule, during the parsing phase, the reduction of the source rule is assumed to be valid all the time.

Pro → *José*:[CAT:*pro*;NUM:*sg*;GEN:*masc*,SEM:*hum*] {[若澤 ; ∅]} (18)

n → *livro*:[CAT:*n*;NUM:*sg*;GEN:*masc*;SEM:*artifact+book*] {[書 ; ∅]} (19)

Where the features set is being bracketed, and separated by a semi-colon, the name and the value of a feature are delimited by a colon to represent the feature pair. Another way to enhance the CSG formalism is to apply the soft preferences other than hard constraints in the process of features unification. Our consideration is two-fold: first, we found that more than one combination of feature values engaged to a single lexical item is very common in the process of natural language, i.e. one word may have several translations according to the different senses and the pragmatic uses of the word, and this has been the problem of word senses disambiguation [15]. Secondly, the conventional feature unification method can only tell us if the process successes or not. In case of a minor part of conditions get failed during the unification, all the related candidates are rejected without any flexibility to choosing the next preferable or probable candidate. In order to resolve these problems, each feature structure is associates with a weight. It is then possible to rank the matching features according to the linear ordering of the weights rather than the order of lexical items expressed in grammars or dictionary. In our prototyping system, each symbol has its original weight, and according to preference measurement at the time in checking the feature constraints, a penalty is used to reduce from the weight to give the effective weight of associated features in a particular context. Features with the largest weight are to be chosen as the most preferable content.

4 Application to Portuguese-Chinese MT

CSG formalism can be parsed by any known CFG parsing algorithm including the Earley [16] and generalized LR algorithms [17] augmented by taking into account the features constraints and the inference of target structure. In the prototyping system, the parsing algorithm for our formalism is based on the generalized LR algorithm that we have development for MT system, since the method uses a parse table, it achieves a considerable efficiency over the Earley's non-complied method which has to compute a set of LR items at each stage of parsing [17]. Generalized LR algorithm was first introduced by Tomita for parsing the augmented Context-Free grammar that can ingeniously handle non-determinism and ambiguity through the use of graph-structured stack while retaining much of the advantages of standard LR parsing[5]. It takes a shift-reduce approach using an extended LR parse table to guide its actions by allowing the multiple actions entries such as shift/reduce and reduce/reduce hence to handle the nondeterministic parse with pseudo-parallelism. In order to adapt to our formalism, we further extend the parse table by engaging with the features constraints and the target rules into the actions table. Our strategy is thus to parse the source rules of CSG productions through the normal shift actions proposed by the parsing table, while at the time reduce action to be fired, the associated conditions are checked to determine if the active reduction is a valid action or not depending on if the working symbols of patterns fulfill the constraints on features.

[5] Especially when the grammar is close to the LR grammars.

4.1 The CSG Parse Table

Fig. 1 shows an extended LR(1) parsing table for Productions (5)-(17)[6] as constructed using the LR table construction method described in [18] extended to consider the rule components of productions by associating the corresponding target rules with constraints, which are explicitly expressed in table. The parsing table consists of two parts: a compact ACTION-GOTO table[7] and CSONTRAINT-RULE table. The ACTION-GOTO table s indexed by a state symbol s (row) and a symbols $x \in V_N \cup V_T$, including the end marker "⊥". The entry ACTION[s, x] can be one of the following: s n, r m, *acc* or blank. s n denotes a shift action representing GOTO[s, x]=n, defining the next state the parser should go to; r m means a reduction by the mth production located in the entry of CONSTRAINT-RULE in state s, and *acc* denotes the accept action and blank indicates a parsing error. The CONSTRAINT-RULE table is indexed by state symbol s (row) and the number of productions m that may be applied for reduction in state s. The entry CONSTRAINT-RULE[s, m] consists of a set of involved productions together with the target rules and features constraints that are used for validating if the active parsing node can be reduced or not, then try to identify the corresponding target generative rule for reduced production.

4.2 The CSG Parser

In the parsing process, the algorithm operates by maintaining a number of parsing processes in parallel, each of which represents an individual parsed result, hence to handle the case of non-deterministic. In general, there are two major components in the process, *shift*(i) and *reduce*(i), which are called at each position i=0, 1, …, n in an input string $I = x_1x_2\ldots x_n$. The *shift*(i) process with top of stack vertex v shifts on x_i from its current state s to some successor state s' by creating a new leaf v'; establishing edge from v' to the top of stack v; and making v' as the new top of stack vertex.

The *reduce*(i) executes a reduce action on a production p by following the chain ofparent links down from the top of stack vertex v to the ancestor vertex from which the process began scanning for p earlier, then popping intervening vertices off the stack. Now, for every reduction action in *reduce*(i), there exists a set C of ordered constraints, $c_1 \prec \ldots \prec c_m$, with the production, each of which is associated with a target rule that may be the probable corresponding target structure for the production, depending on whether the paired constraint gets satisfied or not according to the features of the parsed string p. Before reduction takes place, the constraints c_j ($1 \le j \le m$) are tested in order started from the most specific one, the evaluation process stops once a positive result is obtained from evaluation. The corresponding target rule for the parsed string is determined and attached to the reduced syntactic symbol, which will be used for rewriting the target translation in phase of generation. At the mean while, the features information will be inherited from the designated head element of production. The parsing algorithm for CSG formalism is given in Fig. 2.

---

[6] For simplicity, the productions used for building the parse table are deterministic, so no conflict actions such as shift/reduce and reduce/reduce appear in the parse table in Fig.1.

[7] Original version introduced in [17] maintains two tables, ACTION and GOTO.

Ste	ACTIONs/GOTOs																			Reduced Rules Constraints/Target Rules
	pro	*num*	*n*	*v*	*det*	*p*	*NP*	*VP*	*PP*	*S*	⊥	*o*	*a*	*um*	*ele*	*José*	*livro*	*deu*	*comprou*	
0	s8	s9	s10		s11		s7			s6		s5		s2	s1	s4	s3			
1															r1					(1) pro → *ele* {[他 ; ∅]}
2														r1						(1) num → *um*
3																	r1			(1) n → *livro* {[書 ; ∅]}
4																r1				(1) n → *José* {[若澤 ; ∅]}
5												r1								(1) det → *o*
6											acc									
7				s14				s15										s12	s13	
8	r1																			(1) NP → pro
9	s8	s9	s10		s11		s16					s5		s2	s1	s4	s3			
10			r1																	(1) NP → n
11	s8	s9	s10		s11		s17					s5		s2	s1	s4	s3			
12																		r1		(1) v → *deu* {[給了 ; ∅]}
13																			r1	(1) v → *comprou* {[向, 買了 ;∅]}
14				r1																(1) VP → v
15	s8	s9	s10		s11		s18					s5		s2	s1	s4	s3			
16							r1													(1) NP → *num* NP* {[num 本NP; NP_{sem}=$SEM_{\_book}$]}
17							r1													(1) NP → det NP* {[NP ; ∅]}
18						s21			s20				s19							
19													r1							(1) p → *a*
20	s8	s9	s10		s11		s22					s5		s2	s1	s4	s3			
21						r1														(1) PP → p
22										r1										(1) S → NP_1 VP* NP_2 PP NP_3 {[...]}

Fig. 1. Extended LR(1) parse table

```
PARSE(grammar, x_1 … x_n)
 x_{n+1} ⇐ ⊥
 U_i ⇐ ∅  (0 ≤ i ≤ n)
 U_0 ⇐ v_0
 for each terminal symbol x_i (1 ≤ i ≤ n)
   P ⇐ ∅
   for each node v ∈ U_{i-1}
     P ⇐ P ∪ v
     if ACTION[STATE(v),x_i] = "shift s'", SHIFT(v,s')
     for each "reduce p" ∈ ACTION[STATE(v),x_i], REDUCE(v,p)
     if "acc" ∈ ACTION[STATE(v),x_i], accept
   if U_i = ∅, reject

SHIFT(v,s)
 if v' ∈ U_i s.t. STATE(v')=s and ANCESTOR(v',1)=v and state
    transition δ(v,x)=v'
  do nothing
```

```
  else
    create a new node v'
    s.t.  STATE(v')=s and ANCESTOR(v',1)=v and state tran-
        sition δ(v,x)=v'
    U_i⇐U_i ∪ v'

REDUCE(v,p)
  for each possible reduced parent v_1'∈ANCESTOR(v,RHS(p))
    if UNIFY(v,p)="success"
      s" ⇐ GOTO(v_1',LHS(p))
      if node v"∈U_i-1 s.t. STATE(v")=s"
        if δ(v_1', LHS(p))=v"
          do nothing
        else
        if node v_2'∈ANCESTOR(v",1)
          let v_c" s.t. ANCESTOR(v_c",1)=v_1' and STATE(v_c")=s"
          for each "reduce p" ∈ ACTION[STATE(v_c"),x_i]
             REDUCE(v_c",p)
        else
          if v"∈P
            let v_c" st. ANCESTOR(v_c",1)=v_1' and STATE(v_c")=s"
            for each "reduce p" ∈ ACTION[STATE(v_c"),x_i]
               REDUCE(v_c",p)
          else
            create a new node v_n
            s.t. STATE(v_n)=s" and ANCESTOR(v_n,1)=v_1' and
            state transition δ(v_n,x)=v_1'
            U_i-1⇐U_i-1 ∪ v_n
    else current reduction failed

UNIFY(v,p)
  for "constraint c_j" ∈ CONSTRAINT(STATE(v))  (1 ≤ j ≤ m,
  c_1≺...≺c_m)
    if ξ(c_j,p)="true"                    (ξ(∅,p)="true")
      TARGET(v)⇐j
      return "success"
```

Fig. 2. Modified generalized LR Parsing algorithm

The parser is a function of two arguments PARSE(*grammar*, $x_1 \ldots x_n$), where the grammar is provided in form of parsing table. It calls upon the functions SHIFT(v, s) and REDUCE(v, p) to process the shifting and rule reduction as described. The UNIFY(v, p) function is called for every possible reduction in REDUCE(v, p) to verify the legal reduction and select the target rule for the source structure for synchronization. The function TARGET(v) after unification passed is to dedicate the jth target rule as correspondence.

4.3 Translation as Parsing

Our Portuguese-to-Chinese translation (PCT) system is a transfer-based translation system by using the formalism of Constraint-Based Synchronous Grammar (CSG) as its analytical grammar. Unlike other transfer-based MT systems that the major components: analysis, transfer and generation are carried out individually in pipeline by using different sets of representation rules to achieve the tasks of structure analysis and transformation [19], in PCT, only a single set of CS grammar is used to dominate the translation task. Since the structures of parallel languages are synchronized in formalism, as well as the deviations of their structures are also captured and described by the grammar. Hence, to the translation of an input text, it essentially consists of three steps. First, for an input sentence *s*, the structure of string is analyzed by using the rules of source components from the CSG productions; by using the augmented generalized LR parsing algorithm as described. Secondly, the link constraints that are determined during the rule reduction process are propagated to the corresponding target rules *R* (as selection of target rules) to construct a target derivation sequence *Q*. And finally, based on the derivation sequence *Q*, translation of the input sentence *s* is generated by referencing the set of generative rules *R* that attached to the corresponding constituent nodes in the parsed tree, hence to realize the translation in target language.

5 Conclusion

In this paper, we have proposed a variation of synchronous grammar based on the syntax of context-free grammar, called Constraint-based Synchronous Grammar (CSG). The source components of CSG are being generalized for representing the common structure of language. Different from other synchronous grammars, each source rule is associated with a set of target productions, where each of the target rules is connected with a constraint over the features of source patterns. The set of target rules are grouped and maintained in a vector ordered by the specificity of constraints. The objective of this formalism is to allow parsing and generating algorithms to inference different possible translation equivalences for an input sentence being analyzed according to the linguistic features. We have presented a modified generalized LR parsing algorithm that has been adapted to the parsing our formalism that we have developed for analyzing the syntactic structure of Portuguese in the machine translation system.

References

1. Rambow, O., Satta, G.: Synchronous Models of Language. In Proceedings of 34th Annual Meeting of the Association for Computational Linguistics, University of California, Santa Cruz, California, USA, Morgan Kaufmann (1996) 116-123.
2. Lewis, P.M., Stearns, R.E.: Syntax-directed transduction. Journal of the Association for Computing Machinery, 15(3), (1968) 465-488.
3. Shieber, S.M., Schabes, Y.: Synchronous Tree Adjoining Grammar. Proceedings of the 13th International Conference on Computational Linguistic, Helsinki (1990)
4. Seki, H., Matsumura, T., Fujii, M., Kasami, T.: On multiple context-free grammars. Theoretical Computer Science, 88(2) (1991) 191-229

5. Melamed, I.D.: Multitext Grammars and Synchronous Parsers. In Proceedings of NAACL/HLT 2003, Edmonton, (2003) 79-86
6. Wong, F., Hu, D.C., Mao, Y.H., Dong, M.C. A Flexible Example Annotation Schema: Translation Corresponding Tree Representation. In Proceedings of the 20th International Conference on Computational Linguistics, Switzerland, Geneva (2004) 1079-1085
7. Wu, D.: Grammarless extraction of phrasal translation examples from parallel texts. In Proceedings of TMI-95, Sixth International Conference on Theoretical and Methodological Issues in Machine Translation, v2, Leuven Belgium (1995) 354-372
8. Aho, A.V., Ullman, J.D.: Syntax Directed Translations and the Pushdown Assembler. Journal of Computer and System Sciences, 3, (1969) 37-56
9. Melamed, I.D., Satta. G., Wellington, B.: Generalized Multitext Grammars. In Proceedings of 42th Annual Meeting of the Association for Computational Linguistics, Barcelona, Spain (2004) 661-668
10. Kaplan, R.M., Bresnan, J.: Lexical-Functional Grammar: A Formal System for Grammatical Representation. In Joan Bresnan, The Mental Representation of Grammatical Relations, Cambridge, Mass, MIT Press, (1982) 173-281
11. Kaplan, R.M.: The Formal Architecture of Lexical-Functional Grammar. Information Science and Engineering, 5. (1989) 30-322
12. Wong, F., Mao, Y.H.: Framework of Electronic Dictionary System for Chinese and Romance Languages. Automatique des Langues (TAL), 44(2), (2003) 225-245
13. Wong, F., Mao, Y.H., Dong, Q.F., Qi, Y.H.: Automatic Translation: Overcome the Barriers between European and Chinese Languages. In Proceedings (CD Version) of First International UNL Open Conference, SuZhou China (2001)
14. Pollard, C., Sag, I.: Head-Driven Phrase Structure Grammar. University of Chicago Press, (1994)
15. Ide, N., Veronis, J.: Word Sense Disambiguation: The State of the Art. Computational Linguistics, 24, (1), (1998) 1-41
16. Earley, J.: An Efficient Context-Free Parsing Algorithm. CACM, 13(2), (1970) 94-102
17. Tomita, M.: Computational Linguistics, 13(1-2), (1987) 31-46
18. Aho, A.V., Sethi, R., Ullman, J.D.: Compiler: Principles, Techniques and Tools. Addison-Wesley, (1986)
19. Hutchins, W.J., Somers, H.L.: An Introduction to Machine Translation. Academic Press, (1992)

A Machine Learning Approach to Sentence Ordering for Multidocument Summarization and Its Evaluation

Danushka Bollegala, Naoaki Okazaki, and Mitsuru Ishizuka

University of Tokyo, Japan

Abstract. Ordering information is a difficult but a important task for natural language generation applications. A wrong order of information not only makes it difficult to understand, but also conveys an entirely different idea to the reader. This paper proposes an algorithm that learns orderings from a set of human ordered texts. Our model consists of a set of ordering experts. Each expert gives its precedence preference between two sentences. We combine these preferences and order sentences. We also propose two new metrics for the evaluation of sentence orderings. Our experimental results show that the proposed algorithm outperforms the existing methods in all evaluation metrics.

1 Introduction

The task of ordering sentences arises in many fields. Multidocument Summarization (MDS) [5], Question and Answer (QA) systems and concept to text generation systems are some of them. These systems extract information from different sources and combine them to produce a coherent text. Proper ordering of sentences improves readability of a summary [1]. In most cases it is a trivial task for a human to read a set of sentences and order them coherently. Humans use their wide background knowledge and experience to decide the order among sentences. However, it is not an easy task for computers. This paper proposes a sentence ordering algorithm and evaluate its performance with regard to MDS.

MDS is the task of generating a human readable summary from a given set of documents. With the increasing amount of texts available in electronic format, automatic text summarization has become necessary. It can be considered as a two-stage process. In the first stage the source documments are analyzed and a set of sentences are extracted. However, the document set may contain repeating information as well as contradictory information and these challenges should be considered when extracting sentences for the summary. Researchers have already investigated this problem and various algorithms exist. The second stage of MDS creates a coherent summary from this extract. When summarizing a single document, a naive strategy that arranges extracted sentences according to the appearance order may yield a coherent summary. However, in MDS the extracted sentences belong to different source documents. The source documents

R. Dale et al. (Eds.): IJCNLP 2005, LNAI 3651, pp. 624–635, 2005.

may have been written by various authors and on various dates. Therefore we cannot simply order the sentences according to the position of the sentences in the original document to get a comprehensible summary.

This second stage of MDS has received lesser attention compared to the first stage. Chronological ordering; ordering sentences according to the published date of the documents they belong to [6], is one solution to this problem. However, showing that this approach is insufficient, Barzilay [1] proposed an refined algorithm which integrates chronology ordering with topical relatedness of documents. Okazaki [7] proposes a improved chronological ordering algorithm using precedence relations among sentences. His algorithm searches for an order which satisfies the precedence relations among sentences. In addition to these studies which make use of chronological ordering, Lapata [3] proposes a probabilistic model of text structuring and its application to the sentence ordering. Her system calculates the conditional probabilities between sentences from a corpus and uses a greedy ordering algorithm to arrange sentences according to the conditional probabilities.

Even though these previous studies proposed different strategies to decide the sentence ordering, the appropriate way to combine these different methods to obtain more robust and coherent text remains unknown. In addition to these existing sentence ordering heuristics, we propose a new method which we shall call *succession* in this paper. We then learn the optimum linear combination of these heuristics that maximises readability of a summary using a set of human-made orderings. We then propose two new metrics for evaluating sentence orderings; *Weighted Kendall Coefficient* and *Average Continuity.* Comparing with an intrinsic evaluation made by human subjects, we perform a quantitative evaluation using a number of metrics and discuss the possiblity of the automatic evaluation of sentence orderings.

2 Method

For sentences taken from the same document we keep the order in that document as done in single document summarization. However, we have to be careful when ordering sentences which belong to different documents. To decide the order among such sentences, we implement five ranking experts: Chronological, Probabilistic, Topical relevance, Precedent and Succedent. These experts return precedence preference between two sentences. Cohen [2] proposes an elegant learning model that works with preference functions and we adopt this learning model to our task. Each expert e generates a pair-wise preference function defined as following:

$$\mathrm{PREF}_e(u, v, Q) \in [0, 1]. \tag{1}$$

Where, u, v are two sentences that we want to order; Q is the set of sentences which has been already ordered. The expert returns its preference of u to v. If the expert prefers u to v then it returns a value greater than 0.5. In the extreme case where the expert is absolutely sure of preferring u to v it will return 1.0. On the other hand, if the expert prefers v to u it will return a value lesser than

0.5. In the extreme case where the expert is absolutely sure of preferring v to u it will return 0. When the expert is undecided of its preference between u and v it will return 0.5.

The linear weighted sum of these individual preference functions is taken as the total preference by the set of experts as follows:

$$\mathrm{PREF}_{total}(u, v, Q) = \sum_{e \in E} w_e \mathrm{PREF}_e(u, v, Q). \tag{2}$$

Therein: E is the set of experts and w_e is the weight associated to expert $e \in E$. These weights are normalized so that the sum of them is 1. We use the Hedge learning algorithm to learn the weights associated with each expert's preference function. Then we use the greedy algorithm proposed by Cohen [2] to get an ordering that approximates the total preference.

2.1 Chronological Expert

Chronological expert emulates conventional chronological ordering [4,6] which arranges sentences according to the dates on which the documents were published and preserves the appearance order for sentences in the same document. We define a preference function for the expert as follows:

$$\mathrm{PREF}_{chro}(u, v, Q) = \begin{cases} 1 & T(u) < T(v) \\ 1 & [D(u) = D(v)] \wedge [N(u) < N(v)] \\ 0.5 & [T(u) = T(v)] \wedge [D(u) \neq D(v)] \\ 0 & \text{otherwise} \end{cases} . \tag{3}$$

Therein: $T(u)$ is the publication date of sentence u; $D(u)$ presents the unique identifier of the document to which sentence u belongs; $N(u)$ denotes the line number of sentence u in the original document. Chronological expert gives 1 (preference) to the newly published sentence over the old and to the prior over the posterior in the same article. Chronological expert returns 0.5 (undecided) when comparing two sentences which are not in the same article but have the same publication date.

2.2 Probabilistic Expert

Lapata [3] proposes a probabilistic model to predict sentence order. Her model assumes that the position of a sentence in the summary depends only upon the sentences preceding it. For example let us consider a summary T which has sentences $S_1, \ldots, S_n$ in that order. The probability $P(T)$ of getting this order is given by:

$$P(T) = \prod_{i=1}^{n} P(S_n | S_1, \ldots, S_{n-i}). \tag{4}$$

She further reduces this probability using bi-gram approximation as follows.

$$P(T) = \prod_{i=1}^{n} P(S_i | S_{i-1}) \tag{5}$$

She breaks each sentence into features and takes the vector product of features as follows:

$$P(S_i|S_{i-1}) = \prod_{(a_{<i,j>}, a_{<i-1,k>}) \in S_i \times S_{i-1}} P(a_{<i,j>}, a_{<i-1,k>}). \quad (6)$$

Feature conditional probabilities can be calculated using frequency counts of features as follows:

$$P(a_{<i,j>}|a_{<i-1,k>}) = \frac{f(a_{<i,j>}, a_{<i-1,k>})}{\sum_{a_{<i,j>}} f(a_{<i,j>}, a_{<i-1,k>})}. \quad (7)$$

Lapata [3] uses nouns,verbs and dependency structures as features. Where as in our expert we implemented only nouns and verbs as features. We performed back-off smoothing on the frequency counts in equation 7 as these values were sparse. Once these conditional probabilities are calculated, for two sentences u,v we can define the preference function for the probabilistic expert as follows:

$$\text{PREF}_{prob}(u, v, Q) = \begin{cases} \frac{1+P(u|r)-P(v|r)}{2} & Q \neq \oslash \\ \frac{1+P(u)-P(v)}{2} & Q = \oslash \end{cases}. \quad (8)$$

Where, Q is the set of sentences ordered so far and $r \in Q$ is the lastly ordered sentence in Q. Initially, Q is null and we prefer the sentence with higher absolute probability. When Q is not null and u is preferred to v, i.e. $P(u|r) > P(v|r)$, according to definition 8 a preference value greater than 0.5 is returned. If v is preferred to u, i.e. $P(u|r) < P(v|r)$, we have a preference value smaller than 0.5. When $P(u|r) = P(v|r)$, the expert is undecided and it gives the value 0.5.

2.3 Topical Relevance Expert

In MDS, the source documents could contain multiple topics. Therefore, the extracted sentences could be covering different topics. Grouping the extracted sentences which belong to the same topic, improves readability of the summary. Motivated by this fact, we designed an expert which groups the sentences which belong to the same topic. This expert prefers sentences which are more similar to the ones that have been already ordered. For each sentence l in the extract we define its topical relevance, topic(l) as follows:

$$\text{topic}(l) = \max_{q \in Q} \text{sim}(l, q). \quad (9)$$

We use cosine similarity to calculate sim(l, q). The preference function of this expert is defined as follows:

$$\text{PREF}_{topic}(u, v, Q) = \begin{cases} 0.5 & [Q = \oslash] \vee [\text{topic}(u) = \text{topic}(v)] \\ 1 & [Q \neq \oslash] \wedge [\text{topic}(u) > \text{topic}(v)] \\ 0 & \text{otherwise} \end{cases}. \quad (10)$$

Where, $\oslash$ represents the null set, u,v are the two sentences under consideration and Q is the block of sentences that has been already ordered so far in the summary.

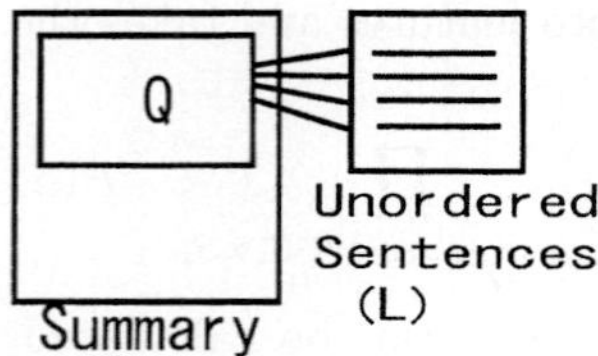

Fig. 1. Topical relevance expert

2.4 Precedent Expert

When placing a sentence in the summary it is important to check whether the preceding sentences convey the necessary background information for this sentence to be clearly understood. Placing a sentence without its context being stated in advanced, makes an unintelligible summary. As shown in figure 2, for each extracted sentence l, we can compare the block of text that appears before it in its source document (P) with the block of sentences which we have ordered so far in the summary (Q). If P and Q matches well, then we can safely assume that Q contains the necessary background information required by l. We can then place l after Q. Such relations among sentences are called precedence relations. Okazaki [7] proposes precedence relations as a method to improve the chronological ordering of sentences. He considers the information stated in the documents preceding the extracted sentences to judge the order. Based on this idea, we define precedence pre(l) of the extracted sentence l as follows:

$$\mathrm{pre}(l) = \max_{p \in P, q \in Q} \mathrm{sim}(p, q). \tag{11}$$

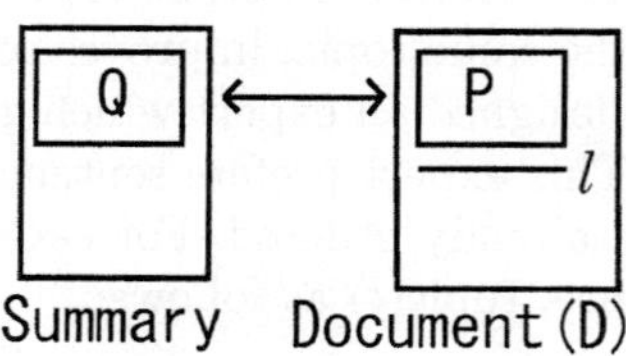

Fig. 2. Precedent expert

Here, P is the set of sentences preceding the extract sentence l in the original document. We calculate sim(p, q) using cosine similarity. The preference function for this expert can be written as follows:

$$\mathrm{PREF}_{pre}(u, v, Q) = \begin{cases} 0.5 & [Q = \emptyset] \vee [\mathrm{pre}(u) = \mathrm{pre}(v)] \\ 1 & [Q \neq \emptyset] \wedge [\mathrm{pre}(u) > \mathrm{pre}(v)] \\ 0 & \text{otherwise} \end{cases} . \tag{12}$$

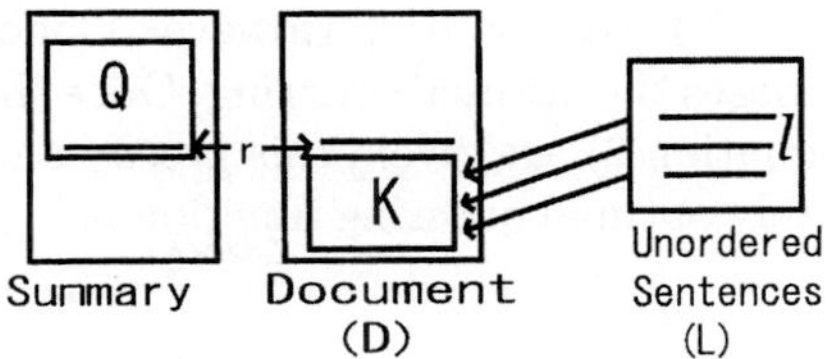

Fig. 3. Succedent expert

2.5 Succedent Expert

When extracting sentences from source documents, sentences which are similar to the ones that are already extracted, are usually ignored to prevent repetition of information. However, this information is valuable when ordering sentences. For example, a sentence that was ignored by the sentence extraction algorithm might turn out to be more suitable when ordering the extracted sentences. However, we assume that the sentence ordering algorithm is independent from the sentence extraction algorithm and therefore does not possess this knowledge regarding the left out candidates. This assumption improves the compatibility of our algorithm as it can be used to order sentences extracted by any sentence extraction algorithm. We design an expert which uses this information to order sentences.

Let us consider the siuation depicted in Figure 3 where a block Q of text is orderd in the summary so far. The lastly ordered setence r belongs to document D in which a block K of sentences follows r. The author of this document assumes that K is a natural consequence of r. However, the sentence selection algorithm might not have selected any sentences from K because it already selected some sentences with this information from some other document. Therefore, we search the extract L for a sentence that best matches with a sentence in K. We define succession as a measure of this agreement(13) as follows:

$$\mathrm{succ}(l) = \max_{k \in K} \mathrm{sim}(l, k). \tag{13}$$

Here, we calculate sim(l, k) using cosine similarity. Sentences with higher succession values are preferred by the expert. The preference function for this expert can be written as follows:

$$\mathrm{PREF}_{succ}(u, v, Q) = \begin{cases} 0.5 & [Q = \oslash] \vee [\mathrm{succ}(u) = \mathrm{succ}(v)] \\ 1 & [Q \neq \oslash] \wedge [\mathrm{succ}(u) > \mathrm{succ}(v)] \\ 0 & \text{otherwise} \end{cases} . \tag{14}$$

2.6 Ordering Algorithm

Using the five preference functions described in the previous sections, we compute the total preference function of the set of experts as defined by equation 2. Section 2.7 explains the method that we use to calculate the weights assigned to each expert's preference. In this section we will consider the problem of finding an order that satisfies the total preference function. Finding the optimal order for a given total preference function is NP-complete [2]. However, Cohen [2] proposes a greedy algorithm that approximates the optimal ordering. Once the unordered extract X and total preference (equation 2) are given, this greedy algorithm can be used to generate an approximately optimal ordering function $\hat{\rho}$.

let $V = X$
for each $v \in V$ **do**

$$\pi(v) = \sum_{u \in V} \text{PREF}(v, u, Q) - \sum_{u \in V} \text{PREF}(u, v, Q)$$

while V is non-empty **do**
  let $t = \arg\max_{u \in V} \pi(u)$
  let $\hat{\rho}(t) = |V|$
  $V = V - \{t\}$
  for each $v \in V$ **do**
    $\pi(v) = \pi(v) + \text{PREF}(t, u) - \text{PREF}(v, t)$
endwhile

2.7 Learning Algorithm

Cohen [2] proposes a weight allocation algorithm that learns the weights associated with each expert in equation 2. We shall explain this algorithm in regard to our model of five experts.

Rate of learning $\beta \in [0, 1]$, initial weight vector $\boldsymbol{w}^1 \in [0, 1]^5$, s.t. $\sum_{e \in E} \boldsymbol{w}_e^1 = 1$.

Do for $t = 1, 2, \ldots, T$ where T is the number of training examples.

1. Get X^t; the set of sentences to be ordered.
2. Compute a total order $\hat{\rho}^t$ which approximates,

$$\text{PREF}_{total}^t(u, v, Q) = \sum_{e \in E} \text{PREF}_e^t(u, v, Q).$$

   We used the greedy ordering algorithm described in section 2.6 to get $\hat{\rho}^t$.
3. Order X^t using $\hat{\rho}^t$.
4. Get the human ordered set F^t of X^t. Calculate the loss for each expert.

$$\text{Loss}(\text{PREF}_e^t, F^t) = 1 - \frac{1}{|F|} \sum_{(u,v) \in F} \text{PREF}_e^t(u, v, Q) \quad (15)$$

5. Set the new weight vector,

$$w_e^{t+1} = \frac{w_e^t \beta^{\text{Loss}(\text{PREF}_e^t, F^t)}}{Z_t} \quad (16)$$

where, Z_t is a normalization constant, chosen so that, $\sum_{e \in E} w_e^{t+1} = 1$.

In our experiments we set $\beta = 0.5$ and $w_i^1 = 0.2$. To explain equation 15 let us assume that sentence u comes before sentence v in the human ordered summary. Then the expert must return the value 1 for PREF(u,v,Q). However,if the expert returns any value less than 1, then the difference is taken as the loss. We do this for all such sentence pairs in F. For a summary of length N we have $N(N-1)/2$ such pairs. Since this loss is taken to the power of β, a value smaller than 1, the new weight of the expert gets changed according to the loss as in equation 16.

3 Evaluation

In addition to Kendall's τ coefficient and Spearman's rank correlation coefficient which are widely used for comparing two ranks, we use sentence continuity [7] as well as two metrics we propose; Weighted Kendall and Average Continuity.

3.1 Weighted Kendall Coefficient

The Kendall's τ coefficient is defined as following:

$$\tau = 1 - \frac{2Q}{{}^nC_2}. \tag{17}$$

Where, Q is the number of discordant pairs and ${}^nC_2$ is the number of combinations that can be generated from a set of n distinct elements by taking two elements at a time with replacement. However, one major drawback of this metric when evaluating sentence orderings is that, it does not take into consideration the relative distance d between the discordant pairs. However, when reading a text a human reader is likely to be more sensitive to a closer discordant pair than a discordant pair far apart. Therefore, a closer discordant pair is more likely to harm the readability of the summary compared to a far apart discordant pair. In order to reflect these differences in our metric, we use an exponentially decreasing weight function as follows:

$$h(d) = \begin{cases} \exp(1-d) & d \geq 1 \\ 0 & \text{else} \end{cases}. \tag{18}$$

Here, d is the number of sentences that lie between the two sentences of the discordant pair. Going by the traditional Kendall's τ coefficient we defined our weighted Kendall coefficient as following, so that it becomes a metric in $[1, -1]$ range.

$$\tau_w = 1 - \frac{2\sum_d h(d)}{\sum_{i=1}^{n} h(i)} \tag{19}$$

3.2 Average Continuity

Both Kendall's τ coefficient and the Weighted Kendall coefficient measure discordants between ranks. However, in the case of summaries, we need a metric which expresses the continuity of the sentences. A summary which can be read continuously is better compared to a one that cannot. If the ordered extract contains most of the sentence blocks of the reference summary then we can safely assume that it is far more readable and coherent to a one that is not. Sentence n-gram counts of continuous sentences give a rough idea of this kind of continuity.

For a summary of length N there are $N - n + 1$ possible sentence n-grams of length n. Therefore, we can define a precision P_n of continuity length n as:

$$P_n = \frac{\text{number of matched n-grams}}{N - n + 1}. \tag{20}$$

Due to sparseness of higher order n-grams P_n decreases in an exponential-like curve with n. Therefore, we define Average Continuity as the logrithmic average of P_n as follows:

$$\text{Average Continuity} = \exp\left(\frac{1}{3}\sum_{n=2}^{4} \log(P_n)\right) \tag{21}$$

We add a small quantity α to numerator and denominator of P_n in equation 20 so that the logarithm will not diverge when n-grams count is zero. We used $\alpha = 0.01$ in our evaluations. Experimental results showed that taking n-grams up to four gave contrasting results because the n-grams tend to be sparse for larger n values. BLEU(BiLingual Evaluation Understudy) proposed by Papineni [8] for the task of evaluating machine translations has an analogical form to our average continuity. In BLEU, a machine translation is compared against multiple reference translations and precision values are calculated using word n-grams. BLEU is then defined as the logarithmic average of these precision values.

4 Results

We used the 3rd Text Summarization Challenge (TSC) corpus for our experiments. TSC[1] corpus contains news articles taken from two leading Japanese newspapers; Mainichi and Yomiuri. TSC-3 corpus contains human selected extracts for 30 different topics. However, in the TSC corpus the extracted sentences are not ordered to make a readable summary. Therefore, we first prepared 30 summaries by ordering the extraction data of TSC-3 corpus by hand. We then compared the orderings by the proposed algorithm against these human ordered summaries. We used 10-fold cross validation to learn the weights assigned to each expert in our proposed algorithm. These weights are shown in table 1. According to table 1, succedent, chronology and precedent experts have the highest weights among the five experts and therefore almost entirely control the process of ordering. Whereas probabilistic and topical relevance experts have almost no influence on their decisions. However, we cannot directly compare Lapata's [3] approach with our probabilistic expert as we do not use dependency

[1] http://lr-www.pi.titech.ac.jp/tsc/index-en.html

Table 1. Weights learned

Expert	Chronological	Probabilistic	Topical Relevance	Precedent	Succedent
Weights	0.327947	0.000039	0.016287	0.196562	0.444102

Table 2. Comparison with Human Ordering

	Spearman	Kendall	Continuity	Weighted Kendall	Average Continuity
RO	-0.267	-0.160	-0.118	-0.003	0.024
PO	0.062	0.040	0.187	0.013	0.029
CO	0.774	0.735	0.629	0.688	0.511
LO	0.783	0.746	0.706	0.717	0.546
HO	1.000	1.000	1.000	1.000	1.000

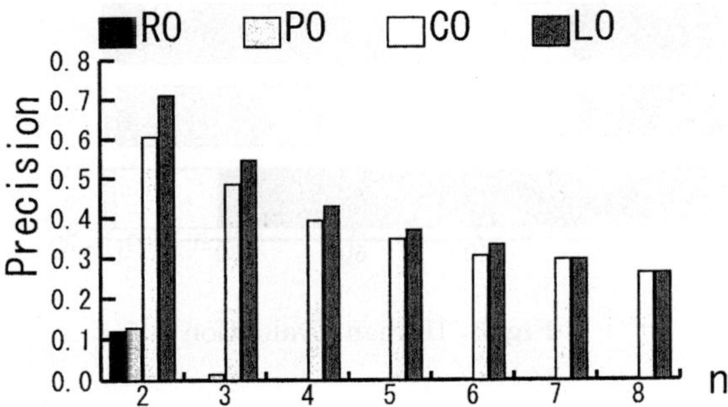

Fig. 4. Precision vs sentence n-gram length

structure in our probability calculations. Moreover, Topical relevance, Precedent and Succedent experts require other experts to guide them at the start as they are not defined when Q is null. This inter-dependency among experts makes it difficult to interpret the results in table 1. However, we could approximately consider the values of the weights in table 1 as expressing the reliability of each expert's decisions.

We ordered each extract by five methods: Random Ordering (RO); Probabilistic Ordering (PO); Chronological Ordering (CO); Learned Ordering (LO); and HO (Human-made Ordering) and evaluated the orderings. The results are shown in table 2. Continuity precision, defined in equation 20, against the length of continuity n, is shown in figure 4.

According to table 2 LO outperforms RO,PO and CO in all metrics. ANOVA test of the results shows a statistically significant difference among the five methods compared in table 2 under 0.05 confidence level. However, we could not find a statistically significant difference between CO and LO. Topical relevance, Precedent and Succedent experts cannot be used stand-alone to generate a total ordering because these experts are not defined at the start, where Q is null. These experts need Chronological and Probabilistic experts to guide them at the beginning. Therefore we have not compared these orderings in table 2.

According to figure 4, for sentence n-grams of length up to 6, LO has the highest precision (defined by equation 20) among the compared orderings. PO did not possess sentence n-grams for n greater than two. Due to the sparseness of the higher order n-grams, precision drops in an exponential-like curve with the length of sentence continuity n. This justifies the logarithmic mean in the definition of average continuity in equation 21. A similar tendency could be observed for the BLEU metric [8].

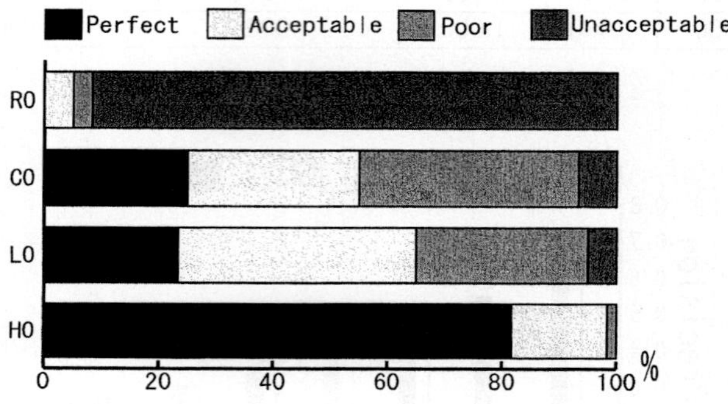

Fig. 5. Human Evaluation

We also performed a human evaluation of our orderings. We asked two human judges to grade the summaries into four categories. The four grades are; *perfect*: no further adjustments are needed, *acceptable*: makes sense even though there is some room for improvement, *poor*: requires minor amendments to bring it up to the acceptable level, *unacceptable*: requires overall restructuring rather than partial revision. The result of the human evaluation of the 60 (2×30) summaries is shown in figure 5. It shows that most of the randomly ordered summaries (RO) are unacceptable. Although both CO and LO have same number of perfect summaries, the acceptable to poor ratio is better in LO. Over 60 percent of LO is either perfect or acceptable. Kendall's coefficient of concordance (W), which assesses the inter-judge agreement of overall ratings, reports a higher agreement between judges with a value of $W = 0.937$.

Although relatively simple in implementation, the chronological orderings works satisfactorily in our experiments. This is mainly due to the fact that the TSC corpus only contains news paper articles. Barzilay [1] shows chronological ordering to work well with news summaries. In news articles, events normally occur in a chronological order. To evaluate the true power of the other experts in our algorithm, we need to experiment using other genre of summaries other than news summaries.

5 Conclusion

This paper described a machine learning approach to sentence ordering for multidocument summarization. Our method integrated all the existing approaches to sentence ordering while proposing new techniques like succession. The results of our experiments revealed that our algorithm for sentence ordering did contribute to summary readability. We plan to do further study on the sentence ordering problem in future work, extending our algorithm to other natural language generation applications.

References

1. Regina Barzilay, Noemie Elhadad, and Kathleen McKeown. Inferring strategies for sentence ordering in multidocument news summarization. *Journal of Artificial Intelligence Research*, 17:35–55, 2002.
2. W. W. Cohen, R. E. Schapire, and Y. Singer. Learning to order things. *Journal of Artificial Intelligence Research*, 10:243–270, 1999.
3. Mirella Lapata. Probabilistic text structuring: Experiments with sentence ordering. *Proceedings of the annual meeting of ACL, 2003.*, pages 545–552, 2003.
4. C.Y. Lin and E. Hovy Neats:a multidocument summarizer. *Proceedings of the Document Understanding Workshop(DUC)*, 2001.
5. Inderjeet Mani and Mark T. Maybury, editors. *Advances in automatic text summarization.* The MIT Press, 2001.
6. Kathleen McKeown, Judith Klavans, Vasileios Hatzivassiloglou, Regina Barzilay, and Eleazar Eskin. Towards multidocument summarization by reformulation: Progress and prospects *AAAI/IAAI*, pages 453–460, 1999.
7. Naoaki Okazaki, Yutaka Matsuo, and Mitsuru Ishizuka. An integrated summarization system with sentence ordering using precedence relation. *ACM-TALIP*, to appear in 2005.
8. Kishore Papineni, Salim Roukos, Todd Ward, and Wei-Jing Zhu. Bleu:a method for automatic evaluation of machine translation. *Proceedings of the 40th Annual Meeting of the Association for Computational Linguistics (ACL)*, pages 311–318, 2002.

Significant Sentence Extraction by Euclidean Distance Based on Singular Value Decomposition

Changbeom Lee[1], Hyukro Park[2], and Cheolyoung Ock[1]

[1] School of Computer Engineering & Information Technology, University of Ulsan, Ulsan 680-749, South Korea
{chblee1225, okcy}@mail.ulsan.ac.kr

[2] Department of Computer Science, Chonnam National University, 300, Youngbong-dong, Buk-gu, Kwangju 500-757, South Korea
hyukro@chonnam.ac.kr

Abstract. This paper describes an automatic summarization approach that constructs a summary by extracting the significant sentences. The approach takes advantage of the cooccurrence relationships between terms only in the document. The techniques used are principal component analysis (PCA) to extract the significant terms and singular value decompostion (SVD) to find out the significant sentences. The PCA can quantify both the term frequency and term-term relationship in the document by the eigenvalue-eigenvector pairs. And the sentence-term matrix can be decomposed into the proper dimensional sentence-concentrated and term-concentrated marices which are used for the Euclidean distances between the sentence and term vectors and also removed the noise of variability in term usage by the SVD. Experimental results on Korean newspaper articles show that the proposed method is to be preferred over random selection of sentences or only PCA when summarization is the goal.

keywords: Text summarization; Principal component analysis; Singular value decomposition.

1 Introduction

Automatic text summarization is the process of reducing the length of text documents, while retaining the essential qualities of the orginal. Many search engines have tried to solve the problem of information overflowing by showing either the title and beginning of of a document. However, such the title and beginning are insufficient to decide the relevance of the documents which user wants to search, and this is the reason that the text summarization is required to resolve this problem.

The process of text summarization could consist of two phases: a document interpretation phase and a summary generation phase. The primary goal of a document interpretation phase is to find the main theme of a document and its

R. Dale et al. (Eds.): IJCNLP 2005, LNAI 3651, pp. 636–645, 2005.

corresponding significant words. Since the significant words collectively represent the main theme of a document, it is important to find them more reasonably. For the purpose of this doing , the word frequency of a document might be utilized[4,8]. But this approach is limited in that cooccurrence relationships among words are not considered at all. In contrast to word frequency, the other method by using WordNet or a thesaurus[2] makes good use of word relationships such as NT(narrow term), RT(related term), and so on. However such resources require a large cost to compile, and often represent too general relationships to fit a specific domain.

In this paper, we propose a new summarization approach by both principal component analysis (PCA) and singular value decomposition (SVD) that are called quantification methods or statistical analysis methods. PCA is utilized to find significant words or terms in the document by term-relationships. Since the necessary term-relationships can be acquired only from the given document by linear transformation of PCA, the proposed method need not exploit the additional information such as WordNet or a thesaurus. And the SVD is used to extract the significant sentences. After performing SVD, a sentence-term matrix is decomposed into three matrices; that is, a sentence-concentrated matrix, a term-concentrated matrix, and a singular value matrix. The distances between significant term vectors and sentence vectors can be calculated by using a sentence-concentrated matrix and a term-concentrated matrix. The shorter the distance is, the more important the sentence is. In a word, to produce the summary of a document, we first identify significant terms by the term-term relationships of being generated by PCA, and second extract the significant sentences by the distances betweeen significant term vectors and all sentence vectors.

This paper is organized as follows. Section 2 and 3 describe the way to identify the significant terms by PCA, and extract the significant sentences by SVD, respectively. Section 4 reports experimental results. A brief conclusion is given in Section 5. And this paper enlarges [7] whose main content is to find out the significant terms by PCA.

2 Significant Term Extraction by PCA

2.1 PCA Overview and Its Application

In this subsection, we will outline PCA which is adapted from [6] and which is used to extract the significant terms in the document.

PCA is concerned with explaining the variance–covariance structure through a few linear combinations of the original variables. Its general objective is data reduction and interpretation. Algebraically, principal components are particular linear combinations of the p random variables $X_1, X_2, \cdots, X_p$. Geometrically, these linear combinations represent the selection of a new coordinate system obtained by rotating the orginal system with $X_1, X_2, \cdots, X_p$ as the coordinate axes.

PCA uses the covariance matrix (i.e., term-term correlation or cooccurrence matrix) instead of the obsevation-variable matrix (i.e., sentence-term matrix) such as Table 2. Let Σ be the covariance matrix associated with the random vector $X^T = [X_1, X_2, \cdots, X_p]$. Let Σ have the eigenvalue-eigenvector pairs (λ_1, e_1), (λ_2, e_2), ..., (λ_p, e_p) where $\lambda_1 \geq \lambda_2 \geq \ldots \lambda_p \geq 0$. The ith principal component(PC) is given by

$$Y_i = e_i^T X = e_{1i}X_1 + e_{2i}X_2 + \cdots + e_{pi}X_p, \qquad i = 1, 2, \ldots, p \tag{1}$$

The first PC is the linear combination with maximum variance, and has the widest spread in a new coordinate system geometrically. Consequently, we can say that it can cover the distribution of term frequency of a document as wide as possible, and also say that it has the power of explanation of the distribution as large as possible (but, not considering the meaning).

The PCs are uncorrelated and have variances equal to the eigenvalues of Σ, and the proportion of total population variance due to the ith PC, ρ_i, is

$$\rho_i = \frac{\lambda_i}{\lambda_1 + \lambda_2 + \ldots + \lambda_p}, \qquad i = 1, 2, \ldots, p \tag{2}$$

If most ($80 \sim 90\%$) of the total population variance, for large p, can be attributed to the first one, two, or three components, then these components can "replace" the original p variables without much loss of information. The first i PCs have also maximal mutual information with respect to the inputs among projections onto all possible i directions, and mutual information is given by $I(X, Y) = H(X) - H(X|Y)$ [5].

As we expected, all terms of the document are not necessary to represent the content (i.e., term frequency distribution) of the document by using a few first i PCs, because they have most of the total population variance and maximal mutual information as noted earlier. In addition, since PCA exploits a covariance matrix, we can use the term-term relationships by eigenvalues and eigenvectors without additional information resources. In the next subsection, we will describe how to extract the significant terms by eigenvalue-eigenvector pairs of a few first i PCs.

2.2 Extracting Significant Terms by Eigenvalue-Eigenvector Pairs

We assume that the candidates for the significant terms are confined only to nouns occurred more than 2 times in a document. We also regard the sentences as observations, the extracted nouns (terms) as variables, and the value of variables as the number of occurrence of terms in each sentence (cf. cumulative frequency of the document in [7]) .

Table 1 shows the term list extracted from one of the Korean newspaper articles composed of 12 sentences, and all of these terms have the occurrences more than twice in the document. Since the terms occurred just once are not reasonable to be representative nouns, we do not consider such terms. In our sample article, 9 terms are extracted for the cadidates for the significant ones as shown in Table 1. The sample article has 12 sentences (observations) originally, but there

Table 1. Variable (term) list

variable	notation
dae-tong-ryeong (president)	X_1
mun-je (problem)	X_2
guk-ga (nation)	X_3
sa-ram (person)	X_4
bu-jeong-bu-pae (illegality and corruption)	X_5
gyeong-je (economy)	X_6
guk-min (people)	X_7
bang-beop (method)	X_8
dan-che-jang (administrator)	X_9

Table 2. Observation-variable (sentence-term) matrix

obs. \ var.	X_1	X_2	X_3	X_4	X_5	X_6	X_7	X_8	X_9
1	1	0	0	0	0	0	0	0	0
2	2	1	0	0	0	0	0	0	0
3	0	0	1	1	0	0	0	0	0
4	0	0	1	1	1	0	0	0	0
5	0	0	0	0	1	2	0	0	0
6	0	0	1	0	0	0	1	0	0
7	0	1	0	0	0	0	1	1	0
8	1	1	0	0	0	0	0	0	0
9	0	0	0	0	0	0	0	1	2

are 9 ones in sentence-term matrix as shown in Table 2. The only reason for this difference was that the sentences, which did not include the 9 extracted terms at all, were omitted. In Table 2, the column under the head X_1 shows the freqeuncy of X_1, that is, X_1 occurred once in first sentence, twice in second sentence, once in eighth sentence. In Table 3, the 9 PCs are obtained after performning PCA with the 9 variables. The column under the head PC_1 shows the eigenvector of the first PC, for instance, $\overrightarrow{PC_1} = (-0.713, -0.417, \cdots, 0.025, 0.111)$. Its eigenvalue is 0.871, and its proportion of total population is 32.34% computed by Eq. (2).

There are two steps to extract the significant terms by eigenvales and eigenvectors as shown in Table 3. First we need to decide how many PCs are selected, and second to find out how to express the each selected PC. In order to select a few most salient PCs, we can make good use of cumulative ratio of eigenvalues. For example, the first four PCs can justify more than 90% (91.28%) of the total sample variance, we can choose them without much loss information. In other words, sample variance is summarized very well by these four PCs and the data from 9 observations on 9 variables can be reasonably reduced to 9 observations on 4 PCs. Until now, we could not know what the selected PCs represent exactly, but we could describe them by their coefficients approximately. A PC can be represented by linear combination of variables multiplied by their respective coefficient. For instance,

Table 3. Eigenvector and corresponding eigenvalue of each PC

var. \ PC	PC_1	PC_2	PC_3	PC_4	PC_5	PC_6	PC_7	PC_8	PC_9
X_1	-0.713	0.220	0.068	-0.334	0.131	0.300	0.035	-0.467	0.000
X_2	-0.417	-0.003	0.010	0.337	-0.596	0.044	0.518	0.295	0.000
X_3	**0.303**	0.151	-0.490	-0.083	0.144	0.289	0.529	-0.139	-0.485
X_4	0.234	0.149	-0.333	-0.292	-0.498	-0.248	0.074	-0.421	0.485
X_5	0.278	0.268	0.212	-0.096	-0.396	0.726	-0.309	0.134	0.000
X_6	0.281	**0.337**	**0.710**	0.135	0.076	-0.151	0.402	-0.310	0.000
X_7	0.038	-0.111	-0.181	**0.653**	0.258	0.375	0.038	-0.288	0.485
X_8	0.025	-0.464	0.092	0.236	-0.358	-0.028	-0.236	-0.548	-0.485
X_9	0.111	-0.703	0.234	-0.416	0.050	0.267	0.362	0.043	0.243
eigenvalue(λ_i)	0.871	0.676	0.563	0.349	0.134	0.049	0.035	0.017	0.000
cumulative ratio(%)	32.34	57.42	78.31	**91.28**	96.25	98.07	99.38	100.00	100.00

$$PC_1 = -0.713 \times X_1 - 0.417 \times X_2 + 0.303 \times X_3 + \cdots + 0.111 \times X_9 \quad (3)$$

Since the coefficients represent the degree of relationship between variables and a PC, the variables with coefficient higher than 0.5 can be reasonably used to express the PC. When the PC has not such coefficient higher than 0.5, the variable with the highest coefficient can be also used to represent the PC. For example, in table 3, the correlation coefficient between PC_1 and X_3 is 0.303, so X_3 can be selected for the description of PC_1. As the most part variance of a document justified by some of the PCs, we selected variables which have a strong correlation ($\geq 0.5\, or\ highest$) with one of these PCs as significant terms. In our example, the extracted significant terms from PC_1 to PC_4 are X_3, X_6 and X_7.

3 Significant Sentence Extraction by SVD

3.1 SVD Overview and Its Application

We will give an outline of SVD adapted from [3,9] and how to make good use of extracting the significant sentences.

Let A be any rectangular matrix, for instance an $S \times T$ matrix of sentences and terms, such as Table 2. The matrix A can be written as the product of an $S \times R$ column-orthogonal matrix U, an $R \times R$ daigonal matrix W with positive or zero elements (i.e., the singular values), and the transpose of a $T \times R$ orthogonal matrix V. Here, R is the rank of the matrix A ($R \leq min(S,T)$). The SVD decompositon is shown in Eq. (4).

$$A = U \cdot W \cdot V^T \quad (4)$$

where $U^T U = I$, $V^T V = I$, and W is the diagonal matrix of singualr values. In contrast to our usage of SVD, [3] used term-document matrix: our sentence-term matrix can be regarded as the transpose of term-document matrix, since the documents can be thought of the sentences in the summarization fields.

In this regard, the matrix A can be regarded as the sentence-term matrix like Table 2, U as the sentence-concentrated matrix whose number of rows is equal to the number of rows of the matrix A, and V as the term-concentrated matrix whose number of rows is equal to the number of columns of the matrix A. Then, the sentence vector $\boldsymbol{s}_i$ is defined as $\boldsymbol{s}_i = (u_{i1}, u_{i2}, \cdots, u_{iR})$ where R is the rank of the matrix A. As before, the vector for a term $\boldsymbol{t}_j$ is represented by $\boldsymbol{t}_j = (v_{j1}, v_{j2}, \cdots, v_{jR})$. Consequently, both the sentence and term vectors can be used to calculate the distances between them.

Actually the reduced dimensionality can be used instead of the full rank, R, by the cumulative ratio of the singular values. The cumulative ratio, σ_k, can be calculated by Eq. (5). When the σ_k is more than 90%, k can be selected for the reduced dimensionality. And this is large enough to capture most of the important underlying structure in association of sentences and terms, and also small enough to remove the noise of variability in term usage.

$$\sigma_k = \frac{\sum_{i=1}^{k} w_i}{w_1 + w_2 + \ldots + w_R}, \quad k = 1, 2, \ldots, R \tag{5}$$

To extract the significant sentences, in the first step, the Euclidean distances can be computed between all the sentence vectors and the significant term vectors (not all the term vectors). In this regard, the shorter the distance is, the more important the sentence is, since the significant terms can be described as representative words of a document. In the second step, the sentences are extracted by means of these Euclidean distances, and then these are included in the summary in the order of their sequences. And the number of the included sentences is depend on the compression rate of user's need.

3.2 Extracting Significant Sentences by the Decomposed Matrices

In this subsection, we will illustrate how to extract the significant sentences by examples. In [7], the importance of each sentence is computed by repeatedly summing 1 for each occurrence of significant terms in the sentence. However, the proposed method can be regarded as more formal or reasonable, since the Euclidean distance between vectors is used to calculate the degree of importance of each sentence.

Computing the SVD of the sentence-term matrix as shown in Table 2 results in the following three matrices for U', W', V'. The matrices are reduced by the cumulative ratio of the singular values computed by Eq. (5). Since the first six singular values can justify 92.31% of the total, the 9-dimension can be reduced to 6-dimension. Thus, the sentence-concentrated matrix, U', and the term-concentrated matrix, V', can be represented only by 6-dimensional vectors. The U' and V' are the vectors for the 9 sentences and 9 terms respectively. The diagonal matrix W' shows the first six values (originally, nine values).

$$\mathbf{U}' = \begin{pmatrix} -0.289 & 0.032 & -0.086 & 0.022 & -0.195 & 0.293 \\ -0.771 & 0.063 & -0.153 & 0.033 & -0.182 & 0.094 \\ -0.015 & -0.367 & -0.019 & -0.441 & -0.209 & -0.077 \\ -0.017 & -0.577 & -0.067 & -0.366 & -0.260 & -0.344 \\ -0.006 & -0.657 & -0.189 & 0.704 & 0.118 & 0.085 \\ -0.052 & -0.269 & 0.070 & -0.363 & 0.354 & 0.767 \\ -0.280 & -0.101 & 0.320 & -0.094 & 0.750 & -0.371 \\ -0.481 & 0.031 & -0.067 & 0.011 & 0.013 & -0.198 \\ -0.094 & -0.115 & 0.904 & 0.181 & -0.340 & 0.092 \end{pmatrix}$$

$$\mathbf{W}' = \begin{pmatrix} 2.826 & 2.424 & 2.314 & 2.117 & 1.672 & 0.984 \end{pmatrix}$$

$$\mathbf{V}' = \begin{pmatrix} -0.818 & 0.078 & -0.199 & 0.047 & -0.326 & 0.288 \\ -0.542 & -0.003 & 0.043 & -0.024 & 0.348 & -0.483 \\ \mathbf{-0.030} & \mathbf{-0.500} & \mathbf{-0.007} & \mathbf{-0.553} & \mathbf{-0.069} & \mathbf{0.352} \\ -0.011 & -0.389 & -0.037 & -0.381 & -0.281 & -0.427 \\ -0.008 & -0.509 & -0.111 & 0.160 & -0.085 & -0.263 \\ \mathbf{-0.004} & \mathbf{-0.542} & \mathbf{-0.163} & \mathbf{0.666} & \mathbf{0.141} & \mathbf{0.173} \\ \mathbf{-0.118} & \mathbf{-0.153} & \mathbf{0.168} & \mathbf{-0.216} & \mathbf{0.660} & \mathbf{0.402} \\ -0.132 & -0.089 & 0.529 & 0.041 & 0.245 & -0.284 \\ -0.066 & -0.095 & 0.781 & 0.171 & -0.407 & 0.187 \end{pmatrix}$$

The Euclidean distances between the significant term vectors and the sentence vectors can be computed by above two matrices, V' and U', to extract the significant sentences. The significant term vectors are the third, sixth and seventh rows in the V'. The significant sentence by X_3, for instance, is the third sentence of the document, since the distance between them is the shortest. All the distances from X_3, X_6 and X_7 vectors are shown in Table 4. Consequently, the three significant sentences (third, fifth and sixth) can be included in the summary of our sample article. When the number of the selected sentences are less than that of user's need, the summary can be supplemented with the other sentences by their distances.

4 Experiments

We compared the proposed method with both only PCA[7] and random selection of sentences.

The [7] selected the significant sentences by the appearance of the significant terms. The [7] also exploited from one to three consecutive sentences for the observation of PCA; however, the performance of extracting the significant sentences was similar. In this paper, we used each sentence within a document for the observation of PCA.

To extract sentences randomly, first, random numbers amounting to 30% of the total number of sentences in a document were created, and then the sentences were extracted by these random numbers.

We tried out the proposed method with two ways. First, the sentences were extracted by the distances of each significant term as described in subsection

Table 4. Euclidean distances between all the sentence vectors and the significant term vectors (X_3, X_6 and X_7)

num. of the sentence	distance		
	X_3	X_6	X_7
1	0.841	0.979	0.904
2	1.144	1.210	1.201
3	**0.484**	1.209	1.062
4	0.752	1.226	1.293
5	1.321	**0.154**	1.279
6	0.668	1.260	**0.526**
7	1.317	1.322	0.821
8	1.057	1.071	1.026
9	1.289	1.342	1.341

Table 5. Evaluation result

Measure	Method			
			PCA & SVD	
	Random	PCA	All	Each
Average Precision	0.256	0.386	0.395	0.407
Average Recall	0.413	0.451	0.486	0.500
F-Measure	0.316	0.416	0.436	0.449

3.2. Second, the sentences were selected by all the distances of all the significant terms. In Table 5, "All" and "Each" denote the latter and the former, respectively.

We used 127 documents of Korean newspaper articles for the evaluation, which were compiled by KISTI(Korea Institute of Science & Technology Information). Each document consists of orginal article and manual summary amounting to 30% of the source text. We regarded the sentences within this manual summary as correct ones.

We use three measures to evaluate the methods: precision, recall, and F-measure. Let

- Count(SystemCorrect) denote the number of correct sentences that the system extracts.
- Count(SystemExtract) denote the number of sentences that the system extracts.
- Count(Correct) denote the number of correct sentences provided in the test collection.

The measures are defined respectively as follows.

$$Precision = \frac{Count(SystemCorrect)}{Count(SystemExtract)}$$

$$Recall = \frac{Count(SystemCorrect)}{Count(Correct)}$$

$$F - Measure = \frac{2 * Precision * Recall}{Precision + Recall}$$

Table 5 shows that, by means of F-measure, the proposed method has improved the performance by about 2% ∼ 3.3% over only PCA, and by about 12% ∼ 13.3% over random selection. Table 5 also shows that the "Each" method is superior to "All". Furthermore, the performance of using PCA is better than that of using term frequency or a thesaurus [7].

5 Conclusion

In this paper, we have proposed a summarization approach that constructs a summary by extracting sentences in a single document. The particular techniques used are PCA and SVD for extracting the significant terms and sentences respectively.

PCA can quantify the information on both the term frequency and the term-term cooccurrence in the document by the eigenvalue-eigenvector pairs. These pairs were used to find out the significant terms among the nouns in the document. In addition, these terms can be regarded as those extracted by relationships between terms in the document, since PCA exploits the variance-covariance structure.

In contrast to PCA, SVD has the inforamtion on the sentences and terms after computing it of sentence-term matrix. In this regard, we can use the decomposed matrices to calculate the distances between the sentence and term vectors, and to make an effective removal of the noise of variability in term usage.

Experimental results on Korean newspaper articles show that the proposed method is superior to the methods of both random selection and only using PCA, and that extracting sentences by the distances per each term is better performance than extracting by all the distances of all the terms.

In conclusion, the information on the cooccurrence relationships between the terms by the PCA and the vector expressions of the sentences and terms by the SVD can be helpful for the text summarization. Furthermore, the proposed methods only exploited the pattern of the statistical occurrences within a document without the additional resources like a thesaurus to find out the relationships between the terms, and the proper dimension of the vectors.

Acknowledgements

This research was supported by the MIC(Ministry of Information and Communication), Korea, under the ITRC(Information Technology Research Center) support program supervised by the IITA(Institute of Information Technology Assessment)

References

1. Baeza-Yates, R., Ribeiro-Neto, B.: Modern Information Retrieval. New York: ACM Press (1999)
2. Barzilay, R., Elhadad, M. : Using Lexical chains for Text Summarization. In: I. Mani, & M. T. Maybury (eds.): Advances in automatic text summarization. Cambridge, MA: The MIT Press (1999) 111–121.
3. Deerwester, S., Dumais, S. T., Harshman, R.: Indexing by latent semantic analysis. Journal of the American Society for Information Science, 41 (6). (1990) 381–407
4. Edmundson, H. P.: New Methods in Automatic Extracting. In: I. Mani, & M. T. Maybury (eds.): Advances in automatic text summarization. Cambridge, MA: The MIT Press (1999) 23–42.
5. Haykin, S. S.: Neural networks: A comprehensive foundation. 2nd edn. Paramus, NJ: Prentice Hall PTR (1998)
6. Johnson, R. A., Wichern, D. W.: Applied Multivariate Statistical Analysis. 3rd edn. NJ: Prentice Hall (1992)
7. Lee, C., Kim, M., Park, H.: Automatic Summarization Based on Principal Component Analysis. In: Pires, F.M., Abreu, S. (eds.): Progress in Artificial Intelligence. Lecture Notes in Artificial Intelligence, Vol. 2902. Springer-Verlag, Berlin Heidelberg New York (2003) 409–413
8. Luhn, H. P.: The Automatic Creation of Literature Abstracts. In: I. Mani, & M. T. Maybury (eds.): Advances in automatic text summarization. Cambridge, MA: The MIT Press (1999) 15–21.
9. Press, W. H., Teukolsky, S. A., Vetterling, W. T., Flannery, B. P.: Numerical recipes in C++. 2nd edn. New York: Cambridge University Press (1992)

Two-Phase Biomedical Named Entity Recognition Using A Hybrid Method

Seonho Kim[1], Juntae Yoon[2], Kyung-Mi Park[1], and Hae-Chang Rim[1]

[1] Dept. of Computer Science and Engineering, Korea University, Seoul, Korea
[2] NLP Lab. Daumsoft Inc. Seoul, Korea

Abstract. Biomedical named entity recognition (NER) is a difficult problem in biomedical information processing due to the widespread ambiguity of terms out of context and extensive lexical variations. This paper presents a two-phase biomedical NER consisting of term boundary detection and semantic labeling. By dividing the problem, we can adopt an effective model for each process. In our study, we use two exponential models, conditional random fields and maximum entropy, at each phase. Moreover, results by this machine learning based model are refined by rule-based postprocessing implemented using a finite state method. Experiments show it achieves the performance of F-score 71.19% on the JNLPBA 2004 shared task of identifying 5 classes of biomedical NEs.

1 Introduction

Due to dynamic progress in biomedical literature, a vast amount of new information and research results have been published and many of them are available in the electronic form - for example, like the PubMed MedLine database. Thus, automatic knowledge discovery and efficient information access are strongly demanded to curate domain databases, to find out relevant information, and to integrate/update new information across an increasingly large body of scientific articles. In particular, since most biomedical texts introduce specific notations, acronyms, and innovative names to represent new concepts, relations, processes, functions, locations, and events, automatic extraction of biomedical terminologies and mining of their diverse usage are major challenges in biomedical information processing system. In these processes, biomedical named entity recognition (NER) is the core step to access the higher level of information.

In fact, there has been a wide range of research on NER like the NER task on the standard newswire domain in the Message Understanding Conference (MUC-6). In this task, the best system reported 95% accuracy in identifying seven types of named entities (person, organization, location, time, date, money, and percent). While the performance in the standard domain turned out to be quite good as shown in the papers, that in the biomedical domain is not still satisfactory, which is mainly due to the following characteristics of biomedical terminologies: First, NEs have various naming conventions. For instance, some entities have descriptive and expanded forms such as "*activated B cell lines, 47 kDa sterol*

R. Dale et al. (Eds.): IJCNLP 2005, LNAI 3651, pp. 646–657, 2005.

regulatory element binding factor", whereas some entities appear in shortened or abbreviated forms like "*EGFR*" and "*EGF receptor*" representing epidermal growth factor receptor. Second, biomedical NEs have the widespread ambiguity out of context. For instance, "*IL-2*" can be doubly classified as "protein" and "DNA" according to its context. Third, biomedical NEs often comprise a nested structure, for example "*⟨DNA⟩⟨protein⟩TNF alpha⟨/protein⟩gene⟨/DNA⟩*". According to [13], 16.57% of biomedical terms in GENIA have cascaded constructions. In the case, recognition of the longest terms is the main target in general. However, in our evaluation task, when the embedded part of a term is regarded as the meaningful or important class in the context, the term is labeled only with the class of embedded one. Thus, identification of internal structures of NEs is helpful to recognize correct NEs. In addition, more than one NE often share the same head noun with a conjunction/disjunction or enumeration structure, for instance, "*IFN-gamma and GM-CSF mRNA*", "*CD33+, CD56+, CD16- acute leukemia*"or "*antigen- or cAMP-activated Th2 cell*". Last, there is a lot of inter-annotator disagreement. [7] reported that the inter-annotator agreement rate of human experts was just 77.6% when performing gene/protein/mRNA classification task manually.

Thus, a lot of term occurrences in real text would not be identified with simple dictionary look-up, despite the availability of many terminological databases, as claimed in [12]. That is one of the reasons why machine learning approaches are more dominant in biomedical NER than rule-based or dictionary-based approaches [5], even though existence of reliable training resources is very critical.

Accordingly, much work has been done on biomedical NER, based on machine learning techniques. [3] and [13] have used hidden Markov Model (HMM) for biomedical NER where state transitions are made by semantic trigger features. [4] and [11] have applied maximum entropy plus Markovian sequence based models such as maximum entropy markov model (MEMM) and conditional random fields (CRFs), which present a way for integrating different features such as internal word spellings and morphological clues within an NE string and contextual clues surrounding the string in the sentence.

These works took an one-phase based approach where boundary detection of named entities and semantic labeling come together. On the other hand, [9] proposed a two-phase model in which the biomedical named entity recognition process is divided into two processes of distinguishing biomedical named entities from general terms and labeling the named entities with semantic classes that they belong to. They use support vector machines (SVM) for each phase. However, the SVM does not provide an easy way for labeling Markov sequence data like B following O and I following B in named entities. Furthermore, since this system is tested on the GENIA corpus rather than JNLPBA 2004 shared task, we cannot confirm the effectiveness of this approach on the ground of experiments for common resources.

In this paper, we present a two-phase named entity recognition model: (1) boundary detection for NEs and (2) term classification by semantic labeling. The advantage of dividing the recognition process into two phase is that we can select separately a discriminative feature set for each subtask, and moreover can measure effectiveness of models at each phase. We use two exponential models for this work, namely conditional random fields for boundary detection having Markov sequence, and the maximum entropy model for semantic labeling. In addition, results from the machine learning based model are refined by a rule-based postprocessing, which is implemented using a finite state transducer (FST). The FST is constructed with the GENIA 3.02 corpus. We here focus on identification of five classes of NEs, i.e. “protein”, “RNA”, “DNA”, “cell line”, and “cell type” and experiments are conducted on the training and evaluation set provided by the shared task in COLING 2004 JNLPBA.

2 Training

2.1 Maximum Entropy and Conditional Random Fields

Before we describe the features used in our model, we briefly introduce the ME and CRF model which we make use of. In the ME framework, the conditional probability of predicting an outcome o given a history h is defined as follows:

$$p_\lambda(o|h) = \frac{1}{Z_\lambda(h)} exp\left(\sum_{i=1}^{k} \lambda_i f_i(h,o)\right) \tag{1}$$

where $f_i(h,o)$ is a binary-valued feature function, λ_i is the weighting parameter of $f_i(h,o)$, k is the number of features, and $Z_\lambda(h)$ is a normalization factor for $\Sigma_o p_\lambda(o|h)$=1. That is, the probability $p_\lambda(o|h)$ is calculated by the weighted sum of active features. Given an exponential model with k features and a set of training data, empirical distribution, weights of the k features are trained to maximize the model's log-likelihood:

$$L(p) = \sum_{o,h} \tilde{p}(h,o) log(o|h) \tag{2}$$

Although the maximum entropy model above provides a powerful tool for classification by integrating different features, it is not easy to model the Markov sequence data. In this case, the CRF is used for a task of assigning label sequences to a set of observation sequences. Based on the principle of maximum entropy, a CRF has a single exponential model for the joint probability of the entire sequence of labels given the observation sequence. The CRF is a special case of the linear chain that corresponds to conditionally trained finite-state machine and define conditional probability distributions of a particular label sequence $\mathbf{s}$ given observation sequence $\mathbf{o}$

$$\begin{aligned} p_\lambda(\mathbf{s}|\mathbf{o}) &= \tfrac{1}{Z(\mathbf{o})} exp(\textstyle\sum_{j=1}^{k} \lambda_j F_j(\mathbf{s},\mathbf{o})) \\ F_j(\mathbf{s},\mathbf{o}) &= \textstyle\sum_{i=1}^{n} f_j(s_{i-1}, s_i, \mathbf{o}, i) \end{aligned} \tag{3}$$

where $\mathbf{s} = s_1 \ldots s_n$, and $\mathbf{o} = o_1 \ldots o_n$, $Z(\mathbf{o})$ is a normalization factor, and each feature is a transition function [8]. For example, we can think of the following feature function.

$$f_j(s_{i-1}, s_i, \mathbf{o}, i) = \begin{cases} 1 \text{ if } s_{i-1}\text{=B and } s_i\text{=I}, \\ \quad \text{and the observation word at position i is ``}\textit{gene}\text{''} \\ 0 \ \textit{otherwise} \end{cases} \quad (4)$$

Our CRFs for term boundary detection have a first-order Markov dependency between output tags. The label at position i, s_i is one of B, I and O. In contrast to the ME model, since B is the beginning of a term, the transition from O to I is not possible. CRFs constrain results to consider only reasonable paths. Thus, total 8 combinations are possible for (s_{i-1}, s_i) and the most likely $\mathbf{s}$ can be found with the Viterbi algorithm. The weights are set to maximize the conditional log likelihood of labeled sequences in the training set using a quasi-Newton method called L-BFGS [2].

2.2 Features for Term Boundary Detection

Table 1 shows features for the step of finding the boundary of biomedical terms. Here, we give a supplementary description of a part of the features.

Table 1. Feature set for boundary detection (+:conjunction)

Model	Feature	Description
CRF, ME_{markov}	Word	$w_{i-1}, w_{i-2}, w_i, w_{i+1}, w_{i+2}$
CRF, ME_{markov}	Word Normalization	normalization forms of the 5 words
CRF, ME_{markov}	POS	$POS_{w_{i-1}}$, POS_{w_i}, $POS_{w_{i+1}}$
CRF, ME_{markov}	Word Construction form	WF_{w_i}
CRF, ME_{markov}	Word Characteristics	$WC_{w_{i-1}}, WC_{w_i}, WC_{w_{i+1}}$
CRF, ME_{markov}	Contextual Bigrams	$w_{i-1} + w_i$
		$w_i + w_{i+1}$
		$w_{i+1} + w_{i+2}$
CRF, ME_{markov}	Contextual Trigrams	$w_{i-1} + w_i + w_{i+1}$
CRF, ME_{markov}	Bigram POS	$POS_{w_{i-1}} + POS_{w_i}$
		$POS_{w_i} + POS_{w_{i+1}}$
CRF, ME_{markov}	Trigram POS	$POS_{w_{i-1}} + POS_{w_i} + POS_{w_{i+1}}$
CRF, ME_{markov}	Modifier	MODI(w_i)
CRF, ME_{markov}	Header	HEAD(w_i)
CRF, ME_{markov}	SUFFIX	SUFFIX(w_i)
CRF, ME_{markov}	Chunk Type	$CType_{w_i}$
CRF, ME_{markov}	Chunk Type + Pre POS	$CType_{w_i} + POS_{w_{i-1}}$
ME_{markov}	Pre label	$label_{w_{i-1}}$
ME_{markov}	Pre label + Cur Word	$label_{w_{i-1}} + w_i$

- **word and POS:** 5 words(target word(w_i), left two words, and right two words) and three POS($POS_{w_{i-1}}$, POS_{w_i}, $POS_{w_{i+1}}$) are considered.

- **word normalization:** This feature contributes to word normalization. We attempt to reduce a word to its stem or root form with a simple algorithm which has rules for words containing plural, hyphen, and alphanumeric letters. Specifically, the following patterns are considered.
  (1) "lymphocytes", "cells" → "lymphocyte", "cell"
  (2) "il-2", "il-2a", "il2a" → "il"
  (3) "5-lipoxygenase", "v-Abl" → "lipoxygenase", "abl"
  (4) "peri-kappa" or "t-cell" has two normalization forms of "peri" and "kappa" and "t" and "cell" respectively.
  (5) "Ca2+-independent" has two roots of "ca" and "independent".
  (6) The root of digits is "D".
- **informative suffix:** This feature appears if a target word has a salient suffix for boundary detection. The list of salient suffixes is obtained by relative entropy [10].
- **word construction form:** This feature indicates how a target word is orthographically constructed. Word shapes refer to a mapping of each word on equivalence classes that encodes with dashes, numerals, capitalizations, lower letters, symbols, and so on. All spellings are represented with combinations of the attributes[1]. For instance, the word construction form of "*IL-2*" would become "IDASH-ALPNUM".
- **word characteristics:** This feature appears if a word represents a DNA sequence of "A","C","G","T" or Greek letter such as beta or alpha, ordinal index such as I, II or unit such as BU/ml, micron/mL. It is encoded with "ACGT", "GREEK", "INDEX", "UNIT".
- **head/modifying information:** If a word prefers the rightmost position of terminologies, we regard it has the property of a head noun. On the other hand, if a word frequently occurs in other positions, we regard it has the property of a modifying noun. It can help to establish the beginning and ending point of multi-word entities. We automatically extract 4,382 head nouns and 7,072 modifying nouns from the training data as shown in Table 2.
- **chunk-type information:** This feature is also effective in determining the position of a word in NEs, "B", "I", "O" which means "begin chunk", "in chunk" and "others", respectively. We consider the chunk type of a target word and the conjunction of the current chunk type and the POS of the previous word to represent the structure of an NE.

We also tested an ME-based model for boundary detection. For this, we add two special features : previous state (label) and conjunction of previous label

[1] "IDASH" (inter dash), "EDASH" (end dash), "SDASH" (start dash), "CAP"(capitalization), "LOW"(lowercase), "MIX"(lowercase and capitalization letters), "NUM"(digit), "ALPNUM"(alpha-numeric), "SYM"(symbol), "PUNC"(punctuation),and "COMMA"(comma)

Table 2. Examples of Head/Modifying Nouns

Modifying Nouns	Head Nouns
nf-kappa	cytokines
nuclear	elements
activated	assays
normal	complexes
phorbol	macrophages
viral	molecules
inflammatory	pathways
murine	extracts
electrophoretic	glucocorticoids
acute	levels
intracellular	responses
epstein-barr	clones
cytoplasmic	motifs

and current word to consider **state transition**. That is, a previous label can be represented as a feature function in our model as follows:

$$f_i(h,o) = \begin{cases} 1 \; if \; \text{pre\_label+tw=B+gene,o=I} \\ 0 \; otherwise \end{cases} \quad (5)$$

It means that the target word is likely to be inside a term (I), when the word is "gene" and the previous label is "B". In our model, the current label is deterministically assigned to the target word with considering the previous state with the highest probability.

2.3 Features for Semantic Labeling

Table 3 shows features for semantic labeling with respect to recognized NEs.

- **word contextual feature:** We make use of three kinds of internal and external contextual features: words within identified NEs, their word normalization forms, and words surrounding the NEs. In Table 3, NE_{w_0} denotes the rightmost word in an identified NE region. Moreover, the presence of specific head nouns acting as functional words takes precedence when determining the term class, even though many terms do not contain explicit term category information. For example, functional words, such as "*factor*", "*receptor*", and "*protein*" are very useful in determining *protein* class, and "*gene*", "*promoter*", and "*motif*" are clues for classifying *DNA* [5]. In general, such functional words are often the last word of an entity. This is the reason we consider the position where a word occurs in NEs along with the word. For inside context features, we use non-positional word features as well. As non-positional features, all words inside NEs are used.
- **internal bigrams and trigrams:** We consider the rightmost bigrams/trigrams inside identified NEs and the normalized bigrams/trigrams.

Table 3. Feature Set for Semantic Classification

Feature	description
Word Features (positional)	$NE_{w_{others}}, NE_{w_{-3}}, NE_{w_{-2}}, NE_{w_{-1}}, NE_{w_0}$
Word Features (non-positional)	All_{NE_w}
Word Normalization (positional)	$WF_{NE_{w_{-3}}}, WF_{NE_{w_{-2}}}, WF_{NE_{w_{-1}}}, WF_{NE_{w_0}}$
Left Context(Words Surrounding an NE)	LCW_{-2}, LCW_{-1}
Right Context	RCW_{+1}, RCW_{+2}
Internal Bigrams	$NE_{w_{-1}} + NE_{w_0}$
Internal Trigrams	$NE_{w_{-2}} + NE_{w_{-1}} + NE_{w_0}$
Normalized Internal Bigrams	$WF_{NE_{w_{-1}}} + WF_{NE_{w_0}}$
Normalized Internal Trigrams	$NE_{w_{-2}} + NE_{w_{-1}} + NE_{w_0}$
IDASH-word related Bigrams/Trigrams	
Keyword	KEYWORD(NE_i)

- **IDASH-word related bigrams/trigrams:** This feature appears if NE_{w_0} or $NE_{w_{-1}}$ contains dash characters. In this case, the bigram/trigram are additionally formed by removing all dashes from the spelling. It is useful to deal with lexical variants.
- **keywords:** This feature appears if the identified NE is informative keyword with respect to a specific class. The keywords set comprises terms obtained by the relative entropy between general and biomedical domain corpora.

3 Rule-Based Postprocessing

A rule-based method can be used to correct errors by NER based on machine learning. For example, the CRFs tag "*IL-2 receptor expression*" as "B I I", since the NEs ended with "*receptor expression*" in training data almost belong to "*other_name*" class even if the NEs ended with "*receptor*" belong to "*protein*" class. It should be actually tagged as "B I O". That kind of errors is caused mainly by the cascaded phenomenon in biomedical names. Since our system considers all NEs belonging to other classes in the recognition phase, it tends to recognize the longest ones. That is, in the term classification phase, such NEs are classified as "other" class and are ignored. Thus, the system losts embedded NEs although the training and evaluation set in fact tends to consider only the embedded NE when the embedded one is more meaningful or important.

This error correction is conducted by the rule-based method, i.e. **If** *condition* **THEN** *action*. For example, the rule '**IF** w_{i-2}=IL-2, w_{i-1}=receptor and w_i=expression **THEN** replace the tag of w_i with O' can be applied for the above case. We use a finite state transducer for this rule-based transformation, which is easy to understand with given lexical rules, and very efficient. Rules used for the FST are acquired from the GENIA corpus. We first retrieved all NEs including embedded NEs and longest NEs from GENIA 3.02 corpus and change

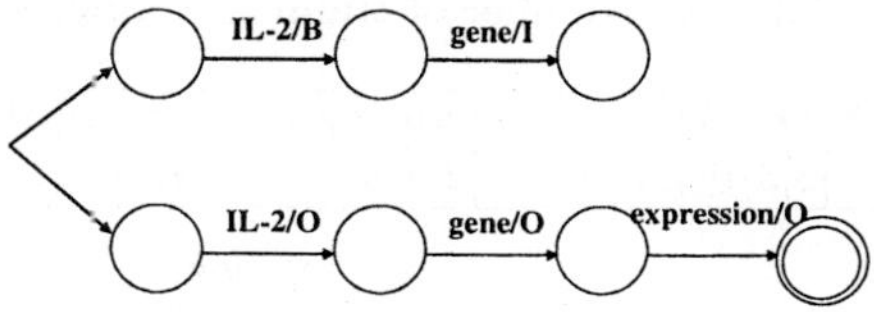

Fig. 1. Non-Deterministic FST

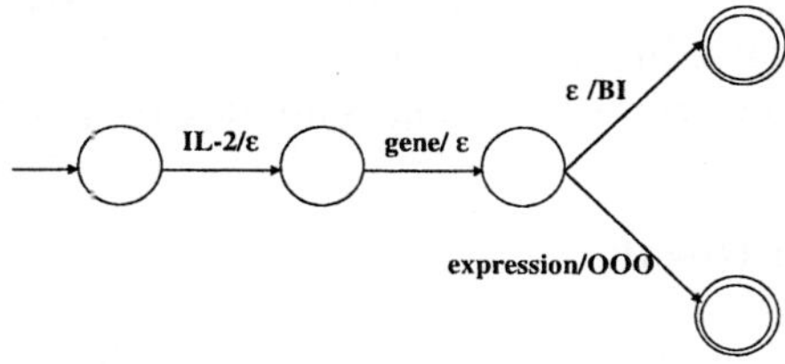

Fig. 2. Deterministic FST

the outputs of all other classes except the target 5 classes to O. That is, the input of FST is a sequence of words in a sentence and the output is categories corresponding to the words.

Then, we removed the rules in conflict with NE information from the training corpus. These rules are non-deterministic (Figure 1), and we can change it to the deterministic FST (Figure 2) since the lengths of NEs are finite. The deterministic FST is made by defining the final output function for the deterministic behavior of the transducer, delaying the output. The deterministic FST is defined as follows: $(\Sigma_1, \Sigma_2, Q, i, F, \otimes, *, \rho)$, where Σ_1 is a finite input alphabet; Σ_2 is a finite output alphabet; Q is a finite set of states or vertices; $i \in Q$ is the initial state; $F \subseteq Q$ is the set of final states; $\otimes$ is the deterministic state transition function that maps $Q \times \Sigma_1$ on Q; $*$ is the deterministic emission function that maps $Q \times \Sigma_1$ on Σ_2^* and $\rho : F \rightarrow \Sigma_2^*$ is the final output function for the deterministic behavior of the transducer.

4 Evaluation

4.1 Experimental Environments

In the shared task, only biomedical named entities which belong to 5 specific classes are annotated in the given training data. That is, terms belonging to other classes in GENIA are excluded from the recognition target. However, we consider all NEs in the boundary detection step since we separate the NER task into two phases. Thus, in order to utilize other class terms, we additionally annotated "O" class words in the training data where they corresponds to other classes such as *other_organic_compound*, *lipid*, and *multi_cell* in GENIA 3.02p version corpus. During the annotation, we only consider the longest NEs on

Table 4. Number of training examples

RNA	DNA	cell_line	cell_type	protein	other
472	5,370	2,236	2,084	16,042	11,475

GENIA. As a consequence, we find all biomedical named entities in text at the term detection phase. Then, biomedical NEs classified as *other* class are changed to *O* at the semantic labeling phase. The total words that belong to *other* class turned out to be 25,987. Table 4 shows the number of NEs with respect to each class on the training data. In our experiments, a quasi-Newton method called the L-BFGS with Gaussian Prior smoothing is applied for parameter estimation [2].

4.2 Experimental Results

Table 5 shows the overall performance on the evaluation data. Our system achieves an F-score of 71.19%. As shown in the table, the performance of NER for cell_line class was not good, because its boundary recognition is not so good as other classes. Also, Table 6 shows the results of semantic classification. In particular, the system often confuses *protein* with *DNA*, and *cell_line* with *cell_type.* Among the correctly identified 7,093 terms, 790 terms were misclassified.

Table 7 shows the performance of each phase. Our system obtains 76.88% F-score in the boundary detection task and, using 100% correctly recognized terms from annotated test data, 90.54% F-score in the semantic classification task. Currently, since we cannot directly assess the accuracy of the term detection process on the evaluation set because of *other* class words, the 75% of the training data were used for training and the rest for testing.

Table 5. Overall performance on the evaluation data

	Fully Correct			Left Correct	Right Correct
Class	**Recall**	**Precision**	**F-score**	**F-score**	**F-score**
protein	76.30	69.71	72.85	77.60	79.15
DNA	67.80	64.91	66.33	68.36	74.57
RNA	73.73	63.04	67.97	71.09	74.22
cell_line	57.40	54.88	56.11	59.04	65.69
cell_type	70.12	77.64	73.69	74.89	81.51
overall	**72.77**	**69.68**	**71.19**	**74.75**	**78.23**

Table 6. Confusion matrix over evaluation data

gold/sys	protein	DNA	RNA	cell_line	cell_type	other
protein	0	72	3	1	4	267
DNA	97	0	0	0	0	49
RNA	11	0	0	0	0	0
cell_line	10	1	0	0	63	37
cell_type	21	0	0	92	0	57

Table 7. Performance of term detection and semantic classification

	Recall	Precision	F-score
term detection (ME_{Markov})	74.03	75.31	74.67
term detection (CRF)	76.14	77.64	76.88
semantic classification	87.50	93.81	90.54
overall NER	72.77	69.68	71.19

Table 8. Performance of NE recognition methods (one-phase vs. two-phase)

method	Recall	Precision	F-score
one-phase	64.23	63.13	63.68
two-phase(*baseline*2) (only 5 classes)	66.24	64.54	65.38
two-phase(*baseline*2) **(5 classes+other class)**	68.51	67.58	68.04

Also, we compared our model with the one-phase model. The detailed results are presented in Table 8. Both of them have pros and cons. The best-reported system presented by [13] uses one-phase strategy. In our evaluation, the two-phase method shows a better result than the one-phase method, although direct comparison is not possible since we tested with a maximum entropy based exponential models in all cases. The features for one-phase method are identical with the recognition features except that the local context of a word is extended as previous 4 words and next 4 words. In addition, we investigate whether the consideration of "other" class words is helpful in the recognition performance. Table 8 shows explicit annotations of other NE classes much improve the performance of existing entity types.

In the next experiment, we test how individual methods have an effect on the performance in the term detection step. Table 9 shows the results obtained by combining different methods in the NER process. At the semantic labeling phase, all methods employed the ME model using the features described in 2.3. Baseline1 is the two-phase ME model which restrict the inspection of NE candidates to the NPs which include at least one biomedical salient word. Baseline2 is the two-phase ME model considering all words. In order to retrieve domain salient words, we utilized a relative frequency ratio of word distribution in the domain corpus and that in the general corpus [10]. We used the Penn II raw corpus as out-of-domain corpus. Both models do not use the features related to previous labels. As a result, usage of salient words decrease the performance and it only speeds up the training process. Baseline2+FST indicates boundary extension/contraction using FST are applied as postprocessing step in baseline2 recognition. In addition, we compared use of CRFs and ME with Markov process features. For this, we added features of previous labels to the feature set for ME. Baseline2+ME_{Markov} is the two-phase ME model considering all features including previous label related features. Baseline2+CRF is a model exploiting CRFs and baseline2+CRF+FST is a model using CRF and FST as postprocessing. As shown in Table 9, the CRFs based

Table 9. F-score for different methods

Method	Recall	Precision	F-score
$baseline1(salientNP)$	66.21	66.34	66.27
$baseline2(all)$	68.51	67.58	68.04
$baseline2 + FST$	68.89	68.53	68.71
$baseline2 + ME_{Markov}$	70.30	67.65	68.95
$baseline2 + ME_{Markov} + FST$	70.61	68.40	69.49
$baseline2 + CRF$	72.44	68.77	70.56
$baseline2 + CRF + FST$	72.77	69.68	71.19

Table 10. Comparisons with other systems

System	Precision	Recall	F-score
Zhou et. al (2004)	69.42	75.99	72.55
Our system	72.77	69.68	71.19
Finkel et. al (2004)	71.62	68.56	70.06
Settles (2004)	70.0	69.0	69.5

model outperforms the ME based model. Our system reached F-score 71.19% on the $baseline2 + CRF + FST$ model.

Table 10 shows the comparison with top-ranked systems in JNLPBA 2004 shared task. The top-ranked systems made use of external knowledge from gazetteers and abbreviation handling routines, which were reported to be effective. Zhou et. al reported the usage of gazetteers and abbreviation handling improves the performance of the NER system by 4.8% in F-score [13]. Finkel et. al made use of a number of external resources, including gazetteers, web-querying, use of the surrounding abstract, abbreviation handling, and frequency counts from BNC corpus [4]. Settles utilized semantic domain knowledge of 17 kinds of lexicons [11]. Although the performance of our system is a bit lower than the best system, the results are very promising since most systems use external gazetteers, and abbreviation and conjunction/disjunction handling scheme. This suggests areas for further work.

5 Conclusion and Discussion

We presented a two-phase biomedical NE recognition model, term boundary detection and semantic labeling. We proposed two exponential models for each phase. That is, CRFs are used for term detection phase including Markov process and ME is used for semantic labeling. The benefit of dividing the whole process into two processes is that, by separating the processes with different characteristics, we can select separately the discriminative feature set for each subtask, and moreover measure effectiveness of models at each phase. Furthermore, we use the rule-based method as postprocessing to refine the result. The rules are extracted from the GENIA corpus, which is represented by the deterministic FST. The rule-based approach is effective to correct errors by cascading structures of biomedical NEs. The experimental results are quite promising. The system achieved 71.19% F-score without Gazetteers or abbreviation handling process. The performance could be improved by utilizing lexical database and testing various classification models.

Acknowledgements

This work was supported by Korea Research Foundation Grant, KRF-2004-037-D00017.

References

1. Thorten Brants. TnT A Statistical Part-of-Speech Tagger. In *Proceedings of the 6th Applied Natural Language Processing.*; 2000.
2. Stanley F. Chen and Ronald Rosenfeld. A Gaussian prior for smoothing maximum entropy models. *Technical Report CMUCS-99-108, Carnegie Mellon University.*
3. Nigel Collier, Chikashi Nobata and Jun-ichi Tsujii. Extracting the Names of Genes and Gene Products with a Hidden Markov Model. In *Proceedings of COLING 2000*; 201-207.
4. Jenny Finkel, Shipra Dingare, and Huy Nguyen. Exploiting Context for Biomedical Entity Recognition From Syntax to thw Web. In *Proceedings of JNLPBA/BioNLP 2004*; 88-91.
5. K. Fukuda, T. Tsunoda, A. Tamura, and T. Takagi. Toward information extraction: identifying protein names from biological papers. In *Proceedins of the Pacific Symposium on Biocomputing 98*; 707-718.
6. Junichi Kazama, Takaki Makino, Yoshihiro Ohta and Junichi Tsujii. Tuning Support Vector Machines for Biomedical Named Entity Recognition, *Proceedings of the ACL Workshop on Natural Language Processing in the Biomedical Domain* 2002; 1-8.
7. Michael Krauthammer and Goran Nenadic. Term Identification in the Biomedical literature. Journal of Biomedical Informatics. 2004; 37(6):512-526.
8. John Lafferty, Andrew McCallum, and Fernando Pereira. Conditional Random Fields: probabilistic models for segmenting and labeling sequence data. In *Proceedings of ICML-01*; 282-289.
9. Ki-Joong Lee, Young-Sook Hwang, Seonho Kim, Hae-Chang Rim. Biomedical named entity recognition using two-phase model based on SVMs. *Journal of Biomedical Informatics* 2004; 37(6):436-447.
10. Kyung-Mi Park, Seonho Kim, Ki-Joong Lee, Do-Gil Lee, and Hae-Chang Rim. Incorportating Lexical Knowledge into Biomedical NE Recognition. In *Proceedings of Natural Language Processing in Biomedicine and its Applications Post-COLING Workshop* 2004; 76-79.
11. Burr Settles. Biomedical Named Entity Recognition Using Conditional Random Fields and Rich Feature Sets. In *Proceedings of JNLPBA/BioNLP* 2004; 104-107.
12. Olivia Tuason, Lifeng Chen, Hongfang Liu, Judith A. Blake, Carol Friedman. Biological Nomenclatures: A Source of Lexical Knowledge and Ambiguity. In *Pacific Symposium on Biocomputing* 2004; 238-249.
13. GuoDong Zhou, Jie Zhang, Jian Su, Chew-Lim Tan. Exploring Deep Knowledge Resources in Biomedical Name Recognition. In *Proceedings of JNLPBA/BioNLP* 2004; 99-102.

Heuristic Methods for Reducing Errors of Geographic Named Entities Learned by Bootstrapping

Seungwoo Lee and Gary Geunbae Lee

Department of Computer Science and Engineering,
Pohang University of Science and Technology,
San 31, Hyoja-dong, Nam-gu, Pohang, 790-784, Republic of Korea

Abstract. One of issues in the bootstrapping for named entity recognition is how to control annotation errors introduced at every iteration. In this paper, we present several heuristics for reducing such errors using external resources such as WordNet, encyclopedia and Web documents. The bootstrapping is applied for identifying and classifying fine-grained geographic named entities, which are useful for applications such as information extraction and question answering, as well as standard named entities such as PERSON and ORGANIZATION. The experiments show the usefulness of the suggested heuristics and the learning curve evaluated at each bootstrapping loop. When our approach was applied to a newspaper corpus, it could achieve 87 F1 value, which is quite promising for the fine-grained named entity recognition task.

1 Introduction

A bootstrapping process for named entity recognition is usually as follows. In the initial stage, it selects seeds and annotates a raw corpus using the seeds. From the annotation, internal and contextual patterns are learned and applied to the corpus again to obtain new candidates of each type. Several methods are adopted to reduce over-generation and incorrect annotation and accept only correct ones. *One sense per discourse* heuristic may also be adopted to expand the annotated instances. It repeats until no more new patterns and entities are learned.

There are several issues in bootstrapping approaches for named entity recognition task to achieve successful performance. One of them is how to control annotation errors introduced in the bootstrapping process, on which we are focusing in this paper. As iteration continues, the bootstrapping expands previous annotation to increase recall. But this expansion may also introduce annotation errors and, as a result, decrease the precision. Ambiguous entities may be misclassified since learning speed per class depends on seeds. For example, *'New York'* may be misclassified to a city name before the patterns that correctly classify it to a state name are learned. Especially such errors in the early stage of the bootstrapping are quite harmful because the errors are accumulated. The

R. Dale et al. (Eds.): IJCNLP 2005, LNAI 3651, pp. 658–669, 2005.

annotation errors are classified into following four cases: *inclusion*, *crossing*, *type conflict* and *spurious*. The first three errors occur when a learned entity overlaps a true entity whereas the last one occurs when a learned entity does not overlap any true entity. Most previous works depend only on the statistics (e.g., scores of patterns) obtained from the previous annotation to control such errors. However, this strategy is not always the best because some trivial errors can also be corrected by simple heuristics. We suggest several heuristics that control the annotation errors in Section 4. The heuristics are embedded in a bootstrapping algorithm, which is modified and improved from [4] and shortly described in Section 3.

Unlike the traditional named entity task, we deal with sub-categorized geographic named entities (i.e., locations) in addition to PERSON and ORGANIZATION. Geographic named entities can be classified into many sub-types that are critical for applications such as information extraction and question answering. As a first step, we define their ten sub-classes: COUNTRY, STATE, COUNTY, CITY, MOUNTAIN, RIVER, ISLAND, LAKE, CONTINENT and OCEAN. We attempt to identify and classify all instances of the eleven classes as well as PERSON and ORGANIZATION in plain text. Annotation of geographic named entities is a formidable task. Geographic named entities are frequently shared between their sub-classes as well as with person names. For example, *'Washington'* may indicate a person in one context but may also mean a city or state in another context. Even country names cannot be exceptions. For some Americans, *'China'* and *'Canada'* may be cities where they live. Geographic named entities such as *'Turkey'* and *'Chile'* can also be shared with common nouns. Contextual similarity among geographic named entities is much higher than the one between PLO (Person-Location-Organization) entities since they are much closer semantically. These make geographic named entity annotation task more difficult than that of the traditional named entity task.

The remainder of this paper is as follows. Section 2 presents and compares related works to our approach. The bootstrapping algorithm is shortly described in Section 3 and several heuristics for controlling the annotation errors are explained in Section 4. Section 5 gives some experimental results verifying our approach, which is followed by conclusions and future works in Section 6.

2 Related Works

Most bootstrapping approaches start with incomplete annotations and patterns obtained from selected seeds and learn to obtain more complete annotations and patterns. However, the incompleteness is apt to cause annotation errors to be introduced in each bootstrapping iteration. Most previous works have designed their own statistical measures to control such errors. Phillips and Riloff [9] developed *evidence* and *exclusivity* measures to filter out ambiguous terms and Yangarber et al. [12] calculated *accuracy*, *confidence* and *score* of their patterns to select better patterns. However, those statistical measures are calculated only using data obtained from their training corpus which cannot often give enough information. Instead, other resources like World Wide Web as well as a gazetteer can be incorporated to compensate the lack of information from the training corpus.

Research on analysis of geographic references recently started to appear and has two directions. One is to focus on building gazetteer databases [6,11] and the other is to focus on classifying geographic entity instances in text [5].

Manov et al. [6] presented KIM (Knowledge and Information Management) that consists of an ontology and a knowledge base. They used it for information extraction but did not show notable results. Uryupina [11] presented a bootstrapping method to obtain gazetteers from the internet. By searching for seed names on the internet, she obtained lexical patterns and learned each classifier for six location sub-types, such as COUNTRY, CITY, ISLAND, RIVER, MOUNTAIN and REGION. Then she obtained and classified candidate names by searching the patterns in the internet. Li et al. [5] suggested a hybrid approach to classify geographic entities already identified as location by an existing named entity tagger. They first matched local context patterns and then used a maximum spanning tree search for discourse analysis. They also applied a default sense heuristic as well as one sense per discourse principle. According to their experiments, the default sense heuristic showed the highest contribution.

3 Bootstrapping

Our bootstrapping algorithm was modified and improved from [4] and the bootstrapping flow has one initial step and four iterative steps, as shown in Figure 1. In the initial step, we annotate a raw corpus with seeds automatically obtained from various gazetteers. Starting and ending boundary patterns are learned from the annotation and applied to the corpus again to obtain new candidates of each type. Then we eliminate annotation errors in the candidates using several

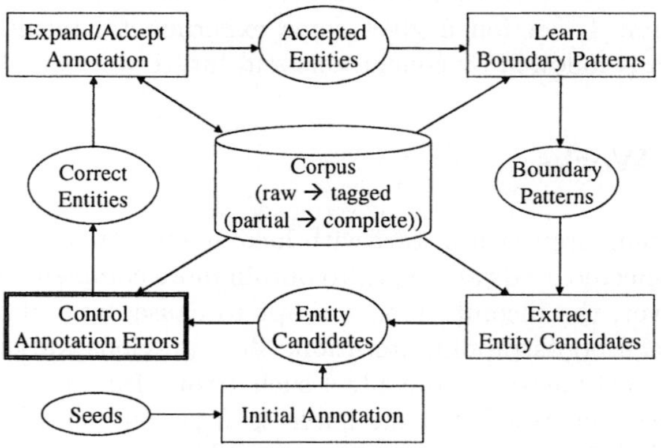

Fig. 1. The bootstrapping overview

linguistic heuristics, which is described in detail in Section 4. Finally, the remaining entity candidates propagate their annotations into other occurrences within the same document by *one sense per discourse* principle [2]. This loop continues until there are no new patterns learned. The algorithm is summarized as follows:

Step 0: Seed Preparation and Initial Annotation

We prepare seeds from the gazetteer and obtain initial entity candidate set, C_1, by marking occurrences of the seeds in the training raw corpus.

$C_1 = \{e_i | e_i$ is an entity candidate obtained from seeds but not accepted yet$\}$;

And we initialize the number of iteration (k), the set of accepted boundary patterns (P_0) and the set of accepted entities (E_0) as follows:

$k = 1;\ P_0 = \phi;\ E_0 = \phi;$

Step 1: Controlling the Annotation Errors

We filter out annotation errors among the entity candidates (C_k) using several heuristics with external resources and construct E_k, a set of entities checked as correct (see Section 4).

$E_k = \{e_i | e_i \in C_k$ and e_i is checked as correct by heuristics$\}$;

Step 2: Expanding and Accepting the Annotation

After removing erroneous candidates, we expand the correct entities by applying *one sense per document* heuristic and then accept M[1] top-ranked entities to construct a new E_k, the set of currently accepted entities.

$E_k = \{e_i | e_i \in E_k$ or is an instance expanded from $e_j \in E_k$, and $Rank(e_i) \geq Rank(e_{i+1}),\ 1 \leq i \leq M\}$;
$E_k = E_{k-1} \cup E_k$;

The rank of an entity candidate, $Rank(e_i)$, is computed as follows:

$$Rank(e_i) = 1 - \{1 - Score(BP_s(e_i))\} \times \{1 - Score(BP_e(e_i))\} \quad (1)$$

$BP_s(e)$ and $BP_e(e)$ indicate starting and ending boundary patterns of an entity e, respectively.

[1] M was set to 300 in our experiment.

Step 3: Learning Boundary Patterns

From the currently accepted entity set, E_k, we learn a new boundary pattern candidate set, $\tilde{P}_k$. We generate starting and ending boundary patterns and compute the accuracy ($Acc(p_i)$) of each pattern p_i which is used to filter out inaccurate patterns below Θ_a[2] and construct $\tilde{P}_k$. Then we compute the score ($Score(p_i)$) of each pattern p_i and add new N[3] top-scored patterns among $\tilde{P}_k$ to the accepted boundary pattern set, P_k, if there exist new patterns in $\tilde{P}_k$. Otherwise, the bootstrapping process stops.

$\tilde{P}_k = \{p_i | p_i = BP(e),\ e \in E_k \text{ and } p_i \notin P_{k-1} \text{ and } Acc(p_i) \geq \Theta_a\}$;
If $\tilde{P}_k = \phi$ then stop;
Otherwise, $P_k = P_{k-1} \cup \{p_i | p_i \in \tilde{P}_k \text{ and } Score(p_i) \geq Score(p_{i+1}),\ 1 \leq i \leq N\}$;

The accuracy, $Acc(p)$ and the score, $Score(p)$, of a boundary pattern, p, are computed as follows:

$$Acc(p) = \frac{pos(p)}{pos(p) + neg(p)} \times \frac{1 - \frac{1}{pos(p)^2+1}}{1 - \frac{1}{Np^2+1}}, \tag{2}$$

$$Score(p) = \frac{pos(p)}{pos(p) + 2 \times neg(p) + unk(p)} \times \frac{1 - \frac{1}{\ln(pos(p)+3)}}{1 - \frac{1}{\ln(Np+3)}}, \tag{3}$$

where $pos(p)$ is the number of instances that are matched to p and already annotated with the same entity type; $neg(p)$ is the number of instances that are matched to p but already annotated with a different type or previously filtered out; $unk(p)$ is the number of instances that are matched to p but not annotated yet; Np is the maximum value of $pos(p)$.

Step 4: Applying Boundary Patterns and Extracting Candidates

We extract new entity candidates, C_{k+1}, for the next iteration by applying the accepted boundary patterns, P_k, to the training corpus and then go to Step 1.

$C_{k+1} = \{e_i | BP_s(e_i) \in P_k \text{ and } BP_e(e_i) \in P_k \text{ and } e_i \notin E_k\}$;
$k := k + 1$;
Go to Step 1.

Since each pattern determines only one – i.e., *starting* or *ending* – boundary, a candidate is identified and classified by a pair of starting and ending boundary patterns with the same type.

---

[2] Θ_a was set to 0.1 in our experiment.
[3] N was set to 700 in our experiment.

4 Error Controls

The annotation errors introduced in the bootstrapping process are classified into following four cases, based on the inconsistency between an erroneous entity candidate and a true entity: *inclusion*, *crossing*, *type conflict* and *spurious*. *Inclusion* occurs when a candidate is a sub-phrase of a true entity – e.g., *'U.S.'* in *'U.S. Army'*. *Crossing* occurs when a candidate partially overlaps with a true entity – e.g., *'Columbia River'* in *"British Columbia River"*, which means a river in *'British Columbia'*. *Type conflict* occurs when a candidate has the same text span but different type from a true entity – e.g., *'New York'* may be misclassified into STATE but it is CITY. *Spurious* indicates that a candidate is spurious and does not interfere with any true entities.

To resolve these inconsistencies, we basically use statistical measures such as the score of a boundary pattern, $Score(p)$, and the rank of an entity candidate, $Rank(e)$, as in most previous works. However, this strategy is not always the best because some trivial errors can also be removed by simple heuristics and linguistic knowledge. Especially, the strategy cannot be applied to erroneous entities whose inconsistencies cannot be detected since their true entities are not identified yet. We call it *potential* inconsistency. We examine *potential inclusion* and *potential type conflict* for each entity candidate using the gazetteer and Web resources. To overcome this limitation of statistical measures obtained from the training corpus, we design several methods that incorporate linguistic knowledge and external resources, which are described in the following subsections.

4.1 Co-occurrence Information

Co-occurrence information (CI) has been widely used to resolve word sense ambiguity [3,8,10] and also can be employed to resolve *crossing* and *type conflict* inconsistencies, which can be regarded as word sense ambiguity problem. We assume that two instances of an ambiguous entity that occur in different texts can be classified into the same class if they share their CI. CI can be collected from definition statements of an entity of an encyclopedia. For example, the underlined phrases are collected as CI of an entity *'Clinton'* with class CITY from a statement *"Clinton is a city in Big Stone County, Minnesota, USA"*. In this way, we could construct initial CI for 18000 entities from the Probert Encyclopedia (http://www.probertencyclopaedia.com/places.htm), most of which are geographic entities. We also augment CI from the accepted entity instances during the bootstrapping process. We consider capitalized nouns or noun phrases in the window of up to left/right 60 words, within sentence boundary, from an entity as its CI. Then, the score of an entity e with class t, $Coinfo(e,t)$, is calculated as the similarity of CI:

$$Coinfo(e,t) = \frac{\sum_{i=1}^{N} freq(cw_i, e, t) \times count(cw_i, e)}{N}, \quad (4)$$

where N is the number of co-occurrence information cw_i, $freq(cw_i, e, t)$ means the frequency of cw_i co-occurring with an entity e of class t in the learned co-occurrence information and $count(cw_i, e)$ means the frequency of cw_i co-occurring with the entity in the current pending context. When two candidates cause *crossing* or *type conflict*, the candidate having smaller $Coinfo$ is considered to be incorrect and removed.

4.2 Gazetteer with Locator

Most entities are often mentioned with geographic entities where they are located, especially when they are not familiar to general readers. For example, *'Dayton'* in *"the Dayton Daily News, Dayton, Ohio"* is restricted to an entity in *'Ohio'*. This means that we can classify *'Dayton'* into CITY if we know a fact that there is a city named *'Dayton'* and located at *'Ohio'*. We can say that the locator information is a special case of the co-occurrence information. The locator information was also collected from the Probert Encyclopedia. If one of two entity candidates causing *crossing* or *type conflict* has a verified locator, the other can be regarded as an error and removed.

4.3 Prior Probability

Ambiguous entities often have different prior probability according to each class. For example, *'China'* appears frequently in general text as a country name but rarely as a city name. *'Canada'* is another example. This means that when two entity candidates cause *type conflict* we can remove one having lower prior probability. It is hard to acquire such probabilities if we do not have a large annotated corpus. However, WordNet [7] can give us the information that is needed to infer the relative prior probability since the sense order in WordNet reflects the frequency that the sense appears in text. According to WordNet, for example, *'New York'* is more frequently mentioned as a city name than as a state name and, therefore, is classified into CITY if its context does not give strong information that it is a state name. We could construct relative prior probabilities for 961 ambiguous gazetteer entries from WordNet. The prior probability of entity e with type t based on WordNet, $Prior_{WN}(e,t)$, is calculated as follows:

$$Prior_{WN}(e,t) = \begin{cases} \frac{1}{N+1} + \alpha_{WN} \times \frac{(m+1) - Sense\#_{WN}(e,t)}{\sum_{i=1}^{m} i} & \text{if there exist in WordNet} \\ \frac{1}{N+1} - \beta_{WN} & \text{otherwise,} \end{cases} \quad (5)$$

where N is the number of possible types of entity candidate e, m is the number of types of entity candidate e registered in WordNet, and $Sense\#_{WN}(e,t)$ means the WordNet sense no. of entity candidate e with type t. α_{WN} and β_{WN} are calculated as follows:

$$\alpha_{WN} = \beta_{WN} \times (N - m) + \frac{1}{N+1}$$

$$\beta_{WN} = \frac{m}{(N+1)^2}$$

Based on these formulas, the prior probabilities of an entity '*New York*' are given as follows according to its type: (CITY, 0.44), (STATE, 0.32), (TOWN, 0.12), and (COUNTY, 0.12).[4]

Although this prior probability is quite accurate, it does not have sufficient applicability. Therefore, we need to develop another method that can acquire prior probabilities of much more entities and Web can be one alternative. For each ambiguous entity X, we query *"X is a/an"* to at least two Web search engines[5] and extract and collect a noun phrase Y matching to *"X is a/an Y"*. Then, we determine a type, which Y belongs to, using WordNet and count its frequency. This frequency for each possible type of the entity X is regarded as sense order information. That is, we can assign to each possible type a sense number in the descending order of the frequency. Now, the prior probability of an entity e with type t based on the Web, $Prior_{Web}(e,t)$, can be similarly calculated. Then, the final prior probability, $Prior(e,t)$, is computed by arithmetic mean of $Prior_{WN}(e,t)$ and $Prior_{Web}(e,t)$. Combined with the Web search, the prior probabilities of the above example are changed as follows: (CITY, 0.36), (STATE, 0.29), (TOWN, 0.18), and (COUNTY, 0.17).

4.4 Default Type

When an ambiguous candidate causing *type conflict* is not registered in WordNet and cannot be detected by the Web search, we can apply default type heuristic. Unlike the prior probability, default type indicates a priority between any two target classes regardless of each individual entity. In general, we can say that, for an ambiguous entity between COUNTRY and CITY, COUNTRY is more dominant than CITY since a country name is more familiar to common people. We built up default types between all pairs of target classes using human linguistic knowledge and prior probability described in the previous subsection.

4.5 Part of Other Entity

Potential inclusion is often not exposed at a bootstrapping iteration since boundary patterns for each class are generated at different speeds and, in addition, all required boundary patterns cannot be generated from seeds. For this, we design two methods in addition to gazetteer consulting.

First, we check if there exists an acronym for a super-phrase. [1] says that we can consult a commonly-used *acronym* to determine extent of a named entity. In other words, *"University of California, Los Angeles"*, for example, must

[4] WordNet does not have COUNTY and TOWN senses of '*New York*'.

[5] We used eight well-known Web search engines such as Google (http://www.google.com/), Ask Jeeves (http://web.ask.com/), AltaVista (http://www.altavista.com/), LookSmart (http://search.looksmart.com/), Teoma (http://s.teoma.com/), AlltheWeb (http://www.alltheweb.com/), Lycos (http://search.lycos.com/), and Yahoo! (http://search.yahoo.com/). We specially thank to the service providers.

be annotated as a unique organization name since the university is commonly referred to as 'UCLA'. As an another example, *'U.S.'* in *"U.S. Navy"* should not be annotated as a country name but *'U.S.'* in *"U.S. President"* should be since *"U.S. Navy"* is represented as the acronym 'USN' but *"U.S. President"* is not represented as 'USP'. To check the existence of their acronyms, we can consult Web search engines by querying the suspected phrases with their possible acronyms, such as *"U.S. Navy* (USN)*"* and *"U.S. President* (USP)*"*, respectively, with exact match option.

Another solution is to check if a super-phrase beginning with a candidate whose class is one of geographic classes can be modified by a prepositional phrase which is derived by *in* or *comma (,)* plus the candidate (denoted as *in-loc*). For example, we can decide that *'Beijing'* in *"Beijing University"* is a part of the university name, since the phrase *"Beijing University* in Beijing*"* is found by Web search engines. If the *'Beijing'* denotes CITY, *"Beijing University"* means *a university* in Beijing and is not modified by the prepositional phrase "in Beijing" duplicately.

5 Experiments

The bootstrapping algorithm was developed and trained on part of New York Times articles (the first half of June, 1998; 28MB; 5,330 articles) from the AQUAINT corpus. We manually annotated 107 articles for test and the counts of annotated instances were listed in Table 1. A gazetteer composed of 80,000 entries was compiled from several Web sites[6]. This includes non-target entities as well as various aliases of entity names.

Table 1. The counts of instances annotated in the test corpus

COUNTRY	STATE	COUNTY	CITY	RIVER	MOUNT.	ISLAND	CONTI.	OCEAN	LAKE	PERSON	ORGAN.	Total
596	422	61	868	26	15	29	74	19	9	2,660	1,436	6,215

We first examined the usefulness of the heuristics, based on the instances (i.e., key instances) annotated in the test corpus. Applicability (*app.*) is defined as the number of key instances (denoted as *#app*), to which the heuristic can be applied, divided by the number of ambiguous ones (denoted as *#ambi*). Accuracy (*acc.*) is defined as the number of instances correctly resolved (denoted as *#corr*) divided by *#app*. There were 2250 ambiguous key instances in the test corpus.

[6] http://www.census.gov/, http://crl.nmsu.edu/Resources/resource.htm, http://www.timeanddate.com/, http://www.probertencyclopaedia.com/places.htm, http://www.world-of-islands.com/, and http://islands.unep.ch/isldir.htm

Applicability and accuracy of the first four heuristics for resolving *type conflict* are summarized in Table 2. As shown in the table, the first two heuristics – *co-occurrence information* and *gazetteer with locator* – have very low applicability but very high accuracy. On the contrary, the last two heuristics – *prior probability* and *default type* – show moderate accuracy with relatively high applicability. Based on this result, we combine the four heuristics in sequence such as high accurate one first and high applicable one last.

We also examined how well the heuristics such as *acronym* and *in-loc* can detect *potential inclusion* of an entity. In case of *acronym*, there were 2,555 key instances (denoted as *#app*) composed of more than one word and we searched the Web to check the existence of any possible acronym of each instance. As a result, we found out the correct acronyms for 1,143 instances (denoted as *#corr*). On the contrary, just 47 instances were incorrectly matched when we tried to search any acronyms of super-phrases of each key instance. In other words, *acronym* can detect *potential inclusion* at 46.58 applicability and 96.05 accuracy. In case of *in-loc*, 1,282 key instances beginning with a geographic word are tried to be checked if they appear with *in-loc* pattern in Web documents and 313 instances of them were confirmed. On the contrary, only 1 super-phrase of a key instance was incorrectly detected. Therefore, *in-loc* can detect *potential inclusion* at 24.49 applicability and 99.68 accuracy. These are summarized in Table 3. It says that the heuristics can detect quite accurately the extent of named entities although they do not have high applicability.

Finally, we evaluated the bootstrapping with the heuristics by investigating the performance change at every iteration. 50,349 seeds were selected from the gazetteer after removing ambiguous ones and only 3,364 seeds among them, which could be applied to the training corpus, were used for training. The recall and precision were measured using the standard MUC named entity scoring scheme and plotted in Figure 2. Starting at low recall and high precision, it gradually increases recall but slightly degrades precision, and it arrived at 87 F1

Table 2. Applicability and accuracy of the heuristics for resolving the inconsistency of 2,250 ambiguous instances (*#ambi*=2,250)

	#app	*#corr*	*app.*	*acc.*
co. info.	44	42	1.96	95.45
gaz. loc.	148	141	6.58	95.27
prior prob.	2,072	1,741	92.09	84.03
def. type	2,225	1,367	98.89	61.44

Table 3. Applicability and accuracy of the heuristics for detecting *potential inclusion*

	#ambi	*#app*	*#corr*	*app.*	*acc.*
acronym	2,555	1,190	1,143	46.58	96.05
in-loc	1,282	314	313	24.49	99.68

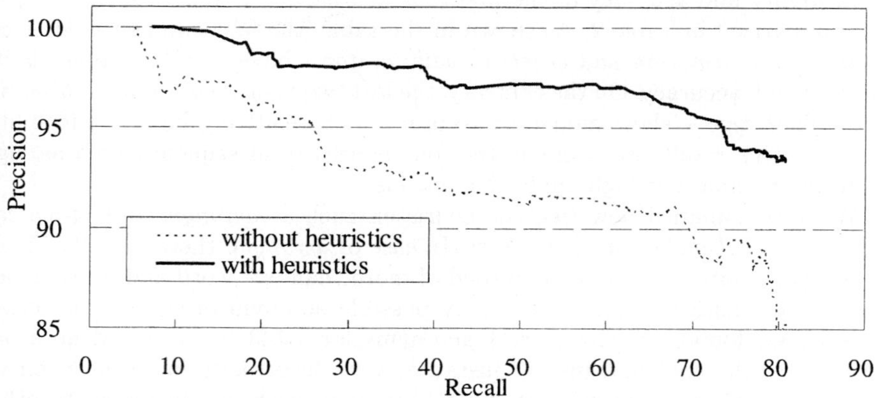

Fig. 2. The learning curve of the bootstrapping with the heuristics

(81 recall and 93 precision) after 1,100 iterations. We think that this performance is quite notable considering our fine-grained target classes, and the suggested heuristics work well to prevent incorrect entity candidates from being accepted during bootstrapping process.

6 Conclusions

In this paper, we observed four kinds of inconsistencies that degrade the performance of bootstrapping for named entity recognition with fine-grained geographic classes. To resolve such inconsistencies, we suggested several heuristics incorporating human linguistic knowledge and external resources like encyclopedia and Web documents. By analyzing the capability of each heuristic, we combined them in sequence. The bootstrapping with the heuristics was evaluated. Starting at low recall and high precision, the bootstrapping largely increased recall at a small cost of precision, and finally it achieved 87 F1. This means that the suggested approach is quite promising for the fine-grained named entity recognition task and the suggested heuristics can effectively reduce incorrect candidates introduced at the intermediate bootstrapping steps. In future, we plan to design a uniform statistical method that can augment the suggested heuristics especially using Web resources and also incorporate our heuristic knowledge used for filtering into the statistical model.

Acknowledgements

This work was supported by 21C Frontier Project on Human-Robot Interface (MOCIE) and by BK21 Project (Ministry of Education).

References

1. Chinchor, N., Brown, E., Ferro, L., Robinson, P.: 1999 Named Entity Recognition Task Definition (version 1.4). http://www.nist.gov/speech/tests/ie-er/er_99/doc/ne99_taskdef_v1_4.pdf (1999)
2. Gale, W.A., Church, K W., Yarowsky, D.: One Sense Per Discourse. In: Proceedings of the 4th DARPA Speech and Natural Language Workshop. (1992) 233–237
3. Guthrie, J.A., Guthrie, L., Wilks, Y., Aidinejad, H.: Subject-dependent Co-occurrence and Word Sense Disambiguation. In: Proceedings of the 29th Annual Meeting of the Association for Computational Linguistics (ACL), Berkeley, CA (1991) 146–152
4. Lee, S., Lee, G.G.: A Bootstrapping Approach for Geographic Named Entity Annotation. In: Proceedings of the 2004 Conference on Asia Information Retrieval Symposium (AIRS2004), Beijing, China (2004) 128–133
5. Li, H., Srihari, R.K., Niu, C., Li, W.: InfoXtract location normalization: a hybrid approach to geographic references in information extraction. In: Proceedings of the HLT-NAACL 2003 Workshop on Analysis of Geographic References, Alberta, Canada (2003) 39–44
6. Manov, D., Kirjakov, A., Popov, B., Bontcheva, K., Maynard, D., Cunningham, H.: Experiments with geographic knowledge for information extraction. In: Proceedings of the HLT-NAACL 2003 Workshop on Analysis of Geographic References, Alberta, Canada (2003) 1–9
7. Miller, G.A.: WordNet: A lexical database for English. Communications of the ACM **38** (1995) 39–41
8. Niwa, Y., Nitta, Y.: Co-occurrence Vectors from Corpora vs Distance Vectors from Dictionaries. In: Proceedings of the 15th International Conference on Computational Linguistics (COLING'94), Kyoto, Japan (1994) 304–309
9. Phillips, W., Riloff, E.: Exploiting Strong Syntactic Heuristics and Co-Training to Learn Semantic Lexicons. In: Proceedings of the 2002 Conference on Empirical Methods in Natural Language Processing (EMNLP2002), Philadelphia, PA (2002) 125–132
10. Shin, S., soek Choi, Y., Choi, K.S.: Word Sense Disambiguation Using Vectors of Co-occurrence Information. In: Proceedings of the Sixth Natural Language Processing Pacific Rim Symposium (NLPRS2001), Tokyo, Japan (2001) 49–55
11. Uryupina, O.: Semi-supervised learning of geographical gazetteers from the internet. In: Proceedings of the HLT-NAACL 2003 Workshop on Analysis of Geographic References, Alberta, Canada (2003) 18–25
12. Yangarber, R., Lin, W., Grishman, R.: Unsupervised Learning of Generalized Names. In: Proceedings of the 19th International Conference on Computational Linguistics (COLING 2002), Taipei, Taiwan (2002) 1135–1141

Building a Japanese-Chinese Dictionary Using Kanji/Hanzi Conversion

Chooi-Ling Goh, Masayuki Asahara, and Yuji Matsumoto

Graduate School of Information Science, Nara Institute of Science and Technology, 8916-5 Takayama, Ikoma, Nara 630-0192, Japan
{ling-g, masayu-a, matsu}@is.naist.jp

Abstract. A new bilingual dictionary can be built using two existing bilingual dictionaries, such as Japanese-English and English-Chinese to build Japanese-Chinese dictionary. However, Japanese and Chinese are nearer languages than English, there should be a more direct way of doing this. Since a lot of Japanese words are composed of kanji, which are similar to hanzi in Chinese, we attempt to build a dictionary for kanji words by simple conversion from kanji to hanzi. Our survey shows that around 2/3 of the nouns and verbal nouns in Japanese are kanji words, and more than 1/3 of them can be translated into Chinese directly. The accuracy of conversion is 97%. Besides, we obtain translation candidates for 24% of the Japanese words using English as a pivot language with 77% accuracy. By adding the kanji/hanzi conversion method, we increase the candidates by 9%, to 33%, with better quality candidates.

1 Introduction

Bilingual dictionaries have unlimited usage. In order for one to learn a new language, a bilingual dictionary can never be absent. In natural language processing community, bilingual dictionaries are useful in many areas, such as machine translation and cross language information retrieval.

In this research, we attempt to build a Japanese-Chinese dictionary using public available resources. There are already some existing Japanese-Chinese dictionaries, such as Shogakukan's Ri-Zhong Cidian [1], but they are not publicly available in electronic form. Our purpose is to build an electronic dictionary from public resources and make it public available.

The first dictionary that we use is IPADIC [2], a Japanese dictionary used by ChaSen [3], a Japanese morphological analyzer. We extract only nouns, verbal nouns and verbs from this dictionary, and try to search for their translation equivalents in Chinese.

One can build a new bilingual dictionary for a new pair of languages using two bilingual lexicons [4–8]. Since it is always easier to get bilingual dictionaries that involve English as one of the languages, using English as a pivot language is possible. In this case, we first look for the English translations of one language, and then try to find the possible candidates in the other language through English. Then we rank the candidates according to the similarities between the two words

R. Dale et al. (Eds.): IJCNLP 2005, LNAI 3651, pp. 670–681, 2005.

using some linguistic knowledge and statistical information. In our research, we make use of two public resources, EDICT [9] - a Japanaese-English dictionary and CEDICT [10] - a Chinese-English dictionary, to create the new language pair Japanese-Chinese dictionary using English as a pivot language. We obtain 77% accuracy. However, this method extracts only translations for about 24% of the Japanese words in IPADIC because the EDICT and CEDICT dictionaries are smaller compared with IPADIC. Therefore, we also look into the possibility to get the translation words using kanji/hanzi conversion. In Japanese, there are three types of characters, namely hiragana, katakana and kanji. Kanji characters are similar to Chinese ideographs. In Chinese, all characters are written in hanzi. Since most of the kanji characters are originally from China, the usage should remain unchangeable in certain contexts. The kanji/hanzi conversion method works only on Japanese words that consist only kanji characters. We obtain a high accuracy of 97% using this conversion. By combining the two methods, we increase the number of translation candidates by 9%, from 24% to 33%.

2 Previous Work

Tanaka and Umemura [4] used English as an intermediate language to link Japanese and French. They are the first who proposed the inverse consultation. The concept behind is that a translation sometimes may have wider or narrower meaning than the source word. They first look up the English translations of a given Japanese word, then the French translations of these English translations. This step gives a set of French candidates equivalent to the Japanese word. For each French candidate, its translations in English is collected. The similarity between the Japanese word and the French word is measured by the number of matches in their English translation. The more matches show the better candidate. This is referred to as "one time inverse consultation". The extension can be furthered by looking up all the Japanese translations of all the English translation of a given French word and seeing how many times the Japanese word appears; this is referred to as "two times inverse consultation".

Bond at al. [6] applied the "one time inverse consultation" in constructing a Japanese-Malay dictionary using a Japanese-English dictionary and a Malay-English dictionary. They also applied the semantic matching using part of speech and second-language matching. Matching only compatible parts of speech could cut down a lot of false matches. The second-language matching score used Chinese as a second intermediate language. If a word pair could be matched through two different languages, it is considered a very good match. Their research showed that about 80% of the translations are good if only highest rank pairs are considered, and 77% for all pairs.

Shirai and Yamamoto [7] used English as an intermediate language to link Korean and Japanese. They tried on 1,000 Korean words and were able to obtain the translations for 365 of them. They achieved an accuracy of 72% when the degree of similarity calculated by one time inverse consultation is higher than a predefined threshold.

Zhang et al. [8] used the same approach, that is using English as a pivot language, for constructing Japanese-Chinese pairs. They used the one time inverse consultation method and also the part of speech information for ranking. Since there is similarity between Japanese kanji and Chinese hanzi, they have further improved on the method by using the kanji information [11]. First they searched for the Chinese translations of single character words in Japanese into using one time inverse consultation. If the Unicode of the two characters are the same, then the ranking is higher. After getting this list of character pairs, the similarity between the Japanese word and the Chinese word is calculated using the edit distance algorithm [12]. Finally, the score obtained from the kanji information is added to the final score function. Their ranking method was improved and the precision increased from 66.67% to 81.43%. Since only about 50% of their Japanese words can be translated into Chinese, they also searched for other approaches to translate the remaining words [13] using web information and machines translation method.

Our work is quite similar to Zhang et al. [11] in the way they constructed the kanji/hanzi conversion table. The difference is that instead of calculating the similarity between kanji and hanzi using Unicode and one time inverse consultation, we make a direct conversion from kanji to hanzi based on the ideographs. Our method sounds more intuitive and direct because kanji and hanzi are of the same origin. Later on, they made use of this conversion table to calcutate the similarity between a Japanese word and a Chinese word from the output of using English as the pivot language. Their method can make the similar Chinese words to have higher ranking but cannot generate new translation candidates. On the other hand, our methods works for both.

3 The Proposed Methods

We propose to combine two methods to find the translations of Japanese entries in IPADIC version 2.7.0 [2]. IPADIC is a monolingual dictionary and consists of 239,631 entries. We only extract nouns, verbal nouns and verbs (a total of 85,553 entries) in our survey. First, we use English as the pivot languege. Second, we make direct conversion from kanji to hanzi for kanji word translation. We now describe in detail the both methods.

3.1 Using Third Language: English

First, we use English as the pivot language to find the translations from Japanese to English, and then from English to Chinese. Since IPADIC is a monolingual dictionary, we use EDICT as the Japanese-English dictionary. The EDICT version (V05-001) consists of 110,424 entries. There exist some words that are polysemous with multiple entries. After combining the multiple entry words, we have 106,925 unique entries in the dictionary. For English to Chinese, we use the CE-DICT dictionary. It consists of 24,665 entries. A word can be polysemous in both dictionary, meaning that for each word there is only one entry but with multiple translations. All the English translations of different senses are in the same record. We assume that a bilingual dictionary should be bi-directional, therefore we reverse the CEDICT dictionary to obtain an English-Chinese dictionary.

The ranking method is the one time inverse consultation [4, 6–8]. Since a word can be polysemous in both dictionaries, if a source word shares more English translations with the target translation word, then they can be considered nearer in meaning. The score is calculated as in equation (1): Let $S_E(J, C_i)$ denotes the similarity between the Japanese word J and the Chinese translation word candidate C_i, where $E(J)$ and $E(C_i)$ are the sets of English translations for J and C_i, respectively:

$$S_E(J, C_i) = \frac{2 \times (|E(J) \cap E(C_i)|)}{|E(J)| + |E(C_i)|} \tag{1}$$

Currently we do not apply the part of speech information in the scoring because this method requires linguistic experts to decide on the similarity between two part of speech tags for different languages[1]. However, this will become part of our future work.

Table 1 shows the results of using English as the pivot language and one time inverse consultation as the scoring function. Using the EDICT and CEDICT only, 32,380 Japanese words obtain their Chinese translation candidates. In total, we obtain 149,841 pairs of translation. We get maximum 90 candidates for a Japanese word, and 4.6 candidates per word by average. Then we check the Japanese words in IPADIC to get their part of speech tags. We only investigate on three categories of part of speech tags from the IPADIC, which are nouns, verbal nouns and verbs. We randomly selected 200 Japanese words from each category for evaluation. The results are judged using 4 categories: **Correct** means that the first rank word is correct (if there are multiple words in the first rank, it is considered correct if any one of the words is correct), **Not-first** means that the correct word exists but not at the first rank, **Acceptable** means that the first rank word is acceptable, and **Wrong** means that all candidates are wrong. All the categories are exclusive of each other.

Table 1. Ranking results

POS	Total	Translated	Correct	Not-first	Acceptable	Wrong
Nouns	58,793	14,275 (24.3%)	152	4	20	24
Verbal nouns	12,041	3,770 (31.3%)	90	12	37	61
Verbs	14,719	2,509 (17.0%)	101	18	27	54

There are about 24.3% of nouns, 31.3% of verbal nouns and 17.0% of verbs in IPADIC that give us some translation candidates in Chinese. For the evaluation

[1] There are 120 part of speech tags (13 categories) in IPADIC, and 45 in Peking University dictionary. Both define some quite specialized part of speech tags which only exist within the dictionary itself.

using 200 randomly selected words, we obtain 88%, 69.5% and 73% accuracy, respectively. The accuracy is 76%, 45% and 50.5%, respectively, if we considered only the first rank. The accuracy is a bit lower compared with previous work as we did not apply other linguistic resources such as parts of speech for scoring. Although improving scoring function can make the rank of the correct words higher, it cannot further increase the number of candidates. Since both EDICT and CEDICT are prepared by different people, the way they translate the words also varies. Furthermore, there is no standization on the format. For example, to represent a verb in English, sometimes it is written in base form (e.g. "discuss"), and sometimes in infinitive form (e.g. "to discuss"). In Chinese, and sometimes in Japanese too, a word shown in the dictionary can be a noun and a verb without inflection. The part of speech category can only be decided based on the usage in contexts. Therefore the same word may be translated into a noun in English too (e.g. "discussion"). It happened too that we cannot find the matches just because of singular form or plural form (e.g. "discussions") of the English translation. With these non-standardization of the English translation, we cannot match the exact words unless we do a morphological analysis in English. Therefore, we also look for other ways to increase to number of candidates. Since Japanese and Chinese share some common characters (kanji in Japanese and hanzi in Chinese), we are looking into the possibility of direct conversion to create the translations. We discuss this method in the following section.

3.2 Direct Conversion of Kanji/Hanzi

Using English as the pivot language is a good starting point to construct a new language pair. However, there remain a lot of words for which the translations cannot be obtained. In Chinese, all the characters are hanzi, but in Japanese, there are hiragana, katakana and kanji. The kanji characters are originated from ancient China. This group of characters, used in China, Japan and Korea, are referred to as Han characters. The Han characters capture some semantic information which should be common in those languages. One can create a new word by combining the existing characters but it is hardly that one can create a new character. Therefore, these characters are stable in their meaning. Due to the common sharing on these Han characters, there might be a more straightforward way to translate a word in Japanese into Chinese if all the characters in the word are made up from kanji only. We refer to this kind of words as kanji words.

A Chinese word can be a noun or a verb without changes of morphological forms. There is no inflection to differenciate them. EDICT and CEDICT make no difference on the parts of speech and therefore the translations in English can be in any form. For example, the following Japanese words and Chinese words exist for the translations of "discussion/discussions/to discuss/discuss".

Japanese: 会談, 議論, 協議, 言論, 商量, 相談, 討議, 討論, 付議, 論議, 交渉, 座談, 詮議, 談論, 評議, 弁論, 話し合う, 話合い, 論, 論う, 論じる, 論ずる

Chinese: 辩, 会谈, 论, 评, 评论, 洽谈, 商谈, 商讨, 谈, 谈论, 讨论, 议, 议论

If we were to match each Japanese word to each of the Chinese words (in fact, we can say that some of them are acceptable translations), then we will get a redundency of 286 (22×13) pairs. Although these words have similar translation, but in fact they have slight differences in meaning. For example, "会談" means the conference amongst the ministers, "交渉" means negotiations. However, "discussion" is one of the translations in English as provided by EDICT. Since the Japanese kanji characters are originated from China, translating Japanese kanji words directly to Chinese can be more accurate than going through a third language like English. If we look from the Japanese side, 12 out of 22 words (会談, 議論, 協議, 言論, 商量, 討論, 交渉, 座談, 談論, 評議, 弁論, 論) could get their exact translations by just simple conversion of kanji/hanzi (会谈, 议论, 协议, 言论, 商量, 讨论, 交涉, 座谈, 谈论, 评议, 辩论, 论), in which some of them cannot get the translations using English. On the other hand, there also exist some words that are not translated into the semantic meaning "discuss" in Japanese but in Chinese, such as "评论" which should be the same as "評論" in Japanese[2]. For the single character words in Chinese (辩, 评, 谈, 议), they are seldom used in Japanese but they do exist with the same meaning (弁, 評, 談, 議).

There exist equivalent characters between Japanese kanji and Chinese hanzi. Both type of characters (Han characters in general) capture significant semantic information. Although the pronunciation varies across languages, the visual form of the characters retains certain level of similarity. Furthermore, Chinese characters can be divided into the characters used by mainland China (referred to as Simplified Chinese) and Taiwan (including Hong Kong and Macao, referred to as Traditional Chinese). Although the ideographs may be different, they are originally the same characters. Most of the Japanese characters are similar to Traditional characters.

Table 2. Successful Traditional-Simplified examples

English	love	garden	rice	fly	kill	talk	fill up	post	excellent	sun
Japanese	愛	園	飯	飛	殺	話	補	郵	優	陽
Traditional Chinese	愛	園	飯	飛	殺	話	補	郵	優	陽
Simplified Chinese	爱	园	饭	飞	杀	话	补	邮	优	阳

Our original Japanese characters are coded in EUC and Chinese characters are coded in GB-2312 codes. To convert a kanji to a hanzi is not a trivial task. Of course most of the characters share the same ideographs. In this case, we can use the Unicode for the conversion as these characters share the same Unicode. However, there exist also quite a number of characters in Japanese that are written in Traditional Chinese ideographs. We have to convert these characters from Traditional Chinese to Simplified Chinese (see Table 2). Finally, there are

[2] The meaning of "商談" (a business talk) in Japanese is different from the meaning of '商谈'" (to discuss verbally) in Chinese.

Table 3. Unsuccessful Traditional-Simplified examples

English	gas	hair	deliver	check	home	pass by	burn	bad	money	whole
Japanese	気	髪	発	検	郷	経	焼	悪	銭	総
Traditional Chinese	氣	髮	發	檢	鄉	經	燒	惡	錢	總
Simplified Chinese	气	发	发	检	乡	经	烧	恶	钱	总

Table 4. Japanese-GBK examples

English	sardine	hackberry	maple	kite	inclusive
Japanese	鰯	榎	椛	凧	込
English	crossroad	field/patch	rice bowl	carpentry	chimera
Japanese	辻	畑	丼	杢	鵺

also some characters in Japanese having similar ideographs, but they are neither Traditional Chinese nor Simplified Chinese (see Table 3). We manually convert these characters by hand. The following shows the steps to convert the characters from Japanese to Chinese.

1. Convert from EUC to Unicode using iconv.
2. Convert from Unicode to Unicode-simplified using a Chinese encoding converter[3]. This step converts possible Traditional characters to Simplified characters.
3. Convert from Unicode-simplified to GB-2312.
4. Those failed to be converted are edited manually by hand.
5. Those characters that do not exist in GB-2312 are converted into GBK using the Chinese encoding converter.

From IPADIC, we extract 36,069 and 8,016 kanji words from noun and verbal noun categories[4], respectively. From these words, we get 4,454 distinct kanji characters. Out of these characters, only 2,547 characters can be directly converted using Unicode without changes of ideographs. 1,281 characters are converted from Traditional Chinese to Simplified Chinese using the Chinese encoding converter. Finally 626 characters are manually checked and 339 characters can be converted to Simplified Chinese. 287 remain in Japanese ideographs but are converted into GBK codes [5]. Most of these words are the names of plants, fish, and things invented by Japanese (see Table 4). While these GBK coded words may not be used in Chinese, we just leave them in the conversion table for the sake of completeness.

---

[3] http://www.madarintools.com/zhcode.html

[4] These two categories consist of most of the kanji words in Japanese. However, verbs are normally hiragana only or a mixture of kanji plus hiragana. Therefore, we omit verbs in this survey.

[5] GBK codes consist of all simplified and traditional characters, including their variants. Therefore, Japanese characters can also be coded in GBK. However, they are rarely used in Chinese.

About 61% of nouns and 67% of verbal nouns in Japanese are kanji words as shown in Table 5. Using the conversion table described above, we convert the kanji words into Chinese words. Then, we consult these words using a Chinese dictionary provided by Peking University [14]. There are about 80,000 entries in this dictionary. About 33% of the nouns and 44% of the verbal nouns are valid words in Chinese. We randomly select 200 words for evaluation. We evaluate the results by 3 categories: **Correct** means that the translation is good, **Part-of** means that either the Japanese word or the Chinese word has a wider meaning, and **Wrong** means that the meanings are not the same though they have the same characters. The accuracies obtained are 97% for nouns and 97.5% for verbal nouns. The pairs that have part-of meaning and different meaning are listed in Table 6 and Table 7 for references.

Table 5. Kanji/Hanzi conversion results

POS	Total	Kanji words	Translated	Correct	Part-of	Wrong
Nouns	58,793	36,069 (61%)	11,743 (33%)	189	5	6
Verbal nouns	12,041	8,016 (67%)	3,519 (44%)	190	5	5

Table 6. Part-of translation examples

Japanese	Chinese
被害 (damage; casualty; victim)	被害 (be murdered; victimization)
侍 (samurai; warrior; servant)	侍 (servant)
一角 (a corner; competent)	一角 (a corner; a unit used for money;)
熨斗 (charcoal iron; noshi - greeting paper)	熨斗 (charcoal iron)
会意 (character formation type)	会意 (character formation type; knowing; understanding)
苦学 (work one's way)	苦学 (hardship study)
安置 (set in place - Buddha statue or corpse)	安置 (set in place - for anything)
作為 (artificiality; deliberateness; aggressive action)	作为 (action; acomplishment; regard as)
下落 (fall; drop)	下落 (fall; drop; whereabouts; find a place for; reprove)
供奉 (attend on the Emperor in his travels; accompany in the imperial trains)	供奉 (offer sacrifice to; people gave commend performances in an imperial palace)

The advantage of this method is that we can get exact translation for those borrowed words from Chinese, especially idioms. We all know that it is always difficult to translate idiomatic phrases from one language to another due to the different cultural background. If we were to use English as the pivot language to translate from Japanese to Chinese, it is difficult to have two different bilin-

Table 7. Wrong translation examples

Japanese	Chinese
本当 (true; really)	本当 (ought; should)
員外 (nonmember)	员外 (ministry councillor; landlord)
流竄 (deportation; banishment; exile)	流窜 (flee hither and thither)
花色 (light indigo)	花色 (variety; designs and colors)
野菜 (vegetables)	野菜 (potherb)
画幅 (picture scroll)	画幅 (size of a picture)
折半 (divide into halves)	折半 (reduce by half)
自訴 (self-surrender)	自诉 (private prosecution)
打算 (selfish; calculating)	打算 (plan; intend; calculate)
開立 (search for cube root)	开立 (draw; issue; open)
勾引 (take a person into custody)	勾引 (seduce; tempt)

gual dictionaries from two different publishers that translate them in the same wordings. Since a lot of the idioms in Japanese are originally from China, the conversion of kanji/hanzi will make the translation process faster and more accurate. Some examples are given below.

同床異夢 (same bed different dream - cohabiting but living in different worlds)
鶏口牛後 (better to be the beak of a rooster than the rump of a bull - better to be the leader of a small group than a subordinate in a large organization)
神出鬼没 (appearing in unexpected places and at unexpected moments)

The difficulty of this method is the translation of single character words. Single character words normally have wider meaning (multiple senses) and the usage is usually based on the context. It is fair enough if we translate the single character words using the conversion table. However, these characters should have more translations of other multi-character words. There are 2,049 single character nouns in Japanese and 1,873 of them exist in Chinese after the conversion. For verbal nouns, there are 128 Japanese words and 127 words exist in Chinese (only 噂 (gossip, rumor) does not exist in Chinese).

3.3 Intergration

We combine both using English as the pivot language and kanji/hanzi conversion method to get the final list of translation candidates. Table 8 shows the results in details. We obtain 20,630 for nouns and 5,356 for verbal nouns. In total, we obtain 28,495 words, in which 7,941 words are new translations. Furthermore, we add in high quality translation candidates into the new bilingual dictionary. 2,428 of the candidates obtained using kanji/hanzi conversion method already exist in the translation candidates using English as the pivot language. This can help to double check on the list of translation candidates and make them rank higher. 4,893 candidates are served as extra and better quality candidates on top of the translation candidates obtained using English as the pivot language.

Table 8. Integration results

POS	Kanji/ hanzi	Acc.	Est.	Using English	Acc.	Est.	Total	In	Extra	New
Nouns	11,743	97%	11,391	14,275	88%	12, 562	20,630	2,008	3,380	6,355
Verbal nouns	3,519	97.5%	3,431	3,770	69.5%	2,620	5,356	420	1,513	1,586
Verbs	-	-	-	2,509	73%	1,832	2,509	-	-	-
Total	15,262		14,822	20,554		17,014	28,495	2,428	4,893	7,941

As an estimation, we will get about 17,014 Japanese words with correct translations in Chinese using English as the pivot language. By using kanji/hanzi conversion method, we could get about 14,822 words with correct translation.

4 Discussion and Future Work

In our survey, only 33% of nouns and 44% of verbal nouns created by kanji/hanzi conversion method exist in the Peking University dictionary. However, this may be due to the incompleteness of the Chinese dictionary that we used. We also found some words after the conversion which are acceptable in Chinese though they do not exist in the dictionary. Some of the examples are as follows: "自闭症(autism), 护法(the defense of Constituition or religion), 第六感(sixth sense), 先帝(the preceding emperor), 玄奥(deep sense), 误信(misbelief)". Therefore, we can further verify the validity of the Chinese words using other resources such as the information from the web.

The current work consider only kanji/hanzi conversion for Japanese words that consists on kanji only. There are a lot of words in Japanese that are mixture of kanji and hiragana. This happens normally with verbs and adjectives. For example, "食べる(eat), 逃げる(escape), 生み出す(produce), 難しい(difficult), 嬉しい(happy), 静か(quite)". We should be able to get some acceptable translations of these words after removing the hiragana parts, but most of the cases we cannot obtain the best or good translations. From the 200 verbs that we used for the evaluation, 139 words exist in Chinese but only 35 are good and 43 are acceptable. The single characters used in these words are normally used only in ancient Chinese but not in contemporary Chinese. For example, 食べる = 吃 (eat) and 捨てる = 丢掉 (throw away), but 食 (eat) and 舍 (throw away) in Chinese are also possible translation in certain contexts. Furthermore, the contemporary Chinese uses two character words more often than single character words even they have the same meaning. This is to reduce the semantic ambiguity as single character words tend to be polysemous. Therefore, direct kanji/hanzi conversion is not so appropriate and we need another approach to handle this type of words.

We can apply the kanji/hanzi conversion method directly to most of the Japanese proper nouns, such as person names, organization names and place names because these names are normally written in kanji characters. Therefore, we do not need any effort to translate these words from Japanese to Chinese if we have the character conversion table. This will ease a lot in the processing of machine translation and cross language information retrieval.

The Unicode Consortium encoded the Han characters in Unicode[6]. Till date, all the languages that use Han characters have their own encoding systems. For example, Japanese is encoded in EUC-JP or JIS, Simplified Chinese is in GB-2312, Traditional Chinese is in Big 5 etc. The same character that is used in different languages is assigned with different codes. Therefore it is difficult to convert from one code to another without a conversion table. The Unicode Consortium solved the problem by unifying the encoding. The same character with the same ideograph has only one code no matter in which language it is used. With this unification, it eased a lot on the CJK research, especially in the area of cross language information retrieval. Currently, they have increased the number of Han characters from 27,496 characters (version 3.0) to 70,207 characters (version 4.0). Such a huge increment is done by the addition of a large amount of unusual characters that only have been used in either person names or place names. With this new version, it covers almost all possible characters used in hanzi (Chinese), kanji (Japanese) and hanja (Korean). The Unihan (unicode for Han characters) provides a lot of information such as the origin, the specific language using that character, conversion to other encodings etc. The most useful information in Unihan to our research is the relationship between the characters. It embeds the links for the variants of characters which are useful for the conversion from one encoding to the others (Japanese, Traditional Chinese, Simplified Chinese or Korean). If we can make use of this table, then we can build a complete conversion table that includes all Han characters.

Zhang et al. [11] proposed to use kanji information to find the similarity between a Japanese word and a Chinese word. They matched on the Unicode and calculated the similarity using the one time inverse consultation. Since they did not make any conversion such as traditional characters to simplified characters, some of the characters have the same meaning but different Unicodes. Therefore, they could not be matched. If they could use the conversion table that we proposed, then it would help to increase the score of the kanji words.

To convert from Japanese kanji to Simplified characters is easier than the reverse. It is because some characters in Traditional characters are simplified into the same characters in Simplified Chinese. For example, 髪 (hair) and 発 (deliver) are simplified to 发. Therefore, it has to depend on the contexts to decide which Japanese character to use if we were to convert the Chinese Simplified characters back to Japanese kanji.

5 Conclusion

As a conclusion, we proposed a method to compile a Japanese-Chinese dictionary using English as the pivot language as a starting point. We made use of the public available resources such as EDICT, CEDICT and IPADIC for the construction

[6] http://www.unicode.org/chart/unihan.html

of the new language pair. The accuracy obtained is 77%. Since Japanese and Chinese share common Han characters which are semantically heavy loaded, the same characters used should carry the same meaning. Therefore, we also proposed a kanji/hanzi conversion method to increase the translation candidates. The accuracy obtained is 97%. The increment of translation candidates is 9%, from 24% to 33%. The conversion table created can also be used in other fields like machine translation and cross language information retrieval.

Acknowledgements

This research uses EDICT file which is the property of the Electronic Dictionary Research and Development Group at Monash University. Thanks go to http://www.mandarintools.com/zhcode.html for their Chinese Encoding Converter.

References

1. Shogakukan and Peking Shomoinshokan, editors: Ri-Zhong Cidian [Japanese-Chinese Dictionary] (1987)
2. Asahara, M., Matsumoto, Y.: IPADIC version 2.7.0. Users Manual. Nara Institute of Science and Technology, Nara, Japan. (2003) http://chasen.naist.jp/.
3. Matsumoto, Y., Kitauchi, A., Yamashita, T., Hirano, Y., Matsuda, H., Takaoka, K., Asahara, M.: Morphological Analysis System ChaSen version 2.2.9 Manual. Nara Institute of Science and Technology, Nara, Japan. (2002) http://chasen.naist.jp/.
4. Tanaka, K., Umemura, K.: Construction of a bilingual dictionary intermediated by a third language. In: Proc. of COLING. (1994) 297–303
5. Lafourcade, M.: Multilingual dictionary construction and services - case study with the fe* projects. In: Proc. of PACLING. (1997) 289–306
6. Bond, F., Sulong, R.B., Yamazaki, T., Ogura, K.: Design and construction of a machine-tractable japanese-malay dictionary. In: Proc. of MT Summit VIII. (2001) 53–58
7. Shirai, S., Yamamoto, K.: Linking english words in two bilingual dictionaries to generate another language pair dictionary. In: Proc. of ICCPOL. (2001) 174–179
8. Zhang, Y., Ma, Q., Isahara, H.: Automatic acquisition of a japanese-chinese bilingual lexicon using english as an intermediary. In: Proc. of NLPKE. (2003) 471–476
9. Jim Breem: EDICT, Japanese-English Dictionary (2005) http://www.csse.monash.edu.au/~jwb/edict.html.
10. Paul Denisowski: CEDICT, Chinese-English Dictionary (2005) http://www.mandarintools.com/cedict.html.
11. Zhang, Y., Ma, Q., Isahara, H.: Use of kanji information in constructing a japanese-chinese bilingual lexicon. In: Proc. of ALR Workshop. (2004) 42–49
12. Levenshtein, V.: Binary codes capable of correcting deletions, insertions and reversals. Doklady Akademii Nauk SSSR **163** (1965) 845–848
13. Zhang, Y., Isahara, H.: Acquiring compound word translation both automatically and dynamically. In: Proc. of PACLIC 18. (2004) 181–185
14. Peking University: (Peking University Dictionary) http://www.icl.pku.edu.cn/.

Automatic Acquisition of Basic Katakana Lexicon from a Given Corpus

Toshiaki Nakazawa, Daisuke Kawahara, and Sadao Kurohashi

University of Tokyo, 7-3-1 Hongo Bunkyo-ku, Tokyo, 113-8656, Japan
{nakazawa, kawahara, kuro}@kc.t.u-tokyo.ac.jp

Abstract. Katakana, Japanese phonogram mainly used for loan words, is a trou-blemaker in Japanese word segmentation. Since Katakana words are heavily domain-dependent and there are many Katakana neologisms, it is almost impossible to construct and maintain Katakana word dictionary by hand. This paper proposes an automatic segmentation method of Japanese Katakana compounds, which makes it possible to construct precise and concise Katakana word dictionary automati-cally, given only a medium or large size of Japanese corpus of some domain.

1 Introduction

Handling words properly is very important for Natural Language Processing. Words are basic unit to assign syntactic/semantic information manually, basic unit to acquire knowledge based on frequencies and co-occurrences, and basic unit to access texts in Information Retrieval.

Languages with explicit word boundaries, like white spaces in English, do not suffer from this issue so severely, though it is a bit troublesome to handle compounds and hyphenation appropriately. On the other hand, languages without explicit boundaries such as Japanese always suffer from this issue.

Japanese character set and their usage. Here, we briefly explain Japanese character set and their usage. Japanese uses about 6,000 ideogram, Kanji characters, 83 phonogram, Hiragana, and another 86 phonogram, Katakana.

Kanji is used for Japanese time-honored nouns (including words imported from China ancient times) and stems of verbs and adjectives; Hiragana is used for function words such as postpositions and auxiliary verbs, and endings of verbs and adjectives; Katakana is used for loan words, mostly from the West, as transliterations.

Japanese is very active to naturalize loan words. Neologisms in special/technical domains are often transliterated into Katakana words without translations, or even if there are translations, Katakana transliterations are more commonly used in many cases. For example, コンピュータ, transliteration of "computer" is more commonly used than the translation, 計算機(*keisanki*).

Even for some time-honored Japanese nouns, both Japanese nouns and translitera-tions of their English translations are used together these days, and the use of

R. Dale et al. (Eds.): IJCNLP 2005, LNAI 3651, pp. 682 – 693, 2005.

translit-erations is increasing, such as デスクワーク, transliteration of "desk work" vs. 机仕事(*tsukue shigoto*). Furthermore, some Japanese nouns, typically the names of animals, plants, and food, which can be written in Kanji or Hiragana, are also written in Katakana sometimes [4, 6].

Word segmentation and Katakana words. Let us go back to the word segmentation issue. Japanese word segmentation is performed like this: Japanese words are registered into the dictionary; given an input sentence, all possible words embedded in the sentence and their connections are checked by looking up the dictionary and some connectivity grammar; then the most plausible word sequence is selected. The criteria of selecting the best word sequence were simple heuristic rules preferring longer words in earlier times, and some cost calculation based on manual rules or using some training data, these days.

Such a segmentation process is in practice not so difficult for Kanji-Hiragana string. First of all, since Kanji words and Hiragana words are fairly stable excepting proper nouns, they are most perfectly registered in the dictionary. Then, the orthogonal usage of Kanji and Hiragana mentioned above makes the segmentation rather simple, as follows:

彼	は	大学	に	通う
(Kare	wa	daigaku	ni	kayou)
he	postp.	Univ.	postp.	go

Kanji compound words can cause a segmentation problem. However, since large num-ber of Kanji characters lead fairly sparse space of Kanji words, most Kanji compounds can be segmented unambiguously.

A real troublemaker is Katakana words, which are sometimes very long compounds such as エクストラバージンオリーブオイル "extra vergin olive oil" and ジャパンカップサイクルロードレース "Japan cup cycle road race". As mentioned above, many neologisms are written in Katakana, it is almost impossible to register all or most Katakana words into a dictionary by hand. To handle such an insufficiency of a dictionary, conventional Japanese word segmentation incorporates a fall-safe method, which considers a whole continuous Katakana string as a word, when it is neither a registered-word, nor a combination of registered-words. And, Japanese word segmentation basically prefers longer registered words. These mechanism leads that, for example, the Katakana string トマトソース "tomato sauce" is properly segmented to トマト "tomato" and ソース "sauce", only when トマト and ソース are in the dictionary and トマトソース is not. When ソース alone is in the dictionary (means an imperfect dictionary) or トマトソース is in the dictionary (means a redundant dictionary), トマトソース is regarded as one word.

Considering the importance of words as a basic unit of NLP, it is quite problematic to handle トマトソース as a single word. We cannot use information that トマトソース is a kind of ソース, which is very important for deeper/semantic processing of texts; a text including トマトソース cannot be retrieved with the word トマトor ソース. Note that a rough treatment using partial string matching causes a tragedy that リソース(*risōsu*) "resource" matches ソース "sauce" and スライス(*suraisu*) "slice" matches ライス(*raisu*)"rice" and イス(*isu*)"chair"!

To solve this severe problem, this paper proposes a method of constructing precise and concise Japanese Katakana word dictionary, by automatically judging a given

Katakana string is a single-word or compound, and registering only single-words to the dictionary. We suppose only a medium or large size of Japanese corpus is given, and Katakana strings and their frequencies in the corpus are extracted as follows. We call this data as a *word-occurrence data* hereafter.

ラーメン(*rāmen*):28727 "noodle"
スープ(*sūpu*):20808 "soup"
レシピ(*resipi*):16436 "recipe
カレー(*karē*):15151 "curry"
メニュー(*meny ū*):14766 "menu"
エスニック(*esunikku*):14190 "ethnic"
サラダ(*sarada*):13632 "salad"
トップ(*toppu*):11642 "top"
トマトソース(*tomatosōsu*):11641 "tomato sauce"
...
トマト(*tomato*):7887 "tomato"
...
ソース(*sōsu*):7570 "sauce"
...

Our proposed method consists of the following three methods, which utilize only a word-occurrence data and publicly available resources:[1]

– A method using a Japanese-English dictionary.
– A method using a huge English corpus and a Japanese-English dictionary.
– A method using relation in a word-occurrence data.

Since most Katakana words are transliterations of English words, we exploit Japanese-English translation information as much as possible, using a Japanese-English dictio-nary and a huge English corpus. Since these methods, however, cannot achieve high-recall, the third method uses a word-occurrence data itself: a Katakana word is regarded as a compound if it is a combination of other, frequent Katakana words in the word-occurrence data. These three methods vary from high-precision to high-recall, and their appropriate combination leads to high-precision, high-recall analysis.

We explain these three methods in detail, and then report the experimental results and discussion.

2 A Method Using a Japanese-English Dictionary

The first method utilizes a Japanese-English dictionary, judging some Katakana words as compounds and others as single-words. Words that are judged here will not be pro-cessed by the next two methods.

The basic idea using a dictionary is as follows. Suppose the input word is トマトソース and the dictionary provides the following information:

[1] There are some Katakana words that are not loan words, such as the names of animals, plants and food. We deal with these words as single-words exceptionally, if they are registered in a Japanese dictionary.

トマトソース= tomato sauce
トマト= tomato
ソース= sauce

If the translation of the input word consists of multi-words and those words correspond to Katakana substrings just enough based on the dictionary information, the input word is considered as a compound. In the case of the above example, トマトソース is divided into トマト+ ソース by these criteria.

On the other hand, if the translation of the input word is one word in the dictionary, it is considered as a single-word (that is, the other two methods are not applied to the input word any more), like the following example:

サンドウィッチ(*sandowicchi*) = sandwich

The Japanese-English dictionary can be used in such a straightforward way. In prac-tice, however, we handle some exceptional cases more carefully as follows:

- When the dictionary provides multi-word translation for an input, and all of them are capitalized, the input is regarded as a proper noun and treated as a single-word.

  ブエノスアイレス(*Buenosuairesu*) = Buenos Aires
  ミルキーウェイ(*Mirukīwei*) = Milky Way
  サザンクロス(*Sazankurosu*) = Southern Cross

- When the dictionary provides multi-word translation for an input, but the alignment of translation words and Katakana substrings fails, still if the final translation word corresponds to the Katakana suffix-string, the input is regarded as a compound, as follows:

  モルネソース(*Morunesōsu*) = Mornay sauce
  ソース= sauce

  スモークハム(*sumōkuhamu*) = smoked ham
  ハム(*hamu*) = ham

- The judgment of being a single-word is invalidated, when the translation corre-sponds to only a partial Katakana string by another dictionary entry as follows:

  シフォンケーキ(*shifonkēki*) = chiffon
  シフォン(*shifon*) = chiffon

  キャッチボール(*kyacchibōru*) = catch
  キャッチ(*kyacchi*) = catch

  シフォンケーキand キャッチボールare not disposed in this method and transfered to the next methods.

3 A Method Using a Huge English Corpus and a Japanese-English Dictionary

A dictionary contains only basic compounds, but there are many more Katakana compounds in real texts. That is, the direct use of dictionary is not enough to handle real Katakana compounds.

Therefore, we have developed a method which utilizes a Japanese-English dictionary to get a basic translation relation, and judges whether a Katakana string is a compound or not by referring to a huge English corpus.

Given an input Katakana string, all possible segmentations to Katakana words registered in the Japanese-English dictionary are detected, and those words are translated into English words. Then, the frequencies of those possible English translations are checked by referring to a huge English corpus, and the most frequent translation is selected as a resultant segmentation. As an English corpus, we use the web, and the hit number of a search engine is used as the frequency.

Forexample, パセリソース(*paserisōsu*) can be segmented in two ways, and the first segmentation can have two different translations, totaling to the three possible translation as follows:

パセリ(*paseri*)+ ソース(*sōsu*) parsley source:554
パセリ(*paseri*)+ ソース(*sōsu*) parsley sauce:20600
パセ(*pase*)+ リソース(*risōsu*) pase resource:3

The web search shows that the second translation, "parsley sauce" is by far the most frequent, supporting パセリソースis a compound パセリ+ ソース.

The important issue is how much we believe the frequency of the web. Some web pages are very messy, and even inappropriate segmentation and its mad translation has some frequency in the web, as follows:

デミ(*demi*)+ グラス(*gurasu*) demi glass:207
バン(*ban*)+ バンジー(*banjī*) van bungee:159

In order to exclude such inappropriate segmentations, we need to set up some threshold to accept the segmentation. Considering that the longer the Katakana word is, the more probable it is a compound, we set the following threshold:

$$C/N^L,$$

where L denotes the length of the Katakana word, and C and N are constant, optimized using some development data set.

4 A Method Using Relation in a Word-Occurrence Data

Though the method using an English corpus is reliable and accurate, it can be applied only when the constituent words are in the dictionary, and the compound is a natural term in English. However, some neologisms and some words that are not usually written in Katakana are not registered in the dictionary. Furthermore, there are many

Japanese-made English-like compounds like "gasoline stand" (means "service station"), which are rarely found in native English corpus.

To handle such cases robustly, we try to find compounds only based on the infor-mation in a word-cccurrence data. For example, if トマト and ソース are sufficiently frequent in the word-occurrence data, we consider トマトソース as a compound, トマト+ ソース.

Again, we have to carefully design the threshold to accept the segmentation. Since the word-occurrence data contains very many varieties of Katakana strings, most single-words can be somehow divided into two or more Katakana strings. For example, even イタリアン(*itarian*) "Italian" can be divided into イタ *ita*)+ リアン(*rian*).

Then, we established the basic criteria as follows: if the geometric mean of fre-quencies of possible constituent words (Fg) is larger than the frequency of the original Katakana word (Fo), then we accept the segmentation. Similar to the method using an English corpus, considering that the longer the Katakana word is, the more probable it is a compound, we modified the condition as follows:

$$F_o < F'_g, \qquad F'_g = F_g/(C/N^l + \alpha)$$

where l denotes the average length of constituent words (equal to the length of the Katakana word divided by the number of constituent words), C, N and α are constant, optimized using some development data set. α is a term to provide the upper bound of F'_g when l becomes large.

When there are segmentations into different number of words, the coarse segmenta-tion, that is, the segmentation into a small number of words is selected. When there are two or more possible segmentations into the same number of words, that of the largest F_g is selected.

Here are some examples in the cooking corpus (the details of this corpus are de-scribed in Section 6.1):

イタリアンレストラン(*itarianresutoran*):207
↔イタリアン(*itarian*):1421 + レストラン(*resutoran*):7922 (Fg= 3355)

スパイスライス(*supaisuraisu*):3
↔スパイ(*supai*):9 + スライス(*suraisu*):2000 (Fg= 134)
↔スパイス(*supaisu*):2203 + ライス(*raisu*):980 (Fg= 1896)

イタリアン(*itarian*):421
↔イタ(*ita*):91 + リアン(*rian*):11 (Fg= 31)
↔イタリ(*itari*):7 + アン(*an*):301 (Fg= 45)

イタリアンレストラン"Italian restaurant" and スパイスライス "spice rice" are not segmented by the English corpus method, because イタリアン is not registered in the Japanese-English dictionary, and "spice rice" does not occur frequently (though "spicy rice" is frequent). However, they are properly segmented by this method. On the other hand, イタリアン is not segmented, since neither of two possible segmentations イタ+ リアンor イタリ+ アン have large Fg.

5 Registration to Katakana Word Dictionary

Given a word-occurrence data, the three methods are applied to exclude compounds, and the remaining single-words are registered to the dictionary of Japanese segmenta-tion program.

In order to handle the ambiguity of compound segmentation, the word is registered with the cost, $C - \log f$, where f is its frequency in the word-occurrence data. Since the Japanese segmentation program JUMAN[4] selects the segmentation with the minimum cost, this cost assignment is consistent with the segmentation selected by the method using relation in the word-occurrence data. For example, the cost of segmenting スパイスライスis calculated as follows:

スパイ+スライス:

$$(C - \log 9) + (C - \log 2000) = 2C - \log (9 \times 2000)$$

スパイス+ライス:

$$(C - \log 2203) + (C - \log 980) = 2C - \log (2203 \times 980)$$

As a result, スパイス+ライス, whose cost is smaller than that of スパイ+スライス, is selected.

This cost calculation is not necessarily consistent with the segmentation supported by the English corpus method. To handle this, Katakana words are once registered into the dictionary with these costs, and then Katakana compounds handled by the English corpus method are fed to the segmentation program. Then, if the segmentation is incorrect, the compound word is registered into the compound word dictionary with its correct segmentation position.[2] All of these treatments can be done automatically based on the results of our compound detection methods.

Note that how much frequent words should be registered into the dictionary depends on the policy of the dictionary maintenance, and the system capability of handling unknown words. These issues are out of the scope of this paper.

6 Evaluation and Discussion

6.1 Experimental Results

We prepared two data sets for experiments: 87K Katakana words appearing more than once in 12-year volume of newspaper articles (5.8M sentences), and 43K Katakana words appearing more than once in web pages of cooking domain (2.8M sentences).

For both data sets, we randomly selected 500 Katakana words, and assigned correct segmentation positions to those words by hand. Then, these manual segmentation posi-tions were compared with automatic segmentation positions, calculating precision and recall scores. Note that the unit of evaluation is not words, but segmentation

---

[2] Japanese segmentation system has a compound dictionary to deal with exceptional (hard-to-segment) compound words, which are not limited to Katakana words. It is one possible way to reigster all Katakana compounds to the compound dictionary, but it is not reasonable from the view point of the dictionary maintenance.

positions. The average number of segmentation positions of 500 words in news domain was 1.39; that in cooking domain was 1.62.

As explained so far, our proposed methods consist of the following three methods:

– A method using a Japanese-English dictionary (D).
– A method using a huge English corpus and a Japanese-English dictionary (C).
– A method using relation in a word-occurrence data (R).

To see the effectiveness of each method, we tested four types of their combination: D, D+C, D+R, D+C+R. In all types, the D method is applied first. Then both C and R method are applied to the words which are not dealt with in D method. Results of C method are prior to those of R method. The parameters were set to $400{,}000/2^L$ for the second method and $F'_g = F_g/(2{,}500/4^l + 0.7)$ for the third method. As a Japanese-English dictionary, we used two free-to-use dictionary: Eijiro (931K all entries and 137K Katakana entries) and Edict (140K all entries and 14K Katakana entries). Table 1 shows the results, indicating that the combination of D+C+R achieved both highprecision and high-recall.

Table 1. Experimental results

News domain

	D	D+C	D+R	D+C+R
Precision/Recall	1.0/0.822	0.996/0.909	0.986/0.945	0.985/0.949
F-measure	0.902	0.950	0.965	0.966

Cooking domain

	D	D+C	D+R	D+C+R
Precision/Recall	1.0/0.717	1.0/0.836	0.990/0.948	0.991/0.956
F-measure	0.835	0.910	0.968	0.973

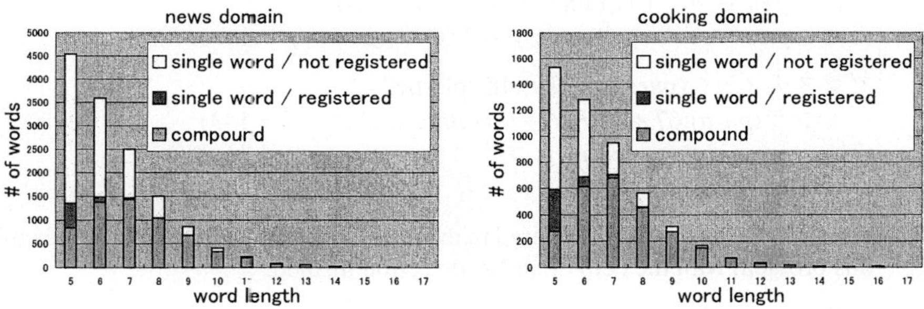

Fig. 1. Statistics of compounds and single-words

Figure 1 shows, among 10 or more frequent words of each length in news domain and cooking domain, the number of compounds, the number of single words registered in the dictionary of the segmentation program JUMAN, and the number of single words not registered in JUMAN. In total, 6K words were judged as compounds out of 13.8K words in news domain; 2.5K words out of 4.9K words in cooking domain.

6.2 Discussion

As shown in Table 1, the method using the dictionary is precise, but the recall is not high enough. Combining it with the methods of using the English corpus and the relation in the word-occurrence data leads to both high-precision and high-recall.

The causes of the incorrect results can be analyzed as follows. When a word is incorrectly segmented, the Japanese-English dictionary overlooks the word as a single word. Then, it is passed to the next methods, and segmented incorrectly. The overlook of the dictionary took place in the following cases:

- **Neologisms or words rarely written in Katakana**

  セル(*seru*)+ ライト(*raito*) cell light:15100 >12500
  (セルライト(*seruraito*) is "cellulite")

  シュレッドチーズ(*syureddochīzu*):24 "shred cheese"
  ↔シュ(*syu*):41 + レッド(*reddo*):112 + チーズ(*chīzu*):7199 (F'_g **= 143)**

- **Not original forms**
  Transliterations of words in not original forms are often used in Katakana com-pounds, but they are not usually listed in the Japanese-English dictionary.

  セーフ(*sēfu*) + ティー(*thī*)safe tea:16500>6250
  (セーフティー(*sēfuthī*)is "safety")

  リストラクチャリング(*risutorakucyaringu*):150 "restructuring"
  ↔リストラ(*risutora*):5081 + クチャ(*kucya*):3 + リング(*ringu*):743 ($F'_g = 238$)

- **Spelling variation problem**
  Though representative Katakana spellings are in the dictionary, their spelling variations are not. Handling of spelling variation is a target of our future work.

  レイン(*rein*)+ ボー(*bō*)rain bow:22100 >12500
  (The representative spelling is レインボウ(*reinbou*) "rainbow")

  プラスティック(*purasuthikku*):48 "plastic"
  ↔プラ(*pura*):67 + スティック(*suthikku*):224 ($F'_g = 143$)
  (The representative spelling is プラスチック(*purasuchikku*))

- **Proper nouns**
  Proper nouns are not well covered in the dictionary. We are planning to reexamine this problem with the help of an NE detection method.

  パス(*pasu*)+ ツール(*tūru*)path tool:13700 >12500
  (パスツール(*pasutūru*) is "Pasteur")

  コネティカット(*konethikatto*):108 "Connecticut"
  ↔コネ(*kone*):177 + ティ(*thi*):166 + カット(*katto*):4144 ($F'_g = 108$)

On the other hand, the reason of lowering recall, that is, the overlook of compounds, can be summarized as follows:

– Especially for shorter words, it is actually very hard to set up clear criteria for compounds. In constructing the test sets, we regarded a word as a compound when the head (the last constituent) has an independent meaning and an is-a relation with the original word. However, whether an English translation is one word or not is not necessarily consistent with these criteria.

バイオサイエンス(*baiosaiensu*) = bioscience
フレックスタイム(*furekkusutaimu*) = flextime
プールサイド(*pūrusaido*) = poolside

– Similar to the precision problem, when the constituent word is not in the dictionary, the compound could not be handled by the English corpus method, and the third method overlooked it sometimes.

ベイエリア(*beieria*):163 "bay area"
↔ベイ(*bei*):116+ エリア(*eria*):1377 (F'_g=127)
(ベイ is not in the dictionary)

シュガーローフ(*syug⁻ofu*):19 "sugar loaf"
↔シュガー(*syuga⁻*):40 + ローフ(*rōfu*):6 (F'_g = 18)
(ローフis not in the dictionary)

– Sometimes segmentation score cannot pass the threshold.

ペパー(*pepa⁻*)+ミント(*minto*) pepper mint:5400 < 6250
ペパーミント(*pepāminto*):41
↔ペパー:8+ミント:56 (F'_g = 16)

ヘア(*hea*)+ケア(*kea*)+チェック(*chekku*)
hair care check:397 < 1562
ヘアケアチェック(*heakeachekku*):458
↔ヘアケア(*heakea*):32+チェック:1350 (F'_g = 281)

Some Katakana strings are ambiguous and their segmentation depends on the context, such as タコス(*takosu*)+ライス(*raisu*) "tacos rice" and タコ(*tako*)+スライス (*suraisu*) "octopus slice". However, there were few such cases in our experiments.

7 Related Work

To our knowledge, there has been no work so far handling the automatic segmentation of phonogram compounds in such a real large-scale. German compound nouns have a similar problem, like Lebensversicherungsgesellschaftsangestellter ("life insurance company employee" in English), and can be a target of our method.

There are several related work which can contribute the modification and extension of our methods. When using a Japanese-English dictionary, if we understand the translation is transliteration, we can utilize the information more effectively, handling inflections. In this sense, work by Knight and Graehl can be incorporated into our method [2].

In order to handle spelling variation problems, there have been many methods proposed [3], and we can utilize recently proposed robust treatment of Japanese Katakana spelling variation by Masuyama et al. [5].

Our second method using Japanese-English dictionary and the English corpus can be considered as a translation acquisition method. It is interesting to compare these results with other web-based methods, such as Utsuro et al. [8, 1].

There have been many studies that extract compound nouns. Nakagawa et al. focused on the tendency that most of technical terms are compound nouns, and proposed a method of extracting technical terms by using frequency and variety of its neiboring words [10, 7].

In view of information retrieval, Yamada et al. aimed at imporving information retrieval using matching of compounds [9]. It is similar to our study in handling compounds.

8 Conclusion

This paper proposed an automatic segmentation method of Japanese Katakana compounds, which makes it possible to construct precise and concise Katakana word dictionary automatically, given only a medium or large size of corpus of some domain. Since Katakana is often used for English transliteration, our method exploited a Japanese-English dictionary and a huge English corpus. Combining translation-based high-precision method with more robust, monolingual, frequency-based method, we could achieve both high-precision and high-recall compound segmentation method.

The results of this method were already successfully used to enhance a Japanese word segmentation program. We are planning to handle Katakana spelling variation and to incorporate our method with an NE detection method.

References

1. Mitsuhiro Kida, Takehito Utsuro, Kohei Hino, and Satoshi Sato. Estimating bilingual term correspondences from japanese and english documents. In *Information Processing Society of JAPAN*, pages 65–70, 2004.
2. Kevin Knight and Jonathan Graehl.Machine transliteration. *Computational Linguistics*, 24(4):599–612, 1998.
3. Junichi Kubota, Yukie Shoda, Masahiro Kawai, Hirofumi Tamagawa, and Ryoichi Sugimura. A method of detecting KATAKANA variants in a document. *Information Processing Society of JAPAN*, 35(12):2745–2751, 1994.
4. Sadao Kurohashi, Toshihisa Nakamura, Yuji Matsumoto, and Makoto Nagao. Improvements of Japanese morphological analyzer JUMAN. In *Proceedings of The International Workshop on Sharable Natural Language*, pages 22–28, 1994.
5. Takeshi Masuyama, Satoshi Sekine, and Hiroshi Nakagawa.Automatic construction of Japanese katakana variant list form large corpus. In *Proceedings of the 20th International Conference on Computational Linguistics*, pages 1214–1219, 2004.

6. Yuji Matsumoto, Akira Kitauchi, Tatsuo Yamashita, Yoshitaka Hirano, Hiroshi Matsuda, Kazuma Takaoka, and Masayuki Asahara. *Morphological Analysis System ChaSen version 2.3.3 Users Manual*, 2003.
7. Hirokazu Ohata and Hiroshi Nakagawa. Automatic term recognition by the relation between compound nouns and basic nouns. In *Information Processing Society of JAPAN*, pages 119–126, 2000.
8. Takehito Utsuro, Kohei Hino, Mitsuhiro Kida, Seiichi Nakagawa, and Satoshi Sato.Inte-grating cross-lingually relevant news articles and monolingual web documents in bilingual lexicon acquisition. In *Proceedings of the 20th International Conference on Computational Linguistics*, pages 1036–1042, 2004.
9. Koichi Yamada, Tatsunori Mori, and Hiroshi Nakagawa.Information retrieval based on combination of japanese compound words matching and co-occurrence based retrieval. *Information Processing Society of JAPAN*, 39(8):2431–2439, 1998.
10. Hiroaki Yumoto, Tatsunori Mori, and Hiroshi Nakagawa.Term extraction based on occurrence and concatenation frequency. In *Information Processing Society of JAPAN*, pages 111–118, 2001.

CTEMP: A Chinese Temporal Parser for Extracting and Normalizing Temporal Information

Wu Mingli, Li Wenjie, Lu Qin, and Li Baoli

Department of Computing,
The Hong Kong Polytechnic University,
Kowloon, Hong Kong
{csmlwu, cswjli, csluqin, csblli}@polyu.edu.hk

Abstract. Temporal information is useful in many NLP applications, such as information extraction, question answering and summarization. In this paper, we present a temporal parser for extracting and normalizing temporal expressions from Chinese texts. An integrated temporal framework is proposed, which includes basic temporal concepts and the classification of temporal expressions. The identification of temporal expressions is fulfilled by powerful chart-parsing based on grammar rules and constraint rules. We evaluated the system on a substantial corpus and obtained promising results.

1 Introduction

Temporal information processing is valuable in many NLP applications, such as information extraction, machine translation, question-answering and multi-document summarization. However, a wide scope of linguistic means, from lexical to syntactic phenomena, can represent this information. It is hard to catch the internal temporal meanings which are behind surface texts. The potential applications and the flexibilities of temporal representations motivate our research in this direction.

In this paper, temporal information is defined as the knowledge about time or duration. This information is crucial for both temporal reasoning and anchoring events on the time line. Temporal expressions are defined as chunks of text which convey direct or indirect temporal information. TIMEX2 annotating guidelines [4, 6] give good descriptions about temporal expressions. According to the guidelines, temporal expressions include dates, times of day, durations, set-denoting expressions, event-anchored expressions, and so on. To retrieve the useful temporal information contained in these temporal expressions, we need to identify the extents of temporal expressions in raw text and then represent temporal information according to some standard. The two tasks are called temporal extraction and temporal normalization, respectively. We have implemented a full system CTEMP, which consists of two modules: extractor and normalizer. The two modules fulfill temporal extraction and temporal normalization, respectively.

A comprehensive temporal framework is investigated to analyze the elements involved in the mapping procedure, from surface text to internal temporal information. This framework includes basic temporal objects and relations, the measurement of time, and the classification of temporal expressions from Chinese texts. To cope with

R. Dale et al. (Eds.): IJCNLP 2005, LNAI 3651, pp. 694 – 706, 2005.

the flexibilities of the temporal expressions, we have built the temporal parser based on chart-parsing and effective constraints. Experiments with respect to a substantial corpus show that the temporal parser achieves promising results. We took part in TERN 2004 Chinese temporal expression extraction with this temporal parser and our performance is the highest in that track.

The rest of the paper is organized as follows: In Section 2 we give a brief discussion on related works; Section 3 describes the temporal framework, which is the basis of the whole temporal parser; extractor and normalizer of the temporal parser are discussed in Section 4 and Section 5, respectively; Section 6 gives the description about experiments and evaluations. Finally, conclusion and future work are presented in Section 7.

2 Related Work

Motivated by the potential applications, temporal information processing has absorbed more attention recently than ever, such as ACL 2001 workshop on temporal and spatial information processing, LREC 2002 and TERN 2004 [14]. Mani [10] gives a good review about the recent trend. Research works in this area can be classified into four types: designing annotation scheme for temporal information representation [4, 6, 12]; developing temporal ontology which covers temporal objects and their relationships between each other [2, 7]; Identifying time-stamps of events or temporal relationships between events [5, 9]; Identifying and normalizing temporal expressions from different languages [1, 3, 8, 11, 13, 15].

Temporal annotation, temporal ontology and temporal reasoning are not the focuses in this paper. Among the research works on temporal expression extraction and normalization, most of them are based on hand-written rules or machine-learnt rules. Mani and Wilson [11] resolve temporal expressions by hand-crafted and machine-learnt rules. Their focus is resolving temporal expressions, especially indexical expressions, which designate times that are dependent on the speaker and some reference time. We concentrate on the procedure of extraction and normalization, and try to cover more temporal expressions. Schilder and Habel [13] employ several finite state transducers based on hand-written rules to extract and normalize time-denoting and event-denoting temporal expressions. Evaluation of the system is presented on a small corpus.

Vazov [15] identifies temporal expressions based on context constraints and regular expressions, but temporal expression normalization is not investigated. Estela et al. [3] present a temporal parser on Spanish based on grammar rules and evaluate the tagger on a small corpus. Jang [8] reports a time tagger for Korean based on a human-edited, automatically-derived dictionary of patterns. The dictionary is induced from training data and is used to extract and normalize temporal expressions in texts. Ahn et al. [1] adopt the task of TERN 2004 evaluation and investigate machine learning methods for extraction of temporal expression and rule based methods for normalization. However, they focus on Korean and English text respectively and may not consider some characteristics of Chinese language.

3 Temporal Framework

The goal of the temporal parser is to extract and normalize temporal expressions. First we should realize the elements involved in this procedure. We propose a temporal framework to describe temporal concepts, the measurement and all kinds of temporal expressions in the surface text. Our temporal parser is based on this comprehensive framework.

3.1 Basic Objects and Relations

In the field of time, basic objects are just time and durations. Time is a point or interval on the time line. Given the origin and a measurement, it can be evaluated with a real number. If there is no extra specification in Chinese text, the calendar is the Gregorian calendar. Duration is the distance between some two times. We can anchor duration by the start time and the end time, or by one of them and the length of the duration. However, if duration is referred to just length, it cannot be anchored on the time line. In temporal field, relations between objects are also defined. Between two times, relations are "before", "same", "include", "after". These objects and relationships are internal concepts behind surface text and we hope to fetch them.

3.2 The Measurement

To represent lengths on the time line, a measurement should be given. The temporal units consist of two types, macro units and micro units, shown in Fig. 1. To represent a time, the scope of the numbers which can be combined with temporal units is limited. "Century" and "Year" are two special time units, because only these two time units can help to anchor a time concept on the time line. If there is no help from contexts, other time units can not anchor a time concept on the time line. These limitations are valuable in normalization of temporal expression.

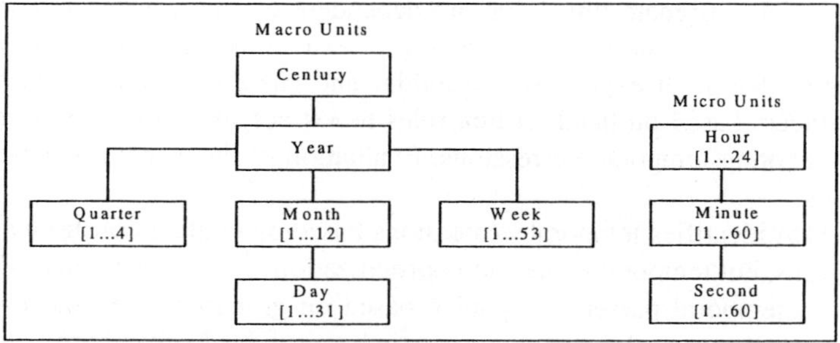

Fig. 1. The scheme of time units

3.3 Representation in Chinese Text

According to our observation on Chinese texts and the annotation standards of TIMEX2 [4, 6] and TIMEX3 [12], temporal expressions can be classified into different classes. They are shown in Fig. 2.

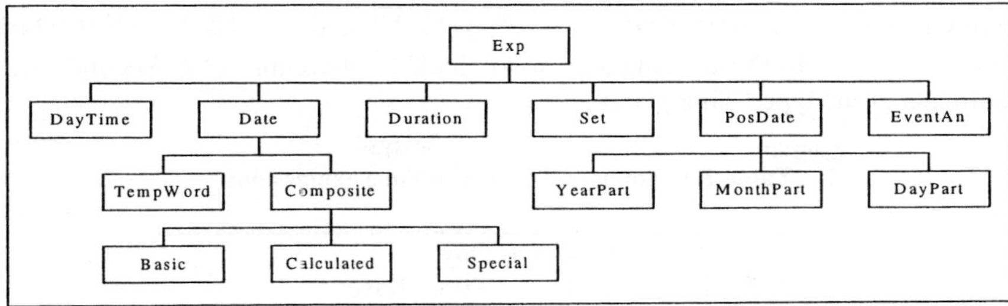

Fig. 2. The classification of temporal expression

In Chinese, if people do not know the exact number at an inferior time level, they may append an imprecise description to denote a position in a larger scope, such as "去年春天/the spring of last year". We named these temporal expressions "PosDate". These expressions consist of date expressions and imprecise appendix.

"TempWord" expressions are some Chinese words which contained temporal meanings, such as "春节/the lunar new year", "目前/now". "Composite" expressions include basic temporal expressions, calculated expressions and special expressions, such as "1999年4月28日/April 28, 1999", and "两年后/after two years" and "1999 财年/ the fiscal year 1999". "Set" expressions denote a set of time and most of them are about frequency, such as "每年/every year" and "每两天/every two days". "EventAn" expressions are relevant to the times of events, such as "当他演讲时/when he was speaking". "EventAn" expressions can be anchored on the time line only after the times of the events are resolved.

4 Extractor Based on Grammar and Constraints

The task of extractor is to identify the extents of temporal expressions in the surface text. A set of context free grammar rules is designed to describe the basic form of all kinds of temporal expressions and a bottom-up chart parser is employed to parse temporal expressions. Word segmentation is a preliminary step in many Chinese NLP applications. However, the performance of word segmentation is not perfect and it may introduce some extra errors. In our system, each possible combination of Chinese characters in a sentence will be looked up, and then all of the constituents are fed into the char parser. If the dictionaries are comprehensive enough, then all the possible explanations of all the possible combinations of characters can be gotten. Ambiguities and overlaps between multiple temporal expressions are left to constraint rules and combination rules.

4.1 Temporal Grammar Rules

A set of grammar rules is designed for each type of temporal expressions. In order to catch more temporal expressions, the grammar rules are given loosely. Some pseudo temporal expressions may be introduced and this problem is addressed in the next section.Given these grammar rules, "15时24分/15:24" and "15时24分39秒/15:24:39" can be recognized. In these examples, "时/o'clock", "分/minute", "秒/second" are all constituents of the type "Time_Unit".

Table 1. Grammar rules for DayTime expressions

No.1.	Exp -> Time_Of_Day
No.2.	Time_Of_Day -> Time_Base
No.3.	Time_Base -> Time_Temp +
No.4.	Time_Temp -> Integer Time_Unit
No.5.	Integer -> Digit +

4.2 Constraint Rules

There are many complex and variable phenomena in natural language. Even the domain is narrowed down to the temporal field, grammar rules are not enough to extract exact temporal expressions. There are some pseudo expressions which satisfy grammar rules, so constraint rules are designed to specify the true temporal expressions according to the context. These constraint rules are developed by analyzing thedata set.

A constraint rule will be triggered after the right part of the corresponding grammar rule is satisfied. If the constraint rule is satisfied, then the grammar rule can be applied; otherwise, it cannot be applied. Examples of constraint rules are shown in Table 2 and the following two examples show the constraint checking procedure step by step.

Table 2. Examples of constraint rules

Grammar rule 3:	Time_Base -> Time_Temp +
Constraint rule 3:	IF There is only one constituent of the type "Time_Temp", THEN the constituent "Time_Unit" which is contained in "Time_Temp", should not be "分/ minute".
Grammar rule 4:	Time_Temp -> Integer Time_Unit
Constraint rule 4:	The constituent "Integer" can not end up with "个/ (a quanti fier)".

(1) 这家新闻机构十分迅速地报道了这次事件。
(This news agency reported the event very quickly.)

Step 1. Look up dictionary.
[十/Digit] [分/Time_Unit]
Step 2. Apply the grammar rule No.5.
[十 /Integer] [分/Time_Unit]
Step 3. Check constraint rule No.4.
Pass.
Step 4. Apply grammar rule No.4.
[十分/Time_Temp]
Step 5. Check constraint rule No.3.
Fail and then terminate parsing.

(2) 晚上7时30分西弗吉尼亚州和俄亥俄州投票结束。

(The ballot ended at 7:30 p.m. in Western Virginia and Ohio.)

Step 1. Look up dictionary.
[7/Digit] [时/Time_Unit][3/Digit] [0/Digit][分/Time_Unit]

Step 2. Apply the grammar rule No.5.
[7/Integer] [时/Time_Unit] [30/Integer][分/Time_Unit]

Step 3. Check constraint rule No.4.
Pass.

Step 4. Apply grammar rule No.4.
[7时/Time_Temp] [30分/Time_Temp]

Step 5. Check constraint rule No.3.
Pass.

Step 6. Apply grammar rule No.3.
[7时30分/Time_Base]

Step 7. Apply grammar rule No.2.
[7时30分/Time_Of_Day]

Step 8. Apply grammar rule No.1.
[7时30分/Exp]

Step 9. Recognize the temporal expression successfully.

In the first example "十分/very" is an adverb and has no temporal meaning. However the character "十/ten" and "分/minute" can be looked up and satisfy the grammar rule. Constraint rules are necessary to filter the pseudo expression.

4.3 Combination of Temporal Expressions

Because each possible substring in a sentence is tried, multiple nested, overlap or adjacent temporal expressions may exist in the sentence. However, some of these expressions are just parts of the optimal answers. So combination is necessary to get the integrated temporal expression. After applying grammar rules, if any two temporal expressions are nested, overlapped or adjacent, our system will combine them and keep the final result. This procedure is shown by the following examples.

(3) 这次列车将于次日早上到达南昌。

(This train will arrive at Nan Chang next morning.)

First recognized temporal expressions are [次日/tomorrow] and [早上/morning]. After the combination, the correct answer [次日早上/next morning] will appear.

(4) 晚上8时篮球比赛开始。

(The basketball game starts at 8:00 p.m.)

First recognized expressions are [晚上/night], [8时/8:00], [晚上8时/8:00 p.m.]. The final result is [晚上8时/ 8:00 p.m.].

4.4 Temporal/Non-temporal Disambiguation

Some strings of characters are temporal expressions in given contexts, but in other contexts they are not. The context should be browsed to extract the true temporal expressions. Some constraint rules are designed to check the context and fulfill disambiguation. Three kinds of ambiguities are founded. The first kind is the ambiguities caused by numbers, such as example 5. In this case, the expression "15：10" contains temporal information, but in sports news messages it may be a score of a game. The second kind is the ambiguities caused by the combination of numbers and time units, such as "十号". In example 6, the expression "十号" just refers to a football team member. However, in many news messages it is a date. The third kind is the ambiguities caused by Chinese words, such as "前". In example 7, the expression means "former" and its explanations in other contexts may be "in front of".

(5) 本次列车将于15：10到达终点站。

(6) 然而6分钟后，10号宿茂臻冲顶即将比分扳平。

(7) 俄罗斯前总统叶利钦等政府首脑为人类和平欣然提笔。

There are multiple explanations for the same one phrase or word, so ambiguities may be caused. To discriminate these expressions, heuristics for disambiguation are embedded in corresponding constraint rules.

5 Normalizer Based on Mapping Procedure

The goal of normalizer is to represent the temporal information of contained in temporal expressions, according to some standard. The normalizer is based on the mapping procedure, in which temporal expressions are explained and represented by values of temporal attributes. In this procedure, the objects number, unit, time and duration are employed to store and represent temporal information.

5.1 Introduction to Normalization

TERN 2004 evaluation [14] is a public evaluation on the extraction and normalization of temporal expressions. To evaluate our temporal parser in a real task, we express temporal information according to the standard of TERN 2004 evaluation. Any temporal expression will be explained by a possible combination of the values of the six attributes. These attributes are described in table 3.

Table 3. Temporal attributes

Attribute	Function
VAL	Contains the value of a time or duration
MOD	Captures temporal modifications
SET	Designates set-denoting expressions
ANCHOR_VAL	Contains a normalized form of the reference time
ANCHOR_DIR	Capture the relative direction/orientation between VAL and ANCHOR_VAL
NON_SPECIFIC	Designates a generic, essensially nonreferencial expression

5.2 Normalization of Temporal Expressions

After the procedure of extraction, the chart parser keeps all the applied grammar rules and recognized intermediate constituents. Semantic meanings of temporal expressions can be achieved by the explanation of these grammar rules. In this procedure, some basic objects, such as "number", "unit", "time" and "duration", can be employed to store and convey temporal information. Applying grammar rules means creations or updates of basic temporal objects. Based on our temporal framework, we explain how to normalize the temporal expression extracted, i.e. mapping the expressions to the values of six attributes. The mapping procedure is different for different kinds of temporal expressions. A general description about the mapping procedure is shown in Fig. 3.

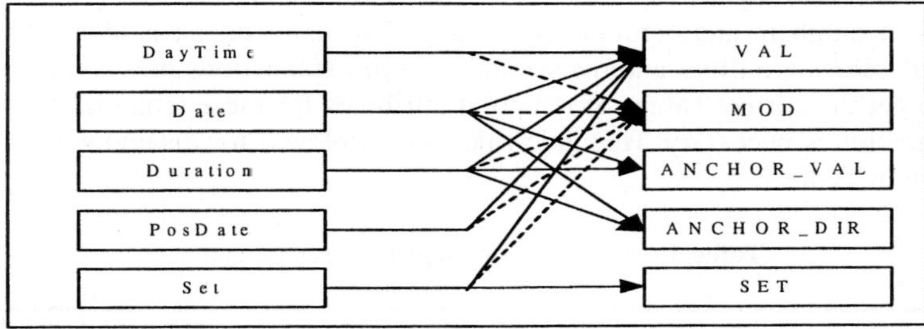

Fig. 3. Mapping temporal expressions to attributes

According to the classification scheme in Section 3.3, all temporal expressions can be mapped to the six attributes. The mapping procedures are complicated and selected examples are shown in Table 4. It is difficult to tell whether a temporal expression is "specific" or not, and few expressions are set a value at this attribute, we do not map expression to the attribute "NON_SPECIFIC".

Table 4. Examples of normalization

Expressions	Attributes
目前/now	val="PRESENT_REF" anchor_val="2000-10-05" anchor_dir="AS_OF"
晚上8时20分/20: 20 p.m.	val="1999-04-26 T20:20"
后两年/the next two years	val="P2Y" anchor_val="2000" anchor_dir="STARTING"
每两天/every two days	val="P2D" set="YES"
明天下午/ next afternoon	val="2000-10-07TAF"

"MOD" attribute of temporal expressions may be set as "YES" if there are some modifying descriptions about the expressions, such as "将近/about", "早于/before" and so on. So any kind of temporal expressions may be mapped on this attribute. "Set" expressions can be explained as set of times, such as "每年/each year", or set of durations, such as "每两年/every two years", so the attributes "VAL" and "SET" will be filled. "ANCHOR_VAL" and "ANCHOR_DIR" refer to reference times and we adopt the publishing times of news articles as the default reference times. Event expressions are relevant with a specific event and it is hard to represent the exact meaning of them. In our system event expressions are not normalized.

5.3 Time/Duration Disambiguation

Sometimes people omit a part of a full temporal expression for convenience in Chinese texts. For example, "4月/April" and "97年/ '97" are used to instead "2000年4月/April, 2000" and "1997年/the year 1997". However, "4月/four months" and "97年/97 years" are also legal temporal expressions. These temporal expressions are combinations of numbers and common time units. The first kind of explanations means these expressions are times and the second kind of explanations means they are durations. To get the correct values of temporal attributes for these temporal expressions, disambiguation is necessary. Heuristic rules are employed for disambiguation, which are shown in Table 5.

Table 5. Some heuristic rules for disambiguation

IF a 3-digit or four-digit number is combined with the unit "年/year", THEN this expression is time; IF a 2-digit number is combined with the unit "年/year" and the number is bigger that 70, THEN this expression is time. IF a 1-digit number is combined with the unit "年/year", THEN this expression is duration.

6 Evaluation and Analysis

In this section we report the results about evaluating our temporal parser on a manually annotated corpus, which consist of 457 Chinese news articles. The data collection contains 285,746 characters/142,872 words and 4,290 manually annotated temporal expressions. We will evaluate the boundaries of expressions and the values of the six temporal attributes.

Table 6. Experiment configuration

Experiment No.	Conditions
1	No constraints, combination of nested expressions
2	No constraints, combination of nested, overlapped and adjacent expressions
3	Constraints, combination of nested expressions
4	Constraints, combination of nested, overlapped and adjacent expressions

In our temporal parser, we embedded constraints to restrict grammar rules. In addition, we combine the nested, overlapped and adjacent temporal expressions. In Chinese, many temporal expressions contain nested temporal expressions. If we do not combine these nested components into the optimal answer, there will be so many mismatched expressions. So the combination of nested temporal expressions is necessary. In the experiments, we try to evaluate two factors: the constraint rules, and the combination of overlapped and adjacent temporal expressions. Four experiments are set up, which are described in Table 6. Given these conditions, the results of the experiments are shown in Table 7.

Table 7. Experiment results

Attributes		NO. 1.	NO. 2.	NO. 3.	NO. 4.
	P	0.717	0.758	0.810	0.856
TEXT	R	0.838	0.850	0.830	0.843
	F	0.773	0.801	0.820	0.849
	P	0.730	0.750	0.787	0.807
VAL	R	0.693	0.681	0.742	0.732
	F	0.711	0.714	0.764	0.768
	P	0.563	0.565	0.629	0.626
MOD	R	0.586	0.550	0.616	0.574
	F	0.574	0.557	0.622	0.599
	P	0.698	0.662	0.879	0.867
SET	R	0.606	0.589	0.611	0.598
	F	0.649	0.624	0.720	0.707
	P	0.680	0.750	0.681	0.687
ANCHOR_VAL	R	0.658	0.681	0.662	0.652
	F	0.669	0.714	0.672	0.669
	P	0.724	0.727	0.733	0.737
ANCHOR_DIR	R	0.682	0.669	0.694	0.682
	F	0.702	0.697	0.713	0.708

Several related works are designed to extract and normalize temporal expressions, however they are about English, Spanish, French, Korea and so on. We take part in TERN 2004 evaluation on Chinese temporal expression extraction and achieve the highest performance in this task. There is no public result on Chinese temporal expression normalization, for reference we compare our normalization result of Experiment NO. 4 with the English normalization result in TERN 2004. Our performance is medium among their results.

Table 7 compares the Precision, Recall and F-measure for different attributes in different experiments. "TEXT" means the performance of exact boundaries of temporal expressions and other attributes are explained in Section 5.1. For attributes "TEXT" and "VAL", we achieve the highest performance in Experiment 4. The F-scores are 0.849 and 0.768, respectively. For other attributes, we also achieved nearly highest score in Experiment 4. From the trend of performance on these two attributes, we can see the constraints and the procedure of combination have positive effects to performance of the temporal parser, especially on "TEXT" and "VAL". At the same time, the procedure of combination is not significant to other attributes. Based on the assumption that two adjacent or overlapped temporal expressions refer to the same temporal concept, we combined them. However, the procedure of combination can not help to explain the meaning of the expressions.

After the evaluation we collect the errors of Experiment NO. 4 and try to summary the reasons. Wrong attribute values include missed, incorrect and spurious cases. The reason for errors on the attributes "ANCHOR_VAL" and "ANCHOR_DIR" is that the system did not give correct reference times. Table 8 gives the error distributions according to different attributes. From this table, it can be seen that temporal Chinese words and events are difficult to extract and normalize.

Table 8. Error distributions

Attributes	Reasons	Number	Percentage
TEXT	Boundaries of temporal Chinese words	366	37.4%
	Boundaries of events	193	19.7%
	Grammar rules	161	16.4%
	Boundaries of temporal noun phrase	89	9.1%
	Combination procedure	76	7.8%
	Annotation inconsistence	75	7.7%
	Temporal/non-temporal ambiguities	19	1.9%
VAL	Explained semantics	299	27.6%
	Explanation of temporal Chinese word	180	16.6%
	Errors introduced by extraction	177	16.3%
	Specification/generalization characteristic	148	13.7%
	Wrong reference times	122	11.3%
	Annotation inconsistence	80	7.4%
	Point/duration ambiguities	63	5.8%
	Explanation of events or noun phrase	14	1.3%
MOD	Errors introduced by extraction	44	33.3%
	Annotation inconsistence	35	26.5%
	Explanation of temporal Chinese word	27	20.5%
	Explained semantics	23	17.4%
	Ambiguities	3	2.1%
SET	Explained semantics	35	81.4%
	Errors introduced by extraction	3	7.0%
	Annotation inconsistence	5	11.6%

7 Conclusion

In this paper, we present the temporal parser that extract and normalize comprehensive temporal expressions from Chinese texts. We also propose a temporal framework, which include basic temporal objects and relations, the measurement and classification of temporal expressions. To cope with kinds of temporal expressions, constraint rules are employed to retrieve genuine expressions and resolve ambiguities. The temporal parser CTEMP is fully implemented, which is based on the chart parsing and constraint checking scheme. We have evaluated the temporal parser on a manually annotated corpus and achieved promising results of F-measures of 85.6% on extent and 76.8% on value. We took part in TERN-2004 Chinese temporal expression extraction with this parser and achieved the highest performance in that track.

In our experiments the temporal parser is also evaluated with/without constraints, combination of nested and overlapped temporal expressions. We find that constraints are significant to the task extraction and normalization. At the same time, combination has positive influence on the task extraction. Error analysis shows that temporal Chinese words and events are more difficult to extract and normalize. To improve the performance of extraction, we plan to decide whether to keep any temporal Chinese words as a genuine temporal expression automatically according to the contribution of the word. We also plan to improve the performance of normalization by more precise semantic explanation.

Acknowledgement

The work presented in this paper is supported by Research Grants Council of Hong Kong (reference number: CERG PolyU 5085/02E and 5181/03E).

References

1. Ahn, D., Adafre, S. F., and Rijke, M. de.: Towards Task-Based Temporal Extraction and Recognition. Proceedings Dagstuhl Workshop on Annotating, Extracting, and Reasoning about Time and Events (2005)
2. Allen, J. F.: Towards a General Theory of Action and Time. Artificial Intelligence, Vol. 23, Issue 2, (1984) 123-154
3. Estela, S., Martinez-Barco, Patricio, and Munoz, R.: Recognizing and Tagging Temporal Expressions in Spanish. Workshop on Annotation Standards for Temporal Information in Natural Language, LREC 2002
4. Ferro, L., Gerber, L., Mani, I., Sundheim, B., And Wilson, G.: TIDES 2003 standard for the annotation of temporal expressions (2004). timex2.mitre.org
5. Filatove E. and Hovy E.: Assigning Time-Stamps to Event-Clauses. Proceedings of the ACL Workshop on Temporal and Spatial Information Processing, Toulouse (2001), 88-95
6. Gerber, L., Huang, S., and Wang, X.: TIDES 2003 standard for the annotation of temporal expressions. Chinese supplement draft (2004). timex2.mitre.org
7. Hobbs, J. R. and Pan, F.: An Ontology of Time for the Semantic Web. ACM Transactions on Asian Language Information Processing (2004), Vol. 3, Issue 1, 66-85
8. Jang, S.B., Baldwin, J. and Mani, I.: Automatic TIMEX2 Tagging of Korean News. ACM Transactions on Asian Language Information processing (2004), Vol. 3, No. 1, 51-65
9. Li, W., Wong, K.-F., and Yuan, C.: A Model for Processing Temporal References in Chinese. Proceedings of the ACL 2001 Workshop on Temporal and Spatial Information Processing (2001)
10. Mani, I., Pustejovsky, J., and Sundheim, B.: Introduction to the special issue on temporal information processing. ACM Transactions on Asian Language Information Processing (2004), Vol. 3, Issue 1, 1-10
11. Mani, I. and Wilson G.: Robust Temporal Processing of News. Proceedings of the 38th Annual Meeting of the Association for Computational Linguistics. New Brunswick, New Jersey (2000)
12. Sauri, R., Littman, J., Knippen, B., Gaizauskas, R., Setzer, A., and Pustejovsky, J.: TimeML Annotation Guidelines (2004). cs.brandeis.edu

13. Schilder, F. and Habel, C.: From temporal expressions to temporal information: semantic tagging of news messages. Proceedings of the ACL 2001 Workshop on Temporal and Spatial Information Processing. Toulouse (2001), 65-72
14. TERN-2004. http://timex2.mitre.org/tern.html 2005
15. Vazov N.: A System for Extraction of Temporal Expressions from French Texts based on Syntactic and Semantic Constraints. Proceedings of the ACL Workshop on Temporal and Spatial Information Processing (2001), 96-103

French-English Terminology Extraction from Comparable Corpora

Béatrice Daille and Emmanuel Morin

University of Nantes, LINA - FRE CNRS 2729,
2, rue de la Houssinière - BP 92208, 44322 Nantes Cedex 3, France
{beatrice.daille, emmanuel.morin}@univ-nantes.fr

Abstract. This article presents a method of extracting bilingual lexica composed of single-word terms (SWTs) and multi-word terms (MWTs) from comparable corpora of a technical domain. First, this method extracts MWTs in each language, and then uses statistical methods to align single words and MWTs by exploiting the term contexts. After explaining the difficulties involved in aligning MWTs and specifying our approach, we show the adopted process for bilingual terminology extraction and the resources used in our experiments. Finally, we evaluate our approach and demonstrate its significance, particularly in relation to non-compositional MWT alignment.

1 Introduction

Traditional research into the automatic compilation of bilingual dictionaries from corpora exploits parallel texts, i.e. a text and its translation [17]. From sentence-to-sentence aligned corpora, symbolic [2], statistical [11], or combined [7] techniques are used for word and expression alignments.
The use of parallel corpora raises two problems:

- as a parallel corpus is a pair of translated texts, the vocabulary appearing in the translated text is highly influenced by the source text, especially for technical domains;
- such corpora are difficult to obtain for paired languages not involving English.

New methods try to exploit comparable corpora: texts that are of the same text type and on the same subject without a source text-target text relationship. The main studies concentrate on finding in such corpora translation candidates for one-item words. For example, the French SWT *manteau* is translated in English by *mantle* in the domain of forestry, *shield* in the domain of marine activities, and by *coat* in the domain of clothing. The method is based on lexical context analysis and relies on the simple observation that a word and its translation tend to appear in the same lexical contexts. Thus, for our three possible translations of *manteau*, three different lexical contexts are encountered which are expressed below by English lexical units:

R. Dale et al. (Eds.): IJCNLP 2005, LNAI 3651, pp. 707–718, 2005.

- *manteau/mantle* : vegetation, forest, wood...
- *manteau/shield* : boat, sea, shipbuilding...
- *manteau/coat* : cloth, cold, wear...

These contexts can be represented by vectors, and each vector element represents a word which occurs within the window of the word to be translated. Translation is obtained by comparing the source context vector to each translation candidate vector after having translated each element of the source vector with a general dictionary. This method is known as the "direct context-vector approach". Using this method, [10] extracts English-Chinese one-item candidate translations from two years of English and Chinese newspaper articles by matching the context vector with 76% precision on the first 20 candidates. From English-German newspaper corpora of 85 million words, [14] improves the precision to 89% on the first one-item 10 candidates using the same techniques. [4] obtain 50% precision on the first one-item 10 candidates from a French/English corpus of 1.2 million words. [1] adapted this approach to deal with many-to-many word translations. In extracting English-Chinese nominal phrases belonging to general domains from the web, they obtain a precision of 91% on the first 3 candidates.

Some improvements have been proposed by [9] to avoid the insufficient coverage of bilingual dictionary and thus not to get context vectors with too many elements that are not translated. This method is called "similarity-vector approach": it associates to the word to be translated the context vectors of the nearest lexical units that are in the bilingual dictionary. With this method, they obtain for one-item French-English words 43% and 51% precision on the ten and twenty first candidates applied on a medical corpus of 100 000 words (respectively 44% and 57% with the direct method) and 79% and 84% precision on the ten and twenty first candidates applied on a social science corpus of 8 millions words (respectively 35% and 42% with the direct method).

If the results obtained in the field of bilingual lexicon extraction from comparable corpora are promising, they only cover either bilingual single words from general or specialised corpora, or bilingual nominal phrases from general corpora. Our goal is to find translation for multi-word terms (MWTs) from specialised comparable corpora.

If MWTs are more representative of domain specialities than single-word terms (SWTs), pinpointing their translations poses specific problems:

- SWTs and MWTs are not always translated by a term of the same length. For example, the French MWT *peuplement forestier* (2 content words) is translated into English as the SWT *crop* and the French term *essence d'ombre* (2 content words) as *shade tolerant species* (3 content words). This well-known problem, referred to as "fertility", is seldom taken into account in bilingual lexicon extraction, a *word-to-word* assumption being generally adopted.
- When a MWT is translated into a MWT of the same length, the target sequence is not typically composed of the translation of its parts [13]. For example, the French term *plantation énergétique* is translated into English as *fuel plantation* where *fuel* is not the translation of *énergétique*. This property is referred to as "non-compositionality".

– A MWT could appear in texts under different forms reflecting either syntactic, morphological or semantic variations [12],[5]. Term variations should be taken into account in the translation process. For example, the French sequences *aménagement de la forêt* and *aménagement forestier* refer to the same MWT and are both translated into the same English term: *forest management.*

We propose tackling these three problems, fertility, non-compositionality, and variations, by using both linguistic and statistical methods. First, MWTs are identified in both the source and target language using a monolingual term extraction program. Second, a statistical alignment algorithm is used to link MWTs in the source language to single words and MWTs in the target language. Our alignment algorithm extracts the words and MWT contexts and proposes translations by comparing source and target words and MWT contexts.

2 Extraction Process

We present in this section the bilingual extraction process which is composed of two steps:

1. Identification in source and target languages of MWTs and their variations;
2. Alignment of theses MWTs using a method close to the "similarity-vector approach".

2.1 MWT Identification

MWTs are extracted using a terminology extraction program available for French and English: *ACABIT*[1]. This program is open source and one of its characteristics is to take into account variants of MWTs (graphical, inflectional, syntactic, and morphosyntactic)[6]. It does not need any external linguistic resources and is domain-independent. ACABIT applies on a corpus with the following pre-processing:

– tokenisation and sentence segmentation;
– part-of-speech and lemma tagging.

First, ACABIT carries out shallow parsing: it scans the corpus, counts and extracts strings whose tag sequences characterise patterns of MWTs or one of their variants. The different occurrences referring to a MWT or one of its variants are grouped and constitute an unique candidate MWT. Thus the candidate MWT *produit forestier* 'forest product' appears under the following forms:

[1] http://www.sciences.univ-nantes.fr/info/perso/permanents/daille/ and LINUX Mandrake release

- **base form:** *produit forestier* ;
- **graphical variant:** *produit fo-restier*, *pro-duit forestier* ;
- **inflexional variant:** *produits forestiers* ;
- **syntatic variant: modification:** *produit non forestier*, *produit alimentaire forestier*, *produit fini d'origine forestiére*, *produit ligneux non forestier* ;
- **syntactic variant: coordination:** *produit halieutique et forestier*, *produit agricole ou forestier*, *le produit et le service forestier.*

The MWT candidates *produit de la forêt*, *produit agroforestier*, *non-produit agroforestier*, and *sous-produit forestier*, *sous-produit de la forêt* have also been identified.

Second, ACABIT performs semantic grouping thanks to the following operations:

Merging of two MWTs. Two MWT candidates are merged if they are synonymic variants obtained by derivation or conversion. Such variants include a relational adjective: either a denominal adjective, i.e. morphologically derived from a noun thanks to a suffix, such as *forêt/forestier* 'forest', or an adjective having a noun usage such as *mathématique* 'mathematical/mathematics'.

Dissociation of some MWT variants. Syntactical variants that induce semantic discrepancies are retrieved from the set of the candidate variants and new MWT candidates are created. Modification variants with the insertion of an adverb of negation denoting an antonymy link such as *produit non forestier* 'non forest product' and *produit forestier* 'forest product', or insertion of a relational adjectives denoting an hyperonymy link such as *produit alimentaire forestier* 'food forest product' with *produit forestier* 'forest product' [6].

Grouping of MWTs. All MWT candidates linked by derivational morphology or by variations inducing semantic variations are clustered. For example, the following MWT candidates constitutes a cluster of MWTs: *produit forestier/produit de la forêt*, *produit non forestier*, *non-produit agroforestier*, *produit agroforestier*, *sous-produit forestier/sous-produit de la forêt*, *produit alimentaire forestier* and*produit forestier.*

In the following steps, we do not consider a unique sequence reflecting a candidate MWT but a set of sequences. We consider only term variants that are grouped under a unique MWT. This grouping of term variations could be interpreted as a terminology normalisation in the same way as lemmatisation at the morphological level.

2.2 MWT Alignment

The goal of this step, which adapts the similarity vector-based approach defined for single words by [9] to MWTs, is to align source MWTs with target single words, SWTs or MWTs. From now on, we will refer to lexical units as words, SWTs or MWTs.

Context Vectors. First, we collect all the lexical units in the context of each lexical unit i and count their occurrence frequency in a window of n sentences around i. For each lexical unit i of the source and the target language, we obtain a context vector v_i which gathers the set of co-occurrence units j associated with the number of times that j and i occur together occ_j^i. We normalise context vectors using an association score such as Mutual Information or Log-likelihood. (cf. equations 1 and 2 and table 1). In order to reduce the arity of context vectors, we keep only the co-occurrences with the highest association scores.

Table 1. Contingency table

	j	$\neg j$
i	$a = occ(i, j)$	$b = occ(i, \neg j)$
$\neg i$	$c = occ(\neg i, j)$	$d = occ(\neg i, \neg j)$

$$MI(i, j) = log \frac{a}{(a + b)(a + c)} \tag{1}$$

$$\begin{aligned} \lambda(i, j) = \; & a \log(a) + b \log(b) + c \log(c) + d \log(d) \\ & +(a + b + c + d) \log(a + b + c + d) - (a + b) \log(a + b) \\ & -(a + c) \log(a + c) - (b + d) \log(b + d) - (c + d) \log(c + d) \end{aligned} \tag{2}$$

Similarity Vectors. For each lexical unit k to be translated, we identify the lexical units which the context vectors are similar to v_k thanks to a vector distance measure such as Cosine [15] or Jaccard [16] (cf. equations 3 and 4). From now, we call "similarity vector" of the unit k a vector that contains all the lexical units which the context vectors are similar to v_k. To each unit l of the similarity vector v_k, we associate a similarity score $simil_{v_l}^{v_k}$ between v_l and v_k. In order to reduce the arity of similarity vectors, we keep only the lexical units with the highest similarity scores. Up to now, similarity vectors have only been built for the source language.

$$simil_{v_l}^{v_k} = \frac{\sum_t assoc_t^l \, assoc_t^k}{\sqrt{\sum_t {assoc_t^l}^2 \, {assoc_t^k}^2}} \tag{3}$$

$$simil_{v_l}^{v_k} = \frac{\sum_t min(assoc_t^l, assoc_t^k)}{\sum_t {assoc_t^l}^2 + \sum_t {assoc_t^k}^2 - \sum_t assoc_t^l \, assoc_t^k} \tag{4}$$

Translation of the Similarity Vectors. Using a bilingual dictionary, we translate the lexical units of the similarity vector and identify their context vectors in the target language. Figure 1 illustrates this translation process.

Depending the nature of the lexical unit, two different treatments are carried out:

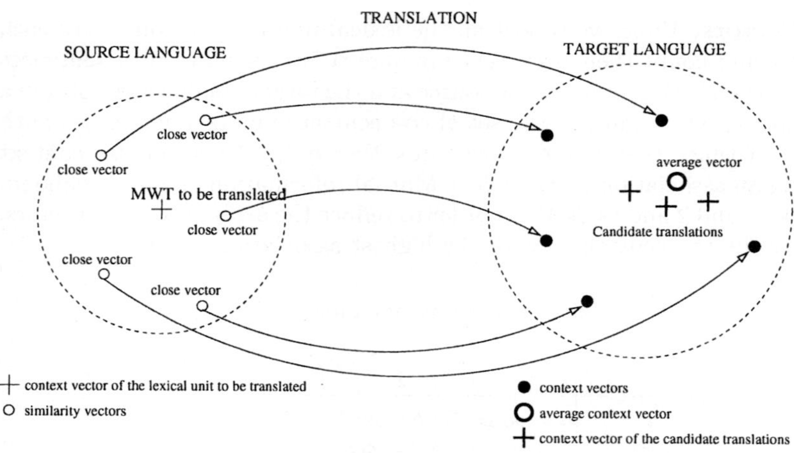

Fig. 1. Transfer procedure of similarity vectors from source to target language

Translation of a SWT. If the bilingual dictionary provides several translations for a word belonging to the similarity vector, we generate as many target context vectors as possible translations. Then, we calculate the union of these vectors to obtain only one target context vector.

Translation of a MWT. If the translation of the parts of the MWT are found in the bilingual dictionary, we generate as many target context vectors as translated combinations identified by *ACABIT* and calculate their union. When it is not possible to translate all the parts of a MWT, or when the translated combinations are not identified by *ACABIT*, the MWT is not taken into account in the translation process.

Finding the MWT Translations. We calculate the barycentre of all the target context vectors obtained in the preceding step in order to propose a target average vector. The candidate translations of a lexical unit are the target lexical units closest to the target average vector according to vector distance.

3 Resources Presentation

We present in this section the different resources used for our experiments:

3.1 Comparable Corpus

Our comparable corpus has been built from the *Unasylva* electronic international journal published by FAO[2] and representing 4 million words. This journal deals

[2] http://www.fao.org/forestry/foris/webview/forestry2/

with forests and forest industries and is available in English, French and Spanish. In order to constitute a comparable corpus, we only select texts which are not the translation of each other.

3.2 Bilingual Dictionary

Our bilingual dictionary has been built from lexical resources on the Web. It contains 22,300 French single words belonging to the general language with an average of 1.6 translation per entry.

3.3 Reference Bilingual Terminology

The evaluation of our bilingual terminology extraction method has been done from a reference bilingual terminology. This reference list has been built from three different terminological resources:

1. a bilingual glossary of the terminology of silviculture[3]. It contains 700 terms of which 70% are MWTs.
2. the Eurosilvasur multilingual lexicon[4]. It contains 2,800 terms of which 66% are MWTs.
3. the multilingual AGROVOC thesaurus[5]. It contains 15,000 index terms of which 47% are MWTs.

These three terminological resources are complementary, the glossary being the most specialised, the thesaurus the least. From these resources, we automatically select 300 terms with the constraint that each French term should appear at least 5 times in our corpus. These terms are divided into three sub-lists:

- [list 1] 100 French SWTs of which the translation is an English SWT. Of course, this translation is not given by our bilingual dictionary.
- [list 2] 100 French MWTs of which the translation could be an English SWT or a MWT. In the case of MWTs, the translation could not be obtained by the translation of the MWT's parts.
- [list 3] 100 MWT of which the translation is an English MWT. The translation of these MWTs is obtained by the translation of their parts.

This reference list contains a majority of terms with low frequency (cf. Table 2). Two main reasons explain this fact: on the one hand, the different resources which have been used to build this reference list are either specific or generic; on the other hand, our corpus covers several domains linked to forestry and does not constitute a highly specialised resource.

[3] http://nfdp.ccfm.org/silviterm/silvi_f/silvitermintrof.htm

[4] http://www.eurosilvasur.net/francais/lexique.php

[5] http://www.fao.org/agrovoc/

Table 2. Frequency in the corpus of the French terms belonging to the reference list

# occ.	< 50	≤ 100	≤ 1 000	> 1 000
[list 1]	50	21	18	11
[list 2]	54	21	25	0
[list 3]	51	18	29	2

4 Evaluation

We present now the evaluation of the bilingual terminology extraction. We have to deal with 55 013 SWTs and MWTs, but only 7 352 SWTs and 6 769 MWTs appear both in the reference bilingual terminology and in the corpus.

4.1 Parameter Estimation

Several parameters appear in the extraction process presented in Section 2. The most interesting results have been obtained with the following values:

- **Size of the context window** is 3 sentences around the lexical unit to be translated;
- **Context vectors** are built only with one-item words to increase representativity. For example, the context vector of the French term *débardage* 'hauling' includes the MWT *tracteur à chenille* 'crawler tractor' which is more discriminating than its parts, *tracteur* or *chenille*. But including MWTs into context vectors increases the vectorial space dimension and reduces the representativity of the terms appearing both in the corpus and the reference bilingual terminology. The term *débardage* 'hauling' has a frequency of 544 as a SWT and only a frequency of 144 as part of a MWT as it appears in several MWTs. The context vector size are limited to the first 100 values of the Log-likelihood association score.
- **Similarity vectors** are the first 30 values of Cosine distance measure.
- **Finding translations** is done with Cosine distance measure.

4.2 Result Analysis

Table 3 gives the results obtained with our experiments. For each sublist, we give the number of translations found (NB_{trans}), and the average and standard deviation position for the translations in the ranked list of candidate translations (AVG_{pos}, $STDDEV_{pos}$).

We note that translations of MWTs belonging to [list 3] which are compositionally translated are well-identified and often appear in the first 20 candidate translations. The translations belonging to [lists 1 and 2] are not always found and, when they are, they seldom appear in the first 20 candidate translations.

The examination of the candidate translations of a MWT regardless of the list to which it belongs shows that they share the same semantic field (cf. table 5).

Table 3. Bilingual terminology extraction results

	NB_{trans}	AVG_{pos}	$STDDEV_{pos}$
[list 1]	56	32.9	23,7
[list 2]	63	30.7	26,7
[list 3]	89	3.8	7,9

Table 4. Bilingual MWT extraction with parameter combination

	NB_{trans}	AVG_{pos}	$STDDEV_{pos}$	**Top 10**	**Top 20**
[list 1]	59	16.2	15.9	41	51
[list 2]	63	14.8	22.3	45	55
[list 3]	89	2.4	3.7	87	88

Table 5. Exemples of candidate translations obtained for 3 terms belonging to [list 2]

degré de humidité (# occ. 41)	gaz à effet de serre (# occ. 33)	papeterie (# occ. 178)
humidity	carbon	newsprint
saturation	carbon cycle	paper production
aridity	atmosphere	raw material
evaporation	**greenhouse gas**	mill
saturation deficit	greenhouse	pulp mill
rate of evaporation	global carbon	raw
atmospheric humidity	atmospheric carbon	manufacture
water vapor	emission	**paper mill**
joint	sink	manufacturing
dry	carbon dioxide	capacity
hot	fossil fuel	printing
rainy	fossil	paper manufacture
temperature	carbon pool	factory
moisture control	mitigate	paperboard
meyer	global warming	fiberboard
party	climate change	bagasse
atmospheric	atmospheric	paper-making
dryness	dioxide	board
monsoon	sequestration	material supply
joint meeting	quantity of carbon	paper pulp

As noted above, our results differ widely according the chosen parameter values. Because of time constraints, we cannot evaluate all the possible values of all the different parameters, but manual examination of the candidate translations for a few different configurations shows:

- Some good translations obtained for one parameter configuration are not found for another, and, inversely, some terms which are not translated in the first configuration could be correctly translated by another. So, it is difficult to choose the best configuration, especially for [lists 1 and 2].
- More precisely, for a given term, the first candidate translations are different for different configurations. For example, for the French MWT *pâte à papier* (*paper pulp*), the first 50 candidate translations of 20 different configurations have only 30 items in common.
- The right translation appears in different positions for different configurations.

In order to identify more correct translations, we decided to take into account the different results proposed by different configurations by fusing the first 20 candidate translations proposed by each configuration. The different configurations concern the size of the context and similarity vectors, and the association and similarity measures. The results obtained and presented in Table 4 show a slight improvement in the position of the correct translations among the set of candidate translations.

The results for [list 3] are still very satisfactory. The results for [list 1] improve, but remain a little below the results obtained by [8] who obtained 43% and 51% for the first 10 and 20 candidates respectively for a 100,000-word medical corpus, and 79% and 84% for a multi-domain 8 million word corpus.

4.3 Comment

In a general way, it is difficult to compare our experiments to previous ones [3],[8] as the corpora are different. Indeed, our comparable corpus covers several domains belonging to forestry, and does not constitute a very specialised resource on the contrary of the medical corpus of [3] built thanks to the key words "symptoms, pathological status". Moreover, half of the terms of the reference bilingual terminological database have a frequency of less than 50 occurrences in the corpus that lead to non-discriminating context vectors. [8] use for their experiments a social sciences corpora of 8 millions words and a reference bilingual terminological database of 180 words with high frequencies in the corpus: from 100 to 1000. Our automatic evaluation is also more constrained than manual evaluation. For example, our reference list gives *haulage road* as the translation of *piste de débardage*. In our candidate translation list, *haulage road* is not present. We find an acceptable translation, *skid trail*, in the first 20 candidates, but this is never considered valid by our automatic evaluation.
Our results for MWTs are better than those for single words. The method seems promising, especially for MWTs for which translation is not compositional.

5 Conclusion

In this paper, we proposed and evaluated a combined method for bilingual MWT extraction from comparable corpora which takes into account three main characteristics of MWT translation: fertility, non-compositionality, and variation clustering. We first extracted monolingually MWTs and clustered synonymic variants. Secondly, we aligned them using a statistical method adapted from similarity-vector approach for single words which exploits the context of these MWTs. This combined approach for MWTs gives satisfactory results compared to those for single word. It also allows us to obtain non compositional translations of MWTs. Our further works will concentrate on the interaction parameters, the combining of the source-to-target and target-to-source alignment results, and the handling of non-synonymic term variations.

Acknowledgements

We are particularly grateful to Samuel Dufour-Kowalski, who undertook the computer programs. This work has also benefited from his comments.

References

1. Cao, Y., Li, H.: Base Noun Phrase Translation Using Web Data and the EM Algorithm. In: Proceeding of the 19th International Conference on Computational Linguistics (COLING'02), Tapei, Taiwan (2002) 127–133
2. Carl, M., Langlais, P.: An intelligent Terminology Database as a pre-processor for Statistical Machine Translation. In Chien, L.F., Daille, B., Kageura, L., Nakagawa, H., eds.: Proceeding of the COLING 2002 2nd International Workshop on Computational Terminology (COMPUTERM'02), Tapei, Taiwan (2002) 15–21
3. Chiao, Y.C.: Extraction lexicale bilingue à partir de textes médicaux comparables : application à la recherche d'information translangue. PhD thesis, Université Pierre et Marie Curie, Paris VI (2004)
4. Chiao, Y.C., Zweigenbaum, P.: Looking for candidate translational equivalents in specialized, comparable corpora. In: Proceedings of the 19th International Conference on Computational Linguistics (COLING'02), Tapei, Taiwan (2002) 1208–1212
5. Daille, B.:. Conceptual Structuring through Term Variations. In Bond, F., Korhonen, A., MacCarthy, D., Villacicencio A., eds.: Proceedings of the ACL 2003 Workshop on Multiword Expressions: Analysis, Acquisition and Treatment (2003) 9–16
6. Daille, B.: Terminology Mining. In Pazienza, M., ed.: Information Extraction in the Web Era. Springer (2003) 29–44
7. Daille, B., Gaussier, E., Langé, J.-M..: Towards Automatic Extraction of Monolingual and Bilingual Terminology. Proceedings of the 15th International Conference on Computational Linguistics (COLING'94) **1** (1994) 515–521
8. Déjean, H., Sadat, F., Gaussier, E.: An approach based on multilingual thesauri and model combination for bilingual lexicon extraction. In: Proceedings of the 19th International Conference on Computational Linguistics (COLING'02). (2002) 218–224
9. Déjean, H., Gaussier, E.: Une nouvelle approche à l'extraction de lexiques bilingues à partir de corpus comparables. Lexicometrica, Alignement lexical dans les corpus multilingues (2002) 1–22
10. Fung, P.: A Statistical View on Bilingual Lexicon Extraction: From Parallel Corpora to Non-parallel Corpora. In Farwell, D., Gerber, L., Hovy, E., eds.: Proceedings of the 3rd Conference of the Association for Machine Translation in the Americas (AMTA'98), Springer (1998) 1–16

11. Gaussier, E., Langé, J.M.: Modèles statistiques pour l'extraction de lexiques bilingues. Traitement Automatique des Langues (TAL) **36** (1995) 133–155
12. Jacquemin, C.: Spotting and Discovering Terms through Natural Language Processing. Cambridge: MIT Press (2001)
13. Melamed, I.D.: Empirical Methods for Exploiting Parallel Texts. MIT Press (2001)
14. Rapp, R.: Automatic Identification of Word Translations from Unrelated English and German Corpora. In: Proceedings of the 37th Annual Meeting of the Association for Computational Linguistics (ACL'99). (1999) 519–526
15. Salton, G., Lesk, M.E.: Computer Evaluation of Indexing and Text Processing. Journal of the Association for Computational Machinery **15** (1968) 8–36
16. Tanimoto, T.T.: An elementary mathematical theory of classification. Technical report, IBM Research (1958)
17. Veronis, J., ed.: Parallel Text Processing. Kluwer Academic Publishers (2000)

A Twin-Candidate Model of Coreference Resolution with Non-Anaphor Identification Capability

Xiaofeng Yang[1,2], Jian Su[1], and Chew Lim Tan[2]

[1] Institute for Infocomm Research,
21, Heng Mui Keng Terrace, Singapore, 119613
{xiaofengy, sujian}@i2r.a-star.edu.sg
[2] Department of Computer Science,
National University of Singapore, Singapore, 117543
{yangxiao, tancl}@comp.nus.edu.sg

Abstract. Although effective for antecedent determination, the traditional twin-candidate model can not prevent the invalid resolution of non-anaphors without additional measures. In this paper we propose a modified learning framework for the twin-candidate model. In the new framework, we make use of non-anaphors to create a special class of training instances, which leads to a classifier capable of identifying the cases of non-anaphors during resolution. In this way, the twin-candidate model itself could avoid the resolution of non-anaphors, and thus could be directly deployed to coreference resolution. The evaluation done on newswire domain shows that the twin-candidate based system with our modified framework achieves better and more reliable performance than those with other solutions.

1 Introduction

In recent years supervised learning approaches have been widely used in coreference resolution task and achieved considerable success [1,2,3,4,5]. Most of these approaches adopt the single-candidate learning model, in which coreference relation is determined between a possible anaphor and one individual candidate at a time [1,3,4]. However, it has been claimed that the reference between an anaphor and its candidate is often subject to the other competing candidates [5]. Such information is nevertheless difficult to be captured in the single-candidate model. As an alternative, several researchers proposed a twin-candidate model [2,5,6]. Instead of directly determining coreference relations, this model would judge the preference between candidates and then select the most preferred one as the antecedent. The previous work has reported that such a model can effectively help antecedent determination for anaphors [5,6].

However, one problem exits with the twin-candidate model. For every encountered NP during resolution, the model would always pick out a "best" candidate as the antecedent, even if the current NP is not an anaphor. The twin-candidate

R. Dale et al. (Eds.): IJCNLP 2005, LNAI 3651, pp. 719–730, 2005.

model itself could not identify and block such invalid resolution of non-anaphors. Therefore, to apply such a model to coreference resolution, some additional efforts have to be required, e.g., using an anaphoricity determination module to eliminate non-anaphors in advance [5], or using threshold to prevent the selection of a candidate if the confidence it wins other competitors is low [6].

In this paper, we explore how to effectively apply the twin-candidate model to the coreference resolution task. We propose a modified learning framework with the capability of processing non-anaphors. In the framework, we make use of non-anaphors to create training instances. This special class of instances would enable the learned classifier to identify the test instances formed by non-anaphors during resolution. Thus, the resulting model could avoid resolving a non-anaphor to a non-existent antecedent by itself, without specifying a threshold or using an additional anaphoricity determination module. Our experiments on MUC data set systematically evaluated effectiveness of our modified learning framework. We found that with this new framework, the twin-candidate based system could not only outperform the single-candidate based one, but also achieve better and more reliable results than those twin-candidate based systems using the two mentioned solutions.

The rest of the paper is organized as follows. Section 2 describes the original framework of the twin-candidate model. Section 3 presents in details the modified framework, including the training and resolution procedures. Section 4 reports and discusses the experimental results and finally Section 6 gives the conclusions.

2 The Original Framework of the Twin-Candidate Model

The basic idea of the twin-candidate model is to learn a binary classifier which could judge the preference between candidates of an anaphor. In this section we will describe a general framework of such a model.

2.1 Instance Representation

In the twin-candidate model, an instance takes a form like $i\{C_1, C_2, M\}$, where M is a possible anaphor and C_1 and C_2 are two of its antecedent candidates. We stipulate that C_2 should be closer to M than C_1 in distance. An instance is labelled as "10" if C_1 is preferred to C_2 to be the antecedent, or "01" if otherwise.

A feature vector would be specified for an instance. The features may describe the lexical, syntactic, semantic and positional relationships between M and each one of the candidates, C_1 or C_2. In addition, inter-candidate features could be used to represent the relationships between the pair of candidates, e.g. the distance between C_1 and C_2 in position.

2.2 Training Procedure

For each anaphor M_{ana} in a given training text, its closet antecedent, C_{ante}, would be selected as the anchor candidate to compare with other candidates.

A set of "10" instances, $i\{C_{ante}, C_p, M_{ana}\}$, is generated by pairing M_{ana} and C_{ante}, as well as each of the interning candidates C_p. Also a set of "01" instances, $i\{C_a, C_{ante}, M_{ana}\}$, is created by pairing C_{ante} and each non-antecedental candidate C_a before C_{ante}.

Table 1. An example text

[$_1$ Globalstar] still needs to raise [$_2$ \$600 million], and [$_3$ Schwartz] said [$_4$ that company] would try to raise [$_5$ the money] in [$_6$ the debt market] .

Consider the example in Table 1. In the text segment, [$_4$ that company] and [$_5$ the money] are two anaphors with [$_1$ Globalstar] and [$_2$ \$600 million] being their antecedents respectively. Thus the training instances to be created for this text would be:

$i\{$[$_1$ Globalstar], [$_2$ \$600 million], [$_4$ that company]$\}$	:	10
$i\{$[$_1$ Globalstar], [$_3$ Schwartz], [$_4$ that company]$\}$	:	10
$i\{$[$_1$ Globalstar], [$_2$ \$600 million], [$_5$ the money]$\}$	:	01
$i\{$[$_2$ \$600 million], [$_3$ Schwartz], [$_5$ the money]$\}$	:	10
$i\{$[$_2$ \$600 million], [$_4$ that company], [$_5$ the money]$\}$	:	10

Based on the training instances, a classifier is trained using a certain machine learning algorithm. Given the feature vector of a test instance, the classifier would return "10" or "01" indicating which one of the two candidates under consideration is preferred.

2.3 Resolution

After the classifier is ready, it could be employed to select the antecedent for an encountered anaphor. The resolution algorithm is shown in Figure 1. In the algorithm, a round-robin model is employed, in which each candidate is compared with every other candidate and the final winner is determined by the won-lost records. The round-robin model would be fair for each competitor and the result is reliable to represent the rank of the candidates.

As described in the algorithm, after each match between two candidates, the record of the winning candidate (i.e., the one judged as preferred by the classifier) will increase and that of the loser will decrease. The algorithm simply uses a unit of one as the increment and decrement. Therefore, the final record of a candidate is its won-lost difference in the round-robin matches. Alternatively, we can use the confidence value returned by the classifier as the in(de)crement, while we found no much performance difference between these two recording strategies in experiments.

```
algorithm ANTE-SEL
input:
M: the anaphor to be resolved
candidate_set: the set of antecedent candidates of M,
{C1, C2, ..., Ck}

for i = 1 to K
    Score[ i ] = 0;
for j = K downto 2
    for i = j - 1 downto 1
        /*CR returns the classification result*/
        if CR(i{Ci, Cj, M}) ) = = 10 then
            Score[ i ]++;
            Score[ j ]−−;
        if CR(i{Ci, Cj, M}) ) = = 01 then
            Score[ i ]−−;
            Score[ j ]++;
SelectedIdx = arg_i max_{Ci∈candidate_set} Score[i];
return C_SelectedIdx
```

Fig. 1. The original antecedent selection algorithm

3 Modified Framework for Coreference Resolution Task

3.1 Non-anaphor Processing

In the task of coreference resolution, it is often that an encountered NP is non-anaphoric, that is, no antecedent exists among its possible candidates. However, the resolution algorithm described in the previous section would always try to pick out a "best" candidate as the antecedent for each given NP, and thus could not be applied for coreference resolution directly.

One natural solution to this is to use an anaphoricity determination (AD) module to identify the non-anaphoric NPs in advance (e.g. [5]). If an NP is judged as anaphoric, then we deploy the resolution algorithm to find its antecedent. Otherwise we just leave the NP unresolved. This solution, however, would heavily rely on the performance of the AD module. Unfortunately, the accuracy that most state-of-the-art AD systems could provide is still not high enough (around 80% as reported in [7]) for our coreference resolution task.

Another possible solution is to set a threshold to avoid selecting a candidate that wins with low confidence (e.g. [6]). Specifically, for two candidates in a match, we update their match records only if the confidence returned from the classifier is above the specified threshold. If no candidate has a positive record in the end, we deem the NP in question as non-anaphoric and leave it unresolved. In other words, a NP would be resolved to a candidate only if the candidate won at least one competitor with confidence above the threshold.

The assumption under this solution is that the classifier would return low confidence for the test instances formed by non-anaphors. Although it may be true, there exist other cases for which the classifier would also assign low confidence values, for example, when the two candidates of an anaphoric NP both have strong or weak preference. The solution of using threshold could not discriminate these different cases and thus may not be reliable for coreference resolution.

In fact, the above problem could be addressed if we could teach the classifier to explicitly identify the cases of non-anaphors, instead of using threshold implicitly. To do this, we need to provide a special set of instances formed by the non-anaphors to train the classifier. Given a test instance formed by a non-anaphor, the newly learned classifier is supposed to give a class label different from the instances formed by anaphors. This special label would indicate that the current NP is a non-anaphor, and no preference relationship is held between the two candidates under consideration. In this way, the twin-candidate model could do the anaphoricity determination by itself, without any additional pre-possessing module. We will describe the modified training and resolution procedures in the subsequent subsections.

3.2 Training

In the modified learning framework, an instance also takes a form like $i\{C_1, C_2, M\}$. During training, for an encountered anaphor, we create "01" or "10" training instances in the same way as in the original learning framework, while for a non-anaphor M_{non_ana}, we

- From the candidate set, randomly select a candidate C_{rand} as the anchor candidate.
- Create an instance by pairing M_{non_ana}, C_{rand}, and each of the candidates other than C_{rand}.

The above instances formed by non-anaphors would be labelled as "00". Note that an instance may have a form like $i\{C_a, C_{rand}, M_{non\_ana}\}$ if candidate C_a is preceding C_{rand}, or like $i\{C_{rand}, C_p, M_{non\_ana}\}$ if candidate C_p is following C_{rand}.

Consider the text in Table 1 again. For the non-anaphors [$_3$ Schwartz] and [$_6$ the debt market], supposing the selected anchor candidates are [$_1$ Globalstar] and [$_2$ \$600 million], respectively. The "00" instances generated for the text are:

i\{[$_1$ Globalstar], [$_2$ \$600 million], [$_3$ Schwartz]\} : 00
i\{[$_1$ Globalstar], [$_2$ \$600 million], [$_6$ the debt market]\} : 00
i\{[$_2$ \$600 million], [$_3$ Schwartz], [$_6$ the debt market]\} : 00
i\{[$_2$ \$600 million], [$_4$ that company], [$_6$ the debt market]\} : 00
i\{[$_2$ \$600 million], [$_5$ the money], [$_6$ the debt market]\} : 00

3.3 Resolution

The "00" training instances are used together with the "01" and "10" ones to train a classifier. The resolution procedure is described in Figure 2. Like in the original algorithm, each candidate is compared with every other candidate. The difference is that, if two candidates are judged as "00" in a match, both candidates would receive a penalty of -1 in their respective record; If no candidate has a positive final score, then the NP would be deemed as non-anaphoric and left unresolved. Otherwise, it would be resolved to the candidate with highest score as usual. In the case when an NP has only one antecedent candidate, a pseudo-instance is created by paring the candidate with itself. The NP would be resolved to the candidate if the return label is not "00".

Note that in the algorithm a threshold could still be used, for example, to update the match record only if the classification confidence is high enough.

```
algorithm ANTE-SEL
input:
M: the new NP to be resolved
candidate_set: the candidates set of M, {C1, C2, ..., Ck}
for i = 1 to K
    Score[ i ] = 0;
for j = K downto 2
    for i = j - 1 downto 1
        if CR(i{Ci, Cj, M}) ) = = 10 then
            Score[ i ]++;
            Score[ j ]−−;
        if CR(i{Ci, Cj, M}) ) = = 01 then
            Score[ i ]−−;
            Score[ j ]++;
        if CR(i{Ci, Cj, M}) ) = = 00 then
            Score[ i ]−−;
            Score[ j ]−−;

SelectedIdx = arg_i max_{Ci∈candidate_set} Score[i];
if (Score[SelectedIdx] <= 0)
    return nil;
return C_SelectedIdx;
```

Fig. 2. The new antecedent selection algorithm

4 Evaluation and Discussion

4.1 Experiment Setup

The experiments were done on the newswire domain, using MUC coreference data set (Wall Street Journal articles). For MUC-6 [8] and MUC-7 [9], 30 "dry-run" documents were used for training as well as 20-30 documents for testing. In addition, another 100 annotated documents from MUC-6 corpus were also prepared for the purpose of deeper system analysis. Throughout the experiments, C5 was used as the learning algorithm [10]. The recall and precision rates of the coreference resolution systems were calculated based on the scoring scheme proposed by Vilain et al. [11].

Table 2. Features for coreference resolution using the twin-candidate model

Feature	Description
Features describing the new markable M:	
1. M_DefNP	1 if M is a definite NP; else 0
2. M_IndefNP	1 if M is an indefinite NP; else 0
3. M_ProperNP	1 if M is a proper noun; else 0
4. M_Pronoun	1 if M is a pronoun; else 0
Features describing the candidate, C_1 or C_2, of M	
5. candi_DefNp_1(2)	1 if C_1 (C_2) is a definite NP; else 0
6. candi_IndefNp_1(2)	1 if C_1 (C_2) is an indefinite NP; else 0
7. candi_ProperNp_1(2)	1 if C_1 (C_2) is a proper noun; else 0
8. candi_Pronoun_1(2)	1 if C_1 (C_2) is a pronoun; else 0
Features describing the relationships between $C_1(C_2)$ and M :	
9. Appositive_1(2)	1 if C_1 (C_2) and M are in an appositive structure; else 0
10. NameAlias_1(2)	1 if C_1 (C_2) and M are in an alias of the other; else 0
11. GenderAgree_1(2)	1 if C_1 (C_2) and M agree in gender; else 0 if disagree; -1 if unknown
12. NumAgree_1(2)	1 if C_1 (C_2) and M agree in number; else 0 if disagree; -1 if unknown
13. SentDist_1(2)	Distance between C_1 (C_2) in sentences
14. HeadStrMatch_1(2)	1 if C_1 (C_2) and M match in head string; else 0
15. NPStrMatch_1(2)	1 if C_1 (C_2) and M match in full strings; else 0
16. StrSim_1(2)	The ratio of the common strings between C_1 (C_2) and M, over the strings of C_1 (C_2)
17. SemSim_1(2)	The semantic agreement of C_1 (C_2) against M in WordNet
Features describing the relationships between C_1 and C_2	
18. inter_SentDist	Distance between C_1 and C_2 in sentences
19. inter_StrSim	0, 1, 2 if $StrSim\_1(C_1, M)$ is equal to, larger or less than $StrSim\_1(C_2, M)$
20. inter_SemSim	0, 1, 2 if $SemSim\_1(C_1, M)$ is equal to, larger or less than $SemSim\_1(C_2, M)$

The candidates of a markable to be resolved were selected as follows. During training, for each encountered markable, the preceding markables in the current and previous four sentences were taken as the candidates. During resolution, for a non-pronoun, all the preceding markables were included into the candidate set, while for a pronoun, only the markables in the previous four sentences were used, as the antecedent of a pronoun usually occurs in a short distance.

For MUC-6 and MUC-7, our modified framework generated 207k training training instances, three times larger than the single-candidate based system by Soon et al [3]. Among them, the ratio of '00","01" and "10" instances was around 8:2:1. The distribution of the class labels was more balanced than in Soon et al.'s system, where only 5% training instances were positive while others were all negative.

In our study we only considered domain-independent features that could be obtained with low computational cost but with high reliability. Table 2 summarizes the features with their respective possible values. Features $f1$-$f17$ record the properties of a new markable and its two candidates, as well as their relationships. Most of these features could be found in previous systems on coreference resolution (e.g. [3], [4]). In addition, three inter-candidate features, $f18$-$f20$, mark the relationship between the two candidates. The first one, *inter_SentDist*, records the distance between the two candidates in sentences, while the latter two, *inter_StrSim* and *inter_SemSim* compare the similarity scores of the two candidates, in string-matching and semantics respectively.

To provide necessary information of feature computation, an input raw text was preprocessed automatically by a pipeline of NLP components. Among them, the chunking component was trained and tested for the shared task for CoNLL-2000 and achieved 92% F-score. The HMM based NE recognition component was capable of recognizing the MUC-style NEs with F-scores of 96.9% (MUC-6) and 94.3% (MUC-7).

4.2 Results and Discussion

In the experiment we compared four systems:

SC. The system based on the single-candidate model. It was a duplicate of the system by Soon et al. [3]. The feature set used in the baseline system was similar to those listed in Table 2, except that no inter-candidate feature would be used and only one set of features related to the single candidate was required.

TC_AD. The system based on the twin-candidate mode with the original learning framework, in which non-anaphors were eliminated by an anaphoricity determination module in advance. We built a supervised learning based AD module similar to the system proposed by Ng and Cardie [7]. We trained the AD classifier on the additional 100 MUC-6 documents. By adjusting the misclassification cost parameter of C5, we obtained a set of classifiers capable of identifying "positive" anaphors with variant recall and precision rates.

TC_THRESH. The system based on the twin-candidate mode with the original learning framework, using threshold to discard the low-confidenced comparison results between candidates.

TC_NEW. The system based on the twin-candidate mode, with our modified learning framework.

The results of the four systems on MUC-6 and MUC-7 are summarized in Table 3. In these experiments, five-fold cross-evaluation was performed on the training data to select the resolution parameters, for example, the threshold for systems TC_THRESH and TC_NEW, and final AD classifier for TC_AD.

As shown in the table, the baseline system SC achieves 66.1% and 65.9% F-measure for MUC-6 and MUC-7 data sets. This performance is better than that reported by Soon et al. [3], and is comparable to that of the state-of-the-art systems on the same data sets.

From the table we could find system TC_AD achieves a comparatively high precision but a low recall, resulting in a F-measure worse than that of SC. The analysis

Table 3. The performance of different coreference resolution systems

	30 Docs						100 Docs					
	MUC-6			MUC-7			MUC-6			MUC-7		
Experiments	R	P	F	R	P	F	R	P	F	R	P	F
SC	70.4	62.4	66.1	69.8	62.5	65.9	67.9	62.1	64.9	69.8	62.5	65.9
TC_AD	62.6	66.4	64.4	60.8	64.7	62.7	61.6	65.4	63.4	60.8	64.6	62.7
TC_THRESH	**70.7**	59.1	64.4	**70.0**	61.7	65.6	**71.0**	60.7	65.4	**70.6**	60.9	65.4
TC_NEW	64.8	**70.1**	**67.3**	66.0	**68.6**	**67.2**	67.0	**70.2**	**68.5**	67.0	**69.2**	**68.1**

of the AD classifier reveals that it successfully identifies 79.3% anaphors (79.48% precision) for MUC-6, and 70.9% anaphors (76.3% precision) for MUC-6. That means, although the pre-processing AD module could partly avoid the wrong resolution of a non-anaphor, it eliminates many anaphors at the same, which leads to the low recall for coreference resolution. Although in resolution different AD classifiers could be applied, we only observe the tradeoff between recall and precision, with no effective resolution improvement in F-measure.

In contrast to TC_AD, system TC_THRESH yields large gains in recall. The recall, up to above 70%, is higher than all the other three systems. However, the precision at the same time is unfortunately the lowest. Such a pattern of high recall and low precision indicates that using threshold could reduce, to some degree, the risk of eliminating true anaphors, but it would be too lenient to effectively block the resolution of non-anaphors.

Compared with TC_AD and TC_THRESH, TC_NEW produces large gains in the precision rates, which rank the highest among all the four systems. Although the recall also drops at the same time, the increase in the precision could compensate it well; we observe a F-measure of 67.3% for MUC-6 and 67.2% for MUC-7, significantly better ($p \leq 0.05$, by a sign test) than the other twin-candidate based systems. These results suggest that with our modified framework, the twin-candidate model could effectively identify non-anaphors and block their invalid resolution, without affecting the accuracy of the antecedent determination for anaphors.

In our experiment we were interested to evaluate the resolution performance of TC_NEW under different sizes of training data. For this purpose, we used the additional 100 annotated documents for training, and plotted the learning curve in Figure 3. The curve indicates that the system could perform well with a small number of training data, while the performance would get further improved with more training data (the best performance is obtained on 90 documents).

In Table 3, we also summarized the results of different systems trained on 100 documents. In contrast to TC_NEW, we find for system SC, there is no much performance difference between using 30 and 100 training documents. This is consistent with the report by Soon et al. [3] that the single-candidate model would achieve the peak performance with a moderate size of data. In the table we could also find that the performance improvement of TC_NEW against the other three systems is apparently larger on 100 training documents than on 30 documents.

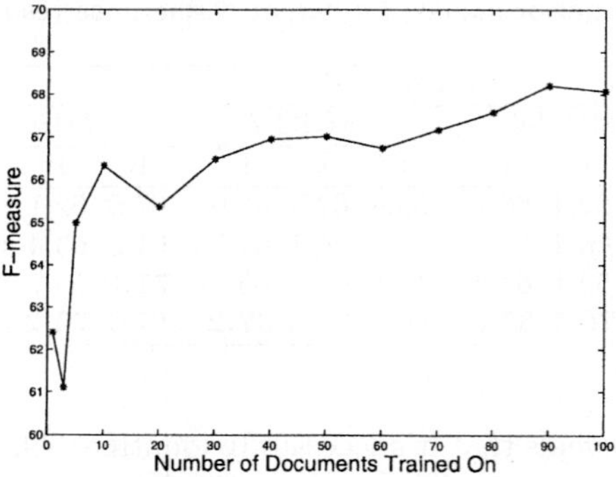

Fig. 3. Learning curve of system TC_NEW on MUC-7

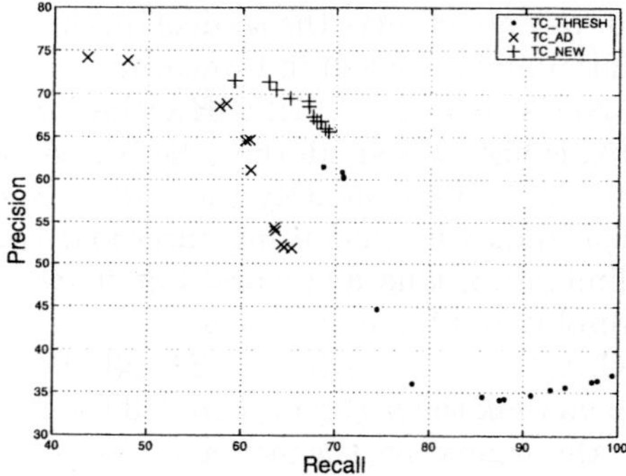

Fig. 4. Recall and precision results for the twin-candidate based systems

In Figure 4, we plotted the variant recall and precision scores that the three twin-candidate based systems were capable of producing when trained on 100 documents. (Here we only showed the results for MUC-7. Similar results could be obtained for MUC-6). In line with the results in Table 3, system TC_AD tends to obtain a high precision but low recall, while system TC_THRESH tends to obtain a high recall but low precision. Comparatively, system TC_NEW produces even recall and precision. For the range of recall within which the three systems coincide, TC_NEW yields higher precision than the other two systems. This figure further proves the effectiveness of our modified learning framework.

As mentioned, in systems TC_THRESH and TC_NEW the threshold parameter could be adjusted. It would be interesting to evaluate the influence of different thresholds on the resolution performance. In Figure 5 we compared the recall and precision of two systems, with thresholds ranging from 65 to 100.

In TC_THRESH, when the threshold is low, the recall is almost 100% while the precision is quite low. In such a case, all the markables, regardless anaphors or

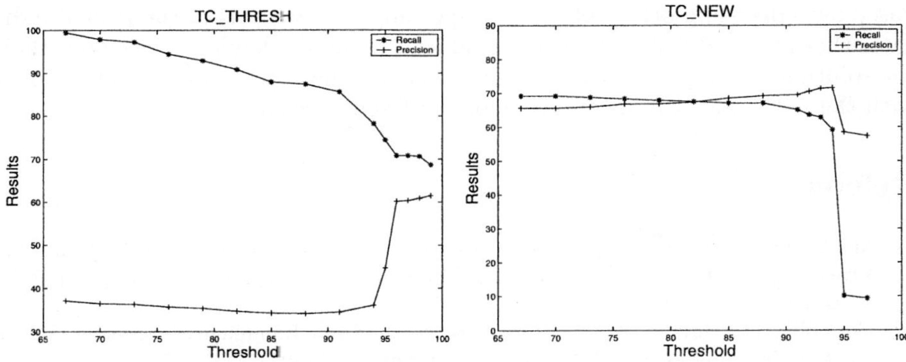

Fig. 5. Performance of TC_THRESH and TC_NEW under different thresholds

non-anaphors, will be resolved. As a consequence, all the occurring markables in a document tends to be linked together. In fact, the effective range of the threshold that leads to an acceptable performance is quite short. The threshold would only work when it is considerably high (above 95). Before that, the precision remains very low (less than 40%) while the recall keeps going down with the increase of the threshold.

By contrast, in TC_NEW, both the recall and precision vary little unless the threshold is extremely high. That means, the threshold would not impose much influence on the resolution performance of TC_NEW. This should be because in the modified framework, the cases of non-anaphors are determined by the special class label "00", instead of the threshold as in TC_THRESH. The purpose of using threshold in TC_NEW is not to identify the non-anaphors, but to improve the accuracy of class labelling. Indeed, we could obtain a good result without using any threshold in TC_NEW. These further confirm our claims that the modified learning framework could perform more reliably than the solution of using threshold.

5 Conclusions

In this paper we aimed to find an effective way to apply the twin-candidate model into coreference resolution task. We proposed a modified learning framework in which non-anaphors were utilized to create a special class of training instances. With such instances, the resulting classifier could avoid the invalid resolution of non-anaphors, which enables the twin-candidate model to be directly deployed to coreference resolution, without using an additional anaphoricity determination module or using a pre-defined threshold.

In the paper we evaluated the effectiveness of our modified framework on the MUC data set. The results show that the system with the new framework outperforms the single-candidate based system, as well as the twin-candidate based systems using other solutions. Especially, the analysis of the results indicates that our modified framework could lead to more reliable performance than the solution of using threshold. All these suggest that the twin-candidate model with the new framework is effective for coreference resolution.

References

1. McCarthy, J., Lehnert, Q.: Using decision trees for coreference resolution. In: Proceedings of the 14th International Conference on Artificial Intelligences. (1995) 1050–1055
2. Connolly, D., Burger, J., Day, D. New Methods in Language Processing. In: A machine learning approach to anaphoric reference. (1997) 133–144
3. Soon, W., Ng, H., Lim, D.: A machine learning approach to coreference resolution of noun phrases. Computational Linguistics **27** (2001) 521–544
4. Ng, V., Cardie, C.: Improving machine learning approaches to coreference resolution. In: Proceedings of the 40th Annual Meeting of the Association for Computational Linguistics, Philadelphia (2002) 104–111
5. Yang, X., Zhou, G., Su, J., Tan, C.: Coreference resolution using competition learning approach. In: Proceedings of the 41st Annual Meeting of the Association for Computational Linguistics, Japan (2003)
6. Iida, R., Inui, K., Takamura, H., Matsumoto, Y.: Incorporating contextual cues in trainable models for coreference resolution. In: Proceedings of the 10th Conference of EACL, Workshop "The Computational Treatment of Anaphora". (2003)
7. Ng, V., Cardie, C.: Identifying anaphoric and non-anaphoric noun phrases to improve coreference resolution. In: Proceedings of the 19th International Conference on Computational Linguistics (COLING02). (2002)
8. MUC-6: Proceedings of the Sixth Message Understanding Conference. Morgan Kaufmann Publishers, San Francisco, CA (1995)
9. MUC-7: Proceedings of the Seventh Message Understanding Conference. Morgan Kaufmann Publishers, San Francisco, CA (1998)
10. Quinlan, J.R.: C4.5: Programs for machine learning. Morgan Kaufmann Publishers, San Francisco, CA (1993)
11. Vilain, M., Burger, J., Aberdeen, J., Connolly, D., Hirschman, L.: A model-theoretic coreference scoring scheme. In: Proceedings of the Sixth Message understanding Conference (MUC-6), San Francisco, CA, Morgan Kaufmann Publishers (1995) 45–52

Improving Korean Speech Acts Analysis by Using Shrinkage and Discourse Stack

Kyungsun Kim[1], Youngjoong Ko[2], and Jungyun Seo[3]

[1] Information Retrieval Division, Diquest.Inc, Seocho-dong, Seocho-gu, Seoul, 137-070, Korea
kksun@diquest.com

[2] Dept. of Computer Engineering, Dong-A University, 840, Hadan 2-dong, Saha-gu, Busan, 604-714, Korea
yjko@dau.ac.kr

[3] Dept. of Computer Science and Interdisciplinary Program of Integrated Biotechnology, Sogang University, Seoul, 121-742, Korea
seojy@sogang.ac.kr

Abstract. A speech act is a linguistic action intended by a speaker. It is important to analyze the speech act for the dialogue understanding system because the speech act of an utterance is closely tied with the user's intention in the utterance. This paper proposes to use a speech acts hierarchy and a discourse stack for improving the accuracy of classifiers in speech acts analysis. We first adopt a hierarchical statistical technique called shrinkage to solve the data sparseness problem. In addition, we use a discourse stack in order to easily apply discourse structure information to the speech acts analysis. From the results of experiments, we observed that the proposed model made a significant improvement for Korean speech acts analysis. Moreover, we found that it can be more useful when training data is insufficient.

1 Introduction

To understand a natural language dialogue, a dialogue system must be able to make out the speaker's intentions indicated by utterances. Since the speech act of an utterance is very important in understanding a speaker's intentions, it is an essential part of a dialogue system. However, it is difficult to infer the speech act from a surface utterance because the utterance may represent more than one speech act according to the context [5][7].

Various machine learning models have been used to efficiently classify speech acts such as MEM (Maximum Entropy Model) [1], HMM (Hidden Markov Model) with Decision Tree [8][11], Neural Network Model [5]. And there are also studies on methods of automatically selecting efficient features with useful information for speech acts analysis [5][10]. Since the machine learning models can efficiently analyze a large quantity of data and consider many different feature interactions, they can provide a means of associating features of utterances with particular speech acts.

Generally, it is hard to create enough the number of examples for each speech act in the training examples. Thus this situation has been one of the main causes for errors occurred in speech acts analysis. That is, the sparse data problem from low

R. Dale et al. (Eds.): IJCNLP 2005, LNAI 3651, pp. 731 – 741, 2005.

frequency of some speech acts has commonly occurred in the previous research [8]. Due to the problem, the accuracy of each speech act in previous research tends to be proportional to the frequency of each speech act in the training data. Therefore, we first focus on how to scale up statistical learning methods to solve the sparseness problem of training data in speech acts analysis. Then we propose to construct the commonly-available hierarchies of speech acts and apply a well-understood technique from Statistics called shrinkage to our speech acts analysis system. It provides improved estimates of parameters that would otherwise be uncertain due to limited amounts of training data [3]. The technique uses a hierarchy to shrink parameter estimates in data sparse children toward the estimates of the data-rich ancestors in ways that are probably optimal under the appropriate conditions [9]. We employ a simple form of shrinkage that creates new parameter estimates for a child by a linear interpolation of all hierarchy nodes from the child to the root.

In addition, discourse structure information can be used to identify the speech acts of utterances [1]. But most previous research has used only speech acts of previous utterances without considering discourse structure information to determine the speech act of current utterance. Therefore, in order to use discourse structure information for analyzing speech acts, we design a simple discourse stack. By using the discourse stack, the discourse structure information is easily applied to speech acts analysis.

In this paper, we propose a new speech acts analysis model to improve the performance by using shrinkage and discourse structure information. From the results of experiments, the proposed system showed significant improvement in comparison with previous research.

The rest of this paper is organized as follows. Section 2 explains the proposed speech acts analysis system in detail. In section 3, we discuss the empirical results in our experiments. The final section presents conclusions.

2 The Proposed Speech Acts Analysis System

The proposed system consists of two modules as shown in Fig. 1: one module to extract features from training data and the other module to build up a hierarchy of

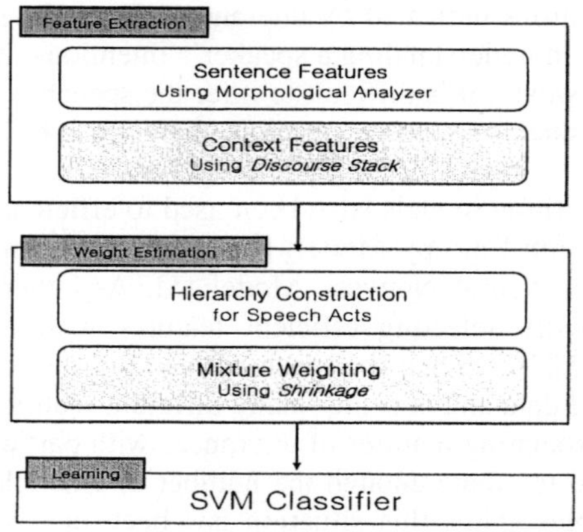

Fig. 1. The overview of the proposed system

speech acts and estimate weights of each feature on the hierarchy by shrinkage. Each process of Fig. 1 is explained in the following sections.

2.1 Feature Extraction

2.1.1 Sentence Features Extraction

We assume that clue words and a sequence of POS tags in an utterance provide very effective information for analyzing the speech act of the current utterance. We extract informative features for speech acts analysis using a Morphological analyzer; they are called the sentence features. The sentence features consist of content words annotated with POS tags and POS bi-grams of all words in an utterance. Fig. 2 shows an example of sentence feature extraction.

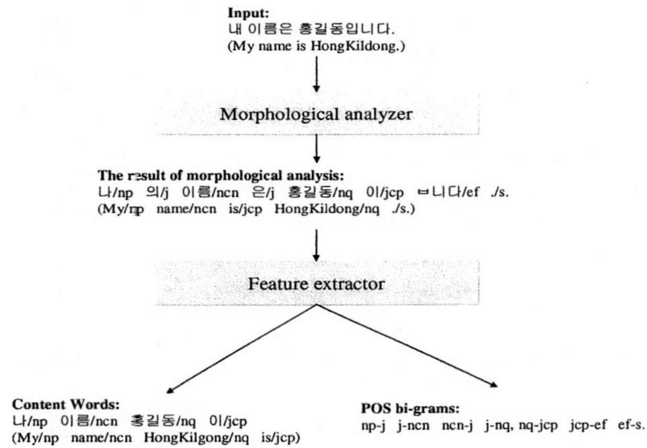

Fig. 2 An example of sentence feature extraction

```
For each utterance

Begin
   if(Move a sub-dialogue?)
        Use speech acts of previous utterance and Sub-dialogue Start (SS)
        Push speech acts of current utterance.
   else if(Return from a sub-dialogue?)
        Use speech acts that pop in discourse stack and Sub-dialogue End (SE)
   else
        Use speech acts of previous utterance and Dialogue Continue (DC)
End
```

2.1.2 Context Features Extraction

Most previous research uses the speech act of previous utterance as context feature (CF1 in Table 1) [5][8]. Since discourse structure information represents the relationship between two consecutive utterances, it is efficient to use discourse structure information for speech acts analysis [1]. Especially, the speech act of seventh utterance in Table 1 (UID: 7) is tied with that of second utterance (UID: 2). In our system, we first design a discourse stack to easily detect discourse structure information and extract the discourse structure information from the discourse stack for context features. Context features of our system consist of speech acts of previous utterance and markers of discourse structure information (CF2 in Table 1). An algorithm for discourse stack is described as the following:

Table 1. An example of Context Feature

UID	DS	Utterance	Speech Acts	CF1	CF2
1	1	방을 하나 예약하고 싶은데요 (I would like to reserve a room)	Inform	Dialog-start	Dialog-start, NULL
2	1.1	어떤 방을 원하시죠? (What kind of room do you want?)	Ask-ref	Inform	Inform, SS
3	1.1.1	어떤 종류의 방이 있습니까? (What kind of room do you have?)	Ask-ref	Ask-ref	Ask-ref, SS
4	1.1.1	더블룸과 싱글룸이 있습니다. (We have single and double rooms)	Response	Ask-ref	Ask-ref, DC
5	1.1.2	방값이 얼마죠? (How much are those rooms?)	Ask-ref	Re-sponse	Response, DC
6	1.1.2	싱글은 삼만원이고 더블은 사만원 입니다. (Singles cost 30,000 won and doubles cost 40,000 won.)	Response	Ask-ref	Ask-ref, DC
7	1.1	싱글룸으로 해주세요. (A single room, please)	Response	Re-sponse	Ask-ref, SE

* UID: ID of utterances, DS: Discourse Structure, CF1: Using speech acts of previous utterances as features (Context Feature Type1), CF2: Using Discourse Structure Information by Discourse Stack as features (Context Feature Type2), Speech acts and discourse structure information were annotated by human.

2.2 The Feature Weight Calculation by Shrinkage in a Hierarchy of Speech Acts

Data sparseness is a common problem in mechanical learning fields. For speech acts analysis, the problem becomes more serious because it is a time-consuming and difficult task to collect dialogue examples and construct dialogue training data tagged with a lot of information for various application areas. Therefore, we apply the shrinkage technique to solve this data sparseness problem in speech acts analysis. The shrinkage technique was verified in its efficiency for text classification tasks learned with insufficient training data. Therefore, we first build up a hierarchy of speech acts to estimate the weight of features for each speech act by the shrinkage technique.

2.2.1 The Hierarchy Construction for Speech Acts

To model a dialogue system, the dialogue grammar has commonly used and it has observed that dialogues consist of adjacency pairs of the types of utterances such as

Table 2. The Hierarchy of Speech Acts

	Parent	Child
Root	Type1: Utterances of request type	Ask-if
		Ask-ref
		Ask-confirm
		Offer
		Suggest
		Request
	Type2: Utterances of response type	Accept
		Response
		Reject
		Acknowledge
	Type3: Utterances with a speaker emotion	Expressive
		Promise
		Closing
	Type4: Utterances of usually life	Opening
		Introducing-oneself
		Correct
		Inform

request-type and response-type [2][8]. Therefore, our speech acts hierarchy is built up according to this grammar. Table 2 shows the structure of our speech acts hierarchy.

2.2.2 Mixture Weighting Model by Shrinkage in a Hierarchy of Speech Acts

The shrinkage technique estimates the probability of a word as the weighted sum of the maximum-likelihood estimates from leaf to root in a hierarchy [9]. This estimate process can give us a possibility to resolve the data sparseness problem in some speech acts with insufficient examples. Fig.3 shows that the shrinkage-based estimate of the probability of a feature ("나/np") given a speech act class ("Accept") is calculated from a weighted sum of the maximum-likelihood estimates from leaf to root.

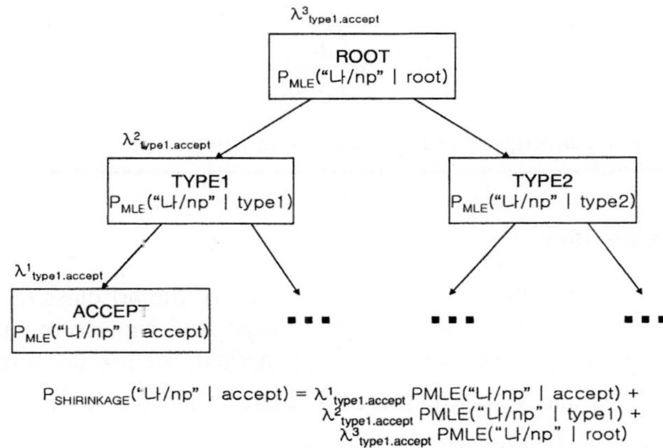

Fig. 3. An example of the shrinkage-based estimate of the probability of features

Let $\{\hat{\theta}_j^1, \hat{\theta}_j^2, ..., \hat{\theta}_j^k\}$ be k such estimates, where $\hat{\theta}_j^k = \theta_j$ is the estimate at the leaf, and k-1 is the depth of speech acts s_t in a hierarchy of Speech Acts. The interpolation weights among the ancestors of speech acts s_t are written $\{\lambda_j^1, \lambda_j^2, ..., \lambda_j^k\}$, where $\sum_{i=1}^{k} \lambda_j^i = 1$. We write $\breve{\theta}_j$ for the new estimate of the speech act-conditioned feature probabilities based on shrinkage. The new estimate for the probability of feature f_t given speech act s_j is as follows:

$$\breve{\theta}_{jt} = P(f_t | s_j; \breve{\theta}_j) = \lambda_j^1 \hat{\theta}_{jt}^1 + \lambda_j^2 \hat{\theta}_{jt}^1 + ... + \lambda_j^k \hat{\theta}_{jt}^1 . \tag{1}$$

We derive empirically optimal weights using the following iterative procedure:

Initialize:

Set the λ_j 's to some initial values, say $\lambda_j^i = \dfrac{1}{k}$

Iterate:

1. Calculate the degree to which each estimate predicts the features f_t in the held-out feature set, H_j, from speech acts s_j :

$$\beta_j^i = \sum_{w_t \in H_j} P(\hat{\theta}_j^i \text{ was used to generate } f_t) = \sum_{w_t \in H_j} \frac{\lambda_j^i \hat{\theta}_{jt}^i}{\sum_m \lambda_j^m \hat{\theta}_{jt}^m} \tag{2}$$

2. Compensate the degree for loss that is caused by large variation of each degree :

$$\beta_i^j = \beta_i^j + \frac{\sum_m \beta_j^m}{m} \tag{3}$$

3. Derive new weights by normalizing the β's :

$$\lambda_j^i = \frac{\beta_j^i}{\sum_m \beta_j^m} \tag{4}$$

Terminate: Upon convergence of the likelihood function

2.3 The SVM Classifier

Support Vector Machines (SVM) is one of the state-of-the-art classifiers for classification tasks [6][12]. Since SVM has shown the high performance in various research areas, we also employ it in our method. In our method, we use the linear models offered by SVM^{light} [4] and $\breve{\theta}_{jt}$, which are calculated by formula (1), are used as the feature weights of speech acts for the SVM classifier.

Table 3. The part of mixture weights learned by shrinkage-based estimation

# training documents	Speech Acts			Mixture Weights		
	Root	Parent	Child	Root	Parent	Child
250	Root	Type1	Ask-ref	0.289	0.32	0.39
			Suggest	0.257	0.275	0.467
		Type2	Expressive	0.263	0.335	0.4
		Type3	Reject	0.259	0.269	0.47
		Type4	Inform	0.297	0.336	0.366
8349	Root	Type1	Ask-ref	0.282	0.295	0.422
			Suggest	0.217	0.22	0.562
		Type2	Expressive	0.229	0.279	0.49
		Type3	Reject	0.212	0.215	0.571
		Type4	Inform	0.26	0.332	0.406

3 Empirical Evaluation

3.1 Experimental Data

We used the Korean dialogue corpus which has used in previous research [1][5][8]. This corpus was transcribed from recordings in real fields such as hotel reservation, airline reservation and tour reservation and consists of 528 dialogues, 10,285 utterances (19.48 utterances per dialogue). Each utterance in dialogues is manually annotated with a speaker (SP), a speech act (SA) and a discourse structure (DS). This annotated dialogue corpus has 17 types of speech acts. Table 4 shows a part of the annotated dialog corpus and Table 5 shows the distribution of speech acts in the annotated dialogue corpus.

Table 4. A part of the annotated dialogue corpus

Tag	Values
SP	Customer
KS	미국 조지아대 어학연수에 참가 신청을 한 학생인데요.
EN	I'm a student and registered for a language course at University of Georgia in U.S.
SA	Introducing-oneself
DS	[2]
SP	Customer
KS	숙소에 관해서 문의할 사항이 있어서요.
EN	I have some questions about lodgings.
SA	Request
DS	[2]

Table 5. The distribution of speech acts in corpus

Speech act type	Ratio (%)	Speech act type	Ratio (%)
Accept	2.49	Introducing-oneself	6.75
Acknowledge	5.75	Offer	0.4
Ask-confirm	3.16	Opening	6.58
Ask-if	5.36	Promise	2.42
Ask-ref	13.39	Reject	1.07
Closing	3.39	Request	4.96
Correct	0.03	Response	24.73
Expressive	5.64	Suggest	1.98
Inform	11.9	Total	100

We divided the annotated dialogue corpus into the training data with 428 dialogues, 8,349 utterances (19.51 utterances per dialogue), and the testing data with 100 dialogues, 1,936 utterances (19.36 utterances per dialogue).

3.2 Primary Experimental Results

3.2.1 The Performances of Speech Acts Analysis Model Using Shrinkage and Discourse Stack

In order to verify the proposed method, we made four kinds of speech acts analysis systems which use different kind of features. The Baseline System used default features such as sentence features and context features [5]. The Second system (Type 1) was built up to verify the shrinkage technique. Its features were the same as those of the first system but they were weighted by the shrinkage technique. The third System (Type 2) used the discourse structure information from the proposed discourse stack without shrinkage. Finally, the fourth system (Type 3) combined the discourse structure information and the shrinkage technique.

Table 6 shows the results of four speech acts analysis systems. As shown in Table 6, the performances of the proposed systems (Type 1,2,3) are better than the baseline system. The proposed system of Type 3 reported the best performance.

3.2.2 The Improvement of the Proposed System Using the Shrinkage Technique in Sparse Data

Here, we verify the facts that the shrinkage technique can improve the speech acts analysis when training data is sparse. We first compare the system with shrinkage (Type 3) and the system without shrinkage (Type 2). Fig. 4 shows the changes of performance in each number of training data from 250 to 8439. The proposed system with shrinkage obtains the better performance over all intervals in Fig. 4. Especially, the shrinkage technique provides more improvement when the amount of training data is small. This is a proof that the shrinkage technique can become an effective solution for sparse data problem from insufficient training data.

Table 6. The results of four speech acts analysis systems (precision %)

Speech acts	Baseline System	Proposed System (Type1)	Proposed System (Type2)	Proposed System (Type3)
Accept	36.00%	50.00%	38.00%	50.00%
Acknowledge	91.30%	91.30%	92.75%	95.65%
ask-confirm	92.68%	96.34%	93.90%	95.12%
ask-if	84.16%	86.14%	86.14%	89.11%
ask-ref	89.88%	91.05%	90.66%	91.44%
Closing	60.00%	61.43%	67.14%	71.43%
Correct	0.00%	0.00%	0.00%	0.00%
Expressive	85.84%	83.19%	87.61%	83.19%
Inform	70.00%	70.00%	76.00%	75.60%
Introducing-oneself	98.58%	98.58%	97.87%	98.58%
Offer	12.50%	12.50%	12.50%	12.50%
Opening	97.60%	96.80%	96.80%	96.80%
Promise	92.50%	92.50%	87.50%	90.00%
Reject	68.18%	72.73%	68.18%	68.18%
Request	71.43%	73.81%	70.24%	69.05%
Response	96.49%	96.07%	96.07%	96.07%
Suggest	56.76%	56.76%	56.76%	62.16%
TOTAL	85.18%	85.85%	86.31%	87.04%

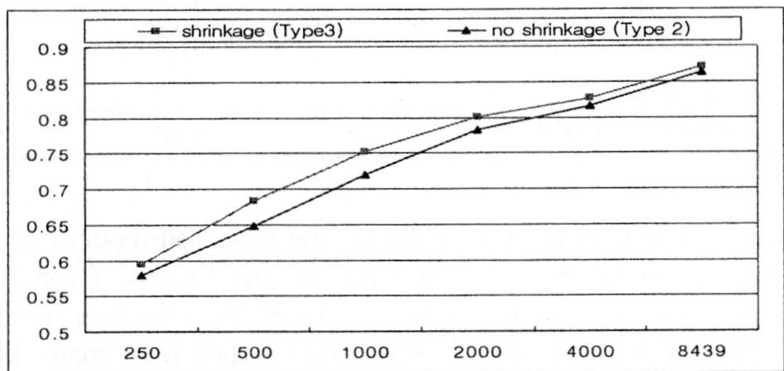

Fig. 4. The performance according to different number of training data

We then compare performances between the system of Type 2 and the system of Type 3 according to distribution of each speech act. As shown in Fig. 5, the proposed system (Type 3) with the shrinkage technique shows higher performance in speech acts with insufficient examples such as ‘Accept’, ‘Closing’, ‘Promise’ and ‘Suggest’.

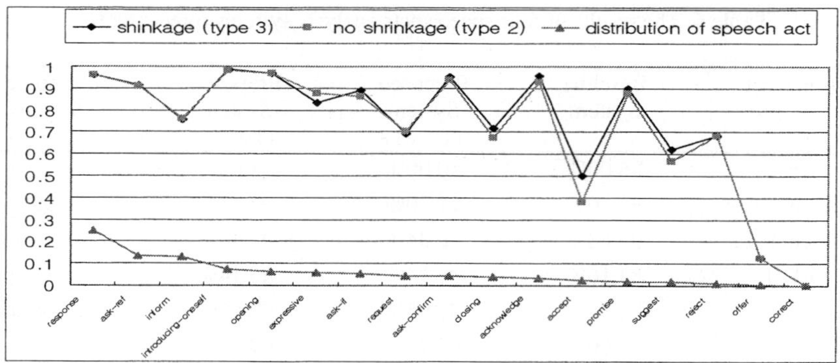

Fig. 5. The comparison of the performances for the shrinkage technique according to the distribution of speech acts

3.2.3 The Comparison of Performance with Other Speech Acts Analysis Models

Table 7 shows results from the proposed model and previous speech acts analysis models: the maximum entropy model (MEM) [1], the decision tree model (DTM) [8], and the neural network model (NNM) [5]. We report the performance of each system when using the same test data set as that of this paper. As a result, the proposed model achieved the highest performance.

Table 7. The experimental results of the proposed model and other previous models

Model	Precision (%)
MEM	83.4%
DTM	81.7%
NNM	85.2%
The propose model	87.0%

In the experiment, it is difficult to compare the proposed model directly with the other models because input features are different respectively. Even though direct comparisons are impossible, we think that the proposed model is more robust and efficient than MEM and DTM. In MEM and DTM, they used many kinds of high level linguistic knowledge than ours such as sentence type, tense, modality and so on. Nevertheless, the performances of them are lower than that of the proposed model. Moreover, the proposed model is more effective than NNM because the performance of the proposed model is better than that of NNM in spite of using same features.

4 Conclusions

In this paper, we proposed the new speech analysis model to improve speech acts analysis by using the shrinkage technique and the discourse stack. We first made a hierarchy of speech acts by dialogue grammar for shrinkage and then estimate the probability of each feature on the hierarchy by the shrinkage technique. In experimental results, the proposed model is more effective for classifying speech acts. Especially, the shrinkage technique achieved more improvement when training data is sparse. Therefore, the shrinkage technique can be applied to the real applications that suffer from the data sparseness problem. We also proposed to use the discourse stack for easily extracting discourse structure information. As a result, the proposed model with shrinkage and the discourse stack showed the better performance than other speech acts analysis models.

Acknowledgement

This research was supported as a Brain Neuroinformatics Research Program sponsored by the Ministry of Commerce, Industry and Energy of Korea.

References

1. Choi, W., Cho, J. and Seo, J.: Analysis System of speech acts and Discourse Structures Using Maximum Entropy Model, In Proceedings of COLING-ACL99, (1999), 230-237
2. Grosz, B.: Discourse and Dialogue, In Survey of the State of the Art in Human Language Technology, Center for Spoken Language Understanding, (1995), 227-254
3. James, W. and Stein, C.: Estimation with Quadratic Loss, In Proceedings of the Fourth Berkeley Symposium on Mathematical Statistics and Probability 1, University of California Press, 361-379
4. Joachims, T.: Text Categorization with Support Vector Machines: Learning with Many Relevant Features. In European conference on machine learning (ECML), (1998), 137-142
5. Kim, K., Kim, H. and Seo, J.: A Neural Network Model with Feature Selection for Korean Speech Act Classification, International Journal of Neural System, VOL. 14 NO. 6, (2004), 407-414
6. Ko, Y., Park, J, Seo, J.: Improving Text Categorization Using the Importance of Sentences, Information Processing & Management, Vol. 40, No. 1, (2004), 65-79
7. Lee, J., Kim, G., and Seo, J.: A Dialogue Analysis Model with Statistical Speech Act Processing for Dialogue Machine Translation, In Proceedings of ACL Workshop on Spoken Language Translation, (1997), 10-15
8. Lee, S. and Seo, J.: A Korean Speech Act Analysis System Using Hidden Markov Model with Decision Trees, International Journal of Computer Processing of Oriental Languages. VOL. 15, NO. 3, (2002), 231-243
9. MacCallum, A., Rosenfeld, R., Mitchell, T. and Ng, A.Y.: Improving Text Classification by Shrinkge in a Hierarchy of Classes, In Proceedings of the International Conference on Machine Learning. (1998)
10. Samuel, K., Caberry, S., and Vijay-Shanker, K.: Automatically Selecting Useful Phrases for Dialogue Act Tagging, In Proceedings of the Fourth Conference of the Pacific Association for Computational Linguistics, (1999)
11. Tanaka, H. and Yokoo, A.: An Efficient Statistical Speech Act Type Tagging System for Speech Translation Systems, In Proceedings of COLING-ACL99, (1999), 381-388
12. Vapnik, V.: The Nature of Statistical Learning Theory, Springer Verlag, New York, (1995)

Anaphora Resolution for Biomedical Literature by Exploiting Multiple Resources

Tyne Liang and Yu-Hsiang Lin

National Chiao Tung University, Department of Computer and Information Science, Hsinchu, Taiwan 300, ROC
{tliang, gis91534}@cis.nctu.edu.tw

Abstract. In this paper, a resolution system is presented to tackle nominal and pronominal anaphora in biomedical literature by using rich set of syntactic and semantic features. Unlike previous researches, the verification of semantic association between anaphors and their antecedents is facilitated by exploiting more outer resources, including UMLS, WordNet, GENIA Corpus 3.02p and PubMed. Moreover, the resolution is implemented with a genetic algorithm on its feature selection. Experimental results on different biomedical corpora showed that such approach could achieve promising results on resolving the two common types of anaphora.

1 Introduction

Correct identification of antecedents for an anaphor is essential in message understanding systems as well as knowledge acquisition systems. For example, efficient anaphora resolution is needed to enhance protein interaction extraction from biomedical literature by mining more protein entity instances which are represented with pronouns or general concepts.

In biomedical literature, pronominal and nominal anaphora are the two common types of anaphora. In past literature, different strategies to identify antecedents of an anaphor have been presented by using syntactic, semantic and pragmatic clues. For example, grammatical roles of noun phrases were used in [9] [10]. In addition to the syntactic information, statistical information like co-occurring patterns obtained from a corpus is employed during antecedent finding in [3]. However, a large corpus is needed for acquiring sufficient co-occurring patterns and for dealing with data sparseness.

On the other hand, outer resources, like WordNet[1], are applied in [4][12][15] and proved to be helpful to improve the system like the one described in [12] where animacy information is exploited by analyzing the hierarchical relation of nouns and verbs in the surrounding context learned from WordNet. Nevertheless, using WordNet alone for acquiring semantic information is not sufficient for solving unknown words. To tackle this problem, a richer resource, the Web, was exploited in [16]

[1] http://wordnet.princeton.edu/

R. Dale et al. (Eds.): IJCNLP 2005, LNAI 3651, pp. 742 – 753, 2005.

where anaphoric information is mined from Google search results at the expense of less precision.

The domain-specific ontologies like UMLS[2] (Unified Medical Language System) has been employed in [2] in such a way that frequent semantic types associated to agent (subject) and patient (object) role of subject-action or action-object patterns can be extracted. The result showed such kind of patterns could gain increase in both precision (76% to 80%) and recall (67% to 71%). On the other hand, Kim and Park [11] built their BioAR to relate protein names to SWISS-Prot entries by using the centering theory presented by [7] and salience measures by [2].

In this paper, a resolution system is presented for tackling both nominal anaphora and pronominal anaphora in biomedical literature by using various kinds of syntactic and semantic features. Unlike previous approaches, our verification of the semantic association between anaphors and their antecedents is facilitated with the help of both general domain and domain-specific resources. For example, the semantic type checking for resolving nominal anaphora can be done by the domain ontology UMLS and PubMed[3], the search engine for MEDLINE databases. Here, UMLS is used not only for tagging the semantic type for the noun phrase chunks if they are in UMLS, but also for generating the key lexicons for each type so that we can use them to tag those chunks if they are not in UMLS. If no type information can be obtained from an chunk, then its type finding will be implemented through the web mining of PubMed. On the other hand, the domain corpus, GENIA 3.02p corpus [20] is exploited while we solve the semantic type checking for pronominal anaphora. With simple weight calculation, the key SA/AO (subject-action or action-object) patterns for each type can be mined from the corpus and they turn out to be helpful in resolution. Beside the semantic type agreement, the implicit resemblance between an anaphor and its antecedents is another evidence useful for verifying the semantic association. Hence, the general domain thesaurus, WordNet, which supporting more relationship between concepts and subconcepts, is also employed to enhance the resemblance extraction.

The presented resolution system is constructed on a basis of a salience grading. In order to boost the system, we implemented a simple genetic algorithm on its selection of the rich feature set. The system was developed on the small evaluation corpus MedStract[4]. Nevertheless, we constructed a larger test corpus (denoted as '100-MEDLINE') so that more instances of anaphors can be resolved. Experimental results show that our resolution on MedStract can yield 92% and 78% F-Scores on resolving pronominal and nominal anaphora respectively. Promising results were also obtained on the larger corpus in terms of 87.43% and 80.61% F-scores on resloving pronominal and nominal anaphora respectively.

2 Anaphora Resolution

Figure 1 is the overview of the presented architecture, including the extraction of biomedical SA/AO patterns and semantic type lexicons in background processing

[2] http://www.nlm.nih.gov/research/umls/
[3] http://www.pubmedcentral.nih.gov/
[4] http://www.medstract.org/

(indicated with dotted lines), as well as the document processing, anaphor recognition and antecedent selection in foreground processing (indicated with solid lines).

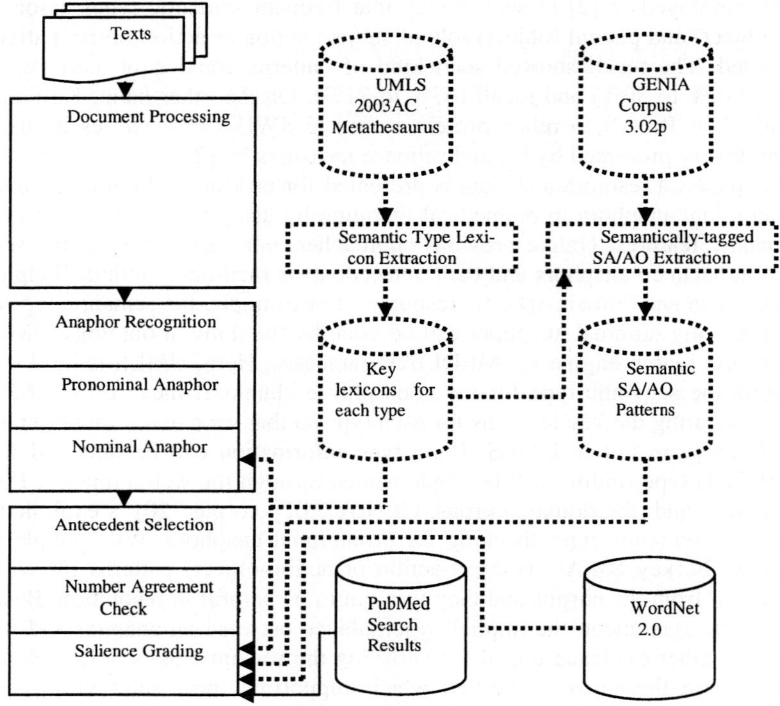

Fig. 1. System architecture overview

2.1 Syntactic Information Extraction

Being important features for anaphora resolution, syntactic information, like POS tags and base NP chunks, is extracted from each document by using the Tagger[5]. Meanwhile, each NP will be tagged with its grammatical role, namely, 'Oblique', 'Direct object', 'Indirect object', or 'Subject' by using the following rules which were adopted from [22] by adding rules 5 and 6.

Rule1:	Prep NP (Oblique)
Rule2:	Verb NP (Direct object)
Rule3:	Verb $[NP]^+$ NP (Indirect object)
Rule4:	NP (Subject) [",[^Verb], "|Prep NP]* Verb
Rule5:	NP1 Conjunction NP2 (Role is same as NP1) Conjunction]
Rule6:	[Conjunction] NP1 (Role is same as NP2) Conjunction NP2

[5] http://tamas.nlm.nih.gov/tagger.html

Rules 5 and 6 are presented for dealing those plural anaphors in such a way that the syntactic agreement between the first antecedent and its anaphora is used to find other antecedents. For example, without rules 5 and 6, 'anti-CD4 mAb' in Example 1 will not be found when resolving anaphora 'they'.

> Example1: "Whereas different anti-CD4 mAb or HIV-1 gp120 could all trigger activation of the ..., they differed..."

2.2 Semantic Information Extraction

Beside the syntactic clues, the semantic agreement between an anaphor and its antecedents can also facilitate anaphora resolution in domain-specific literature. In this paper, the semantic information for each target noun phrase chunk can be extracted with the help of the domain ontology, UMLS, which supports the semantic type for the chunk. However, the semantic types for those chunks which are not in UMLS are needed to be predicted. Therefore we need to extract the key lexicons from UMLS for each semantic type in background processing and use them to tag unknown chunk with predicted types. On the other hand, the semantic type checking for pronominal anaphors is done through the extraction of the key verbs for each semantic type. Hence, a domain corpus GENIA 3.02p is exploited in background processing.

2.2.1 Key Lexicons for Each Semantic Type

For each UMLS semantic type, its key lexicons are mined as the following steps in Figure 2:

A. Collect all UMLS concepts and their corresponding synonyms as type lexicon candidates.

B. Tokenize the candidates. For example, concept 'interleukin-2' has synonyms 'Costimulator', 'Co-Simulator', 'IL 2', and 'interleukine 2'. Then 'interleukin', 'costimulator', 'simulator', 'IL', and 'interleukine' will be treated as lexicon candidates.

C. For each candidate, calculate its weight w_{ij} for each type by using Eq. (1) which takes into account its concentration and distribution. A predefined threshold is given for the final selection of the candidates.

$$w_{i,j} = \frac{w_i}{Max\ c_j} \times \frac{1}{tw_i} \quad (1)$$

$w_{i,j}$:	score of word i in semantic type j
w_i :	count of word i in semantic type j
Max c_j :	Max count of word k in semantic type j
tw_i :	count of semantic types that word i occurs in

Fig. 2. Procedure to mine key lexicons for each semantic type

2.2.2 Semantic SA/AO Patterns

As indicated previously in Section 2.2, the semantic type checking for pronominal anaphors can be done through the extraction of the co-occurring SA/AO patterns extracted from GENIA 3.02p. We tagged each base noun phrase chunk from the corpus with its grammatical role and tagged it with UMLS-semantic type. Then we used Eq. 2 to score each pattern. At resolution, an antecedent candidate is concerned if its scores are greater than a given threshold. Table 1 is an example to show the key lexicons and verbs for two semantic types when the semantically-typed chunk is tagged with the role of subject.

$$score(type_i, verb_j) = \frac{frequency(type_i, verb_j)}{frequency(verb_j)} \times \frac{1}{No.\ of\ types(verb_j)} \tag{2}$$

Table 1. Some key lexicons and verbs for two semantic types

Semantic types	key lexicons for each type	key verbs for each type
Amino Acid, Peptide, or Protein	protein, product, cerevisiae, endonuclease, kinase, antigen, receptor, synthase, reductase, arabidopsis	bind, function, derive, raise, attenuate, abolish, present, signal, localize, release
Gene or Genome	gene, oncogenes	activate, compare, locate, regulate, remain, transcribe, encode, distribute, indicate, occupy

2.3 Anaphora Recognition

Anaphor recognition is to recognize the target anaphors by filtering strategies. Pronominal anaphora recognition is done by filtering pleonastic-it instances by using the set of hand-craft rules presented in [12]. On two corpora, namely, Medstract and the new 100-Medline corpus, 100% recognition accuracy was achieved. The remaining noun phrases indicated with 'it', 'its', 'itself', 'they', 'them', 'themselves' or 'their' are considered as pronominal anaphor. Others like 'which' and 'that' used in relative clauses are treated as pronominal anaphors and are resolved by the following rules.

Rule 1: 'that' is treated as pleonastic-that if it is paired with pleonastic-it.
Rule 2: For a relative clause with 'which' or 'that', the antecedents will be the noun phrases preceding to 'which' or 'that'.

On the other hand, noun phrases shown with 'either', 'this', 'both', 'these', 'the', and 'each' are considered as nominal anaphor candidates. Nominal anaphora recognition is approached by filtering those anaphor candidates, which have no referent antecedents or which have antecedents but not in the target biomedical semantic types. Following are two rules used to filter out those non-target nominal anaphors.

Rule 1: Filter out those anaphor candidates if they are not tagged with one of the target UMLS semantic types (the same types in [2])
Rule 2: Filter out 'this' or 'the' + proper nouns with capital letters or numbers.

We treated all other anaphors indicated with 'this' or 'the + singular-NP' as singular anaphors which have one antecedent only. Others are treated as plural nominal anaphors and their numbers of antecedents are shown in Table 2. At antecedent selection, we can discard those candidates whose numbers differ from the corresponding anaphors.

Table 2. Number of Antecedents

Anaphor	Antecedents #
Either	2
Both	2
Each	Many
They, Their, Them, Themselves	Many
The +Number+ noun	Number
Those +Number+ noun	Number
These +Number+ noun	Number

2.4 Antecedent Selection

2.4.1 Salience Grading

The antecedent selection is based on the salience grading as shown in Table 3 in which seven features, including syntactic and semantic information, are concerned.

Table 3. Salience grading for candidate antecedents

Features		Score
F1	recency 0, if in two sentences away from anaphor 1, if in one sentence away from anaphor 2, if in same sentence as anaphor	0-2
F2	Subject and Object Preference	1
F3	Grammatical function agreement	1
F4	Number Agreement	1
F5	Semantic Longest Common Subsequence	0 to 3
F6	Semantic Type Agreement	-1 to +2
F7	Biomedical antecedent preference	-2 if not or +2

The first feature *F1* is recency which measures the distance between an anaphor and candidate antecedents in number of sentences. From the statistics of the two corpora, most of antecedents and their corresponding anaphors are within in two sentence distance, so a window size for finding antecedent candidates is set to be two sentences in the proposed system. The second feature *F2* concerns the grammatical roles that an anaphor plays in a sentence. Since many anaphors are subjects or objects so antecedents with such grammatical tags are preferred. Furthermore, the antecedent candidates will receive more scores if they have grammatical roles (feature *F3*) or number agreement (feature *F4*) with their anaphors.

On the other hand, features *5, 6,* and *7* are related to semantic association. Feature *5* concerns the fact that the anaphor and its antecedents are semantical variants of each other, so antecedents will receive different scores (as shown below) on the basis of their variation:

If there is total match of the semantic lexicons between an antecedent's head word and its anaphor
Then salience score = salience score + 3
Else If any antecedent component, other than head word, is matched with its anaphor
Then salience score = salience score + 2
Else If any antecedent component is matched with its anaphor's hyponym by WordNet 2.0
Then salience score = salience score + 1

Following are examples to show the cases:

Example 2
case 1: total match:
<anaphor: each *inhibitor*, antecedent: PAH alkyne metabolism-based *inhibitors*>
case 2: partial match:
<Anaphor: both *receptor types*, antecedent: the ETB *receptor* antagonist BQ788>
case 3: component match by using WordNet 2.0:
<Anaphor: this protein (hyponym: growth *factor*), antecedent: Cleavage and polyadenylation specificity *factor*>

If the antecedent can be found by UMLS,
Then record its semantic types;
Else If the antecedent contains the mined key lexicons of the anaphor's semantic type, then record the semantic type;
Else mine the semantic type by web mining in such a way that searching PubMed by issuing {anaphor *Ana*, antecedent A_i } pair and applying Eq. 3 to grade its semantic agreement for A_i.

$$Score(A_i) = Score(A_i) - 1 + \left[\frac{\#of\ pages\ containing(Ana, A_i)}{\#of\ pages\ containing(A_i)} \times 10 \right] \times 0.3 \quad (3)$$

Fig. 3. Procedure to find semantic types for antecedent candidates

Feature 6 is the semantic type agreement between anaphors and antecedents. As described in figure 3, the type finding for each antecedent can implemented with the help of UMLS. When there is no type information can be obtained from an antecedent, the type finding can be implemented with the help of PubMed, and the grading on such antecedent will be as Eq. 3. Feature 7 is biomedical antecedent preference. That is an antecedent which can be tagged with UMLS or the key lexicons database will receive more score.

2.4.2 Antecedent Selection Strategies

The noun phrases which precede a recognized anaphor in the range of two sentences will be treated as candidates and will be assigned with zero at initial state by the presented salience grader. Antecedents can be selected by the following strategies.

(1) Best First: select antecedents with the highest salience score that is greater than a threshold

(2) Nearest First: select the nearest antecedents whose salience value is greater than a given threshold

For plural anaphors, their antecedents are selected as follows:

(1) If the number of the antecedents is known, then select the same number of top-score antecedents.

(2) If the number of antecedents is unknown, then select those antecedent candidates whose scores are greater than a threshold and whose grammatical patterns are the same as the top-score candidate.

2.5 Experiments and Analysis

As mentioned in previous sections, a larger corpus was used for testing the proposed system. The corpus, denoted as '100-Medline', contains 100 MEDLINE abstracts including 43 abstracts (denoted as '43-Genia' in Table 6) randomly selected from GENIA 3.02p and another 57 abstracts (denoted as '57-PubMed' in Table 6) collected from the search results of PubMed (by issuing 'these proteins' and 'these receptors' in order to acquire more anaphor instances). There is no common abstract in the public MedStract and the new corpus. Table 4 shows the statistics of pronominal and nominal anaphors for each corpus.

Table 4. Statistics of anaphor and antecedent pairs

	Abstracts	Sentences	Pronominal instances	Nominal instances	Total
MedStract	32	268	26	47	73
43-GENIA	43	479	98	63	161
57-PubMed	57	565	69	118	187

The proposed approach was verified with experiments in two ways. One is to investigate the impact of the features which are concerned in the resolution. Another is to compare different resolution approaches. In order to boost our system, a simple generic algorithm is implemented to yield the best set of features by choosing best parents to produce offspring.

In the initial state, we chose features (10 chromosomes), and chose crossover feature to produce offspring randomly. We calculated mutations for each feature in each chromosome, and evaluated chromosome with maximal F-Score. Top 10 chromosomes were chosen for next generation and the algorithm terminated if two contiguous generations did not increase the F-score. The time complexity associated with such approach is *O(MN)* where *M* is the number of candidate antecedents, *N* is number of anaphors.

Table 5. F-Score of Medstract and 100-Medlines

	Medstract						100-Medlines					
	Nominal			Pronominal			Nominal			Pronominal		
	P	R	F	P	R	F	P	R	F	P	R	F
Total	33/56	33/47		23/26	23/26		130/184	130/178		145/167	145/167	
Features	58.93	70.21	64.08	88.46	88.46	88.46	70.65	73.34	71.33	86.82	86.82	86.82
	F5, F6, F7			All-F5			F5, F6, F7			All-F5		
	P	R	F	P	R	F	P	R	F	P	R	F
Genetic	37/47	37/47		24/26	24/26		156/212	156/178		146/167	146/167	
Features	78.72	78.72	78.72	92.31	92.31	92.31	73.58	87.64	80.61	87.43	87.43	87.43

Table 6. Feature impact experiments

	Medstract		43-GENIA		57-PubMed	
	Nominal	Pronominal	Nominal	Pronominal	Nominal	Pronominal
All	64.08%	88.46%	67.69%	93.58%	73.28%	76.81%
All – F1	61.05%	73.08%	60.14%	83.87%	75.44%	75.36%
All – F2	65.96%	88.00%	70.22%	93.58%	78.40%	76.81%
All – F3	72.00%	80.77%	69.68%	84.46%	73.45%	76.81%
All – F4	64.65%	81.48%	68.33%	91.54%	73.73%	76.81%
All – F5	48.00%	92.31%	52.55%	93.58%	56.59%	78.26%
All – F6	44.04%	88.46%	46.42%	81.63%	57.14%	78.26%
All – F7	38.26%	59.26%	47.19%	71.96%	60.44%	50.72%

Table 5 shows that anaphora resolution implemented with the genetic algorithm indeed achieves higher F-scores than the one when all features are concerned. Table 5 also shows that the semantic features play more important role than the syntactic features for nominal anaphora resolution. Similar results can be also found in Table 6 where the impact of each feature is justified. Moreover, Table 6 indicates that the pronominal anaphora resolution on 43-Genia is better than that on the other two corpora. It implies that the mined SA/AO patterns from GENIA 3.02p corpus are helpful for pronominal anaphora resolution. Moreover, Table 7 proves that the key lexicons mined from UMLS for semantic type finding indeed enhance anaphora resolution, yet a slight improvement is found with the usage of PubMed search results. One of the reasons is few unknown instances in our corpora.

On the other hand, comparisons with evaluation corpus, Medstract, were shown in Table 8 where the best-first strategy yielded higher F-score than the results by the nearest-first strategy. It also shows that the best-first strategy with the best selection by genetic approach achieves higher F-scores than the approach presented in [2].

Table 7. Impacts of the mined semantic lexicons and the use of PubMed

	With semantic lexicons		w/o semantic lexicons	
	Medstract.	100-Medlines	Medstract.	100-Medlines
With PubMed	78%	80.62%	59%	72.16%
Without PubMed	76%	80.13%	58%	71.33%

Table 8. Comparisons among different strategies on Medstract

	Best-First		Nearest-First		Castaño et al. [2]	
F-score	Nominal	Pronominal	Nominal	Pronominal	Nominal	Pronominal
Total Features	64.08%	88.46%	50.49%	73.47%		
Genetic Features	F5, F6, F7	All - F5	F5, F6, F7	All-(F2,F5)	F4, F5, F6	F4, F6, F7
	78.72%	92.31%	61.18%	79.17%	74.40%	75.23%

3 Conclusion

In this paper, the resolution for pronominal and nominal anaphora in biomedical literature is addressed. The resolution is constructed with a salience grading on various kinds of syntactic and semantic features. Unlike previous researches, we exploit more resources, including both domain-specific and general thesaurus and corpus, to verify the semantic association between anaphors and their antecedents. Experimental results on different corpora prove that the semantic features provided with the help of the outer resources indeed can enhance anaphora resolution. Compared to other approaches, the presented best-first strategy with the genetic-algorithm based feature selection can achieve the best resolution on the same evaluation corpus.

References

1. Baldwin, B.: CogNIAC: high precision coreference with limited knowledge and linguistic resources. In Proceedings of the ACL'97/EACL'97 workshop on Operational factors in practical, robust anaphora resolution (1997) 38-45
2. Castaño, J., Zhang J., Pustejovsky, H.: Anaphora Resolution in Biomedical Literature. In International Symposium on Reference Resolution (2002)

3. Dagan, I., Itai, A.: Automatic processing of large corpora for the resolution of anaphora references. In Proceedings of the 13th International Conference on Computational Linguistics (COLING'90) Vol. III (1990) 1-3
4. Denber, M.: Automatic resolution of anaphora in English. Technical report, Eastman Kodak Co. (1998)
5. Gaizauskas, R., Demetriou, G., Artymiuk, P.J., Willett, P.: Protein Structures and Information Extraction from Biological Texts: The PASTA System. Bioinformatics (2003)
6. Gasperin, C., Vieira R.: Using word similarity lists for resolving indirect anaphora. In ACL Workshop on Reference Resolution and its Applications, Barcelona (2004)
7. Grosz, B.J., Joshi, A.K., Weinstein, S.: Centering: A framework for modelling the local coherence of discourse. Computational Linguistics (1995) 203-225
8. Hahn, U., Romacker, M.: Creating Knowledge Repositories from Biomedical Reports:The MEDSYNDIKATE Text Mining System. In Pacific Symposium on Biocomputing (2002)
9. Hobbs, J.: Pronoun resolution, Research Report 76-1. Department of Computer Science, City College, City University of New York, August (1976)
10. Kennedy, C., Boguraev, B.: Anaphora for everyone: Pronominal anaphora resolution without a parser. In Proceedings of the 16th International Conference on Computational Linguistics (1996) 113-118
11. Kim, J., Jong, C.P.: BioAR: Anaphora Resolution for Relating Protein Names to Proteome Database Entries. ACL Workshop on Reference Resolution and its Applications Barcelona Spain (2004) 79-86
12. Liang, T., Wu, D.S.: Automatic Pronominal Anaphora Resolution in English Texts. Computational Linguistics and Chinese Language Processing Vol.9, No.1 (2004) 21-40
13. Mitkov, R.: Robust pronoun resolution with limited knowledge. In Proceedings of the 18th International Conference on Computational Linguistics (COLING'98)/ACL'98 Conference Montreal Canada (1998) 869-875
14. Mitkov, R.: Anaphora Resolution: The State of the Art. Working paper (Based on the COLING'98/ACL'98 tutorial on anaphora resolution) (1999)
15. Mitkov, R., Evans, R., Orasan, C.: A new fully automatic version of Mitkov's knowledge-poor pronoun resolution method. In Proceedings of CICLing- 2000 Mexico City Mexico (2002)
16. Modjeska, Natalia, Markert, K., Nissim, M.: Using the Web in Machine Learning for Other-Anaphora Resolution. In Proceedings of the Conference on Empirical Methods in Natural Language Processing (EMNLP2003) Sapporo Japan
17. Navarretta, C.: An Algorithm for Resolving Individual and Abstract Anaphora in Danish Texts and Dialogues. ACL Workshop on Reference Resolution and its Applications Barcelona, Spain (2004) 95-102
18. Ng, V., Cardie, C.: Improving Machine Learning Approaches to Coreference Resolution. In Proceedings of the 40th Annual Meeting of the Association for Computational Linguistics, Association for Computational Linguistics (2002)
19. Oh, I.S., Lee, J.S., Moon, B.R.: Hybrid Genetic Algorithms for Feature Selection. IEEE Transactions on pattern analysis and machine Vol. 26. No. 11 (2004)
20. Ohta, T., Tateisi, Y., Kim, J.D., Lee, S.Z., Tsujii, J.: GENIA corpus: A Semantically Annotated Corpus in Molecular Biology Domain. In Proceedings of the ninth International Conference on Intelligent Systems for Molecular Biology (ISMB 2001) poster session (2001) 68

21. Pustejovsky, J., Rumshisky, A., Castaño, J.: Rerendering Semantic Ontologies: Automatic Extensions to UMLS through Corpus Analytics. LREC 2002 Workshop on Ontologies and Lexical Knowledge Bases (2002)
22. Siddharthan, A.: Resolving Pronouns Robustly: Plumbing the Depths of Shallowness. In Proceedings of the Workshop on Computational Treatments of Anaphora, 11th Conference of the European Chapter of the Association for Computational Linguistics (EACL 2003) (2003) 7-14
23. Yang, X., Su, J., Zhou, G., Tan, C.L.: Improving Pronoun Resolution by Incorporating Coreferential Information of Candidates. In Proceedings of ACL 2004 (2004) 127-134

Automatic Slide Generation Based on Discourse Structure Analysis

Tomohide Shibata and Sadao Kurohashi

Graduate School of Information Science and Technology, University of Tokyo,
7-3-1 Hongo, Bunkyo-ku, Tokyo 113-8656, Japan
{shibata, kuro}@kc.t.u-tokyo.ac.jp

Abstract. In this paper, we describe a method of automatically generating summary slides from a text. The slides are generated by itemizing topic/non-topic parts that are extracted from the text based on syntactic/case analysis. The indentations of the items are controlled according to the discourse structure, which is detected by cue phrases, identification of word chain and similarity between two sentences. Our experiments demonstrates generated slides are far easier to read in comparison with original texts.

1 Introduction

A presentation with slides is so effective to pass information to people in many situations, such as an academic conference or business. Although some softwares, such as PowerPoint and Keynote, help us with making presentation slides, it is still cumbersome to make them from scratch.

Some researchers have developed a method of (semi-)automatically making presentation slides from a technical paper or a news article [1, 2]. However, input texts of their systems were supposed to be documents whose structure is annotated: in [1], TEX source and in [2], semantically annotated documents by GDA tag.

In this paper, we propose a method of automatically generating summary slides from a raw text. An example of a text is shown in Figure 1 and an example slide that is generated from the text is shown in Figure 2 (the translated slide is shown in Figure 3). In a slide, topic/non-topic parts that are extracted from the original text are itemized and each item is indented based on the discourse structure of the text. In particular, a big contrast/list structure in the text is an important clue for producing an easy-to-read slide.

The outline of our procedure is as follows:

1. Input sentences are processed by Japanese morphological analyzer, JUMAN [3], and are parsed by Japanese syntactic analyzer, KNP [4].
2. Each sentence is segmented into clauses and the discourse structure of the text is analyzed.
3. Topic/non-topic parts are extracted from the text.
4. Summary slides are generated by displaying the topic/non-topic parts based on the discourse structure.

R. Dale et al. (Eds.): IJCNLP 2005, LNAI 3651, pp. 754–766, 2005.

大阪と神戸を結ぶＪＲ神戸線、阪急電鉄神戸線、阪神電鉄本線の３線の不通により、一日４５万人、ラッシュ時最大１時間１２万人の足が奪われた。ＪＲ西日本東海道・福知山・山陽線、阪急宝塚・今津・伊丹線、神戸電鉄有馬線の不通区間については、震災直後から代替バスによる輸送が行われた。国道２号線が開通した１月２３日から、同国道と山手幹線を使って、大阪〜神戸間の代替バス輸送が実施された。１月２８日からは、国道２号、４３号線に代替バス優先レーンが設置され、効率的・円滑な運行が確保された。(Due to the interruption of the three train services, JR Kobe-line, Hankyu Express Kobe-line and Hanshin Electric Railway, which connected between Osaka and Kobe, 450,000 people per day, 120,000 people per hour at the peak of rush, had no transportation. At the interruption sections in West Japan Railway Toukaidou Line, Sannyou Line, Hankyu Takarazuka, Imazu and Itami Line and Kobe-Electric Arima-line, transportation by alternate-bus was provided just after the earthquake occurred. From January 23th, when National Route 2 was opened, transportation by alternate-bus between Osaka and Kobe was provided. From January 28th, the alternate-bus priority lane was set up and smooth transportation was maintained.)

Fig. 1. An example of a text

鉄道の復旧 (1)

– 大阪と神戸を結ぶＪＲ神戸線、阪急電鉄神戸線、阪神電鉄本線の３線の不通
    • 一日 45 万人、ラッシュ時最大 1 時間 12 万人の足が奪われた
– ＪＲ西日本東海道・福知山・山陽線、阪急宝塚・今津・伊丹線、神戸電鉄有馬線の不通区間
    • 震災直後から
        * 代替バスによる輸送
    • 国道２号線が開通した 1 月 23 日から
        * 同国道と山手幹線を使って、大阪〜神戸間の代替バス輸送が実施
    • 1 月 28 日から
        * 国道２号、43 号線に代替バス優先レーンが設置され、円滑な運行が確保

Fig. 2. An example of a slide

Our method not only helps us with making presentation slides but also creates a full-automatic presentation. That is to say, input texts are spoken via text-to-speech engine while presenting automatically generated summary slides. We call this system "text-to-presentation", as illustrated in Figure 4. For the input of text-to-speech engine, written texts are not appropriate, because unnatural speech might be produced due to difficult words or long compound nouns, which are unsuitable for speech synthesis. Therefore, written texts are automatically converted into spoken texts based on paraphrasing technique [5, 6] and then are inputted into speech synthesis.

The rest of this paper is organized as follows. Section 2 introduces how to analyze discourse structure. Section 3 explains how to extract topic/non-topic parts and Section 4 introduces how to generate a slide. Next, in Section 5, we describe our implemented system and report the evaluation. Finally, in Section 6, we discuss the related work, and in Section 7, we conclude this paper.

Railway Recovery (1)

- Interruption of the three train services, JR Kobe-line, Hankyu Express Kobe-line and Hanshin Electric Railway
  - 450,000 people per day, 120,000 people per hour at the peak of rush, had no transportation
- Interruption sections in West Japan Railway Toukaidou Line, Sannyou Line, Hankyu Takarazuka, Imazu and Itami Line and Kobe-Electric Arima-line
  - after the earthquake occurred
    * transportation by alternate-bus was provided
  - from January 23th, when National Route 2 was opened
    * transportation by alternate-bus between Osaka and Kobe was provided
  - from January 28th
    * the alternate-bus priority lane was set up and smooth transportation was maintained.

Fig. 3. An example of a slide (in English)

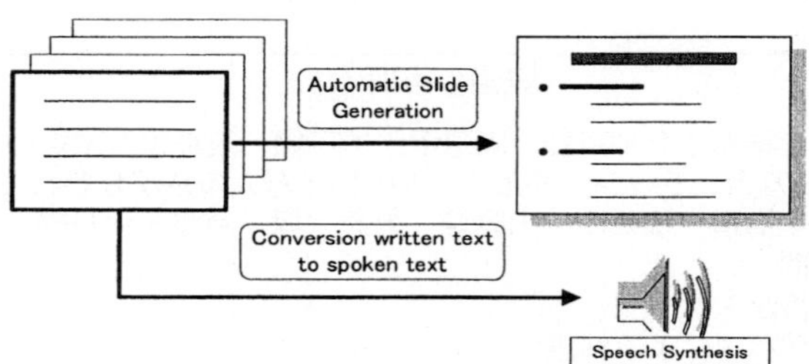

Fig. 4. Overview of text-to-presentation system

2 Discourse Structure Analysis

2.1 Model of Discourse Structure

We consider a clause and a sentence as a discourse unit and take into account the following two types of coherence relations:

1. coherence relations between two clauses in a sentence (four types)
   list, contrast, additive, adversative
2. coherence relations between two sentences (eight types)
   list, contrast, topic-chaining, topic-dominant chaining, elaboration, reason, cause, example

An example of discourse structure is shown in Figure 5. The arrows mean connection of clauses/sentences and the labels on the arrows mean coherence relation.

In our model, as an initial state, the discourse structure has a starting node. A sentence connecting to the starting node has the coherence relation "start", which means this sentence is the beginning of a new topic.

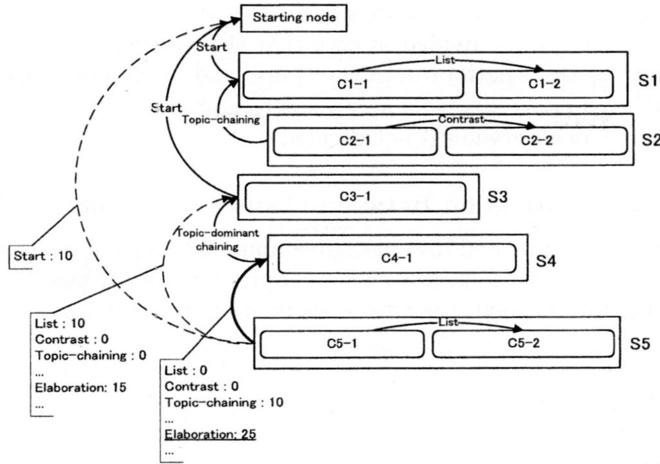

Fig. 5. The model of discourse structure

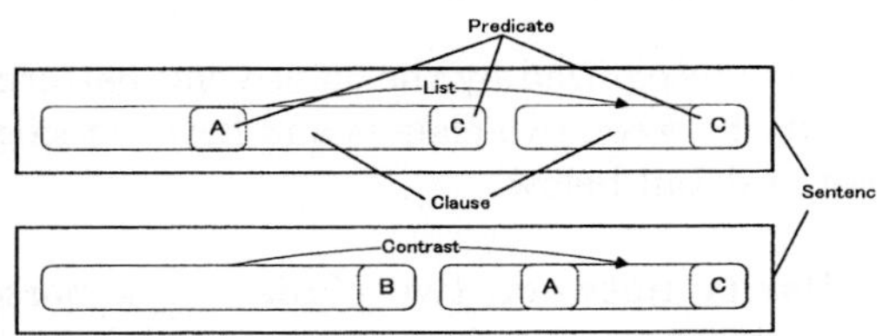

Fig. 6. Segmenting a sentence into discourse units

In the subsequent subsections, we describe how to analyze the discourse structure. This method is based on [7]. We start with the starting node and build a discourse tree in an incremental fashion. An input sentence is first parsed and segmented into clauses, and relations between clauses in a sentence are analyzed. Then, the sentence is connected to the most related preceding sentence and the coherence relation between the sentences is determined.

2.2 Segmenting a Sentence into Discourse Units

First, an input sentence is parsed by KNP and segmented into discourse units, which are the basic units of not only discourse structure but also extraction of topic/non-topic parts described in Section 3.

Japanese is a head-final language and a predicate is placed at the end of the clause. Therefore, each predicate in a sentence can be a discourse-unit boundary. We determine whether the predicate is regarded as a discourse-unit boundary according to the strength of the clause, which is classified into three levels depending on the subsuming relation of the scope[1]. The strength of a clause can be detected by clause-end patterns.

[1] The level A has the narrowest scope and the level C has the broadest scope.

Level C (e.g., ...*ga*(although)) always divided

Level B (e.g., ...*te*(and)) divided in case that the clause and its parent clause are similar[2] or the length of both the clause and its parent clause exceeds a threshold[3].

Level A (e.g., ...*nagara*(while)) not divided

2.3 Detection of Relation Between Clauses in a Sentence

After a sentence is segmented into discourse units, we analyze relations between clauses. First, the parent of each clause is simply determined based on syntactic structure of a sentence. Next, the coherence relation of two clauses is determined as follows:

- Two clauses are similar
  - contrast/list
- Two clauses are not similar
  - additive (...*te*(and),renyou-form)
  - adversative (...*ga*,*keredomo*(although))

Additive or adversative is recognized by the clause-end patterns. The method of calculating the similarity between two clauses and how to recognize contrast/list relation are described in detail below.

Calculation of similarity between two clauses. The parser calculates similarity between two arbitrary word-strings to detect coordinate structures in a sentence. Similarity between clauses is calculated as follows. First, the similarity value between two words is calculated according to exact matching, matching of their parts of speech, and their closeness in a thesaurus dictionary [8]. Then, the similarity value between two word-strings is calculated by the dynamic programming method: combining the similarity values between words in the two word-strings [4].

If two clauses have a certain similarity, the coherence relation between clauses can be two cases: list or contrast. In case of list relation, a thing/person has two different properties, as shown in (1-a), and, in case of contrast relation, two similar but different things have similar properties, as shown in (1-b).

(1) a. <u>John had a beer</u> and <u>eat martini</u>. (list)
b. <u>John went to Paris</u> and <u>Mary went to London</u>. (contrast)

The judgment whether the coherence relation is contrast or list is performed according to similarity between topics of two clauses: if the similarity exceeds a threshold, the coherence relation is determined to contrast relation, otherwise list relation. In Japanese, topics are often marked with *wa*. In the example (2),

[2] The parser calculates similarity between two clauses. The method of calculating similarity is described in the next subsection.

[3] This threshold depends on a width of a slide and a font size.

Table 1. Examples of rules for discourse structure analysis

Coherence relation	Score	Applicable range	Patterns for a connected sentence	Patterns for a new sentence
start	10	*	*	*sate*(then)···
list	5	1	*	*soshite*(and)···
list	30	1	*daiichini*(first)···	*dainini*(second)···
contrast	30	1	*	*mushiro*(rather than)···
elaboration	15	1	*	*tokuni*(especially)···
reason	30	1	*	···*karada*(because)

because *tousho* (at first) and *3-gatsusue-made* (until the end of March) have a certain similarity, the coherence relation is determined to contrast.

(2) *Daitaibus riyousya-wa* *tousho-wa* *1-nichi atari*
Alternate-bus user number-TOP first-TOP per day

3 kara 5 mannin-deattaga *3-gatsusue made-wa* *1-nichi*
from 30 to 50 thousands people the end of March-until per day

yaku 20-mannin-ga *riyoushita*
about 20 thousands people used

(The number of alternate-bus users per day was from 30 to 50 thousands at first and was about 20 thousands until the end of March.)

2.4 Detection of Relation Between Two Sentences

As a new sentence comes in, by checking surface information, we find a connected sentence and the coherence relation between them by calculating reliable scores for all relations by the following three points: (1) cue phrases, (2) word/phrase chain, and (3) similarity between two sentences. As a final result, we choose the connected sentence and the relation that have the maximum score. Note that we make the assumption that a new sentence can be connected to the sentences on the right most edge in the discourse tree (in Figure 5, S5 is not allowed to connect to S1 and S2).

(1) Cue phrases. Examples of rules for matching cue phrases are shown in Table 1. Each rule specifies a condition for a pair of a new sentence and a possible connected sentence: the range of possible connected sentences (how far from the new sentence) and patterns for the two sentences. If a pair meets these condition, the relation and score in the rule are given to it.

(2) Word/phrase chain. A sentence consists of a topic part and a non-topic part. Words in a phrase whose head word is marked with "*wa*" are regarded as a topic part, and words except a topic part as a non-topic part.

In two sentences, if word-chaining is identified between a topic of a connected sentence and a topic of a new sentence, some score is given to topic chaining relation. Similarly, if word-chaining is identified between a non-topic of a connected sentence and a topic of a new sentence, some score is given to topic-dominant relation.

(3) Similarity between two sentences. Similarity between two sentences is calculated by the similar method to one utilized for calculating similarity between two clauses in a sentence described in subsection 2.3. If the topics of two sentences have a certain similarity, the normalized similarity score between two sentences is given to contrast relation: otherwise, list relation.

In the following example, because *1-gatsu-23-nichi-kara*(from January 23th) in the sentence (3-a) and *1-gatsu-28-nichi-kara*(from January 28th) in the sentence (3-b) have a certain similarity, some score is given to contrast relation.

(3) a. *1-gatsu-23-nichi kara* *Oosaka Kobe kan-no*
January 23th-kara Osaka Kobe between

daitai bus yusou-ga *jisshisareta*
alternate bus transportation-NOM provided

(From January 23th, transportation by alternate-bus between Osaka and Kobe was provided.)

b. *1-gatsu-28-nichi-kara-TOC* *enkatuna unten-ga* *kakuho-sareta*
January 28th-kara smooth transportation maintained

(From January 28th, the alternate-bus priority lane was set up and smooth transportation was maintained.)

3 Extraction of Topic Part / Reduction of Non-Topic Part

In this section, we describe how to extract what are displayed in a slide from an original text. As mentioned in Subsection 2.4, a sentence consists of a topic part and a non-topic part. Considering a clause as a basic unit, we extract a topic part and a non-topic part. Since, in general, non-topic part is relatively long, we reduce a non-topic part to make the produced slide easy-to-read. These procedures are illustrated in Figure 7 (T denotes the topic part and N denotes the non-topic part).

3.1 Extraction of Topic Part

A phrase whose head word is marked with a topic marker *wa* is extracted as a topic. A topic is extracted also by several cue phrases. When there are multiple

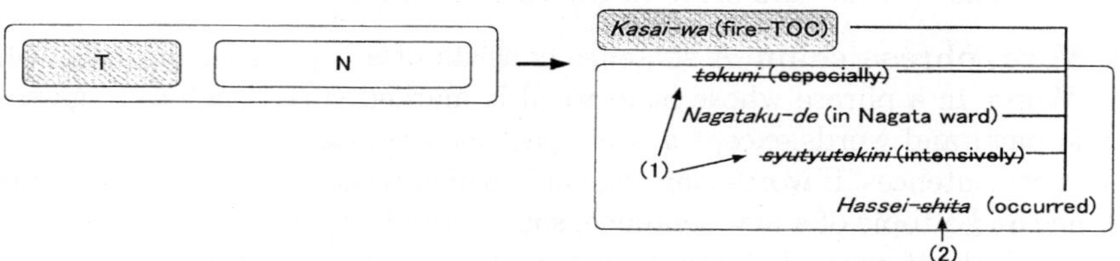

Fig. 7. Extraction of a topic part and reduction of a non-topic part

Table 2. Predicates and their case for key points

Case	Predicate
ga	*zyuuyouda*(important), *kagi-da*(key factor), *taisetsuda*(important), *yuuekida*(beneficial)
wo	*jyuushi-suru*(attach importance to), *akirakani-suru*(clarify)
ni	*tyakumoku-suru*(focus attention on), *jyuutenwo-oku*(stress)

cue phrases in a clause, a topic is extracted only by the first cue phrase. Some of them are shown below:

- *syukkagenin-ga-hanmei-shita-kasai* ni-oite ... (In the fire whose cause was revealed, ...)
- *3-sen-no-futsuu* ni-yori ... (Due to the interruption of the three train services, ...)

Note that the following cases are not regarded as a topic:

- phrases such as "wareware-wa" (we are) and "honronbun-dewa" (in this paper)
- a phrase does not depend on the end of the clause

3.2 Reduction of Non-Topic Part

In order to make a slide easy-to-read, it is important to reduce a text as long as the original meaning is preserved. We reduce a non-topic part by (1) pruning extraneous words/phrases based on syntactic/case structure and (2) deleting extraneous parts of the main predicate by some rules.

1. Pruning extraneous words/phrases
   Extraneous words/phrases are pruned based on syntactic/case structure. The following materials are pruned:
   - conjunction
   - adverb
   - A-level clause
   - adverb phrase
     e.g., *computer-teishi-no-tame data-hikitsugi-mo-konnandatta.* (Because of the computer down, it is difficult to turn over the data.)
   - appositive phrases
     e.g., *nourinsuisansyou, kokudotyou-nado kuni-no-kakukikan.* (Agencies, such as Agriculture, Forestry and Fisheries Ministry and National Land Agency)
2. Removing extraneous parts of a main predicate
   Extraneous parts of a main predicate are removed by the following rules:
   - deverbative noun-*suru*/*sareta* -> *suru*/*sareta* is deleted
     ex.) *jisshi-sareta* -> *jisshi* (carried out)
   - deverbative noun-*ga-okonawareta* -> *ga-okonawareta* is deleted
     ex.) *yusou-ga-okonawareta* -> *yusou* (transport)
   - noun-copula -> copula is deleted
     ex.) *genin-da* -> *genin* (cause)

Note that extraneous parts of the main predicate are not removed if the predicate has a negation expression.

3.3 Extraction of Key Points

When the main predicate of the clause is the one listed in Table 2 and has the specified case component, we regard the non-topic part as key points. Key points are emphasized when they are placed in the slides as described in the next section.

4 Slide Generation

As illustrated in Figure 8, topic/non-topic parts that are extracted in Section 3 are placed in a slide based on the discourse structure that is detected in Section 2. Heuristic rules for generating slides are the following:

- If the text has a title, it is adopted as the title of the slide; otherwise, let the first topic in the text be the title of the slide.
- If there is a topic in a clause, the topic is displayed and in the next line the non-topic parts are displayed in the subsequent indented level. If there is not a topic in a clause, only non-topic parts are displayed. If non-topic parts are regarded as key points, they are emphasized.
- The level of the clause in the same sentence is set to be equal and the indent of each sentence is determined according to the coherence relation to its parent sentence:
  - **start:** the level is set to 0 because a new topic starts.
  - **contrast/list:** the same level.
  - **topic chaining:** if a topic is equal to that of the parent sentence, the level is set to the same level and the topic is not displayed; otherwise, the level is decreased by one and the topic and non-topic parts are displayed.
  - **otherwise:** the level is increased by one.

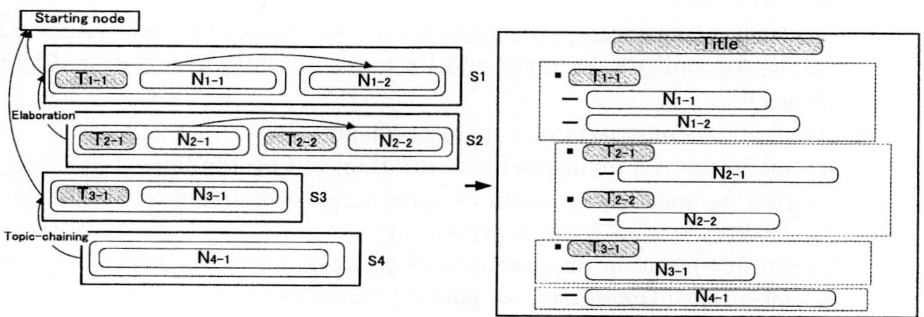

Fig. 8. Slide generation based on discourse structure

Table 3. Evaluation of discourse structure analysis

	accuracy
relation between clauses	30 / 39 (76.9%)
relation between sentences	60 / 89 (67.4%)

If the quantity of displayed texts exceeds a threshold, multiple slides are generated by splitting so that the number of lines in each slide is less than 12.

As a number of researchers have pointed out [9, 10], the discourse structure can be a clue to summarization: units found closer to the root of a discourse structure tree are considered to be more important than those found at lower levels in the tree. Along with such an idea, it can be considered that topic/non-topic parts in a lower unit (deep in a discourse structure) are not placed in a slide. However, in case that automatically generated slides are presented along with speech synthesis, the above treatment is not applied because speech without any corresponding description in the slide is not natural.

5 Implementation and Evaluation

5.1 Implementation of Text-to-Presentation System

We implemented a text-to-presentation system, in which a user can ask a question and enjoy the presentation about the query. We adopted *Hanshin-Awaji Daishinsai Kyoukunn Siryousyuu* (The Collection of Data Regarding the Lessons from the Great Hanshin-Awaji Earthquake Disaster)[4] as a collection of text. The number of the unit of text is 400, which contains an average of 3.7 sentences with an average length of 50 characters.

First, the system retrieves a text that is the most similar to the user's query [11]. Then, the system converts the (written) text into spoken languages and feeds them to a speech synthesis engine, while presenting summary slides generated by the method described in this paper. The system runs on a Web browser as shown in Figure 9. When multiple slides are generated from a text, the system switches the slide to the next slide in synchronization with speech synthesis.

5.2 Evaluation

We generated slides from 30 queries and performed two evaluations: one is evaluation of discourse structure detection, the other is evaluation of automatically generated slides. As for evaluation of paraphrasing and retrieving texts, see [6], [11]. The average reduction rate when comparing the original texts to the generated slides was 0.797.

The accuracy of detecting discourse structure is shown in Table 3. Performance was evaluated by labeled attachment of clauses/sentences. Major errors of discourse structure detection are caused by word-chain mis-identification due to

[4] http://www.hanshin-awaji.or.jp/kyoukun/

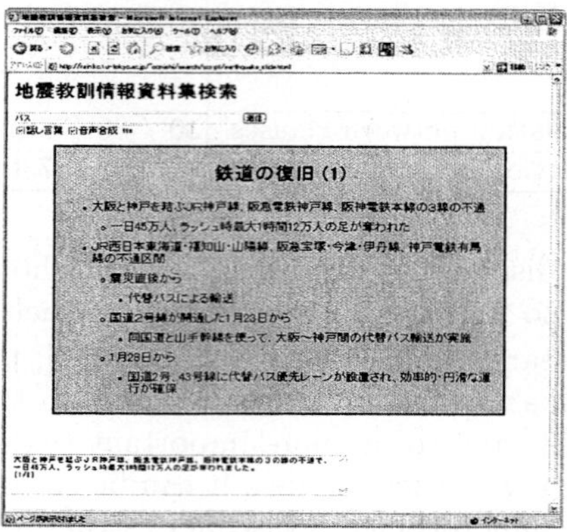

Fig. 9. A screenshot of our system

expression gaps. To deal with this problem, we are planning to apply a method of recognizing semantic equivalence of these gaps. Recognition errors of contrast relations between two clauses/sentences are attributed to a large variety of sentence structure and calculation failure of similarities between topics of two clauses/sentences by thesaurus.

The work of Marcu et al. is well known in the field of discourse parsing [12, 13]. They developed a discourse-annotated corpus and learned a discourse-parsing algorithm from it. In contrast, our discourse analyzer was based on generic heuristic rules. Actually, its application to the earthquake domain texts worked well for producing a summary slide. We do not have any plan for constructing discourse-annotated corpus in this domain because annotating discourse structure of texts takes much costs.

As for automatically generated slides, out of 30 texts, 15 was good, 12 was partially good and 3 was bad (judged by authors). The criterion for evaluation is whether a slide prevents a user to understand a presentation or not. Errors of generating slides are caused by the failure of detecting discourse structure and deleting non-topic part because of syntactic/case analysis errors. The heuristic rules of generating slides described in Section 4 do not cause an error.

Converting original texts into multimodal presentation (summary slides and speech synthesis) is significantly better in comparison with presenting original texts, even if there are some errors in generated slides. In particular, a slide in which a contrast/list structure is detected is far easier to read than an original text, as shown in Figure 9.

6 Related Work

Utiyama and Hasida presented a method of generating slide shows from documents which are semantically annotated by GDA [2]. The GDA is an XML tagset which allows machines to automatically infer the semantic structure underlying the raw documents. The system picks up important topics in the input document on the basis of the semantic dependencies and coreferences identified from the tags and generates a slide by extracting relevant sentences and paraphrasing them to an itemized summary. Although it is possible to generate slide shows from semantically annotated documents even if they are relatively long, the manual annotation costs too much.

In the field of automatic summarization, for improving the quality of summarization, the sentence reduction system has been proposed [14]. Their system was constructed from pairs of articles and human-written summaries. This idea can be applied into our system, utilizing an alignment technique between technical papers and presentation sheets [15].

7 Conclusion

In this paper, we have proposed the method of automatically generating a summary slide from a text. Our method of generating slides consists of discourse structure analysis, extraction of topics/non-topic parts and displaying them based on discourse structure.

While we are improving the accuracy of detecting discourse structure and reducing the non-topic parts, we are planing to integrate text-to-presentation system with embodied conversational agents to enhance the presentation contents.

References

1. Yoshiaki, Y., Masashi, T., Katsumi, N.: A support system for making presentation slides (in japanese). Transactions of the Japanese Society for Artificial Intelligence **18** (2003) 212–220
2. Utiyama, M., Hasida, K.: Automatic slide presentation from semantically annotated documents. In: 1999 ACL Workshop on Coreference and Its Applications. (1999)
3. Kurohashi, S., Nakamura, T., Matsumoto, Y., Nagao, M.: Improvements of Japanese morphological analyzer JUMAN. In: Proceedings of the International Workshop on Sharable Natural Language. (1994) 22–28
4. Kurohashi, S., Nagao, M.: A syntactic analysis method of long japanese sentences based on the detection of conjunctive structures. Computational Linguistics **20** (1994)
5. Kaji, N., Kawahara, D., Kurohashi, S., Sato, S.: Verb paraphrase based on case frame alignment. In: Proceedings of the 40th Annual Meeting of the Association for Computational Linguistics. (2002) 215–222
6. Kaji, N., Okamoto, M., Kurohashi, S.: Paraphrasing predicates from written language to spoken language using the web. In: Proceedings of the Human Language Technology Conference. (2004) 241–248
7. Kurohashi, S., Nagao, M.: Automatic detection of discourse structure by checking surface information in sentences. In: Proceedings of 15th COLING. Volume 2. (1994) 1123–1127
8. Ikehara, S., Miyazaki, M., Shirai, S., Yokoo, A., Nakaiwa, H., Ogura, K., Oyama, Y., Hayashi, Y., eds.: Japanese Lexicon. Iwanami Publishing (1997)

9. Ono, K., Sumita, K., Miike, S.: Abstract generation based on rhetorical structure extraction. In: Proceedings of the 15th COLING. (1994) 344–348
10. Marcu, D.: Discourse trees are good indicators of importance in text. In I.Mani, M.Maybury, eds.: Advances in Automatic Text Summarization. The MIT Press (1999) 123–136
11. Kiyota, Y., Kurohashi, S., Kido, F.: Dialog navigator: A question answering system based on large text knowledge base. In: Proceedings of 19th COLING. (2002) 460–466
12. Marcu, D.: The rhetorical parsing of unrestricted texts: A surface-based approach. Computational Linguistics **26** (2000) 395–448
13. Carlson, L., Marcu, D., Okurowski, M.E.: Building a discourse-tagged corpus in the framework of rhetorical structure theory. In: Proceedings of the 2nd SIGDIAL Workshop on Discourse and Dialogue. (2001)
14. Jing, H.: Sentence reduction for automatic text summarization. In: Proceedings of the sixth conference on Applied natural language processing. (2000) 310–315
15. Hayama, T., Nanba, H., Kunifuji, S.: Alignment between a technical paper and presentation sheets using hidden markov model. In: Proceedings of the 2005 International Conference on Active Media Technology. (2005)

Using the Structure of a Conceptual Network in Computing Semantic Relatedness

Iryna Gurevych

EML Research gGmbH, Schloss-Wolfsbrunnenweg 33, 69118, Heidelberg, Germany
http://www.eml-research.de/~gurevych

Abstract. We present a new method for computing semantic relatedness of concepts. The method relies solely on the structure of a conceptual network and eliminates the need for performing additional corpus analysis. The network structure is employed to generate artificial conceptual glosses. They replace textual definitions *proper* written by humans and are processed by a dictionary based metric of semantic relatedness [1]. We implemented the metric on the basis of GermaNet, the German counterpart of WordNet, and evaluated the results on a German dataset of 57 word pairs rated by human subjects for their semantic relatedness. Our approach can be easily applied to compute semantic relatedness based on alternative conceptual networks, e.g. in the domain of life sciences.

1 Introduction

Semantic relatedness of words represents important information for many applications dealing with processing of natural language. A more narrowly defined phenomenon of semantic similarity has been extensively studied in psychology, cognitive science, artificial intelligence, and computational linguistics. In the context of linguistics, it is typically defined via the lexical relation of synonymy. While synonymy is indeed an example of extreme similarity (suggesting that two words are interchangeable in a certain context), many natural language processing applications require knowledge about semantic relatedness rather than just similarity [2]. Departing from that, we define semantic relatedness as any kind of lexical or functional association that may exist between two words. For example, the words "car" and "journey" apparently display a close semantic relationship, while they are not synonymous.

Many natural language processing applications, e.g. word sense disambiguation or information retrieval, do not need to determine the exact type of a semantic relation, but rather to judge if two words are closely semantically related or not. For example, for an application in the domain of career consultancy it might be important to conclude that the words "baker" and "bagel" are closely related, while the exact type of a semantic relation does not need to be assigned.

Metrics of semantic relatedness are increasingly embedded into natural language processing applications for English due to the availability of free software, e.g. [3] and pre-computed information content values from English corpora. The evaluation of all approaches to compute semantic relatedness has so far been done for the task of semantic similarity. The underlying data was based on the English language [4,5]. We propose the following classification of the metrics of semantic relatedness:

R. Dale et al. (Eds.): IJCNLP 2005, LNAI 3651, pp. 767–778, 2005.

- *intrinsic or extrinsic*. Intrinsic metrics employ no external evidence, i.e. no knowledge sources except for the conceptual network itself [1,6,7]. Extrinsic metrics require additional knowledge, e.g. information content values of concepts computed from corpora [8,9,10].
- *the type of knowledge source employed, e.g. a dictionary or a conceptual network*. Metrics can either employ a machine readable dictionary, i.e. textual definitions of words therein as an underlying knowledge base [1,11], or operate on the structure of a conceptual network, whereby textual definitions themselves are not available [9,7].

Researchers working on the processing of languages such as English, for which many resources exist, have a large choice of options for choosing a metric or a knowledge source. This is, however, not the case for many other languages. Extrinsic metrics relying on a conceptual network and additional corpus data cannot always be applied. It is difficult and time-consuming to find and process a corpus, which is substantially large to compute information content of concepts for a new language. The same is true for domain-specific corpora, e.g. in the domain of life sciences. Before information content of domain concepts, e.g. protein names can be computed, a considerable effort has to be invested in compiling and processing a substantially large corpus in the respective domain. This makes it difficult to apply corpus-based metrics. At the same time, many domains already have a kind of domain model in the form of thesauri or at least taxonomies, which appear to be instances of conceptual networks.

For dictionary based metrics, the difficulty is that textual definitions of word senses in dictionaries are often inconsistent. [12] note that dictionary definitions often do not contain enough words to be effectively deployed in dictionary based metrics. Furthermore, an important dimension is the portability of a metric to new domains, i.e. whether the metric can be applied e.g. to medical or biological domains. They typically have well developed taxonomies, but are lacking language based descriptions (definitions). Therefore, the application of both extrinsic and dictionary based metrics is problematic.

Simultaneously, in this and in many other cases elaborated conceptual networks or taxonomies are available. One of the most prominent examples of that is the Open Directory Project (http://www.dmoz.com). Therefore, we propose a method for computing semantic relatedness which overcomes the constraints related to previous metrics and is completely intrinsic. It exploits solely the structure of a conceptual network, while the need for both external statistical data and textual definitions of concepts is completely eliminated. Thus, our method is language independent and can be applied to different knowledge bases represented as conceptual networks.

We conducted an experiment with human subjects to determine the upper bound of performance for automatic metrics of semantic relatedness. While this task is more difficult than computing semantic similarity, human judgments display a high interclass correlation. We evaluated our approach against this dataset, see Section 4, and compared it with baseline systems. The proposed metric achieves the same performance as a popular extrinsic (information content based) metric by [8], and is significantly better than the results of a conventional dictionary based measure [1] employing a machine-readable dictionary compiled by human writers. To exhaustively evaluate the metric, we introduced an additional baseline based on co-occurrences of words in the Web. A summary of the results is given in Section 5.

2 Definitions in Dictionaries and Conceptual Networks

Definitions of words and their distinct senses are essential to our approach. What is the definition of a good definition? This question has been disputed in philosophy since the days of Platon and Euklid, recently also in the disciplines such as cognitive science and linguistics. Different types of definitions were proposed, whose names are expressed in various terminologies, e.g. lexical, theoretical, circular and the definition by genus and difference to name just a few. Lexical definitions are what we typically find in a dictionary. They often suffer from inaccuracies as they are confined to established meanings and can prove to be confusing for example in legal matters. According to [13], a good definition should include several indisposable components: a *functional part* describing what the concept is intended for, the characteristics of the definiendum contrasting *the general* with *particular*, and *context* (time, place, cultural and mental). For example, "window" is a planar discontinuity in a solid artificial (context) surface (genus), which allows to look through it, or for the penetration of light or air (when not covered or open) (differentia). Without the differentia – with the genus alone – the definition can well fit the door; without the context, the definition can well fit a hole in a rock.

When human writers create definitions, they take care of the structural elements and requirements described above. On the other hand, when creating conceptual networks, dictionaries and language based examples are often employed as knowledge sources to determine lexical and semantic relations between words. Therefore, information about functions, general terms, and context is integrated into a conceptual network. The main idea explored in the present paper is, then, the possibility to extract knowledge about concepts from the conceptual network based on known properties of definitions and how they are encoded in the network. We call extracted pieces of knowledge *pseudo glosses*. Pseudo glosses can be used in the situations when textual definitions *proper* are not available. The information encoded in the network as lexical semantic relations is transformed into artificially generated glosses. Those can be employed in NLP applications. An additional advantage of pseudo glosses as opposed to real glosses is the possibility to include or exclude certain types of information from a gloss. This way, glosses can be easily tailored to a specific task at hand. In our application, this amounts to experimentally determining the types of information crucial for computing semantic relatedness.

The knowledge base employed in our experiments is GermaNet [14], the German counterpart of WordNet [15]. Direct re-implementation of semantic relatedness metrics developed for WordNet on the basis of GermaNet is not a trivial task. While sharing many design principles with WordNet, GermaNet displays a number of divergent features [16]. Some of them, such as the lack of conceptual glosses, make it impossible to apply dictionary based metrics in a straightforward manner. Therefore, pseudo glosses are generated directly from the conceptual network.

We experimented with different parameters that control which concepts are included in a pseudo gloss:

- *size* determines the length of a path for the hypernyms to be included in a pseudo gloss. The values of *size* range over the interval $[1, depth_{max}]$, where $depth_{max}$ is the maximum path length in a conceptual network. The depth is equivalent to the height in this context.
- *limit* determines the length of a path from the root node of a hierarchy (i.e. the most abstract concept) towards a given concept. The concepts of the path are excluded from the pseudo gloss. The values of *limit* range over the interval $[0, depth_{max}]$. Given $limit = 0$ no concepts will be excluded from the pseudo gloss, and given $limit = depth_{max}$ the resulting pseudo gloss contains solely the given word sense itself. If $size$ and $limit$ are conflicting (e.g. the concept A should be included according to $size$, and excluded according to $limit$), the latter takes precedence over the former.
- *one_sense_per_synset* (OSPS) parameter, either true or false. A synset is often represented by multiple synonymous word senses. If the parameter is set to true, only one word sense from a synset will be included into a pseudo gloss (this is also the case in paper dictionaries). Otherwise, all word senses of a synset are included.
- *lexical semantic relations* control the type of relations in a conceptual network which are involved in generating pseudo glosses, i.e. hypernymy, hyponymy, synonymy, meronymy, association, etc.

Table 1 presents examples of pseudo glosses generated according to two different system configurations: a radial gloss (all lexical semantic relations of a given concept are taken into account, except hyponyms, $OSPS = true$, $size = 3$), and a hypernym gloss (only hypernymy relation is considered, $OSPS = true$, $size = 3$, $limit = 2$).

Table 1. Examples of pseudo glosses for "Bruder – Bursche"

Radial glosses	*Hypernym glosses*
Bursche	
1. junger Mensch, Erwachsener, Bursche, Bub, Junge, Knabe, Bube, Kind, Jüngling	1. Bursche, Junge, Kind
Bruder	
1. Bruder, Geschwister, Mitmensch, Familie, Verwandter	1. Bruder
2. LaienpredigerIn, Fachkraft, unausgebildeter Mensch, Geistlicher, Prediger, ausgebildeter Mensch, Bruder, Berufstätiger, Laie, Laienprediger	2. unausgebildeter Mensch, Geistlicher, Prediger, Laie, Laienprediger
3. christlicher Sakralbau, Kloster, Geistlicher, Mönch, Bruder, Mönchskloster, Ordensangehöriger, Berufstätiger, Glaubensgemeinschaft, Orden, Laie	3. Geistlicher, Ordensangehöriger, Mönch

3 Dictionary Based Metrics

Dictionary based metrics of semantic relatedness were introduced by [1] and received a lot of attention in the context of work on word sense disambiguation. The main idea of this work is to permutate all textual definitions of the senses of two words and to assign them a score based on the number of word overlaps in glosses. Thus, the context which matches best the combination of the two words is assumed to be the disambiguated sense. This can also be viewed as a metric of how the two words are semantically related.

A dictionary gloss is typically represented by textual definitions of word senses corresponding to a given word. E.g. in the Digital Dictionary of the German Language[1] we find the following definitions of "Bruder" (Engl. *brother*), s. Example (1) and "Bursche" (Engl. *fellow* or *lad*), s. Example (2).

(1) *Bruder, der; -s, Brüder /Verkl.: Brüderchen, Brüderlein/*
(1_1) jede männliche Person einer Geschwisterreihe in ihrer Beziehung zu jedem anderen Kind derselben Geschwisterreihe
(1_2) a) enger Freund, Gesinnungsgenosse: b) scherzh. unter Brüdern offen, ehrlich gesprochen: c) Rel. kath. Mönch: d) scherzh. /bezeichnet allgemein einen Mann/ e) salopp abwertend Bursche, Kerl

(2) *Bursche, der; -n, -n /Verkl.: Bürschchen, Bürschlein/*
(2_1) männliche Person a) Knabe, Junge b) junger Mann c) vertraul. alter B. (Freund)! d) Studentenspr. Student einer Verbindung e) veraltend Diener, der einem anderen für persönliche Dienstleistungen zur Verfügung steht
(2_2) umg. kräftiges Tier

In Table 2, we present the results of the Lesk algorithm applied to this word pair. The overlaps are counted on the basis of stems because the German language is highly inflected. The sense combination $1_2 - 2_1$ turns out to be the best fitting one resulting in three overlaps of stems *friend, man, lad.* [17] adopts the algorithm by Lesk and apply

Table 2. The Lesk algorithm applied to "Bruder–Bursche"

Sense combin.	*Stem overlaps*	*Score*
$1_1 - 2_1$	männlich, Person	2
$1_1 - 2_2$	–	0
$1_2 - 2_1$	Freund, Mann, Bursch	3
$1_2 - 2_2$	Bursch	1

it to the task of computing semantic relatedness of WordNet concepts. Their metric is based on the number of shared words in the glosses of concepts available through WordNet. They extend the metric to include the glosses of other concepts, to which they are related according to the WordNet hierarchy. Those are encoded in WordNet as semantic relations, but can be found in any dictionary via synonyms, antonyms, and see-also references. The relatedness score rel_{w_1,w_2} is formally defined in Equation 3:

$$rel_{c_1,c_2} = \sum score(R_1(c_1), R_2(c_2)) \quad (3)$$

where c_1 and c_2 are the compared word senses, R is a set of lexical semantic relations, $score()$ is a function which receives the definitions of word senses and their related

[1] http://www.iai.uni-sb.de/iaide/de/dwds.htm

concepts and returns a numeric score of word overlaps in them. [17] reports a correlation of .67 to the Miller and Charles human study, and one of .60 to the Rubenstein and Goodenough's experiment, which is below the performance of other semantic relatedness metrics reported in [2]. E.g. the metric by Resnik yielded a correlation of .774 and .779 on the datasets respectively.

4 Experimental Work

In this section, we detail the process of generating artificial glosses from GermaNet. We discuss the set of parameters, their consequences for the creation of glosses and the application of artificially generated glosses to the task of computing semantic relatedness. The evaluation, then, measures the performance of semantic relatedness algorithms based on pseudo glosses with respect to human judgments of semantic relatedness. We apply the Lesk algorithm to pseudo glosses and compute a semantic relatedness score for each sense combination of a word pair. The scores are related to average human ratings by means of interclass correlation analysis.

As no datasets for evaluating semantic relatedness are available, we translated 65 word pairs from the dataset by [4] to German. Their word pairs were selected to cover a range of semantic distances. We asked 24 subjects (native speakers of German) to rate the word pairs on the scale from 0 to 4 for their semantic relatedness. Semantic relatedness was defined in a broader sense than just similarity. To determine the upper bound of performance for automatic semantic relatedness metrics, we computed a summarized correlation coefficient for a set of 24 judges. This means that we computed correlations for all judges pairwise, transformed them to a Z-score, computed the average and transformed back to a correlation coefficient yielding $r = .8098$, which is statistically significant at $p = .01$. The evaluation results for relatedness metrics are reported on the basis of 57 from 65 word pairs in the test dataset compared with average human judgments. The remaining words were not covered in GermaNet.

4.1 Experiment 1

We evaluated different methods to generate pseudo glosses according to the parameters: *lexical semantic relations* and *size*. The range of values for *size* was set from 2 to 6. The four system configurations for generating pseudo glosses were the following:

1. a *radial* gloss based on all types of lexical semantic relations in GermaNet;
2. a *hypernymy* gloss based exclusively on the hypernymy relation;
3. a *hyponymy* gloss utilizing the hyponymy relation only;
4. a gloss consisting of *coordinate sisters* of a given concept, i.e. the immediate hyponyms of the concepts' hypernyms.

Table 3 presents the results for the four system configurations (Column "Config."), whereby the best result for each configuration is printed in bold. *Radial* and *hypernymy* glosses yield better results as *hyponymy* and *coordinate sisters* glosses. This happens because pseudo glosses generated by these system configurations resemble the structural components of conventional glosses more accurately. In Examples 1 and 2, we hardly find hyponyms in the definitions. At the same time, e.g. *Lausbube* would be included in the gloss as a hyponym and *Boy* as a coordinate of *Bursche*. Summarizing this experiment, we conclude that the information on hyponymy and coordinate word senses for computing semantic relatedness is not very relevant. The remaining system configurations will be further analyzed in the following.

4.2 Experiment 2

The aim of the experiment was to examine the performance of *radial* glosses under different experimental conditions. We observed that many high scores of semantic relatedness were caused by a large number of hyponyms that some of the words, e.g. *Edelstein* (Engl. *gem*) and *Juwel* (Engl. *jewel*) have. Due to this effect, e.g. at $size = 3$, the number of overlaps for *radial* glosses increases to 199, whereas it is only 7 for *hypernym* glosses. As there exist no well-defined guidelines or criteria as to what number of hyponyms a synset should have, it is rather arbitrary and heavily skews the distribution of semantic relatedness scores.

Another parameter $one\_sense\_per\_synset$ (OSPS) controls whether all of the word senses belonging to a synset are included in a pseudo gloss or only one. The motivation to investigate this effect is similar to the one described previously, i.e. the number of synonyms (word senses) for a given synset is arbitrary. This means that counting overlaps according to the Lesk algorithm will "favour" those word pairs, whose synsets have a large number of word senses.

Table 4 shows the results of the $hyponyms = true/false$ parameter variation. We also varied the $size$ while $OSPS$ was set to *true* and *false*. The data makes evident that ignoring hyponyms in generating pseudo glosses consistently improves the performance. It eliminates the bias in the counts of overlaps due to hyponyms, which do not skew the overall distribution of scores any more. Table 5 further explores the effects of the $size$ parameter and $OSPS = true/false$ variation. For *radial* glosses, the results of $OSPS = true$ are better for $size$ from 3 to 6.

Table 3. Evaluation results for different types of pseudo glosses

Config.	*Size=2*	*Size=3*	*Size=4*	*Size=5*	*Size=6*
1	.3885	**.4570**	.4377	.4027	.4021
2	.5936	.6350	**.6682**	.6072	.6279
3	.3167	.3296	.3244	.3322	**.3538**
4	**.3140**	.2560	.2474	.2062	.1305

Table 4. Hyponyms true/false for *radial* glosses

	Hypo_true	*Hypo_false*
OSPS_true, size 1	.3939	.4513
OSPS_true, size 2	.4235	.5494
OSPS_false, size 1	.3885	.4945
OSPS_false, size 2	.4570	**.5567**

4.3 Experiment 3

We explored the application of *hypernym* glosses to computing semantic relatedness. Several issues were checked, such as the use of the *one_sense_per_synset* true versus false in glosses, the use and interaction of *size* and *limit* as well as the optimal settings for those. The results of this experiment are presented in Figure 1, which shows the correlation values for different combinations of *size* and *limit* settings. The value $OSPS = true$ leads to consistently better results for the parameter combinations of *size* and *limit*. Furthermore, the performance of the system rapidly drops for the *limit* range [4,6]. However, the use of limit is generally justified as it improves the performance for $size = 2$ and $size = 3$. At these points the performance is most optimal, s. Table 6 for exact results.

If neither *size* nor *limit* are in use (which corresponds to the case when all hypernyms of a concept become part of the gloss), the correlation drops to .568. These parameters, therefore, turn out to be necessary to control the choice of concepts in a gloss. As a consequence, the most abstract (close to the root) concepts of the hierarchy will not appear in the gloss.

Table 5. Evaluation results with OSPS true/false for *radial* glosses

	Size 1	Size 2	Size 3	Size 4	Size 5	Size 6
OSPS_false	.4945	**.5567**	.5507	.5299	.5247	.4871
OSPS_true	.4513	.5494	**.5525**	.5444	.5309	.5075

Table 6. Scope/limit in *hypernym* pseudo glosses

Scope;limit	(2;0)	(2;1)	(2;2)	(2;3)
r	.6192	.6456	.6768	.6581
Scope;limit	(3;0)	(3;1)	(3;2)	(3;3)
r	.6682	.6735	**.6914**	.6842

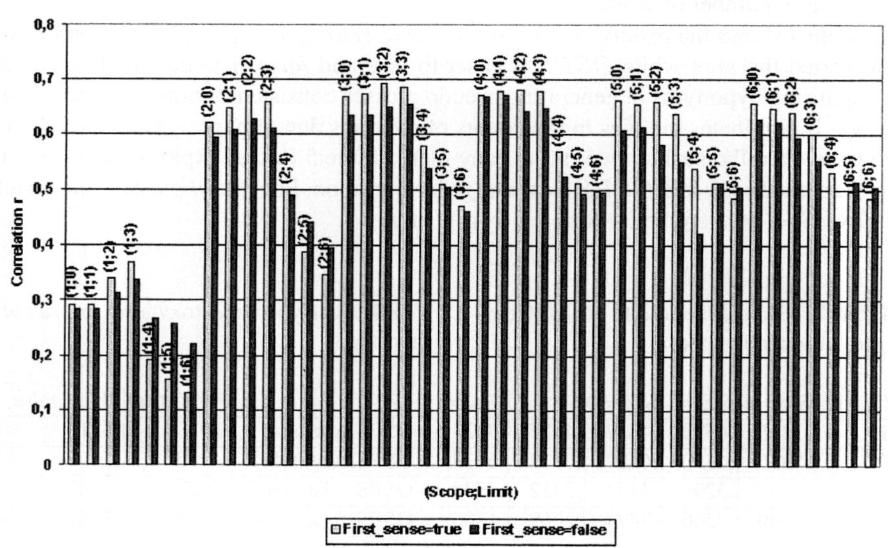

Fig. 1. Correlation r for $one\_per\_synset = true/false$. $r_{(scope,limit)}$ is plotted for $scope = [1;6]$, $limit = [0;6]$.

5 Evaluation Summary

To our knowledge, no datasets are available for validating the results of semantic relatedness metrics.[2] The results obtained for semantic similarity with WordNet are not directly comparable due to differences in the underlying knowledge bases, and – most importantly – in the task definition (changed from similarity to relatedness). The dataset designed during the present study is based on the German language. We opted for GermaNet as the underlying semantic network. Testing the results of metrics for another language, e.g. English, would involve an experiment with native speakers to collect judgments of semantic relatedness and employing an appropriate semantic resource for the chosen language and the domain of interest. However, our evaluation results can be extrapolated to other languages and similar semantic resources, as semantic relatedness metrics themselves are not tied to a particular language or resource. Experimental verification of this fact remains beyond the scope of our paper.

To better understand the performance of the semantic relatedness metrics, we designed and implemented several baselines. The first baseline compares the performance of our system to the original version of the Lesk algorithm operating on the glosses from traditional dictionaries written by human authors. As GermaNet itself does not contain a sufficient number of textual definitions of word senses, they were retrieved from the Digital Dictionary of the German Language.[3] We excluded all additional information from definitions, such as citations and examples of usage. The remaining "pure" definitions were stemmed. The resulting correlation with human judgments yielded $r = .5307$.

The second baseline for the evaluation was represented by word co-occurrence counts obtained by means of querying the Web through Google. This baseline is based on the assumption that the Web can be used as a corpus. [18] provide estimates of the Web size in words, as indexed by Altavista, for the German language: 7,035,850,000. This exceeds the size of freely available German corpora by a large margin. We constructed Google queries, where the query string was represented by a particular word pair. Semantic relatedness of words was, then, computed according to Equation 4, where $hits_{w1}$ and $hits_{w2}$ are the frequencies of words $w1$ and $w2$. The correlation of Google based results with human judgments of semantic relatedness was .5723, which is quite impressive if we consider that the method does not employ any sophisticated knowledge sources. It should be noted that we tried several other established measures of lexical association, e.g. PMI and log-likelihood on Google counts, but the results were worse than those achieved by Equation 4.

$$sim_{w1,w2} = hits_{joint}/hits_{w1} + hits_{joint}/hits_{w2} \tag{4}$$

The third baseline is a conventional approach by [8] to compute semantic relatedness via the information content of the lowest common subsumer of the two concepts. Information content of concepts was calculated on the basis of a German newspaper corpus with 172 million tokens (www.taz.de).

[2] English datasets were designed with semantic similarity in mind as described in Section 4.

[3] In fact, any other machine-readable dictionary for German could have been employed instead.

In Figure 2, we summarize the results of our experimental work. These results are based on the most optimal system configurations as described in Section 4: $OSPS = true$, $hyponyms = false$, $size = 3$ for radial glosses, $OSPS = true$, $size = 4$, $limit = 2$ for hypernym glosses. The results show that radial pseudo glosses perform approximately on the same level ($r = .5525$) as the stemmed glosses created by humans ($r = .5307$). This suggests that radial pseudo glosses mimic the behavior of "real" glosses rather well. Hypernym pseudo glosses outperform their radial counterparts and both the Lesk and the Google based baselines by a large margin, yielding $r = .6914$. Their performance is comparable to that of a conventional method by [8] based on external corpus evidence ($r = .7152$).

As the method operates exclusively on pseudo glosses generated on the basis of the hypernymy relation, this type of information from definitions turns out to be the most important one for computing semantic relatedness. In other words, *definitio per genus proximum* is superior to *definitio per differentia specifica* in this task. It should be noted that the situation can change for different types of tasks where the knowledge from a conceptual network is employed, e.g. in word sense disambiguation. As opposed to using textual definitions from traditional dictionaries, generating them automatically from a conceptual network has a great advantage: we can easily control the usage of specific types of information with the help of a set of parameters. In naturally occurring texts, this is problematic, as the required information should be first extracted from free text, a task not trivial to achieve.

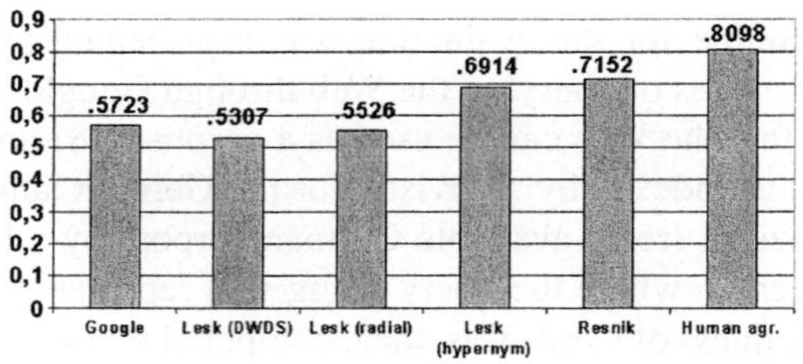

Fig. 2. A summary of evaluation results

If compared to results reported for the task of computing semantic similarity on the basis of WordNet, we note that our numbers are lower due to a number of reasons:

- The upper bound for the performance of computational algorithms is lower for our task ($r = .8089$) as the one given by [8] ($r = .8848$). Semantic relatedness is not as well defined as semantic similarity. The results have to be interpreted according to this lower upper bound.
- The performance of the metrics is dependent on the underlying knowledge base, i.e. WordNet versus GermaNet. Apparently, GermaNet has a lower coverage than WordNet. E.g. no lowest common subsumers are found for some word pairs whereas those exist in WordNet, and some links are missing. Of course, the quality of a conceptual knowledge base and the quality of resulting glosses are strongly correlated.

6 Conclusions

We proposed a method to generate artificial definitions of concepts from a conceptual network. The method was applied to the task of computing semantic relatedness of words and tested on the basis of word senses defined in GermaNet. This approach bridges the gap between gloss based algorithms and the cases, when textual definitions of concepts are not available. This is the case for languages, which do not have well developed machine readable dictionaries, and in many applications which do have domain-specific taxonomies, but no additional descriptions of concepts. The main idea is to compensate for the lack of definitions in a conceptual hierarchy by generating a textual definition of the concept automatically from a knowledge base. NLP applications can then employ the resulting glosses.

We have restricted ourselves to nouns in this work, since this part of speech is very important in NLP and thus represents a good starting point. However, the metrics are applicable to other parts of speech represented in a conceptual network. The results of a semantic relatedness metric operating on automatically generated glosses correlate very well with human judgments of semantic relatedness. The metric performs significantly better than the Lesk algorithm itself, employing a traditional dictionary, and the baseline based on word co-occurrences in Web pages (Google hits). It performs on the same scale as the information content based metric, while no additional processing of corpus data is necessary.

We expect to enhance the work presented here in a number of respects. First of all, we are working on a considerably larger dataset including 350 word pairs with corresponding semantic relatedness judgments. The word pairs involve not only nouns, but verbs and adjectives as well. The reliability of human judgments as well as the performance of semantic relatedness metrics based on the new dataset remain to be studied. Also, we have to find our what kind of modifications may be necessary to make the metrics applicable across different parts-of-speech.

Acknowledgments

This work has been funded by the Klaus Tschira Foundation. I would like to thank Hendrik Niederlich who contributed implementations as a part of an internship and Michael Strube for his valuable comments concerning draft versions of this paper.

References

1. Lesk, Michael: Automatic sense disambiguation using machine readable dictionaries: How to tell a pine cone from an ice cream cone. In Proceedings of the 5th Annual International Conference on Systems Documentation, *Toronto, Ontario, Canada*, June, 1986, pages 24–26.
2. Hirst, Graeme and Budanitsky, Alexander: Correcting real-word spelling errors by restoring lexical cohesion. In Natural Language Engineering, 11(1):87–111, 2005.
3. Pedersen, Ted and Patwardhan, Siddharth and Michelizzi, Jason: WordNet::Similarity – Measuring the relatedness of concepts. In Intelligent Systems Demonstrations of the Nineteenth National Conference on Artificial Intelligence (AAAI-04), *San Jose, CA, 25–29 July 2004*.

4. Rubenstein, Herbert and Goodenough, John: Contextual Correlates of Synonymy. In Communications of the ACM, 8(10), 1965, pages 627–633.
5. Miller, George A. and Charles, Walter G.: Contextual correlates of semantic similarity. In Language and Cognitive Processes, 6(1), 1991, pages 1–28.
6. Leacock, Claudia and Chodorow, Martin: Combining local context and WordNet similarity for word sense identification. In Fellbaum, Christiane (Ed.) WordNet: An Electronic Lexical Database, Cambridge: MIT Press, 1998, pages 265–283.
7. Seco, Nuno and Veale, Tony and Hayes, Jer: An Intrinsic Information Content Metric for Semantic Similarity in WordNet. In Proceedings of the 16th European Conference on Artificial Intelligence, *Valencia, Spain, 22–27 August 2004*, pages 1089–1090.
8. Resnik, Phil: Using information content to evaluate semantic similarity in a taxonomy. In Proceedings of the 14th International Joint Conference on Artificial Intelligence, *Montréal, Canada, 20–25 August 1995*, Volume 1, pages 448–453.
9. Jiang, Jay J. and Conrath, David W.: Semantic similarity based on corpus statistics and lexical taxonomy. In Proceedings of the 10th International Conference on Research in Computational Linguistics (ROCLING), *Tapei, Taiwan*, 1997.
10. Lin, Dekang: An information-theoretic definition of similarity. In Proceedings of the 15th International Conference on Machine Learning, *San Francisco, Cal.*, pages 296–304, 1998.
11. Patwardhan, Siddharth and Banerjee, Satanjeev and Pedersen, Ted: Using measures of semantic relatedness for word sense disambiguation. In Proceedings of the Fourth International Conference on Intelligent Text Processing and Computational Linguistics, *Mexico City, Mexico*, pages 241–257, 2003.
12. Ekedahl, Jonas and Golub, Koraljka: Word Sense Disambiguation using WordNet and the Lesk algorithm, http://www.cs.lth.se/EDA171/Reports/2004/jonas_koraljka.pdf, 2004.
13. Vaknin, Sam: The definition of definitions, http://samvak.tripod.com/define.html, 2005.
14. Kunze, Claudia: Lexikalisch-semantische Wortnetze. In Carstensen, K.-U. and Ebert, C. and Endriss, C. and Jekat, S. and Klabunde, R. and Langer, H. (eds.) Computerlinguistik und Sprachtechnologie. Eine Einführung. Heidelberg, Germany: Spektrum Akademischer Verlag, 2004, pages 423–431.
15. Fellbaum, Christiane (Ed.): WordNet: An Electronic Lexical Database. MIT Press, Cambridge, Mass., 1998.
16. Kunze, Claudia and Lemnitzer, Lothar: GermaNet - representation, visualization, application. In Proceedings of the International Conference on Language Resources and Evaluation (LREC), *Las Palmas, Canary Islands, Spain, 29 - 31 May*, 2002, pages 1485-1491.
17. Banerjee, Satanjeev and Pedersen, Ted: Extended gloss overlap as a measure of semantic relatedness. In Proceedings of the 13th International Joint Conference on Artificial Intelligence, *Chambery, France, 28 August – 3 September*, 1993.
18. Kilgarriff, Adam and Grefenstette, Gregory: Introduction to the special issue on the Web as a corpus. In Computational Linguistics, 29(3), 2003, pages 333–348.

Semantic Role Labelling of Prepositional Phrases

Patrick Ye[1] and Timothy Baldwin[1,2]

[1] Department of Computer Science and Software Engineering,
University of Melbourne, VIC 3010, Australia
[2] NICTA Victoria Laboratories,
University of Melbourne, VIC 3010, Australia
{jingy, tim}@cs.mu.oz.au

Abstract. We propose a method for labelling prepositional phrases according to two different semantic role classifications, as contained in the Penn treebank and the CoNLL 2004 Semantic Role Labelling data set. Our results illustrate the difficulties in determining preposition semantics, but also demonstrate the potential for PP semantic role labelling to improve the performance of a holistic semantic role labelling system.

1 Introduction

Prepositional phrases (PPs) are both common and semantically varied in open English text. Learning the semantics of prepositions is not a trivial task in general. It may seem that the semantics of a given PP can be predicted with reasonable reliability independent of its context. However, it is actually common for prepositions or even identical PPs to exhibit a wide range of semantic fuctions in different open English contexts. For example, consider the PP *to the car*: this PP will generally occur as a directional adjunct (e.g. *walk to the car*), but it can also occur as an object to the verb (e.g. *refer to the car*) or contrastive argument (e.g. *the default mode of transport has shifted from the train to the car*); to further complicate the situation, in *key to the car* it functions as a complement to the N-bar *key*. Based on this observation, we may consider the possibility of constructing a semantic tagger specifically for PPs, which uses the surrounding context of the PP to arrive at a semantic analysis. It is this task of PP semantic role labelling that we target in this paper.

A PP semantic role labeller would allow us to take a document and identify all adjunct PPs with their semantics. We would expect this to include a large portion of locative and temporal expressions, e.g., in the document, providing valuable data for tasks such as information extraction and question answering. Indeed our initial foray into PP semantic role labelling relates to an interest in geospatial and temporal analysis, and the realisation of the importance of PPs in identifying and classifying spatial and temporal references.

The contributions of this paper are to propose a method for PP semantic role labelling, and evaluate its performance over both the Penn treebank (including comparative evaluation with previous work) and also the data from the CoNLL Semantic Role Labelling shared task. As part of this process, we identify the

R. Dale et al. (Eds.): IJCNLP 2005, LNAI 3651, pp. 779–791, 2005.

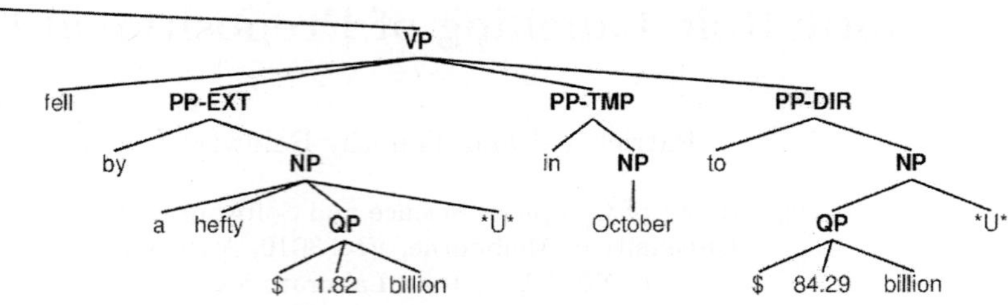

Fig. 1. An example of the preposition semantic roles in Penn Teebank

level of complementarity of a dedicated PP semantic role labeller with a conventional holistic semantic role labeller, suggesting PP semantic role labelling as a potential avenue for boosting the performance of existing systems.

2 Preposition Semantic Role Disambiguation in Penn Treebank

Significant numbers of prepositional phrases (PPs) in the Penn treebank [1] are tagged with their semantic role relative to the governing verb. For example, Figure 1, shows a fragment of the parse tree for the sentence *[Japan's reserves of gold, convertible foreign currencies, and special drawing rights] fell by a hefty $1.82 billion in October to $84.29 billion [the Finance Ministry said]*, in which the three PPs governed by the verb *fell* are tagged as, respectively: `PP-EXT` ("extend"), meaning how much of the reserve fell; `PP-TMP` ("temporal"), meaning when the reserve fell; and `PP-DIR` ("direction"), meaning the direction of the fall.

According to our analysis, there are 143 preposition semantic roles in the treebank. However, many of these semantic roles are very similar to one another; for example, the following semantic roles were found in the treebank: `PP-LOC`, `PP-LOC-1`, `PP-LOC-2`, `PP-LOC-3`, `PP-LOC-4`, `PP-LOC-5`, `PP-LOC-CLR`, `PP-LOC-CLR-2`, `PP-LOC-CLR-TPC-1`. Inspection of the data revealed no systematic semantic differences between these PP types. Indeed, for most PPs, it was impossible to distinguish the subtypes of a given superclass (e.g. `PP-LOC` in our example). We therefore decided to collapse the PP semantic roles based on their first semantic feature. For example, all semantic roles that start with `PP-LOC` are collapsed to the single class `PP-LOC`. Table 1 shows the distribution of the collapsed preposition semantic roles.

[2] describe a system[1] for disambiguating the semantic roles of prepositions in the Penn treebank according to 7 basic semantic classes. In their system, O'Hara and Weibe used a decision tree classifier, and the following types of features:

- **POS tags of surrounding tokens:** The POS tags of the tokens before and after the target preposition within a predefined window size. In O'Hara and Wiebe's work, this window size is 2.

[1] This system was trained with WEKA's J48 decision tree implementation.

Table 1. Penn treebank semantic role distribution (top-9 roles)

Semantic Role	Count	Frequency	Meaning
PP-LOC	21106	38.2	Locative
PP-TMP	12561	22.7	Temporal
PP-CLR	11729	21.2	"Closely related" (somewhere between an argument and an adjunct)
PP-DIR	3546	6.4	Direction (*from/to* X)
PP-MNR	1839	3.3	Manner (incl. instrumentals)
PP-PRD	1819	3.3	Predicate (non-VP)
PP-PRP	1182	2.1	Purpose or reason
PP-CD	654	1.2	Cardinal (numeric adjunct)
PP-PUT	296	0.5	Locative complement of *put*

- **POS tag of the target preposition**
- **The target preposition**
- **Word collocation:** All the words in the same sentence as the target preposition; each word is treated as a binary feature.
- **Hypernym collocation:** The WordNet hypernyms [3] of the open class words before and after the target preposition within a predefined window size (set to 5 words); each hypernym is treated as a binary feature.

O'Hara and Wiebe's system also performs the following pre-classification filtering on the collocation features:

- **Frequency constraint:** $f(coll) > 1$, where *coll* is either a word from the word collocation or a hypernym from the hypernym collocation
- **Conditional independence threshold:** $\frac{p(c|coll)-p(c)}{p(c)} >= 0.2$, where c is a particular semantic role and *coll* is from the word collocation or a hypernym from the hypernym collocation

We began our research by replicating O'Hara and Wiebe's method and seeking ways to improve it. Our initial investigation revealed that there were around 44000 word and hypernym collocation features even after the frequency constraint filter and the conditional independence filter have been applied. We did not believe all these collocation features were necessary, and we deployed an additional ranking-based filtering mechanism over the collocation features to only select collocation features which occur in the top N frequency bins. Algorithm 1 shows the details of this filtering mechanism.

This ranking-based filtering mechanism allows us to select collocation feature sets of differing size, and in doing so not only improve the training and tagging

Algorithm 1. Ranking based filtering algorithm

1. Let s be the list that contains the frequency of all the collocation features
2. Sort s in descending order
3. $minFrequency = s[N]$
4. Discard all features whose frequency is less than $minFrequency$

Table 2. Penn treebank preposition semantic role disambiguation results

Ranking	Accuracy (%)	
	Classifier 1	Classifier 2
10	74.75	81.28
20	76.53	83.52
50	79.21	86.34
100	80.13	87.02
300	81.32	87.62
1000	82.34	87.71
all	82.76	87.45
O'Hara & Wiebe	N/A	85.8

speed of the preposition semantic role labelling, but also observe how the number of collocation features affects the performance of the PP semantic role labeller and which collocation features are more important.

2.1 Results

Since some of the preposition semantic roles in the treebank have extremely low frequencies, we decided to build our first classifier using only the top 9 semantic roles, as detailed in Table 1. We also noticed that the semantic roles `PP-CLR`, `PP-CD` and `PP-PUT` were excluded from O'Hara's system which only used `PP-BNF`, `PP-EXT`, `PP-MNR`, `PP-TMP`, `PP-DIR`, `PP-LOC` and `PP-PRP`, therefore we built a second classifier using only the semantic roles used by O'Hara's system[2]. The two classifiers were trained with a maximum entropy [4] learner[3].

Table 2 shows the results of our classifier under stratified 10-fold cross validation[4] using different parameters for the rank-based filter. We also list the accuracy reported by O'Hara and Wiebe for comparison.

The results show that the performance of the classifier increases as we add more collocation features. However, this increase is not linear, and the improvement of performance is only marginal when the number collocation features is greater than 100. It also can be observed that there is a consistent performance difference between classifiers 1 and 2, which may suggest that PP-CLR may be harder to distinguish from other semantic roles. This is not totally surprising given the relatively vague definition of the semantics of PP-CLR. We return to analyse these results in greater depth in Section 4.

3 Preposition Semantic Role Labelling over the CoNLL 2004 Dataset

Having built a classifier which has reasonable performance on the task of treebank preposition semantic role disambiguation, we decided to investigate

[2] PP-BNF with only 47 counts was not used by the second classifier.

[3] `http://homepages.inf.ed.ac.uk/s0450736/maxent_toolkit.html`

[4] O'Hara's system was also evaluated using stratified 10-fold cross validation.

whether we could use the same feature set to perform PP semantic role labelling over alternate systems of PP classification. We chose the 2004 CoNLL Semantic Role Labelling (SRL) dataset [5] because it contained a wide range of semantic classes of PPs, in part analogous to the Penn treebank data, and also because we wished to couple our method with a holistic SRL system to demonstrate the ability of PP semantic role labelling to enhance overall system performance.

Since the focus of the CoNLL data is on SRL relative to a set of pre-determined verbs for each sentence input,[5] our primary objective is to investigate whether the performance of SRL systems in general can be improved in any way by an independent preposition SRL system. We achieve this by embedding our PP classification method within an existing holistic SRL system—that is a system which attempts to tag all semantic role types in the CoNLL 2004 data—through the following three steps:

1. Perform SRL on each preposition in the CoNLL dataset;
2. Merge the output of the preposition SRL with the output of a given verb SRL system over the same dataset;
3. Perform standard CoNLL SRL evaluation over the merged output.

The details of preposition SRL and combination with the output of a holistic SRL system are discussed below.

3.1 Breakdown of the Preposition Semantic Role Labelling Problem

Preposition semantic role labelling over the CoNLL dataset is considerably more complicated than the task of disambiguating preposition semantic roles in the Penn treebank. There are three separate subtasks which are required to perform preposition SRL:

1. **PP Attachment:** determining which verb to attach each preposition to.
2. **Preposition Semantic Role Disambiguation**
3. **Argument Segmentation:** determining the boundaries of the semantic roles.

The three subtasks are not totally independent of each other, as we demonstrate in the results section, and improved performance over one of the subtasks does not necessarily correlate with an improvement in the final results.

3.2 PP Attachment Classification

PP attachment (PPA) classification is the first step of preposition semantic role labelling and involves determining the verb attachment site for a given preposition, i.e. which of the pre-identified verbs in the sentence the preposition is

[5] Note that the CoNLL 2004 data identifies certain verbs as having argument structure, and that the semantic role annotation is relative to these verbs only. This is often not the sum total of all verbs in a given sentence: the verbs in relative clauses, e.g., tend not to be identified as having argument structure.

governed by. Normally, this task would be performed by a parser. However, since the CoNLL dataset contains no parsing information[6] and we did not want to use any resources not explicitly provided in the CoNLL data, we had to construct a PPA classifier to specifically perform this task.

This classifier uses the following features, all of which are derived from information provided in the CoNLL data:

- **POS tags of surrounding tokens:** The POS tags of the tokens before and after the target preposition within a window size of 2 tokens ($[-2, 2]$).
- **POS tag of the target preposition**
- **The target preposition**
- **Verbs and their relative position (VerbRelPos):** All the (pre-identified) verbs in the same sentence as the target preposition and their relative positions to the preposition are extracted as features. Each (verb, relative position) tuple is treated as a binary feature. The relative positions are determined in a way such that the 1st verb before the preposition will be given the position -1, the 2nd verb before the preposition will be given the position -2, and so on.
- **The type of the clause containing the target preposition**
- **Neighbouring chunk type:** The types (NP, PP, VP, etc.) of chunks before and after the target preposition within a window of 3 chunks.
- **Word collocation (WordColl):** All the open class words in the phrases before and after the target preposition within a predefined window of 3 chunks.
- **Hypernym collocation (HyperColl):** All the hypernyms from the open class words in the phrases before and after the target preposition within a predefined window of 3 chunks.
- **Named Entity collocation NEColl:** All the named entity information from the phrases before and after the target preposition within a predefined window of 3 chunks.

The PPA classifier outputs the relative position of the governing verb to the target preposition, or `None` if the preposition does not have a semantic role.

We trained the PPA classifier over the CoNLL 2004 training set, and tested it on the testing set. Table 3 shows the distribution of the classes in the testing set.

The same maximum entropy learner used in the treebank SRL task was used to train the PPA classifier. The accuracy of this classifier on the CoNLL 2004 testing set is 78.99%.

3.3 Preposition Semantic Role Disambiguation

For the task of preposition semantic role disambiguation (SRD), we constructed a classifier using the same features as the PPA classifier, with the following differences:

[6] The CoNLL 2005 SRL data does contain parse trees for the sentences, possibly obviating the need for independent verb attachment classification.

Table 3. PPA class distribution

PPA	Count	Frequency
None	3005	60.71
-1	1454	29.37
1	411	8.30
-2	40	0.81
2	29	0.59
3	8	0.16
-3	2	0.04
-6	1	0.02

Table 4. CoNLL 2004 semantic role distribution in the CoNLL 2004 test dataset(top-14 roles)

Semantic Role	Count	Frequency	Meaning
A1	424	21.79	Argument 1
A2	355	18.24	Argument 2
AM-TMP	299	15.36	Temporal adjunct
AM-LOC	188	9.66	Locative adjunct
A0	183	9.40	Argument 0
AM-MNR	125	6.42	Manner adjunct
A3	106	5.45	Argument 3
AM-ADV	71	3.65	General-purpose adjunct
A4	44	2.26	Argument 4
AM-CAU	40	2.06	Causal adjunct
AM-PNC	32	1.64	Purpose adjunct
AM-DIS	32	1.64	Discourse marker
AM-DIR	19	0.97	Directional adjunct
AM-EXT	7	0.36	Extent adjunct

1. The window size for the POS tags of surrounding tokens is 5 tokens.
2. The window sizes for the **WordColl**, the **HyperColl** and the **NeColl** features are set to include the entire sentence.

We trained the SRD classifier once again on the CoNLL 2004 training set, and tested it on the testing set. Table 4 shows the distribution of the classes in the testing set.

We used the same maximum entropy leaner as for the PPA classifier to train the SRD classifier. The accuracy of the SRD classifier on the CoNLL 2004 testing set is 58.68%.

3.4 Argument Segmentation

In order to determine the extent of each NP selected for by a given preposition (i.e. the span of words contained in the NP), we use a simple regular expression over the chunk parser analysis of the sentence provided in the CoNLL 2004 data, namely: `PP NP+`. We additionally experimented with a robust statistical parser [6] to determine PP extent, but found that the regular expression-based method performed equally well or marginally better, without requiring any resources external to the original task data.

We make no attempt to perform separate evaluation of this particular subtask because without the semantic role information, no direct comparison can be made with the CoNLL data.

3.5 Combining the Output of the Subtasks

Once we have identified the association between verbs and prepositions, and disambiguated the semantic roles of the prepositions, we can begin the process of creating the final output of the preposition semantic role labelling system. This takes place by identifying the data column corresponding to the verb governing each classified PP in the CoNLL data format (as determined by the PPA classifier), and recording the semantic role of that PP (as determined by the SRD classifier) over the full extent of the PP (as determined by the segmentation classifier).

3.6 Merging the Output of Preposition SRL and Verb SRL

Once we have generated the output of the preposition SRL system, we can proceed to the final stage where the semantic roles of the prepositions are merged with the semantic roles of an existing holistic SRL system.

It is possible, and indeed likely, that the semantic roles produced by the two systems will conflict in terms of overlap in the extent of labelled constituents and/or the semantic role labelling of constituents. To address any such conflicts, we designed three merging strategies to identify the right balance between the outputs of the two component systems:

S1 When a conflict is encountered, only use the semantic role information from the holistic SRL system.

S2 When a conflict is encountered, if the start positions of the semantic role are the same for both SRL systems, then replace the semantic role of the holistic SRL system with that of the preposition SRL system, but keep the holistic SRL system's boundary end.

S3 When a conflict is encountered, only use the semantic role information from the preposition SRL system.

3.7 Results

To evaluate the performance of our preposition SRL system, we combined its outputs with the 3 top-performing holistic SRL systems from the CoNLL 2004 SRL shared task.[7] The three systems are [7], [8] and [9]. Furthermore, in order to establish the upper bound of the improvement of preposition SRL on verb

[7] Using the test data outputs of the three systems made available at `http://www.lsi.upc.edu/~srlconll/st04/st04.html`.

Table 5. Preposition SRL results before merging with the holistic SRL systems, (P = precision, R = recall, F = F-score; above-baseline results in **boldface**)

	SRD$_{AUTO}$						SRD$_{ORACLE}$					
	SEG$_{NP}$			SEG$_{ORACLE}$			SEG$_{NP}$			SEG$_{ORACLE}$		
	P	R	F	P	R	F	P	R	F	P	R	F
VA$_{AUTO}$	38.77	4.58	8.2	55.12	6.96	12.36	62.68	7.42	13.27	**91.41**	11.53	20.48
VA$_{ORACLE}$	42.2	6.96	11.95	56.64	10.36	17.51	71.64	11.81	20.28	**99.37**	18.15	30.69

Table 6. Preposition SRL combined with [7] (P = precision, R = recall, F = F-score; above-baseline results in **boldface**)

		SRD$_{AUTO}$						SRD$_{ORACLE}$					
		SEG$_{NP}$			SEG$_{ORACLE}$			SEG$_{NP}$			SEG$_{ORACLE}$		
		P	R	F	P	R	F	P	R	F	P	R	F
ORIG		72.43	66.77	69.49	72.43	66.77	69.49	72.43	66.77	69.49	72.43	66.77	69.49
S1	VA$_{AUTO}$	72.00	**66.84**	69.32	72.08	**66.91**	69.40	72.13	**66.95**	69.44	72.31	**67.11**	**69.61**
	VA$_{ORACLE}$	71.92	**67.02**	69.38	71.97	**67.30**	**69.55**	72.29	**67.39**	**69.75**	**72.81**	**68.12**	**70.39**
S2	VA$_{AUTO}$	71.34	66.22	68.68	70.66	65.60	68.04	**73.12**	**67.89**	**70.41**	**73.42**	**68.16**	**70.69**
	VA$_{ORACLE}$	71.01	66.16	68.50	69.78	65.21	67.42	**73.68**	**68.67**	**71.08**	**74.35**	**69.55**	**71.87**
S3	VA$_{AUTO}$	70.10	65.00	67.46	72.25	**66.83**	69.43	**73.12**	**67.84**	**70.38**	**77.16**	**71.39**	**74.16**
	VA$_{ORACLE}$	70.38	65.91	68.07	**73.10**	**68.67**	**70.81**	**75.58**	**70.82**	**73.12**	**81.42**	**76.55**	**78.91**

Table 7. Preposition SRL combined with [8] (P = precision, R = recall, F = F-score; above-baseline results in **boldface**)

		SRD$_{AUTO}$						SRD$_{ORACLE}$					
		SEG$_{NP}$			SEG$_{ORACLE}$			SEG$_{NP}$			SEG$_{ORACLE}$		
		P	R	F	P	R	F	P	R	F	P	R	F
ORIG		70.07	63.07	66.39	70.07	63.07	66.39	70.07	63.07	66.39	70.07	63.07	66.39
S1	VA$_{AUTO}$	68.50	**63.79**	66.06	69.17	**64.44**	**66.72**	69.37	**64.60**	**66.90**	**70.58**	**65.73**	**68.07**
	VA$_{ORACLE}$	68.18	**64.59**	66.33	68.93	**65.57**	**67.21**	69.75	**66.09**	**67.87**	**71.65**	**68.18**	**69.87**
S2	VA$_{AUTO}$	68.21	**63.52**	65.79	68.31	**63.64**	65.89	**70.53**	**65.68**	**68.02**	**71.87**	**66.94**	**69.32**
	VA$_{ORACLE}$	67.77	**64.19**	65.93	67.50	**64.19**	65.81	**71.43**	**67.68**	**69.51**	**73.51**	**69.95**	**71.69**
S3	VA$_{AUTO}$	67.14	62.30	64.63	69.39	**64.23**	**66.71**	**70.19**	**65.14**	**67.57**	**74.34**	**68.81**	**71.47**
	VA$_{ORACLE}$	66.79	**63.22**	64.96	69.58	**66.05**	**67.76**	**71.98**	**68.14**	**70.01**	**77.87**	**73.93**	**75.85**

SRL, and investigate how the three subtasks interact with each other and what their respective limits are, we also used oracled outputs from each subtask in combining the final outputs of the preposition SRL system. The oracled outputs are what would be produced by perfect classifiers, and are emulated by inspection of the gold-standard annotations for the testing data.

Table 5 shows the results of the preposition SRL systems before they are merged with the verb SRL systems. These results show that the coverage of our preposition SRL system is quite low relative to the total number of arguments

Table 8. Preposition SRL combined with [9] (P = precision, R = recall, F = F-score; above-baseline results in **boldface**)

		SRD$_{AUTO}$						SRD$_{ORACLE}$					
		SEG$_{NP}$			SEG$_{ORACLE}$			SEG$_{NP}$			SEG$_{ORACLE}$		
		P	R	F	P	R	F	P	R	F	P	R	F
ORIG		71.81	61.11	66.03	71.81	61.11	66.03	71.81	61.11	66.03	71.81	61.11	66.03
S1	VA$_{AUTO}$	70.23	**61.87**	65.78	70.74	**62.43**	**66.32**	71.13	**62.65**	**66.62**	**72.34**	**63.83**	**67.82**
	VA$_{ORACLE}$	69.61	**62.63**	65.94	70.20	**63.60**	**66.74**	71.57	**64.38**	**67.79**	**73.49**	**66.60**	**69.87**
S2	VA$_{AUTO}$	69.92	**61.60**	65.50	69.91	**61.69**	65.54	**72.10**	**63.50**	**67.53**	**73.39**	**64.75**	**68.80**
	VA$_{ORACLE}$	69.14	**62.19**	65.48	68.84	**62.35**	65.43	**72.79**	**65.47**	**68.94**	**74.83**	**67.82**	**71.15**
S3	VA$_{AUTO}$	69.01	60.66	64.57	71.31	**62.57**	**66.65**	**72.24**	**63.49**	**67.58**	**76.54**	**67.15**	**71.54**
	VA$_{ORACLE}$	68.77	**61.86**	65.13	71.59	**64.81**	**68.03**	**74.19**	**66.74**	**70.27**	**80.25**	**72.67**	**76.27**

in the testing data, even when oracled outputs from all three subsystems are used (recall = 18.15%). However, this is not surprising because we expected the majority of semantic roles to be noun phrases.

In Tables 6, 7 and 8, we show how our preposition SRL system performs when merged with the top 3 systems under the 3 merging strategies introduced in Section 3.6. In each table, ORIG refers to the base system without preposition SRL merging.

We can make a few observations from the results of the merged systems. First, out of verb attachment, SRD and segmentation, the SRD module is both: (a) the component with the greatest impact on overall performance, and (b) the component with the greatest differential between the oracle performance and classifier (AUTO) performance. This would thus appear to be the area in which future efforts should be concentrated in order to boost the performance of holistic SRLs through preposition SRL.

Second, the results show that in most cases, the recall of the merged system is higher than that of the original SRL system. This is not surprising given that we are generally relabelling or adding information to the argument structure of each verb, although with the more aggressive merging strategies (namely S2 and S3) it sometimes happens that recall drops, by virtue of the extent of an argument being aversely affected by relabelling. It does seem to point to a complementarity between verb-driven SRL and preposition-specific SRL, however.

Finally, it was somewhat disappointing to see that in no instance did a fully-automated method surpass the base system in precision or F-score. Having said this, we were encouraged by the size of the margin between the base systems and the fully oracle-based systems, as it supports our base hypothesis that preposition SRL has the potential to boost the performance of holistic SRL systems, up to a margin of 10% in F-score for S3.

4 Analysis and Discussion

In the previous 2 sections, we presented the methodologies and results of two systems that perform statistical analysis on the semantics of prepositions, each using a different data set. The performance of the 2 systems was very different. The SRD system trained on the treebank produced highly credible results, whereas the SRL system trained on CoNLL 2004 SRL data set produced somewhat negative results. In the remainder of this section, we will analyze these results and discuss their significance.

There is a significant difference between the results obtained by the treebank classifier and that obtained by the CoNLL SRL classifier. In fact, even with a very small number of collocation features, the treebank classifier still outperformed the CoNLL SRL classifier. This suggests that the semantic tagging of prepositions is somewhat artificial. This is evident in three ways. First, the proportion of prepositional phrases tagged with semantic roles is small – around 57,000 PPs out of the million-word Treebank corpus. This small proportion suggests that the preposition semantic roles were tagged only in certain prototypical situations. Second, we were able to achieve reasonably high results even when we used a collocation feature set with fewer than 200 features. This further suggests that the semantic roles were tagged for only a small number of verbs in relatively fixed situations. Third, the preposition SRD system for the CoNLL data set used a very similar feature set to the treebank system, but was not able to produce anywhere near comparable results. Since the CoNLL dataset is aimed at holistic SRL across all argument types, it incorporates a much larger set of verbs and tagging scenarios; as a result, the semantic role labelling of PPs is far more heterogeneous and realistic than is the case in the treebank. Therefore, we conclude that the results of our treebank preposition SRD system are not very meaningful in terms of predicting the success of the method at identifying and semantically labelling PPs in open text.

A few interesting facts came out of the results over the CoNLL dataset. The most important one is that by using an independent preposition SRL system, the results of a general verb SRL system can be significantly boosted. This is evident because when the oracled results of all three subtasks were used, the merged results were around 10% higher than those for the original systems, in all three cases. Unfortunately, it was also evident from the results that we were not successful in automating preposition SRL. Due to the strictness of the CoNLL evaluation, it was not always possible to achieve a better overall performance by improving just one of the three subsystems. For example, in some cases, worse results were achieved by using the oracled results for PPA, and the results produced by SRD classifier than using the PPA classifier and the SRD classifiers in conjunction. The reason for the worse results is that in our experiments, the oracled PPA always identifies more prepositions attached to verbs than the PPA classifier, therefore more prepositions will be given semantic roles by the SRD classifier. However, since the performance of the SRD classifier is not high, and the segmentation subsystem does not always produce the same semantic role boundaries as the CoNLL data set, most of these additional prepositions would either be given a wrong semantic role or wrong phrasal extent (or both), thereby causing the overall performance to fall.

Finally, it is evident that the merging strategy also plays an important role in determining the performance of the merged preposition SRL and verb SRL systems: when the performance of the preposition SRL system is high, a more preposition-oriented merging scheme would produce better overall results, and vice versa.

5 Conclusion and Future Work

In this paper, we have proposed a method for labelling preposition semantics and deployed the method over two different data sets involving preposition semantics. We have shown that preposition semantics is not a trivial problem in general, and also that has the potential to complement other semantic analysis tasks, such as semantic role labelling.

Our analysis of the results of the preposition SRL system shows that significant improvement in all three stages of preposition semantic role labelling—namely verb attachment, preposition semantic role disambiguation and argument segmentation—must be achieved before preposition SRL can make a significant contribution to holistic SRL. The unsatisfactory results of our CoNLL preposition SRL system show that the relatively simplistic feature sets used in our research are far from sufficient. Therefore, we will direct our future work towards using additional NLP tools, information repositories and feature engineering to improve all three stages of preposition semantic role labelling.

Acknowledgements

We would like to thank Phil Blunsom and Steven Bird for their suggestions and encouragement, Tom O'Hara for providing insight into the inner workings of his semantic role disambiguation system, and the anonymous reviewers for their comments.

References

1. Marcus, M.P., Marcinkiewicz, M.A., Santorini, B.: Building a large annotated corpus of English: the Penn treebank. Computational Linguistics **19** (1993) 313–330
2. O'Hara, T., Wiebe, J.: Preposition semantic classification via treebank and FrameNet. In: Proc. of the 7th Conference on Natural Language Learning (CoNLL-2003), Edmonton, Canada (2003)
3. Miller, G.A.: WordNet: a lexical database for English. Communications of the ACM **38** (1995) 39–41
4. Berger, A.L., Pietra, V.J.D., Pietra, S.A.D.: A maximum entropy approach to natural language processing. Computational Linguistics **22** (1996) 39–71
5. Carreras, X., Màrquez, L.: Introduction to the CoNLL-2004 shared task: Semantic role labeling. In: Proc. of the 8th Conference on Natural Language Learning (CoNLL-2004), Boston, USA (2004) 89–97

6. Briscoe, T., Carroll, J.: Robust accurate statistical annotation of general text. In: Proc. of the 3rd International Conference on Language Resources and Evaluation (LREC 2002), Las Palmas, Canary Islands (2002) 1499–1504
7. Hacioglu, K., Pradhan, S., Ward, W., Martin, J.H., Jurafsky, D.: Semantic role labeling by tagging syntactic chunks. In: Proc. of the 8th Conference on Natural Language Learning (CoNLL-2004), Boston, USA (2004)
8. Punyakanok, V., Roth, D., Yih, W.T., Zimak, D., Tu, Y.: Semantic role labeling via generalized inference over classifiers. In: Proc. of the 8th Conference on Natural Language Learning (CoNLL-2004), Boston, USA (2004)
9. Carreras, X., Màrquez, L., Chrupa, G.: Hierarchical recognition of propositional arguments with perceptrons. In: Proc. of the 8th Conference on Natural Language Learning (CoNLL-2004), Boston, USA (2004)

Global Path-Based Refinement of Noisy Graphs Applied to Verb Semantics

Timothy Chklovski and Patrick Pantel

Information Sciences Institute,University of Southern California,
4676 Admiralty Way,Marina del Rey, CA 90292
{timc, pantel}@isi.edu

Abstract. Recently, researchers have applied text- and web-mining algorithms to mine semantic resources. The result is often a noisy graph of relations between words. We propose a mathematically rigorous refinement framework, which uses path-based analysis, updating the likelihood of a relation between a pair of nodes using evidence provided by multiple indirect paths between the nodes. Evaluation on refining temporal verb relations in a semantic resource called VERBOCEAN showed a 16.1% error reduction after refinement.

1 Introduction

Increasingly, researchers are creating broad-coverage semantic resources by mining text corpora [1][5] and the Web [2][6]. These resources typically consist of a noisy collection of relations between words. The data is typically extracted on a per link basis (i.e., the relation between two nodes is determined without regard to other nodes). Yet, little work has taken a global view of the graph of relations, which may provide additional information to refine local decisions by identifying inconsistencies, updating confidences in specific edges (relations), and suggesting relations between additional pairs of nodes.

For example, observing the temporal verb relations "discover *happens-before* refine" and "refine *happens-before* exploit" provides evidence for the relation "discover *happens-before* exploit," because the *happens-before* relation is transitive.

We conceptualize a semantic resource encoding relations between words as a graph where words are nodes and binary relations between words are edges. In this paper, we investigate the refinement of such graphs by updating the confidence in edges using a global analysis relying on link semantics. Our approach is based on the observation that some paths (chains of relations) between a pair of nodes x_i and x_j imply the presence or absence of a particular direct relation between x_i and x_j. Despite each individual path being noisy, multiple indirect paths can provide sufficient evidence for adding, removing, or altering a relation between two nodes. As illustrated by the earlier example, inferring a relation based on the presence of an indirect path relies on the semantics of the links that make up the path, like transitivity or equivalence classes.

As an evaluation and a sample practical application, we apply our refinement framework to the task of refining the temporal precedence relations in VERBOCEAN, a broad-coverage noisy network of semantic relations between verbs extracted by mining the Web [2]. Examples of new edges discovered (added) by applying the

R. Dale et al. (Eds.): IJCNLP 2005, LNAI 3651, pp. 792 – 803, 2005.

framework include: "ascertain *happens-before* evaluate", "approve *happens-before* back", "coat *happens-before* bake", "plan *happens-before* complete", and "interrogate *happens-before* extradite".

Examples of edges that are removed by applying our framework include: "induce *happens-before* treat", "warm *happens-before* heat", "halve *happens-before* slice", and "fly *happens-before* operate".

Experiments show that our framework is particularly good at filtering out the incorrect temporal relations in VERBOCEAN. Removing incorrect relations is particularly important for inference systems.

2 VerbOcean

We apply our path-based refinement framework to VERBOCEAN [2], a web-extracted lexical semantics resource with potential applications to a variety of natural language tasks such as question answering, information retrieval, document summarization, and machine translation. VERBOCEAN is a graph of semantic relations between verbs, with 3,477 verbs (nodes) and 22,306 relations (edges). Although the framework applies whenever some paths through the graph imply presence or absence of a relation, for the evaluation we focus on the *temporal precedence* relation in VERBOCEAN, and, in an ancillary role, on the *similarity* relation. Senses are not discriminated and an edge indicates that the relation is believed to hold between some senses of the verbs in this relation.

The five semantic relations present in VERBOCEAN are presented in Table 1. *Temporal precedence (happens-before)* is a transitive asymmetric temporal relation between verbs. *Similarity* is a relation that suggests two nodes are likely to be in the same equivalence class, although polysemy makes it only weakly transitive.

Table 1. Types, examples and frequencies of 22,306 semantic relations in VERBOCEAN

Semantic Relation	Example	Transitive	Symmetric	# in VERBOCEAN
temporal precedence	*marry :: divorce*	*Y*	*N*	4,205
similarity	*produce :: create*	*Y*	*Y*	11,515
strength	*wound :: kill*	*Y*	*N*	4,220
antonymy	*open :: close*	*N*	*Y*	1,973
enablement	*fight :: win*	*Y*	*N*	393

In VERBOCEAN, asymmetric relations between two nodes are enforced to be unidirectional (i.e., presence of an edge x_i *happens-before* x_j guarantees absence of an edge x_j *happens-before* x_i). Larger, inconsistent loops are possible, however, as extraction is strictly local. Taking advantage of the global picture to refine the edges of the graph can improve quality of the resource, helping performance of any algorithms or applications that rely on the resource.

3 Global Refinement

Our approach relies on a global view of the graph to refine a relation between a given pair of nodes x_i and x_j, based on multiple indirect paths between the two nodes. The analysis processes triples <x_i, r, x_j> for the relation r to output r, its opposite (which we will denote q), or *neither*. The opposite of *happens-before* is the same relation in the reverse direction (*happens-after*). The refinement is based on evidence provided by indirect paths, over a probabilistic representation of the graph.

Section 3.1 introduces the steps of the refinement, Section 3.2 details which paths are used as evidence, and Section 3.3 derives the statistical model used for combining evidence from multiple unreliable paths.

3.1 Overview of the Refinement Algorithm

We first introduce some notation. Let $R_{i,j}$ denote the event that the relation r is present between nodes x_i and x_j in the original graph – i.e., the graph indicates (perhaps spuriously) the presence of the relation r between x_i and x_j. Let $r_{i,j}$ denote the relation r actually holding between x_i and x_j. Let $\psi_{i,j}$ denote an acyclic path from x_i to x_j of (possibly distinct) relations $\{R_{i,i+1} \,..\, R_{j\text{-}1,j}\}$. For example, the path "x_1 *similar* x_2 *happens-before* x_3" can be denoted $\psi_{1,3}$. If the edges of $\psi_{i,j}$ indicate the relation r between the nodes x_i and x_j, we say that $\psi_{i,j}$ *indicates* $r_{i,j}$.

Given a triple <x_i, r, x_j>, we identify the set $\boldsymbol{\Psi}_r^{full}$ of all paths $\psi_{i,j}$ such that $\psi_{i,j}$ indicates $r_{i,j}$ and $\psi_{i,j}$'s sequence of relations $\{R_{i,i+1} \,..\, R_{j\text{-}1,j}\}$ matches one of the allowed sequences. That is, we only consider certain *path types*. The restriction on types of paths considered is introduced because identifying and processing all possible paths indicating $r_{i,j}$ is too demanding computationally in a large non-sparse graph. The path types considered are detailed in Section 3.2. Note that the intermediate nodes of paths can range over the entire graph.

For each $\psi_{i,j}$ in the above set $\boldsymbol{\Psi}_r^{full}$, we compute the estimated probability that $r_{i,j}$ holds given the observation of (relations that make up) $\psi_{i,j}$. Each edge in the input graph is treated as a probabilistic one, with probabilities $P(r_{i,j})$ and $P(r_{i,j}|R_{i,j})$ estimated from human judgments on a representative sample. Generally, longer paths and paths made up of less reliable edges will have lower probabilities. Section 3.3 presents the full model for estimating these probabilities.

Next, we form the set $\boldsymbol{\Psi}_r$ by selecting from $\boldsymbol{\Psi}_r^{full}$ only the paths which have no common intermediate nodes. This is done greedily, processing all paths in $\boldsymbol{\Psi}_r^{full}$ in order of decreasing score, placing each in $\boldsymbol{\Psi}_r$ iff it does not share any intermediate nodes with any path already in $\boldsymbol{\Psi}_r$. This is done to avoid double-counting the available evidence in our framework, which operates assuming conditional independence of paths.

Next, we compute $P(r_{i,j} \mid \boldsymbol{\Psi}_r)$, the probability of $r_{i,j}$ given the evidence provided by the paths in $\boldsymbol{\Psi}_r$. The model for computing this is described in Section 3.3. Similarly, $\boldsymbol{\Psi}_q$ and $P(q_{i,j} \mid \boldsymbol{\Psi}_q)$ are computed for $q_{i,j}$, the opposite of $r_{i,j}$. Next, the evidence for r and q are reconciled by computing $P(r_{i,j} \mid \boldsymbol{\Psi}_r, \boldsymbol{\Psi}_q)$ and, similarly, $P(q_{i,j} \mid \boldsymbol{\Psi}_r, \boldsymbol{\Psi}_q)$.

Finally, the more probable of the two relations $r_{i,j}$ and $q_{i,j}$ is output if its probability exceeds a threshold value P_{min} (i.e., $r_{i,j}$ is output if $P(r_{i,j} \mid \boldsymbol{\Psi}_r, \boldsymbol{\Psi}_q) > P(q_{i,j} \mid \boldsymbol{\Psi}_r, \boldsymbol{\Psi}_q)$ and $P(r_{i,j} \mid \boldsymbol{\Psi}_r, \boldsymbol{\Psi}_q) > P_{min}$. In Section 4.2, we experiment with varying values of P_{min}.

3.2 Paths Considered

The enabling observation behind our approach is that in a graph in which edges have certain properties such as transitivity, some paths $\boldsymbol{\Psi}_{i,j}$ indicate the presence of a relation between the first node x_i and the last node x_j. In the paths we consider, we rely on two kinds of inferences: transitivity and equivalence. Also, we do not consider very long paths, as they tend to become unreliable due to accumulation of chance of false detection of each edge and sense drift in each intermediate node. The set of paths to consider was not rigorously motivated. Rather, we aimed to cover some common cases. Refining the sets of paths is a possible fruitful direction for future work.

For the presence of *happens-before*, a transitive asymmetric relation, we considered all 11 path types of length 3 or less which imply *happens-before* between the end nodes based on transitivity and equivalence:

"happens-before"
"happens-before, similar"
"similar, happens-before"
"happens-before, happens-before"
"happens-before, similar, similar"
"similar, happens-before, similar"
"similar, similar, happens-before"
"happens-before, happens-before, similar"
"similar, happens-before, happens-before"
"happens-before, similar, happens-before"
"happens-before, happens-before, happens-before"

3.3 Statistical Model for Combining Evidence

This section presents a rigorous derivation of the probabilistic model for computing and combining probabilities with which indirect paths indicate a given edge.

3.3.1 Estimating from a Single Path

We first derive probability of $r_{1,n}$ given single path $\psi_{1,n}$:

$$P(r_{1,n} \mid \psi_{1,n})$$

If n is 2, i.e. $\psi_{1,n}$ has only one edge $R_{1,2}$, we have simply the probability that the edge actually holds given its presence in the graph:

$$P(r_{1,2} \mid \psi_{1,2}) = P(r_{1,2} \mid R_{1,2}) \tag{1}$$

Otherwise, $\psi_{1,n}$ has intermediate nodes, in which case $P(r_{1,n} \mid \psi_{1,n})$ can be estimated as follows:

$$\begin{aligned}P(r_{1,n} \mid \psi_{1,n}) = P(r_{1,n} \mid R_{1,2},\ldots,R_{n-1,n}) = P(r_{1,n} \mid R_{1,2},\ldots,R_{n-1,n},r_{1,2},\ldots,r_{n-1,n})P(r_{1,2},\ldots,r_{n-1,n} \mid R_{1,2},\ldots,R_{n-1,n}) +\\ P(r_{1,n} \mid R_{1,2},\ldots,R_{n-1,n},\neg(r_{1,2},\ldots,r_{n-1,n}))P(\neg(r_{1,2},\ldots,r_{n-1,n}) \mid R_{1,2},\ldots,R_{n-1,n})\end{aligned}$$

Because $r_{1,n}$ is conditionally independent from $R_{i,i+1}$ given $r_{i,i+1}$ or $\neg r_{i,i+1}$, we can simplify:

$$\begin{aligned}P(r_{1,n} \mid \psi_{1,n}) = P(r_{1,n} \mid r_{1,2},\ldots,r_{n-1,n})P(r_{1,2},\ldots,r_{n-1,n} \mid R_{1,2},\ldots,R_{n-1,n}) +\\ P(r_{1,n} \mid \neg(r_{1,2},\ldots,r_{n-1,n}))P(\neg(r_{1,2},\ldots,r_{n-1,n}) \mid R_{1,2},\ldots,R_{n-1,n})\end{aligned}$$

Assuming independence of a given relation $r_{i,i+1}$ from all edges in $\psi_{1,n}$ except for the edge $R_{i,i+1}$ yields:

$$P(r_{1,n} \mid \psi_{1,n}) = P(r_{1,n} \mid r_{1,2},\ldots,r_{n-1,n}) \prod_{i=1..n-1} P(r_{i,i+1} \mid R_{i,i+1}) + \\ P(r_{1,n} \mid \neg(r_{1,2},\ldots,r_{n-1,n}))\left(1 - \prod_{i=1..n-1} P(r_{i,i+1} \mid R_{i,i+1})\right)$$

Let P_{match} denote the probability that there is no significant shift in meaning at a given intermediate node. Then, assume that path $r_{1,2},\ldots, r_{n-1,n}$ indicates $r_{1,n}$ iff the meanings at $n - 2$ intermediate nodes match:

$$P(r_{1,n} \mid r_{1,2},\ldots,r_{n-1,n}) = P_{match}^{\;n-2}$$

Also, when one or more of the relations $r_{i,i+1}$ do not hold, nothing is generally implied[1] about $r_{1,n}$, thus

$$P(r_{1,n} \mid \neg(r_{1,2},\ldots,r_{n-1,n})) = P(r_{1,n})$$

Plugging these in, we have:

$$P(r_{1,n} \mid \psi_{1,n}) = P_{match}^{\;n-2} \prod_{i=1..n-1} P(r_{i,i+1} \mid R_{i,i+1}) + P(r_{1,n})\left(1 - P_{match}^{\;n-2} \prod_{i=1..n-1} P(r_{i,i+1} \mid R_{i,i+1})\right)$$

which can be rewritten as:

$$P(r_{1,n} \mid \psi_{1,n}) = P(r_{1,n}) + (1 - P(r_{1,n}))P_{match}^{\;n-2} \prod_{i=1..n-1} P(r_{i,i+1} \mid R_{i,i+1}) \quad (2)$$

where the prior $P(r_{1,n})$ and the conditional $P(r_{i,i+1} \mid R_{i,i+1})$ can be estimated empirically by manually tagging the relations $R_{i,j}$ in a graph as correct or incorrect: $P(r_{1,n})$ is the probability that an edge will be labeled with relation r by a human judge, and $P(r_{i,i+1} \mid R_{i,i+1})$ is the precision with which the system could identify R. While P_{match} can be estimated empirically we have not done so. We experimentally set $P_{match} = 0.9$.

3.3.2 Combining Estimates from Multiple Paths

In this subsection we derive an estimate of the validity of inferring $r_{1,n}$ given the set $\boldsymbol{\Psi}_r$ of m paths $\psi_{1,n}^{\;1}, \psi_{1,n}^{\;2}, \ldots, \psi_{1,n}^{\;m}$:

$$P(r_{1,n} \mid \psi_{1,n}^1, \psi_{1,n}^2, \ldots, \psi_{1,n}^m) \quad (3)$$

In the case of zero paths, we use simply $P(r_{1,n})=P(r)$, the probability of observing r between a pair of nodes from a sample set with no additional evidence. The case of one path has been treated in the previous section. In the case of multiple paths, we derive the expression as follows (omitting for convenience subscripts on paths, and distinguishing them by their superscripts). We assume conditional independence of any two paths ψ^k and ψ^l given r or $\neg r$. Using Bayes' rule yields[2]:

$$P(r_{1,n} \mid \psi^1,\ldots,\psi^m) = \frac{P(r)P(\psi^1,\ldots,\psi^m \mid r)}{P(\psi^1,\ldots,\psi^m)} = \frac{P(r)\prod_{k=1..m} P(\psi^k \mid r)}{P(\psi^1,\ldots,\psi^m)} \quad (4)$$

---

[1] This is not the case for paths in which the value of one edge, given the other edges, is correlated with the value of the end-to-end relation. The exception does not apply for happens-before edges if there are other happens-before edges in the path, nor does it ever apply for any similar edges.

[2] Here and afterward, the denominators must be non-zero; they are always so when we apply this model.

The above denominator can be rewritten as:

$$P(\psi^1,\ldots,\psi^m) = P(r)P(\psi^1,\ldots,\psi^m \mid r) + P(\neg r)P(\psi^1,\ldots,\psi^m \mid \neg r) = \\ P(r)\prod_{k=1..m} P(\psi^k \mid r) + P(\neg r)\prod_{k=1..m} P(\psi^k \mid \neg r) \tag{5}$$

Using Bayes' rule again, the expressions in the above products can be rewritten as follows:

$$P(\psi^k \mid r) = \frac{P(r \mid \psi^k)P(\psi^k)}{P(r)} \tag{6}$$

$$P(\psi^k \mid \neg r) = \frac{P(\neg r \mid \psi^k)P(\psi^k)}{P(\neg r)} = \frac{(1 - P(r \mid \psi^k))P(\psi^k)}{1 - P(r)} \tag{7}$$

Substituting into Eq. 5 the Eqs. 6 and 7 yields:

$$P(\psi^1,\ldots,\psi^m) = P(r)\prod_{k=1..m} P(\psi^k \mid r) + P(\neg r)\prod_{k=1..m} P(\psi^k \mid \neg r) = P(r)\prod_{k=1..m}\left(\frac{P(r \mid \psi^k)P(\psi^k)}{P(r)}\right) + (1 - P(r))\prod_{k=1..m}\left(\frac{(1 - P(r \mid \psi^k))P(\psi^k)}{1 - P(r)}\right) =$$

$$\left(\prod\nolimits_{k=1..m} P(\psi^k)\right) \times \left(\frac{\prod_{k=1..m} P(r \mid \psi^k)}{(P(r))^{m-1}} + \frac{\prod_{k=1..m}(1 - P(r \mid \psi^k))}{(1 - P(r))^{m-1}}\right)$$

Using the above for the denominator of Eq. 4, using Eq. 6 in the numerator of Eq. 4, and simplifying, we have:

$$P(r \mid \psi^1,\ldots,\psi^m) = \frac{P(r)\prod_{k=1..m} P(\psi^k \mid r)}{P(\psi^1,\ldots,\psi^m)} = \frac{\dfrac{\prod_{k=1..m} P(r \mid \psi^k)}{(P(r))^{m-1}}}{\dfrac{\prod_{k=1..m} P(r \mid \psi^k)}{(P(r))^{m-1}} + \dfrac{\prod_{k=1..m}(1 - P(r \mid \psi^k))}{(1 - P(r))^{m-1}}}$$

which can be rewritten as

$$P(r \mid \psi^1,\ldots,\psi^m) = \frac{\prod_{k=1..m} P(r \mid \psi^k)}{\prod_{k=1..m} P(r \mid \psi^k) + \left(\dfrac{P(r)}{1 - P(r)}\right)^{m-1} \prod_{k=1..m}(1 - P(r \mid \psi^k))} \tag{8}$$

where $P(r \mid \psi^k)$ is as in Eq. 2 and $P(r)$ can be estimated empirically.

3.3.3 Estimating from Supporting and Opposing Paths

Recall that q denotes the opposite of r. The previous section has shown how to compute $P(r \mid \Psi_r)$ and, similarly, $P(q \mid \Psi_q)$. We now derive how to estimate r given both Ψ_r, Ψ_q:

$$P(r \mid \Psi_r, \Psi_q) \tag{9}$$

We assume that r and q are disjoint, $P(r,q) = P(r|q) = P(q|r) = 0$. We also assume that q is conditionally independent from Ψ_r given $\neg r$, i.e.,

$P(q \mid \neg r, \Psi_r) = P(q \mid \neg r)$ and $P(q \mid \neg r, \Psi_r, \Psi_q) = P(q \mid \neg r, \Psi_q)$, and similarly

$P(r \mid \neg q, \Psi_q) = P(r \mid \neg q)$ and $P(r \mid \neg q, \Psi_r, \Psi_q) = P(r \mid \neg q, \Psi_r)$

We proceed by deriving the following, each consequent relying on the previous result:

LEMMA 1: $P(q \mid \neg r)$, in Eq. 10
LEMMA 2: $P(\neg q \mid \Psi_r)$, in Eq. 12
LEMMA 3: $P(r \mid \neg q, \Psi_r)$ and $P(q \mid \neg r, \Psi_q)$, in Eqs. 13 and 14
THEOREM 1: $P(r \mid \Psi_r, \Psi_q)$, in Eq. 18.

LEMMA 1. From P(r | q) = 0, we observe:

$$P(q) = P(r)P(q \mid r) + P(\neg r)P(q \mid \neg r) = P(\neg r)P(q \mid \neg r)$$

Solving for $P(q \mid \neg r)$, we obtain:

$$P(q \mid \neg r) = \frac{P(q)}{P(\neg r)} \tag{10}$$

LEMMA 2. Using an approach similar to that of Lemma 1 and noting that P(q | r, Ψr) = P(q | r) = 0 yields:

$$P(q \mid \Psi_r) = P(r \mid \Psi_r)P(q \mid r, \Psi_r) + P(\neg r \mid \Psi_r)P(q \mid \neg r, \Psi_r) = 0 + P(\neg r \mid \Psi_r)P(q \mid \neg r, \Psi_r)$$

Invoking the assumption $P(q \mid \neg r, \Psi_r) = P(q \mid \neg r)$, we can simplify:

$$P(q \mid \Psi_r) = P(\neg r \mid \Psi_r)P(q \mid \neg r)$$

Substituting the result of Lemma 1 (Eq. 10) into the above yields:

$$P(q \mid \Psi_r) = \frac{P(\neg r \mid \Psi_r)P(q)}{P(\neg r)} \tag{11}$$

And thus

$$P(\neg q \mid \Psi_r) = \frac{P(\neg r) - P(\neg r \mid \Psi_r)P(q)}{P(\neg r)} \tag{12}$$

LEMMA 3. We derive P(r | ¬q, Ψr), using P(¬q | r, Ψr) = 1:

$$P(r \mid \neg q, \Psi_r) = \frac{P(r, \neg q, \Psi_r)}{P(\neg q, \Psi_r)} = \frac{P(r, \neg q \mid \Psi_r)P(\Psi_r)}{P(\neg q \mid \Psi_r)P(\Psi_r)} = \frac{P(r, \neg q \mid \Psi_r)}{P(\neg q \mid \Psi_r)} = \frac{P(r \mid \Psi_r)}{P(\neg q \mid \Psi_r)}$$

Substituting the result of Lemma 2 (Eq. 12) into the above yields:

$$P(r \mid \neg q, \Psi_r) = \frac{P(\neg r)P(r \mid \Psi_r)}{P(\neg r) - P(\neg r \mid \Psi_r)P(q)} \tag{13}$$

Similarly,

$$P(q \mid \neg r, \Psi_q) = \frac{P(\neg q)P(q \mid \Psi_q)}{P(\neg q) - P(\neg q \mid \Psi_q)P(r)} \tag{14}$$

THEOREM 3

$$P(r \mid \Psi_r, \Psi_q) = \frac{P(\neg r)P(r \mid \Psi_r)P(\neg q \mid \Psi_q)}{(1 - P(r))(1 - P(q)) - (P(r \mid \Psi_r) - P(r))(P(q \mid \Psi_q) - P(q))}$$

$P(r \mid \Psi_r, \Psi_q)$ can be derived using the above Lemmas, as follows:

$$P(r \mid \Psi_r, \Psi_q) = P(q \mid \Psi_r, \Psi_q)P(r \mid q, \Psi_r, \Psi_q) + P(\neg q \mid \Psi_r, \Psi_q)P(r \mid \neg q, \Psi_r, \Psi_q)$$

The assumption $P(r \mid q) = 0$ implies $P(r \mid q, \Psi_r, , \Psi_q) = 0$. Also, since r is conditionally independent of Ψ_q given $\neg q$, we have $P(r \mid \neg q, \Psi_r, \Psi_q) = P(r \mid \neg q, \Psi_r)$. Thus, we can simplify:

$$P(r \mid \Psi_r, \Psi_q) = P(\neg q \mid \Psi_r, \Psi_q)P(r \mid \neg q, \Psi_r) = (1 - P(q \mid \Psi_r, \Psi_q))P(r \mid \neg q, \Psi_r) \quad (15)$$

Similarly,

$$P(q \mid \Psi_r, \Psi_q) = P(\neg r \mid \Psi_r, \Psi_q)P(q \mid \neg r, \Psi_q) = (1 - P(r \mid \Psi_r, \Psi_q))P(q \mid \neg r, \Psi_q) \quad (16)$$

Substituting, Eq. 16 into Eq. 15 yields:

$$\begin{aligned} P(r \mid \Psi_r, \Psi_q) &= (1 - (1 - P(r \mid \Psi_r, \Psi_q))P(q \mid \neg r, \Psi_q))P(r \mid \neg q, \Psi_r) \\ &= P(r \mid \neg q, \Psi_r)(1 - P(q \mid \neg r, \Psi_q)) + P(r \mid \Psi_r, \Psi_q)P(q \mid \neg r, \Psi_q)P(r \mid \neg q, \Psi_r) \end{aligned}$$

Solving for $P(r \mid \Psi_r, \Psi_q)$, we get:

$$P(r \mid \Psi_r, \Psi_q) = \frac{P(r \mid \neg q, \Psi_r) - P(r \mid \neg q, \Psi_r)P(q \mid \neg r, \Psi_q)}{1 - P(r \mid \neg q, \Psi_r)P(q \mid \neg r, \Psi_q)} \quad (17)$$

Expanding and simplifying, we establish our Theorem 1:

$$P(r \mid \Psi_r, \Psi_q) = \frac{P(\neg r)P(r \mid \Psi_r)P(\neg q \mid \Psi_q)}{(1 - P(r))(1 - P(q)) - (P(r \mid \Psi_r) - P(r))(P(q \mid \Psi_q) - P(q))} \quad (18)$$

4 Experimental Results

In this section, we evaluate our refinement framework on the temporal precedence relations discovered by VERBOCEAN, and present some observations on applying the refinement to other VERBOCEAN relations.

4.1 Experimental Setup

Following Chklovski and Pantel [2], we studied 29,165 pairs of verbs obtained from a paraphrasing algorithm called DIRT [4]. We applied VERBOCEAN to the 29,165 verb pairs, which tagged each pair with the semantic tag *happens-before*, *happens-after* and *no temporal precedence*[3].

---

[3] VERBOCEAN actually produces additional relations such as *similarity, antonymy, strength* and *enablement*. For our purposes, we only consider the temporal relations.

For our experiments, we randomly sampled 1000 of these verb pairs, and presented them to two human judges (without revealing the VERBOCEAN tag). The judges were asked to classify each pair among the following tags:

Happens-before with entailment
Happens-before without entailment
Happens-after with entailment
Happens-after without entailment
Another semantic relation
No semantic relation

For the purposes of our evaluation, tags *a* and *b* align with VERBOCEAN's *happens-before* tag, tags *c* and *d* align with the *happens-after* tag, and tags *e* and *f* align with the *no temporal relation* tag[4]. The Kappa statistic [7] for the task was $\kappa = 0.78$.

4.2 Refinement Results

Table 2 shows the overall accuracy of VERBOCEAN tags on the 1000 verb pairs randomly sampled from DIRT. Each row represents a different refinement. The number in parentheses is P_{min}, the threshold value for the strength of the relation from Section 3.1. As the threshold is increased, the refinement algorithm requires greater evidence (more supporting paths and absence of opposing evidence) to trigger a temporal relation between a pair of verbs.

Table 2. Accuracy (95% confidence) of VERBOCEAN on a random sample of 1000 verb pairs tagged by two judges

	Accuracy		
	Judge1	Judge2	Total
Unrefined	80.7%	74.8%	77.7% ± 2.0%
Refined (0.5)	66.0%	63.7%	64.8% ± 2.6%
Refined (0.66)	75.4%	71.7%	73.5% ± 2.4%
Refined (0.9)	83.1%	77.2%	80.2% ± 2.1%
Refined (0.95)	84.5%	78.0%	81.3% ± 1.9%
Refined (Combo)*	86.8%	81.3%	84.0% ± 2.4%

* Combo combines the *no temporal relation* from the 0.5 and the *happens-before* and *happens-after* from the and 0.95 refinements, where the reported accuracy is computed on the subset of 716 verb pairs for which the algorithm is most confident.

Table 3 shows the reassignments due to refinement. At the 0.5 level, the refinement left 76 of 81 relations unchanged, revising 3 to *happens-after* and 2 to *no temporal relation*. Similarly, only two of the original *happens-after* relations were changed with refinement. However, of the 849 originally tagged *no temporal relation*, the

[4] In future work, we plan to use the judges' classifications to evaluate the extraction of entailment relations using VERBOCEAN.

Table 3. Allocation change between semantic tags due to refinement

	Happens-Before	Happens-After	No Temporal Relation
Unrefined	81	70	849
Refined (0.5)	190	180	630
Refined (0.66)	118	124	758
Refined (0.9)	53	66	881
Refined (0.95)	40	46	914

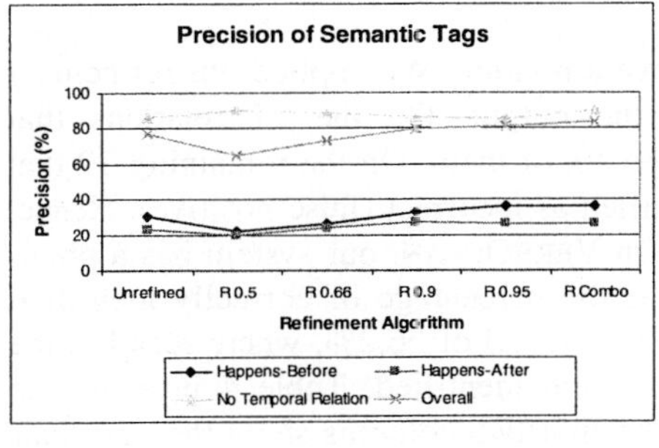

Fig. 1. Refinement precision on each semantic tag

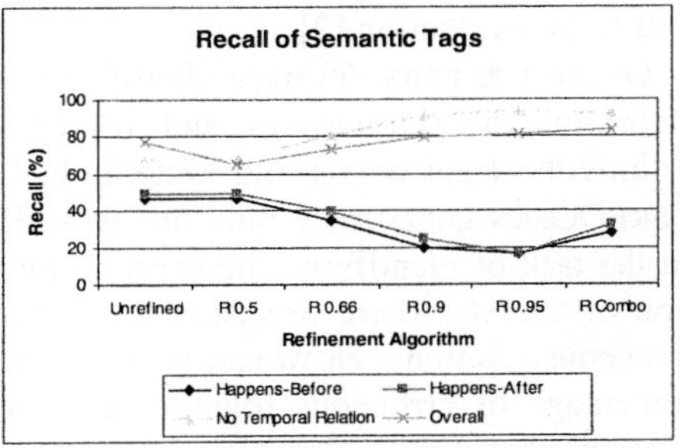

Fig. 2. Refinement recall on each semantic tag

refinement moved 113 to *happens-before* and 109 to *happens-after* The precision of the 0.5 refinement on the *no temporal relation* tag increased by 4%; however, the precision on the temporal relations decreased by 5.7%. At the 0.95 refinement level, 54 of the 81 relations originally tagged *happens-before* and 45 of the 70 relations originally tagged *happens-after* were changed to *no temporal relation*. Only 34 of the 849 *no temporal relations* were changed. At this level, the precision of *no temporal relation* tag decreased by 0.8% and the temporal relations' precision increased by 4%.

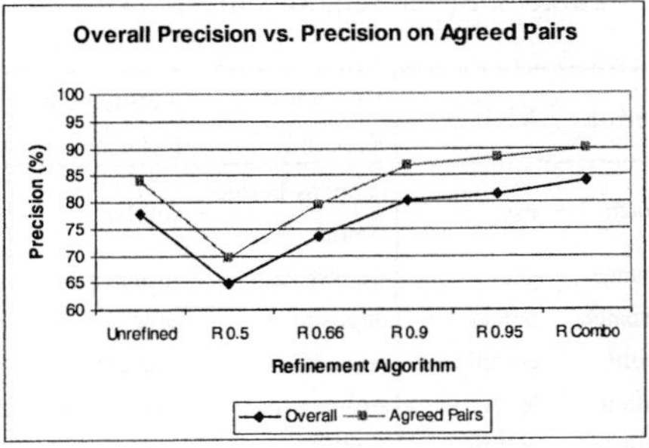

Fig. 3. Refinement precision on all 1000 verb pairs vs. on the 819 verb pairs on which the annotators agree on tag

Hence, at the 0.5 level, pairs classified as *no temporal relation* were improved while at the 0.95 level, pairs classified as a temporal relation were improved. To leverage benefits of the two, we applied both the 0.5 and 0.95 level refinements and kept *happens-before* and *happens-after* classifications from the 0.95 level, and kept the *no temporal relation* classification from the 0.5 level.[5] 284 verb pairs were left unclassified. On the 716 classified verb pairs, refinement improved accuracy by 6.3%.

[5] This combination is guaranteed to be free of conflicts in classification because it is impossible for a relation to be classified as temporal at the 0.95 threshold level while being classified as non-temporal at the 0.5 level.

Figures 1 and 2 illustrate the refinement precision and recall for each semantic tag. Both annotators have agreed on 819 verb pairs, and we examined performance on these. Figure 3 shows a higher precision on these pairs as compared to the overall set, illustrating that what is easier for the annotators is easier for the system.

4.3 Observations on Refining Other Relations

We have briefly investigated refining other semantic relations in VERBOCEAN. The extent of the evaluation was limited by availability of human judgments. We randomly sampled 100 pairs from DIRT and presented the classifications to three human judges for evaluation [2].

Of the 100 pairs, 66 were identified to have a relation. We applied our refinement algorithm to VERBOCEAN and inspected the output. On the 37 relations that VERBOCEAN got wrong, our system identified six of them. On the remaining 29 that VERBOCEAN got correct, only one was identified as incorrect (false positive). Hence, on the task of identifying incorrect relations in VERBOCEAN, our system has a precision of 85.7%, where precision is defined as the percentage of correctly identified erroneous relations. However, it only achieved a recall of 16.2%, where recall is the percentage of erroneous relations that our system identified. Table 4 presents the relations that were refined by our system. The first two columns show the verb pair while the next two columns show the original relation in VERBOCEAN.

Table 4. Seven relations in VERBOCEAN refined by a small test run on other relations

Verb 1	Verb 2	VERBOCEAN Relation	Refinement Relation	Judge 1 Relation	Judge 2 Relation	Judge 3 Relation
attach	use	happens-before similar	similar	none	none	none
bounce	get	weaker than	stronger than	none	none	none
dispatch	defeat	opposite	none	none	none	happens-before
doom	complicate	opposite	similar*	none	stronger-than	stronger-than
flatten	level	stronger than	no relation*	similar	similar	similar
outlaw	codify	similar	opposite	none	none	opposition
privatize	improve	happens-before	none	happens-before	happens-before	happens-before

* only revision of relation to its opposite or "none" was attempted here

4.4 Discussion

Our evaluation focused on the presence or absence of relations after refinement, without exploiting the fact that our framework also updates confidences in a given relation. The additional information about confidence can benefit probabilistic inference approaches (e.g., [3]).

Possible extensions to the algorithm include a more elaborate inference from graph structure, for example treating the absence of certain paths as counter-evidence. Suppose that relations A *happens-before* B and A *similar* A' were detected, but the relation A' *happens-before* B was not. Then, the *absence* of a path

A similar A' happens-before B
suggests the absence of A *happens-before* B.

Other important avenues of future work include applying our framework to other relations (e.g., *strength* in VERBOCEAN) and to better characterize the refinement thresholds.

5 Conclusions

We presented a method for refining edges in graphs by leveraging the semantics of multiple noisy paths. We re-estimated the presence of an edge between a pair of nodes from the evidence provided by multiple indirect paths between the nodes. Our approach applies to a variety of relation types: transitive symmetric, transitive asymmetric, and relations inducing equivalence classes. We applied our model to refining temporal verb relations in a semantic resource called VERBOCEAN. Experiments showed a 16.1% error reduction after refinement. On the 72% refinement decisions that it was most confident, the error reduction was 28.3%.

The usefulness of a semantic resource is highly dependent on its quality, which is often poor in automatically mined resources. With graph refinement frameworks such as the one presented here, many of these resources may be improved automatically.

References

1. Berland, M. and E. Charniak, 1999. Finding parts in very large corpora. In *ACL-1999*. pp. 57-64. College Park, MD.
2. Chklovski, T., and Pantel, P. 2004. VERBOCEAN: Mining the Web for Fine-Grained Semantic Verb Relations. In *Proceedings of 2004 Conference on Empirical Methods in Natural Language Processing (EMNLP 2004)*, Barcelona, Spain, July 25-26.
3. Domingos, P. and Richardson, M. 2004. Markov Logic: A unifying framework for statistical relational learning. In *Proceedings of ICML Workshop on Statistical Relational Learning and its Connections to Other Fields*. Banff, Canada.
4. Lin, D. and Pantel, P. 2001. Discovery of inference rules for question answering. Natural Language Engineering, 7(4):343-360.
5. Pantel, P. and Ravichandran, D. 2004. Automatically labeling semantic classes. In *Proceedings HLT/NAACL-04*. pp. 321-328. Boston, MA.
6. Shinzato, K. and Torisawa, K. 2004. Acquiring hyponymy relations from web documents. In *Proceedings of HLT-NAACL-2004*. pp. 73-80. Boston, MA.
7. Siegel, S. and Castellan Jr., N. 1988. Nonparametric Statistics for the Behavioral Sciences. McGraw-Hill.

Semantic Role Tagging for Chinese at the Lexical Level

Oi Yee Kwong and Benjamin K. Tsou

Language Information Sciences Research Centre, City University of Hong Kong,
Tat Chee Avenue, Kowloon, Hong Kong
{rlolivia, rlbtsou}@cityu.edu.hk

Abstract. This paper reports on a study of semantic role tagging in Chinese, in the absence of a parser. We investigated the effect of using only lexical information in statistical training; and proposed to identify the relevant headwords in a sentence as a first step to partially locate the corresponding constituents to be labelled. Experiments were done on a textbook corpus and a news corpus, representing simple data and complex data respectively. Results suggested that in Chinese, simple lexical features are useful enough when constituent boundaries are known, while parse information might be more important for complicated sentences than simple ones. Several ways to improve the headword identification results were suggested, and we also plan to explore some class-based techniques for the task, with reference to existing semantic lexicons.

1 Introduction

As the development of language resources progresses from POS-tagged corpora to syntactically annotated treebanks, the inclusion of semantic information such as predicate-argument relations is becoming indispensable. The expansion of the Penn Treebank into a Proposition Bank [11] is a typical move in this direction. Lexical resources also need to be enhanced with semantic information (e.g. [5]). In fact the ability to identify semantic role relations correctly is essential to many applications such as information extraction and machine translation; and making available resources with this kind of information would in turn facilitate the development of such applications.

Large-scale production of annotated resources is often labour-intensive, and thus needs automatic labelling to streamline the work. The task can essentially be perceived as a two-phase process, namely to *recognise* the constituents bearing some semantic relationship to the target verb in a sentence, and then to *label* them with the corresponding semantic roles.

In their seminal proposal, Gildea and Jurafsky approached the task using various features such as headword, phrase type, and parse tree path [6]. Such features have remained the basic and essential features in subsequent research, irrespective of the variation in the actual learning components. In addition, parsed sentences are often required, for extracting the path features during training and providing the argument boundaries during testing. The parse information is deemed important for the performance of role labelling [7, 8].

More precisely, in semantic role labelling, parse information is rather more critical for the identification of boundaries for candidate constituents than for the extraction

R. Dale et al. (Eds.): IJCNLP 2005, LNAI 3651, pp. 804 – 814, 2005.

of training data. Its limited function in training, for instance, is reflected in the low coverage reported (e.g. [21]). However, given the imperfection of existing automatic parsers, which are far from producing gold standard parses, many thus resort to shallow syntactic information from simple chunking, though results often turn out to be less satisfactory than with full parses.

This limitation is even more pertinent for the application of semantic role labelling to languages which do not have sophisticated parsing resources. In the case of Chinese, for example, there is considerable variability in its syntax-semantics interface; and when one has more nested and complex sentences such as those from news articles, it becomes more difficult to capture the sentence structures by typical examples.

It is therefore worthwhile to investigate alternatives to the role labelling task for Chinese under the parsing bottleneck, both in terms of the features used and the short-cut or compromise to at least partially pin down the relevant constituents. A series of related questions deserve consideration here:

1. how much could we achieve with only parse-independent features in the role labelling process;
2. with constituent boundaries unknown in the absence of parse information, could we at least identify the headwords in the relevant constituents to be tagged; and
3. whether the unknown boundary problem varies with the nature of the dataset, e.g., will the degradation in performance from known boundaries to unknown boundaries be more serious for complicated sentences than for simple sentences.

So in the current study we experiment on the use of parse-independent features for semantic role labelling in Chinese, for locating the headwords of the constituents corresponding to arguments to be labelled. We will also compare the results on two training and testing datasets.

In Section 2, related work will be reviewed. In Section 3, the data used in the current study will be introduced. Our proposed method will be explained in Section 4, and the experiment reported in Section 5. Results and future work will be discussed in Section 6, followed by conclusions in Section 7.

2 Related Work

The definition of semantic roles falls on a continuum from abstract ones to very specific ones. Gildea and Jurafsky [6], for instance, used a set of roles defined according to the FrameNet model [2], thus corresponding to the frame elements in individual frames under a particular domain to which a given verb belongs. Lexical entries (in fact not limited to verbs, in the case of FrameNet) falling under the same frame will share the same set of roles. Gildea and Palmer [7] defined roles with respect to individual predicates in the PropBank, without explicit naming. To date PropBank and FrameNet are the two main resources in English for training semantic role labelling systems.

The theoretical treatment of semantic roles is also varied in Chinese. In practice, for example, the semantic roles in the Sinica Treebank mark not only verbal arguments but also modifier-head relations within individual constituents, following a head-driven principle [4]. In our present study, we use a set of more abstract semantic roles, which are generalisable to most Chinese verbs and are not dependent on particular predicates. They will be further introduced in Section 3.

The major concerns in automatic semantic role labelling include the handling of alternations (as in "the window broke" and "John broke the window", where in both cases "the window" should be tagged as "patient" despite its appearance in different positions in the sentences), and generalisation to unseen constituents and predicates. For the latter, clustering and semantic lexicons or hierarchies have been used (e.g. [6]), or similar argument structures are assumed for near-synonyms and verbs under the same frame (e.g. [11]).

Approaches in automatic semantic role labelling are mostly statistical, typically making use of a number of features extracted from parsed training sentences. In Gildea and Jurafsky [6], the features studied include phrase type (*pt*), governing category (*gov*), parse tree path (*path*), position of constituent with respect to the target predicate (*position*), voice (*voice*), and headword (*h*). The labelling of a constituent then depends on its likelihood to fill each possible role *r* given the features and the target predicate *t*, as in the following, for example:

$$P(r \mid h, pt, gov, position, voice, t)$$

Subsequent studies exploited a variety of implementation of the learning component, including Maximum Entropy (e.g. [1, 12]), Support Vector Machines (e.g. [9, 16]), etc. Transformation-based approaches were also used (e.g. [10, 19]). Swier and Stevenson [17] innovated with an unsupervised approach to the problem, using a bootstrapping algorithm, and achieved 87% accuracy.

While the estimation of the probabilities could be relatively straightforward, the key often lies in locating the candidate constituents to be labelled. A parser of some kind is needed. Gildea and Hockenmaier [8] compared the effects of Combinatory Categorial Grammar (CCG) derivations and traditional Treebank parsing, and found that the former performed better on core arguments, probably due to its ability to capture long range dependencies, but comparable for all arguments. Gildea and Palmer [7] compared the effects of full parsing and shallow chunking; and found that when constituent boundaries are known, both automatic parses and gold standard parses resulted in about 80% accuracy for subsequent automatic role tagging, but when boundaries are unknown, results with automatic parses dropped to 57% precision and 50% recall. With chunking only, performance further degraded to below 30%. Problems mostly arise from arguments which correspond to more than one chunk, and the misplacement of core arguments.

A couple of evaluation exercises for semantic role labelling were organized recently, such as the shared task in CoNLL-2004 using PropBank data [3], and the one in SENSEVAL-3 using the FrameNet dataset [15]. Most systems in SENSEVAL-3 used a parser to obtain full syntactic parses for the sentences, whereas systems participating in the CoNLL task were restricted to using only shallow syntactic information. Results reported in the former tend to be higher. Although the dataset may be a factor affecting the labelling performance, it nevertheless reinforces the usefulness of full syntactic information.

According to Carreras and Màrquez [3], for English, the state-of-the-art results reach an F_1 measure of slightly over 83 using gold standard parse trees and about 77 with real parsing results. Those based on shallow syntactic information is about 60.

The usefulness of parse information for semantic role labelling would be especially interesting in the case of Chinese, given the flexibility in its syntax-semantics interface (e.g. the object after 吃 'eat' could refer to the *Patient* as in 吃蘋果 'eat apple', *Location* as in 吃食堂 'eat canteen', *Duration* as in 吃三年 'eat three years', etc.). In the absence of sophisticated parsing resources, however, we attempt to investigate how well one could simply use a set of parse-independent features and backward guess the likelihood of headwords to partially locate the candidate constituents to be labelled.

3 The Data

3.1 Materials

As mentioned in the introduction, we attempted to investigate the difference between labelling simple sentences and complex ones. For this purpose, sentences from primary school textbooks were taken as examples for simple data, while sentences from a large corpus of newspaper texts were taken as complex examples.

Two sets of primary school Chinese textbooks popularly used in Hong Kong were taken for reference. The two publishers were Keys Press [22] and Modern Education Research Society Ltd [23]. Texts for Primary One to Six were digitised, segmented into words, and annotated with parts-of-speech (POS). The two sets of textbooks amount to a text collection of about 165K character tokens and upon segmentation about 109K word tokens (about 15K word types). There were about 2,500 transitive verb types, with frequency ranging from 1 to 926.

The complex examples were taken from a subset of the LIVAC synchronous corpus[1] [13, 18]. The subcorpus consists of newspaper texts from Hong Kong, including local news, international news, financial news, sports news, and entertainment news, collected in 1997-98. The texts were segmented into words and POS-tagged, amounting to about 1.8M character tokens and upon segmentation about 1M word tokens (about 47K word types). There were about 7,400 transitive verb types, with frequency ranging from 1 to just over 6,300.

3.2 Training and Testing Data

For the current study, a set of 41 transitive verbs common to the two corpora (hereafter referred to as textbook corpus and news corpus), with frequency over 10 and over 50 respectively, was sampled.

Sentences in the corpora containing the sampled verbs were extracted. Constituents corresponding to semantic roles with respect to the target verbs were annotated by a trained annotator, whose annotation was verified by another. In this study, we worked with a set of 11 predicate-independent abstract semantic roles. According to the *Dictionary of Verbs in Contemporary Chinese* (*Xiandai Hanyu Dongci Dacidian*, 現代漢語動詞大詞典) [14], our semantic roles include the necessary arguments for most

---

[1] http://www.livac.org

verbs such as *Agent* and *Patient*, or *Goal* and *Location* in some cases; and some optional arguments realised by adjuncts, such as *Quantity*, *Instrument*, and *Source*. Some examples of semantic roles with respect to a given predicate are shown in Fig. 1.

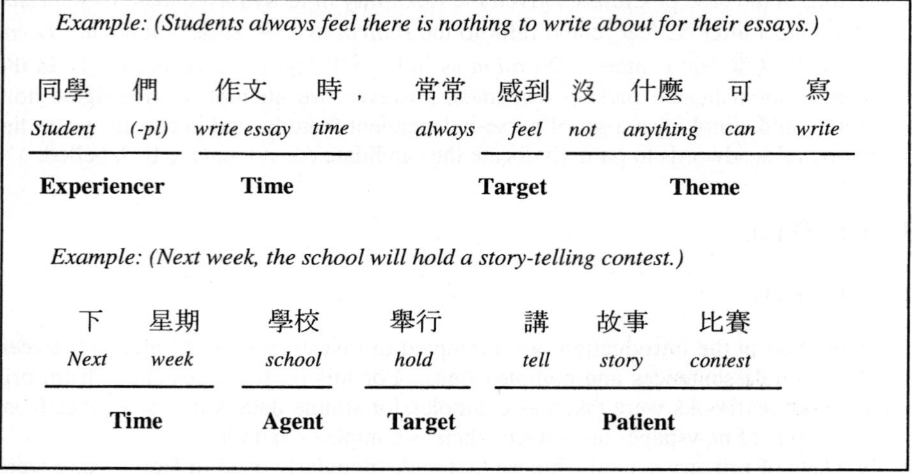

Fig. 1. Examples of semantic roles with respect to a given predicate

Altogether 980 sentences covering 41 verb types in the textbook corpus were annotated, resulting in 1,974 marked semantic roles (constituents); and 2,122 sentences covering 41 verb types in the news corpus were annotated, resulting in 4,933 marked constituents[2].

The role labelling system was trained on 90% of the sample sentences from the textbook corpus and the news corpus separately; and tested on the remaining 10% of the respective corpora.

4 Automatic Role Labelling

The automatic labelling was based on the statistical approach in Gildea and Jurafsky [6]. In Section 4.1, we will briefly mention the features employed in the training process. Then in Sections 4.2 and 4.3, we will explain our approach for locating headwords in candidate constituents associated with semantic roles, in the absence of parse information.

4.1 Training

In this study, our probability model was based mostly on parse-independent features extracted from the training sentences, namely:

---

[2] These figures only refer to the samples used in the current study. In fact over 35,000 sentences in the LIVAC corpus have been semantically annotated, covering about 1,500 verb types and about 80,000 constituents were marked.

Headword (head): The headword from each constituent marked with a semantic role was identified. For example, in the second sentence in Fig. 1, 學校 (school) is the headword in the constituent corresponding to the *Agent* of the verb 舉行 (hold), and 比賽 (contest) is the headword of the noun phrase corresponding to the *Patient*.

Position (posit): This feature shows whether the constituent being labelled appears before or after the target verb. In the first example in Fig. 1, the *Experiencer* and *Time* appear on the left of the target, while the *Theme* is on its right.

POS of headword (HPos): Without features provided by the parse, such as phrase type or parse tree path, the POS of the headword of the labelled constituent could provide limited syntactic information.

Preposition (prep): Certain semantic roles like *Time* and *Location* are often realised by prepositional phrases, so the preposition introducing the relevant constituents would be an informative feature.

Hence for automatic labelling, given the target verb *t*, the candidate constituent, and the above features, the role *r* which has the highest probability for *P(r | head, posit, HPos, prep, t)* will be assigned to that constituent. In this study, however, we are also testing with the unknown boundary condition where candidate constituents are not available in advance, hence we attempt to partially locate them by identifying their headwords to start with. Our approach is explained in the following sections.

4.2 Locating Candidate Headwords

In the absence of parse information, and with constituent boundaries unknown, we attempt to partially locate the candidate constituents by trying to identify their corresponding headwords first. Sentences in our test data were segmented into words and POS-tagged. We thus divide the recognition process into two steps, locating the headword of a candidate constituent first, and then expanding from the headword to determine its boundaries.

Basically, if we consider every word in the same sentence as the target verb (both to its left and to its right) a potential headword for a candidate constituent, what we need to do is to find out the most probable words in the sentence to match against individual semantic roles. We start with a feature set with more specific distributions, and back off to feature sets with less specific distributions. Hence in each round we look for

$$\arg\max_{r} P(r \mid feature\ set)$$

for every candidate word. Ties are resolved by giving priority to the word nearest to the target verb in the sentence.

Fig. 2 shows an example illustrating the procedures for locating candidate headwords. The target verb is 發現 (discover). In the first round, using features *head*, *posit*, *HPos*, and *t*, 時候 (time) and 問題 (problem) were identified as *Time* and *Patient* respectively. In the fourth subsequent round, backing off with features *posit* and *HPos*, 我們 (we) was identified as a possible *Agent*. In this round a few other words were identified as potential *Patients*. However, since *Patient* was already located in the previous round, those come up in this round are not considered. So in the end the headwords identified for the test sentence are 我們 (we) for *Agent*, 問題 (problem) for *Patient* and 時候 (time) for *Time*.

Sentence:
溫習的時候，我們發現了許多平時沒有想到，或是未能解決的問題，於是就去問爸爸。
During revision, we discover a lot of problems which we have not thought of or cannot be solved, then we go and ask father.

Candidate Headwords	Round 1 …	Round 4	Final Result
溫習 (revision)		~~Patient~~	
時候 (time)	Time	----	**Time**
我們 (we)		Agent	**Agent**
平時 (normally)			
想到 (think)		~~Patient~~	
能 (can)			
解決 (solve)		~~Patient~~	
問題 (problem)	Patient	----	**Patient**
去 (go)		~~Patient~~	
問 (ask)		~~Patient~~	
爸爸 (father)		~~Patient~~	

Fig. 2. Example illustrating the procedures for locating candidate headwords

4.3 Constituent Boundary

Upon the identification of headwords for potential constituents, the next step is to expand from these headwords for constituent boundaries. Although we are not doing this step in the current study, it can potentially be done via some finite state techniques, or better still, with shallow syntactic processing like simple chunking if available.

5 The Experiment

5.1 Testing

The system was trained and tested on the textbook corpus and the news corpus respectively. The testing was done under the "known constituent" and "unknown constituent" conditions. The former essentially corresponds to the known-boundary condition in related studies; whereas in the unknown-constituent condition, which we will call "headword location" condition hereafter, we tested our method of locating candidate headwords as explained above in Section 4.2. In this study, every noun, verb, adjective, pronoun, classifier, and number within the test sentence containing the target verb was considered a potential headword for a candidate constituent corresponding to some semantic role. The performance was measured in terms of the precision (defined as the percentage of correct outputs among all outputs), recall (defined as the percentage of correct outputs among expected outputs), and F_1 score which is the harmonic mean of precision and recall.

5.2 Results

The results are shown in Table 1, for testing on both the textbook corpus and the news corpus under the known constituent condition and the headword location condition.

Table 1. Results on two datasets for known constituents and headword location

	Textbook Data			**News Data**		
	Precision	*Recall*	F_1	*Precision*	*Recall*	F_1
Known Constituent	93.85	87.50	90.56	90.49	87.70	89.07
Headword Location	46.12	61.98	52.89	38.52	52.25	44.35

Under the known constituent condition, the results were good on both datasets, with an F_1 score of about 90. This is comparable or even better to the results reported in related studies for known boundary condition. The difference is that we did not use any parse information in the training, not even phrase type. Our results thus suggest that for Chinese, even without more complicated syntactic information, simple lexical information might already be useful in semantic role tagging.

Comparison of the known constituent condition with the headword location condition shows that performance for the latter has expectedly dropped. However, the degradation was less serious with simple sentences than with complex ones, as is seen from the higher precision and recall for textbook data than for news data under the headword location condition. What is noteworthy here is that recall apparently deteriorated less seriously than precision. In the case of news data, for instance, we were able to maintain over 50% recall but only obtained about 39% precision. The surprisingly low precision is attributed to a technical inadequacy in the way we break ties. In this study we only make an effort to eliminate multiple tagging of the same role to the same target verb in a sentence on either side of the target verb, but not if they appear on both sides of the target verb. This should certainly be dealt with in future experiments. The differential degradation of performance between textbook data and news data also suggests the varied importance of constituent boundaries to simple sentences and complex ones, and hence possibly their varied requirements for full parse information for the semantic labelling task.

6 Discussion

According to Carreras and Màrquez [3], the state-of-the-art results for semantic role labelling systems based on shallow syntactic information is about 15 lower than those with access to gold standard parse trees, i.e., around 60. Our experimental results for the headword location condition, with no syntactic information available at all, give an F_1 score of 52.89 and 44.35 respectively for textbook data and news data. This further degradation in performance is nevertheless within expectation, but whether this is also a result of the difference between English and Chinese remains to be seen.

In response to the questions raised in the introduction, firstly, the results for the known constituent condition (F_1 of 90.56 and 89.07 for textbook data and news data respectively) have shown that even if we do not use parse-dependent features such as governing category and parse tree path, results are not particularly affected. In other words, lexical features are already very useful as long as the constituent boundaries are given. Secondly, in the absence of parse information, the results of identifying the relevant headwords in order to partially locate candidate constituents were not as satisfactory as one would like to see. One possible way to improve the results, as suggested above, would be to improve the handling of ties. Other possibilities including a class-based method could also be used, as will be discussed below. Thirdly, results for news data degraded more seriously than textbook data from the known constituent condition to the headword location condition. This suggests that complex sentences in Chinese are more affected by the availability of full parse information. To a certain extent, this might be related to the relative flexibility in the syntax-semantics interface of Chinese; hence when a sentence gets more complicated, there might be more intervening constituents and the parse information would be useful to help identify the relevant ones in semantic role labelling.

In terms of future development, apart from improving the handling of ties in our method, as mentioned in the previous section, we plan to expand our work in several respects, the major part of which is on the generalization to unseen headwords and unseen predicates. As is with other related studies, the examples available for training for each target verb are very limited; and the availability of training data is also insufficient in the sense that we cannot expect them to cover all target verb types. Hence it is very important to be able to generalize the process to unseen words and predicates. To this end, we will experiment with a semantic lexicon like *Tongyici Cilin* (同義詞詞林, a Chinese thesaurus) in both training and testing, which we expect to improve the overall performance.

Another area of interest is to look at the behaviour of near-synonymous predicates in the tagging process. Many predicates may be unseen in the training data, but while the probability estimation could be generalized from near-synonyms as suggested by a semantic lexicon, whether the similarity and subtle differences between near-synonyms with respect to the argument structure and the corresponding syntactic realisation could be distinguished would also be worth studying. Related to this is the possibility of augmenting the feature set with semantic features. Xue and Palmer [20], for instance, looked into new features such as syntactic frame, lexicalized constituent type, etc., and found that enriching the feature set improved the labelling performance.

Another direction of future work is on the location of constituent boundaries upon the identification of the headword. As mentioned earlier on, this could probably be tackled by some finite state techniques or with the help of simple chunkers.

7 Conclusion

The study reported in this paper has thus tackled the unknown constituent boundary condition in semantic role labelling for Chinese, by attempting to locate the corresponding headwords first. We experimented with both simple and complex data. Using only parse-independent features, our results on known boundary condition are comparable to those reported in related studies. Although the results for headword location condition were not as good as state-of-the-art performance with shallow syntactic information, we have nevertheless suggested some possible ways to improve the results. We have further observed that the influence of full syntactic information is more serious for complex data than simple data, which might be a consequence of the characteristic syntax-semantics interface of Chinese. As a next step, we plan to explore some class-based techniques for the task, with reference to existing semantic lexicons.

Acknowledgements

This work is supported by Competitive Earmarked Research Grants (CERG) of the Research Grants Council of Hong Kong under grant Nos. CityU1233/01H and CityU1317/03H.

References

1. Baldewein, U., Erk, K., Padó, S. and Prescher, D. (2004) Semantic Role Labelling With Chunk Sequences. In *Proceedings of the Eighth Conference on Computational Natural Language Learning (CoNLL-2004)*, Boston, Massachusetts, pp.98-101.
2. Baker, C.F., Fillmore, C.J. and Lowe, J.B. (1998) The Berkeley FrameNet Project. In *Proceedings of the 36th Annual Meeting of the Association for Computational Linguistics and the 17th International Conference on Computational Linguistics (COLING-ACL '98)*, Montreal, Quebec, Canada, pp.86-90.
3. Carreras, X. and Màrquez, L. (2004) Introduction to the CoNLL-2004 Shared Task: Semantic Role Labeling. In *Proceedings of the Eighth Conference on Computational Natural Language Learning (CoNLL-2004)*, Boston, Massachusetts, pp.89-97.
4. Chen, F-Y., Tsai, P-F., Chen, K-J. and Huang, C-R. (1999) Sinica Treebank (中文句結構樹資料庫的構建). *Computational Linguistics and Chinese Language Processing, 4(2)*: 87-104.
5. Fellbaum, C., Palmer, M., Dang, H.T., Delfs, L. and Wolf, S. (2001) Manual and Automatic Semantic Annotation with WordNet. In *Proceedings of the NAACL-01 SIGLEX Workshop on WordNet and Other Lexical Resources*, Invited Talk, Pittsburg, PA.
6. Gildea, D. and Jurafsky, D. (2002) Automatic Labeling of Semantic Roles. *Computational Linguistics, 28(3)*: 245-288.
7. Gildea, D. and Palmer, M. (2002) The Necessity of Parsing for Predicate Argument Recognition. In *Proceedings of the 40th Meeting of the Association for Computational Linguistics (ACL-02)*, Philadelphia, PA.
8. Gildea, D. and Hockenmaier, J. (2003) Identifying Semantic Roles Using Combinatory Categorial Grammar. In *Proceedings of the 2003 Conference on Empirical Methods in Natural Language Processing*, Sapporo, Japan.

9. Hacioglu, K., Pradhan, S., Ward, W., Martin, J.H. and Jurafsky, D. (2004) Semantic Role Labeling by Tagging Syntactic Chunks. In *Proceedings of the Eighth Conference on Computational Natural Language Learning (CoNLL-2004)*, Boston, Massachusetts, pp.110-113.
10. Higgins, D. (2004) A transformation-based approach to argument labeling. In *Proceedings of the Eighth Conference on Computational Natural Language Learning (CoNLL-2004)*, Boston, Massachusetts, pp.114-117.
11. Kingsbury, P. and Palmer, M. (2002) From TreeBank to PropBank. In *Proceedings of the Third Conference on Language Resources and Evaluation (LREC-02)*, Las Palmas, Canary Islands, Spain.
12. Kwon, N., Fleischman, M. and Hovy, E. (2004) SENSEVAL Automatic Labeling of Semantic Roles using Maximum Entropy Models. In *Proceedings of the Third International Workshop on the Evaluation of Systems for the Semantic Analysis of Text (SENSEVAL-3)*, Barcelona, Spain, pp.129-132.
13. Kwong, O.Y. and Tsou, B.K. (2003) Categorial Fluidity in Chinese and its Implications for Part-of-speech Tagging. In *Proceedings of the Research Note Session of the 10th Conference of the European Chapter of the Association for Computational Linguistics*, Budapest, Hungary, pp.115-118.
14. Lin, X., Wang, L. and Sun, D. (1994) *Dictionary of Verbs in Contemporary Chinese*. Beijing Language and Culture University Press.
15. Litkowski, K.C. (2004) SENSEVAL-3 Task: Automatic Labeling of Semantic Roles. In *Proceedings of the Third International Workshop on the Evaluation of Systems for the Semantic Analysis of Text (SENSEVAL-3)*, Barcelona, Spain, pp.9-12.
16. Moldovan, D., Girju, R., Olteanu, M. and Fortu, O. (2004) SVM Classification of FrameNet Semantic Roles. In *Proceedings of the Third International Workshop on the Evaluation of Systems for the Semantic Analysis of Text (SENSEVAL-3)*, Barcelona, Spain, pp.167-170.
17. Swier, R.S. and Stevenson, S. (2004) Unsupervised Semantic Role Labelling. In *Proceedings of the 2004 Conference on Empirical Methods in Natural Language Processing*, Barcelona, Spain, pp.95-102.
18. Tsou, B.K., Tsoi, W.F., Lai, T.B.Y., Hu, J. and Chan, S.W.K. (2000) LIVAC, A Chinese Synchronous Corpus, and Some Applications. In *Proceedings of the ICCLC International Conference on Chinese Language Computing*, Chicago, pp. 233-238.
19. Williams, K., Dozier, C. and McCulloh, A. (2004) Learning Transformation Rules for Semantic Role Labeling. In *Proceedings of the Eighth Conference on Computational Natural Language Learning (CoNLL-2004)*, Boston, Massachusetts, pp.134-137.
20. Xue, N. and Palmer, M. (2004) Calibrating Features for Semantic Role Labeling. In *Proceedings of the 2004 Conference on Empirical Methods in Natural Language Processing*, Barcelona, Spain, pp.88-94.
21. You, J-M. and Chen, K-J. (2004) Automatic Semantic Role Assignment for a Tree Structure. In *Proceedings of the 3rd SigHAN Workshop on Chinese Language Processing*, ACL-04, Barcelona, pp.109-115.
22. 啓思中國語文 *Qisi Zhongguo Yuwen*. Primary 1-6, 24 volumes, 2004. Hong Kong: Keys Press.
23. 現代中國語文 *Xiandai Zhongguo Yuwen*. Primary 1-6, 24 volumes, 2004. Hong Kong: Modern Education Research Society Ltd.

Detecting Article Errors Based on the Mass Count Distinction

Ryo Nagata[1], Takahiro Wakana[2], Fumito Masui[2], Atsuo Kawai[2], and Naoki Isu[2]

[1] Hyogo University of Teacher Education, 942-1 Shimokume, Yashiro, 673-1494 Japan
rnagata@info.hyogo-u.ac.jp
[2] Mie University, 1577, Kurimamachiya, Tsu, 514-8507, Japan
{wakana, masui, kawai, isu}@ai.info.mie-u.ac.jp

Abstract. This paper proposes a method for detecting errors concerning article usage and singular/plural usage based on the mass count distinction. Although the mass count distinction is particularly important in detecting these errors, it has been pointed out that it is hard to make heuristic rules for distinguishing mass and count nouns. To solve the problem, first, instances of mass and count nouns are automatically collected from a corpus exploiting surface information in the proposed method. Then, words surrounding the mass (count) instances are weighted based on their frequencies. Finally, the weighted words are used for distinguishing mass and count nouns. After distinguishing mass and count nouns, the above errors can be detected by some heuristic rules. Experiments show that the proposed method distinguishes mass and count nouns in the writing of Japanese learners of English with an accuracy of 93% and that 65% of article errors are detected with a precision of 70%.

1 Introduction

Although several researchers [1,2,3] have shown that heuristic rules are effective to detecting grammatical errors in the English writing of second language learners, it has been pointed out that it is hard to write heuristic rules for detecting article errors [1]. To be precise, it is hard to write heuristic rules for distinguishing mass and count nouns which are particularly important in detecting article errors. The major reason for this is that whether a noun is a mass noun or a count noun greatly depends on its meaning or its surrounding context (Refer to Pelletier and Schubert [4] for detailed discussion on the mass count distinction).

Article errors are very common among Japanese learners of English [1,5]. This is perhaps because the Japanese language does not have an article system similar to that of English. Thus, it is favorable for error detecting systems aiming at Japanese learners of English to be capable of detecting article errors. In other words, such systems need to somehow distinguish mass and count nouns in the writing of Japanese learners of English.

R. Dale et al. (Eds.): IJCNLP 2005, LNAI 3651, pp. 815–826, 2005.

In view of this background, we propose a method for automatically distinguishing mass and count nouns in context to complement the conventional heuristic rules for detecting grammatical errors. In this method, mass and count nouns are distinguished by words surrounding the target noun. Words surrounding the target noun are collected from a corpus and weighted based on their occurrences. The weighted words are used for distinguishing mass and count nouns in detecting article errors.

Given the mass count distinction, errors concerning singular/plural usage, which are also common in the writing of Japanese learners of English, can be detected as well as article errors. For example, given that the noun *information* is a mass noun, *informations* can be detected as an error. Considering this, we include errors concerning singular/plural usage in the target errors of this paper. Hereafter, to keep the notation simple, the target errors[1] will be referred to as article errors.

The next section describes related work on distinguishing mass and count nouns. Section 3 proposes the method for automatically distinguishing mass and count nouns. Section 4 describes heuristic rules for detecting article errors based on the mass count distinction given by the proposed method. Section 5 discusses results of experiments conducted to evaluate the proposed method.

2 Related Work

Several researchers have proposed methods for distinguishing mass and count nouns in the past. Allan [6] has presented an approach to distinguishing nouns that are used only as either mass or count based on countability environments. This distinction is called countability preferences. Baldwin and Bond [7,8] have proposed several methods for learning the countability preferences from corpora[2]. Bond and Vatikitis-Bateson [9] have shown that nouns' countability can be predicted using an ontology[3]. O'Hara et al. [10] have proposed a method for classifying mass and count nouns based on semantic information (Cyc ontological types [11]).

Unfortunately, it is difficult to apply the above methods to complement the conventional heuristic rules for detecting grammatical errors. The methods [6,7,8,9] are not enough for the purpose, because the majority of nouns can be used as both mass and count depending on the surrounding context [12]. The methods [9,10] cannot be readily applicable to the purpose because they work only when semantic information on nouns is given. It would be difficult to extract semantic information from nouns in the writing of learners of English.

[1] The details of the target errors are shown in Sect. 4.

[2] They define four way countability preferences: fully countable, uncountable, bipartite, and plural only.

[3] They define five way countability preferences: fully countable, strongly countable, weakly countable, uncountable, and plural only.

3 Distinguishing Mass and Count Nouns

In the proposed method, decision lists [13] are used to distinguish mass and count nouns. Generally, decision lists are learned from a set of manually tagged training data. In the proposed method, however, training data can be automatically generated from a raw corpus.

Section 3.1 describes how to generate training data. Section 3.2 describes how to learn decision lists from the training data. Section 3.3 explains the method for distinguishing mass and count nouns using the decision lists.

3.1 Generating Training Data

To generate training data, first, instances of the target noun that head their noun phrase (NP) are collected from a corpus with their surrounding words. This can be simply done by an existing chunker or parser.

Then, the collected instances are tagged with mass or count by tagging rules. For example, the underlined *chicken*:

Example 1. ... are a lot of <u>*chicken*</u>s in the roost ...

is tagged as

Example 2. ... are a lot of <u>*chickens/count*</u> in the roost ...

because it is in plural form.

We have made tagging rules based on linguistic knowledge [6,14,12]. Figure 1 and Table 1 represent the tagging rules. Figure 1 shows the framework of the tagging rules. Each node in Fig. 1 represents a question applied to the instance in question. For example, the root node reads "Is the instance in question plural?". Each leaf represents a result of the classification. For example, if the answer is 'yes' at the root node, the instance in question is tagged with count. Otherwise, the question at the lower node is applied and so on. The tagging rules do not classify instances as mass or count in some cases. These unclassified instances are tagged with the symbol '?'. Unfortunately, they cannot readily be included in training data. For simplicity of implementation, they are excluded from training data.

Table 1. Words used in the tagging rules

(a)	(b)	(c)
the indefinite article	much	*the definite article*
another	less	*demonstrative adjectives*
one	enough	*possessive adjectives*
each	all	*interrogative adjectives*
—	sufficient	*quantifiers*
—	—	*'s genitives*

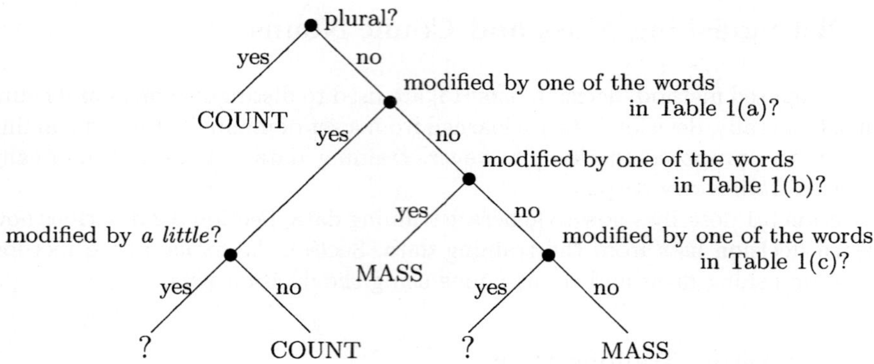

Fig. 1. Framework of the tagging rules

Note that the tagging rules can be used only for distinguishing mass and count nouns in texts containing no errors. They cannot be used in the writing of Japanese learners of English that may contain errors including article errors; they are based on article and the distinction between singular and plural.

Finally, the tagged instances are stored in a file with their surrounding words. Each line in the file consists of one of the tagged instances and its surrounding words as shown in *Example 2*. The file is used as training data for learning a decision list.

3.2 Learning Decision Lists

A decision list consists of a set of rules that are learned from training data. Each rule matches with the template as follows:

$$\text{If } \textit{a condition is true}, \text{ then } \textit{a decision}. \quad (1)$$

To define the template in the proposed method, let us have a look at the following two examples:

Example 3. I read the <u>paper</u>.

Example 4. The <u>paper</u> is made of hemp pulp.

The underlined *paper*s in both sentences cannot simply be classified as mass or count by the tagging rules presented in Sect. 3.1 because both are singular and modified by the definite article. Nevertheless, we can tell that the former is a count noun and that the latter is a mass noun from the contexts. This suggests that the mass count distinction is often determined by words surrounding the target noun. In *Example 3*, we can tell that the *paper* refers to something that can be read from *read*, and therefore it is a count noun. Likewise, in *Example 4*, the *paper* refers to a certain substance from *made* and *pulp*, and therefore it is a mass noun.

Taking this observation into account, we define the template based on words surrounding the target noun. To formalize the template, we will use a random variable MC that takes either *mass* or *count* to denote that the target noun is a mass noun or a count noun, respectively. We will also use w and C to denote a word and a certain context around the target noun, respectively. We define three types of C: np, $-k$, and $+k$ that denote the contexts consisting of the noun phrase that the target noun heads, k words to the left of the noun phrase, and k words to its right, respectively. Then the template is formalized by

If a word w appears in the context C of the target noun,
then the target noun is distinguished as MC.

Hereafter, to keep the notation simple, the template is abbreviated to

$$w_C \rightarrow MC. \tag{2}$$

Now rules that match with the template can be learned from the training data generated in Sect. 3.1. All we need to do is to collect words in C from the training data. Here, the words in Table 1 are excluded. Also, function words such as pronouns and auxiliary verbs, cardinal and quasi-cardinal numerals, and the target noun are excluded. All words are reduced to their morphological stem and converted entirely to lower case when collected. For example, the following tagged instance:

Example 5. She ate a piece of fried <u>*chicken*/mass</u> for dinner.

would give a set of rules that match with the template:

Example 6.
$piece_{-3} \rightarrow mass, \quad fry_{np} \rightarrow mass, \quad dinner_{+3} \rightarrow mass$

for the target noun *chicken* being *mass* when $k = 3$.

In addition to the above rules, a default rule is defined. It is based on the target noun itself and used when no other confident rules[4] are found in the decision list for the target noun. It is defined by

$$t \rightarrow MC_{\text{major}} \tag{3}$$

where t and MC_{major} denote the target noun and the major case of MC in the training data, respectively. Equation (3) reads "If the target noun appears, then it is distinguished as the major case".

The log-likelihood ratio [15] decides in which order rules in a decision list are applied to the target noun in novel context. It is defined by

$$log \frac{p(MC|w_C)}{p(\overline{MC}|w_C)} \tag{4}$$

[4] Confidence is given by the log-likelihood ratio, which will be defined by (4).

where $\overline{MC}$ is the exclusive event of MC and $p(MC|w_C)$ is the probability that the target noun is used as MC when w appears in the context C. For the default rule, the log-likelihood ratio is defined by

$$log \frac{p(MC_{\text{major}}|t)}{p(\overline{MC_{\text{major}}}|t)} \tag{5}$$

It is important to exercise some care in estimating $p(MC|w_C)$. In principle, we could simply count the number of times that w appears in the context C of the target noun used as MC in the training data. However, this estimate can be unreliable, when w does not appear often in the context. To solve this problem, using a smoothing parameter α [16], $p(MC|w_C)$ is estimated by

$$p(MC|w_C) = \frac{f(w_C, MC) + \alpha}{f(w_C) + m\alpha} \tag{6}$$

where $f(w_C)$ and $f(w_C, MC)$ are occurrences of w appearing in C and those in C of the target noun used as MC, respectively. The constant m is the number of possible classes, that is, $m = 2$ (*mass* or *count*) in our case, and introduced to satisfy $p(MC|w_C) + p(\overline{MC}|w_C) = 1$. In this paper, α is set to 0.5. Likewise, $p(MC_{\text{major}}|t)$ is estimated by

$$p(MC_{\text{major}}|t) = \frac{f(t, MC_{\text{major}}) + \alpha}{f(t) + m\alpha} \tag{7}$$

Rules in a decision list are sorted in descending order by (4) and (5). They are tested on the target noun in novel context in this order. Rules sorted below the default rule are discarded because they are never used as we will see in Sect. 3.3.

Table 2 shows part of a decision list for the target noun *chicken* that was learned from a subset of the BNC (British National Corpus) [17]. Note that the rules are divided into two columns for the purpose of illustration in Table 2; in practice, they are merged into one just as shown in Table 3.

On one hand, we associate the words in the left half with food or cooking. On the other hand, we associate those in the right half with animals. From this observation, we can say that *chicken* is a count noun in the sense of an animal but a mass noun when referring to food or cooking, which agrees with the knowledge presented in previous work [18].

Table 2. Rules in a decision list (target noun: *chicken*, $k = 3$)

	Mass		Count
w_C	Log-likelihood ratio	w_C	Log-likelihood ratio
$piece_{-3}$	1.49	$count_{-3}$	1.49
$fish_{-3}$	1.28	$peck_{+3}$	1.32
$dish_{-3}$	1.23	pig_{np}	1.23
$skin_{+3}$	1.23	run_{-3}	1.23
$serve_{+3}$	1.18	egg_{np}	1.18

Table 3. An example of a decision list (target noun: *chicken*, $k = 3$)

Rules	Log-likelihood ratio
$piece_{-3} \rightarrow mass$, $count_{-3} \rightarrow count$	1.49
$peck_{+3} \rightarrow count$	1.32
$fish_{-3} \rightarrow mass$	1.28
$dish_{-3} \rightarrow mass$, $pig_{np} \rightarrow count$, $\cdots$	1.23
:	:

3.3 Distinguishing the Target Noun in Novel Context

To distinguish the target noun in novel context, each rule in the decision list is tested on it in the sorted order until the first applicable one is found. It is distinguished by the first applicable one. If two or more applicable rules (e.g., "$piece_{-3} \rightarrow mass$" and "$count_{-3} \rightarrow count$" in Table 3) are found, it is distinguished by the major decisions of the two or more applicable rules. For example, suppose there are three applicable rules and two of them are for mass nouns (one of them is for count nouns). In this case, the target noun is distinguished as mass. Ties are broken by rules sorted below the ties. If ties include the default rule, it is distinguished by the default rule.

The following is an example of distinguishing the target noun *chicken*. Suppose that the decision list shown in Table 3 and the following sentence are given:

Example 7. I ate a piece of <u>*chicken*</u> with salad.

It turns out that the first rule "$piece_3 \rightarrow mass$" in Table 3 is applicable to the instance. Thus, it is distinguished as a mass noun.

It should be noted that rules sorted below the default rule are never used because the default rule is always applicable to the target noun. This is the reason why rules sorted below the default rule are discarded as mentioned in Sect. 3.2.

4 Heuristic Rules for Detecting Article Errors

So far, a method for distinguishing mass and count nouns has been described. This section describes heuristic rules for detecting article errors based on the mass count distinction given by the method.

Article errors are detected by the following three steps. Rules in each step are examined on each target noun in the target text.

In the first step, any mass noun in plural form is detected as an article error. If an article error is detected in the first step, the rest of the steps are not applied.

In the second step, article errors are detected by the rules described in Table 4. The symbol "$\star$" in Table 4 denotes that the combination of the corresponding row and column is erroneous. For example, the third row denotes that

Table 4. Detection rules used in the second step

Pattern	Count Singular	Count Plural	Mass Singular	Mass Plural
{another, each, one}	—	⋆	⋆	⋆
{a lot of, all, enough, lots of, sufficient}	⋆	—	—	⋆
{much}	⋆	⋆	—	⋆
{kind of, sort of, that, this}	—	⋆	—	⋆
{few, many, these,those}	⋆	—	⋆	⋆
{countless, numerous, several, various}	⋆	—	⋆	⋆
cardinal number except one	⋆	—	⋆	⋆
{any, some, no, *'s genitives*}	—	—	—	⋆
{*interrogative adjectives*, *possessive adjectives*}	—	—	—	⋆

Table 5. Detection rules used in the third step

	Singular a	Singular the	Singular ϕ	Plural a	Plural the	Plural ϕ
Mass	⋆	–	–	⋆	⋆	⋆
Count	–	–	⋆	⋆	–	–

plural count nouns, singular mass nouns, and plural mass nouns that are modified by *another*, *each*, or *one* are erroneous. The symbol "—" denotes that no error can be detected by the table. If one of the rules in Table 4 is applied to the target noun, the third step is not applied.

In the third step, article errors are detected by the rules described in Table 5. The symbols "a", "the", and "ϕ" in Table 5 denote the indefinite article, the definite article, and no article, respectively. The symbols "⋆" and "—" are the same as in Table 4. For example, "⋆" in the third row and second column denotes that the singular mass nouns modified by the indefinite article is erroneous.

In addition to the three steps, article errors are detected by exceptional rules. The indefinite article that modifies other than the head noun is judged to be erroneous (e.g., *an expensive). Likewise, the definite article that modifies other than the head noun and adjectives is judged to be erroneous (e.g., *the them).

5 Experiments

5.1 Experimental Conditions

A subset of essays[5] written by Japanese learners of English were used as the target texts in the experiments. The subset contained 30 essays (1747 words). A native speaker of English who was a professional rewriter of English recognized 62 article errors in the subset.

[5] http://www.lb.u-tokai.ac.jp/lcorpus/index-j.html

The British National Corpus (BNC) [17] was used to learn decision lists. Spoken data were excluded from the corpus. Also, sentences the OAK system[6], which was used to extract NPs from the corpus, failed to analyze were excluded. After these operations, the size of the corpus approximately amounted to 80 million words (the size of the original BNC is approximately 100 million words). Hereafter, unless otherwise specified, the corpus will be referred to as the BNC.

Performance of the proposed method was evaluated by accuracy, recall, and precision. Accuracy is defined by

$$\frac{\text{No. of mass and count nouns distinguished correctly}}{\text{No. of distinguished target nouns}}. \tag{8}$$

Namely, accuracy measures how accurately the proposed method distinguishes mass and count nouns. Recall is defined by

$$\frac{\text{No. of article errors detected correctly}}{\text{No. of article errors in the target essays}}. \tag{9}$$

Recall measures how well the proposed method detects all the article errors in the target essays. Precision is defined by

$$\frac{\text{No. of article errors detected correctly}}{\text{No. of detected article errors}}. \tag{10}$$

Precision measures how well the proposed method detects only the article errors in the target essays.

5.2 Experimental Procedures

First, decision lists for each target noun in the target essays were learned from the BNC. To extract noun phrases and their head nouns, the OAK system was used[7]. An optimal value for k (window size of context) was estimated as follows. For 23 nouns[8] shown in [12] as examples of nouns used as both mass and count nouns, accuracy was calculated using the BNC and ten-fold cross validation. As a result of setting $k = 3, 10, 50$, it turned out that $k = 3$ maximized the average accuracy. Following this result, $k = 3$ was selected in the experiments.

Second, the target nouns were distinguished whether they were mass or count by the proposed method, and then article errors were detected by the mass

[6] OAK System Homepage: http://nlp.cs.nyu.edu/oak/

[7] We evaluated how accurately training data can be generated by the tagging rules using the OAK system. It turned out that the accuracy was 0.997 against 2903 instances of 23 nouns shown in [12] which were randomly selected from the BNC; 1694 of those were tagged with mass or count by the tagging rules and 1689 were tagged correctly. The five errors were due to the OAK system.

[8] In [12], 25 nouns are shown. Of those, two nouns (*hate* and *spelling*) were excluded because they only appeared 12.1 and 15.6 times on average in the ten-fold cross validation, respectively.

count distinction and the heuristic rules described in Sect. 4. As a preprocessing, spelling errors in the target essays were corrected using a spell checker.

Finally, the results of the detection were compared to those done by the native-speaker of English. From the comparison, accuracy, recall, and precision were calculated.

Comparison of performance of the proposed method to that of other methods is difficult because there is no generally accepted test set or performance baseline [19]. Given this limitation, we compared performance of the proposed method to that of Grammarian[9], a commercial grammar checker. We also compared it to that of a method that used only the default rules in the decision lists. We tested them on the same target essays to measure their performances.

5.3 Experimental Results and Discussion

In the experiments, the proposed method distinguished mass and count nouns in the target essays with accuracy of 0.93. This means that the proposed method is effective to distinguishing mass and count nouns in the writing of Japanese learners of English. From this result, we can say that the proposed method can complement the conventional heuristic rules for detecting grammatical errors.

Because of the high accuracy of the proposed method, it detected more than half of the article errors in the target essays (Table 6). Of the undetected article errors (22 out of 62), only four were due to the misclassification of mass and count nouns by the proposed method. The rest were article errors that were not detected even if the mass count distinction was given. For example, extra definite articles such as "I like *the gardening." cannot be detected even if whether the noun "gardening" is a mass noun or a count noun is given. Therefore, it is necessary to exploit other sources of information than the mass count distinction to detect these kinds of article error. For instance, exploiting the relation between sentences could be used to detect these kinds of article error.

The proposed method outperformed the method using only the default rules in both recall and precision. This means that words surrounding the target nouns are good indicators of the mass count distinction. For example, the proposed method correctly distinguished the target noun *place* in the phrase *beautiful place* as a count noun by "$beautiful_{np} \rightarrow count$" and detected an article error from it whereas the method using only the default rules did not.

Table 6. Experimental results

Method	Recall	Precision
Proposed	0.65	0.70
Default only	0.60	0.69
Grammarian	0.13	1.00

[9] Grammarian Pro X ver. 1.5: http://www.mercury-soft.com/

In precision, the proposed method was outperformed by Grammarian; since Grammarian is a commercial grammar checker, it seems to be precision-oriented. The proposed method made 17 false-positives. Of the 17 false-positives, 13 were due to the misclassification of mass and count nouns by the proposed method. Especially, the proposed method often made false-positives in idiomatic phrases (e.g., by plane). This result implies that some methods for handling idiomatic phrases may improve the performance. Four were due to the chunker used to analyze the target essays. Since the chunker is designed for analyzing texts that contain no errors, it is possible that a chunker designed for analyzing texts written by Japanese learners of English reduces this kind of false-positive.

6 Conclusions

This paper has proposed a method for distinguishing mass and count nouns to complement the conventional heuristic rules for detecting grammatical errors. The experiments have shown that the proposed method distinguishes mass and count nouns with a high accuracy (0.93) and that the recall and precision are 0.65 and 0.70, respectively. From the results, it follows that the proposed method can complement the conventional heuristic rules for detecting grammatical errors in the writing of Japanese learners of English.

The experiments have also shown that approximately 35% of article errors in the target essays are not detected by the mass count distinction. For future work, we will study methods for detecting the undetected article errors.

Acknowledgments

The authors would like to thank Sekine Satoshi who has developed the OAK System. The authors also would like to thank three anonymous reviewers for their advice on this paper.

References

1. Kawai, A., Sugihara, K., Sugie, N.: ASPEC-I: An error detection system for English composition. IPSJ Journal (in Japanese) **25** (1984) 1072–1079
2. McCoy, K., Pennington, C., Suri, L.: English error correction: A syntactic user model based on principled "mal-rule" scoring. In: Proc. 5th International Conference on User Modeling. (1996) 69–66
3. Schneider, D., McCoy, K.: Recognizing syntactic errors in the writing of second language learners. In: Proc. 17th International Conference on Computational Linguistics. (1998) 1198–1204
4. Pelletier, F., Schubert, L.: Two theories for computing the logical form of mass expressions. In: Proc.10th International Conference on Computational Linguistics. (1984) 108–111

5. Izumi, E., Uchimoto, K., Saiga, T., Supnithi, T., Isahara, H.: Automatic error detection in the Japanese learners' English spoken data. In: Proc. 41st Annual Meeting of the Association for Computational Linguistics. (2003) 145–148
6. Allan, K.: Nouns and countability. J. Linguistic Society of America **56** (1980) 541–567
7. Baldwin, T., Bond, F.: A plethora of methods for learning English countability. In: Proc. 2003 Conference on Empirical Methods in Natural Language Processing. (2003) 73–80
8. Baldwin, T., Bond, F.: Learning the countability of English nouns from corpus data. In: Proc. 41st Annual Meeting of the Association for Computational Linguistics. (2003) 463–470
9. Bond, F., Vatikiotis-Bateson, C.: Using an ontology to determine English countability. In: Proc. 19th International Conference on Computational Linguistics. (2002) 99–105
10. O'Hara, T., Salay, N., Witbrock, M., Schneider, D., Aldag, B., Bertolo, S., Panton, K., Lehmann, F., Curtis, J., Smith, M., Baxter, D., Wagner, P.: Inducing criteria for mass noun lexical mappings using the Cyc KB, and its extension to WordNet. In: Proc. 5th International Workshop on Computational Semantics. (2003) 425–441
11. Lenat, D.: CYC: A large-scale investment in knowledge infrastructure. Communications of the ACM **38** (1995) 33–38
12. Huddleston, R., Pullum, G.: The Cambridge Grammar of the English Language. Cambridge University Press, Cambridge (2002)
13. Rivest, R.: Learning decision lists. Machine Learning **2** (1987) 229–246
14. Gillon, B.: The lexical semantics of English count and mass nouns. In: Proc. Special Interest Group on the Lexicon of the Association for Computational Linguistics. (1996) 51–61
15. Yarowsky, D.: Unsupervised word sense disambiguation rivaling supervised methods. In: Proc. 33rd Annual Meeting of the Association for Computational Linguistics. (1995) 189–196
16. Yarowsky, D.: Homograph Disambiguation in Speech Synthesis. Springer-Verlag (1996)
17. Burnard, L.: Users Reference Guide for the British National Corpus. version 1.0. Oxford University Computing Services, Oxford (1995)
18. Ostler, N., Atkins, B.: Predictable meaning shift: Some linguistic properties of lexical implication rules. In: Proc. of 1st SIGLEX Workshop on Lexical Semantics and Knowledge Representation. (1991) 87–100
19. Chodorow, M., Leacock, C.: An unsupervised method for detecting grammatical errors. In: Proc. 1st Meeting of the North America Chapter of the Association for Computational Linguistics. (2000) 140–147

Principles of Non-stationary Hidden Markov Model and Its Applications to Sequence Labeling Task

JingHui Xiao, BingQuan Liu, and XiaoLong Wang

School of Computer Science and Techniques,
Harbin Institute of Technology, Harbin, 150001, China
{xiaojinghui, liubq, wangxl}@insun.hit.edu.cn

Abstract. Hidden Markov Model (Hmm) is one of the most popular language models. To improve its predictive power, one of Hmm hypotheses, named *limited history hypothesis*, is usually relaxed. Then Higher-order Hmm is built up. But there are several severe problems hampering the applications of high-order Hmm, such as the problem of parameter space explosion, data sparseness problem and system resource exhaustion problem. From another point of view, this paper relaxes the other Hmm hypothesis, named *stationary (time invariant) hypothesis*, makes use of time information and proposes a non-stationary Hmm (NSHmm). This paper describes NSHmm in detail, including its definition, the representation of time information, the algorithms and the parameter space and so on. Moreover, to further reduce the parameter space for mobile applications, this paper proposes a variant form of NSHmm (VNSHmm). Then NSHmm and VNSHmm are applied to two sequence labeling tasks: pos tagging and pinyin-to-character conversion. Experiment results show that compared with Hmm, NSHmm and VNSHmm can greatly reduce the error rate in both of the two tasks, which proves that they have much more predictive power than Hmm does.

1 Introduction

Statistical language model plays an important role in natural language processing and great efforts are devoted to the research of language modeling. Hidden Markov Model (Hmm) is one of the most popular language models. It was first proposed by IBM in speech recognition [1] and achieved great success. Then Hmm has a wide range of applications in many domains, such as OCR [2], handwriting recognition [3], machine translation [4], Chinese pinyin-to-character conversion [5] and so on.

To improve Hmm's predictive power, one of Hmm hypotheses [6] named *limited history hypothesis*, is usually relaxed and higher-order Hmm is proposed. But as the order of Hmm increases, its parameter space explodes at an exponential rate, which may result in several severe problems, such as data sparseness problem [7], system resource exhaustion problem and so on. From another point of view, this paper relaxes the other Hmm hypothesis, named *stationary hypothesis*, makes use of time information and proposes non-stationary Hmm (NSHmm). This paper first defines NSHmm in a formalized form, and then discusses how to represent time information in NSHmm. After that, the algorithms of NSHmm are provided and the parameter space complexity is calculated. Moreover, to further reduce the parameter space, a

R. Dale et al. (Eds.): IJCNLP 2005, LNAI 3651, pp. 827 – 837, 2005.

variant form of NSHmm (VNSHmm) is proposed later. At last, NSHmm and VNSHmm are applied to two sequence labeling tasks: pos tagging and pinyin-to-character conversion. As the experiment results show, compared with Hmm, NSHmm and VNSHmm can greatly reduce the error rate in the both two tasks.

The rest of this paper is structured as follows: in section 2 we briefly review the definition of standard Hmm. In section 3, NSHmm is proposed and the relative questions are discussed in detail. Experiments and results are discussed in section 4. Finally, we give our conclusions in section 5 and plan the further work in section 6.

2 Hidden Markov Model

Hmm is a function of Markov process and can be mathematically defined as a five-tuple $M = <\Omega, \Sigma, \rho, \alpha, \theta>$ which consists of:

1. A finite set of (hidden) states Ω.
2. A finite set of (observed) symbols Σ.
3. A state transition function ρ: $\Omega \times \Omega$-> [0, 1].
4. A symbol emission function α: $\Omega \times \Sigma$-> [0, 1].
5. And an initial state probability function θ: Omega -> [0, 1].

The functions of ρ, α and θ are usually estimated by MLE principle on large scale corpus. Based on the above definition, Hmm makes two hypotheses at the same time:

1. *Limited history hypothesis*: the current state is completely decided by the last state before, but irrelative to the entire state history.
2. *Stationary hypothesis*: the state transition function ρ is completely determined by states, but irrelative to the time when state transition occurs. So it is with the symbol emission function.

There are three fundamental questions and a series of corresponding algorithms for Hmm:

1. Given Hmm, how to calculate the probability of a sequence observation? Forward algorithm and backward algorithm can handle that question.
2. Given Hmm and an observation sequence, how to find the best state sequence to explain the observation? Viterbi algorithm can fulfill that task.
3. Given an observation sequence, how to estimate the parameters of Hmm to best explain the observed data? Baum-Welch algorithm can solve that problem.

Hmm is a popular language model and has been applied to many tasks in natural language processing. For example, in pos tagging, the word sequence is taken as the observation of Hmm, and the pos sequence as the hidden state chain. Viterbi algorithm can find the best pos sequence corresponding to the word sequence.

3 Non-stationary Hidden Markov Model

3.1 Motivation

There are many approaches to improve the predictive power of Hmm in practice. For example, factorial Hmm [8] is proposed by decomposing the hidden state representation into multiple independent Markov chains. In speech recognition, a factorial Hmm can represent the combination of multiple signals which are produced independently and the characteristics of each signal are described by a distinct Markov chain. And some Hmms use neural networks to estimate phonetic posterior probability in speech recognition [9]. The input layer of the network typically covers both the past states and the further states. However, from the essential definition of Hmm, there are two ways to improve the predictive power of Hmm. One approach is to relax the limited history hypothesis and involve more history information into language model. The other is to relax the stationary hypothesis and make use of time information. In recent years, much research focuses on the first approach [10] and higher-order Hmm is built up. But as the order increases, the parameter space explodes at such an exponential rate that training corpus becomes too sparse and system resource exhausts soon. This paper adopts the second approach and tries to make good use of time information. Then NSHmm is proposed. Since there is no theoretical conflict between NSHmm and high-order Hmm, the two models can be combined together in proper conditions.

3.2 Definition for NSHmm

Similarly with Hmm, NSHmm is also mathematically defined as a five-tuple M = $<\Omega, \Sigma, \rho', \alpha', \theta'>$ which consists of:

1. A finite set of (hidden) states Ω.
2. A finite set of (observed) symbols Σ.
3. A state transition function $\rho': \Omega\times \Omega\times t \text{ -> } [0, 1]$.
4. A symbol emission function $\alpha': \Omega\times \Sigma\times t \text{ -> } [0, 1]$.
5. And an initial state probability function $\theta': \Omega\times t \text{ -> } [0, 1]$.

In the above definition, *t* is the time variable indicating when state transition or symbol emission occurs. Different from Hmm's definition, ρ', α' and θ' are all the functions of *t*. And they can still be estimated by MLE principle on large scale corpus. This key question of NSHmm is how to represent time information. We'll discuss that question in the next section.

3.3 Representation of Time Information

Since time information is to describe when the events of Hmm (e.g. state transition or symbol emission) occur, a natural way is to use the event index in Markov chain to represent the time information. But there are two serious problems with that method. Firstly, index has different meanings in the Markov chains of different length. Secondly, since a Markov chain may have arbitrary length, the event index can be any natural number. However, computer system can only deal with finite value. A refined method is to use the ratio of the event index and the length of Markov chain which is a real number of the range [0, 1]. But there are infinite real numbers in the range [0, 1]. In this paper, we divide the range [0, 1] into several equivalence classes (bins) and each class share the same time information. When training NSHmm, the functions of ρ', α' and θ' should be estimated in each bin respectively according to their time information. And when they are accessed, they should also get the value in the according bin. For example, the state transition function ρ' can be estimated by the formula below:

$$p_{ijt} = \frac{C(i,j,t)}{C(i,t)} \tag{1}$$

where $C(i,j,t)$ is the co-occurrence frequency of state i and state j at time t and it can be estimated by counting the co-occurrence times of state i and state j in the tth bin in each sentence of corpus. $C(i,t)$ is the frequency of state i at time t and can be estimated by counting the occurrence times of state i in the tth bin in the sentence of corpus. And the result P_{ijt} is the transition probability between state i and j at time t. It's similar to estimate the functions of α' and θ'.

3.4 Algorithms on Non-stationary Hidden Markov Model

The three fundamental questions of Hmm also exist in NSHmm. The corresponding algorithms, such as forward algorithm, viterbi algorithm and Baum-Welch algorithm, can work well in NSHmm, except that they have to first calculate the time information and then compute the function values of ρ', α' and θ' according to the statistical information in the corresponding bins.

3.5 Space Complexity Analysis

In this section, we will analyze the space complexity of NSHmm. Compared with Hmm, some conclusions can be drawn at the end of this section. For simplicity and convenience, we define some notations below:

- The hidden state number n
- The observed symbol number m
- The bin number for NSHmm k

In Hmm and NSHmm, all system parameters are devoted to simulate the three functions of ρ, α and θ. For Hmm, a vector of size n is usually used to store the initial probability of each state. An $n \times n$ matrix is adopted to store the transition probabilities between every two states, and $n \times m$ matrix to record the emission probabilities between states and observed symbols. The space complexity for Hmm is the sum of these three parts which is $O(n+n\times n+n\times m)$. For NSHmm, since ρ', α' and θ' are all the functions of time t, time information should be counted in. An $n \times k$ matrix is used to store the initial probability of each state at different time. An $n \times n\times k$ matrix is used to store the transition probability between each state at different time and $n \times m \times k$ matrix to keep the emission probability. Thus, the space complexity of NSHmm is $O((n+n\times n+n\times m)\times k)$ which is k times than that of Hmm. As the analysis shows, the space complexity of NSHmm increases at a linear speed with k, rather than at an exponential speed as high-order Hmm dose. Moreover, as k is usually far below than n, NSHmm is much easier to avoid the problem of parameter space explosion.

3.6 Variant Form of NSHmm

In this section, this paper proposes a variant form of NSHmm (VNSHmm). It's based on these facts: for some applications, such as on mobile platform, there is not enough system resource to build up a whole NSHmm. Then NSHmm has to be compressed. This paper constructs some statistical variables for time information and uses these statistical variables to substitute concrete time information in NSHmm. When computing the probability in VNSHmm, these statistical variables are combined together to calculate a coefficient for normal probability of Hmm.

Two statistical variables, expectation and variance of time information, are adopted in VNSHmm. And such assumptions are made that more weight should be awarded if the time of event occurring fits better with the training corpus, and less weight vice versa. The probability function in VNSHmm is defined as below:

$$p_t = \frac{1}{Z} e^{\alpha \times V / ((t-E)^2 + \beta)} \times p \tag{2}$$

where Z is a normalizing factor, and is defined as:

$$Z = \sum_{t=1}^{t=k} e^{\alpha \times V / ((t-E)^2 + \beta)} \times p \tag{3}$$

The notations in the formulation (2) and (3) are described in the following:

- Current time information t
- Expectation of time information E
- Variance of time information V
- State transition probability (or symbol emission probability) p
- Adjusted coefficients α and β

p_t is descendent with the term t-E which defines the difference between current time and time expectation in training corpus. As the value of t-E decreases, t fits for training corpus better and more weight is added to p_t. For example, we take a Chinese sentence as a state chain of Markov process. The word "首先"(first of all) usually leads a sentence in training corpus. For test corpus, more weight should be given to p_t if 首先(first of all) appears at the beginning of the sentence, whereas less weight if at the sentence end. p_t is ascendant with the variance V. The item V is mainly used to balance the value of term t-E for some active states. For example, in Chinese, some adjectives, such as "美丽"(beautiful), can appear at any position of the sentence. Then it's unreasonable to decrease p_t just because the term t-E increases. In such a situation, the value of item V for "美丽"(beautiful) is usually bigger than that of those inactive states (e.g.首先(first of all)). Then the item V can provide a balance for the value of t-E.

Since VNSHmm just makes use of expectation and variance, rather than the whole time information, its space complexity is equal to that of the NSHmm with only two bins, which is $O((n + n \times n + n \times m) \times 2)$.

4 Experiments

In the experiments, NSHmm and VNSHmm have been applied to two sequence labeling tasks: pos tagging and pinyin-to-character conversion. This paper will describe them in detail in the following two sections.

4.1 Pos Tagging

For pos tagging, this paper chooses the People's Daily corpus in 1998 which has been labeled by Peking University [11]. The first 5 month corpus is taken as training corpus and the 6th month as test corpus. Since most of pos-taggers are based on 2-order Hmm (trigram), 2-order NSHmm and 2-order VNSHmm are constructed respectively in the experiments.

We first calculate KL distances between the emission probability distribution of Hmm and the distributions of NSHmm at different time. Only when the distances are great, could NSHmm be expected to outperform Hmm; otherwise NSHmm would have similar performance as Hmm has. Since there are totally k different distance values for NSHmm with k bins, we just calculate the average distance for each NSHmm. The results are presented in table 1 as below:

Table 1. Average KL Distances between Emission Probability Distributions of NSHmm and Hmm

Bin Number	K=1	K=2	K=3	K=4	K=5	K=6	K=7	K=8
Aver KL Dis	0	0.08	0.12	0.15	0.17	0.19	0.21	0.22

From table 1 we can see that as the bin number increases, the average KL distance become bigger and bigger, which indicates there is more and more difference between the emission probability distributions of Hmm and that of NSHmm. Similar results can be gotten by comparing state-transition-probability distributions of the two models. And as time information increases, we expect more predictive power for NSHmm.

To prove the effectiveness of NSHmm and VNSHmm, in the rest of this section, two sets of experiments, close test and open test, are performed. The results of close test are showed in table 2, figure 1 and the results of open test are presented in table 3, figure 2 as below.

Table 2. Pos Tagging Close Test

Bin Number		K=1	K=2	K=3	K=4	K=5	K=6	K=7	K=8
Hmm (baseline)		6.04%	---	---	---	---	---	---	---
NSHmm	**Error Rate**	6.04%	5.63%	5.55%	5.52%	5.47%	5.44%	**5.42%**	5.47%
	Reduction	---	6.79%	8.11%	8.61%	9.44%	9.93%	**10.26%**	9.43%
VNSHmm	**Error Rate**	6.04%	**5.85%**	5.85%	5.85%	5.85%	5.85%	5.85%	5.85%
	Reduction	---	**3.15%**	3.15%	3.15%	3.15%	3.15%	3.15%	3.15%

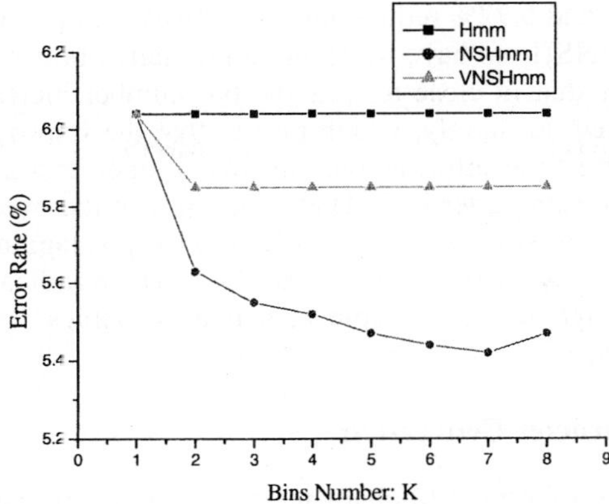

Fig. 1. Pos Tagging Close Test

Table 3. Pos Tagging Open Test

Bin Number		K=1	K=2	K=3	K=4	K=5	K=6	K=7	K=8
Hmm (baseline)		6.99%	---	---	---	---	---	---	---
NSHmm	**Error Rate**	6.99%	6.44%	**6.39%**	6.42%	6.40%	6.43%	6.47%	6.58%
	Reduction	---	7.87%	**8.58%**	8.15%	8.44%	8.01%	7.44%	5.87%
VNSHmm	**Error Rate**	6.99%	**6.59%**	6.59%	6.59%	6.59%	6.59%	6.59%	6.59%
	Reduction	---	**5.72%**	5.72%	5.72%	5.72%	5.72%	5.72%	5.72%

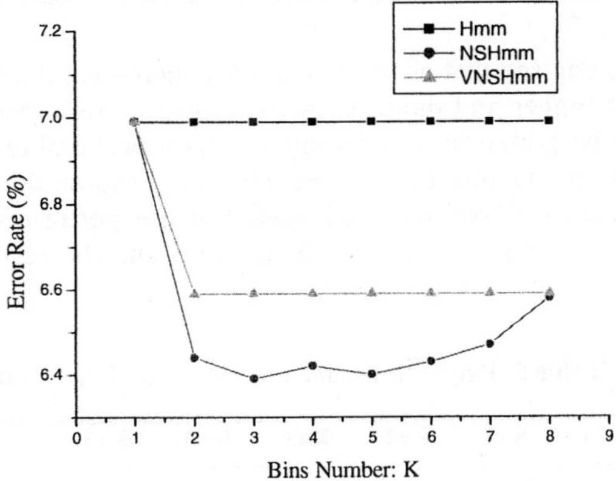

Fig. 2. Pos Tagging Open Test

As table 2 and table 3 have showed, no matter in close test or in open test, NSHmm and VNSHmm achieve much lower error rates than Hmm. NSHmm gets at most 10.26% error rate reduction and VNSHmm obtains 3.15% reduction in close test; and they achieve 8.58% and 5.72% reductions respectively in open test. These facts prove that NSHmm and VNSHmm have much more predictive power than Hmm has. From figure 1 we can see that in close test, as the bin number increases, the error rate of NSHmm is decreased constantly, which proves that the improvement of NSHmm is due to the increasing time information. But in the open test as figure 2 shows, the error rate stops decreasing after k=3. That is because of the overfitting problem. As a consequence, this paper suggests k=3 in NSHmm for pos tagging task. From figure 1 and figure 2, VNSHmm performs stably after k=2, which indicates a small number of parameters are enough to stat reliable statistical variables for VNSHmm and get improved performance.

4.2 Pinyin-to-Character Conversion

For the experiments of pinyin-to-character conversion, this paper adopts the same training corpus and test corpus as in pos tagging experiments. And 6763 Chinese frequent characters are chosen as the lexicon. This paper firstly converts all raw Chinese corpuses to the pinyin corpuses. Then based on the both kinds of corpuses, Hmm, NSHmm and VNSHmm are built up.

In the experiments, we first calculate KL distances between the state-transition-probability distributions of Hmm and the distributions of NSHmm at different time. As we have done in the pos tagging experiments, we just calculate the average KL distance for each NSHmm. The results are presented in table 4.

Table 4. Average KL Distances between State-Transition-Probability Distributions of NSHmm and Hmm

Bin Number	K=1	K=2	K=3	K=4	K=5	K=6	K=7	K=8
Aver KL Dis	0	0.08	0.12	0.15	0.17	0.18	0.19	0.21

From table 4 we can see that as the bin number increases, the average KL distance become bigger and bigger and more predictive power is expected for NSHmm. And similar results can be gotten by comparing emission probability distributions of the two models. Then in the rest of this section, we perform the pinyin-to-character conversion experiments. Close test and open test are performed respectively. The results of close test are showed in table 5, figure 3 and the results of open test are presented in table 6, figure 4 respectively.

Table 5. Pinyin-to-Character Conversion Close Test

Bin Number		K=1	K=2	K=3	K=4	K=5	K=6	K=7	K=8
Hmm (baseline)		8.30%	---	---	---	---	---	---	---
NSHmm	Error Rate	8.30%	7.17%	6.55%	6.08%	5.74%	5.43%	5.19%	**4.98%**
	Reduction	---	13.61%	21.08%	26.75%	30.84%	34.58%	37.47%	**40.00%**
VNSHmm	Error Rate	8.30%	**8.28%**	8.27%	8.28%	8.28%	8.28%	8.28%	8.28%
	Reduction	---	**0.24%**	0.24%	0.24%	0.24%	0.24%	0.24%	0.24%

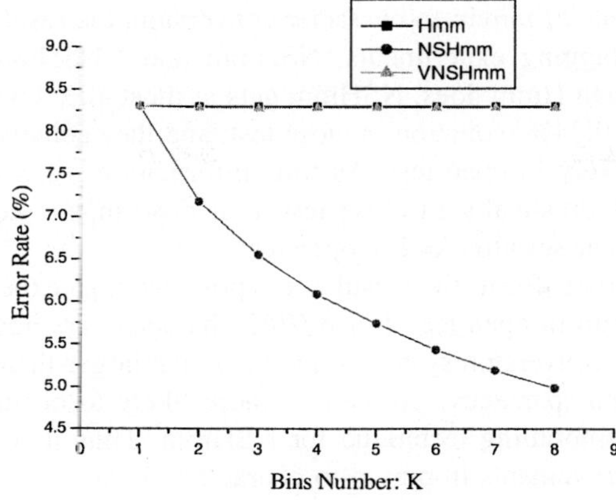

Fig. 3. Pinyin-to-Character Conversion Close Test

Table 6. Pinyin-to-Character Conversion Open Test

Bin Number		K=1	K=2	K=3	K=4	K=5	K=6	K=7	K=8
Hmm (baseline)		14.97%	---	---	---	---	---	---	---
NSHmm	**Error Rate**	14.97%	**12.62%**	13.16%	13.61%	13.93%	14.23%	14.52%	14.81%
	Reduction	---	**15.70%**	12.09%	9.08%	6.95%	4.94%	3.01%	1.07%
VNSHmm	**Error Rate**	14.97%	11.98%	**11.96%**	11.96%	11.96%	11.97%	11.97%	11.97%
	Reduction	---	19.97%	**20.11%**	20.11%	20.11%	20.04%	20.04%	20.04%

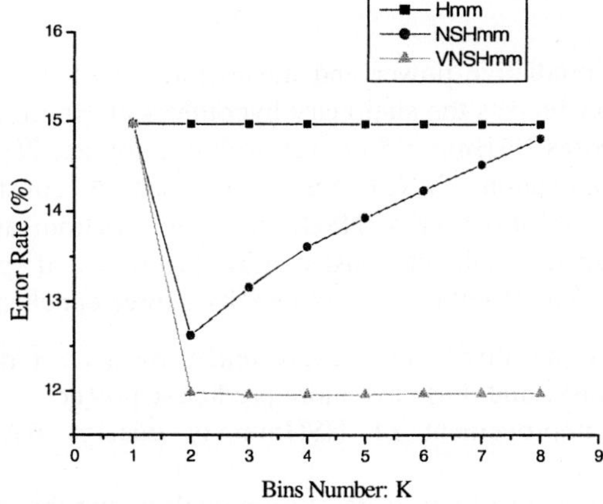

Fig. 4. Pinyin-to-Character Conversion Open Test

In the experiments of pinyin-to-character conversion, the results are very similar to those in the pos tagging experiments. NSHmm and VNSHmm show much more predictive power than Hmm does. NSHmm gets at most 40% error rate reduction and VNSHmm obtains 0.24% reduction in close test; and they achieve 15.7% and 20.11% reductions respectively in open test. As time information increases, the error rate of NSHmm decreases drastically in close test as it dose in pos tagging task. And the overfitting problem arises after k=2 in open test.

However, different from the results of pos tagging experiments, VNSHmm outperforms NSHmm in open test. Since 6763 characters are adopted as states set in pinyin-to-character conversion system, which is much larger than the states set in pos tagging system, data sparseness problem is more likely to occur. VNSHmm can be view as a natural smoothing technique for NSHmm. Thus it works better. We also notice that the improvements in pinyin-to-character conversion experiments are more significant than those in pos-tagging experiments. In pinyin-to-character conversion task, the state chain is the Chinese sentence. Intuitively, some Chinese characters and words are much more likely to occur at some certain positions in the sentence, for instance, the beginning or the end of a sentence. As we discuss in section 3.3, in practice the time information of events in NSHmm is defined as the position information where the events occur. Then NSHmm and VNSHmm can capture those characteristics straightforwardly. But in pos-tagging, the state chain is the pos tag stream. Pos is a more abstract concept than word, and their positional characteristics are not as apparent as words'. Henceforth, the improvements in pos-tagging experiments are less significant than those in pinyin-to-character conversion experiments. But NSHmm and VNSHmm can still model and make good use of those positional characteristics, and notable improvements have been achieved.

In a word, NSHmm and VNSHmm achieve much lower error rates in both of the two sequence labeling tasks and show much more predictive power than Hmm.

5 Conclusions

To improve Hmm's predictive power and meanwhile avoid the problems of high-order Hmm, this paper relaxes the stationary hypothesis of Hmm, makes use of time information and proposes NSHmm. Moreover, to further reduce NSHmm's parameter space for mobile applications, VNSHmm is proposed by constructing statistical variables on the time information of NSHmm. Then NSHmm and VNSHmm are applied to two sequence labeling tasks: pos tagging and pinyin-to-character conversion. From the experiment results, we can draw three conclusions in this paper:

- Firstly, NSHmm and VNSHmm achieve much lower error rates than Hmm in both of the two tasks and thus have more predictive power.
- Secondly, the improvement of NSHmm is due to the increasing time information.
- Lastly, a small number of parameters are enough to stat the statistical variables for VNSHmm.

6 Further Research

Since NSHmm is an enhanced Hmm, some problems of Hmm also exist in NSHmm. For example, data sparseness problem is arising as time information increases in NSHmm. Some smoothing algorithms should be designed to solve it in our further work. Also it's difficult to describe long distance constraint for NSHmm and further research should be devoted to this problem. To construct more compact NSHmm, proper prone techniques should be further studied and be compared with VNSHmm.

Acknowledgements

This investigation was supported emphatically by the National Natural Science Foundation of China (No.60435020) and the High Technology Research and Development Programme of China (2002AA117010-09).

We especially thank the three anonymous reviewers for their valuable suggestions and comments.

References

1. F. Jelinek. Self-Organized Language Modeling for Speech Recognition. IEEE ICASSP, 1989.
2. George Nagy. At the Frontier of OCR. Processing of IEEE. 1992, 80(7).
3. ZhiMing Xu, XiaoLong Wang, Kai Zhang, Yi Guan. A Post Processing Method for Online Handwritten Chinese Character recognition. Journal of Computer Research and Development. Vol.36, No. 5, May 1999.
4. Peter F. Brown, Stephen A. Della Pietra, Vincent J. Della Pietra, and Robert L. Mercer. The Mathematics of Statistical Machine Translation: Parameter Estimation. Computational Linguistics. 1992, 19(2).
5. Liu Bingquan, Wang Xiaolong and Wang Yuying, Incorporating Linguistic Rules in Statistical Chinese Language Model for Pinyin-to-Character Conversion. High Technology Letters. Vol.7 No.2, June 2001, P:8-13
6. Christopher D. Manning and Hinrich Schutze. Foundation of Statistic Natural Language Processing. The MIT Press. 1999.
7. Brown, Peter F., Vincent J. Della Pietra, Peter V. deSouza, Jenifer C. Lai, and Robert L. Mercer. Class-based n-gram models of natural language. Computational Linguistics, 18(4):467-479. 1992.
8. Z. Ghahramani and M. Jordan. Factorial hidden Markov models. Machine Learning, 29, 1997.
9. J. Fritsch. ACID/HNN: A framework for hierarchical connectionist acoustic modeling. In Proc. IEEE ASRU, Santa Barbara, December 1997.
10. Goodman, J. A bit of progress in language modeling. Computer Speech and Language, 403-434. 2001.
11. http://www.icl.pku.edu.cn

Integrating Punctuation Rules and Naïve Bayesian Model for Chinese Creation Title Recognition

Conrad Chen and Hsin-Hsi Chen

Department of Computer Science and Information Engineering,
National Taiwan University, Taipei, Taiwan
drchen@nlg.csie.ntu.edu.tw; hhchen@csie.ntu.edu.tw
http://nlg.csie.ntu.edu.tw/

Abstract. Creation titles, i.e. titles of literary and/or artistic works, comprise over 7% of named entities in Chinese documents. They are the fourth large sort of named entities in Chinese other than personal names, location names, and organization names. However, they are rarely mentioned and studied before. Chinese title recognition is challenging for the following reasons. There are few internal features and nearly no restrictions in the naming style of titles. Their lengths and structures are varied. The worst of all, they are generally composed of common words, so that they look like common fragments of sentences. In this paper, we integrate punctuation rules, lexicon, and naïve Bayesian models to recognize creation titles in Chinese documents. This pioneer study shows a precision of 0.510 and a recall of 0.685 being achieved. The promising results can be integrated into Chinese segmentation, used to retrieve relevant information for specific titles, and so on.

1 Introduction

Named entities are important constituents to identify roles, meanings, and relationships in natural language sentences. However, named entities are productive, so that it is difficult to collect them in a lexicon exhaustively. They are usually "unknown" when we process natural language sentences. Recognizing named entities in documents is indispensable for many natural language applications such as information retrieval [2], summarization [3], question answering [7], and so on.

Identifying named entities is even harder in Chinese than in many Indo-European languages like English. In Chinese, there are no delimiters to mark word boundaries and no special features such as capitalizations to indicate proper nouns, which constitute huge part of named entities. In the past, various approaches [1, 4, 10] have been proposed to recognize Chinese named entities. Most of them just focused on MUC-style named entities [8], i.e., personal names, location names, and organization names. The extensive studies cover nearly 80% of named entities in real documents [1]. Although the performance of such kinds of named entity recognizers is satisfiable, the rest 20% of named entities are so far rarely mentioned and often ignored in previous studies.

These rarely mentioned ones belong to various sorts, such as terminologies, aliases and nicknames, brands, etc. These sorts may not occur as frequently as personal names or location names in a corpus, but the importance of the former in documents

R. Dale et al. (Eds.): IJCNLP 2005, LNAI 3651, pp. 838 – 848, 2005.

of specific domains is no less than that of the latter. For example, knowing names of dishes would be very important to understand articles about cooking. Among these rarely addressed named entities, titles of creations, such as book names, song titles, sculpture titles, etc., are one of the most important sorts. According to Chen & Lee (2004)'s study [1] of Academia Sinica Balanced Corpus (abbreviated ASBC corpus hereafter), about 7% of named entities are titles of creations. In other words, more than one-third of rarely mentioned named entities are titles of creations.

Chinese title recognition is challenging for the following reasons. There are no limitations in length and structures of titles. They might be a common word, e.g. "錯誤" (Mistakes, a Chinese poem), a phrase, e.g. "挪威的森林" (Norwegian Wood, a song), a sentence, e.g. "阿根廷別為我哭泣" (Don't Cry for Me Argentina, a song), or even like nothing, e.g. "摩擦・無以名狀" (Rub • Undescribable, a Chinese poetry collection). Besides, the choice of characters to name titles has no obvious preferences. Till now, few publications touch on Chinese title recognition. There are even no available corpora with titles being tagged.

Several QA systems, such as Sekine and Nobata (2004) [9], used fixed patterns and dictionaries to recognize part of titles in English or Japanese. Lee et al. (2004) [6] proposed an iterative method that constructs patterns and dictionaries to recognize English titles. Their method cannot be adapted to Chinese, however, because the most important feature employed is capitalization, which does not exist in Chinese.

In this paper, we propose a pioneer study of Chinese title recognition. An approach of integrating punctuation rules, lexicon, and naïve Bayesian models is employed to recognize creation titles in Chinese documents. Section 2 discusses some cues for Chinese title recognition. Section 3 gives a system overview. Punctuation rules and title gazetteer identify part of titles and filter out part of non-titles. The rest of undetermined candidates are verified by naïve Bayesian model. Section 4 addresses which features may be adopted in training naïve Bayesian model. Section 5 lists the training and testing materials, and shows experimental results. Section 6 concludes there marks.

2 Cues for Chinese Creation Title Recognition

Titles discussed in this paper cover a wide range of creations, including literature, music, painting, sculpture, dance, drama, movies, TV or radio programs, books, newspapers, magazines, research papers, albums, PC games, etc. All of these titles are treated as a single sort because they share the same characteristics, i.e., they are named by somebody with creativity, and thus there are nearly no regularity or limitations on their naming styles.

The challenging issue is that, unlike MUC-style named entities (MUC7, 1998), titles are usually composed of common words, and most of them have no internal features like surnames or entity affixes, e.g. "市" (City) in "台北市" (Taipei City). In other words, most titles might look just like common strings in sentences. Thus it is even more difficult to decide which fragment of sentences might be a title than to determine if some fragment is a title.

For the lack of internal features, external features or context information must be found to decide boundaries of titles. Table 1 shows some words preceding or following titles in one-tenth sampling of ASBC corpus with titles tagged manually. We can observe that quotation marks are widely used. This is because writers usually quote titles with punctuation marks to make them clear for readers. The most common used ones are the two pairs of quotation marks "「」" and "『』". About 40% of titles are quoted in "「」" or "『』" in our test corpus. However, labeling proper nouns is only one of their functions. Quotation marks are extensively used in various purposes, like dialogues, emphasis, novel words, *etc*. In our analysis, only less than 7% of strings quoted in "「」" or "『』" are creation titles. It means the disambiguation of the usages of quotation marks is necessary.

Table 1. Preceding and Following Words of Titles in One-tenth Sampling of ASBC Corpus

Preceding Word	Frequency	Following Word	Frequency
「	450	」	442
《	216	》	216
(	44	、	56
。	31	，	32
、	25	(	26
，	24	』	16
的	19	的	13
『	16	。	11
是	9	中	7
在	7	)	6
·	6	】	6
【	6	裡	6

The most powerful external feature of creation titles is French quotes "《》", which is defined to represent book names in the set of standard Simplified Chinese punctuation marks of China [5]. However, they are not standard punctuation marks in Traditional Chinese. Besides the usage of French quotes to mark book names, writers often use them to label various types of creation titles. According to our analysis on Web searching and the sampling corpus, about 20% of occurrences of titles in Traditional Chinese documents are quoted in "《》", and nearly no strings other than titles would be quoted in "《》". This punctuation mark shows a very powerful cue to deal with title recognition.

Nevertheless, there are still 40% of titles without any marks around. These unmarked titles usually stand for widely known or classic creations. In other words, these famous works are supposed to be mentioned in many documents many times. Such kinds of titles are extensively known by people like a common vocabulary. A lexicon of famous creations should cover a large part of these common titles.

3 System Overview

Based on the analyses in Section 2, we propose some punctuation rules that exploit the external features of titles to recognize possible boundaries of titles in Chinese documents. Most strings that cannot be titles are filtered by these rules. Titles with strong evidences like "《 》" are also identified by these rules. The rest undecided strings are denoted as "possible titles." To verify these candidates is somewhat similar to solve word sense disambiguation problem. Naïve Bayesian classifier is adopted to tell whether a candidate is really a title or not. The overview of our system is shown in Figure 1.

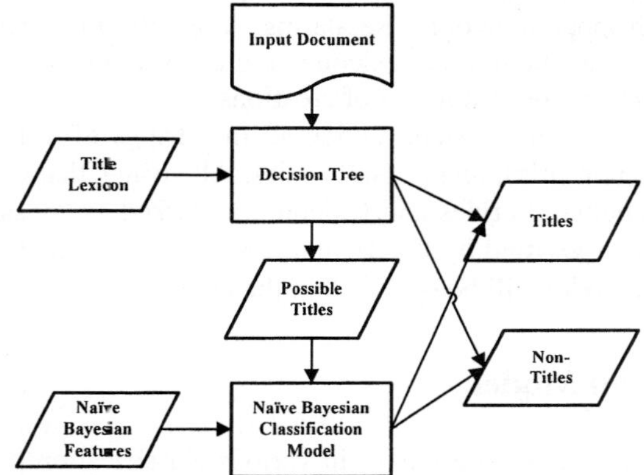

Fig. 1. System Overview

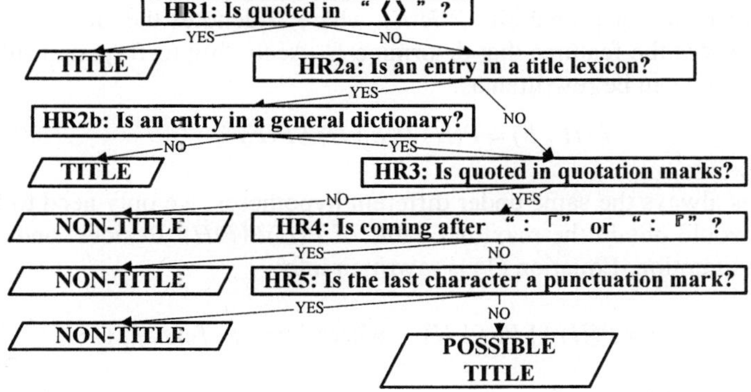

Fig. 2. Decision Tree of Punctuation Rules and Lexicon

Figure 2 shows the applications of the punctuation rules and the title lexicon, which are illustrated as a decision tree. HR1 exploits French quotes "《》" to identify titles like "《桃花扇》" (Taohua Shan, a traditional Chinese drama by Kong, Shang-Ren) and "《迷宮中的將軍》" (El General En Su Laberinto, a novel by Garcia Marquez). HR2a and HR2b then look up the title lexicon to find famous titles like "百年孤寂" (Cien Anos de Soledad) and "三國演義" (Romance of Three Kingdoms). HR3 limits our recognition scope to strings quoted in quotation marks, and HR4 and

HR5 filter out a major sort of non-titles quoted in quotation marks, dialogues, such as "我說：「觀眾小心了！」" (I said, "the audience should be careful!") and "笛卡兒說：「我思，故我在。」" (Rene Descarte said, "I think, therefore I am.").

The title lexicon we use is acquired from the catalogues of the library of our university. These titles are sent to *Google* as query terms. Only the ones that have ever been quoted in "《 》" in the first 1,000 returned summaries are kept. The remained titles are checked manually and those ones that possibly form a fragment of a common sentence are dropped to avoid false alarms. After filtering, there are about 7,200 entries in this lexicon. Although the lexicon could cover titles of books only, it is still useful because books are the major sort of creations.

The punctuation rules and lexicon divide all the strings of a document into three groups – say, titles, non-titles, and possible titles. All strings that cannot be definitely identified by the punctuation rules and lexicon are marked as "possible" titles. These possible titles are then verified by the second mechanism, the naïve Bayesian model. The naïve Bayesian model will be specified in the next section.

4 Naïve Bayesian Model

Naïve Bayesian classifier is widely used in various classification problems in natural language processing. Since it is simple to implement and easy to train, we adopt it in our system to verify the possible titles suggested by the decision tree.

Naïve Bayesian classification is based on the assumption that each feature being observed is independent of one another. The goal is to find the hypothesis that would maximize the posterior probability $P(H|F)$, where H denotes the classifying hypotheses and F denotes the features that determine H. According to Bayesian rule, the posterior probability can be rewritten as:

$$P(H \mid F) = P(H)\, P(F \mid H) \,/\, P(F) \qquad (1)$$

Since $P(F)$ is always the same under different hypotheses, we only need to find which hypothesis would obtain the maximal value of $P(H)P(F|H)$. Besides, under the independence assumption, Equation (1) is rewritten into:

$$P(H \mid F) = P(H) \prod P(f_i \mid H) \quad \text{where } F = \{ f_1, f_2, \ldots, f_n \} \qquad (2)$$

In our system, we have two hypotheses:

H1: candidate S is a title
H2: candidate S is not a title

Four features shown below will be considered. The detail will be discussed in the subsequent paragraphs.

F1: Context
F2: Component
F3: Length
F4: Recurrence

Context. To exploit contextual features, our system adopts a word-based, position-free unigram context model with a window size of 5. In other words, our context model can be viewed as a combination of ten different contextual features of the naïve Bayesian classifier, five of them are left context and the other five are right context. It can be represented as:

$$P(F_{context}|H) = P(L_5, L_4, L_3, L_2, L_1, R_1, R_2, R_3, R_4, R_5 \mid H) \quad (3)$$

Where L_i and R_i denote preceding and following words of the possible title we want to verify, and H denotes the hypothesis.

If we postulate that the contextual features are independent of each other, then equation (3) can be transformed to:

$$P(F_{context}|H) = \prod P(L_i \mid H) \prod P(R_i \mid H) \quad (4)$$

Equation (4) assumes that the distance from a contextual word to a possible title is not concerned both in training and testing. The reason is that we do not have a realistic, vast, and well-tagged resource for training. On the other hand, if we want to exploit it in testing, we need a well-tagged corpus to learn the best weights we should assign to contextual words of different distances.

Component. *Context* deals with features surroundings titles. In contrast, *Component* further considers the features within titles. Similar to the above discussion, our component model is also a word-based, position-free unigram model. A possible title will be segmented into a word sequence by standard maximal matching. The words in the segmentation results are viewed as the "components" of the possible title, and the component model can be represented as:

$$P(F_{comp}|H) = P(C_1 \ldots C_n \mid H) = \prod P(C_i \mid H) \quad (5)$$

Where C_i denotes the component of the possible title we want to verify, and H denotes the hypothesis.

Similar to the context model, the position of a component word is not concerned both in training and testing. Besides the availability issue of large training corpus, the lengths of possible titles are varied so that positional information is difficult to be exploited. Different titles consist of different number of component words. There are no straightforward or intuitive ways of using positional information.

Length. The definition of *Length* feature is the number of characters that constitute the possible title. It can be represented as:

$$P(F_{length}|H) = P(\textit{the length of } S \mid H) \quad (6)$$

Where S denotes the possible title to be verified and H denotes the hypothesis that S is a title.

Recurrence. The definition of *Recurrence* feature is number of occurrences of the possible title in the input document. It can be represented as:

$$P(F_{Rec}|H) = P(\textit{the appearing times of } S \mid H) \quad (7)$$

Where S denotes the possible title to be verified and H denotes the hypothesis that S is a title.

5 Experiment Results

The estimation of $P(H)$ and $P(F|H)$ is the major issue in naïve Bayesian model. There are no corpora with titles being tagged available. To overcome this problem, we used two different resources in our training process. The first one is a collection of about 300,000 titles, which is acquired from library catalogues of our university. This collection is used to estimate *Component* and *Length* features of titles. Besides, these titles are regarded as queries and submitted to *Google*. The returned summaries are segmented by maximal matching and then used to estimate *Context* features of titles. Since titles are usually composed of common words, not all query terms in retrieved results by *Google* are a title. Therefore, only the results with query terms quoted in French quotes " 《》 " are adopted, which include totally 1,183,451 web page summaries. Recall that French quotes are a powerful cue to recognize creation titles, which was discussed in Section 2.

The second resource used in training is ASBC corpus. Since titles in ASBC corpus are not specially tagged and we are short-handed to tag them by ourselves, a compromised approach is adopted. First, the decision tree shown in Figure 2 is used to group all strings of the training corpus into titles, non-titles, and possible titles. All titles thus extracted are used to estimate the *Recurrence* feature of titles, and all possible titles are treated as non-titles to estimate all features of non-titles. Since the probability of possible titles being titles are much less than being non-titles, the bias of the rough estimation is supposed to be tolerable.

We separate one-tenth of ASBC corpus and tag it manually as our testing data. The rest nine-tenth is used for training. There are totally 610,760 words in this piece of data, and 982 publication or creation titles are found. During execution of our system, the testing data are segmented by maximal matching to obtain context and component words of possible titles. To estimate $P(H)$, we randomly select 100 possible titles from the training part of ASBC corpus, and classify them into titles and non-titles manually. Then we count the probability of hypotheses from this small sample to approximate $P(H)$.

Table 2 shows the performance of the decision tree proposed in Figure 2 under the testing data. If we treat HR2a and HR2b as a single rule that asks "Is the string an entry in the title lexicon and not in a general dictionary?", we could view our rules as an ordered sequence of decisions. Each rule tells if a part of undecided strings are titles or non-titles, which is denoted in the column "Decision Type" of Table 2. The column "Decided" shows how many strings can be decided by the corresponding rules, while the columns of "Undecided Titles" and "Undecided Non-Titles" denote how many titles and non-titles are remained in the testing data after applying the corresponding rule. The correctness of the decision is denoted in the columns of "Correct" and "Wrong".

Table 2 shows that these five rules are very good clues to recognize titles. HR1, HR2, HR4 and HR5 have precisions of 100%, 94.01%, 99.15%, and 100% respectively. Because the number of non-titles is much larger than that of titles, the actual precision of HR3 is comparatively meaningless. These rules could efficiently solve a large part of the problem. The rest possible titles are then classified by the naïve Bayesian classifier. The performance is listed in Table 3. We try different combinations of the four features. F1, F2, F3, and F4 denote *Context*, *Component*, *Length*, and *Recurrence*, respectively. The number of True Positives, True Negatives, and False Positives are listed. Precision, recall and F-measure are considered as metrics to evaluate the performance.

Table 2. Performance of Decision Tree in Figure 2

	Decision Type	Decided	Correct	Wrong	Undecided Titles	Undecided Non-Titles
HR1	Title	216	216	0	766	~|corpus|^2/2
HR2	Title	167	126	41[1]	640	~|corpus|^2/2
HR3	Non-Title	~|corpus|^2/2	~|corpus|^2/2	186	454	5812
HR4	Non-Title	1997	1980	17	437	3832
HR5	Non-Title	372	372	0	437	3458

Note that there are two different numbers in the False Positive, Precision, and F-measure columns in Table 3. The left number shows the total number of false positive errors, and the right one ignores the errors caused by other sorts of named entities. This is because many false positive errors come from other types of named entities. For example, in the sentence "參加「一九九四年第三十五屆國際數學奧林匹克競賽」" (attend 1994 35th International Mathematical Olympiad), "一九九四年第三十五屆國際數學奧林匹克競賽" ("1994 35th International Mathematical Olympiad") is a contest name, however, ill-recognized as a title by our system. Because there are various sorts of ill-recognized named entities and most of them have not been thoroughly studied, there are no efficient ways available to solve these false alarms. Fortunately, in many applications, there would be little harm incorrectly recognizing these named entities as titles.

The other major source of false positive errors is appearances of monosyllabic words. For example, in the sentence "「以德報怨」是老子的話" ("Render Good for Evil" is Lao Tzu's speech), "以德報怨" ("Render Good for Evil") are ill-recognized as titles. The reason might be that many context and component words of titles are named entities or unknown words. During training, these named entities are neither tagged nor recognized, so that most of these named entities are segmented into sequences of monosyllabic words. Therefore, while the naïve Bayesian classifier encounters monosyllabic context or component words, it would prefer recognizing the possible title as a title.

From Table 3, we could observe that *Context* and *Component* are supportive in both precision and recall. *Length* boosts precision but decreases recall while *Recurrence* is on the contrary. The combination of F1+F2+F3 obtains the best F-measure, but the combination of all features might be more useful in practical applications,

[1] Total 31 of them can be easily corrected by a maximal-matching-driven segmentation. For example, "心經" (xīn jīng, Heart Sutra, a Buddha book) in "用心經營" (yòng xīn jīng yíng) is an entry in the title lexicon. However, maximal matching prefers the segmentation of "用心 / 經營" (yòng xīn/jīng yíng) than "用 / 心經 / 營" (yòng/xīn jīng/yíng), so that this false alarm would be recovered.

since it only sacrifices 1.4% of precision but gains 3% of recall in comparison with the former. Table 4 summaries the total performance of our creation title recognition system. It achieves the F-measure of 0.585.

Table 3. Performance of the Naïve Bayesian Classifier Using Different Features

	True Positive	True Negative	False Positive	Precision	Recall	F-measure
F1	277	160	959 / 772	0.224 / 0.264	0.634	0.331 / 0.373
F2	153	284	532 / 332	0.223 / 0.315	0.350	0.273 / 0.332
F1 + F3	273	164	859 / 676	0.241 / 0.288	0.625	0.348 / 0.394
F2 + F3	148	289	453 / 247	0.246 / 0.375	0.339	0.285 / 0.356
F1 + F2	288	149	976 / 722	0.228 / 0.285	0.659	0.339 / 0.398
F1 + F4	289	148	1067 / 867	0.213 / 0.250	0.661	0.322 / 0.363
F2 + F4	169	268	695 / 467	0.196 / 0.266	0.387	0.260 / 0.315
F1 + F2 + F3	286	151	888 / 631	0.244 / 0.312	0.654	0.355 / 0.422
F1 + F3 + F4	285	152	946 / 750	0.232 / 0.275	0.652	0.342 / 0.387
F2 + F3 + F4	164	273	542 / 320	0.232 / 0.339	0.375	0.287 / 0.356
All	299	138	967 / 703	0.236 / 0.298	0.684	0.351 / 0.416

Table 4. Performance of the Title Recognition System

	True Positive	True Negative	False Positive	Precision	Recall	F-measure
Decision Tree	342	203	41 / 10	0.915 / 0.978	0.685	0.783 / 0.806
Naïve Bayesian	299	138	967 / 703	0.236 / 0.298	0.684	0.351 / 0.416
Total	641	341	1008 / 713	0.424 / 0.510	0.685	0.524 / 0.585

6 Conclusion

This paper presents a pioneer study of Chinese title recognition. It achieves the precision of 0.510 and the recall of 0.685. The experiments reveal much valuable information and experiences for further researches.

First, the punctuation rules proposed in this paper are useful to recognize creation titles with a high precision. They can relief our burdens in building more resources, make supervised learning feasible, and give us some clues in similar studies like recognition of other sorts of named entities. These useful rules are also helpful for those applications needing high accuracies. For example, we can exploit these rules on an information retrieval system to filter out noises and show only the information about the requested creation or the publication.

Second, naïve Bayesian classifier could achieve a comparable recall on the verification of possible titles. Since we only adopt simple features and use a rough estimation in feature model building, the result shows that naïve Bayesian classifier is practicable in recognizing creation titles. In future works, we may find other useful features and adopt more sophisticated models in naïve Bayesian classifier to seek a higher performance, especially in precision.

Third, our result shows that recognizing rarely seen sorts of named entities is practicable. Because un-recognized named entities might significantly affect subsequent applications in Chinese, in particular, segmentation, we should not ignore the problems introduced by Non-MUC style named entities. Our study suggests that the recognition of these rarely mentioned named entities is promising. The performances of many applications, such as natural language parsing and understanding, might be boosted through adding the mechanism of recognizing these rare named entities.

Finally, our research can also be extended to other oriental languages, such as Japanese, in which there are no explicit features like specialized delimiters or capitalizations to mark creation titles. Just as Chinese, un-recognized named entities in these languages might affect the performances of natural language applications. Recognizing Non-MUC style named entities is an indispensable task to process these languages.

Acknowledgement

Research of this paper was partially supported by National Science Council, Taiwan, under the contract NSC94-2752-E001-001-PAE.

References

1. Chen, Conrad and Lee, Hsi-Jian. 2004. A Three-Phase System for Chinese Named Entity Recognition, Proceedings of ROCLING XVI, 2004, 39-48.
2. Chen, Hsin-Hsi, Ding, Yung-Wei and Tsai, Shih-Chung. 1998. Named Entity Extraction for Information Retrieval, Computer Processing of Oriental Languages, Special Issue on Information Retrieval on Oriental Languages, 12(1), 1998, 75-85.
3. Chen, Hsin-Hsi, Kuo, June-Jei, Huang, Sheng-Jie, Lin, Chuan-Jie and Wung, Hung-Chia. 2003. A Summarization System for Chinese News from Multiple Sources, Journal of American Society for Information Science and Technology, 54(13), November 2003, 1224-1236.
4. Chen, Zheng, W. Y. Liu, and F. Zhang. 2002. A New Statistical Approach to Personal Name Extraction, Proceedings of ICML 2002, 67-74.
5. Gong, Chian-Yian and Liu, Yi-Ling. 1996. Use of Punctuation Mark. GB/T15834-1995. http://202.205.177.129/moe-dept/yuxin-/content/gfbz/ managed/020.htm
6. Lee, Joo-Young, Song, Young-In, Kim, Sang-Bum, Chung, Hoojung and Rim, Hae-Chang. 2004. Title Recognition Using Lexical Pattern and Entity Dictionary, Proceedings of AIRS04, 342-348.
7. Lin, Chuan-Jie, Chen, Hsin-Hsi, Liu, Che-Chia, Tsai, Ching-Ho and Wung, Hung-Chia. 2001. Open Domain Question Answering on Heterogeneous Data, Proceedings of ACL Workshop on Human Language Technology and Knowledge Management, July 6-7 2001, Toulouse France, 79-85.

8. MUC7. 1998. Proceedings of 7th Message Understanding Conference, Fairfax, VA, 1998, http://www.itl.nist.gov/iaui/894.02/related_projects/muc/index.html.
9. Sakine, Satoshi and Nobata, Chikashi. 2004. Definition, Dictionaries and Tagger for Extended Named Entity Hierarchy, Proceedings of LREC04.
10. Sun, Jian, J. F. Gao, L. Zhang, M. Zhou, and C. N. Huang. 2002. Chinese Named Entity Identification Using Class-based Language Model, Proceedings of the 19th International Conference on Computational Linguistics, Taipei, 967-973

A Connectionist Model of Anticipation in Visual Worlds

Marshall R. Mayberry, III, Matthew W. Crocker, and Pia Knoeferle

Department of Computational Linguistics,
Saarland University, Saarbrücken, Germany
{martym, crocker, knoferle}@coli.uni-sb.de

Abstract. Recent "visual worlds" studies, wherein researchers study language in context by monitoring eye-movements in a visual scene during sentence processing, have revealed much about the interaction of diverse information sources and the time course of their influence on comprehension. In this study, five experiments that trade off scene context with a variety of linguistic factors are modelled with a Simple Recurrent Network modified to integrate a scene representation with the standard incremental input of a sentence. The results show that the model captures the qualitative behavior observed during the experiments, while retaining the ability to develop the correct interpretation in the absence of visual input.

1 Introduction

There are two prevalent theories of language acquisition. One view emphasizes syntactic and semantic bootstrapping during language acquisition that enable children to learn abstract concepts from mappings between different kinds of information sources [1,2]. Another view emerges from connectionist literature and emphasizes the learning of linguistic structure from purely distributional properties of language usage [3,4]. While the perspectives are often taken to be diametrically opposed, both can be seen as crucially relying on correlations between words and their immediate context, be it the sentence as a whole or extra-linguistic input, such as a scene.

We combine insights from both distributional and bootstrapping accounts in modelling the on-line comprehension of utterances in both the absence and presence of a visual scene. This is an important achievement in at least two regards. First, it emphasizes the complementarity between distributional and bootstrapping approaches–discovering structure across linguistic and scene contexts [5]. Further, it is an important first step in linking situated models of on-line utterance comprehension more tightly to accounts of language acquisition, thus emphasizing the continuity of language processing.

We present results from two simulations on a Simple Recurrent Network (SRN; [3]). Modification of the network to integrate input from a scene together with the characteristic incremental processing of such networks allowed us to model people's ability to adaptively use the contextual information in order to more rapidly interpret and disambiguate a sentence. The model draws on recent studies that appeal to theories of language acquisition to account for the comprehension of scene-related utterances [6,7]. Recent research within the *visual worlds* paradigm, wherein participants' gazes to a scene while listening to an utterance are monitored, provides support for this view. Findings from this paradigm support an account of scene-related utterance comprehension in

R. Dale et al. (Eds.): IJCNLP 2005, LNAI 3651, pp. 849–861, 2005.

which the rapid coordinated interaction of information from the immediate scene, and linguistic knowledge plays a major role in incremental and anticipatory comprehension.

2 Simulation 1

In Simulation 1, we simultaneously model four experiments that show the rapid influence of diverse informational sources–linguistic and world knowledge as well as scene information – on utterance comprehension. All experiments were conducted in German, a language that allows both subject-verb-object (SVO) and object-verb-subject (OVS) sentence types. In the face of word order ambiguity, case marking indicates the subject or object grammatical function, except in the case of feminine and neuter noun phrases where the article does not distinguish the nominative and accusative cases.

2.1 Anticipation Depending on Stereotypicality

The first two experiments that we modeled examined how linguistic and world knowledge or stereotypicality enabled rapid thematic role assignment in unambiguous sentences, thus determining who-does-what-to-whom in a scene.

Fig. 1. Selectional Restrictions

Experiment 1: Morphosyntactic and lexical verb information. To examine the influence of case-marking and verb plausibility on thematic role assignment, [8] presented participants with utterances such as (1) or (2) that described a scene showing a hare, a cabbage, a fox, and a distractor (see Figure 1) :

(1) *Der Hase frisst gleich den Kohl.*
The hare$_{nom}$ eats shortly the cabbage$_{acc}$.

(2) *Den Hasen frisst gleich der Fuchs.*
The hare$_{acc}$ eats shortly the fox$_{nom}$.

After hearing "The hare$_{nom}$ eats ..." and "The hare$_{acc}$ eats ...", people made anticipatory eye-movements to the cabbage and fox respectively. This reveals that people were able to predict role fillers in a scene through linguistic/world knowledge that identified who-does-what-to-whom.

Experiment 2: Verb type information. To further investigate the role of verb information, the authors replaced the agent/patient verbs like *frisst* ("eats") with experiencer/theme verbs like *interessiert* ("interests"). This manipulation interchanged agent (experiencer) and patient (theme) roles from Experiment 1. For Figure 1 and the subject-first (3) or object-first sentence (4), participants showed gaze fixations complementary to those of Experiment 1, confirming that both case and semantic verb information are used to predict relevant role fillers.

(3) *Der Hase interessiert ganz besonders den Fuchs.*
The hare$_{nom}$ interests especially the fox$_{acc}$.
(4) *Den Hasen interessiert ganz besonders der Kohl.*
The hare$_{acc}$ interests especially the cabbage$_{nom}$.

2.2 Anticipation Depending on Depicted Events

The second set of experiments investigated whether depicted events showing who-does-what-to-whom can establish a scene character's role as agent or patient when syntactic and thematic role relations are temporarily ambiguous in the utterance.

Fig. 2. Depicted Events

Experiment 3: Verb-mediated depicted role relations. [9] presented such initially ambiguous spoken SVO (5) and OVS sentences (6) together with a scene in which a princess both paints a fencer and is washed by a pirate (Figure 2):

(5) *Die Princessin malt offensichtlich den Fechter.*
The princess$_{nom}$ paints obviously the fencer$_{acc}$.
(6) *Die Princessin wäscht offensichtlich der Pirat.*
The princess$_{acc}$ washes obviously the pirate$_{nom}$.

Linguistic disambiguation occurred on the second NP; disambiguation prior to the second NP was only possible through use of the depicted events. When the verb identified an action, the depicted role relations disambiguated towards either an agent-patient (5) or patient-agent (6) role relation, as indicated by anticipatory eye-movements to the patient (pirate) or agent (fencer) respectively for (5) and (6). This gaze-pattern showed the rapid influence of verb-mediated depicted events on the assignment of thematic roles to a temporarily ambiguous sentence-initial noun phrase.

Experiment 4: Weak temporal adverb constraint. [9] also investigated German verb-final active (7) and passive (8) constructions. In this type of sentence, the initial subject noun phrase is role-ambiguous, and the auxiliary *wird* can have a passive or future interpretation.

(7) *Die Princessin wird sogleich den Pirat washen.*
The princess$_{nom}$ will right away wash the pirate$_{acc}$.
(8) *Die Princessin wird soeben von dem Fechter gemalt.*
The princess$_{acc}$ is just now painted by the fencer$_{nom}$.

To evoke early linguistic disambiguation, temporal adverbs biased the auxiliary *wird* toward either the future ("will") or passive ("is -ed") reading. Since the verb was sentence-final, the interplay of scene and linguistic cues (e.g., temporal adverbs) were rather more subtle. When the listener heard a future-biased adverb such as *sogleich*, after the auxiliary *wird*, he interpreted the initial NP as agent of a future active construction, as evidenced by anticipatory eye-movements to the patient in the scene. Conversely, listeners interpreted the passive-biased construction *soeben* with these roles exchanged.

2.3 Architecture

The Simple Recurrent Network is a type of neural network typically used to process temporal sequences of patterns such as words in a sentence. A common approach is for the modeller to train the network on prespecified targets, such as verbs and their arguments, that represent what the network is expected to produce upon completing a sentence. Processing is incremental, with each new input word interpreted in the context of the sentence processed so far, represented by a copy of the previous hidden layer serving as additional input or *context* to the current hidden layer. Because these types of associationist models automatically develop correlations among the data they are trained on, they will generally develop expectations about the output even before processing is completed because sufficient information occurs early in the sentence to warrant such predictions. Moreover, during the course of processing a sentence these expectations can be overridden with subsequent input, often abruptly revising an interpretation in a manner reminiscent of how humans seem to process language. Indeed, it is these characteristics of incremental processing, the automatic development of expectations, seamless integration of multiple sources of information, and nonmonotonic revision that have endeared neural network models to cognitive researchers.

In Simulation 1, the four experiments described above have been modelled simultaneously using a single network. The goal of modelling all experimental results by a single architecture required enhancements to the SRN, the development and presentation of the training data, as well as the training regime itself. We describe these next.

In two of the experiments, only three characters are depicted, the representation of which can be propagated directly to the network's hidden layer. In the other two experiments, the scene featured three characters involved in two events (e.g., **pirate-washes-princess** and **princess-paints-fencer**, as shown in Figure 3). The middle character was

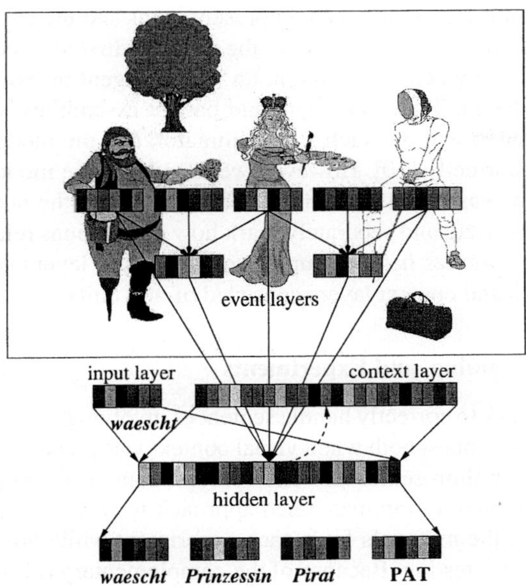

Fig. 3. Scene Integration

involved in both events, either as an agent or a patient (e.g., **princess**). Only one of the events, however, corresponded to the spoken linguistic input.

The representation of this scene information and its integration into the model's processing was the primary modification to the SRN. Connections between representations for the depicted characters and the hidden layer were provided. Encoding of the depicted events, when present, required additional links from the characters and depicted actions to **event** layers, and links from these event layers to the SRN's hidden layer. Representations for the events were developed in the event layers by compressing the scene representations of the involved characters and depicted actions through weights corresponding to the action, its agent and its patient for each event. This event representation was kept simple and only provided conceptual input to the hidden layer: who did what to whom was encoded for both events, when depicted; richer grammatical information (e.g., case and gender on articles) only came from the linguistic input.

Neural networks will usually encode any correlations in the data that help to minimize error. In order to prevent the network from encoding regularities in its weights regarding the position of the characters and events given in the scene (such as, for example, that the central character in the scene corresponds to the first NP in the presented sentence) which are not relevant to the role-assignment task, one set of weights was used for all characters, and another set of weights used for both events. This weight-sharing ensured that the network had to access the information encoded in the event layers, or determine the relevant characters itself, thus improving generalization. The representations for the characters and actions were the same for both input (scene and sentence) and output.

The input assemblies were the scene representations and the current word from the input sentence. The output assemblies were the verb, the first and second nouns, and an assembly that indicated whether the first noun was the agent or patient of the sentence (token **PAT** in Figure 3). Typically, agent and patient assemblies would be fixed in a case-role representation without such a discriminator, and the model required to learn to instantiate them correctly [10]. However, we found that the model performed much better when the task was recast as having to learn to isolate the nouns in the order in which they are introduced, and separately mark how those nouns relate to the verb. The input and output assemblies had 100 units each, the event layers contained 200 units each, and the hidden and context layers consisted of 400 units.

2.4 Input Data, Training, and Experiments

We trained the network to correctly handle sentences involving non-stereotypical events as well as stereotypical ones, both when visual context was present and when it was absent. As over half a billion sentence/scene combinations were possible for all of the experiments, we adopted a grammar-based approach to randomly generate sentences and scenes based on the materials from each experiment while holding out the actual materials to be used for testing. Because of the complementary roles that stereotypicality played in the two sets of experiments, there was virtually no lexical overlap between them. In order to accurately model the first two experiments involving selectional restrictions on verbs, two additional words were added to the lexicon for each character selected by a verb. For example, in the sentence *Der Hase frisst gleich den Kohl*, the nouns *Hase1*, *Hase2*, *Kohl1*, and *Kohl2* were used to develop training sentences. These were meant to represent, for example, words such as "rabbit" and "jackrabbit" or "carrot" and "lettuce" in the lexicon that have the same distributional properties as the orignal words "hare" and "cabbage". With these extra tokens the network could learn that *Hase*, *frisst*, and *Kohl* were correlated without ever encountering all three words in the same training sentence. The experiments involving non-stereotypicality did not pose this constraint, so training sentences were simply generated to avoid presenting experimental items.

Some standard simplifications to the words have been made to facilitate modelling. For example, multi-word adverbs such as *fast immer* were treated as one word through hyphenation so that sentence length within a given experimental set up is maintained. Nominal case markings such as *-n* in *Hasen* were removed to avoid sparse data as these markings are idiosyncratic, and the case markings on the determiners are more informative overall. More importantly, morphemes such as the infinitive marker *-en* and past participle *ge-* were removed, because, for example, the verb forms *malt*, *malen*, and *gemalt*, would all be treated as unrelated tokens, again contributing unnecessarily to the problem with sparse data. The result is that one verb form is used, and to perform accurately, the network must rely on its position in the sentence (either second or sentence-final), as well as whether the word *von* occurs to indicate a participial reading rather than infinitival. All 326 words in the lexicon for the first four experiments were given random representations.

We trained the network by repeatedly presenting the model with 1000 randomly generated sentences from each experiment (constituting one epoch) and testing every

100 epochs against the held-out test materials for each of the five experiments. Scenes were provided half of the time to provide an unbiased approximation to linguistic experience. The network was initialized with weights between -0.01 and 0.01. The learning rate was initially set to 0.05 and gradually reduced to 0.002 over the course of 15000 epochs. Four splits took a little less than two weeks to complete on 1.6Ghz PCs.

2.5 Results

Figure 4 reports the percentage of targets at the network's output layer that the model correctly matches, both as measured at the adverb and at the end of the sentence. The model clearly demonstrates the qualitative behavior observed in all four experiments in that it is able to access the information either from the encoded scene or stereotypicality and combine it with the incrementally presented sentence to anticipate forthcoming arguments.

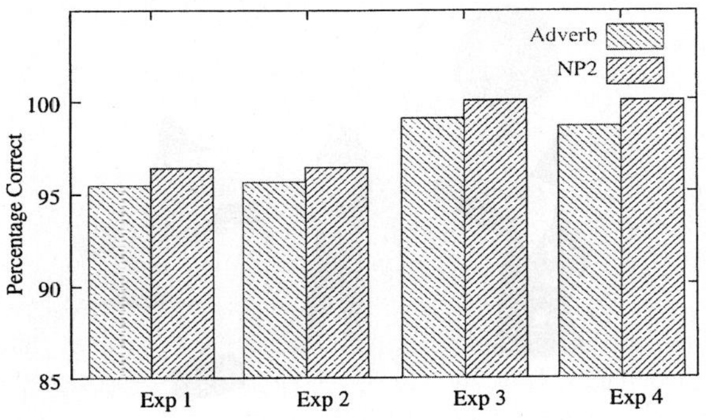

Fig. 4. Results

For the two studies using stereotypical information (experiments 1 and 2), the network achieved just over 96% at sentence end, and anticipation accuracy was just over 95% at the adverb. Because these sentences are unambiguous, the model is able to correctly identify the role of the upcoming argument, but makes errors in token identification, confusing words that are within the selectionally restricted set, such as, for example, *Kohl* and *Kohl2*. Thus, the model has not quite mastered the stereotypical knowledge, particularly as it relates to the presence of the scene.

In the other two experiments using non-stereotypical characters and depicted events (experiments 3 and 4), accuracy was 100% at the end of the sentence. More importantly, the model achieved over 98% early disambiguation on experiment 3, where the sentences were simple, active SVO and OVS. Early disambiguation on experiment 4 was somewhat harder because the adverb is the disambiguating point in the sentence as opposed to the verb in the other three experiments. As nonlinear dynamical systems, neural networks sometimes require an extra step to settle after a decision point is reached due to the attractor dynamics of the weights. For both experiments, most errors occurred on role-assignment due to the initially-ambiguous first noun phrase.

The difference in performance between the first two experiments and second two experiments can be attributed to the event layer that was only available in experiments 3 and 4. Closer inspection of the model's behavior during processing revealed that finer discrimination was encoded in the links between the event layers and hidden layer than that encoded in the weights between the characters and the hidden layer.

3 Simulation 2

The previous set of experiments demonstrated the rapid use of either linguistic knowledge or depicted events to anticipate forthcoming arguments in a sentence. A further important question is the relative importance of these two informational sources when they conflict. We first review an experimental study by [6] designed to address this issue and then report relevant modelling results.

Fig. 5. Scene vs Stored Knowledge

Scene vs Stored Knowledge. One goal of the study by [6] was to verify that stored knowledge about non-depicted events and information from depicted, but non-stereotypical, events each enable rapid thematic interpretation. Case-marking on the first NP always identified the pilot as a patient. After hearing the verb in (9) more inspections to the only food-serving agent (detective) than to the other agent showed the influence of depicted events. In contrast, when people heard the verb in condition two (10), a higher proportion of anticipatory eye-movements to the only stereotypical agent (wizard) than to the other agent revealed the influence of stereotypical knowledge (see Figure 5).

(9) *Den Piloten verköstigt gleich der Detektiv.*
The pilot$_{acc}$ serves-food-to shortly the detective$_{nom}$.

(10) *Den Piloten verzaubert gleich der Zauberer.*
The pilot$_{acc}$ jinxes shortly the wizard$_{nom}$.

Second, the study determined the *relative importance* of depicted events and verb-based thematic role knowledge when these information sources competed. In conditions three and four ((11) & (12)) participants heard an utterance in which the verb identified both a stereotypical (detective) and a depicted agent (wizard). In this case, people preferred to rely on the immediate event depictions over stereotypical knowledge, and looked more often at the wizard, the agent of the depicted event, than at the other, stereotypical agent of the spying-action (the detective).

(11) *Den Piloten bespitzelt gleich der Zauberer.*
The pilot$_{acc}$ spies-on shortly the wizard$_{nom}$.
(12) *Den Piloten bespitzelt gleich der Detektiv.*
The pilot$_{acc}$ spies-on shortly the detective$_{nom}$.

3.1 Architecture, Data, Training, and Results

In simulation 1, we modelled experiments that depended on stereotypicality or depicted events, but not both. The experiment modelled in simulation 2, however, was specifically designed to investigate how these two information sources interacted. Accordingly, the network needed to learn to use either information from the scene or stereotypicality when available, and, moreover, favor the scene when the two sources conflicted, as observed in the empirical results. Recall that the network is trained only on the final interpretation of a sentence. Thus, capturing the observed behavior required manipulation of the frequencies of the four conditions described above during training. In order to train the network to develop stereotypical agents for verbs, the frequency that a verb occurs with its stereotypical agent, such as *Detektiv* and *bespitzelt* from example (12) above, had to be greater than for a non-stereotypical agent. However, the frequency should not be so great as to override the influence from the scene.

The solution we adopted is motivated by theories of language acquisition that take into account the importance of early linguistic experience in a visual environment (see the General Discussion). We found a small range of frequencies that permitted the network to develop an early reliance on the information from the scene while it gradually learned the stereotypical associations. Figure 6 shows the effect this training regime had over 6000 epochs on the ability of the network to accurately anticipate the missing argu-

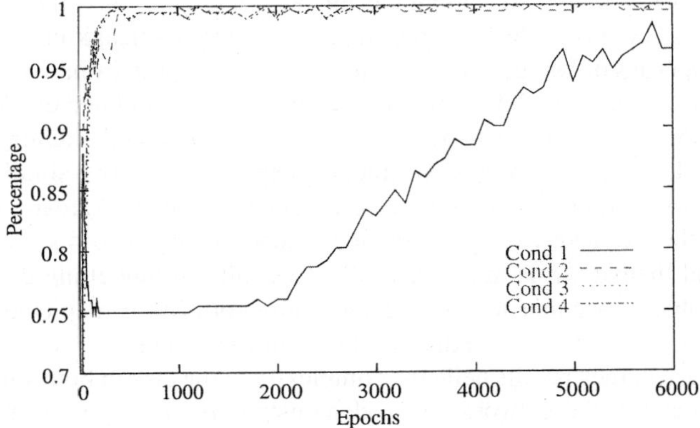

Fig. 6. Acquisition of Stereotypicality

ment in each of the four conditions described above when the ratio of non-stereotypical to stereotypical sentences was 8:1. The network quickly learns to use the scene for conditions 2-4 (examples 10-12), where the action in the linguistic input stream is also depicted, allowing the network to determine the relevant event and deduce the missing argument. (Because the graph shows the accuracy of the network at anticipating the upcoming argument at the adverb, the lines for conditions 3 and 4 are, in fact, identical.) But condition 1 (sentence 9) requires only stereotypical knowledge. The accuracy of condition 1 remains close to 75% (correctly producing the verb, first NP, and role discriminator, but not the second NP) until around epoch 1800 or so and then gradually improves as the network learns the appropriate stereotypical associations.

Results from several separate runs with different training parameters (such as learning rate and stereotypicality ratio) show that the network does indeed model the observed experimental behavior. The best results thus far exceed 99% accuracy in correctly anticipating the proper roles and 100% accuracy at the end of sentence.

As in simulation 1, the training corpus was generated by exhaustively combining participants and actions for all experimental conditions while holding out all test sentences. However, we found that we were able to use a larger learning rate, 0.1, than 0.05 as in the first simulation.

Analysis of the network after successful training suggests why this training policy works. Early in training, before stereotypicality has been encoded in the network's weights, patterns are developed in the hidden layer once the verb is read in from the input stream that enable the network to accurately decode that verb in the output layer. Not surprisingly, the network uses these same patterns to encode the stereotypical agent; the only constraint for the network is to ensure that the scene can still override this stereotypicality when the depicted event so dictates.

4 General Discussion and Future Work

The model demonstrates that reliance on correlations from distributional information in the linguistic input and the scene during training of the model enabled successful modelling of on-line utterance comprehension both in the presence and absence of rich visual contexts. The model that we present acquires stereotypical knowledge from distributional properties of language during training. The mapping from words to the scene representations is established through cooccurrence of scene-related utterances and depicted events during training. The network that emerges from this training regime successfully models five *visual worlds* eye-tracking experiments in two simulations. A first simulation of four experiments models the influence of either thematic and syntactic knowledge in the utterance [8], or of depicted events showing who-does-what-to-whom on incremental thematic role assignment [9]. Crucially in modelling the fifth experiment we are able to account for the greater relative priority of depicted events when event depictions and event knowledge conflict with each other.

The simple accuracy results belie the complexity of the task in both simulations. For experiments 3 and 4, the network has to demonstrate *anticipation* of upcoming roles when the scene is present, showing that it can indeed access the proper role and filler from the compressed representation of the event associated with the verb processed in the linguistic stream when available. This task is rendered more difficult because the appropriate event must be extracted from the superimposition of the two events in the scene, which is what is propagated into the model's hidden layer. In addition, it must also still be able to process all sentences correctly when the scene is not present.

Simulation 2 is more challenging still. The experiment shows that information from the scene takes precedence when there is a conflict with stereotypical knowledge; otherwise, each source of knowledge is used when it is available. In the training regime used in this simulation, the dominance of the scene is established early because it is much more frequent than the more particular stereotypical knowledge. As training progresses, stereotypical knowledge is gradually learned because it is sufficiently frequent for the network to capture the relevant associations. As the network weights gradually saturate, it becomes more difficult to retune them. But encoding stereotypical knowledge requires far fewer weight adjustments, so the network is able to learn that task later during training.

According to the "Coordinated Interplay" account in [7,6,11], the rapid integration of scene and utterance information and the observed preferred reliance of the comprehension system on the visual context over stored knowledge might best be explained by appealing to bootstrapping accounts of language acquisition. The development of a child's world knowledge occurs in a visual environment, which accordingly plays a prominent role during language acquisition. The fact that the child can draw on two informational sources (utterance and scene) enables it to infer information that it has not yet acquired from what it already knows. Bootstrapping accounts for the fact that a child can correlate event structure from the world around it with descriptions of events. When a child perceives an event, the structural information it extracts from it can determine how the child interprets a sentence that describes the event in question. The incremental interpretation of a sentence can in turn direct the child's attention to relevant entities and events in the environment. Events are only present for a limited time when utterances refer to such events during child language acquisition. This time-limited presence might determine the tight coordination with which attention in the scene interacts with utterance comprehension and information extracted from the scene during adult language comprehension. This contextual development may have shaped both our cognitive architecture (i.e., providing for rapid, seamless integration of scene and linguistic information), and comprehension mechanisms (e.g., people rapidly avail themselves of information from the immediate scene when the utterance identifies it).

The model presented in this paper extends current models of on-line utterance comprehension when utterances relate to a scene [12] in several ways. Existing models account for processes of establishing reference in scene-sentence integration when scenes contain only objects. Our network accounts for processes of establishing reference, and furthermore models the rapid assignment of thematic roles based on linguistic and world knowledge, as well as scene events. In this way, it achieves rapid scene-utterance integration for increasingly rich visual contexts, including the construction of propositional representations on the basis of scene events. It models the integration of utterances and relatively rich scenes (that contain actions and events) in addition to objects. Furthermore, the model–in line with experimental findings – successfully accounts for the relative priority of depicted events in thematic interpretation. It importantly achieves this through a modification of the training regime that prioritizes scene information. This confirms suggestions from [7] that a rapid interplay between utterance comprehension and the immediate scene context during acquisition is one potential cause for the relative priority of depicted events during on-line comprehension.

Connectionist models such as the SRN have been used to model aspects of cognitive development, including the time-course of emergent behaviors [13], making them highly suitable for simulating developmental stages in child language acquisition (e.g., first learning names of objects in the immediate scene, and later proceeding to the acquisition of stereotypical knowledge). The finding that modelling this aspect of development provides an efficient way to naturally reproduce the observed adult comprehension behavior promises to offer deeper insight into how adult performance is at least partially a consequence of the acquisition process.

Future research will focus on combining all of the experiments in one model, and expand the range of sentence types and fillers to which the network is exposed. The architecture itself is being redesigned to scale up to much more complex linguistic constructions and have greater coverage while retaining the cognitively plausible behavior described in this study [14].

Acknowledgements

The first two authors were supported by SFB 378 (project "ALPHA"), and the third author by a PhD studentship (GRK 715), all awarded by the German Research Foundation (DFG).

References

1. Steven Pinker. How could a child use verb syntax to learn verb semantics? In Lila Gleitman and Barbara Landau, editors, *The acquisition of the lexicon*, pages 377–410. MIT Press, Cambridge, MA, 1994.
2. Cynthia Fisher, D. G. Hall, S. Rakowitz, and Lila Gleitman. When it is better to receive than to give: Syntactic and conceptual constraints on vocabulary growth. In Lila Gleitman and Barbara Landau, editors, *The acquisition of the lexicon*, pages 333–375. MIT Press, Cambridge, MA, 1994.
3. Jeffrey L. Elman. Finding structure in time. *Cognitive Science*, 14:179–211, 1990.
4. Martin Redington, Nick Chater, and Steven Finch. Distributional information: A powerful cue for acquiring syntactic categories. *Cognitive Science*, 22:425–469, 1998.
5. Deb Roy and Alex Pentland. Learning words from sights and sounds: A computational model. *Cognitive Science*, 26(1):113–146, 2002.
6. Pia Knoeferle and Matthew W. Crocker. Stored knowledge versus depicted events: what guides auditory sentence comprehension. In *Proceedings of the 26th Annual Conference of the Cognitive Science Society*. Mahawah, NJ: Erlbaum, 2004. 714–719.
7. Pia Knoeferle and Matthew W. Crocker. The coordinated interplay of scene, utterance, and world knowledge: evidence from eye-tracking. submitted.
8. Yuki Kamide, Christoph Scheepers, and Gerry T. M. Altmann. Integration of syntactic and semantic information in predictive processing: Cross-linguistic evidence from German and English. *Journal of Psycholinguistic Research*, 32(1):37–55, 2003.

9. Pia Knoeferle, Matthew W. Crocker, Christoph Scheepers, and Martin J. Pickering. The influence of the immediate visual context on incremental thematic role-assignment: evidence from eye-movements in depicted events. *Cognition*, 95:95–127, 2005.
10. Risto Miikkulainen. Natural language processing with subsymbolic neural networks. In Antony Browne, editor, *Neural Network Perspectives on Cognition and Adaptive Robotics*, pages 120–139. Institute of Physics Publishing, Bristol, UK; Philadelphia, PA, 1997.
11. Pia Knoeferle and Matthew W. Crocker. The coordinated processing of scene and utterance: evidence from eye-tracking in depicted events. In *Proceedings of International Conference on Cognitive Science*, Allahabad, India, 2004.
12. Deb Roy and Niloy Mukherjee. Towards situated speech understanding: Visual context priming of language models. *Computer Speech and Language*, 19(2):227–248, 2005.
13. Jeffrey L. Elman, Elizabeth A. Bates, Mark H. Johnson, Annette Karmiloff-Smith, Domenico Parisi, and Kim Plunkett. *Rethinking Innateness: A Connectionist Perspective on Development*. MIT Press, Cambridge, MA, 1996.
14. Marshall R. Mayberry and Matthew W. Crocker. Generating semantic graphs through self-organization. In *Proceedings of the AAAI Symposium on Compositional Connectionism in Cognitive Science*, pages 40–49, Washington, D.C., 2004.

Automatically Inducing a Part-of-Speech Tagger by Projecting from Multiple Source Languages Across Aligned Corpora

Victoria Fossum[1] and Steven Abney[2]

[1] Dept. of EECS, University of Michigan, Ann Arbor MI 48105
vfossum@umich.edu
[2] Dept. of Linguistics, University of Michigan, Ann Arbor MI 48105
abney@umich.edu

Abstract. We implement a variant of the algorithm described by Yarowsky and Ngai in [21] to induce an HMM POS tagger for an arbitrary target language using only an existing POS tagger for a source language and an unannotated parallel corpus between the source and target languages. We extend this work by projecting from *multiple* source languages onto a single target language. We hypothesize that systematic transfer errors from differing source languages will cancel out, improving the quality of bootstrapped resources in the target language. Our experiments confirm the hypothesis. Each experiment compares three cases: (a) source data comes from a single language A, (b) source data comes from a single language B, and (c) source data comes from both A and B, but half as much from each. Apart from the source language, other conditions are held constant in all three cases – including the total amount of source data used. The null hypothesis is that performance in the mixed case would be an average of performance in the single-language cases, but in fact, mixed-case performance always exceeds the maximum of the single-language cases. We observed this effect in all six experiments we ran, involving three different source-language pairs and two different target languages.

1 Introduction

1.1 Background

Statistical NLP techniques typically require large amounts of annotated data. Labelling data by hand is time-consuming; a natural goal is therefore to generate text analysis tools automatically, using minimal resources. Yarowsky et al. [22] present methods for automatically inducing various monolingual text analysis tools for an arbitrary target language, using only the corresponding text analysis tool for a source language and a parallel corpus between the source and target languages. Hwa et al. [15] induce a parser for Chinese text via projection from English using a similar method to that of [22]. Cucerzan and Yarowsky [8] present a method for bootstrapping a POS tagger for an arbitrary target language using

R. Dale et al. (Eds.): IJCNLP 2005, LNAI 3651, pp. 862–873, 2005.

only a bilingual dictionary between the source and target languages, a "basic library reference grammar" for the target language, and an existing corpus in the target language.

While automatically induced text analysis tools use fewer resources, their accuracy lags behind that of more resource-intensive tools. One solution to the problem of error reduction on NLP tasks is to train multiple classifiers, then compute a consensus classifier. Combining multiple classifiers is an effective way to reduce error if the errors made by each classifier are independently distributed. Such approaches have been successfully applied to a range of NLP tasks. Brill and Wu [4], van Halteren et al. [19], and Zavrel and Daelemans [23] investigate various methods for improving the performance of statistical POS taggers by combining multiple such taggers. Henderson and Brill [14] combine the Charniak, Collins, and Ratnaparkhi parsers to achieve an accuracy surpassing the best previous results on the WSJ. Gollins and Sanderson [10] apply projection via multiple source languages to reduce error in cross-linguistic information retrieval.

1.2 Motivation

We hypothesize that a large component of the error rate in the automatically induced text analysis tools generated by [22] is due to morphosyntactic differences between the source and target languages that are specific to each source-target language pair. Therefore, training POS taggers on additional source languages should result in multiple classifiers which produce independently distributed errors on the target language.

Previous research in classifier combination for POS tagging has focused primarily on combining various statistical classifiers trained on data in the same language. Thus, our approach is novel in its exploitation of differences across languages, rather than differences across statistical methods, to improve performance on POS tagging. Our method is general in that it does not rely on language-specific information, and requires no annotated resources in the target language.

Our method is easily extensible to new languages. While it requires a parallel corpus between each source language and the target language, the corpora used to train each single-source tagger need not be translations of the same text. Furthermore, our algorithm is applicable even to target languages belonging to distinct language families from those of the source languages.

1.3 Task Overview

Using existing POS taggers for English, German, and Spanish, we generate single-source taggers for Czech and French via projection across parallel translations of the Bible. To obtain a theoretical upper bound on the performance improvement that is possible by combining multiple POS taggers, we measure the *complementarity* between each pair of single-source taggers. We examine various ways to combine the output of these single-source taggers into a consensus tagger, and measure the resulting performance improvement.

2 Methods

2.1 Single-Source POS Tagger Induction

We implement a variant of the algorithm described in [21] for constructing a single-source bigram-based HMM POS tagger for a target language. First, we identify a language (the "source language") for which a POS tagger exists, and a sentence-aligned parallel corpus consisting of text in the source language and its translation in the target language. We then align the parallel corpora at the word-level using GIZA++ [1]. Next, we annotate the source text using an existing POS tagger. Finally, we project these annotations across the parallel text from the source text to the target text, smooth these projections, and use the projected annotations to train an HMM POS tagger for the target language.

In more detail, we implement the following procedure, based on [21]:

1. Obtain a sentence-aligned parallel corpus in the source and target languages (see Section 2.4).
2. Align the parallel corpus at the word-level using GIZA++[1].

English: He(1) likes(2) cats(4).
French: Il(1) aime(2) les(3) chats(4).

3. Tag the source portion of the parallel corpus using an existing POS tagger for the source language[2]. We use the Brill tagger[3] for English [3], the TNT tagger[4] for German, and the SVMTool tagger[5] for Spanish.

English: He/PRP likes/VBP cats/NNS.

Since the POS tagger for each source language uses its own distinct tagset, we convert the output of each tagger to a "generic" tagset for comparison purposes. Additionally, we label each POS tag as belonging to one of several more general "core" tagset categories (see Table 1).
4. Using the mapping induced by the word-level alignments, project the POS tags from the source language onto the target language.

French: Il/PRP aime/VB les/NULL chats/NNS.

[1] GIZA++ is a component of EGYPT, an open-source implementation of IBM's statistical machine translation system [1].
[2] For all existing POS taggers, we use the default models provided with the tagger for training in the source language. For taggers with variable parameter settings, we use the default settings for all parameters.
[3] A transformation-based tagger [3].
[4] A bigram-based Markov tagger[2].
[5] An SVM-based tagger [9].

Note that tag projection is complicated by the occurrence of many-to-one word alignments from source to target. To handle such cases, we compute two estimates of tag probabilities, $P(t_i|w_i)$: one using only 1-to-1 alignments, and the other using 1-to-n alignments. We then linearly combine the two estimators.
5. Before computing the $P(w_i|t_i)$ model, several steps must be taken to smooth the initial, noisy tag projections. First, $P(w_i|t_i)$ can be decomposed as follows:

$$P(w_i|t_i) = \frac{P(t_i|w_i) * P(w_i)}{P(t_i)}$$

To smooth $P(t_i|w_i)$, the simplifying assumption is made that in most natural languages, each word has at most two possible POS tags at the core tagset granularity. We count the relative frequency of each tag that is assigned to that French word by the tag projection from English, then discard all but the two most frequently assigned core tags. We then recursively smooth the tag probabilities in favor of the two most probable subtags for each of the core tags, where the subtags are members of the more finely grained "generic" tagset. We compute $P(t_i)$ and $P(w_i)$ using corpus frequency.
6. We estimate the probability of unknown words using the probability of words appearing only once in the training corpus. We replace all words occurring only once in the training corpus by the "UNK" token.
7. Before computing the $P(t_j|t_i)$ model, we filter the training data to remove those sentence pairs whose alignment score (as determined by GIZA++) falls into the lowest 25% of alignment scores. To estimate the probability of unknown state transitions, we perform Witten-Bell smoothing [20] on $P(t_j|t_i)$ to assign non-zero probabilities to state transitions not seen in the training data.
8. The resulting model defines an HMM bigram-based tagger in the target language. We use the Viterbi algorithm to determine the most likely sequence of tags given a sentence in the target language [17].

2.2 Multiple-Source POS Tagger Induction

To compute a multiple-source consensus tagger, we train n single-source taggers using n parallel texts, each pairing one of the source languages with the target language. We then apply each single-source tagger to the test sentences. For each word in the test sentences, we record the probability distribution $P_i(t|w)$ over possible tags that the ith single-source tagger produces. We then compute two consensus taggers, *Majority Tag* and *Linear Combination*, by combining the output from each of the n taggers, $P_1(t|w) \dots P_n(t|w)$ as follows:

Majority Tag: Each tagger outputs the most likely tag

$$t_i^{best} = \underset{t}{\operatorname{argmax}}(P_i(t|w))$$

for w. We select the tag from $t_1^{best}, \dots, t_n^{best}$ that receives the greatest number of votes from single-source taggers. To break ties, we select the tag chosen with the highest probability by the taggers that selected it.

Linear Combination: Each tagger outputs a vector of probabilities over possible tags t given w. We take a linear combination of these vectors to compute $P_{linear}(T|w)$, then select the tag t_{linear} with the highest probability.

$$P_{linear}(T|w) = \sum_{i=1}^{n} k_i * (P_i(T|w))$$

$$t_{linear} = \operatorname*{argmax}_t(P_{linear}(t|w))$$

In our experiments, we set $k_i = \frac{1}{n}$, so we effectively average the probability distributions of each tagger over possible tags t for w.

2.3 Tagsets

Two tagsets of different granularities are used in the experiments: the coarse-grained "core" and fine-grained "generic" tagsets (see Table 1). While it can be difficult to map fine-grained POS tags from one language directly onto another another because of morphological differences between languages, languages tend to agree on tags at a coarse-grained level.

2.4 Data Sets

We use two corpora in our experiments: the Bible (with translations in English, Czech, French, German, and Spanish), and the Hansards parallel corpus of Canadian parliamentary proceedings (with translations in English and French). For

Table 1. Generic and Core Tagsets

POS	Generic	Core
Noun	NN	N
Proper Noun	NNP	N
Verb, Inf.	VB	V
Verb, Present	VBP	V
Verb, Present Part.	VBG	V
Verb, Past Part.	VBN	V
Verb, Past	VBD	V
Determiner	DT	D
Wh-Determiner	WDT	D
Conjunction	CC	C
Number	CD	NUM
Adverb	RB	R
Wh-Adverb	WRB	R
Adjective	JJ	J
Pronoun	PRP	P
Preposition	IN	I

the Bible experiments, we use the entire 31,100-line text: training data consists of either one 31,000-line excerpt or two 15,500-line excerpts, while testing data consists of a held-out 100-sentence excerpt. For the Hansards experiments, training data consists of a 85,000-line excerpt; testing data consists of a held-out 100-sentence excerpt.

We perform the following pre-processing steps. Each text is filtered to remove punctuation and converted to lower case; accents are preserved. The English, French, German, and Spanish texts are tokenized to expand elisions.[6]

3 Results

We report percent agreement with the correct tags, determined by comparison with the output of the Treetag tagger[7] for French, and a hybrid rule-based/HMM-based tagger[8] for Czech. For French, agreement with the correctly tagged text is measured on the generic and core tagsets. For Czech, agreement is measured on the core tagset only, since this is the POS tagset provided by the tagger we use for evaluation purposes. All experiments use 5-fold cross-validation. For each iteration, the parallel corpus is divided randomly into training and testing sets. The accuracy of each single-source tagger is limited by the accuracy of the tagger used to tag the source training text; the accuracy of the evaluation of each tagger's performance on French and Czech text is limited by the accuracy of the reference tagger against which it is compared (Table 2).

Table 2. Reported Accuracy of Existing POS Taggers used to Train Single-Source Taggers

Tagger	Language	% Accuracy	F-measure	Test Corpus
Brill	English	96.6%	—	Penn Treebank (English)
TNT	German	—	—	—
SVMTool	Spanish	96.89%	—	LEXESP (Spanish)
TreeTag	French	96.36%	—	Penn Treebank (English)
Rules + HMM	Czech	—	95.38%	PDT (Czech)

3.1 Single-Source

For each single-source tagger, we train on 31,000 lines of the parallel Bible between the source and target languages and test on 100 held-out lines of the Bible in the target language. We report the accuracy of the induced taggers on French (Tables 5 and 4) and Czech (Table 6).

[6] e.g. "doesn't" → "does not", "qu'il" → "que il", "zum" → "zu dem", and "del" → "de el". This tokenization represents the only step of our algorithm that requires additional language-specific knowledge beyond the resources already given.

[7] A decision-tree-based tagger [18].

[8] [13].

To compare our baseline single-source tagger performance against that of [21], we conduct the following experiment, after the experimental procedure used by [21]. We train a single-source English-projected tagger for French on a 2,000,000-word (approximately 85,000-line) excerpt of the French-English Hansards corpus and test it on a 100-line excerpt of the same corpus. We obtain accuracies of 86.5% and 91.1% on the generic and core tagsets, respectively; [21] report accuracies of 91% and 94% on the "English Equivalent" and "core" tagsets, respectively.[9]

3.2 Multiple-Source

Complementarity: We compute the pairwise *complementarity* of each pair of single-source taggers. Brill and Wu [4] define the complementarity of a pair of taggers i and j as the percentage of cases when tagger i is wrong that tagger j is correct (See Table 3):

$$Comp(i, j) = (1 - \frac{errors_i \cup errors_j}{errors_i}) * 100$$

Table 3. Complementarity (row,col) of Single-Source Taggers

	French Bible						Czech Bible		
	Generic Tagset			Core Tagset			Core Tagset		
Source	English	German	Spanish	English	German	Spanish	English	German	Spanish
English	0	38.95	32.87	0	32.75	37.13	0	22.08	18.71
German	42.40	0	44.93	30.49	0	38.95	15.47	0	17.31
Spanish	41.12	48.83	0	35.64	39.51	0	19.95	24.98	0

Pairwise Combination: To determine whether tagger performance improves by using training data from two different source languages, without increasing the total amount of training data, we perform the following experiments. For each possible combination of two single-source taggers, we partition the Bible into two 15,500-line training sets (the first, a parallel corpus between one source language and the target language; the second, a parallel corpus between the other source language and the target language), and a 100-line held-out testing set. We train the first single-source tagger on one half, train the second single-source tagger on the second half, combine their output using the methods described in Section 2.2, and test the resulting consensus tagger on a held-out 100-line excerpt of the French (Tables 4 and 5) or Czech (Table 6) Bibles. For each pairwise combination of taggers, we report the percent error reduction of the combined tagger in comparison to the average accuracy of the constituent single-source taggers.

[9] Our "generic" and "core" tagsets correspond approximately to the "English Equivalent" and "core" tagsets used by [21]. Since we do not have access to the same testing set used by [21], we report results on a held-out excerpt of the Hansards corpus.

Table 4. % Accuracy of Single-Source, Pairwise-Combined, and n-way Combined Taggers Using Generic Tagset on French Bible

Sources	% Accuracy		% Error Rate Reduction
	Linear	Majority	
English	81.95	81.95	–
German	81.21	81.21	–
Spanish	79.76	79.76	–
Eng. + Ger.	**84.52**	84.30	15.96
Eng. + Span.	84.42	**84.48**	18.91
Ger. + Span.	83.89	**84.09**	18.45
E. + G. + S.	**85.80**	85.61	25.38

Table 5. % Accuracy of Single-Source, Pairwise-Combined, and n-way Combined Taggers Using Core Tagset on French Bible

Sources	% Accuracy		% Error Rate Reduction
	Linear	Majority	
English	85.67	85.67	–
German	86.66	86.66	–
Spanish	86.54	86.54	–
Eng. + Ger.	**88.06**	88.05	13.67
Eng. + Span.	**88.13**	88.12	14.54
Ger. + Span.	89.12	**89.19**	19.33
E. + G. + S.	**89.87**	89.43	26.11

n-Way Combination: To examine how much tagger performance can be improved by increasing the total amount of training data n-fold and training each of n single-source taggers on the full 31,000 lines of the Bible, then computing a consensus tagger, we perform the following experiment. We train each single-source tagger on 31,000 lines of the Bible, then compute the consensus output of all 3 single-source taggers on a held-out 100-line excerpt of the French (Tables 4 and 5) or Czech (Table 6) Bibles. For each n-way combination of taggers, we report the percent error reduction of the combined tagger in comparison to the average accuracy of the constituent single-source taggers.

4 Discussion

All multiple-source taggers outperform the corresponding single-source taggers–thus, incorporating multiple source languages improves performance, even when the total amount of training data is held constant (as in the pairwise combination experiments).

4.1 Single-Source Taggers

We expect performance to be highest for those source-target language pairs that are most similar to each other, linguistically. At the generic tagset level, the

Table 6. % Accuracy of Single-Source, Pairwise-Combined, and n-way Combined Taggers Using Core Tagset on Czech Bible

Sources	% Accuracy		% Error Rate Reduction
	Linear	Majority	
English	62.53	62.53	–
German	65.27	65.27	–
Spanish	63.27	63.27	–
Eng. + Ger.	65.44	**65.98**	5.76
Eng. + Span.	**65.41**	65.28	6.77
Ger. + Span.	67.18	**67.75**	9.74
E. + G. + S.	67.13	**67.36**	10.12

poor performance of the Spanish-projected single-source tagger on French text is partially due to a discrepancy between the SVMTool tagset [9] and our generic tagset[10]. At the core tagset level, the distinction between verb tenses becomes irrelevant, and the performance of the Spanish-projected tagger matches that of the other single-source taggers more closely on French data; still, its performance is lower than expected given the close morphosyntactic correspondence between Spanish and French.[11]

For several reasons, we expect single-source tagger performance to be poorer on Czech (Table 6) than on French (Tables 5 and 4). First, Czech is a "highly inflected" language: the role of function words in the Germanic and Romance languages is typically filled by suffixes in Czech. Second, Czech exhibits a "relatively free word order" [7]. Since a great deal of the POS information exploited by an HMM tagger is contained in sequences of function words[12], these features of Czech hinder the performance of an HMM POS tagger.[13] Finally, Czech belongs to the Slavic language family, and is therefore further removed than French from the Germanic and Romance families of the source languages used to train the single-source taggers.

Although our single-source taggers do not replicate the performance results reported by [21] (91% and 94% accuracy on generic and core tagsets, respectively), our primary concern is not their absolute performance but rather their

[10] e.g., SVMTool [9] does not make certain distinctions in verb tense that we make in our generic tagset.

[11] One likely explanation for this discrepancy is that we do not optimize the parameters of the Spanish POS tagger used to annotate the source corpus to suit the input format of our data set, but instead use the default settings. We estimate that optimizing these parameters to match our data set could result in an increase of 1-2% accuracy in the Spanish-projected source tagger for French and Czech; however, such an increase in performance of one of the baseline experiments would not change our conclusion in a significant way.

[12] e.g., a "DT" is likely to be followed by a "NN" in English.

[13] The Czech tagger we use for reference [13] combines a rule-based morphological analyzer with an HMM POS tagger to combat these problems; our induced HMM POS taggers, lacking any morphological analysis component, may not exploit the correct type of information for such languages.

performance relative to the multiple-source taggers. We think it plausible that the improvements we observe would also be observed with Yarowsky's single-source taggers, but it remains an open question.

4.2 Multiple-Source Taggers

Complementarity. Pairwise complementarity among single-source taggers is relatively high on French at both tagset granularities (Table 3). The low pairwise complementarity of taggers on Czech may indicate the existence of a ceiling on the performance of the single-source tagger induction algorithm, imposed by the limited degree of similarity between any of the source languages with the target language. Even under such circumstances, we still see improvement (though diminished) by combining single-source taggers for Czech.

One factor whose influence upon tagger complementarity must be acknowledged is the diversity of the statistical models underlying each of the POS taggers used to tag the source portion of the training text. Since we use a different type of tagger to tag each source language, we cannot separate the component of complementarity that is caused by the difference in statistical models among sources from the component caused by the difference in languages.

Pairwise Combination. All pairwise combined taggers outperform the corresponding single-source taggers, though the total amount of training data is unchanged. We observe this improvement on both French and Czech. This suggests that our approach is likely to improve performance over single-source taggers on a wide range of target languages, and does *not* depend upon a close correspondence between any of the source and target languages.

***n*-Way Combination.** As expected (given the n-fold increase in training data), all n-way combined taggers outperform the corresponding single-source taggers, suggesting that when parallel training data between a particular source-language pair is limited, the performance of a POS tagger projected across that language pair can be improved by the use of a parallel corpus between the target language and a different source language.

5 Conclusion

Projection from multiple source languages significantly improves the performance of automatically induced POS taggers on a target language. We observe performance gains from incorporating multiple source taggers even when the total amount of training data is held constant, indicating that multiple languages provide sources of information whose errors are independent and randomly distributed to a large extent. The approach presented here is general in that it does not depend on any language-specific resources in the target language beyond parallel corpora. Our results suggest that the performance of text analysis tools induced using parallel corpora can benefit from the incorporation of resources in other languages, even in the case of source languages belonging to distinct linguistic families from the target language.

6 Future Work

To further improve the accuracy of induced multiple-source taggers, we plan to investigate other methods for combining the output of single-source POS taggers. We hypothesize that combining the models constructed by each tagger *before* applying each tagger to the testing set would result in greater performance gains.

References

1. Yasser Al-Onaizan , Jan Curin, Michael Jahr, Kevin Knight, John Lafferty, Dan Melamed, Franz-Josef Och, David Purdy, Noah Smith and David Yarowsky: Statistical machine translation. Johns Hopkins University 1999 Summer Workshop on Language Engineering (1999)
2. Thorsten Brants: TnT – a statistical part-of-speech tagger. In Proceedings of the 6th Applied NLP Conference, ANLP-2000, April 29 – May 3, 2000, Seattle, WA. (2000)
3. Eric Brill: Transformation-Based Error-Driven Learning and Natural Language Processing: A Case Study in Part-of-Speech Tagging. Computational Linguistics Vol. 21 No. 4 (1995) 543-565
4. Eric Brill and Jun Wu: Classifier Combination for Improving Lexical Disambiguation. Proceedings of the ACL (1998)
5. Peter F. Brown, John Cocke, Stephen Della Pietra, Vincent J. Della Pietra, Frederick Jelinek, John D. Lafferty, Robert L. Mercer, and Paul S. Roossin: A Statistical Approach to Machine Translation. Computational Linguistics Vol. 16 No. 2 (1990) 79–85
6. S. Clark, J. Curran, and M. Osborne: Bootstrapping POS taggers using unlabelled data. In Walter Daelemans and Miles Osborne, editors, Proceedings of CoNLL-2003, Edmonton, Canada (2003) 49–55
7. Michael Collins, Jan Hajic, Lance Ramshaw, and Christoph Tillmann: A Statistical Parser for Czech. Proceedings of the 37th Annual Meeting of the ACL, College Park, Maryland (1999)
8. Silviu Cucerzan and David Yarowsky: Bootstrapping a Multilingual Part-of-speech Tagger in One Person-day. Proceedings of the Sixth Conference on Natural Language Learning (CoNLL) (2002)
9. Jesus Gimenez and Lluis Marquez: SVMTool: A general POS tagger generator based on Support Vector Machines. Proceedings of the 4th International Conference on Language Resources and Evaluation (LREC'04), Lisbon, Portugal (2004)
10. Tim Gollins and Mark Sanderson: Improving Cross Language Information Retrieval with Triangulated Translation. Proceedings of the 24th annual international ACM SIGIR conference 90–95 (2001)
11. French-English Hansards Corpus of Canadian Parliamentary Proceedings.
12. Jan Hajic and Barbora Hladka: Tagging Inflective Languages: Prediction of Morphological Categories for a Rich, Structured Tagset, COLING-ACL (1998) 483–490
13. Jan Hajic, Pavel Krbec, Pavel Kevton, Karel Oliva, and Vladimir Petkevic: Serial Combination of Rules and Statistics: A Case Study in Czech Tagging. Proceedings of the ACL (2001)
14. John C. Henderson and Eric Brill: Exploiting Diversity in Natural Language Processing: Combining Parsers. Proceedings of the 1999 Joint SIGDAT Conference on Empirical Methods in Natural Language Processing and Very Large Corpora (1999) 187–194

15. Rebecca Hwa, Philip Resnik, and Amy Weinberg: Breaking the Resource Bottleneck for Multilingual Parsing. Proceedings of the Workshop on Linguistic Knowledge Acquisition and Representation: Bootstrapping Annotated Language Data (2002)
16. Gideon Mann and David Yarowsky: Multipath translation lexicon induction via bridge languages. In Proceedings of NAACL 2001: 2nd Meeting of the North American Chapter of the Association for Computational Linguistics (2001) 151–158
17. Lawrence Rabiner: A tutorial on hidden Markov models and selected applications in speech recognition. Proceedings of the IEEE Vol. 77 No. 2 (1989)
18. Helmut Schmid: Probabilistic Part-of-Speech Tagging Using Decision Trees. International Conference on New Methods in Language Processing, Manchester, UK. (1994)
19. Hans van Halteren, Jakub Zavrel, and Walter Daelemans: Improving Data Driven Wordclass Tagging by System Combination. Proceedings of the Thirty-Sixth Annual Meeting of the Association for Computational Linguistics (1998) 491–497
20. Ian Witten and Timothy Bell: The zero-frequency problem: Estimating the probabilities of novel events in adaptive text compression. IEEE Transactions in Information Theory, Vol. 37 No. 4 1085–1094 (1991)
21. David Yarowsky and Grace Ngai: Inducing Multilingual POS Taggers and NP Bracketers via Robust Projection Across Aligned Corpora. Proceedings of NAACL (2001) 200–207
22. David Yarowsky, Grace Ngai, and Richard Wicentowski: Inducing Multilingual Text Analysis Tools via Robust Projection across Aligned Corpora. Proceedings of HLT (2001)
23. Jakub Zavrel and Walter Daelemans: Bootstrapping a Tagged Corpus through Combination of Existing Heterogeneous Taggers. Proceedings of LREC-2000, Athens (2000)

The Verbal Entries and Their Description in a Grammatical Information-Dictionary of Contemporary Tibetan

Jiang Di, Long Congjun, and Zhang Jichuan

Dept. of Phonetics and Computational Linguistics, Institute of Ethnology & Anthropology, Chinese Academy of Social Sciences, Beijing, 100081
jiangdi@cass.org.cn

Abstract. This paper discusses verb information items in the grammatical knowledge dictionary of Tibetan language. The verb information items include morphology, word-formation and syntax, in which the core is the verb classification with syntactic and semantic features. So the influences on clause structures of 12 types of verbs have been discussed. Also the paper designs an information table to compile the verb items and their related knowledge, in which most of the details of verbs have been described. At last some newly-found phenomena have been discussed and the paper therefore proposes that there are still some special tokens or constructs need to be mined out in Tibetan.

1 The Background of Constructing a Grammatical Knowledge Dictionary

Segmentation is one of the important tasks of text-processing in Tibetan. In order to gain satisfactory results we have proposed a suggestion, in which most of chunks can be identified with markers of chunks, and words can be segmented within chunks. Although the proposal achieved well in our sample of small scale data,[1] yet the wrong match and ambiguous phenomenon still obstruct our future work in the real texts. The reasons, we think, are in two aspects. One is lack of a perfect Tibetan grammatical system which is now still not constructed for information processing. Another is deficient in useful resources, especially a Tibetan knowledge dictionary of high quality with morphological and syntactic information.

A grammatical knowledge dictionary means a base with some essential information of the morphological and syntactic grammar, including pragmatic and rhetorical information as well. With such a dictionary, most phenomenon of mistaken word matching and recognizing, to some extent, may perhaps be eliminated during the word-segmenting. As to Tibetan, there are three main types of lexical information. Firstly, the lexical item itself is a kind of grammatical functional markers, such as, the genitive markers; secondly, the lexical item serves as a formal marker of some grammatical sections, such as, in *sku gdung* "Buddha's bone", "sku" acted as the prefix morpheme of the honorific words can construct amounts of honorific vocabulary;[2] last, the grammatical function of words may be ascertained after being analyzed, such as the verb *yid ches byed* "trust" belongs to the cognition verbs, which

R. Dale et al. (Eds.): IJCNLP 2005, LNAI 3651, pp. 874 – 884, 2005.

specify case markers for their subjects and objects. Nevertheless, no matter which information types, they all need previously be tagged as information attributives in a grammatical knowledge dictionary.

It should be pointed out, all the above information of lexical types may regard as the principle to construct a grammar knowledge dictionary. No matter how widely an item is used or how many its function includes, each item is equal in information. That is to say, equal attention should be paid to every lexical item with filling its information contents in every field of the dictionary, no matter much or few phenomenon of items involve.

Finally, the source of information attributives of Tibetan grammatical dictionary should be mentioned. Generally speaking, all the information of lexical items stem from language material or real texts. But the information contents and information attributives of each lexical item should be ascertained through the Tibetan grammatical system. So, we will take verbs as examples and discuss information contents of lexical items in our Tibetan grammatical system, which we call GIDCT (a Grammatical Information-Dictionary of Contemporary Tibetan).

2 Grammatical Features of Verbs

The most important features of Tibetan verbs embodied three dimensions, the morphology, word-formation and syntax. These three dimensions influence each other and condition each other. So the relationship and the forms of grammatical representation among them need to be ascertained gradually.

2.1 Morphological Features

The morphological features only refer to the forms of tense and mood remained from the ancient original forms of Tibetan monosyllabic verbs. That is to say, each monosyllabic verb may have four forms, the present tense form (also named proto-form), future tense form, past tense form and imperative mood form. However, the paradigm of Tibetan monosyllabic verbs, by no means, only adds the affixes or exhibits the regular inflection to construct. From the following examples, we can clearly comprehend the morphological conception of Tibetan verbs in table 1.

Obviously, the paradigm is of irregularity, as is the irregular change of verbs in English. It is quite difficult to analogize for this reason. But on the other hand, there are amount of Tibetan verbs which never change their forms. Related with the syntax, those sentences with prospective aspect markers always use the future tense forms of verbs, and sentences with realis markers always use past tense forms. That means morphology and syntax restrictively interacts each others. In addition, according to H.A.Jäschke's views[3], the present and the future forms always appear together with the negative particle "mi", and the past and imperative forms with negative particle "ma", which also have influences on the orders words. From the above, we know that the morphological features of Tibetan monosyllabic verbs still remain some restrictions on the syntactic function in the contemporary Tibetan, though Tibetan verbal morphemes are the remains of ancient times.

Table 1. Tibetan verbs with inflection forms

states of changes	present	furure	past	imperative	
no change for the whole verb	bstod	bstod	bstod	bstod	acclaim
change by affixing and vowel alternati	lta	blta	bltas	ltos	see
change by affixing	srung	bsrung	bsrungs	srungs	abide by
alternation of consonant forms of root	vtshong	btsong	btsongs	tshong	sold
alternation of consonant forms and aff	vchad	bshad	bshad	shod	say
alternation of affixes and vowels	gcog	gcag	bcag	chog	break off

2.2 Word-Formation Features

Most of the verbs in contemporary Tibetan are polysyllabic verbs, which appears in high frequency, and their meanings trend to be complicated. Tibetan polysyllabic verbs have stronger regularity in word-formation. They consist of nouns and verbs or adjectives and verbs. Among them, most of the verbal morphemes in compounds are common verbs without substantive sense. Please observer the following words in table 2.

Table 2. Compound Verbs in Tibetan

verbal morpheme	noun-verb compound		noun-verb compound		adjective-verb compound	
gtong	jus gtong	make ideas	bstod ra gtong	praise	byams po byed	love
rgyag	glo rgyag	cough	vphya las rgyag	sneer at	yag po byed	be kind
byed	dpang byed	testify	lta rnogs byed	look after	vtshub po byed	act widely
shor	khrag shor	bleed	rgyab vdre shor	fight	dgav po byed	like
vdebs	khrid vdebs	explain	go nor thebs	misunderstand		
gnang	bzo ba gnang	make	thugs khral gnang	be worry about		

One of the most important features of compound verbs is formal markers, namely, the verbal morphemes within words. Because of the productivity of compound verbs, dictionaries always fall behind. So it is possible to resolve the problem of recognition of verbs if verbal morphemes be regarded as morphological markers and rules of compound word-formation be built up in compounds.

Taking *ngal gso rgyag* "relax" as an example, it is always viewed as a phrase, so the compound word and the likes can not enter into *A Tibetan-Chinese Dictionary*[4]. In this case, the segmentation of the word may be *ngal-gso/ rgyag* with the dictionary, in which the former is a noun with meaning "relaxation", the latter is a monosyllabic verb with not-thorough-going meaning "doing, making". The real reason led to such a grammatical conception is that many compound verbs can be inserted some other grammatical constituents, such as *ngal-gso yag-po rgyag* "take a good rest", *ngal-gso tog-tsham rgyag* "take a short break". In our opinion, Tibetan polysyllabic compound verbs are still in progress and not yet fall into a pattern in mind. Anyway, when engaged in computer processing, we can not give up an undertaking on account of a small obstacle. So while we put compound verbs in the dictionary we make some other rules to process the verbal phrases with inserted constituents.

Quite few are another type of common disyllabic compound verbs in Tibetan, which are non-productive in word-formation. For instance, *ha go* "understand", *kha nor* "make an indiscreet remark", *ngo tsha* "be shy", *blo'gel* "trust in", *khas'che* "promise", *ha las* "amaze", *ya mtshan* "be strange at". Those words were formed from phrases in history and are unmarked forms. So we can put them all into the dictionary directly without morphological analysis.

2.3 Syntactic Features

The Tibetan verb syntactic features cover many categories. Such as, whether or not they take objects, what kind of objects they take, which types of case markers they require to subject and object constituents, and so on. On the other hand, The attributions of verbs themselves are very important, which determine the quantity of arguments and the frame of sentences, such as attribution of human verbs, of volition verbs, of controllable verbs, causative verbs, and so on. In addition, some other syntactic features are also of importance. e.g. the formal markers of normalization for each verb, and the position relationships between verbs and adverbial modifiers and so on.

In our project, an effective way to analysis Tibetan verb syntax has been found that is classification for verbs according to the types of syntactic features and semantic features of verbs. With this method we can describe those grammatical information for each verb and compile verbs into the knowledge dictionary in different types. The following are some description of 12 types of verbs.[5]

Verbs of possession: This type of verbs indicates those which contain the meaning "to possess, to gain, to come being to, to form" and so on. For example, *yod /dug* "have", *vthob* "gain", *byung/ yong* "take place", *rag* "obtain", *'dzams* "belong to", *'chor/ shor* "appear, emerge" and so on. The basic format of verbs of possession is "NP+[POS]+NP+$V_{(VOP)}$, which requires that the subjects take possessive case markers, and that the objects take absolutive case marker (zero form). So the syntactic information items of verbs of possession are like these {$V_{(VOP)}$, $NP_{(S)}$+POS, $NP_{(O)}$+Ø}. Also, most of the verbs of possession possess the characteristic of {HMN}(subjects are human being).

Existential verb: This type of verbs expresses the meaning of someone or something being somewhere. For instance, *yod/ 'dug/ yog red* "exist, be". Existential verbs demand the subjects take absolutive case marker, and the objects take locative case marker. The basic syntactic format of existential verbs is "NP+NP+[LOC] +$VP_{(EXI)}$". Existential verbs and verbs of possession do not obligatorily demand the characteristics of {HMN} and {CTR}(subjects can control actions) for subjects. The grammatical information items of existential verbs include {$V_{(EXI)}$, NP+LOC}.

Verbs of change: The verbs of change indicate those which take resultant complement constituents. Such as *sprul* "change", *sgyur* "make to change", *'gyur* "turn to", *'gro* "change", *'dul* "domesticate" and so on. The basic format of the verbs of change is "NP+$VP_{(adj, v)}$+[COP]+$VP_{(CHA)}$". That means verbs of change require complements of adjectives or verbal phrases which express the results of verb changes and there is a complement particle between complement constituents(COP) and verbs. So in the information dictionary, the characteristics of {$V_{(CHA)}$, VP+COP} should be described.

Perception verbs: This type of verbs indicates responses and feelings human being perceives from things or events by sight, by hearing and by aesthesia. Such as, *mthong* "see", *go* "hear", *ha go* "understand", *dran* "remember", *brjed* "forget", *ngo shes* "recognize" and so on. Perception verbs possess the characteristic of {HMN} and {INV}(non-volition). Except of a few words such as *brjed* "forget", the action outcome of the perception verbs can not be controlled by human being with consciousness. So they are non-controllable verbs. The basic format of the perception verbs is "NP+[AG]+NP+$VP_{(PER)}$". That means the subject may take an agentive case marker. So the information items in the dictionary are {$V_{(PER)}$, $NP_{(S)}$+AG, HMN, UCT(=non-control)}, but the information items for verbs like *brjed* "forget" are {$V_{(PER)}$, $NP_{(S)}$+AG, HMN, CTR}.

Directional verbs: This type of verbs indicates those which express moving action concepts or staying status concepts. The common verbs are *'gro* "go", *phyin* "go", *yong* "come", *phebs* "come", *bsdad* "stay", *bzhag* "lay up" and so on. The directional verbs can construct directional-predicate structure: "NP+$VP_{(DIR)}$", or construct directional complement: NP+VP+$VP_{(DIR)}$, in which the verbs are called directional constituents, or construct serial verbal phrases: NP+VP+[TAP]+$VP_{(DIR)}$. The information items of directional verbs in the dictionary are {$V_{(DIR)}$, VP+$V_{(DIR)}$, VP+TAP+$VP_{(DIR)}$}. There are no obligatory demands on the characteristics of {HMN}, {CTR}, or {VOL} for subjects in directional verb structures.

Cognition verbs: This type of verbs indicates those which express non-action psychological activity. The common verbs are *brtsi 'jog byed* "respect", *dga' zhen byed* "like", *ngo tsha* "be shy", *sems shor* "be infatuated with", *mthong tchung byed* "belitter", *ngo rgol byed* "be object to", *dogs* "be suspicious of" and so on. The basic syntactic structure of the cognition verbs is NP+[AG]+NP +[OBJ]+$VP_{(COG)}$, namely the subjects can take agentive case markers, and objects can take objective case markers. The information items of cognition verbs is {$V_{(COG)}$, $NP_{(S)}$+AG, $NP_{(O)}$+OBJ} in the dictionary.

Narrate verbs: The narrate verbs indicate the verbs expressing the meaning of citation and thinking in mind. Such as *bshad* "say", *zer* "speak", *'dri* "ask", *lan slog* "answer", *bsam* "think", *dgongs* "think over", *shes* "know" and so on. The narrate verbs require clausal objects or objects of normalization phrases, the basic structures are "NP+[AG]+[NP+VP]+$VP_{(NAR)}$, or [NP+VP] +NP +[AG]+$VP_{(NAR)}$, in which the clausal objects of citation verbs unusually attaches clause particle "se". The information items of narrate verbs in the dictionary include {$V_{(NAR)}$}.

Interrelation verbs: This type of verbs indicates those which interconnect two or more things or events on logic, or social rules, or common senses, which correspond or subordinate each other. For instance, *'dre* "mix up", *'gal* "violate", *mthun* "be in consensus", *kha bral* "separate", *stun* "fit", *kha thug rgyag* "meet". The syntactic format of the interrelation verbs is NP+NP+[ITP]+$VP_{(REL)}$, namely the interrelation verbs need attach an interrelation case marker "*dang*" to the nouns related. Therefore the information items of interrelation verbs should include {$V_{(REL)}$, NP+ITP}.

Causative verbs: The causative verbs include the meaning of "cause to do", such as *bcug* "let to do", *byed* "let to do, make sth. appear", *bzo* "make sb. do" and so on.

Generally, the subjects of causative verbs attach agentive case marker to subjects, and sometimes possessive case marker to subjects in object-clause. Usually, there is a causative particle "ru" between the object-clause and the causative verbs. The basic syntactic structure of causative verbs are "NP+[AG]+NP+[POS]+(NP+)VP +[CAU]+$VP_{(CAV)}$". The information items of causative verbs in the dictionary are {$V_{(CAV)}$, $NP_{(S)}$+AG, $NP_{(PCC)}$+POS, PCC+CAV}.

Stative verbs: This type of verbs indicates those which express the state of actions. Such as *shi* "die", *bzi* "drunk", *snyun* "be ill", *yal* "disappear" and so on. The basic syntactic structure of the stative verbs is "NP+(NP+) $VP_{(STA)}$", namely the subject and object should be with absolutive case marker. The information items of the stative verbs in the dictionary are {$V_{(STA)}$}.

Action verbs: Action verbs include several types. Some express the meaning of rendering and take two objects, some express the meaning of objects changing and take a result object. The objects' types of action verbs include accusative objects, indirect objects, resultative objects. The subject of action verbs are often attached an agentive case marker. Action verbs can be divided into transitive and intransitive verbs. The basic syntactic structure of intransitive action verb is "NP+$VP_{(ACT)}$", and that of transitive is "NP+NP+$VP_{(ACT)}$", or that of bi-objects is "NP+NP+[DAT]+NP +VP", or that of resultative objects is "NP+[AG]+NP+NP+[FAT]+$VP_{(ACT)}$".

Copula: Copula denotes verbs *yin / red* "be" which express the classes of grammatical subjects. The basic structure of copula is "NP+NP+$VP_{(COU)}$", namely both of the subject and the object use absolutive case marker.[6]

As space is limited, the above description about verbal syntax and semantics is quite simple. We believe more and more grammatical information phenomena will be mined out and be collected into grammatical information dictionary one by one in our future work.

3 Descriptions of the Information Items Related to Verbs and Some Samples

In this section, we will describe the information items of verbs which are in our GIDCT. For the sake of a clear statement, we will illustrate some representative samples as well.

<Number>, it denotes the order location of a word entry in GIDCT.

<Word form>, it denotes Tibetan characters (orthography) of written words, e.g. |རླུང་ལངས

<Transliteration of Word Form>, it denotes transliteration forms of Tibetan words with roman letters according to a scheme designed. E.g. rlung langs.

<Lhasa pronunciation>, it denotes the phonetic transcription of words according to Lhasa pronunciation. E.g. lungf langw or luŋ^{55} laŋ^{132}.

<Meaning$_{(Chinese)}$>, it denotes the basic meaning of entries with Chinese or other languages, this sample is "anger, rage".

<Homograph>, it denotes the homographs of entries, namely dividing a polysemous word into different words, then giving their other meanings here. E.g. "blow".

<Variant>, it provides a different entry forms in spelling. There is no variant for this sample.

<Syllabic Numbers of Entries>, There are about 1300 monosyllabic verbs, and about 100 disyllabic verbs in Tibetan, which are classic forms. A number of modern Tibetan verbs are polysyllable with a noun and a monosyllabic verb, which shows the value and importance of the syllabic numbers in computer processing. This sample is a two syllabic verb.

<Types of word-formation>, it let choose one item from the four: mono-morphemic words, non-productive compounds, productive compounds, reduplicative compounds. Mono-morphemic verbs are monosyllabic verbs; non-productive compound verbs are classic disyllables, both of which are unmarked. Compound verbs are polysyllabic verbs with verbs serving as markers. Reduplicative compound verbs are too complicated, which have been discussed in another paper.[7] For this sample, word-formation type is a non-productive compound.

<Word-formation structure>, it let choose one from types of subject-predicate, predicate-object (verb-object), modifier-head, complement-verb, and co-ordination constituents. Different structures of word-formation of compound verbs have effects on syntactic structures in processing, as in the case of compound verbs with accusative objects. In the format of "noun +noun+ (monosyllabic)verb" (namely: N1+N2+V), the "N1" may be an object of compound verb "N2+V", or a part of the compound verb. On the other, the difference of the inner structure of compound verbs may cause different object types. Such as, the subject-predicate compound verbs usually require accusative objects with zero marker, and verbs of predicate-object type generally require objective objects with objective marker. Therefore, the inner structural relationship of compound verbs may produce influence on the objects and their types.[8] This sample is a non-productive compound verb.

<Word-formation productivity>, it denotes the ability of monosyllabic verbs serving as verbal morpheme in word-formation. The chosen items are strong one, weak one, and null. E.g., classic disyllabic compound verbs possess no capability of combining new-type compound verbs, which are null. The sample is null.

<Classic Tense form>, it denotes the forms of classic monosyllabic verbs, some of which show different forms survived from old time. One of the four forms can be chosen from present form, past form, future form, and imperative form. The sample is present form.

<Formative structure>, it denotes the reduplicative form of verbs only. The sample is not reduplicative form.

<Root>, it let write down directly the transliteration forms of verb root or stem. The sample is "rlung".

<Meaning of verb root 1>, it let write down directly the meaning in Chinese or other language. The sample is "air, wind".

<Meaning of verb root 2>, it let write down directly the meaning in Chinese or other language. The sample is null.

<Word-formation or formative morpheme>, it let write down the transliteration form of word-formation morpheme. The sample is "langs".

<Meaning of word-formation or formative morpheme>, it let write down the meaning of the word-formation or formative morpheme. The sample is "happen".

<Honorific form>, it let write down the honorific forms of some verbs. The sample is null.

<Parts of Speech>, it defines parts of speech of every verb entry, in which there are two main types: transitive and intransitive. The sample is transitive one.

<Verbal Types of syntax and semantics>, it defines the syntactic and semantic types of verbs, and choose one from following: stative verb, action verb, cognition verb, perception verb, verb of change, directional verb, narrate verb, copula, verb of possession, existential verb, interrelation verb, causative verb. The sample is cognition verb.

<Person>, it denotes the agreement between person and copula verbs or existential verbs. The sample is null.

<HMN/UMN>, it denotes whether a verb is a human verb or not. The sample is HMN.

<CTR/NTR>, it denotes whether a verb is a controllable verb or not. The sample is CTR.

<VOL/NOL>, it denotes whether a verb is a volitional verb or non-volitional verb. The sample is volitional verb.

<CAV/NAV>, it denotes whether a verb is a causative or non-causative verb. The sample is NAV.

<Subject case type>, it denotes what type of case markers the verb requires for a subject (including absolutive /agentive/ possessive). The sample is agentive (AG).

<Object case type>. it denotes what type of case markers the verb requires for object (including accusative / objective / resultative). The sample is objective one.

<Indirect object case type>, it denotes what type of case markers the verb requires for indirect objects. The sample is null.

<Cases for noun phrases>, it denotes what type of case markers the verb demands for specific noun phrases (including locative, ablative, allative, instrumental, comparative, exclusive, genitive, factitive and so on).

<Argument value>, it denotes the quantity of arguments the verb refers to. The sample is 2.

<Negative form and the position>, it let choose one from the two negative forms (mi, ma), and ascertain the distributing position in verb phrases, before verbs, or following verbs, or between syllables of verbs. The sample is between two syllables.

<Normalization marker>, it let write down the form of normalization markers of the verb. The sample is "mkhan, dus".

As to the examples, it is better to collect one or more phrases or clauses as examples from real texts, which can illustrate morphological or syntactic phenomenon.

<Example>, sku rlung ma gnang "Don't be angry." (honorific)
pha-ma-s nga-r rlung-langs-song. "My parents are angry with me."
parents-AG me-OBJ angry-PEF(perfect aspect)

The following are two verbal examples. "#" denotes this item is null, and "√" denotes the function may exists.

Sample 1 <No. xxxx >

<word form>	ངལ་གསོ་རྒྱག	<transliteration>	ngal-gso-rgyag
<Lhasa pronunciation>	ngaevsof gyaw	<meaning>	rest
<homograph>	#	<variant>	#
<syllabic number>	3	<types of word-formation >	compound
<word-formation structure>	VO	<word-formation productivity>	strong
<tense form>	present tense	<formative structure>	#
<root>	ngal gso	<meaning of morph 1>	tired , exhausted
<meaning of morph 2>	#	<honorific form >	#
<word-formation／formative morpheme>	rgyag	<meaning of word-formation／formative morpheme>	recuperate
<parts of speech >	vi	<type of verbs>	action
<person>	#	<HMN/UMN>	Y
<CTR/NTR>	Y	<VOL/NOL>	Y
<CAV/NAV>	N	<subject case type>	#
<object case type>	#	<indirect case type>	#
<case for noun phrases>		<argument vaule>	1
<negative form>	mi	<negative position>	postposition
<normalization marker >	#	<as complement>	#
<corresponding prototype>		other features	

<example>: ngal-gso yag-po rgyag "have a good rest";
ngal gso tog tsam brgyab "have a short break"

nga da-lta ngal-gso-rgyag gi-yod.
I now rest DUR
I am resting now.

nad-pa-tsho ngal-gso yag-po rgyag-ru bcug dgos.
Patient-PL rest good V-CAV cause AUX
Let the patients have a good rest.

Sample 2 <No. xxxx>

<word form>	བཅུག	<transliteration>	bcug
<Lhasa pronunciation>	juh	<meaning>	make, allow
<homograph>	#	<variant>	√
<syllabic number>	1	<types of word-formation >	mono-
<word-formation structure>	root/ etyma	<word-formation productivity>	null
<tense form>	past tense	<formative structure>	null
<root>	bcug	<meaning of morph 1>	make, allow
<meaning of morph2>	Insert, install	<honorific form >	bcug gnang
<word-formation／formative morpheme>	null	<meaning of word-formation／formative morpheme>	null
<parts of speech >	vt	<type of verbs>	CAV
<person>	#	<HMN/UMN>	Y
<CTR/NTR>	Y	<VOL/NOL>	Y
<CAV/NAV>	Y	<subject case type>	Agentive

<object case type>	Cl-O+CAV	<indirect case type>	#
<case for noun phrases>	√	<argument vaule>	3
<negative form>	ma	<negative position>	preposition
<normalization marker >	#	<as complement>	#
<corresponding prototype>	'jug	other features	

<Syntactic example>
rgan-lags kyis nga-tsho-r sbyong-tshan bri-ru bcug-gnang-byung.
teacher AG us-PL-POS homework write-CAU make-HON-PEF
The teacher makes us write /do our homework.
khyed-rang-gis nga mi mang-po 'di-'dras dkyil-la ngo-tsha-ru bjug.
you-AG me people many so among-LOC shame-CAU make
You let me lose face in front of so many people.

4 Conclusions and the Problems to Be Solved

The data in this project is in construction. Although the data bulk is still not large, some special problems of data has appeared which are somewhat difficult to enter GIDCT base. For instance, *ngal rtsol byed gi yod mdog mdog byed* "to pretend to work", in which *mdog* criginally means "color", after being reduplicated, it means "false appearance". But it can not be used alone, it is the same with the verb form of *mdog mdog byed* which is constructed by reduplicating form plus verb form. And its object is always a clause (e.g. *grwa pa yin mdog mdog byed* "pretend to be a lama") or a verb phrase (e.g. *mi shes pa shes mdog mdog byed* "pretend to know when one does not know"). There is not any markers between the verb and clause-objects or verb-phrase-objects. Obviously, when processing this kind of forms, we should add some new information items of morphology to the dictionary, such as verbal bound forms or non-absolute verb phrase structures. In addition, some scattered phenomenon can not be overlooked, because as information items of the dictionary, they are of the same value.

Professor Yu Shiwen has made very careful annotation for Chinese word items in *The Grammatical Knowledge-base of Contemporary Chinese*.[9] By contrast, GIDCT is impossible to reach such depth for the time being. There are many reasons, but the essential one is still lack of extensive and thorough researches on grammatical infrastructures. On the other hand, Tibetan language information processing is quite different from Chinese, it is not suitable to make a dictionary by copying the description method of Chinese grammar simply. Take Chinese resultative verbs for an example, this type of verbs always extend to syntactic resultative phrases, such as *记住* (remember-fixed) "remember" to *记得住* (remember-able-fixed) "able to remember". Yet the type of verbs only contains some of Chinese verbs, so it is worth to list their information in the dictionary. For Tibetan polysyllabic compound verbs, nearly all of them can accept modifiers or complements between nominal and verbal morphemes, it is difficult to compile them or describe them in the dictionary.

In true texts, there are close connection among verbs and other constituents, especially predicate endings, including aspect markers, evidential markers and mood markers. But these information may list separately in GIDCT, which is quite different from Yu's GKBCC, in which Chinese "着zhuo, 了le, 过guo" are listed as verbs' information items.[10] Also, some other information, such as information of verbs modified by adverbs and of the relations with auxiliary verbs, etc, have not yet been described in GIDCT temporarily. All in all, it will be an important task to mine information as much as possible in Tibetan grammatical information dictionary construction.

Now the infrastructure of languages and construction of electronic dictionaries has been attached more and more great importance to, including classifying syntax dictionary and semantic dictionary.[11][12] The GIDCT is also a good beginning to Tibetan natural language processing.

Acknowledgement

This research is supported by NSFC of China. No. 60173024, 60473135.

References

1. Jiang Di: The Method and Processs of the Definition to Grammatical Chunks in Modern Tibetan. Minority Languages of China (Minzu Yuwen), Vol.3, (2003) 30-39
2. Zhou Jiwen, Xie Houfang: *A Grammar of Lha Sa Dialect of Tiebtan Language*. Beijing: Minzu Press (2003)
3. Jäschke, H. A. (Heinrich August,1817-1883): *Tibetan grammar*. addenda by A.H. Francke, assisted by W.Simon. [monograph] monograph 1929
4. Zhang Yisun (eds.): *A Tibetan-Chinese Dictionary*. Minzu Press (1993)
5. Huang Xing, Jiang Di: The Lexicographic Principles for Compound Verbs in Tibetan Electronic Dictionary. In: JiangDi, Kong Jiangping (eds.): *Advances on the Minority Language Processing of China*. Beijing: Social Sciences Academic press (2005) 94-107
6. Huang Xing, Jiang Di: Automatic Recognition of the Subject and Object of Linking Verbal Sentences in Tibetan. In: Sun Maosong, Chen Qunxiu (eds.): *Language calculation and content-based text processing*. Beijing: Tsinghua University Press (2003) 167-172
7. Yu Shiwen (eds.). *The Grammatical Knowledge-base of Contemporary Chinese----A Complete Specification*. Beijing: Tsinghua University Press (2003)
8. Yin Yiling, Chen Qunxiu: The Research & Implementation of the machine Tractable Dictionary of Contemporary Chinese Predicate Adjectives. In: Sun Maosong, Chen Qunxiu (eds.): *Language calculation and content-based text processing*. Beijing: Tsinghua University Press (2003) 357-363
9. Zhan Weidong: An Overview of Large Scale Semantic Lexicons for NLP. In: Xu Bo, Sun Maosong, Jin Guangjin (eds.): *Some important Issues of Chinese language processing*. Beijing: Sciences Academic Press (2003)107-121

Tense Tagging for Verbs in Cross-Lingual Context: A Case Study

Yang Ye[1] and Zhu Zhang[2]

[1] Department of Linguistics, University of Michigan, USA
[2] School of Information and Department of Electrical Engineering and Computer Science, University of Michigan, USA
yye@umich.edu, zhuzhang@umich.edu

Abstract. The current work applies Conditional Random Fields to the problem of temporal reference mapping from Chinese text to English text. The learning algorithm utilizes a moderate number of linguistic features that are easy and inexpensive to obtain. We train a tense classifier upon a small amount of manually labeled data. The evaluation results are promising according to standard measures as well as in comparison with a pilot tense annotation experiment involving human judges. Our study exhibits potential value for full-scale machine translation systems and other natural language processing tasks in a cross-lingual scenario.

1 Introduction

Temporal resolution is a crucial dimension in natural language processing. The fact that tense does not necessarily exist as a grammatical category in many languages poses a challenge on cross-lingual applications, e.g. machine translation. The fact that English tenses and Chinese aspect markers align at word level on one hand and sub-word level on the other hand poses a challenge for temporal reference distinction translation in a statistical machine translation (MT) system. A word-based alignment algorithm will not be able to capture the temporal reference distinction when mapping between Chinese and English. Being able to successfully map the temporal reference distinction in Chinese text through disparate features onto the most appropriate tenses for the parallel English text is an important criterion for good translation quality. Languages have various levels of time reference distinction representation: some have finer grained tenses than others, as typological studies have shown. When facing the unbalanced levels of temporal reference distinction between a pair of languages, we have to optimize the mapping between the two temporal systems through intelligent learning. Most machine translation systems do not have a separate temporal reference resolution module, but if we can integrate a special module into them, the temporal reference resolution of the system could be corrected accordingly and yield a better translation. Other than machine translation, in cross-lingual question answering (CLQA) with English as the target language, the ability to successfully formulate queries and maintain the temporal reference information in the original questions is desirable.

R. Dale et al. (Eds.): IJCNLP 2005, LNAI 3651, pp. 885 – 895, 2005.

2 Related Work

2.1 Temporal Reference Modeling in Cross-Lingual Scenario

The nature of being past, present or future is highly relative and hence the information contained in tenses is often referred to as temporal reference distinction. While there is a large body of research on temporal reference in formal semantics and logic as well as in other disciplines of Linguistics, works in cross-lingual temporal reference mapping remain inadequate.

Campbell et. al. [1] proposed a language-neutral framework for representing semantic tense. This framework is called the Language Neutral Syntax (LNS). Based on the observation that grammatical or morphological tenses in different languages do not necessarily mean the same thing, they interpret semantic tense to be largely a representation of event sequence; their work did not attempt direct and explicit representations of tenses. The tense node in the LNS tree contains either global tense feature (also known as "absolute tense") or anchorable tense feature (also known as "relative tense"). This work treated compound tenses as being represented by primary and secondary tense features. The tense in an embedded clause is anchored to the tense in the matrix clause. Campbell's work attempted neither a strict nor a deep semantic representation of tenses, but rather a syntactic representation that is language-neutral. In addition, similar to most of its peer works in tense modeling, it only attacked the problem in a scope of individual sentences.

Pustejovsky et. al. [2] reported an annotation scheme, the TimeML metadata for markup of events and their anchoring in documents. The challenge of human labeling of links among eventualities were discussed to the full fledge in their paper showing that inter-annotator consistency for links is a hard-to-reach ideal. The automatic "time-stamping" was attempted earlier on a small sample of text in an earlier work of Mani [3]. The result was not particularly promising showing need for bigger size of training data as well as more predictive features, especially on the discourse level. At the word level, semantic representation of tenses could be approached in various ways depending on different applications. None of the previous works were designed particularly for cross-lingual temporal reference distinction mapping and the challenges of this mapping for some language pairs have not received full attention.

2.2 Temporal Reference Mapping Between Chinese and English

Since temporal reference distinction mapping is of particular interest of cross-lingual natural language processing tasks, the pilot works for tense classification in Chinese were naturally motivated by machine translation scenario. Olsen et. al. [4] attacked tense reconstructing for Chinese text in the scenario of Chinese to English MT. On top of the more overt features, their work made use of the telicity information encoded in the lexicons through the use of Lexical Conceptual Structures (LCS). Based on the dichotomy of grammatical aspect and lexical aspect, they proposed that past tense corresponds to the telic LCS which is either inherently telic or derived telic. While grammatical aspect markings supersede the LCS, in the absence of grammatical aspect marking, verbs that have telic LCS are translated into past tense and present tense otherwise. This work, while pushing tense reconstruction one step further towards the semantics embedded in the events, is subject to the risk of adopting one-to-one mapping between grammatical aspect markings and tenses hence oversimplifies the temporal reference situation in Chinese text. Additionally, their binary tense taxonomy is oversimplifying the rich temporal reference system that exists in Chinese.

Li et. al. [5] proposed a computational model based on machine learning and heterogeneous collaborative bootstrapping for analyzing temporal relations in a Chinese multiple-clause sentence. The core model is a set of rules that map the combinational effects of a set of linguistic features to one class of temporal relations for one event pair. Their work showed promising results for combining machine learning algorithms and linguistic features to achieve temporal relation resolution, but did not directly address cross-lingual temporal reference information mapping. The nature of the task they were attacking is B Series temporal resolution in Mctaggart's terminology.

3 Problem Definition

3.1 The Taxonomy of Tenses

In the current literature, the taxonomy of tenses typically includes the three basic tenses (present, past and future) plus their combination with the progressive and perfect grammatical aspects, because in English tense and aspect are morphologically merged. This yields a taxonomy of 13 tenses. We collapse these 13 tenses into a taxonomy of three classes: present, past and future. The reason for this collapse is twofold: linguistically, this three-class taxonomy conforms more strictly with the well defined tripartite temporal reference distinction [6]; and in practice, only nine tenses occurred in our data set: simple past, simple future, simple present, present perfect,

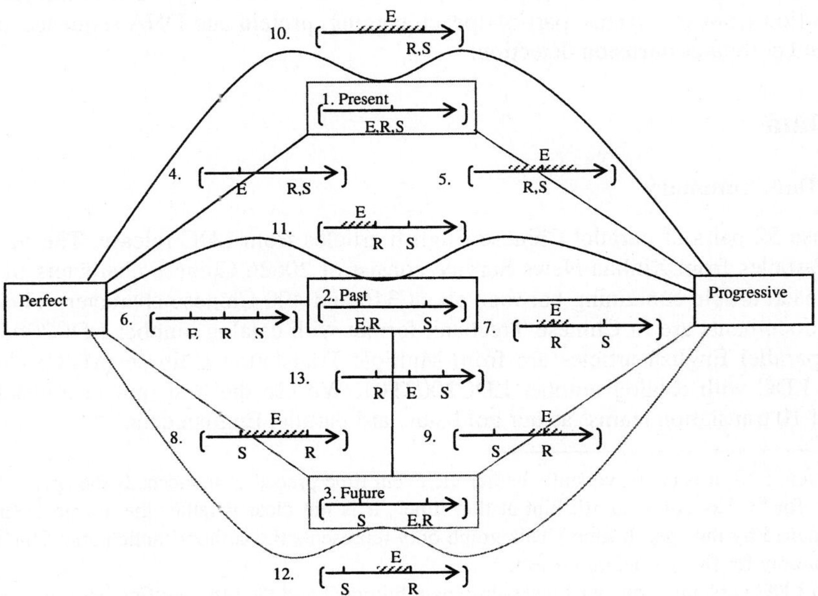

Fig. 1. Tense Taxonomy

present progressive, past perfect, past progressive, past future and present perfect progressive. Some tenses are very sparse in the data set yielding little value from the learning perspective. Figure 1[1] shows the tense taxonomy. In the graph, for each of the thirteen tenses, we provide the timeline representation for the configuration of the three time points under Reichenbachian system. E stands for the event time, R stands for the reference time and S stands for the speech time. It is observed that in terms of the relationship between the speech time and the event time, the thirteen tenses could be grouped into three categories: tense 1 and tense 5 have the event time overlapping with the speech time; tense 2, 4, 6, 7, 10, 11 and 13 have the event time being prior to the speech time; tense 3, 8, 9 and 12 have the event time being later than the speech time. These three categories form our collapsed tense taxonomy.

3.2 Problem Formulation

In general, the tense tagging problem for verbs can be formalized as a standard classification or labeling problem, in which we try to learn a classifier

$$C: V \rightarrow T$$

where V is the set of verbs (each described by a feature vector), and T is the set of possible tense tags (defined by the taxonomy above).

This is, however, a somewhat simplistic view of the picture. Just as temporal events are usually sequentially correlated, verbs in adjacent linguistic utterances are not independent. Therefore the problem should be further formalized as a sequential learning problem, where we try tag a sequence of verbs ($V_1, \ldots, V_n$) with a sequence of tense tags ($t_1, \ldots, t_n$). This formalization shares similarities with many other problems inside and outside the computational linguistics community, such as information extraction from web pages, part-of-speech tagging, protein and DNA sequence analysis, and computer intrusion detection.

4 Data

4.1 Data Summary

We use 52 pairs of parallel Chinese-English articles from LDC release. The 52 Chinese articles from Xinhua News Service consist of 20626 Chinese characters in total with each article containing between about 340 and 400 Chinese characters The Chinese documents are in Chinese Treebank format with catalog number LDC2001T11. The parallel English articles are from Multiple-Translation Chinese (MTC) Corpus from LDC with catalog number LDC2002T01. We use the best human translations out of 10 translation teams[2] as our gold-standard parallel English data.

[1] For tense 13, it is controversial whether the event time precedes or succeeds the speech time. (e.g. for "I was going to ask him at that time", it is not clear whether the asking event has happened by the speech time.) This graph only represents the authors' hunch about the tense taxonomy for this particular project.

[2] Two LDC personnel, one a Chinese-dominant bilingual and the other an English-dominant bilingual, performed this ranking. There was overall agreement on the ranking between the two and minor discrepancies were resolved through discussion and comparison of additional files.

4.2 Obtaining Tense Tags from the Data

The decision of the granularity level of the data points in the current project is a non-trivial issue. Recently it has been argued that tense should be regarded as a category of the whole sentence, or in logical terms of the whole proposition, since it relates to the truth value of the proposition as a whole, rather than just some property of the verb. While we agree with this assertion, in the interest of focusing on our immediate goal of assigning an appropriate tense tag to the parallel verb in the target language, we adopt the more traditional analysis of tense as a category of the verb on the basis of its morphological attachment to the verb.

There are a total of 1542 verbs in the 52 Chinese source articles. We manually aligned these verbs in the Chinese source article with their corresponding verbs in English; this yields a subset of 712 verbs out of the 1542 verbs being translated into English as verbs. We see a dramatic nominalization (i.e. verbal expressions in Chinese are translated into nominal phrases in English) process in Chinese-to-English translation through the dramatic contrast between these two numbers. We excluded the verbs that are not translated as verbs into the parallel English text. This exclusion is based on the rationale that another choice of syntactic structure might retain the verbal status in the target English sentence, but the tense of those potential English verbs would be left to the joint decision of a set of disparate features. Those tenses are unknown in our training data.

5 Tense Tagging by Learning

5.1 Temporal Reference Distinction in Chinese Text

Assigning accurate tense tags to the English verbs in Chinese-to-English Machine Translation is equivalent to understanding temporal reference distinction in the source Chinese text. Since there are no morphologically realized tenses in Chinese, the temporal reference distinction in Chinese is encoded in disparate linguistic features. Figure 2 shows how various features in simple Chinese sentences jointly represent the temporal reference distinction information. For complex sentences with an embedding structure, these features will behave in a more complicated way in that the anaphoric relations

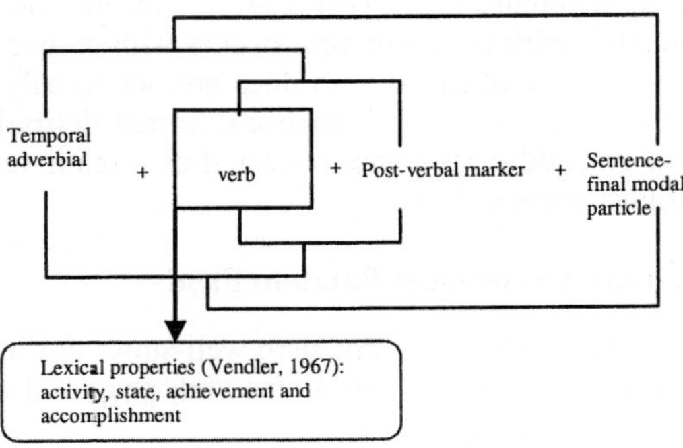

Fig. 2. Temporal Structure for a Simple Chinese Sentence

between the reference time and speech time hold differently for main verbs and verbs in embedded structure. While world knowledge is beyond the scope of our computational capacity at this stage, we expect that the various linguistic features will be able to approximately reconstruct the temporal reference distinction for Chinese verbs.

5.2 The Feature Space

There are a big variety of heterogeneous features that contribute to the temporal reference semantics of Chinese verbs. Tenses in English, while manifesting temporal reference distinction, do not always reflect the distinction at the semantic level, as is shown in the sentence "I will leave when he comes." Hornstein [7] accounted for this type of phenomenon by proposing the Constraints on Derived Tense Structures. Hence the feature space we propose to use consists of the features that contribute to the semantic level temporal reference construction as well as those contributing to the tense generation from that semantic level.

The feature space includes the following 11 features:

feature1: whether the current sentence contains a temporal noun phrase, a temporal location phrase or a temporal prepositional phrase;
feature2: whether or not the current verb is in quoted speech;
feature3: whether the current verb appears in relative clause or sentential complement;
feature4: whether or not the current verb is in news headlines;
feature5: previous word's POS;
feature6: current verb's POS, there are three types of verbs in the corpora: the regular verbs (VV); the copula "shi4"[3] (VC) and the verb "you3" (VE);
feature7: next word's POS;
feature8: whether or not the verb is followed by the aspect marker "le";
feature9: whether or not the verb is followed by the aspect marker "zhe";
feature10: whether or not the verb is followed by the aspect marker "guo";
feature11: whether or not the verb is a main verb;

The above 11 features include lexical features as well as syntactic features. None of the above features is expensive to obtain. We aim to show that the temporal reference distinction classe, as a semantic feature of the verb, could be predicted by learning from inexpensive linguistic features that are easily available. Feature 11 is motivated by the observation that tense in English is used to inform the reader (listener) of when the event associating with the main verb occurs with respect to the time of utterance while the tense of an embedded verb does not necessarily indicate this relationship directly. In the current paper, we have a different definition for main verb: any verb that is not in embedded structure is treated as a main verb including those verbs appearing in adjunct clauses.

5.3 Learning Algorithm: Conditional Random Field

Conditional Random Fields (CRF) is a formalism well-suited for learning and prediction on sequential data. It is a probabilistic framework proposed by Lafferty [8] for

---

[3] The digit at the end of the syllable here indicates the tone. "Shi4" means "be" and "you3" means "have".

labeling and segmenting structured data, such as sequences, trees and lattices. The conditional nature of CRFs relaxes the independence assumptions required by traditional Hidden Markov Models (HMMs); CRFs also avoid the label bias problem exhibited by maximum entropy Markov models (MEMMs) and other conditional Markov models based on directed graphical models. CRFs have been shown to perform well on a number of real-world problems, in particular, NLP problems such as shallow parsing [9], table extraction [10], and named entity recognition [11].

For our experiments, we use the off-the-shelf implementation of CRFs provided by MALLET [12].

6 Experiments and Evaluation

6.1 Preliminary Experiment with Tense Annotation by Human Judges

In order to evaluate the empirical challenge of tense generation in a Chinese-to-English Machine Translation system, a pilot experiment of tense annotation for Chinese text by native judges was carried. The annotation experiment was carried out on 20 news articles from LDC Xinhua News release with category number LDC2001T11. The articles were divided into 4 groups with 5 articles in each group. For each group, three native Chinese speakers annotated the tense of the verbs in the articles. Prior to annotating the data, the judges underwent brief training during which they were asked to read an example of a Chinese sentence for each tense and make sure they understand the examples. During the annotation, the judges were asked to read whole articles first and then select a tense tag based on the context of each verb. In cases where the judges were unable to decide the tense of a verb, they were instructed to tag it as "unknown".

Kappa scores were calculated for the three human judges' annotation results. Kappa score is the de facto standard for evaluating inter-judge agreement on tagging tasks. It is defined by the following formula (1), where P(A) is the observed agreement among the judges and P(E) is the expected agreement:

$$k = \frac{P(A) - P(E)}{1 - P(E)} \tag{1}$$

The annotation was originally carried out on the taxonomy of 13 tenses. We collapsed these 13 tenses into three tenses as discussed in section 3.1. Table 1 summarizes the kappa statistics for the human annotation results after we collapse the tenses:

Table 1. Kappa Scores for Human Tense Annotation for Xinhua News on Collapsed Tense Classes

	Xinhua news 1	Xinhua news 2	Xinhua news 3	Xinhua news 4
Kappa score for 3 judges	0.409	0.440	0.317	0.325

There are different interpretations as to what is a good level of agreement and what kappa scores are considered low. But generally, a kappa score of lower than 0.40 falls into the lower range of agreement[4]. Even if we consider the meta-linguistic nature of the task, the kappa scores we observe belong to the poor-fair range of agreement, illustrating the challenge of temporal reference mapping across Chinese and English. The difficulty of tense classification demonstrated by these experiments with human judges provides an upper bound on the performance of automatic machine classification. As challenging a task as it is, tense generation for English verbs in a Chinese-to-English Machine Translation system must address this cross-lingual mapping problem in order to obtain an accurate translation result.

6.2 Experimental Setup and Evaluation Metrics

It is conceivable that the granularity of sequences may matter in learning from data with sequential relationship, and in the context of verb tense tagging, it naturally maps to the granularity of discourse. Based on this conjecture, we experiment with two different sequential granularities:

— Sentence-level sequence: each sentence is treated as a sequence;
— Paragraph-level sequence: each sentence is treated as a sequence, and there is no boundary between sentences within the paragraph.

All results are obtained by 5-fold cross validation. The classifier's performance is evaluated against the tenses from the best-ranked human translation parallel English text.

To evaluate the performance of classifiers, we measure the standard classification accuracy where accuracy is defined as in equation (2):

$$accuracy = \frac{number \quad of \quad correct \quad predictions}{total \quad number \quad of \quad predictions} \tag{2}$$

To measure how well the classifier does on each class respectively, we compute precision, recall, and F-measure, which are defined respectively in equation (3), (4) and (5):

$$\Pr ecision = \frac{number \quad of \quad correct \quad hits}{total \quad number \quad of \quad hits} \tag{3}$$

$$\mathrm{Re}\, call = \frac{number \quad of \quad correct \quad hits}{size \quad of \quad perfect \quad hitlist} \tag{4}$$

$$F - measure = \frac{2 \times \Pr ecision \times \mathrm{Re}\, call}{\Pr ecision + \mathrm{Re}\, call} \tag{5}$$

[4] http://www.childrens-mercy.org/stats/definitions/kappa.htm

6.3 Experimental Results

The evaluation is carried on the collapsed tense taxonomy that consists of three tense classes: present, past and future. This collapse is motivated by two reasons: linguistically, this collapse reflects the accommodation of the "gray area" that exists in the 13-way tense taxonomy; practically, the collapse helps to alleviate the sparse data problem. Ideally, with a large enough data set that could cover the less-common tenses, the full-fledged tense taxonomy is desirable given that the "gray area" could be analyzed and included into the evaluation. The CRF-based tense classifier yielded the performance in Table 2 and Table 3:

Table 2. Sentence-level sequence: overall accuracy 58.21%

	Precision	Recall	F-measure
Present	42.50%	27.48%	32.07%
Past	67.57%	79.55%	72.10%
Future	29.66%	25.56%	21.56%

Table 3. Paragraph-level sequence: overall accuracy 58.05%

	Precision	Recall	F-measure
Present	38.79%	32.44%	33.96%
Past	69.12%	75.72%	71.59%
Future	33.16%	30.25%	26.59%

An accuracy of around 60% seems not satisfactory if viewed in isolation, but when contrasted with the kappa score of human tense annotating discussed above, the current evaluation indicates promising results for our algorithm. Even though the human judges underwent only minimal training, their poor-to-fair kappa scores indicate that this is a very hard problem. Therefore while there is certainly room for improvement, the tagging performance of our algorithm is quite promising.

It is noticed that the granularity of sequences does not seem to yield significantly different performance based on the current data. However, whether this is true in general remains an open question.

7 Discussions

There are four important dimensions for any natural language processing tasks:

— The data: ideally, the data used should be as representative as possible of a wide range of genres unless the target application is focused on a certain narrow domain;
— The feature space: ideally, the features should be easily available and have wide coverage over the predicting space of the target problem; the more so-

phisticated and the more expensive the features are, the less we could claim to gain from the learning algorithms.

— The learning algorithm: nowadays, various machine-learning algorithms have been proposed and applied in different natural language task domains. A learning algorithm should be chosen to appropriately explore the feature space.
— The evaluation: ideally, evaluation from multiple perspectives is desired to resolve disagreements.

Reflecting upon these dimensions for the current paper, from the data perspective, we focused on news report genre where the temporal thread progression is relatively simpler than many other genres. When facing temporal reference classification for more complicated genres, larger amounts of training data would be necessary for learning a more sophisticated classifier. Fortunately, the amount of accessible parallel data is growing and it is always possible to obtain the tense tags for the Chinese verbs automatically using an off-the-shelf aligning tool although this might introduce a certain amount of noise.

As for the choice of the predicting features, the current project does not utilize any lexical semantic features owing to the limited lexical semantic knowledge resources for Chinese. We expect such knowledge resources, if available, would enhance the feature vector and boost the classification performance. Additionally, it is observed that for a Chinese-to-English MT system, tense generation in English is significantly subject to the syntactic constraints. Hence when integrating into a MT system, the current learning algorithm might have opportunity to employ additional features from other parts of the system, for example, syntactic features for English could be added to the current feature space.

Regarding the choice of learning algorithm, we chose CRFs, a learning algorithm for sequential data, based on the fact that tenses for verbs in a certain discourse unit are not independent of each other.

From the evaluation point of view, the current work evaluates the classifier against the tenses from a certain human translation team. The frequent disagreements among the human annotators illustrate the difficulty of constructing a gold standard against which to evaluate the performance of our classifier. Lastly, measuring BLEU score change brought about by integrating the current classifier into a statistical MT system would be desirable, such that we can better understand the practical implications of this study for MT systems.

8 Conclusions and Future Work

The current work has shown how a moderate set of shallow and inexpensive linguistic features can be combined with a standard machine learning algorithm for learning a tense classifier trained on a moderate number of data points, with promising results. A tense resolution module built upon the current framework could enhance a MT system with its temporal reference distinction resolution.

Several issues to be explored in future work are the following: First, our current training corpus of Xinhua News articles is rather homogeneous, hence the classifier trained exclusively on this data set may not be robust when carried over to data from different source. This will become particularly important if we want to integrate the current work into a general-domain MT system. Secondly, related to the homogeneity of our training data, we only explored a limited number of features, while the feature space could be expanded to include a richer and wider scope. For example, discourse structure features have not been explored. Finally, we are very interested in evaluating our work against existing MT systems with regard to temporal mapping.

References

1. Campbell, R., Aikawa, T., Jiang, Z., Lozano, C., Melero, M and Wu, A.: A Language-Neutral Representation of Temporal Information. In Proceedings of the Workshop on Annotation Standards for Tempora Information in Natural Language, LREC 2002, Las Palmas de Gran Canaria, Spain (2002) 13-21.
2. Pustejovsky, J., Ingria, B., Sauri, R., Castano, J., Littman, J., Gaizauskas, R., Setzer, A., Katz, G. and Mani, I.: The Specification Language TimeML. In Mani, I., Pustejovsky, J., and Gaizauskas, R (eds.). (2004) The Language of Time: A Reader. Oxford University Press, to appear
3. Mani, I.: "Recent Developments in Temporal Information Extraction (Draft)", In Nicolov, N., and Mitkov, R. Proceedings of RANLP'03, John Benjamins, to appear.
4. Olson, M., Traum, D., Van-ess Dykema, C. and Weinberg, A.: Implicit Cues for Explicit Generation: Using Telicity as a Cue for Tense Structure in a Chinese to English MT System, in proceedings Machine Translation Summit VIII, Santiago de Compostela (Spain) (2001)
5. Li, W., Wong, K. F., Hong, C. and Yuan, C.: Applying Machine Learning to Chinese Temporal Relation Resolution, Proceedings of the 42nd Annual Meeting of the Association for Computational Linguistics (2004) 582-588
6. Reichenbach, H.: Elements of Symbolic Logic, The Macmillan Company (1947)
7. Dorr, B. J. and Gaasterland, T.: "Constraints on the Generation of Tense, Aspect, and Connecting Words from Temporal Expressions," Technical Report CS-TR-4391, UMIACS-TR-2002-71, LAMP-TR-091, University of Maryland, College Park, MD (2002)
8. Lafferty, J., McCallum, A. and Pereira, F.: Conditional random fields: Probabilistic models for segmenting and labeling sequence data. In Proceedings of ICML-01, (2001) 282-289
9. Sha, F. and Pereira, F.: Shallow Parsing with Conditional Random Fields, In Proceedings of the 2003 Human Language Technology Conference and North American Chapter of the Association for Computational Linguistics (HLT/NAACL-03) (2003)
10. Pinto, D., McCallum, A., Lee, X. and Croft, W. B.: Table Extraction Using Conditional Random Fields. In Proceedings of the 26th Annual International ACM SIGIR Conference on Research and Development in Information Retrieval (SIGIR 2003) (2003)
11. McCallum, A. and Li, W.: Early Results for Named Entity Recognition with Conditional Random Fields, Feature Induction and Web-Enhanced Lexicons. In Proceedings of the Seventh Conference on Natural Language Learning (CoNLL) (2003)
12. McCallum, A. K.: MALLET: A Machine Learning for Language Toolkit http://mallet.cs.umass.edu. (2002)

Regularisation Techniques for Conditional Random Fields: Parameterised Versus Parameter-Free

Andrew Smith and Miles Osborne

School of Informatics, University of Edinburgh, United Kingdom
a.p.smith-2@sms.ed.ac.uk, miles@inf.ed.ac.uk

Abstract. Recent work on Conditional Random Fields (CRFs) has demonstrated the need for regularisation when applying these models to real-world NLP data sets. Conventional approaches to regularising CRFs has focused on using a Gaussian prior over the model parameters. In this paper we explore other possibilities for CRF regularisation. We examine alternative choices of prior distribution and we relax the usual simplifying assumptions made with the use of a prior, such as constant hyperparameter values across features. In addition, we contrast the effectiveness of priors with an alternative, parameter-free approach. Specifically, we employ **logarithmic opinion pools** (LOPs). Our results show that a LOP of CRFs can outperform a standard unregularised CRF and attain a performance level close to that of a regularised CRF, without the need for intensive hyperparameter search.

1 Introduction

Recent work on Conditional Random Fields (CRFs) has demonstrated the need for regularisation when applying these models to real-world NLP data sets ([8], [9]). Standard approaches to regularising CRFs, and log-linear models in general, has focused on the use of a Gaussian prior. Typically, for simplicity, this prior is assumed to have zero mean and constant variance across model parameters. To date, there has been little work exploring other possibilities. One exception is Peng & McCallum [8]. They investigated feature-dependent variance for a Gaussian prior, and explored different families of feature sets. They also compared different priors for CRFs on an information extraction task.

In the first part of this paper, we compare priors for CRFs on standard sequence labelling tasks in NLP: NER and POS tagging. Peng & McCallum used variable hyperparameter values only for a Gaussian prior, based on feature counts in the training data. We use an alternative Bayesian approach to measure confidence in empirical expected feature counts, and apply this to all the priors we test. We also look at varying the Gaussian prior mean. Our results show that: (1) considerable search is required to identify good hyperparameter values for all priors (2) for optimal hyperparameter values, the priors we tested perform roughly equally well (3) in some cases performance can be improved using feature-dependent hyperparameter values.

R. Dale et al. (Eds.): IJCNLP 2005, LNAI 3651, pp. 896–907, 2005.

As can be seen, a significant short-coming of using priors for CRF regularisation is the requirement for intensive search of hyperparameter space. In the second part of the paper we contrast this parameterised prior approach with an alternative, parameter-free method. We factor the CRF distribution into a weighted product of individual **expert** CRF distributions, each focusing on a particular subset of the distribution. We call this model a **logarithmic opinion pool** (LOP) of CRFs (LOP-CRFs).

Our results show that LOP-CRFs, which are unregularised, can outperform the unregularised standard CRF and attain a performance level that rivals that of the standard CRF regularised with a prior. This performance may be achieved with a considerably lower time for training by avoiding the need for intensive hyperparameter search.

2 Conditional Random Fields

A linear chain CRF defines the conditional probability of a label sequence $\mathbf{s}$ given an observed sequence $\mathbf{o}$ via:

$$p(\mathbf{s} \mid \mathbf{o}) = \frac{1}{Z(\mathbf{o})} \exp\left(\sum_{t=1}^{T+1} \sum_{k} \lambda_k f_k(s_{t-1}, s_t, \mathbf{o}, t)\right) \tag{1}$$

where T is the length of both sequences, λ_k are parameters of the model and $Z(\mathbf{o})$ is the partition function that ensures (1) represents a probability distribution. The functions f_k are feature functions representing the occurrence of different events in the sequences $\mathbf{s}$ and $\mathbf{o}$.

The parameters λ_k can be estimated by maximising the conditional log-likelihood of a set of labelled training sequences. The log-likelihood is given by:

$$LL(\lambda) = \sum_{\mathbf{o}} \tilde{p}(\mathbf{o}) \sum_{\mathbf{s}} \tilde{p}(\mathbf{s}|\mathbf{o}) \left[\sum_{t=1}^{T+1} \lambda \cdot \mathbf{f}(\mathbf{s}, \mathbf{o}, t)\right] - \sum_{\mathbf{o}} \tilde{p}(\mathbf{o}) \log Z(\mathbf{o}; \lambda)$$

where $\tilde{p}(\mathbf{s}|\mathbf{O})$ and $\tilde{p}(\mathbf{o})$ are empirical distributions defined by the training set. At the maximum likelihood solution the model satisfies a set of feature constraints, whereby the expected count of each feature under the model is equal to its empirical count on the training data:

$$E_{\tilde{p}(\mathbf{o},\mathbf{s})}[f_k] - E_{p(\mathbf{s}|\mathbf{o})}[f_k] = 0, \ \forall k$$

In general this cannot be solved for the λ_k in closed form so numerical routines must be used. Malouf [6] and Sha & Pereira [9] show that gradient-based algorithms, particularly limited memory variable metric (LMVM), require much less time to reach convergence, for some NLP tasks, than the iterative scaling methods previously used for log-linear optimisation problems. In all our experiments we use the LMVM method to train the CRFs.

For CRFs with general graphical structure, calculation of $E_{p(\mathbf{s}|\mathbf{o})}[f_k]$ is intractable, but for the linear chain case Lafferty et al. [5] describe an efficient dynamic programming procedure for inference, similar in nature to the forward-backward algorithm in hidden Markov models.

Given a trained CRF model defined as in (1), the most probable labelling under the model for a new observed sequence **o** is given by $\text{argmax}_{\mathbf{s}} p(\mathbf{s}|\mathbf{o})$. This can be recovered efficiently using the Viterbi algorithm.

3 Parameterised Regularisation: Priors for CRFs

Most approaches to CRF regularisation have focused on the use of a prior distribution over the model parameters. A prior distribution encodes prior knowledge about the nature of different models. However, prior knowledge can be difficult to encode reliably and the optimal choice of prior family may vary from task to task. In this paper we investigate the use of three prior families for the CRF.

3.1 Gaussian Prior

The most common prior used for CRF regularisation has been the Gaussian. Use of the Gaussian prior assumes that each model parameter is drawn independently from a Gaussian distribution. Ignoring terms that do not affect the parameters, the regularised log-likelihood with a Gaussian prior becomes:

$$LL(\lambda) - \frac{1}{2} \sum_k \left(\frac{\lambda_k - \mu_k}{\sigma_k} \right)^2$$

where μ_k is the mean and σ_k the variance for parameter λ_k. At the optimal point, for each λ_k, the model satisfies:

$$E_{\tilde{p}(\mathbf{o},\mathbf{s})}[f_k] - E_{p(\mathbf{s}|\mathbf{o})}[f_k] = \frac{\lambda_k - \mu_k}{\sigma_k^2} \quad (2)$$

Usually, for simplicity, each μ_k is assumed zero and σ_k is held constant across the parameters. In this paper we investigate other possibilities. In particular, we allow the means to take on non-zero values, and the variances to be feature-dependent. This is described in more detail later. In each case values for means and variances may be optimised on a development set.

We can see from (2) that use of a Gaussian prior enforces the constraint that the expected count of a feature under the model is discounted with respect to the count of that feature on the training data. As discussed in [1], this corresponds to a form of logarithmic discounting in feature count space and is similar in nature to discounting schemes employed in language modelling.

3.2 Laplacian Prior

Use of the Laplacian prior assumes that each model parameter is drawn independently from the Laplacian distribution. Ignoring terms that do not affect the parameters, the regularised log-likelihood with a Laplacian prior becomes:

$$LL(\lambda) - \sum_k \frac{|\lambda_k|}{\beta_k}$$

where β_k is a hyperparameter, and at the optimal point the model satisfies:

$$E_{\tilde{p}(\mathbf{o},\mathbf{s})}[f_k] - E_{p(\mathbf{s}|\mathbf{o})}[f_k] = \frac{\text{sign}(\lambda_k)}{\beta_k},\ \lambda_k \neq 0 \tag{3}$$

Peng & McCallum [8] note that the exponential prior (a one-sided version of the Laplacian prior here) represents applying an absolute discount to the empirical feature count. They fix the β_k across features and set it using an expression for the discount used in absolute discounting for language modelling. By contrast we allow the β_k to vary with feature and optimise values using a development set.

The derivative of the penalty term above with respect to a parameter λ_k is discontinuous at $\lambda_k = 0$. To tackle this problem we use an approach described by Williams, who shows how the discontinuity may be handled algorithmically [13]. His method leads to sparse solutions, where, at convergence, a substantial proportion of the model parameters are zero. The result of this pruning effect is different, however, to feature induction, where features are included in the model based on their effect on log-likelihood.

3.3 Hyperbolic Prior

Use of the hyperbolic prior assumes that each model parameter is drawn independently from the hyperbolic distribution. Ignoring constant terms that do not involve the parameters, the regularised log-likelihood becomes:

$$LL(\lambda) - \sum_k \log\left(\frac{e^{\beta_k\lambda_k} + e^{-\beta_k\lambda_k}}{2}\right)$$

where β_k is a hyperparameter, and at the optimal point the model satisfies:

$$E_{\tilde{p}(\mathbf{o},\mathbf{s})}[f_k] - E_{p(\mathbf{s}|\mathbf{o})}[f_k] = \beta_k\left(\frac{e^{\beta_k\lambda_k} - e^{-\beta_k\lambda_k}}{e^{\beta_k\lambda_k} + e^{-\beta_k\lambda_k}}\right) \tag{4}$$

3.4 Feature-Dependent Regularisation

For simplicity it is usual when using a prior to assume constant hyperparameter values across all features. However, as a hyperparameter value determines the amount of regularisation applied to a feature, we may not want to assume equal values. We may have seen some features more frequently than others and so be more confident that their empirical expected counts are closer to the true expected counts in the underlying distribution.

Peng & McCallum [8] explore feature-dependent variance for the Gaussian prior. They use different schemes to determine the variance for a feature based on its observed count in the training data. In this paper we take an alternative, Bayesian approach motivated more directly by our confidence in the reliability of a feature's empirical expected count.

In equations (2), (3) and (4) the level of regularisation applied to a feature takes the form of a discount to the expected count of the feature on the training data. It is natural, therefore, that the size of this discount, controlled through a hyperparameter, is related to our confidence in the reliability of the empirical expected count. We formulate a measure of this confidence. We follow the approach of Kazama & Tsujii [4], extending it to CRFs.

The empirical expected count, $E_{\tilde{p}(\mathbf{o},\mathbf{s})}[f_k]$, of a feature f_k is given by:

$$\begin{aligned}\sum_{\mathbf{o},\mathbf{s}} \tilde{p}(\mathbf{o},\mathbf{s}) \sum_t f_k(s_{t-1}, s_t, \mathbf{o}, t) &= \sum_{\mathbf{o}} \tilde{p}(\mathbf{o}) \sum_{\mathbf{s}} \tilde{p}(\mathbf{s}|\mathbf{o}) \sum_t f_k(s_{t-1}, s_t, \mathbf{o}, t) \\ &= \sum_{\mathbf{o}} \tilde{p}(\mathbf{o}) \sum_{t,s',s''} \tilde{p}(s_{t-1}{=}\, s', s_t{=}\, s''|\mathbf{o}) f_k(s', s'', \mathbf{o}, t)\end{aligned}$$

Now, our CRF features have the following form:

$$f_k(s_{t-1}, s_t, \mathbf{o}, t) = \begin{cases} 1 \text{ if } s_{t-1} = s_1,\ s_t = s_2 \text{ and } h_k(\mathbf{o}, t) = 1 \\ 0 \text{ otherwise} \end{cases}$$

where s_1 and s_2 are the labels associated with feature f_k and $h_k(\mathbf{o}, t)$ is a binary-valued predicate defined on observation sequence $\mathbf{o}$ at position t. With this feature definition, and contracting notation for the empirical probability to save space, $E_{\tilde{p}(\mathbf{o},\mathbf{s})}[f_k]$ becomes:

$$\begin{aligned}\sum_{\mathbf{o}} \tilde{p}(\mathbf{o}) \sum_{t,s',s''} \tilde{p}(s', s''|\mathbf{o}) \delta(s', s_1) \delta(s'', s_2) h_k(\mathbf{o}, t) &= \sum_{\mathbf{o}} \tilde{p}(\mathbf{o}) \sum_t \tilde{p}(s_1, s_2|\mathbf{o}) h_k(\mathbf{o}, t) \\ &= \sum_{\mathbf{o}} \tilde{p}(\mathbf{o}) \sum_{t:h_k(\mathbf{o},t)=1} \tilde{p}(s_1, s_2|\mathbf{o})\end{aligned}$$

Contributions to the inner sum are only made at positions t in sequence $\mathbf{o}$ where the $h_k(\mathbf{o}, t) = 1$. Suppose that we make the assumption that at these positions $\tilde{p}(s', s''|\mathbf{o}) \approx \tilde{p}(s', s''|h_k(\mathbf{o}, t) = 1)$. Then:

$$E_{\tilde{p}(\mathbf{o},\mathbf{s})}[f_k] = \sum_{\mathbf{o}} \tilde{p}(\mathbf{o}) \sum_{t:h_k(\mathbf{o},t)=1} \tilde{p}(s_1, s_2|h_k(\mathbf{o}, t) = 1)$$

Now, if we assume that we can get a reasonable estimate of $\tilde{p}(\mathbf{o})$ from the training data then the only source of uncertainty in the expression for $E_{\tilde{p}(\mathbf{o},\mathbf{s})}[f_k]$ is the term $\tilde{p}(s_{t-1} = s_1, s_t = s_2|h_k(\mathbf{o}, t) = 1)$. Assuming this term is independent of sequence $\mathbf{o}$ and position t, we can model it as the parameter θ of a Bernoulli random variable that takes the value 1 when feature f_k is active and 0 when the feature is not active but $h_k(\mathbf{o}, t) = 1$. Suppose there are a and b instances of these two events, respectively. We endow the Bernoulli parameter with a uniform prior Beta distribution Be(1,1) and, having observed the training data, we calculate the variance of the posterior distribution, Be$(1 + a, 1 + b)$. The variance is given by:

$$\mathrm{var}[\theta] = V = \frac{(1+a)(1+b)}{(a+b+2)^2(a+b+3)}$$

The variance of $E_{\tilde{p}(\mathbf{o},\mathbf{s})}[f_k]$ therefore given by:

$$\mathrm{var}\left[E_{\tilde{p}(\mathbf{o},\mathbf{s})}[f_k]\right] = V \left[\sum_{\mathbf{o}} \sum_{t:h_k(\mathbf{o},t)=1} \tilde{p}(\mathbf{o})^2 \right]$$

We use this variance as a measure of the confidence we have in $E_{\tilde{p}(\mathbf{o},\mathbf{s})}[f_k]$ as an estimate of the true expected count of feature f_k. We therefore adjust hyperparameters in the different priors according to this confidence for each feature. Note that this value for each feature can be calculated off-line.

4 Parameter-Free Regularisation: Logarithmic Opinion Pools

So far we have considered CRF regularisation through the use of a prior. As we have seen, most prior distributions are parameterised by a hyperparameter, which may be used to tune the level of regularisation. In this paper we also consider a parameter-free method. Specifically, we explore the use of logarithmic opinion pools [3].

Given a set of CRF model **experts** with conditional distributions $p_\alpha(\mathbf{s}|\mathbf{o})$ and a set of non-negative weights w_α with $\sum_\alpha w_\alpha = 1$, a **logarithmic opinion pool** is defined as the distribution:

$$\bar{p}(\mathbf{s}|\mathbf{o}) = \frac{1}{\bar{Z}(\mathbf{o})} \prod_\alpha [p_\alpha(\mathbf{s}|\mathbf{o})]^{w_\alpha}, \text{ with } \bar{Z}(\mathbf{o}) = \sum_\mathbf{s} \prod_\alpha [p_\alpha(\mathbf{s}|\mathbf{o})]^{w_\alpha}$$

Suppose that there is a "true" conditional distribution $q(\mathbf{s}|\mathbf{o})$ which each $p_\alpha(\mathbf{s}|\mathbf{o})$ is attempting to model. In [3] Heskes shows that the KL divergence between $q(\mathbf{s}|\mathbf{o})$ and the LOP can be decomposed as follows:

$$K(q, \bar{p}) = \sum_\alpha w_\alpha K(q, p_\alpha) - \sum_\alpha w_\alpha K(\bar{p}, p_\alpha) = E - A \tag{5}$$

This explicitly tells us that the closeness of the LOP model to $q(\mathbf{s}|\mathbf{o})$ is governed by a trade-off between two terms: an E term, which represents the closeness of the individual experts to $q(\mathbf{s}|\mathbf{o})$, and an A term, which represents the closeness of the individual experts to the LOP, and therefore indirectly to each other. Hence for the LOP to model q well, we desire models p_α which are individually good models of q (having low E) and are also diverse (having large A).

Training LOPs for CRFs. The weights w_α may be defined a priori or may be found by optimising an objective criterion. In this paper we combine pre-trained expert CRF models under a LOP and train the weights w_α to maximise the likelihood of the training data under the LOP. See [10] for details.

Decoding LOPs for CRFs. Because of the log-linear form of a CRF, a weighted product of expert CRF distributions corresponds to a single CRF distribution with log potentials given by a linear combination (with the same weights) of the corresponding log potentials of the experts. Consequently, it is easy to form the LOP given a set of weights and expert models, and decoding with the LOP is no more complex than decoding with a standard CRF. Hence LOP decoding can be achieved efficiently using the Viterbi algorithm.

5 The Tasks

In this paper we compare parametric and LOP-based regularisation techniques for CRFs on two sequence labelling tasks in NLP: **named entity recognition** (NER) and **part-of-speech tagging** (POS tagging).

5.1 Named Entity Recognition

All our results for NER are reported on the CoNLL-2003 shared task dataset [12]. For this dataset the entity types are: persons (PER), locations (LOC), organisations (ORG) and miscellaneous (MISC). The training set consists of 14,987 sentences and 204,567 tokens, the development set consists of 3,466 sentences and 51,578 tokens and the test set consists of 3,684 sentences and 46,666 tokens.

5.2 Part-of-Speech Tagging

For our experiments we use the CoNLL-2000 shared task dataset [11]. This has 48 different POS tags. In order to make training time manageable, we collapse the number of POS tags from 48 to 5 following the procedure used in [7]. In summary: (1) All types of noun collapse to category **N**. (2) All types of verb collapse to category **V**. (3) All types of adjective collapse to category **J**. (4) All types of adverb collapse to category **R**. (5) All other POS tags collapse to category **O**. The training set consists of 7,300 sentences and 173,542 tokens, the development set consists of 1,636 sentences and 38,185 tokens and the test set consists of 2,012 sentences and 47,377 tokens.

5.3 Experts and Expert Sets

As we have seen, our parameter-free LOP models require us to define and train a number of expert models. For each task we define a single, complex CRF, which we call a **monolithic** CRF, and a range of **expert sets**. The monolithic CRF for NER comprises a number of word and POS features in a window of five words around the current word, along with a set of orthographic features defined on the current word. The monolithic CRF for NER has 450,345 features. The monolithic CRF for POS tagging comprises word and POS features similar to those in the NER monolithic model, but over a smaller number of orthographic features. The monolithic model for POS tagging has 188,488 features.

Each of our expert sets consists of a number of CRF experts. Usually these experts are designed to focus on modelling a particular aspect or subset of the distribution. The experts from a particular expert set are combined under a LOP-CRF with the unregularised monolithic CRF.

We define our expert sets as follows: (1) **Simple** consists of the monolithic CRF and a single expert comprising a reduced subset of the features in the monolithic CRF. This reduced CRF models the entire distribution rather than focusing on a particular aspect or subset, but is much less expressive than the monolithic model. The reduced model comprises 24,818 features for NER and 47,420 features for POS tagging. (2) **Positional** consists of the monolithic CRF and a partition of the features in the monolithic CRF into three experts, each consisting only of features that involve events either behind, at or ahead of the current sequence position. (3) **Label** consists of the monolithic CRF and a partition of the features in the monolithic CRF into five experts, one for each label. For NER an expert corresponding to label X consists only of features that involve labels B-X or I-X at the current or previous positions, while for POS tagging an expert corresponding to label X consists only of features that involve label X at the current or previous positions. These experts therefore focus on trying to model the distribution of a particular label. (4) **Random** consists of the monolithic CRF and a random partition of the features in the monolithic CRF into four experts. This acts as a baseline to ascertain the performance that can be expected from an expert set that is not defined via any linguistic intuition.

6 Experimental Results

For each task our baseline model is the **monolithic** model, as defined earlier. All the smoothing approaches that we investigate are applied to this model. For NER we report F-scores on the development and test sets, while for POS tagging we report accuracies on the development and test sets.

6.1 Priors

Feature-Independent Hyperparameters. Tables 1 and 2 give results on the two tasks for different priors with feature-independent hyperparameters. In the case of the Gaussian prior, the mean was fixed at zero with the variance being the adjustable hyperparameter. In each case hyperparameter values were optimised on the development set. In order to obtain the results shown, extensive search of the hyperparameter space was required. The results show that: (1) For each prior there is a performance improvement over the unregularised model. (2) Each of the priors gives roughly the same optimal performance.

These results are contrary to the conclusions of Peng & McCallum in [8]. On an information extraction task they found that the Gaussian prior performed

Table 1. F-scores for priors on NER

Prior	Development	Test
Unreg. monolithic	88.33	81.87
Gaussian	89.84	83.98
Laplacian	89.56	83.43
Hyperbolic	89.84	83.90

Table 2. Accuracies for priors on POS tagging

Prior	Development	Test
Unreg. monolithic	97.92	97.65
Gaussian	98.02	97.84
Laplacian	98.05	97.78
Hyperbolic	98.00	97.85

significantly better than alternative priors. Indeed they appeared to report performance figures for the hyperbolic and Laplacian priors that were lower than those of the unregularised model. There are several possible reasons for these differences. Firstly, for the hyperbolic prior, Peng & McCallum appeared not to use an adjustable hyperparameter. In that case the discount applied to each empirical expected feature count was dependent only on the current value of the respective model parameter and corresponds in our case to using a fixed value of 1 for the β hyperparameter. Our results for this value of the hyperparameter are similarly poor. The second reason is that for the Laplacian prior, they again used a fixed value for the hyperparameter, calculated via an absolute discounting method used language modelling [1]. Having achieved poor results with this value they experimented with other values but obtained even worse performance. By contrast, we find that, with some search of the hyperparameter space, we can achieve performance close to that of the other two priors.

Feature-Dependent Hyperparameters. Tables 3 and 4 give results for different priors with feature-dependent hyperparameters. Again, for the Gaussian prior the mean was held at 0. We see here that trends differ between the two tasks. For POS tagging we see performance improvements with all the priors over the corresponding feature-independent hyperparameter case. Using McNemar's matched-pairs test [2] on point-wise labelling errors, and testing at a significance level of 5% level, all values in Table 4 represent a significant improvement over the corresponding model with feature-independent hyperparameter values, except the one marked with *. However, for NER the opposite is true. There is a performance degradation over the corresponding feature-independent hyperparameter case. Values marked with † are significantly worse at the 5% level. The hyperbolic prior performs particularly badly, giving no improvement over the unregularised **monolithic**. The reasons for these results are not clear. One possibility is that defining the degree of regularisation on a feature specific basis is too dependent on the sporadic properties of the training data. A better idea may be to use an approach part-way between feature-independent hyperparameters and feature-specific hyperparameters. For example, features could be clustered based on confidence in their empirical expected counts, with a single confidence being associated with each cluster.

Varying the Gaussian Mean. When using a Gaussian prior it is usual to fix the mean at zero because there is usually no prior information to suggest penalising large positive values of model parameters any more or less than large mag-

Table 3. F-scores for priors on NER

Prior	Development	Test
Gaussian	89.43	83.27†
Laplacian	89.28	83.37
Hyperbolic	88.34†	81.63†

Table 4. Accuracies for priors on POS tagging

Prior	Development	Test
Gaussian	98.12	97.88*
Laplacian	98.12	97.92
Hyperbolic	98.15	97.92

nitude negative values. It also simplifies the hyperparameter search, requiring the need to optimise only the variance hyperparameter. However, it is unlikely that optimal performance is always achieved for a mean value of zero.

To investigate this we fix the Gaussian variance at the optimal value found earlier on the development set, with a mean of zero, and allow the mean to vary away from zero. For both tasks we found that we could achieve significant performance improvements for non-zero mean values. On NER a model with mean 0.7 (and variance 40) achieved an F-score of 90.56% on the development set and 84.71% on the test set, a significant improvement over the best model with mean 0. We observe a similar pattern for POS tagging. These results suggest that considerable benefit may be gained from a well structured search of the joint mean and variance hyperparameter space when using a Gaussian prior for regularisation. There is of course a trade-off here, however, between finding better hyperparameters values and suffering increased search complexity.

6.2 LOP-CRFs

Tables 5 and 6 show the performance of LOP-CRFs for the NER and POS tagging experts respectively. The results demonstrate that: (1) In every case the LOPs significantly outperform the unregularised **monolithic**. (2) In most cases the performance of LOPs is comparable to that obtained using the different priors on each task. In fact, values marked with ‡ show a significant improvement over the performance obtained with the Gaussian prior with feature-independent hyperparameter values. Only the value marked with † in Table 6 significantly under performs that model.

Table 5. LOP F-scores on NER

Expert set	Development set	Test set
Unreg. monolithic	88.33	81.87
Simple	90.26	84.22‡
Positional	90.35	84.71‡
Label	89.30	83.27
Random	88.84	83.06

Table 6. LOP accuracies on POS tagging

Expert set	Development set	Test set
Unreg. monolithic	97.92	97.65
Simple	98.31‡	98.12‡
Positional	98.03	97.81
Label	97.99	97.77
Random	97.99	97.76†

We can see that the performance of the LOP-CRFs varies with the choice of expert set. For example, on NER the LOP-CRFs for the **simple** and **positional** expert sets perform better than those for the **label** and **random** sets. Looking back to equation 5, we conjecture that the **simple** and **positional** expert sets achieve good performance in the LOP-CRF because they consist of experts that are diverse while simultaneously being reasonable models of the data. The **label** expert set exhibits greater diversity between the experts, because each expert focuses on modelling a particular label only, but each expert is a relatively poor model of the entire distribution. Similarly, the **random** experts are in general better models of the entire distribution but tend to be less diverse because they do not focus on any one aspect or subset of it. Intuitively, then, we want to devise experts that are simultaneously diverse and accurate.

The advantage of the LOP-CRF approach over the use of a prior is that it is "parameter-free" in the sense that each expert in the LOP-CRF is unregularised. Consequently, we are not required to search a hyperparameter space. For example, to carefully tune the hyperbolic hyperparameter in order to obtain the optimal value we report here, we ran models for 20 different hyperparameter values. In addition, in most cases the expert CRFs comprising the expert sets are small, compact models that train more quickly than the **monolithic** with a prior, and can be trained in parallel.

7 Conclusion

In this paper we compare parameterised and parameter-free approaches to smoothing CRFs on two standard sequence labelling tasks in NLP. For the parameterised methods, we compare different priors. We use both feature-independent and feature-dependent hyperparameters in the prior distributions. In the latter case we derive hyperparameter values using a Bayesian approach to measuring our confidence in empirical expected feature counts. We find that: (1) considerable search is required to identify good hyperparameter values for all priors (2) for optimal hyperparameter values, the priors we tested perform roughly equally well (3) in some cases performance can be improved using feature-dependent hyperparameter values.

We contrast the use of priors to an alternative, parameter-free method using logarithmic opinion pools. Our results show that a LOP of CRFs, which contains unregularised models, can outperform the unregularised standard CRF and attain a performance level that rivals that of the standard CRF regularised with a prior. The important point, however, is that this performance may be achieved with a considerably lower time for training by avoiding the need for intensive hyperparameter search.

References

1. Chen, S. and Rosenfeld, R.: A Survey of Smoothing Techniques for ME Models. IEEE Transactions on Speech and Audio Processing (2000) 8(1) 37–50
2. Gillick, L., Cox, S.: Some statistical issues in the comparison of speech recognition algorithms. ICASSP (1989) 1 532–535
3. Heskes, T.: Selecting weighting factors in logarithmic opinion pools. NIPS (1998)
4. Kazama, J. and Tsujii, J.: Evaluation and Extension of Maximum Entropy Models with Inequality Constraints. EMNLP (2003)
5. Lafferty, J. and McCallum, A. and Pereira, F.: Conditional Random Fields: Probabilistic Models for Segmenting and Labeling Sequence Data. ICML (2001)
6. Malouf, R.: A comparison of algorithms for maximum entropy parameter estimation. CoNLL (2002)
7. McCallum, A., Rohanimanesh, K. Sutton, C.: Dynamic Conditional Random Fields for Jointly Labeling Multiple Sequences. NIPS Workshop on Syntax, Semantics, Statistics (2003)

8. Peng, F. and McCallum, A.: Accurate Information Extraction from Research Papers using Conditional Random Fields. HLT-NAACL (2004)
9. Sha, F. and Pereira, F.: Shallow Parsing with Conditional Random Fields. HLT-NAACL (2003)
10. Smith, A., Cohn, T., Osborne, M.: Logarithmic Opinion Pools for Conditional Random Fields. ACL (2005)
11. Tjong Kim Sang, E. F. and Buchholz, S.: Introduction to the CoNLL-2000 shared task: Chunking. CoNLL (2000)
12. Tjong Kim Sang, E. F. and De Meulder, F.: Introduction to the CoNLL-2003 Shared Task: Language-Independent Named Entity Recognition. CoNLL (2003)
13. Williams, P.: Bayesian Regularisation and Pruning using a Laplace Prior. Neural Computation (1995) 7(1) 117–143

Exploiting Lexical Conceptual Structure for Paraphrase Generation

Atsushi Fujita[1], Kentaro Inui[2], and Yuji Matsumoto[2]

[1] Graduate School of Informatics, Kyoto University
fujita@pine.kuee.kyoto-u.ac.jp
[2] Graduate School of Information Science, Nara Institute of Science and Technology
{inui, matsu}@is.naist.jp

Abstract. Lexical Conceptual Structure (LCS) represents verbs as semantic structures with a limited number of semantic predicates. This paper attempts to exploit how LCS can be used to explain the regularities underlying lexical and syntactic paraphrases, such as verb alternation, compound word decomposition, and lexical derivation. We propose a paraphrase generation model which transforms LCSs of verbs, and then conduct an empirical experiment taking the paraphrasing of Japanese light-verb constructions as an example. Experimental results justify that syntactic and semantic properties of verbs encoded in LCS are useful to semantically constrain the syntactic transformation in paraphrase generation.

1 Introduction

Automatic paraphrasing has recently been attracting increasing attention due to its potential in a broad range of natural language processing tasks. For example, a system that is capable of simplifying a given text, or showing the user several alternative expressions conveying the same content, would be useful for assisting a reader.

There are several classes of paraphrase that exhibit a degree of regularity. For example, paraphrasing associated with verb alternation, lexical derivation, compound word decomposition, and paraphrasing of light-verb constructions (LVC(s)) all fall into such classes. Examples[1] (1) and (2) appear to exhibit the same transformation pattern, in which a compound noun is transformed into a verb phrase. Likewise, paraphrases involving an LVC as in (3) and (4) (from [4]) have considerable similarities.

(1) s. **His machine operation** is very **good**.
t. **He operates the machine** very **well**.

(2) s. My **son's bat control** is **unskillful** yet.
t. My **son controls his bat poorly** yet.

(3) s. Steven **made an attempt** to stop playing.
t. Steven **attempted** to stop playing.

(4) s. It **had a noticeable effect** on the trade.
t. It **noticeably affected** the trade.

[1] For each example, "s" and "t" denote an original sentence and its paraphrase, respectively. Note that our target language is Japanese. English examples are used for an explanatory purpose.

R. Dale et al. (Eds.): IJCNLP 2005, LNAI 3651, pp. 908–919, 2005.

However, the regularity we find in these examples is not so simple that it cannot be captured only in syntactic terms. For example, the transformation pattern as in (1) and (2) does not apply to another compound noun "machine translation." We can also find a range of varieties in paraphrasing of LVCs as we describe in Section 3.

In spite of this complexity, the regularity each paraphrase class exhibits were explained by recent advances in lexical semantics, such as the Lexical Conceptual Structure (LCS) [8] and the Generative Lexicon [17]. According to the LCS, for instance, a wide variety of paraphrases including word association within compounds, transitivity alternation, and lexical derivation, were explained by means of the syntactic and semantic properties of the verb involved. The systematicity underlying such linguistic accounts is intriguing also from the engineering viewpoint as it could enable us to take a more theoretically motivated but still practical approach to paraphrase generation.

The issue we address in this paper is to empirically clarify (i) what types of regularities underlying paraphrases can be explained by means of lexical semantics and how, and (ii) how lexical semantics theories can be enhanced with feedback from practical use, namely, paraphrase generation. We make an attempt to exploit the LCS among several lexical semantics frameworks, and propose a paraphrase generation model which utilizes LCS combining with syntactic transformation.

2 Lexical Conceptual Structure

2.1 Basic Framework

Among several frameworks of lexical semantics, we focus on the Lexical Conceptual Structure (LCS) [8] due to the following reasons. First, several studies [9,3,19] have shown that the theory of the LCS provides a systematic explanation of semantic decomposition as well as syntax determines. In particular, Kageyama [9] has shown that even a simple typology of LCS can explain a wide variety of linguistic phenomena including word association within compounds, transitivity alternation, and lexical derivation. Second, large-scale LCS dictionaries have been developed through practical use on machine translation and compound noun analysis [3,19]. The LCS dictionary for English [3] (4,163-verbs with 468 LCS types) was tailored based on a verb classification [12] with an expansion for the semantic role delivered to arguments. For Japanese, Takeuchi *et al.* [19] developed a 1,210-verbs LCS dictionary (with 12 LCS types) called the T-LCS dictionary, following Kageyama's analysis [9]. In this paper, we make use of the current version of the T-LCS dictionary, because it provides a set of concrete rules for LCS assignment, which ensures the reliability of the dictionary.

Examples of LCS in the T-LCS dictionary are shown in Table 1. An LCS consists of a combination of semantic predicates ("CONTROL," "BE AT," etc.) and their argument slots (x, y, and z). Each argument slot corresponds to a semantic role, such as "Agent," "Theme," and "Goal," depending on its surrounding semantic predicates. Let us take "*yakusu* (to translate)" as an example. The inner structure "[y BE AT z]" denotes the state of affairs where z ("Goal") indicates the state or physical location of y ("Theme"). The predicate "BECOME" expresses a change of y. In the case of example phrase in Table 1, the change of the language of the book is represented. The leftmost

Table 1. Examples of LCS

LCS for verb (example verb)
example Japanese phrase
[y BE AT z] (*ichi-suru* (to locate), *sonzai-suru* (to exist))
gakkou-ga kawa-no chikaku-ni ichi-suru.
school-NOM river-GEN near-DAT to locate-PRES
The school (Theme) locates near the river (Goal).
[BECOME [y BE AT z]] (*houwa-suru* (to become saturate), *bunpu-suru* (to be distributed))
kono-hana-ga sekaiju-ni bunpu-suru.
this flower-NOM all over the world-DAT to distribute-PRES
This flower (Theme) is distributed all over the world (Goal).
[x CONTROL [BECOME [y BE AT z]]] (*yakusu* (to translate), *shoukai-suru* (to introduce))
kare-ga hon-o nihongo-ni yakusu.
he-NOM book-ACC Japanese-DAT to translate-PRES
He (Agent) translates the book (Theme) into Japanese (Goal).
[x ACT ON y] (*unten-suru* (to drive), *sousa-suru* (to operate))
kare-ga kikai-o sousa-suru.
he-NOM machine-ACC to operate-PRES
He (Agent) operates the machine (Theme).
[y MOVE TO z] (*ido-suru* (to move), *sen'i-suru* (to propagate))
ane-ga tonarimachi-ni ido-suru.
my sister-NOM neighboring town-DAT to move-PRES
My sister (Theme) moves to a neighboring town (Goal).

part "[x CONTROL ...]" denotes that the "Agent" causes the state change. The difference between "BECOME BE AT" and "MOVE TO" is underlying their telicity: the former indicates telic, and thus the verb can be perfective, while the latter atelic. Likewise, "CONTROL" implicates a state change, while "ACT ON" merely denotes an action. The following are examples of syntactic and semantic properties represented in LCS:

- Semantic role of argument (e.g. "[x CONTROL ...]" indicates x="Agent")
- Syntactic case particle pattern (e.g. "[y MOVE TO z]" indicates y=NOM, z=DAT)
- Aspectual property (e.g. "MOVE TO" is atelic ("**ket-tearu* (to kick-PERF)"), while "BECOME BE AT" is telic ("*oi-tearu* (to place-PERF)."))
- Focus of statement
  (e.g. x is focused in "[x CONTROL ...]", while z in "[z BE WITH ...]")
- Semantic relations in lexical derivation
  - transitivity alternation ("*kowasu* (to break (vt))" ⇔ "*kowareru* (to break (vi))")
  - lexical active-passive alternation ("*oshieru* (to teach)" ⇔ "*osowaru* (to be taught)")

2.2 Disambiguation in LCS Analysis

In principle, a verb is associated with more than one LCS if it has multiple senses. The mapping from syntactic case assignments to argument slots in LCS is also many-to-many in general. In the case of Japanese, the case particle "*ni*" tends to be highly ambiguous as demonstrated in (5).

(5) a. *shuushin-jikan-o* ***yoru-11ji-ni*** *henkou-shita.*
bedtime-ACC 11 p.m.-DAT (complement) to change-PAST
I changed my bedtime to 11 p.m.

b. ***yoru-11ji-ni*** ***yuujin-ni*** *mail-o* *okut-ta.*
11 p.m.-DAT (adjunct) friends-DAT (complement) mail-ACC to send-PAST
I sent a mail to my friends at 11 p.m.

Resolution of these sorts of ambiguity is called semantic parsing and has been actively studied by many researchers recently [6,2] as semantically annotated corpora and lexical resources such as the FrameNet [1] and the Proposition Bank [16] have become available. Relying on the promising results of this trend of research, we do not address the issue of semantic parsing in this paper to focus our attention on the generation side of the whole problem.

3 Paraphrasing of Light-Verb Constructions

In this paper, we focus our discussion on one class of paraphrases, i.e., paraphrasing of light-verb constructions (LVCs). Sentence (6s) shows an example of an LVC. An LVC is a verb phrase ("*kandou-o atae-ta* (made an impression)," c.f., Figure 1) that consists of a light-verb ("*atae-ta* (to give-PAST)") that syntactically governs a deverbal noun ("*kandou* (an impression)"). A paraphrase of (6s) is shown in sentence (6t), where the deverbal noun functions as the main verb with its verbalized form ("*kandou-s-**ase**-ta* (to be impressed-CAUSATIVE-PAST)").

(6) s. *eiga-ga* *kare-**ni*** *saikou-no* ***kandou-o*** ***atae**-ta.*
film-NOM him-DAT supreme-GEN impression-ACC to give-PAST
The film made an supreme impression on him.

t. *eiga-ga* *kare-**o*** *saikou-ni* ***kandou-s-ase**-ta.*
film-NOM him-ACC supreme-DAT to be impressed-CAUSATIVE-PAST
The film supremely impressed him.

Example (6) indicates that we need an information to determine how the voice of target sentence must be changed and how the case particles of the nominal elements must be reassigned. These decisions depend not only on the syntactic and semantic attributes of the light-verb, but also on those of the deverbal noun [14]. LVC paraphrasing is thus a novel challenging material for exploiting LCS.

Figure 1 demonstrates tree representations of source and target expressions involved in LVC paraphrasing, taking (6) as an example. To generate this type of paraphrase, we need a computational model that is capable of the following operations:

Change of the dependence: Change the dependences of the elements (a) and (b) due to the elimination of the original modifiee, the light-verb. This operation can be done by just making them dependent on the resultant verb.

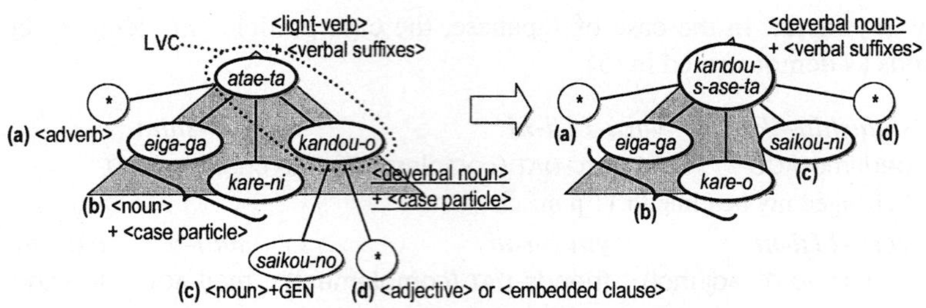

Fig. 1. Dependency structure showing the range which the LVC paraphrasing affects. The oval objects denote Japanese base-chunks so-called *bunsetsu.*

Re-conjugation: Change the conjugation form of the elements (d) and occasionally (c), according to the syntactic category change of their modifiee: the given deverbal noun is verbalized. This operation can be carried out independently of the LVC paraphrasing.

Selection of the voice: Choose the voice of the target sentence among active, passive, causative, etc. In example (6), the causative (the auxiliary verb "*ase*") is chosen. The decision depends on the syntactic and semantic attributes of both the given light-verb and the deverbal noun [14].

Reassignment of the cases: Assign the case particles of the elements (b) and (c), the arguments of the main verb. In (6), the syntactic case of "*kare* (him)," which was originally assigned dative case "*ni*" is changed to accusative "*o*."

Among these operations, this paper focuses on the last two, namely handling the element (b), the sibling cases of the deverbal noun. Triangles in both trees in Figure 1 indicate the range which we handle. Henceforth, elements outside of the triangles, namely, (a), (c), and (d), are used only for explanatory purposes.

4 LCS-Based Paraphrase Generation Model

Figure 2 illustrates how our model paraphrases the LVC, taking (7) as an example.

(7)	s.	*Ken-ga*	*eiga-ni*	***shigeki-o***	***uke**-ta.*
		Ken-NOM	film-DAT	inspiration-ACC	to receive-PAST
		Ken received an inspiration from the film.			
	t.	*Ken-ga*	*eiga-ni*	***shigeki-s-are**-ta.*	
		Ken-NOM	film-DAT	to inspire-PASSIVE-PAST	
		Ken was inspired by the film.			

The generation process consists of the following three steps:

Step 1. Semantic analysis: The model first analyzes a given input sentence including an LVC to obtain its LCS representation. In Figure 2, this step generates LCS_{V1} by filling arguments of LCS_{V0} with nominal elements.

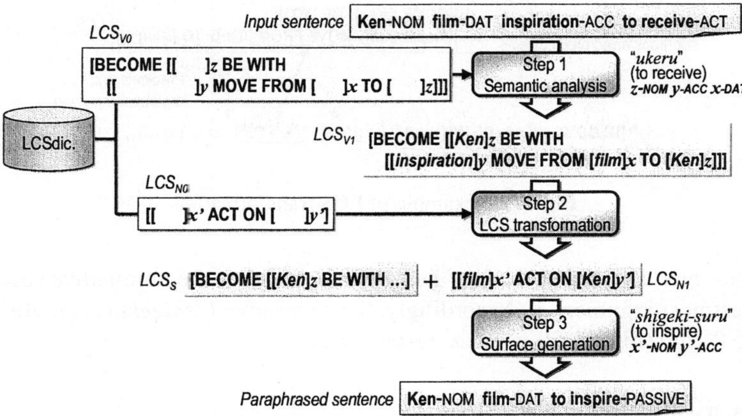

Fig. 2. LCS-based paraphrase generation model

Step 2. Semantic transformation (LCS transformation): The model then transfers the obtained semantic structure to another semantic structure so that the target structure consists of the LCS of the verbalized form of the deverbal noun. In our example, this step generates LCS_{N1} together with the supplement "[BECOME [...]]". We refer to such a supplement as LCS_S.

Step 3. Surface generation: Having obtained the target LCS representation, the model finally generates the output sentence from it. LCS_S triggers another syntactic alternation such as passivization and causativization.

The idea is to use the LCS representation as a semantic representation and to retrieve semantic constraints to relieve the syntactic underspecificity underlying the LVC paraphrasing. Each step consists of a handful of linguistically explainable rules, and thus is scalable when the typology and resource of LCS is given. The rest of this section elaborates on each step, differentiating symbols to denote arguments; x, y, and z for LCS_V, and x', y', and z' for LCS_N.

4.1 Semantic Analysis

Given an input sentence (a simple clause with an LVC), the model first looks up the LCS template LCS_{V0} for the given light-verb in the T-LCS dictionary, and then applies the case assignment rule below to obtain its LCS representation LCS_{V1}:

- In the case of the LCS_{V0} having argument x, fill the leftmost argument of the LCS_{V0} with the nominative case of the input, the second leftmost with the accusative, and the rest with the dative case.
- Otherwise, fill arguments y and z of the LCS_{V0} with the nominative and the dative cases, respectively.

This rule is proposed in [19] instead of semantic parsing in order to tentatively automate LCS-based processing. In the example shown in Figure 2, LCS_{V0} for the

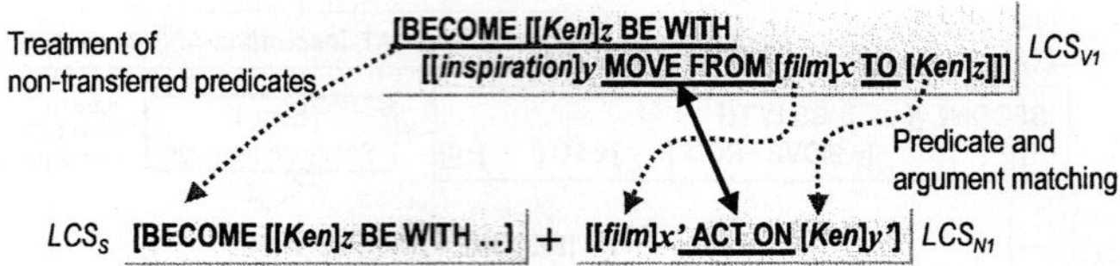

Fig. 3. An example of LCS transformation

given light-verb "*ukeru* (to receive)" has argument x, thus the nominative case, "*Ken*," fills the leftmost argument z. Accordingly, the accusative ("*shigeki* (inspiration)") and the dative ("*eiga* (film)") fill y and x, respectively.

4.2 LCS Transformation

The second step matches LCS_{V1} with the another LCS for the verbalized form of the deverbal noun LCS_{N0} to generate the target LCS representation LCS_{N1}. Figure 3 shows a more detailed view of this process for the example shown in Figure 2.

Muraki [14] described that the direction of action and the focus of statement are important clues to determine the voice in LVC paraphrasing. We therefore incorporate the below assumptions into matching process. The model first matches predicates in LCS_{V1} and LCS_{N0}, assuming that the agentive argument x is relevant to the direction of action. We classify the semantic predicates into the following three groups: (i) agentive predicates (involve argument x): "CONTROL," "ACT ON," "ACT TO," "ACT," and "MOVE FROM TO," (ii) state of affair predicates (involve only argument y or z): "MOVE TO," "BE AT," and "BE WITH," and (iii) aspectual predicates (with no argument): "BECOME," and allowed any pair of predicates in the same group to match. In our example, "MOVE FROM TO" matches "ACT ON" as shown in Figure 3.

Having matched the predicates, the model then fills each argument slot in LCS_{N0} with its corresponding argument in LCS_{V1}. In Figure 3, argument z is matched with y', and x with x'. As a result, "*Ken*" and "*eiga*" come to y' and x' slots, respectively. When an argument is filled with another LCS, arguments within the inner LCS are also taken into account. Likewise, we introduced some exceptional rules assuming that the input sentences are periphrastic. For instance, arguments filled with the implicit filler (e.g. "name" for "to sign" is usually not expressed in Japanese) and the deverbal noun, which is already represented by LCS_{N0} are never matched. Argument z in LCS_{V1} is allowed to match with y' in LCS_{N0}.

LCS representations have right-embedding structures, and inner-embedded predicates denote the state of affairs. We thus prioritize the rightmost predicates in this matching process. In other words, the proceeds from the rightmost inner predicates to the outer ones, and the matching process is repeated until the leftmost predicate in LCS_{N0} or that in LCS_{V1} matched.

If LCS_{V1} has any non-transferred part LCS_S when the predicate and argument matching has been completed, it represents the semantic content that is not expressed by LCS_{N1} and needs to be expressed by auxiliary linguistic devices such as voice auxiliaries. As described in Section 2.1, the leftmost part specifies the focus of statement. The model thus attaches LCS_S to LCS_{N0} as a supplement, and then use it to determine auxiliaries in the next step, the surface generation. In the case of Figure 3, "[BECOME [[*Ken*]$_z$ BE WITH]]" in LCS_{V1} remains non-transferred and be attached.

4.3 Surface Generation

The model again applies the aforementioned case assignment rule to generate a sentence from the resultant LCS. From the LCS_{N1} in Figure 2, sentence (8) is generated.

(8) ***eiga-ga*** *Ken-o* ***shigeki-shi****-ta.*
film-NOM Ken-ACC to inspire-PAST
The film inspired Ken.

The model then makes the final decision on the selection of the voice and the reassignment of the cases. As we described above, the attached structure LCS_S is a clue to determine what the focus is. We therefore use the following decision list:

1. If the leftmost argument of LCS_S has the same value as the leftmost argument in LCS_{N1}, the viewpoints of LCS_S and LCS_{N1} are same. Thus, the active voice is selected and the case structure is left as is.
2. If the leftmost argument of LCS_S has the same value as either z' or y' in LCS_{N1}, the model makes the argument a subject (nominative). That is, the passive voice is selected and case alternation (passivization) is applied.
3. If LCS_S has "BE WITH" and its argument has the same value as x' in LCS_{N1}, the causative voice is selected and case alternation (causativization) is applied.
4. If LCS_S has an agentive predicate, and its argument is filled with a value different from those of the other arguments, then the causative voice is selected and case alternation (causativization) is applied.
5. Otherwise, active voice is selected and thus no modification is applied.

The example in Figure 2 satisfies the second condition, thus the model chooses "***s-are****-ru* (PASSIVE)" and passivizes the sentence (8). As a result, "*Ken*" becomes to be the nominative "*ga*" as in (7t).

5 Experiment

5.1 Paraphrase Generation and Evaluation

To conduct an empirical experiment, we collected the following data sets. Note that more than one LCS was assigned to a verb if it was polysemous.

Deverbal nouns: We regard "*sahen*-nouns" and adverbial forms of verbs as deverbal nouns. We retrieved 1,210 deverbal nouns from the T-LCS dictionary. The set consists of (i) activity nouns (e.g., "*sasoi* (invitation)" and "*odoroki* (surprise)"), (ii) Sino-Japanese verbal nouns (e.g., "*kandou* (impression)" and "*shigeki* (inspiration)"), and (iii) English borrowings (e.g., "drive" and "support").

Tuples of light-verb and case particle: A verb takes different meanings when it constitutes LVCs with different case particles, and not every tuple of a light-verb v and a case particle c functions as an LVC. We therefore tailored an objective collection of tuples $\langle v, c\rangle$ from corpus in the following manner:

Step 1. From a corpus consisting of 25 million parsed sentences of newspaper articles, we collected 876,101 types of triplet $\langle v, c, n\rangle$, where v, c, and n denote a base form of verb, a case particle, and an deverbal noun.
Step 2. For each of the 50 most frequent $\langle v, c\rangle$ tuples, we extracted the 10 most frequent triplets $\langle v, c, n\rangle$.
Step 3. Each $\langle v, c, n\rangle$ was manually evaluated to determine whether it functioned as an LVC. If any of 10 triplets functioned as an LVC, the tuple $\langle v, c\rangle$ was merged into the list of light-verbs, assigning an LCS according to the linguistic tests examined in [19]. As a result, we collected 40 types of $\langle v, c\rangle$ for light-verbs.

Paraphrase examples: A collection of paraphrase examples, pairs of an LVC and its correct paraphrase, were constructed in the following way:

Step 1. From the 876,101 types of triplet $\langle v, c, n\rangle$ collected above, 23,608 types of $\langle v, c, n\rangle$ were extracted, whose components, n and $\langle v, c\rangle$, were in the dictionaries.
Step 2. For each of the 245 most frequent $\langle v, c, n\rangle$, the 3 most frequent simple clauses including the $\langle v, c, n\rangle$ were extracted from the same corpus.
Step 3. Two native speakers of Japanese, adults graduated from university, were employed to build a gold-standard collection. 711 out of 735 sentences were manually paraphrased in the manner of LVC, while the remaining 24 sentences were not because $\langle v, c, n\rangle$ within them did not function as LVCs.

The real coverage of these 245 $\langle v, c, n\rangle$ with regard to all LVCs among the corpus falls in the range between the below two:

Lower bound: If every $\langle v, c, n\rangle$ is an LVC, the coverage of the collection is estimated at 6.47% (492,737 / 7,621,089) of tokens.
Upper bound: If the dictionaries cover all light-verbs and deverbal nouns, the collection covers 24.1% (492,737 / 2,044,387) of tokens.

In the experiment, our model generated all the possible paraphrases when a given verb was polysemous with multiple entries in the T-LCS dictionary. As a result, the model generated 822 paraphrases from the 735 input sentences, at least one for each input. We then classified the resultant paraphrases as correct and incorrect by comparing them with the gold-standard, where we ignored ordering of syntactic cases, and obtained 624 correct and 198 incorrect paraphrases Recall, precision, and F-measure ($\alpha = 0.5$) were 0.878 (624 / 711), 0.759 (624 / 822), and 0.814, respectively.

As the baseline, we employed a statistical language model developed in [5]. Among all the combinations of the voice and syntactic cases, the baseline model selects the one that has the highest probability. Although the model is trained on a large amount of data, the generated expression often falls out of the vocabulary. In such a case, the probability cannot be calculated, and the model outputs nothing for the given sentence. As a result of an application of this baseline model to the same set of input sentences, we obtained 320 correct and 215 incorrect paraphrases (Recall: 0.450 (320 / 711), Precision: 0.598 (320 / 535), and F-measure: 0.514). The significant improvement indicates that our lexical-semantics-based account benefited on the decisions we considered.

The language model can also be complementary used to our LCS-based paraphrase generation. By filtering implausible paraphrases out, 66 incorrect and 15 correct paraphrases were filtered, and the performance was further improved (Recall: 0.857, Precision: 0.822, and F-measure: 0.839).

5.2 Discussion

Although the performance has room for further improvement, we think the performance is reasonably high under the current stage of the T-LCS dictionary. In other words, the tendency of errors does not so differ from our expectation. As we expected in Section 2.2, the ambiguity of dative case "*ni*" (c.f. (5)) occupied the largest portion of errors (78 / 198). This was because the case assignment was performed by a rule instead of semantic parsing. Each rule in our model has been created relying on a set of linguistic tests used in the theory of LCS and our linguistic intuition on handling LCS. However, the rule set was not sufficiently sophisticated, so that led to 59 errors. Equally, 30 errors occurred due to the immature typology of the T-LCS dictionary.

We consider the improvement of the LCS typology as the primal issue, because our transformation rules depend on it. For the moment, we have the following two suggestions. First, more variety of semantic roles should be handled step by step. For example, we need to handle the object of "*eikyou-suru* (to affect)," which is marked by not accusative but dative. Second, the necessity of "Source" is inconsistent. Verbs such as "*hairu* (to enter)" do not require this argument ("BECOME BE AT") , while some other verbs, such as "*ukeru* (to receive)," explicitly require it ("MOVE FROM TO"). The telicity of "MOVE FROM TO" should also be discussed. With such a feedback from the application and an extensive investigation into lexicology, we have to enhance the typology, and enlarge the dictionary preserving its consistency.

6 Related Work

The paraphrases associated with LVCs are not idiosyncratic to Japanese but also appear commonly in other languages such as English, French, and Spanish [13,7,4] as shown in (3) and (4). Our approach raises an interesting issue of whether the paraphrasing of LVCs can be modeled in an analogous way across languages.

Iordanskaja *et al.* [7] proposed a set of paraphrasing rules including one for LVC paraphrasing based on the Meaning-Text Theory introduced by [13]. The model seemed to properly handle LVC paraphrasing, because their rules were described according to the deep semantic analysis and heavily relied on what were called lexical functions, such as lexical derivation (e.g., $S_0(affect) = effect$) and light-verb generation (e.g., $Oper_1(attempt) = make$). To take this approach, however, a vast amount of lexical knowledge to form each lexical function is required, because they only virtually specify all the choices relevant to LVC paraphrasing for every combination of deverbal noun and light-verb individually. In contrast, our approach is to employ lexical semantics to provide a general account of those classes of choices, and thus contributes to the knowledge development in terms of reducing human-labor and preserving consistency.

Kaji *et al.* [10] proposed a paraphrase generation model which utilized an monolingual dictionary for human. Given an input LVC, their model paraphrases it referring to the glosses of both the deverbal noun and light-verb, and a manually assigned semantic feature of the light-verb. Their model looks robust due to the availability of resource. However, their model fails to explain the difference between examples (7) and (9) in the voice selection, because it selects the voice based only on the light-verb irrespective of the deverbal noun: the light-verb "*ukeru* (to receive)" is always mapped to the passive voice.

(9) s. *musuko-ga* *kare-no* *hanashi-ni* ***kandou-o*** ***uke**-ta.*
son-NOM his-GEN talk-DAT impression-ACC to receive-PAST
My son was given a good impression by his talk.
t. *musuko-ga* *kare-no* *hanashi-ni* ***kandou-shi**-ta.*
son-NOM his-GEN talk-DAT to be impressed-PAST
My son was impressed by his talk.

In their model, the target expression is restricted only to the LVC itself (c.f., Figure 1). Hence, their model is unable to reassign the case particles as we saw in example (6).

There is another trend in the research of paraphrase generation: i.e., the automatic paraphrase acquisition from existing lexical resources such as ordinary dictionaries, parallel/comparable corpora, and non-parallel corpora. This type of approach may be able to reduce the cost of resource development. However, there are drawbacks that must be overcome before they can work practically. First, automatic methods require large amounts of training data. The issue is how to collect enough large size of data at low cost. Second, automatically extracted knowledge tends to be rather noisy, requiring manual correction and maintenance. In contrast, our approach, which focuses on the regularity underlying paraphrases, is a complementary avenue to develop and maintain knowledge resources that cover a sufficiently wide range of paraphrases.

Previous case studies [14,18,11] have employed some syntactic properties of verbs to constrain syntactic transformations in paraphrase generation: e.g. subject agentivity, aspectual property, passivizability, and causativizability. Several classifications of verbs have also been proposed [12,15] based on various types of verb alternation and syntactic case patterns. In contrast, the theory of lexical semantics integrates syntactic and semantic properties including those above, and gives a perspective to formalize and maintain the syntactic and semantic properties of words.

7 Conclusion

In this paper, we explored what sorts of lexical properties encoded in LCS can explain the regularity underlying paraphrases. Based on an existing LCS dictionary, we built an LCS-based paraphrase generation model, and conducted an empirical experiment on paraphrasing of LVC. The experiment confirmed that the proposed model was capable of generating paraphrases accurately in terms of selecting the voice and reassigning the syntactic cases, and revealed potential difficulties that we have to overcome toward a practical use of our lexical-semantics-based account. To make our model more accurate, we need further discussion on (i) the enhancement of the T-LCS dictionary with feedback from experiments, (ii) the LCS transformation algorithm, and (iii) the semantic parsing. Another goal is to practically clarify what extent can be done by LCS for other classes of paraphrase, such as those exemplified in Section 1.

References

1. C. F. Baker, C. J. Fillmore, and J. B. Lowe. The Berkeley FrameNet project. In *Proceedings of the 36th Annual Meeting of the Association for Computational Linguistics and the 17th International Conference on Computational Linguistics (COLING-ACL)*, pages 86–90, 1998.
2. X. Carreras and L. Màrques. Introduction to the CoNLL-2004 shared task: semantic role labeling. In *Proceedings of 8th Conference on Natural Language Learning (CoNLL)*, pages 89–97, 2004.
3. B. J. Dorr. Large-scale dictionary construction for foreign language tutoring and interlingual machine translation. *Machine Translation*, 12(4):271–322, 1997.
4. M. Dras. *Tree adjoining grammar and the reluctant paraphrasing of text.* Ph.D. thesis, Division of Information and Communication Science, Macquarie University, 1999.
5. A. Fujita, K. Inui, and Y. Matsumoto. Detection of incorrect case assignments in automatically generated paraphrases of Japanese sentences. In *Proceedings of the 1st International Joint Conference on Natural Language Processing (IJCNLP)*, pages 14–21, 2004.
6. D. Gildea and D. Jurafsky. Automatic labeling of semantic roles. *Computational Linguistics*, 28(3):245–288, 2002.
7. L. Iordanskaja, R. Kittredge, and A. Polguère. Lexical selection and paraphrase in a meaning-text generation model. In C. L. Paris, W. R. Swartout, and W. C. Mann, editors, *Natural Language Generation in Artificial Intelligence and Computational Linguistics*, pages 293–312. Kluwer Academic Publishers, 1991.
8. R. Jackendoff. *Semantic structures.* The MIT Press, 1990.
9. T. Kageyama. *Verb semantics.* Kurosio Publishers, 1996. (in Japanese).
10. N. Kaji and S. Kurohashi. Recognition and paraphrasing of periphrastic and overlapping verb phrases. In *Proceedings of the 4th International Conference on Language Resources and Evaluation (LREC) Workshop on Methodologies and Evaluation of Multiword Units in Real-world Application*, 2004.
11. K. Kondo, S. Sato, and M. Okumura. Paraphrasing by case alternation. *IPSJ Journal*, 42(3):465–477, 2001. (in Japanese).
12. B. Levin. *English verb classes and alternations: a preliminary investigation.* Chicago Press, 1993.
13. I. Mel'čuk and A. Polguère. A formal lexicon in meaning-text theory (or how to do lexica with words). *Computational Linguistics*, 13(3-4):261–275, 1987.
14. S. Muraki. *Various aspects of Japanese verbs.* Hitsuji Syobo, 1991. (in Japanese).
15. A. Oishi and Y. Matsumoto. Detecting the organization of semantic subclasses of Japanese verbs. *International Journal of Corpus Linguistics*, 2(1):65–89, 1997.
16. M. Palmer, D. Gildea, and P. Kingsbury. The Proposition Bank: an annotated corpus of semantic roles. *Computational Linguistics*, 31(1):71–106, 2005.
17. J. Pustejovsky. *The generative lexicon.* The MIT Press, 1995.
18. S. Sato. Automatic paraphrase of technical papers' titles. *IPSJ Journal*, 40(7):2937–2945, 1999. (in Japanese).
19. K. Takeuchi, K. Kageura, and T. Koyama. An LCS-based approach for analyzing Japanese compound nouns with deverbal heads. In *Proceedings of the 2nd International Workshop on Computational Terminology (CompuTerm)*, pages 64–70, 2002.

Word Sense Disambiguation by Relative Selection

Hee-Cheol Seo[1], Hae-Chang Rim[2], and Myung-Gil Jang[1]

[1] Knowledge Mining Research Team,
Electronics and Telecommunications Research Institute (ETRI),
Daejeon, Korea
{hcseo, mgjang}@etri.re.kr
[2] Dept. of Computer Science and Engineering, Korea University,
1, 5-ka, Anam-dong, Seongbuk-Gu, Seoul, 136-701, Korea
rim@nlp.korea.ac.kr

Abstract. This paper describes a novel method for a word sense disambiguation that utilizes relatives (i.e. synonyms, hypernyms, meronyms, etc in WordNet) of a target word and raw corpora. The method disambiguates senses of a target word by selecting a relative that most probably occurs in a new sentence including the target word. Only one co-occurrence frequency matrix is utilized to efficiently disambiguate senses of many target words. Experiments on several English datum present that our proposed method achieves a good performance.

1 Introduction

With its importance, a word sense disambiguation (WSD) has been known as a very important field of a natural language processing (NLP) and has been studied steadily since the advent of NLP in the 1950s. In spite of the long study, few WSD systems are used for practical NLP applications unlike part-of-speech (POS) taggers and syntactic parsers. The reason is because most of WSD studies have focused on only a small number of ambiguous words based on sense tagged corpus. In other words, the previous WSD systems disambiguate senses of just a few words, and hence are not helpful for other NLP applications because of its low coverage.

Why have the studies about WSD stayed on the small number of ambiguous words? The answer is on sense tagged corpus where a few words are assigned to correct senses. Since the construction of the sense tagged corpus needs a great amount of times and cost, most of current sense tagged corpora contain a small number of words less than 100 and the corresponding senses to the words. The corpora, which have sense information of all words, have been built recently, but are not large enough to provide sufficient disambiguation information of the all words. Therefore, the methods based on the sense tagged corpora have difficulties in disambiguating senses of all words.

R. Dale et al. (Eds.): IJCNLP 2005, LNAI 3651, pp. 920–932, 2005.

In this paper, we proposed a novel WSD method that requires no sense tagged corpus[1] and that identifies senses of all words in sentences or documents, not a small number of words. Our proposed method depends on raw corpus, which is relatively very large and on WordNet [1], which is a lexical database in a hierarchical structure.

2 Related Works

There are several works for WSD that do not depend on a sense tagged corpus, and they can be classified into three approaches according to main resources used: raw corpus based approach [2], dictionary based approach [3,4] and hierarchical lexical database approach. The hierarchical lexical database approach can be reclassified into three groups according to usages of the database: gloss based method [5], conceptual density based method [6,7] and relative based method [8,9,10]. Since our method is a kind of the relative based method, this section describes the related works of the relative based method.

[8] introduced the relative based method using International Roget's Thesaurus as a hierarchical lexical database. His method is conducted as follows: 1) Get relatives of each sense of a target word from the Roget's Thesaurus. 2) Collect example sentences of the relatives, which are representative of each sense. 3) Identify salient words in the collective context and determine weights for each word. 4) Use the resulting weights to predict the appropriate sense for the target word occurring in a novel text. He evaluated the method on 12 English nouns, and showed over than 90% precision. However, the evaluation was conducted on just a small part of senses of the words, not on all senses of them.

He indicated that a drawback of his method is on the ambiguous relative: just one sense of the ambiguous relative is usually related to a target word but the other senses of the ambiguous relatives are not. Hence, a collection of example sentences of the ambiguous relative includes the example sentences irrelevant to the target word, which prevent WSD systems from collecting correct WSD information. For example, an ambiguous word *rail* is a relative of a meaning *bird* of a target word *crane* at WordNet, but the word *rail* means *railway* for the most part, not the meaning related to *bird*. Therefore, most of the example sentences of *rail* are not helpful for WSD of *crane*. His method has another problem in disambiguating senses of a large number of target words because it requires a great amount of time and storage space to collect example sentences of relatives of the target words.

[9] followed the method of [8], but tried to resolve the ambiguous relative problem by using just unambiguous relatives. That is, the ambiguous relative *rail* is not utilized to build a training data of the word *crane* because the word *rail* is ambiguous. Another difference from [8] is on a lexical database: they utilized WordNet as a lexical database for acquiring relatives of target words

[1] Strictly speaking, our method utilizes bias of word senses at WordNet, which is acquired a sense tagged corpus. However, our method does not access a sense tagged corpus directly. Hence, our method is a kind of a weakly supervised approach.

instead of International Roget's Thesaurus. Since WordNet is freely available for research, various kinds of WSD studies based on WordNet can be compared with the method of [9]. They evaluated their method on 14 ambiguous nouns and achieved a good performance comparable to the methods based on the sense tagged corpus. However, the evaluation was conducted on a small part of senses of the target words like [8].

However, many senses in WordNet do not have unambiguous relatives through relationships such as synonyms, direct hypernyms, and direct hyponyms.[2] A possible alternative is to use the unambiguous relatives in the long distance from a target word, but the way is still problematic because the longer the distance of two senses is, the weaker the relationship between them is. In other words, the unambiguous relatives in the long distance may provide irrelevant examples for WSD like ambiguous relatives. Hence, the method has difficulties in disambiguating senses of words that do not have unambiguous relatives near the target words in the WordNet. The problem becomes more serious when verbs, which most of the relatives are ambiguous, are disambiguated. Like [8], the method also has a difficulty in disambiguating senses of many words because the method collects the example sentences of relatives of many words.

[10] reimplemented the method of [9] using a web, which may be a very large corpus, in order to collect example sentences. They built training datum of all noun words in WordNet whose size is larger than 7GB, but evaluated their method on a small number of nouns of lexical sample task of SENSEVAL-2 as [8] and [9].

3 Word Sense Disambiguation by Relative Selection

Our method disambiguates senses of a target word in a sentence by selecting only a relative among the relatives of the target word that most probably occurs in the sentence. A flowchart of our method is presented in Figure 1 with an example[3]: 1) Given a new sentence including a target word, a set of relatives of the target word is created by looking up in WordNet. 2) Next, the relative that most probably occurs in the sentence is chosen from the set. In this step, co-occurrence frequencies between relatives and words in the sentence are used in order to calculate the probabilities of relatives. Our method does not depend on the training data, but on co-occurrence frequency matrix. Hence in our method, it is not necessary to build the training data, which requires too much time and space. 3) Finally, a sense of the target word is determined as the sense that is related to the selected relative. In this example, the relative *stork* is selected with the highest probability and the proper sense is determined as *crane#1*, which is related to the selected relative *stork*.

[2] In this paper, direct hypernyms and direct hyponyms mean parents and children at a lexical database, respectively.

[3] In WordNet 1.7.1, a word *crane* contains four senses, but in this paper only two senses (i.e. *bird* and *device*) are described in the convenience of description.

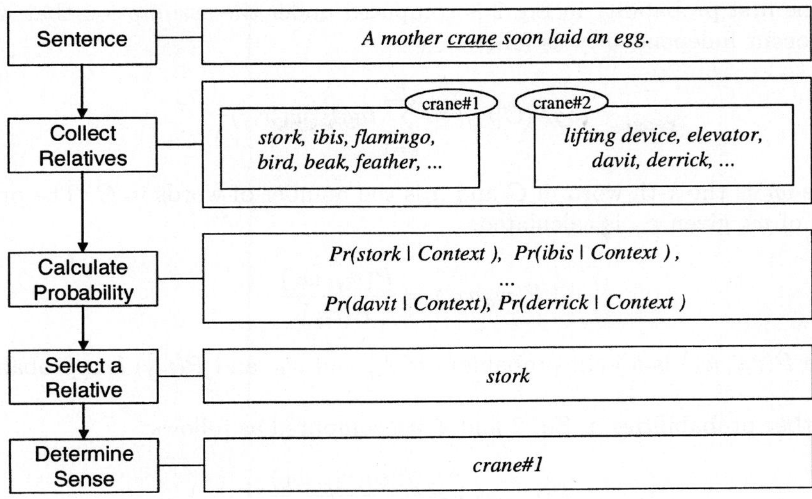

Fig. 1. Flowchart of our proposed method

Our method makes use of ambiguous relatives as well as unambiguous relatives unlike [9] and hence overcomes the shortage problem of relatives and also reduces the problem of ambiguous relatives in [8] by handling relatives separately instead of putting example sentences of the relatives together into a pool.

3.1 Relative Selection

The selected relative of the i-th target word tw_i in a sentence C is defined to be the relative of tw_i that has the largest co-occurrence probability with the words in the sentence:

$$SR(tw_i, C) \stackrel{\text{def}}{=} \arg\max_{r_{ij}} P(r_{ij}|C)P(S_{r_{ij}})W(r_{ij}, tw_i) \quad (1)$$

where SR is the selected relative, r_{ij} is the j-th relative of tw_i, $S_{r_{ij}}$ is a sense of tw_i that is related to the relative r_{ij}, and W is a weight of r_{ij}. The right hand side of Eq. 1 is logarithmically calculated by Bayesian rule:

$$\begin{aligned} &\arg\max_{r_{ij}} P(r_{ij}|C)P(S_{r_{ij}})W(r_{ij}, tw_i) \\ &= \arg\max_{r_{ij}} \frac{P(C|r_{ij})P(r_{ij})}{P(C)} P(S_{r_{ij}})W(r_{ij}, tw_i) \\ &= \arg\max_{r_{ij}} P(C|r_{ij})P(r_{ij})P(S_{r_{ij}})W(r_{ij}, tw_i) \\ &= \arg\max_{r_{ij}} \{logP(C|r_{ij}) + logP(r_{ij}) \\ &+ logP(S_{r_{ij}}) + logW(r_{ij}, tw_i)\} \end{aligned} \quad (2)$$

The first probability in Eq. 2 is computed under the assumption that words in C occur independently as follows:

$$logP(C|r_{ij}) \approx \sum_{k=1}^{n} logP(w_k|r_{ij}) \tag{3}$$

where w_k is the k-th word in C and n is the number of words in C. The probability of w_k given r_{ij} is calculated:

$$P(w_k|r_{ij}) = \frac{P(r_{ij}, w_k)}{P(r_{ij})} \tag{4}$$

where $P(r_{ij}, w_k)$ is a joint probability of r_{ij} and w_k, and $P(r_{ij})$ is a probability of r_{ij}.

Other probabilities in Eq. 2 and 4 are computed as follows:

$$P(r_{ij}, w_k) = \frac{freq(r_{ij}, w_k)}{CS} \tag{5}$$

$$P(r_{ij}) = \frac{freq(r_{ij})}{CS} \tag{6}$$

$$Pr(S_{r_{ij}}) = \frac{0.5 + WNf(S_{r_{ij}})}{n * 0.5 + WNf(tw_i)} \tag{7}$$

where $freq(r_{ij}, w_k)$ is the frequency that r_{ij} and w_k co-occur in a raw corpus, $freq(r_{ij})$ is the frequency of r_{ij} in the corpus, and CS is a corpus size, which is the sum of frequencies of all words in the raw corpus. $WNf(S_{r_{ij}})$ and $WNf(tw_i)$ is the frequency of a sense related to r_{ij} and tw_i in WordNet.[4] In Eq. 7, 0.5 is a smoothing factor and n is the number of senses of tw_i. Finally, in Eq. 2, the weights of relatives, $W(r_{ij}, tw_i)$, are described in following Section 3.1.

Relative Weight. WordNet provides relatives of words, but all of them are not useful for WSD. That is to say, it is clear that most of ambiguous relatives may bring about a problem by providing example sentences irrelevant to the target word to WSD system as described in the previous section.

However, WordNet as a lexical database is classified as a fine-grained dictionary, and consequently some words are classified into ambiguous words though the words represent just one sense in the most occurrences. Such ambiguous relatives may be useful for WSD of target words that are related to the most frequent senses of the ambiguous relatives. For example, a relative *bird* of a word *crane* is an ambiguous word, but it usually represents one meaning, *"warm-blooded egg-laying vertebrates characterized by feathers and forelimbs modified as wings"*,

[4] WordNet provides the frequencies of words and senses in a sense tagged corpus (i.e. SemCor), and WNf is calculated with the frequencies in WordNet. That represents bias of word senses in WordNet.

which is closely related to *crane*. Hence, the word *bird* can be a useful relative of the word *crane* though the word *bird* is ambiguous. But the ambiguous relative is not useful for other target words that are related to the least frequent senses of the relatives: that is, a relative *bird* is never helpful to disambiguate the senses of a word *birdie*, which is related to the least frequent sense of the relative *bird*.

We employ a weighting scheme for relatives in order to identify useful relatives for WSD. In terms of weights of relatives, our intent is to provide the useful relative with high weights, but the useless relatives with low weights. For instance, a relative *bird* of a word *crane* has a high weight whereas a relative *bird* of a word *birdie* get a low weight.

For the sake of the weights, we calculate similarities between a target word and its relatives and determine the weight of each relative based on the degree of the similarity. Among similarity measures between words, the total divergence to the mean (TDM) is adopted, which is known as one of the best similarity measures for word similarity [11].

Since TDM estimates a divergence between vectors, not between words, words have to be represented by vectors in order to calculate the similarity between the words based on the TDM. We define vector elements as words that occur more than 10 in a raw corpus, and build vectors of words by counting co-occurrence frequencies of the words and vector elements.

TDM does measure the divergence between words, and hence a reciprocal of the TDM measure is utilized as the similarity measure:

$$Sim(\vec{w_i}, \vec{w_j}) = \frac{1}{TDM(\vec{w_i}, \vec{w_j})}$$

where $Sim(\vec{w_i}, \vec{w_j})$ represents a similarity between two word vectors, $\vec{w_i}$ and $\vec{w_j}$.

A weight of a relative is determined by the similarity of a target word and its relative as follows:

$$W(r_{ij}, tw_i) = Sim(\vec{r_{ij}}, \vec{tw_i})$$

3.2 Co-occurrence Frequency Matrix

In order to select a relative for a target word in a given sentence, we must calculate probabilities of relatives given the sentence, as described in previous section. These probabilities as Eq. 5 and 6 can be estimated based on frequencies of relatives and co-occurrence frequencies between each relative and each word in the sentence.

In order to acquire the frequency information for calculating the probabilities, the previous relative based methods constructed a training data by collecting example sentences of relatives. However, to construct the training data requires a great amount of time and storage space. What is worse, it is an awful work to construct training datum of all ambiguous words, whose number is over than 20,000 in WordNet.

Instead, we build a co-occurrence frequency matrix (CFM) from a raw corpus that contains frequencies of words and word pairs. A value in the i-th row and

j-th column in the CFM represents the co-occurrence frequency of the i-th word and j-th word in a vocabulary, and a value in the i-th row and the i-th column represents the frequency of the i-th word.

The CFM is easily built by counting words and word pairs in a raw corpus. Furthermore, it is not necessary to make a CFM per each ambiguous word since a CFM contains frequencies of all words including relatives and word pairs. Therefore, our proposed method disambiguates senses of all ambiguous words efficiently by referring to only one CFM.

The frequencies in Eq. 5 and 6 can be obtained through a CFM as follows:

$$freq(w_i) = cfm(i,i) \tag{8}$$

$$freq(w_i, w_j) = cfm(i,j) \tag{9}$$

where w_i is a word, and $cfm(i,j)$ represents the value in the i-th row and j-th column of the CFM, in other word, the frequency that the i-th word and j-th word co-occur in a raw corpus.

4 Experiments

4.1 Experimental Environment

Experiments were carried out on several English sense tagged corpora: SemCor and corpora for both lexical sample task and all words task of both SENSEVAL-2 & -3.[5] SemCor [12][6] is a semantic concordance, where all content words (i.e. noun, verb, adjective, and adverb) are assigned to WordNet senses. SemCor consists of three parts: *brown1, brown2* and *brownv*. We used all of the three parts of the SemCor for evaluation.

In our method, raw corpora are utilized in order to build a CFM and to calculate similarities between words for the sake of the weights of relatives. We adopted Wall Street Journal corpus in Penn Treebank II [13] and LATIMES corpus in TREC as raw corpora, which contain about 37 million word occurrences.

Our CFM contains frequencies of content words and content word pairs. In order to identify the content words from the raw corpus, Tree-Tagger [14], which is a kind of automatic POS taggers, is employed.

WordNet provides various kinds of relationships between words or synsets. In our experiments, the relatives in Table 1 are utilized according to POSs of target words. In the table, *hyper3* means 1 to 3 hypernyms (i.e. parents, grandparents and great-grandparent) and *hypo3* is 1 to 3 hyponyms (i.e. children, grandchildren and great-grandchildren).

[5] We did not evaluate on verbs of lexical sample task of SENSEVAL-3 because the verbs are assigned to senses of WordSmyth, not WordNet.

[6] In this paper, SemCor 1.7.1 is adopted.

Table 1. Used Relative types

POS	relatives
noun	synonym, hyper3, hypo3, antonym, attribute, holonym, meronym, sibling
adjective	synonym, antonym, similar to, alsosee, attribute, particle, pertain
verb	synonym, hyper2, tropo2, alsosee, antonym, causal, entail, verbgroup
adverb	synonyms, antonyms, derived

4.2 Experimental Results

Comparison with Other Relative Based Methods. We tried to compare our proposed method with the previous relative based methods. However, both of [8] and [9] did not evaluate their methods on a publicly available data. We implemented their methods and compared our method with them on the same evaluation data.

When both of the methods are implemented, it is practically difficult to collect example sentences of all target words in the evaluation data. Instead, we implemented the previous methods to work with our CFM. WordNet was utilized as a lexical database to acquire relatives of target words and the sense disambiguation modules were implemented by using on Naïve Bayesian classifier, which [9] adopted though [8] utilized International Roget's Thesaurus and other classifier similar to decision lists. Also the bias of word senses, which is presented at WordNet, is reflected on the implementation in order to be in a same condition with our method. Hence, the reimplemented methods in this paper are not exactly same with the previous methods, but the main ideas of the methods are not corrupted. A correct sense of a target word tw_i in a sentence C is determined as follows:

$$\begin{aligned} &Sense(tw_i, C) \\ &\stackrel{\text{def}}{=} \arg\max_{s_{ij}} P(s_{ij}|C)P_{wn}(s_{ij}) \end{aligned} \tag{10}$$

where $Sense(tw_i, C)$ is a sense of tw_i in C, s_{ij} is the j-th sense of tw_i. $P_{wn}(s_{ij})$ is the WordNet probability of s_{ij}. The right hand side of Eq. 10 is calculated logarithmically under the assumption that words in C occur independently:

$$\begin{aligned} &\arg\max_{s_{ij}} P(s_{ij}|C)P_{wn}(s_{ij}) \\ &= \arg\max_{s_{ij}} \frac{P(C|s_{ij})P(s_{ij})}{P(C)} P_{wn}(s_{ij}) \\ &= \arg\max_{s_{ij}} P(C|s_{ij})P(s_{ij})P_{wn}(s_{ij}) \\ &= \arg\max_{s_{ij}} \{logP(C|s_{ij}) + logP(s_{ij})) \\ &+ logP_{wn}(s_{ij})\} \\ &\approx \arg\max_{s_{ij}} \{\sum_{k=1}^{n} logP(w_k|s_{ij}) + logP(s_{ij})) \\ &+ logP_{wn}(s_{ij})\} \end{aligned} \tag{11}$$

where w_k is the k-th word in C and n is the number of words in C. In Eq. 11, we assume independence among the words in C.

Probabilities in Eq. 11 are calculated as follows:

$$P(w_k|s_{ij}) = \frac{P(s_{ij}, w_k)}{P(s_{ij})} = \frac{freq(s_{ij}, w_k)}{freq(s_{ij})} \quad (12)$$

$$P(s_{ij}) = \frac{freq(s_{ij})}{CS} \quad (13)$$

$$P_{wn}(s_{ij}) = \frac{0.5 + WNf(s_{ij})}{n * 0.5 + WNf(tw_i)} \quad (14)$$

where $freq(s_{ij}, w_k)$ is the frequency that s_{ij} and w_k co-occur in a corpus, $freq(s_{ij})$ is the frequency of s_{ij} in a corpus, which is the sum of frequencies of all relatives related to s_{ij}. CS means corpus size, which is the sum of frequencies of all words in a corpus. $WNf(s_{ij})$ and $WNf(tw_i)$ are the frequencies of a s_{ij} and tw_i in WordNet, respectively, which represent bias of word senses. Eq. 14 is the same with Eq. 7 in Section 3.

Since the training data are built by collecting example sentences of relatives in the previous works, the frequencies in Eq. 12 and 13 are calculated with our matrix as follows:

$$freq(s_{ij}, w_k) = \sum_{r_l \ related \ to \ s_{ij}} freq(r_l, w_k)$$

$$freq(s_{ij}) = \sum_{r_l \ related \ to \ s_{ij}} freq(r_l)$$

where r_l is a relative related to the sense s_{ij}. $freq(r_l, w_k)$ and $freq(r_l)$ are the co-occurrence frequency between r_l and w_k and the frequency of r_l, respectively, and both frequencies can be obtained by looking up the matrix since the matrix contains the frequencies of words and word pairs.

The main difference between [8] and [9] is whether ambiguous relatives are utilized or not. Considering the difference, we implemented the method of [8] to include the ambiguous relatives into relatives, but the method of [9] to exclude the ambiguous relatives.

Table 2. Comparison results with previous relative-based methods

	S2 LS	S3 LS	S2 ALL	S3 ALL	SemCor
All Relatives	38.86%	42.98%	45.57%	51.20%	53.68%
Unambiguous Relatives	27.40%	24.47%	30.73%	33.61%	30.63%
our method	40.94%	45.12%	45.90%	51.35%	55.58%

Table 3. Comparison results with top 3 systems at SENSEVAL

	S2 LS	S2 ALL	S3 ALL
[15]	40.2%	56.9%	.
[16]	29.3%	45.1%	.
[5]	24.4%	32.8%	.
[17]	.	.	58.3%
[18]	.	.	54.8%
[19]	.	.	48.1%
Our method	40.94%	45.12%	51.35%

Table 2 shows the comparison results.[7] In the table, *All Relatives* and *Unambiguous Relatives* represent the results of the reimplemented methods of [8] and [9], respectively. It is observed in the table that our proposed method achieves better performance on all evaluation data than the previous methods though the improvement is not large. Hence, we may have an idea that our method handles relatives and in particular ambiguous relatives more effectively than [8] and [9].

Compared with [9], [8] obtains a better performance, and the difference between the performance of them are totally more than 15 % on all of the evaluation data. From the comparison results, it is desirable to utilize ambiguous relatives as well as unambiguous relatives.

[10] evaluated their method on nouns of lexical sample task of SENSEVAL-2. Their method achieved 49.8% recall. When evaluated on the same nouns of the lexical sample task, our proposed method achieved 47.26%, and the method of [8] 45.61%, and the method of [9] 38.03%. Compared with our implementations, [10] utilized a web as a raw corpus that is much larger than our raw corpus, and employed various kinds of features such as bigram, trigram, part-of-speeches, etc.[8] Therefore, it can be conjectured that a size of a raw corpus and features play an important role in the performance. We can observe that in our implementation of the method of [9], the data sparseness problem is very serious since unambiguous relatives are usually not frequent in the raw corpus. In the web, the problem seems to be alleviated. Further studies are required for the effects of various features.

[7] Evaluation measure is a *recall*, which is utilized for evaluating systems at SENSEVAL. In the table, S2 means SENSEVAL-2, LS means lexical sample task, and ALL represents all words task.

[8] [10] also utilized the bias information of word senses at WordNet.

Comparison with Systems Participated in SENSEVAL. We also compared our method with the top systems at SENSEVAL that did not use sense tagged corpora.[9] Table 3 shows the official results of the top 3 participating systems at SENSEVAL-2 & 3 and experimental performance of our method. In the table, it is observed that our method is ranked in top 3 systems.

5 Conclusions

We have proposed a simple and novel method that determines senses of all contents words in sentences by selecting a relative of the target words in WordNet. The relative is selected by using a co-occurrence frequency between the relative and the words surrounding the target word in a given sentence. The co-occurrence frequencies are obtained from a raw corpus, not from a sense tagged corpus that is often required by other approaches.

We tested the proposed method on SemCor data and SENSEVAL data, which are publicly available. The experimental results show that the proposed method effectively disambiguates many ambiguous words in SemCor and in test data for SENSEVAL all words task, as well as a small number of ambiguous words in test data for SENSEVAL lexical sample task. Also our method more correctly disambiguates senses than [8] and [9]. Furthermore, the proposed method achieved comparable performance with the top 3 ranked systems at SENSEVAL-2 & 3.

In consequence, our method has two advantages over the previous methods ([8] and [9]): our method 1) handles the ambiguous relatives and unambiguous relatives more effectively, and 2) utilizes only one co-occurrence matrix for disambiguating all contents words instead of collecting training data of the content words.

However, our method did not achieve good performances. One reason of the low performance is on the relatives irrelevant to the target words. That is, investigation of several instances which assign to incorrect senses shows that relatives irrelevant to the target words are often selected as the most probable relatives. Hence, we will try to devise a filtering method that filters out the useless relatives before the relative selection phase. Also we will plan to investigate a large number of tagged instances in order to find out why our method did not achieve much better performance than the previous works and to detect how our method selects the correct relatives more precisely. Finally, we will conduct experiments with various features such as bigrams, trigrams, POSs, etc, which [10] considered and examine a relationship of a size of a raw corpus and a system performance.

---

9 At SENSEVAL, unsupervised systems include the weakly supervised systems though there are some debates. In this paper, our methods are compared with the systems that are classified into the unsupervised approach at SENSEVAL.

References

1. Fellbaum, C.: An WordNet Electronic Lexical Database. The MIT Press (1998)
2. Schütze, H.: Automatic word sense discrimination. Computational Linguistics **24** (1998) 97–123
3. Lesk, M.: Automatic sense disambiguation using machine readable dictionaries: How to tell a pine cone from an ice cream cone. In: Proceedings of the 5th annual international conference on Systems documentation, Toronto, Ontario, Canada (1986) 24–26
4. Karov, Y., Edelman, S.: Similarity-based word sense disambiguation. Computational Linguistics **24** (1998) 41–59
5. Haynes, S.: Semantic tagging using WordNet examples. In: Proceedings of SENSEVAL-2 Second International Workshop on Evaluating Word Sense Disambiguation Systems, Toulouse, France (2001) 79–82
6. Agirre, E., Rigau, G.: Word sense disambiguation using conceptual density. In: Proceedings of COLING'96, Copenhagen Denmark (1996) 16–22
7. Fernandez-Amoros, D., Gonzalo, J., Verdejo, F.: The role of conceptual relations in word sense disambiguation. In: Proceedings of the 6th International Workshop on Applications of Natural Language for Information Systems, Madrid, Spain (2001) 87–98
8. Yarowsky, D.: Word-sense disambiguation using statistical models of Roget's categories trained on large corpora. In: Proceedings of COLING-92, Nantes, France (1992) 454–460
9. Leacock, C., Chodorow, M., Miller, G.A.: Using corpus statistics and WordNet relations for sense identification. Computational Linguistics **24** (1998) 147–165
10. Agirre, E., Martinez, D.: Unsupervised wsd based on automatically retrieved examples: The importance of bias. In: Proceedings of the Conference on Empirical Methods in Natural Language Processing (EMNLP), Barcelona, Spain (2004)
11. Lee, L.: Similarity-Based Approaches to Natural Language Processing. PhD thesis, Harvard University, Cambridge, MA (1997)
12. Miller, G.A., Leacock, C., Tengi, R., Bunker, R.: A semantic concordance. In: Proceedings of the 3 DARPA Workshop on Human Language Technology. (1993) 303–308
13. Marcus, M.P., Santorini, B., Marcinkiewicz, M.A.: Building a large annotated corpus of english: The penn treebank. Computational Linguistics **19** (1994) 313–330
14. Schmid, H.: Probabilistic part-of-speech tagging using decision trees. In: Proceedings of the Conference on New Methods in Language Processing, Manchester, UK (1994)
15. Fernandez-Amoros, D., Gonzalo, J., Verdejo, F.: The UNED systems at SENSEVAL-2. In: Proceedings of SENSEVAL-2 Second International Workshop on Evaluating Word Sense Disambiguation Systems, Toulouse, France (2001) 75–78
16. Litkowski, K.: SENSEVAL-2:overview. In: Proceedings of SENSEVAL-2 Second International Workshop on Evaluating Word Sense Disambiguation Systems, Toulouse, France (2001) 107–110

17. Strapparava, C., Gliozzo, A., Giuliano, C.: Pattern abstraction and term similarity for word sense disambiguation: Irst at senseval-3. In: Proceedings of SENSEVAL-3: Third International Workshop on the Evaluation of Systems for the Semantic Analysis of Text, Barcelona, Spain (2004) 229–234
18. Fernandez-Amoros, D.: Wsd based on mutual information and syntactic patterns. In: Proceedings of SENSEVAL-3: Third International Workshop on the Evaluation of Systems for the Semantic Analysis of Text, Barcelona, Spain (2004) 117–120
19. Buscaldi, D., Rosso, P., Masulli, F.: The upv-unige-ciaosenso wsd system. In: Proceedings of SENSEVAL-3: Third International Workshop on the Evaluation of Systems for the Semantic Analysis of Text, Barcelona, Spain (2004) 77–82

Towards Robust High Performance Word Sense Disambiguation of English Verbs Using Rich Linguistic Features

Jinying Chen and Martha Palmer

Department of Computer and Information Science,
University of Pennsylvania, Philadelphia, PA, 19104, USA
{jinying, mpalmer}@cis.upenn.edu

Abstract. This paper shows that our WSD system using rich linguistic features achieved high accuracy in the classification of English SENSEVAL2 verbs for both fine-grained (64.6%) and coarse-grained (73.7%) senses. We describe three specific enhancements to our treatment of rich linguistic features and present their separate and combined contributions to our system's performance. Further experiments showed that our system had robust performance on test data without high quality rich features.

1 Introduction

Word sense disambiguation (WSD) has been regarded as essential or necessary in many high-level NLP applications that require a certain degree of semantic interpretation, such as machine translation, information retrieval (IR) and question answering, *etc.* However, previous investigations into the role of WSD in IR have shown that low accuracy in WSD negated any possible performance increase from ambiguity resolution [1,2]. This suggests that improving the performance of WSD systems is crucial for applications to attain benefits from WSD.

Much effort has been aimed at the creation of sense tagged corpora that can be used to develop supervised WSD systems with high accuracy.[1] However, highly polysemous words with subtle sense distinctions still pose major challenges for automatic systems, as evidenced in SENSEVAL2 [3]. This problem seems more serious for verbs, as indicated by the relatively poorer performance achieved by the best system in the SENSEVAL2 English lexical sample task for verbs: 56.6% accuracy, in contrast with the 64.2% accuracy for all parts-of-speech [4,5]. On the other hand, disambiguating verb senses accurately is very important for lexical selection in MT. It is also helpful for information retrieval, especially for fact retrieval systems that take full-sentence queries as their input. Therefore, this paper will focus on improving the accuracy of our supervised WSD system for verbs.

We are using a linguistically rich approach for verb sense disambiguation. Linguistically rich approaches [5-9] utilize syntactic and/or semantic features, e.g., syntactic relations, selectional preferences, and semantic information of NP arguments of verbs,

[1] http://www.senseval.org/

R. Dale et al. (Eds.): IJCNLP 2005, LNAI 3651, pp. 933–944, 2005.

etc. In verb sense disambiguation, Dang and Palmer's work [5] demonstrated that their system, which achieved 59.6% accuracy (62.5% in a recent report [10]) in disambiguating the SENSEVAL2 English verbs, benefited substantially from using rich linguistic features that capture information about a verb's lexical semantics.

On the other hand, the performance of a system using rich linguistic features relies heavily on the quality of preprocessing, such as part-of-speech tagging, parsing, feature extraction and generation, *etc.* How accurate and how robust can such a system be? In particular, we are interested in the following three questions: *How much advantage can we gain from the rich-feature approach by careful extraction and treatment of the rich features? How much will a relatively poor quality of preprocessing negatively affect the system's performance? Which strategies can we adopt to alleviate these negative effects?*

To address the first question, we enhance the feature extraction and generation of our original system, which was inspired by Dang's system[10], in three ways. First, to increase the recall of the extraction of a verb's subject, we carefully handle relative clauses, nonfinite clauses, and verbs within prepositional phrases by using linguistic knowledge and heuristics. Second, to treat semantic features of NP arguments of verbs and prepositions in a more uniform way, we incorporate a rule-based pronoun resolver and also unify the semantic features generated by WordNet [11] and by a named entity tagger. Third, we treat sentential complements of verbs in a verb-specific way. Our evaluation on the SENSEVAL2 English verbs shows that our new system achieves 64.6% accuracy, which is significantly better than the best system on English verbs in SENSEVAL2 (57.6%) and also outperforms Dang's system (62.5%). Further experiments indicate that the three enhancements are all beneficial. They each boost the system's performance by 1.0~1.2 percent and the combined gain is 2.6 percent. A similar performance improvement is achieved for coarse-grained senses: 73.7% vs. Dang's 71.7%. The data analysis of the results suggests that further improvements may come from disambiguating WordNet synsets and from using statistical methods for subject extraction and pronoun resolution.

We address the last two robustness questions in two more experiments. To investigate how the parser's performance affects our system, we divide the test data into an easy set that is similar to the parser's training material and a hard set that is not. The evaluation shows that although our system's accuracy is lower on the hard set, it is still high (62.2%). In the second experiment, our system is trained with rich features and tested on data with linguistically impoverished features. The results show little penalty from missing rich features at the test phase. The observations from this experiment also suggest the following strategy for using WSD systems that utilize rich linguistic features. When good parsers are not available at the time of application, the use of topical features and any available, accurate rich features (e.g., features associated with the verb's direct object) will alleviate penalties.

The rest of the paper is organized as follows. We introduce our system and the three major enhancements we made in Section 2. In Section 3, we show the evaluation results on SENSEVAL2 English verbs and show how much the three enhancements improve our system's performance. We then discuss the potential improvements of our system in the future. In Section 4, we investigate the robustness of our system and propose our strategy for alleviating the negative effects of poor preprocessing. We conclude our discussion in Section 5.

2 System Description

Our original WSD system was inspired by the successful MaxEnt WSD system of Dang [5,10]. We used the same machine learning model, Mallet, that implements a smoothing maximum entropy (ME) model with a Gaussian prior [12]. An attractive property of ME models is that there is no assumption of feature independence [13]. Empirical studies have shown that a ME model with a Gaussian prior generally outperforms ME models with other smoothing methods [14]. In addition to topical and collocation features, we also used similar rich syntactic and semantic features, although we implemented them in different ways. Furthermore, we enhanced the treatment of certain rich linguistic features, which we believed would boost the system's performance. Before discussing these enhancements, we first briefly describe the basic syntactic and semantic features used by our system:

Syntactic features:

1. Is the sentence passive, semi-passive[2] or active?
2. Does the target verb have a subject or object? If so, what is the head of its subject or/and object?
3. Does the target verb have a sentential complement?
4. Does the target verb have a PP adjunct? If so, what is the preposition and what is the head of the NP argument of the preposition?

Semantic features:

1. The Named Entity tags of proper nouns and certain types of common nouns
2. The WordNet synsets and hypernyms of head nouns of the NP arguments of verbs and prepositions

To better explore the advantage of using rich syntactic and semantic features, we enhanced our original system in three primary aspects: increasing the recall of the extraction of a verb's subject; unifying the treatment of semantic features of pronouns, common nouns and proper nouns; and providing a verb-specific treatment of sentential complements. These are each described in more detail below.

2.1 Increasing Subject Extraction Recall

To extract a subject, our original system simply checks the left NP siblings of the highest VP that contains the target verb and is within the innermost clause (see Figure 1). This method has high precision but low recall. Typical examples from SENSEVAL2 data that are not handled by this approach are shown in (1a-c).[3]

(1) a. **Relative clauses:** For Republicans$_{sbj}$ [$_{SBAR}$ who began$_{verb}$ this campaign with such high hopes], ...

b. **Nonfinite clauses:** I$_{sbj}$ didn't ever want [$_{S}$ to see$_{verb}$ that woman again].

c. **Verbs within PP's:** Karipo and her women$_{sbj}$ had succeeded [$_{PP}$ in driving$_{verb}$ a hundred invaders from the isle ...]

---

[2] Verbs that are past participles and are not preceded by *be* or *have* verbs are semi-passive.

[3] The target verb and its subject or subject candidates are underlined and the innermost clause or the PP containing the verb is bracketed.

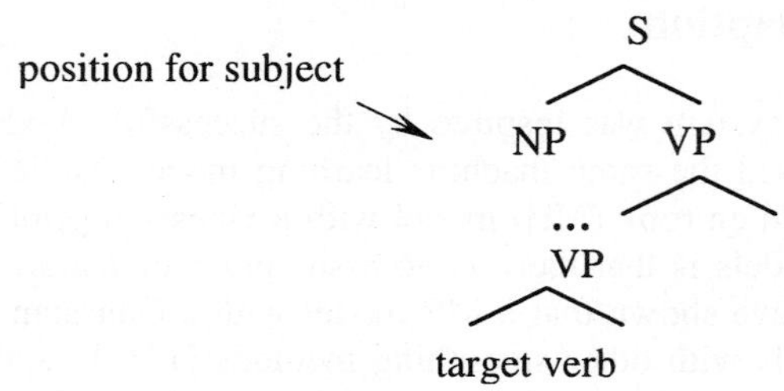

Fig. 1. position for verb's subject

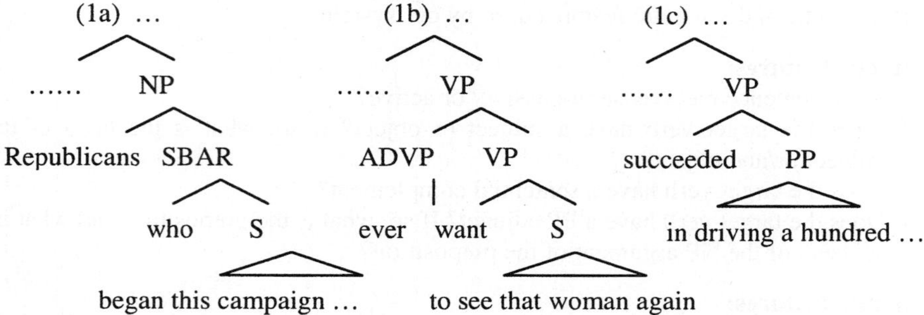

To increase the recall, we refined the procedure of subject extraction by adding rules based on linguistic knowledge and bracketing labels that can handle relative clauses, nonfinite clauses, and verbs within prepositional phrases (PP's). For example, for cases like (1a), if a clause containing the target verb has a bracketing label SBAR and an NP parent, and is headed by a relative pronoun such as *that, which* or *who*, then check its left NP siblings for the verb's subject. For cases like (1b) and (1c), if the parent node of a nonfinite clause S or a PP is a VP, then continue searching positions outside the S or PP. For the last case, we also use a heuristic, i.e., a check as to whether the subject candidate is a person or an organization, to filter out non-person-and-organization candidate NPs whose parent nodes are not labeled as S or SBAR. Many cases like (2a-b) can be handled correctly using this heuristic.

(2) a. A number of accounts of the events accused the ministry$_{\text{sbj}}$ [$_{\text{PP}}$ of pulling$_{\text{verb}}$ the plug on the UAL deal ...].

b. Mr. Wolf$_{\text{sbj}}$ faces a monumental task [$_{\text{PP}}$ in pulling$_{\text{verb}}$ the company back together again].

The above rule-based approach does not handle difficult cases like (3a-b) very well.

(3) a. Freddy's instinct was [$_{\text{S}}$ to keep$_{\text{verb}}$ growing by stock mergers and small expenditure of cash ...]

b. The arrangement I had with him was [$_{\text{S}}$ to work$_{\text{verb}}$ four hours a day].

With this enhancement, our new system extracts about 35% more subjects than before.

2.2 Unifying Semantic Features

In this section we describe the changes to the use of semantic features. In order to provide a more uniform treatment for the semantic features of the NP arguments of verbs and prepositions, we first merge the semantic features associated with proper nouns and common nouns. We then extend our treatment to include pronouns by adding a pronoun resolution module.

2.2.1 Merging Semantic Features

Our system used an automatic named entity tagger, *IdentiFinder*^{TM} [15], to tag proper nouns with **Person, Organization** and **Location** and common nouns with **Date, Time, Percent** and **Money**. Additional semantic features are all WordNet synsets and hypernyms[4] of the head nouns of NP arguments, i.e., the system does not disambiguate different WordNet senses of a head noun.

To utilize semantic features more efficiently, we refine their treatment. Previously there was no overlap between semantic features generated by the named entity tagger and by WordNet. For example, a personal proper noun only has a **Person** tag that has no similarity to the WordNet synsets and hypernyms associated with similar common nouns such as *specialist* and *doctor, etc.* This is likely to be a problem for many WSD tasks that usually have small amounts of training data, such as SENSEVAL2. To overcome this problem, our new system associates a common noun (or a noun phrase) with each Named Entity tag (see 4) and adds the WordNet semantic features of these nouns (or noun phrases) to the original semantic feature set.

(4) Person – someone, Organization – organization, Location – location
Time – time unit, Date – time period, Percent – percent, Money – money

2.2.2 Adding Pronoun Resolution

Our original system has no special treatment for pronouns, although a rough count shows that about half of the training instances contain pronominal arguments. Lacking a high performance automatic pronoun resolution module, we adopt a hybrid approach. For personal pronouns, we simply treat them as personal proper nouns. For the rest of the pronouns including *they, them, it, themselves* and *itself*, which occur in about 13% of the training instances, we programmed a rather simple rule-based pronoun resolver. In brief, the resolver searches the parse tree for antecedent candidates similarly to Hobb's algorithm as exemplified in [16] and uses several syntactic and semantic constraints to filter out impossible candidates. The constraints include syntactic constraints for anaphora antecedents [16], number agreement, and whether the candidate is a person. The first candidate that survives the filtering is regarded as the antecedent of the pronoun and its semantic features are added to the original feature set.

2.3 Verb-Specific Sentential Complements

The different types of sentential complements can be very useful for distinguishing certain verb senses. (5a-b) shows two sentences containing the verb *call* in the SENSEVAL2 training data. *Call* has WordNet Sense 1 (name) in (5a) and Sense 3

---

[4] A unique number defined in WordNet represents each synset or hypernym.

(ascribe) in (5b). In both cases, *call* takes a small clause as its sentential complement, i.e., it has the subcategorization frame X *call* Y Z. The difference is that Z is a Named Entity when *call* is in Sense 1, and Z is usually a common NP or an adjective phrase (ADJP) when *call* is in Sense 3.

(5) a. The slender, handsome fellow was $\underline{\text{called}}_{\text{verb}}$ [$_S$ Dandy Brandon].
b.The White House is purposely not $\underline{\text{calling}}_{\text{verb}}$ [$_S$ the meeting a summit] …

Another example is shown in (6). The verb *keep* has WordNet Sense 1 (maintain) in (6a) and Sense 2 (continue) in (6b). In Sense 1, *keep* often takes a small clause and has the subcategorization frame X *keep* Y ADJP. In contrast, *keep* takes a sentential complement the head verb of which is in the present tense when it is in Sense 2.

(6) a. He shook his head, $\underline{\text{kept}}_{\text{verb}}$ [$_S$ his face expressionless].
b. We $\underline{\text{keep}}_{\text{verb}}$ [$_S$ wondering what Mr. Gates wanted to say].

Our original system uses a single feature *hasSent* to represent whether the target verb has a sentential complement or not, which cannot capture the rich information that is crucial to distinguishing certain verb senses but is deeply embedded in the sentential complements, as described above. Therefore, we treat sentential complements in a more fine-grained, verb-specific way. We resort to WordNet and PropBank [17] for the information about verb subcategorization frames. Another advantage of this verb-specific treatment is that it can filter out illegal sentential complements generated by the parser.

3 System Evaluation

Since the more recent SENSEVAL3 data were collected over the internet and had a relatively low quality of annotation, we decided to evaluate our new system on the SENSEVAL2 English verbs. Ratnaparkhi's MaxEnt sentence boundary detector and POS tagger [18], Bikel's parsing engine [19], and a named entity tagger, *IdentiFinder*[TM] [15], were used to preprocess the training and test data automatically.

3.1 Experimental Results

Table 1 shows the performance of our system (MX-RF) on the 29 verbs with fine-grained WordNet senses. Columns 2 and 3 show the number of senses and normalized sense perplexity[5] for each verb in the test data respectively. It also gives the performance of the best system on English verbs in SENSEVAL2, KUNLP [5], and Dang's system [10]. As we see, our system achieves an average accuracy of 64.6%, which is significantly better than KUNLP (57.6%) that only uses linguistically impoverished features (topical and collocation features). Our system also outperforms Dang's system (62.5%). Recall that the types of rich linguistic features used by our system were originally inspired by Dang's system, although we implemented them in different ways. Therefore, we attribute the more success of our new system mainly to the three

[5] It is calculated as the entropy of the sense distribution of a verb in the test data divided by the largest possible entropy, i.e., $\log_2$ (the number of senses of the verb in the test data).

specific enhancements we made. To our best knowledge, the accuracy our system achieved is the best result for this task at present.

To investigate exactly how much we gain by enhancing the system in the three ways discussed in Section 2, we tested our system by removing our refinements (subject extraction, pronoun coreferences, and verb-specific sentential complements) separately and all together. The results (columns 8-11) show that each refinement boosts the system's performance by 1.0~1.2 percent and that together they achieve an improvement of 2.6 percent. This confirms the utility of these enhancements.

In addition to fine-grained verb senses, we also evaluated our system on coarse-grained senses (see Table 2). Previous work [20] suggested that not all NLP applications need fine-grained sense distinctions; in some cases coarser granularities will suffice. Furthermore, it has been demonstrated that annotation with coarser senses is much faster and more accurate [21]. The SENSEVAL2 verb senses have been grouped by using both syntactic and semantic criteria, with a resulting inter-annotator agreement (ITA) of 82% (column 4). As we expected, the accuracy of our system increases by about 9 percent on the coarse-grained senses to 73.7%, which again consistently outperforms Dang's system (71.7%).

3.2 Discussion

Compared verb-by-verb, the performance of our system is better than or comparable to Dang's on most verbs, except that it has notably lower accuracy on *develop, dress* and *serve*. It is not obvious why, since although our features are similar to Dang's, the implementations are different. Nevertheless, an investigation of the specific features our system generated for these three verbs gives us a few clues. The semantic categories of the direct objects of the three verbs are very diverse, so there are not enough instances of similar categories for the model to generalize. Therefore, the system performance benefits little from our enhancements. In fact, our system may be more susceptible to noisy data introduced by the pronoun resolver for these three verbs. Erroneous antecedents found by the resolver are indistinguishable from the actual direct objects that occur rarely in the training data, and therefore they get the same treatment from the machine learning algorithm.

The experimental results and the above data analysis suggest that our system can be improved further by increasing the accuracy of subject extraction and pronoun resolution. We expect a state-of-the-art pronoun resolution module and a statistical subject finder to do better jobs in the future. Our current system does not distinguish senses of nouns when using WordNet synsets and hypernyms as semantic features, which introduces many irrelevant features (associated with the irrelevant senses). The machine learning algorithm sometimes cannot generalize well using these features. A potential solution for this problem is to distinguish the senses of the target verb and its NP arguments simultaneously. Furthermore, we need to have a better generalization, or clustering, of WordNet synsets and hypernyms, especially when the subject or object of a verb has semantic versatility. More performance improvements will bring us closer to our goal of an overall level of accuracy of 80%, especially with respect to coarse-grained senses, that should finally be more beneficial to NLP applications.

Table 1. Evaluation of MX-RF on the SENSEVAL2 English verbs, with fine-grained senses

Verb	#of Sen	Sen Per-plex.	ITA	KUNLP	Dang 2004	MX-RF	MX-RF w/o sbj extract.	MX-RF w/o pron.	MX-RF w/o verb spec sent-comp	MX-RF w/o all three
begin	**7**	**0.63**	**81.2**	**81.4**	**89.3**	**91.2**	**90.0**	**90.4**	**89.3**	**88.6**
call	**17**	**0.86**	**69.3**	**48.5**	**54.5**	**56.8**	**56.8**	**55.3**	**53.8**	**52.3**
carry	**19**	**0.87**	**60.7**	**45.5**	**39.4**	**44.7**	**45.5**	**40.2**	**43.2**	**42.4**
collab-orate	**2**	**0.47**	**75.0**	**90.0**	**90.0**	**90.0**	**90.0**	**90.0**	**90.0**	**90.0**
develop	**14**	**0.82**	**67.8**	**42.0**	**58.0**	**49.3**	**49.3**	**50.7**	**49.3**	**49.3**
draw	**21**	**0.95**	**76.7**	**34.1**	**31.7**	**41.5**	**39.0**	**34.1**	**41.5**	**36.6**
dress	**12**	**0.79**	**86.5**	**71.2**	**72.9**	**64.4**	**64.4**	**69.5**	**67.8**	**64.4**
drift	**9**	**0.89**	**50.0**	**53.1**	**40.6**	**67.2**	**51.6**	**60.9**	**64.1**	**48.4**
drive	**13**	**0.84**	**58.8**	**54.8**	**59.5**	**60.7**	**60.7**	**58.3**	**60.7**	**58.3**
face	**6**	**0.38**	**78.6**	**82.8**	**83.9**	**81.2**	**82.3**	**83.3**	**81.2**	**83.3**
ferret	**0**	**0.00**	**1.00**	**100.0**	**100.0**	**100.0**	**100.0**	**100.0**	**100.0**	**100.0**
find	**17**	**0.94**	**44.3**	**27.9**	**36.8**	**41.2**	**36.8**	**36.8**	**36.8**	**33.8**
keep	**20**	**0.79**	**79.1**	**44.8**	**61.2**	**64.2**	**61.9**	**65.7**	**61.2**	**57.5**
leave	**10**	**0.86**	**67.2**	**50.0**	**60.6**	**57.6**	**57.6**	**54.5**	**53.0**	**50.0**
live	**9**	**0.70**	**79.7**	**59.7**	**70.1**	**69.4**	**69.4**	**67.9**	**69.4**	**67.9**
match	**7**	**0.79**	**56.5**	**52.4**	**50.0**	**59.5**	**61.9**	**57.1**	**59.5**	**57.1**
play	**20**	**0.85**	**N/A**	**37.9**	**53.0**	**62.1**	**59.1**	**62.1**	**62.1**	**62.1**
pull	**25**	**0.89**	**68.1**	**45.0**	**50.0**	**58.3**	**56.6**	**58.3**	**53.3**	**56.7**
replace	**4**	**0.85**	**65.9**	**55.6**	**60.0**	**61.1**	**60.0**	**55.5**	**61.1**	**57.8**
see	**13**	**0.84**	**70.9**	**39.1**	**39.1**	**44.2**	**39.9**	**42.8**	**41.3**	**35.5**
serve	**11**	**0.85**	**90.8**	**68.6**	**74.5**	**68.6**	**66.7**	**64.7**	**68.6**	**66.7**
strike	**20**	**0.89**	**76.2**	**40.7**	**38.9**	**51.9**	**50.0**	**53.7**	**51.9**	**55.6**
train	**8**	**0.87**	**28.8**	**58.7**	**63.5**	**60.3**	**60.3**	**63.5**	**60.3**	**63.5**
treat	**5**	**0.88**	**96.9**	**56.8**	**50.0**	**50.0**	**50.0**	**52.3**	**50.0**	**56.8**
turn	**26**	**0.93**	**74.2**	**37.3**	**49.3**	**48.5**	**44.0**	**47.8**	**47.0**	**46.3**
use	**6**	**0.65**	**74.3**	**65.8**	**71.1**	**69.7**	**72.4**	**68.4**	**69.7**	**68.4**
wander	**5**	**0.47**	**65.0**	**82.0**	**80.0**	**82.0**	**82.0**	**82.0**	**82.0**	**82.0**
wash	**7**	**0.94**	**87.5**	**83.3**	**66.7**	**75.0**	**75.0**	**75.0**	**75.0**	**75.0**
work	**18**	**0.84**	**N/A**	**45.0**	**45.0**	**53.3**	**51.7**	**50.0**	**53.3**	**43.3**
average	**12**	**0.77**	**71.3**	**57.6**	**62.5**	**64.6**	**63.4**	**63.6**	**63.4**	**62.0**

Table 2. Evaluation of MX-RF on coarse-grained senses of the SENSEVAL2 English verbs

	# of grp	ITA grp	Acc. of Dang 2004	Acc. of MX-RF
Ave. on 29 verbs	**5.9**	**82.0**	**71.7**	**73.7**

4 System Robustness

A frequent criticism of systems using rich linguistic features is that they do not port well to domains for which accurate preprocessors are not available. In this section we discuss two experiments designed to address the following two questions: How much will a relatively poor quality of preprocessing negatively affect the system's performance? Which strategies can we adopt to alleviate these negative effects?

4.1 Experiment I

Since the parser is the most critical component of our preprocessing and is more likely to have lower performance when it is used in an unfamiliar data set, we investigate how the performance of the parser on different test data sets affects our system. We divided the SENSEVAL2 test data into two sets: an easy set and a hard set. The test data from the Wall Street Journal (wsj) sections of Penn Treebank (PTB) [22] are put into the easy set because they are similar to the parser's training data: 02-21 wsj sections. The hard set contains test data from the Brown sections of PTB and BNC data. It is expected that the parser and therefore the system will perform better on the easy set. We trained our system on the whole SENSEVAL2 training data set and evaluated its performance on the easy and hard test sets separately. The results are shown in Table 3.

Table 3. Performance on different test data sets

Test data set	Hard	Easy	Whole Set
Num. of test inst.	**895**	**911**	**1806**
Average Acc.	**62.2**	**66.9**	**64.6**

As we expected, the system's performance on the hard test set is 4.7 percent lower than on the easy set. On the other hand, even on the hard set, its accuracy (62.2%) is still high and is comparable to Dang's system. It is worth noting that the experiment is preliminary because the easy set and the hard set are most likely to be different not only on whether they are familiar to the parser but also on the subtlety and distributions of their senses. Nevertheless, it is evidence of our system's robustness.

4.2 Experiment I I

There will be situations where systems trained with rich linguistic features extracted from high quality parses will be run on applications where such rich features will not be available. It is most likely that systems in such situations will go back to a position similar to where rich features are not available in both the training and test phases. However, could things get even worse? A machine learning model often tends to favor informative features (e.g., rich linguistic features in our case) and fit the distribution of these features well in its training phase. Therefore, it is expected that the model will be penalized more heavily when these informative features are used in its training phase but are not accessible in its test phase. In this subsection, we discuss a second experiment to test the robustness of our system in such situations and explore possible strategies for alleviating penalties.

We trained our system with rich features of the SENSEVAL2 training data and tested its performance on the SENSEVAL2 test data with three different feature sets: a rich set containing topical, collocation, syntactic and semantic features (top+col+syn+sem), a poor set containing topical and collocation features (top+col) and a medium set containing topical and collocation features plus features for direct objects (top+col+obj). The reason we include the medium set is that a parser can usually find the direct object of verbs. Furthermore, we trained and tested our system on SENSEVAL2 data with linguistically impoverished features (top+col) and used this result as a control. As shown in Table 4, the system's accuracy drops to the same level as the control (58.0% vs. 58.1%) when it is trained with rich features but tested with poor features. When the features associated with the verb's direct object are added, the system's performance improves (59.1%).

The experimental results here suggest that our system has not been penalized very much when rich linguistic features are only available in its training phase. Intuitively, the topical features[6] our system uses alleviate the penalty. As expected, when the topical features of the test data were excluded, the performance of our system dropped to 54.8%. But this will be a common problem for all systems using topical features, not only for systems using rich linguistic features.[7] These results suggest a strategy for using our system and other similar systems in a more robust way. When a state-of-art parser is not available for the application data, topical features can be used to alleviate the penalty. Rich features that can be obtained more easily and reliably, e.g., features associated with the direct object of verbs, can also be used whenever they are available.

Table 4. Performance of our system trained and tested on data sets with different features

Training set / Test set	top+col+syn+sem	top+col
top+col+syn+sem	**64.6**	
top+col	**58.0**	**58.1**
top+col+obj	**59.1**	

5 Conclusion

We have shown that our system using rich linguistic features was more successful, compared with the previous best systems, in classifying the fine-grained and coarse-grained SENSEVAL2 verb senses. The three enhancements to the system's treatment

[6] Our system uses all the contextual nouns, verbs, adjectives and adverbs that are not in a stop word list as topical features.

[7] In fact, the performance of our system trained with (top+col) features and tested with only collocation features also dropped to 55.8%, in contrast to the control accuracy 58.1%.

of rich linguistic features were beneficial. Further improvements may come from disambiguating WordNet synsets and improving the accuracy of subject extraction and pronoun resolution. Furthermore, our system was robust when it was applied to test data that had a relatively poor quality of rich features. Based on the experimental results, we proposed a strategy for using systems with rich features in a more robust way. Our goal is to continue to improve the performance of our current WSD system, with respect to both fine-grained and coarse-grained senses, so that it becomes increasingly beneficial to NLP applications.

References

1. Mark Sanderson: Word sense disambiguation and information retrieval. In Proceedings of the 17th Int. ACM SIGIR, Dublin, IE (1994).
2. Christopher Stokoe, Michael P. Oakes, John Tait: Word sense disambiguation and information retrieval revisited. In Proceedings of the 26th annual int. ACM SIGIR conference on research and development in information retrieval. Toronto, Canada (2003).
3. Philip Edmonds and Scott Cotton: SENSEVAL-2: Overview. In Proceedings of SENSEVAL-2: 2nd Int. Workshop on Evaluating WSD Systems. ACL-SIGLEX, Toulouse, France (2001).
4. David Yarowsky, Silviu Cucerzan, Radu Florian, Charles Schafer and Richard Wicentowski: The Johns hopkins SENSEVAL2 system description. In Proceedings of SENSEVAL-2: 2nd Int.Workshop on Evaluating WSD Systems. Toulouse France (2001).
5. Hoa T. Dang and Martha Palmer: Combining contextual features for word sense disambiguation. In Proceedings of the SIGLEX/SENSEVAL Workshop on WSD: Recent Successes and Future Directions, in conjunction with ACL-02, Philadelphia (2002).
6. Martínez David, Agirre Enek. and Màrquez Liuis: Syntactic Features for High Precision Word Sense Disambiguation. In Proceedings of the 19th International COLING. Taipei (2002).
7. Dekang Lin: Using Syntactic Dependency as Local Context to Resolve Word Sense Ambiguity In Proceedings of ACL-97, Madrid, Spain (1997).
8. Yoong Keok Lee and Hwee Tou Ng: An empirical evaluation of knowledge sources and learning algorithms for word sense disambiguation. In Proceedings of the Conference on Empirical Methods in Natural Language Processing (EMNLP) (2002) pages 41–48.
9. Rada Mihalcea and Ehsanul Faruque: Sense Learner: Minimally Supervised Word Sense Disambiguation for All Words in Open Text. In Proceedings of SENSEVAL-3: Third International Workshop on the Evaluation of Systems for the Semantic Analysis of Text, Barcelona, Spain (2004).
10. Hoa T. Dang: Investigations into the role of lexical semantics in word sense disambiguation. PhD Thesis. University of Pennsylvania (2004).
11. Christiane Fellbaum: WordNet - an Electronic Lexical Database. The MIT Press, Cambridge, Massachusetts, London, UK (1998).
12. Andrew K. McCallum: MALLET: A Machine Learning for Language Toolkit. http://www.cs. umass.edu/~mccallum/mallet (2002).
13. Adam L. Berger, Stephen A. Della Piertra, and Vincent J. Della Pietra: A maximum entropy approach to natural language processing. Compuational Linguistics, (1996) 22(1): 39-71.
14. Stanley. F. Chen and Ronald Rosenfeld: A Gaussian prior for smoothing maximum entropy models. Technical Report CMU-CS-99-108, CMU (1999).

15. Daniel M. Bikel, Richard Schwartz and Ralph M. Weischedel: An algorithm that learns what's in a name. Machine Learning, (1999) 34(1-3). Special Issue on Natural Language Learning.
16. Shalom Lappin and Herbert Leass: An algorithm for pronominal anaphora resolution. Computational Linguistics, (1994) 20(4): 535-561.
17. Paul Kingsbury, Martha Palmer, and Mitch Marcus: Adding semantic annotation to the Penn Tree-Bank. In Proceedings of HLT 2002, San Diego, CA (2002).
18. Adwait Ratnaparkhi: Maximum entropy models for natural language ambiguity resolution. Ph.D. thesis, University of Pennsylvania (1998).
19. 19 Daniel M. Bikel: Design of a multi-lingual, parallel-processing statistical parsing engine.In Proceedings of HLT 2002. San Diego, CA (2002).
20. Paul Buitelaar: Reducing lexical semantic complexity with systematic polysemous classes and underspecification. In Poceedings of the ANLP Workshop on Syntactic and Semantic Complexity in NLP Systems. Seattle, WA (2000).
21. Martha Palmer, Olga B. Malaya and Hoa T. Dang: Different sense granularities for different appli-cations. In Proceedings of HLT/NAACL-04. Boston (2004).
22. Mitchell Marcus, Grace Kim, Mary A. Marcinkiewicz, Robert MacIntyre, Mark Ferguson, Karen Katz and Britta Schasberger: The Penn Treebank: annotating predicate argument structure. In Proceedings of the ARPA'94 HLT Workshop (1994).

Automatic Interpretation of Noun Compounds Using WordNet Similarity

Su Nam Kim[1,2] and Timothy Baldwin[2,3]

[1] Computer Science, University of Illinois, Chicago, IL 60607 USA
sunamkim@gmail.com
[2] Computer Science and Software Engineering,
University of Melbourne, Victoria 3010 Australia
[3] NICTA Victoria Lab, University of Melbourne, Victoria 3010 Australia
tim@csse.unimelb.edu.au

Abstract. The paper introduces a method for interpreting novel noun compounds with semantic relations. The method is built around word similarity with pretagged noun compounds, based on `WordNet::Similarity`. Over 1,088 training instances and 1,081 test instances from the Wall Street Journal in the Penn Treebank, the proposed method was able to correctly classify 53.3% of the test noun compounds. We also investigated the relative contribution of the modifier and the head noun in noun compounds of different semantic types.

1 Introduction

A **noun compound** (NC) is an $\bar{\mathrm{N}}$ made up of two or more nouns, such as *golf club* or *paper submission*; we will refer to the rightmost noun as the **head noun** and the remainder of nouns in the NC as **modifiers**. The interpretation of noun compounds is a well-researched area in natural language processing, and has been applied in applications such as question answering and machine translation [1,2,3]. Three basic properties make the interpretation of NCs difficult [4]: (1) the compounding process is extremely productive; (2) the semantic relationship between head noun and modifier in the noun compounds is implicit; and (3) the interpretation can be influenced by contextual and pragmatic factors.

In this paper, we are interested in recognizing the semantic relationship between the head noun and modifier(s) of noun compounds. We introduce a method based on word similarity between the component nouns in an unseen test instance NC and annotated training instance NCs. Due to its simplicity, our method is able to interpret NCs with significantly reduced cost. We also investigate the relative contribution of the head noun and modifier in determining the semantic relation.

For the purposes of this paper, we focus exclusively on binary NCs, that is NCs made up of two nouns. This is partly an empirical decision, in that the majority of NCs occurring in unrestricted text are binary,[1] and also partly due to there being existing methods for disambiguating the syntactic structure of higher-arity NCs, effectively decomposing them into multiple binary NCs [3]. Note also that in this paper, we

[1] We estimate that 88.4% of NCs in the Wall Street Journal section of the Penn Treebank and 90.6% of NCs in the British National Corpus are binary.

R. Dale et al. (Eds.): IJCNLP 2005, LNAI 3651, pp. 945–956, 2005.

distinguish semantic relations from semantic roles. The semantic relation in an NC is the underlying relation between the head noun and its modifier, whereas its semantic role is an indication of its relation to the governing verb and other constituents in the sentence context.

There is a significant body of closely-related research on interpreting semantic relations in NCs which relies on hand-written rules. [5] examined the problem of interpretation of NCs and constructed a set of hand-written rules. [6] automatically extracted semantic information from an on-line dictionary and manipulated a set of hand-written rules to assign weights to semantic relations. Recently, there has been work on the automatic (or semi-automatic) interpretation of NCs [4,7,8]. However, most of this work is based on a simplifying assumption as to the scope of semantic relations or the domain of interpretation, making it difficult to compare the performance of NC interpretation in a broader context.

In the remainder of the paper, we detail the motivation for our work (Section 2), introduce the `WordNet::Similarity` system which we use to calculate word similarity (Section 3), outline the set of semantic relations used (Section 4), detail how we collected the data (Section 5), introduce the proposed method (Section 6), and describe experimental results (Section 7).

2 Motivation

Most work related to interpreting NCs depends on hand-coded rules [5]. The first attempt at automatic interpretation by [6] showed that it was possible to successfully interpret NCs. However, the system involved costly hand-written rules involving manual intervention. [9] estimated the amount of world knowledge required to interpret NCs and claimed that the high cost of data acquisition offsets the benefits of automatic interpretation of NCs.

Recent work [4,7,8] has investigated methods for interpreting NCs automatically with minimal human effort. [10] introduced a semi-automatic method for recognizing noun–modifier relations. [4] examined nominalizations (a proper subset of NCs) in terms of whether the modifier is a subject or object of the verb the head noun is derived from (e.g. *language understanding* = *understand language*). [7] assigned hierarchical tags to nouns in medical texts and classified them according to their semantic relations using neural networks. [8] used the word senses of nouns to classify the semantic relations of NCs. However, in all this work, there has been some underlying simplifying assumption, in terms of the domain or range of interpretations an NC can occur with, leading to questions of scalability and portability to novel domains/NC types.

In this paper, we introduce a method which uses word similarity based on WordNet. Word similarity has been used previously in various lexical semantic tasks, including word sense disambiguation [11,12]. [11] showed that term-to-term similarity in a context space can be used to disambiguate word senses. [12] measured the relatedness of concepts using similarity based on WordNet. [13] examined the task of disambiguating noun groupings with respect to word senses using similarity between nouns in NCs. Our research uses similarities between nouns in the training and test data to interpret the semantic relations of novel NCs.

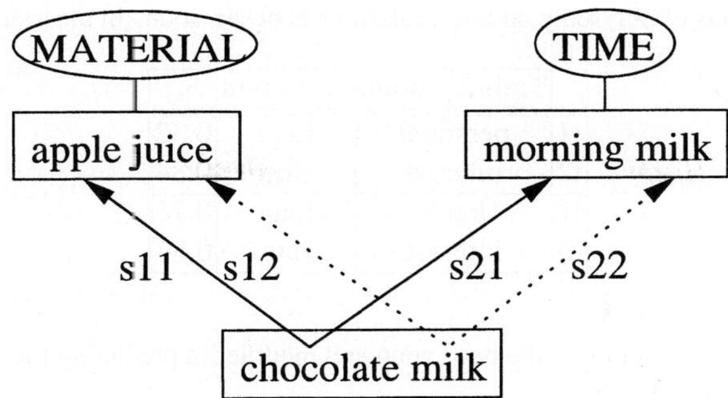

Fig. 1. Similarity between test NC *chocolate milk* and training NCs *apple juice* and *morning milk*

Table 1. WordNet-based similarities for component nouns in the training and test data

	Training noun	Test noun	S_{ij}
t1	apple	chocolate	0.71
t2	juice	milk	0.83
t1	morning	chocolate	0.27
t2	milk	milk	1.00

Figure 1 shows the correspondences between two training NCs, *apple juice* and *morning milk*, and a test NC, *chocolate milk*; Table 1 lists the noun pairings and noun–noun similarities based on WordNet. Each *training* noun is a component noun from the training data, each *test* noun is a component noun in the input, and S_{ij} provides a measure of the noun–noun similarity in *training* and *test*, where $t1$ is the modifier and $t2$ is the head noun in the NC in question. The similarities in Table 1 were computed by the WUP method [14] as implemented in `WordNet::Similarity` (see Section 3).

The simple product of the individual similarities (of each modifier and head noun, respectively) gives the similarity of the NC pairing. For example, the similarity between *chocolate milk* and *apple juice* is 0.60, while that between *chocolate milk* and *morning milk* is 0.27. Note that although *milk* in the input NC also occurs in a training exemplar, the semantic relations for the individual NCs differ. That is, while *apple juice* is *juice* made from *apples* (MATERIAL), *morning milk* is *milk* served in the *morning* (TIME). By comparing the similarity of both elements of the input NC, we are able to arrive at the conclusion that *chocolate milk* is more closely related to *chocolate milk*, which provides the correct semantic relation of MATERIAL (i.e. *milk* made from/flavored with *chocolate*). Unlike word sense disambiguation systems, our method does not need to determine the particular sense in which each noun is used. The next example (Table 2) shows how our method interprets NCs containing ambiguous nouns correctly.

One potential pitfall when dealing with WordNet is the high level of polysemy for many lexemes. We analyze the effects of polysemy with respect to *interest*. Assume that we have the two NCs *personal interest* (POSSESSION) and *bank interest* (CAUSE/TOPIC) in the training data. Both contain the noun *interest*, with the meaning of a state of cu-

Table 2. The effects of polysemy on the similarities between nouns in the training and test data

	Training noun	Test noun	S_{ij}
t1	personal	loan	0.32
t2	interest	rate	0.84
t1	bank	loan	0.75
t2	interest	rate	0.84

Table 3. Varying contribution of the head noun and modifier in predicting the semantic relation

Relative contribution of modifier/head noun	Relation	Example
modifier < head noun	PROPERTY	*elephant seal*
modifier = head noun	EQUATIVE	*composer arranger*
modifier > head noun	TIME	*morning class*

riosity or concern about something in *personal interest*, and an excess or bonus beyond what is expected or due in *bank interest*. Given the test NC *loan rate*, we would get the desired result of *bank interest* being the training instance of highest similarity, leading to *loan rate* being classified with the semantic relation of CAUSE/TOPIC. The similarity between the head nouns *interest* and *rate* for each pairing of training and test NC is identical, as the proposed method makes no attempt to disambiguate the sense of a noun in each NC context, and instead aggregates the overall word-to-word similarity across the different sense pairings. The determining factor is therefore the similarity between the different modifier pairings, and the fact that *bank* is more similar to *loan* than is the case for *personal*.

We also investigate the weight of the head noun and the modifier in determining overall similarity. We expect for different relations, the weight of the head noun and the modifier will be different. In the relation EQUATIVE, e.g., we would expect the significance of the head noun to be the same as that of the modifier. In relations such as PROPERTY, on the other hand, we would expect the head noun to play a more important role than the modifier. Conversely, with relations such as TIME, we would expect the modifier to be more important, as detailed in Table 3.

3 WordNet::Similarity

`WordNet::Similarity`[2] [12] is an open source software package developed at the University of Minnesota. It allows the user to measure the semantic similarity or relatedness between a pair of concepts (or word senses), and by extension, between a pair of words. The system provides six measures of similarity and three measures of relatedness based on the WordNet lexical database [15]. The measures of similarity are based on analysis of the WordNet `isa` hierarchy.

[2] `www.d.umn.edu/~tpederse/similarity.html`

The measures of similarity are divided into two groups: path-based and information content-based. We chose four of the similarity measures in `WordNet::Similarity` for our experiments: WUP and LCH as path-based similarity measures, and JCN and LIN as information content-based similarity measures. LCH finds the shortest path between nouns [16]; WUP finds the path length to the root node from the least common subsumer (LCS) of the two word senses that is the most specific word sense they share as an ancestor [14]; JCN subtracts the information content of the LCS from the sum [17]; and LIN scales the information content of the LCS relative to the sum [18].

In `WordNet::Similarity`, relatedness goes beyond concepts being similar to each other. That is, WordNet provides additional (non-hierarchical) relations such as `has-part` and `made-of`. It supports our idea of interpretation of NCs by similarity. However, as [19] point out, information on relatedness has not been developed as actively as conceptual similarity. Besides, the speed of simulating these relatedness effects is too slow to use in practice. Hence, we did not use any of the relatedness measures in this paper.

4 Semantic Relations

A semantic relation in the context of NC interpretation is the relation between the modifier and the head noun. For instance, *family car* relates to POSSESSION whereas *sports car* relates to PURPOSE. [20] defined complex nominals as expressions that have a head noun preceded by one or more modifying nouns or denominal adjectives, and offered nine semantic labels after removing opaque compounds and adding nominal non-predicating adjectives. [5] produced a diverse set of NC interpretations. Other researchers have identified alternate sets of semantic relations, or conversely cast doubts on the possibility of devising an all-purpose system of NC interpretations [21]. For our work, we do not intend to create a new set of semantic relations. Based on our data, we chose a pre-existing set of semantic relations that had previously been used for automatic (or semi-automatic) NC interpretation, namely the 20-member classification of [10] (see Appendix). Other notable classifications include that of [6] which contains 13 relations based on WH questions, making it ideally suited to question answering applications. However, some relations such as TOPIC are absent. [7] proposed 38 relations for the medical domain. Such relations are too highly specialized to this domain, and not suitable for more general applications. [8] defined 35 semantic relations for complex nominals and adjective phrases.

5 Data Collection

We retrieved binary NCs from the Wall Street Journal component of the Penn treebank. We excluded proper nouns since WordNet does not contain even high-frequency proper nouns such as *Honda*. We also excluded binary NCs that are part of larger NCs. In tagging the semantic relations of noun compounds, we hired two annotators: two computer science Ph.D students. In many cases, even human annotators disagree on the tag allocation. For NCs containing more than one semantic relation, the annotators were judged to have agreed is there was overlap in at least one of the relations specified by them for a given NC. The initial agreement for the two annotators was 52.31%. From the disagreement of tagged relations, we observed that decisions between SOURCE and CAUSE, PURPOSE and TOPIC, and OBJECT and TOPIC frequently have lower agreement. For the NCs where there was no agreement, the annotators decided on a set of relations through consultation. The distribution of semantic relations is shown in the Appendix. Overall, we used 1,088 NCs for the training data and 1,081 NCs for the test data.

6 Method

Figure 2 shows how to compute the similarity between the ith NC in the test data and j^{th} NC in the training data. We calculate similarities for the component nouns of the ith NC in the test data with all NCs in the training data. As a result, the modifier and head noun in the ith test NC are each associated with a total of m similarities, where m is the number of NCs in the training data. The second step is to multiply the similarities of the modifier and head noun for all NCs in the training data; we experiment with two methods for calculating the combined similarity. The third step is to choose the NC in the training data which is most similar to the test instance, and tag the test instance according to the semantic relation associated with that training instance.

Formally, S_A is the similarity between NCs $(N_{i,1}, N_{i,2})$ and $(B_{j,1}, B_{j,2})$:

$$S_A((N_{i,1}, N_{i,2}), (B_{j,1}, B_{j,2})) = \frac{((\alpha S1 + S1) \times ((1-\alpha)S2 + S2))}{2} \quad (1)$$

where $S1$ is the modifier similarity (i.e. $S(N_{i,1}, B_{j1})$) and $S2$ is head noun similarity (i.e. $S(N_{i,2}, B_{j2})$); $\alpha \in [0, 1]$ is a weighting factor.

S_B is an analogous similarity function, based on the F-score:

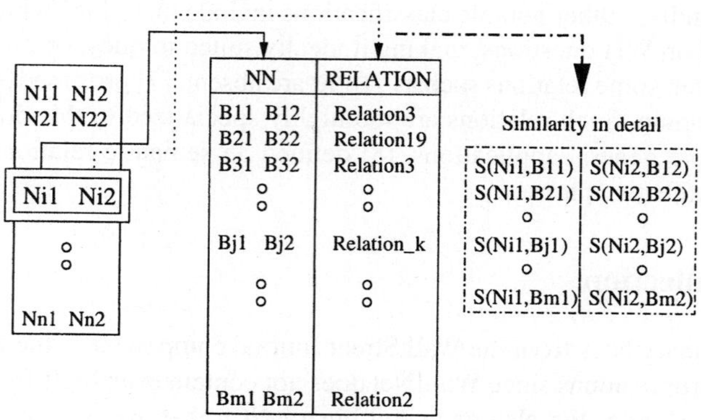

Fig. 2. Similarity between the ith NC in the test data and j^{th} NC in the training data

$$S_B((N_{i,1}, N_{i,2}), B(_{j,1}, B_{j,2})) = 2 \times \frac{(S1 + \alpha S1) \times (S2 + (1 - \alpha)S2)}{(S1 + \alpha S1) + (S2 + (1 - \alpha S2))} \quad (2)$$

The semantic relation is determined by rel:

$$rel(N_{i,1}, N_{i,2}) = rel(B_{m,1}, B_{m,2}) \quad (3)$$
$$\text{where } m = \underset{j}{\text{argmax}}\, S((N_{i,1}, N_{i,2}), (B_{j,1}, B_{j,2}))$$

7 Experimental Results

7.1 Automatic Tagging Using Similarity

In our first experiment, we tag the test NCs with semantic relations using four different measures of noun similarity, assuming for the time being that the contribution of the modifier and head noun is equal (i.e. $\alpha = 0.5$). The baseline for this experiment is a majority-class classifier, in which all NCs are tagged according to the TOPIC class.

Table 4. Accuracy of NC interpretation for the different WordNet-based similarity measures

Basis	Method	S_A	S_B
majority class	Baseline	465 (43.0%)	465 (43.0%)
path-based	WUP	**576 (53.3%)**	557 (51.5%)
path-based	LCH	572 (52.9%)	**565 (52.3%)**
information content-based	JCN	505 (46.7%)	470 (43.5%)
information content-based	LIN	512 (47.4%)	455 (42.1%)
human annotation	Inter-annotator agreement	565 (52.3%)	565 (52.3%)

Table 4 shows that WUP, using the S_A multiplicative method of combination, provides the highest NC interpretation accuracy, significantly above the majority-class baseline. It is particularly encouraging to see that WUP performs at or above the level of inter-annotator agreement (52.3%), which could be construed as a theoretical upper bound for the task as defined here. Using the F-score measure of similarity, LCH has nearly the same performance as WUP. Among the four measures of similarity used in this first experiment, the path-based similarity measures have higher performance than the information content-based methods over both similarity combination methods.

Compared to prior work on the automatic interpretation of NCs, our method achieves relatively good results. [7] achieved about 60% performance over the medical domain. [8] used a word sense disambiguation system to achieve around 43% accuracy interpreting NCs in the open domain. Our accuracy of 53% compares favourably to both of these sets of results, given that we are operating over open domain data.

7.2 Relative Contribution of Modifier and Head Noun

In the second experiment, we investigated the relative impact of the modifier and head noun in determining the overall similarity of the NC. While tagging the NCs, we got

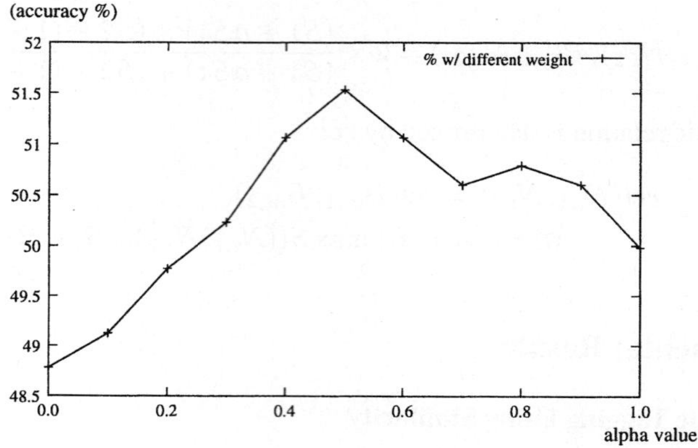

Fig. 3. Classifier accuracy at different α values

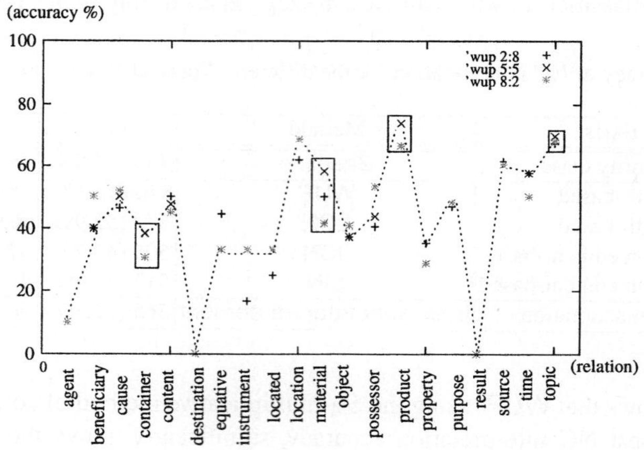

Fig. 4. Classification accuracy for each semantic relation at different α values

a sense of modifiers and head nouns having variable impact on the determination of the overall NC semantic relation. For this test, we used the WUP method based on our results from above and also because it operates over the scale $[0, 1]$, removing any need for normalization. In this experiment, modifiers and head nouns were assigned weights (α in Equations 1 and 2) in the range $0.0, 0.1, ...1.0$.

Figure 3 shows the relative contribution of the modifier and head noun in the overall NC interpretation process. Interestingly, the head noun seems to be a more reliable predictor of the overall NC interpretation than the modifier, and yet the best accuracy is achieved when each noun makes an equal contribution to the overall interpretation (i.e. $\alpha = 0.5$). Thus suggests that, despite any localized biases for individual NC interpretation types, the modifier and head noun have an equal impact on NC interpretation overall.

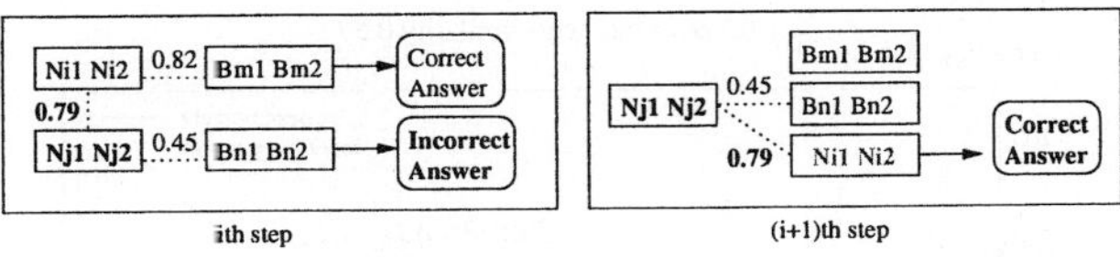

Fig. 5. Accumulating correctly tagged data

Figure 4 shows a breakdown of accuracy across the different semantic relation types for different weights. In Figure 4, we have shown only the weights 0.2, 0.5 and 0.8 (to show the general effect of variation in α). The dashed line shows the performance when the weight of modifiers and head nouns is the same ($\alpha = 0.5$). The $\times$ symbol shows the results of modifier-biased interpretation ($\alpha = 0.8$) and the $+$ symbol shows the results of head noun-biased interpretation ($\alpha = 0.2$). From Figure 4, we can see that for relations such as CAUSE and INSTRUMENT, the modifier plays a more important role in the determination of the semantic relation of the NC. On the other hand, for the CONTENT and PROPERTY relations, the head noun contributes more to NC interpretation. Unexpectedly, for EQUATIVE, the head noun contributes more than the modifier, although only 9 examples were tagged with EQUATIVE, such that the result shown may not be very representative of the general behavior.

8 Discussion

We have presented a method for interpreting the semantic relations of novel NCs using word similarity. We achieved about 53% interpretation accuracy using a path-based measure of similarity. Since our system was tested over raw test data from a general domain, we demonstrated that word similarity has surprising potential for interpreting the semantic relations of NCs. We also investigated using different weights for the head noun and modifier to find out how much the modifier and head noun contributes in NC interpretation and found that, with the exception of some isolated semantic relations, their relative contribution is equal.

Our method has advantages such its relative simplicity and ability to run over small amounts of training data, but there are also a few weaknesses. The main bottleneck is the availability of training data to use in classifying test instances. We suggest that we could use a bootstrap method to overcome this problem: in each step of classification, NCs which are highly similar to training instances, as determined by some threshold on similarity, are added to the training data to use in the next iteration of classification. One way to arrive at such a threshold is to analyze the relative proportion of correctly- and incorrectly-classified instances at different similarity levels, through cross-validation over the training data. We generate such a curve for the test data, as detailed in Figure 6.

If we were to use the crossover point (similarity ≥ 0.57), we would clearly "infect" the training data with a significant number of misclassified instances, namely 30.69% of the new training instances; this would have an unpredictable impact on classification performance. On the other hand, if we were to select a higher threshold based on a higher estimated proportion of correctly-classified instances (e.g. 70%), the relative

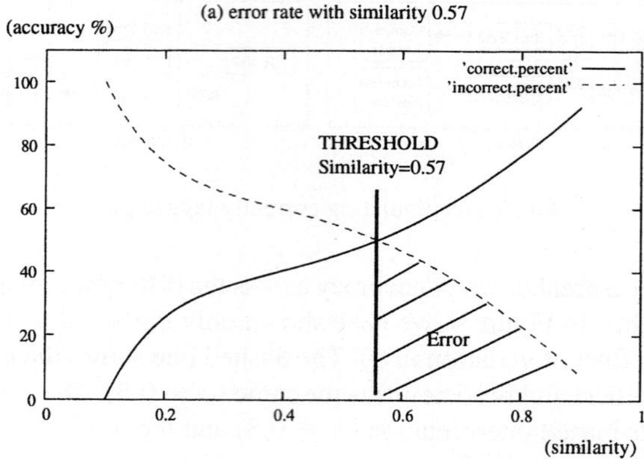

Fig. 6. The relative proportion of correctly- and incorrectly-classified NCs at different similarity values, and the estimated impact of threshold-based bootstrapping

increase in training examples would be slight, and there would be little hope for much impact on the overall classifier accuracy. Clearly, therefore, there is a trade-off here between how much training data we wish to acquire automatically and whether this will impact negatively or positively on classification performance. We leave investigation of this trade-off as an item for future research. Interestingly, in Figure 6 the proportion of misclassified examples is monotonically decreasing, providing evidence for the soundness of the proposed similarity-based model.

In the first experiment (where the weight of the modifier and head noun was the same), we observed that some of the test NCs matched with several training NCs with high similarity. However, since we chose only the NC with the highest similarity, we ignored any insight other closely-matching training NCs may have provided into the semantics of the test NC. One possible workaround here would be to employ a voting strategy, for example, in taking the k most-similar training instances and determining the majority class amongst them. Once again, we leave this as an item for future research.

Acknowledgements

We would like to express our thanks to Bharaneedharan Rathnasabapathy for helping to tag the noun compound semantic relations, and the anonymous reviewers for their comments and suggestions.

References

1. Cao, Y., Li, H.: Base noun phrase translation using web data and the em algorithm. In: COLING2002. (2002)
2. Baldwin, T., Tanaka, T.: Translation by machine of compound nominals: Getting it right. In: ACL2004-MWE, Barcelona, Spain (2004) 24–31

3. Lauer, M.: Designing Statistical Language Learners: Experiments on Noun Compounds. PhD thesis, Macquarie University (1995)
4. Lapata, M.: The disambiguation of nominalizations. Comput. Linguist. **28** (2002) 357–388
5. Finin, T.W.: The semantic interpretation of compound nominals. PhD thesis, University of Illinois, Urbana, Illinois, USA (1980)
6. Vanderwende, L.: Algorithm for automatic interpretation of noun sequences. In: Proceedings of the 15th conference on Computational linguistics. (1994) 782–788
7. Rosario, B., Marti, H.: Classifying the semantic relations in noun compounds via a domain-specific lexical hierarchy. In: Proceedings of the 2001 Conference on Empirical Methods in Natural Language Processing. (2001) 82–90
8. Moldovan, D., Badulescu, A., Tatu, M., Antohe, D., Girju, R.: Models for the semantic classification of noun phrases. HLT-NAACL 2004: Workshop on Computational Lexical Semantics (2004) 60–67
9. Fan, J., Barker, K., Porter, B.W.: The knowledge required to interpret noun compounds. In: Seventh International Joint Conference on Artificial Intelligence. (2003) 1483–1485
10. Barker, K., Szpakowicz, S.: Semi-automatic recognition of noun modifier relationships. In: Proceedings of the 17th international conference on Computational linguistics. (1998) 96–102
11. Artiles, J., Penas, A., Verdejo, F.: Word sense disambiguation based on term to term similarity in a context space. In: Senseval-3: Third International Workshop on the Evaluation of Systems for the Semantic Analysis of Text. (2004) 58–63
12. Patwardhan, S., Banerjee, S., Pedersen, T.: Using measures of semantic relatedness for word sense disambiguation. In: Proceedings of the Fourth International Conference on Intelligent Text Processing and Computational Linguistics. (2003)
13. Resnik, P.: Disambiguating noun groupings with respect to wordnet senses. In: Proceedings of the 3rd Workship on Very Large Corpus. (1995) 77–98
14. Wu, Z., Palmer, M.: Verb semantics and lexical selection. In: 32nd. Annual Meeting of the Association for Computational Linguistics. (1994) 133 –138
15. Fellbaum, C., ed.: WordNet: An Electronic Lexical Database. MIT Press, Cambridge, USA (1998)
16. Leacock, C., Chodorow, N.: Combining local context and wordnet similarity for word sense identification. [15]
17. Jiang, J., Conrath, D.: Semantic similarity based on corpus statistics and lexical taxonomy. In: Proceedings on International Conference on Research in Computational Linguistics. (1998) 19–33
18. Lin, D.: An information-theoretic definition of similarity. In: Proceedings of the International Conference on Machine Learning. (1998)
19. Banerjee, S., Pedersen, T.: Extended gloss overlaps as a measure of semantic relatedness. In: Proceedings of the Eighteenth International Joint Conference on Artificial Intelligence. (2003) 805–810
20. Levi, J.: The syntax and semantics of complex nominals. In: New York:Academic Press. (1979)
21. Downing, P.: On the creation and use of English compound nouns. Language **53** (1977) 810–42

Appendix

Table 5. The Semantic Relations in Noun Compounds (N_1 = modifier, N_2 = head noun)

Relation	*Definition*	*Example*	*# of test/training*
AGENT	N_2 is performed by N_1	*student protest, band concert*	10(2)/5
BENEFICIARY	N_1 benefits from N_2	*student price, charitable compound*	10(1)/7(1)
CAUSE	N_1 causes N_2	*printer tray, flood water*	54(10)/74(11)
CONTAINER	N_1 contains N_2	*exam anxiety*	13(6)/19(5)
CONTENT	N_1 is contained in N_2	*paper tray, eviction notice*	40(5)/34(7)
DESTINATION	N_1 is destination of N_2	*game bus, exit route*	2(1)/2
EQUATIVE	N_1 is also head	*composer arranger, player coach*	9/17(3)
INSTRUMENT	N_1 is used in N_2	*electron microscope, diesel engine*	6/11(2)
LOCATED	N_1 is located at N_2	*building site, home town*	12(2)/16(4)
LOCATION	N_1 is the location of N_2	*lab printer, desert storm*	29(10)/24(5)
MATERIAL	N_2 is made of N_1	*carbon deposit, gingerbread man*	12(1)/15(2)
OBJECT	N_1 is acted on by N_2	*engine repair, horse doctor*	88(16)/88(21)
POSSESSOR	N_1 has N_2	*student loan, company car*	32(3)/22(4)
PRODUCT	N_1 is a product of N_2	*automobile factory, light bulb*	27(1)/32(9)
PROPERTY	N_2 is N_1	*elephant seal*	76(5)/85(7)
PURPOSE	N_2 is meant for N_1	*concert hall, soup pot*	160(23)/160(23)
RESULT	N_1 is a result of N_2	*storm cloud, cold virus*	7(4)/8(1)
SOURCE	N_1 is the source of N_2	*chest pain, north wind*	86(21)/99(18)
TIME	N_1 is the time of N_2	*winter semester, morning class*	26(2)/19
TOPIC	N_2 is concerned with N_1	*computer expert, safety standard*	465(51)/446(60)

The 4th column gives us the number of words tagged with the corresponding relation in the 1st column. The numbers within the parenthesis gives us the number of words that are tagged with multiple relations(i.e. those that are tagged with the relation in the 1st column and other relations as well). In the training data, 94 NCs have multiple relations and in test data, 81 NCs have multiple relations.

An Empirical Study on Language Model Adaptation Using a Metric of Domain Similarity

Wei Yuan[1], Jianfeng Gao[2], and Hisami Suzuki[3]

[1] Shanghai Jiao Tong University, 1954 Huashan Road, Shanghai 200030
sunnyuanovo@sjtu.edu.cn
[2] Microsoft Research, Asia, 49 Zhichun Road, Haidian District, Beijing 100080
jfgao@microsoft.com
[3] Microsoft Research, One Microsoft Way, Redmond WA 98052
hisamis@microsoft.com

Abstract. This paper presents an empirical study on four techniques of language model adaptation, including a maximum *a posteriori* (MAP) method and three discriminative training models, in the application of Japanese Kana-Kanji conversion. We compare the performance of these methods from various angles by adapting the baseline model to four adaptation domains. In particular, we attempt to interpret the results given in terms of the character error rate (CER) by correlating them with the characteristics of the adaptation domain measured using the information-theoretic notion of cross entropy. We show that such a metric correlates well with the CER performance of the adaptation methods, and also show that the discriminative methods are not only superior to a MAP-based method in terms of achieving larger CER reduction, but are also more robust against the similarity of background and adaptation domains.

1 Introduction

Language model (LM) adaptation attempts to adjust the parameters of a LM so that it performs well on a particular domain of data. This paper presents an empirical study of several LM adaptation methods on the task of Japanese text input. In particular, we focus on the so-called *cross-domain* LM adaptation paradigm, i.e. to adapt a LM trained on one domain to a different domain, for which only a small amount of training data is available.

The LM adaptation methods investigated in this paper can be grouped into two categories: maximum *a posterior* (MAP) and discriminative training. Linear interpolation is representative of the MAP methods [1]. The other three methods, including the boosting [2] and perceptron [3] algorithms and minimum sample risk (MSR) method [4], are discriminative methods, each of which uses a different training algorithm.

We carried out experiments over many training data sizes on four distinct adaptation corpora, the characteristics of which were measured using the information-theoretic notion of cross entropy. We found that discriminative training methods

[1] This research was conducted while the author was visiting Microsoft Research Asia.

R. Dale et al. (Eds.): IJCNLP 2005, LNAI 3651, pp. 957 – 968, 2005.

outperformed the LI method in all cases, and were more robust across different training sets of different domains and sizes. However, none of the discriminative training methods was found to outperform the others in our experiments.

The paper is organized as follow. Section 2 introduces the task of IME and the role of LM. In Section 3, we review related work. After a description of the LM adaptation methods in our experiments in Section 4, Sections 5 and 6 present experimental results and their discussions. We conclude our paper in Section 7.

2 Language Model and the Task of IME

Our study falls into the context of Asian language (Japanese in this study) text input. The standard method for doing this is that the users first input the phonetic strings, which are then converted into the appropriate word string by software. The task of automatic conversion is called *IME* in this paper, which stands for *Input Method Editor*, based on the name of the commonly used Windows-based application.

The performance of IME is typically measured in terms of the *character error rate* (CER), which is the number of characters wrongly converted from the phonetic string divided by the number of characters in the correct transcript. Current Japanese IME systems exhibit about 5-15% CER in conversion of real-world data in a wide variety of domains. In the following, we argue that the IME is a similar problem to speech recognition but is a better choice for evaluating language modeling techniques.

Similar to speech recognition, IME can also be viewed as a Bayesian decision problem. Let A be the input phonetic string (which corresponds to the acoustic signal in speech). The task of IME is to choose the most likely word string W^* among those candidates that could have been converted from A:

$$W^* = \arg\max_{W \in GEN(A)} P(W \mid A) = \arg\max_{W \in GEN(A)} \frac{P(W, A)}{P(A)} = \arg\max_{W \in GEN(A)} P(W)P(A \mid W) \tag{1}$$

where **GEN**(A) denotes the candidate set given A.

Unlike speech recognition, there is almost no acoustic ambiguity in IME, because the phonetic string is provided directly by users. Moreover, we can assume a many-to-one mapping from W to A in IME, i.e. $P(A|W) = 1$. So the decision of Equation (1) depends solely upon $P(W)$, making IME a more direct evaluation test-bed for LM than speech recognition. Another advantage is that it is relatively easy to convert W to A, making it possible to obtain a large amount of training data for discriminative learning, as described later.

3 Related Work

Our goal is to quantify the characteristics of different domains of text, and to correlate them with the performance of various techniques for LM adaptation to compare their effectiveness and robustness. This relates our work to the study of domain similarity calculation and to different techniques for LM adaptation.

3.1 Measuring Domain Similarity

Statistical language modeling (SLM) assumes that language is generated from underlying distributions. When we discuss different domains of text, we assume that the text from each of these domains is generated from a different underlying distribution. We therefore consider the problem of distributional similarity in this paper.

Cross entropy is a widely used measure in evaluating LM. Given a language L with its true underlying probability distribution p and another distribution q (e.g. a SLM) which attempts to model L, the cross entropy of L with respect to q is

$$H(L,q) = -\lim_{n\to\infty}\frac{1}{n}\sum_{w_1...w_n} p(w_1...w_n)\log q(w_1...w_n) \quad (2)$$

where $w_1...w_n$ is a word string in L. However, in reality, the underlying p is never known and the corpus size is never infinite. We therefore make the assumption that L is an ergodic and stationary process [5], and approximate the cross entropy by calculating it for a sufficiently large n instead of calculating it for the limit.

$$H(L,q) \approx -\frac{1}{n}\log q(w_1...w_n) \quad (3)$$

This measures how well a model approximates the language L.

The KL divergence, or relative entropy, is another measure of distributional similarity that has been widely used in NLP and IR [6]. Given the two distributions p and q above, the KL divergence is defined as

$$D(p(w_1...w_n) \parallel q(w_1...w_n)) = \sum_{w_1...w_n} p(w_1...w_n)\log\frac{p(w_1...w_n)}{q(w_1...w_n)} \quad (4)$$

The cross entropy and the KL divergence are related notions. Given the notations of L, p and q above, [5] shows that

$$H(L,q) = H(L) + D(p \parallel q) \quad (5)$$

In other words, the cross entropy takes into account both the similarity between two distributions (given by KL divergence) and the entropy of the corpus in question, both of which contribute to the complexity of a LM task. In this paper we are interested in measuring the complexity of the LM adaptation task. We therefore define the similarity between two domains using the cross entropy. We will also use the metric that approximates the entropy of the corpus to capture the in-domain diversity of a corpus in Section 5.2.[2]

3.2 LM Adaptation Methods

In this paper, two major approaches to cross-domain adaptation have been investigated: maximum *a posteriori* (MAP) estimation and discriminative training methods.

---

[2] There are other well-known metrics of similarity within NLP literature, such as the mutual information or cosine similarity [7], which we do not discuss in this paper.

In MAP estimation methods, adaptation data is used to adjust the parameters of the background model so as to maximize the likelihood of the adaptation data [1]. Discriminative training methods to LM adaptation, on the other hand, aim at using the adaptation data to directly minimize the errors on the adaptation data made by the background model. These techniques have been applied successfully to the task of language modeling in non-adaptation [8] as well as adaptation scenarios [9] for speech recognition. But most of them focused on the investigation of performance of certain methods for LM adaptation, without analyzing in detail the underlying reasons of different performance achieved by different methods. In this paper we attempt to investigate the effectiveness of different discriminative methods in an IME adaptation scenario, with a particular emphasis on correlating their performance with the characteristics of adaptation domain.

4 LM Adaptation Methods

We implement four methods in our experiments. The Linear Interpolation (LI) falls into the framework of MAP while the boosting, the perceptron and the MSR methods fall into that of discriminative training.

4.1 Linear Interpolation (MAP)

In MAP estimation methods, adaptation data is used to adjust the parameters of the background model so as to maximize the likelihood of the adaptation data.

The linear interpolation is a special case of MAP according to [10]. At first, we generate trigram models on background data and adaptation data respectively. The two models are then combined into one as:

$$P(w_i \mid h) = \lambda P_B(w_i \mid h) + (1-\lambda) P_A(w_i \mid h) \tag{6}$$

where P_B is the probability of the background model, P_A is the probability of the adaptation model and the history h corresponds to two preceding words. For simplicity, we chose a single λ for all histories and tuned it on held-out data.

4.2 Discriminative Training

Discriminative training follows the general framework of linear models [2][3]. We use the following notation in the rest of the paper.

- Training data is a set of example input/output pairs $\{A_i, W_i^R\}$ for $i = 1 \ldots M$, where each A_i is an input phonetic string and each W_i^R is the reference transcript of A_i.
- We assume a set of D+1 features, $f_d(W)$, for d=0…D, where each feature is a function that maps W to a real value. Using vector notation, we have $\mathbf{f}(W)=\{f_0(W), f_1(W) \ldots f_D(W)\}$ and $\mathbf{f}(W) \in R^{D+1}$. Without loss of generality, $f_0(W)$ is called the base model feature, and is defined in this paper as the log probability that the background trigram model assigns to W. $f_d(W)$, for d=1…D, are defined as the counts of the word n-gram in W, where n = 1 and 2 in our case.

- Finally, the parameters of the model form a vector of $D + 1$ dimensions, each for one feature function, $\boldsymbol{\lambda} = \{\lambda_0, \lambda_1 \ldots \lambda_D\}$. The likelihood score of a word string W is

$$Score(W, \boldsymbol{\lambda}) = \boldsymbol{\lambda}\mathbf{f}(W) = \sum_{d=0}^{D} \lambda_d f_d(W) \tag{7}$$

Then the decision rule of Equation (1) can be re-written as

$$W^*(A, \boldsymbol{\lambda}) = \arg\max_{W \in \mathbf{GEN}(A)} Score(W, \boldsymbol{\lambda}) \tag{8}$$

Assume that we can measure the number of conversion errors in W by comparing it with a reference transcript W^R using an error function Er(W^R, W), which is an edit distance in our case. We call the sum of conversion errors over the training data as *sample risk* (SR). Discriminative training methods strive to minimize the SR by optimizing the model parameters, as defined in Equation (9).

$$\boldsymbol{\lambda}^* = \arg\min_{\boldsymbol{\lambda}} SR(\boldsymbol{\lambda}) = \arg\min_{\boldsymbol{\lambda}} \sum_{i=1 \ldots M} Er(W_i^R, W_i(A_i, \boldsymbol{\lambda})) \tag{9}$$

However, SR(.) cannot be optimized easily since Er(.) is a piecewise constant (or step) function of $\boldsymbol{\lambda}$ and its gradient is undefined. Therefore, discriminative methods apply different approaches that optimize it approximately. As we shall describe below, the boosting and perceptron algorithms approximate SR(.) by loss functions that are suitable for optimization, while MSR uses a simple heuristic training procedure to minimize SR(.) directly without applying any approximated loss function. We now describe each of the discriminative methods in turn.

The boosting algorithm [2] uses an exponential function to approximate SR(.). We define a ranking error in a case where an incorrect candidate conversion W gets a higher score than the correct conversion W^R. The margin of the pair (W^R, W) with respect to the model $\boldsymbol{\lambda}$ is estimated as

$$M(W^R, W) = Score(W^R, \boldsymbol{\lambda}) - Score(W, \boldsymbol{\lambda}) \tag{10}$$

Then we define an upper bound to the number of ranking errors as the loss function,

$$\text{ExpLoss}(\boldsymbol{\lambda}) = \sum_{i=1 \ldots M} \sum_{W_i \in \mathbf{GEN}(A_i)} \exp(-M(W_i^R, W_i)) \tag{11}$$

Now, ExpLoss(.) is convex with respect to $\boldsymbol{\lambda}$, so there are no problems with local minima when optimizing it. The boosting algorithm can be viewed as an iterative feature selection method: at each iteration, the algorithm selects from all possible features the one that is estimated to have the largest impact on reducing the ExpLoss function with respect to the current model, and then optimizes the current model by adjusting only the parameter of the selected feature while keeping the parameters of other features fixed.

The perceptron algorithm [3] can be viewed as a form of incremental training procedure that optimizes a *minimum square error* (MSE) loss function, which is an approximation of SR(.). As shown in Figure 1, it starts with an initial parameter setting and adapts it each time a training sample is wrongly converted.

1 Initialize all parameters in the model, i.e. $\lambda_0 = 1$ and $\lambda_d = 0$ for d=1...D
2 For t = 1...T, where T is the total number of iterations
  For each training sample (A_i, W_i^R), i = 1...M
    Use current model $\boldsymbol{\lambda}$ to choose some W_i from GEN(A_i) by Equation (8)
    For d = 1 ... D
      $\lambda_d = \lambda_d + \eta(f_d(W_i^R) - f_d(W_i))$, where η is the size of the learning step

Fig. 1. The standard perceptron algorithm with delta rule

In our experiments, we used the average perceptron algorithm in [3], a simple refinement to the algorithm in Figure 1, which has been proved to be more robust. Let $\lambda_d^{t,i}$ be the value for the dth parameter after the ith training sample has been processed in pass t over the training data. Then the "average parameters" are defined as in Equation (12).

$$(\lambda_d)_{avg} = (\sum_{t=1}^{T}\sum_{i=1}^{M}\lambda_d^{t,i})/(T \cdot M) \tag{12}$$

The minimum sample risk (MSR) method [4] can be viewed as a greedy stage-wise learning algorithm that minimizes the sample risk SR(.) directly as it appears in Equation (9). Similar to the boosting method, it is an iterative procedure. In each iteration, MSR selects a feature that is estimated to be most effective in terms of reducing SR(.), and then optimizes the current model by adjusting the parameters of the selected feature. MSR, however, differs from the boosting method in that MSR tries to optimize the sample risk directly while the boosting optimizes the loss function that is an upper bound of the sample risk.

As mentioned earlier, SR(.) can be optimized using regular gradient-based optimization algorithms. MSR therefore uses a particular implementation of line search, originally proposed in [11], to optimize the current model by adjusting the parameter of a selected feature while keeping other parameters fixed.

Assuming f_d is the selected feature, its parameter λ_d is optimized by line search as follows. Recall that Er(W^R,W) is the function that measures the number of conversion errors in W versus its reference transcript W^R. The value of SR(.) is the sum of Er(.) over all training samples. For each A in training set, let **GEN**(A) be the set of n-best candidate word strings that could be converted from A. By adjusting λ_d, we obtain for each training sample an ordered sequence of λ_d intervals. For λ_d in each interval, a particular candidate would be selected according to Equation (8). Then the corresponding Er(.) is associated with the interval. As a result, for each training sample, we obtain a sequence of λ_d intervals and their corresponding Er(.) values. By combining the sequences over all training samples, we obtain a global sequence of λ_d intervals, each of which is associated with a SR(.) value. Therefore we can find the optimal interval of λ_d as well as its corresponding sample risk by traversing the sequence and taking the center of the interval as the optimal value of λ_d.

5 Experimental Results

5.1 Data

The data used in our experiments stem from five distinct sources of text. A 36-million-word *Nikkei* newspaper corpus was used as the background domain. We used four adaptation domains: *Yomiuri* (newspaper corpus), *TuneUp* (balanced corpus containing newspaper and other sources of text), *Encarta* (encyclopedia) and *Shincho* (collection of novels).

For the computation of domain characteristics (Section 5.2), we extracted 1 million words from the training data of each domain respectively (corresponding to 13K to 78K sentences depending on the domain). For this experiment, we also used a lexicon consisting of the words in our baseline lexicon (167,107 words) plus all words in the corpora used for this experiment (that is, 1M words times 5 domains), which included 216,565 entries. The use of such a lexicon was motivated by the need to eliminate the effect of out-of-vocabulary (OOV) items.

For the experiment of LM adaptation (Section 5.3), we created training data consisting of 72K sentences (0.9M~1.7M words) and test data of 5K sentences (65K~120K words) from each adaptation domain. The first 800 and 8,000 sentences of each adaptation training data were also used to show how different sizes of adaptation training data affected the performances of various adaptation methods. Another 5K-sentence subset was used as held-out data for each domain. For domain adaptation experiments, we used our baseline lexicon consisting of 167,107 entries.

5.2 Computation of Domain Characteristics

The first domain characteristic we computed was the similarity between two domains for the task of LM. As discussed in Section 3, we used the cross entropy as the metric: we first trained a word trigram model using the system described in [12] on the 1-million-word corpus of domain B, and used it in the computations of the cross entropy $H(L_A, q_B)$ following equation (3). For simplicity, we denote $H(L_A, q_B)$ as $H(A,B)$.

Table 1 displays the cross entropy between two domains of text. Note that the cross entropy is not symmetric, i.e., $H(A,B)$ is not necessarily the same as $H(B,A)$. In order to have a representative metric of similarity between two domains, we computed the *average cross entropy* between two domains, shown in Table 2, and used this quantity as the metric for domain similarity.

Along the main diagonal in the tables below, we also have the cross entropy computed for $H(A,A)$, i.e., when two domains we compare are the same (in boldface). This value, which we call *self entropy* for convenience, is an approximation of the entropy of the corpus A, and measures the amount of information per word, i.e., the *diversity* of the corpus. Note that the self entropy increases in the order of Nikkei → Yomiuri → Encarta → TuneUp → Shincho. This indeed reflects the in-domain variability of text: Nikkei, Yomiuri and Encarta are highly edited text, following style guidelines; they also tend to have repetitious content. In contrast, Shincho is a collection of novels, on which no style or content restriction is imposed. We expect that the LM task to be more difficult as the corpus is more diverse; we will further discuss the effect of diversity in Section 6.[3]

Table 1. Cross entropy (rows: corpora; column: models)

	Nikkei	Yomiuri	TuneUp	Encarta	Shincho
Nikkei	**3.94**	7.46	7.65	9.81	10.10
Yomiuri	7.93	**4.09**	7.62	9.26	9.97
TuneUp	8.25	8.03	**4.41**	9.04	9.06
Encarta	8.79	8.66	8.60	**4.40**	9.30
Shincho	8.70	8.61	8.07	9.10	**4.61**

Table 2. Average cross entropy

	Nikkei	Yomiuri	TuneUp	Encarta	Shincho
Nikkei	**3.94**	7.69	7.95	9.30	9.40
Yomiuri		**4.09**	7.82	8.96	9.29
TuneUp			**4.41**	8.82	8.56
Encarta				**4.40**	9.20
Shincho					**4.61**

5.3 Results of LM Adaptation

We trained our baseline trigram model on our background (Nikkei) corpus using the system described in [12]. The CER (%) of this model on each adaptation domain is in the second column of Table 3. For the LI adaptation method (the third column of Table 3), we trained a word trigram model on the adaptation data, and linearly combined it with the background model, as described in Equation (6).

For the discriminative methods (the last three columns in Table 3), we produced a candidate word lattice for each input phonetic string in the adaptation training set using the background trigram model mentioned above. For efficiency purposes, we kept only the best 20 hypotheses from the lattice as the candidate conversion set for discriminative training. The lowest CER hypothesis in the lattice, rather than the reference transcript, was used as the gold standard.

To compare the performances of different discriminative methods, we fixed the following parameter settings: we set the number of iterations N to be 2,000 for the boosting and MSR methods (i.e., at most 2,000 features in the final models); for the perceptron algorithm, we set T = 40 (in Figure 1). These settings might lead to an

[3] Another derivative notion from Table 1 is the notion of *balanced* corpus. In Table 1, the smallest cross entropy for each text domain (rows) is the self entropy (in boldface), as expected. Note, however, that the second smallest cross entropy (underlined) is always obtained from the TuneUp model (except for Nikkei, for which Yomiuri provides the second smallest cross entropy). This reflects the fact that the TuneUp corpus was created by collecting sentences from various sources of text, in order to create a representative test corpus. Using the notion of cross entropy, such a characteristic of a test corpus can also be quantified.

unfair comparison, as the perceptron algorithm will select far more features than the boosting and MSR algorithm. However, we used these settings as they all converged under these settings. All other parameters were tuned empirically.

In evaluating both MAP and discriminative methods, we used an N-best rescoring approach. That is, we created N best hypotheses using the background trigram model (N=100 in our experiments) for each sentence in test data, and used domain-adapted models to rescore the lattice. The oracle CERs (i.e., the minimal possible CER given the hypotheses in the lattice) ranged from 1.45% to 5.09% depending on the adaptation domain. Table 3 below summarizes the results of various adaptation methods in terms of CER (%) and CER reduction (in parentheses) over the baseline model. In the first column, the numbers in parentheses next to the domain name indicates the number of training sentences used for adaptation.

Table 3. CER (%) and CER reduction over Baseline

Domain	Baseline	LI	Boosting	Perceptron	MSR
Yomiuri (800)	3.70	3.70 (0.00%)	3.13 (15.41%)	3.18 (14.05%)	3.17 (14.32%)
Yomiuri (8K)	3.70	3.69 (0.27%)	2.88 (22.16%)	2.85 (22.97%)	2.88 (22.16%)
Yomiuri (72K)	3.70	3.69 (0.27%)	2.78 (24.86%)	2.78 (24.86%)	2.73 (26.22%)
TuneUp (800)	5.81	5.81 (0.00%)	5.69 (2.07%)	5.69 (2.07%)	5.70 (1.89%)
TuneUp (8K)	5.81	5.70 (1.89%)	5.47 (5.85%)	5.47 (5.85%)	5.47 (5.85%)
TuneUp (72K)	5.81	5.47 (5.85%)	5.33 (8.26%)	5.20 (10.50%)	5.15 (11.36%)
Encarta (800)	10.24	9.60 (6.25%)	9.82 (4.10%)	9.43 (7.91%)	9.44 (7.81%)
Encarta (8K)	10.24	8.64 (15.63%)	8.54 (16.60%)	8.34 (18.55%)	8.42 (17.77%)
Encarta (72K)	10.24	7.98 (22.07%)	7.53 (26.46%)	7.44 (27.34%)	7.40 (27.73%)
Shincho (800)	12.18	11.86 (2.63%)	11.91 (2.22%)	11.90 (2.30%)	11.89 (2.38%)
Shincho (8K)	12.18	11.15 (8.46%)	11.09 (8.95%)	11.20 (8.05%)	11.04 (9.36%)
Shincho (72K)	12.18	10.76 (11.66%)	10.25 (15.85%)	10.18 (16.42%)	10.16 (16.58%)

6 Discussion

6.1 Domain Similarity and CER

The first row of Table 2 shows that the average cross entropy with respect to the background domain (Nikkei) increases in the following order: Yomiuri → TuneUp → Encarta → Shincho. This indicates that among the adaptation domains, Yomiuri is the most similar to Nikkei, closely followed by TuneUp; Shincho and Encarta are the least similar to Nikkei. This is consistent with our intuition, since Nikkei and Yomiuri are both newspaper corpora, and TuneUp, which is a manually constructed corpus from various representative domains of text, contains newspaper articles.

This metric of similarity correlates perfectly with the CER. In Table 3, we see that for all sizes of training data for all adaptation methods, the following order of CER performance is observed, from better to worse: Yomiuri → TuneUp → Encarta → Shincho. In other words, the more similar the adaptation domain is to the background domain, the better the CER results are.

6.2 Domain Similarity and the Effectiveness of Adaptation Methods

The effectiveness of a LM adaptation method is measured by the relative CER reduction over the baseline model. Figure 3 shows the CER reduction of various methods for each domain when the training data size was 8K.[4]

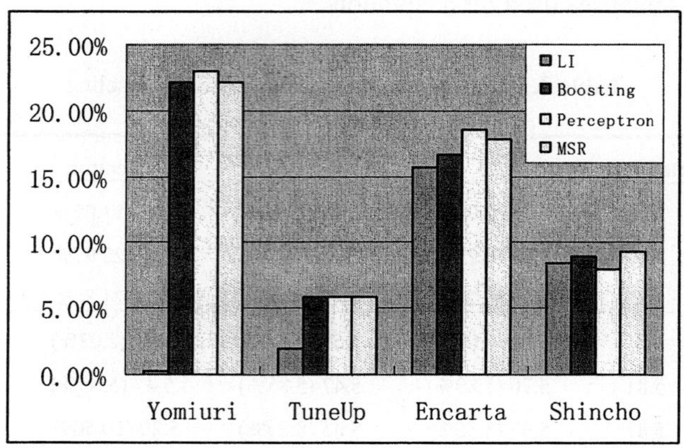

Fig. 2. CER reduction by different adaptation methods

In Figure 2 the X-axis is arranged in the order of domain similarity with the background domain, i.e., Yomiuri → TuneUp → Encarta → Shincho. The first thing we note is that the discriminative methods outperform LI in all cases: in fact, for all rows in Table 3, MSR outperforms LI in a statistically significant manner ($p < 0.01$ using *t*-test);[5] the differences among the three discriminative methods, on the other hand, are not statistically significant in most cases.

We also note that the performance of LI is greatly influenced by domain similarity. More specifically, when the adaptation domain is similar to the background domain (i.e., for Yomiuri and TuneUp corpora), the contribution of the LI model is extremely limited. This can be explained as follows: if the adaptation data is too similar to the background, the difference between the two underlying distributions is so slight that adding adaptation data leads to no or very small improvements.

Such a limitation is not observed with the discriminative methods. For example, all discriminative methods are quite effective on Yomiuri, achieving more than 20% CER reduction. We therefore conclude that discriminative methods, unlike LI, are robust against the similarity between background and adaptations domains.

[4] Essentially the same trend is observed with other training data sizes.

[5] The only exception to this was Shincho (800).

6.3 Adaptation Data Size and CER Reduction

We have seen in Table 3 that in all cases, discriminative methods outperform LI. Among the discriminative methods, an interesting characteristic regarding the CER reduction and the data size is observed. Figure 3 displays the self entropy of four adaptation corpora along the X-axis, and the improvement in CER reduction when 72K-sentence adaptation data is used over when 800 sentences are used along the Y-axis. In other words, for each adaptation method, each point in the figure corresponds to the CER reduction ratio on a domain (corresponding to Yomiuri, Encarta, TuneUp, Shincho from left to right) when 90 times more adaptation data was available.

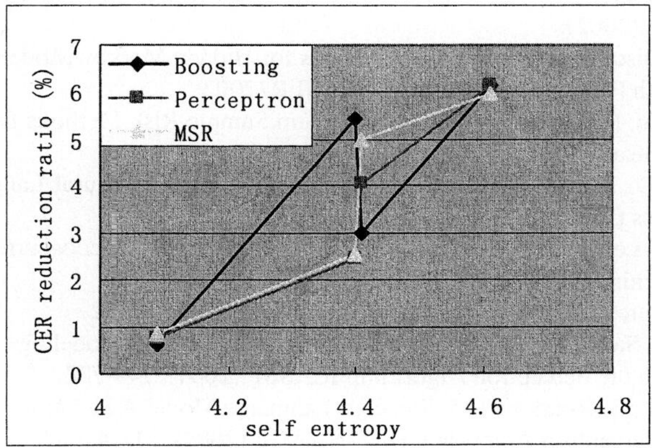

Fig. 3. Improvement in CER reduction for discriminative methods by increasing the adaptation data size from 800 to 72K sentences

From this figure, we can see that there is a positive correlation between the diversity of the adaptation corpus and the benefit of having more training data available. This has an intuitive explanation: the less diverse the adaptation data is, the less distinct training examples it will include for discriminative training. This result is useful in guiding the process of adaptation data collection.

7 Conclusion and Future Work

In this paper, we have examined the performance of various LM adaptation methods in terms of domain similarity and diversity. We have found that (1) the notion of cross-domain similarity, measured by the cross entropy, correlates with the CER of all models (Section 6.1), and (2) the notion of in-domain diversity, measured by the self entropy, correlates with the utility of more adaptation training data for discriminative training methods (Section 6.3). In comparing discriminative methods with a MAP-based method, we have also found that (1) the former uniformly achieve better CER performance than the latter, and (2) are more robust against the similarity of background and adaptation data (Section 6.2).

Though we believe these results are useful in designing the future experiments in domain adaptation, some results and correlations indicated in the paper are still inconclusive. We hope to run additional experiments to confirm these findings. We also did not fully investigate into characterizing the differences among the three discriminative methods; such an investigation is also left for future research.

References

1. Bellagarda, J. An Overview of Statistical Language Model Adaptation. In ITRW on Adaptation Methods for Speech Recognition (2001): 165-174.
2. Collins, M. Ranking Algorithms for Name-Entity Extraction: Boosting and the Voted Perceptron. ACL (2002).
3. Collins, M. Discriminative Training Methods for Hidden Markov Models: Theory and Experiments with Perceptron Algorithms. EMNLP (2002).
4. Gao. J., H. Yu, P. Xu, and W. Yuan. Minimum Sample Risk Methods for Language Modeling. To Appear (2005).
5. Manning, C.D., and H. Schütze. Foundations of Statistical Natural Language Processing. The MIT Press (1999).
6. Dagan, I., L. Lee, and F. Pereira. Similarity-based models of cooccurrence probabilities. Machine Learning, 34(1-3): 43-69 (1999).
7. Lee, L. Measures of distributional similarity. ACL (1999): 25-32.
8. Roark, B, M. Saraclar and M. Collins. Corrective Language Modeling for Large Vocabulary ASR with the Perceptron Algorithm. ICASSP (2004): 749-752.
9. Bacchiani, M., B. Roark and M. Saraclar. Language Model Adaptation with MAP Estimation and the Perceptron Algorithm. HLT-NAACL (2004): 21-24.
10. Bacchiani, M. and B. Roark. Unsupervised language model adaptation. ICASSP (2003): 224-227
11. Och, F.J. Minimum error rate training in statistical machine translation. ACL (2003): 160-167.
12. Gao, J., J. Goodman, M. Li, and K.F. Lee. Toward a unified approach to statistical language modeling for Chinese. ACM Transactions on Asian Language Information Processing l-1 (2002): 3-33.

A Comparative Study of Language Models for Book and Author Recognition

Özlem Uzuner and Boris Katz

MIT,Computer Science and Artificial Intelligence Laboratory,
Cambridge, MA 02139
{ozlem, boris}@csail.mit.edu

Abstract. Linguistic information can help improve evaluation of similarity between documents; however, the kind of linguistic information to be used depends on the task. In this paper, we show that distributions of syntactic structures capture the way works are written and accurately identify individual books more than 76% of the time. In comparison, baseline features, e.g., tfidf-weighted keywords, function words, etc., give an accuracy of at most 66%. However, testing the same features on authorship attribution shows that distributions of syntactic structures are less successful than function words on this task; syntactic structures vary even among the works of the same author whereas features such as function words are distributed more similarly among the works of an author and can more effectively capture authorship.

1 Introduction

Expression is an abstract concept that we define as "the way people convey particular content". Copyrights protect an author's expression of content where *content* refers to the information contained in a work and *expression* refers to the linguistic choices of authors in presenting this content. Therefore, capturing expression is important for copyright infringement detection.

In this paper, we evaluate *syntactic elements of expression* in two contexts: book recognition for copyright infringement detection and authorship attribution. Our first goal is to enable identification of individual books from their expression of content, even when they share content, and even when they are written by the same person. For this purpose, we use a corpus that includes translations of the same original work into English by different people. For the purposes of this study, we refer to the translations as *books* and an original work itself as a *title*.

Given the syntactic elements of expression, our second goal is to test them on authorship attribution, where the objective is to identify all works by a particular author. Our syntactic elements of expression capture differences in the way people express content and could be useful for authorship attribution. However, the experiments we present here indicate that syntactic elements of expression are more successful at identifying expression in individual books while function words are more successful at identifying authors.

R. Dale et al. (Eds.): IJCNLP 2005, LNAI 3651, pp. 969–980, 2005.

2 Related Work

In text classification literature, similarity of works has been evaluated, for example, in terms of genre, e.g., novels vs. poems, in terms of the style of authors, e.g., Austen's novels vs. Kipling's novels, and in terms of topic, e.g., stories about earthquakes vs. stories about volcanoes. In this paper, we compare several different language models in two different classification tasks: book recognition based on similarity of expression, and authorship attribution. Authorship attribution has been studied in the literature; however, evaluation of similarity of expression, e.g., Verne's *20000 Leagues* vs. Flaubert's *Madame Bovary*, is a novel task that we endeavor to address as a first step towards copyright infringement detection.

We define expression as "the linguistic choices of authors in presenting content": content of works and the linguistic choices made while presenting it together constitute expression. Therefore, capturing expression requires measuring similarity of works in terms of both of these components.

To classify documents based on their content, most approaches focus on keywords. Keywords contain information regarding the ideas and facts presented in documents and, despite being ambiguous in many contexts, have been heavily exploited to represent content. In addition to keywords, subject–verb and verb–object relationships [12], noun phrases [12,13], synonym sets of words from WordNet [12], semantic classes of verbs [12] from Levin's studies [21], and proper nouns have all been used to capture content.

Linguistic choices of authors have been studied in stylometry for authorship attribution. Brinegar [7], Glover [9] and Mendenhall [22], among others, used distribution of word lengths to identify authors, e.g., Glover and Hirst studied distributions of two- and three-letter words [9]. Thisted et al. [33] and Holmes [14] studied the idea of richness of vocabulary and the rate at which new words are introduced to the text. Many others experimented with distributions of sentence lengths [9,18,24,30,31,32,38,40], sequences of letters [17,20], and syntactic classes (part of speech) of words [9,20,19].

Mosteller and Wallace [25] studied the distributions of function words to identify the authors of 12 unattributed Federalist papers. Using a subset of the function words from Mosteller and Wallace's work, Peng [26] showed that verbs (used as function words, e.g., be, been, was, had) are important for differentiating between authors. Koppel et al. [19] studied the "stability" of function words and showed that the features that are most useful for capturing the style of authors are "unstable", i.e., they can be replaced without changing the meaning of the text. Koppel et al.'s measure of stability identified function words, tensed verbs, and some part-of-speech tag trigrams as unstable.

Syntactically more-informed studies of the writings of authors came from diMarco and Wilkinson [39] who treated style as a means for achieving particular communicative goals and used parsed text to study the syntactic elements associated with each goal, e.g., clarity vs. obscurity. Adapting elements from Halliday and Hasan [10,11], diMarco et al. studied the use of cohesive elements of text, e.g., anaphora and ellipsis, and disconnective elements of text, e.g., parenthetical constructions, as well as the patterns in the use of relative clauses, noun embeddings, and hypotaxis (marked by subordinating conjunctions) when authors write with different communicative goals.

Expression is related to both content and style. However, it is important to differentiate expression from style. Style refers to the *linguistic elements that, independently of content, persist over the works* of an author and has been widely studied in authorship attribution. Expression involves the *linguistic elements that relate to how an author phrases particular content* and can be used to identify potential copyright infringement.

3 Syntactic Elements of Expression

We hypothesize that, given particular content, authors choose from a set of semantically equivalent syntactic constructs to create their own expression of it. As a result, different authors may choose to express the same content in different ways. In this paper, we capture the differences in expression of authors by studying [34,35,36]:

- sentence-initial and -final phrase structures that capture the shift in focus and emphasis of a sentence due to reordered material,
- semantic classes and argument structures of verbs such as those used in START for question answering [16] and those presented by Levin [21],
- syntactic classes of embedding verbs, i.e., verbs that take clausal arguments, such as those studied by Alexander and Kunz [1] and those used in START for parsing and generation [15], and
- linguistic complexity of sentences, measured both in terms of depths of phrases and in terms of depths of clauses, examples of which are shown in Table 1.

Table 1. Sample sentences broken down into their clauses and the depth of the top-level subject (the number on the left) and predicate (the number on the right)

Sentence	**Depth of Clauses**
$[\text{I}]_a$ [would not think that $[\text{this}]_b$ $[\text{was possible}]_b]_a$	0, 2
$[\text{I}]_a$ [have found $[\text{it}]_b$ [difficult to say that $[\text{I}]_c$ $[\text{like it}]_c]_b]_a$.	2, 2
[That $[\text{she}]_b$ $[\text{would give such a violent reaction}]_b]_a$ $[\text{was unexpected}]_a$.	1, 1
[For $[\text{her}]_b$ $[\text{to see this note}]_b]_a$ $[\text{is impossible}]_a$.	1, 1
$[\text{Wearing the blue shirt}]_a$ $[\text{was a good idea}]_a$.	1, 1
$[\text{It}]_a$ [is not known whether $[\text{he}]_b$ $[\text{actually libelled the queen}]_b]_a$.	0, 2
$[\text{He}]_a$ [was shown that $[\text{the plan}]_b$ $[\text{was impractical}]_b]_a$.	0, 2
$[\text{They}]_a$ [believed $[\text{him}]_b$ $[\text{to be their only hope}]_b]_a$.	0, 2
$[\text{I}]_a$ [suggest $[\text{he}]_b$ $[\text{go alone}]_b]_a$.	0, 2
$[\text{I}]_a$ [waited for $[\text{John}]_b$ $[\text{to come}]_b]_a$.	0, 2

We extracted all of these features from part-of-speech tagged text [5] and studied their distributions in different works. We also studied their correlations with each other, e.g., semantic verb classes and the syntactic structure of the alternation [21] in which they occur. The details of the relevant computations are discussed by Uzuner [34].

3.1 Validation

We validated the syntactic elements of expression using the chi-square (and/or likelihood ratio) test of independence. More specifically, for each of sentence-initial and -final phrase structures, and semantic and syntactic verb classes, we tested the null hypothesis that these features are used similarly by all authors and that the differences observed in different books are due to chance. We performed chi-square tests in three different settings: on different translations of the same title (similar content but different expression), on different books by different authors (different content and different expression), and on disjoint sets of chapters from the same book (similar content and similar expression).

For almost all of the identified features, we were able to reject the null hypothesis when comparing books that contain different expression, indicating that regardless of content, these features can capture expression. For all of the features, we were unable to reject the null hypothesis when we compared chapters from the same book, indicating a certain consistency in the distributions of these features throughout a work.

4 Evaluation

We used the syntactic elements of expression, i.e., sentence-initial and sentence-final phrase structures, semantic and syntactic classes of verbs, and measures of linguistic complexity [34,35,36], for book recognition and for authorship attribution.

4.1 Baseline Features

To evaluate the syntactic elements of expression, we compared the performance of these features to baseline features that capture content and baseline features that capture the way works are written. Our baseline features that capture content included tfidf-weighted keywords [27,28] excluding proper nouns, because for copyright infringement purposes, proper nouns can easily be changed without changing the content or expression of the documents and a classifier based on proper nouns would fail to recognize otherwise identical works. Baseline features that focus on the way people write included function words [25,26], distributions of word lengths [22,40], distributions of sentence lengths [14], and a basic set of linguistic features, extracted from tokenized, part-of-speech tagged, and/or syntactically parsed text. This basic set of linguistic features included the number of words and the number of sentences in the document; type–token ratio;

average and standard deviation of the lengths of words (in characters) and of the lengths of sentences (in words) in the document; frequencies of declarative sentences, interrogatives, imperatives, and fragmental sentences; frequencies of active voice sentences, be-passives, and get-passives; frequencies of 's-genitives, of-genitives, and of phrases that lack genitives; frequency of overt negations; and frequency of uncertainty markers [9,34].

4.2 Classification Experiments

We compared the syntactic elements of expression with the baseline features in two separate experiments: recognizing books even when some of them are derived from the same title (different translations) and recognizing authors. For these experiments, we split books into chapters, created balanced sets of relevant classes, and used boosted [29] decision trees [41] to classify chapters into books and authors. We tuned parameters on the training set: we determined that the performance of classifiers stabilized at around 200 rounds of boosting and we eliminated from each feature set the features with zero information gain [8,37].

Recognizing Books: Copyrights protect original expression of content for a limited time period. After the copyright period of a work, its derivatives by different people are eligible for their own copyright and need to be recognized from their unique expression of content. Our experiment on book recognition focused on and addressed this scenario.

Data: For this experiment, we used a corpus that included 49 *books* derived from 45 *titles*; for 3 of the titles, the corpus included multiple books (3 books for the title *Madame Bovary*, 2 books for *20000 Leagues*, and 2 books for *The Kreutzer Sonata*). The remaining titles included works from J. Austen, F. Dostoyevski, C. Dickens, A. Doyle, G. Eliot, G. Flaubert, T. Hardy, I. Turgenev, V. Hugo, W. Irving, J. London, W. M. Thackeray, L. Tolstoy, M. Twain, and J. Verne. We obtained 40–50 chapters from each book (including each of the books that are derived from the same title), and used 60% of the chapters from each book for training and the remaining 40% for testing.

Results: The results of this evaluation showed that the syntactic elements of expression accurately recognized books 76% of the time; they recognized each of the paraphrased books 89% of the time (see right column in Table 2). In either case, the syntactic elements of expression significantly outperformed all individual baseline features (see Table 2).

The syntactic elements of expression contain no semantic information; they recognize books from the way they are written. The fact that these features can differentiate between translations of the same title implies that translators add their own expression to works, even when their books are derived from the same title, and that the expressive elements chosen by each translator help differentiate between books derived from the same title.

Despite recognizing books more accurately than each of the individual baseline features, syntactic elements of expression on their own are less effective

Table 2. Classification results on the test set for recognizing books from their expression of content even when some books contain similar content

Feature Set	Accuracy on complete corpus	Accuracy on paraphrases only
Syntactic elements of expression	76%	89%
Tfidf-weighted keywords	66%	88%
Function words	61%	81%
Baseline linguistic	42%	53%
Dist. of word length	29%	72%
Dist. of sentence length	13%	14%

than the combined baseline features in recognizing books; the combined baseline features give an accuracy of 88% on recognizing books (compare this to 76% accuracy by the syntactic elements of expression alone). But the performance of the combined baseline features is further improved by the addition of syntactic elements of expression (see Table 3). This improvement is statistically significant at $\alpha = 0.05$.

Table 3. Classification results of combined feature sets on the test set for book recognition even when some books contain similar content

Feature Set	Accuracy on complete corpus	Accuracy on paraphrases only
All baseline features + syntactic elements of expression	92%	98%
All baseline features	88%	97%

Ranking the combined features based on information gain for recognizing books shows that the syntactic elements of expression indeed play a significant role in recognizing books accurately; of the top ten most useful features identified by information gain, seven are syntactic elements of expression (see rows in italics in Table 4).

In the absence of syntactic elements of expression, the top ten most useful features identified by information gain from the complete set of baseline features reveal that the keywords "captain" and "sister" are identified as highly discriminative features. Similarly, the function words "she", "her", and "'ll" are highly discriminative (see Table 5). Part of the predictive power of these features is due to the distinct contents of most of the books in this corpus; we expect that as the corpus grows, these words will lose predictive power.

Recognizing Authors: In Section 2, we described the difference between style and expression. These concepts, though different, both relate to the way people write. Then, an interesting question to answer is: Can the same set of features help recognize both books (from their unique expression) and authors (from their unique style)?

Table 4. Top ten features identified by information gain for recognizing books even when some books share content. Features which are syntactic elements of expression are in italics; baseline features are in roman.

Features
Std. dev. of the depths of the top-level left branches (measured in phrase depth)
Std. dev. of the depths of the top-level right branches (measured in phrase depth)
Std. dev. of the depths of the deepest prepositional phrases of sentences (measured in phrase depth)
% of words that are one character long
Average word length
% of sentences that contain unembedded verbs
% of sentences that contain an unembedded verb with noun phrase object (0-V-NP)
Frequency of the word "the" (normalized by chapter length)
Avg. depth of the subordinating clauses at the beginning of sentences (measured in phrase depth)
% of sentences that contain equal numbers of clauses in left and right branch
Type-token ratio

Table 5. Top ten baseline features identified by information gain that recognize books even when some books share content

Features
% words that are one character long
Average word length
Frequency of the word "the" (normalized by chapter length)
Type-token ratio
Frequency of the word "captain" (tfidf-weighted)
Probability of Negations
Frequency of the word "sister" (tfidf-weighted)
Frequency of the word "she" (normalized by chapter length)
Frequency of the word "her" (normalized by chapter length)
Frequency of the word "'ll" (normalized by chapter length)

Data: In order to answer this question, we experimented with a corpus of books that were written by native speakers of English. This corpus included works from eight authors: three titles by W. Irving, four titles by G. Eliot, five titles by J. Austen, six titles by each of C. Dickens and T. Hardy, eight titles by M. Twain, and nine titles by each of J. London and W. M. Thackeray.

Results: To evaluate the different sets of features on recognizing authors from their style, we trained models on a subset of the titles by each of these authors and tested on a different subset of titles by the same authors. We repeated this experiment five times so that several different sets of titles were trained and tested on. At each iteration, we used 150 chapters from each of the authors for training and 40 chapters from each of the authors for testing.

Table 6. Results for authorship attribution. Classifier is trained on 150 chapters from each author and tested on 40 chapters from each author. The chapters in the training and test sets come from different titles.

Feature Set	Accuracy Run 1	Accuracy Run 2	Accuracy Run 3	Accuracy Run 4	Accuracy Run 5
Function words	86%	89%	87%	90%	81%
Syntactic elements of expression	64%	63%	64%	55%	62%
Distribution of word length	33%	37%	44%	53%	35%
Baseline linguistic	39%	39%	41%	48%	28%
Distribution of sentence length	33%	41%	31%	41%	25%

Table 7. Average classification results on authorship attribution

Feature Set	Avg. Accuracy
Function words	87%
Syntactic elements of expression	62%
Distribution of word length	40%
Baseline linguistic	39%
Distribution of sentence length	34%

The results in Table 7 show that function words capture the style of authors better than any of the other features; syntactic elements of expression are not as effective as function words in capturing the style of authors. This finding is consistent with our intuition: we selected the syntactic elements of expression for their ability to differentiate between individual works, even when some titles are written by the same author and even when some books were derived from the same title. Recognizing the style of an author requires focus on the elements that are similar in the works written by the same author, instead of focus on elements that differentiate these works. However, the syntactic elements of expression are not completely devoid of any style information: they recognize authors accurately 62% of the time. In comparison, the function words recognize authors accurately 87% of the time. Top ten most predictive function words identified by information gain for authorship attribution are: `the`, `not`, `of`, `she`, `very`, `be`, `her`, `'s`, `and`, and `it`.

Combining the baseline features together does not improve the performance of function words on authorship attribution: function words give an accuracy of 87% by themselves whereas the combined baseline features give an accuracy of 86%.[1] Adding the syntactic elements of expression to the combination of baseline features hurts performance (see Table 8).

We believe that the size of the corpus is an important factor in this conclusion. More specifically, we expect that as more authors are added to the corpus, the contribution of syntactic elements of expression to authorship attribution will increase. To test this hypothesis, we repeated our experiments with up to thirteen authors. We observed that the syntactic elements of expression improved the

[1] This difference is not statistically significant.

Table 8. Average classification results of combined feature sets on authorship attribution

Feature Set	Average Accuracy for 8 Authors
All baseline features + syntactic elements of expression	81%
All baseline features	86%
Function words	87%
Syntactic elements of expression	62%

Table 9. Average classification results of combined feature sets on authorship attribution. For these experiments, the original corpus was supplemented with works from W. Ainsworth, L. M. Alcott, T. Arthur, M. Braddon, and H. James.

Feature Set	Average Accuracy for 8-13 Authors					
	8	9	10	11	12	13
All baseline features + syntactic elements of expression	81%	88%	88.4%	87.6%	88%	88%
All baseline features	86%	86%	87.8%	86.6%	86%	86.8%
Function words	87%	86.4%	85.4%	85.2%	84.8%	82.6%
Syntactic elements of expression	62%	65.6%	68.2%	67.4%	66%	64.4%

performance of the baseline features: as we added more authors to the corpus, the performance of function words degraded, the performance of syntactic elements of expression improved, and the performance of the combined feature set remained fairly consistent at around 88% (see Table 9).

4.3 Conclusion

In this paper, we compared several different language models on two classification tasks: book recognition and authorship attribution. In particular, we evaluated syntactic elements of expression consisting of sentence-initial and -final phrase structures, semantic and syntactic categories of verbs, and linguistic complexity measures, on recognizing books (even when they are derived from the same title) and on recognizing authors. Through experiments on a corpus of novels, we have shown that syntactic elements of expression outperform all individual baseline features in recognizing books and when combined with the baseline features, they improve recognition of books.

In our authorship attribution experiments, we have shown that the syntactic elements of expression are not as useful as function words in recognizing the style of authors. This finding highlights the need for a task-dependent approach to engineering feature sets for text classification. In our experiments, feature sets that have been engineered for studying expression and the language models based on these feature sets outperform all others in identifying expression. Similarly, feature sets that have been engineered for studying style and the language models based on these feature sets outperform syntactic elements of expression in authorship attribution.

References

1. D. Alexander and W. J. Kunz. *Some Classes of Verbs in English.* Linguistics Research Project. Indiana University, 1964.
2. J. C. Baker. A Test of Authorship Based on the Rate at which New Words Enter an Author's Text. *Journal of the Association for Literary and Linguistic Computing*, 3(1), 36–39, 1988.
3. D. Biber. A Typology of English Texts. *Language*, 27, 3–43, 1989.
4. D. Biber, S. Conrad, and R. Reppen. *Corpus Linguistics: Investigating Language Structure and Use.* Cambridge University Press, 1998.
5. E. Brill. A Simple Rule-Based Part of Speech Tagger. *Proceedings of the 3rd Conference on Applied Natural Language Processing*, 1992.
6. M. Diab, J. Schuster, and P. Bock. A Preliminary Statistical Investigation into the Impact of an N-Gram Analysis Approach based on Word Syntactic Categories toward Text Author Classification. In Proceedings of *Sixth International Conference on Artificial Intelligence Applications*, 1998.
7. C. S. Brinegar. Mark Twain and the Quintus Curtius Snodgrass Letters: A Statistical Test of Authorship. *Journal of the American Statistical Association*, 58, 85–96, 1963.
8. G. Forman. An Extensive Empirical Study of Feature Selection Metrics for Text Classification. *Journal of Machine Learning Research*, 3, 1289–1305, 2003.
9. A. Glover and G. Hirst. Detecting stylistic inconsistencies in collaborative writing. In *Sharples, Mike and van der Geest, Thea (eds.), The new writing environment: Writers at work in a world of technology.* London: Springer-Verlag, 1996.
10. M. Halliday and R. Hasan. *Cohesion in English.* London: Longman, 1976.
11. M. Halliday. *An introduction to functional grammar.* London; Baltimore, Md., USA : Edward Arnold, 1985.
12. V. Hatzivassiloglou, J. Klavans, and E. Eskin. Detecting Similarity by Applying Learning over Indicators. *37th Annual Meeting of the ACL*, 1999.
13. V. Hatzivassiloglou, J. Klavans, M. Holcombe, R. Barzilay, M.Y. Kan, and K.R. McKeown. SimFinder: A Flexible Clustering Tool for Summarization. *NAACL'01 Automatic Summarization Workshop*, 2001.
14. D. I. Holmes. Authorship Attribution. *Computers and the Humanities*, 28, 87–106. Kluwer Academic Publishers, Netherlands, 1994.
15. B. Katz. Using English for Indexing and Retrieving. *Artificial Intelligence at MIT: Expanding Frontiers.* P. H. Winston and S. A. Shellard, eds. MIT Press. Cambridge, MA., 1990.
16. B. Katz and B. Levin. Exploiting Lexical Regularities in Designing Natural Language Systems. In *Proceedings of the 12th International Conference on Computational Linguistics*, COLING '88, 1988.
17. D. Khmelev and F. Tweedie. Using Markov Chains for Identification of Writers. *Literary and Linguistic Computing*, 16(4), 299–307, 2001.

18. G. Kjetsaa. *The Authorship of the Quiet Don.* ISBN 0391029487. International Specialized Book Service Inc., 1984.
19. M. Koppel, N. Akiva, and I. Dagan. A Corpus-Independent Feature Set for Style-Based Text Categorization. Proceedings of *IJCAI'03 Workshop on Computational Approaches to Style Analysis and Synthesis,* 2003.
20. O. V. Kukushkina, A. A. Polikarpov, and D. V. Khemelev. Using Literal and Grammatical Statistics for Authorship Attribution. Published in *Problemy Peredachi Informatsii,*37(2), April-June 2000, 96–108. Translated in "Problems of Information Transmission", 172–184.
21. B. Levin. *English Verb Classes and Alternations. A Preliminary Investigation.* ISBN 0-226-47533-6. University of Chicago Press. Chicago, 1993.
22. T. C. Mendenhall. Characteristic Curves of Composition. *Science,* 11, 237–249, 1887.
23. G. A. Miller, E. B. Newman, and E. A. Friedman.: Length-Frequency Statistics for Written English. *Information and Control,*1(4), 370–389, 1958.
24. A. Q. Morton. The Authorship of Greek Prose. *Journal of the Royal Statistical Society (A),* 128, 169–233, 1965.
25. F. Mosteller and D. L. Wallace. Inference in an authorship Problem. *Journal of the American Statistical Association,* 58(302), 275–309, 1963.
26. R. D. Peng and H. Hengartner. Quantitative Analysis of Literary Styles. *The American Statistician,* 56(3), 175–185, 2002.
27. G. Salton and C. Buckley. Term-weighting approaches in automatic text retrieval. *Information Processing and Management,* 24(5), 513–523, 1998.
28. G. Salton, A. Wong, and C. S. Yang. A vector space model for automatic indexing. *Communications of the ACM,* 18(11), 613–620, 1975.
29. R. E. Schapire. The Boosting Approach to Machine Learning. In *MSRI Workshop on Nonlinear Estimation and Classification,* 2002.
30. H. S. Sichel. On a Distribution Representing Sentence-Length in Written Prose. *Journal of the Royal Statistical Society (A),* 137, 25–34, 1974.
31. M. W. A. Smith. Recent Experience and New Developments of Methods for the Determination of Authorship. *Association for Literary and Linguistic Computing Bulletin,* 11, 73–82, 1983.
32. D. R. Tallentire. *An Appraisal of Methods and Models in Computational Stylistics, with Particular Reference to Author Attribution.* PhD Thesis. University of Cambridge, 1972.
33. R. Thisted and B. Efron. Did Shakespeare Write a Newly-discovered Poem? *Biometrika,* 74, 445–455, 1987.
34. Ö. Uzuner. *Identifying Expression Fingerprints using Linguistic Information.* Ph.D. Dissertation. Massachusetts Institute of Technology, 2005.
35. Ö. Uzuner and B. Katz. Capturing Expression Using Linguistic Information. In *Proceedings of the 20th National Conference on Artificial Intelligence (AAAI-05),* 2005.
36. Ö. Uzuner, B. Katz and Thade Nahnsen. Using Syntactic Information to Identify Plagiarism. In *Proceedings of the Association for Computational Linguistics Workshop on Educational Applications (ACL 2005),* 2005.
37. Y. Yang and J. O. Pedersen. A Comparative Study on Feature Selection in Text Categorization. In *Proceedings of ICML-97, 14th International Conference on Machine Learning.* 412–420, 1997.

38. G. U. Yule. On Sentence-Length as a Statistical Characteristic of Style in Prose, with Application to Two Cases of Disputed Authorship. *Biometrika*, 30, 363–390, 1938.
39. J. Wilkinson and C. diMarco. Automated Multi-purpose Text Processing. In *Proceedings of IEEE Fifth Annual Dual-Use Technologies and Applications Conference*, 1995.
40. C. B. Williams. Mendenhall's Studies of Word-Length Distribution in the Works of Shakespeare and Bacon. *Biometrika*, 62(1), 207–212, 1975.
41. I. H. Witten and E. Frank. Data Mining: Practical machine Learning Tools with Java Implementations. Morgan Kaufmann, San Francisco, 2000.

Lexical Choice via Topic Adaptation for Paraphrasing Written Language to Spoken Language

Nobuhiro Kaji[1] and Sadao Kurohashi[2]

[1] Institute of Industrial Science, The University of Tokyo,
4-6-1 Komaba, Meguro-ku, Tokyo 153-8505, Japan
kaji@tkl.iis.u-tokyo.ac.jp

[2] Graduate School of Information Science and Technology,
The University of Tokyo, 7-3-1 Hongo,
Bunkyo-ku, Tokyo 113-8656, Japan
kuro@kc.t.u-tokyo.ac.jp

Abstract. Our research aims at developing a system that paraphrases written language text to spoken language style. In such a system, it is important to distinguish between appropriate and inappropriate words in an input text for spoken language. We call this task lexical choice for paraphrasing. In this paper, we describe a method of lexical choice that considers the topic. Basically, our method is based on the word probabilities in written and spoken language corpora. The novelty of our method is topic adaptation. In our framework, the corpora are classified into topic categories, and the probability is estimated using such corpora that have the same topic as input text. The result of evaluation showed the effectiveness of topic adaptation.

1 Introduction

Written language is different from spoken language. That difference has various aspects. For example, spoken language is often ungrammatical, or uses simplified words rather than difficult ones etc. Among these aspects this paper examines difficulty. Difficult words are characteristic of written language and are not appropriate for spoken language.

Our research aims at developing a system that paraphrases written language text into spoken language style. It helps text-to-speech generating natural voice when the input is in written language. In order to create such a system, the following procedure is required: (1) the system has to detect inappropriate words in the input text for spoken language, (2) generate paraphrases of inappropriate words, and (3) confirm that the generated paraphrases are appropriate. This paper examines step (1) and (3), which we call lexical choice for paraphrasing written language to spoken language.

Broadly speaking, lexical choice can be defined as binary classification task: the input is a word and a system outputs whether it is appropriate for spoken

R. Dale et al. (Eds.): IJCNLP 2005, LNAI 3651, pp. 981–992, 2005.

language or not. This definition is valid if we can assume that the word difficulty is independent of such factors as context or listeners. However, we think such assumption is not always true. One example is business jargon (or technical term). Generally speaking, business jargon is difficult and inappropriate for spoken language. Notwithstanding, it is often used in business talk. This example implies that the word difficulty is dependent on the topic of text/talk.

In this paper, we define the input of lexical choice as a word and text where it occurs (= the topic). Such definition makes it possible for a system to consider the topic. We think the topic plays an important role in lexical choice, when dealing with such words that are specific to a certain topic, e.g., business jargon. Hereafter, those words are called *topical words*, and others are called non-topical words. Of course, in addition to the topic, we have to consider other factors such as listeners and so on. But, the study of such factors lies outside the scope of this paper.

Based on the above discussion, we describe a method of lexical choice that considers the topic. Basically, our method is based on the word probabilities in written and spoken language corpora. It is reasonable to assume that these two probabilities reflect whether the word is appropriate or not. The novelty of the method is topic adaptation. In order to adapt to the topic of the input text, the corpora are classified into topic categories, and the probability is estimated using such corpora that have the same topic category as the input text. This process enables us to estimate topic-adapted probability. Our method was evaluated by human judges. Experimental results demonstrated that our method can accurately deal with topical words.

This paper is organized as follows. Section 2 represents method overview. Section 3 and Section 4 describe the corpora construction. Section 5 represents learning lexical choice. Section 6 reports experimental results. Section 7 describes related works. We conclude this paper in Section 8.

2 Method Overview

Our method uses written and spoken language corpora classified into topic categories. They are automatically constructed from the WWW. The construction procedure consists of the following two processes (Figure 1).

1. **Style Classification**
   Web pages are downloaded from the WWW, and are classified into written and spoken language style. Those pages classified as written/spoken language are referred as written/spoken language corpus. In this process, we discarded ambiguous pages that are difficult to classify.
2. **Topic Classification**
   The written and spoken language corpora are classified into 14 topic categories, such as arts, computers and so on.

Both classification methods are represented in Section 3 and Section 4.

Given an input word and a text where it occurs, it is decided as follows whether the input word is appropriate or inappropriate for spoken language.

1. The topic category of the input text is decided by the same method as the one used to classify Web pages into topic categories.
2. We estimate the probabilities of the input word in the written and spoken language corpora. We use such corpora that have the same topic as the input text.
3. Using the two probabilities, we decide whether the input word is appropriate or not. Section 5 describes this method.

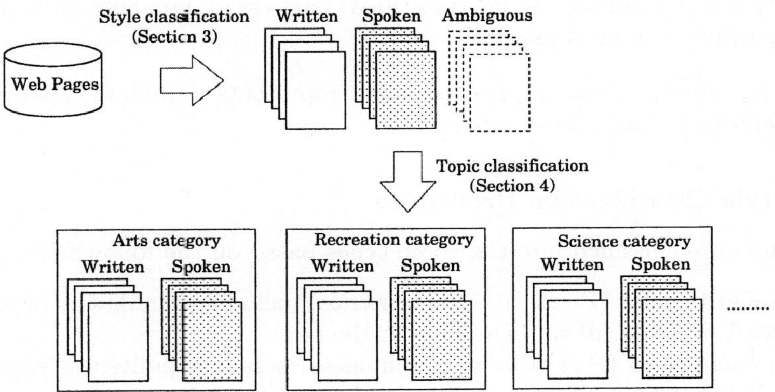

Fig. 1. Written and spoken language corpora construction

3 Style Classification

In order to construct written and spoken language corpora classified into topic categories, first of all, Web pages are classified into written and spoken language pages (Figure 1). Note that what is called spoken language here is not real utterance but chat like texts. Although it is not real spoken language, it works as a good substitute, as some researchers pointed out [2,11].

We follow a method proposed by Kaji et al (2004). Their method classifies Web pages into three types: (1) written language page, (2) spoken language page, and (3) ambiguous page. Then, Web pages classified into type (1) or (2) are used. Ambiguous pages are discarded because classification precision decreases if such pages are used. This Section summarizes their method. See [11] for detail. Note that for this method the target language is Japanese, and its procedure is dependent on Japanese characteristics.

3.1 Basic Idea

Web pages are classified based on interpersonal expressions, which imply an attitude of a speaker toward listeners, such as familiarity, politeness, honor or contempt etc. Interpersonal expressions are often used in spoken language, although not frequently used in written language. For example, when spoken language is used, one of the most basic situations is face-to-face communication. On the other hand, such situation hardly happens when written language is used.

Therefore, Web pages containing many interpersonal expressions are classified as spoken language, and vice versa. Among interpersonal expressions, such expressions that represent familiarity or politeness are used, because:

- Those two kinds of interpersonal expressions frequently appear in spoken language,
- They are represented by postpositional particle in Japanese and, therefore, are easily recognized as such.

Hereafter, interpersonal expression that represents familiarity/politeness is called familiarity/politeness expression.

3.2 Style Classification Procedure

Web pages are classified into the three types based on the following two ratios:

- Familiarity ratio (F-ratio): '# of sentences including familiarity expressions' divided by '# of all the sentences in the page'.
- Politeness ratio (P-ratio): '# of sentences including politeness expressions' divided by '# of all the sentences in the page'.

The procedure is as follows. First, Web pages are processed by Japanese morphological analyzer JUMAN[3]. And then, in order to calculate F-ratio and P-ratio, sentences which include familiarity or politeness expressions are recognized in the following manner. A sentence is considered to include the familiarity expression, if it has one of the following six postpositional particles: *ne*, *yo*, *wa*, *sa*, *ze*, *na*. A sentence is considered to include the politeness expression, if it has one of the following four postpositional particles: *desu*, *masu*, *kudasai*, *gozaimasu*.

After calculating the two ratios, the page is classified according to the rules illustrated in Figure 2. If F-ratio and P-ratio are equal to 0, the page is classified as written language page. If F-ratio is more than 0.2, or if F-ratio is more than 0.1 and P-ratio is more than 0.2, the page is classified as spoken language page. The other pages are regarded as ambiguous and are discarded.

3.3 The Result

Table 1 shows the number of pages and words (noun, verb, and adjective) in the corpora constructed from the WWW. About 8,680k pages were downloaded from the WWW, and 994k/1,338k were classified as written/spoken language. The rest were classified as ambiguous page and they were discarded. The precision of this method was reported by Kaji et al (2004). According to their experiment, the precision was 94%.

[3] http://www.kc.t.u-tokyo.ac.jp/nl-resource/juman-e.html

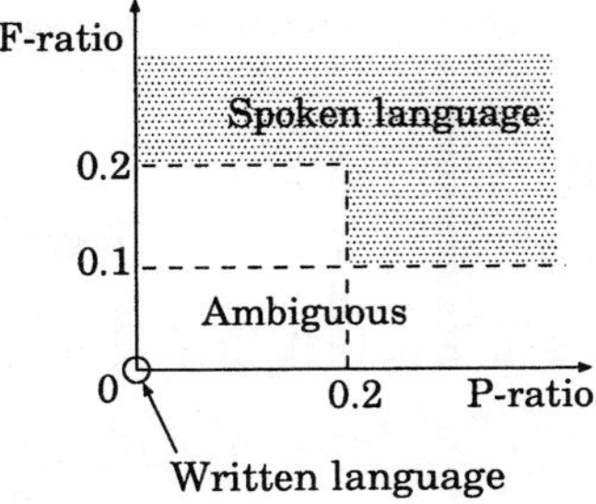

Fig. 2. Style classification rule

Table 1. The size of the written and spoken language corpora

	# of pages	# of words
Written language	989k	432M
Spoken language	1,337k	907M

Table 2. The size of the training and test data

Topic category	Training	Test
Arts	2,834	150
Business & Economy	5,475	289
Computers & Internet	6,156	325
Education	2,943	155
Entertainment	6,221	328
Government	3,131	165
Health	1,800	95
News	2,888	152
Recreation	4,352	230
Reference	1,099	58
Regional	4,423	233
Science	3,868	204
Social Science	5,410	285
Society & Culture	5,208	275

4 Topic Classification

The written and spoken language corpora are classified into 14 topic categories (Figure 1). This task is what is called text categorization. We used Support Vector Machine because it is reported to achieve high performance in this task.The training data was automatically built from Yahoo! Japan[4].

The category provided by Yahoo! Japan have hierarchy structure. For example, there are Arts and Music categories, and Music is one of the subcategories of Arts. We used 14 categories located at the top level of the hierarchy. We downloaded Web pages categorized in one of the 14 categories. Note that we did not use Web pages assigned more than one categories. And then, the Web pages were divided them into 20 segments. One of them was used as the test data, and the others were used as the training data (Table 2). In the Table, the

[4] http://www.yahoo.co.jp/

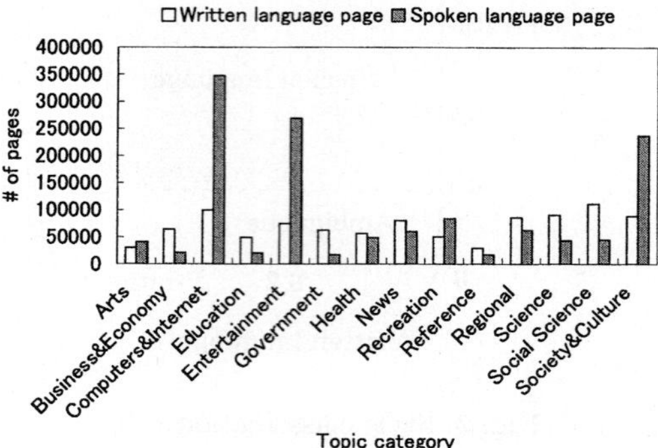

Fig. 3. The size of written and spoken language corpora in each topic category

first column shows the name of the 14 topic categories. The second/third column shows the number of pages in the training/test data.

SVM was trained using the training data. In order to build multi-class classifier, we used One-VS-Rest method. Features of SVM are probabilities of nouns in a page. Kernel function was linear. After the training, it was applied to the test data. The macro-averaged accuracy was 86%.

The written and spoken language corpora constructed from the WWW were classified into 14 categories by SVM. Figure 3 depicts the number of pages in each category.

5 Learning Lexical Choice

We can now construct the written and spoken language corpora classified into topic categories. The next step is discrimination between inappropriate and appropriate words for spoken language using the probabilities in written and spoken language corpora (Section 2). This paper proposes two methods: one is based on Decision Tree (DT), and the other is based on SVM. This Section first describes the creation of gold standard data, which is used for both training and evaluation. Then, we describe the features given to DT and SVM.

5.1 Creation of Gold Standard Data

We prepared data consisting of pairs of a word and binary tag. The tag represents whether that word is inappropriate or appropriate for spoken language. This data is referred as gold standard data. Note that the gold standard is created for each topic category.

Gold standard data of topic T is created as follows.

1. Web pages in topic T are downloaded from Yahoo! Japan, and we sampled words (verbs, nouns, and adjectives) from those pages at random.
2. Three human judges individually mark each word as INAPPROPRIATE, APPROPRIATE or NEUTRAL. NEUTRAL tag is used when a judge cannot mark a word as INAPPROPRIATE or APPROPRIATE with certainty.

3. The three annotations are combined, and single gold standard data is created. A word is marked as INAPPROPRIATE/APPROPRIATE in the gold standard, if
   - All judges agree that it is INAPPROPRIATE/APPROPRIATE, or
   - Two judges agree that it is INAPPROPRIATE/APPROPRIATE and the other marked it as NEUTRAL.

   The other words are not used in the gold standard data.

5.2 The Features

Both DT and SVM use the same three features: the word probability in written language corpus, the word probability in spoken language corpus, and the ratio of the word probability in spoken language corpus to that in written language. Note that when DT and SVM are trained on the gold standard of topic T, the probability is estimated using the corpus in topic T.

6 Evaluation

This Section first reports the gold standard creation. Then, we show that DT and SVM can successfully classify INAPPROPRIATE and APPROPRIATE words in the gold standard. Finally, the effect of topic adaptation is represented.

6.1 The Gold Standard Data

The annotation was performed by three human judges (Judge1, Judge2 and Judge3) on 410 words sampled from Business category, and 445 words sampled from Health category. Then, we created the gold standard data in each category (Table 3). The average Kappa value [3] between the judges was 0.60, which corresponds to substantial agreement.

Table 3. Gold standard data

	Business	Health
INAPPROPRIATE	49	38
APPROPRIATE	267	340
Total	316	378

Table 4. # of words in Business and Health categories corpora

	Business	Health
Written language	29,891k	30,778k
Spoken language	9,018k	32,235k

6.2 Lexical Choice Evaluation

DT and SVM were trained and tested on the gold standard data using Leave-One-Out (LOO) cross validation. DT and SVM were implemented using C4.5[5] and TinySVM[6] packages. The kernel function of SVM was Gaussian RBF. Table

[5] http://www.rulequest.com/Personal/

[6] http://chasen.org/ taku/software/TinySVM/

Table 5. The result of LOO cross validation

Topic	Method	Accuracy	# of correct answers	Precision	Recall
Business	DT	.915 (289/316)	31 + 258 = 289	.775	.660
	SVM	.889 (281/316)	21 + 260 = 281	.750	.429
	MCB	.845 (267/316)	0 + 267 = 267	—	.000
Health	DT	.918 (347/378)	21 + 326 = 347	.600	.552
	SVM	.918 (347/378)	13 + 334 = 347	.684	.342
	MCB	.899 (340/378)	0 + 340 = 340	—	.000

4 shows the number of words in Business and Health categories corpora. Three features described in Section 5 were used.

The result is summarized in Table 5. For example, in Business category, the accuracy of DT was 91.5%. 289 out of 316 words were classified successfully, and the 289 consists of 31 INAPPROPRIATE and 258 APPROPRIATE words. The last two columns show the precision and recall of INAPPROPRIATE words. MCB is Majority Class Baseline, which marks every word as APPROPRIATE.

Judging from the accuracy in Health category, one may think that our method shows only a little improvement over MCB. However, considering other evaluation measures such as recall of INAPPROPRIATE words, it is obvious that the proposed method overwhelms MCB. We would like to emphasize the fact that MCB is not at all practical lexical choice method. If MCB is used, all words in the input text are regarded as appropriate for spoken language and the input is never paraphrased.

One problem of our method is that the recall of INAPPROPRIATE words is low. We think that the reason is as follows. The number of INAPPROPRIATE words in the gold standard is much smaller than that of APPROPRIATE words. Hence, we think a system that is biased to classify words as APPROPRIATE often achieves high accuracy. It is one of future works to improve the recall while keeping high accuracy.

We examined discrimination rules learned by DT. Figure 4 depicts the rules learned by DT when the whole gold standard data of Business category is used as a training data. In the Figure, the horizontal/vertical axis corresponds to the probability in the written/spoken language corpus. Words in the gold standard can be mapped into this two dimension space. INAPPROPRIATE/ APPROPRIATE words are represented by a cross/square. The line represents discrimination rules. Words below the line are classified as INAPPROPRIATE, and the others are classified as APPROPRIATE.

6.3 Effect of Topic Adaptation

Finally, we investigated the effect of topic adaptation by comparing our method to a baseline method that does not consider topic.

Our method consists of two steps: (1) mapping from a word to features, and (2) applying discrimination rules to the features. In the step (1), the probability is estimated using the written and spoken language corpora in a certain topic

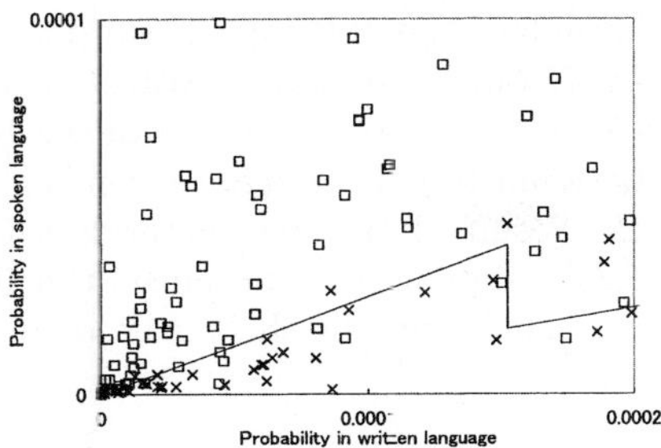

Fig. 4. Decision tree rules in Business category

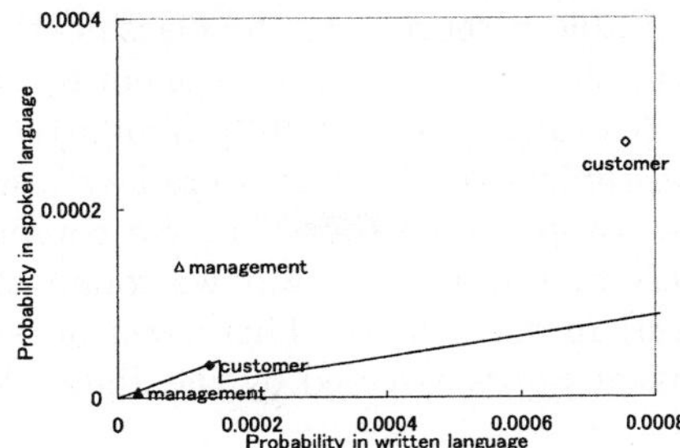

Fig. 5. Examples in Business category

T. In the step (2), discrimination rules are learned by DT using the whole gold standard data of topic T. We used DT rather than SVM because rules are easy for humans to understand. On the other hand, the baseline uses the same discrimination rules as our method, but uses the whole written and spoken language corpora to map a word to features. Hereafter, the two methods are referred as PROPOSED and BASELINE. Both methods use the same discrimination rules but map a word to features in a different way. Therefore, there are such words that are classified as INAPPROPRIATE by PROPOSED and are classified as APPROPRIATE by BASELINE, and vice versa. In the evaluation, we compared the classification results of such words.

We evaluated the results of topical words and non-topical words separately. This is because we think PROPOSED is good at dealing with topical words and hence we can clearly confirm the effectiveness of topic adaptation. Here, a word is regarded as topical word in topic T, if its probabilities in the written and spoken language corpora assigned topic category T are larger than those in the whole corpora with statistical significance (the 5% level). Otherwise it is regarded as non-topical word in topic T. As a statistical test log-likelihood ratio [4] was used. The evaluation procedure is as follows.

1. Web pages in Business category were downloaded from Yahoo! Japan, and words in those pages were classified by the two methods. If the results of the two methods disagree, such words were stocked.
2. From the stocked words, we randomly sampled 50 topical words in Business and 50 non-topical words. Note that we did not use such words that are contained in the gold standard.
3. Using Web pages in Health category, we also sampled 50 topical words in Health and 50 non-topical words in the same manner.
4. As a result, 100 topical words and 100 non-topical words were prepared. For each word, two judges (Judge-A and Judge-B) individually assessed which method successfully classified the word. Some classification results were difficult even for human judges to assess. In such cases, the results of the both methods were regarded as correct.

Table 6 represents the classification accuracy of the 100 topical words. For example, according to assessment by Judge-A, 75 out of 100 words were classified successfully by PROPOSED. Similarly, Table 7 represents the accuracy of the 100 non-topical words. The overall agreement between the two judges according to the Kappa value was 0.56. We compared the result of the two methods using McNemar's test [8], and we found statistically significant difference (the 5% level) in the results. There was no significant difference in the result of non-topical words assessed by the Judge-A.

Table 6. Accuracy of topical words classification

Judge	Method	Accuracy
Judge-A	PROPOSED	75% (75/100)
	BASELINE	52% (52/100)
Judge-B	PROPOSED	72% (72/100)
	BASELINE	53% (53/100)

Table 7. Accuracy of non-topical words classification

Judge	Method	Accuracy
Judge-A	PROPOSED	48% (48/100)
	BASELINE	66% (66/100)
Judge-B	PROPOSED	38% (38/100)
	BASELINE	78% (78/100)

6.4 Discussion and Future Work

PROPOSED outperformed BASELINE in topical words classification. This result indicates that the difficulty of topical words depends on the topic and we have to consider the topic. On the other hand, the result of PROPOSED was not good when applied to non-topical words. We think this result is caused by two reasons: (1) the difficulty of non-topical words is independent of the topic, and (2) BASELINE uses larger corpora than PROPOSED (see Table 1 and Table 4). Therefore, we think this result does not deny the effectiveness of topic adaptation. These results mean that PROPOSED and BASELINE are complementary to each other, and it is effective to combine the two methods: PROPOSED/BASELINE is applied to topical/non-topical words. It is obvious from the experimental results that such combination is effective.

We found that BASELINE is prone to classify topical words as inappropriate and such bias decreases the accuracy. Figure 5 depicts typical examples sampled from topical words in Business. Both judges regarded 'management' and 'customer'[7] as appropriate for spoken language in Business topic. The white triangle and diamond in the Figure represent their features when the probability is estimated using the corpora in Business category. They are located above the line, which corresponds to discrimination rules, and are successfully classified as appropriate by PROPOSED. However, if the probability is estimated using the whole corpora, the features shift to the black triangle and diamond, and BASELINE wrongly classified the two as inappropriate. In Health category, we could observe similar examples such as 'lung cancer' or 'metastasis'.

[7] Our target language is Japanese. Examples illustrated here are translation of the original Japanese words.

These examples can be explained in the following way. Consider topical words in Business. When the probability is estimated using the whole corpora, it is influenced by the topic but Business, where topical words in Business are often inappropriate for spoken language. Therefore, we think that BASELINE is biased to classify topical words as inappropriate.

Besides the lexical choice method addressed in this paper, we proposed lexical paraphrase generation method [10]. Our future direction is to apply these methods to written language texts and evaluate the output of text-to-speech. So far, the methods were tested on a small set of reports.

Although the main focus of this paper is lexical paraphrases, we think that it is also important to deal with structural paraphrases. So far, we implemented a system that paraphrases compound nouns into nominal phrases. It is our future work to build a system that generates other kinds of structural paraphrases.

7 Related Work

Lexical choice has been widely discussed in both paraphrasing and natural language generation (NLG). However, to the best of our knowledge, no researches address topic adaptation. Previous approaches are topic-independent or specific to only certain topic.

Lexical choice has been one of the central issues in NLG. However, the main focus is mapping from concepts to words, (e.g., [1]). In NLG, a work by Edmonds and Hirst is related to our research [5]. They proposed a computational model that represents the connotation of words.

Some paraphrasing researches focus on lexical choice. Murata and Isahara addressed paraphrasing written language to spoken language. They used only probability in spoken language corpus [12]. Kaji et al. also discussed paraphrasing written language to spoken language, and they used the probabilities in written and spoken language corpora [11]. On the other hand, Inkpen et al. examined paraphrasing positive and negative text [9]. They used the computational model proposed by Edmonds and Hirst [5].

The proposed method is based on the probability, which can be considered as a simple language model. In language model works, many researchers have discussed topic adaptation in order to precisely estimate the probability of topical words [6,7,13]. Our work can be regarded as one application of such language model technique.

8 Conclusion

This paper proposed lexical choice method that considers the topic. The method utilizes written and spoken language corpora classified into topic categories, and estimate the word probability that is adapted to the topic of the input text. From the experimental result we could confirm the effectiveness of topic adaptation.

References

1. Berzilay, R., Lee, L.: Bootstrapping Lexical Choice via Multiple-Sequence Alignment. Proceedings of EMNLP. (2002) 50–57
2. Bulyko, I., Ostendorf, M., and Stolcke, A.: Getting More Mileage from Web Text Sources for Conversational Speech Language Modeling using Class-Dependent Mixtures. Proceedings of HLT-NAACL (2003) 7–9
3. Carletta, J.: Assessing Agreement on Classification Tasks: The Kappa Statistic. Computational Linguistics. **22** (2). (1996) 249–255
4. Dunning, T.: Accurate Methods for the Statistics of Surprise and Coincidence. Computational Linguistics. **19** (1). (1993) 61–74
5. Edmonds, P., Hirst, G.: Near-Synonymy and Lexical Choice. Computational Linguistics. **28** (2). (2002) 105–144
6. Florian, R., Yarowsky, D.: Dynamic Nonlocal Language Modeling via Hierarchical Topic-Based Adaptation: Proceedings of ACL. (1999) 167–174
7. Gildea, D., Hofmann, T.; TOPIC-BASED LANGUAGE MODELS USING EM. Proceedings of EUROSPEECH. (1999) 2167–2170
8. Gillick, L., Cox, S.: Some Statistical Issues in the Comparison of Speech Recognition Algorithms. Proceedings of ICASSP. (1989) 532–535
9. Inkpen, D., Feiguina, O., and Hirst, G.: Generating more-positive and more-negative text. Proceedings of AAAI Spring Symposium on Exploring Attitude and Affect in Text. (2004)
10. Kaji, N., Kawahara, D., Kurohashi, S., and Satoshi, S. : Verb Paraphrase based on Case Frame Alignment. Proceedings of ACL. (2002) 215–222
11. Kaji, N., Okamoto, M., and Kurohasih, S.: Paraphrasing Predicates from Written Language to Spoken Language Using the Web. Proceedings of HLT-NAACL. (2004) 241–248
12. Murata, M., Isahara, H.: Automatic Extraction of Differences Between Spoken and Written Languages, and Automatic Translation from the Written to the Spoken Language. Proceedings of LREC. (2002)
13. Wu, J., Khudanpur, S.: BUILDING A TOPIC-DEPENDENT MAXIMUM ENTROPY MODEL FOR VERY LARGE CORPORA. Proceedings of ICASSP. (2002) 777–780

A Case-Based Reasoning Approach for Speech Corpus Generation

Yandong Fan and Elizabeth Kendall

School of Network Computing, Faculty of IT, Monash University, Australia
yandong.fan@infotech.monash.edu.au
Kendall@infotech.monash.edu.au

Abstract. Corpus-based stochastic language models have achieved significant success in speech recognition, but construction of a corpus pertaining to a specific application is a difficult task. This paper introduces a Case-Based Reasoning system to generate natural language corpora. In comparison to traditional natural language generation approaches, this system overcomes the inflexibility of template-based methods while avoiding the linguistic sophistication of rule-based packages. The evaluation of the system indicates our approach is effective in generating users' specifications or queries as 98% of the generated sentences are grammatically correct. The study result also shows that the language model derived from the generated corpus can significantly outperform a general language model or a dictation grammar.

1 Introduction

Stochastic language models have achieved significant success in speech recognition since the last decade [1, 2]. The main underlying technique in stochastic approaches is the use of corpora. The successful utilization of corpora has been proven by many researchers [3,4,5]. However, construction of a corpus pertaining to a specific application is a difficult task, given that there is no pre-knowledge on how users might communicate with the application before the deployment of a system. Research [6] has been conducted to explore the effectiveness of Web-based text corpus generation. Although the proliferation of eText has made the collection of textual material easier than ever, Thompson [7] argues that actually locating eText appropriate to your needs can be quite difficult. Moreover, in the context of conversational systems, the suitability of corpora purely collected from the Internet is controversial due to the difference of written text and spoken language.

Although generally there is a lack of spoken material pertaining to a new application, ample transcriptions do exist in some well-established domains, such as the Air Traffic Information System (ATIS) domain. User modeling has been studied for long and conversations between users and agents of spoken language systems have been recorded and accumulated for decades in these domains. In our project, we seek to develop a speech-enabled mobile commerce application, which we called the MCCS (Mobile Car City system). The system allows a mobile-phone user to specify preferences or initiate queries by speech at the beginning of the conversation. Then all

R. Dale et al. (Eds.): IJCNLP 2005, LNAI 3651, pp. 993 – 1003, 2005.

car models conforming to the preferences or queries are retrieved to guide the user in finding specific car models that meet his/her needs. Through carefully examining the spoken transcriptions from the ATIS domain, we believe that user specifications or queries in the MCCS system should share significant similarity in sentence syntactic structure with their counterparts in the ATIS domain. Motivated by this assumption, we believe that the MCCS system can learn a set of sample sentences from the ATIS domain, which can then be used as the knowledge base for case-based reasoning (CBR) to generate a speech corpus pertaining to the MCCS domain.

NLG (Natural Language Generation) research has been dominated by two approaches in the past three decades: template-based and rule-based [8, 9]. Some claim that template-based approaches are not flexible enough while others criticize the sophistication of linguistic grammars implemented in rule-based approaches [8]. A new strand in the arena is learning-based NLG, in which the objective is to learn the mapping from semantics to surface realization through sample sentences. Research [10, 11, 12] suggests that learning-based approaches can balance the inflexibility of template-based methods and the linguistic sophistication of rule-based NLG packages when developing domain-specific generation systems.

In this paper, we explore an incremental learning approach for speech corpus generation. Firstly, a set of sample sentences pertaining to user specifications or queries in the MCCS application are learnt from the ATIS domain. Secondly, a CBR system is built to generate a corpus based on those sample sentences. Finally, an n-gram language model is derived from the corpus by learning the statistical distribution of tokens. The paper is structured as follows. Section 2 introduces the general structure of the corpus generation system. Detailed implementation of the system is described through Section 3-5. Section 6 presents the evaluation results of the generated corpus. Related work is discussed in Section 7. We conclude the study and briefly discuss potential future work in Section 8.

2 System Overview

Our aim is to develop a case-based, domain-specific generation system that can significantly reduce complexity in comparison to rule-based solutions. Case-based reasoning (CBR) systems have long been applied for problem solving in many areas, such as classification, diagnosis, configuration and design, and planning, but only recently has it attracted significant attention from researchers in NLG. Like any other CBR system, a CBR-based NLG system has to include the following components:

- Sample sentence set (Case Base)
- Schema for sentence structure, includes semantic and syntactic (Knowledge Representation)
- Similarity measurement (Acceptance Function)
- Sentence generation (Case Retrieval and adaptation algorithms)

Figure 1 represents the overall structure of our CBR-based corpus generation system. The system implements a pipeline architecture consisting of three stages. Firstly, an initial sample sentence set is created manually to integrate an ATIS sentence base (ASB) and a MCCS phrasal base (MPB). The ASB is a collection of sentences from a well-established corpus in the ATIS domain. The MPB collects phrases in describing car model features, which are abstracted from car manufacturers' websites and marketing brochures. Through careful analysis on the sentences in the ASB and the phrases in the MPB, sample sentences for user queries or specifications pertaining to the MCCS system can be created to form a case sentence base (CSB). The examples (2.1)-(2.3) show an ATIS sentence from the ASB, a MCCS phrase from the MPB, and a sample sentence from the CSB, respectively.

I prefer [**PluralObject** flights] [**ServiceFeature** serve lunch] (2.1)

[**SingularObject** A car] with [**NumOfDoorFeature** four doors] (2.2)

I prefer **cars** with **four doors.** (2.3)

Secondly, these sample sentences in the CSB are annotated to abstract semantic structure and corresponding syntactic structure, which become the case representation for instance learning. Finally, based on the understanding of the characteristics of user queries and specifications, a new input that represents a unique semantic meaning passes through the CBR system. The similarity between the input and a case is calculated and examined. If the distance is within the predefined threshold, adaptation is conducted to generate a new syntactic structure for the semantic input. This procedure is continuously performed until all possible inputs are enumerated. The resultant corpus is then ready for creating an n-gram language model.

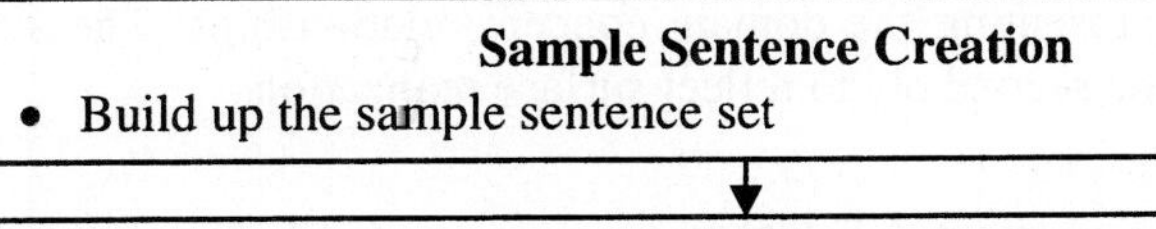

Sample Sentence Creation
• Build up the sample sentence set
Case Sentence Annotation
• Implement the schema for representing the semantic and syntactic structure of sample sentences
Corpus Generation
• Retrieve cases from the set
• Calculate the distance between a new input and a case
• Perform adaptation to generate new sentences

Fig. 1. Main procedures of the CBR-based corpus generation system

3 Sample Sentence Set

We collect utterances pertaining to user preference specifications or queries from the ATIS domain. The utterances are classified into four categories [13] according to their sentence acts. The followings are examples for each category:

Declarative: I prefer a [**TimeFeature** morning] [**SingularObject** flight]. (3.1)

Imperative: Show me the [**PriceFeature** cheapest] [**SingularObject** flight]. (3.2)

Yes-no-question: Can you give me some information for [**Carrier** United]? (3.3)

Wh-question: What [**PluralObject** flights] [**ServeFeature** serve breakfast] and [**HaveFeature** have stops]? (3.4)

Each sentence in the ASB has been annotated by assigning conceptual categories [14] to domain concepts reflecting semantic meanings. Such simple annotations can help us create sample sentences in the MCCS domain by substituting or adjoining operations. The examples (3.5)-(3.8) show the corresponding cases in the CSB rooted from (3.1)-(3.4). There are in total 114 cases in the CSB.

Declarative: I prefer a white car. (3.5)

Imperative: Show me the cheapest sedan. (3.6)

Yes-no-question: Can you give me some information for Honda? (3.7)

Wh-question: What cars can seat more than 5 passengers and have 4 doors? (3.8)

4 Case Sentence Annotation

In our corpus generation system, we implement an annotation scheme for sample sentences in the CSB. Each sample sentence is annotated in two plies. The first ply is the semantic structure representing the domain concept relationships. The syntactic structure is abstracted in the second ply to reflect surface realization.

QueryObject CAT_Color CAT_NumOfDoor
CAT_NumOfCylinder CAT_Make CAT_BodyStyle
CAT_Transmission CAT_DriveWheel
NUM_MadeYearStartValue NUM_MadeYearEndValue
NUM_EngineLiterStartValue NUM_EngineLiterEndValue
NUM_PriceStartValue NUM_PriceEndValue
NUM_NumOfPassengerStartValue NUM_NumOfPassengerEndValue

Note: *CAT means categorical feature while NUM means numeric feature*

Fig. 2. Conceptual category set

We utilize a set of conceptual categories to abstract conceptual meanings in our application domain (Figure 2). The benefit of introducing conceptual categories is that each concept in a case sentence can be instantiated with different values to satisfy word coverage. The semantic ply indicates the sentence act and the number type (singular or plural) of the query object. It also catches the relations between those conceptual categories involved in the annotated sentence. For instance, the semantic ply of Example (3.8) can be described in a Query Language [15] as:

$$\{x|x.\text{Act='wh-question'} \wedge x.\text{QueryObject='car'} \wedge x.\text{ObjectType='Plural'} \wedge car.\text{NumOfDoor='four'} \wedge car.\text{NumOfPassenger.StartValue=5}\} \quad (4.1)$$

The syntactic ply analyzes the syntactic structure of the sentence, which is the formalism for surface realization. The structure of the formalism is adapted from the systemic functional grammar [16], which consists of three layers: clause, phrase and token. Figure 3 represents the syntactic structure of the example (3.8).

```
<SynStructure type="ComplexClause">
 <SynClause localID="c1">
  <SynPhrase type="Simple" fc="CannedText" value="What" />
  <SynPhrase type="Simple" fc="ObjectThing" ref="Head" value="VALUE" />
  <SynPhrase type="Simple" fc="Predicate" value="can seat" />
  <SynPhrase type="Complex" fc="NUMFeature" ref="NumOfPassenger">
    <SynToken type="Simple" fc="CannedText" value="more than" />
    <SynToken type="Simple" fc="Feature" value="StartValue" />
    <SynToken type="Simple" fc="Quantifier" value="passengers" />
  </SynPhrase>
  <SynPhrase type="Simple" fc="PredicateConj" value="and" />
  <SynPhrase type="Simple" fc="Predicate" value="have" />
  <SynPhrase type="Complex" fc="CATFeature" ref="NumOfDoor" />
    <SynToken type="Simple" fc="Feature" value="VALUE" />
    <SynToken type="Simple" fc="Quantifier" value="doors" />
  </SynPhrase>
 </SynClause>
</SynStructure>
```

Fig. 3. The syntactic structure of Example (3.8) in XML

5 Corpus Generation

The general principles for creating a corpus are semantic coverage, syntactic coverage, prosodic coverage and word coverage [11]. As the target outcome of our system is a sentence corpus for language modeling, prosodic coverage is not our focus.

- *Semantic coverage*: the corpus should cover domain concepts and relationships as completely as possible;
- *Syntactic Coverage*: the corpus should reflect many rich syntactic variations, as found in natural language;
- *Word Coverage*: the corpus should cover as many words as possible in the vocabulary.

In this Section, we demonstrate how these three principles have been considered and satisfied during the corpus generation. Although case sentences marked with domain-specific conceptual categories can be used directly for surface natural language generation, as was suggested in [17], it is only capable of handling certain circumstances, such as simple applications (as the NLG1 in [17]) or under the assumption that the corpus is large enough for statistical analysis (as the NLG2 and NLG3 in [17]). In our project, we seek to create a corpus based on a sample sentence set with a limited size. Therefore, a CBR approach with adaptability is more appropriate [11]. An input to the sentence generator is a semantic structure represented in an AVM (attribute value matrix) form, including a sentence act, the query object and its features. Figure 4 shows a typical example of inputs.

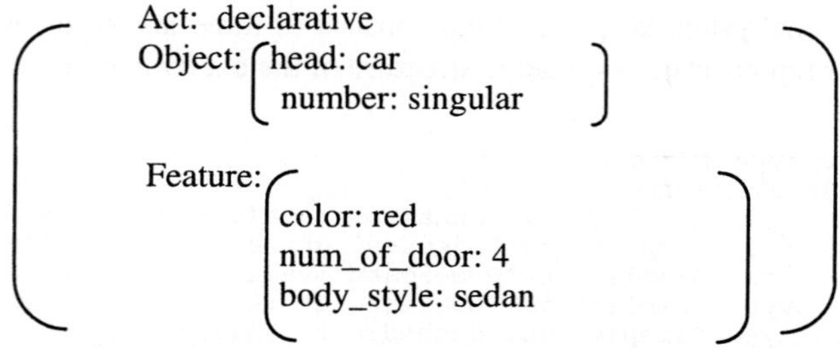

Fig. 4. An example input showing the semantic meaning of a user's specification: "I would prefer a red sedan with four doors"

In order to satisfy the semantic coverage, we explore all possible combinations of features related to the car object. We made a decision to include only those combinations with less than 5 features so that the generated sentence can be kept in a reasonable length. In terms of syntactic coverage, we consider all sentence acts to express a feature combination. In addition, the variations of syntax in describing a numeric feature are explored. The examples (5.1)-(5.4) show four types of phrases with different foci to specify the price of a car. The word coverage is achieved through enumerating all possible values of each feature.

a price no less than [**PriceStartValue** 15,000] dollars (5.1)

a price no more than [**PriceEndValue** 30,000] dollars (5.2)

a price from [**PriceStartValue** 15,000] to [**PriceEndValue** 30,000] dollars (5.3)

a price around [**PriceStartValue=PriceEndValue** 20,000] dollars (5.4)

The generation of sentences is performed according to a procedural algorithm. The algorithm consists of four procedures:

- *Distance measuring*: An input is compared with the semantic representation of an instance in the CSB. Candidates above the threshold are selected for further processing.
- *Feature categorizing*: Through examining the difference between the feature set of the input and that of the case, features are categorized into four groups: *OldFeatures*, *AdjustFeatures*, *OtioseFeatures* and *NewFeatures*. Old features are those shared by the input and the case. Adjust features are those numeric features belonging to both but with different focuses. Features in the case but not in the input are called otiose features, and new features are those that appeared in the input but not in the case.

Sentence Generation Algorithm

Input: The semantic structure of a new sentence: I ;
An instance of cases retrieved from the sentence base: C;
Output: a generated sentence if it's successful; otherwise null.

1. If (I.act == C.act) then proceed to 2;
2. If (isCompatible (I.object, C.object)) then proceed to 3;
3. Calculate Dis (I, C);

Denote I (F) as the input, where $F=\{F_1,F_2,..F_n\}$ represents the feature set of the input.
Denote C (A) as the case, where $A=\{A_1,A_2,\ldots A_m\}$ represents the feature set of the case.
Denote k as the number of features $\in F\cap A$.
If we define:

$$d(f_i, C) = \begin{cases} \alpha & \text{if } f_i \in C \\ \beta & \text{if } f_i \notin C \end{cases}$$

$$d(a_i, F) = \begin{cases} \alpha & \text{if } a_i \in F \\ \gamma & \text{if } a_i \notin F \end{cases}$$

then $Dis(I, C) = \Sigma\, d(f_i, C) + \Sigma\, d(a_i, F) = 2\alpha k + (n-k)\beta + (m-k)\gamma$
The distance function (metric) should satisfy the following conditions:

(1) $0 \le Dis(I,C) \le 1$;
(2) if n=m=k then Dis (I,C)=0;
(3) if k=0 then Dis (I, C) =1;
(4) $\beta > \gamma > 0$, given that insertion is a more difficult operation than deletion;

Thus $\alpha=0$;
$1/(m+n) < \beta < 1/n$;
and $\gamma = (1-n\beta)/m$.

Choose $\beta = 1/(n+1)$ then $Dis(I, C) = (n-k)*(1/(n+1)) + (m-k)*(1/(n+1))/m$

4. If (Dis(I,C) <0.5) then proceed to 5;
5. For each feature $f_i \in$ {oldFeatures||adjustFeatures}$=F\cap A$, perform value substitution or adjustment operation;
   For each feature $f_j \in$ {otioseFeatures}$=(F\cup A)-F$, perform deletion operation;
   For each feature $f_k \in$ {newFeatures}$=(F\cup A)-A$, perform insertion operation.
6. Surface realize the sentence according to the adaptive syntactic structure.

Fig. 5. Sentence generation algorithm

- *Case adapting*: For each type of features, different adaptations to the case are performed to generate a syntactic structure corresponding to the semantic structure of the input.
- *Surface realizing*: A sentence is generated according to the adapted syntactic structure.

Figure 5 depicts the details of the sentence generation algorithm.

6 Evaluation

The evaluation is done at two levels. Firstly, the generated sentences are scored by human evaluators using three ratings: no grammatical error, minor grammatical error and major grammatical error. The ratios generally represent the quality of sentence generation. Secondly, the generated corpus is divided into two sets: a training set and a test set. We use the training set to build an n-gram language model. The language model is applied to a speech recognition engine to test recognition effectiveness. The sentences from the test set are used for this testing. We measure the word error rate to verify the acceptability of the language model.

Table 1. Testing results of language models

Testing Engine	Language Model	I	O	S	N_{sol}	Percent correct	Accuracy
Sphinx 4, No speaker training	Our Domain Specific Model	84	16	154	1024	83.4%	75.2%
Sphinx 4, No speaker training	WSJ5K Model (Vocabulary size: 5,000)	82	10	568	1024	43.6%	34.6%
Sphinx 4, No speaker training	HUB4 Model (Vocabulary size: 64,000)	56	28	704	1024	28.5%	23.1%
Dragon Naturally Speaking Preferred (version 3.52), Speaker training	Dictation Grammar	99	26	327	1024	65.5%	55.9%

I: Number of *inserted* symbols **O: Number of *omitted* symbols**
S: Number of *substituted* symbols **N_{sol} : Total Number of symbols for testing**

Two hundred sentences are randomly selected from the generated corpus for grammatical evaluation. Of these sentences, 196 sentences are grammatically correct. Three sentences have major grammatical errors and one has minor error. The effectiveness of the system in generating user specifications and queries is supported by the high percentage of correctness. We then follow the methods introduced in [1] to test the performance of the language model derived from the corpus. We utilize the Sphinx 4 Recognition Engine [18] without speaker training to test our language model and two general models. A further test is conducted to compare our model with the dictation grammar used in the Dragon Naturally Speaking Preferred (version 3.52) Engine with speaker training. Table 1 details the test results, which suggest the language model specific to the MCCS can significantly outperform a general language model or a dictation grammar.

7 Related Work

Generating natural language through learning is a relatively new endeavor. Trainable methods for surface NLG are introduced in [17] to learn the mapping between semantic meaning and syntactic structure so that sophisticated grammars can be avoided. The implicative assumption of trainable systems is the existence of a large corpus. In our project, we can only create a sample sentence set of a limited size, which is not appropriate for training. Our CBR approach differs from trainable methods in that instances in the case base are used for adaptation to generate new sentences directly, instead of for calculating statistical distribution. [10, 12] introduce an approach for instance-based natural language generation. However, instead of adapting instances to generate sentences, instances are just used to compare with sentences generated by a rule-based system for choosing the final output. No adaptation is performed during the generation procedure. [11] presents a surface natural language generator in the real estate domain that employs a case-based paradigm. Its adaptation-guided retrieval makes it ultimately similar to our system. However, our approach differs from it in two respects. Firstly, we employ a quantitative distance measurement for acceptance function. Compared with the qualitative cost-analysis method used in [11], our method provides a numeric value for similarity comparison, which we believe is more straightforward. Secondly, the syntactic structure of cases in our system is represented in systemic functional formalism while graphical tree structure is utilized in [11] to represent the syntactic, lexical, prosodic and acoustic realizations. Our method is simpler and less prone to grammatical error in generating structured sentences.

8 Conclusions

This paper presents a CBR system to generate a speech corpus for the MCCS application. In comparison to traditional NLG approaches, this system overcomes the inflexibility of template-based methods while avoiding the linguistic sophistication of rule-based packages. Our research indicates that CBR learning techniques can perform effectively in generating structured sentences. This approach is particularly useful if the size of the sample sentence set is relatively small. The study results also suggest that a language model pertaining to a specific application is a necessity as general models or dictation grammar cannot satisfy the requirements for recognition accuracy.

This study is part of research to incorporate natural language understanding capacity into a framework to develop speech-enabled mobile commerce applications. We only explore natural language models for understanding user specifications or queries at the beginning of a conversation in the context of mobile commerce. After that, users would be guided by a system-directed dialogue to continue their search for desired products. When a user shows interest in a particular product and selects to listen to the detailed description of the product, the system will play a pre-recorded audio file. We believe speech for product description can be generated through CBR-based NLG system in a similar manner. A NLG method can provide much more flexibility in generating product descriptions in comparison to pre-recorded audio files. In future work, the CBR approach introduced in this paper should be able to be extended for product description generation.

Acknowledgements

The authors would like to thank Benny Nasution and Adrian Ryan for examining the sample sentences, grammatically evaluating the generated sentences and testing the performance of different language models.

References

1. Becchetti, C. and Ricotti, L.P. (1999): Speech Recognition: Theory and C++ Implementation, John Wiley & Sons.
2. Somers, H. (2000): Empirical Approaches to Natural Language Processing, in Handbook of Natural Language Processing (Eds., Dale, R. et al.), pp.377-384. New York, Marcel Dekker.
3. Jurafsky, D. et al. (1994): The Berkeley Restaurant Project. In Proceedings of ICSLP-94, Yokohama, Japan, pp.2139-2142.
4. Lesher, G.W. et al. (1999): Effects of ngram order and training text size on word prediction, In Proc. of the RESNA'99 Annual Conference, Arlington, VA. pp.52-54.
5. Rudnicky, A.I. et al. (2000): Task and Domain Specific Modeling in the Carnegie Mellon Communicator System, in ICSLP2000, Beijing, China.
6. Lesher, G.W. and Sanelli, C. (2000): A Web-Based System for Autonomous Text Corpus Generation, In Proceedings of ISSAAC 2000, Washington DC, U.S.A.
7. Thompson, H.S. (2000): Corpus Creation for Data-Intensive Linguistics. In Handbook of Natural Language Processing (Eds, Dale R. et al.), pp.385-401. New York, Marcel Dekker.
8. Reiter, E. (1995): NLG vs. Templates, In Proceedings of the 5th European Workshop on Natural Language Generation, Leiden, the Netherlands.
9. Oh, A.H. and Rudnicky, A. (2000): Stochastic Language Generation for Spoken Dialogue Systems, In Proceedings of the ANLP/NAACL Workshop on Conversational Systems, May 2000, pp.27-32.
10. Varges, S. and Mellish, C. (2001): Instance-based Natural Language Generation, In Proceedings of the 2nd Meeting of the North America Chapter of the Association for Computational Linguistics (NAACL-2001), Pittsburgh, PA, June 2001.
11. Pan, S. and Weng, W. (2002): Designing a speech corpus for instance-based spoken language generation. In Proceedings of INLG2002, New York, U.S.A.

12. Varges, S. (2003): Instance-based Natural Language Generation, PhD thesis, Institute for Communicating and Collaborative Systems, School of Informatics, University of Edinburgh.
13. Jurafsky, D. and Martin, J.H. (2000): Speech and Language Processing: An Introduction to Natural Language Processing, Computational Linguistics, and Speech Recognition, Prentice Hall.pp.332-334.
14. Sun, J. et al. (2000): A Robust Speech Understanding System Using Conceptual Relational Grammar, In Proceedings of ICSLP'2000, Oct 2000, Beijing, China.
15. Minock, M.J. (2003): A Phrasal Generator for Describing Relational Database Queries, In Proceedings of the 9th European Association of Computational Linguistics workshop on Natural Language Generation, Apr 2003, Budapest, Hungary.
16. Halliday, M.A.K. and Matthiessen, M.I.M. (2004) An Introduction to Functional Grammar, 3rd Edition, ARNOLD.
17. Ratnaparkhi, A. (2000): Trainable Methods for Surface Natural Language Generation, In proceedings of the ANLP/NAACL'00, Seattle, WA. pp.194-201.
18. The CMU Sphinx Group Open Source Speech Recognition Engines. Retrieved Dec 12, 2004. From http://cmusphinx.sourceforge.net/html/cmusphinx.php

Web-Based Terminology Translation Mining

Gaolin Fang, Hao Yu, and Fumihito Nishino

Fujitsu Research and Development Center, Co., LTD. Beijing 100016, China
{glfang, yu, nishino}@frdc.fujitsu.com

Abstract. Mining terminology translation from a large amount of Web data can be applied in many fields such as reading/writing assistant, machine translation and cross-language information retrieval. How to find more comprehensive results from the Web and obtain the boundary of candidate translations, and how to remove irrelevant noises and rank the remained candidates are the challenging issues. In this paper, after reviewing and analyzing all possible methods of acquiring translations, a feasible statistics-based method is proposed to mine terminology translation from the Web. In the proposed method, on the basis of an analysis of different forms of term translation distributions, character-based string frequency estimation is presented to construct term translation candidates for exploring more translations and their boundaries, and then sort-based subset deletion and mutual information methods are respectively proposed to deal with subset redundancy information and prefix/suffix redundancy information formed in the process of estimation. Extensive experiments on two test sets of 401 and 3511 English terms validate that our system has better performance.

1 Introduction

The goal of Web-based terminology translation mining is to mine the translations of terminologies or proper nouns which cannot be looked up in the dictionary from the Web using a statistical method, and then construct an application system for reading/writing assistant (e.g. Mont Blanc→万宝龙, 白朗峰). Translators and technical researchers cannot yet obtain an accurate translation after many lookup efforts when they encounter terminology or proper noun during translating or writing foreign language. According to Web statistics by Google, 76.59% of Web pages are English. In China, statistical results by China Internet Network Information Center in July 2004 show that the number of Internet users has reached 94 million, and nearly 87.4% of users have educational backgrounds beyond high school. These users can smoothly read general English pages, but some terminologies in the Web hamper them to exactly understand the whole content. Some skilled users perhaps resort to a Web search engine, but they cannot obtain effective information from a large amount of retrieved irrelevant pages and redundancy information. Thus, it is necessary to provide a system to automatically mine translation knowledge of terms or proper nouns using abundant Web information so as to help users accurately read or write foreign language.

The system of Web-based terminology translation mining has many applications. 1) Reading/writing assistant, as one part of computer-assisted language learning (CALL) used in the E-learning. During reading or writing, users often meet terms

R. Dale et al. (Eds.): IJCNLP 2005, LNAI 3651, pp. 1004 – 1016, 2005.

whose translations cannot be found in the dictionary, but this system can help them mine native and accurate translations from the Web. 2) The tool for constructing bilingual dictionary. The system can not only provide translation candidates for compiling bilingual lexicon, but also evaluate or rescore the candidate list of the dictionary. The constructed dictionary can be further applied in cross-language information retrieval (CLIR) and machine translation. 3) As one of the typical application paradigms of the combination of CLIR and Web mining.

There are some issues that need to be solved using Web information to mine terminology translation: 1) How to find more comprehensive results, i.e. mining all possible forms of annotation pairs in the Web. 2) How to obtain the boundary of candidate translations, especially for the language without the boundary mark such as Chinese and Japanese. Because we don't know the translation is at left or right, and what is between the pair, and where is the candidate endpoint? 3) How to remove the noises formed in the statistics and rank the remained candidates.

On the basis of reviewing all possible methods of acquiring translations, a feasible statistics-based method is proposed to mine terminology translation from the Web. In the proposed method, after analyzing different forms of term translation distributions, character-based string frequency estimation is employed to construct term candidate translations for exploring more translations and their boundaries, and then the candidate noises formed in the process of statistics are defined as two categories: subset redundancy information and prefix/suffix redundancy information. Sort-based subset deletion and mutual information methods are respectively proposed to deal with two redundancy information. Experiments on two test sets of 401 and 3511 English terms show that our system has better performance. In all reported literatures, our experiment is the first time for the extensive research on Web-based terminology translation mining on the largest scale.

2 Related Work

Automatic acquisition of bilingual word pairs or translations has been extensively researched in the literature. The methods of acquiring translations are usually summarized as four categories: 1) acquiring translation from parallel corpora, 2) acquiring translation from a combination of translations of constituent words, 3) acquiring translation from bilingual annotation in the Web, and 4) acquiring translation from non-parallel corpora.

1) Acquiring translation from parallel corpora.
Acquiring bilingual lexicon or translations from parallel corpora (including sentence alignment and paragraph alignment) is to utilize statistics information such as co-occurrence, position, and length between source word and translation equivalence in parallel texts as an evaluation criterion to obtain one-to-one map word pairs. Many previous researches focused on extracting bilingual lexicon from parallel corpora, and readers can refer to the reviews [1], [2] for the details. However, due to the restriction of current available parallel corpora of different languages, together with the fact that corpus annotation requires a lot of manpower and resources, researchers have attempted to extract translations from non-parallel corpus or Web data. As opposed to extracting from parallel corpora, there are no corresponding units in non-parallel

corpora so that statistics information such as co-occurrence, position and length become unreliable. New statistical clues have to be proposed to build the relationship for acquiring translation pairs from non-parallel corpora, which is more difficult to handle than in parallel corpora.

2) Acquiring translation from a combination of translations of constituent words. Grefenstette [3] employed an example-based approach to obtain compound word translations. His method first combined possible translations of each constituent, and then searched them in WWW, where the retrieved number was viewed as an evaluation criterion. Experiments on a set of 724 German words and a set of 1140 Spanish terms showed that the accuracies of English translations were about 87% and 86%, respectively.

Cao and Li [4] proposed a dictionary-based translation combination method to collect translation candidates of English base noun phrases, and then employed a naive Bayesian classifier and TF-IDF vector constructed with EM algorithm as evaluation criterions for translation selection. In an experiment with 1000 English base noun phrases, the coverage of acquiring translations was 91.4%, and the accuracy of top 3 choices was 79.8%. The system was further improved in the literature [5].

Navigli et al. [6] proposed an ontology learning method for acquiring terminology translations from English to Italian. His method was based on bilingual lexicon and semantic relation between the constituents of source language derived from ontology learning, where disambiguated terms dramatically reduced the number of alternative translations and their combinations. This system can automatically extract the translations of 405 complex terms in the tourism domain.

Using the translation combination of each constituent to acquire the translation of a multiword term is very suitable for translation acquisitions of base noun phrases. However, terminologies and technical terms often consist of unknown words, and their translations are seldom the combination of each constituent. Thus, the result of direct combination is not very desirable for terminology translation acquisition.

3) Acquiring translation from bilingual annotation in the Web. Nagata et al. [7] proposed an empirical function of the byte distance between Japanese and English terms as an evaluation criterion to extract the translation of Japanese word, and their results could be used as a Japanese-English dictionary. Preliminary experiments on the 50 word pairs showed that an accuracy of top 50 candidates reached 56%. The reasons for such experimental results have two aspects: first, the system didn't further deal with candidate noises for mining useful knowledge; second, this system only handled top 100 Web pages retrieved from search engine. In fact, previous 100 Web pages seldom contain effective bilingual annotation information only directly using keyword search rather than imposing other restrictions. Thus, this problem should be further researched for practical applications. Since his research focused on finding English translation given a Japanese term, the segmentation of Japanese could be avoided. However, our problem is to find Chinese equivalent using English term, so we have to cope with how to obtain the correct boundary of Chinese translations. Therefore, the issue and the proposed method in this paper are distinctly different with Nagata's.

4) Acquiring translation from non-parallel corpora.
Acquiring translation from non-parallel corpora is based on the clue that the context of the source term is very similar to that of the target translation in a large amount of corpora. In 1995, Rapp [8] assumed that there is a correlation between the patterns of word co-occurrence in non-parallel texts of different languages, and then proposed a matrix permutation method to match these patterns. However, computational limitation hampered further extension of this method. In 1996, Tannaka and Iwasaki [9] demonstrated how to extract lexical translation candidates from non-aligned corpora using the similar idea. In 1999, this method was developed and improved by Rapp [10]. Rather than computing the co-occurrence relation matrix between one word and all words, the matrix between one word and a small base lexicon are estimated. Experiments on 100 German words indicated that an accuracy of top 1 English translation was 72%, and top 10 was 89%. This system was only suitable for the situation of one word to one word, and didn't further research on the translation acquisition from multiword to multiword.

In 1995, Fung [11] proposed a "context heterogeneity" method to compute the measure similarity between word and its translation for finding translation candidates. In the experiment with 58 English words, an accuracy of 50% is obtained in the top 10 Chinese word candidates. Based on this work, Fung presented the word relation matrix to find the translation pair in 1997 [12]. This method respectively computed the correlation vectors between source word and seed word, target word and seed word. In 19 Japanese term test set, the accuracy of English translations reached 30%. In 1998, the method was improved to extend to non-parallel, comparable texts for translation acquisition [13]. This system use TF/IDF as the feature, and different measure functions as the similarity computation between the candidate pair. However, the system was restricted to the assumption that there are no missing translations and all translations are included in the candidate word list.

Shahzad et al. [14] first extracted the sentence corpora that are likely to contain the target translation using bilingual dictionary and transformation table. And then, the heuristics method was employed to obtain the correct candidate by analyzing the relations of source compound nouns and using partial context information. Experiments on the 10 compound nouns showed that the average accuracy and recall were respectively 34% and 60%.

As shown from the current situation of translation acquisition from non-parallel corpora, all experiments above are basically performed on small-scaled word set, and their results are very inspiring but difficult to put into practical use. Furthermore, most experimental methods are only suitable for one word translation, i.e. the word number ratio of translation pair is on a basis of 1:1. Thus, there are many issues to be further researched before it is used to explore new translation in the application area.

From the review above, we know that Method 1 requires a large number of parallel corpora, and Method 2 and Method 4 have some limitations when they are applied to acquire the terminology translation, and Method 3 makes the best of mass Web resources and is a feasible approach. When people use Asia language such as Chinese, Japanese, and Korean to write, especially scientific article or technical paper, they often annotate the associated English meaning after the terminology. With the development of Web and the open of accessible electronic documents, digital library, and scientific articles, these resources will become more and more abundant. Thus, Method 3 is a feasible way to solve the terminology translation acquisition, which is also validated by the following experiments.

3 The Framework of the Terminology Translation Mining System

The Web-based terminology translation mining system is depicted in Fig. 1 as follows:

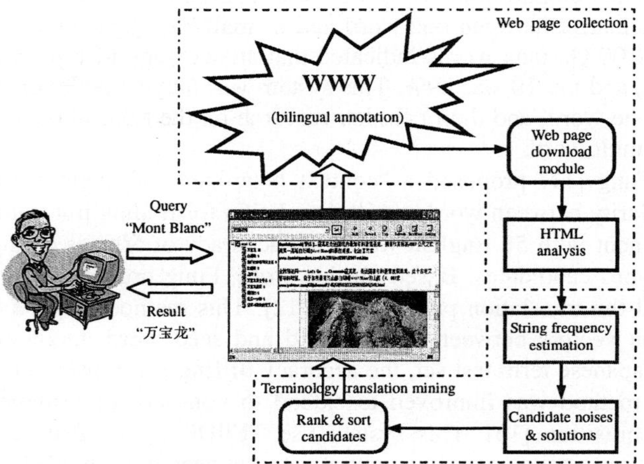

Fig. 1. The Web-based terminology translation mining system

The system consists of two parts: Web page collection and terminology translation mining. Web page collection includes download module and HTML analysis module. The function of download module is to collect these Web pages with terms' associated bilingual annotations, and then the pages are inputted into HTML analysis module. In HTML analysis, Web pages are built as a tree structure from which possible features for the bilingual pair and text information in the HTML page are simultaneously extracted.

Terminology translation mining includes string frequency estimation, candidate noises and their solutions, and rank & sort candidates. Translation candidates are constructed through string frequency estimation module, and then we analyze their noises and propose the corresponding methods to handle them. At last, the approach combining the possible features such as frequency, distribution, length proportion, distance, keywords and key symbols is employed to rank these candidates.

In Web pages, there are a variety of bilingual annotation forms. Correctly exploring all kinds of forms can make the mining system extract the comprehensive translation results. After analyzing a large amount of Web page examples, we summarize translation distribution forms as the following six categories: 1) Direct annotation 2) Separate annotation 3) Subset form 4) Table form 5) List form 6) Explanation form. Direct annotation is the most widely used form in the Web, where English meaning often follows after Chinese terminology, and some have symbol marks such as bracket parentheses and bracket, and some have nothing, e.g. "白朗峰Mont Blanc". Separate annotation is referred to as the case that there are some Chinese words or English letters between the translation pair, e.g. "万能寿险,英文称universal life insurance". Subset form is that the extracted translation pair is a subset of existing bilingual pair, for example, during searching the term "Mont Blanc", the term pair "夏蒙尼·勃朗峰 (Chamonix Mont Blanc)" also provides the valid information. Table or list form is the Web page in the form of table or list. Explanation form is the explanation and illustration for technical terms.

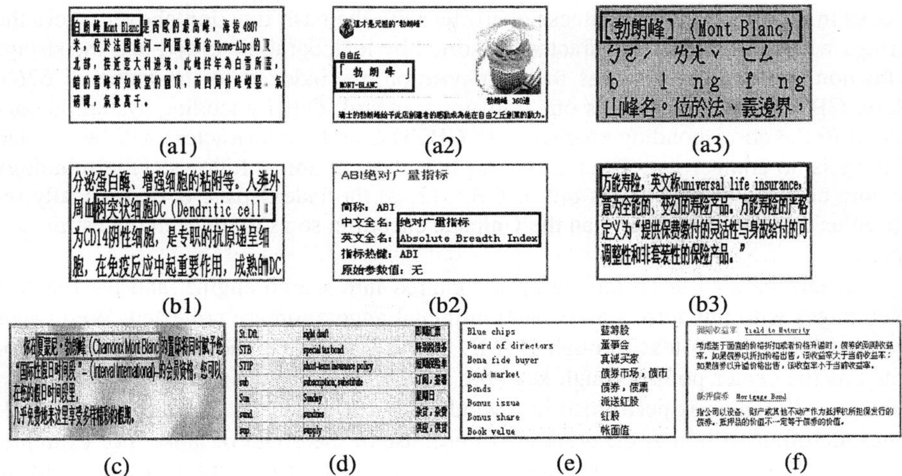

Fig. 2. The examples of translation distribution forms, (a) Direct annotation, some has no mark (a1), and some have some symbol marks (a2, a3) (b) Separate annotation, there are English letters (b1) or some Chinese words (b2, b3) between the translation pair (c) Subset form (d) Table form (e) List form (f) Explanation form

4 Statistics Based Translation Finding

4.1 Character-Based String Frequency Estimation

All kinds of possible translation forms of terminologies in the Web can be effectively and comprehensively mined through character-based string frequency estimation. The proposed method with Chinese character as the basic unit of statistics can not only obtain the correct boundary of the translation candidate, but also conveniently explore these Chinese candidate terminologies that usually consist of unknown words or unknown compound words.

String frequency information is one of the important clues during extracting candidate translations. Its estimation method has a direct influence on the system performance efficiency. The method combing hash index and binary search is employed to construct the index for all translation candidates. The definition of hash function is calculated according to 6763 Chinese characters in GB2312 system with a one-to-one map. Hash function is formulized as:

$$Y = \begin{cases} 94(c_0 - 176) + (c_1 - 161) & 215 \geq c_0 \geq 176 \\ 94(c_0 - 176) + (c_1 - 161) - 5 & c_0 > 215 \\ 6763 & otherwise \end{cases} , \quad (1)$$

where c_0, c_1 are respectively the unsigned encoding values of the first, second bytes of first Chinese character of candidate items. All strings are partitioned into different blocks in terms of the first Chinese character with the hash function above, where the strings with the same first character are sorted by lexicographic order, and the strings with non-Chinese character as the first position are indexed to the value of 6763. Here, GB2312 is employed as our statistics standard. Other encoding system is converted to the corresponding characters in GB2312, and the characters will be omitted if there is no counterpart. The reasons for this strategy are as follows: 1) terminology seldom consists of rare words out of GB2312, 2) the index space is dramatically reduced using GB2312 rather than the Unicode encoding so as to quicken the estimation speed.

The terminology to be looked up is inputted into search engine, and the relevant Web pages with this term's associated bilingual annotation are collected. Web pages are transformed into text through HTML analysis module. The term position is located as the center point through keyword search, and then string frequency and distribution estimation is performed in a window of 100 bytes. In Web pages, terminologies are often written as different forms because of the effect of noise. For example, the term "Mont Blanc" may be written as "MONT BLANC", "Mont-Blanc", "Mont ??Blanc", and "MontBlanc". For finding different forms of keywords in the Web, the fuzzy string matching approach is proposed. This method takes 26 English letters in the keyword as effective matching symbols, while ignoring the blank space and other symbols. In the matched text, only these English letters are viewed as effective items for comparison. Using this method can effectively locate different forms of terms and therefore obtain comprehensive translation candidates.

The process of string frequency estimation is described as follows. In the windows with keyword as the center, each character is built as a beginning index, and then the string candidates are constructed with the increase of the string in the form of one Chinese character unit. Since terminology translation usually consists of unknown words or compound words, character is employed as the basic unit of statistics rather than word so as to explore these unknown term translations as more as possible. String candidates are indexed in the database with hash and binary search method, if there exists the same item as the inputted candidate, its frequency is increased by 1, otherwise, this candidate is added to the database at this position. After handling one Web page, the distribution information is also estimated at the same time. In the programming implementation, the table of stop words and some heuristic rules of the beginning and end with respect to the keyword position are constructed to accelerate the statistics process.

4.2 Translation Noises and Their Solutions

All possible forms of terminology translations can be comprehensively mined after character-based string frequency estimation. However, there are many irrelevant items and redundancy noises formed in the process of mining. These noises are defined as the following two categories.

1) Subset redundancy information. The characteristic of this kind information is that this item is a subset of one item, but its frequency is lower than that item. For example: "Mont Blanc万宝龙(38) 万宝(27) 宝龙(11)", where "万宝", "宝龙" belong to subset redundancy information. They should be removed.

2) Prefix/suffix redundancy information. The characteristic of this kind information is that this item is the prefix or suffix of one item, but its frequency is greater than that item. For example: 1. "Mont Blanc 朗峰(16) 白朗峰(9) 勃朗峰(8)", 2. "Credit Rating 信用(12) 信用等级(10)", 3. "Knowledge Portal 知识门户(33) 企业知识门户(30)". In Example 1, the item "朗峰" is suffix redundancy information and should be removed. In Example 2, the item "信用" is prefix redundancy information and should also be removed. In Example 3, the term "知识门户" is in accord with the definition of suffix redundancy information, but this term is a correct candidate. Thus, the problem of prefix/suffix redundancy information is so complex that we need an evaluation method to decide to retain or drop this candidate.

```
Sort by entropy value
Sort by boundary[*] for the same entropy
Sort by length and lexical sort for the same entropy and boundary
int nNum = 0;   //record the number of remained candidates
for(int i=0; i<m_nDataNum; i++) {
        int nIsSubString = FALSE;
        if(nNum == 0)   //for the first item to be remained
              Judge whether to remain this item using boundary and length proportion
              information;
        else {
              for(int j=0; j< nNum; j++)  {
                      Judge if the ith candidate is a subset of the jth, and doesn't emerge in
                      the isolated form, if yes
                      {   nIsSubString = TRUE;   break;   }
              }
        }
        if(!nIsSubString)  {
              Move the ith candidate information to nNum position, and save;
              The saved number nNum++;
        }
}
m_nDataNum = nNum; //Save the total number.
[*]Note: refer to the case that the string has the distinct left and right boundary in the Web
```

Fig. 3. The description of the sort-based subset deletion algorithm

4.2.1 Sort-Based Subset Deletion Method

Aiming at subset redundancy information, we propose sort-based subset deletion method to handle it. Because subset redundancy information is an intermediate of estimating terminology translations, its information is basically contained by the longer string candidate with higher frequency. Therefore, this problem can be well solved by first sorting and then judging if this item is a subset of the preceding candidates. The detailed algorithm is described in Fig. 3.

4.2.2 Mutual Information Based Method

Prefix/suffix redundancy information is very complicated to deal with. In some cases, previous candidate is a correct translation and should be retained, while in other cases, it is a noise and should be deleted. In this paper, mutual information based method is proposed to decide if the candidate should be retained or deleted.

The concept of information entropy is first proposed by Shannon in 1948. Entropy is a measure of uncertainty of a random variable, and defined as:

$$H(X) = -\sum_{i=1}^{k} p(x_i) \log_2 p(x_i)\,, \tag{2}$$

where $p(x_i)$ is a probability function of a random variable $X=x_i$.

Mutual information is a concept of information theory, and is a measure of the amount of information that one random variable contains about another variable. The mutual information of two events X and Y is defined as:

$$I(X,Y) = H(X) + H(Y) - H(X,Y)\,, \tag{3}$$

where $H(X)$ and $H(Y)$ are respectively the entropies of the random variables of X and Y, and $H(X,Y)$ is the co-occurrence entropy of X and Y.

Mutual information reflects a closeness degree of the combination of X and Y. If there is no interesting relationship between X and Y, I(X,Y)=0, that is, X and Y are independent each other. If there is a genuine association between X and Y, the co-occurrence of XY will be bigger than the random individual occurrence chance of X or Y, and consequently I>>0. In this case, the possibility as a fixed compound phrase of XY becomes very big. Small mutual information hints that the combination of X and Y is very loose, and therefore there is a great possibility of a boundary between two words X, Y.

String frequency estimation is performed on different Web pages. In each Web page there is more than one occurrence for a candidate translation. Mapping this estimation process to the entropy calculation, we define $p(x_i) = n_i / N$, where n_i denotes the number of a translation candidate in one Web page, and N represents the total number of this candidate. We define k as the number of the estimated Web pages. The calculation of entropy is rewritten as:

$$H(X) = -\sum_{i=1}^{k} \frac{n_i}{N} \log_2 \frac{n_i}{N} = -\frac{1}{N} \sum_{i=1}^{k} n_i \log_2 n_i + \log_2 N\,. \tag{4}$$

Through this formula, the candidate entropy can be computed directly rather than after counting all Web data. Therefore, it can reduce the time of statistics.

Entropy can not only reflect the frequency information N, but also the distribution information in different Webs. The higher the frequency is, and the larger the entropy is. If the distribution is more uniform, this entropy value will become bigger. This is also in accord with our intuition.

Given two candidate patterns of t_1 , t_2 in the set of translation candidates, $C(t_1) > C(t_2)$, where C denotes the frequency of estimation. For suffix redundancy information, $t_1 = suff(t_2)$; for prefix redundancy information, $t_1 = pref(t_2)$. According to the definition of mutual information, $I(t_2) = H(t_1) + H(t_2 - t_1) - H(t_2)$.

The mutual information based method for prefix/suffix redundancy information is described as follows. First, judge if the condition of $\sum_i C(t_1t_i)/C(t_1) \geq 0.95$ or $\sum_i C(t_it_1)/C(t_1) \geq 0.95$ is satisfied, where the candidates t_1t_i represent the items that do not contained each other in the windows of 10 candidates after the candidate t_1 . If the condition is met, then delete t_1 . In an example of "Dendritic Cell 细胞(62) 树突状细胞(40) 树突细胞(15) 树枝状细胞(4)", because (40+15+4)/62=0.952>0.95, the candidate "细胞" is deleted. If prefix/suffix redundancy information don't satisfy the condition above, then judge the condition of $\lambda I(t_1) < I(t_2)$, if yes, then delete t_1 , otherwise retain it. The value of λ is determined by the experiments, and the following experimental results demonstrate that λ=0.85 is the best parameter.

5 Experiments

Our experimental database consists of two sets of 401 English-Chinese term pairs and 3511 English-Chinese term pairs in the financial domain. There is no intersection between two sets. Each terminology often consists of 1-6 English words, and the associated translation contains 2-8 Chinese characters. In the test set of 401 terms, there are more than one Chinese translation for one English term, and only one Chinese translation for 3511 term pairs. The top n accuracy is defined as the percentage of terms whose top n translations include correct translation in the term pairs.

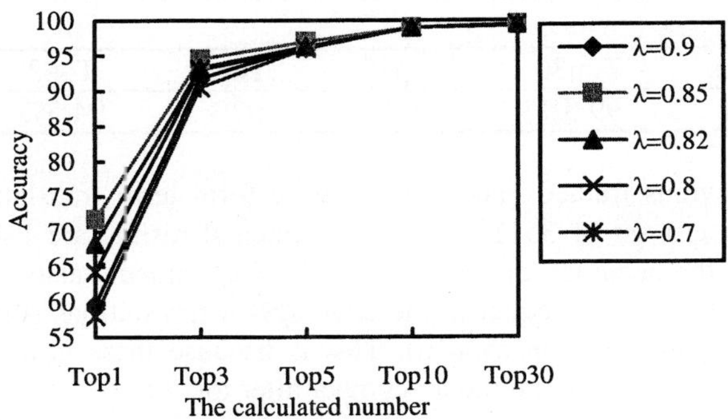

Fig. 4. The relationship between the parameter λ and the accuracy

For testing in what condition, mutual information based method is the best to deal with the prefix/suffix redundancy information. The parameter of λ is respectively set to 0.7, 0.8, 0.82, 0.85, and 0.9 in the experiment on the test set of 401 terms. Experimental results are shown in Fig. 4. From the figure, we know that λ=0.85 is the best parameter.

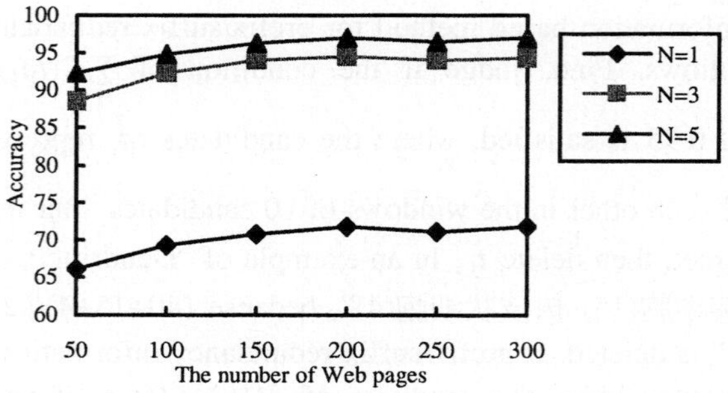

Fig. 5. The relationship between the number of Web pages and the accuracy

A second experiment is to analyze the number of Web pages influencing the term translation accuracy. The experiments are respectively performed on 50, 100, 150, 200, 250, and 300 Web pages retrieved from the Web. Experimental results are illustrated in Fig. 5, where N=1, 3, 5 represent the results of top 1, top 3, and top 5. As seen from the figure, the result of using 200 Web pages is best. When the Web pages increase more than 200 Web pages, the performance isn't improved distinctly, while the computation cost grows. In the case of 200 Web pages, the Chinese translation accuracy of top 1 is 71.8%, and top 3 is 94.5%, and top 5 is 97% on the test set of 401 English terms (see Table 1).

Table 1. Experimental results on a test set of 401 terms

Candidates	Top30	Top10	Top5	Top3	Top1
Accuracy	99.5%	99%	97%	94.5%	71.8%

Using the previous trained parameters, we perform term translation mining experiments in the test set of 3511 terms. Experimental results are listed in Table 2. From this table, the accuracy of top 3 is 83.6%. Experiments also validate that the accuracy of top 30 is nearly equal to the coverage of translations (the percentage of term translations found by our system). This is because there is no change on the accuracy when increasing the candidate number after top 30.

Table 2. Experimental results on a test set of 3511 terms

Candidates	Top30	Top10	Top5	Top3	Top1
Accuracy	95.4%	93.8%	89.1%	83.6%	56.4%

6 Conclusions

In this paper, after reviewing and analyzing all possible methods of acquiring translations, a statistics-based method is proposed to mine terminology translation from the Web. In the proposed method, character-based string frequency estimation is first presented to construct term translation candidates, and then sort-based subset deletion and mutual information methods are respectively proposed to deal with two redundancy information formed in the process of estimation. Experiments on two vocabularies of 401 and 3511 English terms show that our system has better performance, about 94.5% and 83.6% in the top 3 Chinese candidates. The contributions of this paper focus on the following two aspects: 1) On the basis of reviewing all possible methods of acquiring translations and analyzing different forms of term translation distribution, a statistics-based method is proposed to mine terminology translation from the Web. 2) The candidate noises are defined as two categories: subset redundancy information and prefix/suffix redundancy information. Sort-based subset deletion and mutual information methods are respectively proposed to deal with two redundancy information.

References

1. Somers, H.: Bilingual Parallel Corpora and Language Engineering. Proc. Anglo-Indian Workshop "Language Engineering for South-Asian languages", (2001)
2. Véronis, J.: Parallel Text Processing - Alignment and Use of Translation Corpora. The Netherlands: Kluwer Academic Publishers, (2000)
3. Grefenstette, G.: The WWW as a Resource for Example-Based MT Tasks. Proc. ASLIB Translating and the Computer 21 Conference, (1999)
4. Cao, Y., Li, H.: Base Noun Phrase Translation Using Web Data and the EM Algorithm. Proc. 19th Int'l Conf. Computational Linguistics, (2002) 127-133
5. Li, H., Cao, Y., Li, C.: Using Bilingual Web Data to Mine and Rank Translations. IEEE Intelligent Systems. 4 (2003) 54-59
6. Navigli, R., Velardi, P., Gangemi, A.: Ontology Learning and Its Application to Automated Terminology Translation. IEEE Intelligent Systems. 1 (2003) 22-31
7. Nagata, M., Saito, T., Suzuki, K.: Using the Web as a Bilingual Dictionary. Proc. ACL 2001 Workshop Data-Driven Methods in Machine Translation, (2001) 95–102
8. Rapp, R.: Identifying Word Translations in Nonparallel Texts. Proc. 33th Annual Meeting of the Association for Computational Linguistics, (1995) 320-322
9. Tanaka, K., Iwasaki, H.: Extraction of Lexical Translation from Non-Aligned Corpora, Proc. 16th Int'l Conf. Computational Linguistics, (1996) 580-585
10. Rapp, R.: Automatic Identification of Word Translations from Unrelated English and German Corpora. Proc. 37th Annual Meeting Assoc. Computational Linguistics, (1999) 519-526
11. Fung, P.: Compiling Bilingual Lexicon Entries from a Non-Parallel English-Chinese Corpus. Proc. Third Annual Workshop on Very Large Corpora, (1995) 173-183

12. Fung, P.: Finding Terminology Translations from Nonparallel Corpora. Proc. Fifth Annual Workshop on Very Large Corpora (WVLC'97), (1997) 192-202
13. Fung P., Yee, L.P.: An IR Approach for Translation New Words from Nonparallel, Comparable Texts. Proc. 17th Int'l Conf. Computational Linguistics and 36th Annual Meeting of the Association for Computational Linguistics, (1998) 414-420
14. Shahzad, I., Ohtake, K., Masuyama, S., Yamamoto, K.: Identifying Translations of Compound Nouns Using Non-Aligned Corpora. Proc. Workshop on Multilingual Information Processing and Asian Language Processing, (1999) 108-113

Extracting Terminologically Relevant Collocations in the Translation of Chinese Monograph*

Byeong-Kwu Kang, Bao-Bao Chang, Yi-Rong Chen, and Shi-Wen Yu

The Institute of Computational Linguistics, Peking University, Beijing, 100871, China
{kbg43, chbb, chenyr, yusw}@pku.edu.cn

Abstract. This paper suggests a methodology which is aimed to extract the terminologically relevant collocations for translation purposes. Our basic idea is to use a hybrid method which combines the statistical method and linguistic rules. The extraction system used in our work operated at three steps: (1) Tokenization and POS tagging of the corpus; (2) Extraction of multi-word units using statistical measure; (3) Linguistic filtering to make use of syntactic patterns and stop-word list. As a result, hybrid method using linguistic filters proved to be a suitable method for selecting terminological collocations, it has considerably improved the precision of the extraction which is much higher than that of purely statistical method. In our test, hybrid method combining "Log-likelihood ratio" and "linguistic rules" had the best performance in the extraction. We believe that terminological collocations and phrases extracted in this way, could be used effectively either to supplement existing terminological collections or to be used in addition to traditional reference works.

1 Introduction

Communication between different individuals and nations is not always easy, especially when more than one language is involved. This kind of communication can include translation problems, which can be solved by the translators who bridge the gap between two different languages.

Through the past decade, China and Korea have been undergoing large economic, cultural exchange, which invariably affects all aspects of communication, particularly translation. New international contacts, foreign investments as well as cross-cultural communication have caused an enormous increase in the volume of translations produced and required. But by now, most of all this translation work has been conducted by translators alone, which bears the burden of an enormous translation task to them.

In order to accomplish these tasks with maximum efficiency and quality, a new translation method supported by computer technology has been suggested. MAHT, also known as computer-assisted translation involves some interaction between translator and the computer. It seems to be more suited for the needs of many

* This work has been supported by The National Basic Research Program of China(973 program, No. 2004CB318102) and the 863 program (No. 2001AA114210, 2002AA117010).

R. Dale et al. (Eds.): IJCNLP 2005, LNAI 3651, pp. 1017 – 1028, 2005.

organizations which have to handle the translation of the documents. Computer-assisted translation systems are based on "translation memory" and "terminology databases". With translation memory tools, translators have immediate access to previous translations of the text, which they can then accept or modify.

Terminology management systems also can prove very useful in supporting translator's work [2, 11]. Most translators use some sort of glossary or terminology database, especially in the translation of the technical documents or academic monograph. Many translation bureaux have the collection of the terminology data bases. But time pressure and costs make it difficult to get glossary building task done fully manually. Thus there is a pressing need for the tool which is computationally supported. For Chinese, other than for English, terminology management tools are not so sophisticated that they could provide wide enough coverage to be directly usable for the translators.

We are contemplating, in this article, situations where computational support is sought to extract the term candidate, construct or enhance such terminology databases. Our work will be more focused on the problem of terminologically relevant collocation extraction.

In order to extract multiword terms from the domain corpus, three main strategies have been proposed in the literature. First, linguistic rule-based systems propose to extract relevant terms by making use of parts of speech, lexicons, syntax or other linguistic structure [2, 4]. This methodology is language dependent rather than language independent, and the system requires highly specialized linguistic techniques to identify the possible candidate terms. Second, purely statistical systems extract discriminating multiword terms from the text corpora by means of association measures [5, 6, 7]. As they use plain text corpora and only require the information appearing in texts, such systems are highly flexible and extract relevant units independently from the domain and the language of the input text. Finally, hybrid methodologies define co-occurrences of interest in terms of syntactical patterns and statistical regularities [1, 3, 9].

There is no question that the term extraction work comes into play when the tools are parameterized in such a way as to provide as much relevant material (maximizing recall and precision), and as little "noise" as possible. As seen in the literature, neither purely rule-based approach nor statistic based approach could bring an encouraging result alone[3, 4]. The main problem is the "noise". So we need to find a combined technique for reducing this "noise". In this paper, we have taken a hybrid approach which combines the linguistic rules and statistical method. First, we applied a linguistic filter which selects candidates from the corpus. Second, the statistical method was used to extract the word class combinations. And then, the results of several experiments were evaluated and compared with each other.

2 Methodology Overview

The basic idea in our work is that the extraction tool operates on pre-processed corpus which contains the results of tokenizing word and word class annotation (POS-tagging). Figure1 contains an annotated sentence from one of the Chinese academic monograph[18].

<s id=2>
随着/p 社会/n 生活/n 的/u 日益/d 信息化/v ， /w 人们/n 越来越/d 强烈/a 地/u 希望/v 用/p 自然/n 语言/n 同/p 计算机/n 交流/v 信息/n 。/w

Fig. 1. Sample annotated text (tagged by the Peking University Tagger)

And the extraction routine used in our work operated at three steps: (1)Tokenization and POS Tagging; (2)Extraction of the candidates from the corpus; (3)Linguistic filtering(making use of syntactic patterns and stop-word list). The schema in Figure2 summarizes the three steps of pre-processing and extracting the term candidate. The extraction is automatic once the appropriate templates are designed.

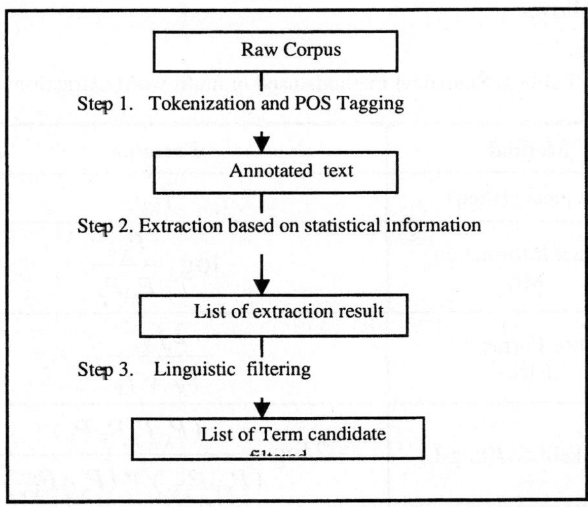

Fig. 2. Simplified schema of term extraction from a corpus

3 Statistical Method

Statistical methods in computational linguistics generally share the fundamental approach to language viewed as a string of characters, tokens or other units, where patterns are discovered on the basis of their recurrence and co-occurrence. Accordingly, when we approach the extraction of multi-word terms from a statistical point of view, we initially retrieve the word sequences which are not only frequent in their occurrence but also collocating each other.

Before a statistical methodology could be developed, some characteristics of terms in Chinese had to be established. In Chinese, the length of terms can vary from single word to multi-words(n-gram), with the majority of entries being less than 4-word items, usually two word items(bi-gram) (See in 4.3). The number of n-grams with n>4 is very small, and the occurrence of which is also rare. Therefore, the problems of bi-grams, tri-grams and 4-grams are primarily taken into considerations in our work.

Now let us consider the correlation between two neighboring words A and B. Assuming that these two words are terminologically relevant units, we can intuitively expect that they occur more often than random chance. From a statistical point of view, this probability can be measured by several statistical methods, such as "co-occurrence frequency", "Mutual Information", "Dice coefficient", "Chi-square test", "log-likelihood", etc[1, 6, 15].

Table 1 lists several statistical measures which have been widely used in extracting collocations. In table 1: XY represents any two word item; $\overline{X}$ stands for all words except X; N is the size of corpus; f_X and P_X are frequency and probability of X respectively; f_{XY} and P_{XY} are frequency and probability of XY respectively。And assuming that two words X and Y are independent of each other, the formulas are represented as follows:

Table 1. Statistical methods used in multi word extraction

Method	Formula
Frequency(Freq)	f_{XY}
Mutual Information (MI)	$\log_2 \frac{P_{XY}}{P_X P_Y}$
Dice Formula (Dice)	$\frac{2 f_{XY}}{f_X + f_Y}$
Log-likelihood(Log-L)	$-2\log \frac{(P_X P_Y P_{\overline{X}} P_{\overline{Y}})^{f_Y}}{(P_{XY} P_{\overline{XY}})^{f_{XY}} (P_{X\overline{Y}} P_{\overline{X}Y})^{f_{\overline{X}Y}}}$
Chi-squared(Chi)	$\frac{N(f_{XY} f_{\overline{XY}} - f_{X\overline{Y}} f_{\overline{X}Y})^2}{(f_{XY}+f_{X\overline{Y}})(f_{XY}+f_{\overline{X}Y})(f_{\overline{XY}}+f_{X\overline{Y}})(f_{\overline{XY}}+f_{\overline{X}Y})}$

For the purposes of this work, we used these five statistics to measure the correlation of neighboring words. The statistical criterion of judgments is the value of measures which can judge the probability whether they belong to the rigid collocations or not. From a statistical point of view, we can say that if the value of measure is high, the two word combination is more likely to be a rigid collocation. And XY could be accepted as a collocation if its statistical value is larger than a given threshold. Those bi-gram candidates with correlation coefficient smaller than a pre-defined threshold are considered to occur randomly and should be discarded. Others are sorted according to their correlation coefficient in descending order.

Tri-gram and 4-gram candidates were processed in the same way. To compute the correlation coefficient of all tri-grams, we just considered a tri-gram as the combination of one bi-gram and one word, and then calculated their correlation coefficient. Similarly, a 4-gram was considered either as the combination of a tri-gram and a word, or the combination of two bi-grams [12].

As mentioned before, our methodology was tested on pre-processed corpus which contained the result of word class annotation. The extraction test was delivered on word sequence (POS tags) combinations. And the test corpus was a Chinese academic monograph [18]. The size of this corpus is 0.2 million Chinese characters, including about 5,000 sentences. In our test, the extraction of multi-word units was based on 65,663 candidate bi-grams. Among these candidates, when their correlation coefficients were higher than a given threshold, they were considered as multi-word unit, and then sorted in descending order. The results of experiment are shown in Figure3.

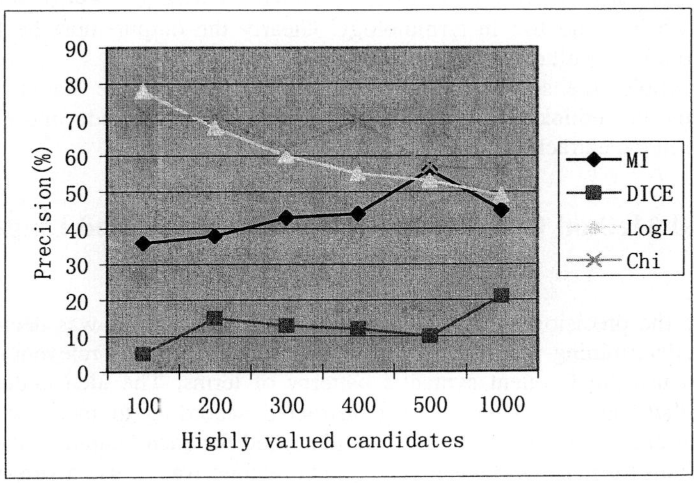

Fig. 3. Comparison of Extraction Performance between different statistical measures

Table 2. The sample result sorted by Chi Square value

1stWord	2ndWord	Chi	LogL	DICE	MI
信息	词典	7822. 14	1278. 48	517. 581	5. 28183
显现	出来	4233. 43	42. 8348	2520	10. 4636
集体	量词	3085. 64	160. 647	4560	7. 59925
字段	填	1461. 41	424. 818	767. 36	3. 90891
概括	地	809. 168	38. 2226	844	7. 66964
趋向	动词	752. 637	124. 353	787. 243	5. 16173
增加	了	619. 694	111. 527	1600	5. 02194
转换	为	582. 425	52. 0341	516. 444	6. 40501
不同	的	549. 119	286. 884	17037. 1	2. 66906
状态	词	336. 283	58. 0757	2166. 67	5. 13281
查	词典	296. 196	52. 8541	544. 348	4. 96744
也	是	228. 596	122. 119	523. 597	2. 2667

An examination of the results first showed a significant difference in precision. Checked by hand, the precisions of Chi-square value and Log-likelihood ratio were relatively high. In contrast, the precisions of Mutual information and Dice formula were not so ideal.

Considering the size of the corpus and the terminological richness of the texts, this result is not very encouraging. Regardless of any statistical measure, the precision and coverage of the extraction are not so high that could be directly used in the application system.

More over, as shown in table 2, the purely statistical system extracts all multi-word units regardless of their types, so that we can also find sequences like "增加[zengjia](add) 了 [le](auxiliary word)", "不同 [butong](different) 的 [de](auxiliary word)", "也[ye](also)是[shi](be)", "转换[zhuanhuan](change)为[wei](become)", etc., for which we have no use in terminology. Clearly the output must be thoroughly filtered before the result can be used in any productive way.

On the whole, the somewhat disappointing outcome of the statistical method provoked us to rethink the methodology and tried to include more linguistic information in the extraction of terminology.

4 Hybrid Method Combining Statistical Method and Linguistic Rules

To improve the precision and recall of the extraction system, it was decided to use two criteria determining whether a sequence was terminologically relevant or not. The first was to use the frequent syntactic patterns of terms. The idea underlying this method is that multi-word terms are constructed according to more or less fixed syntactic patterns, and if such patterns are identified for each language, it is possible to extract them from a POS tagged corpus. The second was to use a stop-word filter that a term can never begin or end in a stop-word. This would filter out things not relevant with the domain-specific collocation or term.

4.1 Syntactic Patterns of Terms in Chinese

Before a methodology for extracting the terminologically relevant word units could be developed, some characteristics of terms in Chinese had to be established. We were especially interested in the following: How many words do terms usually have in Chinese? What is the structure of multi-word units in terms of syntax and morphology? What kind of terms can be successfully retrieved by computational methods?

To find answers to the above questions, an existing terminology database could be used as a sample. Because the source text to be tested in our work is related with computational or linguistic domain, we selected the terminology database of computational linguistics which was constructed by Peking University. This term bank currently contains over 6,500 entries in English and Chinese.

An analysis of 6,500 term entries in Chinese showed that the length of terms can vary from 1 to over 6 words, with the majority of entries being two-word items, usually a "noun+noun" sequence. The second most frequent type is a single-word term. As less than 5% of all entries exceed 4 words and single word terms can be identified with the use of monolingual or bilingual dictionary[1], we decided that automatic extraction should be limited to sequences of 2-4 words.

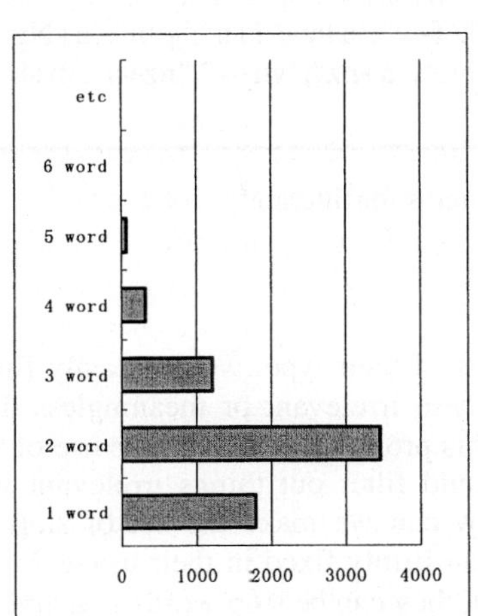

Fig. 4. Length of Chinese terms

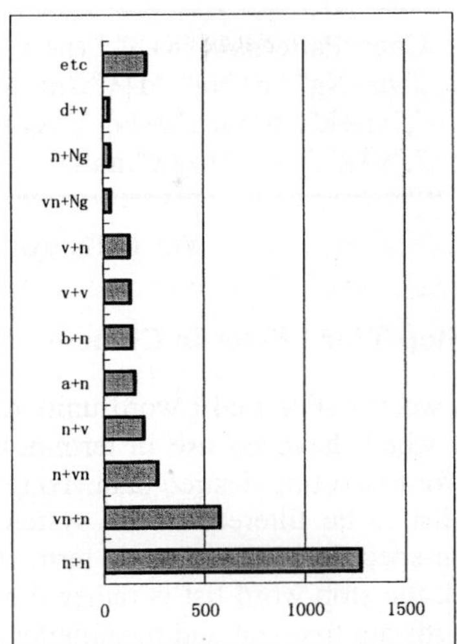

Fig. 5. Syntactic patterns of two word terms

As the next step we manually analyzed the syntactic patterns of Chinese terms and ordered them according to frequency. These patterns were needed for the second part of the experiment, the "linguistically motivated" filtering. According to the analysis of the existing terms, multi-word terms have some kinds of fixed syntactic patterns. In many cases, these syntactic patterns are based on the combinations of different two word classes, such as "noun+noun", "gerend verb+noun", "adjective+noun", "noun+suffix" etc. We found that there were about 30 syntactic patterns which covered almost 95% in the two word combinations. Therefore, we decided that these patterns could be used filtering in the extraction. In figure 6, certain types of word combinations are more typical for technical vocabulary than for general language.

More than three word combinations also can be divided into two small parts whose syntactic structures are the same as those of two word terms. For example: "(n+n)+n", "(vn+n)+n", "(v+n)+(n+vn)", "(a+n)+(vn+n)", etc. Therefore when we extracted three-word or four-word units, we didn't set another syntactic rule for them. We just considered tri-gram as the combination of one bi-gram and one word. Similarly, 4-gram was considered as the combination of different two bi-grams.

Although we admit that these syntactic patterns are typical for certain type of technical prose only, we don't think that they could filter out all the irrelevant units. If

[1] To extract a glossary of terms from a corpus, we must first identify single-word terms. But it might be slightly confusing for the computer to identify the single word terms alone. So we would like to set aside this problem for the sake of achieving efficiency. But we believe that the translator might not be troubled with single terms if he has some kind of dictionary in the translation of the source text.

we extract all combinations of a certain POS-shape, additional filters are needed afterwards, to identify those combinations which are terminologically relevant.

```
Char*Patterns={"n+n","vn+n","n+vn","n+v","a+n","b+n","v+v","v+n"
,"vn+Ng","n+Ng","d+v","m+n","h+n","f+v","a+v","f+n","j+n","a+Ng
","vn+k","b+vn","b+Ng","Ag+n","v+Ng","a+nz","vn+v","nz+n","b+k
","v+k","j+n","nz+v",null};
```

Fig. 6. The syntactic patterns for filtering[2]

4.2 Stop-Word Filter in Chinese

When we examine multi word units regardless of their type, we can easily find some words which have no use in terminology. These irrelevant or meaningless data is a noise for extracting desired data. To resolve this problem, we can make use of the stop word list to be filtered. In the system, it would filter out things irrelevant with the domain-specific collocation or term. But how can we make the set of stop words? Indeed, the stop word list is rather flexible than firmly fixed in their usage. Whenever the words are frequent and meaningless in text, they can be stop words in a given task.

For practical purposes, we used the word frequency data of the large technical domain corpora which was constructed by Beijing Language and Cultural University. In this data, we randomly selected the 2,000 words most highly frequent in their usage. And then we examined whether the frequent words were terminologically relevant or not. The analysis of the word data showed that 77.6% were domain dependent which could be the part of term, and 22.4% were general words. It means that terminologically irrelevant words amounted to about 450 words of the highly frequent 2000 words in technical corpora. The results are shown in Table 3.

Table 3. The results of analysis on the high frequency words

Frequency	Terminologically Relevant words	Terminologically Irrelevant words	Example
1-100	44(44%)	56(56%)	的(aux), 是(be), 和(and), 在(at), 中(middle), etc.
101-200	58(58%)	42(42%)	提供(provide),给(to),当(serve as),具有(possess), etc.
201-500	229(76.3%)	71(23.7%)	好(good),为了(for),某(some),只(only),其它(other), etc.
501-1000	408(81.6%)	92(18.4%)	相当 (quite), 看 (see), 引起(arose), 指出(indicate),etc.
1001-2000	813(81.3%)	187(18.7%)	出发(leave),从事(engage),甚至(even),不必(need not),etc
Total	1552(77.6%)	448(22.4%)	

[2] These POS patterns are based on the tag sets of Peking University.

According to these analyzed data, we made the set of stop words which amounted to about 450 words. And we used them for filtering out the frequent, meaningless words in a given text before the output can be used in any productive way.

5 Experiments

The hybrid methods combining statistical measure and linguistic rules were tested on pre-processed corpus. Based on the statistical method, the extraction test was limited to the boundary of the frequent syntactic patterns first, and then filtered out by the stop word list. Three different statistical measures were used to enhance the precision of the extraction, such as Log-likelihood ratio, Chi-square test and Mutual information. Because of the poor performance in our first test, Dice formula was not used in hybrid method any more. Therefore, we have delivered three different experiments using like "LogL + Liguistic Filter", "Chi + Liguistic Filter", "MI + Liguistic Filter" methods.

In Figure 7, we present the comparative results of precision rate among these different experiments. In order to measure the precision rate of the result, we used the grammatical criterion: A multi word n-gram could be considered as accurate result if it is grammatically appropriate. By grammatical appropriation, we refer to compound noun phrase or compound verb phrase, since with majority of multi-word terms have these structures.

As a result, hybrid method using linguistic filters proved to be a suitable method for selecting terminological collocations, and it has considerably improved the precision of the extraction. The precision was much higher than that of purely statistical method, retrieving appropriate result almost 10%-20% higher than in the first experiment. In our test, hybrid method combining "Log-likelihood ratio" and "linguistic rules" had the best performance in the extraction. The precision was higher than 90%. According to their performance, the results of different experiments can be arranged like:

LogL+Filter > Chi+Filter > MI+Filter > LogL > Chi > MI > Dice

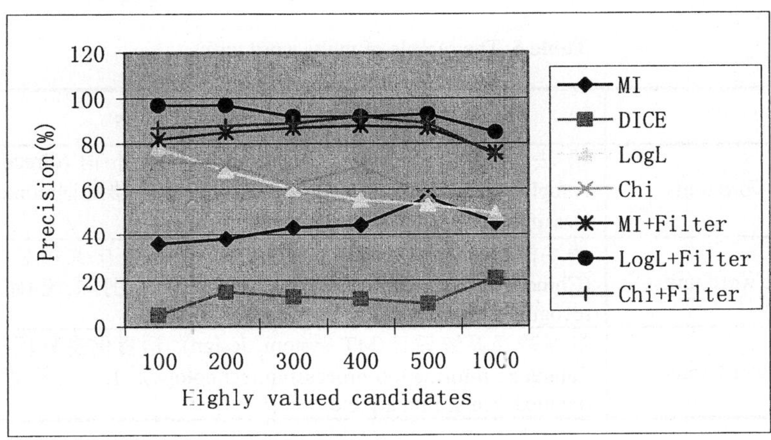

Fig. 7. Comparison of Extraction Performance between statistical measures and hybrid measure

In the analysis of the extraction data, we examined the precision of every 100 multi-word candidates which sorted in descending order. Considering the size of corpus, we compared the results within the highly valued 1000 candidates. A sample of the highly valued output is seen in Table 4.

Table 4. The sample result sorted by Log-likelihood ratio

1stWord	2ndWord	LogL+Filter	CHI+Filter	MI+Filter
语法	信息	1026.38	3748.65	4.20189
信息	处理	1020.43	5102.98	4.93017
信息	词典	981.323	3651.52	4.23672
自然	语言	899.731	7805.59	6.16647
汉语	语法	734.213	2284.06	3.76964
计算	语言学	718.016	14931.3	7.80401
语言学	研究所	557.888	13569.4	8.11656
语法	功能	537.196	2361.49	4.60008
本	字段	500.011	12919.7	8.26776
前接	成分	363.259	3535.04	6.19858
电子	词典	355.499	2053.22	5.29117
单	音节	345.551	6733.13	7.55539
趋向	补语	339.45	6092.73	7.41208
语言	信息	329.536	1061.09	3.76944
专有	项目	316.792	8130.74	8.08733

As seen in Table 4, although not all these units would be considered terms in the traditional sense of the word, most of them either contain terms or include terminologically relevant collocations. Besides, our extraction started from these two word items, expanded to extract multi-word units like three word or four word units. Finally we could extract multi word units such as the following sample:

Table 5. The sample of multi-word terms

	Terminologically relevant units
Two word units	语法功能(grammatical function), 趋向补语(directional complement), 规格说明书(specification), 容器量词(container classifier), 使用频度(usage frequency), etc.
Three word units	语法信息词典(grammatical knowledge-base), 中文信息处理(Chinese Information Processing), 语音识别系统(speech recognition system), etc.
Four word units	机器翻译系统设计(MT system design), 语言信息处理技术(language information processing technology), 上下文无关语法(context free grammar), etc.

On the whole, as we think that the performance of the extraction was quite good, this method could be applicable in the translation system.

6 Conclusions and Future Work

The paper presents a methodology for the extraction of terminological collocations from academic documents for translation purposes. It shows that statistical methods are useful because they can automatically extract all the possible multi word units according to the correlation coefficient. But the purely statistical system extracts all multi-word units regardless of their types, so that we also find sequences which are meaningless in terminology. Clearly the output must be thoroughly filtered before the result can be used in any productive way. To improve the precision of the extraction system, we decided to use linguistic rules determining whether a sequence was terminologically relevant or not. The frequent syntactic patterns of terminology and the stop-word list were used to filter out the irrelevant candidates. As a consequence, hybrid method using linguistic filters proved to be a suitable method for selecting terminological collocations, and it has considerably improved the precision of the extraction. The precision was much higher than that of purely statistical method.

We believe that terminological collocations and phrases extracted in this way, could be used effectively either to supplement existing terminological collections or to be used in addition to traditional reference works.

In future we envisage the development of techniques for the alignment of exact translation equivalents of multi-word terms in Chinese and Korean, and one way of doing so is by finding correspondences between syntactic patterns in both languages. Translation memory systems already store translations in a format similar to a parallel corpus, and terminology tools already involve functions such as "auto-translate" that statistically calculate the most probable translation equivalent. By refining these functions and making them language specific, we could soon be facing a new generation of tools for translators. It remains to be seen, however, whether they can really be implemented into translation environments on broad scale.

References

1. Chang Bao-Bao, Extraction of Translation Equivalent Pairs from Chinese-English Parallel Corpus, Terminology Standardization and Information Technology, pp24-29, 2002.
2. Bourigault, D. Lexter, A Natural Language Processing Tool for Terminology Extraction. In Proceedings of 7th EURALEX International Congress, 1996.
3. Daille, B. Study and Implementation of Combined Techniques for Automatic Extraction of Terminology. In The balancing act combining symbolic and statistical approaches to language. MIT Press, 1995.
4. Ulrich Heid, A linguistic bootstrapping approach to the extraction of term candidates from German text, http://www.ims.uni-stuttgart.de/~uli/papers.html, 2000 .
5. Sayori Shimohata, Toshiyuki Sugio, JunjiI Nagata, Retrieving Domain-Specific Collocations By Co-Occurrences and Word Order Constraints, Computational Intelligence, Vol 15, pp92-100, 1999.
6. Shengfen Luo, Maoseng Sun Nation,Two-Character Chinese Word Extraction Based on Hybrid of Internal and Contextual Measures, 2003
7. Smadja, F. Retrieving Collocations From Text: XTRACT. In Computational Linguistics, 19(1) (pp 143--177).1993.

8. David Vogel, Using Generic Corpora to Learn Domain-Specific Terminology, Workshop on Link Analysis for Detecting Complex Behavior, 2003
9. Dias, G. & Guilloré, S. & Lopes, J.G.P. Multiword Lexical Units Extraction. In Proceedings of the International Symposium on Machine Translation and Computer Language Information Processing. Beijing, China. 1999.
10. Feng Zhi-Wei, An Introduction to Modern Terminology, Yuwen press, China, 1997.
11. Gaël Dias etc, Combining Linguistics with Statistics for Multiword Term Extraction, In Proc. of Recherche d'Informations Assistee par Ordinateur, 2000.
12. Huang Xuan-jing & Wu Li-de & Wang Wen-xin, Statistical Acquisition of Terminology Dictionary, the Fifth Workshop on Very Large Corpora, 1997
13. Jiangsheng Yu, Automatic Detection of Collocation, http://icl.pku.edu.cn/yujs/, 2003
14. Jong-Hoon Oh, Jae-Ho Kim, Key-Sun Choi, Automatic Term Recognition Through EM Algorithm, http://nlplab.kaist.ac.kr/, 2003
15. Patrick Schone and Daniel Jurafsky, Is Knowledge-Free Induction of Multiword Unit Dictionary Headwords a Solved Problem?, In proceedings of EMNLP, 2001.
16. Philip Resnik, I. Dan Melamed, Semi-Automatic Acquisition of Domain-Specific Translation Lexicons, Proceedings of the fifth conference on Applied natural language processing, pp 340-347, 1997.
17. Sui Zhi-Fang, Terminology Standardization using the NLP Technology, Issues in Chinese Information Processing,pp341-352, 2003.
18. Yu Shi-wen, *A Complete Specification on The Grammatical Knowledge-base of Contemporary Chinese,* Qinghua Univ. Press, 2003

Author Index

Lecture Notes in Artificial Intelligence (LNAI)

Vol. 3717: B. Gramlich (Ed.), Frontiers of Combining Systems. X, 321 pages. 2005.

Vol. 3702: B. Beckert (Ed.), Automated Reasoning with Analytic Tableaux and Related Methods. XIII, 343 pages. 2005.

Vol. 3698: U. Furbach (Ed.), KI 2005: Advances in Artificial Intelligence. XIII, 409 pages. 2005.

Vol. 3690: M. Pěchouček, P. Petta, L.Z. Varga (Eds.), Multi-Agent Systems and Applications IV. XVII, 667 pages. 2005.

Vol. 3684: R. Khosla, R.J. Howlett, L.C. Jain (Eds.), Knowledge-Based Intelligent Information and Engineering Systems, Part IV. LXXIX, 933 pages. 2005.

Vol. 3683: R. Khosla, R.J. Howlett, L.C. Jain (Eds.), Knowledge-Based Intelligent Information and Engineering Systems, Part III. LXXX, 1397 pages. 2005.

Vol. 3682: R. Khosla, R.J. Howlett, L.C. Jain (Eds.), Knowledge-Based Intelligent Information and Engineering Systems, Part II. LXXIX, 1371 pages. 2005.

Vol. 3681: R. Khosla, R.J. Howlett, L.C. Jain (Eds.), Knowledge-Based Intelligent Information and Engineering Systems, Part I. LXXX, 1319 pages. 2005.

Vol. 3673: S. Bandini, S. Manzoni (Eds.), AI*IA 2005: Advances in Artificial Intelligence. XIV, 614 pages. 2005.

Vol. 3662: C. Baral, G. Greco, N. Leone, G. Terracina (Eds.), Logic Programming and Nonmonotonic Reasoning. XIII, 454 pages. 2005.

Vol. 3661: T. Panayiotopoulos, J. Gratch, R. Aylett, D. Ballin, P. Olivier, T. Rist (Eds.), Intelligent Virtual Agents. XIII, 506 pages. 2005.

Vol. 3658: V. Matoušek, P. Mautner, T. Pavelka (Eds.), Text, Speech and Dialogue. XV, 460 pages. 2005.

Vol. 3651: R. Dale, K.-F. Wong, J. Su, O.Y. Kwong (Eds.), Natural Language Processing – IJCNLP 2005. XXI, 1031 pages. 2005.

Vol. 3642: D. Ślezak, J. Yao, J.F. Peters, W. Ziarko, X. Hu (Eds.), Rough Sets, Fuzzy Sets, Data Mining, and Granular Computing, Part II. XXIII, 738 pages. 2005.

Vol. 3641: D. Ślezak, G. Wang, M. Szczuka, I. Düntsch, Y. Yao (Eds.), Rough Sets, Fuzzy Sets, Data Mining, and Granular Computing, Part I. XXIV, 742 pages. 2005.

Vol. 3632: R. Nieuwenhuis (Ed.), Automated Deduction – CADE-20. XIII, 459 pages. 2005.

Vol. 3630: M.S. Capcarrere, A.A. Freitas, P.J. Bentley, C.G. Johnson, J. Timmis (Eds.), Advances in Artificial Life. XIX, 949 pages. 2005.

Vol. 3626: B. Ganter, G. Stumme, R. Wille (Eds.), Formal Concept Analysis. X, 349 pages. 2005.

Vol. 3625: S. Kramer, B. Pfahringer (Eds.), Inductive Logic Programming. XIII, 427 pages. 2005.

Vol. 3620: H. Muñoz-Avila, F. Ricci (Eds.), Case-Based Reasoning Research and Development. XV, 654 pages. 2005.

Vol. 3614: L. Wang, Y. Jin (Eds.), Fuzzy Systems and Knowledge Discovery, Part II. XLI, 1314 pages. 2005.

Vol. 3613: L. Wang, Y. Jin (Eds.), Fuzzy Systems and Knowledge Discovery, Part I. XLI, 1334 pages. 2005.

Vol. 3607: J.-D. Zucker, L. Saitta (Eds.), Abstraction, Reformulation and Approximation. XII, 376 pages. 2005.

Vol. 3596: F. Dau, M.-L. Mugnier, G. Stumme (Eds.), Conceptual Structures: Common Semantics for Sharing Knowledge. XI, 467 pages. 2005.

Vol. 3593: V. Mařík, R. W. Brennan, M. Pěchouček (Eds.), Holonic and Multi-Agent Systems for Manufacturing. XI, 269 pages. 2005.

Vol. 3587: P. Perner, A. Imiya (Eds.), Machine Learning and Data Mining in Pattern Recognition. XVII, 695 pages. 2005.

Vol. 3584: X. Li, S. Wang, Z.Y. Dong (Eds.), Advanced Data Mining and Applications. XIX, 835 pages. 2005.

Vol. 3581: S. Miksch, J. Hunter, E. Keravnou (Eds.), Artificial Intelligence in Medicine. XVII, 547 pages. 2005.

Vol. 3577: R. Falcone, S. Barber, J. Sabater-Mir, M.P. Singh (Eds.), Trusting Agents for Trusting Electronic Societies. VIII, 235 pages. 2005.

Vol. 3575: S. Wermter, G. Palm, M. Elshaw (Eds.), Biomimetic Neural Learning for Intelligent Robots. IX, 383 pages. 2005.

Vol. 3571: L. Godo (Ed.), Symbolic and Quantitative Approaches to Reasoning with Uncertainty. XVI, 1028 pages. 2005.

Vol. 3559: P. Auer, R. Meir (Eds.), Learning Theory. XI, 692 pages. 2005.

Vol. 3558: V. Torra, Y. Narukawa, S. Miyamoto (Eds.), Modeling Decisions for Artificial Intelligence. XII, 470 pages. 2005.

Vol. 3554: A. Dey, B. Kokinov, D. Leake, R. Turner (Eds.), Modeling and Using Context. XIV, 572 pages. 2005.

Vol. 3550: T. Eymann, F. Klügl, W. Lamersdorf, M. Klusch, M.N. Huhns (Eds.), Multiagent System Technologies. XI, 246 pages. 2005.

Vol. 3539: K. Morik, J.-F. Boulicaut, A. Siebes (Eds.), Local Pattern Detection. XI, 233 pages. 2005.

Vol. 3538: L. Ardissono, P. Brna, A. Mitrovic (Eds.), User Modeling 2005. XVI, 533 pages. 2005.

Vol. 3533: M. Ali, F. Esposito (Eds.), Innovations in Applied Artificial Intelligence. XX, 858 pages. 2005.

Vol. 3528: P.S. Szczepaniak, J. Kacprzyk, A. Niewiadomski (Eds.), Advances in Web Intelligence. XVII, 513 pages. 2005.

Vol. 3518: T.B. Ho, D. Cheung, H. Liu (Eds.), Advances in Knowledge Discovery and Data Mining. XXI, 864 pages. 2005.

Vol. 3508: P. Bresciani, P. Giorgini, B. Henderson-Sellers, G. Low, M. Winikoff (Eds.), Agent-Oriented Information Systems II. X, 227 pages. 2005.

Vol. 3505: V. Gorodetsky, J. Liu, V. Skormin (Eds.), Autonomous Intelligent Systems: Agents and Data Mining. XIII, 303 pages. 2005.

Vol. 3501: B. Kégl, G. Lapalme (Eds.), Advances in Artificial Intelligence. XV, 458 pages. 2005.

Vol. 3492: P. Blache, E. Stabler, J. Busquets, R. Moot (Eds.), Logical Aspects of Computational Linguistics. X, 363 pages. 2005.

Vol. 3488: M.-S. Hacid, N.V. Murray, Z.W. Raś, S. Tsumoto (Eds.), Foundations of Intelligent Systems. XIII, 700 pages. 2005.

Vol. 3487: J. Leite, P. Torroni (Eds.), Computational Logic in Multi-Agent Systems. XII, 281 pages. 2005.

Vol. 3476: J. Leite, A. Omicini, P. Torroni, P. Yolum (Eds.), Declarative Agent Languages and Technologies II. XII, 289 pages. 2005.

Vol. 3464: S.A. Brueckner, G.D.M. Serugendo, A. Karageorgos, R. Nagpal (Eds.), Engineering Self-Organising Systems. XIII, 299 pages. 2005.

Vol. 3452: F. Baader, A. Voronkov (Eds.), Logic for Programming, Artificial Intelligence, and Reasoning. XI, 562 pages. 2005.

Vol. 3451: M.-P. Gleizes, A. Omicini, F. Zambonelli (Eds.), Engineering Societies in the Agents World V. XIII, 349 pages. 2005.

Vol. 3446: T. Ishida, L. Gasser, H. Nakashima (Eds.), Massively Multi-Agent Systems I. XI, 349 pages. 2005.

Vol. 3445: G. Chollet, A. Esposito, M. Faundez-Zanuy, M. Marinaro (Eds.), Nonlinear Speech Modeling and Applications. XIII, 433 pages. 2005.

Vol. 3438: H. Christiansen, P.R. Skadhauge, J. Villadsen (Eds.), Constraint Solving and Language Processing. VIII, 205 pages. 2005.

Vol. 3430: S. Tsumoto, T. Yamaguchi, M. Numao, H. Motoda (Eds.), Active Mining. XII, 349 pages. 2005.

Vol. 3419: B. Faltings, A. Petcu, F. Fages, F. Rossi (Eds.), Constraint Satisfaction and Constraint Logic Programming. X, 217 pages. 2005.

Vol. 3416: M. Böhlen, J. Gamper, W. Polasek, M.A. Wimmer (Eds.), E-Government: Towards Electronic Democracy. XIII, 311 pages. 2005.

Vol. 3415: P. Davidsson, B. Logan, K. Takadama (Eds.), Multi-Agent and Multi-Agent-Based Simulation. X, 265 pages. 2005.

Vol. 3403: B. Ganter, R. Godin (Eds.), Formal Concept Analysis. XI, 419 pages. 2005.

Vol. 3398: D.-K. Baik (Ed.), Systems Modeling and Simulation: Theory and Applications. XIV, 733 pages. 2005.

Vol. 3397: T.G. Kim (Ed.), Artificial Intelligence and Simulation. XV, 711 pages. 2005.

Vol. 3396: R.M. van Eijk, M.-P. Huget, F. Dignum (Eds.), Agent Communication. X, 261 pages. 2005.

Vol. 3394: D. Kudenko, D. Kazakov, E. Alonso (Eds.), Adaptive Agents and Multi-Agent Systems II. VIII, 313 pages. 2005.

Vol. 3392: D. Seipel, M. Hanus, U. Geske, O. Bartenstein (Eds.), Applications of Declarative Programming and Knowledge Management. X, 309 pages. 2005.

Vol. 3374: D. Weyns, H. V.D. Parunak, F. Michel (Eds.), Environments for Multi-Agent Systems. X, 279 pages. 2005.

Vol. 3371: M.W. Barley, N. Kasabov (Eds.), Intelligent Agents and Multi-Agent Systems. X, 329 pages. 2005.

Vol. 3369: V. R. Benjamins, P. Casanovas, J. Breuker, A. Gangemi (Eds.), Law and the Semantic Web. XII, 249 pages. 2005.

Vol. 3366: I. Rahwan, P. Moraitis, C. Reed (Eds.), Argumentation in Multi-Agent Systems. XII, 263 pages. 2005.

Vol. 3359: G. Grieser, Y. Tanaka (Eds.), Intuitive Human Interfaces for Organizing and Accessing Intellectual Assets. XIV, 257 pages. 2005.

Vol. 3346: R.H. Bordini, M. Dastani, J. Dix, A.E.F. Seghrouchni (Eds.), Programming Multi-Agent Systems. XIV, 249 pages. 2005.

Vol. 3345: Y. Cai (Ed.), Ambient Intelligence for Scientific Discovery. XII, 311 pages. 2005.

Vol. 3343: C. Freksa, M. Knauff, B. Krieg-Brückner, B. Nebel, T. Barkowsky (Eds.), Spatial Cognition IV. XIII, 519 pages. 2005.

Vol. 3339: G.I. Webb, X. Yu (Eds.), AI 2004: Advances in Artificial Intelligence. XXII, 1272 pages. 2004.

Vol. 3336: D. Karagiannis, U. Reimer (Eds.), Practical Aspects of Knowledge Management. X, 523 pages. 2004.

Vol. 3327: Y. Shi, W. Xu, Z. Chen (Eds.), Data Mining and Knowledge Management. XIII, 263 pages. 2005.

Vol. 3315: C. Lemaître, C.A. Reyes, J.A. González (Eds.), Advances in Artificial Intelligence – IBERAMIA 2004. XX, 987 pages. 2004.

Vol. 3303: J.A. López, E. Benfenati, W. Dubitzky (Eds.), Knowledge Exploration in Life Science Informatics. X, 249 pages. 2004.

Vol. 3301: G. Kern-Isberner, W. Rödder, F. Kulmann (Eds.), Conditionals, Information, and Inference. XII, 219 pages. 2005.

Vol. 3276: D. Nardi, M. Riedmiller, C. Sammut, J. Santos-Victor (Eds.), RoboCup 2004: Robot Soccer World Cup VIII. XVIII, 678 pages. 2005.

Vol. 3275: P. Perner (Ed.), Advances in Data Mining. VIII, 173 pages. 2004.

Vol. 3265: R.E. Frederking, K.B. Taylor (Eds.), Machine Translation: From Real Users to Research. XI, 392 pages. 2004.

Vol. 3264: G. Paliouras, Y. Sakakibara (Eds.), Grammatical Inference: Algorithms and Applications. XI, 291 pages. 2004.

Vol. 3259: J. Dix, J. Leite (Eds.), Computational Logic in Multi-Agent Systems. XII, 251 pages. 2004.